D1074679

THE CAMBRIDGE HISTORY OF THE BRITISH EMPIRE

General Editors:

THE LATE E. A. BENIANS
SIR JAMES BUTLER
P. N. S. MANSERGH
E. A. WALKER

VOLUME EIGHT

THE CAMBRIDGE HISTORY OF THE BRITISH EMPIRE

VOLUME VIII

SOUTH AFRICA, RHODESIA AND THE HIGH COMMISSION TERRITORIES

General Editor

ERIC A. WALKER

Professor Emeritus of Imperial and Naval History in the University of Cambridge

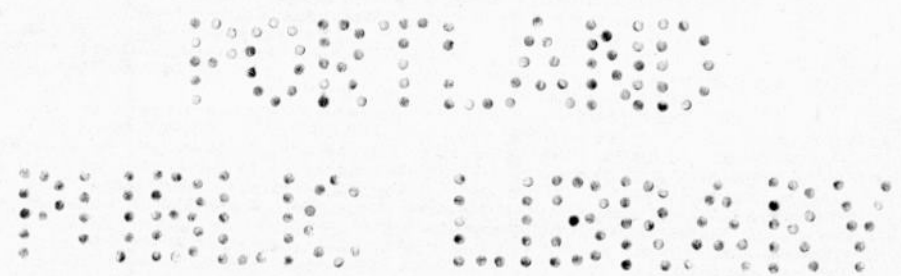

CAMBRIDGE
AT THE UNIVERSITY PRESS
1963

PUBLISHED BY

THE SYNDICS OF THE CAMBRIDGE UNIVERSITY PRESS

Bentley House, 200 Euston Road, London, N.W.1
American Branch: 32 East 57th Street, New York 22, N.Y.
West African Office: P.O. Box 33, Ibadan, Nigeria

Printed by Spottiswoode, Ballantyne & Co. Ltd., London and Colchester

PREFACE TO THE FIRST EDITION

WITH this, the third and last of our Dominion volumes, we complete that portion of our work. According to the policy set out in our former prefaces, the guiding purpose of the first three volumes of the series is to describe British expansion and imperial policy from the point of view of the Empire as a whole, while each Dominion volume deals with them only so far as they affect the fortunes of the Dominion concerned. In this volume, we treat not only the history of the territories now united in the Union of South Africa, but the whole of the African sub-continent to the south of the River Zambesi. Both geographically and historically the area is one, and the development of each part of it has affected that of the others.

Southern Africa stands apart from the regions of tropical Africa which lie beyond the Zambesi, its natural northern limit. But it is a part of the Old World, and, unlike Canada, Australia and New Zealand, has been visited by civilised men of European and Asiatic stock for many centuries. Neither the Greeks nor the Arabs knew the extreme south, but they knew a good deal about the coast of East Africa, washed by the Ocean beyond which were the ancient kingdoms of India, and they often speculated as to what lay further to the south. Our story begins long before the coming of the Portuguese under Dias and da Gama, and our earliest historical chapter surveys the knowledge which Europe had of Africa in ancient and medieval times. Many of the relevant passages in the ancient authors are assembled here in an exact English translation for the first time. Examined thus, we find that South African history has roots deep in the ancient past. Those roots were never completely broken, for while in the Dark Ages Europe's knowledge of African geography dwindled away, Arabian navigators carried on the old Roman trades of the Indian Ocean and found valuable sources of profit in the gold and ivory of South-eastern Africa. In the thirteenth century Marco Polo brought some of their knowledge back to Europe, and when in the fifteenth Vasco da Gama followed Dias round the Cape of Good Hope and reach Sofala, he was not searching blindly like the explorers of the American coasts. He knew that Sofala was the port through which supplies of gold came down from the African interior, and from Arabian sources he learned of the routes that led northwards from it and across the sea to the marts of Southern India. He began the Portuguese efforts to exploit South-eastern Africa and thenceforward its history has been continuous. The activities of the Portuguese in India and the Spiceries have overshadowed their activities in Southern Africa, but the story of the latter is full of interest and forms an integral part of the history of European relations with the sub-continent. In Mozambique and Angola the Portuguese showed the way to other nations, and, both as missionaries, explorers and conquerors, they anticipated many of the discoveries of more recent times.

It was they who first came into contact with the Native inhabitants, and our first accounts of the Southern Bantu, whom the Portuguese called Kaffirs after the fashion of the Arabs, are derived from their narratives. The history of South Africa differs from that of the other British Dominions by reason of the essential part played by the Natives which appears in almost every part of our work. During the first hundred years after the Netherlands East India Company had occupied the Cape of Good Hope as a refreshment station for their ships trading with the East Indies, their settlers had little or no contact with the Bantu, and their Native policy was only concerned with the Bushmen and Hottentots of the south-west corner of the sub-continent. Not until the period after the first British occupation of 1795 did the government of the colony become seriously concerned with the Bantu. One of our earliest chapters describes the tribal life and practices of the Bushmen, Hottentots and Southern Bantu—an essential explanatory introduction to the events narrated in the main body of our history.

From the latter part of the eighteenth century began those conflicts between the eastward-pressing settlers and the Kaffirs moving south-westward to fresh land which were to influence South African history for the next hundred years. In the search for satisfactory methods of establishing stable relations with Xhosas, Basuto, Bechuana and Zulus British officials gained an experience of the government of Native peoples living in tribal societies which has moulded British policy in many parts of the Empire. Even beyond the British Empire that experience has had influence, and many of its lessons are seen in the principles of Native government since laid down in international covenants. The difficult story dealt with in the middle chapters of our volume, with its many unfamiliar names of Bantu tribes and chiefs, is thus a highly significant part of the history of European expansion oversea.

The concurrent story of the political and constitutional development of the Cape Colony, and later of the Republics and of Natal, is traced in detail down to the formation of the Union of South Africa and the period immediately after the War of 1914–18. It is a story of bold and progressive development, to which men both of Afrikander and British stock have contributed of their best, and the editors consider themselves peculiarly fortunate in having secured the collaboration of so many South African scholars in the work.

The stream of South African culture flows deep and wide with dual currents in Afrikaans and English, and the list of our contributors shows that we have been able to draw from both. Nearly every one of the South African universities is represented in the list, while the names of Senator Malan, Mr J. H. Hofmeyr, Minister of the Interior, Mr Justice Watermeyer and Dr S. F. N. Gie, Minister of the Union of South Africa in Berlin, give evidence of the assistance we have received from men of outstanding position in the public services of the Union. While the work was in progress, historical scholarship suffered severe losses by the death of three of our most valued contributors, Sir George Cory, the doyen of South African historians, Cecil Headlam, the accomplished editor of *The Milner Papers*, and Professor John Ewing. Fortunately their chapters were already completed, except for the final proof correction, for which the editors have been responsible.

We desire to express our warmest acknowledgments and thanks to all our contributors, to Mr A. C. G. Lloyd and Mr A. T. Milne for their work in connection with the bibliography and particularly to our Advisor in South Africa, Professor Eric Walker of the University of Cape Town, whose assistance and advice at every stage of the work, placed at our service without stint, have been invaluable.

For the spelling of South African place-names we have, where possible, taken the *Post Office Guide* of the Union of South Africa as our criterion. In regard to Native names, both of persons and places, we have taken a middle course. An exact rendering of Bantu names according to the latest decisions of linguistic experts would have been puzzling to most of our readers, and many traditional names would have been almost unrecognisable. In Professor Schapera's chapter on the natives we have adopted the most accurate forms ascertainable, with the necessary peculiarities of type-setting, but elsewhere throughout the work we have adopted a compromise. If the name is well known and has acquired a traditional form of spelling, we have retained it in the text, but have added the other forms in the index. In other cases we have used an approximately correct spelling in the text without the addition of clicks and other minor points. We trust that in this difficult and somewhat debatable matter we may receive the indulgence of our readers.

A. P. N.
E. A. B.

July 1936

PREFACE TO THE SECOND EDITION

THE volume of the *Cambridge History of the British Empire* devoted to Southern Africa was first published in 1936 under the general editorship of A. P. Newton and E. A. Benians, and has now been out of print for some years. This new edition incorporates the results of recent research. Many chapters contain a fair number of revisions and corrections; two are rewritten (Professor L. Schapera has provided entirely new material for his chapter on "The Native Inhabitants", and the final chapter, on "Cultural Development", has been rewritten by Professors O. Doughty and E. A. Walker); and two other chapters have entirely new sections (chapter XXIV (b) on "Rhodesia" is now contributed by Professor K. Kirkwood, and chapter XXI (b) and (c) on "The Jameson Raid and its Consequences" by Professor Walker).

The second edition, like its predecessor, treats not only the history of the territories now forming the Republic of South Africa, but the whole of the African sub-continent south of the River Zambesi. The work covers the period from ancient and medieval times to 1921.

E. A. W.

January 1963

ABBREVIATIONS OF TITLES OF WORKS AND SOURCES QUOTED IN THIS VOLUME

A.O.	Audit Office Records, Public Record Office, London.
B.M. Add. MSS.	British Museum, Additional Manuscript.
B.T.	Board of Trade Records, Public Record Office, London.
Cape V. & P., H.A.	Cape Colony, Votes and Proceedings, House of Assembly.
C.H.B.E.	Cambridge History of the British Empire.
C.J.	Great Britain, Parliament, House of Commons Journals.
C.O.	Colonial Office Records, Public Record Office, London.
C.O. (Cape Archives)	Colonial Office Records, Cape Archives, Cape Town.
F.O.	Foreign Office Records, Public Record Office, London.
Hansard	Hansard's Parliamentary Debates.
Parl. Pap.	Great Britain, Parliament, House of Commons, Parliamentary Papers. The references are to the Session, the volume, the sessional or command number of the paper, and the pages of the paper.
P.R.O.	Public Record Office, London.
S.C.	Union of South Africa, Parliament, Select Committee Report.
U.G.	Union of South Africa, Union Government Report.

TABLE OF CONTENTS

CHAPTER I

THE GEOGRAPHICAL ENVIRONMENT

By P. Serton, Litt.D., Professor of Geography in the University of Stellenbosch, South Africa.

CHAPTER II

THE NATIVE INHABITANTS

By I. Schapera, M.A., Ph.D., Professor of Social Anthropology in the University of London.

CHAPTER III

AFRICA IN ANCIENT AND MEDIEVAL TIMES

By E. H. Warmington, M.A., Professor of Classics in the University of London (Birkbeck College).

CHAPTER IV

THE PORTUGUESE IN SOUTH AFRICA

By EDGAR PRESTAGE, D.Litt., Camoens Professor of Portuguese Literature and History in the University of London, and the late A. P. NEWTON, D.Litt., F.S.A., Rhodes Professor of Imperial History in the University of London.

CHAPTER V

FOUNDATION OF THE CAPE COLONY, 1652–1708

By the late LEO FOUCHÉ, B.A., Ph.D., Litt.D., sometime Professor in the University of Pretoria, and sometime Professor of History in the University of the Witwatersrand, Johannesburg, South Africa.

CHAPTER VI

THE CAPE COLONY UNDER COMPANY RULE, 1708–1795

By the late S. F. N. Gie, B.A., Ph.D., sometime Professor of South African History in the University of Stellenbosch, Minister Plenipotentiary for the Union of South Africa at Berlin.

CHAPTER VII

THE BRITISH OCCUPATIONS, 1795–1806

By the late Vincent T. Harlow, D.Litt., sometimes Beit Lecturer on Colonial History, Beit Professor of Imperial History in the University of Oxford, Keeper of the Library, Rhodes House, Oxford.

CHAPTER VIII

CAPE COLONY, 1806–1822

By the late VINCENT T. HARLOW, D.Litt.

CHAPTER IX

THE BRITISH SETTLERS OF 1820

By the late Sir GEORGE CORY, M.A., Litt.D., sometime Professor at the Rhodes University College, Grahamstown, South Africa, and Honorary Archivist of the Union of South Africa.

CHAPTER X

POLITICAL DEVELOPMENT, 1822–1834

By W. M. Macmillan, M.A., Research Fellow and sometime Professor of History in the University of Witwatersrand, Johannesburg, South Africa.

CHAPTER XI

SLAVERY AT THE CAPE, 1652–1838

By A. F. Hattersley, M.A., D.Litt., Emeritus Professor of History, University of Natal.

CHAPTER XII

THE PROBLEM OF THE COLOURED PEOPLE, 1792–1842

By W. M. Macmillan, M.A.

CHAPTER XIII

THE FRONTIER AND THE KAFFIR WARS, 1792–1836

By W. M. Macmillan, M.A.

CHAPTER XIV

THE FORMATION OF NEW STATES, 1835–1854

By Eric A. Walker, M.A., sometime King George V Professor of History in the University of Cape Town, South Africa, Professor Emeritus of Imperial History in the University of Cambridge.

CHAPTER XV

CONSTITUTIONAL DEVELOPMENT, 1834–1858

By H. J. MANDELBROTE, M.A., LL.B., King George V Professor of History in the University of Cape Town, South Africa.

CHAPTER XVI

THE PERIOD OF TRANSITION IN SOUTH AFRICAN POLICY, 1854–1870

By C. W. de Keiwiet, M.A., Ph.D., Assistant Professor of History in the State University of Iowa, U.S.A. and President of Rochester University, N.Y.

CHAPTER XVII

THE ESTABLISHMENT OF RESPONSIBLE GOVERNMENT IN CAPE COLONY, 1870–1872

By C. W. DE KIEWIET, M.A., Ph.D.

CHAPTER XVIII

THE FAILURE OF CONFEDERATION, 1871–1881

By the late CECIL HEADLAM, M.A., Editor of the *Calendar of State Papers, Colonial Series.*

CHAPTER XIX

POLITICAL DEVELOPMENT, 1872–1886

By the late J. H. Hofmeyr, M.A., M.P., sometime Minister of the Interior of the Union of South Africa.

CHAPTER XX

THE RACE FOR THE INTERIOR, 1881–1895

By the late Cecil Headlam, M.A.

CHAPTER XXI

THE PROBLEM OF CO-OPERATION, 1886–1895

(*a*) RAILWAYS, CUSTOMS AND THE NON-EUROPEAN QUESTION

By the late J. H. HOFMEYR, M.A., M.P.

(*b*) THE JAMESON RAID

By the late CECIL HEADLAM, M.A. and Professor E. A. WALKER

CHAPTER XXII

THE STRUGGLE FOR SUPREMACY, 1896–1902

By Professor Eric A. Walker, M.A.

CHAPTER XXIII

THE FORMATION OF THE UNION, 1901–1910

By the Lord Leconfield, B.A.

CHAPTER XXIV

SOUTH AFRICA AFTER THE UNION, 1910–1921

(*a*) THE UNION OF SOUTH AFRICA

By the late Rt. Hon. Senator F. S. Malan, P.C., B.A., LL.D., sometime Minister of Mines and Industries of the Union of South Africa.

(*b*) RHODESIA

By Professor Kenneth Kirkwood, M.A., Rhodes Professor of Race Relations, University of Oxford.

(*c*) THE HIGH COMMISSION TERRITORIES

By W. M. Macmillan, M.A.

CHAPTER XXV

THE UNION CONSTITUTION AND ITS WORKING

By H. J. Mandelbrote, M.A., LL.B.

CHAPTER XXVI

THE GERMANS IN SOUTH-WEST AFRICA, 1883–1914

(*a*) THE MILITARY OCCUPATION, 1883–1907

By H. Vedder, Ph.D., Okahandja, South-West Africa.

(*b*) CIVIL ADMINISTRATION AND ECONOMIC CONDITIONS

By Veit Valentin, Ph.D., sometime Professor of History in the University of Freiburg-im-Breisgau.

CHAPTER XXVII

SOUTH AFRICA IN THE WORLD WAR

By the late John Ewing, M.A., sometime Professor of History at the Rhodes University College, Grahamstown, South Africa.

CHAPTER XXVIII

SOUTH AFRICA AND THE EMPIRE

By Professor Eric A. Walker, M.A.

CHAPTER XXIX

ECONOMIC DEVELOPMENT, 1795–1921

By Sir Arnold Plant, B.Sc., B.Com., sometime Professor of Commerce in the University of Cape Town, Professor of Commerce in the University of London.

CHAPTER XXX

SOCIAL AND ECONOMIC DEVELOPMENTS IN NATIVE TRIBAL LIFE

By C. W. de Kiewiet, M.A., Ph.D.

CHAPTER XXXI

THE ROMAN-DUTCH LAW IN SOUTH AFRICA

By the late Rt. Hon. Chief Justice E. F. Watermeyer, M.A., South Africa.

CHAPTER XXXII

CULTURAL DEVELOPMENT

By Professor Oswald Doughty and Professor E. A. Walker.

CHAPTER I

THE GEOGRAPHICAL ENVIRONMENT

SOUTH Africa is one of the four self-governing Dominions of the British Commonwealth which belong to the great continental mass of the Old World.[1] This fact has been of fundamental importance in the country's early history. Age after age culture elements from the North have slowly but persistently trickled down from tribe to tribe, making even the southernmost corner of the continent less foreign to the white man than America or Australia. Cattle and sheep that could be obtained by barter from the Natives were one of the chief inducements towards the founding of a permanent settlement in a country otherwise singularly poor in commercial attractions, although iron tools and weapons had reached the remote south of the continent before the period of European discovery.

Nevertheless, it is clear that, in relation to Europe, South Africa has a comparatively isolated position. The early Arab trade in the Indian Ocean did not reach beyond Cape Correntes and only the extreme north-east of the region has undergone any marked influence from this side. On the west the climatic barrier of the Sahara and the political barrier of Islam have proved so effective against European expansion that Central and South Africa were in the Middle Ages quite as far off and unknown as America and Australia. They were discovered by sea; practically the whole of their foreign trade still goes by sea, and their political relations with Europe have until recent times been exclusively maritime.

Tropical Africa has until recently been a negligible factor in the economic development of South Africa, while Australia and South America show so much similarity in production with South Africa that the possibilities of trade with these regions are very limited. Even to-day no special shipping lines are required for the purpose: the more or less incidental communications maintained by steamers passing the Cape from Great Britain and the Far East are quite sufficient. The different subantarctic islands which are the nearest fragments of land to the subcontinent have importance only as meteorological and as whaling stations. Less than 2000 miles separate Cape Agulhas from the average northern limit of the pack-ice, beyond which lies the most inaccessible part of the polar wastes, and the intervening ocean, beset with storms and icebergs, is avoided by shipping, even at the cost of substituting the long east-west courses for the great circle routes.

In short, South Africa is one of the southern outposts of the habitable world. The isolation of the country was to a certain extent

[1] South Africa became a republic outside the Commonwealth on 31 May 1961.

masked in the pre-Suez-Canal days by the position of the Cape on the sailing routes to southern Asia. Though there was little export trade, the farmer found some kind of an outside market in the passing ships and in the often considerable garrison which the strategic importance of the settlement made necessary. The special significance of the Cape dated only from the rise of Dutch and English trade in the Indian Ocean, and more particularly from 1611, when Hendrik Brouwer proved the superior value of the southerly route leading to the Straits of Sunda. From that time sailing ships trading between western Europe and the Indies made their outward and homeward voyages through entirely different waters, seeking to avoid as much as possible regions where winds and currents were unfavourable. In the Java trade there were only two points on the surface of the ocean which a ship must pass both on the outward and the homeward voyage—one of them in the middle of the Atlantic, the other the Cape. The routes to ports of mainland India were more complicated by seasonal differences due to the monsoons. In all cases, however, the South African coast was the only shore within easy reach of East Indiamen, both outward and homeward bound, at every season of the year. No other point than the Cape of Good Hope was suitable for a permanent refreshment station—a fact commonly overlooked in the explanation of the founding of the Cape settlement as a "halfway-house". The halfway-point, reckoned in steamship miles, lies somewhere between Table Bay and the island of St Helena; but reckoned in sailing days St Helena is itself the exact middle point of the voyage from Batavia to the English Channel, and was actually in use by the home-bound ships of the Dutch East India Company before the Directors of that body chose the Cape in its place.

The reason for the Directors' preference is indicated in the *Remonstrantie* of Janszoon and Proot (1649).[1] They wanted a port that could also serve on the outward voyage, when winds and currents forced the ships to sail round to the south-westward of St Helena in a semicircular curve of 1200 miles' radius. During the century of Portuguese predominance in the Indian trade the position of the Cape was far less important on account of the different system of navigation then prevailing. In the Atlantic the Portuguese had soon discovered the correct routes, which are, with minor changes only, still followed by present-day sailing vessels. In the Indian Ocean, on the other hand, they followed the more primitive Arab system of monsoon navigation, sailing out and back by more or less the same route, which meant that they had to wait in each case for the favourable season. Consequently they might have used any point on the African coast between the Cape and Mozambique as a port of call in either direction. But the Portuguese held numerous possessions in different parts of the Atlantic. On the outward voyage they could

[1] *Vide infra*, p. 113.

call at Madeira, the Cape Verde Islands and, in case of necessity, Brazil; on the homeward at St Helena and the Azores. With this favourable distribution of their Atlantic settlements, they had little need of a new station at the south-western extremity of Africa, and naturally founded their South African headquarters far up the east coast in Mozambique at the other end of their 2000-mile coasting trip, where monsoon navigation began and often made it necessary to wait for the right season.

The unique strategic and commercial significance of the Cape passed away rapidly when the general use of steamships made it possible for sailors to follow nearly identical routes outward and homeward at the very time that the opening of the Suez Canal in 1869 took away the bulk of the eastern trade.

The coast of South Africa is not favourable for traffic. Long stretches of sandy beach alternate with rocks and cliffs, which in a few instances run out to sea in proud headlands. The bays behind these capes are wide and open, giving free entrance to the swell and affording very little shelter to shipping. Not a single river mouth in the Union has sufficient depth in its natural state to admit sea-going vessels of modest dimensions. The drowned valley of Saldanha Bay was the only real harbour on the whole coast, but its value as a port of call and potential site for a settlement was greatly diminished by a low rainfall and the absence of fresh water, while its situation up the west coast was unfavourable for outward-bound East Indiamen. Only after the middle of the nineteenth century did artificial harbours become financially possible, so that for the first two hundred years of the Cape Colony's existence port facilities were very primitive.

The Agulhas Bank competes with the Cape Horn region for the honour of having the highest waves in the world. No wonder that South Africa had a bad reputation among the old seafarers, and that shipwrecks play a prominent part in its early history. Shipwrecks occurred frequently even in Table Bay itself before the construction of the breakwater in the eighteen-sixties.

The ocean currents have had their influence in shaping both the old sailing routes and those of the modern steamship. Down the east and south coast runs the strong Agulhas Current with a speed varying from 30 to 100 miles a day. Some remarkable instances are recorded of its puzzling effects on the movements of sailing vessels in the days before its peculiarities were well known. Its strength is greatest in the deep water outside the Agulhas Bank; inshore it is much weaker, and counter-currents may even be found. For this reason eastward-bound steamers keep near the coast, while westward-bound ships stand well out. A branch of this current runs all along the south coast and even passes Cape Point; the main body, however, curves round to the east on encountering the great Antarctic Drift, which encircles the earth south of latitude 40°. The Benguela Current, which runs up the west coast, is partly fed by a branch from this drift originating near Cape Point.

The steamship routes between England and Australia *via* the Cape well illustrate the influence which currents and wind conditions have on navigation even at the present day. Outward-bound ships in the Indian Ocean keep well south of 40°, and usually have Cape Town as their only South African port of call. On the return voyage the best route lies in about latitude 30° and leads straight to Durban.

The Agulhas Current coming from the tropics is warm; the Antarctic Drift and the Benguela Current are cold. Along the west coast of South Africa this low temperature is accentuated by the rising of very cold water from the depths of the ocean. In the region where warm and cold water meet and intermingle, currents, waves and weather conditions are very irregular, and this seems to be the principal reason why the Cape seas were so dangerous for the old sailing ships. The difference in sea-water temperature between the west and east coasts is very marked and has a profound influence on climate.

On the basis of human geography no definite boundary can be drawn between South and Central Africa. At present one would be inclined to choose the Kunene-Zambesi line.[1] The geographical concept of "South" Africa is more or less vague, but there is at least one good reason why the Kunene-Zambesi line should be taken as a fairly satisfactory northern limit.

Typically South African conditions may be said to exist as far north as the country is fit for permanent settlement of both the white and the black races. The sandy coast-belt and the tropical northern corner of South-West Africa are inhospitable, and even within the Union there are districts which can hardly be called fit for Europeans. In Southern Rhodesia these undesirable regions become more extensive, but there is still an important area of high altitude and cool climate, which leaves the general character of the country distinctly South African. The farther north we go, the more these favourable parts of the country become isolated patches, but even in Kenya there is a region whose social and economic conditions show affinities with South Africa. On the plateau lands to the north of the Zambesi, however, seasonal differences in temperature which contribute so much to the well-being of a white population, become small though not negligible. Moreover, it should be remembered that our meteorological tables give only the temperature of the air measured in the shadow, a very different thing from the heating power and chemical effect of the direct rays of the sun as experienced by a man working on the land. Both these last are greater on the plateaux than in coastal lowlands of the same latitude whose air temperature is much

[1] I.e. the northern frontiers of South-West Africa and Southern Rhodesia.

higher. Life in the tropical highlands may be very pleasant to the white man whose work permits him to protect himself from the worst effects of the sunshine, but a white labour-class is hardly possible there and Europeans will always form a far smaller percentage of the population than in the Union. Southern Rhodesia experiences these difficulties to a certain extent, but that territory must certainly be included within any boundary selected. The copperfields of Northern Rhodesia have a comparatively large white population, which is, however, insufficient to change the general character of the country. For the present it does not seem advisable to extend the geographical notion of South Africa to the country beyond the Zambesi.

If we exclude the low-lying Portuguese territory on the east coast, the country south of the Kunene-Zambesi line comprises 1·25 million square miles, an imposing figure on the European scale, more than double the combined area of France, Germany and the British Isles, but far behind the 3 million square miles of Australia or the 3·7 million of Canada. It should be borne in mind, however, that fully one-half of South Africa, as here defined, is fit for effective occupation by white men against little more than one-quarter in Australia.

The area of a country forms one of the important geographical controls in its history, and it has been particularly potent in South Africa. In Australia the area that is neither too dry nor too hot for active European farming is scarcely 30 per cent larger than in South Africa, and it would be a mistake to consider difference in area as a reason why the Australian immigration figures are so much higher than those for the Union and Rhodesia. Canada and Australia carry an immense dead weight of undeveloped territory without much historical importance.[1] Space and distance have played in South African history quite as large a part as they have done in the development of the other Dominions.

The area of a country may be compared with that of others to form an estimate of its importance among the nations of the world, but we may also compare the number of square miles with that of the people living on them to find how much room there is for each individual. In South Africa this figure has always been high. From an early date the farm of 6000 acres has been typical, not only in dry regions but also in districts which are to-day fit for intensive methods of production. This means that in South Africa a given area has been considered to be fully occupied far sooner than it would have been for instance in Canada, and that the individual farmer has always been far more isolated. The results have been slow communications, poor markets, imperfect control by Government, difficulty of keeping in touch with Church and school, a conservative frame of mind and strong self-reliance.

[1] Valuable minerals are now being worked in Canada north of the settled agricultural and industrial transcontinental belt.

Before the days of mechanical transport travelling was done on horseback or, where road conditions permitted, in horse-drawn vehicles. Typical for the old districts was the two-wheeled "kapkar" i.e. hooded cart for passenger traffic (by misunderstanding usually called "Cape cart" in English). It is drawn by two horses or mules and is still in use by some country people who cannot afford a motor car.

Far more important historically is the ox-waggon, which served for the transport of heavy goods and for human travel over long distances when a great load of baggage was necessary. It moved slowly, but with a supreme disregard for minor obstructions. It needed no elaborate road system; twelve or fourteen strong oxen would pull a waggon anywhere so long as water and grass were available. At night there was, under the great white hood, a comfortable bed consisting of a wooden frame spanned with intertwined thongs (another often swinging below between the wheels) with prepared antelope skins for mattress and blankets, an ideal conveyance for a pastoral people always on the move but not inclined to attach much value to time. More than a mere conveyance: a home, and in native warfare, when at every halting place the waggons would be drawn up into a "laager" or waggon-ring, a movable fortification.

When the travellers came to a mountain range, there was no question of climbing a pass in easy zigzags; they searched about for the lowest place and the best gradients offered by nature and set their oxen to pull. At difficult spots the ox-spans of two or three waggons would be joined to bring their loads over by turns, and for this purpose, as well as for mutual safety, people tried to avoid travelling alone. Downhill the waggons were often lowered with ropes. In very bad cases they were taken to pieces and everything was carried over, as on a Canadian portage. The historian, who sees the remains of old waggon tracks still visible on many mountain passes, no longer wonders why ideas spread slowly among people who depended upon such roads for communication with the outside world.

Less serious were the difficulties of rivers; even the largest had their "drifts" i.e. fords, which were impassable only during high-water periods. To-day the main routes are provided with bridges over all rivers of any importance, but on secondary roads the drift problem still exists and often causes more trouble for the modern motor driver than for the old-time waggon traffic.

The ox-waggon belongs to the past; it is still in use for farm work and local transport, but railway and motor traffic have done away with its romantic prominence in South African life. Moreover, the cheaper donkey is often used as draft animal for heavy waggons (in teams of up to sixteen), since most transport is now done over smooth roads and reasonable gradients.

The interior of South Africa is an extensive plateau, for the most part from 4000 to 6000 feet above sea-level, either undulating or forming wide plains, but even in its flattest parts dotted with isolated hills (*kopjes* or *koppies*). The lowest part of this area (3000 feet and less) runs in a wide strip through the Kalahari from the Orange River to the Zambesi, and from this low-lying belt the land rises gradually in all directions towards the high rim of the plateau. This rim consists of rather irregular mountain masses in South-West Africa; but within the Union it forms on the whole a regular escarpment running from the Roggeveld Mountains in the south-west to the Drakensberg in the east, where it offers most serious obstacles to all forms of transport and culminates in the gigantic eastern ramparts of the natural fortress of Basutoland.

The watercourses in the south of the great plateau belong to the Orange River system. The valleys are shallow, the rivers themselves are comparatively slow, and, except during the short high-water periods, offer no serious hindrance to primitive ox-waggon traffic. In Basutoland and the adjoining districts alone, where thick layers of basaltic lava have been piled upon the old land surface to Alpine heights, there are swift and deep valleys, cutting up the whole region into wild mountains, where communications are difficult and military defence is easy. There lies the stronghold of the Basuto like a pocket edition of Abyssinia.

The Limpopo and Zambesi Rivers far away to the north have cut into the great plateau far more deeply than has the Orange River. Lower altitude and tropical situation make their valleys very unhealthy and constitute them two broad belts which are inimical to settlement and traffic and thereby in great measure isolate the plateau of Southern Rhodesia.

Still more pronounced is the contrast between the Orange system and the short but swift rivers that run towards the south and south-east coasts from the escarpment of the central plateau, at whose foot the altitude is still 3000–4000 feet and, here and there, even more. Many of these rivers in their lower reaches flow through deep gorges with steep, densely wooded sides. The country drained by them can be divided into a south-western and a south-eastern section, differing markedly from one another. In the south-eastern the land descends towards the coast in terraces, but orographical conditions are by no means simple. The rainfall is high when measured by South African standards; the rivers are perennial; erosion is strong, the country is deeply dissected by a network of valleys, and outlying parts of the plateau help to complicate the relief.

Towards the south-west and south coasts the transition area has a different character. The Great Karoo, a second plateau of lower altitude (2000–3000 feet), lies here at the foot of the escarpment and is bordered in its turn by a folded mountain system, which stretches under various names from the Olifants River to the Fish River. These ranges, though higher and steeper on the coastal than on the landward side, are not mere escarpments but real mountain chains. The highest summits reach 6000–7000 feet. Among these mountains there is room for settlement and traffic in a number of basins and wide longitudinal valleys, like those of the Olifants and Breede Rivers, the Basin of Tulbagh, the surroundings of Oudtshoorn (Little Karoo), Langkloof, etc. The transverse valleys are unfavourable for transport. They mostly form deep, narrow gorges, where road-making was impossible before the nineteenth century brought dynamite and greater financial resources. Man and beast could cross the ranges by difficult footpaths, but for waggons the obstacles were often almost insurmountable. Consequently this mountain system has formed a serious barrier between the coastal regions and the interior. The expansion of settlement followed the foot of the mountains, but only slowly crossed them. When finally white settlers established themselves in the Karoo, the farmers found it very difficult to bring their products to the Cape Town market. Not before the middle of the nineteenth century did modern roads cross the passes, and even then the construction of railways was handicapped because at the very beginning of the undertaking the difficulties of these mountain ranges had to be overcome.

The coastal region in the south has the character of a low plateau, in parts badly cut up by river valleys. In the west, from Cape Town northward, we find a true coastal plain with isolated hills. In contrast with the south-western mountains and the south-eastern terrace lands the Great Karoo and the central plateau have been favourable for all forms of human movement, wherever the water supply was sufficient. The only river in South Africa that has any value for shipping is the Zambesi, and then only for its last three hundred miles or so. A number of other streams are navigable for launches for a few miles in their lower reaches, but they are nowhere of commercial importance. Consequently the country was entirely without modern means of traffic before the building of the railways. Until that time the ox-waggon was supreme. But the rivers furnished water for farms and domestic use, which gave them some importance, for before the era of boreholes and wind-pumps, settlement in South Africa was often dependent on running water.

The relief of South Africa is doubtless the same to-day as when Jan van Riebeeck landed in Table Bay, for geological processes are almost always too slow to have any appreciable effect in a few hundred years. On the other hand far-reaching climatic changes are possible in historical time. Small changes, occupying a short series of years, can be detected by the study of meteorological records. Such changes are mostly of an oscillating character, often showing a certain rhythmical periodicity. It has been maintained, however, that South Africa's rainfall is diminishing at a quite extraordinary rate. The historical foundations of this hypothesis are very weak, the arguments being based on a few disconnected scraps of information. Investigation of the climatic data for the Eastern Karoo in all the available records of eighteenth- and early nineteenth-century travellers suggests that one trait at least of South Africa's climate is the same today as in the eighteenth century: its irregularity. The great difference in the rainfall and the appearance of vegetation from one year to another explains why two authors, who visited the same spot at only a few years' interval, may describe it in the most divergent terms, one depicting as a paradise what to the other seems little better than a desert.

The general impression left by a study of this kind is that the essential characteristics of the climate have not changed during the last two centuries, but that minor modifications are by no means improbable. The popular belief that formerly the rainfall used to be less torrential and more steady in character finds a good deal of support in the descriptions of the eighteenth-century writers. And though there is no sufficient reason to believe that the amount of precipitation has diminished, such a change of character would have a decided influence on the usefulness of the rainfall. There is further little doubt that the flow of the rivers has become more irregular, that many "fountains" have dried up, and that the vegetation in different regions has deteriorated; but these phenomena can be explained from human causes: over-stocking, veld-burning, carelessness in stopping erosion, etc. Good results are being obtained where these evils have been fought systematically. Sensational statements representing South Africa as a country condemned to die of thirst have never yet been supported by sound arguments.[1]

The continent of Africa is almost evenly divided by the Equator. The latitudes between which South Africa is situated correspond very closely with those of the various North African countries. Cape Agulhas, for example, may be compared with the Moroccan Rif, Cape Town with Fez, Durban with Cairo, the Rand with Assiut. Both the northern Transvaal and the extreme south of Egypt are just inside the tropics. It would be very misleading, however, to make such comparisons the basis for an estimate of temperature conditions. The southern hemisphere is, latitude for latitude, cooler than the northern, and the "thermic equator" crosses Africa between 10° and 20° north. Moreover, the altitude of the South African plateaux forms an additional reason why the climate is not so warm as might be expected. To find the average temperatures corresponding to those of the Union, we have to look towards southern Europe and not to

[1] See Schumann, T. E. W. and Thompson, W. R., *A Study of South African Rainfall*. Also *Report of the Desert Encroachment Committee*, 1951.

the Nile Valley and the Sahara. Moreover, the comparatively low averages are primarily caused by moderate summer temperatures which are lower in Cape Town than in Lyons or Budapest. The winters of the Cape Peninsula correspond to those of Gibraltar.

In discussing the possibilities of emigration to a warmer country, the summer temperatures are the main factor to be taken into account. Nearly all the ancestors of the present white population of South Africa came from temperate lands: the Netherlands, France, Germany and the British Isles, and they found far more tolerable summer-conditions than they would have found under the same latitude in North Africa. If they missed the colder winters of Europe, yet the seasonal differences remained great enough for the physical well-being of a white population. The high proportion of healthy, strongly built men and women and their success in every branch of sport give ample evidence on this point. Whether such a soft and sunny climate is equally auspicious for mental activities seems less certain.

It has been of great historical importance that the colonist, trekking northward, found for long distances no appreciable rise in average temperature, the increase in insolation being compensated by that in altitude. Johannesburg is actually cooler than Cape Town, and even Salisbury in the tropics is not very much warmer. The temperature conditions most nearly approaching those of western Europe are not found on the south coast but in the Upper Karoo.

The principal difference between two stations, which like Nantes and Sutherland in the Upper Karoo are closely similar in their yearly average of temperature, is the greater daily variation on the South African plateau.[1] A bitterly cold winter night is often followed by an afternoon suggestive of English summer weather.

The narrow strip of lowland along the east coast, strongly influenced by the Agulhas Current, is very warm and from Zululand northward malarious. This has greatly hindered the development of the Portuguese settlements and goes far to explain their slow advance towards the interior. The healthy plateau remained unoccupied and lay open to political influence from the south. The low-lying portions of the Transvaal and Southern Rhodesia and the northern parts of the Kalahari and of South-West Africa are also unhealthy. Malaria has been even more important than temperature itself in limiting the extension of white settlement. As the boundaries of the malarious regions are being slowly but continuously pushed back, there is room for a certain amount of expansion in so far as the land is not reserved for non-Europeans.

[1] *Comparison of European and South African Temperatures.*

Average temperature in ° F.	Year	Warmest month	Coldest month	Difference	Mean yearly Minimum	Mean yearly Maximum
Sutherland (Upper Karoo)	52·3	64·9	39·2	25·7	14·9	94·3
Nantes (France)	52·2	65·7	40·1	25·6	17·1	93·6

The west coast, washed by cold seas, has a cool climate and, except in the extreme north, is free from malaria, but it is useless for farming on account of drought. From Port Nolloth to the Kunene River the coast belt is absolute desert.

The remarkable degree of uniformity in average temperature, which is characteristic of large areas in South Africa, causes climatic regions to be distinguished mainly on the basis of rainfall data. On the east and south coasts above the surface of the Agulhas Current, there is warm air heavily laden with water vapour. When carried landwards by the prevailing south-east winds of the summer months, this air is easily cooled and gives large amounts of rain. Above the cold sea on the west coast the cool air has little water vapour. If this reaches the land, it is usually warmed and hence no condensation is possible. Even in winter, when the land is at its coldest, conditions in these parts are seldom sufficiently favourable for rainfall. Northward, as the temperature of the land rises and that of the sea falls at first, the greatest contrast between them is found on the coast of South-West Africa. This fact, combined with the distribution of barometric pressure, gives the neighbourhood of Walvis Bay the lowest rainfall of the continent south of the Equator, and a comparatively dry climate continues till near the Congo estuary.

Ocean temperatures and seasonal changes in barometric pressure form the main controls in the distribution of South African rainfall. Over a large area in the centre of the sub-continent, summer rains are experienced in conjunction with low pressure. These rains are strongest on the east coast, and diminish gradually towards the west. A small region of winter rains is found in the extreme south-western corner of the continent, where the contrast between sea and land temperatures is not yet too marked and the influence of the winterly cyclones is strongly felt. This is the only part of the west coast that receives any appreciable amount of rain. The south coast, from the Breede River to East London, has its rains more or less evenly distributed over the year, but the amount varies a good deal from one place to another. The wettest part is found in the middle round the Knysna forest lands.

Locally these rainfall conditions are modified by relief. Many steep mountain sides facing the rain-bearing winds receive a large amount of precipitation. On the other hand, in the rain shadow of the coastal ranges there are very dry areas even in the vicinity of the warm sea, e.g. the western Karoo, which receives less rain than any part of the Kalahari.

While the probability of climatic changes in historical times remains an open question, there is no doubt that the vegetation of South Africa differs a good deal to-day from that which the first colonists found, yet the general character of the geographical distribution remains the same, the changes taking the form of a deterioration of existing plant associations. Over-grazing destroys the grasses and valuable bushes but leaves the inedible plants free to develop; veld-burning kills trees and large bushes, while the smaller shrubs and grasses soon recover after a fire.

Trees need on the whole more water than grasses and certainly a more regular supply. Grass veld can easily stand a long dry season; forests cannot. A given amount of winter rain has, moreover, a higher value than an equal amount in summer, because during the cold season there is less evaporation and the water soaks deeper into the subsoil. With the exception of a few remarkable examples of relief rain, the precipitation in South Africa, as we have said, is nowhere very high; nearly everywhere there is a long dry season, and by far the greater part of the country gets its rain in summer. For these reasons there are no extensive forests. Natural forests are found in favoured localities only—in the small area of abundant and evenly distributed rainfall on the south coast round Knysna, in deep moist river valleys and on mountain sides with strong relief rains. It is a well-known fact that the extension of natural forests is by no means an indication of the possibilities of tree planting. A little care on the part of man will help the trees over the first difficult years, and is often sufficient to establish large woods in the moister parts of the grass veld. In most cases these consist of European firs or Australian eucalypt and wattle trees; the indigenous South African species give excellent hard timbers, but as they are nearly all slow growers there is no profit in cultivating them. The commercial possibilities of tree planting are only now being realised by landowners.

The natural type of vegetation for a country like South Africa is the steppe, either in the form of grasslands or of Karoo veld, which is even better adapted to withstand long droughts. The meaning of the term "veld" in South Africa differs widely from that of its English etymological equivalent "field". Here, as in so many cases, the geographical terminology of the country reflects the mind of the stock-farmer. Veld means originally land with a natural vegetation more or less fit for grazing purposes. The term is not applied to cultivated ground, nor is it used to indicate true forest. In Great Britain only moorlands, heaths and other half-waste areas could be called veld in this sense. The term is used with different qualifications, indicating specialised forms of localities. Expressions like grass veld, bush veld, Karoo veld, high veld, low veld, sand veld, mountain veld, sour veld (deficient in lime), sweet veld and many others are of frequent occurrence. It should be borne in mind that different names may be applied to the same stretch of veld according to the point of view from which it is being considered. Grass veld may be sour or sweet; but sour veld need not always be covered with grass.

It may also carry a vegetation of shrubs. The same holds good for mountain veld and sand veld.

The Karoo vegetation is composed of small shrubs and makes no favourable impression at first sight. There is a superficial resemblance to a European heath in a very dry and poor condition, but many of the bushes have high nutritive qualities for sheep and goats, and thus the region is fit for stock-farming on extensive lines. Grass veld, poor in trees, occupies the eastern and north-eastern interior of the Union, Karoo veld is found in the west; the boundary between the two runs through the south-western Free State. The grass veld is comparable to the prairies of North America or the pampas of the Argentine. After heavy summer rains the colour of the landscape may for a short time approach the rich green of English meadows, but the impression is deceptive; the grass is coarser than in western Europe, it grows higher and in the dry season soon withers into a natural hay of yellow-brown colour. In tropical and sub-tropical regions the grass veld is often interspersed with numerous trees and is then indicated as bush veld, a savanna formation. This consists of open parklands, which must be clearly distinguished from true forest, as there is always enough grass for stock-farming. The combination of trees and grass on the same ground would be of great importance if health conditions were better. Bush veld is mostly malarious and therefore not so well settled as economic circumstances would permit.

Bush veld covers the better part of the northern and eastern Transvaal, and continues in a modified and impoverished form westward into the Kalahari. Apart from the worst sand-dune areas, this lonely country has far more tree growth than the designation "desert" on our maps would suggest. Grass veld with isolated trees is also found over a large part of Natal and the Eastern Province of the Cape; it is sometimes described as thorn veld. Furthermore, even in the driest parts of the Karoo the river banks are usually clothed with thorn trees. Though many of these "rivers" have no visible water for eleven months out of twelve, there is always some moisture left in their depths.

In South Africa, as in many other steppe regions, it is open to discussion how far the absence of trees is a natural phenomenon and how far it may be ascribed to the influence of man. The Bantu enjoy a very bad reputation as destroyers of tree growth, and the first white men were little better. In certain areas the disappearance of trees has taken place in recent historic times. On the whole, however, we may take it that the interior of South Africa was always a wide open country, poor in trees, even if we cannot be positively certain how poor.[1]

[1] According to Acocks there has been an appreciable diminution of forest in the eastern and southern coastal regions during the last five centuries, while the Karoo has been advancing into the grass veld, and good karoo veld in the west has become little better than desert. These processes are believed to be still actively going on, but to be reversible under

The winter-rain area of the south-west, the region of oldest colonisation, is not very favourable for grass growth. Characteristic of its natural vegetation are numerous kinds of shrubs and bushes, growing to a height of about six feet. Where undisturbed by fire, they clothe the mountain sides with a dense jungle of bronze-green colour, sharply distinguished from the low, sparse and greyish Karoo vegetation. It is the "maquis" of Mediterranean lands. In the moistest localities small patches of forest are found. Stock-farming is less important here than agriculture.

It should be remembered that, even inside the Union, owing to climatic conditions and partly also for economic reasons, less than 10 per cent of the land consists of either cultivated ground or forest. In the rest of the subcontinent the percentage must be lower. If we add to this certain areas of very dense scrub, useless sand, etc., there still remain fully nine-tenths of South Africa that may be described as veld of one form or another. Lonely farmhouses with their patches of cultivation, surrounded by vast stretches of grazing land, are typical of most parts of the country. Thus the character of the landscape depends to a far greater extent on *natural* vegetation than is the case in western Europe, and this explains why the names of different types of veld have been taken over for whole geographical regions.

Bush Veld as a proper name indicates the region with this type of vegetation in the northern Transvaal, regardless of the fact that there are large areas of bush veld in Rhodesia, Bechuanaland and the Mandated Territory. It is clear that in this secondary sense the term does not exclude the cultivated land and small forests found within the area. In the same way the High Veld is by no means all veld in the original sense of the word, as it has an important agricultural production.

It is somewhat confusing that local names given by farmers, who felt no need for systematic classification, have been taken over in maps and books, where their meaning often has to be modified to a certain extent. The high plateau of the southern Transvaal is the best part of that province for European occupation. In its eastern districts there is a rather sudden change to lower altitudes, higher temperature and bad health conditions, and it was along this border that the names high veld and low veld originated. Towards the north the change in altitude is less marked, and here the difference in vegetation was decisive for the choice of a local name: bush veld. It was only when people began to make maps that difficulties of delimitation arose. Much of the low veld is bush veld when considered from the standpoint of vegetation. Treeless grass veld covers a large part of the Free State as well as the southern Transvaal, and continues even into the Cape Province. On maps all this country is often called

scientific veld management. See *Report of the Desert Encroachment Committee* 1951; Acocks, J. P. H., *Veld Types of South Africa. Botanical Survey, Memoir* 28, 1953.

high veld, but anyone using the word in this extended sense in everyday life would probably be misunderstood.

The term "Karoo" is also used with various meanings, dependent on the point of view, topographical, geological, botanical or agricultural. As topographical names we have the Great Karoo, that is, the plateau between the Roggeveld Escarpment and the Zwartberg Range, and the lower-lying Little Karoo between the latter mountains and the coastal ranges. The climate of the Little Karoo is more varied and on the whole somewhat less dry; but more important for explaining the greater density of population is the comparative wealth of this region in irrigation water derived from the bordering mountains. This gives rise to intensive forms of agriculture side by side with extensive stock-farming of true Karoo type.

North of the Roggeveld Mountains the vegetation is very similar in general appearance and economic usefulness to that of the Great Karoo, but the scientific eye detects a great deal of difference, and in botanical works this region is often alluded to as the Karoid Plateau. It is hardly to be expected that such a name would have come into common use. The farmer calls all this country Karoo, even north of the Orange River. When it is desired to designate this northern part with a name of its own, it is sometimes called Upper Karoo.

The rainfall of the Little, Great and Upper Karoos diminishes from east to west, and in the same direction the vegetation becomes poorer, the population scantier, the farms larger. In the eastern Karoo districts 6000 acres are enough for a sheep farm; in the western 10,000 are considered a minimum, and farms of more than 20,000 acres are not exceptional. It is rather remarkable that the whole area is divided up into farms. There is no free land and consequently none of the problems about its use that give so much trouble in similar regions in North America (e.g. Utah, Nevada). Migratory movements of stock are common in the Karoo, but are due to commercial arrangements between different landowners.

On the basis of Köppen's classification of climates the greater part of the Karoo must undoubtedly be called desert.[1] Apart from climate however, a number of other geographical conditions are remarkably favourable for human settlement. The soil is extremely fertile; the natural vegetation is drought-resisting and of high value for small stock; underground water is as a rule within easy reach and railway facilities are comparatively good, because the main line to the north had to cross the region in its full breadth. For all these reasons the geographer can hardly classify the Karoo as desert; he will rather speak of a semi-desert region developed to the limits of its modest possibilities.

The Kalahari is at present a real desert as far as settlement, production and traffic are concerned. The reason is the absence of

[1] Köppen, W., *Grundriss der Klimakunde* (2nd impr. of *Die Klimate der Erde*).

permanent surface water, largely caused by the deep sandy soil. Climate and vegetation on the contrary do not justify the use of the term "desert", except in a small, south-western corner near the Orange River. The driest parts have a decidedly better climate than corresponding areas in the Karoo. Nature and man, however, while co-operating to develop the Karoo, have conspired to retard progress in the Kalahari. The region has little relief; there are no mountain chains to catch the rain and make irrigation possible along the resulting watercourses. The size of the unfavourable area is larger than in the Karoo, no lines of communication cross it, and little has yet been done to make underground water available. The best lands in the east are locked up in Native reserves, and the moister regions of the north-west, near Lake Ngami, are very unhealthy.

Probably the Kalahari will be a temporary desert only. Railway construction and systematic water-boring may be expected to bring a certain amount of development. At present, however, it remains a dangerous thirstland for any man who lacks intimate knowledge of the places where ground water can be reached.

The extraordinary richness of South Africa in big game is to-day largely a matter of the past, at least in so far as the Union is concerned. When van Riebeeck landed in 1652, lion and elephant, rhinoceros and hippopotamus were common in the immediate vicinity of Table Bay. Within the Union these are now found only in a few of the remotest districts. Game reserves have become a necessity to prevent the total destruction of many interesting species. Historically the wild fauna has been very important in the opening of the country to European influence. The numerous antelopes especially formed a never failing supply of food to any man who could handle a rifle. They enabled trader and missionary to travel with limited provisions; they made it unnecessary for the trek-boer to slaughter his own animals, and generally have contributed to that ease of movement which is so remarkable in South African history.

Some of the smaller carnivora are still fairly general. The most dangerous among these is the leopard, which is by no means extinct even in the mountains of the south-western Cape Province. Harmless to human beings, but serious as an economic problem, is the jackal, the enemy of the sheep farmer. Among the insects which have influenced the course of settlement may be named the malaria mosquito in the northern and eastern Transvaal and Zululand, the tsetse fly in restricted areas near the Portuguese border, and the locust.

In the south-western corner of the country the aborigines practised no agriculture; all cultivated plants have been directly imported by the white man. European grains, vegetables and fruit were grown from the start; as a matter of fact their cultivation was the chief reason for the founding of the new settlement, which was to serve as a "refreshment" station. When van Riebeeck left the Cape after ten years of office, viticulture, though still in its infancy, was already an established industry. The popular belief, which ascribes its introduction to the French refugees, may be explained by the improvement of local methods resulting from the arrival of experienced wine farmers. Wheatfields, orchards and vineyards remain typical of this winter-rain area to the present day. Combined with extensive planting of oaks and fir trees they give to the landscape the aspect of southern Europe. The fruit exports of this region consist mainly of pears, peaches, plums, apricots and grapes. A product of some importance in the south-west, which was introduced later, is Turkish tobacco.

The agricultural possibilities of the larger and more recently developed summer rain area are very different. Here the principal grain is maize, locally called "mealies". This was introduced into Africa only after the discovery of America, but is now of great importance both for the Natives and the white farmers. Millet has been grown all over the Dark Continent from time immemorial. The plant is hardy and the grain very nourishing, so that it deserves more attention from the white man than it receives; at present it is so much a Native product that the South African variety is known as "kaffir corn". Citrus fruit forms an important article of export. In the warmer parts of the summer rain area, sub-tropical and tropical products are found, such as cotton, groundnuts, pineapples, bananas, etc. The small but highly developed cane-sugar region on the coast of Natal is interesting. Even here the climate is not very favourable for this industry; neither heat nor moisture is quite sufficient, with the result that the cane grows and matures very slowly. The same climatic conditions, however, make this region more desirable from the human standpoint than ordinary tropical sugar countries. Combined with the advantages of a highly protected and comparatively extensive market, this explains the large production. Towards the north of the Natal coast there have been a number of tea plantations, but the acreage has dwindled to practically nothing, because sugar is more profitable.

Native cattle and sheep, obtained by barter from the Hottentots, formed the basis for the stock of the early colonists. The breeds that were developed were in both cases indicated as "Afrikaners" to distinguish them from imported European types. Afrikaner cattle are hardy and strong and unsurpassed as draught animals, a most important consideration in the pre-railway era. For dairying and meat production their value is not so high, and in modern times they have largely been replaced by Frisians and English beef cattle. Most of the animals in the hands of the Native population are of poor quality and little economic value.

Afrikaner sheep have hair instead of wool and are kept for their meat and fat only. In the beginning of the nineteenth century merinos began to replace the native breed, but even to-day this process has not yet led to its complete disappearance. It is especially adapted to drought conditions and holds its own in the more unfavourable regions. An imported race of haired sheep, also kept for meat only, are the Persians. Karakul sheep for astrakhan lamb-skins predominate in South-West Africa.

Goats, too, are used for slaughter purposes. They are numerous in the same districts as haired sheep and for the same reasons. The number of Angora goats has fallen far below the figures of forty years ago, but the Union remains even to-day the principal rival of Turkey in the production of Angora hair.

The ostrich, tamed in South Africa and the pride and glory of the Little Karoo for half a century from 1869 onwards, is comparatively unimportant nowadays. Only the best birds are still being kept by optimists, who hope for a return of high prices on the feather market.

South Africa is rich in mineral resources, but their distribution is rather remarkable. Practically nothing has been found within the old dominions of the Dutch East India Company, though the Directors were eager enough for mineral discoveries that might have made the Cape Colony financially self-supporting. As early as 1685 the Commander, Simon van der Stel, reached the copper deposits of Namaqualand, but he found that transport difficulties were too great for profitable working, and it was only recently that the highly portable diamond was discovered in the same area. Apart from the very poor coal of the Stormberg area, all other mines or diggings of any importance are situated north of the Orange River. Thus the mining industry could not begin in the interior till the Trekkers had established organised states in the middle of the nineteenth century, or in South-West Africa till the Germans had taken control. Unlike less valuable minerals, alluvial gold and diamonds need not wait for the railway to make their working possible. They are true pioneer industries that can be started under very primitive circumstances and are thus specially fitted to revolutionise social and political conditions. The fact that coal was near at hand greatly facilitated the quick development of the gold and, to a less extent, diamond mines in the Transvaal. The nature of the gold deposits may be mentioned as another geographical fact that helped to give the industry its revolutionary character. There is very little alluvial gold in South Africa. Gold diggings, where the individual worker tried his luck, have been exploited in Lydenburg and Barberton, but they have never reached the importance of those in Australia and California or of the diamond diggings in South Africa itself. The great field of the Witwatersrand, responsible for half the world's yearly production, has no room for the small man because its gold is finely distributed in a very hard rock that can only be obtained by deep mining, and has to undergo a long process of crushing and chemical treatment in expensive installations. Hence the Rand was a capitalistic field from the start, and there was nothing to ease the social transition from simple subsistence farming to modern economic conditions. Uranium has recently become a very important by-product of many of the gold mines.

The principal trade of South Africa is with western Europe and eastern North America, and carriage over distances of 6000 and 7000 miles forms even to-day a considerable handicap to the export of bulky or perishable products. Before the great fall in transport costs which characterised the nineteenth century, the export of farm produce was hardly possible on a commercial basis. An illuminating calculation is found in the memorandum wherein De Mist, Commissioner-General for the Batavian Republic in 1802,[1] explaining how conditions at the Cape might be improved by agricultural exports, gave figures for a cargo of wheat, with some wine, talc and aloes, sent to Holland in 1792 on board a troopship that would otherwise have returned in ballast. On sale these goods fetched two and a half times their Cape Town price. Yet the margin of profit was only $16\frac{1}{2}$ per cent; the rest went on cost of transport. Thus the Cape farmer had to be content with two-fifths of the European market price, if he wanted to sell for export. Seeing that these figures were given by way of encouragement, it is not astonishing that the efforts to send Cape products overseas should have met with so little success in the eighteenth century.

Comparative isolation is more advantageous to southern Africa from the point of view of political than of economic geography. The great problems of the Pacific, so vitally important to many other Dominions, are still relatively as remote from her as are the perils of the North Atlantic storm centre. It is true that entirely new means of destruction have been invented and the protective value of distance has been greatly reduced since the first edition of this volume was published in 1936; but there is still a certain amount of safety in being far removed from the chief sources of trouble. New dangers, nearer home, may arise from political developments in tropical Africa, but it is too early yet to estimate accurately their nature and extent.

[1] *Vide infra*, p. 195.

CHAPTER II

THE NATIVE INHABITANTS

WHEN the first Dutch settlers landed at Table Bay in 1652, the south-western parts of the modern Cape Province were occupied by two kinds of native peoples, afterwards known to Europeans as Bushmen and Hottentots. The Bushmen were short yellow-skinned hunters, who lived scattered about in small nomadic groups and spoke languages with peculiar "click" consonants. The Hottentots resembled them closely in appearance and speech, but were predominantly pastoral and lived in much larger communities.

The Hottentots had come into contact with Europeans as far back as 1497, when Vasco da Gama encountered them at St Helena Bay, and their slaughter of Francisco d'Almeida and many of his companions at Table Bay in 1510 showed that they could not be offended with impunity. Later callers at the Cape were usually more fortunate in relations with them, and recorded much interesting, if not always accurate, information about their customs and beliefs; consequently they were already known to some extent by the time that the settlement was founded.

The Bushmen are not mentioned in the Cape records as a separate people until about 1682. In general the first settlers did not distinguish them clearly from the Hottentots, apart from noting that the latter kept cattle and sheep, whereas the former lived entirely upon game and wild plants. The main reason for this early confusion is that the two peoples look very much alike, differing only in certain features not readily apparent to the casual observer.[1] The Bushmen are typically short, averaging about five feet in height, and have slender bodies with short arms and legs; they are often hollow-backed, and steatopyga is common in women. Their skin is yellowish-brown and wrinkles easily; the hair is short and woolly, and gathered into small "peppercorn" tufts; the head is small and relatively broad, and the face characterised by bulging forehead, prominent cheekbones, short lobeless ears, and extremely flat nose, with eyes narrow and often slightly oblique. The Hottentots resemble them in colour and build, and have the same kind of hair and facial features, but in general are taller, with narrower and higher heads, and faces more pointed and projecting.

It is now commonly accepted that the Hottentots are of the same racial origin as the Bushmen, but have been affected by the intrusion of alien blood. The standard theory is that they developed from an early mixture of Bushmen with people of Hamitic stock to whom

[1] See Schapera, I., *The Khoisan Peoples of South Africa* (1930), pp. 51–64.

they are said also to owe certain distinctive features of language and culture.[1] Consequently, although Bushmen and Hottentots are usually classed as belonging to one ethnic group, termed "Khoisan" by Schultze,[2] it is both more convenient and more accurate to regard them as two separate divisions of that group.

BUSHMEN

It was formerly believed that the present-day Bushmen were the original human inhabitants of South Africa, and that they had occupied the country from times of remote antiquity. This view, held for example by Stow, was based chiefly on the occurrence of "Bushman" stone implements and other remains in underground deposits, and on the seemingly great age of certain "Bushman" rock engravings.[3] It has now been established that the Bushmen were in fact preceded by other peoples. At Saldanha Bay there were discovered in 1953 fragments of a skull, of the same type as *Homo rhodesiensis*, which represents a far older branch of humanity.[4] In addition, stone-age deposits earlier than those usually associated with them have yielded skeletal remains, which "because of their pedomorphic or infantile character" are assumed to constitute the ancestral stock from which they themselves are derived. Similar remains have been found in Kenya and elsewhere in East Africa. Even to-day, moreover, there are in Tanganyika peoples, such as the Sandawe and Hadzapi, whose languages are akin to Bushman and who have "Khoisan" physical characteristics; here, too, rock paintings have been found very like some of those in South Africa. Because of all this, some archaeologists argue that the ancestors of the Bushmen entered Africa from the north and spread southwards; others, however, regard the parent "Bushmanoid" stock as native to South Africa, whence it spread to the north.[5]

Whichever view is correct, it is at least certain that the Bushmen have been in South Africa for a very long time, that they were the earliest of its present-day inhabitants, and that they once extended over almost the whole region from the Zambesi River down to the south coast. Their relics, in the form of skeletal remains, culture deposits, pictorial art and place-names, are found widely scattered throughout, and afford clear evidence of their former presence in many parts where they are no longer seen. Even well within historical times Bushmen were living in districts from which they have now

[1] See discussion and references in Schapera, *Khoisan Peoples*, pp. 42 *sqq*, 63 *sqq*.

[2] Schultze, L., *Zur Kenntnis des Körpers der Hottentotten und Buschmänner* (1928), p. 211.

[3] Stow, G. W., *The Native Races of South Africa* (1905), chs. I–II.

[4] Cf. Drennan, M. R., "Saldanha Man and his Associations", *Amer. Anthrop.* LVI (1954), 879–84.

[5] Cole, S., *The Prehistory of East Africa* (1954), pp. 111–13; cf. Galloway, A., "Man in Africa in the light of recent discoveries", *S. Afr. J. Sci.* XXXIV (1937), 89–120; Bleek, D. F., "The Hadzapi . . . of Tanganyika Territory", *Africa*, IV (1931), 273–86; Trevor, J. C., "The Physical Characters of the Sandawe", *J.R. Anthrop. Inst.* LXXVII (1947), 61–78.

completely disappeared, or where perhaps only a few individuals still survive. This applies, for example, to Natal, Basutoland, Orange Free State and especially the Cape, in all of which, as recently as the middle of last century, Bushmen were still fairly numerous.

In their native conditions the Bushmen were divided into many "tribes", each with its own language and name. These tribes have been classified, primarily on linguistic grounds, into three separate groups: Southern, Northern, and Central.[1] (*a*) The Southern Group lived mainly in the central and western districts south of the Tropic of Capricorn. Its best-known tribe was the */xam-ka !k'e* (*/xam* people[2]), formerly spread in great numbers over much of the Cape Colony. They were the Bushmen with whom the early settlers first came into contact, and who suffered so severely from conflict with them, and with other invaders, as to have become almost completely extinct. Other representative tribes, still in existence though much broken up, are the */auni* in the waterless regions of the Lower Nosob, and the */nu-//en* (*Nusan*) of the Upper Nosob and Auob valleys, bordering on the south-west Kalahari. (*b*) The Northern Group is still relatively intact and has retained much of its traditional culture, though not without traces of foreign influence. It is spread over the northern parts of South-West Africa, extending into south-east Angola, and includes, amongst others, three large well-known tribes: *//kau-//en* (*Auen*) in the Kaukauveld of South-West Africa, *!Khu* (*Kung*) reaching north-west of them into Angola, and *Hei-//kum* (*Heikum*) in the north-central districts of South-West Africa. (*c*) The Central Group, finally, consists of many different tribes scattered over the central and northern Kalahari. Among them are the *//aikwe* (*Naron*) and allied groups, reaching up north and east from the vicinity of Sandfontein to Lake Ngami; */tannekwe* in the Okovango marshes north of Lake Ngami; *Hukwe* and *Galikwe*, extending north-east of them into Northern Rhodesia; *Tserekwe*, *Kabakwe* and others along the Botletle River south-east of Lake Ngami, and *Hiechware*, in the Tati (Francistown) district of the Bechuanaland Protectorate. Most of these tribes have been considerably influenced in physique and culture by intermixture with adjoining Bantu peoples, especially Tswana, to whom they are collectively known as *Masarwa*.

Wherever the Bushmen lived undisturbed by other peoples, their social organisation was very simple.[3] Every "tribe" consisted of several bands, each containing on the average from about fifty to one hundred persons, all of whom were usually related by blood or

[1] Bleek, D. F., "The distribution of Bushman languages", *Festschrift Meinhof* (1927), pp. 55–64; Schapera, "The tribal divisions of the Bushmen", *Man*, XXVII (1927), 68–73.

[2] The following special symbols are conventionally used to represent the "clicks" in Bushman and Hottentot: / (dental), ‡ (alveolar), ! (palato-alveolar), and // (lateral).

[3] A comprehensive summary and critical discussion of the literature relating to Bushman culture, with full references to sources, is given by Schapera, *Khoisan Peoples*, chs. IV–VIII.

by marriage. Each band managed its own affairs independently of the rest; there was no central authority to whom they were all subject. Stow speaks of Chiefs who were "looked upon as paramount over the whole territory belonging to the tribe";[1] but this view is mistaken, though, to meet aggression by stronger peoples, neighbouring bands did occasionally unite for a while under a common war-leader. The "tribe" was in fact a loose aggregate of bands linked together only by a common language and name. The affairs of each band were usually managed by an informal camp council of all the men, among whom experienced elders, good hunters and other outstanding individuals tended to have special influence. In the north-west each band also had a headman, whose position was hereditary from father to son. His authority was slight, and although in some groups he had certain ritual duties, his main task was to take the lead in carrying out the decisions of the men's council. He had no judicial functions and no special means of enforcing his own wishes. Among all Bushmen adult men had great freedom of action and, for such wrongs as theft, adultery and homicide, the only recognized remedy was self-help (*lex talionis*) exercised directly by the victim himself or by his next of kin.

Each band also had its own territory, whose limits were clearly defined by such natural features as riverbeds, sand-dunes, hills and belts of trees. If neighbouring bands were friendly, people went freely from one to another to trade, seek a wife or visit relatives; but any stranger caught wandering through the land or poaching was ruthlessly punished, and might even be killed. In consequence, adjoining bands were often in a state of feud. Special importance was attached to water-holes, and only members of the band were entitled to live, hunt and gather wild foods in their vicinity. These rights were shared equally by all, individual- or family-holdings being unknown; but camps were never located very close to the water, lest the game be scared away, and the position of the huts was often changed.

These circumstances [Miss Bleek remarks] have given rise to many misconceptions. Travellers passing through the country, and seeing the Bushmen appear from nowhere and disappear again, have often written that they had no fixed homes or property, and were mere wanderers, erecting crude bush screens wherever they happened to be. The writers would have been surprised to learn that they were themselves trespassers and poachers in the Bushman landowner's eyes, camping at his water and shooting his buck....If the white man were a passing hunter and friendly, if he shared his bag with the Bushmen, he was welcomed and could travel through the territory in peace; but when the settlers came in, permanently occupying the land at the springs, and doing great execution among the game, then the Bushmen retaliated by shooting the intruders or killing their stock. Whereupon the white man, unaware of any unfriendly behaviour on his part, unhesitantly dubbed the Bushman an untamable savage and a thief, and did his best

[1] Stow, *Native Races*, p. 33.

to imprison or shoot him. Hence the war of extermination, which has reduced the race of Colonial Bushmen to its present vanishing figure.[1]

Within a band, the only division was into families, each consisting of a man and his wife or wives and their dependent children. Polygamy was practised, but not extensively, and generally only a few of the older men had two or three wives. People were not allowed to marry within their own band. In some regions wives were acquired by capture, but usually this happened only if neighbouring bands were unfriendly. Elsewhere marriages were arranged in advance. The prospective bridegroom then had to kill a big-game animal for the wedding-feast, and thus show that he was able to support a wife. For a year or so afterwards he lived in her band, hunting for her parents, but once she had borne him a child he would move with her back to his former home.

Owing largely to lack of other suitable foods, children were not weaned until three or four years old, and in the northern tribes babies born while their predecessors were still being nursed were usually killed at once. This was also the fate of one of twins. Because of these customs and of the high infant-mortality due to the natural hardships and strenuous conditions of Bushman life, relatively few children survived: it was seldom that more than two or three in a family grew to maturity. On reaching the age of puberty, they were ceremonially initiated into the status of adult. A girl when she first menstruated was secluded in a small hut, and observed various food taboos and other restrictions; in the north-western tribes a special fertility dance, representing the courtship of the eland bull, formed part of the ceremony. Boys were initiated in groups. They were kept in the bush for about a month, during which time they were instructed in the traditional lore of their people and subjected to arduous hunting-tests. They were also taught religious dances in which animal masquerades predominated, and towards the end of their stay special marks were cut on their forehead by the officiating magicians.

Once initiated, young people participated fully in the routine activities of their community. All Bushmen depended for subsistence upon the natural resources of their environment. They had no domestic animals except dogs, and they cultivated no crops. Their vegetable-food consisted of wild roots, plants and fruits, and meat was obtained primarily by hunting, supplemented where possible by fishing. They ate all animals except baboons and hyenas. Frogs, snakes, lizards and locusts were greatly relished and, in times of need, even scorpions, beetles and termites were welcome.

Hunting was done by the men. Their principal weapons were the bow and small arrows, whose detachable points were coated with a mixture of animal and vegetable poisons, the deadly effects of which

[1] Bleek, D. F., *The Mantis and his Friends* (1923), p. vii.

were sometimes felt by the Dutch colonists. Traps, snares and pitfalls were used everywhere, and the northern tribes also had throwing sticks and spears. Vegetable foods were collected by the women, who dug up tubers and roots with a pointed stick of hard wood, which in the south was often weighted by a perforated stone ball and tipped with a buck's horn. Theirs, too, was the daily task of gathering firewood and fetching water. A buck's stomach made a handy water-bag, and ostrich egg-shells were also used for carrying and storing water. Fire was made by drilling one piece of wood into another, and cooking was done in crude pots of clay.

Game meat was shared among all members of the band, but a man kept the skin of any animal that he killed. From it he made bags for holding his personal equipment, and also the clothing for himself and his family. Men wore a triangular piece of hide drawn between the legs and tied round the waist, women a small apron in front and a larger one behind. Both sexes also had cloaks tied round the shoulders and waists, and when travelling donned skin caps and sandals. Women wore leather bangles and chains of ostrich egg-shell beads as ornaments, and on festive occasions decorated their faces with black or red paint.

The nature of their food supply made all Bushmen wanderers. When game and edible plants in the vicinity of one water-hole grew scarce, the people moved on to another. They seldom remained at any place for more than a few weeks. In the dry season they frequented localities where water could be found, but when the rains came they roamed about all over their own area, often in dispersed family groups. In consequence, they had no settled homes. Their dwellings, erected by the women, were generally crude semicircular shelters of branches stuck into the ground and covered with grass; these were easily put together, and were lightly abandoned when camp was moved. Those living in mountainous parts used natural caves and rock shelters, from which they could survey the surrounding country and observe both the movements of game and the approach of enemies. Many caves still have their walls decorated with paintings, relics of the former Bushman occupation. These paintings, made chiefly with mineral earths, constituted a notable feature in the culture of the southern and eastern Bushmen. They were highly artistic studies, often in polychrome, and remarkable for their vivid impressionism; the subjects depicted included cattle raids, hunts, battles, dances and incidents from mythology, but the most common were representations of single animals or human beings.

In their home environment, undisturbed by alien invaders, the Bushmen were a cheerful, merry people, especially when meat was plentiful. They were very fond of dancing, which among them all was common both as a social pastime and as part of the religious ritual. Many dances took the form of masquerades in which the manners, appearance and cries of animals or persons were mimicked with wonderful fidelity. Several kinds of musical instruments were used to accompany them, and also for solo performances, the most common being variants of the musical bow.

About the religious beliefs and practices of the Bushmen little detail has been recorded. They prayed to the moon and other celestial bodies, which in the south featured prominently in a rich and extensive mythology. They believed also in certain supernatural beings. One of these, known in the south as */kaggen* (the Mantis) and in the north as *Huwe*, *Hishe*, or *Thora*, was looked upon as the creator: he controlled rain, thunder and lightning, and to him were directed prayers and ceremonies for abundance and good luck in hunting, recovery from illness and protection from danger. Some north-western groups held that the souls of dead people went to live with him in the sky. The southern Bushmen also spoke of an afterworld of the dead, but did not connect it specially with any supernatural being. It was everywhere believed that the dead became mischievous ghosts that were harmful to their surviving relatives; hence, whenever a person was buried, the people abandoned the spot and always avoided it in future. In the north there was another deity, *//gaua*, who was closely connected with the ghosts of the dead and consequently regarded as a source of illness and death, reputedly often inflicted through the media of thunder, lightning, shooting stars and similar natural phenomena. He does not seem to have been worshipped.

Omens, charms and divination also featured prominently in the lives of the Bushmen. Among them all, too, there were professional magicians, both male and female, who were held to be in special contact with the ghosts and hence had the power to cure the sickness that these caused. The magicians also charmed hunters for success in the chase, officiated at the puberty ceremonies, performed rain-making rites in times of drought and communicated with the deities, whose wishes they revealed to the people. In their own field they had special authority, but they were not otherwise distinguished in status or mode of life, and they carried on the same routine subsistence activities as all other Bushmen.

HOTTENTOTS

By the time that Europeans began to settle in southern Africa, the Bushmen in the western Cape had been reduced to living in isolated groups among the more powerful Hottentots. The latter, according to their own traditions, came originally from the vicinity of the Great Lakes of East Africa. Owing to pressure from the north, they gradually pushed south-westwards across the high plateau of Central Africa "with their faces towards the setting sun", until they reached the "great waters", i.e. the Atlantic. Then they turned south, crossing the Kunene, and, moving slowly down the west coast, entered the Cape Peninsula and passed on to the east. At different stages on their route south of the Kunene, sections remained behind, each in time becoming a separate tribe.[1] As they advanced, they gradually dispossessed their Bushman predecessors, driving them into the arid plateaus of the interior but occasionally also mixing with them. Relations between the two peoples remained on the whole unfriendly or even actively hostile, although, as for example around the Cape Peninsula, Bushmen sometimes became subjects of the local Hottentots. We do not know how long the Hottentots had been in the coastal regions of the Cape before the Portuguese first came into contact with them. Stow says that they reached the Atlantic at the end of the fourteenth century[2], but the fact that they were in lengthy and intimate contact with the Bantu far to the east suggests that the date must have been at least a century or so earlier.

The first colonists found the Hottentots thinly scattered all along the western and southern coastal regions. Later expeditions revealed their presence beyond the Orange River to the north and as far as the Kei River in the east, but nowhere had they penetrated far into the interior. Many different tribes existed, all speaking one or other of four closely-related languages. These linguistic differences form the basis for the usual classification of the Hottentots into four main divisions: Cape Hottentots, Eastern Hottentots, Korana, and Nama.[3]

The Cape Hottentots were the people found by the settlers in the vicinity of Table Bay.[4] Of the tribes mentioned in the old Cape records and the reports of early travellers, the *Goringhaiqua* (with their offshoot the *Goringhaikona*) and the *Gorachouqua* lived in and about the Cape Peninsula. The Gorachouqua moved away inland from the neighbourhood of the Dutch settlement about the end of the seventeenth century, and are commonly said to have been the ancestors of what afterwards became the Korana division. Farther north along the west coast, from near Table Bay to Saldanha Bay, roamed the *Kochoqua*, who at the time when the settlement was founded were the strongest of the local groups. Beyond them, and extending

[1] Stow, *Native Races*, pp. 267 *sqq.*; Hoernle, A. W., "South-West Africa as a primitive culture area", *S. Afr. Geog. J.* VI (1923), 23; Theal, G. M., *Ethnography and Condition of South Africa before A.D. 1505* (1910), pp. 83–90. Against the traditional view, H. Vedder has more recently argued that the Hottentots migrated into the Cape from the north-east and then slowly pushed upwards through the western coastal regions into South-West Africa (*Das alte Südwestafrika*, 1934, pp. 119–26).

[2] Stow, *Native Races*, p. 267.

[3] Fritsch, G., *Die Eingeborenen Süd-Afrika's* (1872), pp. 265 *sqq.*; Stow, *Native Races*, pp. 238 *sqq.*; Schapera, *Khoisan Peoples*, pp. 44 *sqq.*

[4] The relevant early sources are summarised in Maingard, L. F., "The lost tribes of the Cape", *S. Afr. J. Sci.* XXVIII (1931), 487–504.

north of the Olifants River, were the *Chariguriqua* (from whom the modern "Griquas" derive their name). To the east, beyond the Hottentots-Holland mountains, lived the *Chainoqua* (sometimes known, after one of their chiefs, as *Soeswaqua*); then came the *Hessequa* (in the modern district of Swellendam), *Gouriqua* (about Mossel Bay and the Gouritz River), *Attaqua* (extending north of them to near the present town of George), *Houteniqua* (eastwards as far as the Kromme River), and *Inqua* (to the north in the present district of Aberdeen).

Still farther east were the various tribes of Eastern Hottentots. They included the *Damaqua* and *Hoengeiqua*, located between the Gamtoos and Keiskamma Rivers. Beyond these were the *Gonaqua*, who during the eighteenth century became the most powerful tribe and, expanding westwards, incorporated scattered fragments of all the others. They were the first Hottentots to come into contact with the Bantu, and early travellers noted that, because of intermixture with them, they were taller and darker than the people at the Cape. In course of time they became almost completely absorbed by the Bantu; the Gqunukhwebe, one of the leading Xhosa (Bantu) tribes, are indeed said to be partly of Hottentot origin and to have retained, in modified form, the old name of Gonaqua.

In the west, north of the Chariguriqua, were the tribes of the Nama division. The early settlers classified them into the "Little Namaqua" living south of the Orange River in what is now Little Namaqualand, and the "Great Namaqua" occupying the southern parts of South-West Africa. Members of both groups at times visited the settlement at Table Bay. The "Little Namaqua", like the Cape and Eastern Hottentots, have now disappeared as separate entities, but several "Great Namaqua" tribes survive. Among those that figured prominently in the history of South-West Africa during the nineteenth century were the *Gei-//Khauan* (commonly known as "Rooi Nasie"), *//Khau-/Goan* ("Swartboois"), *//Haboben* ("Velskoendräers"), *!Gami-/nun* ("Bondelswarts"), *//O-gein* ("Groot Doode"), *!Khara-gei-khoin* ("Fransmanns") and *‡Aunin* ("Topnaars").[1]

Like the Bushmen, the Hottentots did not cultivate crops, but in other respects they had a more advanced standard of living.[2] They were essentially a pastoral people with herds of long-horned cattle and flocks of fat-tailed sheep, and their principal food was the milk of their cattle, which they kept in wooden pots and dishes or in skin bags and drank once it had thickened. The milking was done by the women, but all other work relating to the animals was in the

[1] A very detailed history of this division, with many incidental references to culture, is given by Vedder, H., *Das alte Südwestafrika* (1934), *passim*.

[2] For a comprehensive account of Hottentot culture, based on all the available sources, see Schapera, *Khoisan Peoples*, chs. IX–XIV.

hands of the men. Women also gathered wild fruits and other vegetable foods of many different kinds, which were eaten either raw or prepared in various ways by baking or roasting. Meat, a luxury, was obtained chiefly by hunting, the methods and weapons employed being generally similar to those of the Bushmen. In times of scarcity all sorts of rodents and reptiles were eaten. The domestic animals were not killed for food except on ceremonial occasions, but all dying of disease or other causes were eaten with relish. Young oxen were trained for riding and to carry burdens, and there is good evidence that sometimes they were even stampeded into battle against the tribe's enemies.

The Hottentots, unlike the Bushmen, also smelted iron and copper from which they made implements, weapons and certain ornaments. They likewise carved pails, dishes and other vessels from wood, wove mats and baskets of reeds and rushes, and from skins made bags of various kinds, including some for holding milk and water. Their clothing consisted entirely of skins prepared by scraping and softening; men wore a loin-skin with perhaps a small kaross, women a well-ornamented apron with larger karosses before and behind. Both sexes adorned their heads with copper trinkets and smeared their bodies with ochre and fat; women also had shell ornaments and sewed leather strips round their legs, and men often wore armlets of ivory and copper.

Owing to the grazing- and water-needs of their livestock, the Hottentots were necessarily a nomadic people, but their dwellings were more substantial than those of the Bushmen. They lived in spacious and airy beehive-shaped huts made of reed mats covering a framework of long slender poles planted in the ground, bent inwards and joined together by cross-pieces. When camp was moved, the huts were taken apart and transported on ox-back until needed again, when they were easily reassembled. The camp itself had a circular fence of thorn bushes, along whose inner circumference the huts were located. The great open space in the centre was the scene of many daily activities, and served at night as a fold for the cattle and sheep.

Their mode of life also prevented the Hottentots from living together permanently in great numbers. The largest unit in their social system was the tribe containing perhaps from about 500 to 2500 people. Although each tribe had its own land, there were no rigidly-defined tribal boundaries. The members of a tribe usually ranged round certain fountains or other permanent water-holes, which they regarded as theirs because of habitual and continuous exploitation. Occasionally they all camped together, but seldom for long; normally they were dispersed over the country in several small groups, each wandering about on its own. There were no individual or family titles to land; everybody grazed and watered his cattle wherever he wished. Strangers trekking through the country were allowed the same privileges, and no attempt was made to exclude them; but, if they intended to remain anywhere for long, they had to seek permission from the local people and pay annual tribute, usually in cattle, in token of allegiance. Failing this, there might be fighting, the usual outcome of which was that the weaker group moved somewhere else.

Each of the local communities in a tribe consisted as a rule of a single clan or part of a clan, a group the heads of whose constituent households all claimed descent in the male line from a common ancestor. Every clan had its own headman, whose office was hereditary from father to son. He was helped by an informal council composed of all the other men of his group. Together with them he settled internal disputes, tried and punished criminals, and decided upon such matters as moving to new pasture grounds; in time of war, he led them into battle.

The clans were graded in order of rank, and the hereditary head of the senior clan was also the acknowledged Chief of the whole tribe. He presided over a council composed of all the other clan-heads, whom he summoned to his camp whenever occasion arose. This council dealt with all intertribal relations, and also acted as a court of justice in disputes involving members of different clans. Without its co-operation and support the Chief had little real power; hence, his authority over its members depended largely upon his personality. Clan loyalty was always stronger than tribal loyalty, and often enough a powerful clan would break away under its headman and claim full independence. Clan solidarity was reflected also in the law relating to homicide: if anybody was killed, his nearest relatives were obliged to avenge him, even against a fellow-tribesman, and if the murderer himself could not be found, one of his clansmen might be killed instead.

Within the clan, the principal social unit was the family, consisting of a man with his wife or wives and their dependent children. As a rule only the more powerful and wealthy men were polygamists, and even they seldom had more than two or three wives. The first wife married was the chief wife, and her eldest son was the main heir to his father's position and property. Each wife had her own hut in which she lived with her children, and she had sole control over its contents and food; sometimes she also had her own cattle, given to her by her parents, which her husband might not barter or slaughter without her consent. Marriages were arranged by the parents of the children concerned. Members of the same clan were forbidden to intermarry, but otherwise there were no special regulations governing the choice of a wife. The marriage was celebrated by a feast at the bride's home, the animals for slaughter being provided by the groom's people. The young couple then lived there for a year or so, during which time the husband served his parents-in-law; after the birth of his first child, however, he took his wife to his parental home, where they established a separate household of their own.

Children were nursed until about two or three years old. Before very long, they gradually became useful at home. Little boys early began to herd sheep and calves, and with small bows and arrows hunted birds, lizards, mice etc., which they ate. As they grew older, they were put to herding the cattle, and also joined the men on hunting expeditions. After a boy had killed his first big game animal, he was ceremonially initiated into the ranks of adult hunters. Little girls remained with their mother, learning to help her in such daily tasks as fetching firewood and water, preparing food and ointment for the body, making reed mats, and keeping the hut in repair.

The children were also taught various rules of conduct to be observed in family life. Respect for age was strongly emphasised and deference was always expected towards elders. Even after he had set up his own household, a man acknowledged the authority of his eldest brother and consulted him on all matters of domestic importance. Boys were taught also to be "shy" of their sisters, in whose presence they had to behave with much decorum; special respect was due to the eldest sister, who in consequence exercised much influence over her brothers and their children.

The attainment of puberty was marked by special rites, after which the children were regarded as adults and allowed to marry. Every boy, when his father thought him old enough, was put for a month or so under the care of a specially chosen old man, who systematically taught him various moral rules; a feast was then held, after which the boy was free to associate habitually with the men, and to eat and smoke in their company. A girl when she first menstruated was similarly secluded in a hut, and while there had to observe many food and other restrictions, including above all the complete avoidance of cold water. The ceremony was brought to an end by feasting and by a long series of purificatory rites, some of which were designed to promote fertility in men, domestic animals and plants.

Other domestic ceremonies in Hottentot life were associated with such events as birth, menstruation, sickness and bereavement. In every instance the person affected was secluded for a while, during which, among other restrictions, all contact with cold water had to be avoided. Dead people were usually buried, though, like the Bushmen, the Hottentots sometimes abandoned old and helpless persons, who ultimately either died of starvation or were devoured by wild beasts. When burial took place, the near relatives underwent a special ceremony of purification; the dead person's hut was then abandoned and the camp moved to another site.

The Hottentots had no definite conception of an afterworld or special land of the dead. They believed that the soul of a dead person went with him into the grave, from which it was able to emerge at will in human or animal guise. These ghosts, termed *|hei-|nun* ("fawn feet") or *||gaunagu* (sing. *||gaunab*), were thought to be mischievous or harmful, and in particular were held to cause sickness and death; consequently they were much dreaded and the graves of the dead were avoided.

The word *||gaunab* was used also as the name of a supernatural being closely associated with the ghosts of the dead and, like them, a source of sickness and death. Whirlwinds, eclipses of the sun or moon, shooting stars and similar natural phenomena were all omens of great misfortune for which he was responsible. In Hottentot mythology he figured as a malevolent chief always in conflict with *Tsui-||goab*, the great national hero. *Tsui-||goab* was regarded as the creator, the guardian of health, the source of prosperity and abundance and, above all, as the controller of rain and its associated phenomena. To him was directed the great annual rain-making ceremony, the most important public ritual in Hottentot life; and since, as giver of the rain, he was also the source of good pastures and edible roots and berries, prayers were often addressed to him for food. Another conspicuous figure in ritual and belief was *Heitsi-Eibib*, the central personage of a great cycle of myths, in which he and members of his family had many wonderful adventures. All the actions ascribed to him were those of a man, but one endowed with supernatural powers: he died and rose again many times, he was a rich and powerful chief, a seer and a great hunter, but he was also a trickster and by no means blameless in character. His "graves", large mounds of stone, were found all over the country, and no Hottentot would pass one without adding to it a stone or a twig, sometimes also uttering a prayer for good luck in hunting. Early writers state also that at new moon and full moon the people spent the night in dancing, singing and merrymaking; some add that on such occasions prayers were addressed to the moon, but others deny this. The moon figured too in Hottentot mythology in connection with the origin of death: it promised immortality to men, and when its message was irrevocably distorted by the hare, it was also the avenger, punishing the fateful deceiver.

As among the Bushmen, there were among the Hottentots specialists in the art of magic. Their main function was to cure people who had been "bewitched", but they also officiated at ritual ceremonies and practised divination. Great faith was likewise placed in such omens as dreams, the flight and cry of birds, the direction of the wind and celestial phenomena; the sight of the mantis, especially, heralded very good fortune. The wearing of amulets was common; herdsmen, warriors, hunters and others tied round their necks small pieces of wood, fangs, beads and similar objects obtained from the magicians and believed to ward off danger, maintain health or deliver the possessor from evil.

BANTU

In the first years of the eighteenth century the Dutch settlers in the course of their eastward excursions had established fleeting contact with a type of native inhabitant differing markedly in appearance and culture from Bushmen and Hottentots. The Bantu, as those people are now called, are basically Negroes mixed with Hamitic, negrillo and other types. They vary considerably amongst themselves, but, in general, have lighter skin, lower stature, broader head, flatter forehead, less projecting jaws and narrower noses than the true Negro. They practise both animal husbandry and agriculture, have well-developed systems of social and political organisation, and speak languages of a family extending far beyond South Africa.

The Bantu did not seriously affect the lives of the European settlers until towards the end of the eighteenth century. Ever since, the relations between the two peoples have constituted one of the most vital problems of South Africa. Unlike the Bushmen and Hottentots, who, except in South-West Africa and the Bechuanaland Protectorate, have disappeared as separate entities, the Bantu are still vigorous and powerful. They not only greatly outnumber the white population, but seem to be increasing steadily; and, despite some far-reaching changes due to contact with Western civilisation, they have in many instances retained the principal features of their tribal system.

At present they are found living as separate communities in most parts of southern Africa except the central and western Cape and the southern districts of South-West Africa, although even there, and especially in the western Cape, many of them have recently settled as labourers in European industrial and farming areas. Despite many basic similarities, they vary sufficiently in details of language and culture to be classified into four major groups: Eastern, Central, Northern, and Western.[1]

The Eastern Group occupies the coastal region east of the Drakensberg mountains and south of the Sabi River. It consists of two main divisions: Nguni and Tsonga. The former include the Cape Nguni of the Transkei and Ciskei (Xhosa, Thembu, Mpondo, etc.,[2] together with the "Fingo", the fugitive remnants of tribes broken up in Natal during the great intertribal wars at the beginning of the nineteenth century); the Natal Nguni or "Zulu" of Natal and Zululand,

[1] The names used above for the four groups relate to their geographical location in southern Africa. In the conventional classification of the Bantu languages generally, what are here called the Eastern and Central groups constitute the "South-eastern Zone", the Northern group constitutes the "South-central Zone", and the Western group forms part of the "Western Zone". Cf. Doke, C. M., *Bantu* (1945), pp. 2, 73–105.

[2] In accordance with modern scientific practice, the names of Bantu tribes are given here in their root form, without the prefixes (*umu-uba*, *mo-ba*, etc.) that distinguish number.

with their offshoot the Ndebele (Tebele) of Southern Rhodesia; the Swazi of Swaziland and eastern Transvaal, and the Ndebele of central and northern Transvaal (who, despite the similarity of name, are historically distinct from the people now in Southern Rhodesia). The Tsonga are found chiefly in Mozambique (Portuguese East Africa) with relatively recent offshoots in eastern and northern Transvaal. Their main linguistic subdivisions are the Ronga (south), Tonga (centre and west) and Tswa (north).[1]

The Central Group, occupying the greater portion of the interior plateau north of the Orange River and west of the Drakensberg, also consists of two main divisions: Sotho and Venda. The former include the southern Sotho of Basutoland and adjoining districts, the western Sotho or Tswana (Tlhaping, Rolong, Hurutshe, Kwena, etc.) of Bechuanaland and western Transvaal, and the northern Sotho (Pedi and many others) of central and northern Transvaal. The Venda are a much smaller and very homogeneous division inhabiting the Soutpansberg district of north-eastern Transvaal.[2]

The Northern Group embraces the Shona peoples of Southern Rhodesia (Mashonaland) and Portuguese East Africa (Mozambique). Its main linguistic divisions are the Kalanga (western), Korekore (northern), Zezuru (central), Karanga (southern), Manyika (north-eastern) and Ndau (south-eastern).[3]

The Western Group comprises the Herero in the central, and the Ambo in the northern, districts of South-West Africa. Both divisions, like those in each of the other groups, are politically subdivided into different tribes, although under German rule (1884–1914) the Herero were united under a single Paramount Chief.[4]

All four groups are descended from immigrants who travelled overland from the north. It is generally assumed that they originally came from somewhere in the region of the Great Lakes of East Africa, where the Bantu peoples as a whole are thought to have had their main focus of development; but it is difficult to state with any certainty when, why and how their southward migrations occurred. The relevant evidence consists mainly of tribal traditions and cultural affinities, and of the former van Warmelo has aptly said that, "at the very best, [it] is weak in chronology and scanty in regard for truth. As a rule, three hundred years is the limit of possibly reliable tradition. Beyond that, legend and fairy-tales begin to luxuriate."[5] Moreover, the Bantu appear to have entered South Africa in successive

[1] A detailed list of the tribes belonging to this group, with notes on their distribution and size, is given by van Warmelo, N. J., *A Preliminary Survey of the Bantu Tribes of South Africa* (1935), pp. 59–95; cf. also his article, "Grouping and Ethnic History", in *The Bantu-speaking Tribes of S. Africa* (ed. Schapera; 1937), pp. 45–57.

[2] For fuller details, cf. van Warmelo, *Survey* (1935), pp. 96–121; van Warmelo, "Grouping" (1937), pp. 57–65.

[3] Doke, C. M., *The Southern Bantu Languages* (1954), p. 205.

[4] Vedder, *Südwestafrika*, ch. II.

[5] "Grouping", p. 44.

waves occupying a fairly long period of time, though the relative order and component elements of those waves have by no means been finally determined. At present, therefore, we cannot do more than mention some of the current hypotheses, which should, however, be treated with great reserve.[1]

It was formerly believed that the earliest Bantu invaders reached southern Africa about the eleventh or twelfth centuries A.D., but recent archaeological investigations have shown that as far back as the eighth or ninth centuries A.D. there was established in Southern Rhodesia the highly-developed culture associated with Zimbabwe and other stone ruins. Its builders, whose identities have given rise to much controversy, are now generally held to have been of Bantu origin, and the cumulative evidence suggests that they were the ancestors of the modern Shona peoples. The Zimbabwe culture attained its zenith during the tenth and eleventh centuries; then it gradually began to decline. Portuguese records of the early sixteenth century (which, incidentally, name many tribes still existing to-day) speak of the great Karanga kingdom of Monomotapa which centred in Zimbabwe, but show that it was already disintegrating owing to internal dissension. After many vicissitudes, it was finally shattered about the end of the seventeenth century, when a new domination was established over the other Shona tribes by the Rozwi (a section of the Kalanga). For the next century and a half the Rozwi remained supreme, but their power collapsed with the arrival of Mzilikazi's Ndebele and other Nguni invaders from the south (*c.* 1825–40).[2]

The Sotho peoples apparently came later than the Shona. The conventional view is that they entered South Africa, probably through the western portions of Southern Rhodesia, in three series of migrations. The first is represented to-day by the people collectively known as Kgalagadi, who settled in the eastern and more fertile parts of Bechuanaland, where they mixed freely with the Bushmen already there. Following them came the ancestors of the modern Rolong, who settled along the upper reaches of the Molopo River, whence they gradually spread south and west. They absorbed some of their Bushman and Kgalagadi predecessors, most of whom, however, retreated before them into the arid zones of the Kalahari Desert. The third and greatest migration brought the ancestors of all the other Sotho

[1] The most useful summaries of the older views are by Barthel, K., "Völkerbewegungen auf der Südhälfte des afrikanischen Kontinents", *Mitt. Ver. Erdk. Leipzig* (1893), pp. 1–90; and Theal, *Ethnography and Condition*, chs. VIII–IX. References to more recent opinions are given below.

[2] On Zimbabwe and its Bantu associations, see Caton-Thompson, G., *The Zimbabwe Culture* (1931), esp. pp. 194 *sqq.* The Portuguese records of the sixteenth and seventeenth centuries are published in Theal, *Records of South-East Africa*. A concise account of the Rozwi and of more recent Shona tribal history is given by Posselt, F. W. T., "Ethnographical sketch of the Natives of Southern Rhodesia", *Official Year Book of S. Rhodesia*, No. 2 (1930), esp. pp. 752–5.

tribes. They settled as a united body in south-western Transvaal and then broke up rapidly into separate clusters, the most important of which were the Hurutshe, Kwena and Kgatla.[1]

Even if the traditions are reasonably reliable, it is impossible to date the migrations that they record. All that can safely be said is that the Sotho were already in the eastern half of their present habitat by about 1600 A.D. During the next two centuries, each of the existing clusters became increasingly subdivided. It was a constantly recurring feature in Bantu history for part of a tribe, led by an ambitious or discontented relative of the ruling Chief, to secede and become independent. The Rolong, for example, are the parent tribe of the modern Tlhaping, Kaa and many others; the Hurutshe, traditional leaders of the final migration from the north, broke up into the modern Hurutshe tribes (Manyana, Moilwa, etc.), Tlharo, Khurutshe and others; the Kgatla, an early offshoot from the Hurutshe, broke up into the modern Kgatla tribes (Mosêtlha, Kgafêla, etc.), Tlôkwa, and Pedi; while the Kwena, another early offshoot from the Hurutshe, broke up into the Fokeng, Mogôpa, Phalane, etc. A section of the Mogôpa subsequently seceded and moved westwards (*c.* 1720); these people, now known as the Kwena of Sechele, were the first important Tswana tribe to settle in the Bechuanaland Protectorate. The Ngwaketse and Ngwato broke away from them not long afterwards, and the Tawana then broke away from the Ngwato (*c.* 1790–1800).[2]

The Venda, said to have come originally from the region of Nyasaland, settled for a long time among the Shona, to whom they owe certain features of language and culture. Then, about three centuries ago, they continued their southward migration and finally became established in the Soutpansberg, which they found inhabited by Sotho peoples whom they brought under their rule.[3]

The early traditions of the Nguni are much more confused. We know from written records that by the end of the sixteenth century they were already inhabiting the coastal regions of Natal, but how long they had then been there it is difficult to ascertain. Soga maintains that they are all derived from three parent stocks: Lala, Nguni and Mbo. The Lala (ancestors of the modern Bele, Hlubi, Zizi and, possibly, also Zulu and Thembu) belonged originally to the Kalanga of Southern Rhodesia, but early broke away in large sections and, travelling south, were the first to enter Zululand and Natal. Next

[1] Stow, *Native Races*, chs. XXI *sqq.*; van Warmelo, *Survey*, pp. 96 *sqq.*; van Warmelo, "Grouping", pp. 57–63.

[2] The main accounts of more recent history of the Sotho tribes are: Ellenberger, D. F., *History of the Basuto* (1912); Schapera, *The Ethnic Composition of Tswana Tribes* (1952); Sillery, A., *The Bechuanaland Protectorate* (1952), pp. 104–94; Hunt, D. R., "An account of the Bapedi", *Bantu Studies*, V (1931), 275–326.

[3] Lestrade, G. P., "Some notes on the ethnic history of the BaVenda", *S. Afr. J. Sci.* XXIV (1927), 486–95; van Warmelo, *Contributions towards Venda History, Religion, and Tribal Ritual* (1932), pp. 5–36.

came the Nguni (ancestors of the modern Xhosa tribes and others), who are thought to have formed part of the Zimba hordes that during the sixteenth century devastated the country between the Zambesi River and Mombasa. The Mbo, remnants of tribes then living in the Lower Zambesi valley, fled before the Zimba, and some of them, cutting their way through the Tsonga and eastern Shona, ultimately crossed the Limpopo River and, pushing south, settled in Natal (*c.* 1620). Here they broke up again into their original elements (including, among others, the ancestors of the modern Mpondo, Mpondomisi, Bomvu, Bomvana, Xesibe and Swazi). The Xhosa and Thembu subsequently pushed south-westwards, one after the other, conquering and partly mixing with the local Hottentots, until, towards the end of the eighteenth century, their vanguard first came into conflict with the advancing European settlers in the vicinity of the Great Fish River.[1]

According to the views just summarised, the focus of Nguni development lay somewhere in Natal, whence the Cape tribes travelled farther south, whereas the Transvaal Ndebele and Swazi offshoots went north-west and north respectively. But, as van Warmelo stresses,[2] all the Nguni languages are distinguished from those of other southern Bantu by the presence of "clicks", almost certainly derived from the Hottentots. This suggests not only that the Nguni must have developed their linguistic peculiarities farther to the south, where alone intensive contact with Hottentots was possible, but also that they got there much earlier than usually supposed, since "clicks" occur even in the language of those Ndebele who have been living in the Transvaal for at least three to four centuries.

Of the Tsonga little more can be said than that the tribes now composing this division entered Mozambique from different directions (north, west and south) and are therefore probably of mixed origins. They have been in the country for a very long time (Portuguese records of the mid-sixteenth century name several chiefs whose people still live round Delagoa Bay), but they were themselves preceded by other Bantu peoples represented to-day by the Chopi and by the Tsonga of Inhambane.[3]

The western tribes, who like most of the others speak of having come from "a land of great waters", seem to have advanced spasmodically to the south-west, until (according to Vedder early in the sixteenth century) they reached the Okovango River in the northwest of Bechuanaland Protectorate. The Ambo then gradually occupied their present territory of Ovamboland. The Herero migrated farther west to the Atlantic coastal region of the Kaokoveld immediately

[1] Soga, J. H., *The South-Eastern Bantu* (1930), pp. 30, 81 *sqq.*, 299 *sqq.*, 395 *sqq.* A different version of early Nguni history is given by Bryant, A. T., *Olden Times in Zululand and Natal* (1929), chs. I and II.

[2] "Grouping", pp. 45 *sqq.*

[3] Junod, H. A., *The Life of a South African Tribe* (1927), I, 20 *sqq.*

south of the Kunene River. Here they remained until about 1750. Then, in small groups, they began moving to the south-east and occupied the central districts of South-West Africa, conquering many of the local Bushmen and Bergdama, a negro people, living mainly on game and wild plants and speaking Hottentot, of whose early history hardly anything is known. In due course (*c.* 1830) they came into conflict with the Nama Hottentots to the south, with whom for the next sixty years they were often at war.[1]

Despite the unreliability of the earlier traditions, it is at least certain that by the end of the eighteenth century most divisions of Bantu had already been living for some time in the regions where they are now found. The early years of the following century saw the creation in southern Africa of several strong native states, when many formerly independent tribes were amalgamated into single political entities. The process began at the end of the eighteenth century in Zululand, where there were then more than one hundred small separate tribes. Dingiswayo, chief of the Mthethwa, began gradually to conquer his neighbours and absorb them under his rule. Under his successor Shaka, originally chief of the Zulu tribe and a despot of outstanding ambition and military ability, the policy of conquest and amalgamation was carried to an extent hitherto unprecedented in Bantu history. By 1820, it has been estimated, Shaka had more than 100,000 warriors, and had added about 500,000 people to his rule, having deprived some three hundred tribes of their independence. His example was followed by several of his generals, who fled with their armies to found kingdoms of their own: Mzilikazi (Moselekatse), after terrorising the central and western Transvaal (*c.* 1821–37), went on to conquer the Shona tribes of Southern Rhodesia, where he established the Ndebele ("Matebele") kingdom; Soshangane (Manukuza) conquered most of the Tsonga peoples of Portuguese East Africa and founded the Gasa ("Shangana") kingdom; and Zwangendaba, "after an amazing march of some thousands of miles", set up the Ngoni kingdom in Nyasaland. In Basutoland a similar result was achieved more or less peacefully by Moshweshwe (Moshesh), who from the remnants of tribes scattered by the wars following in the wake of Shaka's raids built up what is now the "Basuto nation"; Thulare and his son Sekwati welded various northern Sotho tribes into the strong Pedi monarchy, and Sebetwane, leading a horde of Sotho refugees from the south, established in far-off Barotseland the great Kololo kingdom of which David Livingstone wrote.[2]

These wars and conquests led to a considerable disturbance of

[1] The fullest and most convenient historical account of these peoples is by Vedder, *Das alte Südwestafrika* (1934); for the early traditions, see especially ch. III.

[2] Convenient summaries of the developments noted above are given by van Warmelo, "Grouping", *passim*.

tribal conditions in southern Africa during the first half of the nineteenth century; indeed, the wholesale destruction of life and dispersal of people to which they gave rise undoubtedly facilitated the subsequent extension of European settlement over the country. Under the impact of Western civilisation most of the new states were destroyed by the end of the century, but the "kingdoms" of the southern Sotho, Swazi and Ngwato still survive as examples of the political development to which the Bantu could sometimes attain.

Before the upheavals just mentioned, the Bantu were divided politically into very many different tribes, possibly more than a thousand in all.[1] Each tribe occupied its own territory and managed its own affairs under a Chief who was independent of any higher authority. Tribes varied greatly in size; some had as many as 20,000 members or more, others were very much smaller. Normally a man belonged to the same tribe as his father and remained there for life; but almost every tribe had a population of mixed origins, its members having come from several different sources. Some were of the same stock as the Chief himself, others (or their ancestors) were refugees from an invading army or the oppression of a conqueror, others might have submitted voluntarily or been forcibly annexed when their territory was invaded and occupied, and still others might have seceded from their parent tribe because of internal dissension. It was indeed fairly common for malcontents or victims of injustice to change their allegiance from one Chief to another. The tribe was thus not a closed group, membership of which was permanently fixed by birth; it was, rather, an association into which people might be born, be absorbed by conquest, or enter of their own accord, and from which, again, they might depart voluntarily or be expelled.

In the Eastern, Northern and Western Groups the people were normally distributed over their territory in small hamlets or "kraals" separated one from another by distances of, say, a hundred yards to a mile or so. The inmates of each hamlet constituted a single household consisting basically of a man and his married sons, and possibly also his younger brothers, with the wives and unmarried children of them all. In the Central tribes, on the other hand, the people lived in compact villages, often several miles apart. Most villages contained, say, from ten to fifty separate households, but many were much larger; among the Tswana, especially, the capitals of some tribes had populations of more than 5000 inhabitants.

Whatever the type of settlement might be, each household was always clearly marked off from the rest. In the Eastern tribes the

[1] Except where otherwise stated, the description of traditional Bantu culture that follows refers mainly to the Eastern and Central groups, which were the two that figured most prominently in the history of tribal contacts with the European colonists. The principal sources upon which it is based are listed in the bibliography to this chapter.

central feature of its hamlet was the cattle-pen, a strongly-fenced circular enclosure in which the domestic animals were kept at night. Around it were ranged the dwelling-huts; every married woman had her own, and there were also special huts for the older boys and older girls respectively. In other groups the form of domestic enclosure sometimes differed; among the Tswana, for example, the dwelling-huts were contained within a low rectangular courtyard, whereas the cattle, owing to the great size of the villages, were usually kept at special grazing-posts out in the veld. The huts of the Nguni tribes were typically of beehive shape made of wattle and daub; elsewhere they usually had circular walls of wood or earth surmounted by a conical roof of poles covered with thatch.

The number of huts in a household depended mainly upon the number of wives. Polygamy was permitted everywhere, and although most men had only one wife, there were many with two or three, while Chiefs and other wealthy or important men often had ten or more. A man's first wife was generally chosen for him by his parents, who conducted all the elaborate and highly-formalised negotiations on his behalf; his subsequent wives he was free to choose for himself. Marriage was legalised by the transfer to the wife's people of *lobola* (Nguni) or *bogadi* (Sotho), objects normally consisting of cattle, but exceptionally, as among the early Tsonga, of substitutes such as iron hoes. This "payment" was not a form of wife-purchase, as is sometimes asserted; its primary function was to establish the husband's claim to any children borne by the woman. In polygamous households there was always a chief wife, the rest being of minor importance. Sometimes, as among the Xhosa, a second wife also had distinctive rank, being termed the "right-hand wife", and, as among the Zulu, possibly also a third, the "left-hand wife". The chief wife usually had more privileges and a higher status than the others, and her eldest son was the husband's main heir and successor.

Each household produced its own food. The women and girls worked in the fields, where they cultivated sorghum, maize and such minor crops as pumpkins, melons, sweet cane, peas and beans. The corn was converted into porridge or into a mild and much-relished beer; the other crops were eaten either raw or as prepared dishes of various kinds. Wild spinach, fruits and tubers were also gathered when available and, in times of crop-failure, were often the means of preventing starvation. Men and boys looked after the cattle and goats, whose milk, drunk both fresh and sour, was part of the staple diet. The animals were seldom slaughtered except by wealthy owners or on ceremonial occasions, but all dying of disease or other causes were eaten. Meat was more generally obtained by hunting, a pastime much favoured by the men.

Cattle and goats were not merely a source of food; they furnished raw materials for such industries as leatherwork and bone-carving. They were the principal mediums of exchange and of sacrifice to the spirits of the dead. The more cattle a man had, the more wives he could marry. The labour of these women provided him with more corn, which, converted into porridge or beer, he could use to enhance his popularity by entertaining generously. The possession of cattle was itself a source of status; a man's wealth was estimated by the size of his herds, and a large owner was generally respected and influential in tribal affairs. By placing out his cattle on loan, he could also command the labour and allegiance of the holders for various purposes.

The members of a household built their own home and made for themselves most of the articles in common daily use. They wore clothing made chiefly of skins, and ornaments of beadwork, iron, copper or bone, and they used such implements as baskets, clay pots, iron-bladed hoes, spears, axes and knives, skin bags, mats, milk-sacks, and shields, wooden food-bowls, milk-pails, spoons, clubs and head-rests, and calabash cups, scoops and bottles. The men worked in skin, wood and bone, and the women, apart from doing the cooking and housework, made pots and baskets. Metal goods, however, were made by specialist smiths, who bartered them for cattle and grain. Most implements and ornaments could also be exchanged for other commodities, and food was widely used as payment for labour and to satisfy various social obligations towards kinsmen and neighbours. There was, however, no systematic production for exchange nor any organised system of trade.

The tribal territory and all its resources were administered by the Chief through his subordinate local authorities. It was their duty to see that every married man received, free of special charge, a site for his home and land to cultivate. He was entitled only to what he and his children were themselves likely to use and could never claim more. So long as he maintained his home and tilled his land, he had exclusive rights over them and, on his death, they normally passed to his heirs. He could give away or lend land that he did not want at the moment, but he could not claim payment in return; sale and rent of land were both unknown in tribal law. If he moved away permanently, however, he forfeited his rights and his land became available for re-allocation. Pasture-land was not similarly portioned out, but was used freely by all; so, too, anybody could hunt when and where he wished, or take wood, grass, clay, water, earth and wild edible plants wherever he found them.

Beyond the immediate circle of the household was the wider, ill-defined body of kindred, relatives either by blood or by marriage. Kinship ties formed the basis of many social institutions. A man's close relatives, for example, advised and supported him in all his troubles and undertakings; they helped him at work, provided him with hospitality and sent him periodical gifts of meat, beer and other commodities; they contributed towards the *lobola* for his wife, and exchanged with him other specified gifts and ceremonial services, whose nature varied with the type of relationship. In the relative absence of industrial specialisation and consequent economic interdependence, kinship thus served to establish greater social cohesion and wider co-operation than could be obtained within the limits of the household. The so-called "communal system" of the Bantu was largely the manifestation of this close bond of solidarity and reciprocity. Kinship also entered into the marriage regulations. Among Sotho and Venda, for example, a man was expected to marry his maternal uncle's daughter, and the Tswana also permitted marriage with any other kind of first cousin; among Nguni and Tsonga, on the other hand, marriage between all but very distant blood relatives was completely prohibited.

Everywhere, in addition, there were well-defined social groups organised on a kinship basis. The Nguni and Tsonga, for example, were divided into clans and lineages. A clan consisted of people claiming descent in the male line from a common ancestor, who was their eponym (*isibongo*); a lineage comprised those people within a clan who were able to trace their relationship genealogically through a more recent ancestor. Membership of a clan, unlike that of the tribe, was determined solely by descent, but new clans might originate when lineages were considered sufficiently remote from the main stem to permit of intermarriage between them. Clans varied greatly in size, some having several thousand members each. At one time they were local groups; many tribes, indeed, seem to have consisted predominantly of one clan with only a small proportion of foreigners. Owing to warfare and migration, most clans in due course became dispersed over many different tribes; conversely, a single tribe might contain portions of many different clans. Within each tribe, members of the same clan usually clustered together in lineages or segments of large lineages, and sometimes a subdistrict or even a district might be inhabited chiefly by people of one clan.

The Sotho and Venda, similarly, were divided firstly into large patrilineal totemic groups almost all widely dispersed over many different tribes, but each with its own special taboos and other ritual usages. Among the Sotho these groups were not exogamous, nor did people regard one another as kinsmen merely because they had the same totem; among the Venda, on the other hand, members of the same group claimed to be related and were not allowed to intermarry. In both divisions, the largest effective kinship unit was the lineage, usually subdivided into segments of varying span; descent was everywhere traced through the father, and among the Venda and certain northern Sotho, but nowhere else, the group was also exogamous. People of the same lineage or, more commonly, the same segment of a lineage tended to live together, and it was rarely that a man's immediate neighbours did not include some of his close agnates. The relatively small villages characteristic of Venda and southern Sotho were indeed each inhabited mainly by people of one kinship group; only in the large settlements found especially among the Tswana did many different groups of kin normally occur in close proximity, although even here each tended to constitute the whole or part of a "ward" (local subdivision of the settlement).

In every local group of kin, the man senior to the rest in line of birth was their acknowledged head. He arbitrated their internal disputes, the matter being taken to an official court only if agreement could not be reached, and he was the medium through whom all their public dealings with other people and the tribal authorities were conducted. If the group predominated in its area, he was usually also the official local headman with jurisdiction over all the inhabitants; in some of the larger tribes a whole district might be governed by the head of the clan or lineage most strongly represented. Moreover, not only was his office normally hereditary, but his near relatives always shared in his authority; they were his recognised advisers and assistants, and during his absence or illness one of them acted as his deputy.

Apart from these kinship groupings, there were social distinctions between men and women. In tribal law women were treated as perpetual minors, being subject for life to the authority of male guardians. They sat apart from men at feasts and other social gatherings, and were normally excluded from the cattle-pen and its adjoining council-place. Sons were preferred as children, and a woman bearing daughters only was pitied and sometimes even regarded with contempt. Each sex had its own recognised sphere of economic activity; neither would undertake work normally done by the other. Women were debarred from officiating at sacrifices and other religious ceremonies, and except among the Nguni the practice of magic was also essentially a male occupation. Women in general were likewise never consulted on questions of tribal policy, and all political offices were normally held only by men. A Chief's mother occasionally acted as Regent for him during his minority, and among Venda and some northern Sotho there were sometimes also female heads of villages or districts; in one northern Sotho tribe, the Lovhedu, the chieftainship itself was from the beginning of the nineteenth century held continuously by women and is still so held. Nevertheless such instances were decidedly exceptional and in no way enhanced the social status of women generally.

Age and seniority were likewise of considerable importance in Bantu social life. In every household, people were entitled to respect from those younger than themselves, whose services they could freely command. Children were taught to honour and obey their elders, and might be severely chastised for insolence or undue familiarity. In the kinship terms, and in the associated patterns of behaviour, a man distinguished clearly between his older and his younger brothers, and invariably took precedence over the latter. This regard for one's elders was extended beyond the family and kin to the tribe as a whole; in general, people were required to respect and obey all those older than themselves. Breach of this rule was sometimes a penal offence.

Among all divisions of the Central and Eastern Groups except the Cape Nguni, adults were formally grouped into age-sets or "regiments". In the Central Group, each regiment consisted of coevals, and there were separate regiments of men and of women. The Chief created a new regiment every five years or so, when all the eligible youths (aged roughly from fourteen to eighteen) were initiated simultaneously. Among the Sotho, for example, they were secluded for three months or so in a special "lodge" built in the veld, and, after being circumcised, were systematically taught various rules of conduct. Henceforth they were a united body with their own name and leader (usually a son or brother of the Chief), and they could be summoned collectively for public service whenever required. The able-bodied men's regiments fought as separate units in the tribal army and, in times of peace, were often employed on such tasks as rounding up stray cattle, hunting game, destroying beasts of prey, acting as police or working for the chief.

The Zulu and Swazi did not have initiation "schools" like those of the Sotho, but they too formed and used age-regiments for both military purposes and tribal labour. Among the Zulu, in the hey-day of their power, each regiment on active service lived in a separate kraal close to the Chief's home; these kraals, controlled by resident indunas and various subordinates, often had thousands of inhabitants and were thus a conspicuous exception to the traditional Nguni pattern of settlement. The men remained here for several years, until the Chief formally allowed them to return home and marry, and when not at war they were used for any other work that he wanted done. The Swazi did not have a standing army of this type, but some men of each regiment were usually stationed at the royal kraals and available for service, either public or domestic. The military organisation of the Tsonga was likewise based on a system of age-regiments, although (as among the Sotho) the members of a regiment usually lived at their own homes when not at war. Among the Cape Nguni, both the army and tribal labour were organised on a local basis: the men of each district, regardless of age, constituted a separate division of the army and might also be summoned as a unit to work for the Chief.

Other social distinctions were based on the recognition of at least two well-defined classes: aristocrats and commoners. The former included all people of the same ancestral stock as the Chief, although often only members of his own clan or lineage were held to be the true nobility. The rest of the population constituted the commoners, but among them newly-conquered groups and relatively recent immigrants were sometimes distinguished as "foreigners". The class distinctions operated mainly in political life. In general, the more highly placed a man's family was in the tribal hierarchy the greater his authority. The Chief's principal advisers and officers, for example, consisted predominantly of senior aristocrats and a few outstanding commoners, and foreigners were normally excluded both from important executive posts and from the tribe's inner councils. The system of ranking, however, was not rigid. Lowly commoners and even foreigners could acquire prestige through bravery in war, skill in debate, soundness of judgment or knowledge of law and precedent; indeed, men who combined such qualities with conspicuous loyalty and faithful service were often rewarded by being placed in charge of local groups or employed in responsible capacities at the Chief's court.

The Chief himself was the lifelong head of the tribal government. After his death he was usually succeeded by the eldest son of his great wife, or, if there were no male issue in her house, by the eldest son of the wife next in rank; if he had no sons or male descendants of sons, the succession passed to the line of his next younger brother, and so on. If an heir was too young to rule when his father died, a paternal uncle or some other close agnate was chosen to act as Regent during his minority. The order of succession was determined primarily by seniority of descent; but doubts about the relative status of wives often led to the emergence of rival claimants, and Regents sometimes also tried to usurp the chieftainship for themselves. Consequently disputes about the succession were common, and often enough the outcome was that an unsuccessful claimant would secede with his followers and found his own tribe.

The Chief's duties extended over many different spheres of tribal life. He was the representative and spokesman of his people in all their external relations. With the aid of his advisers and councils, he decided questions of public policy, promulgated new laws and amended or abolished others, organised regimental and other large-scale activities, and took whatever action seemed appropriate in case of war, pestilence, famine or some other calamity. He judged all serious crimes and civil disputes, heard appeals from the verdicts of lesser courts, and regulated the distribution and use of land, the cycle of agricultural work and many other economic activities. He often led the tribal army in war, and arranged or personally performed many religious and magical ceremonies on behalf of the tribe. He was expected to watch over the interest of his subjects and to keep himself informed of tribal affairs generally; he therefore spent much time daily at his council-place, where anybody could approach him directly with news, petitions or complaints. He also rewarded with gifts of cattle and other commodities, sometimes including wives, the services of his officers, warriors and other assistants; in addition, he entertained people who came to visit him, supported destitute widows and orphans, slaughtered cattle and provided beer and porridge for all who gathered at his village on great public occasions, and in times of famine distributed corn from his granaries. One quality always required of him was generosity. Should he fail in this respect he soon became unpopular.

The Chief was always treated with great respect. He was ceremonially addressed by distinctive titles of rank, and his deeds were extolled in special praise-poems recited at important assemblies. His installation and marriage were occasions of great public festivity, and his death was universally mourned. He received tribute from his subjects in both labour and kind; for example, hunters gave him specified portions of their spoils, local authorities contributed to the *lobola* for his great wife and gave him cattle at his installation or when he visited them, and ordinary commoners helped to build his huts, cultivate his fields and herd his cattle. He had the first choice of land for his home and fields; he took precedence in all matters of ritual, and he alone could convene tribal assemblies, create new regiments, arrange the tribal ceremonies and sentence people to death. Offences against him personally were usually punished more severely than if committed against other tribesmen, and disloyalty or revolt against his authority often met with death and the confiscation of the culprit's property. If his own conduct was unsatisfactory, he would be warned or even reprimanded by his advisers or at public assemblies. If he ruled despotically or repeatedly neglected his duties, the people would begin to desert him, or a more popular relative would try to oust him by force; as a last resort, he might even be assassinated, as happened, for example, to Shaka in 1828.

In determining tribal policy, the Chief relied first upon confidential advisers, whom he consulted habitually and fairly often individually or collectively. Although he could choose and vary them as he wished, they almost always included some of his senior paternal uncles and brothers, whose traditional right and duty it was to serve him in this capacity. He also had a formal and much wider council, which met as a body at his summons, and to which he referred most important questions. It generally included all subchiefs and headmen and other influential men, and was therefore representative of the tribe as a whole. Among the Nguni, Tsonga and Venda, this council was the main deliberative assembly. Among the Sotho, however, matters of public concern were discussed finally at an assembly, commonly known as *pitso*, open to all the men of the tribe. The assembly was characterised by great freedom of speech and, if the occasion seemed to warrant it, the Chief or his private advisers were openly criticized. It was perhaps largely because of this that Sotho chiefs were seldom as despotic as some Nguni chiefs are reported to have been, notably Shaka and Mzilikazi.

In his judicial and administrative capacities the Chief was served by special officers living at or close to his home. These men, commonly termed his indunas, were seldom closely related to him; indeed the most important were usually commoners. They helped him to administer justice, direct public labour and military operations, and organize the major tribal ceremonies; some of them were his state messengers to other Chiefs. They also supervised the running of his household and court, and controlled the many minor officials who attended to such routine tasks as looking after the council-place, preparing and distributing food at public gatherings, summoning people to meetings or cases, and, if necessary, arresting criminals or enforcing judgments.

Every local division of the tribe also had an official head. There were usually at least two separate grades of local authority: subchiefs, administering major divisions such as districts, and, under them, headmen of smaller units such as subdistricts, villages or wards. Officers of both grades were sometimes appointed directly by the Chief from among his own relatives or favourites, but the majority were the hereditary heads of the local population. Their duties were essentially the same throughout, but all headmen in a district were responsible to the local subchief, who in turn was responsible to the Chief. In each case, the higher official heard appeals from the decisions of his inferiors, tried cases that they could not settle, and had overriding authority in all other respects.

Within his own group every local ruler organised and directed the collective activities of his people, and could freely command their services for public purposes. He saw that they carried out the commands of his political superiors, and collected the tribute due from them to the Chief. He was their official representative and spokesman, supported and protected them in their dealings with outsiders, allotted land to them, prayed to his ancestors on their behalf, and performed various other ceremonies for their welfare and protection. He was also responsible for maintaining law and order in his area, and adjudicated over disputes between any of his people or those involving them as defendants.

In practice, although not in formula, the Bantu distinguished between "criminal" and "civil" offences. The former included offences against rulers in their official capacity, breaches of laws made by the Chief, sorcery, incest, and often also homicide and other cases of bloodshed. Such offences all had to be reported to the nearest local authority, who saw to the arrest and trial of the person accused; if the offence were at all serious, he merely inquired into the facts and then referred the case to the Chief. For civil wrongs, such as breach of marital and filial obligations, seduction, adultery, trespass, unpaid debts and theft, action lay with the person aggrieved. Normally he first tried to reach a settlement by negotiation; many civil disputes were in fact resolved by direct discussion between the people concerned, aided always by their close relatives. If this did not succeed, a formal complaint was lodged with the offender's headman, who then fixed a day for hearing the case.

All trials were held in public and any tribesman might attend and take part in the proceedings. The plaintiff and the defendant successively stated their case, speaking freely and without interruption; they were then questioned closely by anybody who wished. The witnesses were next heard, starting with the plaintiff's, and they too were questioned in turn. When everybody concerned had spoken, the matter was thrown open for general discussion. All those who wished asked further questions or expressed their opinions; the judge's advisers, one by one, then debated the issues and merits of the case, referring if necessary and possible to precedents; the judge himself finally summarized the evidence and the opinions expressed, discussed them, and gave his verdict. In most civil cases, the plaintiff stated what reparation he wanted, and if successful he was awarded either the whole or part of his claim, according to the merits of his case. Crimes were usually punished by a fine in cattle or small stock; one of the animals might be killed for the men at the court, but the others were kept by the judge. For serious offence, such as treason, sorcery and sometimes murder, the penalty was death or banishment, both usually accompanied by confiscation of property. Among the Cape Nguni the standard penalty for homicide was a fine payable to the Chief; among Tsonga and some divisions of Sotho, on the other hand, the culprit had to pay compensation to the relatives of his victim.

The administration of justice was one of the major duties of local rulers and especially of the Chief. The latter was also responsible for various great ceremonies upon whose performance the security and prosperity of his people were held to depend. These included the periodical "doctoring" of the army when all the warriors were inoculated or sprinkled with special medicinal preparations, the boys' initiation rites among Sotho, Venda and Tsonga, and the annual ceremonies associated with the cycle of agricultural activity. In the Eastern Group, especially, the first-fruits festival was an elaborate and picturesque ritual lasting for several days: the whole tribe gathered at the capital, the Chief received magical treatment designed to "strengthen" him, the army was doctored, and the warriors sang and danced in all their finery. Everywhere the Chief was also expected to ensure that the rainfall was adequate, and his popularity might well depend upon his success or failure in this connection. In some tribes he organised annual rain-making ceremonies, in others he usually resorted to them only in times of drought. Some of these ceremonies were public and involved the participation of many people; others were performed in secret either by himself of by specialists whom he employed.

In many of these ceremonies the Chief was the link between the tribe and its deities. His dead ancestors, so it was believed, provided supernatural protection and help to the people they had once ruled, and therefore he visited their graves to pray and sacrifice to them on behalf of all his subjects. This he did, not only regularly on such occasions as the opening of the agricultural season and the eating of the first-fruits, but also in time of war, pestilence, drought and whenever else the diviners decided that his ancestors needed to be appeased. The fact that only he, as Chief, could officiate at the ceremonies was one of the main sanctions for his authority.

Every family was similarly held to be under the guidance of its own agnatic ancestors, who in turn were interested only in the affairs of their own descendants. The head of the family conducted the rites. He sacrificed and prayed to the dead at their graves whenever they revealed themselves through dreams or calamity or in some other form, which the diviners interpreted as a sign that they were offended. He also invoked them on all important domestic occasions such as birth, marriage or the start of some new enterprise, when he offered them libations of beer or sacrifices of fowls, goats and, in emergencies, even cattle, and prayed to them for continued help or thanked them for the blessings they had sent.

Ancestor-worship was perhaps the most conspicuous aspect of Bantu religion, but all groups further had some conception, often rather vague, of a power in the universe not connected with the ancestors. It was known by various names, such as Tilo (Tsonga), Unkulunkulu (Zulu), Modimo (Sotho) and Raluvhimba (Venda), and the beliefs and practices relating to it differed considerably. The Sotho, for example, regarded Modimo as the creator of all things and the moulder of destiny. He was associated with the phenomena of the weather, and punished innovations or departures from established usage by sending wind, hail or heat and withholding the rain; death, if not attributable to sorcery, was spoken of as an "Act of God". He was, however, considered too remote from the world of man to be directly approached in prayer, although at times the ancestral spirits might be implored to intercede with him. The Tsonga, on the other hand, thought of Tilo as an impersonal power presiding over all unaccountable and inevitable phenomena of the atmosphere, of the fields and of human existence, and would attempt to propitiate it in times of drought or other extreme distress. There is little to suggest that these universal powers ever played as intimate a part in the normal religious life of the Bantu as did the spirits of the ancestors.

On the other hand there was considerable and frequent resort to magic, that is, the use of spells and material substances (Sotho *ditlhare*, "medicines") for the attainment of specific ends that could not be achieved by empirical methods alone. Certain people (Nguni *izinyanga*, Sotho *dingaka*, "doctors") were specialists in the art. They treated the sick, divined the riddles of the present and the future, and through inoculation or other use of medicines endowed people, livestock, fields and dwellings with good fortune, or protected them from sorcery and other ills. Any misfortune, and especially sickness or death, was generally attributed to the malevolent use of magic, and the culprit, if found, was severely punished; he might even be killed by order of the Chief. Often enough there were cases of deliberate injustice—an accusation of sorcery was a convenient means of removing a rival—but on the whole prosecutions were inspired by a genuine, and by no means always unfounded, conviction that the sorcerer was consciously trying to harm other people.

In this respect the Bantu did not differ so very much from Europeans of only a few centuries ago. To dismiss them as ignorant and superstitious savages, incapable of knowing better, is both unjust and inaccurate. The belief in magic and sorcery was derived, not from a specific type of inherited mentality, but from a particular form of cultural environment. Once that environment is altered by effective teaching of scientific principles, the belief will be discarded, just as other features of Bantu culture have already been discarded in favour of European cultural institutions and accessories.

Bantu life in the past was no doubt at times savage and harsh. The horrors of sorcery, the constraining fear of the ancestral spirits, the cramping insistence on the hierarchy of age and tribal seniority, the occasional tyranny of a Chief, and the possible destruction of life and property through ruthless warfare or irresistible famine did not always make for happiness. But to the average tribesman, so long as things went well, life was far from unpleasant. Feasting with his companions or debating with keen interest the finer points of a lawsuit, taking part in the many ceremonies and dances that gave so much colour to his yearly routine, listening with pride to the glorification of his Chief or himself boastfully reciting the doings of his ancestors, excitedly going out to war or the chase, and best of all coming back to his home at sunset with his beloved cattle lowing all round him, or sitting contentedly round the fire with his food while nearby some old woman entertained his children with one of the many folktales so abundant in the lore of his people, he might well feel that, in the words of the Tsonga proverb, "it is good to be alive". At heart he was a peasant farmer, interested mainly in his domestic concerns and economic welfare. To ignore this basic factor in his life in favour of the many "quaint" or "savage" customs that separated his culture from our own is to misunderstand completely the values that most directly governed his relations with the colonists.

CHAPTER III

AFRICA IN ANCIENT AND MEDIEVAL TIMES

THE history of Africa, if we except the lower part of the valley of the Nile and the northern and north-eastern regions so far as they were occupied and governed by the Greeks, the Carthaginians, the Romans and the Arabians, is almost entirely modern; for beyond these limits there are scarcely any records of man's activities in the Dark Continent save the traditions of native tribes, which bear relation only to recent events. Even archaeology yields us little; the civilisations of ancient Egypt, of Greece, of Carthage and her fellow-Phoenicians, of Rome, and of ancient and Islamic Arabia have left in Africa scarcely any archaeological remains outside the limits which they directly occupied.

However, these same civilisations have left literary records relating to their activities by sea round the coasts of Africa, and it is on them that we must rely in order to find out how far Africa south of the Equator came within their field of exploration or of knowledge. These records give us only scattered allusions and descriptions, journals and reports of actual travellers being not only rare but exceptional; and even when these reports form the basis, directly or indirectly, of derivative sources, we find that they have often enough been used without due understanding.

While the general movement of successive civilisations has been westwards and eastwards, the African continent runs north and south, and this fact retarded exploration of the coastline. Africa's position in the great ocean causes it to look naturally towards the east, and since the Red Sea was the only sea-way along Africa which led towards some definite goal, it is on this side that the continent has felt most strongly the effects of culture from people outside, and it was of north-eastern and eastern Africa that ancient and medieval peoples came to know most, outside such African regions as they made their own. Only when the Red Sea route was deliberately closed by any people, or its trade subjected to unbearable imposts, did the ancient and medieval world ponder over a possible route to the Indian and Arabian Seas round the western side of Africa.

Any southward approach by land was made extremely difficult by natural barriers. The Sahara, extending just south of the northern coast from the Red Sea to the Atlantic, is the largest desert in the world. Two thousand years ago it was apparently less dry than it is now, but even then it was not easy to traverse its expanse without camels, which were not widely used in North Africa until the systematic introduction of them by the Islamic Arabians. Again exploration of deserts appealed very little to civilised peoples in ancient times, and there was no trade to draw them across the Sahara. We do indeed know of two successful crossings before A.D. 150[1]; but even if men of European stock, of whom no record remains, crossed that desert in ancient times, they were doubtless stopped by the forest which divides central Africa a little south of latitude 10° N. Only those acclimatised peoples who live in and really know inner Africa feel that there are no natural barriers which are insurmountable. In addition to these difficulties, the great heat in the equatorial region and the deadly diseases, especially in the moister places, destroyed the chances of a successful crossing of the forest. The Egyptians, the most highly organised community in Africa in ancient times, had their home in the delta and the valley of the Nile, and might have been expected to make some attempts at exploration of the interior. More still might have been expected from the Greeks and then later the Romans when they became rulers of the land. But Egypt is a very narrow and enclosed country and for many hundreds of miles the only way of travel is the Nile, and the Nile was used much more for irrigation than as a waterway. Further, exploration along this route was stopped by the great marshes produced partly by "sudd" which forms a serious barrier on the White Nile above the place where the Sobat flows in, and so even Greek and Roman knowledge did not extend much beyond Khartum.

We are left then with the coasts and the sea. Here the barriers of the Sahara and of heat were felt less, but they helped to fix firm in the minds of ancient peoples the belief that to push southwards even by sea was neither easy nor safe, while the enormous length of the coastline was a never-ending mystery. Indeed, until the middle of the nineteenth century, Africa was known to Europeans as a series of coastlines rather than a continent. The northern coast was, in ancient times, still more completely a coast of Europe than it is now, while Egypt has always belonged less to Africa than to Asia. Some Greek geographers included Africa in Asia, while the name Arabia was habitually extended so as to include the African coast-region of the Red Sea. Again, the east coast even in ancient times became Arabian and to a slight degree Persian and Indian, just as the southern part of the coast of West Africa, when it was discovered, tended to be connected with America, not with the interior, and the Cape of Good Hope was for long only a calling place between the east and the west and the far south.

In the ancient world, while the urge of scientific enquiry was not entirely lacking, the explorer had only one object—the pursuit of gain. Zeal for religion was utterly absent, and penetration by conquest was, with the exception of small areas in North Africa, confined

[1] *Vide infra*, p. 68.

to Europe and Asia. The goals of the Arab traders were India, Persia and the Levant, and in ancient as in Islamic times they tried to keep their own waters closed and secret from Europeans, while the Phoenicians and the Greeks were Mediterranean peoples with a Mediterranean outlook. Their ways and means of travel were developed to fulfil the demands of that sea, and all travel outside its limits into the "Atlantic" Ocean or in the Sea which the Greeks called "Erythraean" or "Red"—a name which included the Red Sea of modern times, the Persian Gulf and the Arabian Sea—was a desperate adventure into unknown waters. There was no southward lure for any of these races, except to a certain degree for the Arabians, and the various disadvantages under which they lay were magnified when applied to travel in and round Africa. The ancient ships were very small and low in freeboard; their gear, rigging and sails did not allow them to tack across a wind or sail close to it, and a side gale left them helpless or worse; a sinking ship far from shore meant virtually the loss of all on board, for it was unprovided with lifeboats except one or two that could be towed behind. The navigators had no adequate instruments for measuring distance or time or for taking bearings, and no compass or accurate substitute for it; being largely vegetarians, they could manage fairly well on mainly cereal foods, but they found great difficulties in the matter of drinking-water. Their wide knowledge of medicinal plants did not meet the dangers of various diseases, and even the most highly civilised of the ancients were not greatly superior in weapons of war to the primitive races which they might meet. Thus, weak in ships and resources, ancient navigators in general made their voyages only towards some known and definite region. During the period of the early Roman empire, Greek ships sailed regularly from Egypt to India over distances of between two and three thousand miles without a halt[1]; but there was a strong commercial attraction in such voyages, which were taken with the exceptional help of the monsoons. In relation to Europe, therefore, Africa south of the Equator was always isolated, and even in the Middle Ages South Africa was almost as impossible of access for Europeans as were the still undiscovered America and Australia. But, in spite of these facts, there are undoubted traces of ancient attempts to solve the problems of the unknown African seas and lands to the south, and since they were in a sense a prologue to the successful voyages of more modern times which led immediately to the discovery of America and the sea-way to the Far East, and ultimately to European settlement in the subcontinent of South Africa, it is fitting that they should be recorded here.

At an early period the Sabaeans of Southern Arabia established commercial barriers which made it difficult for any other race,

[1] Charlesworth, M. P., *Trade Routes and Commerce of the Roman Empire*, 2nd ed. (Cambridge University Press, 1926), chs. II, IV and VIII.

whether from west or east, to frequent the Arabian coasts or pass through the Gulf of Aden, except under the closest supervision, the object being to keep in Arabian hands the carriage of the precious wares whose origin was in their own land or in India. This commercial barrier was extended later to the Somali coasts; broken only for a short period by the Greeks of the Roman Empire, it was maintained in medieval as in ancient times. But these Arabian restrictions were not extended to the Somali coasts until the end of the second century B.C., and thus there was no resistance offered to the Egyptians on their voyages to the land of Punt,[1] that is, Somaliland west of Cape Guardafui. The farthest limit of Egyptian voyages along the African coast was reached during the eighteenth dynasty (*c.* 1580–1322 B.C.) when Queen Hatshepsut sent an expedition which may have gone beyond Cape Guardafui. There were likewise voyages made by men from India to the same region and to the nearer parts of East Africa, and the Arabians, when they extended the barrier to African coasts, allowed these voyages to continue, while they rigorously excluded all others in the interests of their monopoly. Though they used the monsoons, knowledge of which they kept carefully from other races, in all probability neither Arabians nor Indians sailed to the south beyond Somaliland.

In the tenth century before Christ, Phoenicians of Tarshish in southern Spain were, according to the Hebrew chronicles, employed by King Solomon in voyages to Ophir, which lay between Sheba and Havilah.[2] There have been in the past various theories as to the situation of this mart or district, but the data are too vague to permit of anything more than mere guesses. It has been plausibly suggested that we must look for its site in India or Ceylon or more probably in South Arabia. But other scholars have pressed for the identification of Ophir with Sofala, 130 miles south of the Zambesi, and of Havilah with Rhodesia, where many ancient gold-workings have been found. The renewal of the voyage every three years and the varied nature of the wares which these Phoenicians brought back—silver, precious stones, Indian sandalwood and peacocks, apes, ivory and, above all gold—suggest a trading voyage carried out by Sabaean Arabs of South Arabia like those which even to-day the Arab dhows make from the Red Sea by way of Muscat to Malabar and thence back to Africa and down the east coast to Madagascar and sometimes Sofala.

There was an early and widespread belief, made popular by J. T. Bent[3] and others, that Ophir was the place represented by the extensive ruins at Zimbabwe in Mashonaland, about 200 miles inland from Sofala to which they are connected by blockhouses. But

[1] Cf. Breasted, J. H., *Ancient Records of Egypt*, I, 161, 351, 360–1; II, 246–95.

[2] 1 Kings ix, 28; x, 11, 21–2; 2 Chron. ix, 10, 21; viii, 18; Gen. x, 28; ii, 11; cf. Job xxii, 24; xxviii, 16; Psalm xiv, 9; Isaiah xiii, 12; 1 Chron. xxix, 4.

[3] Bent, J. T., *Ruined Cities of Mashonaland.*

since the beginning of the present century the origin of these great ruins has been much debated. MacIver, Dornan and Schofield held that they were built by Bantu (Africans); Hall and Neal believed that they were the work of pre-Moslem Sabaean or Himyaritic Arabs from Arabia helped by Indians; van Oordt maintained that they were erected by Dravidian Indians.[1]

Recently Caton-Thompson has shown that there can be little doubt that their builders were Africans somewhere between 600 and 1100 A.D.[2] It is still an open question whether these folk were stimulated by Arabs. For the rest, though a certain amount of Indonesian, Malayan and Indian influence has been traced in African ethnography, and, as we have mentioned, the parts round Cape Guardafui were undoubtedly visited by Indians in ancient times, the question of early visits by civilised man to southern Africa remains unsolved.

Out of the wreckage of the "Dorian" invasion of the eleventh century the Greek city-states of history rose in the Aegean, and about 800 B.C. they began to engage in naval adventures. They discovered the "Pillars of Heracles" or Straits of Gibraltar before 630 B.C. but gave way on north-west African and Spanish coasts to the Carthaginians before 500 B.C., so that, since the Egyptians did not encourage or allow them to reach the Red Sea, the non-Mediterranean coasts of Africa remained unknown to them. However, the early conception of the Greeks that the "oikoumene" or "inhabited part of the earth" was surrounded by the Ocean made them believe that Africa was surrounded by sea. The same idea seems to have been prevalent among non-Greeks in the Near East. The Phoenicians, whether Carthaginians and others in the western Mediterranean, or those in the Levant and Egypt, and the Arabians were in a much better position to explore the coast of Africa than were the Greeks; and at the beginning of the sixth century some Phoenicians are said to have circumnavigated Africa from east to west.

According to Herodotus, about the years 600–595 B.C., when Necho was king of Egypt, certain Phoenicians were sent out by him into the Red Sea with definite orders to sail right round Africa. Herodotus says that the Phoenicians sailed out of the Red Sea into the "Southern Sea":

> On each occasion when autumn-time came round, they put to shore, sowed grain in the soil of whatever part of Libya they had reached on their voyage, and waited until reaping-time. They then harvested the corn and sailed on. When two years had passed in this fashion, they doubled the Pillars of Heracles in the third year and came to Egypt. They made a statement which other men may

[1] MacIver, Randall, *Medieval Rhodesia*; Hall, R. W. *Prehistoric Rhodesia*; Hall R. N., and Neal, W. G., *The Ancient Ruins of Rhodesia*. See also *Journ. Anthr. Inst.* 1906, xxxv and *Geogr. Journ.* 1906; *S. A. Journ. of Sci.* 1915–16, pp. 502 *sqq.*; *Vide supra* 35, n. 3. Van Oordt, J., *Who were the Builders of Great Zimbabwe?*

[2] Caton-Thompson, G., *The Zimbabwe Culture* (1931).

believe, of course, but not I, that in sailing round Libya they had the sun on their right hand.[1]

Herodotus looked on this voyage as a proof that the Indian and Atlantic Oceans were one connected body of water.

This is one of the most interesting and at the same time most disappointing records of exploration in ancient literature. Herodotus' statement is based not upon any written records coming from Necho's time, even if any were made, but on his personal conversations with Phoenicians of Tyre or Egypt, and with the priests of Egypt, when he visited that country after 448 B.C. The ultimate source of the story is certainly to be found in the narratives of the Phoenicians, a race notorious for falsehoods, and the whole account of the circumnavigation has been discredited both in ancient and in modern times. No details whatever are given by Herodotus; the leader of the voyagers remains unknown; the voyagers, being Phoenicians, a people which habitually steered by the Great Bear and the Pole Star, would have reported the disappearance of these stars rather than the change in the position of the sun, a fact which could be deduced without experience both by Egyptians and Phoenicians of those days; such a voyage of sixteen thousand miles in the ships of that age, amidst manifold dangers, is very improbable; the proper "autumn-season" or "sowing-season" would be difficult to determine and to utilise successfully—such are the main objections to a belief in this alleged circumnavigation. But such a voyage was not impossible in those days, and the objections to it can be met by parallel and indisputable achievements performed in medieval and early modern times. Yet it is safer to believe merely that in Necho's reign Phoenician navigators sailed down the coast of East Africa into the southern hemisphere; and, for the rest, to keep an open mind.[2]

Within the next century and a half after Herodotus wrote, there were some striking explorations along the coast of western Africa beyond the Pillars of Heracles, which are based upon sounder historical evidence that the voyage of Necho's time. The Phoenicians alone came to know well any part of the Atlantic coast, and they set up barriers of secrecy and falsehood which not only kept the Greeks from sharing in direct commerce with that region, but blocked the Straits of Gibraltar against them. About the middle of the sixth century, and before the Phoenician blockade was set up, Euthymenes,[3] a Greek of Massalia (Marseilles), claimed that he had found on the coast of West Africa a river (the Senegal?), whose stream was being driven back by a wind blowing from the sea and contained

[1] Herodotus, IV, 42.

[2] For the whole question, see Müller, W., *Die Umsegelung Afrikas*; Rennell, J., *Geographical System of Herodotus*, pp. 672–714; Carty and Warmington, *The Ancient Explorers*, pp. 87–95; Thomson, J. O., *History of Ancient Geography*, pp. 71–72.

[3] Jacoby, in Pauly-Wissowa, *Real-Encyklopädie*, VI, I, cols. 1509–11; Cary and Warmington, *Ancient Explorers*, p. 46.

crocodiles. Any Greek attempt to follow in his track was frustrated by the Carthaginians, who had now eclipsed their fellow-Phoenicians, and it is certain that before the end of the sixth century Carthaginian ships were regularly trading along the coast southwards beyond the Straits. About 500 B.C. one of them was blown by a gale to an unknown island, which was almost certainly Madeira.[1]

Then followed one of the greatest explorations recorded in ancient history. Between 500 and 480 B.C. the government of Carthage sent out a man named Hanno, with sixty ships and, according to the record, men and women thirty thousand in number, with orders to found trading colonies on the West African coast. The official report of Hanno's adventures has come down to us in a Greek translation of his own words, which is included in a single manuscript of the tenth century A.D. preserved at Heidelberg.[2] Although the interpretation of this document is not free from difficulties, the identification of the geographical and other features mentioned in it is fairly certain.

After sailing for two days beyond the Pillars, Hanno founded "Thymiaterion" [Mehedia] by a wide plain, and then, having passed a densely wooded headland "Soloeis" [Cape Cantin] and an overgrown and beast-haunted "lagoon" [Tensift marshes], established more towns including "Carian Fort" [Mogador] and "Acra" [Agadir]. Beyond these he discovered next a large river "Lixos" [Wadi Draa]. Along it dwelt a friendly tribe who supplied him with interpreters. Leaving this tribe he coasted to and fro along "the desert" [Sahara] and chose for his next colony an island about nine days' sail from the "Lixos". He named this colony "Cerne" [Herne]. The voyagers sailed on to the delta of a great river the "Chretes" [branch of Senegal], where unfriendly savages [Guanches] prevented them from landing; another wide river [Senegal] beyond was filled with crocodiles and hippopotami. After returning to Cerne, Hanno took his remaining ships southwards for twelve days and put to shore under a high and well wooded headland [Cape Verde]. A two days' sail round this brought him to a great recess [estuary of the Gambia]. After a further five days' sail, he reached a great gulf called by the interpreters "Horn of the West" [Bissagos Bay]. In it lay an island [Orang I.], which contained another island in a lagoon. Here the voyagers landed and saw fires by night and heard much yelling and weird music. After four days' sail beyond, they came to the highest mountain yet seen by them called the "Chariot of the Gods" [Kakulima]. It was all ablaze by night. Three more days brought them to a gulf, the "Horn of the South" [Sherbro Sound]. At

[1] Diodorus, v, 19–20; cf. *de Miris Auscultationibus*, p. 84.

[2] Müller, C., *Geographi Graeci Minores*, I, 1–14; Cary and Warmington, *Ancient Explorers* pp. 47–52; Bunbury, E., *History of Ancient Geography*, I, 318 *sqq.*; Thomson J. O., *op. cit.*, pp. 73–77.

intervals between the great recess or bay and this gulf many fires [grass-fires?] had been seen by night and by day. In the gulf lay another isle-within-isle [Macaulay I.]. Here they found timid hairy men and women [chimpanzees or dog-faced baboons], whom the interpreters called "Gorillas". They captured three females, who bit and scratched. They killed and flayed these captives and brought their hides to Carthage. Hanno did not sail further owing to lack of provisions.[1]

All things considered, we may take it that Hanno reached Sierra Leone and Sherbro Sound, over three thousand miles from home. Since the coast takes a decidedly eastward turn in this region, it was probably Hanno's voyage which caused the Carthaginians to say that Africa could be circumnavigated, but of the southern half of Africa he saw and learned nothing. Though the Carthaginians traded for many years as far as Cerne, no similar effort followed his great voyage, and the new settlements gradually disappeared.

A curious but credible story is told by Herodotus of a Persian noble named Sataspes, who, apparently on a mere whim of the Persian king Xerxes (485–465 B.C.), was sent out to sail round Africa from the Pillars of Heracles to the Red Sea in expiation of some misdeed. Having obtained a ship and a crew in Egypt:

> He sailed out between the Pillars, doubled the headland of Libya which is named Soloeis, and went sailing on towards the south. He traversed much sea in many months, and, finding that there was ever more voyaging before him, turned round and sailed back again to Egypt. From Egypt he came to Xerxes' court and made report that at the furthest limit of his voyage he was sailing by a land of dwarfed men who wore clothes made of palm-leaves. These men, wherever he put his ship to land, left their towns and fled towards the mountains. He and his crew entered the towns but did no harm, taking only cattle from them. As for the reason why he did not circumnavigate Libya, he said that the ship was not able to go on farther, but was stopped.[2]

Sataspes was not believed by Xerxes, but there is little doubt that he spoke the truth. He rounded Cape Spartel (Soloeis in Herodotus), and, avoiding the Phoenician settlements, sailed beyond their limit and discovered, beyond the Sahara, negro tribes who were not too primitive to dwell in large villages. His return may be attributed to an adverse wind or current.

After 448 B.C., when the wars between Greeks and Persians ceased, the former, who hitherto had known nothing beyond the southern end of the Red Sea, began to learn by hearsay something of South Arabia and Somaliland on the borders of the "Southern Sea". But many came to believe that it was impossible to sail round Africa. An astonishing theory arose that eastern Africa, in the unknown regions where the Nile took its source, was joined to North India so that the Nile and the Indus were one river and the Arabian Sea

[1] Müller, *op. cit.* I, 1–14.
[2] Herodotus, IV, 43.

was a great lake. Some also came to believe that the sea along the west coast of Africa was blocked up in some way. Others, however, believed that just beyond the mouth of the Red Sea the coast of Africa bent round to the south-west and west to the Pillars of Heracles, so that the existence of the whole of Africa south of the unknown limits of the Sahara was not even imagined. The West African mart, Herne, to which Greek cities sent their wares through the Carthaginians in exchange for African products, became an object of speculation amongst Athenian and other Greek merchants, who, desirous of avoiding Carthaginian imposts and restrictions, wondered whether it might not be reached by sailing south and west round Africa from the "Erythraean" Sea. But it was assumed that in the south the heat became too great to bear, while the jealous Carthaginians further reported that the Atlantic was a muddy, shallow, weedy sea, not blessed with favourable winds, and that sailings beyond Herne were difficult if not impossible.[1] There was indeed a rumour in the fourth century B.C. that, beyond Herne, the sea went round to Egypt and made Africa a great peninsula,[2] but this idea was based on guesswork, while Aristotle's insistence on a temperate zone in the southern as in the northern hemisphere was due to the Greek love of symmetry.[3] Alexander, by sailing down the Indus to its mouths in 325 B.C., exploded for ever the idea that there was a connection between the Indus and the Nile; but his death prevented his proposed circumnavigation of Africa from east to west.

The Macedonian dynasty of the Ptolemies, which was established in Egypt after Alexander's death, failed to overcome the barriers set up by the Arabians on the way to India, but found the African coast free from restriction during the first two hundred years of their sway. Under the first four Ptolemies trading ports were founded along the Red Sea and successful expeditions were sent out by them to open up commerce and to secure large numbers of African elephants for use in war. The coasts of Somaliland became tolerably well known by the Greeks as far as Cape Guardafui, so that they ceased to make the African coast turn westwards at the mouth of the Red Sea; but by 200 B.C. Ptolemaic activities in these regions had somewhat declined.

In 242–1 B.C. Rome destroyed the sea-power of Carthage and in due course became mistress of Spain. Yet no further voyage of exploration was made down the coast of West Africa, and by the end of the century many thinkers became convinced that the northern hemisphere was the only part of the earth which was inhabited by man, and that it was cut off for ever from the south by great heat.[4]

[1] Cf. "Scylax", *Periplus*, p. 112; Müller, C., *Geog. Graeci Min.* I, 93–4; Ephorus in Pliny, VI, 199.

[2] Aristotle, *Meteorologica*, II, I, 12; "Scylax", *loc. cit.*

[3] *Op. cit.* II, 5.

[4] Strabo, II, 114, 118.

The old belief that Africa was not surrounded by sea at all but continued on and on towards the south and east as land without limit still persisted.[1] Yet others in greater wisdom were following the famous geographer, Eratosthenes (*circa* 210 B.C.), who had maintained that it must be possible to sail round Africa because the tides of the ocean on both sides of Africa were similar.[2] Others, again, like Crates, who died in 145 B.C., pictured to themselves a mass of land beyond known Africa to the south and separated from it by sea. The destruction of Carthage in 146 B.C. enabled Polybius[3] to sail with a fleet beyond the Senegal without difficulty, but, in spite of this, West African commerce was much reduced owing to the decay of the Carthaginian colonies. For merchants who sailed out of the Mediterranean by the Pillars, the attractions lay far more towards the north than the south. The Romans, as they rose to power throughout the Mediterranean, were fully engaged with problems of internal politics and imperial diplomacy and government, and apart from this they had no interest in the exploration of Africa by land or sea. The geographical system of Eratosthenes held good: outside the Straits of Gibraltar the coast, according to him, went due south for some distance and then turned south-eastwards for a long way, and finally eastwards as far as Cape Guardafui, where it then turned (as it does in fact) westwards towards the Red Sea. He held that the whole of Africa, less than one-third of the continent as it really exists, lay north of the Equator.

In spite of the destruction of Carthage and the consequent decay of its western colonies, and in spite of the degeneration of the Ptolemies, the last part of the second century saw another remarkable adventure of which the motive and the circumstances are of peculiar interest. There were rumours that ships of Gadeira or Gades (Cadiz), a still vigorous Phoenician city, were circumnavigating Africa from west to east, and were trading with Somali and Arabian coasts, out of reach of the Ptolemaic exactions which all who passed through Egypt had to bear. Belief in these rumours brought about an attempt to reach India from Spain by sailing round Africa, so as to avoid not only these exactions, but also the Arabian imposts, which were, from *circa* 115 B.C. onwards, levied on merchants by the Himyarites. These now became the ruling power in southern Arabia in place of the Sabaeans, and extended commercial imposts and restrictions to all the Somali coasts.

After 146 B.C. in the reign of Ptolemy Euergetes II there came to Egypt a merchant named Eudoxus, a man of Cyzicus, which was an Asiatic city by the sea of Marmora. He, being a man who was thrilled by thoughts of exploring unknown lands, was sent with

[1] Hipparchus in Strabo, I, 5 *fin.*–6; Polybius, III, 38, 1–2.
[2] Strabo, I, 56.
[3] Pliny, V, 9.

others by the king to discover the route round Arabia to India. Having made two successful voyages to India, on his second return (between 117 and 108 B.C.) he was blown by the north-eastern monsoon some way down the east coast of Africa south of Cape Guardafui. He landed here and there, made friends with the "Ethiopian" natives, and compiled a glossary of some of their words. He found and brought back to Egypt a piece of the prow of a wrecked ship, which experts in Alexandria stated to be a fragment of a ship of Gades. Deprived of his cargo after both voyages, and convinced that Africa could be circumnavigated, he determined to sail for India by a route that would avoid the Ptolemies' monopoly and so satisfy the demands of business. He prepared a ship at Cyzicus, advertised his plans at Puteoli in Italy, Massalia in Gaul and towns on the coasts between Massalia and Gades, and then, at Gades, says Strabo,

> he built a large ship and two tow-boats, like those which pirates use. He put on board girls and boys who were skilled in music, and also surgeons, and artisans besides these, and then sailed for India on the high sea, while constant western breeze blew him on.... [After a wreck, he built a third boat of surviving timbers...] and then sailed on until he found himself among people who used the same words as those on the list which he had made before. He now recognised that these people of this region belonged to the same nation as those other Ethiopians, and that they dwelt on the borders of Bogus's Kingdom. So he abandoned the voyage to India and turned back. As he sailed along the coast he sighted and made note of a well-watered and well-wooded but uninhabited island. He reached Maurusia safely and disposed of his boats [and ultimately returned to Gades.] ... Having built once more a round ship for sailing in the open sea, and a long ship of fifty oars for exploring the coast, he placed in them agricultural implements, seeds and artisans, and set out with the same circumnavigation in view. His intention was, in case the voyage should be delayed, to pass the winter on the island which he had seen before, sow and reap a crop, and then complete the voyage on which he had resolved at the outset.[1]

This story of Eudoxus[2] was doubted even in ancient times, but on quite insufficient grounds; Eudoxus may well have been himself deceived and misled by others in the matter of the ship of Gades on the east coast of Africa, and there may have been, as there are now, natives on both sides of Africa speaking tongues of similar sound; the places at which Eudoxus called in order to gain assistance before his first voyage from Gades were the very places at which good cargoes for the east could be got; the girls and boys whom he took would make very suitable gifts for the harems of Indian potentates; and, lastly, the account, which Strabo quotes from Posidonius, a younger contemporary of Eudoxus, does not make Eudoxus succeed in his final attempt, and moreover is free from obvious falsehoods.

[1] Strabo, II, 98–102.

[2] See Gaffarel, P., in *Mém. de la Soc. d'Émulation du Doubs*, IV Sér., vol. VII, 1872, pp. 13–100; Berger, H., *Geschichte der wissenschaftlichen Erdkunde der Griechen*, 2nd ed., pp. 569 *sqq.* cp. 71 *sqq.*; Cary and Warmington, *Ancient Explorers*, pp. 98–103; Thomson, J. O., *op. cit.*, p. 850.

Eudoxus had published no written record before his disappearance; hence the absence of details. It is possible that Pomponius Mela, of the first century after Christ, has preserved in dim and muddled form some of the yarns told by Eudoxus' sailors about eastern and western Africa—stories of dumb men and mouthless men (timid folk of the west coast?) and of people whose lips were stuck together (by some ornament?), of men with no noses (because almost hidden by thick lips?), and of dwarfs and other strange beings.[1] Again, it is possibly a result of Eudoxus' discoveries on his second return from India that Artemidorus,[2] about 100 B.C., knew that the coast of Africa bends round at the "Horn of the South", which in this case is Cape Guardafui. But we have no real clue to the limits reached by Eudoxus on either coast, beyond the fact that, on his first voyage down West Africa, he reached a point not far south of Mauretania or Morocco, where Bogus or Bocchus ruled. Nor have we any clue to his fate. But we may accept the very credible story told by Strabo. Eudoxus, in spite of the failure of his ultimate plan, is of especial interest to us, since his activities represent the first clear manifestation of that interconnection between East Africa, Arabia and India which has never since been broken.

After the time of Eudoxus we hear little of African voyages for nearly two centuries. The geographer Strabo, writing about 7 B.C., based himself largely on the views of Eratosthenes, and placed the whole of Africa to the north of the Equator; of its southern part he says he could speak by guess-work only; even if it were possible to approach this part of Africa, nobody had done so; and he stated definitely that all who had sailed either out of the Pillars of Heracles or the Red Sea had been forced to return.[3] We must bear in mind the fact that Strabo's unapproached southern part of Africa is not the real continent but the convex hypotenuse of a rough right-angled triangle which runs north-west and south-east and includes the western coast. The eastern turn given to the west coast of Africa, established as a belief for about seventeen centuries by the geography of Eratosthenes, is not the real bend of the Gulf of Guinea, but was drawn to the north-west of this and was entirely imaginary. So far were men from understanding the true geography of the continent on the western side that even Strabo believed that there was an impassable torrid zone which made all human life impossible.

With the establishment of the Roman Empire as a peaceful and prosperous Mediterranean unity, the attention of would-be explorers was drawn in more profitable directions, western Africa being as before largely ignored, since the Romans put the limit of their interests at Sala (Sallee). One isolated adventure along western Africa was

[1] Mela, III, 9.
[2] Strabo, XVI, 774.
[3] Strabo, I, 22; II, 132–3, 120; XVII, 825, etc.

the expedition of King Juga of Mauretania, which, about the beginning of our era, brought back accurate details about the Canary Islands.[1] The Carthaginians had probably discovered these islands long before, because Fuerteventura can be seen from Cape Juby, and the Greeks may have heard vaguely of the group as certain "Fortunate Islands" in the distant west. All were uninhabited and were deemed unworthy of further visits.

The progress of knowledge concerning the eastern coast of Africa was much greater than knowledge of the west. This arose from the annexation of Egypt by the Romans in 30 B.C. and their consequent interest in the commerce of the Red Sea. The Greek merchants who carried on the trade of the Empire sought how to deal in Indian goods without the intervention of Arabian middlemen, and, from the beginning of the Empire in 27 B.C. to the reign of Claudius (A.D. 41–54) these merchants were trading in considerable numbers with the Arabians on both sides of the Gulf of Aden, though very few of them made their way to India. The emperor Augustus (27 B.C.–A.D. 14) made some efforts to break the Arabian monopoly; in 25 B.C. he sent Aelius Gallus with an army to explore southern Arabia and Ethiopia; and Aelius marched to the borders of Yemen, but returned without achieving much. About the year 1 B.C. preparations were made for the circumnavigation of Arabia from Egypt to Mesopotamia by a Roman fleet, and it was decided that the circumnavigation of Africa should also be attempted. Interest seems to have revived in the tales about the African voyages of the ships of Gades; and it was said that when the Roman fleet sailed down the Red Sea, it discovered wreckage of ships which were identified as Spanish,[2] though we have no record of how far the fleet went either along the Arabian or African coast.

But Roman trade with Arabia, East Africa and India increased greatly owing to the ever-growing demand of the Empire for oriental luxuries. We are fortunate in having a first-hand record of this trade in the form of an anonymous merchants' practical guidebook for the "Erythraean" or Arabian Sea, including the Indian coasts as far as the Ganges. It is preserved in the same manuscript as the record of Hanno's voyage, which we have already mentioned, and is entitled "Periplus [i.e. Circumnavigation] of the Erythraean Sea".[3] From internal evidence we may judge that it was written about the year A.D. 60 in Nero's reign. It reveals in striking fashion how the commerce and politics of East Africa, Arabia and India must have created for the Roman emperors one single department of oriental policy. From our point of view, the importance of this document

[1] Pliny, v, 5; vi, 201–5; Müller, C., *Fragm. Hist. Graec.* iii, 472–4.

[2] Pliny, vi, 175; ii, 168.

[3] Text in Müller, *Geog. Graeci Min.* ii, 257 *sqq.*; translation by Schoff, W. H., *The Periplus of the Erythraean Sea.*

lies in its revelation of persistent Graeco-Roman attempts to break down the Arabian monopoly, and of some results of these successful efforts. About A.D. 40 a Greek named Hippalus radically altered Romano-Arabian relations by discovering that by using the monsoon winds, the periodicity of which was common knowledge, a navigator could sail across the open sea, between the Gulf of Aden and north-western India, free from Arab interference. The combined evidence of the *Periplus* and an important passage in Pliny[1] shows how other Greeks, following Hippalus' methods, had, by about A.D. 50, established direct voyages between the Gulf of Aden and every part of the western coast of India, the favourite points of departure being Cape Guardafui and Socotra.

Thus the Arabian monopoly of Indian trade was circumvented. It was inevitable that the use made of the monsoons, and treaties now arranged between the Romans and the Arabians, should have opened up Somaliland on both sides of Cape Guardafui more fully to Westerners. In Nero's time, not only were the Somali coasts explored and all the marts well known, but the Greeks also, like the Arabians, frequently visited Socotra, doubled Cape Guardafui, and sailed down the eastern coast of Africa across the Equator:

Where the land falls away towards the south there is situated the Mart of Spices [Obok] and an abrupt promontory—the furthest headland [Ras Asir, Guardafui] of the Barbaric [Berber] mainland . . . towards the east. . . . When a storm comes . . . all navigators flee before it to the great headland . . . which is called Tabae—[Ras Chenarif?]. . . . After four hundred stades [i.e. 50 geographical miles] from Tabae navigators reach the village Pano [Ras Binna]; then after coasting along a promontory another four hundred stades they reach another mart Opone [by Ras Hafun] . . . [where are obtained cinnamon, slaves, and tortoiseshell.] . . . The voyage to all these far-side marts from Egypt is made in July. Even wares, whose origin is the inner parts of Ariace [Kutch, Kathiawar and Gujarat in India] and Barygaza [Broach], are habitually prepared and transported to these marts across the sea—corn, rice, ghi, gingelly oil, cotton, girdles, and reed-honey which is called "sakchari" [sugar]. . . . There is no king of this region, and each mart is governed by its own potentate. After Opone, the sea-shore bears away more to the south. First come the so-called Little and Great Crags [coast of El Hazin] of Azania [the southern part of Italian Somaliland, Kenya Colony and Tanganyika as far as the Zanzibar Channel]. This coast is destitute of harbours, though there are places where vessels can rest at anchor, the beach being precipitous. This course lasts six days in a direction south-west. Then come Little Strand and Great Strand [Sif el Tauil], extending for six more courses, and next in order after this the Courses of Azania, the first being the so-called Serapion [Magadoxo, Mogdishu?], the next Nicon . . . seven more courses, [ending at the] Pyralaae islands [Patta, Manda, Lamu] and the so-called Channel. A little beyond this, towards the south of south-west, after a course of two days and nights, one comes across Menuthias island [Pemba or Zanzibar]. . . . It is situated about three hundred stades distant from the land and is low and covered with trees. In it there are rivers and very many kinds of birds, and the mountain-tortoise, but it has no beasts except crocodiles who do no harm to man. Round it small boats are met with, some being stitched vessels, others being dug-outs, . . .[fishing and tortoise-hunting.] . . . After two courses from this island is the last mart to be found on the mainland of

[1] *Periplus*, 31–2, 39, 57; Pliny, VI, 100–106.

Azania. This mart is so-called Rhapta [Dar-es-Salaam].... Very great quantities of ivory and tortoiseshell are obtained there. Round this region dwell men who are very large in body; among them each chief rules over his own place like a despot. Its overlord is the despot of Mapharitis [southern Tehama in Arabia]... but with his permission it is held as a tributary possession by the people of Muza [Mokha in Southern Arabia]. These send to it cargo-boats which are for the most part provided with Arab skippers and agents; these latter have intermarriage and intercourse with the natives and have skilled knowledge of their territory and language.... These then may be taken as the very last marts of Azania.... For beyond these regions the ocean, which is unexplored, bends round towards the west, and, stretching out along the remote southern parts of Ethiopia and Libya or Africa mingles with the western Ocean.[1]

In this passage the facts of control by Arabs along the East African coast, and of visits well beyond the Equator by Roman subjects and by Indians, are indisputable. But the precise limits to which their voyages and knowledge reached are not certain. Menuthias Island, described in the *Periplus* apparently from hearsay, should be Pemba; but the description applies better to Zanzibar and includes characteristics of the mainland, while the name Menuthias may survive in Monfiyeh or Mafia, a still more southerly island, and the location of Rhapta depends on that of Menuthias. Comparison of the *Periplus* with the later *Geography* of Ptolemy points to Zanzibar for Menuthias and Dar-es-Salaam for Rhapta. The alleged western bend of the coast is a surmise only, but at any rate it is certain that the Greeks had now traced the southerly continuation of Africa beyond the Equator.

Further advances towards southern Africa on the eastern side are revealed by Ptolemy the geographer in his tables for constructing a map of the known world, and in his prefaces. He compiled his *Geographike Syntaxis*, or Mathematical Geography, between A.D. 125 and 155, incorporating in it much material obtained from Marinus of Tyre who wrote a little earlier. The new discoveries which he records and reflects took place about A.D. 100–140. With regard to eastern Africa, he adds something to the *Periplus* record from the reports of later navigators, and with regard to inner Africa, he reveals, however dimly, some fresh knowledge of great importance and interest obtained largely by Greek merchants.

From those merchants who make the passage from Arabia the Blest [Yemen] to the Cape of Spices [Guardafui] and Azania and Rhapta, calling all this region Barbaria, we learn that the voyage does not lead exactly towards the south; it leads partly west by south, the passage from Rhapta to Prason leading east by south; and that the lakes from which the Nile flows are not situated by the sea, but far inland.[2]

The length of the passage down the Africa coast is indicated in another part of the work:

[1] *Periplus*, 12–18.

[2] Ptolemy, I, 17, 6 and compare IV, 7, 28.

Marinus records that a certain Diogenes, one of those who sail regularly to India, was returning from a voyage thither; and when he was in the region of the Cape of Spices he was driven out of his course by northerly winds. Keeping Troglodytice [the African coast] on his right hand for twenty-five days he came to [the latitude of] the lakes from which the Nile flows; the Cape of Rhapta is a little further south than these. Marinus also says that a certain Theophilus, one of those who sail regularly to Azania, put out from Rhapta with a south wind, and reached the Cape of Spices on the twentieth day. . . . Marinus says that the voyage from Rhapta to Prason, lasting many days, was assumed by one Dioscorus to be one of five thousand stades only, it being reasonable to find that the winds under the equator are changeable because the movement of the sun to one side or the other in the equatorial region are swifter than they are elsewhere.[1]

Of the coast beyond the limits mentioned by the *Periplus* Ptolemy gives some details:

By Cape Rhapton [the merchants say] there is a river Rhapton and a metropolis with the same name Rhapta, situated a short distance from the sea. The bay which extends from Rhapta to Cape Prason is very great but not deep; round the bay dwell savages who are cannibals.[2]

On the other hand, Ptolemy's description of north-western Africa reflects an almost complete falling-off of knowledge since the time of Hanno, of whose *Periplus* we can see hardly a trace in Ptolemy. He makes the coast run continuously south after Cape Spartel, and his southern limit of knowledge is the "Great Gulf on the Western Ocean"—a gulf which is certainly not the Gulf of Guinea and has no place in actual fact.[3] The Graeco-Roman ideas of further Africa are well summed up in the following passages:

Inner Ethiopia, which is situated south of all the rest of Libya, is bounded by that part of the Western Ocean, which forms the Great Gulf; on the south-west it is bounded by unknown land, and on the east by the Barbaric Gulf which is called "The Shallow Sea" because of its shallows and extends from Cape Rhapta to Cape Prason, and by the unknown land which extends from this point. Cape Prason is situated in 80° long.,[4] 15½° south lat. North-east of this point lies the island named Menuthias, whose position is in 85° long., 12½° south lat. Round this gulf dwell cannibal Ethiopians. To the west of these, stretches the Mountain-Range of the Moon, from which the lakes of the Nile receive snow. The two ends of the Mountain-Range of the Moon are situated respectively in 57° long., 12½° south lat., and 67° long., 12½° south lat. South of it dwell Rhapsian Ethiopians. Round the Great Gulf by the Western Ocean dwell fish-eating Ethiopians; farther south than these, up to the unknown land, dwell those Ethiopians who are called by the common name "Western", and farther to the east, Ethiopians called "Athacae". Again, towards the east, along the whole of Libya extends the spacious territory of the Ethiopians in which occur, besides rhinoceroses and leopards, the whole known breed of white elephants. Along the unknown land, moreover, extends an Ethiopian territory for a very long distance called "Agisymba". This territory has mountain ranges, including many great ones, as far

[1] Ptolemy, I, 9, 1–3, on estimating the distances of voyages.

[2] Ptolemy, I, 17, 121; and compare I, 17, 7; IV, 7, 11–12—details Cape of Spices—Rhapta.

[3] Ptolemy, VI, 6, 3 *sqq.*

[4] Ptolemy's longitudes are reckoned from a prime meridian 0° through the Fortunate (i.e. Canary) Islands.

as the unknown land, which are nameless. . . . Between the southernmost part of the inhabited land-mass to the south pole there are 73 and more unknown degrees.[1]

Marinus puts the Ethiopian territory called Agisymba and Cape Prason under the parallel which marks off the southernmost limit of the known earth.[2]

In describing the upper part of the Nile Basin, Ptolemy mentions the White Nile the Blue Nile and the Atbara, which had been known to the Greeks since the third century B.C. He also says:

The place where the Nile unites into one river the rivers which flow from the two lakes lying towards the south is situated in 60° long., 2° north lat. Of the lakes the more westerly is situated in 57° long., 6° south lat., and the more easterly, in 65° long., 7° south lat.[3] Near the lakes the so-called Pylaea or Pylae Mountains are situate in 65° long. and on the equator; and Mount Maste is situated in 68° long., 5° south lat.[4]. . . The Mastitae dwell from here [*sc.* the equator] to the lakes of the Nile.[5]

Reasonable interpretation of these passages is difficult because they deal with regions on the borderland of the known and the unknown, so that enormous distortion of the truth, which is found amongst Greek and Roman cartographic data even for well known regions, is here very prominent. Ptolemy's definite location of geographical features by latitude and longitude is an unreliable guide, because his precise figures are based only on rough and ready calculations of merchants, and are only given in order to fix the most likely location on a map. Again, his location of the known geographical features of further Africa is uniformly too far to the south, so that his latitude of any place is only of value relatively to another place. As far as the voyages down eastern Africa are concerned, Ptolemy produces something like first-hand information accumulated by Marinus from Greek eye-witnesses; but, with regard to the inland regions of eastern Africa, we cannot tell whether these Greeks saw them or obtained their information from Arabs or African natives. Nevertheless, the considerable addition to Greek knowledge of Africa in his day is a positive fact. Greek navigators by the time of Marinus had reached the entrance of the Mozambique Channel, for there is little doubt that Cape Prason is the southern Cape Delgado where Portuguese East Africa begins. The bay extending from Prason northwards to Rhapta would thus be the concave coast of Tanganyika Territory, the River Rhapton would be the Rufu, and Cape Rhapta would be Cape Poonah. Menuthias is again a puzzle, for Ptolemy puts it in 5° long., 3° north lat. from Cape Prason, which leaves it far out to sea. This suggests not Zanzibar but the Great Comoro, and even so we can only fix its north-easterly position relative to Prason if we identify Prason with Mozambique, which, in view of

[1] Ptolemy, IV, 8, 1–7.

[2] *Id.* I, 7, 2; Thomson, J. O., *op. cit.*, pp. 274 *sqq.*

[3] Ptolemy, IV, 7, 23–4.

[4] *Id.* IV, 7, 26.

[5] *Id.* IV, 7, 31; cf. also IV, 7, 3; II, 1, 6; I, 15, 10; I, 10, 1.

the "bay" from Rhapta to Prason, is not a likely conclusion. Ptolemy habitually fixes islands too far out to sea and his directions are often wrong. All we can say is that it is probable that the Greeks possessed some confused hearsay information about the Comoros and even perhaps about the great island of Madagascar itself.

Ptolemy's notices about the Mountains or Mountain-Range of the Moon, which he represents as stretching 500 miles east and west, and of the melted snow which fed two lakes, these being the reservoirs of two streams of the Nile which unite north of the Equator, are of great interest. We think at once of the Ruwenzori range, whose thirty miles of glacier might suggest a lunar landscape; of the Victoria Nyanza which receives, from the Ruwenzori range, the Kagera, headstream of the Nile; and of the smaller Lake Albert which receives and emits the Nile after it has flowed through the marshy Lake Choga. It is true that the Ruwenzori runs north and south and that Lake Albert lies north-north-west of Lake Victoria; but if we turn this part of Ptolemy's map clockwise through one-quarter of a circle (as must be done, for example, counter-clockwise with his map of Scotland, the length of which he represents as running east and west), and include in the "Mountain of the Moon" not only the Ruwenzori but the hills to the west of Lake Tanganyika, we have these hills and Lakes Victoria and Albert roughly in their right relation to each other, and even roughly in their right latitudes. Between the lakes and the coast, according to Ptolemy's location, were the Pylaea or Pylae Mountains and, to the south of these, Mount Maste. If we ignore the actual latitudes given by Ptolemy, and think only of these heights in relation to each other, we can identify the Pylaea with Kenya Mountain and with the heights westward of it to Lake Victoria, and Maste with the great peak of Kilimanjaro.

The reports of Greek merchants concerning the Mountain of the Moon left permanent traces in ancient geography, and until the early part of the nineteenth century the mountains and the twin lakes were delineated in most maps as the sources of the Nile, though the essential truth of the old reports was obscured by the erroneous insistence of some Greek and Roman writers on the identity of the true Nile with the Niger or "Western Nile". This belief is connected with the vague ancient knowledge of the Sahara, wherein lay Agisymba and the mountain Dauchis, Ion, etc. The Sahara was rightly conceived by Ptolemy as mountainous, but it was prolonged too far southwards to an enormous extent. It is worth while mentioning here that before Herodotus' time a party of Nasamones, a Berber tribe, crossed the Sahara and reached the Niger by way of Asben and Timbuktu.[1] A little before the time of Marinus, a Roman

[1] Herodotus, II, 32–3. This is the only certain record of the Niger in antiquity. In Ptolemy, IV, 6, 13–14, Geir and Nigeir appear to be merely the Jedi and Igharghar of north-west Africa.

officer named Julius Maternus, travelling from the Bay of Tripoli, "in four months reached Agisymba, a territory of the Ethiopians, where the rhinoceroses congregate"[1] on the Sudanese steppe, apparently between Asben and Lake Chad. It may be that Ptolemy's notices of Sahara heights are based on information afforded by Maternus.

To sum up—there is little doubt that the southern limits of Greek and Roman knowledge of Africa, though they are fixed by Ptolemy on a line drawn at 20° south latitude, must in reality be placed at about 11° south latitude, and even this applies to the eastern coast only. Here the Greeks had explored as far as Cape Delgado, or possibly Mozambique, but not beyond. There is no space here to discuss the various opinions of scholars adduced in Hall's *Prehistoric Rhodesia* on south-eastern Africa as known to the ancients;[2] it is enough to say that some go beyond the bounds of probability. There have been found two Roman coins which might indicate direct intercourse by Greeks with regions still further distant than Cape Delgado. Thus a coin of the emperor Antoninus Pius (A.D. 138–161) has been found inland at Zimbabwe, and one of Constantine (A.D. 306–337) in Madagascar; but it is most probable that the former was brought thither by some Himyarite Arab, and the latter by some Abyssinian trader, as indicated below. Again, with regard to the western coast of Africa, Ptolemy's description gives no clue to any explorations made under the Roman Empire; yet a Roman coin of the emperor Trajan (A.D. 98–117) has been found on the Congo. It is much more likely that this coin was introduced at a much later date than that there was direct Roman intercourse so far down the western coast. Moreover, no single article unmistakably originating in Africa south of the Equator has been discovered in the Graeco-Roman world or in contemporary Arabia, nor is there any mention of such article in written records, while the coins are the only ancient European or Arabian articles that have been found in the southern parts of Africa.

Of much greater significance for later geographers was an extraordinary belief held by Ptolemy with regard to Africa. Along the western coast he gave no indication of any idea of what lay beyond the known limits; but with regard to the eastern coast he revived and modified an ancient geographic error, as is shown by a passage in his description of the Far East, which was already being visited by Roman subjects in his time. After describing the land of the Sinae or Chinese, Ptolemy says:

> From Cattigara [Hanoi?] in a westward direction the boundary of the country is formed by the unknown land which surrounds the Prasonian sea all the way to Cape Prason where there begins, as we have said, the gulf of the Shallow Sea connecting the land with Cape Rhapton and the southern parts of Azania. . . .[3]

[1] Ptolemy, I, 8, 5; cf. IV, 6, 3.
[2] Hall, R. N., *Prehistoric Rhodesia*, pp. 352 *sqq*.
[3] Ptolemy, VII, 3, 6.

Cattigara itself is placed by Ptolemy in $8\frac{1}{2}°$ south latitude,[1] whereas all China is really north of 20° north latitude. Thus, according to him, the east coast of Africa, as it runs southwards, bends eastwards near Cape Delgado so as to face north, and, forming a southern shore of the Indian Ocean, is joined to a westward-facing China. The eastern coast of Africa in large part became the northern coast of a wholly imaginary southern region. The Erythraean sea was conceived once more as a lake. The plain fact is that the vast length of the coasts of Africa, combined with the lack of any definite commercial goal, caused Ptolemy and those who followed him to give up the hope of finding out the form of Africa in the far south. We must note, however, that Ptolemy's *Geography*, lasting as its influence was, remained a work for the select few; the old Eratosthenic idea that the inhabited part of the world lay wholly within the north temperate zone, with a circumnavigable Africa wholly north of the Equator, was the more popular one.

After the second century A.D. the Roman Empire suffered an appalling economic decline and political collapse, and the loss of its purchasing power struck at the roots of European travel and trade in the east as in other directions; Roman subjects abandoned the Arabian Sea, where the Arabs, and then the Axumites of Abyssinia in conjunction with the Arabs and the Persians, took their place. A partial revival of trade under later Roman emperors of Constantinople, and the activities of the first Christian missionaries, who like their fellows adopted entirely false ideas of the earth, failed in some parts to produce even a re-exploration of regions that had once been known. Thus, in the west, the geographical knowledge embodied in Ptolemy's work faded, like other knowledge, from the minds of the laity, since the clerics and scholars behind the walls of colleges and cloisters kept their learning to themselves, and when a geographical work was published, it was generally a compilation of old classical knowledge and traditions. When, in the seventh century, the Arab conquests completely blocked out Europeans from eastern waters, even South Arabia became utterly remote to western peoples. In this period, from the second century to the seventh, and all through the early Middle Ages, those who interested themselves in the geography of Africa or knew anything about it adopted, with few exceptions, one or other of the following schemes: (i) the scheme of Eratosthenes, including a very limited Africa, as handed down in fragments by Pliny, by Solinus, who copied him, and by less important writers; (ii) the scheme of Ptolemy, including an unlimited Africa; (iii) a combination of both schemes; (iv) the ideas of many Christians who based their views on biblical texts, and, opposing the learned in their oval and circular conceptions, made Ocean flow all round the inhabited world, and foretold an everlasting fire for all

[1] *Id.* VII, 3, 3.

unbelievers. The scheme of Eratosthenes became by far the most popular, largely owing to the widely read work of Solinus dating from the third century. Macrobius, of the early fifth century, also widely read in the Middle Ages, believed that only the torrid zone prevented circumnavigation. Later writers and later maps show similar ideas, and very few authorities show Ptolemy's endless land.

In the seventh century the Arabs swept in; they conquered all the northern parts of Africa from the Red Sea to the Atlantic and Spain and cut off the westerners from access to both sides of Africa. They held some of the chief centres of learning, and ruled over lands which bordered on the unknown parts of Africa. For more than three centuries they were not strong in numbers, and ruled by the might of the sword; however, it was within that period that their first settlement in eastern Africa south of the Equator was made. A band of Muslim heretics, led out from Arabia about A.D. 740 by Zaide, came gradually down the east coast of Africa as far as the Equator, and mixed with the natives;[1] they were followed by a company of "true believers" in three ships; these newcomers about A.D. 930 founded Magadoxo and Borawa or Brava and pushed their Emozaidi forerunners inland to become intermediaries in commerce. At a later period some explorers from Magadoxo reached Sofala, and, obtaining gold in that region, founded a community there. Subsequently a small settlement was made by the River Nyambana, or Inhambane, by Cape Correntes. When Al Masudi[2] of Baghdad wrote his *Meadows of Gold* about A.D. 950, Arabs, Persians and Indians were, by using the monsoons, visiting East Africa as far as Sofala, where the Bushmen traded with them. It is not certain whether the island Kanbalú, another goal of trade, inhabited by Muslims and "Zanj" or Blacks and situated in the "sea of the Zanj", is Madagascar or merely Zanzibar, but it is worth noting that Masudi rejected Ptolemy's idea of an unlimited land down the south and south-east of Africa, and believed that Africa could be circumnavigated. However, the limits of voyages were Kanbalu and the land of Sofala and the Wakwak (Bushmen), "which is on the extremity of the country of the Zanj and the low countries thereabouts".

About A.D. 1020 Persian Muslims from Ormuz, under one Ali, settled at Kilwa and showed themselves bitter enemies of the Arabs. They set up control over all the older settlements and established, or re-established, new ones, not only at Malindi, Mombasa, Pemba, Zanzibar, Mafia, Mozambique, Quilimane, at Sena well inland on the Lower Zambesi, and at Sofala, but also in Madagascar and the Comoros. But they did not know much beyond the mouths of the

[1] Theal, G. M., *Records of South-Eastern Africa*, VII, 465 *sqq*.

[2] Maçudi, *Les Prairies d'Or, Texte et Traduction*, Barbier de Meynard et Pavet de Courteille, I, 230 *sqq*.; III, 6 *sqq*.; also Sprenger, A., *El Masudi's Historical Encyclopaedia*, I, 260 *sqq*. Hall, R. N., *Prehistoric Rhodesia*, pp. 65 *sqq*.

Zambesi. No one indeed sailed beyond Cape Correntes,[1] for men were afraid of the Mozambique current and of certain mermaids, who lured navigators to their doom amidst enchanted waves of mountainous size.

Marco Polo's accounts of Madagascar and of "Zanghibar" are derived from information given to him by Arabs in A.D. 1294, and are of some importance. The main points in his account of "Madeigascar"[2] may be summarised as follows:

By sailing from "Scotra" (Socotra) in a direction south-south west for about a thousand miles one reaches the noble and beautiful island of Madeigascar, which is about four thousand miles in circumference, and is inhabited by Saracens under four Elders or Sheiks. These conduct a great trade in ivory obtained from elephants which, more than anywhere else, abound in the island and in the land of Zanghibar which lies beyond. Their only article of food is camel's flesh. All the forests there consist of sandal-wood. Much ambergris is gathered along the coast, and leopards, bears and lions are found inland. Many ships bring silken and other clothing for trade, resorting only to this island and to Zanghibar, for Madeigascar lies so far towards the south that ships cannot visit some other islands still further south except Zanghibar, because the sea runs with such a swift current southwards that it is impossible to return. Ships which take twenty days in voyaging to Madeigascar and Zanghibar from Malabar must struggle for more than three months on their return voyage.

Polo then describes the alleged appearances in those other islands of that mighty bird the "rukh" or "roc", and how envoys sent by the Great Khan brought back a roc's feather and two heavy tusks of a kind of huge "boar" (teeth of the hippopotamus?). He concludes by mentioning the camelopards (giraffes) and asses of the island.

Examination of this account reveals a confusion of Madagascar with the coastland of eastern Africa. Polo gives an underestimate of the distance from Socotra to Madagascar, but records the direction correctly. Madagascar is about two thousand miles, not four thousand, in circuit. The Muhammadans had, it is clear, firmly established themselves there as rulers and traders, and ships came across thither with the monsoons from India. Polo's remarks about the strong current flowing southwards are quite true, and can only refer to the Mozambique current. On the other hand there are no elephants, leopards, bears, lions, giraffes or wild asses in Madagascar. Polo's remarks about these apply to the African mainland opposite. Ambergris could be obtained on the coasts both of the island and the mainland. The camel's flesh was probably imported from Makdau or Magadoxo, for there, according to Ibn Batuta, many camels were slaughtered every year. Tusks or teeth would likewise be imports into Madagascar, not obtained from any animals there. Madagascar

[1] Theal, *Records*, I, 12; Masudi (trans. Sprenger), 261; Abulfeda, as cited below. Edrisi (A.D. 1100–1154) speaks of Sofala with its gold, iron and furs; near by dwelt the Wakwak, but nobody traded with them.

[2] Marco Polo, III, 33, from which the modern name has been derived.

has much forest, but neither Madagascar nor Africa produces red sandalwood; this must have been brought thither by the ships from Maabar (which is not the modern Malabar, but the Coromandel coastland), unless we are to understand the wood and other parts of the Madagascar spice-tree (*Ravintsara madagascariensis*). The other islands which lay further towards the south than Madagascar (provided that they are not imaginary) can only be Bassas da India and Europa in the Mozambique Channel, or else the Mascarene group (Mauritius and Réunion) east of Madagascar.

What then of "Zanghibar"? On this Polo has a separate chapter[1] of which the main points may here be summarised:

> The great and noble island of Zanghibar is about two thousand miles in circumference. Polo describes the inhabitants in some detail. They are an idolatrous people who live in subjection to an independent King. They are tall, stout and black, and wear only a loin-cloth. They have crisp black hair, large mouths, thick lips, upturned noses, and eyes so large and bloodshot that the people look like demons. Their women are very ugly. Flesh, milk, rice, dates, and wine, made from dates and from spices, rice and sugar, form their food and drink. The island has elephants in abundance, and also giraffes, black-headed white sheep, and black lions. The many ships which visit its coasts carry away ivory as the staple of trade, and ambergris. The inhabitants fight from the backs of elephants and camels, since they have no horses.

This description of Polo's can apply only to the mainland of Africa and the negro people there. The name Zanghibar (which appears as Zanzibar in the Latin versions and as Tangibar in the early epitomes) can be traced back to Azania and to Ptolemy's Zingis not far south of Guardafui, and appears in "Zenj", or Zanj, which is the Arabic name for "blacks", and in the name Zanguebar, which was originally applied to a long strip of coastland both northwards and southwards of modern Zanzibar. It seems to have meant "land" or "coast of the blacks". It is probable that Polo's Arab informants used the name vaguely of the whole of the coastland of East Africa, as far as they knew it—that is, as far as Cape Correntes, roughly opposite to the southern extremity of Madagascar. It is also just possible that, since the Arabic word *jezireh* or *jeziret* means peninsula as well as island, Polo's informants intended to describe the southern extremity of the African continent. This possibility, however, is entirely lacking in confirmatory evidence. Polo's own account gives no clue. There is some falsity in details, such as the natives' methods of warfare, but his description is, as a whole, truthfully applicable to any part of East Africa between Guardafui and Correntes. It has been maintained by Yule, in his edition of Marco Polo, that "Zanghibar" is in fact the island of Zanzibar and the coast opposite to it. He argues that Polo's information about "Madeigascar" is largely confused with details of Magadoxo, so that it is but natural that Polo places "Zanghibar" beyond "Madeigascar". If this plausible

[1] Marco Polo, III, 34.

conclusion be accepted, the islands still further southwards would be the Comoros. In any case, knowledge in Polo of Madagascar and of the Mozambique Channel and current is indisputable.

There is no evidence available to show whether the Islamic Arabians ever sailed round the southern extremity of Africa. There are indeed indications that one or two bold adventurers sailed to some point south of Madagascar in the fourteenth century, but the evidence is very vague.[1] At any rate, none passed the southernmost point of Africa, or, so far as we know, came anywhere near it. This is clear enough from a statement in Abulfeda's *Summary or Description of the Inhabited World*, written early in the fourteenth century. The information which he gives is taken from Al Biruni of the eleventh century, but was equally true of his own age. It states that although men sailed no further than Sofala because of rough waters, yet they had sure proof of a connection between the Indian Ocean and the Atlantic; but no one had confirmed it with his own eyes.[2] Abulfeda himself disagreed with Al Biruni's belief that the southern hemisphere was uninhabitable, but at the same time says that men of his age knew the north-western and south-eastern coasts of the world, but no one had ever visited the south-west. It is safe then to believe that no voyagers ventured beyond Cape Correntes; nor was there any real penetration inland except up the Zambesi. The settlers traded with the Bantu in person when the Africans came down to the coast, or through a large population of half-castes.[3] The interior could only be reached by crossing over a succession of heights, the rivers being very unhelpful.

Of these eastern explorations and settlements, and of their commerce and warfare, both Europeans and the Arabs of North Africa remained long ignorant; it was Ibn Batuta who, by his journey to Mombasa and Kilwa about 1330, first brought accurate knowledge of this new East Africa, as far as Sofala, to the Mediterranean peoples.

Arabian influence and the Muhammadan religion had meanwhile spread southwards across the Sahara, particularly to the regions of Lake Chad, Darfur and Wadai,[4] and by the middle of the twelfth century opened up, even to European knowledge, a strip of land stretching right across Africa south of the Sahara but north of the great forests.[5] In 1353 Ibn Batuta saw Timbuktu, the western Sudan and the Niger, though none found the mouth of that river. Ibn

[1] *Directorium ad Passagium Transmarinum*, Beazley, C. R., *Amer. Hist. Rev.* XII, 821–2; XIII, 67.

[2] Reinaud, M., *Géographie d'Aboulféda*, II, 15–16.

[3] Cf. Theal, *Records*, I, 12; III, 77, 93 *sqq.*; Hall, *Prehistoric Rhodesia*, pp. 73 *sqq.*

[4] La Roncière, C. B. de, *La Découverte de l'Afrique au Moyen Age*, I, 79.

[5] See, for example, Masudi, trans. de Meynard and de Courteille, III, ch. 33, pp. 1 *sqq.*; El Bekri, "Book of Roads and Realms" (eleventh century) in Cooley, *Negroland of the Arabs*, p. 47; Al Edrisi, in *Description de l'Afrique et de l'Espagne*, trans. Dozy and de Goeje, pp. 2 *sqq.*

Batuta thought that the Niger was the Nile, and for ages the Arabs believed in a western Nile flowing from the Mountains of the Moon to the Atlantic—a belief which of course was not based on any knowledge whatever of the Congo, but was a legacy of old Greek misconceptions of the Nile and of the Niger. Arabian progress southwards was checked by fly-infested swamps and by the broad belt of dense forest which extends across Africa. This barrier prevented further advance as effectively as the Sahara had blocked the southward penetration of their predecessors, for among swamps and forests the camel was useless. Thus the Arabs were cut off from the Guinea coast and from all Africa beyond, for they did not explore far down the coast beyond Morocco. Many of them looked on the southern Atlantic as a hot and sticky or coagulated "Green Sea of Darkness" and whirlpools, and thought it was madness to sail thereon,[1] and when Christians began to make trial of its mysteries, said that they would be lost in a vast wilderness of winds and fogs, and that their only fate would be engulfment by the whirlpools. Such ideas as these were a revival of the old Greek traditions, which themselves had their origin in Carthaginian attempts to scare away the Greeks from the West African shores. The Arabs certainly traded as far as "Oulil" or Cape Timiris,[2] whence salt was fetched across Africa, but there was no attempt to explore and to make settlements down the west coast like those on the eastern; it was mere accident which caused Ibn Fatima to round Cape Blanco (before A.D. 1274), and his was an isolated achievement.[3]

The tradition of Eratosthenes, however, was strong enough to prevent a denial, in most cases, that there really was sea all round Africa. Thus Masudi, although he stated that the waters round Africa had never been navigated and were unnavigable in the latitudes beyond the "Copper Idols" or Straits of Gibraltar, yet believed that there was nevertheless water all round the continent, while Edrisi was uncertain whether to follow Ptolemy or not; his map makes the east coast of Africa turn eastwards after Guardafui, so that Sofala and the Wakwak are in longitudes east of India but are not joined to China; yet he is willing to assume an immense blank, circular, southern coastline extending from the Wakwak to a sandy desert south of the Equator and south-west of the Sahara. This unknown coastline is likewise shown on western maps as far apart in time as the maps of Beatus (A.D. 776), the Anglo-Saxon (ninth century) and the Hereford (about 1280). Abulfeda again says that the sea along West Africa runs southwards by uninhabited and

[1] Edrisi, in *Description*, etc., p. 1; Abulfeda, in Reinaud, *Géogr. d'Aboulféda*, II, 24.

[2] This identification is pretty clear from the account of Ibn Said (1214–76); Reinaud, *Géogr. d'Aboulféda*, II, 213; Taylor, E. G. R., *Pactolus*, pp. 137–8. Contrast de Santarem, *Recherches sur la priorité de la découverte des pays situés sur la côte occid. de l'Afr.*, introd. pp. xliii–xliv; cf. also Reinaud, *Géogr. d'Aboulféda*, p. 213; Edrisi, p. 2.

[3] Ibn Said, in Reinaud, *Géogr. d'Aboulféda*, pp. 215–16.

unvisited shores as far as the Equator, and then turns eastward behind the Comr Mountains where the Nile rises, and washes the southern coasts of the world. Thence it continues eastwards past uninhabited lands behind the country of the Zenj and then turns north-eastwards and stretches away to the sea of China and India. This confused idea shows that the translation of Ptolemy's *Geography* into Arabic handed on the belief that Africa went on indefinitely as land and was joined to a southern tract lying to the south of the Indian Ocean. Nevertheless the idea of an insular Africa remained general.[1] Late in the thirteenth century the Italians began to lift the veil of terror and ignorance from the Atlantic and to venture into its strong and sticky waters of "darkness and ghosts". The compass, the astrolabe, the time-piece and marine charts made travel and records thereof much more certain. About 1270 the Canaries were rediscovered, and in 1291 came the attempt of Ugolino Vivaldo and Guido Vivaldo to find a way to India round West Africa. They were lost, as Eudoxus had been. Before 1350 the Azores and Madeira were found again. The Spanish and the French joined in, but the final success was left to the Portuguese, to whom the translation of Ptolemy's *Geography* into Latin in 1410 was no discouragement.

This chapter serves to show that the idea of finding a southern sea-route to India round Africa—an idea which ended in the ultimate discovery and circumnavigation of the southernmost part of the continent—was not only present to the minds of the ancient Greeks, but was even put to the test, though unsuccessfully; and, further, that, owing largely to lack of objectives on the western side of Africa, and to the Mozambique current on the eastern, the Cape of Good Hope and Cape Agulhas, the southernmost point, were apparently not discovered. But, while the extreme south and south-west of Africa thus remained unknown, Asiatics of Arab and Persian origin pushed down in real and permanent discoveries to Cape Correntes, not far from the frontier of British South Africa. If there is one region which was really found by the ancients or the Arabs within South Africa as defined in our first chapter, it is Mashonaland.[2] But the most reasonable conclusion is that even the Muhammadans at Sofala, as at nearly all their other colonies in East Africa, were confined to their settlement and its immediate neighbourhood, and obtained their inland commodities knowledge through intermediaries.

[1] See, for example, Roger Bacon's *Opus Majus*, trans. Burke, R. B., I, IV, 311, 329 *sqq.*; Pope Pius II, *Asiae Europaeque Elegantissima Descriptio*, chs. II, VII.

[2] *Vide supra*, pp. 4 *sqq.*, 35, 54.

CHAPTER IV

THE PORTUGUESE IN SOUTH AFRICA

THOUGH he did not live to see it, the discovery of Africa south of the Sahara may justly be noted as the direct result of the labours of Prince Henry, called by English writers the Navigator (1394–1460). A son of John I of Portugal and Philippa of Lancaster, he devoted his life to a single aim and pursued it with the zeal of an apostle in the face of opposition, disappointment and at least one serious setback. Ocean voyages had been made before his time, but they were sporadic and without lasting results; it was reserved for him to organise them systematically and continuously and to crown them by the permanent occupation of some of the new-found regions.[1]

When Henry died, his mariners had reconnoitred and mapped the coast of West Africa from Cape Bojador in Morocco to Sierra Leone or thereabouts; the Madeira group and the Azores had been rediscovered and most of them colonised, and some of the Cape Verde Islands had been found. During the next ten years little advance was made, but in 1469 King Affonso V leased the trade of Guinea to a wealthy citizen of Lisbon, Fernão Gomes, for five years, with the obligation of exploring annually 100 leagues of unknown coastline.[2] Under this lease between 1470 and 1472 the Equator was crossed, Cape St Catherine was passed and the islands in the Gulf of Guinea were added to the map. On the termination of Gomes' lease, the king transferred the administration of the conquests, as they were termed, to his heir Prince John. The absorption of the energies of Portugal in the war with Castile from 1475 to 1479 prevented further discovery during those years, but, when John ascended the throne in 1481, he resumed the exploration of the African coast with a zeal equal to that of the Navigator and far greater prospects of success, for, as king, John II was in command of all the resources of the Crown, which, by reason of the profits on the gold trade of Guinea, were now very considerable.

The first gold dust from Africa was brought back from the Arguim coast by Henry's servant Antão Gonçalves in 1442 or 1443, but the trade only became important after the establishment of the Portuguese upon the Gold Coast, the source whence gold dust had been carried by the caravans across the Sahara to the Moorish ports upon the Mediterranean for many centuries.[3] Its conquest had been one

[1] For a general discussion of the opening of the age of discovery, see *C.H.B.E.* I, ch. II, and Prestage, E., in Newton, A. P. (ed.), *Travel and Travellers of the Middle Ages* and *The Great Age of Discovery*; Prestage, E., *The Portuguese Pioneers* (Pioneer Series).

[2] I.e. the west coast, so far as then known.

[3] La Roncière, C. B. de, *La Découverte de l'Afrique au Moyen Age*, I, 88, 94–9.

of the main purposes of the Portuguese explorations, and in 1482 a fortress was established at São Jorge de Mina to command the coast and serve as the headquarters of Portuguese power in African waters.

The details of the gold trade are obscure, but there is no doubt that after the middle of the fifteenth century it became an important factor in the economic life of Europe and started the rise of Portugal to wealth. From 1494 to 1498 the gold imported was worth 11,777 *dobras*,[1] and it increased so much that in the three years 1511 to 1513 the Crown drew 4,236,927 *reis* from this source.[2] The 900,000 *cruzados* of dower given by John III to his sister Isabel on her marriage to the Emperor Charles V in 1526 was paid from Mina gold,[3] but the trade fell off, at least from 1531, for reasons not yet ascertained.

John II set himself to overcome the difficulty which had hindered navigation since the Portuguese approached the Equator and were unable to see and determine their latitude by the Pole Star. Under his direction two Jewish mathematicians, Joseph Vizinho and Abraham Zacuto, applied to the southern hemisphere the method of calculating latitude by measuring the height of the sun at midday with the astrolabe or cross-staff. They prepared tables of declination, but these were probably incomplete when the king sent out Diogo Cão to resume exploration along the southward-trending coast beyond the Bight of Biafra and the Equator. In his first voyage of 1482–4 Cão found the mouth of the River Congo and went on to Cape St Mary, setting up stone pillars or *padrões* at both points as marks of his master's possession. In his second voyage of 1485–6 he passed Cape Negro and attained Cape Cross near the modern Walvis Bay, erecting similar pillars. Two of his pillars have been recovered and are now preserved in the museum of the Geographical Society in Lisbon.[4] Cão ascended the River Congo as far as the Yelala Falls, as an extant inscription on the rock testifies, and, according to the historian João de Barros,[5] he visited the King of Congo and took back to Lisbon an ambassador, Caçuta or Nsaku, and some Negroes to be instructed in the Christian faith, though, according to another account, these men only reached Portugal in 1488 with Bartholomew Dias.[6] Until this discovery the Portuguese had only come into contact with the petty chieftains of the Guinea coast, each of whose territories was clearly very limited and whose tribal status could not be mistaken. But round the mouth of the Congo Cão found a somewhat wider form of organisation, for the tribes were associated at the moment

[1] The *dobra* was equal to 120 *reis*. *Vide* J. Lucio de Azevedo, *Epocas de Portugal Economico*, p. 175.

[2] *Ibid.* p. 176. In *c.* 1550, one *real* (pl. *reis*) equalled about three-farthings. One *cruzado* was worth 400 *reis* or, say, £1 5*s.* 0*d.*

[3] *Ibid.* p. 186.

[4] See Ravenstein, E. G., "The Voyages of Dio Cão and Bartholomew Dias", in *Geographical Journal*, December 1900.

[5] Barros, João de, *Da Asia*, Dec. I, Bk. 3, ch. III.

[6] See Ravenstein, *op cit.*

under one of those Paramount Chiefs who have arisen from time to time among the Bantu and by their personal prowess imposed their control over a wider area than their own tribe. The Portuguese saw in such a paramount chief a king such as they knew in Europe, and imagined that they had discovered a fully organised State with which it would be possible to enter into relations. They called the chief the "King of Congo", and thus fell into an error similar to that which, as we shall see later, they made in South-East Africa.

Ruy da Pina and Barros say that Cão returned safely to Portugal after his second voyage, but, according to a legend on the map of Henricus Martellus (1489) and a statement by the Spanish cosmographers at the Junta of Badajoz (1529), he died at Serra Parda near his last *padrão*.

In the lands they discovered John II and his successors naturally looked for trading profit, but being devout Catholics they made it also their aim to evangelise the natives. Indeed it was for this purpose that successive Popes granted them exclusive rights over the new-found parts. The contemporary historians, Ruy da Pina and Garcia de Resende, devote many pages to an account of the baptism of Caçuta and other Negroes brought over from the Congo and to the spread of Christianity in that region. But they say little about the voyages and their geographical results, and the official records were destroyed in the ruins of the India House, where they were preserved, in the Lisbon earthquake of 1755. A recent Portuguese historian has contended with apparent force that this neglect of the explorations by the chroniclers was due to the policy of secrecy deliberately adopted by the Government to conceal its new sources of wealth from its rivals.[1] This has deprived us of clear and accurate information concerning what was accomplished, and much of our knowledge of this foundation period in African history must necessarily therefore be based upon conjecture and inference.

In 1486 João Affonso d'Aveiro first visited the country of Benin and brought back the earliest consignment of Malaguette pepper. He related that there was a great Negro monarch living in the interior, and this prince was identified with the priest-king "Prester John", the situation of whose kingdom had been a subject of discussion in Europe for more than two centuries. The search for Prester John had been an important motive in Prince Henry's schemes. In the legends of the thirteenth and fourteenth centuries his seat had been placed in Central Asia, but by the fifteenth it had moved to Africa and, with vague information concerning the Christian kingdom that we now know as Abyssinia, it had become localised by geographers near the sources of the Egyptian Nile.[2] In 1452 an envoy of Prester John had come to Lisbon, and John II before 1486 had

[1] Cortesão, J., *Lusitania*, I, 45.
[2] Ross, E. D., in Newton, A. P. (ed.), *Travel and Travellers of the Middle Ages.*

been in touch with Abyssinian clerics who visited the Peninsula, probably as pilgrims to Santiago de Compostella.[1] He had also obtained information from Portuguese friars, who had been in Jerusalem, and sent ambassadors to the priest-king, but these failed to get beyond the Holy Land.[2] In 1487 John resolved on a more systematic attempt than ever before to get in touch with Prester John and to open up a direct route to the spice marts of Asia. He planned simultaneous action both by land and sea so that he might obtain complementary information. In May 1487 Pero da Covilhan, a gentleman of his court, and Affonso de Paiva were sent overland to Cairo to obtain detailed particulars concerning the Muslim spice trade. They journeyed together as far as Aden, where they parted company. Paiva died, but Covilhan succeeded in reaching the spice marts on the Malabar coast of western India and thence crossed to the coast of East Africa, where the "Moors", i.e. the Arab traders, had many posts. We know that Covilhan sent home information that was of first-rate importance to the Portuguese when they entered the waters of the Indian Ocean, but unfortunately his letters have not survived.

Meanwhile John II was systematically planning the extension of exploration along the African coast right down to its southern extremity. In 1487 an experienced sailor, Bartholomew Dias, a knight of the king's household, was sent forth from Lisbon with two caravels, each of 50 tons burthen, and a storeship carrying additional supplies of food. He received orders to proceed beyond the limits of the coast discovered by Cão and to press on as far south as possible without delaying to trade. He took with him two Negroes whom Cão had seized and four Negresses from Guinea; they were landed at various points, supplied with samples of silver, gold and spices which they were to exhibit and enquire whether similar things were to be found in the interior. At the same time they were to announce that the ships of the King of Portugal were off the coast, and it was hoped that the news would reach Prester John and that he would send to meet the explorers.

Dias sailed by the familiar route to Guinea and from Elmina across to São Thomé or Principe to water, and thence to the mouth of the Congo. Then, like his predecessor he ran down the coast, keeping close in and naming the capes, bays and other points he discovered. On reaching the Angra do Salto, which may be identified with the modern Port Alexander in the extreme south of Angola, he landed the Negroes and perhaps left his storeship in that safe harbour. On the feast of the Conception, December 8, four months after leaving Lisbon, he came to a bay, which he named Golfo de S. Maria da Conceição, now Walvis Bay, and there he spent some days. A little

[1] Barros, *Da Asia*, Dec. I, Bk. 3, ch. IV.
[2] *Ibid.* Dec. I, Bk. 3, ch. V.

further on at Cabo da Volta, now Dias Point, he erected his first *padrão*, dedicated to St James, and set on shore one of the Negresses.

For the only connected account of the voyage we are dependent upon the historian Barros who wrote more than half a century later;[1] but it may be supplemented by the legends upon the contemporary map of Henricus Martellus (1489), the Portuguese chart of 1502, called after its Italian purchaser the Cantino map, and the Canerio map of the same date. The maps do not agree with one another and in many cases they do not tally with Barros's account. Ravenstein, the most recent investigator of this fundamental voyage, has used the maps to reconstruct its course, but his conclusions drawn from them have not been universally accepted.[2]

According to Barros, Dias stood off and on for five days near Angra das Voltas (Angra Pequeña), and thence a strong wind drove him south for thirteen days. Ravenstein contests this on the ground that northerly winds there are very rare and squalls from the north never last long. He admits that Dias may have met gales off the edge of the Agulhas Bank much further south and been driven out to sea. As there is thus room for doubt, it seems best to adhere to Barros' account, which we shall follow for the rest of the voyage.

As Dias' vessels were small, the waves high and the weather cold in those southerly latitudes, the crews suffered severely and were seized with fear after being so long out of sight of land. When the storm had blown itself out and Dias could hoist all his sails, he steered to the eastward in the hope of picking up the coast. As for several days no land appeared, he altered his course to north. Dias at last saw land once more near a bay he called dos Vaqueiros, or the Bay of the Cowherds, afterwards known as Agoada de São Braz, our Mossel Bay. There he found certain small people of an ashy brown colour herding cattle, but as none of his interpreters, who were familiar with the languages of Guinea, could understand them, he was unable to have speech with them. Indeed, they were so alarmed by the sight of the ships that they drove off their herds in panic, and when the Portuguese landed to take in water, they pelted them with stones and Dias replied by killing one of them with a bolt from a crossbow. Sailing on, the mariners found to their great joy that the coast was unmistakably trending to the east, and a few days later they came to what is now called Algoa Bay. There Dias set up a cross on a rocky island and some miles further on a pillar called after St Gregory on a cliff still known as Cape Padrone.

The crews were now worn out by the rough weather they had experienced, and began to murmur and beg Dias to turn back,

[1] The policy of secrecy explains the unsatisfactory and inadequate account of the voyage of Dias by Barros. The contemporary official chroniclers, Pina and Resende, do not mention it.

[2] Ravenstein, E., *Geographical Journal*, December 1900, p. 645.

saying that the stock of food would hardly last until they reached the storeship and that they had done enough by discovering in one voyage such a large stretch of coast. Moreover, as the coast continued to run to the east, it was certain that while they were out of sight of land, they must have passed some great cape where the long southward-trending coast would end, and his officers urged the commander of the expedition to turn back and search for it. By his *Regimento* or instructions, Dias had been ordered to consult his officers and representatives of the crews on important matters, and he now held a council to discuss the course to be taken. The decision was reached in favour of a return, and a document recording it was drawn up and signed by all present. The facts are recorded by Barros, our only authority, but the document itself has apparently not survived. Dias felt that he had accomplished the main purpose of his voyage and that the sea-way round Africa had been opened, but to make certain he persuaded his officers to continue on an easterly course for two or three days longer, promising that, if nothing then occurred to lead them to alter their decision, he would obey it. This was agreed to and they sailed past the Penedo das Fontes, which is identified by Ravenstein as Ship Rock, and came either to the Kowie or the Great Fish River, which was called Rio do Infante, because João Infante, captain of the *Pantalião*, was the first to land there. At that point, as his crews began again to complain, Dias ordered a return.

Antonio Galvão,[1] writing in the middle of the sixteenth century, compared Dias to Moses, and said that he saw the promised land of India but did not enter it, while Barros states that, when passing the pillar of St Gregory on the way back, he left it with as much sorrow as if it were a son condemned to perpetual exile. His prevision was only too true, for he never saw it again.

We do not know the exact day of the discovery of the Cape, but if, as Ravenstein thinks, Dias dedicated Cape Agulhas, the southernmost point of Africa, to St Brendan, it must have been in May 1488. The name he chose is uncertain; Barros says he called it Cabo Tormentoso, "the Stormy Cape", which name John II changed to the Cape of Good Hope, from the expectation it gave that India would soon be reached. According to Duarte Pacheco, author of *Esmeraldo de situ orbis*, the first sailing guide to the west and south coasts of Africa, written in 1505–6, the present name was actually bestowed by Dias himself.[2] On the shore below the Cape Dias set up the last of his pillars, that of St Philip.

After nine months' absence, Dias rejoined his storeship and found only three survivors of the nine men he had left with it, and one of these, being very weak from illness, died of joy on seeing his returning

[1] Galvão, A., *Discoveries of the World*, p. 77, Hakluyt Society, London, 1862.
[2] *Esmeraldo*, Bk. 3, ch. VII.

comrades. After revictualling his vessels, Dias proceeded northward to Ilha do Principe (Prince's Island) in the Bight of Biafra. There he took in Duarte Pacheco, who had been prevented by illness from executing a commission to explore the rivers on the coast. Passing thence, Dias called at Mina, the headquarters of the Portuguese on the African coast, where he took on board a quantity of gold dust, and after an uneventful passage he reached Lisbon in December 1488. His voyage had lasted sixteen months and seventeen days, and it must be accounted the greatest and most successful of all the long series of African voyages that had begun under Prince Henry's inspiration seventy years before. Dias died in 1500. Sailing in the fleet of Pedro Alvares Cabral, which was dispatched for the Indies voyage upon da Gama's return, his vessel met with a sudden squall and went down with all on board.

Dias had discovered 350 leagues of new coast, but above all he had delimited conclusively the southward extension of Africa. His experience, supplemented by the reports of Covilhan, proved that the sea route to India was possible and that it lay open to Portugal when she was ready to follow it up. The name of Dias must always stand high on the roll of maritime fame, and in the history of South Africa it is pre-eminent along with that of his master, John II. The task that Henry the Navigator had envisaged and begun, they had completed. John had planned and organised, Cão and Dias had carried out the discovery of the African coast and the secrets of its navigation down to its furthest extremity. Henceforth, though subsequent explorers had to fill in the details, the shape of Africa was revealed and fixed upon the maps. The old legends of the impossibility of navigation in the torrid zone were exploded and the oceans were thrown open. Columbus had still to make his fair-weather voyage across the Atlantic and begin the revelation of a New World, but Dias' achievement really surpassed his, for, directed by the scientific plans and equipment of his king, he had with splendid courage and determination fought his way through storm and tempest beyond the southernmost limit of the old "habitable world" and had solved the problem that had baffled geographers since the days of Herodotus.[1] Da Gama and Manoel might reap where Cão, Dias and John II had sown, but it is to these last that the credit of the victory really belongs.

The death of his only son in 1490, which threatened new difficulties over the succession to the throne, the Jewish problem and disputes with Spain prevented John II from proceeding with his maritime plans after Dias' return, and it fell to his successor Manoel, justly called "the Fortunate", to win the prize that had been sought so long. Soon after his accession in October 1495, Manoel submitted the matter to his council, and though some members opposed the

[1] *Vide supra*, ch. III.

Eastern adventure on the ground that it would involve Portugal in distant wars and lead to friction with other powers such as Venice and Egypt by damaging their commercial interests, the king endorsed the opinion of those who favoured it. He ordered an expedition to be prepared carefully and without regard to expense, and since its object was much more than discovery and demanded capacity to negotiate with Asiatic potentates, he passed over Bartholomew Dias and entrusted the leadership to Vasco da Gama, a skilled and able soldier of high rank and considerable administrative experience. Da Gama was given credentials as ambassador to establish friendly relations and make a commercial treaty with the ruler of Calicut, which was then the principal emporium on the western coast of India. Da Gama had no previous maritime experience, but this did not matter since he took with him the two best pilots of the day, Pero de Alemquer and Pero de Escolar, who had served under Dias, and the latter himself accompanied the fleet as far as Mina in his own caravel. The vessels of the expedition numbered four, the *St Gabriel*, *St Raphael*, *Berrio* and a storeship. Dom Diogo Ortiz, the learned Bishop of Tangier, a cosmographer of high reputation, supplied maps and charts, while Abraham Zacuto, the Jewish scientist, provided astronomical instruments and tables of the sun's declination and probably taught da Gama to make observations. The complements of the ships numbered 170 men of all ranks.

Leaving the Tagus on 8 July 1497[1] the expedition passed the Canaries on the 15th and picked up the African coast at Terra Alta; the vessels then parted company in a fog and only came together at the Cape Verde Islands on the 26th, where they provisioned. Starting again on August 3, da Gama stood south-east for 200 leagues and then, to escape the doldrums and currents of the Gulf of Guinea and the rough weather experienced by Dias on his coast-wise voyage, he made the important decision to steer south-west and take a circular course to the Cape. This was the first such course recorded in history, but it has been followed by sailing ships ever since. Save for the appearance of whales and birds, nothing broke the monotony of sea and sky for ninety-six days, that is until November 4, when land was sighted, and three days later he entered St Helena's Bay and remained a week to clean the ships' bottoms, mend the sails and take in wood. When the Portuguese landed, the Hottentots who were encountered were at first friendly and actually took one of the sailors to their kraal, but on his return to the shore they became hostile and, hurling their assegais, they wounded da Gama and some companions who came to his rescue. On the 22nd the fleet doubled the Cape of Good Hope in good weather and on the 25th anchored in the bay of St Braz, where the storeship was broken up and its contents

[1] For the details of da Gama's voyage, see *A Journal of the first Voyage of Vasco da Gama, 1497–9*, translated and edited by Ravenstein, Hakluyt Society, 1898.

transferred to the other vessels. Here again the natives began by showing friendliness, bartered one of their fat oxen for some trifling objects and danced with the newcomers, but they became so angry when the Portuguese took the water they regarded as their own that they demolished a pillar and cross which de Gama had set up on an island in the bay. Between the Cape and the Great Fish River the vessels ran into a heavy storm and were in some danger, and next the Agulhas Current bore them back, but on Christmas Day 1497 da Gama came to the coast of a new country which on that account he called Natal. Leaving there, he stood out to sea until drinking-water began to fail and he had to seek a port; on 11 January 1498 he put in near the mouth of a small stream which he called Copper River from the abundance of that metal which was found in the possession of the natives. They were black men, strikingly different from the brown Hottentots and yellow Bushmen near the Cape. He was so well received by them that he stayed five days at this "land of Good Folk". It lay a short way to the west of Cape das Correntes. Despite the currents from which it derives its name, da Gama passed this cape without difficulty and knew that he was approaching the waters familiar to the "Moors" about which Covilhan had spoken.

The navigators had now left behind them the territory inhabited by primitive savages and were about to come into contact with their ancient foes, Muslims of a mixed race, partly indigenous, partly Arab and Persian, who had established petty states in the island coast towns of East Africa.

On his outward voyage da Gama did not touch at Sofala, the most southerly town of the Arabs, but passed it without realising its exact position. His contact with civilised people in East Africa began at Kilimane, where he landed on 25 February 1498 as the first to reach that coast by sea. He remained for thirty-two days to careen and refit his ships. He was courteously treated there, as at first he was at Mozambique also where he touched next. The Arab traders there did not at once realise that the newcomers were Christians who were coming to dispute their monopoly in those waters, but when they did, their attitude abruptly changed. Da Gama found Arab ships in the harbour laden with Indian goods and the spices for which he was in search, but above all he learned that he was at last approaching the dominions of Prester John to whom he was carrying letters of commendation. The stories that were told him of the priest-king's power along the coast further to the north probably represented a vague knowledge by the coast Arabs that the Abyssinians had relations with some of the coast cities like Magadoxo (Mogdishu), but they were quite indefinite and raised hopes of securing Christian allies against the Moors that were soon dashed. It was not long before da Gama realised that Portugal would have to depend upon her own power, for almost everywhere he touched he was treated as an enemy by the coast sultans, who tried to overcome him either by force or treachery. This happened at Mombasa, which he reached on April 7. At Malindi, however, he received a ready welcome, for the sultan of that place hoped to throw off the supremacy of the neighbouring Muslim power at Kilwa and was anxious to secure the help of the newcomers with their powerful artillery, even though they were Christians. There da Gama remained nine days, and at the end of April he procured the help of Indian or Arab pilots to guide him across the Arabian Sea to Calicut, whither we need not follow him.[1]

The earliest Arab settlement upon the coast of East Africa was at Magadoxo in what was to be Italian Somaliland, but in the fifteenth century the principal power upon the coast of the region, called by the Arabs and Portuguese "Zanguebar", lay in the hands of the sultans of Kilwa.[2] Arab explorations never proceeded further south than Cape Correntes because the violent currents which gave the cape its name rendered navigation too difficult and dangerous for their fragile ships, whose timbers were only held together by strands of coir. The first Arabs to explore the coast came from Magadoxo, but later the sultans of Kilwa made themselves masters of the gold trade which came down to the coast not far north of Cape Correntes. There they developed the port of Sofala, which became the principal mart for the whole commerce of the Bantu tribes of the interior; the silk and cotton cloths, coloured beads and trinkets from Cambay, on the west coast of India, were exchanged there for the small beads of gold and the ivory brought from the region known to the Portuguese as the kingdom of Sofala. With the wealth derived from this traffic, Kilwa made herself mistress of the other principal towns in Zanguebar, Mombasa and Malindi and of the islands of Pemba, Zanzibar and Comoro; but at the end of the fifteenth century her power was in decline owing to the divisions that followed many contested successions to the sultanate.

At that time very few Arabs of pure stock were upon the coast, for there had been a progressive deterioration owing to admixture with Bantu blood. The rulers were still professed adherents of the Muslim faith and called the Bantu "Kaffirs" or unbelievers, a term soon adopted by the Portuguese, but most of the population on the coast was indifferent or actually heathen.

The Portuguese were determined to take advantage of the discontent felt by the other towns at the exactions of Kilwa, which had made Malindi ready to welcome the proffered alliance of Vasco da Gama and rendered it a safe port of call for the Portuguese ships. Kilwa, on the other hand, was hostile to the newcomers from the

[1] For an account of his doings on the Indian coast, see *C.H.B.E.* IV, 3–4.

[2] Barros, *Da Asia*, Dec. I, Bk. 8, ch. IV.

beginning, for its sultan realised that they were anxious to seize Sofala, the principal source of his wealth.

It was not until 7 January 1499 that da Gama was back at Malindi, the Sultan of which had decided to throw in his lot with the Portuguese and henceforward remained one of their staunchest allies in East Africa. Da Gama returned to Mozambique on February 1 and erected a *padrão* on the neighbouring island of St George. He doubled the Cape of Good Hope on March 20, and entered the Tagus on 29 September 1499, two years after his departure. Of the 170 men who had sailed, two-thirds had perished, most of them of scurvy, for the management of long voyages through hot climates was still to be learned. The voyage, however, had been an undeniable success, for though da Gama had failed to secure the alliances he sought, he had proved once and for all that the sea-way to southern Asia round the south of Africa was practicable and that it lay open to the sailors who held the monopoly of the Guinea navigation.

The results of da Gama's voyage made an immediate and outstanding change in the relations between Europe and Asia, and, needless to say, the possibilities of the Indian trade occupied the first place in the plans of King Manoel and the shrewd and experienced advisers who had been trained under his predecessor. Their design was to send the king's ships as rapidly as possible to the marts of Malabar and to see them return safely and expeditiously with cargoes of drugs and spices. But Africa also filled a space in their schemes. Beyond the well-known and valued Guinea coast both Cão and Dias had shown that there were no opportunities of easy profit down to the Cape, and the south coast seemed even more inhospitable. It afforded nothing more than the prospect of conflict with poor and primitive savages, while its stormy seas and powerful currents made navigation difficult.

Beyond Cape Correntes things were different. The fact that the east coast was the source of a trade in gold and ivory that had enriched the Arabs or "Moors" for centuries was well understood, and Manoel planned to secure control of this trade as completely as he held that of the gold trade of Guinea with his fortress of São Jorge da Mina. Ready access to a supply of gold was an essential factor in the rise of Portugal to a rank among the nations far in advance of anything she could attain while solely dependent upon the comparatively slender resources of her own small territory. In the Europe of the Middle Ages the supply of the precious metal was very limited, and the Portuguese knew well that the merchants in the Indian marts would only sell their wares for coin or bullion. The Negroes of Guinea, on the other hand, were willing to trade their gold dust and ivory for manufactured articles which could be purchased in Europe, and it was hoped that the Bantu of south-eastern Africa would be willing to trade in a similar way. But that trade had long been monopolised by the Arabs, and it was fully realised that they would not easily relinquish their hold.

When Pedro Alvares Cabral was dispatched from Lisbon in 1500 with thirteen ships to follow up da Gama's discoveries, he received orders to take possession of Sofala and establish a post there. He could not make the port, however, and only reached Mozambique with very great difficulty and with but a battered remnant of his fleet. After touching at the coast of Brazil, he had lost four of his ships along with Bartholomew Dias in a hurricane in the South Atlantic, possibly near the Cape of Good Hope, and the rest of his fleet was scattered and suffered much damage.[1] Cabral was better received at Mozambique than da Gama had been, but Kilwa was violently hostile and he had to pass on to Malindi and thence to India. At Malindi he met for the first time with certain Abyssinians and received definite information concerning the realm of Prester John in the interior, to whom he sent emissaries, thus continuing the efforts of the Portuguese to open up communication by sea with Abyssinia. Those efforts were persisted in for many years and finally succeeded, but they lie beyond the limits of our subject.

Before Cabral's return to Lisbon, King Manoel dispatched João da Nova with four ships on the Indian voyage. He called at the Agoada or Watering Place of St Braz and there erected a small chapel or hermitage which was the first Christian building in South Africa. Its erection may have indicated an intention to make the bay a regular port of call, but it was rarely visited. On his return voyage da Nova discovered the island of St Helena, which thenceforward became a regular watering place for Portuguese ships. In 1502 Vasco da Gama was sent out for a second time, with a larger fleet than before, to seize control of the trade on the Malabar coast and to keep the sea against his Moorish competitors. He called at Sofala and entered into friendly relations with the local sheik, but could obtain little gold. At Kilwa, however, by a show of force, he compelled the sultan to accept Portuguese suzerainty and pay tribute. One of his captains, Antonio do Campo, is said to have discovered Delagoa Bay on this voyage. It was fully explored in 1544 by Lourenço Marques, whose name the port upon its shores now bears.

In the following year (1503) three separate squadrons sailed for the East; under Francisco de Albuquerque, his brother, Affonso, and Antonio de Saldanha respectively. On his way out Saldanha entered Table Bay, which became known as Agoada de Saldanha, and he was the first European to climb Table Mountain. His task was to close the mouth of the Red Sea against the exit of an Egyptian fleet and to capture any Arab vessels attempting to carry on their old trade. In the course of the cruise one of his captains, Ruy Ravasco, subdued the island of Zanzibar and the town of Brava and compelled

[1] Barros, *Da Asia*, Dec. I, Bk. 5, ch. II.

them to pay tribute, but he could not leave garrisons there and they returned to their commerce with the Arabs as soon as the Portuguese ships sailed away.

In 1505 Portuguese policy entered upon a new stage and larger designs were conceived and put into practice. King Manoel determined to win the monopoly of the maritime trade of the East by securing the complete control of the sea and resting it on a chain of fortresses at strategic points along the shores of the Indian Ocean. The strong points of East Africa which guarded the entrances to the ocean necessarily occupied a prominent place in the scheme. The conception of this great strategic plan, one of the boldest maritime ideas ever formulated, was probably due to Affonso de Albuquerque and to a noble of high rank, Dom Francisco de Almeida. The latter was entrusted with the task of carrying it into effect and was appointed the first Viceroy of the Indies with very extensive powers.[1] He left Lisbon in March 1505 with a fleet of twenty ships carrying besides their crews a force of 1500 trained soldiers who were destined to hold the fortresses that were to be established. Almeida's first care was to dominate the African coast, and while a separate force was sent to secure the gold trade, he attacked each of the Arab strongholds in turn. He seized Kilwa and built a fort there, and took and destroyed Mombasa; so thoroughly did he clear up the coast before he passed on to India that thenceforward Portugal was supreme in those waters. But it was still insecure so long as it was open to external attack, and Almeida's greatest claim to fame rests on his memorable naval victory over the forces of the Sultan of Egypt at Diu in 1509. This triumph established the complete command of the sea for a century and is thus an event of importance in the history of Africa.

Almeida is remembered by this achievement and by his tragic death. On the way home to rest on the laurels he had won, in March 1510 he landed, against his will, at Table Bay to punish some insolent Hottentots, and he and sixty-five of his soldiers, including eleven captains, whose only arms were swords and lances, were slaughtered ingloriously by the natives' assegais. Thus the first Viceroy of India perished on the sandy beach of Salt River near the future site of Cape Town.

At the same time that Almeida was sent out in supreme command, King Manoel dispatched a squadron of six ships under a Spaniard, Pedro d'Anhaya, to occupy Sofala and build a fortress there which should command the gold trade,[2] and thus accomplish another essential part of the broad strategic plan upon which the nation had embarked. Before the show of force which d'Anhaya brought, the local Arab sheik had to give way and allow the fort to be constructed.

[1] Barros, *Da Asia*, Dec. I, Bk. 8, ch. III.
[2] *Ibid.*, Dec. I, Bk. 9, ch. VI.

He consoled himself with his knowledge of the extreme unhealthiness of the site and his belief that it could not fail to weaken the Portuguese who garrisoned it. But though the plan was soundly conceived and efficiently carried out, it failed to yield the results that were hoped for, and the gold trade never became as important a factor in Portugal's advancement as it had promised to be in the days of John II. This was due to the instability of conditions in the interior.

The vast stretch of territory between the Zambesi and the Limpopo from which Sofala drew its trade was then inhabited by a confederation of Bantu tribes known to the Portuguese as Makalanga, or in their own tongue Makaranga. Their paramount chief, who was supposed to possess supernatural powers, was known as the *Monomatapa*, a title of disputed significance, which probably means "chief of the mountain", for his place of residence was near the mountain called Fura which was regarded as sacred. The Portuguese mistook the loose form of Bantu tribal organisation for something more systematic. They took the local chiefs to be "kings" and translated *monomotapa* as "emperor", thus bringing into European geography the erroneous idea of an organised empire covering the whole of the interior of South-East Africa which persisted until the beginning of the nineteenth century. Each of the local chiefs of the many clans, into which the Makaranga were divided, had his seat at a *zimbao*, or collection of kraals, and at some of these there were stone buildings whose origin was due to some earlier people, for the Makaranga had no tradition concerning it. The most extensive of the ruins was that now known as the Great Zimbabwe, concerning whose origin many fantastic legends have been current since the sixteenth century. They have given rise to acute controversy and it cannot be said that any explanation yet commands universal approval.[1]

Gold workings were widespread throughout the territories of the Makaranga, but they were specially rich in Manica and the country now known as Southern Rhodesia. The metal was obtained by the Bantu from the streams by washing, or extracted by shallow digging from alluvial deposits, and sold to peripatetic Arab traders from the coast in exchange for cotton stuffs from the Malabar marts, coloured beads and other trinkets. It was Covilhan's reports concerning this trade that first directed the cupidity of the Portuguese to Sofala, whence most of the gold was exported. There were a few nuggets among the gold, but it was mostly in the form of small beads or flakes, for the Makaranga had not sufficient skill to work it up into ornaments.[2] When d'Anhaya erected his fortress, the Makaranga confederacy was already breaking up. Lesser confederacies were striving to throw off the paramountcy of the *Monomotapa*, especially

[1] For rival theories concerning the matter, *vide supra*, Chapter III, pp. 35, 54-5.

[2] For a description of the circumstances in the region, see Diogo de Alcaçova to King Manoel, 20 November 1506. Theal, *Records of S.E. Africa*, I, 57–68.

in Manica, Barue and Kiteve, and the constant sporadic warfare was stopping the journeys of the Arab pedlars and drying up the flow of trade to Sofala, just when the Portuguese aspired to displace the Moors as masters of the region.

After its occupation the chief captaincy on the African coast was at first established at Sofala, but that port was found very unsuitable owing to its shallowness and the many shoals impeding navigation along the neighbouring coast. The island town of Mozambique, which was much more accessible than Sofala, was occupied in 1508, and thenceforward it became the port where vessels called on the outward voyage and whence they took their departure for Europe. Owing to the occasional uncertainties of the monsoon navigation, vessels often had to pass the winters there. Though at first only a factory with a small fort, Mozambique became the seat of government for the whole coast in 1558, and the construction of the existing great fortress of St Sebastian was then commenced. The commerce of Sofala never fulfilled the high expectations of its conquerors, but the loss of it ruined Kilwa, and that place fell into decay and was abandoned in 1512. Much of the trade that survived the anarchy in the interior trickled down to small places in the delta of the Zambesi which were not yet in Portuguese control, and there Arab adventurers made precarious profits upon a small scale.

During the first twenty years of the sixteenth century Portuguese captains explored all the African seas in search of the precious metals or valuable goods for trade. In 1506 Tristão da Cunha discovered the islands now known by his name in the South Atlantic, and in company with Affonso de Albuquerque he explored the coast of Madagascar. He was told that silver and ginger existed there, and this led to the design of establishing a fort, but, as the information proved untrue, nothing was done; subsequently, São Lourenço, as the Portuguese named the island, was examined with a view to its conquest, but it was never occupied. The same two captains subdued the coast towns north of Mombasa, taking and sacking Oja and Brava, and as Socotra was supposed to be the key of the Red Sea, they seized the Arab fort on the island, but the mistake was soon discovered and the place abandoned.

Military control of the coast south of Cape Delgado was complete by 1509; forts in the principal towns held the half-caste Arabs in subjection, and fear of punishment sufficed for those which had no Portuguese garrison; later experience proved that stockades and guns were enough to keep the 'Kaffirs' in awe. The command of the sea was secured by oared boats manned by slave rowers and by the India ships, which passed up and down the coast yearly and called in according to the needs of the fortresses or their own. Arab dhows could not dispute it, and when the Turks made the attempt in 1589, they were vanquished at Patta by a fleet sent from Goa for the purpose. The Turkish admiral, Ali Beg, was captured by the Portuguese, while men of his crews who fled to the mainland fell into the hands of the cannibal "Muzimbas"[1] and were killed and eaten by them. Native navigation was regulated as in India, but with far less difficulty; the dhows had to call at certain ports to pay customs dues.

The Portuguese displaced the Arabs wherever their authority extended and endeavoured to seize their trade, but they could not prevent smuggling. The commerce of East Africa was made a royal monopoly under the direction of the king's factors at Sofala and Mozambique, who distributed the merchandise, imported from India, to the various coastal and inland stations and received the gold, ivory and ambergris obtained in exchange. In 1595 the trade was farmed out to the captains of the two fortresses, and in 1682 it was thrown open to private merchants, but as the Banyans (i.e. Indian traders) tended to oust the Portuguese, it was then transferred to a council at Mozambique. Portuguese East Africa for long depended economically, as it always did politically, on the State of India, to which it formed the avenue, and it was subject to the Governor or Viceroy, who ruled in the beginning from Cochin and after 1510 from Goa.

To the north of Cape Delgado conditions were different. Although the Portuguese could rely on the friendship of the sultans of Malindi and Zanzibar, and the coast towns were left in the hands of the inhabitants, who paid tribute, risings took place from time to time and had to be suppressed. Patta and Mombasa gave most trouble, especially the latter. Mombasa was situated on a coral reef with an excellent harbour, where a factory was established in 1509. It was conquered and burned, as we have seen, by D. Francisco de Almeida in 1505, and again by Nuno da Cunha in 1529, by D. Martim Affonso de Mello in 1587 and by Thomé de Sousa Coutinho in 1589. In 1593 the fortress of Jesus was built to control the place with stones brought ready cut from Portugal, and the seat of the captaincy, extending from Cape Delgado to Malindi, was moved from the latter place to Mombasa.

The building of the Portuguese fort at Sofala and the break-up of the Makaranga confederacy in the interior caused, as we have said, a diversion of the trade of the interior from about 1510 onwards to the alternative route down the Zambesi to the small ports in its delta.[2]

The first penetration of the interior by the Portuguese was the work of individual merchants and missionaries. At an early date various adventurous spirits, among whom were some of Italian

[1] The AmaZimba of the ethnologists.

[2] See a letter from Affonso de Albuquerque to King Manoel, 10 December 1514. Theal, *Records*, III, 147–8.

extraction, set up trading stations on the coast at Ibo, Inhambane and Delagoa Bay and in the delta of the Zambesi, called by the Portuguese the rivers of Cuama or of Sena. About 1531 they carried their activities up the main stream to Sena and Tete, the head of navigation, where small towns and forts were erected after the middle of the century; and later on they established periodical fairs at the junction of native trails like Masapa, the seat of the *Monomotapa* near Mount Fura, Bocuto and Luanze. Some of the adventurers acquired lands in the delta by conquest or otherwise and took the place of the native chiefs or *fumos*.

The first missionaries in South Africa were Dominicans and that Order became the predominant one, having spiritual charge of the fortresses of Sofala and Mozambique and of churches at Querimba and Ibo on the coast, at Sena and Tete, in the villages in the Makaranga country where fairs existed, and finally at Zimbaoe, the kraal of the *Monomotapa*.

The ecclesiastical government of East Africa was confided to an administrator at Mozambique, who was either a secular priest or a Dominican. The Augustinians and Jesuits also formed missionary centres. By 1591 the Dominicans claimed to have baptised 20,000 persons in the Zambesi delta alone,[1] but their greatest successes were obtained in the seventeenth century. The conversions were usually more apparent than real, and the native practice of polygamy was an obstacle to lasting results, but this must not blind us to the extraordinary courage and spiritual devotion of many of these first Christian missionaries in Africa south of the Equator.

The Jesuits had the glory of furnishing the protomartyr in the person of Frei Gonçalo da Silveira,[2] a missionary of noble family, who in 1560 was sent from Goa in response to an appeal from the *Monomotapa* for Christian instruction. He preached the Gospel for some weeks at Otongwe in the Inhambane country, this being the first mission ever established in South Africa. Silveira made many converts, but they fell away when his presence was removed. It was very difficult to make real progress in the teaching of Christianity to the Bantu, and no one realised this more than the best of the missionaries themselves. The only native religion was a crude form of ancestor-worship, and, as their first teachers said, the blacks were wrapped up in the pleasures of the flesh and had no idea of the soul. From the Inhambane country, whither he had gone on the appeal of the Tongan chief, whose "great place" lay some ninety miles up the Zambesi and who was his first temporary convert, Father Silveira undertook the long journey to the kraal of the *Monomotapa* himself. There he succeeded in baptising the chieftain and some of his wives and headmen; but this apparent success was entirely delusive, for it

[1] Theal, *Records*, I, 392.

[2] English biography by Father H. Chadwick, S.J. (Roehampton, 1910).

was merely due to their desire to secure the help of the powerful King of Portugal or to the traditional courtesy of the Bantu in deferring to the desires of their visitors. When the missionaries attempted to reform the heathen practices of their hosts, they met with stubborn and menacing hostility. The revulsion from his facile baptisms ended this time in tragedy, for certain Muslim traders easily persuaded the *Monomotapa* that Father Silveira was plotting his death by sorcery and poison. In March 1561 Silveira and many of his converts were strangled with heathen barbarities and their bodies thrown into the river. Thus perished the first martyr for the Christian faith in South Africa, to be followed a little later by his Muslim denunciators, who also fell victims to the savagery of heathen superstition. The tragedy led directly to important results, for it was one of the causes of the first serious Portuguese attempt to conquer the South African interior.

The policy of coastal occupation based on fortresses and the command of the sea, which had been inaugurated on the shores of the Indian Ocean under Manoel the Fortunate, was continued by John III, the Pious, who was a zealous promoter of missionary enterprise and a lover of peace. His successor, Sebastian, was a devoted believer in the Counter-Reformation, inspired with the ideal of the Crusaders of the thirteenth century and anxious to devote himself and all the resources of his kingdom to the foundation of an African empire for Christ. His schemes led to the occupation of Angola, which we shall discuss later, and to the campaigns in Morocco ending in his defeat and slaughter with the flower of the Portuguese nobility at Alcaçer-Kebir in 1578, and so to the annexation of Portugal to Spain in 1580 with its momentous consequences.

Before we turn to the events in South-East Africa that resulted from Silveira's murder and King Sebastian's crusading zeal, we must refer to the course of development in south-west Africa during the first part of the sixteenth century.

When the Congo was first discovered by Diogo Cão, the Negro kingdom included the southern portion of the modern Belgian Congo and more than half the area of the territory of Angola as a dependency,[1] but it was already tending to disintegrate. During the first sixty years after its discovery, the Kings of Portugal made genuine efforts to civilise the natives and convert them to Christianity, without any attempt at conquest; but though some initial success was achieved, the inconstant nature, superstitions and vices of the

[1] Ravenstein includes conjectural maps of Congo and Angola to illustrate their history down to the seventeenth century in his edition of *The Strange Adventures of Andrew Battell*. Hakluyt Society, 1901. Among other recent works, the history of these countries to 1635 by Snr Alfredo Felner, entitled *Angola* (Coimbra, 1933), was consulted in proof by the courtesy of the author. It supplements and sometimes corrects Ravenstein's narrative from Portuguese sources.

barbarians prevented any lasting results, and internal disorder then drove away missionaries and traders. Angola on the other hand developed into a colony, which the Congo had never been, and the latter was neglected.

In 1490 John II sent an expedition to explore the Congo under Gonçalo de Sousa accompanied by Franciscan friars chosen for their scientific knowledge, who were to ascertain the way to the land of Prester John, while others were to explore the interior. Ruy de Sousa, a lieutenant of the leader, actually sailed up the River Congo and obtained information as to the upper reaches beyond the Yelala Falls and the great lake which was vaguely rumoured to lie beyond. Before returning to Portugal he established a factory at Pinda, at the mouth of the river, to which the inhabitants of St Thomé resorted to purchase slaves, ivory and copper. Some of them settled down there and even made journeys inland to get merchandise for the vessels that came from the island.

Relations between the two countries later became intimate; Congolese youths regularly repaired to Lisbon to be educated, while Portuguese merchants were able to travel far into the interior and carry on trade. A custom house was established at Pinda, where duties were levied on goods passing in and out for the benefit of Portugal, which assumed the position of suzerain power. Nevertheless, the King of Congo would not allow the Portuguese to work the mines they had found, nor would he give leave for Gregorio de Quadra, the emissary of King Manoel, to explore the Upper Congo and seek a way to Abyssinia.[1] In 1526, however, he came to favour the second project, and in 1536 had wood made ready for two boats which were to serve for the discovery of the great lake; but by then the expedition no longer interested the Portuguese, who had already reached the country of Prester John by sea.

The first recorded visit of the Portuguese to Angola, after the early discoveries along its coast, took place in 1520. The native name for the country was Ndongo, but it was not co-extensive with the modern Portuguese province. In some directions it had influence in territories now a part of the British Empire and so falling within our subject. It was also the scene of the earliest attempts at European colonisation in Africa south of the Equator, and its early history is therefore of direct interest. The paramount chief, called the *Ngola*, from whom the modern name is derived, had before 1520 heard of the liberalities of King Manoel to his protégés in the kingdom of Congo, and desiring a share of them and of trade with the Portuguese, he asked for missionaries as the means of obtaining both, and accompanied his request with a present of silver bracelets. In consequence, Manuel Pacheco and Baltasar de Castro were sent out with orders, first to explore the west coast and rivers from the Cape of

[1] Damião de Goes, *Chronica de D. Manoel*, IV, cap. 54.

Good Hope northward to the Cuanza, and next to visit the *Ngola* and ascertain whether he would accept the Christian faith. They were ordered at the same time to collect information about the mines of silver and other metals which were rumoured to exist in the region.[1] In all probability there was a sound basis for these rumours in the knowledge the natives had of the great copper deposits of the Katanga. Castro actually reached the residence of the *Ngola*, but was held there as a prisoner for six years, and he then owed his liberation to the intercession of the King of Congo. The action of the *Ngola* was probably inspired by some of the Portuguese renegades who had fled into Angola from the small European settlements on the Congo and in their own interests did not wish to see their refuge closed to them. It is worthy of note that during his long residence among the Negroes Castro could never secure confirmation of the existence of silver mines, but the legend persisted for a century, and it was one of the causes which induced the Portuguese to undertake the conquest of the country. Another reason prompting Portuguese designs upon Angola was that it was noted for ample supplies of cheap slaves owing to the overpopulation of the country. Brazil was beginning to be opened up for the cultivation of sugar before 1540, and Negro slaves were needed to work the new estates. The Portuguese had organised the slave trade in Guinea in the second half of the fifteenth century and used the island of St Thomé as one of their entrepôts. When a demand arose for slaves for Brazil, St Thomé was a convenient centre from which to supply it, and soon after 1540 we hear of slave-traders on the coast of Angola bartering European goods for their cargoes. In 1548 the King of Congo caused an enquiry to be made about the vessels which the factor and officials of St Thomé were dispatching to the ports of Angola without his leave and forbade the trade, as it interfered with that carried on with his own country. This prohibition deprived the *Ngola* of his profit and about 1550 he revolted against his overlord. In 1556 he sent an embassy to Lisbon to obtain the recognition of his independence and assistance against the King of Congo, who in that year had dispatched an army against him which was defeated on the River Dande.

The Portuguese Government realised the advantage of entering into direct relations with Angola, which promised greater trading advantages than the Congo, but, owing to the death of the *Ngola* and for other reasons, it delayed taking action for some years. At length, however, in 1560 Paulo Dias de Novais,[2] grandson of Bartholomew Dias, was sent out to study the situation on the spot and find out if the new "king", as the Portuguese called him, was willing to accept Christianity and enter into an agreement. Three Jesuits were

[1] Their instructions are in *Alguns Documentos da Torre do Tombo*, etc., p. 436.

[2] He is often spoken of by English writers as Novais, but the Portuguese always call him Paulo Dias.

sent out with Dias to begin a mission, but the *Ngola*, suspicious of their intentions, held them prisoners for some time, robbed them of their goods and otherwise ill-treated them. However, after some years Dias was able to reassure him and compose the differences between Angola and Congo. He returned to Portugal in 1572 with an envoy of the *Ngola* and rich presents for the King of Portugal as a token of the proffered alliance; but before we deal with the results of this mission we must return to trace what was happening at the same time in south-east Africa.

When Sebastian succeeded John III upon the throne of Portugal he took up seriously the schemes for securing the possession of the gold-mines in the dominions of the *Monomotapa* which had been often discussed in the reign of John III. Sebastian's purpose was to carry out the obligations to spread the Christian faith to which he was bound under the papal grants made to his predecessors from as early a date as 1452,[1] to punish the *Monomotapa* for the murder of Father Silveira and, lastly, to increase the revenue of the Crown. He submitted the question of the morality, or, as we should put it, the propriety according to international law of making war against the *Monomotapa* to a commission of lawyers and theologians, called the Mesa da Consciencia, and in January 1569 they delivered an opinion which is of considerable interest as marking the opinion of the sixteenth century concerning relations with non-Christian peoples. They held that the King of Portugal might justly make war on the *Monomotapa* on account of his murder of Father Silveira and other Portuguese, his robbery of their property and his sheltering of the Moors, the enemies of the Christian faith and the instigators of those crimes. Besides the aforesaid causes there must be "in the King who represents a public person obliged to defend his state and subjects from all injuries, an upright intention of spreading the gospel in those parts. This conversion and salvation of souls must be the principal end in view . . . and not the increase of empire, or the personal glory and profit of the prince, or other private interests." On these grounds the commissioners pronounced the war just.[2] Francisco Barreto, who had been a successful Governor of India, was appointed captain-general of the first expedition and of the lands when gained. He was supplied with three vessels and 550 veteran soldiers, including many members of noble houses, for the fame of the gold-mines, which were popularly identified with the ancient Ophir, led to a general rush to enlist. Barreto left Lisbon in April 1569, called at Bahia, where he remained six months, and reached Mozambique on 11

[1] See Davenport, F. G., *European Treaties bearing on the history of the United States . . . to 1648*, p. 12.

[2] Theal, *Records*, III, 153. From a contemporary copy in Bibl. Nat., Paris, Dept. of MSS., Portugais 8, fo. 266.

March 1570. He had been preceded by his second in command, Vasco Fernandes Homem, who found there the historian Diogo do Conto and the poet Camoens, the latter of whom had been stranded on the homeward voyage owing to lack of means and had spent the time in polishing his great epic, *The Lusiads*, for the press. Instead of proceeding to his destination, Barreto wasted a year and a half in reducing Zanzibar, Patta and other coast towns, and then, instead of taking the route up-country *via* Sofala, was persuaded by Father Monclaros, the leading Jesuit who accompanied him, to go by the Zambesi, as Monclaros desired to obtain satisfaction for the murder of Father Silveira and recover his remains. Finally, in November 1572, he sailed with twenty-two craft for Kilimane and so up the river to Sena, where there was already a small Portuguese settlement, and there he disembarked his "select and well-equipped company, more in the humour to fight Turks than mere Kaffirs". There the traditional Muslim hostility showed itself; they knew that they would lose their trade in gold with the Natives if the Portuguese obtained possession of the mines. The expedition was accompanied by 2000 slaves in charge of the baggage waggons and camels, and by a fleet of boats on the river to carry those who fell ill, and it took a month to traverse the fifty leagues from Sena to the country of the Mongas, a warlike tribe on the Zambesi, "more cruel and dreaded than the Turks in Italy". Such enemies could not safely be left in the rear, and Barreto decided to march inland and subdue them before proceeding further. In two fierce battles against their overwhelming forces, the training, artillery and muskets of his little band won a complete victory; but the climate, foul water and poor food caused daily deaths and so enfeebled the survivors that Barreto had to retreat to the river and return to Sena, after penetrating only some twelve leagues from its banks.

The *Monomotapa* had heard of the expedition and its object, and his envoy now arrived to say that he desired amity with the Portuguese and would welcome trade with them; whereupon Barreto boldly dictated his terms. The *Monomotapa* must expel the Muslims from his dominions, allow the Gospel to be preached and hand over the ownership of some of his mines to the King of Portugal. He then went back to Mozambique to get fresh troops, and after his departure all the officers and men he had left at Sena, except fifty, sickened and died. The *Monomotapa* accepted the demands made on him, but it could not be disguised that the expedition had been a failure. He promised to expel the Arabs, and did so, laying on them the blame for the murder of Father Silveira; he gave leave for the preaching of Christianity, though he would not promise to return to the faith, while, as to the gold-mines, he offered to hand over some of them and also the silver-mines near Tete.

The prestige of the Portuguese in South-East Africa was undeniably weakened by this disaster and it suffered a further blow between 1570 and 1593 from repeated invasions by cannibal "Mumbos" and "Mazimbas" from the north.[1] Father Monclaros, who wrote an account of the expedition,[2] remarks concerning the agreement with the *Monomotapa* that he actually gave some gold-mines to Portuguese traders, but the extraction of the metal proved so costly that they abandoned them, finding it more profitable to get gold from the natives in exchange for cloth. After Barreto's failure, Fernandes Homem, who succeeded him as captain-general, took the Sofala route to the mines, invaded Manica and reached the vicinity of Massikesse, but only found some poor workings from which little gold could be extracted. He retired disillusioned.

In 1597 and the following years the Makaranga territories were invaded by neighbouring tribes and disturbed by internal rebellions, and as the Portuguese settlers at Sena and Tete, and especially Diogo Simões Madeira, captain of the latter place, lent their assistance to the Makaranga, in 1609 the reigning *Monomotapa*, Gasilusere, made a grant of all his mines to King Philip III of Spain, who then ruled over Portugal. He also gave the silver-mines at Chicova above Tete to Madeira in return for his services in restoring him more than once to power, but the latter was never able to obtain possession of them; the native chiefs refused to disclose their whereabouts, fearing that the Portuguese would seize the lands in which they were situated. On hearing of the grant to Madeira, Philip III ordered that an attempt should be made to take possession of the mines, and in 1609 D. Nuno Alvares Pereira was sent as captain-general for the purpose, but achieved nothing. In 1612 D. Estevam de Ataide, his successor, quarrelled with the *Monomotapa* and refused to deliver the *curva* or present of cloth, worth 5000 *cruzados*,[3] which was by custom given to secure liberty of trade in the Makaranga dominions. On this the *Monomotapa* seized the property of the Portuguese residents in the interior and caused some of them to be slain. Philip III disapproved of the agreement made by the Viceroy of India with Ataide for the conquest of the mines and ordered the latter to hand it over to Madeira, who succeeded him as captain-general; Madeira paid the *curva* and, once peace had been restored, lent further aid to the *Monomotapa*. The latter ordered the mines to be disclosed, but then, repenting of his gift, secretly countermanded his instructions. In 1613, therefore, Madeira determined to seek for the mines by himself, and in digging in the hills near Chicova, where he had built a fort in 1612, many large nuggets were found; but owing to the hostility of a judge, Francisco da Fonseca, who had been sent from India to report on the mines and supply his needs, Madeira was

[1] OvAmbo and AmaZimba, *vide supra*, pp. 36 *sqq*.

[2] Theal, *Records*, III, 157–253.

[3] According to Antonio Bocarro, but Barreto de Resende says 15,000. Theal, *Records*, II, 390 and III, 381.

compelled by sickness and lack of food to abandon his post in 1616 and return to Tete. He was reinstated in 1618, and instructed to assist Alvares Pereira, who seems to have made another expedition in search of the mines which proved as unsuccessful as the others. From a report of Father Manuel Barreto made in 1667[1] and other sources, it seems doubtful if gold or even silver existed in the lands under Portuguese control, at least in sufficient quantities to repay the cost of working, but Madeira was for long hopeful and dispatched Gaspar Bocarro with some nuggets of silver to the court of Madrid. This man made an overland journey from Chicova to Kilwa, in the course of which he discovered and crossed Lake Nyasa and the River Rovuma, more than two centuries before Livingstone. In 1624 the Viceroy of India was ordered to find out if there was a route by way of this lake to Abyssinia, where Portuguese influence was then on the decline owing to a nationalist revival founded on suspicion of the Europeans and their creed.

In view of the failure of all attempts to reach the mines, and as these enterprises had only led to a waste of men and money, Philip III in 1622 ordered the search to be abandoned. The monopoly of trade in the dominions of the *Monomotapa* and on the coast south of the Zambesi was leased to the captains of Mozambique for 40,000 *cruzados* on condition that they kept up the fortress and paid the garrisons.[2] By arrangement with the *Monomotapa*, a Portuguese official, called Captain of the Gates, lived at Masapa and acted as intermediary between him and the merchants; he derived his title from the fact that no trader could pass inland thence without his leave.

In 1628 the Makaranga empire was actually conquered by the Portuguese inhabitants of Sena and Tete in company with their compatriots at Luanse and Masapa. In the following year they put on the throne a new *Monomotapa*, Manuza, who became a Christian, acknowledged himself a vassal of King Philip and agreed to the conditions demanded by Francisco Barreto half a century earlier.[3] The dethroned *Monomotapa* made an attempt to recover his throne, but was defeated by forces of Native warriors raised by the Dominican friars, Manuel Sardinha and Damião do Espirito Santo, while Diogo de Sousa de Menesses overran Manica and set up a new king, who accepted Portuguese overlordship and also became a Christian. Twenty years later the Kings of Kiteve and Barue were baptised, but all of these Bantu rulers were only nominal believers. Portuguese influence in East Africa then attained the height of its power and prosperity, and as late as 1694 the Viceroy informed the King of Portugal that he had no dominion in the East so valuable as that

[1] Printed in Theal, *Records*, III, 436.
[2] Theal, *Records*, IV, 185, 193.
[3] The treaty made on this occasion is in Theal, *Records*, V, 287.

of the "rivers of Sena". The Portuguese had a captain and garrison at Zimbaoe, the royal residence, and, according to Father Barreto, elected or deposed emperors at their pleasure, while, as to their profits, he calls the rivers of Cuama "truly rivers of gold". He also says that 3000 *pastas* or 60,000 ounces were exported yearly from Kilimane and only 500 from Sofala, which in Arab days had been the port for the whole trade. Very little of the money, however, reached the royal treasury; indeed, as early as 1552 Simon Betelho, overseer of the revenue, informed the king that even the captains of Sofala and Mozambique, though they received beads and cloth from India to exchange for ivory, sent hardly any, on the ground that the profits of their fortresses belonged to themselves. This was the view held and acted upon, not only by the Portuguese officials in the East, but by their English trading rivals, and it is not therefore surprising to learn that in 1580–4 neither Sofala nor Mozambique yielded any revenue to the State.

In 1590–1 Sofala cost 1,351,400 *reis*,[1] the vicar of the church received 2400 *reis* for the masses he said for the soul of Prince Henry the Navigator, and Mozambique cost 3,829,661 *reis*. The latter fortress was at times in dire need of munitions and its garrison reduced to a hundred men or less, so that, if the Dutch had attacked it on one of these occasions, it would have fallen and with it the dominion of the Portuguese in East Africa, while the State of India could hardly have been held without the halfway station of Mozambique for the annual fleets. The captains of Kilimane, Sena and Tete, if less rich than the captains of Mozambique who could make 200,000 *cruzados* in their three-year term, were more powerful, for they were able to put in the field 12,000 picked Kaffirs with 300 guns.[2]

The only territory actually belonging to the Portuguese Crown in East Africa at the close of the sixteenth century, apart from the coastal fortresses, consisted of a triangle bounded on the north by the Zambesi and running from Chicova to Kilimane, on the south by an imaginary line drawn from Chicova to Sofala, while the coast from Kilimane to Sofala formed the third side. This tract was divided into districts called *moganos*, which had been acquired by Portuguese adventurers, who paid a quit-rent to the king and received from the Natives a tribute on the products of the soil and on the ivory they obtained by hunting. The districts were governed by four captains, the chief of whom was usually the captain of Sena; as the latter was the most important place in the whole territory, decisions of peace or war generally depended on him. He derived his appointment from the captain of Mozambique. The owners of the districts, or *prasos da*

[1] Theal, *Records*, IV, 5. He estimates the value of a *real* as equal to one farthing to-day, but it was more probably worth three.

[2] According to Father Barreto (Theal, *Records*, III, 474); but Barreto de Resende, writing thirty years earlier, says that in the district of Sena alone there were 30,000 armed Kaffirs at the captain's orders.

corõa, which came to number eighty-five, may be compared to feudal lords, and by intermarriage with Natives their European blood became more and more diluted as time went on.

As in the delta, adventurers had also acquired large properties in the Makaranga dominions by purchase from the *Monomotapa*, and with their hordes of slaves they were more powerful than he; in Manica also they held more lands than the King, while Gobira, part of the kingdom of Quiteve, was also in their hands. One of the most daring of these men was Sisnando Dias Bayão, who penetrated as far as the Butua country or Matabeleland, overran it and built forts, which, however, were abandoned on his death. The captains of Mozambique could not control these adventurers, who made wars on their own account and were independent chieftains, and the royal treasury derived no advantage from their exploits. Hence Father Barreto in his report suggested to the King that, if the *Monomotapa* rose in rebellion again, he should take the opportunity of subduing and annexing the whole of his dominions and dividing the land among the Portuguese, who, besides a quit-rent, might be obliged to pay tithes for them. He estimated that these together would bring in more than a million *reis*; but the execution of such a plan was beyond the strength of Portugal, for though Portugal had recovered independence in 1640, and in 1668 had won the war with Spain that had dragged on for twenty-eight years, and had also regained Angola and Brazil from the Dutch, the nation was exhausted by the efforts it had put forth.

In the last decade of the seventeenth century a subject of the *Monomotapa* named Changamira[1] rose from humble origins to be a power in Butua, and between 1693 and 1695 he conquered most of the dominions of his former master, and the political authority of Portugal in the region of the Zambesi was gradually reduced to its present limits. But before that date the Portuguese had lost the command of the sea to the Dutch and dominion on the northern part of the coast to the Oman Arabs,[2] so that they had ceased to play an important part in South-East Africa.

We must now continue the story of Angola from the point where we left it in 1572. The conviction had already been formed in Portugal before that date that Angola was a suitable country for colonisation after the manner of Brazil, to which it would form a useful appendage since it could supply it with slaves.

Paulo Dias de Novais was therefore able to secure without difficulty from the Crown of Portugal a "donation" of territory on similar lines to the captaincies already granted in Brazil.[3] His dona-

[1] The wars of Changamira with the Portuguese are described by Antonio da Conceição in *Chronista de Tirsuary*, II, 105 *sqq*.

[2] *Vide infra*, pp. 110 *sqq*.

[3] The document is printed by Snr Felner, *Angola*, p. 407.

tion was twofold: he received for himself in perpetuity thirty-five leagues of coastline running south from the River Cuanza and inland as far as he could subdue, while the government of the whole of the territory between the Cuanza and the Dande was bestowed upon him for life, and in both regions he was given full civil and criminal jurisdiction. By the terms of the grant he had to meet all the expenses of his expedition and they cost him more than 27,000 *cruzados*,[1] most of which he borrowed. He undertook to occupy the country and build forts and a church in the territory north of the Cuanza, and the revenue he raised in both territories was to be divided between him and the Crown. The King reserved to himself the traffic in slaves, but Dias had the right to export on his own account, free of duty, forty-eight *peças da India*, that is to say ninety-six slaves, every year.

Dias' expedition was the first attempt to establish a colony in this part of Africa. Leaving Lisbon in October 1574 with a small fleet carrying 400 settlers capable of bearing arms, including artisans, a physician and a barber-surgeon, Dias first established himself on Loanda Island and then on the mainland opposite, where the town of St Paul de Loanda soon began to rise. The new colony was named the "realm of Sebaste" in honour of King Sebastian. Dias called together the roving Portuguese adventurers who were already living in Angola and informed them of his rights and powers, which must have been very distasteful to men unaccustomed to obey any settled authority. The *Ngola* sent an envoy to treat with him; for a time harmony reigned between the donatory and the surrounding Native tribes, and trade gradually increased, especially in slaves, purchased from Chiefs in the interior. Between 1575 and 1591, 52,000 *pecas*, or about 104,000 individuals, were exported, notwithstanding the disorders that arose within the Native confederacy after the founding of the settlement. Soon, however, the Natives began to attack and rob Portuguese traders so frequently as to make their journeys into the interior very precarious. Though Dias endeavoured to avoid hostilities against the offending Chiefs and their tribes, he saw that, unless he was prepared to abandon his donation, they would be inevitable.

During the first years of the colony Dias had heard of the existence of what were said to be rich silver-mines at Cambambe in the interior, and he made it his object to mark a trail thither and to establish fortified posts along it to guard his caravan from attack. He actually built three of these posts, the last being at Anzelle. He told the envoys from the *Ngola*, who came down to protest, that the posts were established to defend him from his enemies. But the "great chief" refused to accept this explanation and treated his action as a

[1] About £30,000 of our money, according to Snr Felner, but when he died he left debts amounting to about £117,000 as the result of his colonising efforts, *op. cit.*, pp. 123 *sqq.*

declaration of war. He massacred all the Portuguese traders upon whom he could lay hands and assembled a large army to attack the invaders. Dias had already prepared himself and asked for reinforcements from Portugal. One hundred and fifty well-armed and trained men came out to the colony in 1580, and when the *Ngola* attacked him, the assailants were completely routed near Mocumba on 1 November 1580.

During the next two years many of the Chiefs of Kissama and Ilamba were reduced to obedience, and though one of the lieutenants of Dias, who endeavoured to seize the mines, was defeated and killed, the Jesuit father Baltasar Barreira brought up all the available Portuguese from the coast and thus enabled Dias to undertake another campaign. Thanks in a large measure to the enthusiasm which this patriotic priest roused in the small body of Portuguese soldiers, they won a decisive victory over the *Ngola* in person at Teka-Ndungo on 2 February 1583. In thanksgiving Dias built a church at Massangano, where he established a permanent encampment in a strong position between the Rivers Lucala and Cuanza. The Cambambe Hills being near, specimens of metal could now be obtained, which were sent to Europe with an earnest request for more men and munitions, and at the end of 1584 two hundred soldiers and some miners arrived. In the meantime the effect of the victory of the previous year had worn off, and, seeing that the Portuguese did not move, many of the Chiefs who had submitted revolted again. While engaged in punishing them, Dias was again attacked by the *Ngola*, and, though he defeated him in 1585 near Massangano and in 1586 on the Lucala, he lacked the strength to pursue his conquests and was glad to accept the offer of the residents of Loanda to build a fort at Benguela Velha. Shortly before his death in 1589 its garrison was surprised and slain by the Natives.

At this time nearly all the captaincies of strips of territory granted by the Portuguese Government to its subjects in Brazil had been purchased by and vested in the Crown, because the donatories had proved unable to develop them, and in 1583 a similar policy was applied to Angola. The land between the Cuanza and the Dande was taken over, while the financial and judicial administration of the territory south of the Cuanza was entrusted to royal officials, so that the privileges of Dias were greatly diminished; indeed after his death the Governors of Angola were sent out from home. Before the first royal Governor took over control, his lieutenant Luis Serrão endeavoured to continue his plan of penetrating the interior, and with only 128 Portuguese and 15,000 Native troops made a daring raid as far as Ngwallma a Kitambu beyond Ambaca in the province of Ari. There he was beaten by an overwhelming host of the Chiefs of Angola, Matamba, Congo and Jagas, who had united to oppose him, and was obliged to retreat to Massangano. This defeat showed the folly of attempting to conquer distant provinces with an inadequate force, for it was only by the heroism of his small band that Dias had been able to reduce even those of Kissama and Ilamba near the sea after fiercely contested battles. Moreover, Chiefs who had accepted Portuguese suzerainty were apt to return to their former allegiance when they found that the Europeans were few in number and could not protect them from the vengeance of the *Ngola*. This happened now, and the prestige of the Portuguese arms was only restored by the Governor, João Furtado de Mendonça, who arrived in 1594. It was confirmed for a time by his successor, João Rodrigues Coutinho, who came in 1602 and brought with him 1000 soldiers.

De Mendonça made two expeditions to Bengo, while Baltasar Rebelo de Aragão, a typical *conquistador*, repelled an attack on Massangano and built a fort at Kissama; moreover, knowing that Natives in the service of his countrymen had crossed the continent to Mozambique, he attempted to do likewise in 1606, but was called back before he had gone far on the way. Coutinho received the submission of many Chiefs and routed Agoacoango, one of the most troublesome, and though fever carried him off in the midst of his work, it was completed by Manuel Cerveira Pereira. The chief Caxufe, who had foiled more than one effort to conquer him, now sued for peace and even the *Ngola* came to terms with the Governor. After founding a fortress at Cambambe in 1604, Pereira exploded the legend of the silver-mines, since a careful search showed that the metal did not exist in sufficient quantity to be worth working; but he started another project about rich copper-beds near the south coast, which was to prove equally fantastic. However, he committed such abuses of authority that he was sent home in disgrace.

The death of Dias had raised an important problem of administration; the Crown possessed no vassals, because, when Chiefs submitted, they did so to the donatory, and their services and tribute were granted out to the captains who had helped him in the wars. In 1590 a lawyer, Domingo Abreu a Brito, was sent out to examine the condition of the colony, and he drew up a report which formed the basis for the future government of Angola.[1] Though he alluded only indirectly to the question of vassalage, it was too important to be left without solution. Even before the nomination of D. Manuel Pereira Forjaz to succeed Cerveira Pereira, a royal order had been issued revoking the grants made by Dias, and Forjaz was instructed to publish it and see that it was obeyed. He was also charged to avoid Native wars and to have the mines worked by agreement with the Natives, while slaves were not to be bought outside the fairs and white men were to be present to see that justice was done. The new policy had been communicated to Cerveira Pereira and probably accounts

[1] This important document has been printed by Snr Felner under the title *Um inquerito á vida administrativa e economica de Angola e Brasil* (Coimbra, 1931).

for his peaceful dealings with the *Ngola*, which did not accord with his violent character, though it may have been due to his mining fever. It is doubtful if Forjaz obeyed the instructions he had received, since he seems to have neglected administration for private business; but he initiated trade with Bié, Benguela and Bailundo and brought back from them large quantities of cattle, slaves and ivory, and by so doing contributed to the economic development of the colony.

On the sudden death of Forjaz in 1611, Bento Banha Cardoso became interim Governor; he repulsed the incursions made by the *Ngola* in reply to Portuguese penetration, founded a new fort at Ambaca, repelled attacks from the Congo and made no less than eighty Chiefs tributary. In the meantime Cerveira Pereira had freed himself from the charges made against him and so far persuaded King Philip III of the value of the copper-mines that he was sent out again as Governor of the province of Benguela, which was separated from Angola, and there in 1617 he founded the present town of St Philip. Though the court of Madrid recommended the Governors to live in peace with the Native tribes, Philip III wished to increase the number of his vassals and the tribute they paid, and this necessarily meant a diminution of the authority and revenue of the *Ngola*, who was certain to resist. Such a double-edged policy was therefore impossible of execution. Luis Mendes de Vasconcellos, who assumed the government of the colony in 1616, did not attempt it and not only took up arms against the *Ngola* but strove to depose him and set up a Christian Chief in his stead. Though the Portuguese nominee was not recognised by the Natives, Vasconcellos' military operations resulted in the submission of 109 Chiefs, but they also disorganised trade and as a result of complaints on this head he was recalled. Nevertheless his destruction of the *Ngola's* kraal and the imposition of a tribute on him were the beginning of the end in the struggle between Portuguese and Natives. The Governor found it wiser to make peace with the beaten Chief and his sister Ginga, a remarkable woman, who came as ambassadress to negotiate the treaty and, as a guarantee, accepted baptism.

Two years later, in 1623, Ginga caused her brother to be murdered, and soon after her ascent to the throne she began to foment rebellion among the Chiefs who had accepted Portuguese rule. A force was sent against her which attacked and entered her camp on Ndangi Island in the Cuanza. She escaped, but the Portuguese followed her up as far as Quissuma, defeated her army and captured her two sisters. Escaping once more, she took refuge in distant Songo. Though she afterwards gave trouble, she had ceased to be a danger.

Governor Fernão de Sousa extended Portuguese authority further than any of his predecessors; he kept the Native tribes in check by means of the Jagas, secured the salt-mines of Ndemba and opened fairs in Haco and Bango. According to the estimate of Snr Felner the Portuguese had before 1630 occupied over 70 square miles of territory and reduced 204 Chiefs to obedience, so that a very material enterprise of colonisation had been accomplished.

While the Portuguese were thus active in Angola and Mozambique, they entirely neglected the long coastline between them which now bounds the territory of the Union of South Africa. But, despite their efforts, some knowledge concerning the lands behind it gradually grew, for, again and again during the sixteenth century, ships voyaging out to or homeward bound from the Indies were cast away upon this coast, and the tragic experiences of their castaways brought them into contact with the savages who roamed there. Not all the wrecks can have been recorded in detail, and some ships were lost without a trace, but many tragic narratives have survived,[1] and from them we can derive some idea of the constantly changing relationships between the South African tribes. The Portuguese failed to understand the political nature of Bantu life and called every chieftain of more than a kraal or two a "king", attributing to each the possession of a definite area of land, which was far from being correct. They called the headmen of separate kraals "nobles" and apparently conceived of them as being in something like a feudal relation to the "kings".[2] The use of these terms and ideas led to serious misconceptions among European writers for nearly two centuries and gravely impaired the value of their interpretation of the history of the region.

The so-called "kingdoms" did not stretch further south than the modern Natal, for the Bantu south and west of that territory were split up into numberless little clans without cohesion, and they seem to have been the scattered remnants of tribes fleeing from the invasions of stronger peoples from the north-east. Though their languages, culture and customs were much the same as those of the tribal Bantu of more recent times, there was, according to Theal, nowhere, at least from Sofala southwards, a single tribe of the same name as any now existing.[3] Their grouping was entirely different and in a continual state of flux. Many of their names were sadly mangled in the attempt to transliterate them into Portuguese, and it would be profitless to attempt to recapitulate them. The whole region was, in fact, a vast no-man's-land, roamed over by savages with merely tribal institutions and nothing but a rudimentary and primitive culture. They had no traditions stretching back more than a generation or two, and thus until the coming of the Europeans the extreme south had no systematic history.

[1] They are recorded in the *Historia Tragico-Maritima* (Lisbon, 1735–6).

[2] *Vide supra*, p. 39.

[3] Theal, *The Portuguese in South Africa*, p. 175. But see Garrod in *Report of the S. A. Assoc. for the Advancement of Science*, 1913, pp. 146 *sqq*.

Until the closing years of the sixteenth century Portugal held an unchallenged monopoly of the African waters south of the Equator and of the exploitation of the coasts that bordered them. In the struggle that she waged with the "Moors", she achieved a success that left her without serious competitors for three-quarters of a century, though on rare occasions an isolated French privateer or two found their way round the Cape of Good Hope into the waters of the Indian Ocean. But when she lost her independence in 1580 and was absorbed into the vast dominions of Philip II, Portugal's immunity from interference was ended and competitors of a new and infinitely dangerous sort came to challenge her. A detailed study of the incoming of Dutch and English into African and Indian waters lies beyond our present purpose,[1] but we may appropriately say something of how that vast maritime struggle affected Portugal's position in East and South-West Africa.

The Dutch East India Company founded in 1602 was able to send out ships more numerous, better equipped and better manned than her rival. Moreover, the Dutch possessed other advantages for a struggle in Eastern waters, for, not being Crusaders, they had no quarrel with Muslims as such, nor did they take upon themselves the onerous burden of evangelisation which had absorbed so much Portuguese energy since the accession of Sebastian. Like the English East India Company, they had a hatred of Catholicism, which embittered the struggle with the Portuguese, but did not divert them from their strictly commercial purpose to get valuable cargoes which they could monopolise to the exclusion of all competitors.

The first magnet attracting the Dutch to East Africa was the gold trade of Sofala and Mozambique, and they determined to make themselves master of it by capturing the fortress of Mozambique where it then centred. In 1604 a Dutch fleet under Steven van der Hagen blockaded it for six weeks, and in April 1607 another of eight large vessels, carrying 1060 men under Paulus van Caerden, laid regular siege to the fortress. The small garrison of 184 men, commanded by D. Estevam de Ataide, put up a desperate resistance and at last the Dutch had to sail away baffled, though they burned the houses and churches on the island, cut down the coconut trees and destroyed everything of value they could find. A third attempt against Mozambique was made in 1608 by a still more formidable fleet, and a fourth half a century later, but in both cases with the same lack of success.

The Dutch never succeeded in establishing themselves in East Africa, but, instead, made the island of Mauritius the centre of their operations in those waters. The weakening of the Portuguese hold was brought about by their disasters elsewhere. The African posts could get no assistance from Goa all of whose resources were devoted

[1] See *C.H.B.E.* vol. IV, chapters II and IV.

to trying to keep off the English from Surat or the Dutch from Ceylon. They could get no reinforcements direct from Portugal, for Spain made all Portuguese resources subservient to her disastrous European adventures. The posts were thus cast back upon themselves and there was a progressive decline, an enfeebling of the European stock by admixture with African blood, and a consequent rise in the power of the mixed Swahili-speaking peoples among whom they lived.

On the west coast the Dutch attacks came later than on the east and were closely associated with the ambitious schemes of the Dutch West India Company in Brazil. Count Maurice of Nassau, who was endeavouring to build up a great Dutch colony there, desired to obtain possession of the market which provided slaves for the sugar plantations and to deprive his competitors of their source of supply. In 1641 he sent an expedition against Angola under Admiral Cornelis Jol, which captured the port of Loanda and drove the Governor of Angola, Pedro Cesar de Menezes, with his troops to Massangano in the interior. This loss was followed by that of Benguela. A truce of ten years was concluded in 1641 between the Dutch and Portugal, which had now revolted from Spain, but it was agreed that it should only be effective in the colonies when it had been proclaimed there.[1] News of the signature of the truce arrived early in 1643. Though the Dutch officially intimated it to their rivals, they treacherously attacked the Portuguese camp and took the Governor and 150 men prisoners, slaughtered others and carried away a rich booty in merchandise, metals and slaves. We mentioned above how the fierce chieftainess Ginga had long been in conflict with the Portuguese, and the Dutch now joined hands with her. With their assistance she set out to attack Massangano, but was defeated in January 1646. Some months later the Dutch advanced up the River Cuanza, but failed to take Moxima or overcome the Portuguese adventurers and their African auxiliaries in that region. In 1648, when the great Portuguese revival was driving out the last remnants of Dutch power from Brazil, an expedition from that colony, led by Salvador Correa de Sá e Benevides, retook first Loanda and then Benguela and cleared Angola of the intruders.[2] Ginga, deprived of Dutch aid, withdrew into the remote interior and at last made peace with the Portuguese in 1657; before her death in 1663 she returned to the Christian faith which she had nominally adopted in youth. Thus, by 1663, the Portuguese had fully recovered their power in Angola and their monopoly of the slave trade on which the prosperity of Brazil depended. Between that date and the end of the seventeenth century

[1] Davenport, *European Treaties bearing on the history of the U.S.…to 1648*, p. 329.

[2] The story of the Dutch invasion of and expulsion from Angola is told by the secretary of the colony, Luis Felis Cruz, in *Manifesto das Ostillidades*, etc., Lisbon, 1651, 2nd ed. (Coimbra, 1919).

there were two short Native wars in Angola, which were ended by Portuguese victories at Pungu a Ndongo in 1671 and at Katole in 1683, when the last *Ngola* was taken and beheaded. In 1685 the fortress of Kakonda, over 150 miles from the coast, was founded.

After the Dutch had been driven out, the Portuguese extended their boundaries and strengthened their military hold on the country, but their missionary efforts, in which the Jesuits had been conspicuous, gradually slackened. Angola depended on Brazil, from which it drew its supplies of food, rather than on Portugal, and all the energies of the mother country were given to the development of her South American possession. In Angola only thirty-six friars and twenty-nine secular priests were left by the end of the century, half of whom lived in Loanda. Most of the fifty churches and chapels scattered over the interior had fallen into ruin; as a consequence many of the Native converts abandoned the practice of Christianity and returned to their former superstitions.

There followed a long period of neglect and decline in the civilising work of the Portuguese in Angola and Mozambique, and it was not until the nineteenth century that it was resumed. But the work done in the seventeenth century was not wholly barren, for some lasting benefits were conferred upon the region. The Portuguese colonists are said to have introduced a large number of fruit trees and vegetables from Asia and America,[1] but the evidence for this statement is suspect, and in any case the introduction exerted little influence beyond the coast settlements.

On the east coast the final downfall of Portuguese power was brought about by an Arab revival. In 1651 the Arabs took Muscat through the treachery of an Indian employee, so that the Portuguese were then left without a post either in the Persian Gulf or on the coast of Arabia. In 1631 a Muslim rising broke out in East Africa while the Portuguese at sea were constantly being harassed by Dutch privateers, and Mombasa and other places were lost. In 1636–7 Mombasa was recaptured and the revolting towns punished, but in 1652 the Arabs conquered Zanzibar and Pemba, and, though these were afterwards recovered, the gains were not permanent. In 1698 the Arab Sultan of Oman, who had a large navy, captured Mombasa after a siege of two years and Portuguese sovereignty north of Cape Delgado came to an end.

In Sofala and Mozambique there was a progressive decline in the character of the Portuguese inhabitants and soldiers till few of pure European blood remained. While the Dutch held Angola and monopolised the slave trade, a few slaves were carried from Mozambique to Brazil, but the recovery of the colony by the Portuguese brought this trade to an end, and until the middle of the eighteenth century very few slaves were taken to America from South-East

[1] Johnston, Sir H. H., *A History of the Colonization of Africa by alien races*, p. 92.

Africa. Not until the gold trade was destroyed by the constant Native wars and unrest in the period preceding the Kaffir wars in South Africa did slave-trading become the principal industry of the region from the delta of the Zambesi southwards. It became a very important factor in the history of British policy towards the interior of South Africa, as will appear later in this volume.

Missionary enterprise fell into complete decay in South-East Africa during the eighteenth century, and the Dominican friars, who had made such great efforts in earlier days, sank into languor and indifference. Their stations in the interior were swept away in the devastations of the tribal wars, and only churches at Inhambane, Sofala, Sena and Tete were left, where a handful of secular priests ministered to the few whites and half-caste inhabitants.[1]

The whole story of the first European effort to open up Africa south of the Zambesi is one of extraordinary initial energy sinking away into lassitude and neglect, owing partly to lack of means, but principally to the superior attractions of Brazil. Peoples possessed of greater man-power and wealth were later to take up the work and base it, not upon the fever-ridden tropical coast and the fly-infested rivers, but upon the temperate and fertile valleys of the south-west. But the history of the South African interior, where new European colonies were to be founded in the nineteenth century, has its real beginnings in the depressing story of Portuguese failure, which we have here surveyed.

[1] See Texeira Botelho, J. J., *Historia Militar dos Portugueses em Moçambique*. This work had not been published when this chapter was written for the first edition of the *C.H.B.E.* vol. viii.

CHAPTER V

FOUNDATION OF THE CAPE COLONY 1652–1708

BY the middle of the seventeenth century the power of the Portuguese in and around the Indian Ocean was completely broken, and the Netherlands East India Company, the *Generale Vereenigde Geoctroyeerde Nederlandsche Oost Indische Compagnie*, was supreme in the Archipelago of the Spiceries which had been the goal of European effort for a century and a half.[1] From its headquarters at Batavia in Java the Company dominated the trade of the whole Indian Ocean. Its establishments ranged from Mocha and Aleppo to Timor, and from the Cape of Good Hope to Desima in Japan. It had factories in Ceylon and on the mainland coast of India, in Siam, Cambodia and Tonkin, in Formosa, Borneo and Sumatra, while its servants had begun to explore the coasts of New Guinea and the Great Southland and had visited and named Van Diemen's Land and New Zealand.[2]

During the first half of the seventeenth century the financial position of the Company was very sound; in spite of the enormous expenditure on incessant wars, the average dividend at this period amounted to 25 per cent.[3] The voyage between the Netherlands and India, however, remained a dangerous undertaking. The death-rate was less disastrous than it had been and was never so bad as foreign contemporaries believed;[4] nevertheless heavy losses of life from dysentery and scurvy still occurred every year and were sometimes so serious as to lead to the loss of vessels with valuable cargoes.

The Directors naturally considered the question of refreshment stations on this long and costly voyage. Their ships touched regularly at St Helena, the Cape and Mauritus for this purpose; indeed, Jan Pieterzoon Coen, the great Governor-General who was the real founder of the Dutch Empire in the East, had vainly urged the Directors "to plant a colony" at the Cape.[5] When the temporary *entente* of 1619 was established between the English and the Dutch East India Companies, a scheme was mooted for a joint refreshment station there, and while the two directorates were considering whether to build a joint fort or two separate ones, two English captains,

[1] For some account of the foundation of the company and its struggles with the Portuguese and English see *Camb. Mod. Hist.* IV, ch. XXV and *C.H.B.E.* IV, ch. II. Conditions of space have prevented the inclusion here of an account of the earlier history of the Company. [Ed.]

[2] Heeres, J. E., *The Part borne by the Dutch in the Discovery of Australia*, 1606–1765.

[3] Colenbrander, H. T., *Koloniale Geschiedenis*, II, 245, 246.

[4] Cf. *C.H.B.E.* I, 127; Colenbrander, *Koloniale Geschiedenis*, II, 223.

[5] de Jonge, *Opkomst van het Nederlandsche Gezag in Oost Indie*, IV, 213.

Shillinge and Fitzherbert, took possession of the Cape in the name of King James I, though the English Government did not recognise the action and nothing resulted.[1] The Cape continued to be used indifferently with St Helena and Mauritius by sailors of both nations for taking in fresh water and, if fortune favoured, fresh meat. It also provided wild sorrel, which was very useful against scurvy, and further served as a post office, letters being regularly left behind under slabs of stone for passing friends to take to Europe or to the East.[2]

On 25 March 1647, while a homeward-bound fleet of the Dutch Company was at anchor in Table Bay, one of the ships, the *Haarlem*, was wrecked in a storm. Her valuable cargo was salvaged, but could not be carried home by the remaining vessels. Accordingly, sixty of her crew were left behind, under Leendert Janszoon, to protect the cargo and await later ships.[3] The sailors made a comfortable camp on what is now Green Point Common and amused themselves with shooting and fishing. They also laid out little vegetable gardens and found that the soil was fertile and that everything grew well. With the Natives, who had as yet no distinguishing name among the Europeans, they easily established friendly relations. Far from being intractable cannibals, as the Portuguese had represented, they were found to be peaceable and ready to meet kindness with kindness. They soon got to know the names of the whites and even picked up a few phrases of Dutch—such as, significantly enough "*Eerst hout halen, dan brood eten*" (First fetch wood, then eat bread).[4]

In April 1648, the homeward-bound fleet picked up the *Haarlem*'s cargo and its guardians. Arrived in the Netherlands, Janszoon with another officer, Nicolaas Proot, who had touched at the Cape while the men of the *Haarlem* were ashore there, were asked to present a report to the XVII, the supreme directorate of the Company, on the suitability of the Cape as a refreshment station.

The report of Janszoon and Proot—the first South African state paper—was dated 26 July 1649.[5] The two officers warmly recommended such an undertaking. Vegetables and fruit, they stated, could be produced in abundance, and the sick restored to health quickly. The Natives would not be a danger if kindly treated, and cattle could be obtained from them very cheaply. The expense of such an undertaking would not be very great, and could very probably be met with the proceeds of seal and whale fishery. They laid stress on the great strategic importance of the Cape: "No better place in the world could be found", they say, to waylay the Company's richly laden East Indiamen, as they straggled singly or in twos and

[1] Theal, G. M., *History of South Africa before 1795*, I, 425–7.
[2] Some of these stones are preserved in the South African Museum, Cape Town.
[3] Theal, *op. cit.*, II, 2.
[4] Leibbrandt, *Letters and Documents Received*, 1649–62 (in *Précis of the Archives of the Cape of Good Hope*), I, 13, 15.
[5] *Ibid.* I, 3 *sqq.*

threes into Table Bay. They expressed surprise that their enemies had not yet attempted this.

The Company had already taken possession of St Helena in 1633, but without occupying it permanently; in 1638 again, it had occupied Mauritius, though that island was too close to Batavia to be of much use as a half-way house.[1] In September 1650, the Directors decided to establish a refreshment station at the Cape and offered the command of the undertaking to Nicolaas Proot. On his refusal, they offered it to Jan van Riebeeck, an experienced and widely travelled ship's surgeon, who had been in the Company's service off and on since 1639. On 24 December 1651 van Riebeeck set out with three small ships to found the first European settlement at the Cape. On 6 April 1652 he cast anchor in Table Bay.

The object of the undertaking entrusted to van Riebeeck was explained in his instructions.[2] It was to enable the ships of the Company "to refresh themselves with vegetables, meat, water and other necessities, by which means the sick on board may be restored to health". Immediately on his arrival he was "to erect a little defensive fort", and thereafter to lay out a garden. Cattle and sheep he would have to obtain from the Natives, with whom he was to establish and carefully maintain friendly relations. Van Riebeeck's anxiety on this point is shown by his first ordinance, the first law proclaimed in South Africa, which he published before the expedition disembarked. This forbade provocation or ill-treatment of the Natives on any pretext. All offenders, "whether they be in the right or in the wrong", would receive fifty lashes, in the presence of the Natives, to prove to the latter the friendly intentions of the authorities.[3] All the labour required for building the fort and barracks, for laying out and maintaining the garden and for bartering cattle and breeding from these, was to be supplied by the Company. Van Riebeeck had authority to keep ninety men, soldiers and sailors, and with these he would have to accomplish everything.

It is significant that colonists were not thought of. Fifty years' experience had made the Directors less desirous than ever to encourage colonisation. The handful of colonists, or "free burghers", as they were called, who were settled elsewhere in their dominions—chiefly at Batavia, Banda and Amboyna—had proved a source of continual trouble, since they persistently transgressed the regulations restricting private trade and thereby imperilled the monopoly of the Company. The monopoly of trade was regarded as the corner-stone of the whole magnificent edifice which the Company had built up in the East. Its successful position had been attained only by the violent exclusion of all competitors. As it was, serious inroads were being

[1] Heeringa, in *Indische Gids*, 1896: *De Nederlanders op Mauritius*, etc.
[2] Leibbrandt, *Letters Rec.* I, 29.
[3] *Ibid.* II, 355.

made on the Company's preserves by its own dishonest servants; but, while thieving officials might be a necessary evil, colonists were not. To generation after generation of Directors colonists were anathema.[1]

A formidable task confronted van Riebeeck when he landed in Table Bay. As he himself expressed it, he had "to bring forth everything out of nothing."[2] His tiny labour force, enfeebled by a long voyage and disgusted by the nature of the work they had to undertake, was quite inadequate. The men were not only unwilling, "they were as raw as the whole world had ever seen", and van Riebeeck "had to be his own engineer, delver, gardener, farmer, carpenter, mason, smith, etc." It is not surprising that in these circumstances he longed for a different type of pioneer. A fortnight after landing he begins to talk of "hard-working Chinese or other free men".[3] Again and again in those early days, he reverts to the subject. In his first report, to the Governor-General and Council at Batavia (13 May 1652), he points out how useful "free families" would be for raising crops and cattle and for making butter and cheese.[4] The outbreak of the war with the English Commonwealth strengthened this argument. In asking for reinforcements from Batavia, he again pointed out how useful colonists would be for defence. He adds that he "hopes to put his humble views in this matter before the Honble. Directors".[5] His "humble views" were however not to reach the XVII so soon. A high official, who touched at the Cape a few months later, "enlightened me to such a degree", wrote van Riebeeck ruefully, "that I have kept absolutely mum on the matter to the Lords and Masters, since Their Honours' intentions are merely to provide refreshments here".[6]

In the meantime van Riebeeck's vigorous efforts began to bear some fruit. Gardens had been laid out and all kinds of vegetables and fruit planted. Within a year the homeward-bound fleet could be "supplied reasonably well" with cabbages, carrots and other greens,[7] but the post was still dependent on the Netherlands and India for bread, salt meat, rice, beans and other foodstuffs.[8]

The war with England brought sharp trials for the settlement. The garrison had been strengthened, but the return fleet, which was bringing supplies, did not touch at the Cape, fearing an English ambush.[9] A serious dearth of provisions was the consequence. To

[1] Cf. Heeres, J. E., *Bouwstoffen voor de Geschiedenis der Nederlanders in den Maleischen Archipel*, III, p. lxxiv; and de Jonge, *Opkomst*, IV, pp. cxl *sqq*.

[2] Leibbrandt, *Letters Despatched*, 1652–62 (in *Précis of the Archives of the Cape of Good Hope*), III, 74.

[3] *Dagverhaal van Jan van Riebeeck*, I, 22, 24, 56.

[4] Leibbrandt, *Letters Desp.* I, 27.

[5] *Ibid.* I, 73.

[6] *Ibid.* I, 139, 141.

[7] *Dagverhaal*, I, 199.

[8] *Letters Rec.* I, 93.

[9] *Letters Desp.* I, 181; *Letters Rec.* I, 97.

make matters worse, the Hottentots chose this unpropitious moment to begin hostilities. While the garrison was at church one Sunday, they raided the herds of cattle, killed the herdsman and carried off everything, so that van Riebeeck found himself left with "one milch cow, one ox and four newly born calves".[1] In the course of the year 1654 the garrison was threatened with starvation. The men had to be fed partly on penguins, "most unlovely and disgusting to eat",[2] and seal meat, and were further reduced to two meals a day.[3] In April they actually devoured a dead baboon found on Table Mountain, "since their mess of greens provided but little nourishment".[4]

It was clearly necessary that the post should become self-supporting. Both agriculture and cattle-breeding would have to be undertaken on a much larger scale. But the Hottentots were barring the way to any development. Becoming every day more impudent, since van Riebeeck had not dared to punish them for the cattle robberies, they stole everything they could lay hands on and threatened to kill any Europeans they could get hold of.[5]

Experiment had proved that wheat could not be raised in the immediate vicinity of the fort, owing to the prevalence of fierce summer gales. Further inland more sheltered spots could be found, but "this would cost too much to protect from the savages.".[6] The Commander's perplexities were increased by serious complaints from the XVII and India about the "heavy expenses" of the station[7] coupled with demands for increased production. To which van Riebeeck replied, that "to bring much more land under cultivation would require many more hands, and for this purpose colonists would be best, as also slaves."[8]

His soldier labourers were a constant source of annoyance. They loathed the farm work and stowed away on every passing ship.[9] The Commander had constantly "to take the cane to them, as they think and indeed roundly assert also, that their pay runs the same, whether they do much or little". He had "never been able to use the half of the men for the necessary labour",[10] whereas if farming operations were handed over to colonists, he held that the garrison, and consequently the expense, could be considerably reduced.[11] Furthermore, colonists, with the stimulus of working in their own interests, would produce much more than mutinous soldiers, would require

[1] *Dagverhaal*, I, 256.
[2] Fouché, L., *Journael van Gysbert Heeck*, p. 7.
[3] *Dagverhaal*, I, 340, 342.
[4] *Ibid.* I, 343.
[5] *Ibid.* I, 343; *Letters Desp.* I, 261.
[6] *Letters Desp.* I, 267.
[7] *Letters Rec.* I, 105, 161 *sqq.*
[8] *Letters Desp.* II, 205.
[9] *Ibid.* I, 97 and III, 53.
[10] *Ibid.* I, 99 *sqq.* and II, 290.
[11] *Ibid.* II, 236.

no wages and could help in defence. Logically, therefore, the only means of increasing production and at the same time cutting down expense was the introduction of colonists.

By 1655 the Company had been farming for three years on its own account and the results had been most disappointing. At this juncture, a casual sentence in a letter from the XVII gave van Riebeeck the opportunity for which he had longed so ardently to lay before the Lords and Masters his "humble views" on the need for colonists.[1] Seizing on what had obviously been a mere aside in this letter as an indication that, as he tactfully expressed it, the XVII "seemed minded to establish a colony", he unburdened himself at length on the question of colonisation at the Cape.[2] Colonists alone could do what the Directors desired. The conditions on which such colonists should be permitted were carefully outlined. They would have to be attracted by prospects of gain and be attached to the soil in such a way that they would "in time become weaned from Holland and make this place entirely their fatherland". They should further be bound to sell all their cattle and produce to the Company and to trade with it alone. In any case, the Company must remain "master of everything". He added that there were several servants of the Company at the Cape, who had experience of local conditions and who would be inclined to take their discharges and become colonists, if their wives could be sent out to them.

The XVII, in their reply,[3] again urged him to devote all his energy to developing agriculture, and then, "in order to make an experiment in this direction and because many things can be undertaken better by colonists than by the Company and its servants", they authorised him to discharge such of their servants as had had experience locally, and who might wish to become colonists. They accepted all the points laid down in his letter and promised to provide the new colonists with slaves, as he had asked.

Thus grudgingly and half-heartedly, the XVII consented "to make an experiment" with colonists at the Cape. It was no denial of their principles in regard to colonisation in general; for these Cape colonists would be very few in number, they would have to devote themselves exclusively to agriculture, and since at the Cape there was nothing whatever to arouse cupidity, the monopoly fetish of the Company could remain inviolate. But van Riebeeck was now free to establish colonists on the basis which he had himself proposed. Early in 1657 his preparations were complete, and in February, nine of those who had volunteered were selected as being "the most capable and hopeful" and were duly established on the land.[4]

[1] *Letters Rec.* I, 147.
[2] *Letters Desp.* II, 93.
[3] *Letters Rec.* I, 221 *sqq.* (30 October 1655).
[4] *Dagverhaal*, II, 46, 47, 130, 131.

The conditions on which these first "free burghers" received their lands remained the basis for all future grants and thus affected profoundly the whole subsequent history of colonisation in South Africa. Van Riebeeck had drawn up an elaborate agreement[1] based on the principles he had set forth to the Directors, and this the colonists had to accept. But three weeks later a Commissioner, Ryklof van Goens, arrived to inspect the post and, after consulting the new colonists, he modified the agreement in some points, which he considered too harsh.[2]

The modified conditions were, briefly, that each free burgher received 13½ morgen (about 28 acres) of land free. He was bound to cultivate this land diligently for twelve years and to grow wheat and other grains. During that period the land would be free from taxation. The Company would supply the farmers with trek-oxen and with cows and sheep for breeding at fixed prices, and with farming implements and rations at cost price. Rations would be supplied on credit, the Company taking the wheat crop in payment of the debts so incurred. Garden produce might be sold freely to passing ships, but colonists would not be allowed to go on board until three days after the arrival of the ship.

Van Riebeeck's original agreement had prohibited any barter "of cattle, sheep or anything whatsoever" from the Natives; but van Goens, anxious to see the colonists make a start with cattle-breeding, decided that they might, with special permission of the Commander, barter sheep and cows, provided that all bartering was carried on with articles supplied by the Company and that the colonists did not offer higher prices than the Company.

Tobacco was a favourite article of barter with the Hottentots, and for this reason the majority of the farmers had hoped to cultivate tobacco on a large scale. Van Riebeeck had expressly encouraged it, but the colonists had no sooner planted out their seedlings than the Hottentots came by night and stole them from the fields. The wrathful farmers naturally sat up with muskets in their hands to guard their lands, and to avert the imminent bloodshed the authorities prohibited the cultivation of tobacco.[3] This unfair proceeding aroused much bitterness, for though the excuse advanced—fear of trouble with the Natives—had some grounds, behind it lay the selfish desire to keep this profitable article of barter entirely in the hands of the Company.

The shooting of game, except in the case of noxious animals, was forbidden, and fishing was only permitted for personal use. The colonists had to mount guard in the blockhouses and maintain their arms at their own expense. Most significant of all and the root of most

[1] *Ibid.* II, 133 *sqq.* and Theal, *Abstract of the Debates and Resolutions of the Council of Policy*, 1651–87, pp. 23–5.

[2] *Letters Rec.* II, 219 *sqq.*; *Letters Desp.* II, 314; *Letters Rec.* II, 288 *sqq.*

[3] *Letters Rec.* II, 291.

of their future troubles, they were bound to sell all their grain and all their superfluous cattle exclusively to the Company, at "reasonable" prices to be fixed by the Company alone.

Finally, the colonists were to be subject to all the existing and future laws of the Netherlands and India, and the conditions on which they held their farms could be altered at the pleasure of the Directors. But "in order to maintain the colonists in their rights", van Goens gave instructions that one of their seniors should have a seat on the Council of Justice, whenever a case involving colonists came up for trial.[1] This was the sole representative element at the time. To protect the interests of the colonists further, no servant of the Company was to be permitted to cultivate any land privately. Those already in possession of gardens were deprived of them.[2]

Such were the conditions under which the first handful of pioneers were called upon to lay the foundation of civilisation in South Africa. It would be interesting to compare their circumstances with those of the English and French colonists, who were then engaged in a similar task on the North American continent, but there is a fundamental difference between the settlements, which renders all comparison worthless. The colonist in British North America was free to grow what he liked and to sell his produce at the best possible price, and (the Act of Navigation notwithstanding) in the best possible market.[3] The Cape colonist was to be forced to grow what the Company wanted, and to sell all his produce to the Company alone, and that at prices to be fixed exclusively by the Company.

The colonists set to work to break land and start cultivation. Their first formal petitions are interesting. They ask for permission to plant tobacco and to sell their cattle and produce not merely to the Company at its prices, but freely to passing ships at the best prices obtainable.[4] Thus at the very beginning, before even they had anything to sell, the colonists had realised the fatal weakness of their position. Their request was referred to the XVII, as van Riebeeck considered the matter too serious for him and his Council to decide. The XVII, in reply, ordered the Commander to help the colonists as much as possible "so far as may be done without noticeable prejudice or injury to the Company".[5] But this meant nothing, for a free market was out of the question and therefore nothing was done.

After much insistence on the part of van Riebeeck, slaves were imported from the East Indies for the farmers, but they proved more of a hindrance than a help.[6] They did not understand any language

[1] *Letters Rec.* II, 251.
[2] *Ibid.* II, 291, 292.
[3] Cf. *C.H.B.E.* I, 157, 162, 311.
[4] Leibbrandt, *Resolutiën van Commandeur en Raden van het Fort Goede Hoop*, 1652–62 (in *Précis of the Archives*, etc.), 143.
[5] *Letters Rec.* II, 79.
[6] *Letters Desp.* II, 290, 294, 298; *Letters Rec.* II, 231.

spoken by their masters, and a formal school had to be started to teach them a few words of Dutch.[1] They absconded at every opportunity and caused fresh complications with the Hottentots.[2] There was practically no money in circulation at this time, which caused great inconvenience. The men of the garrison still deserted whenever ships touched at the Cape, and some of the free burghers, discouraged at their prospects, also took to flight to rouse the wrath of the Governor-General and Council at Batavia "with countless complaints that the colonists could not maintain themselves at the Cape, so that they had been forced by hunger and want to flee from there".[3] The Commander hoped that, if wives were provided for the colonists, matters would improve. He therefore insistently called for "lusty farm wenches", not girls from the towns.[4] Meanwhile, determined to make a success of the experiment, which was really his own, he constantly inspected the lands of the farmers and prescribed what should be planted and sown, even such unfamiliar things as rice and vines and maize. If they refused, he threatened to cut off supplies.[5] When a couple of farmers had "proved themselves more and more slack, piling up debts...without showing any proper energy in the growing of wheat", a resolution of Council directed an official "daily to press on the said persons to do their bounden duty on their own lands, as if they were the Company's servants".[6] But the farmers were not servants of the Company: they were free citizens of the Republic, a fact which at the Cape seems at times to have been overlooked. Van Riebeeck's despotism was however thoroughly paternal; he was always ready to help the colonists,[7] but, unfortunately for them, the Company's interests were paramount.

The colonists had taken advantage of the right to barter cattle from the Natives and had soon found that they could get far higher prices for meat from passing ships than those fixed by the Company. To stop this traffic, they were forbidden to slaughter any animal, except with the express permission of the Commander.[8] Naturally, the farmers resorted to subterfuges. Thus, when an English ship was taking in provisions, some farmers came to van Riebeeck with a tale that ten of their sheep had been "drowned", and asked permission to sell the meat to the English; but he, "feeling sure that the sheep had been slaughtered and not drowned", refused the request, "since otherwise they would always pretend to have cattle drowned or died, whenever there were English lying at anchor".[9] Van Riebeeck, in-

[1] Fouch, L., *Onze Eerste Scholen*, p. 2.
[2] *Letters Desp.* III, 41, 42, 49, 50.
[3] *Letters Desp.* III, 21, 52; *Letters Rec.* II, 145.
[4] *Letters Desp.* III, 95, 115.
[5] *Ibid.* III, 16 *et passim*; *Dagverhaal*, II, 465, 602.
[6] *Dagverhaal*, III, 295.
[7] Leibbrandt, *Resolutiën*, etc., pp. 147, 150, 153 *sqq.*
[8] *Dagverhaal*, II, 203.
[9] *Ibid.* II, 284.

deed, had always held that the cattle trade should be reserved to the Company, even after he had been overruled by van Goens.[1] Now, in May 1658, on the plea that the colonists were neglecting their lands for this easier and vastly more profitable pursuit, he arbitrarily forbade all trade with the Hottentots.[2]

This was a terrible blow to the colonists. It robbed them of the one remaining source of profit, since the cultivation of tobacco had already been forbidden, and drove the more venturesome of them into illicit traffic with the Natives.[3] Dissatisfaction at this curtailment of their rights was soon changed to desperation by another anxiety. In December 1658 they reaped their first regular harvest and then found the Commander unwilling to name a definite price for their wheat and barley.[4] This so alarmed them that on 23 December 1658 their representatives laid before the Council of Policy a memorial of complaint, signed by fourteen free burghers, the sum total of colonists in possession of farms.[5] It is a revealing document. "We have become free", they stated, "in order to carry on free cattle trade with the Hottentots, and now that we have undertaken our bloody toil on the land, the barter is forbidden." They demand its restitution and, further, the fixing of prices before they proceed to thresh their crops. "Fix a price immediately, because until we know the prices, we shall not work our land, since we will not be slaves of the Company." They declare they will no longer "be forced" to grow all kinds of unfamiliar seeds. "If we are to remain on the land we will not be forced by anybody, no matter whom, in our farm work." For their wheat they named their own price, failing which they were "minded not to cultivate another foot of land". Nay rather, "we will return all our cattle, slaves and everything else, because we will not remain, like this. Because instead of being helped, we are oppressed."

In face of this bombshell, van Riebeeck acted with tact. He pointed out the enormity of their offence in threatening a strike and dictating to their lawful rulers. He admitted that the price they demanded for their wheat was reasonable. Unfortunately, his orders were to offer only four guilders, less than half of what they wanted. Such was the general dismay when this price was disclosed, that he promised to do his utmost to persuade the XVII to increase their price, and exhorted the farmers vigorously to behave better in future and to stick to their ploughs in the meantime, and finally he ordered "a rummer or two of wine all round". Whereupon, "peace and order being restored, eveyone returned home in cheerful mood".[6]

[1] *Ibid.* II, 203; *Letters Desp.* III, 25.
[2] *Dagverhaal*, II, 379; Theal, *Abstract of Debates*, etc., p. 36.
[3] *Dagverhaal*, II, 542 *et passim*.
[4] *Letters Desp.* III, 79.
[5] *Dagverhaal*, II, 595.
[6] *Ibid.* II, 613.

The episode is very significant. The good faith of the Company was being put to the test for the first time. For the crops which the colonists were forced to deliver to them, the Company promised "reasonable" prices. Would they keep that promise? The Commander's testimony answers that question. When the Company's prices were disclosed, he "saw everyone immediately lose heart and become entirely discouraged".[1] In fixing these prices, the Directors had shown an extraordinary lack of imagination. They had simply taken the prices current in the East for native-grown grain as the basis for the Cape prices. When van Riebeeck pointed out how unreasonable this was, they remained unmoved, and only grudgingly allowed a slight and quite inadequate increase.[2]

The tone of the memorial, "full of sedition and rebellion", shocked the Directors profoundly. They blamed van Riebeeck sharply for listening to it and threatened "hard measures" if the offence were repeated. Nevertheless, they were afraid "to make the colonists unwilling in their labour", and so ordered the Commander "to help them as much as possible", an empty phrase of which they were fond.[3]

The memorial of December 1658 marks a distinct stage in the early history of the colony. With the establishment of colonists a new factor had come into the life of the settlement. Few as they were, they had to be reckoned with, for they were ready to stand up for their rights and openly expressed their determination not to be "slaves of the Company". The refreshment station had become a colony, though the officials of the Company did not realise it.

For years van Riebeeck had been planning to cut off the post on the Peninsula from the mainland by means of a physical barrier of some sort, in order to protect it against the raids of the Hottentots. In true Dutch fashion, a canal had been projected between Table Bay Bay and False Bay.[4] When this proved too big an undertaking, he constructed a line of blockhouses linked up by a fence and hedge of bitter almond, which, together with the Salt River and the Liesbeek, was to form a complete defence against the Natives.[5] Within the *enceinte* formed by this line and Table Mountain some 6000 acres of agricultural land were enclosed to suffice for all future needs. No extension of any kind beyond this barrier was ever to be contemplated. So van Goens had ordained, and van Riebeeck, in complete agreement, instructed his successor in this sense in 1662.[6] The Directors were equally determined to prevent any further development. "We have remarked", they write in 1661,[7] "that you are gradually

[1] *Ibid.* II, 602.
[2] *Letters Rec.* II, 117.
[3] *Letters Rec.* II, 156.
[4] Theal, *History of S. A. before 1795*, II, 54, 69–70.
[5] *Letters Desp.* III, 247; *Dagverhaal*, III, 285.
[6] *Letters Desp.* III, 248.
[7] *Letters Rec.* II, 178.

tending towards the building of a town there, and the enlarging of the colony; but as we look upon it, this idea should be abandoned, and you should get along with the men and the free men whom you have with you at present, without extending any further." None of them realised that, once a considerable body of colonists was established, the settlement could not be confined within any ring-fence. The colonists would labour to extend their holdings and their herds. Their natural increase would burst through van Riebeeck's barrier as easily as a growing seed bursts through its husk. When van Riebeeck settled his first colonists on the land, he had "builded better than he knew."

Another consequence of the coming of colonists was the importation of slaves to provide them with labour.[1] The Cape thus became a slave-holding colony—a tragic circumstance which had a great influence in moulding the customs and character and even the language of the future inhabitants. But the most noticeable consequence at the time of the coming of colonists was that it provoked war with the Hottentots. Van Riebeeck relates that while he was selecting lands for the future colonists, the Hottentots, who were camped in the neighbourhood, "hearing talk of building houses here and there... asked, if we were going to build houses and break land, where they were then to live?" The Commander tried to soothe them, "but", he adds, "it was clearly to be seen that it was not at all to their liking".[2] No sooner had the new farmers begun to break land, than the Natives began systematic reprisals. They stole the tobacco plants[3] and began to steal the cattle of the colonists, especially their trek-oxen, "because", as they long afterwards explained, "the whites were everywhere breaking land with the plough, and they thought to prevent this by taking the oxen with which we were doing this. Also, some of the free burghers had done them much harm."[4]

This latter reason is worthy of remark. It was natural that they colonists became at once embroiled with the Natives. The Hottentots had developed petty thieving to a fine art, since the Commander had never dared to punish them, but had always punished severely any European who had sought revenge on the thieves. The Company servants had been taught to let ill alone. But when the colonists were robbed, they addressed a memorial to the Council unanimously demanding that a thorough revenge be taken on the thieves.[5] Van Riebeeck, always hoping to preserve the peace, refused to act. The molestations became worse, and the clamours of the colonists for war increased in proportion. In vain van Riebeeck warned them of the dangers and losses which hostilities would entail, especially when

[1] *Letters Desp.* II, 93, 95, 101, 290–8; *Letters Rec.* II, 231, 245.
[2] *Dagverhaal*, II, 130.
[3] *Ibid.* II, 148.
[4] *Ibid.* III, 270.
[5] *Ibid.* III, 53.

no help or compensation could be expected from the Company.[1] The colonists "were prepared to take all dangers at their charge", but they asked that the Company's forces might help them, not only defensively but also offensively. Failing this, they demanded leave to avenge their losses independently.[2] At last van Riebeeck gave way and consented to attack the Hottentots.

It is interesting to note how quickly the Hottentots saw the difference between colonists and Company's men. They had disliked the coming of the Company, but had not been really alarmed by it; but as soon as colonists appeared, they instinctively recognised in them a much more serious menace and decided on reprisals. At the Cape, as everywhere else in similar circumstances, the coming of colonists portended the gradual dispossession of the Natives and their ultimate extinction, and the Natives promptly grasped the danger with which this new element threatened them.

The "war" with the Hottentots brought great miseries in its train. By the time the ploughing season arrived, the farmers had been robbed of most of their trek-oxen, and so farm work came to a standstill.[3] The Commander did his best to encourage them, but many gave way to despair.[4] The Natives raided the settlement at every opportunity and evaded the heavy-footed Europeans, who could not overtake them.[5] Horses were therefore imported from Java to run down the Hottentots.[6] The colonists served with the soldiers and bore their full share in the hardships suffered.[7] They did more: they acted at times on their own initiative and pursued cattle thieves without waiting for the soldiers.[8] Before the outbreak of hostilities, they had already taken the law into their own hands, as van Riebeeck afterwards discovered. Having lost some cattle, they seized the chief of the band they suspected and "hanged him by the neck to a beam", until he confessed where the stolen cattle were hidden.[9] These were significant, perhaps ominous, signs of a readiness to take the law into their own hands, which was afterwards to be a marked characteristic of the frontier farmers.

In January 1660, the Hottentots sued for peace, which was formally concluded in the following April.[10] The Natives made valiant and pathetic efforts to regain their rights to the grazing lands now occupied by the whites, "standing upon it, that we [the Dutch] had gradually been taking more and more of their land, which had been

[1] *Ibid.* III, 71.
[2] *Ibid.* III, 72.
[3] *Dagverhaal,* III, 50.
[4] *Letters Desp.* III, 125.
[5] *Dagverhaal,* III, 78, 84, 87.
[6] *Letters Rec.* I, 168; II, 154.
[7] *Dagverhaal,* III, 57.
[8] *Ibid.* III, 59, 73.
[9] *Letters Desp.* III, 192.
[10] *Dagverhaal,* III, 270, 300.

theirs since the beginning of time....Asking also, whether, if they came to Holland, they would be permitted to do the like." The Commander replied that if their lands were restored, there would not be enough grazing for both nations. Whereupon the Hottentots retorted, "Have we then no cause to prevent you from getting more cattle? The more you have, the more lands you occupy. And to say the land is not big enough for us both, who should by right give way, the rightful owner or the foreign invader?" Plainly disconcerted by such logic, the Commander, in accordance with the ideas of his time and the universal practice of colonising peoples,[1] could only adduce the right of conquest.[2] In the end the Hottentots had to accept the situation and promise to cease their molestations.

With the conclusion of peace cattle barter was restarted and the farmers were able to resume their work. Van Riebeeck reported with pride that most of them were "beginning to sit so fast" that they "would not think of getting up again".[3] A Commissioner who inspected the Cape in 1661 found the colonists making good progress. The only serious drawback, he reported, was that their lands had proved much less suitable for wheat than had been expected. Because of the poor yield and the limited amount of arable land available within van Riebeeck's hedge, only half the wheat required to feed the settlement could be produced.[4]

Such was the situation in April 1662, when van Riebeeck relinquished his command on promotion to a post in the East, which he had long been soliciting. According to the Muster Rolls of that year, there were at the Cape 1394 souls all told.[5] Of this number thirty-six were free burghers and fifteen wives of free burghers, mostly of farmers. The colonists had twenty-two children. Fifty-seven Europeans, of whom the majority appear to have been free burghers also, were working as hired servants of colonists. The colonists possessed at least twenty-three slaves—twelve male and eleven female. Of the thirty-six colonists established "on their own account", nineteen were farmers, four were fishermen, two innkeepers and eleven artisans. The farmers owned 300 cattle, over 800 sheep and 100 pigs, the Company 278 cattle, about 600 sheep and 300 pigs. With their lands, gardens and poultry, in addition to their livestock, it is plain that the colonists had accumulated a considerable amount of property in five years. Van Riebeeck, always ready to regard his own geese as swans, considered that they were getting on better at the Cape than they would have done in the Netherlands,[6] and it may at least be conceded that the farmers were making a living. But this

[1] See *C.H.B.E.* I, ch. VI.
[2] *Dagverhaal*, III, 300 *sqq*.
[3] *Letters Desp.* III, 145, 146.
[4] *Letters Rec.* II, 312 *sqq*. and II, 348.
[5] Original in the Royal Archives, the Hague, Koloniaal Archief, No. 3974.
[6] *Letters Desp.* III, 229; *Letters Rec.* II, 158.

living was precarious. Their poultry and vegetables brought in some ready money from passing fleets three or four times a year, provided the latter were in season when a fleet arrived; but their wheat, which demanded the hardest work and the heaviest outlay, brought in no direct return, as it was taken by the Company in repayment of advances, and their cattle had to be sold to the Company at prices which could be improved by six or seven hundred per cent if they were sold clandestinely to others.

Even so, cattle-farming proved so much easier and much more lucrative than wheat-growing that van Riebeeck repeatedly observed that the farmers "do not put much energy into wheat-growing, but devote most of their time and scheming to cattle bartering".[1] When he prohibited further barter—wrongfully as the farmers believed—they continued the forbidden trade in secret in spite of several penalties and "smuggled" the proceeds to ships in the bay. Thus the farmers' living was as yet a hand-to-mouth existence, eked out by constant infractions of the law against "free trade".

By the middle of the seventeenth century, thanks to her two great India Companies, East and West, the Dutch Republic had become a world power. Her commercial supremacy, built up at the expense of Spain and Portugal, was now to be challenged by England and France. Cromwell's Navigation Ordinance, aimed at the Dutch carrying trade, had provoked war between the two republics, and when Charles II continued Cromwell's policy and seized New Amsterdam, a new war broke out (1664).[2] This war had important consequences for the Cape. The Directors came to recognise its strategic importance. If the fate of New Amsterdam overtook it, it would, in English hands, become a deadly menace to the Company's position in the East. The Cape garrison was promptly and strongly reinforced, and a modern fortress, capable of withstanding heavy ordnance, was begun to replace the mud-walled fort of van Riebeeck.

The growing ambitions of Louis XIV brought a new danger. By the Treaty of Dover (1670), England and France agreed to overwhelm the Dutch with simultaneous attacks by land and sea. Fortunately for the Republic, England's share in the war was half-hearted and Charles was forced by Parliament to make peace in 1674. When this new war was threatening, the Directors sent out a military engineer, Ysbrand Goske, with the special rank of Governor, to defend the Cape.[3] Goske pushed on the building of the Castle, which had been suspended after the Peace of Breda, and by 1674 he had brought it into a defensible condition. The Peace of Westminster once more interrupted the work and the Castle was not completed till 1679.[4] Alternating moods of fear and relief are clearly

[1] *Dagverhaal*, II, 292.
[2] See *C.H.B.E.* I, 212–13, 311–14.
[3] Theal, *History of S. A. before 1795*, II, 192, 194.
[4] *Ibid.* II, 219, 244.

traceable in the history of its building. For the isolated little community at the Cape it was a barometer of war; for the Directors it had become the "frontier fortress of India",[1] the precious connecting link between the mother country and their Eastern empire. In grateful memory of the heroic William III who had led his people through the fiery ordeal of 1672, the bastions of the fortress were name after the possessions of his House.[2]

Since the hostilities of 1661, relations with the Hottentots had been peaceful. If the supply of cattle for barter was sometimes interrupted, it was owing to intertribal feuds. In 1672 the inspecting Commissioner, Arnout van Overbeke, sought to regularise the position of the Europeans by concluding a formal contract between the Company and various tribes.[3] All the land as far north and east as the Hottentots-Holland Mountains and Saldanha Bay was ceded in full ownership to the Company. Trade goods to the value of £1600 were to be the price, but in reality less than £10 worth of goods was handed over. In palliation of such cheating, it might be said that the claims of the contracting tribes to the sole ownership of the ceded land were extremely doubtful, for Gonnema, the "Black Captain", who was not included in the bargain, had at least as good a claim to part of the land as some who were. Whether as a result of his exclusion or not, Gonnema began hostilities in November 1672,[4] and by his raids kept friendly tribes and colonists in a state of alarm until 1677, when he sued for peace.

This was the last organised resistance on the part of the Hottentots. Some tribes were beginning to break up. Others moved away from the Cape into the barren interior, hitherto left to the wandering Bushmen, who were now the only enemy that remained to resist the white intruders. The Bushmen were incapable of acting in large groups, but they made up for what they lacked in organisation by untamable hostility. They waged unceasing war against the herds and the lives of the invaders of their hunting grounds. In time they came to be regarded, and to be treated by Hottentots and Europeans alike as noxious animals to be destroyed at sight. Had not Grotius laid down that *justissimum esse bellum in belluas, proximum in homines belluis similes*?[5]

Van Riebeeck's successors during the next twenty years differed widely in character and outlook, but, on one point, they were unanimous: that the colonists were showing more and more aversion to wheat-growing and were becoming more and more addicted to smuggling.[6] The production of wheat remained quite insufficient for

[1] *Ibid.* II, 203.
[2] *Ibid.* II, 244.
[3] *Ibid.* II, 198–200.
[4] Theal, *History of S. A. before* 1795, II, 212, 213, 233.
[5] Grotius, *De Jure Belli et Pacis*, Liber II, Cap. XX, § XLI.
[6] Fouché, L., *Die Evolutie van die Trekboer*, p. 6.

the needs of the settlement in spite of innumerable complaints and exhortations from the XVII. The men on the spot repeatedly recommended that the Company should permit them to offer better prices, but always in vain. They therefore had to fall back on compulsion. The lands of the farmers were inspected regularly to see that enough wheat was being grown, to estimate crops and to prevent fraud. Nevertheless it happened more than once that farmers, after harvesting their wheat, allowed it to rot in the stacks rather than take further pains for prices so inadequate; whereupon the Commander would send soldiers to thresh the wheat "for the common weal",[1] thereby revealing a state of affairs that must be unique in the annals of colonisation. While higher prices, the one thing needful to stimulate wheat-growing, were refused, the mania for fixing prices and regulating business grew apace. Farmers were forbidden to sell anything whatever on their farms. They must offer all their produce for sale in the public market, after the Indian fashion, where prices were fixed for everything down to milk and eggs and were strictly enforced by an official.[2] These prices also were so low that the farmers could easily double them by selling secretly. Indeed Commander Wagenaar excused himself for allowing his officials to keep gardens, against the instructions of the XVII, on the plea that the farmers refused to sell the officials even a pint of milk at the official prices, since they could obtain much more from passing ships or even by smuggling their produce to far-away Batavia.[3]

The repugnance to agriculture as opposed to cattle-rearing is clearly seen in the census figures. In 1679 the acting-Commander, who had been at the Cape since van Riebeeck's time, reported that there were then sixty-two families of colonists, but that only twenty-two could be considered wheat-growers.[4] In other words, while the numbers of colonists had nearly doubled since 1662, the number of wheat farmers had increased only by three.

The other branch of farming, cattle-rearing, was proving infinitely more attractive. There was a big demand for fresh meat for the fleets which brought some six or seven thousand men to Table Bay every year, and although here also the prices fixed by the Company were very low, it was much easier and cheaper to rear cattle than to grow wheat.

Furthermore, cattle-grazing gave endless opportunities of secret trade with the Hottentots. The Natives were always eager to trade with the colonists, who invariably gave far better prices than the Company—generally five or six times as much.[5] The profits were so considerable that the severest penalties could not stop the illicit trade

[1] Fouché, *Trekboer*, p. 6.
[2] *Ibid.*
[3] *Ibid.*
[4] *Ibid.*
[5] *Ibid.* p. 7.

with its double lure of profit and adventure. Laws and regulations were multiplied; special watch-towers were built on the grazing grounds whence sentries watched night and day to prevent meetings between colonists and Natives. No farmer might allow a Hottenott on his land; presently, merely to speak to a Hottentot became a punishable offence; finally, pains and penalties were prescribed for such farmers as allowed their beasts to graze out of sight of a sentry.[1] Legislation so tyrannical, and so futile, defeated its own aims. Farmers and Natives alike laughed at the regulations and continued to smuggle.

The two tendencies so unanimously deplored by all the Commanders—the repugnance to wheat-growing and the addiction to smuggling—sprang from a single cause—the monopoly of the Company. The ban on a free market made smuggling inevitable, if only because the Cape colonists were for the most part Netherlanders, a people whose existence was bound up in trade. The Directors of the Company in a memorial to the States-General remarked complacently, "We are the best traders in the whole world"; yet they expected their fellow-countrymen at the Cape to smother the trading instincts bred in their bones and to produce wheat at a ridiculous price in order to save them unwelcome expense. To keep the colonists at this impossible task, the XVII cut off or controlled every single avenue of gain. But though they might transform free citizens of the Republic into economic slaves, they could not transform their natures. The colonists proposed to fight for a free market as obstinately and as unscrupulously as the Company fought for its monopoly.

In spite of these handicaps, the colony developed. To meet the needs of their children, the first generation of born South Africans, the colonists in 1676 petitioned for farms in Hottentots-Holland, thirty miles island, where the Company had had a cattle station for four years past. This was refused on the ground that they would be too much exposed to attacks from the Natives; but in 1679 a new Commander arrived, who was destined to break down the narrow limits imposed in van Riebeeck's time and to plant new settlements fifty miles further into the interior.

This was Simon van der Stel. Born in Mauritius, where his father had been Commander, van der Stel had developed a patriotism which was probably rendered more sensitive by his own equivocal position, for the belief was generally held that his mother had been a woman of colour.[2] His ambition was to develop the Cape into a great national colony. So far the settlement had been confined to the Peninsula, not so much by van Riebeeck's hedge as by a formidable natural barrier. This was a waste of desolate sandflats, nearly thirty miles wide, stretching from Table Bay in the north to the shores of

[1] *Ibid.*

[2] Theal, *Belangrijke Historische Dokumenten*, III, 11.

False Bay in the south. It was a wilderness, swept in summer by howling south-easters and in winter by north-west gales, that changed the landscape in a few days and raised "impassable great sand dunes" where formerly a road had run.[1] The first step beyond the Peninsula must therefore be a long one, and any settlement beyond the Cape Flats must be large enough to protect itself.

Immediately on his arrival Simon van der Stel started on a tour of inspection. Beyond the barrier of sand, about thirty miles east of the Castle, he found what he had been seeking, a suitable spot for a new settlement. It was a beautiful and fertile valley under the Hottentots-Holland mountains, watered by the Eerste River. Here he laid out a group of farms and named the new colony Stellenbosch.[2] Before the end of the year the first farmer had taken up his allotment, and by 1683 thirty families had been established at Stellenbosch and were petitioning for a minister (sick-comforter) and teacher.[3]

This request was promptly granted, for van der Stel took a keen personal interest in his foundation. Indeed, in 1686 he conferred a great privilege on Stellenbosch by instituting an annual *kermis* or fair from October 1 to 14, during which period free trade was permitted.[4] All the colonists made eager use of this opportunity, The Commander always visited Stellenbosch during fair time to celebrate his birthday with stately ceremonial, to inspect the school and to watch the militia exercise.

The expansion of the settlement made some extension of the simple administrative machinery necessary. The system of government which van Riebeeck had established at the Cape was that which existed throughout the Company's dominions. In territories where the Company exercised sovereignty, the head of the government was a Governor. Less important posts were ruled over by Directors or Commanders, and the smallest were in the charge of an *Opperhoofd* (Chief). In every case the local ruler had a Council of Policy to share his responsibility in the administration, and a Council of Justice as local court. These two bodies were composed of the higher local officials appointed by the Governor-General and Council of India.[5]

Van Riebeeck had come to the Cape as *Opperhoofd*[6] and was only promoted Commander in 1654.[7] At the beginning he had only a Council of Policy, which also functioned as Council of Justice, but in 1656 a separate Council of Justice was instituted.[8] With the coming

[1] Royal Archives, the Hague, Koloniaal Archief, No. 3981.
[2] Theal, *History of S. A. before* 1795, II, 250.
[3] *Ibid.* II, 259.
[4] *Ibid.* II, 316; Fouche, *Onze Eerste Scholen.*
[5] Colenbrander, *Koloniale Geschiedenis,* II, 212.
[6] *Letters Rec.* I, 37, 39.
[7] *Ibid.* I, 131–3.
[8] Leibbrandt, *Resolutiën,* etc., pp. 109, 110.

of the free burghers, a representative of the latter was appointed to sit on the Council of Justice, whenever a case involving colonists was to be heard.[1]

In 1682 van der Stel instituted a Court of Heemraden at Stellenbosch, consisting of four colonists, to settle local disputes.[2] Three years later, a visiting Commissioner created a new post, that of landdrost (or rural magistrate) to represent the Company in the countryside, and to preside at the meetings of the Heemraden. The new Court of Landdrost and Heemraden had a double function. It was a court for petty cases in the country with competence in civil actions involving less than £10, and at the same time a District Council charged with the supervision of roads and water and the destruction of noxious animals. It also controlled the Stellenbosch mill and could raise revenue by means of a local tax.[3]

The colonists were further represented in the Militia Council[4] and the Orphan Chamber,[5] bodies whose functions are explained by their names. Two burghers also sat, with two officials, in the Matrimonial Court,[6] a body which existed in all the Company's posts to enquire into the antecedents of couples wishing to marry lest there be some legal impediment, perhaps a necessary precaution where there were so many passing sailors. Finally, burgher representatives sat at the Castle in the Court of Petty Cases, which had been created in 1683[7] to relieve the Council of Justice of trivial cases.

In matters ecclesiastical, the Company was "master" as in everything else. It paid all the ministers, who were assigned to and removed from their posts entirely at the discretion of the Governor-General and Council. Where congregations were formed, as at Batavia and the Cape, the ordinary presbyterian form of Dutch Reformed Church government was established, but at all meetings of the *Kerkeraad* (consistory) the Company was represented by a *Commissaris Politiek* (Political Commissioner).[8] Furthermore, all correspondence with the Church organisation in the Netherlands was censored by the Company.[9]

In 1687 another settlement was begun further north on the banks of the Berg River. It came to be known as De Paarl. The holdings given out in these new settlements were considerably larger than those originally granted in the Peninsula. The farmer generally received in freehold sixty *morgen* (more than 120 acres) of arable land, with access to water and permission for

[1] *Letters Rec.* II, 251.
[2] Theal, *History of S. A. before 1795*, II, 258.
[3] *Ibid.* II, 271.
[4] *Ibid.* II, 91.
[5] *Ibid.* II, 221, 222.
[6] *Ibid.* II, 238.
[7] *Ibid.* II, 265.
[8] Theal, *History of S. A. before 1795*, II, 149, 318.
[9] Colenbrander *Koloniale Geschiedenis*, II, 241.

his cattle to graze on unoccupied land anywhere in the neighbourhood.[1]

In 1685 Commissioner-General Hendrik Adriaan van Rheede tot Drakenstein arrived at the Cape on a special mission. He had been appointed by the XVII in the previous year and armed with full authority to root out the growing corruption among the officials from the Governor-General downwards.[2] He was to tour the western posts of the Company, inspect every activity minutely and to make any changes he thought desirable. He began his labours at the Cape. After an examination into every branch of the administration lasting three months, he left instructions by which the little colony was regulated for many years to come.[3]

"The aim of the Company—the object of all its activities at the Cape," he stated,[4] "is the assured possession and mastery of the same." A secondary aim was to find the means of paying for the maintenance of its defences against all enemies. "The Cape of Good Hope must therefore be considered a frontier and the Castle a place which, being in daily danger of attack by an enemy, depends entirely on its own resources and strength...."[5] "The great advantage the Company expects in this country consists in planting a good colony of our Nation, and peopling it by that means", so that "by the increase of their numbers, they may become so powerful that they may keep out all enemies and assure its peaceful possession to the Company" and enable the latter as ruler "to draw from their prosperity enough in return to pay for garrison".

Modest as these aims were, they had not been attained. Van Rheede considered that the Cape was not safe against a surprise attack.[6] It had never yielded a penny of profit, but had been a heavy drain on the Company from the start. He calculated that down to 1684 the Company had spent 1,376,932 guilders on the settlement. The annual expenditure in 1685 amounted to 82,181 guilders, while the Company's income at the Cape from all sources was only 53,121 guilders.[7] This was certainly not good business. It made the Commissioner long for "something rich to be discovered or something profitable to be contrived" for the solace of the Company.[8]

As to the colonists, they were making headway. They now had 14,501 sheep and 2297 cattle. Van Rheede found thirty families living round the Castle, who maintained themselves by keeping lodgings or inns and gardens. From Rondebosch to Wynberg there

[1] Cf. Old Cape Freeholds, in Office of Surveyor-General, Cape Town.
[2] Colenbrander, *Koloniale Geschiedenis*, II, 218; Theal, *op. cit.* II, 269, 270.
[3] Theal, *op. cit.* II, 270–8.
[4] Theal, *Belanarijke Hist. Dokumenten*, I, 28, 14.
[5] *Ibid.* I, 14.
[6] *Ibid.* I, 7.
[7] Theal, *Belangrijke Hist. Dokumenten*, I, 38. One guilder was worth one shilling and eightpence.
[8] *Ibid.* I, 39.

were twenty-four households, and at Stellenbosch and the Paarl ninety-nine families, all engaged in farming.

These numbers must be increased if the Company's aim, "the assured possession of the Cape", was to be attained. The Directors now definitely attempted to encourage emigration. They offered farms to Netherlanders willing to go to the Cape, and sought also to obtain wives for settlers from the famous orphanages of Amsterdam and Rotterdam. These girls, carefully trained and educated, would have made excellent colonists, but very few of them could be persuaded to leave their friends and go to that distant and barbarous land. The XVII were not more successful in procuring farmers at home. The Republic was too prosperous and too free from political or religious troubles to provide large numbers of emigrants. Nor were the XVII prepared to take any and every volunteer. Van Rheede gave strict instructions that only men of good conduct and sound Protestantism, subjects of the Republic or of German princes not engaged in sea trade, should be allowed to settle at the Cape.[1]

The result of this selective policy was, that although immigrants came every year, they were very few in number. A more considerable accession was, however, presently forthcoming. The revocation of the Edict of Nantes by Louis XIV had brought about a great emigration of Protestants from France. Of the half million or more who sought refuge abroad, such vast numbers came to the Netherlands that great camps were constructed outside Amsterdam and other towns to receive them. The Directors at once offered to take some of these refugees to the Cape, especially such as were skilled in the cultivation of the vine. From 1688 onwards French refugee families were sent out in driblets, until by 1700 some 200 souls had been brought to the colony.[2] The French were warmly welcomed. Subscriptions were opened for them in the colony and at Batavia and a handsome sum was collected to provide for the destitute. Farms were allocated to the heads of families at Stellenbosch, Paarl and Franschhoek, so called after the refugees. Great care was taken, however, to scatter the French among the Dutch and German farmers. The authorities could not forget that, although they were refugees, they belonged to the nation whose king was still threatening the very existence of the Republic. Moreover, France had latterly become a dangerous rival in the East. Hence the French colonists were not to be allowed to remain French.[3] The sooner they lost their nationality the better the XVII would be pleased. Deliberate efforts to keep them apart from one another and to teach only Dutch to their children naturally incensed the French, and led to bitter protests, some of which were

[1] *Ibid.* I, 36.

[2] Botha, C. G., *The French Refugees at the Cape*; also personal communication to the writer.

[3] Leibbrandt, *Rambles through the Archives...of the Cape of Good Hope*, pp. 10, 21.

successful. The new colonists settled down, but for long kept themselves aloof and would not intermarry with the older settlers.

The 200 French found themselves dispersed among some 600 colonists of Dutch and German blood. Their superior education, moral qualities and great energy soon gave them an influence far greater than their numbers would indicate. The South African people which was to develop in the eighteenth century received from this infusion of new blood a precious accession of strength.

Meanwhile, the quaintly expressed desire of Commissioner van Rheede "to find something rich" to indemnify the Company for its expenditure at the Cape led to an active search for minerals in various directions. Van der Stel himself undertook a great journey of exploration to the semi-desert regions of Namaqualand in an endeavour to find the mountains from which the Hottentots got their supplies of copper, and though he failed to find any workable copper-mine, he added much to the knowledge of those remote regions.[1]

The energetic Governor (for van der Stel had been promoted to that rank in 1691) encouraged the colonists in every way.[2] He enforced tree-planting in his new settlements and took a great interest in improving the wine of the country. He became a farmer himself, and after much experimenting eventually produced at his beautiful Peninsula farm, Constantia, a wine that earned an international reputation. In his hands the Company's garden at the Cape ceased to be a mere vegetable garden and became a famous botanical collection with rare plants collected from every land.[3] Nevertheless, his kindly attitude towards the colonists was not unmarked by suspicion. In his eyes the only good colonist was the *landbouwer*, the tiller of the soil, and he found the colonists too ready to evade their duties as cultivators. In his first report (1679) he observed that "agriculture is not on a good footing. The colonists do not trouble themselves overmuch with the plough",[4] but prefer easier means of making a living, such as cattle-farming. Like all his predecessors, he saw that the cause was the inadequate prices fixed by the Company. When he himself increased prices, as in the case of wine in 1692, he noted how this immediately encouraged the farmers, and he urged the XVII to offer higher prices as the only means of inducing farmers to take pains in preparing their wine.[5]

Secret trading with the Natives still went on. A party of colonists would obtain a permit to shoot hippopotami, which entailed a considerable journey into the interior and thus offered opportunities for barter with the Natives. It was, however, not only the hope of gain that sent the colonists hunting. Established as they were in a hunter's

[1] Theal, *History of S. A. before 1795*, II, 279.
[2] *Ibid.* II, 363.
[3] *Ibid.* II, 319, 320, 381–3.
[4] Fouché, *Trekboer*, p. 7.
[5] *Ibid.*, p. 8.

paradise, swarming with big game and beasts of prey, they lived musket in hand. Van der Stel on his visit to Stellenbosch notes with admiration how "admirably handy" they were with their weapons. They are becoming "daily more enterprising and skilful against lions, tigers[1] and other destructive animals", he declares, and at the target-shooting, "out of a hundred shots...hardly one missed".[2]

The lure of a hunter's life was beginning to draw farmers away from their lands to the evident alarm of the Governor. He complained to the XVII in 1681 that hippopotami had quite disappeared from around the peninsula and that colonists had to travel ten or twelve days into the interior to find them. This he considered a deplorable waste of time. The colonists would do much better to stay at home working their lands, "it being certain, besides, that the shooting of these animals is practised by the free burghers more for amusement than for profit"[3]. The fascination of the hunter's life outweighed the attractions of agriculture, and in 1690 Governor and council lamented "that many of the inhabitants, chiefly among those living in the country, have not scrupled to proceed secretly and by night into the interior, in direct contravention of the laws thereanent to shoot hippopotami and other big game", which will at this rate soon be exterminated, "besides that many of these inhabitants are coming to make this [hunting] their daily occupation, thus playing the sluggard and abandoning altogether the cultivation of the soil". Severe pains and penalties were prescribed for those who might transgress in this fashion.[4]

Van der Stel's ordinances were labour lost. Nowhere in the world had laws been made more numerous and more draconian than at the Cape to keep colonists "on the land". No pains and penalties could force free men to grow wheat in a land where rewards were so inadequate and counter-attractions—the roving life of the grazier and hunter—so strong. Moreover, economic pressure drove the colonists into the interior. As their herds grew, they were compelled to seek new grazing lands. Towards the end of the century, the farmers of Stellenbosch and Paarl were suffering severely from the drawbacks of close settlement. Even the French refugees, whose farms were at least half an hour's walk from those of their nearest neighbours, complained of lack of elbow-room. One would not think, an observer remarked, that they could feel overcrowded, yet "such is the general complaint of these people; they allege that they cannot possibly live like this, as no one has enough grazing for his cattle".[5] It was a general feeling among the farmers, he continues, that when they see the smoke of a neighbour's chimney, they felt crowded.

[1] The South African 'tiger' is a leopard.
[2] *Ibid.* [3] *Ibid.* [4] *Ibid.*
[5] Fouché, *Trekboer*, p. 9. Cf. also W. A. van der Stel's remarks in Leibbrandt, *Letters Desp.* 1696–1708 (in *Précis of the Archives*, etc.), p. 136.

The cattle farmers were thus driven to plunge deeper and deeper into the interior. They ignored the boundaries repeatedly set up by a government anxious to keep them within recognised limits. Simon van de Stel expressly warns his successor to check this type of colonist, since "the whole of Africa would not be sufficient to accommodate and satisfy them".[1] With their increase in numbers, a new system of land tenure developed. A farmer would hire a large tract of unoccupied land on the frontier for six months and graze his cattle there during the summer months, living in a makeshift hut of reeds or simply in his great ox-waggon. If he were satisfied with his grazing farm, he would renew the lease. Soon every well-to-do farmer had one or more "cattle posts" in the interior, the forerunners of the *leenings-plaatsen* (loan farms) of the eighteenth century.

The young farmer would look after his cattle himself. Grown older, he would remain on his freehold farm and send his overseer and his sons to the cattle post. Thus the younger generation grew up accustomed to the roving life and ready to plunge still further into the unknown. The home farm would usually be too small to subdivide among the sons; thus the younger sons were forced to set up for themselves further in the interior. In this way each succeeding generation moved further from civilisation and became of necessity less dependent on its amenities. Owing to the vast distance from Cape Town and the complete absence of roads and bridges, the frontier farmers were forced to concentrate more and more on cattle-farming. It became the rule for the cattle farmer, even when he had a fixed abode, not to cultivate any lands except for his personal needs. Kolbe noted how the graziers in the Berg River valley ate nothing but meat, "which suits them so well that one seldom hears of a sickness". Bread was for them difficult to obtain, but even if they could get it, he says, "they would avoid the trouble".[2] Similarly, van der Stel declares: "they are only inclined to sow enough for themselves, and are always looking out for places far inland, in order to make their living by bartering with the Hottentots".[3]

Thus towards the end of the seventeenth century a new type of colonist was beginning to develop—the cattle farmer. In South Africa, with its long rainless seasons and periodic droughts, the cattle farmer is of necessity a rover. With good reason the language of the country dubs him *trekboer*.

Theal has expressed some doubt of the view here advanced, holding that this type did not develop till the eighteenth century,[4] but it is certain that van der Stel recognised the roving tendency among the colonists and tried to arrest it. A proclamation of 1692[5] illustrated

[1] Leibbrandt, *Rambles*, p. 8.
[2] Fouché, *Trekboer*, p. 10.
[3] Leibbrandt, *Rambles*, p. 8.
[4] Theal, *Catalogue of Books and Pamphlets relating to Africa*, p. 107.
[5] Fouché, *Trekboer*, p. 10.

his fears: it stated that colonists were making a living by grazing cattle and bartering in the interior, thus "leading a lazy, sluggardly life, to the detriment of the common weal", and ordained that no colonist who was not permanently domiciled within the recognised boundaries of the colony might possesss cattle. All who were grazing cattle beyond the frontier were to return within eight months and be registered by their landdrost on pain of confiscation of all their beasts. "And to prevent that any of the free burghers of Stellenbosch and Drakensteyn shall establish themselves beyond the recognised boundaries or keep any cattle there", all farmers were required to return with all their cattle to their homesteads every night, after grazing them during the day. If any farmer were found to have been absent from his home with his cattle for eight days, his cattle were to be confiscated.

This seems clear proof that the *trekboer*, as a distinct type, was coming into existence during the time of van der Stel. This type of colonist was destined to be of the greater importance, for the *trekboer* has been the great pioneer in South African history. Generation after generation of these hardy and self-reliant nomads pushed the frontiers of civilisation further into the wilderness. Incessantly at war with wild beasts and savage men, forcing a passage over great mountain barriers and waterless deserts, they led a self-dependent life of their own—as remote and isolated as any white men have ever lived. In time the *Wanderlust* entered into their blood and developed in their descendants a restlessness which raises grave social problems even in our times. In their day, however, the *trekboeren* performed a mighty task. Their spirit, the trek-spirit, the roving instinct which Simon van der Stel had tried in vain to smother at birth, was during the next century to enter into and possess the frontier farmers, and later prepare the Great Trek of the nineteenth century and mark out the path of the white man from the Cape to the Zambesi.

In 1699 van der Stel resigned and retired to his magnificent estate, Constantia. He had greatly extended the colony, he had founded Stellenbosch, Paarl and Franschhoek, and he had seen the graziers push through the first great mountain barrier into the Breede River valley on the second of the terraces by which the subcontinent rises from the sea.

His successor was his son, Willem Adriaan.[1] The new Governor, who had once occupied a minor post at the Cape and had also been an alderman of Amsterdam,[2] owed his appointment to the respect felt for his father and to the influence of patrons among the all-powerful oligarchy which ruled the Company and the Republic. Later on his enemies among the colonists alleged that he had arrived at the Cape loaded with debts.[3] Whether this be true or not, it is beyond dispute

[1] Theal, *Belangrijke Hist. Dokumenten*, III, 1.
[2] Leibbrandt, *Letters Rec.* 1695–1708, p. 154.
[3] Fouché, *The Diary of Adam Tas*, p. xxii.

that he came with the fixed intention of making money and of sticking at nothing to gain his object. For a man in his situation there was nothing strange in this. Everywhere else in the Company's dominions, officers of his rank abused their position to enrich themselves.[1] The only difference between Willem Adriaan van der Stel and his Eastern colleagues was that they could rob a long-suffering Company and downtrodden natives of a rich and extensive trade, whereas he would have to rob poor and suspicious European farmers. There was a danger here, which he did not realise until it was too late. At the Cape there was no trade and only one industry—agriculture. The official whose bad luck brought him to the Cape had only one means of making money; he had to take to farming. In spite of repeated prohibition by the XVII, it had been an established custom from van Riebeeck's time onward for the Commander and as many of the senior officials as dared follow his example to obtain land and cattle by underhand means and to eke out thus their miserable salaries.[2]

Simon van der Stel had notoriously farmed on a great scale[3] and his two senior officials had done likewise. Willem Adriaan, therefore, at once took to farming as a matter of course. He obtained 400 *morgen* of rich land from a passing Commissioner in flat defiance of the orders of the XVII, and soon added to this by the simple expedient of granting further land to his servant and then "buying" this land from him.[4] The land registers would in this way show no sign of his double-dealing. He began at the same time to gather herds of cattle and sheep, and by means of sharp practice and trickery, soon possessed the biggest herds in the colony. When the XVII, anxious to help the colonists, ordered him to throw open the cattle barter with the Hottentots, he kept this order secret, but made full use of his inside knowledge to barter as many as possible for himself. By the time a visiting Commissioner forced him to make the order public he had the cream of the market.[5]

On his farm, Vergelegen in Hottentots-Holland, he laid out immense vineyards extending over sixty *morgen*—the size of an ordinary farm. Half a million vines were soon established on an improved plan which would give a greater yield than the old-fashioned vineyards of the colonists. Of the 2,000,000 stocks in the colony the Governor possessed one-quarter. His father's famous vineyard counted a further 100,000 stocks.[6]

Willem Adriaan's flocks and herds increased so rapidly that soon eighteen cattle-posts were required to depasture them. Wheat lands

[1] Cf. Colenbrander, *Koloniale Geschiedenis*, II, 217–21.
[2] Fouché, *Diary*, pp. 190–92.
[3] *Letters Desp.* 1695–1708, pp. 287, 288, 333; Fouché, *Diary*, p. 192.
[4] Fouché, *Diary*, p. 192.
[5] *Ibid.* p. 198.
[6] Fouché, *Diary*, pp. 194, 302–4.

were also laid out at Vergelegen on such a scale that the Governor's yield of wheat soon amounted to nearly one-quarter of the total produced by the faming community. These vast enterprises required many hands. The chief gardener and fifty or sixty servants of the Company directed the labours of between 200 and 300 slaves. Van der Stel asserted later that 200 of these were his own property; but the colonists alleged that they had been acquired by writing off as "dead" slaves that had belonged to the Company. The rest, together with the white overseers, he "borrowed" from the Company as required.[1] A great mansion, quarters for overseers and slaves, workshops and a mill were built at Vergelegen. The materials came mostly from the Company's stores. A special fishing station, manned by eight fishermen, was required to help to feed this little army of labourers.

The Governor's example was eagerly followed by his subordinates. Elsevier, the Secunde (Lieutenant-Governor), Berg, the commander of the garrison, Kalden, the senior chaplain, ten Damme, the surgeon and even Blesius, the Independent Fiscal, all had large farms and establishments.[2] It is impossible to arrive at an exact knowledge of the extent of their farming operations, since they took great care to cover up their illegal activities. Such scraps of information as are available enable us to say with certainty that by 1705 the van der Stel family and the four or five senior officials owned and farmed about 12,000 *morgen* of land. As we have seen, the ordinary freehold farm was about sixty *morgen* in extent, so that this area equalled the holdings of 200 colonists. There were at that time 554 free burghers at the Cape, of whom probably less than 400 possessed farms. Thus the Governor and his coterie were illegally farming as much land as half the total number of free farmers in the colony.

The colonists did not object to the farming operations of officials as long as they themselves had a market for their produce. But at this moment the farmers were facing a very serious economic crisis. In the past the local market had been fairly balanced, the demand being sufficient to absorb all their produce. But Simon van der Stel had fought hard to obtain facilities for the export of surplus wheat to Batavia,[3] and had expressly warned his successor against the tendency of the farmers "to an excessive cultivation of the vine".[4] By 1705 Simon van der Stel's forebodings were being realised. The market was hopelessly oversupplied and exportation was made practically impossible by the opposition of the Company's servants in Java. Batavia preferred the cheaper grain of Surat and Bengal and

[1] *Ibid.* pp. 296–306.
[2] *Ibid.* pp. 306–18.
[3] *Letters Desp.* 1696–1708, pp. 11, 18, 33, 37, 39.
[4] Cf. his Instructions to his successor, in Leibbrandt, *Rambles*, p. 7.

only took Cape wheat grudgingly.[1] Cape wines were not wanted in the East, while the distillation of brandy, which would have been a great boon to the farmers, was strictly prohibited by the Company, which preferred to make its profits on European spirits.[2] Further, Simon van der Stel's experimental exports of dried meat had come to nothing.[3] The great flocks of fat-tailed sheep at the Cape yielded no wool, but were kept exclusively for the local butchers.

By 1705 the position was alarming. The farmers had produced 1132 *leggers*[4] of wine, whereas the total sales of wine for that year were not more than 500 *leggers*. They possessed 11,000 head of cattle and 69,485 sheep, and not more than 10,000 sheep had been bought by the butchers that year. Moreover, of this number, the farmers appear to have sold only one-quarter, the rest having been supplied by the farmer-officials.[5] The wheat harvest had been seriously damaged by rains and was nearly one-third below normal, the total returned by the farmers being 4331 bags. Yet 1400 bags were exported to Batavia, an amount equal to one-third of the yield of a bad year.[6]

The farmers were thus face to face with the worst of economic evils—chronic overproduction. Into this overstocked market the officials now stepped as privileged rivals. The Governor possessed 20,000 sheep, produced 1000 bags of wheat and would soon be producing 600 *leggers* of wine. Except for the wheat, he could supply the whole demand by himself alone. And there remained his friends to be reckoned with. It is clear that the condition of the market alarmed the official coterie, for in spite of their favoured position as officials, they might find it difficult to sell their own produce. They therefore took special measures to assure themselves a safe market.

The right to retail meat was farmed out by auction for a term of years. One, Henning Huising, had held this contract for years past and had become the richest man among the colonists. At first he had been the Governor's "best crony", but van der Stel's greed and the blackmail he levied in return for his favour had proved too much for Huising. A serious quarrel between the two had been patched up by the Chaplain, Kalden, who arranged that Huising should give the Governor "3000 ewes and his best slave" as payment for the renewal of his "friendship".[7] Van der Stel's rapacity was not satisfied. He knew how profitable the meat contract was and determined to secure it for himself. He therefore decreed that there were to be four contractors instead of one, and arranged that all of them were his own

[1] Fouché, *Diary*, pp. 320–2.

[2] *Letters Desp.* 1696–1708, pp. 102, 142; Leibbrandt, *Rambles*, p. 159; Fouché, *Diary*, pp. 318–20.

[3] Leibbrandt, *Rambles*, p. 25.

[4] 1 *legger* = 2600 gallons.

[5] Fouché, *Diary*, pp. 318–28.

[6] *Ibid.*

[7] *Ibid.* pp. 106–9.

secret agents.[1] Henceforth not a pound of meat could be legally sold without his consent.

The only remaining source of profit was the wine lease. The right to retail wine and spirits was auctioned in the same way as the meat monopoly, but here the practice was to divide it among four contractors. Van der Stel, remembering his vast vineyards, could not permit four independent contractors to jeopardise his sales. He ordained that henceforth the four wine leases would be combined in the hands of one contractor, Johannes Phyffer, an ex-convict and the most notorious smuggler at the Cape, who had been the Governor's partner in many dishonest schemes.[2] With Phyffer as sole buyer and retailer of wine not a gallon could henceforth be sold except as the Governor willed.

By thus putting his personal agents in possession of the two great contracts, van der Stel had obtained for himself and his friends an enviable position. They represented the Company and bought in its name and with its money. The meat and wine contractors, again, were their dummies who bought and sold only for their principals. Thus there was only a single group of buyers in the entire market—the Governor and his clique.

All this was only half of their design. They expected soon to become the only sellers as well. It was common talk in the Governor's circle at this time that soon "no free burghers would be required at the Cape...and that there was a chance for them, the four or five of them, to provide the Company and the Cape with everything".[3]

The officials had thus set up, within the cast-iron monopoly of the Company, a still more crushing monopoly of their own. How the farmers regarded this is shown by their own words. They felt that the officials "had severed their main artery, the free trade in wine, corn and cattle". Henceforth they would literally have "to feed from one man's hand", the hand of van der Stel, who had apparently determined "to mop the colonists out of the land".[4] Ruin stared them in the face. Those present at the auction of the wine lease no sooner heard the terms of the new lease read out than they departed in uproar and went straight to the house of Huising to plan resistance.[5] Huising himself had already complained of the misgovernment of van der Stel to the latter's patrons in Holland and, in the previous year, with other colonists had addressed complaints to the Governor-General at Batavia.[6] So far, these complaints had been without result. The meeting at his house now resolved to draw up a formal memorial of complaint and to address it direct to the XVII, a serious

[1] Fouché, *Diary*, p. 200.
[2] *Ibid.* pp. 200–2.
[3] *Ibid.* p. 330.
[4] *Ibid.*
[5] *Ibid.* p. 202.
[6] *Ibid.* p. 14 and note.

and, indeed, unprecedented step which would involve those concerned in very grave danger if their design were discovered by van der Stel. The memorial was drawn up by Adam Tas, a nephew by marriage of Huising, and the only man of education among the farmers. Tas kept an entertaining diary at this time, which became famous in the ensuing troubles, and which shows how he collected evidence against the Governor and obtained signatures to the memorial. The memorial itself was a lengthy document of thirty-eight paragraphs.[1] Half of these dealt exclusively with the illegal landholding of the officials, their extensive farming operations, and their monopoly of the sale of wheat, wine and cattle. Article 4 exposed the dishonesty of the Governor in regard to the cattle barter with the Natives. The remaining less important clauses dealt with cases of vexatious treatment meted out to farmers and others by the van der Stels.[2]

While Tas was occupied in this manner, the return fleet arrived from India with news that complaints against the Governor had been received at Batavia.[3] Van der Stel was not unduly perturbed by complaints against himself addressed to that quarter. He probably expected sympathy rather than censure from his seasoned colleagues in the East. But he realised from the commotion at the wine auction that the animosity against himself had grown enormously. He suspected that if the colonists had complained the year before to Batavia, they might very well now be desperate enough to approach the XVII. He determined to forestall any such step. Huising, whom he had grievously wronged, would be the natural leader, and Tas, known as "an elegant writer", was sure to be secretary. He therefore sent Starrenburg, landdrost of Stellenbosch, with a posse of soldiers to surprise Tas in the night of 27 February 1706.[4] They found in his desk a draft of the memorial of complaint, a list of names and the diary. The original memorial, signed by sixty-three colonists, was fortunately safely hidden at Cape Town; but by means of the draft memorial and the diary, van der Stel was fully informed of the movement and of the charges against himself. In wild panic he threw the ringleaders into prison and began a campaign of violence against those colonists whom he suspected of sympathising with the movement with a view to forcing them to withdraw their accusations.

Without the slightest excuse van der Stel now acted as if a state of rebellion had arisen. He summoned a so-called Broad Council[5] consisting of the Cape Council of Justice and the senior officers of the fleet, and then tried, with some success, to set aside the ordinary

[1] Translation in Leibbrandt, "Defence of W. A. van der Stel" in *Précis of the Archives*, pp. 52–65.

[2] Cf. Fouché, *Diary*, pp. 206 *sqq*.

[3] *Ibid*. p. 126.

[4] *Ibid*. pp. 220–22.

[5] *Ibid*. pp. 220–24.

machinery of justice. The imprisoned colonists at once challenged the jurisdiction of the local Council of Justice and demanded to have their case tried in Holland on the entirely reasonable grounds that since the Governor and the other members of the Council of Justice were accused by name in the memorial, they could not sit in judgment on their accusers. The Broad Council admitted the justice of this plea and agreed that five colonists should represent the signatories of the memorial before their competent judges in the Netherlands. Four colonists, Henning Huising, Pieter van der Byl, Ferdinand Appel and Jan van Meerland, were sent off to answer before the Directors themselves, in the name of the colonists, the charges of conspiracy and rebellion which van der Stel was bringing against them.[1] The fifth free burgher, Jacobus van der Heiden, was illegally kept back by van der Stel, because he had shown so much spirit and obstinacy in the preliminary hearing that the Governor was afraid to let him appear before the XVII. Van der Heiden was thrust into the infamous Black Hole of the Castle, where only criminals condemned to death were put to await execution, and threatened with torture in order to make him retract. Only when the surgeon pronounced his life to be in danger as the result of his ill-treatment was he brought back to the ordinary prison. He steadfastly refused to recant.[2]

With the fleet there had gone a vast mass of documents, sworn statements, attestations, extracts from the Company's books, etc., which van der Stel feverishly collected as evidence to rebut the charges of the colonists and to prove their own seditious and rebellious behaviour. On the other hand, the burghers' memorial had been smuggled away under the Governor's nose in the keeping of Abraham Bogaert, a sympathetic ship's surgeon.[3]

Since the Board Council had removed the whole matter from the jurisdiction of the local court, the imprisoned colonists should have been left alone while their case was being tried at Amsterdam. But van der Stel had no intention of letting his enemies out of his clutches. He was incessantly occupied with efforts to intimidate the prisoners into retracting their accusations. Solitary confinement, threats of torture, banishment, every means was tried to terrify them into submission. This travesty of justice, which one of the sufferers rightly described as "Inquisition rather than justice", produced a few insignificant retractations from thoroughly frightened prisoners.[4] The country districts meanwhile were in a state of suppressed rebellion. Nine of the signatories had fled thither and were being hidden by their friends. When all efforts to capture them proved fruitless, they were formally banished.

[1] Fouché, *Diary*, pp. 234–6.
[2] *Ibid.* pp. 230–42.
[3] Cf. Bogaert, *Historische Reizen door d'oostersche deelen van Asia*, etc. (Amsterdam, 1711).
[4] Fouché, *Diary*, pp. 242–65.

In the meantime, three of the burghers' delegates had survived the voyage to the Netherlands, and in due time the anxiously awaited decision of the XVII arrived on 16 April 1707.[1] In a letter, dated 30 October 1706,[2] the Directors expressed annoyance at the "unpalatable news of the excessive commotions and quarrels between a large portion of the colonists and the Cape Government.....We have decided," they wrote, "for the sake of maintaining the general peace in this colony, and for other valid reasons," to remove from their posts, the Governor, the Lieutenant-Governor, the Chaplain and the Landdrost of Stellenbosch, who were to be sent to Holland at the first opportunity. The Governor's land they consider "to have been granted without our knowledge or order and therefore it shall be restored to the Company". All the servants of the Company, "from the highest to the lowest", who possessed land were at once to dispose of it, and no land should henceforth be allowed to fall directly or indirectly into the hands of an official. "Nor shall such servants dare to trade in corn, wine or cattle, personally or by means of others, directly or indirectly." The wine lease given to Phyffer was to be cancelled and divided into four parts. The meat contract was also to be cancelled and half of it granted to Huising. As for the burghers sent to appear before them "accused of mutiny and conspiracy" by van der Stel, the Directors declared that they had "after careful examination of all the evidence collected by you...not been able to find guilty of the crimes mentioned; neither the rest of the subscribers to the memorial". They therefore "order that all the persons mentioned" be liberated immediately.

Having thus done justice, the Directors proceeded to order the Cape Government to take measures that in future no colonist should receive too much land. "Our intention in this respect is, that the various colonists should be able to make an honest living, without the necessity of any one of them rising prominently above his fellows by the possession of more lands and chattels. The more an equality can be secured among them...the more it will please us."

The decision of the XVII was a fair reflection of their policy. The Company had powerful enemies in the mother country, who would welcome a scandal. Hence, in all its activities the utmost secrecy had always been rigidly enforced upon both servants and Directors.[3] A public scandal had to be prevented above all things. Therefore they dismissed their dishonest servants. But if they were to punish them further they must in equity proceed against other dishonest servants, beginning perhaps with their Governor-General, Johan van Hoorn, who was known to be piling up millions for himself by practices more dishonest even than those of van der Stel, and who presently retired

[1] Fouché, *Diary*, p. xxviii.
[2] *Letters Rec.* 1695–1708, pp. 433 *sqq.*
[3] Colenbrander, *Koloniale Geschiedenis*, II, 207.

with a fortune of ten millions.[1] And where would punishment stop? Was there no righteous man among all their servants? And—a much more delicate question—would the dishonesty be found only among the servants? Would not enquiry inevitably reveal that corruption was rampant among the Directors themselves? The vicious circle was aptly demonstrated in this very case, for Wouter Valckenier, who, as visiting Commissioner, had illegally granted van der Stel his first block of land, was now a Director and a member of the committee investigating the misdeeds of his beneficiary.[2] *Quieta non movere*. The hornets' nest stirred up by the Cape colonists had thoroughly frightened the Directors.

The free burghers had proved themselves dangerous subjects. Among the papers of Adam Tas had been found the draft of a memorial to Their High Mightinesses, the States-General.[3] Should the colonists remain unappeased, and dare to appeal unto Caesar—what a coil! Therefore, the colonists had to be upheld and their leader mollified by the renewal of his lost meat contract. But that was as far as the XVII would go. The colonists must not be allowed to get out of hand again. Hence the Cape Government was ordered to see to it that no colonist be in future permitted to become rich. So far, it is true, only one individual had (almost miraculously) succeeded in amassing more than a competence, but he had turned out a very dangerous subject. Finally, the uproar at the Cape confirmed them in their aversion to all colonising experiments. Already, in 1700, on Willem Adriaan's recommendation, they had ceased to send out French refugees: they now decided to send out no more colonists of any description.[4]

The outbreak of 1705 was directly caused by the stranglehold which van der Stel had established on the Cape market. But his unofficial monopoly was the direct result of the monopoly of the Company and the arbitrary powers which it gave to the Governor to control all buying and selling. Without that he could never have abused his authority as he did. Doubtless, he was guilty of the grossest dereliction of duty; but it was the system of the Company which made his misdeeds possible, and the culpable connivance of its servants, high and low, which promised him impunity. It was only the presence of a considerable body of colonists whom his schemes would ruin that brought the scandal to light. For the troubles of 1705, therefore, the Company itself must bear the blame.

For the colonists the movement had important consequences. They were at the time a heterogeneous body: Dutch, both home and South African born, German and French. These diverse elements had not

[1] *Ibid.* II, 219.
[2] Theal, *Belangrijke Hist. Dokumenten*, III, 9; *Letters Rec.* p. 433.
[3] Fouché, *Diary*, p. 358; *Letters Desp.* p. 290.
[4] Theal, *Belangrijke Hist. Dokumenten*, III, 6.

yet amalgamated and some of them, especially the French, were still holding aloof and were themselves regarded with suspicion.[1] The "unsupportable yoke" of van der Stel, the common danger in conspiring against him and the common suffering under his persecutions brought about a sense of unity, which had so far been wanting. The most conspicuous feature of the movement against van der Stel was the solidarity of the colonists. All differences of race were forgotten. Of the sixty-three signatories to the memorial thirty-one were French, the rest were Netherlanders and South Africans. Kolbe, an eyewitness, notes as "an extraordinary circumstance" that of the nine colonists banished for their share in the conspiracy, three were Hollanders, three Afrikaners and three Frenchmen, and that of the three who died during van der Stel's persecutions one was a Hollander, one a South African and one a Frenchman.[2]

Coincidences so striking had a special significance for contemporaries. They symbolised the unanimity of the colonists against the tyrant. For the future they were a happy augury. Henceforth differences of race would no longer form a barrier between the groups of colonists.

A last point remains to be noticed. The movement against van der Stel was exclusively a farmers' movement, sprung from farmers' grievances. The town burghers, a parasitic community, which "lived from God and the stranger", had no hand in it. Van der Stel insisted on all occasions that it was *de boeren* (the farmers) who were attacking him. The memorialists, he declared, were "ignorant farmers" and "insolent, rascally farmers". As he was about to leave the Cape in disgrace, he declared: "It was the farmers [*de boeren*] who cooked my goose."[3] When he was abusing his enemies in this way, he was not merely attacking a class of the community. He was giving a name to the new nation which was beginning to emerge—the nation which his own tyranny had helped to form.[4]

[1] Fouché, *Diary*, p. 358 and note.
[2] *Ibid.* p. 360.
[3] *Ibid.* p. 362.
[4] *Vide infra*, p. 457.

CHAPTER VI

THE CAPE COLONY UNDER COMPANY RULE, 1708–1795

THE main purpose for which a settlement had been established at the Cape, that is to supply the company's fleets with fresh food, was not fully achieved under Jan van Riebeeck. His immediate successors continued his policy of encouraging the farmers to increase their production till, as we have seen, under the van der Stels the problem of production was practically solved as far as the needs of the Company were concerned. The colonisation of Stellenbosch and Drakenstein by Simon van der Stel and the development of wheat growing in the south-western coastal belt, the so-called Zwartland (Black Country), which began also in his time, soon resulted in sufficient agricultural supplies becoming available, and the extension of sheep- and cattle-farming along the frontier, inaugurated by Willem Adriaan van der Stel, made the authorities less dependent on the uncertain barter with the Hottentots which had been hitherto their main source for obtaining fresh meat for the fleets.

The conflict between the second van der Stel and the colonists was marked by the emergence of a new factor in the economic history of the settlement. This was the difficulty which the farmers thenceforth experienced in disposing of their vegetables, wine and cereals. The victory of the colonists relieved the position for a time, but the inability of the Cape market in normal times to absorb the agricultural products of the farmers remained a difficult problem and was an important reason why many pioneers crossed the coastal mountain ranges and applied themselves to a pastoral pursuits in the interior.

For seventy years after the fall of Willem Adriaan van der Stel the occupation of the interior was the main trend in the development of the settlement. In Cape Town and its adjacent rural area the even tenor of life was rarely disturbed by any happenings of major importance. There was the normal succession of Governors, and though few of them made their mark, their names at least with a brief chronicle of events may be recorded.

Louis van Assenburgh, who succeeded Willem Adriaan van der Stel, died in 1711, and Maurits Pasques de Chavonnes arrived in 1714 to take his place. During the interval in 1713 an epidemic of smallpox, brought to Cape Town by the crew of a ship, killed about a quarter of its European inhabitants, wrought even greater havoc amongst the slaves and, spreading into the interior, practically annihilated whole clans of Hottentots, thus further reducing the potential economic value of these tribesmen. An even more virulent visitation of the same disease occurred in 1755. Meanwhile Mauritius, hitherto a dependency of the Cape, had been abandoned in 1709 only to be snapped up by the French six years later. At de Chavonnes' death in 1724 his second-in-command, Jan de la Fontaine, assumed control till the arrival in 1727 of the new Governor, Peter Gysbert Noodt, an unpopular man who only survived his appointment for two years. On his sudden death de la Fontaine at length became Governor. It was during the rule of the three last-named Governors that, from 1721 onwards, the company occupied Delagoa Bay, from which the Portuguese had withdrawn temporarily. The loss of life from disease was heavy, trade proved negligible and, after the occupation had lasted barely ten years, the post was abandoned in 1730. Jan de la Fontaine retired in 1737 and two years later his second-in-command, Hendrik Swellengrebel, was appointed Governor, the first South African born man to achieve that distinction. Long residence at the Cape in high official positions and his resulting local knowledge, connections and sympathies, as well as his lengthy term of office from 1739 to 1751, made Swellengrebel a more important figure in the history of the settlement than any of his immediate predecessors had been. A rebellion, instigated and led by a deserting soldier of French descent, one Estienne Barbier, which arose from Government intervention in border strife with Hottentot tribesmen, received very little support from the colonists and ended with the execution of Barbier in 1739 soon after Swellengrebel's accession to office. More noteworthy in his time were the visit of the reforming Governor-General of the East Indies, Baron van Imhoff, in 1743 and the founding of the village and drostdy of Swellendam in 1743–5, events to which further reference will be made.

In 1751 Swellengrebel was succeeded by his brother-in-law, Ryk Tulbagh, president of the Council of Justice. He was a highly respected and popular public figure at the Cape when he became Governor, and when he died in 1771, he had so enhanced his reputation that his name was long held in grateful memory by the colonists. How circumstances helped him to gain a unique place in their affections will be explained later. His Sumptuary Laws of 1755, which caused some stir, were regulations framed by the Company primarily for the East Indies where officials who had many opportunities of acquiring wealth squandered it in ostentatious extravagance. The application of the regulations to the Cape was not due to any similar extravagance of living, which was impossible in the modest circumstances of the colony, but to the fact that it was part of a single commercial empire ruled over by the Governor-General and High Council of Batavia, and must be subjected to the same rules. Still, the prosperity which the colonists enjoyed in Tulbagh's time enabled them to live more comfortably than they had ever before found possible; under his successor, Joachim van Plettenberg (1771–85), the period of quiet and rapid expansion came to an end.

When the eighteenth century began, the south-western barrier ranges near Cape Town had often been crossed by hunters, traders, and explorers, but it was only in the time of Governor Willem Adriaan van der Stel that they were penetrated by white men driving their flocks and herds before them—the first "Great Trek" into the interior. This happened almost simultaneously at two points, and at both the Governor led the way. In 1699, soon after his arrival, he went on a journey of inspection and, on reaching the northern border of the settlement, entered the present Tulbagh Basin. He regarded the country as very suitable for stock-farming and, after his return to Cape Town, began to issue grazing licences for this area. Where the mountains approach False Bay, the Governor himself was the pioneer. His farm and its contiguous grazing lands reached to the western base of the mountains, and some of his herdsmen and flock-masters were stationed many miles further eastward, where the rocky slopes dissolve into pleasant valleys and downs. During his rule this portal was closed to all competitors, but after his fall not only his farm, but also his sheep-runs and cattle-posts, passed into the hands of a few fortunate burghers. They were soon followed by other pioneers with grazing licences, who pressed further forward into the rolling sheep and grain country of the south coast. At the same time the valleys of the Breede and Zonder Einde Rivers were being taken up. These converging lines of colonisation, having met at the junction of the two rivers, reached Mossel Bay before 1735 and ten years later were nearing the Gamtoos River. In the meantime a new frontier district had been proclaimed (1743) to keep the eastern pioneers within the official confines of the colony. It was called Swellendam after Governor Swellengrebel and his wife, Helena ten Damme. Its administrative centre, the seat of a landdrost, was a little village of the same name founded on the Breede River in 1745.

Meantime from the passes of the long mountain chain which shuts in the Breede River valley on the north, settlers were spreading northward over the plateaux of the interior and had reached the highlands of the Hantam Mountains (Calvinia) in the west in 1735. The general tendency of the interior settlers, however, was to move towards the east and north-east, for the great Karoo plains in those directions have a larger rainfall than towards the west and consequently provide better pasturage. The march over the Karoo, notwithstanding its wide front, proceeded very rapidly. In 1771, Willem Prinsloo, a rugged leading spirit amongst the frontiersmen, established himself at the Boschberg near the banks of the Little Fish River on the site of the present town of Somerset East, and not far behind him, to left and right from the Sneeuwberg in the north, over Bruintjies Hoogte and down to the Zuurveld east of Algoa Bay, settlers were pressing forward in scattered groups and straggling lines.

The first "Great Trek" came to a stop when it met the Xhosa

vanguard of the Bantu peoples in the late 'seventies of the eighteenth century. Down to that time it had hardly been hampered by opposition on the part of the aborigines. The only Natives to be found south of the Orange and west of the Great Fish Rivers and the Zuurveld before 1770 were Hottentots and Bushmen, and border troubles with them after 1700 never seriously retarded the expansion of the Cape settlement.

The Hottentots were probably at no time numerically strong enough to offer a serious obstacle to the progress of European colonisation, and, as has been shown, their numbers were greatly reduced by epidemics of smallpox in the course of the eighteenth century. The survivors were detribalised, even losing their own languages in the process and acquiring Dutch as their new mother tongue. They were excellent herdsmen, for from time immemorial their ancestors were skilled in finding water and feed for their sheep and cattle in arid regions and in defending their stock against the Bushmen and wild beasts. They therefore became a real asset to the farmers in the interior, and though in their natural state they had not, like the Bantu, learned to till the soil, they proved to be adaptable in this as also in other respects. Not very many of them were employed on the wine and grain farms on the south-west, for the labour of imported Malay and African slaves was mainly utilised there; but the colonists beyond the mountains grew grain, fruit and vegetables for their own consumption when circumstances permitted, and the Hottentots with whom they came into contact eventually developed the ability to render them assistance in simple agricultural operations. When not serving European masters, the Hottentots during the eighteenth century did not practise agriculture. They retained their roving propensities and were notoriously averse from sustained manual labour, but as servants they suited the particular needs of the interior settlers. Though stock-thieving on a small scale remained a minor pastime of some Hottentots, their sins in this direction no longer led to military conflicts.

After the termination of the last Hottentot War in 1677, during a full century the only frontier fighting that took place was with the Bushmen. These pigmies of the veld practised neither agricultural nor pastoral pursuits and subsisted upon such vegetable food as nature supplied and the meat that fell to their poison-tipped arrows. They regarded the flocks and herds of the Hottentots and Bantu as fair game, and these peoples retaliated by treating them as wild animals. It was inevitable that the European farmers should suffer from their raids, and that reprisals should follow. Attempts were made to induce the Bushmen to adapt themselves to a more settled form of life; one reads of groups being supplied with sheep to keep them from thieving,[1] and they were sometimes employed as herdsmen;

[1] Theal, *Belangrijke Hist. Dokumenten*, III, 139.

but as a race they proved untamable and, as the settlement grew, they could only escape extermination by retreating northwards.

The main importance of the Bushmen in the history of South African colonisation lies in the fact that in fighting against them the colonists developed a military system which was destined to play a great part in less unequal struggles during the nineteenth century.

From the first introduction of the free burghers it was regarded as an axiom that all white men in the colony able to carry arms could be called upon to defend it; indeed, even before the first Commander left the Cape, the colonists had been made to feel that they were expected to bear the brunt in border warfare. They took a natural pride in their military achievements, and on one occasion in sending a memorial to van Riebeeck they boldly asserted: "For we be the defenders of our land!"[1] Though contact with the garrison soldiers was at first retained, the free men were soon formed into militia units under their own officers and, in the time of Simon van der Stel, the annual militia drills had assumed large and interesting proportions. The first occasion when a purely burgher commando took the field was probably in 1715, when the colonists under a commandant of their own choice were allowed to chastise the Bushmen, who had raided the Drakenstein farms.[2] The commando system did not immediately prove to be very efficient, but it did not take the colonists long to become expert in chasing and rounding up stock thieves and, before the middle of the eighteenth century, they had virtually pushed the Bushmen out of the occupied regions into the interior plains. The ultimate success of the system was due to its simplicity and the fact that it perfectly suited not only the parsimonious policy of the Company but also the circumstances and needs of the colonists. In registers kept for the purpose the authorities in Cape Town and the landdrosts in the rural districts had a record of the able-bodied male Europeans above the age of sixteen years who formed the militia forces, and though these registers tended to become unreliable, there was never any lack of men when occasion demanded that a commando should be called out. Military operations might not be undertaken without the sanction of the Government, but when such approval had been obtained and ammunition supplied from the Company's stores, the burghers were allowed and expected to make their own arrangements. They served under officers of their own selection, who likewise received no remuneration for their services, and every man had to provide for his own subsistence and transport. Commandos consisting wholly of mounted men soon became the rule in the interior, where it seemed natural for every white man to have at least one horse at his disposal. On the Karoo plains the commandos had more elbow-room to develop their tactics, and there also military

[1] *Journal of Jan van Riebeeck*, 23 December 1658.
[2] Theal, *History of S. A.* 1652–1795, I, 432–4.

leaders were trained who afterwards proved their merit in far more difficult warfare against the Bantu. A typical example was Adriaan van Jaarsveld. In 1770 we find him leading a commando against the Bushmen northwards across the Karoo, and ten years later he was commanding the burgher forces on the eastern border in their first clash with the Xhosas.

The military operations of the colonists during the eighteenth century were not due to quarrels with the Natives about land. There was more than sufficient open land for everybody, and it was neither necessary nor even feasible to make special provision by means of reserves for the needs of the Hottentots and Bushmen. The Hottentots had indeed, in negotiating with van Riebeeck and his early successors, claimed the whole country as their own,[1] but being nomads they had no real notion of land ownership or boundaries, and their dispersed tribal remnants, which remained in contact with the whites, continued to wander from place to place without appreciably cramping the colonists. The Bushmen, as we have seen, needed no pastures. The only kind of reserve which could have suited them might have been a game reserve, but they would have used it primarily as a base of operations against the flocks and herds of their pastoral neighbours.

The pioneers occupied the interior under a new form of land tenure, the loan farm.[2] In the time of Governor W. A. van der Stel, the number of grazing licences issued already showed a rapid increase, but this did not yet imply that large numbers of independent loan farms were being occupied. The licensees were in the main still owners of freehold farms, and their sons or overseers were in charge of their stock along the northern border. No charge was originally made for a licence, which was ordinarily restricted to three or, at the most, six months. It was not until the first "Great Trek" had definitely begun that the loan farms emerged clearly. Then for the first time we find large numbers of farmers without any freehold property occupying land on graziers' licences only. From the middle of 1714 it became the rule that a fee of one rix-dollar per month or twelve per year had to be paid for every grazing licence, and in 1732 this was raised to twenty-four rix-dollars per annum (about £5.) The term *recognitie* was used for this payment, the implication being that the licensee "recognised" the Company as the owner of his stock farm, though as a matter of fact he held it on an indeterminate lease. For every new loan farm application had to be made to the nearest landdrost or magistrate, who appointed commissioners to ascertain *in loco* whether or no the proposed licence infringed on existing certified grazing rights. They determined its boundaries by "riding off"

[1] *Journal of Jan van Riebeeck.*

[2] Botha, C. Graham, *Early Cape Land Tenure* (reprint from *S. A. Law Journal*, May and August 1919).

the new farm in four or more directions, i.e. they walked their horses from a central point for half an hour each way and so roughly indicated its extent, which was usually about 6000 acres. These preliminaries having been complied with and the licence granted, the grazier knew that his title was assured provided he paid his *recognitie*; and even if he fell into arrear, as often happened, there was little likelihood of eviction. The squatter built a small adobe house, provided stabling for his horses and constructed kraals for his stocks, all clustered near a spring or, as it is called in South Africa, a "fountain" (hence the many farm names ending in *fontein*). These visible signs of occupacy were called the *opstal*, and regarded as belonging to the licensee. He could sell his *opstal*, and as this implied the transfer of its surrounding grazing rights, the price was calculated on the value of the whole farm. On the rare occasions when a loan farm was taken back by the Government, e.g. for the purposes of establishing a town, compensation was similarly evaluated. Only in one respect was the farmer's ownership limited—he could not subdivide his loan farm and dispose of it in pieces.

The loan-farm system was largely reponsible for the rapid extension of the borders of the settlement. The leaps and bounds by which the pioneers were pressing forward soon began to cause concern in official circles and, when Baron van Imhoff visited the Cape in 1743, he was thoroughly alarmed at their dispersion. He was on his way to Batavia as Governor-General, and it was his duty to report on conditions at the Cape, which was a station under his authority. He expressed himself as gravely perturbed about the future of the colonists in the interior, who, he feared, would shake off all vestiges of control and lose contact with civilisation. He considered ways and means of obviating these dangers, and measures were framed with a view to keeping the foremost pioneers within reasonable bounds and generally retarding their *Wanderlust*. In 1743 van Imhoff introduced a new form of land tenure which was a combination of the freehold and loan-farm systems. The licensee could at small additional expense get full ownership in respect of his *opstal* and sixty morgen of adjoining land (about 120 acres) while still retaining his grazing lands to their full extent on loan. Very few colonists applied for farms under the new system; hence as a means of binding them to particular localities, it proved quite ineffective. Nor did the increase in the rent for loan farms lead to the issue of fewer licences.

A sudden change came over the placid scene of the colony in 1778 and 1779. The long and bloody conflict with the Bantu on the eastern border began, and its opening stages synchronised with a wholly unrelated agitation for reform in Cape Town and the immediately adjacent district. This agitation was primarily due to factors that had somewhat suddenly sprung into operation; but its roots must also be traced to the commercial policy of the Company and its system of government.

The history of the Dutch East India Company during the first three-quarters of the eighteenth century is the uninspiring record of a great and once vigorous and enterprising organisation getting set in its ways, jealously guarding its monopoly, and so fearful of innovations that it allowed its commercial and administrative systems to become obsolete, corrupt and ineffective.[1] It was a period of stagnation and decline. The power that guided the policy of the Company was in the hands of the so-called Patricians, a relatively small number of wealthy families, who also possessed dominating political influence in the Republic and prevented the States-General from enquiring into the Company's affairs. Their main objective was to see to it that their large annual dividends, which averaged 25 per cent during the first half of the century, were paid, and though these dividends were reduced to 12½ per cent in the second half of the century, they were continued at that rate till 1782 whether the Company had made a profit or not. By that time the Company had incurred an enormous debt.[2]

Even under a liberal commercial policy it would probably have proved impossible during the eighteenth century to convert the Cape settlement into a thriving colony with a rapidly growing population. Its wealth and material progress depended on what the farmers could produce and sell, and neither Europe nor the East was at that time to an appreciable extent in need of or able to import the agricultural products of a country situated in the southern temperate zone. This very obvious fact explains why the export of wheat and wine never rose beyond a few thousand *muids* and some hundreds of *leggers* per year.[3] It has been suggested that the Cape pastoralists would have found the export of wool profitable, if they had followed in the footsteps of the second van der Stel and given attention to woolled sheep; but it is open to serious question whether, in view of the high transport costs and the fact that Europe was still growing all the wool it required, it would have paid them to do so. No government at the time could have removed the main economic disadvantages which retarded the progress of the Cape, but the Dutch East India Company undoubtedly aggravated them.

All oversea trade remained an inviolable prerogative of the Company, with the result that in this direction the colony practically made no progress. When the Company's ships reached Table Bay on their return from the East, they were usually already crammed with merchandise. During the first two decades of the eighteenth

[1] Geyer, A. L., *Das wirtschaftliche System der niederländischen ostindischen Kompanie am Kap der guten Hoffnung*, 1785–95.

[2] Klerck de Reus, *Geschichtlicher Ueberblick der Administrativen, Rechtlichen und Finanziellen Entwicklung der niederlandisch-ostindischen Compagnie*, Beilage VI.

[3] 1 *muid* = 2·972 bushels; 1 *legger* = about 133 gallons.

century about forty-five Dutch ships touched at the Cape each year; in the 'thirties an average of about sixty-eight was reached; in the course of the next few decades it fell well below sixty; and the last normal figure—for 1793—was fifty-three.[1] The colonists were therefore in effect debarred from developing an export trade, and Cape Town remained their only market. Here also their prospects were restricted, for the local consumption of the Company for its garrison also remained static, and the only hope left to the colonists was that they would be able to sell their surplus to the crews of foreign vessels—not for export, of course, but for consumption on the voyage. They sometimes succeeded in doing so, when Anglo-French rivalry in India brought great fleets into South African waters and led to the establishment and strengthening of French and English bases at Mauritius and St Helena. But soaring prices were usually soon followed by restrictive measures on the part of the Cape Government, and the colonists were compelled to supply the Company's needs at a fixed tariff. They had furthermore to obtain official permission to sell provisions to foreign ships, the end in view being the protection not of the strangers but of the Company. "We derive our livelihood from God and the stranger", said the burghers; but the stranger was frequently exploited and extortionate prices coupled with uncertainty as regards available supplies tended to keep foreign customers away. The commercial policy of the Company, the worst effects of which were sometimes further vitiated by official corruption and inefficiency, created a thoroughly unsound business atmosphere. No private commercial houses could come into being, and the colonists, though descended from great commercial nations, lost the tradition of doing business. Their attempts in this direction were characterised by furtiveness and pettiness. Clandestine trade was carried on in almost every private dwelling in Cape Town, and even the best families sent their slaves to hawk the produce of their gardens and other minor wares on the streets.

It is interesting to note that early in the century the colonists began to grow perturbed about the future of their children. Of these there was a relatively large number in the settlement; indeed, the increase in the European civilian population, which grew from 1300 in 1700 to 10,000 in 1778, was mainly due to a high local birth-rate. In several respects adequate provision was made for the material and spiritual wants of the rising generation. An Orphan Chamber had been established as far back as 1674. It was controlled by a board, on which the burghers were well represented, and satisfactorily looked after the property of orphaned minors. In passing it may be stated that this institution also served the purposes of a loan bank. Simple parish schools were attached to the various churches, the number of which increased as the settlement grew, and though the standard of

[1] Beyers, C., *Die Kaapse Patriotte*, 1779–91, pp. 237–9.

education was low, complete illiteracy amongst the whites was rare. Farmers also employed vagabond instructors to teach their offspring the three R's, mainly in order that they might be able to read the Bible and the Catechism book with a view to qualifying for church membership. In 1714 a "Latin" school was started in Cape Town, but it could not be maintained and was closed after a few years. No further effort to provide more advanced facilities for education was made before 1793. Missionary work was begun by Georg Schmidt of the Moravian Missionary Society in 1737, but his activities amongst the Hottentots led to a conflict with the Established Church and he had to leave the Cape in 1744. Only in the 'nineties of the eighteenth century was the Christianising of the Hottentots taken up seriously again, and generally speaking non-European education received little or no attention. The colonists, on the other hand, in view of their circumstances were not badly off for churches and schools; but they looked with apprehension at their unsold produce and felt grave concern about the economic prospects of their steadily growing colony.

There was some immigration during the eighteenth century, mainly from Holland and Germany, but attempts to bring larger numbers of new settlers to the Cape proved futile. When this question was receiving special attention, notably in the time of Governor de Chavonnes (1714–24), from van Imhoff in 1743 and from the Directors in 1750, the presence of slaves and other coloured labourers was stressed as the chief retarding factor. Van Imhoff made a great point of it and expressed regret that the slaves had not only made the colonists averse from manual work but were also keeping immigrants out. There was undoubtedly much truth in what he said, but, he like other critics of this kind before and after him, was prone to overrate the economic possibilities of the Cape. Such criticism did not give sufficient attention to the accumulating agricultural surplus which could not be disposed of. As early as 1717 the Cape Government warned the overseas authorities to refrain from sending out more colonists, and in 1751, when the Directors once more suggested increasing the flow of immigrants, the representatives of the rural population begged them not to do so, as the prospects of the rising generation in the colony were already bad enough.[1]

Overproduction of wine and grain, and ultimately also of meat, became chronic, and though the situation was now and again temporarily relieved by droughts or a sudden increased demand, the economic basis of the settlement remained fundamentally unsound. Short periods of almost hectic prosperity were followed by long stretches of severe depression. For a considerable time before the War of the Austrian Succession (1740–8) prosperity was at a very low

[1] Theal, *History of S. A.* 1652–1795, I, 436; II, 55–6. Van Riebeeck Society Publications, No. 1.

ebb. Several large English fleets then sailed into Table Bay for provisions, and Admiral Boscawen on his way to recapture Madras prolonged his visit to encamp his army on land and thoroughly recuperate his forces. The English were officially welcomed as allies, but it was the way they bought up the surplus produce that chiefly endeared them to the burghers. About 1750 times again became very bad, and towards the close of the decade the annual number of bankruptcies was appalling. Fortunately for the Cape, the Seven Years War had already begun and, before the end of 1758, a large French fleet with an army on board made its appearance. It was followed by an increasing number of English vessels, and by agents of the rival nations from St Helena and Mauritius, who remained to compete with each other in the Cape market. Prosperous years followed, even though in 1762 the Government, to ensure a sufficient supply for the Company, temporarily prohibited the sale of wine to strangers. This was in the time of Governor Ryk Tulbagh, whom we have already mentioned. He was an able, just and humane ruler, fully deserving of the high esteem in which he was held, but it was the good times that the Cape enjoyed during the latter part of his governorship that no doubt enhanced the reputation of "Father Tulbagh", as he was called. When he died, the pendulum had started swinging back again and, during the 'seventies, economic conditions rapidly grew worse than they had ever been before.

The recurrence of bad times, even in a very aggravated form, would not alone have led to the seething discontent which began to manifest itself in 1778. In that year, as a direct result of the surreptitious dissemination of revolutionary ideas, the whole system of government at the Cape and in particular the tyranny of some officials were discussed in private conversations and secret gatherings. Political interest was enormously stimulated, and even in quiet farmhouses quotations from Grotius, Pufendorf, Locke and other great constitutional teachers, contained in a couple of pamphlets that were being avidly read, were seriously considered by earnest-minded men, who reminded themselves that they were citizens of the free Dutch Republic, a state which had been liberated from the yoke of Spain by their own ancestors. It has usually been taken for granted that the revolt of the American colonies also exercised considerable influence at this time; but recent research has shown that people at the Cape during the 'seventies knew or thought very little of what was going on in America; they drew their inspiration from nearer home.[1] The fact that they were not unversed in self-government in local affairs made them less willing to submit to the evils of the general situation which they attributed to tyranny. In military matters, as we have seen, they had to a large extent been left to themselves. Their presbyterian church organisation also was strongly democratic, and

[1] Beyers, C., *Die Kaapse Patriotte*, pp. 169–81.

local government, too, was largely in the hands of the heads of families. Each rural district was under the control of an official (landdrost), but he was assisted in his judicial and administrative work by a council of burgher representatives (heemraden),[1] and even the assessment of taxes and the allocation of new farms was to a large extent carried out by them.

In the organs of central government in Cape Town, however, the colonists were far less effectively represented. A few Burgher Councillors had seats in the High Court of Justice, but they could be outvoted by the official members. The Burgher Councillors could exert some influence on the decisions of the Governor and his Council, which consisted of the chief officials, for it was customary to consult them when matters affecting the colonists were under consideration; but the arbitrary power of the bureaucracy in Cape Town, whose decisions were binding upon the whole settlement, was never in principle curtailed by any existing organs of popular government. Whether there was despotism at the Cape or not ultimately depended on the kind of Governor who happened to be in command and the men who occupied positions of authority under him. Unfortunately, Joachim van Plettenberg (1771–85), who succeeded Tulbagh, was inferior to his predecessor in ability and character, and the very important position of Independent Fiscal was filled by one Willem Boers, a narrow-minded, self-seeking and arrogant bureaucrat. As chief fiscal officer Boers had peculiarly wide and full powers, and the way in which he used and abused them caused intense exasperation.[2]

Early in 1779 a disreputable individual, Carel Buitendag, was summarily banished to India by decree of the Governor-in-Council. Excited meetings of protest took place. With increased fervour the political writings of Locke were quoted by the Patriots, as the malcontents styled themselves, to show that opposition to the misgovernment of bad rulers was an inalienable right of the subject, and the burghers with intense approbation heard it reiterated that their liberties were based not only on their citizenship of a free republic but also on the more fundamental laws of "God and Nature". No redress was to be expected from the Cape officials, and before the end of the year a small deputation, which included Tieleman Roos, the leader of the Paarl malcontents, had proceeded to Holland and laid a lengthy petition before the council of the XVII. It consisted partly of bitter complaints against the bureaucrats in Cape Town and particularly Boers, partly of drastic proposals in connection with the consitutional and economic policy of the Company at the Cape.[3] The petitioners begged *inter alia* that judicial reform should make it impossible, as in the case of Buitendag, for a man to be banished

[1] *Vide supra*, p. 130.
[2] Beyers, C., *Die Kaapse Patriotte*, pp. 132–4.
[3] *Ibid.* pp. 8–37.

without trial; that the High Court of Justice should consist of an equal number of civilian and official members; that seven "freely chosen" representatives of the burghers should be added to the Political Council; that these should be permitted to report directly to the overseas authorities on matters affecting the colonists; that the inhabitants of the settlement should be allowed to trade freely with Madagascar, the east coast of Africa and the Indian Archipelago, and that they should be permitted to send one or two ships to Holland every year in order to export their own produce.

Roos and his friends did not effect much. Their petition was referred to the Cape authorities for their remarks, and soon after, when Holland became embroiled in the American War of Independence, the Company was called upon to give its attention to much greater and more pressing worries. The main concession obtained was equal representation in the High Court of Justice. Spurred on by their friends at the Cape, Roos and his fellow-petitioners put the case before the States-General; but their liberal friends, the Dutch Patriots, who warmly sympathised with them, were not yet able to influence the Government of the Republic in their favour; hence their appeal proved fruitless. A second deputation in 1785 met with no more success, and the movement for reform at the Cape did not retain sufficient impetus to carry matters any further, one reason being that the good burghers there were once again, as a result of Anglo-French strife, experiencing a period of unparalleled prosperity.

The depression, which became serious soon after the death of Tulbagh in 1771, reached its climax in the beginning of 1781; but in June of that year a French fleet under Admiral de Suffren brought immediate relief. It had been dispatched to save the Cape from being taken by an English expedition under Commodore Johnstone, and de Suffren, after a brush with his opponent's ships off Santiago in the Cape Verde Islands, had managed to reach Table Bay a month ahead of him and so to strengthen its defences that though Johnstone captured some richly laden Dutch vessels in Saldanha Bay, he did not venture to attack Cape Town. The arrival of the French created a large demand for agricultural products, which had for a number of years been almost unsalable, and even when de Suffren had continued his voyage to India, the Cape market remained exceptionally good, for a French regiment was left behind and more vessels of the anti-British alliance came sailing in. Cape Town became a gay little town with a French theatre and with manners and morals that led to its being described as a miniature replica of Paris. Even after the end of the war by the Peace of Versailles (1783) the good times did not cease. India continued to loom large in the considerations of political and commercial circles, particularly in Great Britain and France, and an increasing number of foreign vessels visited the Cape. The war had furthermore thrown a vivid light on its strategic importance, and a garrison of between 2000 and 3000 men was maintained to ensure its safety. These factors alone would have been sufficient to ensure the prosperity of the colony, and were soon enhanced by the arrival of a new Governor with an ambitious outlook.

Jacob van de Graaff, who succeeded van Plettenberg in 1785, was a military officer of high rank in the army of the United Provinces, and a friend and protégé of the Prince of Orange. Resolved to enhance the importance of his government in the eyes of the world, he initiated building operations on a very large scale, as, for example, extensive fortifications and a large new hospital, and financed them with fiat money. Before the boom began the Cape Government had been so badly off for funds that it had been compelled to issue paper money representing a value of 900,000 rix-dollars; but when things improved, it had withdrawn the notes so rapidly that when van de Graaff arrived there were only 100,000 paper rix-dollars in circulation.[1] The new Governor in the course of five or six years increased this amount to 500,000 rix-dollars, but as in the case of previous issues, they remained practically at par. Though the Company was piling up its debts, the credit of the Cape Government, which guaranteed these issues of paper money, was unquestioned.

However unsound its basis soon proved to be, the pecuniary wealth of the settlement had indeed increased enormously, and a very enhanced standard of living was found in Cape Town and the adjacent agricultural areas. A few stately country residences had been erected previously, e.g. Groot Constantia and Vergelegen by the van der Stels, but it was particularly during this last period of prosperity under the Company that the burghers of Cape Town erected handsome flat-fronted dwellings, and those of Stellenbosch and the Paarl built the many fine gabled farmhouses which still add dignity and charm to their countryside.

The time of prosperity passed with disconcerting suddenness. The Cape had often experienced rapid economic fluctuations, but never had it been subjected to so abrupt a crash as when it was plunged into its last and most serious depression under Dutch rule. The Company, as we have said, had been piling up enormous debts. These grew from $7\frac{1}{2}$ million guilders in 1778 to $26\frac{1}{2}$ million in 1783 and 81 million in 1790,[2] while the Company was getting ever smaller returns from the East Indies with which to pay the interest. During the American War the British frigates had swept up scores of the Company's ships as prizes, and for a number of years its trade oversea was practically at a standstill. No commercial body could stand such losses and the Company was clearly tottering to an inglorious end. The bulk of the loans by which its existence had been prolonged had been provided by the States of Holland, and that dominating legislature in the

[1] One rix-dollar was worth four shillings.

[2] One guilder was worth one shilling and eightpence.

Netherlands insisted on immediate administrative and financial reforms in the Company's affairs.

The Directors at long last were moved to take action; hence in February 1791, they sent the Cape authorities summary instructions to eradicate abuses and reduce expenditure in every possible way. The building operations of the Government were to be stopped forthwith and the slaves and others employed upon them be sold or discharged, the spendthrift Governor was recalled, and the additional regiment with which the garrison had been strengthened since 1779 was ordered to proceed to Batavia. The bubble of spurious prosperity was effectively pricked, and when about fifteen months later two Special Commissioners, Sebastian Nederburgh and Simon Frykenius, took control with a view to applying more effectively the new policy of economy and reform, conditions had become appalling. "We find", they wrote, "the major portion of the population financially ruined; the rolls of the Court of Justice at each session filled with demands for the payment of debts, and piles of orders-of-court awaiting execution, since the dire needs of creditors make it impossible for them to allow debtors any extensions of time; hard currency, so to speak, banished from the colony; fixed property in consequence rendered almost wholly valueless; people of means together with those possessing none threatened with complete ruin, and signs of general dissatisfaction and bitterness everywhere." Faced with this position and the necessity of balancing revenue and expenditure, the Commissioners, even after reducing administrative costs, had to resort to new and increased levies on estates and sales. Trade as a result became even more stagnant, and the income of the Government remained inadequate, for the colonists were already seriously in arrear with such payments as they could evade.

In 1792 barely 25 per cent of the total sums due for rent on loan farms was collected, and with every month the farmers were becoming even less able and willing to strengthen the financial resources of the Government. The Commissioners tried to assist the farming community by instituting a Loan Bank, but as its capital was obtained from additions to the paper currency, this inflation was bringing about rapid depreciation. When in 1793 the Commissioners proceeded to India leaving Abraham Sluysken, newly arrived from Batavia, to carry on as best he could as Commissioner-General, the economic system of the Company at the Cape may be said to have collapsed. Two years later the international storm blowing from Paris whirled the settlement into a financial condition even worse than that which Nederburgh and Frykenius had described and foretold in 1792.

Politically also the régime of the Company at the Cape ended in a débâcle, the reason being its inability to assert itself as a government in the new conflict between Boer and Bantu on the eastern border. The Xhosa vanguard of the Bantu had been living for a considerable time in the vicinity of the Kei River; but on the death in 1775 of their great chief, Palo, the tenth of his line, succession troubles split the tribe into two main sections under Galeka and Rarabe, and the adherents of the latter received the impetus which sent some groups under minor chiefs across the Fish River, where they encroached on ground in the area of European occupation. The two opposing streams of migration, European and Bantu, having met, a clash was inevitable, for both peoples were pastoralists constantly on the look out for new pastures and water-holes, and the fact that the Afrikaner cattle and sheep of the European graziers, a heritage of their barter with the Hottentots, were practically identical with those owned by the Xhosas made stock-lifting easy. As always in frontier troubles, disputes arose over the ownership of cattle and the Xhosas were accused by the Boers of driving into their kraals beasts that did not belong to them.

In 1778 Governor van Plettenberg had visited the eastern borderlands and had agreed with some minor chiefs that the middle reaches of the Fish River should be the dividing line between European and Bantu. In spite of this, trouble broke out in the winter of 1779, when months of drought and further intertribal bickerings brought large numbers of Xhosas on the warpath and eventually led to sudden and extensive raids against the border farmers. As often happened afterwards on similar occasions, these latter were not immediately able to offer much resistance, for they were scattered and must first obtain the consent of the Government for concerted action on their part. A number of whites were killed, many farm dwellings were plundered and burnt, and the Xhosas retired with thousands of looted cattle. In 1781 the tables were turned. A commando under Adriaan van Jaarsveld completely routed the marauders, recovered much booty, dislodged the Xhosas even from the woody fastnesses of the Zuurveld and drove them back over the Fish River.

We may say that the policy adopted with regard to the Xhosas at this stage was one of segregation by force of arms. The Chiefs were told that they must keep their people from crossing the Fish River, and for a number of years there was peace on the border. In other respects also more settled conditions began to prevail. The frontiersmen had begged Governor van Plettenberg, when he visited them in 1778, to establish an administrative and church centre in their midst. This boon was granted them by his successor, van de Graaff, when, in December 1785, the eastern borderlands became a new district. It was called Graaff-Reinet after the Governor and his wife, and the customary procedure of giving the seat of the landdrost the same name was followed. Two loan farms on the Sunday River were expropriated at a valuation of 2650 rix-dollars, and here

Maurits Woeke, the first landdrost, began to preside over a new local Council of Heemraden. The election of elders and deacons soon followed, and a simple church was built and a parish schoolmaster appointed. As regards military matters also Graaff-Reinet became a separate unit under the border commandant, Adriaan van Jaarsveld.

Disturbing reports regarding the Xhosas began to reach Cape Town at this time. Rarabe had died in 1781, leaving an infant grandson, Gaika, to succeed him. During Gaika's minority his uncle Ndlambi was Regent, but the latter's authority was not recognised by all the Rarabes, and their mutual quarrels again threatened to embroil the borderlands in war. An increasing number of Xhosas were crossing the Fish River, and Woeke's suggestion that a commando should be called out to stop this irruption was rejected by the authorities in Cape Town. Not only had they standing instructions from the Company to avoid conflicts with the Natives, but a new and very potent factor was also beginning to influence native policy at the Cape in the late 'eighties of the century. The Rev. Ritzema van Lier, a young religious enthusiast who had come out from Holland in 1786 imbued with the intense fervour for missionary work which was common in devotional circles in Europe at that time, was attracting a zealous following, and Johann Reichel, a representative of the Moravian Missionary Society, who arrived in 1787, strengthened the movement. Influential officials of the Company gave it their support. Amongst them was young Honoratus Maynier, and to him was entrusted the responsibility for settling the difficulties which had again arisen on the border, Thus, in 1789, he went to Graaff-Reinet to demonstrate to Woeke the effectiveness of the new official policy of negrophile philanthropy and to teach the frontiersmen the elements of the rule of law.[1]

The frontiersmen believed that if van Jaarsveld had again been allowed to chastise the intruding Xhosas in accordance with the old policy, he would soon have allayed unrest, for his commando had already driven the marauders back against the Fish River, which was in flood and difficult to cross, and might well hope for a decisive victory. As it was, they were compelled to stay their hand; the commando was disbanded, and Maynier arranged a benevolent peace with the enemy. The Chiefs received presents and, their friendship having thus, as he thought, been assured, they were allowed to retain the fruits of their raids and to remain in the territory where these had been perpetrated. This kind of peace reduced the border farmers to an even worse plight than that of the agriculturists of the west. Many cattle were stolen and an alarming number of homesteads burnt, while the burghers, who, if they had been permitted to organise their forces against the Xhosas, would have been quite capable of

[1] Marais, J. S., *Maynier and the First Boer Republic.*

defending their lives and property, were not allowed to do so. Maynier negotiated a second "peace" in 1793 on similar lines to that of 1789 and with equally disastrous consequences, and when repeated petitions to the authorities in Cape Town had proved fruitless, the border farmers under the leadership of van Jaarsveld at last refused, early in 1795, to submit any longer to the authority of the Dutch East India Company, which by the misguided actions of its representative had brought them to such a serious pass. Maynier was driven out and compelled to return to Cape Town and the frontiersmen set up a government of their own.

Though this revolt of the men of Graaff-Reinet was not really due to any revolutionary influences from oversea, they had a vague idea that they were following in the footsteps of the French revolutionaries, for we find them denouncing their bureaucratic oppressors as "aristocrats", calling the gathering, which placed governing powers in the hands of a council of "representatives of the people", their "national assembly" and electing Carel David Gerotz as president and van Jaarsveld as military leader. The truth was that they refused allegiance to the Company because it had in effect ceased to exercise authority in the chaos which it had allowed to develop on the border, and which it prevented them from terminating, but they stressed their desire to remain loyal subjects of the States-General. Swellendam, the adjacent southern district, immediately followed the example of Graaff-Reinet, so that by August 1795 the control of the Company's government in Cape Town was definitely repudiated over practically the whole wide expanse which had been added to the settlement towards the east by the first "Great Trek".

In the very same week that Graaff-Reinet proclaimed its independence, a British fleet appeared in Simon's Bay in pursuit of the aims of a world war and caring nothing for the internal affairs of the Cape as such. It came with the authority of the Prince of Orange, by that time an exile in England. On 16 September 1795, after a prolonged but half-hearted resistance, which we shall describe in our next chapter, the Company's forces laid down their arms and surrendered the Castle of Cape Town and with it the whole colony into the hands of the British commander.[1] A fresh era began, but before we pass from the old to the new, from the days of the Company to the problems of the new time, it seems fitting to pause for a moment and consider what manner of community it was that thus became associated with the British Empire.

In 1795 the number of European colonists totalled nearly 20,000. According to the census figures for 1798 it was 21,746, divided as follows: in Cape Town and the Cape district 6261, in Stellenbosch 7256, in Swellendam 3967 and in Graaff-Reinet 4262. There were

[1] *Vide infra*, pp. 176 *sqq.*

more than 25,000 slaves, 80 per cent of whom were found in Cape Town and its adjoining rural areas and in Stellenbosch. In Graaff-Reinet there were less than a thousand slaves. In this border district and Swellendam Hottentots were largely employed as farm-labourers, but many of them were not in service. In 1798 it was estimated that 15,000 Hottentots were living within the borders of the colony, and of these, 14,000 were to be found in Swellendam and Graaff-Reinet. They were still largely pastoral nomads, but the erstwhile large tribes had practically all been split up into insignificant groups. Of the Bushmen no numerical records are available, but their number was negligible.

The colony stretched from the west coast to the Great Fish River, a distance of 500 miles, and its northern border ran from the Buffels River, 300 miles north of Cape Town in the arid north-west, to the Stormberg in the east. In this large area Cape Town was the only important urban centre. It had a population of about 15,000, of whom one-third were Europeans. The town of Stellenbosch had a thousand inhabitants and seventy residences. Paarl was a relatively thickly populated rural community with a church in its midst. Zwartlands-Kerk (Malmesbury) and Roodezands-Kerk (Tulbagh), as the names indicate, were merely church centres with only a few dwellings apiece. Swellendam had about thirty houses, and Graaff-Reinet, according to Barrow, who visited it soon after the establishment of British rule at the Cape, consisted of "a dozen mudhouses covered with thatch".[1] The European population was therefore scattered over a large area and was preponderantly rural.

As regards standard of living and culture there was a considerable difference between the settled agriculturalists of the south-west and the pioneers of the interior and the south-east coastal region. The former, notwithstanding their frequent inability to find a satisfactory market for their produce, were on the whole living comfortably, and, as appeared in 1779, they had not lost contact with what was being thought and written in the Netherlands. They lived in good houses, and their farms largely supplied them with what they required for their bodily welfare. Lichtenstein, who spent several years at the Cape during the period of Batavian rule (1803–6), stresses the material self-sufficiency of the agriculturalists, and he quotes examples of farms visited by him, which to his mind could be compared with "small independent states".[2] The owner of such a farm in some cases possessed scores of horses, hundreds of horned cattle and thousands of sheep besides large gardens and tilled lands. His family, servants and slaves sometimes comprised a hundred individuals, and he fed them mainly on what the farm produced, having to purchase only sugar, tea, coffee and other luxuries for this purpose. He had further to

[1] Barrow, Sir John, *Travels into the Interior of Southern Africa*, 1806.
[2] Lichtenstein, M. H. C., *Travels in Southern Africa*, 1812–15.

send to Cape Town for arms, ammunition, textiles, implements, household ware, iron, lead and superior timber; but he had skilled craftsmen on his farm for putting up buildings and making furniture, and he could do without new supplies of imported goods for long periods, when circumstances necessitated his so doing. For several generations these *seigneurs* of the Cape and also the smaller farmers were forced to rely on their own resources, and resourceful self-reliance had become natural to them. They were kindly and simple folk, and all travellers agreed that their hospitality was almost overwhelming, but they were imbued with a spirit of vigorous independence.

The pioneers of Swellendam and Graaff-Reinet generally lived much more primitively. Many of them spent a considerable part of their lives on trek in hooded waggons, and most of their houses were even poorer than those seen in Graaff-Reinet by Barrow and consisted of only a few rooms each. Far removed from the amenities which closer proximity to Cape Town could offer, these graziers learned to subsist largely on the simple diet which the chase, their flocks and herds and milch cows and the somewhat uncertain results of their attempts at wheat-growing and gardening could provide. A supply of coffee, tea and sugar was usually also available. This, as well as other necessities such as ammunition, guns, cloth, etc., was obtained when ox-waggons from all parts of the interior, which annually conveyed salted butter and home-made soap to Cape Town, came lumbering back after months of travel. Droves of sheep and cattle, bought by agents of the Company on the inland farms and making even slower progress on their way to the Cape market, constituted the main source of ready money for the pioneers, who kept their rix-dollars in wooden waggon-chests. They possessed less pecuniary wealth than the agriculturalists and indeed needed it less, the circumstances of their existence having inured them to hard and simple lives. Their cultural contacts were limited, and one reason why they received a stranger with much hospitality was because interesting news could be expected from him. Their literary attainments were small, being generally restricted to the ability to use the Bible and hymn-books for the daily family devotions.

Towards the end of the century the evangelical religious movement of the Rev. Ritzema van Lier, which we mentioned above, began in the south-east to mitigate and humanise the somewhat frigid dogmatism of eighteenth-century Calvinism, but the colonists in the interior in 1795 had not yet experienced this revival of religious fervour. Their creed played a great part in their lives, but it was an austere creed in which missionary zeal had no place. It served rather to strengthen in them a conviction that, compared with the Natives, they were a chosen people, and their primary concern in their dealings first with the Hottentots and later with the Xhosas was to imbue these peoples with a proper sense of the superior authority of the white man. This attitude undoubtedly led to abuses, as was sufficiently proved, for instance, by a judicial investigation, the so-called "Black Circuit" of 1812;[1] nevertheless, the eastern pioneers must as a class be absolved from the charge of having wantonly oppressed the Natives. They defended what they regarded as their rights and just interests, and they did so sometimes with a heavy hand, but cruelty did not become a characteristic trait amongst them. Circumstances imposed upon them the necessity of fending for themselves and inevitably hardened them, but the outcome was not moral deterioration. As could be expected from a virile race, the chief result was that they became even more self-sufficient and self-reliant than their kinsmen nearer to Cape Town.

The differences between the agriculturalists of the south-west and the pastoralists of the interior should not be over-accentuated. They were of the same Dutch, French and German origin and were in fact closely interrelated. There were probably few graziers in the borderlands without kinsfolk in the older settled area, and a frontiersman on his annual visit to Cape Town might use the occasion to exchange greetings with a brother living in Stellenbosch. They spoke the same language, for the transformation of Dutch into a new language, Afrikaans, had been completed and become general before the end of the eighteenth century. This new language was firmly established as regards structure, showed few variations with localities and, except in small official circles, was the only medium of conversation used throughout the settlement. Dutch was still the written language of the colonists and, as has been stated, the ability to read it was fairly general amongst them. They required this ability in order to become church members, for Calvinism presupposes that its adherents must themselves read the Word of God and the Heidelberg Catechism, and no pioneer, however far his wanderings might take him, would forgo the privilege of being enrolled as a member of the Dutch Reformed Church. These two bonds, a common and distinctive language and a common Church, were probably the strongest links that drew the South African colonists together. They were further connected by their experience of and attachment to constitutional arrangements, e.g. the Boards of Heemraden and the Commando system, which gave them an important share in the government of their country, and which tended to increase amongst them all that spirit of independence that their economic conditions and their general environment also promoted.

The colonists were indeed essentially one people. The differences between those living in fine residences in the south-west and those who inhabited little mudhouses on the border were in fact mainly due to temporary differences in environment, and it is interesting to

[1] *Vide infra*, pp. 208, 290 *sqq*.

note that, as soon as circumstances allowed them to do so, the pioneers also started to erect more suitable dwellings and to develop farms, which could bear comparison with those of the south-western agriculturalists. One reads in Lichtenstein of good houses, surrounded by extensive irrigated lands and gardens even in the remote Sneeuwberg area along the northern confines of Graaff-Reinet, and of patriarchal masters, owning great flocks and herds and with many children and servants under their command, exercising lordly sway over such domains. The patriarch of the Sneeuwberg was the border counterpart of the *seigneur* of the Eerste River.

Such, in brief, was the community, the nation of the Boers, which in 1795 for the first time came into intimate contact with the British Empire.

CHAPTER VII

THE BRITISH OCCUPATIONS

1795–1806

THROUGHOUT the eighteenth century the Netherlands were declining from maritime and commercial primacy to comparative impotence. Like their Portuguese predecessors the Dutch found the maintenance of a world-wide commercial system an increasingly rapid drain upon their limited man-power and resources. Their great East India Company, weakened by official corruption within and by the pressure from its rival, the English Company, came in the late 'seventies within sight of bankruptcy. When France developed grandiose schemes in Europe and overseas which brought her into conflict with Britain, the enfeebled Republic of the Netherlands, because of its geographical position and because it held the Cape and Ceylon, the keys of India, was inevitably embroiled in the struggle. For the Cape the days of sluggish peaceful isolation were numbered.

"What was a feather in the hands of Holland", wrote Captain Blankett, "will become a sword in the hands of France."[1] So long as the Cape of Good Hope was merely a half-way house to the Eastern Seas, a useful depot held by a small and friendly power, there was no reason why the Boer farmer should not continue to live his life undisturbed; but when the genius of Clive and Warren Hastings laid the foundations of a vast British-Indian Empire, the Cape became strategically of the first importance. It was an "island" fortress guarding the entrance to the Indian Ocean and, as such, it must be kept at all costs out of the hands of the Gallic rival who was threatening the independence of its Dutch owner. "The importance of the Cape with regard to ourselves", wrote Sir Francis Baring, a Director of the East India Company, "consists more from the detriment which would result to us if it was in the hands of France, than from any advantage we can possibly derive from it as a colony. It commands the passage to and from India as effectively as Gibraltar doth the Mediterranean."[2] But in another letter to Secretary Dundas advocating British intervention, he added a warning: "as a colony it would be rather dangerous (than otherwise), as there is too much encouragement for settlers, and we have already too many drains upon our own population."[3] Until after the end of the Napoleonic War the British regarded the Cape as nothing more than a valuable fortress, an

[1] Capt. John Blankett, R.N., to Under-Secretary (Sir) Evan Nepean, 25 January 1795, *Records of the Cape Colony*, ed. G. M. Theal, I, 26.

[2] Baring to Dundas, 12 January 1795, *ibid.* I, 22–3.

[3] Baring to Dundas, 4 January 1795, *ibid.* I, 17.

outwork of the Indian defence system. For that reason they were most anxious to conciliate the Dutch settlers. The last thing that any of their statesmen desired, while their country was fighting for her existence, was to weaken her resources by pouring British settlers into Cape Colony or to engage in social or political reconstruction there.

In the new British policy of commercial empire which followed the break-up of the old colonial system,[1] India was the focal point, and thus the Cape assumed a strategical importance in the eyes of British statesmen that was commercial as well as military. It lay on the trade route between Europe and the Eastern Seas, but it was also a half-way house between Asia and America. After 1783 Englishmen viewed with concern the penetration of ships from the United States into Indian and Chinese waters, and as regards South America, if the plans of British statesmen came to fruition, the Cape would be a link in a triangular system with its three points at London, the River Plate and India. "The produce as well as the locality of the Cape command the Coast of Africa; . . . Madagascar and the Brazils depend on the system that may be adopted. The Americans who still persevere in their trade to India and China, might be supplied at the Cape and be the means of introducing a beneficial trade instead of the contraband they now strive to continue."[2] Naturally these considerations were not lost upon Henry Dundas, the shrewd and energetic Secretary of State who fathered the new policy, and who from 1784 until his retirement from office in April 1805 was unofficial Minister for India. There can be little doubt that Dundas's interest in the Cape and his appreciation of the importance of acquiring it, should the opportunity arise, dated from the very beginning of his connection with Indian affairs.[3] The causes of the failure of the expedition under Commodore Johnstone in 1781, which was sent to occupy the Cape when the United Provinces joined France in the American War, received his careful attention. The French occupation of the Cape Peninsula in that year under Admiral de Suffren marked the beginning of a new stage in the European invasion of South Africa of which the Dutch settlement had been the advance-guard.[4]

After that war the struggle between Great Britain and France continued in a series of diplomatic battles centring round the Dutch. On the one side, the Orange party in the Netherlands strove to maintain its ascendancy with British assistance: on the other, the "Patriots", the middle-class opposition, sought to gain predominance with the co-operation of France. The political and commercial alliance between Dutch and French in 1785 was a serious blow to the British,

[1] See *C.H.B.E.* vol. II.

[2] Capt. Blankett to Nepean, 25 January 1795, *Recs. of Cape Col.* I, 23–6.

[3] Furber, D., *Henry Dundas, First Viscount Melville*, 1742–1811, p. 63.

[4] *Vide supra*, p. 159. Cf. Harlow, *The Founding of the Second British Empire*, 1763–1793, I, 106–35.

which was, however, temporarily countered by the Triple Alliance of 1788 between the United Kingdom, Prussia and the Netherlands.[1] Under this arrangement the two Powers effected separate reinsurance treaties with the United Provinces. In both cases the system of government represented by the Hereditary Stadtholderate, vested in the House of Orange, was guaranteed against all forms of attack. In the event of war, the British and Dutch pledged themselves to afford each other specified armed assistance, neither side to make peace without the consent of the other. A separate clause provided for naval and military co-operation in the East, where British and Dutch officers were to assist each other in case of attack without orders from home. For the time being British interests in India had been safeguarded. It was under the terms of this treaty that the first British occupation of the Cape of Good Hope subsequently took place. But the unpopularity of an incompetent Stadtholder was enhanced by his dependence upon the protection of a foreign commercial rival, and ultimately enabled the forces of the French Revolution to supersede British influence in the name of liberty. That event opened a struggle between Great Britain and France in which the control of the Scheldt, the Cape of Good Hope and India were questions indissolubly linked.

While thus opposing French influence at the Hague, the British Government endeavoured to protect its eastern empire by two parallel lines of policy—territorially, by substituting British for French alliances with Indian potentates, and, commercially, by effecting a close co-operation between the English and Dutch East India Companies. As evidence of the dangerous weakness of the Dutch colonial empire accumulated at Downing Street and the aggressive propensities of the French revolutionary leaders developed, Dundas in 1791 propounded the terms of a bargain which had been in his mind for some years. Let the Dutch Company place all its settlements within "the benefit of British power and protection" in return for a guaranteed monopoly of the spice trade (which he regarded as of no value to Great Britain) and a share in the trade with China. The Dutch would be relieved of the heavy, and by now futile, expense of maintaining establishments in India itself as well as at places like the Cape of Good Hope, and their spice trade would be protected; while the British would be relieved of the upkeep of Penang[2] and be placed in an impregnable position as against the French. Understandably enough the Dutch declined this, as they had declined previous offers of a similar nature. There matters stood until the psychology of revolution imparted an entirely new vigour to French ambition.

On 16 November 1792, the French Convention issued a decree declaring the navigation of the Scheldt and the Meuse open to and

[1] See Cobban, A., *Ambassadors and Secret Agents: the diplomacy of the First Earl of Malmesbury at the Hague.*

[2] In Malaya; leased in 1786.

from the sea, notwithstanding that by long-standing treaties such navigation was absolutely controlled by the Dutch Republic within its borders; and on the same day General Dumouriez was authorised to pursue the Austrian enemy even into Dutch territory. The direct repercussion upon South Africa of that challenge is to be found in two events which quickly succeeded each other. On 2 February 1793, before war with France had formally begun, Lord Grenville, the British Foreign Secretary, wrote at the instance of the East India Company to Lord Auckland, ambassador at the Hague, instructing him to represent to the Dutch ministers that a French invasion of India from Mauritius or Réunion could be made impossible by cutting off food supplies from the Cape of Good Hope, and to suggest that a British garrison be sent thither from St Helena.[1] Within a fortnight the French point of view had been equally well illustrated by Dumouriez' proclamation to the Batavians, whom he adjured to throw off the tyranny of the Anglophile House of Orange. "Ne livre-t-il pas en ce moment vos Établissemens les plus importans, le Cape de Bonne Esperance, l'Isle de Ceylan, et tout votre commerce des Indes, à la seule nation dont vous avez à craindre l'incessante Rivalité!"[2]

Naturally enough the Stadtholder's party, although threatened with extinction at the hands of the Patriots and their French allies, were somewhat afraid of *Britannicos dona ferentes*. In March the States-General forbade the export of provisions from the Cape to the French islands, but they stood out for naval protection in place of the suggested military force. Towards the end of that month fear of France became temporarily uppermost, and a deputation from the Dutch Company asked Lord Auckland for British troops as well as ships to be sent to the Cape. Negotiations accordingly proceeded "d'agir du plus parfait concert avec l'Angleterre pour garantir les possessions dans l'Inde contre l'Ennemi commun", and the British Cabinet officially promised the desired support.[3] Dundas, with his perennial interest in the Cape in relation to India, watched the proceedings with anxiety. "The preservation of the Cape of Good Hope", he wrote to Grenville, "is an object of so much importance, both to Holland and Great Britain, it is impossible for this country to view with indifference any circumstance that can endanger the safety of that Settlement."[4] He would be glad to learn the military state of the Cape and how far the Dutch were disposed to admit British troops there for defensive and possibly offensive operations. Unfortunately for the realisation of Dundas's hopes, the fortunes of the Allied armies improved during May, June and July, and the Dutch changed their

[1] *Recs. of Cape Col.* I, I.

[2] *Ibid.* p. 3.

[3] For details of these negotiations see the correspondence between Grenville and Lord Auckland, with the Dutch enclosures from the latter, *ibid.* pp. 3–10.

[4] Dundas to Grenville, 23 April 1793, *ibid.* pp. 10–11.

minds. On May 23 P. J. Guepin, Chief Advocate of the Dutch Company, wrote to Lord Auckland supplying the desired information, but much exaggerating the military strength at the Cape and rehearsing all the previous arguments against the dispatch of British troops. If, despite the strong preference of the Dutch for a fleet, Great Britain insisted on sending a military force, then it must remain directly under the orders of the Dutch Company while stationed in a Dutch colony.[1] But to the minds of British ministers the authority of the Stadtholderate overseas was too precarious to admit of such a condition. An impasse had been reached.

The decisive events which occasioned the British occupation of the Cape took place in the winter of 1794–5, when the United Provinces were overrun by the troops of France and Amsterdam was entered in triumph. The Stadtholder and his chief supporters fled to England; the Batavian Republic was proclaimed and rapidly became a French appendage. Early in February 1795, the Company ordered all Dutch vessels to leave British ports and detained British vessels in their own. A month later the Patriots, now in control of the States-General, concluded a defensive and offensive alliance with France which was primarily designed against Great Britain. By this treaty the Dutch surrendered to French control half their naval and military forces and the right to garrison Flushing, and agreed to pay an indemnity of one hundred million Dutch florins.[2] In return they received the recognition of their independence. The imposition of such far-reaching conditions upon an important maritime and colonial power transformed the war from a European affair into a world-wide struggle in which the colonial aspect became increasingly prominent.

It was now clear that, unless the British Government took rapid action, the Cape as the key to India would become a French possession as effectively as Flushing. The necessity for action and the method which should be adopted had already been urged by Dundas in a letter to Grenville in November 1794. "If the French", he wrote, "either by conquest or treaty get possession of the seat and instruments of the Dutch Government, and have their senses about them, their first act will be to send a French force on board the Dutch shipping to the Cape and take possession of it. There are, I am afraid too many democrats and disaffected subjects there to leave any doubt of their being too cordially received. We must be beforehand with them, and the means of it are not difficult. . . . The foundation of the transaction", he continued, "ought to be a liberty to us to lodge at the Cape any force we please, to be protected as a Dutch possession, and for their behoof when peace is restored; but, in the meantime, to be defended at all events against any attempt of a French force to possess it. I am not sure but the Prince of Orange is

[1] Guepin to Lord Auckland, 23 May 1793, *Recs. of Cape Col.* I, 12–16.

[2] Say, £4,166,666 reckoning the florin (guilder) at one shilling and eightpence.

properly the head of the Dutch East India Company, and, as such, perhaps could give the order himself to admit our force at the Cape."[1]

The idea of a temporary occupation of Dutch settlements under the authority of Prince William was based on the Treaty of 1788 with the rehabilitated House of Orange, whereby Great Britain engaged to defend the Republic and its possessions against the French.[2] After some discussion it was adopted. On 1 February 1795, Grenville forwarded to the Duke of York a draft order for the Prince's signature, enjoining all Governors of Dutch colonies and forts to surrender possession of them to Great Britain as a protective measure against the enemy, such colonies and forts to be returned under solemn pledge as soon as independence and "its ancient and established Form of Government" had been restored to his afflicted country.[3] A week later Prince William at Kew issued orders to the Governor of the Cape and the naval officer commanding there to admit British troops and warships under the above conditions.[4] Little time was lost in taking advantage of these instructions. On April 3 two squadrons of six and four vessels, commanded respectively by Admiral Sir George Keith Elphinstone (later Lord Keith) and Commodore Blankett, sailed from England with a military force of close upon 1600 men under Major-General James Henry Craig. Some time later a third and much more formidable force, comprising fourteen ships and 5000 men and artillery under Major-General Alured Clarke, proceeded to San Salvador in Brazil, there to await events.[5] The two divisions of the advance expedition arrived at the same time and anchored off Simonstown in False Bay on June 11. Two days later Elphinstone and Craig sent an officer ashore to Commissioner-General Sluysken with the Prince of Orange's order and letter requesting admittance for the British force in accordance therewith.

Sluysken was in a very difficult position. His troops were approximately equal in number to the newcomers, but they were a motley array: burgher militia, mercenaries, Hottentot Pandours and Malays, and quite inadequate to man the massive system of batteries and earthworks that guarded Cape Town. The districts of Graaff-Reinet and Swellendam were in open revolt, regarding themselves as more or less independent republics.[6] On the other hand, the authority of an ex-Stadtholder was extremely doubtful, especially in view of the impending change over to the side of France of which rumours had reached the Cape. Sluysken therefore temporised to the great dis-

[1] Dundas to Grenville, 16 November 1794, *Hist. MSS. Comm.*, 14th Rept., App. pt. v. Dropmore MSS. II, 645–6 (hereinafter cited as *Dropmore Papers*).

[2] Walker, E. A., *History of S. Africa*, (1957 edn.), p. 120.

[3] *Recs. of Cape Col.* I, 26–8.

[4] *Ibid.* p. 28.

[5] See Elphinstone to Nepean, 4 July 1795, *ibid.* pp. 106–8.

[6] *Vide supra*, p. 164.

appointment of the British commanders, who with only 1500 men, and without cavalry, guns or money had no wish to fight. For the next fortnight a brisk correspondence took place, Elphinstone and Craig urging upon the Council of Policy and the inhabitants the good government and material prosperity that they had to offer in contrast to the Company's régime, and Sluysken playing for time.[1] But when definite news of the Franco-Batavian alliance reached him, the latter terminated negotiations, stopped the sale of fresh provisions to the British, and withdrew his forces to the strongly fortified position at Muizenberg. All hopes of a friendly and peaceful occupation were at an end. Gradually Craig landed his troops on the western shore of False Bay, and at last on August 7 launched an attack on Muizenberg supported by a barrage from the ships' guns. The steadiness of the British regulars and the flight of the German mercenaries, who had no desire to lose their lives in a cause with which they were out of sympathy, decided the day.

The situation for the British with 200 men down with scurvy was, however, very precarious. A frontal attack upon Cape Town and the Castle with its heavily-gunned batteries was out of the question, while Sluysken with his burgher militia was still in a strong position to defend the sandy and difficult tract of land between Muizenberg and Table Bay. Craig, in fact, was being compelled to put his force to a use for which it had not been intended. Within a week of arrival he had reported to Dundas that the attempt to gain admission in the name of the House of Orange had been a mistake and had reminded him that, with his small command, he was incapable of taking the colony by force.[2] On the same day Elphinstone had sent a fast sloop to General Clarke in Brazil, urging his instant departure for the Cape. A friendly British garrison was to be reinforced by an army of conquest. Clarke's instructions (dated 4 May 1795) had been issued only twelve days before the promulgation of the expected Franco-Batavian treaty, and they accordingly ordered him, in the event of Craig having met with a hostile reception, to take Cape Colony in King George III's name, a fact that governed the eventual capitulation.[3]

At San Salvador, where he had been courteously received by the Portuguese governor, Clarke was anxiously awaiting news with his fourteen ships in constant readiness to put to sea. Elphinstone's letter reached him on July 22, and he complied without delay. On September 3 he arrived at the Cape and none too soon[4]: for during the intervening months the small British advance force had suffered

[1] See the despatches of Elphinstone and Craig to Dundas with enclosures (letters to Sluysken, manifestoes to the inhabitants, etc.), *ibid.* pp. 52–108.

[2] Craig to Dundas, 16 June 1795, *Recs. of Cape Col.* pp. 52–6.

[3] See Walker, *Hist. of S. A.* p. 122. In the House of Commons in December Pitt cited the Cape with Martinique as a "conquest", *Parl. Hist.* XXXII, 585.

[4] *Recs. of Cape Col.* I, 109–10, 112–13, 119–21.

reverses at Retreat and the Steenberg, and Craig himself considered that he was getting the worst of it.[1]

With the arrival of Clarke's 5000 men and an ample supply of artillery the issue was virtually decided. After the failure of a final appeal to the Dutch to accept British protection, a general attack was launched. While the fleet threatened to bombard the Castle and batteries in Table Bay, though actually refraining from doing so, the army advanced against Sluysken's force on Wynberg Hill, nine miles from the capital. Deserted once again by the mercenaries (whose commanding officer seems to have received a substantial bribe from the British),[2] the burghers stood for a while and then broke. On September 16 a capitulation was signed at Rustenburg. Apart from the fact that the inhabitants were required to take an oath of allegiance to King George III "for so long a time as His said Majesty shall continue in possession of this colony" and that the rights and property of the Dutch Company were handed over, the conditions were basically the same as those originally offered three months before. The laws and customs of the inhabitants were to remain unaltered; no new taxes were to be levied and, where possible, burdensome ones to be abolished; for the first time the colony was to enjoy free internal trade, and external trade was to be regulated on generous lines—a promise which, as will be noted, was handsomely fulfilled. The paper money circulated by the Dutch Company, which amounted to 1,291,276 rix-dollars, was guaranteed by the new government on the understanding that the lands and buildings of the Company should continue to be the security for that portion of the paper (namely 631,521 rds) not issued on private mortgages.[3] It was not until 1797 that Lord Macartney discovered that the Company had never pledged their property as security, and that that property, if realised, could only redeem about a quarter of the paper. "It follows, therefore," he then wrote, "that the security as it is called of the lands and houses for the paper money is a mere illusion.... This paper is in fact a loan to the English Treasury, and may be annihilated by the Treasury remitting the amount in specie to buy it up."[4] The eventual redemption of the original and subsequent paper issues with a silver and copper coinage backed by Treasury bills in 1825 cost the British Exchequer £92,000.[5] Not the least of the grievances of the colonists against "Jan Compagnie" was this shoddy currency which was only exchangeable into the hard money of foreign merchants at a discount of between 20 and 30 per cent.

The régime of Craig, who was left to hold the Cape when Clarke and Elphinstone departed for India on November 15, is chiefly

[1] *Recs. of Cape Col.* pp. 148–53.
[2] See *Recs. of Cape Col.* I, 83, 230.
[3] Say, £258,255 and £126,304, reckoning the rix-dollar at four shillings.
[4] Macartney to Dundas, 20 October 1797, *ibid.* II, 188–94.
[5] *Vide infra*, p. 261.

important as revealing the nature of the first contact of British officials with the Afrikaner colonists. Craig himself was well fitted for his difficult position. Intensely interested in his task, he showed himself to be a vigorous, humane and scrupulously honest administrator. His lengthy and frequent despatches to Dundas are full of suggestions for conciliating the settlers, developing the prosperity of the Colony and removing abuses. He was a humanitarian Tory, who disliked the cruel treatment of a slave almost as much as he hated a Jacobin.

The Afrikaners with whom he had to deal were roughly divided into three types: the merchant and official class of Cape Town, the settled farmers of the Cape and south-western Stellenbosch districts and, thirdly, the cattle ranchers of Further Stellenbosch, Swellendam and Graaff-Reinet—frontiersmen true to the universal frontier type. These last were about to find themselves in a situation very similar to that of the French *habitants* of Quebec after 1760. Both represented the first wave of a European migration; in both regions there was a considerable interval between the arrival of the original pioneers and the incoming of Anglo-Saxons, an interval long enough for a distinctive French-Canadian and Dutch-South-African conciousness to strike deep roots. In both countries, too, the task, inevitably fraught with friction, of amalgamating the two racial elements into a new and united people has still to be achieved. Unfortunately the turmoil of adjustment in South Africa was to be exacerbated by the existence of a frontier problem of unique difficulty. Little did Ministers in London, with their conception of the Cape as an Indian fortess, realise that they might be undertaking responsibility for a colonial expansion compared with which American westward expansion had been simple. For whereas the American frontier was to be supplied from a broad base of thirteen wealthy and thickly populated communities, the South African—capable too of a vast extension—was manned by a mere handful, maintained from a single point and having no solid population base nearer than Europe.

As long as the British held the Cape under war conditions with an irresistibly strong garrison the implications of this situation did not fully emerge; but glimpses of the future were not lacking, for Cape Town differed in one vital respect from Gibraltar: it was dependent for its meat supply upon the hinterland, especially upon Graaff-Reinet, the home of the most turbulent and mobile frontiersmen. And these men were still maintaining the revolt against authority which they had begun against the Dutch Company. On 29 October 1795, they wrote to Craig explaining the reasons for their previous attitude. They had resisted, on the one hand, the extortionate monopolies and restrictions of the Company, and, on the other, what they called the perverse pro-native policy of Landdrost Maynier and his subordinates, who in the opinion of the burghers had imperilled their safety in face of the Kaffirs.[1] The obnoxious officials had accordingly been expelled and new Heemraden and military officers had been appointed by popular vote. Let Craig accept this arrangement, appoint a Landdrost, and supply them with ammunition with which to defend themselves.[2]

In reply Craig was firm but conciliatory. He accepted their nominee, Gerotz, as provisional Landdrost until Bresler, the man of his own choice, could take over; he had no wish to defend the oppressions of the previous Government: he had been instructed to do everything possible for the happiness and prosperity of the colonists, and he would see to it that the military force under his command was used to maintain order against all disturbers of the peace. Finally he trusted to their good judgment to prevent them from being led astray by "the specious pretence of liberty" which had plunged half Europe into "an abyss of Horror and Misery".[3] But Craig's conception of benevolent yet all-powerful governance from Cape Town was alien to the minds of an isolated community in which (to quote the words of a South African) "everybody would command and nobody would obey".[4] When Bresler arrived at the drostdy on 9 February 1796, a stormy meeting took place. The British flag was torn down and all refused to take the temporary oath of allegiance. After further fruitless negotiations Bresler departed for Cape Town and Craig prepared to use force. Three hundred men under Major King were sent to Stellenbosch in readiness to move against the village of Graaff-Reinet; all supplies of goods and ammunition were cut off, and a corps of Hottentots—successors of the Company's Pandours and a fruitful source of future grievance to the burghers—was enrolled for service in the interior.[5]

At this stage the British occupation of the Cape appeared to be in considerable danger. Although the majority of the people in the Cape, Stellenbosch and Swellendam districts had taken the oath, "nearly every man in the colony", Craig reported, "is our enemy".[6] It was known that a Batavian fleet under Admiral Engelbertus Lucas was on its way from Europe to recover the Cape, and that a French squadron had sailed from La Rochelle for the same destination. Strong naval and military reinforcements were hurried out from England and from Madras. When, therefore, Lucas anchored in

[1] J. S. Marais in his well-documented work, *Maynier and the First Boer Republics* (Cape Town, 1944), shows that Maynier was a humane realist rather than the sentimental visionary as portrayed by G. M. Theal and others. While active in defending the frontier zone, he incurred the hostility of the more turbulent of the Graaff-Reinet farmers by his insistence that durable security depended primarily on avoidance of cruel reprisals against the Xhosas and harsh treatment of Hottentot servants.

[2] Burghers of Graaff-Reinet to Craig, 29 October 1795, *Recs. of Cape Col.* I, pp. 208–10.

[3] Craig to Gerotz and the Burgher Officers of Graaff-Reinet, 23 November 1795, *Recs. of Cape Col.* I, 234–6.

[4] Memorial on the condition of the colony by G. Kersteins, *ibid.* pp. 167–75.

[5] See Theal, G. M., *History of South Africa since 1795*, I, 6 *et sqq.*

[6] Craig to Dundas, 22 September 1795, *Recs. of Cape Col.* I, 156.

Saldanha Bay, he was opposed by an army of 6500 men with eleven field guns and a naval force of fourteen warships. As Craig on land and Elphinstone (who had returned from India) with his ships, closed in upon the Batavian fleet, mutiny broke out among the Dutch crews, the majority of whom were of the Orange party. On August 17 Lucas surrendered. The officers were shipped back to the Netherlands, and a large number of the sailors enlisted under the British flag.[1] As for the French squadron, it proceeded to Mauritius, making no effort to effect a junction with the Batavians.

The news of this decisive display of British power convinced the Graaff-Reinet farmers that resistance for the time being was useless. The proposed march on the drostdy at Swellendam was cancelled, and on November 12 the malcontents offered their submission, provided that they might enter the Kaffir country to recover cattle when stolen and that they might be allowed to occupy land beyond the recognised boundary, that is to say, beyond the Fish River. It was the first of a series of such requests which culminated in the Great Trek.[2] On the following day the frontiersmen acknowledged with gratification the receipt of Craig's proclamation granting full pardon and promise of mild treatment, and appended an urgent appeal for powder and shot to replace that used in a recent commando, which they had been compelled to send out "as it has not yet pleased Providence to extirpate from this colony the rapacious Bosjesmen". The same plea for expansion had been made again and again by American backwoodsmen and was to be repeated by the squatters of New South Wales. And both would have endorsed the point of view of the Graaff-Reinet men about the Natives.

Craig's reply was not peculiar to himself or his generation: it was the standing official answer in respect of colonial frontiers. Not only did he refuse to accept elected Heemraden (on that point he was merely voicing his own generation), but he strictly enjoined the burghers to abstain from acts of hostility or injury to the Kaffirs. As for their request to occupy land beyond the boundary—"with what face can you ask of me to allow you to occupy lands which belong to other people? What right can I have to give you the property of others, and what blessing or protection could I expect from God were I to cause or even to encourage such a gross and glaring act of injustice? . . . Reflect for a moment on what would be your own sensations were you to hear that I was even debating on a proposal . . . to turn you out of your farms, and to give them to others." Make friends with the Kaffirs, he advised, and later on an amicable arrangement might be possible with them if territorial extension were to become necessary. Sardonic laughter must have echoed in the drostdy when that passage was read out. On the other hand, it

[1] For the correspondence between Elphistone and Lucas and other relevant documents, see *Recs. of Cape Col.* I, pp. 428–51.

[2] *Vide infra*, pp. 324 *sqq.*

would have warmed the heart of Lord Glenelg, the philanthrophic Colonial Secretary, thirty years later. The cardinal issue in future South African history was already plain to the eye.

A further illustration of the initial impact of British upon Afrikaner ideas is furnished by Craig's effort to induce the Court of Justice to modify the rigour of the criminal code, which in certain types of murder added to capital punishment the terrors of breaking on the wheel and other tortures. While assuring the Court that the British Government was very much alive to the necessity of maintaining "an exact subordination" among a numerous slave population, he suggested that without formally abolishing torture its application might cease in practice. The reply is reminiscent of some of the answers sent in by British West Indian planters during the slave enquiry of 1788. The mere deprivation of life was not a sufficient deterrent "unless accompanied by such cruel circumstances as greatly aggravate their bodily sufferings". Death by torture could safely be abolished as regards the free folk, but not for slaves who would thereby be encouraged to revolt. Moreover, the colonists would become alarmed for their own safety and would regard such a step as a subtle plan tending towards emancipation. The only sound policy was to encourage kinder treatment, especially in rewarding good work done by slaves, who would then become supporters of order, "instead of seeing it disturbed with pleasure as is the case at present". In a further letter Craig returned to the charge, urging that, if the experiment of a more humane legal procedure was worth trying, it could be done with greater safety then than at any previous time owing to the presence of an unusually strong military force. But the Court was not to be moved. After deep consideration, they replied that they could not feel that the suggested experiment "would be advisable at present" in view of "that misconceived fear of the inhabitants" to which they had previously referred. In other words, Craig himself must take the responsibility for any innovation, and that he was not empowered to do. He said no more, but copies of the correspondence went to London and led to the issue of instructions to Craig's successor, Lord Macartney, to abolish all forms of torture in criminal proceedings.[1]

A useful administrative reform announced by Craig was the replacement of the Committee of the High Court by a more popular body, the Burgher Senate, which consisted of six members, vacancies being filled by the Governor from a fourfold panel supplied by the Senate itself. Its multifarious duties comprised the furnishing of advice on all matters, other than judicial, which had previously fallen

[1] See Macartney's Instructions, 30 December 1796, *Recs. of Cape Col.* II, 3–19. That this reform was due to Craig's initiative is attested by Macartney himself in a letter to the Court of Justice, 17 May 1797, Macartney's Letter-Books, I, p. 5 (Afr. MSS. t. 2, Rhodes House Library, Oxford).

within the purview of the Burgher Councillors and the Commissioners of the High Court. Another measure of Craig's which did much to conciliate the colonists related to the currency problem. On October 1 he issued a proclamation fixing the rates of exchange between paper rix-dollars and British and Spanish coin. It was, of course, impossible to prevent the continued depreciation of the paper by such means, but the proclamation allayed the immediate fears of the colonists. Craig's interim régime, however, was drawing to a close. On 5 May 1797, Earl Macartney on arrival from England took the oaths of office as Military Governor of the colony, and on the following day invested General Craig with a well-deserved K.C.B. as a mark of the British Government's appreciation of his services.

The system of government inaugurated by Macartney was the result of protracted consideration in London. The British Ministers had been animated by the desire to win the loyalty of the Afrikaner colonists by every means in their power. On 15 April 1796 Dundas had written to Craig approving of his removal of the Dutch Company's restrictions. He expressed the hope that these concessions, while attaching the colonists to His Majesty's "just and mild Government", would be accepted "as an earnest of the liberal arrangements which will soon be carried into effect, and cannot fail to promote in a high degree the prosperity of that important colony".[1] Oppressive monopolies were accordingly prohibited, arrears of land-rent incurred before the conquest were cancelled, and liberty of conscience and of public worship were guaranteed. Public institutions were left untouched except for the introduction of necessary reforms in the judiciary and civil services. The High Court was reduced to a President and seven members with fixed salaries; the Governor and Lieutenant-Governor were constituted a Civil Court of Appeal in cases involving sums above £200 with a right of appeal to the Privy Council under certain conditions, and the powers of local Courts in similar cases were enlarged. An extremely important reform, which lack of funds had prevented the Dutch Company from instituting, was the substitution of fixed salaries for fees and perquisites in the case of minor officials. In general, the new Governor was instructed that the administration of justice "should as nearly as circumstances will permit, be exercised by you in conformity to the Laws and Institutions that subsisted under the ancient Government of the said Settlement".[2]

In matters commercial the Cape was accorded an exceptional position in the Empire. When, by Order-in-Council of 7 December 1796, the draft of Macartney's commission was submitted to the Committee for Trade and Plantations, the latter passed it on to the Law Officers of the Crown for their scrutiny and report, accompanied

[1] *Recs. of Cape Col.* I, 361–2.
[2] Macartney's Instructions, 30 December 1796, *ibid.* II, 3–19.

by the instruction: "That the Government intended thereby to be established is merely provisional, and that the question of the future government of the Cape is to be resolved for the consideration of His Majesty or of Parliament, as circumstances may require, and that it is not their Lordships' intention that as far as relates to the Commerce carried on in the Ports of the Cape, the Laws of Navigation should attach."[1] When the Law Officers objected that it was not within the power of His Majesty to exempt any colonial possession from the operation of 7 and 8 William III, cap. 22 and similar statutes by the terms of a commission, the Committee at once drafted a Bill for Parliament, which was enacted forthwith.[2] After reciting the fact that during the Dutch régime ships belonging to nations in amity with the United Provinces had been free to trade at the Cape, the Act authorised His Majesty in Council to make special regulations for a limited period to regulate the commerce of that dependency.[3] Under this authority an Order-in-Council of December 28 provided that goods imported from any part of His Majesty's dominions should have free entry, while the goods of friendly foreign Powers were to be admitted on paying duties to be fixed by the Governor. The only limitation upon this concession was the reservation of the East India Company's monopoly of trade to and from all parts east of the Cape.[4] In other words, Dundas through the Committee for Trade had secured special legislation in order that the Cape colonists should lose no material advantage enjoyed under their previous rulers. The hardship occasioned during Craig's interregnum by the application of the Navigation Laws, which excluded foreign goods at a time when British cargoes had not begun to arrive, had been noted and remedied.[5]

While conciliation and material advantage were thus held out, the Ministry was determined that imperial control should be absolute and direct. All civil and military power was concentrated in the hands of the Governor alone, unhampered even by an Advisory Council. The arrangement was an example of the new Crown Colony system as applied to "Colonies by Conquest" in the West Indies and elsewhere, and was induced by the desire for an impregnable imperial executive after the *débâcle* in North America. The case for a paternal despotism was exceptionally strong as regards the Cape. It continued the Dutch tradition and also appeared to its framers to be the most efficient method of retaining control of a fortress in time of war. In Macartney's commission and in his instructions emphasis was laid on the temporary nature of the system, and elaborate data were

[1] Minutes of the Committee for Trade and Plantations, 13 December 1796, B.T. 5/10 pp. 284–5 (P.R.O.).

[2] *Ibid.* pp. 286–95.

[3] *Statutes at Large*, 37 Geo. III, cap. 21.

[4] *Recs. of Cape Col.* II, 1–3.

[5] See *ibid.* I, 237–40, 266–7, 283–93, 300–2, 331–2, 353–9, 468–72.

called for to assist the Ministry in devising a more permanent form at a future date; but so convenient was this temporary system found to be that it remained substantially unaltered until 1828.

It is indicative of the importance which Dundas attached to the Cape that he selected such an outstanding administrator to be the first British Governor. Successively an Envoy-Extraordinary at St Petersburg, Chief Secretary to the Lord-Lieutenant of Ireland, Governor of Grenada and of Madras, and the head of an official commercial mission to the Emperor of China, Macartney had gained an exceptionally varied experience as a public servant and won a high reputation. He also, as on previous occasions, set a high price on his services, and Dundas was evidently prepared to pay it for the sake of his favourite project at the Cape, and agreed that he should receive the lavish salary of £10,000 a year besides a table allowance of £2000 and the promise of a pension from the Cape Treasury of £2000 on retirement. The emoluments of the Governor taken with the salaries of the other English officials amounted to an annual charge of £24,700 a year, payable in sterling. It is true that this was no immediate hardship to the colonists, since the revenue, which had stood at £25,153 (125,769 rix-dollars) in the year 1795–6, rose to £64,502 (322,512 rds.) two years later, and for the period 1797 to 1802 maintained an average of £73,518 a year. The tradesfolk and merchants of Cape Town enjoyed a period of unparalleled prosperity, but the situation was highly artificial. An impoverished colony with almost negligible exports was called upon to support a heavy superstructure out of the profits of a temporary war boom. When under peace conditions the Cape returned to its normal economic level, hard times were experienced until expenditure was reduced in proportion. Meanwhile, however, Dundas was prepared to spend lavishly to secure the best possible service.

Macartney had been sought as one who could be relied on not only as a strong Governor but also as an expert adviser. From practical knowledge of Far Eastern commerce he would be able to estimate the value of the colony as a British possession and so provide Dundas with evidence to convince Pitt and Grenville and the East India Company of the necessity for its retention. In his first despatch Macartney began to supply the desired information. As a market for British manufactures the Colony was not worth consideration; nor was there much hope of making it an entrepôt for a lucrative trade with equatorial Africa and the Arab merchants of the almost unknown East Coast, an idea which had been frequently urged in recent years by West African adventurers.[1] On the other hand, the colony would prove expensive, for the garrison and the fleet stationed there would involve an annual charge upon the Treasury of approximately a quarter of a million sterling. But he was convinced

[1] Cf. Memo. by Donald Campbell, *Recs. of Cape Col.* I, 137–40.

that, despite the failure of commercial hopes and the heavy expense, it was infinitely worth keeping. "Its chief importance to us", he wrote, "arises from its geographical position, from its forming the master link of connection between the western and eastern world, from its being the great outwork of our Asiatic commerce and Indian Empire." And above all, he continued, if it fell into the hands of a powerful enemy, "it might enable him to shake to the foundation, perhaps overturn and destroy, the whole fabric of our oriental opulence and dominion".[1] Looking at the Cape from this oriental point of view it is not surprising that he repeatedly advocated that on the termination of war it should be transferred to the control of the East India Company, on the ground that the autocratic powers exercised by the Dutch Company could be handed on to its English successor—powers which, if vested in the Crown, might cause resentment among "the ignorant and disaffected".[2] He did, however, propose a partial check on the power of the Governor, which unfortunately was not adopted. He suggested a Council of three "principally to consult, advise, administer, and superintend all the business of the Colony, subject to the control and decision of the Governor whenever he might think fit to assume the responsibility".

Unfortunately for Macartney's plan, the Company was far from being convinced that the acquisition of the Cape was of benefit to them; rather the reverse. The strategical argument, they held, was weak, for if Great Britain retained supremacy by sea there was little need for an intermediate base. Also it was better to have the powerful Cape garrison in India itself than waiting for an emergency on the other side of the Indian Ocean. And the existence of Cape Town as a British free port was directly injurious, because it greatly assisted the swarms of English, Dutch and French, masquerading as neutrals, who stole their trade.[3] The negative attitude which these considerations induced among the Directors aroused considerable irritation in the minds of both Macartney and Dundas. On 27 November 1797 the former complained that he, as well as the Madras Government, was still ignorant of the Company's intentions with regard to the method to be employed in supplying the Cape with Eastern goods, and that the colonists were suffering great inconvenience in consequence. Eight months later he informed Dundas that by letters received from home "it would seem as if there were not wanting some gentlemen in Leadenhall Street, who affected to disparage or undervalue this colony. If this be the real opinion of the Company, and the Cape should slip from us, *Tempus erit magno cum optaverit emptum*."[4] On his

[1] Macartney to Dundas, 10 July 1797, *ibid.* II, 112–21. [2] *Ibid.* p. 214.

[3] The records of this period are full of complaints and reports on this illicit traffic. British interlopers appear to have been the worst offenders, acquiring citizenship in some neutral country to which they brought back their Eastern cargoes.

[4] Macartney to Dundas, *Recs. of Cape Col.* I, pp. 204–6, 265–6. The quotation is from Virgil, *Aeneid* x, l. 503.

side Dundas forwarded Macartney's complaints to the Court of Directors and stirred them to activity in framing the requisite regulations. In reply to the Governor he remarked that since the prejudice of the Court of Directors against the Cape did not appear to involve very serious consequences in time of war, he was not disposed for the present "to bring them to any new issue upon the points on which we differ".[1] Soon, however, the imperialist Secretary was to be involved in a losing battle for the retention of the Cape under any conditions.

While Macartney was taking part in the struggle over the Cape which was developing behind the scenes in London, he was ruling the colonists with inelastic efficiency. The even-handed justice of "the old Lord", as he was called, was respected and admired, but failed to conciliate or gain affection. In private he could be the most charming of men, as his letters to Lady Anne Barnard attest; but as an official he met presumption with hauteur, and disobedience with uncompromising severity. His letter-book containing copies of his official correspondence within the colony provides a clear picture of both these aspects of his régime. On 10 February 1798 he addressed a characteristic letter to the Burgher Senate, who, notwithstanding a previous refusal, had importuned him to permit the importation of slaves (of which there was an acute shortage) from the East Coast. He again refused, with the comment that he would be better pleased, if, instead of petitioning for things which could not be granted, they would devote their energies to the lighting and repair of the streets, which "still continue in a condition disgraceful to the police of a civilised city".[2] The long tussle between the Governor and the disgruntled Burgher Senate on the matter of road repairs and the provision of street lamps engendered considerable friction without achieving much improvement in the desired direction.[3] As for the townsfolk of Cape Town itself, the situation was very similar to that obtaining in French Quebec. One party maintained friendly relations with the officers and officials of the Castle, taking part in musical evenings and other similar social relaxations, and were heartily disliked by the rest, who held sullenly aloof. Now that the British were firmly in the saddle some of the latter evinced a desire to be included in Government circles, but found that their presence was not welcomed by their more successful rivals.[4]

Further afield Macartney was fortunate in having no trouble from Swellendam or Graaff-Reinet, where the burghers, disappointed in

[1] Dundas to Macartney, *ibid.*, pp. 309–13. Cf. the correspondence between Dundas and Hugh Inglis, Chairman of the Court of Directors, Afr. MSS. t. 4, ff. 8–15, Rhodes House Library, Oxford (from the Melville Collection).

[2] Macartney Letter Books, 1, p. 248.

[3] See further letters on this subject to the Burgher Senate, *ibid.* pp. 98, 131–2, 359–61, 386–7.

[4] Fairbridge, D., *Lady Anne Barnard at the Cape of Good Hope*, 1797–1802, p. 146.

their hopes of French or Batavian support, were disposed to accept the situation for the time being. But the banishment of Commandant Delport without trial, although legal under the powers with which his commission vested him, was a tactical blunder. Macartney's frontier policy was aptly summarised by himself, when he instructed Landdrost Bresler of Graaff-Reinet "to restore the tranquillity of that country, to give the inhabitants a proper confidence in the benignity of the present Government towards them, and at the same time impress them with a dread of its resentment in case of their abusing it".[1] Brave words and fairly intended; but they were even more difficult of fulfilment in the case of Kaffirs and Bushmen than of the burghers. The exploratory tour conducted by Bresler and John Barrow across the Great Fish River into Kaffirland as far east as the Keiskamma River provided the latter with the material for his narrative, which, while condemning barbarities inflicted upon unoffending Natives, did little more than reveal the complexities of the frontier situation.[2] Under orders from the Governor they tried to arrange a *modus vivendi* on the basis of non-intercourse between European and Native. The farmers of Tarka, Sneeuwberg and the Zuurveld on the far eastern and north-eastern frontier, who had been driven from their homes, were promised six years' remission of rent if they returned to their farms within four months. Lenient methods were to be employed with the Bushmen, but they were to be reduced to obedience by commandos and, if necessary, be expelled to the Kalahari desert. At the same time a northern as well as an eastern boundary was proclaimed. But the cracks to the eastward were not so easily papered over. Formidable Xhosa clans, in rebellion against their nominal overlord, Gaika, were in occupation of the Zuurveld, and somewhat naturally refused to be persuaded by repeated conferences to surrender their new grazing grounds and to retire across the Great Fish River to face Gaika's wrath. Arrangements were made with Gaika himself for a strict observance of that river as a frontier between his people and the farmers. *Verba et praeterea nihil.* An extensive frontier thinly held by a handful of land-hungry squatters against a numerous population of warlike Natives presents a problem which can only be solved by intensive colonisation or by the presence of a defensive system as elaborate as the Roman Wall.

When Macartney, in November 1798, decided that gout and advancing years demanded his return to England and retirement, the colony was in order and in seeming content. No unrest had come to the surface except the mutiny of part of the naval squadron in October 1797, which belongs to British naval history rather than that of the Cape.[3] Macartney had been able to enforce obedience because

[1] Macartney to Bresler, 30 June 1797, Macartney Letter Books, I, p. 81.

[2] (Sir) John Barrow, *Travels into the Interior of Southern Africa*, 2 vols. (1806 edn.).

[3] For a full documentation of the episode, which, as at Spithead, seems to have been due more to bad food than to bad treatment, see *Recs. of Cape Col.* II, 161–86.

he had the requisite personality and a sufficiently strong military force at his back. Both were removed from the scene at the same time. On November 4 three veteran regiments were sent off from the Cape to Madras against the danger which threatened from Tipu Sultan and his French allies; and the day after Lieutenant-General Francis Dundas had taken charge as Acting Governor (November 22), a disastrous fire destroyed over 130 cavalry horses and a large part of the naval and military stores in the colony. The news quickly spread to the frontier where it was believed that the garrison had been virtually put out of action.[1] Graaff-Reinet rose in rebellion, an event which had been precipitated by the arrest of one of its leaders, Adriaan van Jaarsveld, for forgery. Once begun, the revolt was further encouraged by the reduction of the fleet on the station and the departure for India in January 1799 of further regiments, which were replaced by a weak contingent of youthful recruits from England. The conception of the Cape as nothing more than a convenient maritime fortress was already presenting difficulties.

The Acting-Governor, Francis Dundas, a nephew of the statesman, was honest and efficient in routine, but choleric and overbearing, and tact was a gift withheld from him. "He can determine on nothing", commented Lady Barnard, "unless he is in a passion, and then it is a chance if it is not the wrong way."[2] The rebellion which he was called upon to handle was not only a severe test of his own capacity but a revelation of the difficulties inherent in the South African situation. Fortunately the immediate fear of French intervention from Mauritius in conjunction with the rebels was removed by the capture on 9 February 1799 of the French frigate *Prudente* before it could land its troops and ammunition at Algoa Bay. For a space the problem appeared to have narrowed down to the suppression of some two hundred insurgent farmers, who, having triumphantly rescued van Jaarsveld, were besieging the drostdies of Graaff-Reinet and Swellendam and threatening to carry off Landdrosts Bresler and Faure to the Kaffir country.[3] By the time that General Vandeleur and his cavalry reached Graaff-Reinet on March 19, it was evident that the great majority of the burghers were not prepared to fight. Turning southward, Vandeleur proceeded through the district of Bruintjes Hoogte to the Boschberg, where on April 6 Willem Prinsloo with 112 followers surrendered without fighting. Van Jaarsveld, who had been rearrested, was detained and sent with his son and eighteen other ringleaders to prison at the Cape pending trial for high treason —an unexpected reminder that the new Power intended to be master of the frontier.

[1] See Theal, *History of South Africa since* 1795, p. 43.

[2] Lady Anne Barnard to Lord Macartney, 16 May 1800, Fairbridge, *Lady Anne Barnard*, pp. 206–7.

[3] See Faure to Gen. Dundas, 5 March 1799, and Bresler's Journal, January 17–March 19, *Recs. of Cape Col.* II, 379–80, 389–95.

Had peace coincided with the termination of the rebellion, the episode would have been of slight importance; but the British were about to learn that mastery of the frontier involved infinitely more than the employment of strong measures against a few restless frontiersmen. In order to reach Algoa Bay, where he intended to embark his troops for Cape Town, Vandeleur was obliged to march through the dangerous neighbourhood of the Zuurveld, where the Xhosas, who had refused to move at the instance of Craig's emissaries, had recently been reinforced by new recruits coming over the Fish River under the leadership of Ndlambi. As the Kaffirs advanced, the wretched farmers fled, losing most of their possessions. One clan, that of the Gunukwebes under Cungwa, had not joined in this new devastation, and Vandeleur hoped to pass through their area without a collision. But Cungwa suspected that he was about to be driven back across the Fish River and accordingly ambushed the British column before it reached the Bay, inflicting serious loss. Vandeleur responded by calling out the Graaff-Reinet and Swellendam farmers on commando. Then, as though the situation were not already sufficiently serious, the armed Hottentot auxiliaries deserted their white masters and threw in their lot with the invaders. The opportunity of avenging past cruelties and of indulging their ruling passion for plunder was too good to be missed, for the men of Graaff-Reinet were defenceless, the supply of powder and ball from the Cape having been stopped during the revolt; many of the troops had already returned to the Cape, and some twenty farms on the Zuurveld lay untenanted.[1] A like case would have been a Negro insurrection in the West Indies coupled with a Carib invasion.

Vandeleur himself was eager to teach the Xhosas a stern lesson by driving them out from all territory west of the Fish, but Dundas clung to his instructions. Defensive warfare was justifiable, and he himself was preparing to come to the rescue with a strong force; but a war of expulsion would only start a feud producing endless bitterness. Vandeleur must convince the Kaffirs of British good-will "by conciliatory means, by ambassadors, by presents, and by promises". Protestations of friendship from an apparently beaten foe do not ring convincingly in the ear of fighting men, especially savage men. They did not do so in this case, and the waiting commandos lost heart. By the end of July the Boers were panic-stricken and incapable of offering any resistance to the Hottentots and Kaffirs, who were now in possession of all the southern half of the Graaff-Reinet district and were committing terrible atrocities.[2] On August 7 General Dundas set out for the front with fifty dragoons and some companies of infantry, and after collecting large commandos in Stellenbosch and

[1] See Secretary Barnard to Henry Dundas, 13 September 1799, *Recs. of Cape Col.* II, 479–82.

[2] See the reports of the Field-Cornets, etc., 2–31 July 1799, *ibid.* pp. 444–8, 449–53.

Swellendam arrived on the scene early in September. But he had come to conciliate and only to fight as a last resort. He was furious with Vandeleur for having involved himself in guerilla warfare with the Natives which was certain to result in "disappointment and disgrace".[1] Negotiations with the Hottentot and Xhosa leaders were opened by Honoratus Maynier, the humane but unpopular ex-landdrost, whom Dundas had brought with him; and as the marauders had now plundered everything within reach, it was an easy matter to persuade them to abstain from further depredations in return for a promise (reinforced by large presents) that they would be left undisturbed on the Zuurveld.[2] In October "peace" was proclaimed on this basis and Maynier installed as Resident Commissioner with special powers and with instructions to protect the Hottentots from cruelty and injustice. He was supported by a few dragoons and Hottentot soldiers at Graaff-Reinet. As an advance base in case of future trouble, Fort Frederick, with a garrison of 350 men, was established at Algoa Bay.[3] With that Dundas returned to the Cape, admitting that what he had accomplished was a withdrawal from war rather than a settlement.

Dundas's policy may be summed up in quotations from his own words. "Our possession of the colony", he wrote in August "may possibly be at stake if we do not secure a permanent establishment [at Algoa Bay] for the protection of the Frontier *of this too extensive colony*."[4] Secondly, in response to a query why he had withdrawn his troops so rapidly, he replied, "It became highly necessary to remember the weakness of the garrison at Cape Town".[5] Inevitably, like his Dutch predecessors, the British Governor looked at the Cape with his back to the hinterland and assessed its importance in relation to the sea. The interests of the frontiersmen and of the Cape authorities, whether Dutch or British, were incompatible. Frontiersmen demanded protection on their own terms, which were exorbitant; the authorities required obedience because the Indian Gibraltar could not exist without them.

The collapse of Dundas's system, the first of so many of a like nature, was a foregone conclusion. Maynier was called upon to enforce the rule of law, and humanitarian law at that, without the essential police apparatus. Regulations for enforcing better treatment of the Hottentots and drastic restrictions upon the use of armed parties to recover stolen cattle were particularly resented when the law was helpless to stop the renewed plundering by these same Hottentots, or even to make it safe for the refugees to return to their deserted farms. Anger, stirred by wild rumours, boiled up at last. In October 1801, Maynier was besieged in his drostdy by a large

[1] Cf. Lady Anne Barnard to Lord Macartney, 9 January 1800. Fairbridge, D., *Lady Anne Barnard*, p. 132.

[2] Theal, *op. cit.* I, 54.

[3] The origin of Port Elizabeth.

[4] Gen. Dundas to Secretary Ross, 10 August 1799, *Recs. of Cape Col.* II, 462–3.

[5] See Dundas to Sir George Yonge, 24 February 1800, *ibid.* III, 57–67.

burgher force. On the arrival of troops a series of strongly worded petitions of grievance against the Commissioner was presented, not by the irreconcilables, but by responsible leaders, such as Commandant Tjaart van der Walt. Maynier was accordingly recalled, Bresler and the Heemraden reinstated, and a commission appointed, which presently acquitted Maynier of all charges, adding as a rider that the evidences laid against him were "such as to merit the most serious reprehension."[1] The Colony had had its first taste of the new European humanitarianism; it was soon to have a further instalment under the Dutchman, de Mist.[2] Slowly but inevitably this isolated outpost was being drawn into the troubled orbit of European life and thought.

The removal of Maynier pleased the farmers and they dispersed; but the problem of making life endurable in the presence of victorious and marauding Hottentots and Kaffirs remained. In December 1801, a location or reserve was established on the Zwartkops River, whither Dr J. T. van der Kemp of the London Missionary Society, the first effective missionary at the Cape, conducted several hundreds of Hottentots.[3] This step was followed up by a series of commandos; but the farmers had lost faith in the capacity both of themselves and of the Government to cope with the situation and turned out in poor numbers. The first rally, in February 1802, failed to make any impression on Stuurman's Hottentot bands and dispersed. The second, which assembled in May and remained in the field for two months, enjoyed better success, capturing some 13,000 cattle, until the loss of their trusted leader, van der Walt, sent them home in confusion. It seemed as if much of the eastern districts was about to pass into the hands of the Xhosas and their allies.

Knowing that the Colony was about to be handed over to the Batavian Republic, General Dundas himself returned to the frontier in the hope of effecting a settlement before the transfer took place. Nothing less than a full-dress Kaffir war could, however, accomplish such a settlement. In the end a special commando, drawn from every district outside the Cape itself, was summoned to hold the field while the troops withdrew, and in February 1803 a makeshift peace was agreed upon, whereby farmers, Hottentots and Kaffirs agreed to leave each other alone. But the problem remained. A British Governor had spoken words of conciliation to savages on the warpath because he felt that there was no alternative. His duty was to hold the Cape, not to become an African *conquistador* on behalf of frontiersmen who combined high-handed methods with numerical weakness.[4]

[1] Marais *Maynier*, p. 135.

[2] *Vide infra*, pp. 196 *sqq*.

[3] For an account of his work for the Hottentots at Bethelsdorp and in general, see Martin, A. D., *Doctor Vanderkemp* (1931).

[4] Cf. Dundas to Yonge, 20 February 1800: "It has always been my intention to acquire the friendship of the Savages dwelling on the Confines of the Colony, as I conceive it [i.e. the friendship] to be an essential Object for the British Government to secure to itself under

Moreover, the maximum of friction had been engendered, because, although British power was strong enough to rule the white frontier, it was unprepared to accept the burden of mastering the black.

Meanwhile something in the nature of a comic interlude had been enacted at Cape Town. On 6 April 1799, Sir George Yonge received his commission as Governor and Commander-in-Chief of Cape Colony and duly arrived while General Dundas was still away up-country. On paper he was an experienced public official, having served at the Admiralty, the War Office, in Ireland and as Master of the Mint, but his instability and lack of judgment totally unfitted him to be the successor of Lord Macartney. He had been financially embarrassed, but there is no proof that he enriched himself by dishonest means at the Cape, though he certainly connived at such conduct in his subordinates. Generosity combined with weakness made him an easy mark for unscrupulous self-seekers. "Why, why did they not give him", wrote Lady Anne Barnard, "something in the shape of a Council to influence him right?" Why indeed. Had that precaution been taken, he might well have developed into a successful Governor. His introduction of William Duckitt and his improved methods of agriculture was a costly failure, but it showed an appreciation of a real need. His despatches too are full of eager and sometimes valuable suggestions for reform. The four existing districts into which the Colony was divided were too large for efficient administration. Inspired by the Fiscal Willem van Ryneveld, a staunch Orangeman, he proposed to subdivide them with resident magistrates in control of each. Two members of the High Court were to be sent out on circuit, a proper system of education should be introduced, and the Slave Code be revised to raise the status of slaves "nearly similar to husbandry labourers in England". "It is desirable", he wrote, "to knit and tie this colony to the Mother Country as much as possible", and to abolish its commercial dependence upon the East India Company.[1] However much Henry Dundas might agree with this last point, in an important declaration of policy he imposed a definite veto on Yonge's system of "thorough". As regards the farmers, the wisest course was "to interfere as little as possible in their domestic concerns and interior economy". Treat them as distant clans, dependent upon the British Government, but not directly amenable to British institutions. Let good faith and justice do its gradual work of civilisation and assimilation. Any hasty imposition of British law or customs, he added with prophetic insight, would tend rather "to create a spirit of resistance or a disposition to migrate still further from the seat of Government".[2]

the present circumstances of this Country and the dispositions of the people." *Recs. of Cape Col.* III, 48–57.

[1] See Yonge to Secretary Dundas, *Recs. of Cape Col.* III, 28–30, 37–41, 86–94, 94–100, 356–8.

[2] Secretary Dundas to Yonge, 28 July 1800, *ibid.* pp. 199–206.

Yonge's tenure of office was short, and on 14 January 1801 he was recalled after a governorship of less than two years. Meanwhile in Europe the Cape pawn was being moved about the diplomatic chess-board. In the British Cabinet opinion was divided as to its value. As we have already seen, Dundas had consistently fought for its acquisition and retention as being vital to the security of India. In Lord Grenville he found a consistent ally on this point, if not on others; but Pitt himself, though agreeing that its retention was desirable, was never prepared to jeopardise a possible peace settlement for it. The struggle began in the abortive negotiations with the Directory at Lille in the autumn of 1797.

In his official instructions to Lord Malmesbury, the British plenipotentiary, Grenville laid it down that the Cape must not be returned to the Batavian Republic, now the subservient tool of France. Notwithstanding, Pitt secretly authorised Malmesbury to agree to its restoration if need arose. Both desired peace, but so eager was Pitt that he was prepared to pay a far higher price for it than Grenville. The *coup d'état* of Fructidor (4 September 1797), which led to the triumph of the extreme Jacobin faction in the Directory, doomed the negotiations to failure. The question of the Cape was ostensibly the chief crux at Lille, but in reality it was the domineering spirit of the Directors which occasioned the rupture.[1] Before Fructidor there was some talk of the Dutch being prepared to leave the Cape, which they regarded as a heavy financial burden, in British hands in return for a large cash payment. But the French *coup d'état* ruled out any such accommodation. On September 16 Malmesbury was informed that unless he was authorised to make full restitution of all territory conquered by Great Britain from either France or her allies, he must depart from Lille within twenty-four hours. Yet despite the rupture thus occasioned, Pitt struggled hopefully on. Early in October fresh proposals were considered, which Grenville with very great reluctance was prepared to accept, if Pitt insisted. But against one of the proposals, that the British should pledge themselves to accord free entry to all nations at the Cape and Ceylon, he protested strongly—"a very inconvenient stipulation in point of effect, if France is to be the guarantee to all the World of our conduct to them in our own territories".[2] But it was not to be peace. The nadir of British weakness was passed, and with the rise of Napoleon a new and far more deadly struggle was beginning.

Meanwhile Dundas lost no opportunity of stiffening the Cabinet in favour of retaining the Cape. Taking alarm at a draft despatch forwarded to him by Grenville in November 1799, he wrote: "It is only

[1] J. Holland Rose in *Camb. Hist. of Brit. For. Policy*, I, 280.

[2] Grenville to Pitt, 8 October 1797, Chatham MSS, P.R.O., 30 8/140. Grenville's uneasiness at Pitt's policy of peace at any price was shared by William Windham. See ironic letter to Pitt, dated October 10, *Windham Papers*, II, 61–3.

stated that we are not *likely* to give up Ceylon, the Cape and other places. I really flattered myself we had all felt for a long time that such a cession was impossible." If they did not stand out for the preservation of British imperial interests, they would be "playing the part of spendthrift bankrupts. . . . If the leading members of His Majesty's Government have made up their minds to a different view of the subject, I am sure that they act most unwisely in keeping me among them."[1] In reply Grenville pointed out that, although it was premature to say that *all* conquests would be retained at a price, yet "as to the Cape and Ceylon . . . you will know, my mind was made up when that opinion was far from general even among our colleagues".[2]

Unfortunately for these views the Pitt ministry went out of office on the question of Catholic emancipation, and was replaced in February 1801 by that of Addington. In March pourparlers were begun in London, which eventually resulted in the Treaty of Amiens. These critical negotiations were in the hands of a shadow Cabinet, inept and ill-informed, and dependent on the good-will of Pitt and his followers. By the preliminaries of peace, which were signed in London on October 1, all British conquests overseas were restored with the exception of Trinidad and Ceylon. The Cape was to return to Dutch control, but as a free port.[3] Grenville and Dundas exchanged letters of rage and disgust. In promising to surrender Malta and the Cape, we had lost the keys of Egypt and India.[4] But worse was to follow. Further concessions resulted in the final negotiations including the return of the Cape to the Batavian Republic "in full sovereignty".

The stormy debate in Parliament which ensued revealed considerable division of opinion as to the importance of the Cape to Great Britain. In the Lords, Grenville insisted that in restoring the Cape to the Dutch we had in effect made a present of it to Napoleon; but many speakers, including Lords Nelson and St Vincent, poured contempt on the notion of its strategical importance. Provided maritime supremacy was retained, possession of the Cape was unnecessary and a French occupation was impossible. If we lost that supremacy, the Cape would go also. Why incur vast expense and trouble for an illusory advantage?[5] In the Commons similar arguments for and against the cession of the Cape were repeated, Dundas making an impassioned speech against abandonment. Pitt, consistently with his previous attitude, regretted the loss of the Cape, but supported the treaty as an honourable settlement.[6] Both Houses finally gave their approval with easy majorities.

[1] Dundas to Grenville, 24 November 1799, *Dropmore Papers*, VI, 37–9.
[2] Grenville to Dundas, 25 November 1799, *ibid.* VI, 46–7.
[3] See Lord Hawkesbury's complacent announcement of the terms to Grenville on the same day, *ibid.* VII, 45.
[4] 4 and 10 October 1801, *Dropmore Papers*, VII, 48, 56–7.
[5] *Parliamentary History*, XXXVI, 692–734.
[6] *Ibid.* pp. 739–828.

As if to give point to the absorption of the Cape into the European political system, the very act of transference from British to Batavian authority was interrupted by a turn of the political kaleidoscope in England. Although no longer Prime Minister, Pitt remained convinced that he alone could save the country. Throughout the summer and winter of 1802 he grew increasingly impatient that Addington failed to see the matter in the same light, but he continued to accord support and advice which were received with docility. Expecting an early return to office at the head of a new coalition and a renewal of war with France, Pitt advised the Ministry to postpone the evacuation of Alexandria and the Cape. On October 17 orders were sent out accordingly.[1]

The despatch reached General Dundas at noon on December 31 when the retrocession was actually in progress and the Dutch troops were about to take possession of the batteries and the Castle. The excited townsfolk were hourly expecting to see the Batavian flag hoisted, when to their astonishment the British troops were suddenly hurried back to resume possession. Praiseworthy forbearance on both sides tided over a very delicate situation. Meanwhile Pitt changed his mind. His plan of a coalition with Addington and the Grenville clan, led by himself, had fallen through and the omens in Europe were not propitious for immediate war with France. Alexandria and the Cape should therefore be evacuated. Again the Ministry obsequiously accepted the advice, and the British troops at last departed from Cape Town in February 1803.[2] Thus the conservative burghers of distant Cape Colony found themselves citizens of the revolutionary Batavian Republic and face to face with the reforming zeal of its Commissioner-General de Mist.

The impact of European ideas, as represented by British Toryism, upon Afrikaner society had been slight. Judicial matters had been governed by Roman-Dutch law and Dutch judges, and local government both in Cape Town and in the districts had remained substantially in Dutch hands; but the new Batavian Republic, to which the Cape was ceded in full sovereignty in March 1802, represented a phase of European thought fundamentally different from the conceptions of the British Government. In place of the corrupt oligarchy of the United Provinces and the intensely conservative Dutch East India Company now stood a Republic infused with the advanced ideas of revolutionary France. The cession of the Cape, as it affected the colonists, did not so much represent a transference from British to Dutch control as a sudden removal from a conservative world into a strange and alien one of radicalism. This first contact with a changing Europe was too short to enable a present-day observer to

[1] *Recs. of Cape Col.* IV, 447.
[2] See *Dropmore Papers*, VII, intro. p. xxiii.

do more than hazard a guess as to what the outcome would have been had it continued.

The Council for Asiatic Possessions and Establishments, which the States-General had established in 1800, was anxious to make a clean sweep of past abuses and to open a new era in colonial administration. Before deciding upon the form of government to be established at the Cape, the Council called upon one of its members, Jacob Abraham de Mist, a distinguished lawyer, to examine the relationship of the Cape with the mother country in all its bearings and to report. The memorandum which he submitted in 1802 was an extremely able document that gained the warm approval of the Council. De Mist was appointed Commissioner-General to receive the colony from the British and to establish a system of government along the lines proposed in his report. Lieut.-General Jan Willem Janssens was appointed Governor, and to him de Mist was to hand over as soon as the new machinery was in working order. On 5 August 1802, the Commissioner and Governor set sail from the Texel with a staff of selected officials. A week later three Commissioners, who had been sent on ahead to arrange for the reception of a Batavian garrison, reached Simon's Bay.

The policy which De Mist and Janssens pursued after the final departure of the British on 20 February 1803 aimed at assimilating the Colony to the parent Republic by thorough-going control in every department. It was, in fact, a constructive colonial policy as contrasted with the comparatively negative military policy of the British. As such it provided the colonists with a greatly improved administrative organisation and at the same time attempted to subject the frontiersmen to a form and a degree of interference never previously experienced. In his memorandum de Mist had repudiated the strictures against farmer brutality in Barrow's *Travels*, and even modified his own views after personal observation, but he asserted that isolation had reduced the frontiersmen "to the savage state of the Kaffirs", and insisted that future Governors must be able to enforce their commands "by an army powerful enough to reduce the insolent and rebellious to silent obedience".[1] Administration must be free from corruption, impartial, strong, and directly controlled by the Batavian Government and not from Java as in the Company days. In commercial matters the colony must be bound to the parent State by orthodox mercantilism.[2] Provided that political and economic centralisation was effectively maintained, there was no need to fear a repetition of the American Rebellion, even though the colony be vigorously developed. The gradual substitution of free European

[1] *The Memorandum of Commissary J. A. de Mist, containing recommendations for the form and administration of Government at the Cape of Good Hope*, 1802 (Van Riebeeck Society Publications, No. 3), pp. 192 and 209.

[2] *Ibid.* pp. 248–9.

labour for slaves was both desirable and feasible. In short, all the elements of a centralising and reforming policy, calculated to infuriate frontier opinion, were present in De Mist's mind at the outset.

Whereas the British Government had deliberately refrained from making any but minor changes in the administrative system until the war should be over, Commissioner de Mist had persuaded the Asiatic Council to sanction a drastic overhaul at once. All the sins of the Company régime, he had written, "can now be wiped out as with a damp sponge".[1] Accepting his scheme, the Batavian Government established a central administration consisting of a Governor assisted by a Council of four and a Secretary, a Department of Accountancy, and a reformed Council of Justice consisting of a President and six Councillors, all of them professional lawyers.[2] It was an excellent foundation on which to build a system commanding the respect and affection of the colonists. But organisation at Cape Town could not solve the frontier problem. Only intensive settlement (for which economic conditions were not yet ripe) or the expenditure of vast sums on frontier defence could do that. De Mist and Governor Janssens were the representatives of a poor and not a wealthy Power. The British estimates for the Colony had amounted to well over a quarter of a million sterling, and even then General Dundas had vetoed a Kaffir war because of the inadequacy of his resources. Janssens had rather less than £100,000 a year to spend on defence internal and external, and he accordingly had no alternative but to adopt and continue the peace policy of his British predecessor. During a tour of the southern and eastern parts of the colony in 1803 he completed the pacification of the Hottentots on the lines laid down by Maynier and Dundas. Reserves were provided, the missionary Dr van der Kemp and his followers were established at Bethelsdorp near Algoa Bay, and Hottentot labour was protected by registration and effective supervision of contracts. In handling the Xhosas the Batavians failed as lamentably as the British and for the same reason. As before, solemn palavers proved an inadequate instrument to remove their victorious warriors from the Zuurveld. When de Mist followed the Governor in an independent tour some months later, the Chiefs of these western clans refused even to meet him.

De Mist's quick mind at once saw that until the central administration was underpinned by an efficient local government, nothing of permanent importance could be done to reverse this humiliating impotence. In 1804 the districts were reduced to somewhat smaller and more manageable dimensions by the creation of two new ones: Uitenhage in the south-east and Tulbagh in the north-west. This

[1] *The Memorandum of Commissary J. A. de Mist*, p. 172.

[2] Extract from the "Register of Resolutions by the State Government of the Batavian Republic", 8 March 1802, *ibid.* pp. 289–90.

step was followed by a codification of the functions of the Landdrost and his Heemraden together with an important extension of the civil functions of the *Veld Wachtmeester*, now renamed *Veld Kornet*, whose relation to the central authority became analogous to that of the Tudor Justice of the Peace.[1] These measures were admirable for enforcing the rule of law upon the farmers, but they were merely a preliminary stage in the process of affording them protection. That appeared to be as far off as ever. Instead of increasing the garrison of 150 mercenaries at Fort Frederick in order to overawe the Xhosas of the Zuurveld, Governor Janssens was obliged to reduce it. Chronic lack of money also caused him to resort to unsound finance. In order to meet the cost of new public buildings and other charges he printed off 300,000 additional rix-dollar notes, thus raising the total amount in circulation to 2,086,000. In consequence the exchange value of the rix-dollar fell from a nominal 4*s.* to 3*s.* 4*d.* The colonists were, in fact, paying for their public buildings by inflation, that is to say, by an increase in the price of imports which they could not do without.

In internal social matters the policy of de Mist and of Janssens was as enlightened and as unpalatable to many of the colonists as their handling of the Hottentot problem. De Mist's allowance of "equal protection of the law" to Lutherans, Anglicans, Roman Catholics and even Moslems was followed by the authorisation given to each Landdrost with two Heemraden to solemnise civil marriages; and although provision was made for religious instruction, the establishment of a predominantly secular Board to organise school education free from clerical control deeply shocked a people accustomed to regard education and religion as being one and indivisible. French revolutionary liberalism was attacking the Calvinism of the Boers in its innermost citadel. Had time permitted, the storm which was everywhere brewing would have broken.[2]

But that storm was anticipated by another from overseas. Ever since the news that war had been renewed between Great Britain and France reached him in July 1805, Janssens had been labouring to prepare for the inevitable return of the British. Seriously weakened by the withdrawal of his best troops to Batavia, he had been obliged to rely on the burgher militia, which he accordingly reorganised. As soon as Napoleon's invasion scheme had been checked in July 1805 by Calder off Ferrol, a fleet of sixty-one ships under Sir Home Popham set sail for the Cape with Major-General Baird and 6700 troops on board. The outcome of a contest between such a body of regulars and Janssen's militia and unreliable mercenaries was a foregone conclusion. After a preliminary skirmish at Blaauwberg, sixteen miles north of Cape Town, one section of the Dutch force fled back to the city and on 10 January 1806 capitulated. Nine days later, Janssens, who with

[1] Walker, E. A., *Hist. of S. A.* p. 136.

[2] Cf. van der Merwe, J. P., *Die Kaap onder die Bataafse Republiek.*

the rest had retreated inland to the Hottentots-Holland Pass, surrendered with the honours of war. Under the terms of the capitulation, colonists in arms were to return home forthwith and all private property was to be respected, but the property of the Batavian Government was to be surrendered. The paper money was to remain in circulation on the same terms as before, until the British Government should otherwise determine. Public worship as then existing was to be maintained, and, most important of all, the inhabitants were guaranteed all their former rights and privileges—a stipulation which *inter alia* subjected British merchants resident in the colony to Dutch legal procedure, which they resented.

The Batavian Republic, represented by a Commissioner who was an uncompromising reformer and a capable governor, had thrown itself enthusiastically into the task of transforming the Cape into a model colony on up-to-date lines. In consequence a community with the ideas of the seventeenth century had during a brief interlude been in contact with revolutionary European liberalism and had been sorely disquieted. Batavian zeal for reform was now to be replaced by the Toryism of an England fighting for its existence and for the preservation of its Indian Empire. The newcomers had arrived to occupy a fortress, not to inaugurate a social revolution. Colonial and especially frontier susceptibilities were therefore safe again for the time.

CHAPTER VIII

CAPE COLONY, 1806–1822

THE year 1805 had witnessed the failure of Napoleon's plans for invading England, the vindication of British sea supremacy at Trafalgar, and the ruin of Pitt's last European coalition. In the new phase of the struggle, which was about to begin, Napoleon strove to break the islanders by striking at their commerce. The attempt to eliminate them from the European economic system was defeated by Europe's need of their manufactures and by the same sea-power which had thwarted military invasion. The Emperor's experiment produced two momentous consequences. His interference with the everyday needs of the peoples under his control accelerated the rise of national, as distinct from governmental opposition to his power, which eventually effected his downfall. Secondly, the attempt to drive Great Britain out of Europe accentuated that reliance upon an Asiatic and commercial empire which had increasingly characterised her policy since the time of the Seven Years War.

The eighteenth century witnessed an increase of British interest in the Orient occasioned by maritime supremacy and growing industrial superiority. The loss of the American colonies was more than compensated for in contemporary British opinion by expansion in India, where profits were large and turbulent Assemblies unknown. Napoleonic pressure carried the process an important stage further. By 1815 the focal point of British imperial interest had shifted from the North Atlantic to the Pacific and Indian Oceans. When, therefore, the Cape of Good Hope was reconquered in 1806 the nation was determined upon its permanent incorporation in the imperial system. While the expedition under Sir David Baird was still on its way thither, the Court of Prussia was officially informed that in any peace negotiations the retention of the Cape and Malta by Great Britain was to be considered a *sine qua non*.[1] In 1795 the Cape had been occupied primarily for its strategic importance in relation to India, and its value in that respect had been seriously questioned; the Second Occupation was undertaken with a more comprehensive purpose, as the acquisition of a port which controlled the trade route from the Eastern Seas, not only to Europe, but also to North and South America.

The intimate connection existing in the minds of contemporary Englishmen between the occupation of the Cape and the opening of the ports of Spanish America to British manufacturers is well

[1] Theal, G. M., *S. A. since 1795*, I, p. 151.

illustrated by the escapade of Sir Home Popham, an intimate friend of Henry Dundas. The latter had long cherished the idea of adding a new continent to the British system of commercial empire by liberating the Spanish colonies and so fostering a vast triangular traffic between Great Britain, South America and India. Midway along the base of the triangle lay the Cape of Good Hope. Upon the rupture with Spain in 1804, Popham was employed as a confidential intermediary between the British Government and General Miranda, the Spanish American revolutionary, and by November Popham's proposals had been accepted and he himself had been provisionally appointed to command an expedition to retake the Cape as a preliminary to the invasion of South America. The plan fell through, but within a week of Admiral Calder's victory off Cape Finisterre (22 July 1805), Popham was appointed to command the fleet, which, with the military force under Sir David Baird, finally acquired the Cape for the British Empire.

Popham himself was determined to carry out the original scheme in its entirety. On 6 March 1806, the Batavian leaders evacuated the Colony, and on April 13, Popham also departed from it, taking with him the entire British squadron and some 900 soldiers under General Beresford for an attack on Monte Video and Buenos Aires. He had moreover secured the enthusiastic support of Sir David Baird, who on learning of the capture of Buenos Aires dispatched reinforcements from the Cape to the extent of 2197 officers and men. When disaster overtook the adventure,[1] Popham was court-martialled, but suffered nothing more serious than a reprimand. The proceedings made it clear that he had not acted under authority, but the evidence of Dundas made it equally clear that the acquisition of the South African base had been considered by the Government in relation to South America as well as to India.

The pressure exercised by Napoleon upon the leading manufacturing nation was compelling that Power to consolidate and expand her non-European markets. In the process, the lonely Dutch caravanserai at the Cape of Good Hope became the dependency of a people with a genius for business and government, whose protective instinct was strongly developed, but who showed themselves lacking in the imaginative insight needed if they were to understand and be understood by civilised races different from themselves. Therein lies the strength and weakness of British imperial effort and the key to most of the problems connected with the revolutionary epoch in the history of Southern Africa which the French Emperor unwittingly opened in 1806.

The system of colonial government established in that year by Secretary Windham was virtually identical with that devised by Dundas in 1797. As before, all executive and legislative authority

[1] See *C.H.B.E.* vol. II, chap. IV.

was centralised in the person of the Governor as the delegate of the sovereign power; but a number of circumstances combined to render the actual authority wielded by the new Governor, Lord Caledon, somewhat less extensive than that exercised by his predecessors. One limitation related to patronage. Between them Macartney and Dundas had filled all the senior offices at the Cape with their nominees, and a large part of this patronage had remained with the Governor himself. This practice had deprived certain Government departments at home (notably the Treasury) of the disposal of a number of lucrative places. In 1806 Grenville at the Treasury waged a stubborn and successful campaign with Windham at the Colonial Office to recover the lost ground.[1] By a clause in his instructions Caledon was forbidden to fill any office "which is or shall be granted under the Great Seal of this Kingdom" or to which appointment was usually made by warrant under the royal signet and sign manual.[2] A further restriction on Caledon's authority resulted from the controversy between himself and General Grey with regard to military control, which, as will be seen later, was a source of serious administrative weakness.

Other restrictions upon gubernatorial autocracy existed on paper only; the Governor of the Cape still remained the most powerful of all colonial governors. Customs, audit and ordnance officials looked to their superiors in Whitehall, and naval and military commanding officers asserted their distinctive authority, but the Governor was the Government. His legislative acts were to be transmitted home for approval, with "very full and particular Observations upon each of them", explaining the reasons and occasion for their enactment; yet Lord Charles Somerset, a later Governor, had to complain that proclamations imposing new taxation failed to secure even acknowledgment from the Secretary of State. The power of the Governor was further enhanced by the completeness of his control over the Afrikaner officials, for their appointment and promotion was entirely in his hands, as was their pay, since the Home Government left the arrangement of the salary budget to him.[3] Apart from a few specialised departments the administrative machinery was concentrated in the office of the Colonial Secretary. Its comprehensive functions are well described by a contemporary official.

> The duty of the secretary and, in his absence, of the deputy secretary, is to refer to the Governor the multifarious memorials and occurrences each day, with a précis of every one, and to receive his decisions thereon, causing them to be put in force. A general correspondence with the offices at the Cape, with the magistrates and with all parts of the Colony, is carried on by the secretaries. All deeds of

[1] See Lord Grenville to W. Windham, 5 Sept. 1806. *Dropmore Papers*, VIII, 307–8. For the remainder of the correspondence on this topic, which lasted from June to October, 1806, see *ibid.* pp. 183, 189–91, 208, 361–2, 262–5, 374–5.

[2] Caledon's Instructions, 1 Aug. 1806, *Recs. of Cape Colony*, VI, 6–19.

[3] Manning, H. T., *British Colonial Government after the American Revolution*, pp. 419–20.

mortgage are prepared in their office, excepting those to the loan bank and orphan chamber; as are also transfers of landed property; all of which are passed before commissioners to the court of justice, and entered in the public registers of the office. Grants of land are prepared and issued; the financial arrangements of the government are conducted, and the proclamations and regulations of government emanate hence. The state of the currency, the register of strangers, the detail of vessels arriving and sailing, and all statistical returns of population and of produce, are objects of the duty of the secretaries....The attendance of the secretaries is daily; the entire business of the Colony going through their office, which acts as the main spring of the machine, forcing all into motion.[1]

The intention of the Home Government with regard to the Cape, as with all colonies acquired during the Napoleonic War, was to rule directly from Whitehall, organising the colonial administration as a sub-office, with the Governor as a kind of seconded Permanent Under-Secretary. In practice the central authority showed little inclination to assume the burden of direct supervision, with the result that the colonial administration acquired a substantial, though temporary, independence of either local or imperial control.

Beneath this superstructure the Dutch systems of local government, justice and police, each with its own personnel, were left intact. Landdrosts, Heemraden and Field-cornets were for the most part the same people and ran local affairs as before. Similarly, Roman-Dutch law and the constitution and procedure of the Courts remained for the time being unchanged—to the indignation of the British officials and merchants, who resented proceedings *in camera* and the absence of a jury. Indeed, had not the Afrikaner civil servants loyally accepted the new régime, it would have been impossible to have administered the colony outside Cape Town. Such was the machinery of government as re-established at the Cape in 1806. Under Caledon and his successor, Sir John Cradock, it functioned efficiently and to the satisfaction of the inhabitants.

The circumstances under which Du Pré Alexander, Earl of Caledon, was appointed to the governorship of the Cape are instructive. Among the names mentioned for the appointment were those of Sir Philip Francis and Lord Charles Somerset.[2] In a letter to Windham, Grenville described the latter as "a person for whom it would be extremely convenient to find some provision on many accounts, but I do not know whether you would think him of sufficient calibre for the Cape".[3] It was unfortunate that eight years later the convenience of providing for Lord Charles by this means induced the then Ministers to overlook his insufficiency of calibre. The choice finally fell upon Lord Caledon, a young man of twenty-nine and one of the representative Peers of Ireland, because the Government needed his

[1] *State of the Cape of Good Hope in 1822*, by W. Wilberforce Bird (Comptroller of the Customs at the Cape), pp. 8–9.

[2] See Lord Grenville to the Prince of Wales, 5 March 1806. *Dropmore Papers*, VIII, 48.

[3] Lord Grenville to W. Windham, 24 April 1806. *Ibid.* p. 119–120.

political influence at a forthcoming election in the county of Tyrone.[1]

A bargain of this sort does not usually produce a first-rate administrator, but in this case the Ministry had contrived to make the best of both worlds. They had secured a man of considerable ability, who threw himself into his new work with a great devotion and an honesty of purpose, which gained for him the esteem of the colonists. On arrival at the Cape he took the oaths of office (21 May 1807), superseding the Lieutenant-Governor, General Grey, who had preceded him and had taken over from Sir David Baird in January. When Caledon left England, it had been Grenville's intention to inaugurate a vigorous consolidating and anglicising policy at the Cape, a policy with which the new Governor was in enthusiastic agreement.[2] Such a policy might possibly have been premature before the issue with Napoleon was decided, but as it was, the Ministry of all the Talents had resigned a month before Caledon reached the Cape, to be succeeded by the Tories under the Duke of Portland. The new Secretary of State for War and the Colonies, Lord Castlereagh, did not share the increasingly high value put upon the Cape by the majority of his countrymen and was not prepared to sanction drastic innovation. Requests for a declaration of policy were ignored. Caledon took the hint. At the end of his governorship his cousin was able to write of him: "His maxim in most things was *haud quieta movere* in the absence of positive instruction."[3]

During the war period the Government maintained the customary policy of making no basic change in the administrative system of a conquered colony. Adherence to this attitude was the more marked because of the concentration of effort in the titanic European contest and because under the terms of the capitulation the colonists had been guaranteed their religion, laws and privileges. "Positive instruction" was accordingly wrung from a reluctant Secretary of State only on rare occasions. It is indicative of the situation that the only important reform during the Caledon régime was effected by the Governor himself and by a proclamation which was apparently never even sent to the Colonial Office. This was the proclamation of 26 May 1811, which provided that two justices of the High Court should go on circuit from time to time to the drostdies of the distant districts to hear civil and criminal cases and to draw up a comprehensive report on all matters pertaining to the welfare of the Colony. It is difficult to overestimate the importance of this measure, which, although suggested during the First Occupation, had not been adopted. In all undeveloped communities occupying an extensive

[1] Lord Grenville to W. Windham, 24 April 1806. pp. 145, 148, 164, 175, 185.

[2] H. Alexander to Brig.-Gen. Stewart (Castlereagh's brother), 2 July 1807. *Recs. of Cape Colony*, VI, 164–6.

[3] H. Alexander to Sir John Cradock, 13 Jan. 1812. *Recs. of Cape Colony*, VIII, 244.

area the standing problem is how to extend the rule of law from the environs of the capital to the extremities. Like Henry II's Justices in Eyre, the itinerant judges from Cape Town brought the people of the border country into direct contact with the central government. While the assize linked up the drostdy in all its judicial capacities with Cape Town, Caledon brought the drostdy into closer touch with the individual farm. The Landdrosts were ordered as part of their regular duty to pay an annual visit of enquiry to the station of each Field-cornet in his district. Public warning was to be given of the impending visit to enable the farmers and Hottentot labourers to bring forward any complaints. Contact was thus indirectly established between London and Graaff-Reinet.

The Judges of Assize were not only a travelling court; they were also a Commission of Enquiry. The careful report which they submitted to the Governor at the end of their toilsome progress reviewed the work of the local officials, the condition of public buildings and roads, the needs of the district as regards education and religion, the relations of the farmers with Hottentots and slaves, and the policy of the various mission stations. The information and suggestions supplied were of very great value to the Governor. In 1813 Sir John Cradock, Caledon's successor, paid a high tribute to the usefulness of the system.[1]

In the early years of his governorship Caledon was engaged in reviewing the financial condition of the colony. His investigations led him to suggest a number of drastic reforms. Lack of credit and surplus revenue hampered trade and made expenditure on improvements out of the question. As an initial step he proposed to reform the Loan Bank, which had so far departed from its original purpose of encouraging trade by issuing short loans at low interest that it had lent right and left without making any effort to enforce repayment. Although Caledon's suggestions were not received with favour by Castlereagh, the Governor returned to the charge in October 1809. While existing revenue, he reported, was barely adequate to meet current expenses, the construction of numerous public works was urgent. To meet the situation by increased taxation was in his opinion dangerous in a community which lacked an Assembly to voice its views. As the only possible alternative he asked for authority to issue new paper money up to one million rix-dollars under certain safeguards. Unlike Castlereagh, the new Secretary of State, Lord Liverpool, supported by the Committee for Trade, gave approval to the plan.[2]

Caledon's financial operations amounted to putting the lending activities of the State Bank on a sound footing and of meeting

[1] Cradock to Chief Justice Truter, 20 August 1813, *Recs. of Cape Colony*, IX, 219–22.

[2] Liverpool to Caledon, 3 March 1810. *Recs. of Cape Colony*, VII, 260–3; cf. Minutes of the Committee for Trade. B.T. 5/20, pp. 278 *et sqq.*

increased governmental expenditure by mortgaging the future. The effect of that policy, when the Cape was faced by the post-war depression, will be discussed at a later stage in this chapter. Meanwhile he was able to erect buildings and wharfs, to create three new districts by reducing the unwieldy size of the existing ones, and to provide Cape Town with an up-to-date system of water-supply.

But however interested he might be in further internal improvements, no Governor of the Cape could ignore for long the stern reality of the frontier. The situation at the beginning of the second British occupation urgently demanded strong measures if the Government was to do its duty in providing reasonable security. For the moment there was peace, but only because the farmers had been obliged to admit complete defeat. Farm after farm on the Zuurveld had been abandoned by their disheartened owners to the advancing Xhosas. The colonists had been quite unable to dislodge them, so that by Caledon's time the Xhosas claimed the area as of right. Small bands of Xhosas had now advanced as far as the Lange Kloof, one-third of the distance between the Fish River (the old boundary) and Cape Town. The continued existence of the Colony as a white settlement was in danger. In 1809 Lieut.-Colonel Richard Collins was dispatched on an extensive tour of the frontier districts to investigate and make suggestions. The reports which he submitted on his return embodied the most constructive scheme of frontier policy that had yet been devised. Its essential feature was non-intercourse between Xhosa and farmer. Contact was perilous until the representatives of civilisation were numerically stronger and "more advanced in arts and industry". The savages must be cleared out of the occupied areas into their own country. The region between the colonial boundary and the Keiskamma River should be respected as their territory, but no kraals must be permitted there. Fronting this unoccupied belt there should be an area of dense settlement on the Zuurveld split up into farms of not more than 120 acres each with a nominal rent. For this purpose 6000 new settlers would be required, who could be procured from Great Britain at moderate cost. In face of so formidable a barrier marauding Xhosas would turn their attention to the Bruintjes Hoogte district. Actual frontier defence should be undertaken by the Boers themselves, who were experts at that kind of fighting, with a stiffening of regulars. Previously this had been impossible because of their hostility to the British, but a change had taken place and cordial co-operation could now be expected. Finally treaties should be made with the Xhosa chiefs who should be encouraged to restrain their followers by the award of annual presents.[1]

The idea of maintaining racial segregation was not, of course, new. It had in theory been the policy of the Cape Government from 1652 onwards, although inability to control the frontiersmen had

[1] Collins to Caledon, 6 August 1809. *Recs. of Cape Colony*, VII, 98–139.

prevented its effective application between 1715 and 1778. Attempts had been made to enforce it, notably by Maynier under the Dutch Company and during the first British administration, and non-intercourse had been the declared policy of Lord Macartney and Commissary De Mist. Moreover the Fiscal, W. S. van Ryneveld, in 1797 had suggested the establishment of a close agricultural settlement on Algoa Bay, which should wean the colonists from their trekking habit—the primary source of frontier friction. Collins's suggestions are important because they combined general principles into the comprehensive and practical system which was afterwards in large measure carried out by Lord Charles Somerset.

For several reasons Caledon was not prepared to adopt the forward policy which Collins advocated. To clear the Zuurveld meant a full-dress Kaffir war, which would be expensive, onerous and a fruitful cause of friction with Grey, the General-Officer-Commanding. As it was, Caledon could only ensure the reinforcement of Fort Frederick on Algoa Bay by asking Grey to see to it. Caledon, therefore, determined to pursue a policy "of preserving what we already possess, and leaving to a future period what an increased population and a military force, unshackled by a foreign war, may without risque easily and effectually accomplish".[1] *Haud quieta movere.*

But if Caledon refused to grasp the frontier nettle, he proved himself to be an active reformer with regard to non-Europeans within the colonial borders. His famous Hottentot Code, promulgated by a proclamation dated 1 November 1809, was a practical measure designed to regulate existing conditions. It continued the economic dependence of the Hottentot labourer upon his farmer employer by tying him to "a fixed place of abode" and by withholding the right to own land of his own, but it was also designed to provide him with protection and saved the remnant of this unfortunate people from destruction.[2]

The activity of Caledon in internal affairs and his negative attitude with regard to the frontier problem is partly explained by the unfortunate controversy between himself and General Grey which continued throughout his tenure of office. By the terms of his commission Caledon, like his predecessors at the Cape, was designated as Commander-in-Chief according to the form normally used in the commissions of American and West Indian Governors. The respective spheres of military authority exercised by the Governor and the senior military officer in the old colonies had been precisely defined in accordance with the Governor's constitutional position in relation to the local Assembly, which voted supplies for military defence, and with the military officer's responsibility to the Commander-in-Chief and the War Department at home. But there was no Assembly

[1] Caledon to Castlereagh, 15 October 1809. *Recs. of Cape Colony*, VII, 170–5.
[2] For further discussion *vide infra*, chap. XII.

at the Cape, and with the exception of that for the Hottentot Corps, all military expenditure was defrayed by the Home Government. Governors at the Cape from Lord Macartney onwards had accordingly claimed that they, and they only, as the delegates of the Sovereign Power, were responsible for the direction of defence policy, which it was the Commanding Officer's function to carry out. In the case of Sir George Yonge the claim had been hotly contested by General Dundas, and when the dispute was referred home, the Secretary at War had quoted the instructions issued to the Earl of Halifax in 1765 in respect of North America, which for the above-mentioned reason did not meet the case. When Caledon resurrected the question in February 1807, he was given for his guidance an extract from the same document of 1765. The controversy therefore continued. In 1810 he urged the importance of a proper demarcation of authority in view of the standing menace of the frontier.[1] Failure to secure a definite answer resulted in the passive acceptance of a dangerous frontier situation.

It was not until the controversy threatened to impede the general conduct of the war in the Indian seas that the Home Government made an effort to define the rival authorities. In July 1810 Caledon received from Lord Minto, Governor-General of India, a requisition for 3000 troops from the Cape to co-operate with forces from Bengal and Madras in the conquest of Bourbon and the Île de France, subsequently Mauritius.[2] Grey acquiesced in the desirability of compliance, but endeavoured to reserve to himself the discretionary power in the sending of reinforcements, while Caledon asserted with equal vigour that the decision properly lay with him.[3] The Governor sent Alexander, the Colonial Secretary, home with a further despatch urging the necessity for a definite ruling. When the latter arrived, he found Lord Liverpool in a state of perplexity. The Duke of York as Commander-in-Chief had been writing despatches to Grey supporting his view of the matter and had expressed indignation at Caledon's presumptuous interference. From the Horse Guards also Sir David Dundas pressed Liverpool to give the division in favour of the Army.[4] Liverpool's decision (in February 1811) was a confession of failure to adapt the normal machinery to an exceptional case, and amounted to little more than a recommendation to the two men to solve the difficulty themselves by employing their good sense. When troops from the Cape were requisitioned, as recently by Lord Minto, the occasion must by its importance for the general interest of the Empire preclude the probability of a difference of opinion. In the case of a Kaffir war the declaration of hostilities lay with the Governor as

[1] Caledon to Liverpool, 30 June 1810. *Recs. of Cape Colony*, VII, 296–303.
[2] Same to same, 12 July 1810. *Ibid.* VII, 333–4.
[3] Same to same, 27 August and 12 September 1810. *Ibid.* VII, 357–9, 369–71.
[4] Sir David Dundas to Liverpool, 28 November 1810. *Ibid.* VII, 435–59.

representing the Crown; but as regards the planning and conduct of the campaign the opinion of the commanding officer must be given "the most serious consideration, if not entire predominance". On the whole Liverpool had come down on the side of the War Department[1], but after Caledon had resigned, as he did before the Secretary of State's despatch had reached him, supreme military control was vested in the Governor, who until 1854 was usually a soldier. The controversy had served to illustrate the abnormal position of the Cape in the Empire. As an imperial fortress, manned at the expense of the occupying Power and administered on Crown Colony lines, traditional rules of procedure—in military no less than in commercial matters—could not be applied.

Caledon's successor, Sir John Cradock, who took the oaths of office on 6 September 1811, was a Major-General with a distinguished and varied military career behind him. The vigour and efficiency of his administration of the Cape from 1811 to 1814 earned for him the warm approval of the Secretary of State, while the manner in which he identified himself with the interests and point of view of the colonists won for him an affectionate esteem which they had accorded to none of his predecessors. The new Governor was at once faced by the difficult problem which had been raised by the grave charges of the ill-treatment of Hottentots brought by missionaries and officials against the farmers. A special commission of four Judges was sent out from Cape Town on 23 September 1812 to investigate the charges. The story of the Black Circuit which followed is narrated elsewhere in this volume.[2] Its effect was doubly unhappy. The publicity which it had secured in Great Britain did much to establish in British minds a conception of Boer brutality which was responsible for future misunderstanding; whilst the frontier farmer, whether he had been convicted or acquitted, had been subjected to humiliation which he bitterly resented. With the highest motives and great courage the missionaries had joined battle at an unfortunate juncture. Successive Governors had pursued a policy of amelioration, which, implemented by a growing obedience to the rule of law, was gradually changing the relationship between farmer and Native. Although led astray in some cases by their own credulity, the missionaries succeeded in proving that the general situation was far from being in accord with civilised notions; but in so doing they retarded instead of furthering the course of reform.

Yet it is easy to exaggerate the friction engendered by the "Black" Circuit by viewing it in the light of after events. Every subsequent circuit, in so far as it summoned farmers to answer the complaints of their Hottentot servants, was "black". But the civilising agency was a commission of Dutch judges, adjudicating criminal charges under

[1] Liverpool to Caledon, 28 February 1811. *Ibid.* VII, 493–5.

[2] *Vide infra*, chap. XII.

Roman-Dutch law. The advent of the London Missionary Society represented the evangelism of the middle class in England, which had not yet acquired political power. Official British authority was still Tory in outlook and of the eighteenth century, and it therefore still shared the conservatism of the Afrikaners. The British Governor, the Afrikaner Fiscal and the local Landdrost were at one in advocating justice and kindness and in their detestation of "enthusiasm".

It was very unfortunate that the frontier farmers came into collision with English middle-class opinion at a time when their cry for "security" was being answered by *non possumus*. As we have seen, Caledon's lack of military authority was partly responsible for a negative frontier policy, which left the Xhosas in possession of the Zuurveld and failed to check their growing audacity in murder and thieving. By May 1811, fifty-three loan-places in the Uitenhage district had been abandoned owing to Xhosa raids, and Landdrost Cuyler frankly told Caledon that he was unable to hold his ground against Kaffir intrusion.[1] Similarly Capt. Hawkes reported from the frontier that the Boers were refusing to endure the conditions any longer and were leaving their places.[2] The only effective course, as Cuyler repeatedly urged, was the reconquest of the Zuurveld. Caledon confessed to his successor that his policy of conciliation had been a failure.[3]

Sir John Cradock was an experienced soldier as well as being titular Commander-in-Chief. Within a month of his assumption of office and the departure of Caledon and Grey, he had organised a large combined force of burghers and regulars for the clearance of the Zuurveld and the driving of the Kaffirs across the Fish River.[4] During January and February 1812, the work of expulsion was carried out under the able leadership of Lieut.-Colonel Graham, who was appointed Special Commissioner for all civil and military affairs in the districts of Graaff-Reinet, Uitenhage and George. Skill and determination were responsible for the hustling of 20,000 warlike Kaffirs out of the Eastern Province with surprisingly little bloodshed. By the end of February Graham was able to report that "hardly a Kaffir now remains". Heartened at last by a decisive policy at Cape Town, the farmers had exhibited great endurance and initiative.[5]

The more difficult task, that of securing the regained territory, remained. This Cradock attacked with characteristic vigour. While the preparations were going forward, the great majority of the regular troops were retained on the frontier. The system of defence

[1] *Recs. of Cape Colony*, VIII, 44–8, 56–7, 72–4, 90–1. *Cf.* Landdrost Stockenstrom's protest, *ibid.* VIII, 116–20.

[2] Hawkes to Cuyler, 24 June 1811. *Ibid.* VIII, 88–9.

[3] Caledon to Cradock, 1 July 1811. *Ibid.* VIII, 111.

[4] See his instructions to Lieut.-Col. Graham, 6 Oct. 1811, his proclamation of 18 October, and his despatch to Lord Liverpool, 18 October 1811. *Ibid.* VIII, 159–63, 163–4, 179–81.

[5] Graham to Cradock, 26 February 1912. *Ibid.* VIII, 286–7.

which Cradock and Graham devised consisted of a double chain of fortified posts manned by patrols of ten men each. Behind these lines an embryo garrison town was established on the Zuurveld at Grahamstown, for which a Deputy Landdrost was appointed. While the right wing of the frontier in the Uitenhage district was thus provided for, a similar arrangement was made in the following year for the Graaff-Reinet wing on the left by the establishment of another township, named Cradock, also with a Drostdy and a Deputy Landdrost. To man this frontier system the whole of the Cape Corps with a detachment of cavalry and infantry was employed.[1] For the first time a stong military force was stationed on the frontier as a standing garrison. This change of policy was symptomatic of the transformation of the Cape, which circumstances were gradually effecting, from being a primarily strategic post to a gateway leading to the interior.

While Cradock was using valuable British regulars to defend Afrikaner farmers, Great Britain was holding its own with great difficulty against Napoleon at the height of his power. It was natural therefore that the change from the passive conciliation of Caledon to the offensive measures of Cradock should be viewed with distaste. As soon as the latter's warlike preparations were known, Lord Liverpool sent out a despatch urging caution. Systematic warfare against the Kaffirs, even if completely successful, was an impolitic course from which little benefit could accrue.[2] On hearing of the Zuurveld campaign Earl Bathurst, Liverpool's successor in the Secretaryship for War and the Colonies, used more emphatic language. Cradock was reminded that a great European war was in progress, and that it was his duty to keep the whole of his troops disposable for the defence of the Colony, not against the Xhosas of the hinterland but against the French from the sea. It would give Bathurst great satisfaction to learn that hostilities had ended with a fair prospect of permanent tranquillity, even at the price of surrendering some of the territory regained "if it will not interfere with the rights of other individuals".[3] There, of course, was the rub. The Cape had an imperial value: the price to be paid for its retention was responsibility for an advancing and almost indefensible frontier. Until the colony became responsible for its own defence, every Secretary of State strove to keep the bill within reasonable limits. Bathurst, like many of his successors, had kicked against the pricks, but, as Cradock pointed out, retention of the fortress depended upon the security of the hinterland. The Governor had effected a revolution in frontier policy and had succeeded in carrying the Home authorities with him.

The complementary problem awaiting treatment related to land

[1] For an account of the system see Cory, *Rise of South Africa*, I, 246–53.
[2] Liverpool to Cradock, 20 December 1811. *Recs. of Cape Colony*, VIII, 216–18.
[3] Bathurst to Cradock, 29 July 1812. *Ibid.* VIII, 475–6.

tenure. No less than three thousand applications for Government confirmation of new holdings had accumulated, and, apart from the serious loss of revenue entailed, the farmers were growing restive because of the uncertainty of their situation. Cradock also realised that the future progress of the Colony demanded that the old system of granting extensive leaseholds, which fostered dispersion and therefore weakness, must be superseded. It was clearly impracticable to impose modifications in respect of grants already made. The policy, therefore, which he submitted to the Government, was to establish for the future perpetual quit-rent tenure, which would provide all the advantages of tenure in fee simple and also add a permanent increase to the revenue. Holders of loan-leases were to be persuaded to exchange the old tenure for the new, and in all future grants the area of the allotment was to be contracted. In reply, Bathurst and the Committee for Trade virtually declared their inability to judge the issue and within wide limits left it to the Governor to do what he thought best.[1]

He was, in fact, already working out his own scheme. The necessity for a speedy resettlement of the Zuurveld provided him with an opportunity of making a fresh start in that region. Colonel Graham was told that he must countermand the grants of loan-places which he had begun to make to the burghers, who were flocking back to their old homes. A new system of permanent leasehold and smaller allotment was to be adopted. Cradock was, however, prepared to make large grants to original landholders on the Zuurveld and to forgo rent for several years; but in these as in all other cases there must be proper survey, and the principle of a graded quit-rent must be accepted.[2] He thus adopted in principle the policy of close settlement so strongly advocated by Alexander. The new system was given general application by the proclamation of 6 August 1813. It provided for the voluntary conversion of loan leaseholds into holdings by perpetual hereditable quit-rent, but none must exceed 3000 morgen, the legal extent of the original loan-places which had often been greatly exceeded by gradual encroachment. The rent, which, though small, was to be considerably higher than that paid under the old system, was to be in proportion to the fertility and situation of the land.[3] Two subsidiary proclamations established the perpetual quit-rent principle for all future grants and provided for accurate surveys and for local commissions to investigate and report to the Governor on all applications for land.[4]

Cradock's settlement divides itself into three sections: voluntary

[1] Minutes of the Committee for Trade, 23 September 1812. B.T. 5/20, pp. 457–8.

[2] See Cradock to Col. Graham, 2 April 1812. Printed from the Graham MSS. by Cory, *op. cit.*, I, 255–6. Cf. Alexander's letters to Graham of the same date and of 23 May, *Recs. of Cape Colony*, VII, 370–4, 423–6.

[3] Proclamation of 6 August 1813. *Ibid.* VII, 204–8.

[4] Proclamations of 16 July and 23 July 1813. *Ibid.* VII, 200–3, 203–4.

conversion of old holdings, rules for future grants, and special arrangements for the Zuurveld. As regards the first, the scheme was a failure. The farmer felt himself to be, and in practice was, perfectly secure against the danger of Government resumption of his land, and naturally he failed to see the advantage of paying a considerably higher rent. During the first year not a single application for conversion was received. On the Zuurveld, local conditions were too strong to be overridden: the policy of "group settlement" had to be abandoned. But the general regulations for future grants were of great value, for they provided an ordered system which yielded a reasonable revenue and prevented the worst excesses of land-grabbing. They were received in London with "entire approval", and Cradock's successor was forbidden to deviate thereform "without previous and specific authority from Home".[1]

Cradock's reforming zeal touched every important aspect of colonial life. By bounties and improved regulations he did his utmost to stimulate the production of new commodities for export,[2] for, with the exception of wine, an export trade was virtually non-existent. In order to protect the public, the central government undertook to supervise the Landdrosts' assessments for taxation. Cradock was also responsible for an important and salutary change in legal procedure. British civil servants and merchants strongly resented their subjection to Dutch courts and Roman-Dutch law. The cry, which had been so familiar in Quebec, for the privileges of English law in civil causes was being raised. Not understanding Dutch procedure these merchants were probably unfair in their strictures. "The cause of a foreigner", wrote one, "was always, indeed, considered as hopeless."[3] When the Commission of Circuit recommended that the proceedings of the superior courts at Cape Town should be henceforth heard in public, Cradock seized the opportunity and urged the desirability of the change in a letter to Chief Justice Truter. Such a reform would go far to satisfy the British part of the community, who would regard the grant of "open doors and unconcealed process" as some compensation for the absence of trial by jury.[4] To the Governor's surprise and pleasure Truter was able to secure the consent of his colleagues, and the change was accordingly made.[5]

The terms of the farewell addresses, which were presented to Cradock on his relinquishment of the government in April 1814, attest the hoppy relations which he had established with all sections of the community and the warm regard which his zeal and integrity had gained for him.[6] Under his vigorous and constructive administration the Colony had taken a long step forward.

[1] Bathurst to Somerset, 18 February 1814. *Recs. of Cape Colony*, VII, 410–11.
[2] See Fisher, R. B., *The Importance of the Cape of Good Hope* (London, 1814), p. 71.
[3] *Ibid.* pp. 36, 39.
[4] Cradock to Truter, 20 August 1813. *Recs. of Cape Colony*, IX, 219–22.
[5] See *ibid.* IX, 236–46. [6] *Ibid.* X, 103–10.

The advent of his successor, Lord Charles Somerset, was less happy. On 5 April 1814, H.M.S. *Medway* arrived at the Cape with the new Governor and his numerous suite on board. Somerset landed on the following morning, presented his commission, and demanded to be sworn in at once. Cradock protested that he must continue in office for a few days to wind up an accumulation of administrative business. But Somerset was peremptory. After an interview lasting several hours the retiring Governor, "deeply mortified", gave way, and Somerset at once proclaimed himself. For no discoverable cause, save his own hauteur, he had offered a gratuitous insult to an officer whose policy he had been ordered to regard as a model for imitation. He subsequently treated Sir Rufane Donkin in the same manner, although on that occasion his discourtesy was due to violent anger against his deputy. Cradock at once reported the episode to Bathurst in deep indignation[1] and repeated his protests on arrival in England.[2] It created an unfortunate impression in Cape Town, where Cradock's friends were numerous. Several years later Lady Holland described the new Governor with some venom as "a horse jockey who went to the Cape to make money".[3] The description is not a fair summary of Somerset's attainments, but it does indicate his chief motive in going to the Cape. One of his first acts was to take 45,000 rix-dollars from the Colonial Treasury on account of salary. After a prolonged wrangle with the Commissioners for Auditing Colonial Accounts, he was allowed to compound by paying back one-half—which he did in 1824, when the rix-dollar had depreciated from three shillings to one shilling and sixpence. It has been calculated that his profits on the deal amounted to over £7000.[4] The transaction, though relatively unimportant, illustrates Somerset's general lack of principle in money matters. Avarice combined with vindictiveness against those who opposed his designs introduced an unwholesome atmosphere into his administration, which was in painful contrast to the integrity of Caledon and Cradock. It was particularly unfortunate that the influence of the Beaufort family should at last have succeeded in planting Somerset at the Cape at a time when the Colony was approaching a very critical period in its history.[5] Yet he was not without ability, nor in his own peculiar way

[1] Cradock to Bathurst, 1 May 1814. *Recs. of Cape Colony*, x, 110–11. Somerset to Bathurst, 18 April 1814. *Ibid.* IX, 490–3.

[2] Same to same, 3 December 1814. *Bathurst Papers. Hist. MSS. Comm.*, p. 311.

[3] Goulburn to Bathurst, 17 October 1821. *Ibid.* p. 520.

[4] Cory, *op. cit.* II, 241–3. Cf. *Fifth Report from the Select Committee of the House of Commons on Finance, July* 1819, *Parl. Pap.* 1819, II (539), Appendix IV, 125.

[5] The myth that the Beaufort clan commanded important parliamentary influence which caused Lord Liverpool to agree to the appointment and which was strong enough to protect Somerset when he afterwards came under attack, has been effectively exposed by Professor Michael Roberts, "Lord Charles Somerset and the Beauforts' Influence" (*Archives Year Book for S. African History*, 1951, II, 1–34). The Beauforts were however, socially influential. It would have been "extremely convenient . . . on many accounts" to have sent Somerset to the Cape in 1806. Apparently it still was in 1814.

was he unmindful of the interest of the Colony. His strenuous opposition to the reduction of the Cape garrison and his absorption in the problems of frontier defence bear witness to that fact. His natural propensity to override and to bully those who protested was given full scope for development in a post which carried with it the exercise of autocratic authority. His faults might have passed with less notice before 1815, but his régime coincided with a post-war period when new ideas and a new population were about to invade the colony.

In the meantime the battle of Leipzig had dealt a shattering blow to Napoleon's Empire, and the Peninsular campaign had been crowned with victory for the arms of Wellington. At the Congress of Vienna, Great Britain, under the guidance of Castlereagh, accepted responsibilities she had never previously undertaken. The policy of isolation and the safeguarding of specific British interests, as pursued at the Treaty of Amiens, was abandoned, and Great Britain participated in a new and universally guaranteed equilibrium.[1] The future of the Netherlands and the Dutch Empire was a factor common to both the European settlement and to that overseas. The fulcrum of Castlereagh's new balance of power was a rehabilitated Netherlands reinforced by union with Belgium. It was, therefore, wise statesmanship not to weaken this buffer State by depriving it of the Dutch colonies which had been conquered by British arms. Accordingly by the Convention of London (13 August 1814) Great Britain restored to the Netherlands the East Indies and all other Dutch colonies captured since 1803, with the exception of the Cape of Good Hope and the Guiana settlements of Demerara, Essequibo and Berbice. With regard to the Cape, the new Dutch Government was not sorry to be rid of the expense of its maintenance, and instructed its envoy, Hendrik Fagel, to concentrate his efforts upon retaining the South American colonies, which, unlike the Cape, were a valuable commercial asset.[2] Castlereagh, on his side, was equally unimpressed by the commercial value of Cape Colony, but bowed to popular insistence upon the necessity of its retention in relation to India.[3]

By the middle of July 1814, Castlereagh had become so exasperated by what he regarded as the rapacity and ingratitude of the Dutch Cabinet that he refused to separate the negotiations with respect to the Dutch colonies from the general arrangements to be made at Vienna.[4] Accordingly, a fortnight later, Lord Clancarty in Brussels was instructed to make a formal proposal to the Prince of Orange that the above-mentioned colonies should remain in British hands by way of compensation for certain specified financial commitments,

[1] Cf. Webster, C. K., *The Foreign Policy of Castlereagh*, 1815–1822, pp. 50–3; *Camb. Hist. of Brit. For. Policy*, I, 518–20; and *The Congress of Vienna*, 1814–15, *passim.*

[2] See Colenbrander, H. T., *Gedenkstukken der Algemeene Geschiedenis van Nederland*, XXIII, 614–18.

[3] See Castlereagh to Clancarty, 30 July 1814. *Recs. of Cape Colony*, X, 145.

[4] Same to same, 14 July 1814. *Ibid.* X, 130–2.

involving a total sum of £6,000,000, which Great Britain was prepared to undertake on behalf of the Netherlands. The Prince admitted the force of the argument that, if the British public was to be reconciled "to burthens of such magnitude", it was necessary for Castlereagh to have "something to hold out in the nature of an equivalent for their immediate advantage".[1] By the convention with the Netherlands Great Britain undertook to pay £1,000,000 to Sweden, £2,000,000 to the Netherlands for the fortification of the Belgian frontier (representing a half of the total cost), and a sum not exceeding £3,000,000 "towards the final and satisfactory settlement of the Low Countries, in union with Holland"—a phrase to be elucidated later. The Cape and the three Guiana colonies were ceded to Great Britain "in consideration and in satisfaction of the above engagements".

This arrangement has been inaccurately described by many historians as a "purchase" of the colonies in question for a cash payment of £6,000,000.[2] The payment of £1,000,000 to Sweden was made as compensation for French Guadeloupe, which, after being captured by the British and handed over by them in 1813 to Sweden in exchange for certain trading privileges, was now to be restored to France. The Dutch failed to see why a British debt to Sweden should be liquidated by a payment which was represented as being a Dutch obligation.[3] The second item of British expenditure, namely the £2,000,000 paid directly to the Netherlands Government towards Belgian fortification, was naturally enough not regarded as a boon by the minister Van Nagel and the Dutch "colonials", who disliked the very idea of union with Belgium.

The nature of the third charge undertaken by Great Britain, that of £3,000,000, was revealed in a separate Convention with the Netherlands and Russia, dated 19 May 1815.[4] During the war Russia had raised a loan in Holland through Hope and Co. of Amsterdam, on account of which she owed 80 million florins to bondholders.[5] The Czar's treasury was empty, but he had a large army in France, and his assent to the Belgic settlement was essential. Under the circumstances he decided to sell that assent at the price of relief from the Dutch loan, and instructed his minister, Count Nesselrode, to suggest that Great Britain and Holland should assume joint liability for the debt. Although deeply incensed, Castlereagh persuaded the British Cabinet and the Prince of Orange to accept the proposition rather than imperil the peace settlement. By the Convention with Russia

[1] Clancarty to Castlereagh, 4 August 1814. *Ibid.* x, 147–52.

[2] The details of the arrangement are clearly set out in Walker, E. A., *History of S. A.*, p. 139, n. 1. Cf. Robson, W. H., "New Light on Lord Castlereagh's Diplomacy", *Journal of Modern History*, III, 198–218.

[3] See Colenbrander, *op cit.* XXIII, 632–5, 648–9. Cf. *Correspondence, Dispatches and other Papers of Viscount Castlereagh*, IX, 344–6.

[4] This and the two previous Conventions of 13 August 1814 (with the Netherlands and Sweden respectively) are printed in *Hansard*, XXXI, 707–16.

[5] Say £6,000,000.

Great Britain and the Netherlands undertook responsibility for the Russian debt on account of capital and arrears of interest up to 25 million florins each,[1] but with the stipulation that all payments should cease if the Belgic provinces should be severed from Holland. During the final negotiations the Count de Lieven had tried to have the British contributions made unconditional, leaving the *proviso* to stand with respect to Holland only. Castlereagh retorted that so obnoxious a measure would destroy his whole case in Parliament by enabling his opponents to describe the arrangement "as one not upon the principle of a fair equivalent with Holland but as a gratuitous concession to Russia". The Opposition would rightly maintain that, in view of the danger that Napoleon (now returned from Elba) would reabsorb the Netherlands, Great Britain ought not only "to save its money, but keep the Dutch colonies into the bargain".[2]

In short, Castlereagh was asking his countrymen, at the end of a world war of unparalleled duration and financial strain, to expend a further £6,000,000 to ensure a stable peace. The sum to be expended was—assuming the practicability of his continental system—a benefit to Europe, a form of insurance for British interests, and indirectly a substantial aid to the Netherlands. The diplomatic fiction that Great Britain discharged liabilities which properly belonged to the Dutch was Castlereagh's only chance of obtaining parliamentary approval. After two decades of war with Great Britain, Holland was treated with moderation, if not with generosity, because of her buffer position in Europe. The future of the Cape aroused little discussion during the negotiations. Its acquisition, with Malta and Mauritius, completed Great Britain's strategic control of the trade routes of her Empire.[3]

The Colony was thus retained not merely because of its relation to India, but also because the British public was prejudiced in its favour as a market for their manufactures and as a trade depot. A further reason advanced by Castlereagh was that the Abolitionists desired to maintain control over those conquered colonies which in other hands would be useful for the prosecution of the slave trade. The growing interest in the Cape as a colony rather than a fortress had already been reflected in the legislation of the Governors. Now that it was a part of the Empire and peace conditions obtained, British ideas and British institutions were bound to exert an increasing influence.[4]

While the future destiny of the Cape was being decided on the

[1] Say, £2,083,333.

[2] *Castlereagh Correspondence*, x, 365–7.

[3] Cf. *Camb. Hist. of Brit. For. Policy*, I, 519.

[4] For an advocacy of the Cape as a field for post-war emigration, see Fisher, R. B., *The Importance of the Cape of Good Hope as a Colony to Great Britain independently of the advantages it possess as a Military and Naval Station* (London, 1814). Its value as a centre for trade had been discussed, among others, by Percival, R., *An Account of the Cape of Good Hope* (London, 1804).

battlefields of Europe and at the Vienna Congress, the South African frontier was being steadily subjected to the rule of law. Year by year two Justices perambulated the distant districts investigating charges of disobedience against Hottentot servants and hearing their complaints of ill-usage. A new tradition was gradually being established that neither Boer nor Hottentot was a law unto himself. The work of each succeeding Circuit widened the general acceptance of the principle. The reports of the Commissioners for 1813 and 1814 agreed in stating that the treatment of the slaves was generally good and that the labour contracts of the Hottentots were for the most part conscientiously observed by the burghers. Inevitably, however, there was a minority whose temperament predisposed them to abuse the frontier tradition of self-preservation by each white man acting as judge in his own cause.

The Court of Circuit for 1815 had a number of charges of ill-treatment before it. One of them concerned a frontier farmer of Baviaan's River named Frederik Cornelis Bezuidenhout, who had ignored the summons of two previous Circuit Courts to answer to a charge of cruelty to a Hottentot. The Court issued an order for his arrest, and the Landdrost of Graaff-Reinet secured the services of a white officer and twelve men of the Hottentot Corps to assist the Deputy-Sheriff. As the party approached his house, Bezuidenhout fired on them and was himself killed in the resulting scuffle. At his funeral his brother Johannes swore to avenge his death by driving the British and their Hottentot employees out of the border districts and to establish a republic. The little group of conspirators planned to rid themselves of the humiliating presence of the Hottentot Regiment by calling to their aid the even less civilised Kaffirs. Neither the effort to secure the intervention of Gaika nor that to induce the burghers to rise in general rebellion met with success. Most of those who joined the revolt became disheartened by the evident lack of response, but the ringleaders stubbornly refused to consider submission without the prior release of their comrade, Hendrik Prinsloo, who had been taken by surprise and marched off. Finally a combined force of burghers and soldiers rounded up the insurgents, numbering about sixty, at Slachter's Nek. Some of them quietly surrendered and were conveyed as prisoners to the military post known as Van Aardt's. The rest fled, but were all presently arrested, except Johannes Bezuidenhout who refused to be taken and continued to fire on his pursuers until he was mortally wounded.

The Court of Circuit was ordered to proceed on its normal duties and on November 27 a Special Commission was appointed to try the prisoners. The judges arrived at Uitenhage on December 14 and sat for nearly six weeks. Forty-seven persons were charged, but a number who had obviously been deceived or compelled to take part were released at an early stage. The sentences of the Court condemned six to death and thirty to banishment.[1] When submitted for confirmation to the Governor many of these sentences received considerable mitigation; but except in the case of W. F. Kruger, who was eventually pardoned, Somerset decided that those condemned to death must suffer the extreme penalty as a salutary warning that the old practice of armed rebellion as the normal method of voicing grievances was at an end—a decision with which the Secretary of State fully concurred.

The importance of a historical event frequently lies, not so much in the extent of its influence upon contemporary thought and action, as in its propaganda value for a later generation. The Slachter's Nek episode was intrinsically nothing more than a riotous act committed by some sixty individuals, who supported the cause of a man who had tried to shoot the representatives of the law in the execution of their duty. The mass of the population, so far from participating in the disturbance, took an active part with the troops in suppressing it. But in retrospect it assumed a different complexion. To many Voortrekkers, smarting twenty years later under "the unjustifiable odium which has been cast upon us by interested and dishonest persons, under the cloak of religion, whose testimony is believed in England to the exclusion of all evidence in our favour",[2] Bezuidenhout and the five ringleaders who were executed were martyrs who had championed the same cause as themselves. At the same time the threat of Prinsloo to attack the frontier posts and exterminate the Hottentot garrisons undoubtedly illustrated in an extreme form a general restiveness at being kept in order by a Coloured police, and Somerset urged the desirability of replacing the Hottentot Corps by a British battalion.[3] Moreover, the incident made an undue impression upon the official mind in England. On 6 March 1816, Henry Goulburn, the Under-Secretary for the Colonies, in the House of Commons, defended the maintenance of a garrison 2000 strong at the Cape, not only on the ground that the use of regular troops was the only effective method of holding the frontier, but also because the Boers themselves required constant supervision. He cited Slachter's Nek.[4]

Hitherto the relationship between Great Britain and Cape Colony had subsisted on a war-time basis. A garrison of between four and five thousand men had been regularly stationed there for purposes of defence and as a military depot from which reinforcements could be drafted to India in times of emergency. The presence of so many

[1] For verbatim reports of the respective trials, see Leibbrandt, *The Rebellion of 1815, Generally known as Slachter's Nek* (Cape of Good Hope Archives, Capetown, 1902), *passim.* See also Reyburn, H. A., "Studies in Cape Frontier History", in *The Critic*, January and April 1935.

[2] Manifesto of the Emigrant Farmers, 2 February 1837; *vide infra*, pp. 328, 330. Bell and Morrell, *Select Documents on British Colonial Policy*, 1830–1860, pp. 485–6. Also in Eybers, G. W., *Select Constitutional Documents*, pp. 143–5.

[3] Somerset to Bathurst (with enclosures), 11 December 1815. *Recs. of Cape Colony*, XI, 42–1.

[4] *Hansard*, XXXII, 1255.

mouths to feed had provided the inhabitants with an artificial market, which had become a primary factor in their commercial and financial organisation; but after Waterloo the Liverpool ministry found itself faced by a critical financial situation at home, which was an index of the exhausted condition of the country, and was subjected to a sustained attack by the Opposition. The debates on the Army estimates for 1816, which provided a military force of approximately 100,000 for the defence of the Empire, provoked a number of instructive comments on colonial defence generally and that of the Cape in particular. Ministerialists argued that the Cape was in a position of exceptional importance on the trade routes of the Empire and that the price of controlling a turbulent population and guarding an extended frontier was worth paying. The Opposition, on the other hand, asked if it were not true that Great Britain had won the war and, if so, what sense there was in burdening an exhausted country with the expense of defending colonies against non-existent enemies. Was France or the Netherlands in a position to attack the Cape? As for internal defence, that colony was capable of providing for it out of its own resources.[1] In a further debate in the Lords on 15 March 1816, the Marquis of Lansdowne maintained that the estimate of 3000 men for the Cape was indispensable, having regard to the necessity of detaching seven or eight hundred into the interior to prevent Kaffir incursions; but Lord Grenville poured scorn on the Ministry's proposals, jeering that Britain was supreme in the Indian Ocean and yet was to be called upon to maintain 3000 men at the Cape "to guard against a few Caffres".[2]

The tenor of these debates produced an immediate effect upon the Government departments. On March 29 Bathurst wrote to Somerset instructing him to carry out a minute investigation of public expenditure and to report all possible economy cuts.[3] The Government's intention was to increase the surplus of colonial revenue and to apply it to meet part of the Army Commissariat expenditure. But Somerset, who was assiduously reading his *Hansard*, had already taken alarm. In May he wrote to the Secretary of State referring to a Commons debate on March 4 in which Palmerston had notified the House of a number of peacetime reductions, including the abolition of the office of Commander of the Forces at the Cape then vested in the Governor and the entrusting of the command to the senior officer on the station. He at once pointed out that the impossible situation previously existing between Caledon and General Grey would be reproduced. But worse was to follow. The economy campaign in

[1] Mr Freemantle's speech, 27 February 1816. *Hansard*, XXXII, 915. Cf. previous debates in the Commons, 12 and 19 February, *ibid.* XXXII, 385, 389 *et seq.*, 671, 992—3, and in the Lords, 14 February, *ibid.* XXXII, 510–26.

[2] *Ibid.* XXXIII, 356, 973–8. The same arguments were again repeated in the Commons, 8 and 11 March 1816. *Ibid.* XXXIII, 76–116, 134–57.

[3] Bathurst to Somerset, 29 March 1816. *Recs. of Cape Colony*, XI, 97–8.

Parliament was taken up with fervour by *The Times* and *The Morning Chronicle*. These newspapers made Somerset's administration at the Cape the centre of their onslaught, for it offered them the double advantage of attacking the arrogant Beaufort clan and at the same time the administration of a particularly expensive colony.

The general onslaught put the Colonial Office on the run. Somerset did his best to fend off the worst excesses of economy as regards the Cape by transmitting a reasoned statement of what, in his view, were and what were not practicable reductions in expenditure. A garrison of 4000, he maintained, was the minimum compatible with efficient internal defence; but he proposed certain changes in personnel which would effect a substantial saving. Any reduction in the salaries of the civil service, whether British or Dutch, was not to be thought of: they were inadequately paid already. In conclusion he took higher ground. An arbitrary increase of taxation would be impolitic. An enlargement of the burden, coincident with a restriction of services, and at a time when an extension, particularly as regards education, was urgently called for, would be ungenerous and unwise. Moreover, a drastic reduction in the garrison would deprive the Colony of its chief means of paying for its imports, namely, the Commissary bills on London. For the sake of an inconsiderable economy the Government would constrict the Colony's purchasing power and rob British manufacturers of an expanding market.[1]

But parliamentary pressure was too powerful to be resisted. The insistence of Sir James Mackintosh and other Opposition members that Great Britain would eventually break down under the strain of providing for the internal defence of rapidly growing colonies was taken to heart. It was decided to transfer the whole of the Commissariat charges of the garrison to the Cape Treasury. To enable the colonial revenue to meet this burden, it would be relieved of a total expenditure of 280,000 rix-dollars by the abolition of the Hottentot Corps, the withdrawal of the Lieutenant-Governor and the cessation of public works. The Governor was authorised, as had been his predecessors, to draw upon the British Treasury to an amount not exceeding £5000 in any one year to make up any resulting deficit.[2]

Instead of a military force of 4000, including for frontier work a proportion of cavalry which Somerset had suggested, the garrison was to be reduced to a peacetime footing of 2400 infantry. The Governor must take comfort from the fact that the Commissariat charges would be proportionately diminished. In 1818 and 1819 the Colonial Treasury accordingly paid out 103,000 and 155,000 rix-dollars respectively on account of these charges, which was approximately half of what Bathurst had calculated would be required.

[1] Somerset to Bathurst, 1 September 1816 (2nd despatch of that date). *Recs. of Cape Colony*, XI, 151–64. Cf. same to same, 19 September 1816. *Ibid.* XI, 188.

[2] Bathurst to Somerset, 1 January 1817. *Ibid.* XI, 240–2.

In effect, the British Government had temporarily saved itself the pay of some 1600 soldiers and part of the maintenance of a garrison of 2400 by giving a sharp downward thrust to an already depreciating currency, which it was ultimately obliged to redeem with hard cash.[1] But the plain truth was that the Cape farmer, unless his standard of living was to drop to the level of the African, must inevitably live to some extent at the expense of the taxpayers of the imperial Power. As a British official at the Cape pertinently remarked, his fellow-countrymen must remember that they went there in defence of their interests and not in the expectation of financial or commercial gain.[2]

The year 1817 was an unfortunate time to have inaugurated an economy campaign at the expense of military efficiency. Cradock's lines of military posts, though well conceived, had been unable to present an impassable barrier to the Xhosas. Owing to the easy fordability of the Fish River at almost any point and the dense scrub covering the countryside, it was an easy matter for marauders to slip through. By December 1813, Cradock had admitted his disappointment in the effectiveness of his system, for the Xhosa inroads were continuing.[3] The tide of burgher immigration to the Zuurveld was checked, stopped, and then began to recede. Without the backing of a settled population his chain of posts was in the air. By April 1815 the raiders had been temporarily curbed. Somerset disbanded the farmers, who had been on commando in relays since August 1811, and trusted to the new troops on the frontier to prevent further incursions.[4] But the seeming tranquillity was merely a lull in the storm. Depredations began again and became so serious that in the spring of 1817 Somerset himself made a tour of the frontier in a vigorous effort to find a working solution. What he found there was a state of general panic. The inhabitants had lost 3600 head of cattle. In the Zuurveld (now known as Albany) 90 families out of the 145 which had settled there had abandoned their farms, and the remainder were on the point of flight.[5]

The policy which Somerset adopted was directly opposed to that of his predecessors. Whereas Cradock had denounced all treaties with the Xhosas as useless and had insisted on the complete isolation of African and colonist, Somerset tried to secure the co-operation of the tribal Chiefs by making it to their interest to punish cattle-thieving. At a conference with Gaika and an assembly of lesser Chiefs at the Kat River on 2 April 1817, he propounded the new policy. Rewards

[1] *Vide infra*, p. 261. The total reduction of troops throughout the Empire was 55,802 officers and men. *Second Report from the Select Committee on Finance, April 1819*; *Parl. Pap.* 1819, II (206).

[2] *State of the Cape* . . ., pp. 140–4.

[3] Memorandum by Cradock, 19 December 1813. *Recs. of Cape Colony*, IX, 285–7. Cf. his letters to Colonel Vicars (27 November 1813) and to Bathurst (6 December.), *ibid.* IX, 269–70, 275–6.

[4] Somerset to Bathurst, 3 April 1815. *Ibid.* X, 293.

[5] Same to same, 24 April 1817. *Ibid.* XI, 303–9.

would be paid to Chiefs who returned plunder, provided they protected the colonists; exemplary punishment would be inflicted on "all persons who shall trespass upon or molest the Caffre people or property", and barter for the European goods which the Natives needed would be permitted under regulation at Grahamstown. On the other hand, they were warned that cattle-raids would incur swift punishment by overwhelming armed force, and were subjected to a system of tribal compensation for losses, which was customary among themselves. Gaika as the titular, though far from actual, Paramount Chief was made generally responsible.[1] With regard to the defence of the frontier, Somerset strengthened and increased the chain of posts along the Fish River, reducing the number of those in the rear. Instead of infantry, he relied for the most part on cavalry as being more effective for the swift pursuit of marauders and, therefore, added a hundred horses to the detachment of mounted dragoons. He returned to Cape Town hopeful of the arrangements with Gaika and his subordinates and confident that he had made the frontier impregnable. But the problem of resettling "that fertile spot the Zuurveld", as he called it, remained unsolved. In a letter to the Landdrost and Heemraden of Uitenhage he urged that the surest way of repressing Xhosa depredations was to re-occupy the deserted areas and, by way of encouragement, offered to remit all rent for ten years and to grant a title in perpetual quit-rent after three years' occupancy.[2] But the offer failed to attract, and the anomaly of an expensive garrison guarding an almost empty country persisted.

When Somerset returned from his travels he found Bathurst's "economy" despatch awaiting him. Having just devised a system of frontier defence based on the employment of mounted dragoons, he was now informed that the garrison was reduced to 2400 with no cavalry at all. Small though the future garrison would be, he was determined to station at least 1100 troops on the frontier; for until the Xhosas had been mastered, population, "the natural defence of all countries", could not be expected. To make matters worse, the quality of some of the troops provided was extremely poor. One of the regiments at the Cape was the 60th, which consisted entirely of bad characters drafted from other regiments, and the Governor had just heard that 500 English deserters were being sent out to reinforce it. This regiment had given constant trouble and was quite unfit for frontier duty. The Royal African Corps too, comprising foreign adventurers and captured British deserters, was a constant source of annoyance to the inhabitants. Somerset protested that if he must perforce manage with a dangerously small force, it should at any rate be of dependable quality. The obnoxious 60th Regiment was removed

[1] "Minutes relative to . . . a conference between His Excellency Lord Charles Somerset and the Caffre chief Gaika at the Kat River on the 2nd April 1817" (enclosed in above despatch). *Recs. of Cape Colony*, XI, 310–16.

[2] 29 March 1817. *Ibid.* XI, 296–9.

in January 1819, but Great Britain was suffering too acutely from the post-war depression for any augmentation to be possible. On the one side, the British refused to defend the Cape frontier on a perpetual war-footing in time of peace; and on the other, efforts to remedy the chronic weakness of the Eastern Districts by attracting Boer settlers had failed. An attempt was about to be made to oppose a barrier to Kaffir aggression in the form of surplus population brought from the United Kingdom.

The situation in that country at the end of the Napoleonic wars was such as to make a new wave of emigration inevitable. The normal outflow of population created by conditions attendant upon an industrial revolution had been dammed up since the beginning of the war with the American colonies. Its release occurred at a time when heavy taxation, increased cost of living and post-war dislocation caused it to be greatly augmented by numbers of ex-officers and professional men as well as artisans and farm labourers. Migration on a large scale was thus certain: the only matter in doubt was its destination. From a non-political view the United States, owing to its comparative proximity and established position, offered the greatest attractions; indeed by 1819 British emigrants were sailing for America at the rate of two hundred a week.[1] The loss of so much valuable man-power to a rival naturally evoked efforts to direct the flow to regions within the Empire. The circumstances which ultimately led to the choice of Cape Colony as the favoured receptacle were the existence there of an empty and apparently fertile region, a savage enemy on the frontier with whom a depleted garrison was unable to cope, and an Afrikaner population inclined to be hostile. As early as May 1813, Colonel Graham had urged that no time should be lost in peopling the Zuurveld with Highland crofters, who were being driven from their holdings.[2]

The pressure which was brought to bear upon the Government resulted in the adoption of two distinct and successive policies. From 1817 to 1819 lukewarm support was given to general Empire settlement, that is to say, to settlement in Canada and Cape Colony, the only areas in the Empire suitable for European colonisation other than Australia, which was saddled with the convict problem. The preponderating motive was the disposal of English unemployed. The second phase of policy, which was responsible for the famous Albany Settlement of 1820, was primarily due to the worst Kaffir irruption into Cape Colony which had yet been experienced. The need of easing the distressful situation at home was now subordinated to the desire to plant in the border country a dense population, which would guarantee the security of the Colony and relieve the Mother

[1] *Annual Register* for 1819, "Chronicle", pp. 25–6.

[2] Graham to Alexander, 21 May 1813. *Recs. of Cape Colony*, IX, 182–6. Cf. Graham to Bathurst, 21 November 1814. *Ibid.* X, 206–8.

Country of an onerous burden. The process of converting the Government to the idea of transforming a conquered military post into an area for settlement was long and arduous, and all the more so because assisted immigration even to Canada was still frowned upon. In 1814, while the cession of the Cape was still in doubt, Richard Fisher, a merchant who was interested in the Colony and a close friend of Sir John Cradock, published a pamphlet entitled *The Importance of the Cape of Good Hope as a Colony to Great Britain*. Therein he advocated its development as a market by stimulating its own productiveness. "As it is extremely probable", he wrote, "that the emigration from this country must be very considerable, and the Cape holds out encouragement for settlers, no small number may be induced to try it."[1] For two years he exercised all the influence at his command and bombarded Bathurst and his Secretaries with requests for interviews in an effort to induce the Colonial Office to undertake the transportation of English labour to the Cape, but without result. The economy campaign was in full swing, and the idea had not yet taken hold that the settlement of a British population fronting the Kaffirs might relieve the poor-rates and the Army estimates at one and the same time. Two letters, which Fisher wrote in 1816 to Bathurst and William Wilberforce respectively, provide an excellent picture of the combination of motives which at last induced the Government to move. To Bathurst he repeated his old argument of commercial profit, the relief of British distress and the political necessity for anglicisation; but he added a new one: "In its present defenceless state, it may be taken by any power, but it is most likely, by the reduction of the Cape Regiment and other military force there, to become a prey to the revengeful and bloodthirsty Caffres." And to Wilberforce he painted a horrible and exaggerated picture of Afrikaner brutality to the Hottentots and urged the introduction of English law and English free labour as the only sound remedy.[2] Just as the humanitarians had desired the retention of the conquered colonies as a means of limiting the slave trade of other European powers, so they now began to support emigration to the Cape for the same reason.

With the exception of this last, the arguments in favour of assisted settlement applied equally to South Africa and Canada. British merchants desired the anglicisation of French-Canadian as well as Dutch-Afrikaner institutions, and both countries needed the protection of defensive "marks" on their borders. In 1817 applications from intending settlers became so numerous that the Colonial Office abandoned its negative attitude and adopted a new system.[3] The Govern-

[1] Fisher, R. B., *op. cit.* pp. 59, 71.

[2] Fisher to Bathurst, 13 September 1816. *Recs. of Cape Colony*, XI, 173–5. Fisher to Wilberforce. *Ibid.* XI, 176–83. Cf. Somerset's indignant repudiation of Fisher's charges regarding Dutch cruelty and immorality. *Ibid.* XI, 344–5.

[3] See Office copy of a circular letter embodying the new regulations, dated 1817. *Ibid.* XI, 388–9.

ment was now prepared to encourage the cultivation of larger holdings in the North American Colonies and at the Cape by granting to any individual 100 acres for every settler whom he engaged himself to take out and establish. The prospective proprietor must undertake to transport not less than ten persons. In other words, the minimum grant of land was 1000 acres. On this basis free passages would be provided by the Government for the proprietor and his followers. As security he must pay a deposit of £10 for every settler, which would be repaid as soon as his people had been located on the land assigned to him. In future "free-lance" emigrants must go at their own expense and would receive no assistance beyond the usual grant of twenty-five acres on arrival in the colony of their choice.

On paper the scheme solved the standing problem of labour scarcity and provided a dense population for resistance against attack; but no scheme of systematic colonisation is applicable to both agricultural and pastoral areas, and the only unoccupied region in Cape Colony, namely the Zuurveld or Albany, was and still is predominantly pastoral. A thickly populated cattle-ranch is an economic impossibility.

On 28 July 1817, Bathurst had written to Somerset mentioning the numerous applications which he was receiving from intending emigrants, and asking for the Governor's advice on the prospects of settlement in the colony and whether he advocated large grants conditional upon the transportation of a proportionate number of indentured settlers or the previous system of small independent holdings. Somerset's reply, dated December 18, was not received until 9 February 1818, some months after the new regulations had been adopted. Thus the plan of empire settlement to which the Government had committed itself was not dictated by the strategic needs of Albany but by the normal motives for colonisation. Somerset's despatch was, however, ultimately responsible for the contraction of that general plan into an effort to people the Zuurveld. The Albany scheme was not primarily a palliative for economic distress in Great Britain, as is frequently stated, but an effort to introduce normal self-reliance into an unusually weak colonial frontier.[1]

Somerset's report on the Cape as a general field for colonisation had been deliberately discouraging. All land worthy of cultivation had already been taken up and the remainder was so destitute of water as to be permanently uninhabitable. One possible region remained, the empty Zuurveld, the fertility of which he depicted in glowing colours. Once more he suggested, as he had been doing at frequent intervals ever since his adoption of the idea from Colonel Graham in 1813, that the emigrating impulse should be utilised to solve the Kaffir problem, "not disguising from you that I am much swayed in recommending the plan by a strong wish to be able

[1] On this point see Edwards, I. E., *The 1820 Settlers in South Africa.*

eventually to withdraw the military detachments from that quarter". It would be just to warn intending settlers that vigilance and courage would be necessary to defend their property. In addition to the Albany proposal he pointed out that the remainder of the Colony was capable of absorbing considerable numbers of artisans and labourers, who, being in great demand, would be assured of high wages; and he suggested that it would be an excellent investment to encourage such migration by granting free passages.[1] On receipt of this despatch the Colonial Office began to bring gentle pressure to bear upon their applicants to choose the Cape in preference to other colonies, and by the end of the year (1818) emigrants to Canada were excluded from the assistance provided by the new regulations. Moreover, applications to settle in parts of Cape Colony other than Albany were refused. Somerset's plan had, in fact, been accepted in principle, but it was applied half-heartedly and on a limited scale. In December Henry Atkinson, who proposed to conduct a party of settlers thither, was informed that "proposals for emigrating to the Cape have already been accepted to the fullest extent to which it is in contemplation of the Government to encourage them".[2] Moreover, Somerset's second suggestion of stimulating the migration of indentured labour had been ignored. It seemed that the forward policy of 1817–18 was about to come to a speedy termination.

The advocates of assisted labour transportation as distinct from land settlement were greatly disappointed at the Government's negative attitude. In January 1818, Henry Nourse had submitted a scheme to Lord Sidmouth "for the relief of the numerous distressed objects who crowd our streets". He proposed that a careful selection should be made of persons of good character and ability who should be conveyed to the Cape. On arrival their indentures, embodying reasonable conditions, should be put up for sale. Lack of labour in the colony was so chronic that these articles of agreement would fetch anything from £30 to £100. The amount of the original expenditure on clothing and transport, totalling about £20, should be immediately returned to an emigration fund, the surplus profit being retained at the Cape for the support of emigrants awaiting employment. Thus for a moderate initial outlay all parties concerned would receive permanent benefit.[3] The latter was forwarded by Sidmouth to the Colonial Office for Bathurst's attention, but nothing came of it.[4] Some time later, when Nourse called at the Office, he was merely given a copy of the circular letter and told that no new regulations had been made. But his scheme had attracted attention elsewhere. On 28 June 1819 he was summoned to give evidence before the Select

[1] Somerset to Bathurst, 18 December 1817. *Recs. of Cape Colony*, XI, 425–31.
[2] Quoted by Edwards, *op. cit.* p. 48.
[3] Nourse to Lord Sidmouth, 12 January 1818. *Recs. of Cape Colony*, XI, 445–8.
[4] *Ibid.* XI, 449–50.

Committee of the Commons on the Poor Laws, where he described an elaborated version of his original plan and criticised the Government scheme. Let settlers go out to the Cape independently, obtain their grants of land, and then acquire indentured labour, as provided by his plan, according to need. The questions put by members of the Committee showed that they were considering his proposals, not merely in relation to poor-relief, but as a possible means of replacing slave by free labour at the Cape. It was an interesting proposition which illustrates one aspect of British public opinion in regard to the colony;[1] but it was the examination of the next witness which revealed the dominating trend in political circles. W. J. Burchell,[2] who had travelled extensively in South Africa, blamed the Afrikaner frontiersmen for all the previous troubles with the Kaffirs, and advocated the planting of a British settlement on the border as the most effective means of re-establishing a good understanding. "Would there be any danger", he was asked, "if we conciliated the Caffres at this new settlement, that we might have for enemies the Dutch settlers?" "The Dutch settlers", he replied, "would find themselves circumscribed by this new establishment on the one side and by the authority of the laws of the Cape on the other and would probably not venture to commit any ill-natured acts against them."[3] The new frontier policy derived from a combination of humanitarianism and economy. It aimed by the substitution of a strong British border community for a weak Afrikaner one to put an end to Kaffir wars for ever.

The Committee was evidently aware that a special effort to colonise the Albany District was impending, for members closely questioned Burchell on what he would consider "the essential requisites" for persons "on the point of proceeding to Algoa Bay to settle". The project was made public on July 12 when Vansittart, the Chancellor of the Exchequer, rose in the House to move a grant of £50,000 to assist unemployed persons to emigrate to the Cape of Good Hope. The reason given was that the Government, having successfully experimented on a small scale in settling surplus population in one of the colonies, was desirous of making a more ambitious experiment. The Cape, he explained, had been found to be "more advantageous" than Canada. "The particular part of the Colony selected was the south east coast of Africa... some distance from Cape Town."[4] The statement was, in fact, deliberately veiled, and when the Chancellor was subsequently challenged about this remarkable preference for South Africa rather than Canada, he seems to have descended to

[1] *Second Report from the Select Committee*, 1819, *Parl. Pap.* 1819, II (509), Nourse's evidence, pp. 21–7.

[2] Author of *Travels in the Interior of Southern Africa*, 2 vols. (London, 1822–4). Cf. I, 82.

[3] *Second Report from the Select Committee*, Burchell's evidence, pp. 27–32. A shortened version is printed in the *Annual Register* for 1819, "Chronicle", pp. 331–6.

[4] *Hansard*, XL, 1549, 12 July 1819.

prevarication.[1] No doubt the Government was not anxious to advertise the fact that they were proposing to settle a dangerous area for military purposes, but the precaution seems to have been somewhat futile in view of the fact that news of a fresh Kaffir war was already public property and that the members of the Poor Laws Committee a fortnight previously had considered whether an advance guard of 3000 settlers would be able to protect themselves from Kaffir incursions.[2]

The change from a passive to an active furtherance of the Albany scheme was almost certainly caused by the arrival of alarming news from the Cape. Somerset's recognition of Gaika as Paramount Chief had ignored Bantu ideas of tribal autonomy. The standing feud between Gaika and his uncle Ndlambi broke out afresh when Dushane, son of the latter, deserted Gaika for his father. Feeling themselves strong enough to avenge past wrongs, father and son with other Xhosa chiefs attacked Gaika in force, inflicted on him a bloody defeat and deprived him of a vast quantity of cattle. Gaika thereupon appealed for aid to the Governor, who responded by sending a mixed detachment of troops and burghers under Colonel Brereton. The colonists recaptured most of the cattle but failed to come to grips with Gaika's enemies, who promptly retaliated by instituting a reign of terror on the frontier. The climax was reached on 22 April 1819, when 10,000 Xhosas in three columns swept down from the surrounding heights upon the town and barracks of Grahamstown. The defenders under Colonel Willshire numbered only 320, but their devoted courage and the immense superiority of the musket over the assegai defeated the onslaught. Three of the defenders were killed and five wounded, while the Xhosas lost between seven and eight hundred before they retreated. For a time Willshire's advance was hampered by lack of water and distemper among the horses, but eventually Ndlambi's army was followed and completely broken. In his report Somerset paid a glowing tribute to "that fine body of men", the burgher force.[3] In October he held a conference with Gaika and the defeated Chiefs. The latter were compelled to recognise Gaika once more as Paramount Chief and to restore his territory. To strengthen the colonial boundary Somerset established a neutral zone—an idea which had been suggested by Collins in 1809 and repeated in 1813 by the Court of Circuit.[4] The densely wooded area between the Fish and Keiskamma Rivers, which had provided ideal cover for Xhosa raiders, was declared neutral territory closed to Xhosa and colonist alike. Insulation was to be maintained by a military post (Fort Willshire) on the banks of the Keiskamma and by a system of military patrols.[5]

[1] See Edwards, *op. cit.* p. 53.

[2] *Second Report from the Select Committee*, 1819, p. 32.

[3] Somerset to Bathurst, 22 May 1819. *Recs. of Cape Colony*, XII, 193–202.

[4] Report of the Circuit Commission for 1813. *Ibid.* X, 94.

[5] Somerset to Bathurst, 15 October 1819. *Ibid.* XII, 337–45.

The verbal treaty by which this arrangement was made was destined to be a fruitful source of trouble for the future. From a military point of view the eastward extension of control was sound; but as Somerset urged once more on Bathurst, there could be no solution until the frontier was backed by a dense population. The attempt to provide that desideratum by the famous Albany Settlement is described in a subsequent chapter.[1]

The failure of the 1820 experiment to fulfil its original purpose was due to a faulty premiss in the argument. Obviously the question of success or failure turned on the point whether or not the soil of the Zuurveld was capable of producing regular crops of roots and cereals. A certain Mr Francis, giving evidence before the Commission of Inquiry, stated that Albany was considered by the Boers as being "peculiarly liable to blight, and [they] were never in the habit of permanently occupying such lands. Albany can only succeed in pasture and then requires extensive allotments to admit of changing grounds when the grasses fail."[2] The astounding thing is that no one thought of finding out the truth beforehand. The Colonial Office is not perhaps very blameworthy for accepting Somerset's assurances on the point at their face value. As for the latter it is not credible that he would have staked his reputation upon the colonisation of this particular region had he known its real character. One can only assume that he held himself so aloof from the Afrikaners that he was never told. Some thousands of optimistic settlers were accordingly planted in an area which was notoriously poor and incapable of supporting even the normal number of pastoralists. A heavier charge which lies against the Colonial Office has reference to financial responsibility. The records attest the care bestowed upon the selection and organisation of the settlers, and their own letters are enthusiastic about the comfort of the transport arrangements. But there Bathurst's imagination seems to have stopped short. The leading principle, it was stated, "is that after landing the new Settlers are to be of no expense to the Mother Country. Whatever they receive they must pay for."[3] The failure of three successive harvests and the consequent necessity of feeding some 5000 individuals for two years was, of course, unpredictable; but Somerset was given no chance to explain that Cape Colony had often much ado to feed itself, and that food transports should accompany the emigrant ships. As one British official at Cape Town drily remarked, it was a case of sending *pauperes pauperioribus*.[4] The newcomers were only kept alive by the hasty importation of foodstuffs from abroad, which cost the colonial Government (after

[1] *Vide infra*, chap. IX.

[2] Journal of the Proceedings of the Commissioners of Inquiry commenced at Cape Town, Monday 28 July 1823. Printed in Edwards, *op. cit.* pp. 179–200.

[3] The Colonial Military Secretary to the Commissary General, 2 April 1820. *Recs. of Cape Colony*, XIII, 100. Cf. Bathurst to Somerset. *Ibid.* XII, 259.

[4] Bird, W. W., *State of the Cape*, p. 183.

deducting the second and third instalments of the deposits) 57,000 rix-dollars in 1820, and in 1821 the substantial sum of 195,000 rix-dollars.[1] If the Colonial Department had forgotten the early history of Virginia, it might have recalled the slow and expensive business of putting American Loyalists on their feet in Canada. The close settlement of the eastern borderlands had been advocated by successive Governors and was an inherently sound proposition. It failed of its original purpose through lack of attention to vitally important details; but it incidentally and unknowingly injected an explosive force into a comparative static society.

The years 1806 to 1822 represent a "great divide" in the history of European South Africa, witnessing an infiltration of social and political conceptions from Great Britain which constituted the first stage in the creation of a new Anglo-Afrikaner nation. The same period was responsible for changes in the sphere of commerce and finance which were equally significant. Until the 1820 experiment in colonisation, the Cape, as its previous history has shown, was regarded by Dutch and British Governments in turn as a strategic point and nothing more. It was not a "colony" in the normal connotation of the term. Neither the Dutch nor the English East India Companies desired to see it interfere in the traffic between Europe and Asia by becoming an area of native productivity. The Afrikaners were accordingly a poor community, maintaining a primitive self-sufficiency by producing their own food. Foreign trade as such was virtually non-existent. Cape Town itself was an ocean tavern, which by providing board and lodging for travellers enabled the farmers to buy the few articles of European manufacture which they needed. But population steadily increased—from 62,000 of all colours in 1798 to approximately 120,000 in 1822[2]—and with it the costs of administration. Batavian republicans and British humanitarians pressed for the creation of civilising agencies, which cost money. New drostdies, new churches and schools and roads were called for; and there was no foreign trade to pay for them. During the war of American Independence Governor van Plettenberg had been driven to relieve the prevailing distress by issuing 47,696 rix-dollars of paper money on the good faith of the Government and with a solemn assurance that it would be redeemed as soon as normal intercourse with Holland could be resumed.[3] But once it had been adopted this dangerously easy expedient of relieving governmental penury was not abandoned. By the time of the surrender of the Colony in 1795 the total issue amounted to 1,292,276 rix-dollars—nominally £258,255. 4*s.* 0*d.* in British currency. Commissioner-General Sluysken's disingenousness

[1] Bird, W. W., *State of the Cape*, p. 238. Say, £11,400 and £39,000.
[2] *Ibid.*, p. 354.
[3] Say, £9,540.

in inducing the British to assume responsibility for the debt on the totally inadequate security of the public buildings has already been adverted to.[1] During the First British Occupation additional issues were made, totalling 495,000 rix-dollars, which on the restoration of the Batavian Government were redeemed by the British. In justice to the public, Commissioner de Mist should at once have destroyed paper currency to that amount, but poverty induced him to leave it in circulation unsupported by any tangible assets. The anxiety of de Mist and Governor Janssens to develop the Colony was responsible for further issues amounting to 300,000 rix-dollars. On the return of the British in 1806 Sir David Baird added another 83,197 rix-dollars, thus bringing the gross amount in circulation to 2,169,197 rix-dollars.[2]

So large a currency was far in excess of the needs of a small community whose internal transactions were mostly conducted by barter and bank drafts. None the less, money failed to circulate freely and the colonial revenue was incapable of providing for necessary improvements. Caledon determined to meet the situation by a bold policy which eventually proved to be extremely injurious. After some hesitation the British Government authorised him to issue new money to the extent of one million rix-dollars. Provision was made on paper for the payment of interest and the gradual redemption of the capital outlay for public buildings by the respective districts.[3] "In an ill moment the local government was induced on very mistaken grounds to resolve on its augmentation while its diminution should, on the contrary, have been determined."[4] Soon after Cradock's assumption of office he was alarmed to find that the premium paid for sterling bills on London, which usually stood between parity and 20 per cent below, had risen to the unprecedented figure of 80¾. But much worse was to follow. After remaining at that level for some two years, the premium rate mounted with accumulating momentum from 85 in March 1816 to 195 in May 1822. In other words, the external purchasing power of the rix-dollar depreciated by 57 per cent.[5]

Cradock realised that the Colony was in a dangerous financial position and took active measures to stop the rot by inaugurating a policy of currency contraction. Scarcely was he gone before the worst happened. A large paper currency is not itself an evil, provided that its volume is commensurate with public confidence in the Government to which it has been lent. As long as the colonial Administration used the new money to pay for roads, wharfs, prisons and so on, and then withdrew the paper after it had served its purpose, no internal injury had been inflicted. The transaction was a form of tax upon the

[1] *Vide supra*, p. 176.

[2] Based on the report of a special committee set up by Lord Caledon. *Recs. of Cape Colony*, VI, 273–8. Say, £16,633 and £433,840.

[3] *Recs. of Cape Colony*, VII, 163–8, 260–3.

[4] H. T. Colebrooke's editorial observations, *State of the Cape*, p. 342.

[5] *Vide ibid.* App. I, p. 324, where a detailed table is printed.

inhabitants by which they supplied labour and materials for the construction of permanent assets. But when new paper was not withdrawn from circulation and was treated as revenue, as had been the usual practice in the past, the purchase of benefits therewith (whether cargoes of rice in times of scarcity or permanent buildings) represented a mortgage on the profit-making capacity of the community. Had that been all, an increasing population with a consequently expanding revenue could have met the liability; but the same people who were putting up buildings and developing roads and harbours were also purchasing foreign wares which they could not afford—iron and steel goods from Great Britain, muslin and silks from India and tea from China. Under the double strain the currency collapsed.

The economic situation of the Colony was, indeed, highly artificial. Drawn into the orbit of a world power, the inhabitants of Cape Town imitated the more lavish standards of their visitors and bought from abroad more than the country could pay for with its own products. A permanently adverse balance of trade was the result. The Colony possessed three chief sources of income: the British garrison, the entertainment of invalids from India and the export of Cape wine. But the receipts from these and a few minor sources amounted in 1821 to no more than 4,921,192 rix-dollars, whereas imports totalled 6,666,244 rix-dollars, thus showing an arrear of remittances due to Great Britain of nearly two million rix-dollars on the year's working.[1] The result was an increasing competition at the auctions of the Government bills on London with which the Commissary Department at the Cape paid for army expenses. When the supply of public bills was insufficient, remittances were made by private bills, which were not always honoured. Inevitably the London merchants began to grow shy of hazarding further consignments and, even when they did so, sent articles of inferior quality.[2] "The state of the credit at the Cape", it was said in 1822, "is so desperate that confidence in individuals is gone. There is a host of borrowers and no lenders."[3]

As the colony sank more deeply into debt and the value of its currency declined, prices soared and trade stagnated. Moreover, the inadequate export trade was further contracted by two unexpected occurrences. The economy clamour in England, which caused the Government to reduce the Cape garrison by almost one-half, correspondingly reduced the colony's most important market.[4] The second misfortune was the death of Napoleon in 1821. During his exile, St Helena had been an important market for Cape produce, which was exported thither to an annual value of over 509,000 rix-dollars[5], payment being made in Spanish dollars and by bills on

[1] Say, £984,238 and £1,333,248; Bird, W. W., *State of the Cape* (from the Cape Customs registers), pp. 124–5.

[2] Fisher, R. B., *op. cit.* p. 47.

[3] *State of the Cape*, p. 36.

[4] Cf. Somerset to Bathurst, 19 July 1817. *Recs. of Cape Colony*, XI, 360.

[5] Say, £101,800.

London. When Bonaparte died and the special establishment departed, this source of revenue to the Cape came to an end.

Necessity demanded that the Colony should rectify her trade balance by developing new lines for export and by securing favourable terms of entry for them in markets abroad. To achieve this end successive Governors, together with the Colonial Agent and British merchants interested in the Cape, carried on a long struggle, trying on the one hand to encourage new industries and on the other to defeat the opposition of vested interests to securing concessions in the British market. As being an enemy possession conquered in war, Cape Colony was not included in the general commercial system of the Empire as embodied in the Navigation Laws, but a special discretionary power was temporarily vested in the Crown to regulate its commerce by Orders-in-Council.[1]

The first Order-in-Council after the conquest, that of 11 June 1806,[2] permitted entry to the Cape of foreign goods in either British or foreign ships from any part of His Majesty's Dominions duty free; but this liberality was not destined to last, for the Court of Directors of the East India Company intervened. By the Act of 1806 the Company's monopoly had been specifically safeguarded in relation to the Cape; that is to say, the Colony had been totally debarred from participation in eastern trade within the limits of the Company's charter. As soon as the conquest was known, negotiations took place between the Directors and Lord Castlereagh in regard to the terms upon which the former would be willing to supply the Cape with Indian and China goods. In a letter dated 6 June 1806, they took the opportunity to press not only for discrimination against foreigners, but for higher duties than had been imposed during the First Occupation.[3] The Company, in fact, viewed the Cape with suspicion as a dangerous door through which Americans and other rivals could too easily slip into their preserves. One of the chief reasons put forward for reconquering the Cape had been the advisability of locking that door.[4] It was an attitude stubbornly maintained by the Company until the limitation of its exclusive privileges in India in 1813, and one which robbed the Cape of the opportunity of becoming an emporium for East and West trade.

After considerable delay the Company's proposals were submitted to the Committee of Privy Council for Trade and were eventually accepted.[5] British goods in British ships were to be admitted duty free, while foreign goods in British ships were to pay a duty of 5 per

[1] *Statutes at Large*, 46 Geo. III, cap. 30. The authority so vested was continued by the following short-term Acts: 49 Geo. III, cap. 17; 56 Geo. III, cap. 8; 1 Geo. IV, cap. 11.

[2] Privy Council Register, P.C. 2/170, ff. 353–5.

[3] Committee for Trade, In-Letters, B.T. 1/34, no. 53.

[4] Percival, R., *An Account of the Cape of Good Hope* (London, 1804), p. 334.

[5] For the negotiations see Committee for Trade, Minutes, B.T. 5/17, p. 203 (21 April 1807); *ibid.* p. 246 (8 May); B.T. 1/34, no. 61; Privy Council Register, P.C. 2/173, ff. 47–8.

cent, and foreign goods in foreign ships 15 per cent *ad valorem.*[1] The Company had won its point.

When the further enabling Act of March 1809 was passed, the Order-in-Council of May 1807 automatically expired. A new Order was issued on 12 April, the provisions of which were identical with those of its predecessor.[2] Then the stringent treatment of neutrals in European waters occasioned by Napoleon's Continental System produced repercussions in South Africa. The Committee for Trade came to the conclusion that it was unwise to continue to allow neutrals to participate further in the Cape trade. On 1 October 1811, a fresh Order was issued which ordained that as from 12 April 1812 commerce to and from the Cape must be conducted in British ships only, and that the previous permission to foreign vessels should cease.[3] On 24 September 1814, an Order-in-Council placed the Cape under the general incidence of the Navigation Laws.[4]

At this stage in the hesitant process of incorporating the Cape in the imperial economic system its position was peculiarly unfortunate. Its supporters had not yet secured for it equality of treatment as regards the eastern trade, and it was now subject to all the restrictions of a British colony without enjoying the concomitant privileges. As Thomas Courtenay, the Colonial Agent for the Cape, pointed out, Cape produce (with the exception of wine) was still ranked in the British table of customs duties with that of foreign countries, while other British settlements received preferences as against the foreigner amounting in many cases to a prohibition. He also repeated a previous suggestion that, instead of excluding foreign vessels, the Cape should be declared a free port. By this means the foreigner would be discouraged from going to the East Indies, the products of which, being deposited at the Cape, might be thence conveyed to Europe or America. It would also have the valuable result of checking the serious decline in the colonial currency.[5] It was a policy which steadily gained adherents. "Make the Cape a free port for the nations of Europe", advised *The Times* in 1819, "and we banish North America from the Indian Seas."[6]

But, apart from other considerations, the charter rights of the East India Company stood in the way. The representatives of the Cape interests accordingly concentrated their efforts upon trying to break through the restrictions imposed by the Company on the one side and to secure preferences in the British market on the other. In December 1811 Sir John Cradock pointed out that it was useless for

[1] Caledon's Proclamation, 18 September 1807. *Recs. of Cape Colony*, VI, 203–4.

[2] Privy Council Register, P.C. 2/180, ff. 379–84. Cf. Caledon's Proclamation, 29 September 1809. *Recs. of Cape Colony*, VII, 153–6.

[3] Privy Council Register, P.C. 2/192, ff. 341–2. Printed in *Recs. of Cape Colony*, VIII, 157–8. Cf. B.T. 1/67, no. 16; B.T. 5/21, p. 371.

[4] Privy Council Register, P.C. 2/196, ff. 189–92.

[5] *Recs. of Cape Colony*, X. 221–4. [6] *Ibid.* XII, 234.

the Government to expect agricultural development at the Cape until the colony was able to dispose of its surplus produce in an external market.[1] He also concluded his report on the Cape revenues with the remark that the Company's monopoly was stultifying all improvements.[2]

Yet even after the Company's monopoly had been limited in 1813 to the trade in tea and the China trade, a special provision was made in respect of the Cape, whereby the monopoly remained as to trade between the Cape and Great Britain: any merchant legally qualified could import India goods to the Cape, but such goods could only be re-exported by the Company or by the Company's licence.[3] A strenuous but unsuccessful effort was made by Courtenay, the Colonial Agent, to have this limitation removed.[4] The Colony had thus failed to secure the degree of commercial freedom which it had a right to expect, though it had received a substantial relaxation of the previous restrictions.

Meanwhile Sir John Cradock had scored an important success for the Colony with regard to its wine industry. As the result of his representations, the Committee for Trade, in May 1813, recommended an absolute reduction of the duties on Cape wine to one-third of those previously imposed.[5] The one article which the Cape had as yet been able to produce which Great Britain could absorb on a large scale was thus given a substantial preference. Considerable new capital was accordingly invested and, by 1815, Cape wine was beginning to establish itself in England: by 1817 it was selling on a large scale. Indeed it is not too much to say that without the acquisition of this export trade the Colony would have become totally insolvent. In 1821 the total value of colonial produce export amounted to 1,741,035 rix-dollars; of that sum wines were responsible for no less than 1,095,600 rix-dollars.[6]

With regard to other commodities, however, the Cape was still on the same footing as foreign countries and did not share in the preferences accorded to the North American and West Indian colonies. In 1818 a committee of shipowners and merchants interested in the Colony made a concerted effort to secure colonial privileges for Cape wheat and brandy. They asked that wheat be allowed to be imported into the United Kingdom when the average price rose to 67*s.* per quarter and that brandy be admitted on the same terms as the West Indian spirit. With regard to the former the Committee for Trade remarked that an Act of Parliament would be necessary and were

[1] Cradock to Robt Willimott, 10 December 1811. Committee for Trade, In-Letters, B.T. 1/67, no. 17. Printed in *Recs. of Cape Colony*, VIII, 345–6.

[2] In-Letters, B.T. 1/67, no. 19.

[3] 54 Geo. III, cap. 34, sec. 3.

[4] B.T. 1/90, nos. 40 and 41; B.T. 5/23, p. 336.

[5] Minutes, B.T. 5/22, pp. 267, 329. Cf. M. d'Ecury's memo. stating the case for a reduction of duty, B.T. 1/77, no. 37.

[6] Say, £348,207 and £219,120; *State of the Cape*, p. 325.

evidently not disposed to invite trouble. It was in favour of encouraging Cape brandy, but unfortunately the Customs Commissioners objected on the ground that large quantities of French and Spanish brandy were exported from the United Kingdom to the Cape, and that if the duty were lowered to the West Indian level, this foreign spirit would be mixed with the Cape product and re-exported to England at the lower rate.[1] Not a very convincing argument.

But the pertinacity of Courtenay was about to secure for the Cape a specially privileged position which marked a turning point in its commercial future. In 1819 the ports of Mauritius were opened by Order-in-Council to foreign vessels. Courtenay seized the opportunity of repeating his previous demands on behalf of the Cape. In an extremely cogent letter he pointed out the benefits which would accrue if the colony were made a clearing house between the Orient and those parts of Europe and America from which British ships were excluded. The concession demanded had already been granted to Mauritius. If the Cape were not similarly favoured, it would compete at a disadvantage with that island and find its own less extensive privileges rendered nugatory.[2]

Courtenay wrote his letter to the Colonial Office on 18 August 1819. On 19 April 1820 it was considered by the Committee for Trade, who accepted Courtenay's arguments.[3] The resulting Order for the Cape was issued on 12 July 1820. Under its terms British ships were allowed to import to the Cape foreign goods from the country of origin, except cotton, iron, steel and wool manufactures. Such British ships could reload with cargoes of Cape produce or other articles legally imported there and proceed to foreign ports at will. Any foreign State which gave entry to British ships trading to and from the Cape as aforesaid should receive identical privileges for its own vessels at the Cape. A countervailing duty was to be imposed as need arose to keep the rates of duty charged on foreign vessels at the Cape level with those imposed by foreigners on British ships. Foreign vessels exporting from the Cape were to pay a duty of 8 per cent over and above that paid by exporting British ships, unless and until it was shown that the British received equal treatment in the foreign port.[4]

The use of free ports had long been a weapon in the armoury of British overseas commercial policy: in the Western hemisphere it had been used again in 1818 with the opening under certain conditions of the ports of Halifax in Nova Scotia and St John in New Brunswick.[5]

[1] See the memorials of the Committee of Ship-Owners (Messrs May and Alewyn, Messrs Nourse and Christian, J. D. Maseau, H. T. Colebrooke, etc.), B.T. 5/26, pp. 60, 335, 435; B.T. 1/125, no. 27; B.T. 1/127, nos. 6, 7, 8, 10, 11 and 12.

[2] Courtenay to Goulburn, 18 August 1819. *Recs. of Cape Colony*, XII, 287–9.

[3] Minutes, B.T. 5/28, p. 363 (19 April 1820).

[4] Privy Council Register, P.C. 2/202, ff. 454–7. (Printed in *Recs. of Cape Colony*, XIII, 181–4.)

[5] Manning, H. T., *British Colonial Policy after the American Revolution*, p. 273. The original purpose of the free-port system (initiated in 1766) had been to break through

But the arrangement for the Cape in 1820 introduced the principle of reciprocity. The rise of Great Britain to a position of pre-eminence in industry induced a growing self-confidence which accelerated the advent of more liberal ideas of international exchange. The Cape-Mauritius experiment was among the first of a series which by 1825 constituted a new imperial system and a new conception. The Cape was now free to develop her commerce where she would. A period of profound change in her economic no less than in her social and political life was about to begin.

the Spanish monopoly by establishing entrepôts in the Caribbean whither Spanish settlers from Central America would be induced to come and buy British manufactures in exchange for such of their own commodities that Britain desired (see Armytage, F., *The Free Port System in the British West Indies: A Study in Commercial Policy* 1766–1822). A similar purpose motivated the Free Port Act of 1818. "By making Halifax and St John free ports, it was hoped to make both ports once again distributing centers, not only for British manufacturers to the United States, but for American produce to the West Indies". (Graham, G. S., *Sea Power and British North America*, 1783–1820, p.226).

CHAPTER IX

THE BRITISH SETTLERS OF 1820

UNTIL the year 1820 the vast eastern parts of Cape Colony were very sparsely inhabited. At considerable distances from one another—in some cases many miles—a few Afrikaner people lived in primitive dwellings and carried on the simplest farming operations. The development of this part of the country can scarcely be said to have begun before 1820. In its whole extent there were but four villages—assuming that an insignificant collection of wattle and daub hovels was worthy of such a name. These were Graaff-Reinet (1786), Uitenhage (1804), Grahamstown (1812) and Cradock (1813). To the east, beyond the Great Fish River, which could be crossed without difficulty, was Kaffirland with its restless Bantu tribes.

The Colonial Government had from time to time discussed the strengthening of this frontier by a close settlement of Europeans. In 1812 the Xhosas had been thrust back from the Zuurveld behind the Fish River, but seven years later they had crossed it again and attacked Grahamstown, and had only been repelled with difficulty. In the early part of 1819, while this struggle was actually proceeding, a movement was set on foot in England to send out a number of emigrants. It was hoped that they would at once strengthen the frontier and relieve the Old Country of some of the troubles which were afflicting her as a result of the abrupt ending of the Napoleonic wars in the midst of the Industrial Revolution.

The origin of the scheme was due to Benjamin Moodie, a settler of Scottish extraction who had a large estate in the Swellendam district. There was, and had always been, such a dearth of labour in the colony that work was plentiful and wages good. In 1817, Moodie, who was then in Scotland, conceived the idea of organising and financing a supply of labour as a profitable speculation by sending out at his own risk, unaided by Government, a number of unmarried artisans from Edinburgh. Each man had to provide a sum of £30 and to indenture himself to Moodie for a period of three years. In return, he received a free passage to the Cape and maintenance until the expiry of the contract, unless he obtained work elsewhere before that time. On these terms a party of two hundred young men left Edinburgh for the Cape and most of them soon found such lucrative employment that they were able to pay for the cancellation of their agreements. Thus this scheme was eminently successful.

In the following year, 1818, two other Scottish gentlemen, Peter Tait and James Goslin, engineered a similar venture, which also met with success and did much to advertise Cape Colony as a field for emigration. In 1819, three other enthusiasts actuated by motives of philanthropy devoted themselves to propaganda on behalf of the English labourers and issued a pamphlet describing in alluring terms the advantages of emigration to South Africa. The London *Times* of 18 June 1819 supported the scheme with enthusiasm. "Our noble station at the Cape of Good Hope", it said, "has the finest soil and climate in the world; it produces in unparalleled abundance all the necessaries and all the luxuries of life, whether civilised or savage." The eulogy, however, was somewhat modified by the statement that "the natives in the vicinity of our settlement are now in arms against us". These enticing accounts of the conditions of life in Cape Colony became a common topic of public conversation and excited universal interest.[1] The problem of disposing of the unemployed was at that moment the constant preoccupation of the Cabinet, and the fact that Lord Charles Somerset, Governor of the Cape Colony, was advocating closer settlement along the eastern frontier to strengthen its defence seemed to afford the opportunity of dealing with two problems at once. In the event, on the last business day of the session (July 1819) the House of Commons voted a sum of £50,000 for the purpose of carrying out a large emigration scheme.[2]

In order that no one should arrive in the colony in the penniless state of many emigrants to America, a deposit of £10 was required for each family of man, wife and two children, of £2. 10*s*. 0*d*. for each additional child under fourteen, and £5 for every single person between the ages of fourteen and eighteen. A third of these sums was to be returned to the emigrant on his landing in the colony, another third on his reaching the alloted location and the last third three months later. A free passage with provisions was to be provided, and to each man was to be allotted one hundred acres of land in the new country at a quit-rent, which, however, would be remitted during the first ten years. After three years' continued residence "the land shall be measured at the expense of Government and the holder shall obtain, without fee, his title thereto on a perpetual quit-rent not exceeding two pounds ten shillings per hundred acres". The Crown reserved to itself all gold, silver and precious stones which might be found on any of the locations. In the case of a hundred families of one religious persuasion applying for leave to take out a minister with them, the Government was willing to assign a salary to such minister.

There was a widespread eagerness to reach the supposed Promised Land and it is said that there were ninety thousand applications. The selection of those who eventually emigrated was made in accordance with the following procedure. The first man in a particular town or district who made application to the Secretary of State for permission

[1] For a detailed account of the promotion of the scheme, see Edwards, Isobel, *The 1820 Settlers and the Albany Settlement*.

[2] See *C.H.B.E.* vol. II, and *vide supra*, p. 227.

to emigrate under the scheme was accepted, but he was told that he would have to make up a party of at least ten others with or without families. The further selection was then left to him and he became the recognised "head of the party", through whom all communication between the members of the party and the Government was to take place. Hence some became heads of parties, who, on account of their limited education, former occupations and habits of life, were incapable of exercising any control or influence over others. On the other hand, there were a few heads of parties who were retired officers of the Army and Navy and others of good education and position who possessed considerable means. These saw in the scheme a profitable investment for their capital and looked to the establishment of large and fine estates. They took with them a number of indentured settler servants, for whom they paid the necessary deposits. In these ways fifty-six different parties were formed, comprising 3487 men, women and children, with a combined capital in deposit moneys of £14,054. The average number in a party was about forty. John Carlisle's was the smallest with fifteen, but in William Parker's of Cork there were 220 individuals, in John Bailie's 256, in Thomas Willson's 307 and in Hezekiah Sephton's, the largest, 344.

To transport this crowd of people from England to South Africa twenty-four ships, each of about 400 tons burthen, were chartered. It was arranged that they should leave in pairs and at such intervals of time as to obviate the difficulties arising from too many arrivals in the distant land at one time. For their greater convenience in those days of difficult land travel, the vessels were to start from ports which were as near as possible to the districts from which the emigrants came. The English ports chosen were Deptford, the most important, Portsmouth, Liverpool and Bristol, and, for the Irish, the Cove of Cork.

Before the necessary preparations in the ships were completed emigrants began to arrive and embark. The winter of 1819–20 was exceptionally tempestuous and cold. The Thames was frozen from bank to bank, and the vessels at Deptford were for a time icebound. The consequent delay in commencing the voyage gave many of the emigrants the opportunity of reconsidering the wisdom of leaving England and deciding finally to abandon the venture and get back to land. Their places at the last moment were filled by others. Thus the lists of emigrants originally prepared in London do not agree with the lists of arrivals in Cape Town.

The first move of the emigrant fleet was made by the *Nautilus*, which drifted slowly down through the Thames ice on 5 December 1819; she was followed by the *Chapman* on the 9th and, during the ensuing six weeks, the whole body of the British settlers set forth for the shores of South Africa. The letters and diaries of the emigrants show that every reasonable provision was made for their comfort, and after some early mishaps the voyage was accomplished uneventfully in about ninety days. The destination of the vessels in the first instance was Simonstown, though a few called at Cape Town. At Simonstown, the vessels remained for a few days to take on provisions and water. The bleak hills and desolate stretches of land, as viewed from the decks, did not impress the new-comers favourably. Their disappointment and depression were not lessened when they found that none but heads of parties were allowed to land, the more so as there had been much quarrelling during the voyage, and petitions to break up into smaller parties under other leaders were ready for presentation to the Colonial Government.

The further voyage to Algoa Bay took from five days, in the case of the *Brilliant*, to a month in the case of the *Northampton*. Meanwhile, the Cape Government sent all the available military tents to the shore of Algoa Bay as temporary shelters. Ox-waggons were hired from farmers, far and near—even from distant Graaff-Reinet, to convey the settlers to the locations which had been allotted to them; and stores of farm implements, seeds and other materials to start the emigrants in life were collected in large quantities upon the beach. The *Chapman*, first of the flotilla, reached the eastern anchorage on 10 April 1820, the *Nautilus* four days later.

The first view of the promised land was even more forbidding than that of the Simonstown mountains. The voyagers saw the inhospitable shores of Algoa Bay girt with barren sand-hills and a broad belt of angry surf. There was no sign of human habitation but the solitary Fort Frederick on the top of a distant hill. Fortunately, during the whole of the three months over which the landing stretched, the weather was fine and the sea calm, but even under these circumstances the surf on the shore was dangerous. All were, however, landed without a single casualty.

The emigrants from the *Chapman* were landed on 11 April. Being the first to reach the shore, they found an adequate number of waggons —about ninety—to convey them straight away to their location near the mouth of the Great Fish River, about six days distant. In due course, other vessels arrived, but owing to the vagaries of the wind two or three anchored simultaneously. In consequence of the inadequate number of waggons, the long distances they had to travel and their slow rate of motion, the shore of Algoa Bay became very inconveniently crowded and the tents were filled to their utmost capacity. Not until July did the last party leave the shore.

Thomas Pringle, the poet and head of a party of Scottish settlers, gives us a very good description of the settlers as he observed them waiting on the shore:

> I strolled along the beach [he says] to survey more closely the camp of the settlers, which had looked so picturesque from the sea. On my way I passed two or three marquees, pitched apart among the evergreen bushes which were scattered between the sandhills and the heights behind. These were the encampments of

some of the higher class settlers, and evinced the taste of the occupants by the pleasant situations in which they were placed, and by the neatness and order of everything about them....A little way beyond, I entered the Settlers' Camp. It consisted of several hundred tents, pitched in parallel rows or streets, and occupied by the middling and lower classes of emigrants. These consisted of various descriptions of people; and the air, aspect, and array of their persons and temporary residences were equally various. There were respectable tradesmen and jolly farmers, with every appearance of substance and snug English comfort about them. There were watermen, fishermen, and sailors from the Thames and English seaports, with the reckless and weather-beaten look usual in persons of their perilous and precarious professions. There were numerous groups of pale-visaged artisans and operative manufacturers from London and other large towns, of whom doubtless a certain proportion were persons of highly reputable character and steady habits, but a far larger proportion were squalid in their aspect, slovenly in their attire and domestic arrangements, and discontented and discourteous in their demeanour. Lastly, there were parties of pauper agricultural labourers, sent out by the aid of their respective parishes, healthier perhaps than the class just mentioned but not apparently happier in mind, nor less generally demoralised by the untoward influence of their former social condition. On the whole, they formed a motley and rather unprepossessing collection of people. Guessing vaguely from my observations on this occasion and on subsequent rambles through their locations, I should say that probably about a third part were persons of real respectability of character and possessed of some worldly substance; but that the remaining two-thirds were, for the most part, composed of individuals of a very unpromising description—persons who had hung loose upon society—low in morals and desperate in circumstances.[1]

Sir Rufane Donkin, who was acting in the place of the Governor, Lord Charles Somerset, was on the shore to welcome the strangers. He founded a new town at the landing place and named it Port Elizabeth after his wife, Lady Elizabeth Donkin, who had died shortly before in India.

The locations on which the settlers were placed were some thousands of acres in extent, varying in size according to the number in a party. They were in the present districts of Albany and Bathurst. The general appearance of the country was calculated to arouse a desire in enthusiastic agriculturists to commence cultivation forthwith. For the most part it consisted of undulating grassy lands, presenting an aspect of fertility which needed only determination and industry to cause it to yield all that could be desired. But not all the settlers, in the first instance, were sent to the Albany Zuurveld. With due regard to the susceptibilities of parties arriving from the different parts of the United Kingdom, and to prevent discord arising from differences of tastes, habits and manners, the Irish parties were landed at Saldanha Bay and sent to the arid district of Clanwilliam in the western colony. The small party of Scots under Thomas Pringle went to the Baviaans River in the present Bedford district on the extreme eastern frontier sixty miles to the north of the main English settlement in Albany, while the Welsh were placed at the Zonder Einde River in the Caledon district, a mere hundred miles or

[1] Pringle, T., *Narrative of a Residence in South Africa*, pp. 11 *sqq.*

so from Capetown. Within a few months, however, all those in the west, except some who found work in the locality, had gravitated to Albany.

As each waggon arrived on a location, the homeless people were dumped down and left to shift for themselves as best they could. A few were so fortunate as to have tents, but by far the greater number had to find such shelter as the place afforded until they had constructed the roughest of huts and hovels. For their maintenance until they could support themselves, rations were supplied by the Government; but these had to be paid for out of the second and third instalments of the deposit money which still stood to their credit. These rations, such as flour and groceries, had to be fetched, in the first instance, from Grahamstown, a distance of over thirty miles from some of the locations. Meat was supplied in the form of live sheep. As a more central station for the issue of supplies and at the same time as a seat of magistracy, Sir Rufane Donkin founded a township in a beautiful part of the country and named it Bathurst in honour of the Secretary of State for War and the Colonies, Earl Bathurst.

After the dwellings had been constructed, ploughs were set to work and seed corn and vegetables were sown. It soon became evident, however, that many of the people were not adapted to agricultural pursuits. Having described, and perhaps having believed, themselves to be agriculturists while in England, they, especially the Londoners, found, on discovering the conditions of life in the colony, that they were sadly mistaken. The term "Cockney gardener" came to be a gibe which was levelled at all who showed incompetence. All were prisoners on the locations. They could not leave without permission from the head of the party and then they had to show a pass to the Landdrost in Grahamstown. It was evident that it was useless to keep on the locations some of the men who could find no scope for their abilities there, but who would be useful members of society in other parts; hence, at the end of 1820, an "ornamental trades" proclamation was issued permitting these to leave and go wherever they could find work. Some of the "ornamental trades" which were declared by the pseudo-agriculturists were those of goldsmith, painter on porcelain, designer of armorial bearings, Oxford bootmaker and others. These were the fortunate ones and, like Moodie's people, were soon earning good wages. But, for the others, in December 1820, the first sign of the terrible distress which was to overwhelm them made its appearance. For months the wheat crops had given promise of an abundant harvest, but when the period of fruition approached, the whole was attacked by the rust and rendered useless. The settlers thus saw that their labour had been in vain and the year 1821 opened with the prospect of starvation. The second and third instalments of the deposit money had not only been exhausted, but the people were already in debt to the Government and further advances on their account were absolutely necessary. It was decided, therefore, to continue the supply of rations, to take receipts for them and to allow the amounts to stand as mortgage on the buildings and lands which would belong to the settlers after three years' residence upon them. The total expenditure or advance on this account up to the end of 1821 was £15,364.

Under these circumstances the people took heart and commenced to plough and sow again and to improve their dwellings. At no great distance from the locations was a large and beautiful river, the Kowie. Some of the more enterprising, seeing in this the future Liverpool of South Africa, had it surveyed. For a time it promised well. Small vessels plied between the river and Algoa Bay, but most of them came to untimely ends if only because the Kowie mouth was narrow and swept by currents. The fuller development of the Kowie was a problem for future years. The British settlers, however, have the credit of being the first to exploit the Kowie and also of laying the foundations of the town of Port Elizabeth under the shadow of Fort Frederick.

During 1821 the Xhosas first thrust themselves upon the attention of the settlers. The growing number of cattle tempted marauders from the far side of the Great Fish River. In September, an English boy who was herding cattle was murdered and the cattle were traced far into Kaffirland. Later two other settler children and the cattle of which they were in charge disappeared. The skeletons which were found some time afterwards showed that they had been murdered. Two settlers were attacked while passing through the bush and stabbed to death. This was the beginning of Kaffir trouble yet in store for the newcomers.

Misfortune and disaster seemed to dog the settlers' every step. Towards the end of the year 1821, the wheat crop promised a harvest, but again it was attacked by the rust and destroyed. Gloom, hopelessness and dread of the future beset them, and they found little consolation and encouragement in the return of Lord Charles Somerset to the colony in November 1821. He improved matters somewhat by relieving them of compulsory residence on the locations; but he regarded them with no friendly eye—as "Radicals" and people who could be of no benefit to the country. He forbade public meetings, as it had come to his ears that the free speech which had been the privilege of these people in England had been levelled, in no complimentary terms, against Captain Trappes, the magistrate appointed to their district. He caused the new settlement at Bathurst, which was to have been the "Settlers' City", to be abandoned and seemed determined to undo all that Sir Rufane Donkin had done for their advantage. But in doing this, the Governor had disturbed a hornets' nest. The settlers, or some of them, set on foot investigations into his actions which contributed to bring about his resignation in 1826.[1]

[1] *Vide infra*, pp. 249 *sqq*. The real leaders of the agitation against Somerset, which began in 1821, were in Cape Town.

In spite of the two failures of the wheat crops, a third attempt was made in 1822 with a variety known as Bengal wheat. But, however satisfactory in Bengal, this variety did not withstand the rust of Albany, and a third failure followed—thereby proving that Albany, at least, was not a wheat country. In 1823 there were great distress and misery on the locations. Those settlers who felt they could better themselves elsewhere abandoned their places and went to Grahamstown and other towns. In May 1823, of the 1004 males who arrived in 1820, only 438 remained on the locations; of Bailie's party of 256 individuals a mere 76 remained. The chief sufferers were those who could not follow any useful trade, and some of the capitalist heads of parties, who, by this time, had spent all their money in paying servants and promoting developments which had given no return. So bad were matters at this time that a Distressed Settlers' Fund was started in Cape Town, and extended presently to England, India and St Helena, to provide the starving people with rice and other foodstuffs.

To fill the settlers' cup of sorrow, in October 1823 a tremendous rainstorm deluged the district for ten days. Houses and furniture were destroyed and the soil was washed off the lands leaving bare the underlying rocks. With all these setbacks, the 1820 settlers' emigration scheme seemed to be a great failure. Certainly its original purpose as a scheme for concentrating a large population on the immediate frontier had failed.

From the end of 1823 onwards the tide turned. Government proposed to issue to the survivors titles for farms much larger than those that had been intended originally, and, at the close of 1824, Somerset decided to shut down the state Somerset Farm, which the settlers had always regarded as an unfair competitor. A few months later that farm became the village and magistracy of Somerset East. Meanwhile, at the New Year of 1825, the Governor had visited Albany, spurred on doubtless by the presence of the Commissioners of Enquiry in the colony.[1] He appointed a new and more tactful landdrost at Grahamstown, encouraged the failing township of Bathurst, named Port Frances at the mouth of the Kowie, stationed a magistrate there and another at Port Elizabeth, and proposed to open both ports to direct trade with England. Leave for that desirable measure was only forthcoming from London in July 1826 after Somerset's departure from the colony. In the course of 1825 his Government issued the promised land titles, relieved the labour shortage in Albany by making provision for apprenticing Bechuana refugees to the settlers and forbore to collect direct taxes till January 1826. Finally, the imperial authorities cancelled the settlers' debts for rations in excess of their original deposits.

[1] *Vide infra*, p. 251.

Meanwhile the settlers had discovered unexpected fields of enterprise which only needed courage and determination for their development. The first real opportunity appeared in the trade in ivory.

The thick and extensive Fish River bush or forest abounded in elephants. The Xhosas, with merely their assegais, were daring and successful hunters and secured many tusks with apparent ease. Dealing in ivory with the tribes had been forbidden both by the Dutch and, at first, by the British Government, yet a clandestine traffic was carried on by the soldiers and others on the frontier. In July 1824, the Government, finding that it could not stop the trade, wisely did the next best thing: it sanctioned it under certain rules and regulations and thus inaugurated the commerce of the Eastern Province. Three days in each week traders under licence were allowed to repair to Fort Willshire, which had been built in 1820 on the Keiskamma River, a dozen miles beyond the Fish River frontier. There they exchanged their wares—beads, buttons, highly coloured materials and other gew-gaws—for the ivory, hides and gum which the tribesmen brought. A company of soldiers maintained order and an officer saw that all the dealings were fair.

The trade was a great success and the tide of the settlers' misfortunes seemed to have turned. From 18 August 1824 to 12 March 1825 more than 50,000 lb. or about 20½ Cape tons of ivory were obtained. Besides this the traders gained 16,800 lb. of gum and 15,000 hides. The trade having been so brisk, and all, both white and black, having behaved so well, the Government went further by permitting Europeans to go far into Kaffirland and open trading stations. Thus began what is known as the "Inland Kaffir trade", the value of which soon rose to about £40,000 per annum. This reacted upon the colony, for the importation of "Kaffir truck" and the exportation of ivory, hides and gum necessitated the establishment of big warehouses in Grahamstown and Port Elizabeth and the consequent development not only of these two towns but of the Eastern Province generally.

Another commodity, even more than ivory, was responsible for the further increase of commerce and the encouragement of the struggling settlers. This was wool. In 1827 three enterprising settlers, Lieutenant Richard Daniell, Charles Griffith and Major Thomas White, commenced fine-wool farming in the Eastern Province. Tried in other parts of the colony many years before, it had not been a success. This new attempt, however, succeeded beyond expectation, and thus was inaugurated an industry, characteristically Eastern Province, which has done more than anything else, not excepting ostrich farming, to develop this part of South Africa. In 1830, as a commencement, 4500 lbs. of wool valued at £222 were exported to London; in 1841 the amount had risen to 61,778 lbs. valued at £27,848.

Thus, in this and other directions, the settlers of 1820 discovered, after the first few years of distress, avenues in which their abilities might provide them with daily bread and bring benefit to the colony. In 1824 some joined a small party of adventurers and migrated to Natal and formed the first British settlement there.[1] In after years many of them and their sons occupied some of the most responsible positions in the country as members of the Legislative Council, magistrates and other officials, commandants of forces for the protection of the colony and newspaper editors. Sir Richard Southey became Colonial Secretary and Lieutenant-Governor of Griqualand West; Sir Thomas Scanlen Prime Minister of the Cape Colony; Sir Walter Currie commandant of the Frontier; Sir Walter Stanford chief magistrate of the Transkei; the Hon. John Centlivres Chase member of the Legislative Council and the historian of those times; the Hon. Robert Godlonton, also a member of the Legislative Council, though not the founder, was for many years editor of the first newspaper in the Eastern Province—the *Grahamstown Journal*; the family of the Bowkers were all distinguished either in Parliament or in the field against the Xhosas. Before 1820 the permanent British element in South Africa had been small and confined to Cape Town and its neighbourhood, being mainly composed of retired army and naval officers; but, after the arrival of the 1820 settlers, British influence commenced to radiate from Algoa Bay in all directions, and a strong English-speaking stock was added to join with the earlier Afrikaner settlers in the development of South Africa.

[1] *Vide infra*, p. 330.

CHAPTER X

POLITICAL DEVELOPMENT, 1822–1834

ONE consequence of the coming of the 1820 Settlers was to add to the number of the Colonial Government's critics. Since the days of the instructions to the first regular British Governor, Earl Macartney, in 1796, "all the powers of Government, as well Civil as Military" had in truth rested "solely" in the Governor, there being little exaggeration in the subsequent complaint that there was "no law in the Colony but the will of Lord Charles Somerset".[1] Though even now it needed men of assurance, possibly thick-skinned, to face the notoriety incurred by refusing to submit quietly to arbitrary authority, the new classes and new interests of a more complex society could not indefinitely continue to be subjected to unqualified autocracy. The Settlers also had friends at home to take notice of Cape happenings. Yet it is possible to exaggerate their direct influence. Not many of them were politically experienced. From the beginning the hard task of developing a by no means easy or fertile district, far removed from markets and in close proximity to hostile tribes, made them watchful of their own particular interests; but Grahamstown was never in all its history a great centre of radicalism. Individual settlers like Thomas Pringle, who, having planted his "party" on the frontier, turned his hand to journalism, gave notable help; but the real leaders of the political struggle which presently began lived in the parent settlement, Cape Town.

In the general political history of the country the last months of 1821 and the year 1822 marked the beginning of vital developments. On 30 November 1821 Lord Charles Somerset returned from leave to begin an eventful second term as Governor, and it would almost seem that in England he had imbibed a new impatience of opposition and a special fear of the radicalism which had alarmed Lord Sidmouth and his own aristocratic connection at the time of "Peterloo". He seems indeed to have been followed very shortly by an ill-omened instrument of repression in the person of "Oliver the Spy", and in spite of the secrecy of any such transactions, there is evidence to suppose that he was not unwilling to avail himself of Oliver's services in dealing presently with Cape discontents.[2] On the Governor's first arrival there was a hint of trouble to come. Taking violent offence, partly at his substitute's course of action on the frontiers, but perhaps still more at his cutting down the expenses of the Governor's estab-

[1] Unsigned draft in Philip MSS; *vide infra*, p. 984 for notes on the Philip Papers.

[2] Cory, G. E., *Rise of S. A.* II, 274, 278; Macmillan, W. M., *The Cape Colour Question*, p. 180.

lishment,[1] Lord Charles showed such asperity that the Acting-Governor, Sir Rufane Donkin, left the country in dudgeon without so much as an interview on "handing over" office. Very soon after this Dr John Philip, the notable missionary round whom much of the history of the colony was to centre for twenty years, returned from Bethelsdorp armed with evidence on which he was to start a campaign for a drastic overhaul of the laws affecting coloured people.[2] Absorption in white colonial politics has a little obscured the decisive influence of this campaign and how much it helped, in the first place, to secure a Commission of Inquiry; but recent research has enabled us to estimate more justly Philip's work in general.

This missionary with the interests of a statesman had arrived in the country as agent of the London Missionary Society, but, never a mere curate of souls, in the course of years he developed his task far beyond the ordering of the affairs of his own Society. Born in East Fife in 1775, John Philip was trained at Hoxton for the Congregationalist ministry. He served a long apprenticeship from 1804 to 1818 in Aberdeen, a hard and critical school, where his natural abilities were developed. He was thus a mature man of forty-four when he landed in Cape Town in February 1819 endowed with the added dignity of his recently granted doctor's degree of Columbia University, New York. By the time of Lord Charles Somerset's return, Philip had taken the measure of the social and political situation in the Colony, and, since he was at no pains to hide his opinions, his character and training, with perhaps a certain Scottish pugnacity, could not but earn him a reputation for "meddling" in politics. There is little to support the view that he was a doctrinaire with hard and fast ideas of the way to safeguard the interests of the backward people who were now to become his chief concern. Nor did he come thirsting for battle with the authorities. On the contrary, all his letters show him to be something of a Whig in politics, abhorrent of radicalism, a thorough believer in middle-class respectability, susceptible to friendly attention from those in high places, and deferential to constituted authority—at all times eager to co-operate with the ruling powers if they showed any readiness to help, and turning against them only when convinced that he had no alternative. So little was he disposed to prejudge the situation that within two months of landing he had set out on his first long tour of stations in the interior, being absent from his Cape Town base fully four months, as he was to be thereafter almost every second year for anything from three to eleven months at a time, anxious to see things for himself and never taking action till fully armed with facts. Before his first return to England in 1826 he had made four such ox-waggon treks, that of 1825 taking him far northward into Bechuanaland. Soon, no Governor and few officials or colonists had

[1] Cory, G. E., *Rise of S. A.* II, 119 *seq.*
[2] *Vide infra*, ch. XII.

so wide an experience of South African conditions, or such a grasp of the situation in all its aspects, whether relating to European or Native.

On 25 July 1822, Wilmot Horton, Earl Bathurst's Under-Secretary in the Commons, moved an address asking for a Commission of Inquiry into Cape affairs. The genesis of this motion is rather obscure like a good deal else in those years, when British colonial policy was, to say the least, hesitant, and even important colonies were the concern chiefly of a handful of officials in one room of the Colonial Office. Some caution is necessary and we must not magnify stray references in English newspapers into evidence that the matters to which they referred were issues of high politics. This in sober truth they never were. In 1836, the year following a long "Kaffir" war, there is no single reference to South Africa in the *Annual Register*, and repeatedly, on the annual Colonial Office vote, the House of Commons was counted out.[1] Of this Commission it can only be said that several of the colonies were causing concern, and that, the post-war "Peterloo" panic having spent itself, enquiry was favoured by Downing Street as a guide to policy. New South Wales, like the Cape, had given signs under Governor Macquarie of what may be described as growing pains, and in 1819 John Thomas Bigge, a lawyer with West Indian experience, had been commissioned to inquire and advise. Enquiry was also being suggested for Ceylon, Mauritius and the West Indies. As for the Cape, for some time it had been felt that at least the judicial system and the personnel of the Bench stood in need of reform, this being the theme, for example, of a memorandum sent to London by H. Ellis, Deputy Colonial Secretary, as early as 1821.[2] Finance and currency also caused concern.[3] In Great Britain moreover, both in newspapers and in Parliament the hardships and disabilities of the British Settlers got some notice. The first issue of the *Manchester Guardian*, 5 May 1821, had an article on the principal page on Settler hardships as a topic of general interest. Even if some references may have been inaccurate or tendentious,[4] in one way or another the Cape was giving Downing Street cause to think.

While there is no evidence of formal Settler pressure before a petition to Earl Bathurst dated 10 March 1823,[5] it now appears that missionary influence, though possibly not originating, at least helped to force the issue and to make this enquiry the first thorough review of the Cape situation as a whole. Dr Philip, as we have seen, had at the end of 1821 found new light on the question of Hottentot disabilities. While doing all he could by representations to the Colonial Government, he also took steps to bring the case to the direct notice

[1] See instances cited in Mills, *Colonisation of Australia*, pp. 23 *sqq*.
[2] Ellis to Goulburn, *Records of Cape Colony*, XIV, 183 *seq*.
[3] *Ibid.* Vols. XX–XXV. Correspondence of Commissioners, 1825.
[4] Cory, *Rise of S. A.* II, 154 n. commenting on *Morning Chronicle* of 20 September 1822.
[5] *Ibid.* II, 152.

of Downing Street. Having then no personal contact with British Members of Parliament and no great faith in the influence of the Directors of his own society, he put his trust in Sir Jahleel Brenton, an Evangelical friend, lately Commissioner of the dockyard at Simonstown. Returned home in 1822, Brenton was at once deluged with letters and memorials, which included evidence of the working of forced labour at the Bethelsdorp mission reserve. Convinced from his own experience that "nothing short of a Commission of disinterested and upright men"[1] would meet the need, Sir Jahleel succeeded, not without difficulty, in persuading members of the Clapham Sect in Parliament that the case of slaves and Hottentots was one and the same. One evening in July, just before the debate of the 25th, he met William Wilberforce, Fowell Buxton and Dr Lushington at Wilberforce's house, and pressed his own views and Philip's evidence with such success that the great anti-slavery leader himself took up the case. According to Brenton, it was due to the intervention of Wilberforce that the Commission, mooted only for the West Indies, was now first promised by Under-Secretary Horton for the Cape as well. This claim may be excessive—Wilberforce's speech certainly concentrated on the case of slaves and Hottentots—but the Philip-Brenton intervention had the effect at least of clinching the matter and of making the terms of reference comprehensive.

The personnel of the Commission formally constituted under the Great Seal in January 1823 suggests some regard for experience. Bigge had lately reported, however cautiously, on New South Wales[2]; and Major William Macbean George Colebrooke, though quite a young man, had served some time in the East. Investigation was to include "the general administration of the country, and the immediate control exercised by the Governor himself...local institutions, establishments and regulations, civil and military, and more especially those of a judicial and financial character", besides "the extent of [the Governor's] control over the funds and resources of the Colony... the duties and functions of" officials, and "the amount of their respective salaries and emoluments". The Commissioners would also "fully inform themselves of the condition" of slaves, apprenticed Africans and other Coloured persons and, though they were not to touch individual complaints without specific instructions from the Colonial Office, they were to make full investigation of general grievances, including any concerning land tenure.[3]

The presence of the Commission in itself inspired new hope and, as Dr Philip put it, soon after the arrival of the Commissioners in July 1823 "every mouth was open". It may be, he shrewdly commented, that such a long term of office as that enjoyed by Somerset from 1814

[1] Macmillan, W. M., *The Cape Colour Question*, p. 185, for Brenton's account.
[2] See *C.H.B.E.* VII, 113–15.
[3] For Instructions, see *Records of Cape Colony*, XV, 237 *sqq.*

onwards was itself a mistake: "The people bear while there is a prospect of relief, and with a change of men expect a change of measures; but, seeing no end to their sufferings, they have burst through all restraints."[1]

Down to this time the only semblance of a newspaper at the Cape had been the *Government Gazette*;[2] but on 3 February 1823 Thomas Pringle, one of the Settler leaders, having found a kindred spirit in the Dutch Reformed clergyman, Abraham Faure, had approached the Governor for leave to publish a quarterly magazine in English and Dutch—the collaboration of these two men showing that the older Afrikaner colonists to some extent shared the feelings and aspirations of the newer British settlers. In July of the same year a printer, George Greig, proposed a more ambitious venture, a weekly newspaper. Both sets of applicants moved with caution, Pringle and Faure undertaking to exclude controversial subjects, and Greig "all discussions of matters relating to the policy and administration of the colonial Government". But Lord Charles Somerset was unconvinced. Reporting the applications to Lord Bathurst he gave his own view that permission to publish was inadvisable, adding that Pringle—for a time editor of *Blackwood's Magazine* in Edinburgh—was "an arrant Dissenter who had scribbled". Having renewed their request to the Commissioners, the journalists were advised to wait. At last they were informed in December that "Lord Bathurst was of opinion that there could be no objection...so long as the pledge so distinctly and unequivocally given in the prospectus of the *Journal* was abided by, namely, the strict exclusion from the work of all topics of political or personal controversy". Shortly afterwards Pringle and Faure's *Journal* and *Tydschrift* appeared, to be followed on 7 January 1824 by the first number of the *Commercial Advertiser*, which, though generally known as Greig's newspaper, from the beginning owed more to the drive and inspiration of the same Pringle and his friend John Fairbairn. Fairbairn, destined to nearly a lifetime of editorship, soon became the principal partner: to Pringle he wrote, not long after, that Greig must publish what he (Fairbairn) sends him, or he "will get another printer".[3] Before either paper was four months old the mere existence of a popular press brought the autocratic government of Lord Charles Somerset to a critical test. It so happened that the first months of the *Commercial Advertiser* were marked by an extraordinary sequence of events, which moved Cape Town society to its little depths, furnishing what in a free community would have been first-class press copy, but in the trammelled state of this infant press was only dangerous temptation. For some years a highly

[1] Philip to Sir J. Brenton, 27 August 1823, Philip MSS.

[2] For a first-hand account of the Press controversy see Meurant, L. H., *Sixty Years Ago*, p. 62 *sqq*.

[3] Letters in Philip MSS., especially to Pringle, 29 September 1825.

litigous gentleman, Bishop Burnett, had been involved in a fruitless series of lawsuits with one Robert Hart about Grahamstown farm dealings. By the bungling of the Courts[1] one suit had grown into six or more, and when in desperation Burnett wrote protesting and calling in question the competence and honour of the Judges, he was summoned, early in 1824, to stand his trial in Cape Town on a charge of libel. Soon Burnett's grievance involved him in the affairs of two other men who also regarded themselves, not wholly without reason, as victims of official incompetence and high-handedness. For months Cape Town had been in commotion over alleged official malpractices concerning prize negroes, these being exposed in a memorial, the work of Launcelot Cooke, a merchant, and William Edwards, a clever and irrepressible attorney. On May 4 Edwards, who had already had one month in prison for contempt of court, was due for trial, not for the first time, on a charge of libel. Apprehensive as to the attitude of the *Commercial Advertiser*, the Fiscal sent for the printer, Greig, and reminding him of the conditions on which alone the paper was tolerated, demanded 10,000 rix-dollars (£2000) as security, or, failing this, that proof-sheets be submitted to him before publication. Thus threatened, the proprietors on May 5 announced their intention to suspend publication altogether, and a few days later, despite the sealing of their presses and the Governor's order to Greig to leave the colony within one month, contrived to print off by hand and issue a sheet containing "Facts connected with the stopping of the Press, and the censorship of the Fiscal".[2]

On May 7 also, the second number of Pringle's magazine appeared with an article, greatly daring, on the "Present State and Prospects of the English Emigrants in South Africa". On the 13th Pringle in turn was sent for and warned; whereupon, protesting that to continue the magazine was "inconsistent with our personal safety", he also suspended publication. Thus, short of direct suppression, Somerset made it clear that journalism was a risky trade. For a short time the *Gazette* was supplemented by a quasi-official *Chronicle and Mercantile Advertiser*, which William Bridekirk was officially authorised to print on Greig's press; in other words the Colony was dependent once more on the Government even for its news supply.

Throughout 1824 the Governor behaved with that surprising lack of restraint and touchy intolerance of criticism which from the beginning marked his second term of office. The repeated trials of Cooke, Edwards, Burnett and others for libel did nothing to add to the prestige either of the Government or the courts. Lord Bathurst had to point out that in so far as Somerset had communicated Cooke's memorial to the Collector of Customs (the official alleged to be

[1] Cory, *Rise of S. A.* II, 252–3.

[2] Bound in with vol. I of the *S. A. Commercial Advertiser* in the S. A. Public Library, Cape Town, and reprinted 1924. See also Meurant, *op. cit.* pp. 62 *sqq.*

defamed), he himself was "the Publisher" of one of the alleged libels.[1] The lack of a strong Colonial Secretary as second-in-command may have had something to do with the Governor's conduct. The holder of the office was Colonel Christopher Bird, a man of considerable experience. In 1822, by some accounts on the pretext that he was a Roman Catholic, Somerset pressed for his removal, and this, in a letter of 13 March 1824, Lord Bathurst sanctioned. Colonel Bird, there is reason to suppose, had once, especially under Donkin, been a considerable power, according to Philip even "the real Governor". As late as September 1823 Philip had written: "We gain nothing by the removal of Lord Charles Somerset, if Colonel Bird is left behind"; but his later and maturer view seems more just, that Bird was in truth a sobering influence. "As soon as Lord Charles got rid of Colonel Bird," he wrote in 1831, "he seemed like a boy let loose from school... playing all manner of foolish tricks." It is certainly true that the decisive events of Somerset's governorship fell in those months when the Colonial Secretary was under sentence of dismissal and his influence all but gone.

Thus on June 1, when a scurrilous "placard" attacking the Governor's personal character was found posted on a tree in the main street, there was, on the flimsy and unreliable evidence of the few individuals said to have seen it, a house-to-house visitation of suspects like the printer Greig. This was followed by the handing round of lists of persons branded as obnoxious to Government House. The inquisition, not far removed from the use of general warrants, was such that Grahamstown Settlers were driven to write of a "Reign of Terror" and to resort to indirect channels of communication with their friends in Cape Town.[2] Feelings were so strained that, in August, the Governor fell foul of the committee of a Fund for the Relief of Distressed Settlers over his apparently reasonable wish to add to the committee the Landdrost and two other nominees of his own. The Settlers, led in this instance by their chairman, Philip, stoutly opposed the additions on the ground that the unpopular Landdrost, Harry Rivers, had neglected to make full use of relief funds formerly under his control. The result was a war of pamphlets between Rivers, the Governor's protégé, and Philip—an outbreak of such personal rivalries as at any time cause feeling in a small community. They caused also a definite widening of the breach between Somerset and Philip. Next the Governor stamped on the attempt of Pringle and Fairbairn to found a "Literary and Scientific Society" in Cape Town. Though these "Radicals" got the support of respectable citizens including the Chief Justice, Sir John Truter, this was not enough to commend their scheme to Lord Charles

[1] Cory, *Rise of S. A.* II, 261 n. The "Collector" was Wilberforce Bird, not to be confused with Colonel C. Bird, the Colonial Secretary.

[2] Macmillan, W. M., *The Cape Colour Question*, p. 117.

Somerset. In September, moreover a highly safe and respectable clergyman, the Rev. Alexander Smith of Uitenhage, was sharply snubbed for venturing to propose for his district a "Society for the communication of religious and general instruction to all classes of the people". On behalf of the Governor, Smith was curtly informed that it was "inconsistent with his duty to permit the establishment of an association which could not answer the end of its institution".

The panic and alarm which seized the Governor was that of an old-fashioned anti-Jacobin Tory. This talk of "sedition" was itself absurd. The Afrikaner colonists were on the whole unperturbed: next year many of them subscribed to an address laudatory of the Governor. The only "danger" was to the personal feelings and sense of dignity of an irresponsible Governor who had alienated individuals and classes alike. All these libel actions, the result of his own impatience of restraint or question, sadly strained the powers of the Courts where the authority of the Judges was insufficient to curb the extravagances of Edwards or even of Burnett.[1] These extravagances, indeed found a match in the wild language used by the Governor himself in his private despatches. In July, for example, even before the Settler Fund dispute had developed, he told Earl Bathurst:

> I would rejoice in an opportunity to expose Philip and Wright, but though I am aware of all they do by secret intelligence upon which I depend, I should, if I were to bring their conduct forward, disclose the only source of intelligence upon which I depend and which I consider of too much importance to the safety of my Government to give up.[2]

According to this "secret and confidential" despatch in the Governor's own handwriting, "Philip,—the *Reverend* as he styles himself—Pringle, Fairbairn, and one Wright" were the real source of mischief, Philip in particular, so he was informed, being "the real writer for that seditious Press". Whatever the source of this information, even if it came from "Oliver the Spy", it was at fault. Philip in fact had warned his friend Pringle to be careful and had himself kept aloof from the Press—being actually on tour in the interior on Hottentot and missionary business until the very eve of the crisis. On his return, in all innocence he reclaimed one of the confiscated presses, the property of the London Missionary Society, which had been lent to Greig on condition that he repaired it and was valued later at no more than £18 or £20. Somerset, however, as if convinced that Philip was his most formidable critic, took occasion, first, in defiance of his own ban on printing, to circulate an old attack on Philip for a share in a domestic dispute in the Scots Church in London Wall; later, to drag back to Cape Town two ministers of the Dutch Reformed Church, the Rev. Andrew Murray and Rev. Alexander Smith, in the hope of getting information against him; and, as late

[1] Cory, *Rise of S. A.* II, 269.

[2] C.O.[a] (Cape Archives), Duplicate Despatches, vol. XII, 18 July 1824.

as January 1825, to forward to London a foolish document described as a "Biographical Sketch of John Philip, formerly a journeyman weaver, now head of the Missionary Society at the Cape, and calling-himself *Doctor* Philip".[1] One result was that Dr. Philip came to regard these personal attacks upon himself as arising directly from the Governor's hostility to missions, and to his own attempts to raise the status of the Hottentots.

In May the attorney Edwards had been sentenced to transportation to Botany Bay, whence, as appeared a little later, he had originally come. In September, when a convict ship arrived and his removal was imminent, he contrived to escape with the help of a friend, Captain John Carnall. For two days Edwards was at large, but on his recapture and expulsion to Australia, Carnall in turn was brought to book for aiding and abetting the escape and was sentenced to deportation. In the end he was excused Botany Bay and allowed to go to England. Now a whole host clamoured against the Governor in London—Sir Rufane Donkin, the friends of aggrieved Settlers, Greig the printer—also the missionary interest, as yet perhaps only watchful. Thither also went Burnett. Brought to trial at last in August, after various delays due to appeals and threatened further appeals, he contrived to escape and carry his grievances with him to the further edification of Earl Bathurst and the Home Government. In the course of 1825 Somerset, indeed, showed greater discretion. In January, when he visited Albany, he removed the unpopular Landdrost Rivers and investigated the land grievances. Donald Moodie and others who had been loud against him were quieted, Moodie, according to his friend, Duncan Campbell, being "timid and shy". since he had "become a functionary", that is, magistrate of the little port at the Kowie. In the middle of the same year Philip felt free to go off on one of his longest tours to collect more of the information on the Hottentots, which he was presently to make use of in England. Nevertheless, in the end the outcry against Somerset was greater than the British Government could face.

The reaction to these happenings in England is not easy to trace in detail, but certainly the Colonial Office was kept abnormally busy. The shelves of the Public Record Office witness how heavily the correspondence of the years 1824–7 exceeded the normal in mere bulk with the affairs of Donkin, Burnett, Cooke and Edwards, Fairbairn and Pringle taking whole volumes to themselves. Repeatedly in the session of 1825 allegations against the Governor were referred to, and as early as June 1825 it was announced in Parliament that Lord Charles had been given leave of absence. Somerset's sailing being delayed, on October 26 *The Times* weighed in heavily to suggest that the Government could not be so "borough-ridden" as to shield him by procrastination from the enquiry called for by the public

[1] Macmillan, W. M., *The Cape Colour Question*, pp. 199 *sqq*.

outcry against him. At the Cape the fact of his virtual recall was known by September and this served to make for quiet.[1] Yet it was not until March of the year following that he handed over to General Bourke, by which time Brougham was talking even of impeachment.[2] In view of the political turmoil he had caused, the most surprising fact of all is that he escaped dismissal, resigning quietly only on the fall of the long-lived Tory ministry of Lord Liverpool and the political changes in England that marked the beginning of 1827.

All this time the Crown Commissioners had been at work with little obvious result. Formal reports were actually still longer delayed partly as a result of the work heaped on them by the Colonial Office, which, time and again, took refuge from its embarrassments by referring to them, for example, the complaints of Donkin and of Pringle, and by asking critics to suspend judgment till they had replied.[3] Without waiting for the Commissioners' suggestions, Bathurst himself now thought it wise, by a despatch of 9 February 1825, to appoint an Advisory Council of officials including the Chief Justice, the Colonial Secretary, the General, and the Auditor and Receiver. This council was to discuss only what might be submitted by the Governor, but had power also to minute any points it would like to be considered. In practice it could make little real difference. It is at any time difficult for even high officials of a Crown Colony to take a line strongly independent of the Governor; and though in the unlikely event of their doing so, disregard of their opinion or advice might attract attention and cause inconvenient questions to be asked by the Colonial Office, yet at this slight risk the Governor could, if he chose, ignore his Council and carry on much as before. The inauguration of this new body was no more than the first halting recognition that the Colony's needs were becoming too complex to be left to the unfettered discretion of a single individual. Any really vital changes came later, some of them without much direct influence from the long-deferred reports of the Commissioners.[4]

In essentials the old system of government continued under General Bourke, with a respite from libel trials, but with a renewed fight for the freedom of the Press. In August 1825 the banished Greig had returned, in modified triumph, with permission to resume publication of the *Commercial Advertiser* provided he adhered to the terms of his original non-political prospectus. A lively series of letters from Fairbairn to Pringle shows little enthusiasm for this achievement:

[1] Rev. A. Faure to Philip in September 1825, Philip MSS.

[2] *The Times*, 19 January 1826.

[3] Wilmot Horton in reply to J. Hume, 11 March 1825. Also *Records of Cape Colony*, 1825. Vols. XX–XXV.

[4] The principal reports appear in *Parl. Pap.* 1826, XXIII (438)—Currency: 1826–7, XXI (282)—General Administration and Finance: also 1829, V (300)—Trade: 1830, XXI (584)—Natives and missionary institutions. For these and lesser reports, and correspondence, see *Records of Cape Colony*, index.

"Greig was not the lad to make too good a bargain with such crafty carles as Lord Bathurst and the Attorney General", wrote Fairbairn on 7 October 1825.[1] Bathurst, he continued, was said to fear only for "the endangering of the peace and safety of the colony"; Somerset, "the philosopher of Florence", they were also assured, had only "the good of the Colony at heart". Fairbairn for his part had nothing to do with Somerset's heart. "It may be in the right place...only let him keep off his hands and his ill-scraped tongue"—of which there was "little hope", since he "dabbled with everything". Actually, early in the year 1826, a new venture of Fairbairn's own, the *New Organ*, was suspended by the outgoing Governor. Finally, in May 1827, by the latest direct intervention of Lord Bathurst, probably at the instigation of the ex-Governor, the *Commercial Advertiser* itself was definitely suppressed for daring to reproduce from *The Times* of 25 January 1826 an article which reflected on the doings of Lord Charles Somerset. This time Fairbairn himself went to fight the battle of the Press in London. Aided by the accession to power of a less reactionary Government, he returned triumphant to Cape Town in July 1828 with the guarantee of a Press ordinance based on English law. Subject to paying a deposit surety and stamp duty, printers and publishers were set free from the direct control of the Governor-in-Council and made answerable only to the law of libel as interpreted now by independent Judges. The freedom of the Press was thus very largely won by colonists for themselves.

Freedom became effective only when the Crown Commissioners' reports began at last to underline the need for radical reform of the whole system of government. Far more important than the Advisory Council of 1825 was the Charter of Justice of 1827. Issued by writ of Privy Seal on August 24, this was a real breach in the old autocracy and the first step towards a free constitution. By this Charter, revised in 1832 and promulgated finally in February 1834,[2] the Executive or, in effect, the Governor, though still for a while the sole legislative authority, ceased at last to be also the final Court of Appeal. Consideration of the series of cases which raised such storms in and about 1824 had convinced the King's advisers that reform was necessary to secure not merely the authority of the Cape courts of law but ordinary respect for its administration. Under the old order[3] only the Chief Justice held a whole-time office, the lesser Judges being recruited from almost any source, often from among officials—wharfmasters, collectors of customs, and the like—who had earned or needed some supplementing of the salary paid for duties they continued to exercise. Naturally such men held office only *durante bene placito*: appeals moreover, which lay to the Governor with one or

[1] Philip MSS.

[2] Eybers, G. W., *Select Constit. Docs.* pp. 107 *sqq.*

[3] *Records of Cape Colony*, XXVII, 342 *sqq.*

more of them as assessors, have been described as of the nature of private interviews with that august official. Henceforth the Judges were to be barristers or advocates of at least three years' standing, whole-time officers, appointed by and responsible to the Crown. In civil cases the Chief Justice and two Puisne Judges were to form a quorum, with appeal to the Privy Council where the sum of £1000 (later £5000) was involved. Criminal cases were to be heard by one Judge, with a jury of nine: cases on circuit, by one Judge, with appeal, where more than £100 should be involved, to the full Bench of the Supreme Court. At the same time the duties of the Vice-Admiralty Court were transferred to the new High Court, and, to complete the system, the duties of the old Fiscal were transferred to an Attorney-General, the Court being further supplied with a Registrar, a Sheriff, and, in 1834, a Master to take over the duties of the Orphan Chamber. The last three officials were to be appointed by the Secretary of State on the recommendation of the Governor.

The Commissioners' legal changes on the whole worked out well. The Roman-Dutch civil law remained the basis of the legal system, English practices and rules of court only being introduced with caution. English criminal law served to mitigate the severity of the penalties still prescribed by the old Roman-Dutch system, and the introduction at the same time of the English jury system brought with it the English law of evidence.[1] So far as European interests were concerned, the jury system provided some slight check on a still irresponsible Executive: but its benefits have been perhaps less obvious in those cases where it has fallen to a European jury to judge a fellow-European charged with a crime of violence against a Coloured person or an African.

Some of the administrative changes were more open to criticism. In 1824 English became the language of the government offices to the exclusion of Dutch, and in 1828 of the Courts also,[2] though ignorance of English was not held to be a bar to service as a juryman. This change was due mainly to necessity. The judges and other higher officials were nearly all English, their offices could hardly be manned by Netherlanders, High Dutch was not freely spoken by the people, Afrikaans was far from being a literary language and there were no adequate means of training bilingual recruits within the Colony. True, in 1822, Somerset had imported James Rose-Innes and a few other Scots to staff schools in the larger centres and in 1829 the South African College opened its doors as a private venture; but though this college was destined to be the parent of the University of Cape Town, it was at the moment little more than a school. More to the point, the teaching in all these institutions was almost

[1] *Vide infra*, chapter xxx.

[2] Eybers, *op. cit.*, p. 107.

entirely in English. Doubtless more has been made of the consequent hardships in retrospect than was felt at the time; nevertheless, it cannot be denied that the almost exclusively Dutch or Afrikaans-speaking country folk were placed at a disadvantage. The Dutch East India Company's economic restrictions had already limited the variety of employment open to the youth of the country, and now the rural Afrikaners were confirmed in an isolation which throughout the nineteenth century gave them a sense of inferiority, and in extreme cases helped even to make them "poor whites".

Incidentally, by an early recommendation of the Commissioners the divergent interests of East and West were recognised if not emphasised at this time by the division of the Colony into two Provinces, Captain Andries Stockenstrom becoming Commissioner-General for the Eastern Districts. This able and zealous official, son of a Landdrost of Graaff-Reinet, a man of Swedish origin, had already served full twenty years in frontier districts. He was discovered by Colonel Collins in 1808, and though since 1815 he had done excellent work as Landdrost of Graaff-Reinet, the big part he was to play in affairs was yet to come. A staunch upholder of the civil as against the military authority, which he felt was encroaching in the matters of commandos and reprisals, he resigned the Commissionership in dudgeon in 1833, protesting that as Commissioner-General his position was no better than that of "the fifth wheel to a waggon".

More immediately serious were some of the consequences of substituting Civil Commissioners and Magistrates for Landdrosts. So far as the extended powers of the new officials made civil justice speedier and more accessible and removed some of the anomalies of the old matrimonial law, this was to the good: the removal of the petty judicial powers of the Field-cornets was perhaps also a reform. But when the original salary seemed inadequate to secure efficient Resident Magistrates (and, after 1834, almost entirely for reasons of economy, the offices of Civil Commissioner and Resident Magistrate were combined), there was a growing and unfortunate tendency for the Magistrate to swallow up the Civil Commissioner. For the backward Natives of South Africa, the law thus came to be associated more and more with the Magistrates' Court and the policeman rather than with a fatherly Chief going about among the people themselves, an administrative and, in the true sense, "political" officer. The effect on the European colonists was more immediately unfortunate, for with the Landdrosts there disappeared also the local Boards of Heemraden as well as the Burgher Senate in Cape Town. This, with the concentration of all local revenues in central funds, had the disastrous effect of snapping the only direct link between government and the people governed, weakening fatally, what had much need of fostering, a proper sense of local responsibility. Two unofficial nominees on the Governor's Council of Advice, together with a few Justices of the Peace in country districts, were inadequate substitutes, and the effect of the change in weakening links with central authority about the time of the Great Trek, a few years later, can only be dimly guessed.

Despite such defects the reforms of 1828 marked a definite constitutional and political advance. The right of public meeting was not enjoyed till 1848, but in 1824 the Dutch Reformed Church, reinforced by the Rev. Andrew Murray and other Scottish ministers whom Somerset had brought in, obtained the right of meeting in quinquennial General Synod. Now, under the influence of the British movement for parliamentary reform, even the Cape began to hope for a constitution. As early as 1830, Fairbairn, the leading journalist and a stout believer in self-government, was preaching the old doctrine, "No taxation without consent".[1]

The Commissioners undoubtedly helped to set the country on the road to political progress, but the economic problem was beyond their power to remedy. There was in truth little likelihood of solid prosperity or even solvency whether with representative institutions or without them. Till the mineral developments of the later nineteenth century brought relief, South Africa was by reason of the sparseness of the population, inadequate means of communication and recurrent droughts but a poor country. Home market there was little or none; the most considerable export, wine, was in decline; wool production was in its earliest infancy, though Port Elizabeth in the 'thirties did an increasing trade in hides and skins, largely from Kaffirland. Before 1831, however, there was no publication of accounts and the revenue was commonly supposed to be more elastic than it really was. Overhead expenses from the Governor's salary of £10,000 a year downwards being on a grand scale, there was a constant struggle to make ends meet—except perhaps in times of war when heavy expenditure on the comings and goings of troops to and from Table Bay produced a boom. In the late 'twenties, however, peace had reigned for longer than usual, and Europe itself was suffering sharply from post-war financial disturbance. At the Cape the currency was at once insecure, inflated and heavily depreciated.[2] The standard being the paper rix-dollar of the nominal value of 4*s*., the Crown Commissioners found the amount in circulation risen to 5,587,056 rds. (i.e. £269,029 at par). Of this roughly 1½ million was new debt incurred since 1806 to meet the needs of troops or as loans for public works; another 484,451 rds. were forged notes. Theoretically secured on public property, this total was considerably in excess of the currency needs and spending power of the Colony. The rix-dollar, therefore, had depreciated rapidly from 4*s*., to round about 1*s*. 6*d*., when, in the financial reorganisation following the resumption of specie payments by the Bank of England, the British Government proposed to make British silver current throughout the Empire. With the best will in

[1] E.g. *Commercial Advertiser*, 21 August and 2 October 1830.

[2] *Records of Cape Colony*, XXII, 141 *sqq*.

the world, some people were likely to suffer in the process of the deflation, which began with the stabilisation of the rix-dollar at 1*s*. 6*d*. silver in 1825. The British Government did indeed provide silver to buy in and secure the cancellation of over one million paper rix-dollars, this amounting in effect to a loan of £92,000 without interest. London also cancelled some of the debt due on account of rations provided to the Albany settlers and took over the charge for a reduced Cape Corps of Hottentots. But in the Colony, with the fixed yield of land quit-rents suffering from the depreciation at the same time as new methods of trade heavily reduced the old auction dues, revenue and expenditure were as hard to balance as ever. Even after 1834 retrenchment continued by express orders from home; salaries were heavily cut; worse still, expenditure, which was desirable and necessary to meet the expanding needs of the public administration, was avoided and turned down. Enforced economy or merely short-sighted parsimony added not a little to the difficulties, for example, of the Kaffir frontier, where provision alike for magistrates and for police was long most inadequate.[1]

Generally the creditor classes in the towns were hardest hit by the collapse of the rix-dollar, and for a time economic discontents greatly stimulated the political demand for representative control of finance and taxation. In 1827, and again in May 1830, petitions to the Crown for representative government got so far as being discussed in the House of Commons;[2] but by this time the hope of further constitutional progress was fainter. The agitation against Somerset had been effective as a protest. It even united cautious Settlers, radical pressmen, and liberal Dutch-speaking colonists like the Rev. Abraham Faure for a time under a common leader—John Philip—chairman of the Settlers' Fund, the intimate of Pringle, the father-in-law of Fairbairn, the champion of Hottentot rights and of the missionary interest. Now the Colony, which only a few years earlier had learned to stand united against the autocracy of Lord Charles Somerset, was torn by faction.

The full story of what led to this disturbance of colonial harmony is told in a later chapter.[3] While the colonists at large were absorbed in their own affairs—the conflict with Somerset, the Press affair, the constitutional reforms—Philip was from the beginning concerned above all about Hottentot grievances and disabilities, and in the year 1828 the agitation he had led bore fruit in the famous Fiftieth Ordinance "for improving the condition of the Hottentots and other free persons of colour'. This proved to be a ruder and more widely felt shock even than the attack on slavery which was then nearing its

[1] See e.g. complaint of Capt. C. L. Stretch in "Memorandum on Kaffir Treaties", Gubbins Collection in the library of the University of Witwatersrand, Johannesburg.

[2] *Hansard*, 2nd Ser. XXIV, 1005, reproduced in Eybers, *Select Constit. Docs.*, p. 30.

[3] *Vide infra*, chapter XII.

climax. The Albany settlers had never been allowed predial slaves, and many Afrikaner frontiersmen were too poor to have them: but all had Hottentot servants. The promulgation of the Ordinance led to an outcry that Hottentot labour, at best of poor quality, would now be scarcer and less efficient than ever. A scapegoat was soon found, and the Colony seethed with indignation at the allegations supposed to be made against colonial masters in the *Researches* recently published by Philip, the man whom Lord Charles Somerset himself clearly regarded as the most formidable of all his critics. Now, and for many years to come, "Colonists" were ranged on one side, and, on the other, the "anti-Colonial Party", a group small in numbers but able and highly vocal. With the colony thus divided, the 1830 petition for self-government had no hope of success. East was divided against West, and British settlers and old Dutch colonists were by no means consistently united. Such divisions made the case hopeless.

Outward signs of social progress are, therefore, misleading. When, for example, in 1830 Cape Town acquired a second newspaper, *De Zuid Afrikaan*, and 1831 saw the birth of the *Grahamstown Journal*, these were not really unmixed evidence of what a Grahamstown writer in 1832 described as "our improved state of society". "But for the *Researches*," the same writer complained, "little doubt we should have had a Legislative Assembly, and some legal and constitutional check on the amount of our taxation and the manner of our expenditure."[1] The new journals were really the outward and visible signs of the inward divisions. The Western Province in particular was greatly agitated by the anti-slavery measures which preceded emancipation. There were even hints of rebellion.[2] *De Zuid Afrikaan* and the *Commercial Advertiser* watched and denounced each other, though at one point the former professed to offer gradual emancipation in return for self-government. Meantime, the *Grahamstown Journal* came to life in direct consequence of the unpopularity of the *Advertiser* and of its editor, Fairbairn, who in the course of a visit to the Eastern Province in 1830 had the temerity to promote the prosecution of "half-a-dozen" Albany employers for unlawfully withholding wages from Hottentot servants.[3] For in Grahamstown, though there were no slaves, "Kaffir thieving" was regarded as a formidable menace, and Emancipationists and Humanitarians were as unpopular as in Cape Town. Duncan Campbell, quondam ally of Pringle, whom he assured in 1825 that "powder and ball" were the most effective civilising agents for "Kaffirs", was now Civil Commissioner of Albany, and Philip in 1830 was moved to retort, "In Albany a *civilised* Hottentot is one content to work without wages, or for any trifle,

[1] A.B. in the *Grahamstown Journal*, 24 February 1832.
[2] Walker, E. A., *Hist. of Southern Africa*, p. 167.
[3] Philip MSS. quoted by Macmillan, W. M., *The Cape Colour Question*, p. 221 n.

without complaint."[1] Colonial society, in short, was rent from top to bottom even more about the Fiftieth Ordinance than about slavery itself. Until this breach was healed, constitutional progress was likely to be hampered and slow, even had the years following been less distracted by war and frontier troubles.[2]

The elaborate instructions given to Sir Benjamin D'Urban, who assumed office as Governor in January 1834, would indicate that in spite of frequent changes of Secretary the Colonial Office was giving the Cape quite serious attention. D'Urban was required not only to inaugurate an improved Council and to complete the emancipation of the slaves, but to consider the development of municipal institutions and, above all, the framing of a more satisfactory frontier policy. Unfortunately he was also expressly charged to pursue economy and retrenchment: he had himself to be content with only £5000 a year, as against £10,000, the former salary of the Governor. A soldier like his predecessors, some fifty-six years of age, with experience first in the wars, then as Governor of Barbados and of British Guiana, both his character and experience were to be severely tested by the trials awaiting him.

His first task was straightforward, to substitute for the ineffective Advisory Council of 1825 an official Executive and, in addition, a Legislative Council composed of the same officials and from five to seven nominated citizens. The right of initiation remained with the Governor, but the consent of the Council was required for all legislation, and laws could be set aside only if the King-in-Council withheld consent or failed to approve them within two years. Meetings of the Council soon came to be thrown open to the public and to reporters, and unofficial members were strong enough on occasion to override the officials, as in the matter of the Draft Vagrant Law of 1834.[3] It was also of good omen that, on December 1 of that year, slave emancipation[4] took effect in perfect calm, as if indeed the end of suspense was a relief. But, almost at that moment, the cause of popular self-government was heavily checked by the defection of Fairbairn. In consequence of a dispute at a Cape Town meeting in October 1834, he resigned from the reform committee, sending word to the leader of the Kat River Hottentots through Philip that:

> He authorises you to tell A. Stoffles that he is quite of his opinion now and will not advocate [an elected legislative Assembly] any more till the Hottentots and people of colour are fit to take their place in it along with the white population. But he wishes them to make haste, as he is still anxious that such an Assembly should be introduced.[5]

In the same month began the fiercest of the Kaffir wars.

[1] Macmillan, *The Cape Colour Question*, pp. 121, 224.

[2] For an account of these concurrent troubles, *vide infra*, chapter XIII.

[3] *Vide infra*, pp. 297.

[4] *Vide infra*, pp. 275.

[5] Philip MSS., Mrs Philip to Philip, October 1834.

Self-government was now less likely than ever to be conferred upon a colony where a section even of the "Radicals" opposed it as unsuitable if not dangerous. Nor was it discussed seriously again until, peace being restored, Municipal Councils,[1] Road Boards and Local School Committees had done something to promote in the colonists a habit of association for public purposes, and the Masters and Servants Law of 1842, extending the principle of the Fiftieth Ordinance, had firmly established the legal equality of black and white.

[1] Ordinance of August 1836; Eybers, p. 6

CHAPTER XI

SLAVERY AT THE CAPE, 1652–1838

IN the seventeenth century, slaves were held to be necessary to the development of plantation colonies, and many years before the establishment of a settlement at the Cape of Good Hope, slavery had been introduced into the possessions of the Dutch East India Company. There was little antipathy to slavery on religious and philosophical grounds, whilst the economic argument that colonial prosperity grew with the progressive organisation of a traffic in slaves carried general conviction. The Cape, however, was not a tropical dependency and, in the first few years of the settlement, manual labour was performed by the Company's own free Dutch servants. The experiment was costly and as early as April 1654 van Riebeeck was convinced that slave labour would be less expensive. Visiting Commissioners came to the same conclusion; for instance Van Rheede (1685) was anxious to replace European labourers with slaves born at the Cape. The Company's servants expected to lead an easier life than in the mother country, and slaves would perform the menial tasks at one-quarter the cost to the Company for clothing and provisions. The settlement was so slow to reach a basis of self-sufficiency that, fifty years after its establishment, not more than thirty families were thought to be self-supporting. Under such circumstances the Council of Policy, in 1717 and again in 1743, came to the conclusion that no more European workmen should be dispatched to the Cape.[1]

A few slaves had been brought from Batavia and Madagascar prior to 1658, when desertion by slaves is first mentioned. Since it was already manifest that the Cape Hottentots were averse to regular work the Company resolved on organised importation. West Africa proved disappointing as a source of supply and slaving ships mostly made for Madagascar and the East Coast. The expeditions were not always a success even when their commanders had been furnished with letters of courtesy to Malagasy potentates, and, in the eighteenth century, competition from French and Portuguese slaving vessels sent up the price. The East Coast remained, however, the most reliable source of supply, and, for ten years (1720–30), the Company found it worth while to maintain a station at Delagoa Bay from which slaves were periodically shipped to the Cape. East Coast Africans had the reputation of being intractable and treacherous; hence their employment was mostly for porterage and other laborious work. Asiatic slaves imported from the Malabar coast were found to be more submissive

[1] *Reports of Chavonnes...and of Van Imhoff, on the Cape*, p. 93. (Van Riebeeck Society Publications, No. 1.)

and faithful, but there was also a third class of banished criminals, mostly Malay, from the Company's eastern possessions, who were responsible for the slave insurrections and crimes of violence which endangered colonial life in the more remote districts. Malays indeed were found in useful employment as skilled tailors, carpenters and cobblers, but the majority gave more trouble than they were worth. In 1767, as a result of repeated representations from the Council of Policy, the exportation to the Cape of Asiatic offenders was brought to an end.

The names and places of origin of all slaves disembarked at Cape Town were inscribed in a register. Slaves not needed for the Company's use or bought by officials were put up for sale to the burghers, who were allowed to purchase on credit. Prices ruled low, for African-born slaves were preferred to those imported from abroad. Domestic servants were recruited from the numerous classes of half-breeds, the offspring of intercourse between female slaves and Europeans.

At the beginning of the eighteenth century, Cape burghers owned several hundred slaves, the vast majority of whom were male. Hottentots were nominally free persons, but it was difficult to distinguish them from the servile Coloured population, and intermarriage was apt to lead to the children being claimed as slaves. The total slave population increased at a fairly rapid rate during the century and amounted to 25,754 in 1798.[1] The number would have been greater but for the facilities for manumission which allowed the slave to purchase his own freedom. Manumission was, moreover, compulsory in the not very rare case of children being born to a white man by a female slave. At the same time, owners could not have their slave children baptised without promising ultimate freedom, the profession of the Christian religion and the ability to speak Dutch being considered good reasons for claiming manumission. Emancipated slaves were potential producers of foodstuffs needed for supplying the Company's ships, and it was not until the authorities found by unhappy experience that freed slaves were commonly indolent that these liberal arrangements were modified. In 1682 Governor-General van Goens was moved to legislate against the manumission of non-Christian slaves except for good cause, whilst in 1708 owners were required to give a guarantee that emancipated slaves would not become a burden on the public for a period of ten years.[2] Manumission, usually by will, of slaves born at the Cape continued to be common, but such slaves were few in number, as nearly all imported slaves were males.

At the Cape the largest servile class was that of the domestic or

[1] Bigge, J. T., *Report upon Slaves and State of Slavery at C.G.H.*, 5 April 1831. *Records of Cape Colony*, xxxv, 353. The number of adult slaves owned by the colonists in 1708 had been 1147.

[2] The various restrictions on manumission were repealed between 1823 and 1830. *Records of Cape Colony*. xxxv. 261.

personal slaves. In Cape Town, the slaves of well-to-do burghers led an easy enough life and were in general humanely treated. Many were expert in making up raw materials into shoes and clothing. Poorer burghers made a considerable profit out of their domestic slaves by requiring them to hawk provisions and articles of dress. Others allowed their slaves to work for their own profit on payment of a weekly sum. Many were expert craftsmen and did well at Cape Town, particularly in wood-carving and furniture-making. In the eighteenth century mechanical trades were almost entirely in the hands of slaves from India, Ceylon and the Far East. Slaves were thus allowed to profit by their own exertions, whilst the burghers found it possible to live comfortably on small incomes.

In the country districts and at the Company's Slave Lodge at the capital slavery had few alleviations. The Company's slaves worked long in the warehouses and at porterage to and from the ships. In the outlying districts slaves were much less numerous. There was no mass production and, consequently, no *driving* system, for Cape economy was not that of the tropical plantation. On the other hand, the burghers derived no more than a precarious living from subsistence farming, and slaves necessarily shared the poverty of their masters. They were commonly underfed and overworked, but there is little evidence of brutal treatment as a rule.[1] The severity of the law, which enjoined savage punishments for crimes committed by slaves, was mitigated in practice, save in the most heinous cases. For many offences slaves could be flogged by officials without trial, but legislation against cruel punishment by masters was followed by trial and conviction of European burghers.[2] The Company set a good example by the provision of a liberal diet of fish and rice at the Slave Lodge, and it repeatedly legislated against compulsory work on Sundays. Masters were obliged, as far as possible, to instruct their slaves in the Reformed religion, and schools were provided from time to time for the gratuitous instruction of slave children. In the country districts, little could be done, and Muhammadanism grew apace. In the vain hope of checking this development, a Batavian resolution of 1770 provided that slaves confirmed in the Christian religion could not be sold.[3]

Slaves did not contribute to the welfare of the settlement. At the Cape, there were no tropical plantations needing Negro labour for their cultivation, and the capital expenditure on slaves was largely unremunerative. Moreover, it led to contempt for labour among the

[1] Even Malay slaves were found to speak with gratitude of their masters for generous treatment. Lichtenstein, H., *Travels in Southern Africa in the years* 1803–6, vol. I, pp. 61–2, 206. Percival, T., *Account of the Cape of Good Hope*, p. 284.

[2] Dehérain, H., *Le Cap de Bonne-Espérance au* XVIIe *siècle*, pp. 213–16. By the Statutes of India masters could inflict a flogging up to thirty-nine stripes without informing the judicial authorities.

[3] This prohibition was repealed by Cradock in 1812 as it operated to induce masters to oppose conversion of their slaves to Christianity.

Europeans and increased the burdens on agriculture. As early as 1717 Dominique de Chavonnes pointed out that the wages of white labourers would increase the circulation of money and save unprofitable expenditure on aged and sick slaves and on the upbringing of slave children. In the towns the competition of unfree mechanics and artisans discouraged burghers from entering useful trades. Slaves performed most of the work in carpentry and masonry for the master builder. At a later date, Hermanus Schutte employed a few white masons and plasterers in Cape Town, but good slave masons, carpenters and plasterers could be hired for three rix-dollars a day or less, without food.[1] The white colonial boy learned from the cradle to despise manual work and to expect ready obedience. There was little occasion for the cultivation of qualities of accommodation and self-subordination.

The establishment of British rule at the Cape (1795) came at a time when the protest of the English humanitarians against the slave trade had won powerful support in parliament and country. Thomas Clarkson and William Wilberforce appealed to moral and religious arguments, but there was also the economic plea that the trade helped to build up the prosperity of the French West Indian islands at a time when Britain was at war with France. Under such circumstances, the British Government was disposed to restrict the slaving activities of British subjects. Craig reported on 27 December 1795[2] that the 534 slaves formerly belonging to the Company would more than suffice for the needs of the new government. The British occupation, however, stimulated production and brought about a genuine shortage of labour. Slave importations ceased altogether for four years (1793–7), but in 1797 Craig, who had found slaves indispensable for work on fortifications and transport as well as for employment on public buildings and the gardens of official residences, was constrained to sanction the landing of 350 negroes. Next year Lord Macartney after considering total prohibition as the best means of obliging the European colonists to become "more industrious and useful members to the State", and possibly of stopping their continual trekking,[3] made the importation of slaves without government licence punishable with a heavy fine, and slaves illegally introduced were to be entitled to freedom and repatriation. The Batavian authorities, during the rule of the Republic 1803–6, likewise prohibited the unauthorised landing of slaves, though de Mist was prepared to sanction a limited importation until such time as slaves could be replaced in the labour market by European workers. His colleague, General J. W. Janssens, was of opinion that slave-holding encouraged luxurious habits among

[1] Common European labourers received no more in wages than slaves. Evidence of John Cannon. *Records of Cape Colony*, XXIX.

[2] Craig to Secretary of State, 27 December 1795. *Records*, I, 272.

[3] Replies... by W. S. van Ryneveld, 29 November 1797, quoted Walker, E. A., *The Great Trek*, p. 68.

the colonial youth, and did what he could to secure slaves from injustice and maltreatment, charging the Landdrosts with the duty of protecting their interests. Nevertheless, the importation of slaves continued under licence and subject to the payment of specified duties.

The restoration of British rule (1806) was soon followed by the coming into force on 1 January 1808 of the Act for the abolition of the slave trade.[1] Britain's industrial wealth was now so great that the plantation trade, which slaving had sustained, was relatively of small importance. Under the Act, no slave could be legally landed in any British port after 1 March 1808, and slaves landed contrary to law were to become "prize negroes". The administration of the Act was, from the first, defective. Wholesale slaving by Spanish and Portuguese subjects was connived at by their Governments, and so long as slavery itself remained legal there was a certain market for illicit cargoes. The profits of slaving were larger than they had been whilst the trade remained lawful, and pecuniary penalties were powerless to deter offenders. At the Cape, foreign slavers were allowed for many years to call and revictual. Under the regulations, prize negroes were to be apprenticed until such time as they should be able to maintain themselves by their own labour. In practice they were often assigned to tradespeople under conditions which made it difficult for them to secure release from service.[2] To check illicit importations Governor Caledon secured the appointment of a committee before which all persons having in their possession recently imported slaves could be compelled to attend and to declare how they came to be possessed of them. With these precautions evasion of the law became difficult, and, after 1810, the slave population grew merely by excess of births over deaths and manumission.[3]

The abolition of the trade naturally had the effect of sending up the price of slaves within the Colony. "The purchase of slaves", wrote Cradock, "is at present out of the reach of all persons who do not possess considerable funds."[4] This increase in value brought with it a general improvement in conditions. At Cape Town, it was usual to provide fresh meat, soup and fish in abundance for slaves, and to clothe them well. The salubrity of the climate and the cheapness of provisions contributed to bring about a rapid advancement in their numbers. The betterment of their condition by alteration of the law had been contemplated by Sir George Yonge as early as 1800, and in 1815 the House of Commons recommended colonial legislatures to ameliorate the lot of slaves. The establishment of a complete system

[1] 47 Geo. III, Sess. I, c. 36.

[2] *Papers relating to Prize Slaves at the Cape of Good Hope*, *Parl. Pap.*, 1826–7, XXI (42), p. 19.

[3] There were probably some cases of negroes being brought on shore clandestinely, and sent into the country till enquiry ceased. *Report* (VII) *of the Protector of Slaves*, 25 December 1826—25 June 1827, *Parl. Pap.* 1829, XXV (335), pp. 109–11.

[4] Cradock to Lord Liverpool, 21 July 1812. Bigge wrote in 1826 that the average price of a male slave which was £60, prior to abolition, had risen to £150.

of registration had long been desired and in April 1816 a central registry, with a Protector of Slaves, was set up by proclamation of Lord Charles Somerset. The measure was intended to check, not merely the illicit introduction of slaves, but also the re-enslavement of manumitted persons and the merging of prize negroes in the state of slavery. Non-registered slaves were to be presumed to be free, and all transactions of sale, transfer and manumission were required to be entered. The new system was not a complete success. Registration was not accompanied by any description of the slave's person. The registers were soon found to be defective,[1] and many cases occurred of undue delay in the hearing of claims to freedom. Moreover, the burden of proof fell, not on the master, but on the servant, who was required to show that neither he nor his maternal ancestors had ever been lawfully reduced to slavery.

The Albany settlement scheme of 1820 brought to the eastern districts of the Colony a fairly large body of free European labourers, who were prohibited from holding predial slaves, but the prohibition did not extend to the magistrates and officials in their midst.[2] The sudden introduction of white immigrants into a country where the proletariat was largely unfree involved the menace of social debasement. The new settlers made more widely known in the Mother Country the conditions of slavery at the Cape, and to this extent may be said to have contributed to hasten the abolition of the whole system. In 1822, slaves were still legally incapable of entering into a contract of marriage or of acquiring property without their owners' consent. They were subject to the power of their masters to convict and punish them without the interposition of a legal judgment. Enfranchisement could not be purchased from an unwilling owner. At Cape Town, no slave could walk in the street with a lighted pipe, or go out at night without a lanthorn, on pain of a flogging. Caledon, renewing an enactment of 1794, decreed that slaves should not hawk commodities, other than provisions, for sale through the streets. An earlier proclamation (1800) made it illegal for a slave to hire a house or room and to reside other than with his master or the person to whom he might have been hired out for this master's profit. These regulations indicated an intention to prevent slaves from carrying on a trade or business of their own, but were seldom effective, for slaves competed successfully with Europeans in skilled trades and even employed Europeans, taking white youths as apprentices.[3] By the year 1826 it was a common practice at Cape Town to allow slaves to

[1] The accuracy of the registers was never tested by any process of identification, and numbers of slaves always exceeded the figures entered on the *opgaaf* (tax) rolls.

[2] Bathurst directed that slave labour should be prohibited upon all newly granted land in frontier districts. Albany in 1834 had fewer slaves (247) than any other district.

[3] *Records of Cape Colony*, XXI, 436–49, where a slave is stated to have paid 150 dollars to a European settler for the services of a white boy, Patrick Farrel, for seven years. The slave undertook to feed and clothe the boy and to teach him his trade. He even paid for a tutor to give Patrick, an Irish boy immigrant, schooling.

reside where they wished and to dispose of their own labour, provided they paid an agreed sum to their masters. Outside Cape Town predial slaves were mostly employed in the wine industry and in the herding of farm stock. Stellenbosch wine-producers might have fifty or more slaves, many of whom would be hired out at a harvest-time to the corn farmers. In the more settled areas of the south and west, slave labour was so valuable and so difficult to replace that good treatment was the rule. Manumission, however, was exceptional, despite the abolition of payments on emancipation (1823), since good conduct, earning customarily a premium for the slave, enhanced his pecuniary value, whilst insubordination and idleness were punished by sale to a farmer in a distant part of the colony. There, the frontier cattle-herd was frequently ill-fed and ill-clothed, and slavery had none of the alleviations which were allowed in the western districts.

The *Reports* of the Protector and of the Assistant Guardians in the various districts convinced the imperial authorities that a careful review of the entire slave code was required. It was clear that these officials were not invested with authority sufficient to enforce obedience to laws for the protection of the slave population. Something, however, had already been done to improve the law with the publication by Lord Charles Somerset of the proclamation of 18 March 1823. This proclamation, which to some extent anticipated the views of the Imperial Government, forbade field labour on Sundays, save "such as is ordinarily considered work of necessity", and longer week-day hours in field or garden than ten in winter and twelve in summer. Married slaves and their children under ten years of age were not to be sold separately. Slaves were to be allowed to hold and dispose of property, and were to be supplied with sufficient and wholesome food and good clothing. The evidence of baptised slaves, which the Courts had previously admitted when they found it convenient to do so, was now to be heard on oath. Domestic punishment of a slave was not to exceed twenty-five stripes, and, if an owner were convicted of mal-treatment, the slave could be sold against the wishes of his master. The new regulations were a step in the right direction, but the machinery for their enforcement was defective. Moreover, when a slave had made complaints against his master, failure of proof was made a ground for punishment without the necessity for establishing malice. The proclamation was welcomed by the more enlightened owners, who realised that improvement in the conditions of slavery was beneficial to the interests of the master inasmuch as it enhanced the value of his property. Others appreciated the fact that the colonial authorities had succeeded in defining the scope of the Cape's programme of amelioration.

More unpopular was the Nineteenth Ordinance published by General Bourke in June 1826. This was the measure afterwards stigmatised as "degrading" by the Trekkers and as a principal cause of their decision to leave the Colony.[1] It followed closely the terms of the Trinidad Order-in-Council (1824)[2], allowing a slave to give evidence in criminal cases against his master and to purchase his freedom by tendering his appraised value. This permission was attacked as damaging rights of property; but, as slaves were prohibited from Sunday employment, except on works of necessity, and donations were disallowed, few could have acquired the means to effect their emancipation. Intense irritation was caused by the provision that conviction for serious ill-treatment should involve forfeiture of property in the slave, for masters complained, not altogether without justice, that slaves took advantage of the ordinance to procure their freedom by the exhibition of self-inflicted wounds. During the excitement at Cape Town, the Burgher Senate refused to proclaim the Ordinance. Manumissions were not appreciably affected by the measure, but gross cruelty by masters became more uncommon with improvement in the machinery for detection and redress.

The specific evils in the slave codes had now to some extent been amended in all the slave-owning colonies of Great Britain. It remained to gather up regulations into a consistent code of slave law and to reinforce the law by security for obedience. This was the function of the consolidated Order-in-Council of 1830, supplemented by the Order of 1831, brought into force at the Cape by proclamations of the Governor. Briefly, these proclamations repealed previous legislation and laid down comprehensive rules for the treatment of slaves. The regulations as to hours of labour, what should constitute "necessary operations" on Sundays, and the minimum provision of food and clothing were rendered specific. The flogging of female slaves was prohibited and that of male slaves subjected to various restrictions. Whips were not to be carried in the field. Managers were to keep punishment record books and to make returns twice a year to the Protector of Slaves. Legal incapacity to hold or manage slaves was to follow upon a second conviction for cruelty. The later (1831) Ordinance authorised Protectors to enter slave dwellings and estates at their discretion.

These regulations were drawn up with a view to conditions in the British West Indies. At the Cape farmers might live at a distance of ten days' journey from the nearest seat of magistracy, whilst many would spend several months on trek. Even the Protector, G. J. Rogers, described as "inapplicable and uncalled for here" the keeping of punishment record books, since many proprietors could not write and gaols, workhouses and a police force were totally lacking over the greater part of the Colony. Imprisonment of a slave was punishment for the master. Proprietors complained that it was usually at harvest

[1] *Memorial*, published in *De Zuid Afrikaan*, 7 June 1839. Eybers, G. W., *Select Constitutional Documents*, pp. 154–5.

[2] It nevertheless sanctioned the moderate chastisement of female slaves and deviated in other ways from the Trinidad Order-in-Council.

and other busy seasons that slaves found occasion to resort to the Protector. To meet the difficult situation the authorities permitted the furnishing of returns of punishments to become a dead letter, whilst in cases of discrepancy in the evidence the Protector was content to arrange that the complainant should be hired out to another master. The most violent asperities were thus to some extent softened;[1] nevertheless Sir Lowry Cole was obliged to issue an Ordinance prohibiting meetings likely to endanger good order.

The administration of the law rested largely with the local officials, who were themselves slave owners. In the western districts Governors could claim with some justice that the law afforded security against gross ill-treatment. Cases of great brutality were, however, not altogether uncommon in the east. The sjambok of hippopotamus hide was not a more merciful instrument than the driving whip of the West Indian planter. Many instances of maltreatment doubtless went unrecorded, whilst juries evinced a general reluctance to convict despite the weight of evidence.[2] On the other hand, there was need for protection on both sides, and the new regulations even operated to encourage misconduct, in that a slave might absent himself from work to make complaint of merited punishment.

It may be doubted whether slaves derived much real benefit from the long series of measures which preceded ultimate emancipation. The Cape farmer had strict notions of his right of property in slaves. Resentment at interference with what he held to be his just right of dominion over his slaves prompted him, in many cases, to withdraw indulgences formerly extended to his servants. The attempt to mitigate slavery may thus have aggravated the lot of slaves in individual cases; nevertheless, the regulations prepared the colonial population for the inevitable emancipation.

Suggestions had indeed been made from time to time within the Colony for enfranchisement of the slave population. Lord Charles Somerset had proposed in 1823 the emancipation of slave children by state purchase. Colonial proposals to enfranchise young female slaves were usually accompanied by stipulations as to compensation in one form or another. In 1828, a Cape of Good Hope Philanthropic Society had been established for the purpose of aiding "deserving slaves and slave children to purchase their freedom". In four years the society emancipated by purchase 102 female children, but the great majority of its supporters were well-wishers in England and there was no real prospect of slavery being terminated by such means.[3]

[1] Report of the Protector of Slaves, 1833. C.O. 53/57, P.R.O.

[2] The Protector himself dismissed some cases where the law had been admittedly broken (e.g. in the flogging of female slaves).

[3] *Annual Reports of the Cape of Good Hope Philanthropic Society* (Cape Town, 1828–32). Chase, J. C., *Practical Considerations on the Exact Position of the Slave Question* (Cape Town, 1831). The proposal that slave children should be emancipated at birth took no account of the practical difficulties of a situation in which the older generation would remain unfree.

Even in the critical years 1826–32 births of slaves largely exceeded deaths and manumissions combined. Rogers, the Protector, however believed that the 5660 slave children under six could have been declared free, and at a trifling cost in compensation, provided they were assigned as apprentices until the age of eighteen to their owners with power to transfer their services.

In the Mother Country, emancipation became an important issue at the momentous elections of 1832. In the new Parliament, it figured as a government measure. The Bill for the abolition of slavery throughout British dominions passed the House of Commons on 7 August 1833 and obtained the royal assent three weeks later. It was badly received at the Cape, but not rebelliously, for it was accompanied by the undertaking to pay compensation to proprietors, whilst a period of apprenticeship was prescribed to meet the immediate difficulties of the labour situation. Compensation was to be based on prices at which slaves had been sold over a period of eight years ending on 20 December 1830, aged or disabled slaves (899 in number) being valued at £5. 13*s*. 2¼*d*., whilst the terms and conditions of apprenticeship were to be adjusted by the colonial legislatures. At the Cape, 1 December 1834 was the date ultimately fixed for the emancipation of the 35,742 slaves.[1] A committee sat at Cape Town from 13 May 1834 to receive and investigate claims for compensation. The work was hindered and delayed by the Kaffir irruption into the eastern districts of the Colony in December 1834,[2] with the result that the lists were not closed until 31 October 1840.[3] Only in November 1836 was it known that, instead of the sum of £3,041,290 as originally estimated at Cape Town, the meagre total of £1,247,401 would be available in grants to Cape proprietors. Monetary compensation thus fell far short of the assessed value of the emancipated slaves. Moreover, the distribution of this sum was to be made in London, where the majority of Cape farmers had no business connections. Claims were sold at a heavy discount to agents in the Colony, sometimes not even for cash. These arrangements hastened the foreclosing of mortgages, for slave property had afforded greater facilities than any other species of property for the raising of money by this means.[4] Many families were reduced to distress, but it is not clear that the community as a whole suffered, even in the years immediately following Emancipation. The labour value of the slaves remained what it had been. The scarcity of vacant cultivable land compelled enfranchised slaves,

[1] The latest returns from the Cape (to 31 August 1833) showed the number as 38,257, but a final check at London reduced the figures to 35,742, of whom 8196 lived in eastern districts as compared with 8609 in the single western district of Stellenbosch. T. 71/1523, P.R.O.

[2] *Vide infra*, p. 277.

[3] A balance of nearly £5907 was due to the Cape from the Compensation Fund on 31 December 1842, and one exceptional claim was received as late as 24 February 1844.

[4] *Records of Cape Colony*, XXXV, 375. In 1823 no less than 4089 were pledged in this way. Petitioners (Oct. 1827) against a proposed tax on slaves said 15,000 were mortgaged.

in the majority of cases, to continue to work for their masters, perhaps with a short interval of idleness after the termination of apprenticeship. Wages for many years remained little above the cost of their previous subsistence, Hottentots often serving in remote areas on yearly contracts for food and clothing alone, with perhaps a cow or a few sheep or goats.[1] The frontier farmers complained bitterly of ruined crops, but their position had long been well-nigh desperate for reasons unconnected with the emancipation of the slaves. In the West, there was genuine anxiety as to the supply of labour. Grain and wine farmers alike had suffered in the late 'twenties from the scarcity and high price of slave labour. On the other hand, they were beginning to appreciate the advantages of free labour. The first cost, in the case of slaves, was heavy, the risks considerable, and maintenance expensive in proportion to returns. The cost of keeping a slave in food and clothing averaged 150 dollars a year.[2] Mozambique slaves were usually too old for hard labour at forty, others at fifty. The average income from capital invested in slaves was reckoned in 1826 as no more than 18 per cent for Cape Town and considerably less for the country districts.[3] In the early 'thirties, free European labour had begun to compete in the Cape market, and the value of slaves tended to decline. It is clear, moreover, that the transition to free labour meant an ultimate gain in higher values all round. Money, which had been scarce, became sufficiently plentiful to stimulate expansion of joint-stock banking, "large sums", wrote Fairbairn, "having come into the hands of persons not engaged in business as compensation for their slaves."[4] Individual owners might be ruined, but many used compensation money profitably to purchase woolled sheep or farms abandoned by trekking Boers, and there was no sudden withdrawal of emancipated slave labour from the staple agricultural industries of the country.

Largely as a result of the inadequacy of the compensation, the Act was denounced at the Cape as unjust and tyrannical; but the imperial Parliament had abolished rotten boroughs without compensation, and, though slaves had been legally recognised property, the original title to such property had been no more than the slave trader's bill of sale.[5] Latterly, slave importations had been reluctantly sanctioned in response to colonial clamour, and it was not unreasonable that a part of the burden of enfranchisement should be borne by the community at the Cape.

[1] For rates of wages see Despatch No. 85 of 1841 (Napier to Sec. of State, 26 August 1841), C.O. 1371 (Cape Archives), and the *Blue Book for 1843*, pp. 288–90.

[2] P. M. Brink, a Burgher Senator, estimated the cost at 172 dollars, exclusive of medicine. Clothing might come to 60–100 dollars. The daily cost of food alone was reckoned in 1826, as four *skillings* (ninepence). *Records of Cape Colony*, XXIX, 435–92.

[3] *Records of Cape Colony*, XXIX, 494–6.

[4] *South African Commercial Advertiser*, 30 January 1841.

[5] Cf. the Attorney-General of Jamaica's ruling on the legality of slavery. P.R.O., C.O. 137/192, O'Reilly on the Emancipation Act, 16 August 1834.

Slave emancipation had an important influence on the Great Trek, but the actual loss of property in slaves was not the determining factor among the motives which produced that emigration. Available lists of owners on trek in 1836–7 show that the majority had submitted claims for compensation; and, though the eastern districts had no more than 8196 of the total number of 35,742 slaves, the scarcity of labour would enhance their value and make the compensation offered appear the more inadequate.[1] On the other hand, no awards were made before 17 November 1836, by which time the majority of Trekkers had crossed the colonial frontiers. Slave emancipation must be considered in conjunction with the legislation for improving the status of the Hottentots and other free Coloured persons at the Cape. Letters and memorials from emigrant Boers make a prominent grievance of the manner in which slave emancipation was brought about, but fundamentally the objection lay against the determination of the British authorities to protect the black man against his master. The clauses which offended most in the Act of Emancipation were those which involved the complete extinction of the domestic authority of the master, and the substitution for it of the authority of the magistrate. Emigrants were, in the main, those who believed in the maintenance of "proper relations between master and servant",[2] and were not prepared for the awkward social transition involved in the acceptance of equality before the law.

The real termination of slavery came about in 1838 rather than 1834. Apprenticeship was a condition of semi-servitude designed to avoid the perils of immediate emancipation. The liberated slaves were to be compelled to enter into contracts with their masters under which they would perform stipulated services in return for specific allowances. The Act allowed all Cape slaves to be classified as non-predial with the result that proprietors could claim the whole, and not merely three-fourths, of the time of their apprentices. As a consequence apprentices had no opportunity to gain experience in new occupations, whilst four years was too short a period for them to learn habits of industry and initiative. But the intermediate stage was also intended to help the proprietor, and indeed to serve as part compensation for loss of property. It was unfortunate that the conclusion of apprenticeship should have been fixed for 1 December at the commencement of the busiest farming season. Compulsion to remain at wages for an additional four months would have removed the farmer's immediate anxieties, and enabled the apprentice to enter upon freedom with some accumulated savings.

[1] C. V. Buchner, Field Cornet, Quagga's Vlakte, sent lists of emigrants leaving Oliphant's Hoek and the Winterberg. *Grahamstown Journal*, 2 February 1837. Other parties were enumerated, *Journal*, 2 November 1837.

[2] Manifesto of the emigrant farmers in *Grahamstown Journal*, 2 February 1837. For the influence of slave emancipation on the Great Trek, see Chase, J. C., *A Reprint of all Authentic Notices relating to Natal*, 1, 83, and *vide infra*, pp. 327 *sqq*.

To the ex-slaves the years 1834–8 were a continuation of the period of servitude. Apprentices continued to work for their masters under very much the old conditions with legal compulsion to ensure that the specified amount of toil was duly rendered. Absenteeism and careless work were made severely punishable under the Cape Ordinance of 1835. At the termination of the period, some endeavoured to make a precarious living by methods known to the colonists as "vagabondage". The transition was most awkward for the 8775 slaves over the age of forty-five, many of whom, according to Protector Rogers, would have been "better off as slaves than let loose on the world at an age when apprenticeship will cease".[1] The last vestiges of legal servitude were swept away when the day of full freedom dawned on 1 December 1838.

[1] Report, 20 January 1834, C.O. 53/57. P.R.O.

CHAPTER XII

THE PROBLEM OF THE COLOURED PEOPLE 1792–1842

WE have already described the backward coloured races of South Africa in an earlier chapter,[1] but we must here make it clear that throughout the story the "coloured people" are to be distinguished from the so-called "Kaffirs". The official boundary of the Colony of the Cape of Good Hope was for many years at the Fish River, and the Bantu tribes, whom we now speak of as the "natives" of the country, had not in 1792 penetrated very far west of that boundary. With the exception after 1835 of a few thousand Fingos,[2] any Bantu who entered the Colony were regarded and treated by the Cape Administration as "foreigners" until the annexation of British Kaffraria in 1847.[3] In 1800 the "coloured people" of the colony comprised, besides a handful of Bushmen, a widely scattered population of "free" men, loosely known as "Hottentots", and a roughly equal number of slaves of foreign origin mainly concentrated in the extreme west. Even at that early date the Hottentots were a much mixed people, perhaps predominantly Hottentot in origin, but including also strains of Bushman, Malay, Negro and European. In colour they ranged from black or brown to nearly white. A writer in the *Grahamstown Journal* of 18 March 1838 "did not know a *pure* Hottentot within the Colony", and when we read of "Hottentots" at this period we really have to do with the people—with whom the freed slaves ultimately merged—now distinguished by the epithet Cape Coloured or sometimes Eurafrican.

In the absence of formal census the numbers of these Hottentots are doubtful. Contemporary estimates suggest that in the eighteen-twenties in the Colony proper, an area where white and coloured still roughly balance to-day,[4] they just about equalled the 30,000 Europeans. The numbers of the Hottentots, however, were likely to be underestimated, for the country was so vast and its administration so imperfect that those in remoter parts would escape reckoning altogether. In the older districts a few quasi-tribal centres remained at points which presently became missionary-controlled Institutions like Genadendal and Pacaltsdorp. Of the remainder, a large proportion were employed in some fashion on European farms. As servants, however, their position was precarious and unprofitable, and many of the more venturesome sought to escape restrictions by

[1] *Vide supra*, ch. II. [2] *Vide infra*, p. 317. [3] *Vide infra*, p. 344.
[4] *Census Report* of 1921.

flight. Especially in the remote northern districts, groups of them gained notoriety as "banditti", operating from islands on the Orange River or from mountain fastnesses beyond; it was some of these, trained and civilised by missionaries settled at centres like Griquatown and Philippolis, who came to be known as "Griquas"[1] In addition, numbers of Hottentots remained practically undisturbed in occupation of the remote and inaccessible kloofs and valleys even of European-owned farms within the Colony. By origin nomads, virtual nomads they remained. Living on game, roots and wild honey, they soon came to figure as "vagrants", who, unsettled and homeless, roamed the country—if contemporary reports are to be believed—"stealing and plundering as they went". Enumeration of all these scattered people could hardly be complete. In estimating their numbers, moreover, it should be remembered that colour prejudice was very much weaker than it has since become, so that while the Hottentots in the mass were despised as inferior even to the imported slaves, the better class or light-skinned Eurafrican might occasionally pass as European. The "Hottentots", therefore, may very well have been, if anything, rather more numerous than the Europeans; but unlike the Bantu (Africans), they were neither numerous nor powerful enough to inspire the colonists with fear or with any feeling but contempt.

Down to that time indeed the aboriginal Bushmen and Hottentots had been for the most part disregarded—in the colony, but hardly of it.[2] While the Bushmen were too few to affect the problem, the Hottentots were at best tolerated—tolerance of a poor and despised people being easy just so long as the inconvenient question of their legal rights lay dormant. From motives of policy rather than of principle the Company had refused to make slaves of them; indeed it had sometimes intervened for their protection. Slavery being accepted by all as of the natural order of things, neither Government nor colonists were concerned to make extravagant claims for Coloured people, and thus no problem could arise. Soon after the British Occupation of 1795, however, several factors combined to make Hottentot status a live issue. In the first place, no organised modern state could, like a Company of Merchants, continue merely to ignore so large a proportion of the population. Next, restrictions upon the British slave trade, and in 1807 its abolition, synchronising with a war-time trade boom, created a serious shortage of labour: whereupon almost for the first time colonists began to think of Hottentots as potentially useful servants. The result was that successive Governments, welcoming the idea of finding a suitable substitute for slaves so ready to their hand, were torn between two conflicting motives; laws reflecting an honest desire to protect the Hottentots, but

[1] *Vide supra*, p. 28, *et infra*, pp. 304 *sqq*.
[2] *Vide supra*, p. 127.

administered by farmer Field-cornets, had to contend rather unequally with the exigencies of a policy designed to make them "useful" labourers and servants.

Now also the moral and religious forces, which had combined in Great Britain against the slave trade, began to penetrate the colonies. Though the movement had affinities with the teaching of Rousseau, the spear-head of the attack on slavery was religious, the dominant Evangelical doctrine stressing the value of the individual human soul. In Britain the emotional gospel of Divine Grace preached by the original Methodism appealed especially to the humbler classes; but in time, through upper-class leaders like William Wilberforce, Evangelicalism captured a section also of the Established Church, and by this alliance the Nonconformist bodies gained in influence and in responsibility. The Protestant communities, which ever since the Reformation had with rare exceptions been too much occupied with their own struggle for existence to obey the command to go into all the world and preach the Gospel, now bethought themselves of the backward coloured races in distant colonies. In the Cape Colony, hitherto, the Moravian Brethren alone had made any serious attempt to work among the aboriginal Hottentots, though their pioneer missionary, George Schmidt, had given up the task after a short struggle with adverse circumstances lasting only from 1737 to 1744.[1] From the seventeen-nineties onward, however, the prevailing belief in the essential equality of all men in the sight of God bore fruit, and missionary societies sprang into life, the Baptist, London, Church, Wesleyan and various Scottish societies all being founded within a few years.[2] In 1792 the Moravians returned to Schmidt's old station. They were quickly followed by the London Missionary Society, whose pioneer leader, Dr Johannes Theodosius van der Kemp, arrived in 1798, and was followed by James Read and William Anderson in 1800.

Presently missionaries and philanthropists, who hitherto had concentrated upon the slave trade, began by an inevitable logic to direct their attention to slavery as an institution, and more slowly to the general position of backward races, whether slave or nominally "free". At the very moment when from several angles the interests of the Hottentots were forcing themselves on official attention, the missionaries arrived to live among them, necessarily as close and interested witnesses of the treatment they received. In such human contact the newcomers could not but become their champions and spokesmen. The consequences were momentous. To repudiate slavery, as the new school did, was to raise the whole essential issue. The slave as such had no rights and was therefore no problem; but if the backward peoples are not slaves, what was to be their status—backward as they still were—in a

[1] *Vide supra*, p. 156.

[2] See *C.H.B.E.*, vol. VII, ch. V and p. 330.

civilised community? Battle was soon joined over the attempt to answer this question and define the legal rights and status of the "free" people of colour, sometimes between missionaries and Government, but very often between Government and colonists, since the Government was on the whole more open-minded and disinterested than the latter, a good many of whom were or had been slave-owners. Occasionally the fight was among colonists themselves.

When after the fall of the Dutch East India Company the status of these "free people of colour" first came under serious review, it did not need the missionaries to suggest to the Hottentots that they had grievances. Their lot was hard enough. Deprived of their old grazing lands, they had also lost what wealth they had ever had in cattle; without allotted "reserves", they were too poor to buy land, even had they not also been legally debarred from acquiring it. Untaught, hardly even deemed worthy of employment, the majority of them were of necessity dependent on colonial farmers. While there is no reason to doubt that on most farms masters and servants lived quite peaceably together, it is certain that if, as might occasionally happen, masters should withhold wages or even physically ill-use their servants, the extra-legal position of the Hottentots left them almost wholly without remedy. At best, the country being very poor and undeveloped, there was no fat living either for farmers or for Hottentots, and wages were nominal. Farm service having so few attractions, the Hottentots were easily tempted—as farmers complained—to wander at large, or even to take any opportunities of "plunder" that offered. The disturbances in the eastern part of the Colony at the turn of the century afforded such an opportunity,[1] and while some Hottentots were enrolled in 1796 for general service even against rebellious colonists, others joined the "Kaffirs" in plundering the country about the Gamtoos River till confusion reigned in the interior.

In these circumstances the British Governors of the First Occupation were soon forced to give some thought and attention to a definite Hottentot problem. In 1801 the Fiscal, Willem Stephanus van Ryneveld, deputed for the purpose by the Acting-Governor, General Dundas, made a report which is the earliest considered statement on the working and deficiencies of the old colonial system as it affected the Cape Coloured people.[2] The Hottentots, the Fiscal reported, were actively discontented, even "thinking of revenge". Van Ryneveld also indicated the cause which made reform so difficult. The farmers, he pointed out, were likely to resent any weakening of control over their servants. To meet them he suggested a system of passes as a check on vagrancy or actual desertion of service. Van Ryneveld also saw that, such as it was, the law was ill-administered. The Field-cornets,

[1] *Vide supra*, chapter VIII; *infra*, chapter XIII.
[2] *Records of Cape Colony*, IV, 88 *sqq*.

being farmers living among farmers, were not impartial; therefore, the official class must be strengthened. Landdrosts should make regular tours of their districts; additional Deputy-Landdrosts should be appointed to the larger districts, and an annual Commission or Circuit Court was desirable.

General Dundas thereupon made the first of many attempts to regularise the conditions of Hottentot farm service. As a measure of protection he required contracts of service to be registered, so that relations should be fixed by the terms of written agreements. Later on other of the Fiscal's suggestions were acted upon, but at the time little could be accomplished before British rulers gave way to those of the Batavian Republic. Meanwhile in a letter of 1802 the British Governor's Adjutant had urged the missionary van der Kemp to continue his efforts on behalf of the Hottentots of Graaff-Reinet, promising also to use his good offices with the new Batavian Government on behalf of the Hottentots generally.[1] Whether or not this hint was necessary, the Batavian Government soon showed itself in substantial agreement with Dundas and his colleagues. The views of General Janssens were reflected in a letter to the Landdrost of Swellendam dated 10 April 1803.[2] Anxious that Hottentots should increasingly take the place of "imported slaves, who are dangerous and degrading to morals", he proposed to enable them "to find liberty, safety, and means of subsistence, on the soil which was originally theirs". To this end, "no private person must dare to put them in chains or to chastise them", this being a function of magistrates, and then only "after regular trial". Confirming General Dundas, he concluded that contracts with these "voluntary servants" should be "just, clear and in writing, and be observed with good faith". The essential problem was how to reconcile the human rights and personal freedom of the weaker race with the claims of superior white settlers, whose very existence depended on the labour of the backward natives.

Batavian rule was too short-lived for its enlightened and liberal rulers to make much headway or to see their experiments put to the test; nevertheless, besides thus giving his adherence to the plan of written contracts, General Janssens was soon persuaded to adopt a more important measure of general policy. The disorders about 1799 had been clearly due, so far as Hottentots were concerned, to their being so often landless and homeless. Unwilling as the colonists were to accept the obvious fact, not all Hottentots were fit for farm services; the aged, the infirm, child-bearing women and young children could only be a burden on farms; a few, more enterprising, would demand some independent outlet. In 1802 the later plan of assigning "reserves" to the bulk of a conquered people had not been thought of. Unlike the Bantu, the Hottentots were never agriculturists

[1] Philip MSS. [2] Translated copy in Philip MSS.

and, as nomads, there was no room for them; but once General Dundas and his colleagues had come to realise the evil consequences of Hottentot landlessness, the advent of Christian missionaries suggested "institutions" as a way out—places where teachers might collect the roving Hottentots, train them and make them useful, at the same time providing a refuge for the old or destitute. As early as March 1802 Dr van der Kemp was armed with a "passport" signed by the Fiscal, van Ryneveld, which authorised him to select a site on Government lands near the Zwartkops River, to settle there, and to build a school for such Hottentots "*als zij stil en wel gedragen, en de Ingezetenen geen overlast aandoen*" ("as bear themselves peaceably, and without hurt to settlers").[1] All and sundry were, moreover, warned that van der Kemp was not to be hindered, nor any of his scholars interfered with or injured, since this "*liefde dienst*" (labour of love) was undertaken "with the full approval, and under the special protection of the Government". General Janssens consistently showed himself well disposed to his able if eccentric countryman, van der Kemp, who as a physician and former soldier was a man of education and social standing. The Moravians having already set the fashion in "institutions" at Baviaans Kloof, which Janssens himself later renamed Genadendal, in 1803 van der Kemp's Bethelsdorp came into being as part of a definite Government policy for the settlement of the roaming Hottentots of the frontier districts.[2]

Colonial criticism of Bethelsdorp has obscured the fact that Hottentot "institutions" were thus forced upon the Batavians and their successors as a substitute for the "reserves" of a later day. So far as Bethelsdorp was less satisfactory than Genadendal, this was in large part only a reflex of the unsettled past and of the more difficult agricultural conditions of the Eastern Province.[3] Had there been no missionaries to undertake the task, the Government itself must have been driven to find some home for the economically redundant and wandering Hottentots. As it was, with official approval and help, the Moravians presently extended their work to Groenekloof (Mamre) near Cape Town. In spite of an unfavourable report on Bethelsdorp,[4] the London Mission in 1811 founded the Caledon Institution at Zuurbraak near Swellendam, and in 1813 also began work at Pacaltsdorp near George. In the same year Governor Sir John Cradock personally helped to select the site of Theopolis, near Grahamstown, as a relief station for Bethelsdorp—there being some evidence that this was designed also to make use of Hottentots as a buffer against the Xhosa tribes. In 1814 Lord Charles Somerset granted an addition of one normal-sized Boer farm of some 3000 morgen to Genadendal. In 1819 Pacaltsdorp was granted an extension on the Karoo, at Dys-

[1] Philip MSS.
[2] Theal, G. M., *Belangrijke Hist. Dokumenten*, III, 235.
[3] Macmillan, W. M., *The Cape Colour Question*, pp. 150 *sqq*.
[4] *Records of Cape Colony*, VII, 107, 112.

selsdorp, and shortly afterwards Theopolis was slightly enlarged. In 1822 overcrowded Hottentots of Bethelsdorp were allowed to contribute—obviously from the profits of their transport-riding for the 1820 Settlers—to the purchase of a farm on the Gamtoos; this became known as Hankey, one of the longest-lived and most important of these institutions. Beyond the northern frontier, missionaries secured the location of wandering Griquas at Griquatown and elsewhere. As late as 1829 when the London Missionary Society, the patron of most of the stations, was falling into official disfavour, the Government itself assigned a portion of old "Kaffir" territory to Hottentots drawn mainly from Bethelsdorp and Theopolis, who, within a year, in spite of official frowns, "called" the London missionary, James Read. Thereafter, the Settlement became an important centre of the London Missionary Society's activity.

Thus a whole generation of Governors, Dutch as well as British, recognised that it was highly desirable that Hottentots should have more settled homes. At these institutions alone, and for the first time, some thousands of the Coloured people were given a chance of education and of regular church services. There were still disabilities: while institutions escaped the ordinary labour laws, they were liable not only, like European burghers, to taxation (the *opgaaf*) and to compulsory military service, but, in addition, to continuous calls for labour, supposedly for public purposes;[1] but by the year 1826 an intelligent missionary teacher was able to report, even of Bethelsdorp, that "the Gospel is not now a novelty", and that the Hottentots "normally profess Christianity" and were therefore, as to "results", in the position of "any dissenting congregation in England".[2]

At most the Institutions provided for some thousands of Hottentots—certainly not more than one-third of the total in the country. The major problem of Hottentot legal status remained to be settled—with the difference, now, that the Coloured people had these fixed centres of community life, and, presently, very doughty European champions among the missionaries. Farmers meantime were perforce learning to rely on Hottentot servants, in lieu of slaves, and wanted them under control—more than ever after the abolition of the slave trade in 1807. At least as early as 1808 the missionary Read had begun to take notice of hardship or actual ill-usage and to write to England about it. Hardly needing such prompting, the Government followed up the work begun by van Ryneveld in 1801, and sent Colonel Collins on a tour of inspection. On 1 November 1809, acting on his detailed report,[3] the Governor, Earl Caledon, issued a proclamation,[4] which, if it marked no striking development of policy, at

[1] Philip, John, *Researches in South Africa* (London, 1828), official letters in Appendix XI.
[2] Macmillan, W. M., *The Cape Colour Question*, p. 154.
[3] *Records of Cape Colony*, VI, 340 *sqq.*; VII, 20 *sqq.*
[4] *Proclamations*, etc. 1806–25 (Cape Town, 1827).

least defined the *status quo*. With minor amendments and, in 1812 and 1819, two considerable additions affecting "apprenticeship", the Caledon Code stood as the law of the land till 1828.

The proclamation of 1809 has often been described with complacency as the "Magna Carta of the Hottentots". On any view but that of the scholars who stigmatise King John's famous charter as a piece of feudal class-legislation, this description is misleading. Like Magna Carta, indeed, it sought practical remedies for what practical men of the day believed was in need of remedy, but it aimed little higher. The words of the preamble reflect the almost irreconcilable conflict of motives; it was deemed "necessary" not only that Hottentots "in the same manner as the other Inhabitants, should be subject to proper regularity in regard to their places of abode and occupations, but also that they should find an *encouragement* for preferring entering the service of the Inhabitants to leading an indolent life...." Hottentots, therefore, "*shall have* a fixed place of abode". For their security, contracts, to run only for one year, were to be registered in triplicate with a proviso, in case of dispute, favouring the Hottentot. Wages, moreover, were to be duly paid; payments in kind must be witnessed and registered; wine and brandy must not rank as necessaries of life nor count as wages; no claims to personal service should lie against the servant in respect of debt, anything due to the employer beyond the value of the servant's wages being recoverable only by ordinary process of law.

To prevent "vagrancy", however, and to protect the masters, the "fixed place of abode" was to be registered with the Landdrost, and in the event of the Hottentot removing to another district—"which he was at perfect liberty to do unless bound by contract"[1]—he had to obtain a certificate, better known as a "pass", from the Landdrost on pain of "arrest as a vagabond and treatment accordingly". This provision rather neutralised anything there may have been, on paper, to protect or to improve the economic status of the Hottentots. They were required, for example, to have a "fixed place of abode" without having either the means or the legal right to acquire land of their own. Since the missionary Institutions were small and scattered, this meant, in effect, that they must take service with farmers on such terms as their economic weakness could secure. These were poor enough. Forbidden, as they were, to move without a pass from a Field-cornet or Landdrost, and being thus thoroughly immobilised, they were in no position even to seek the best labour market. Any European could demand to see this pass, and any Hottentot failing to produce it on demand was a "vagrant", liable to be "dealt with" or assigned to labour at the will of the local authorites "after due inquiry as they shall feel incumbent to do".

Later amendments of the Code made in the same direction. Thus,

[1] Cory, G., *Rise of South Africa*, I, 200.

in 1812 Sir John Cradock instituted the so-called "apprenticeship". Since it appeared that farmers had "no interest whatever in young Hottentots",[1] Landdrosts were empowered to "bind" children from their eighth to their eighteenth year to any farmer who had maintained them in their infancy—or if the farmer concerned should be considered unsuitable, then to some other master. In 1819, Somerset completed the system by empowering Landdrosts to apprentice orphans.[2] Apprenticeship, which carried with it no necessity of regular instruction of any kind, was little more than a device for securing long-term indentured servants. The whole practice, excused on the ground that discipline was necessary, was open to grave abuses. As Collins had seen earlier, the expense of maintaining children was exaggerated, for "a child can scarcely crawl before it is turned to some purpose".[3] Since the ages of any such people are rather hard to determine, the service under the indentures was undoubtedly often carried on beyond the eighteenth year, and the result may well have been to bind whole families while a succession of children were coming to maturity. Yet with slight modifications apprenticeship has persisted as a feature of South African farm life, especially in the Transvaal, whither, with other characteristics of the pre-1828 law, it was carried by the Trekkers.

For the rest, something would depend also on the administration of the law. The independent permanent officials, the Landdrosts, being few and scattered, the burden fell on the Field-cornets. These, as farmers among farmers, were interested in suppressing vagrancy by enforcing the pass-laws or in promoting apprenticeship, rather than in carrying out and strengthening the law of contracts and in seeing that Hottentots were fairly treated, fully paid and not unlawfully detained when the period of their contracts had expired. Undoubtedly Landdrosts did their duty on occasion; once, for example in 1824, when it is true that the Crown Commissioners were in the neighbourhood, Colonel Cuyler of Uitenhage fined a Field-commandant and a Field-cornet 100 rds. each "for detention of Hottentots and their property beyond the terms of their contract".[4] On the other hand, even Landdrosts might write and act in the spirit of a letter by this same Cuyler to the Rev. George Barker at Bethelsdorp (12 January 1821).

I beg of you to notify your People, that notwithstanding they may be with their waggons absent from your Institution, they will nevertheless require your Pass as Sanction for their being absent, and Such who may be found even with their waggons, without your Pass will be taken up and treated as a vagrant.[5]

It came to be accepted, moreover, that no Hottentot could be admitted to an Institution without the sanction of the Landdrost, who

[1] *Records of Cape Colony*, VIII, 302 (Report of the Circuit Commission).
[2] *Records of Cape Colony*, XII, 249. [3] *Ibid.* vii, 111.
[4] Report of Crown Commissioners. *Records of Cape Colony*, XXXV, 316.
[5] Philip MSS.

thus came under the suspicion of many of the missionaries as inclined to use his power to force Hottentots into service, and to throw emphasis, like the Field-cornets, on the labour rather than on the protective clauses of the law.

Missionaries were, in fact, the means of bringing the whole question of Hottentot laws and status into the limelight of controversy. The laws themselves and their administration came now to be closely watched as they could hardly have been in earlier days, and where Hottentots' and farmers' interests clashed, friction often arose between colonist and missionary. Inevitably in such a clash the representatives of the London Missionary Society were prominent, and for this they have been unfavourably contrasted by some writers with their Moravian and Wesleyan Methodist colleagues. But the Moravians, who in the first place were foreigners and thus disabled for contest with a hospitable Government, had comparatively few stations, and these being, with one exception, in the longer-settled western districts, had far less direct knowledge of the situation in all its bearings. The Wesleyans, strong and important as they grew to be, were, as a rule, conservative in politics, and also much later in the field; their first preacher was licensed only in 1816, and their missionary work, which only began after 1820, took them for the most part beyond the Colony, certainly beyond the Hottentot zone. In Albany after 1820 the Wesleyans became essentially the "Settlers' Church". The London Missionary Society had the disability, possibly, of being an almost exclusively missionary body with only a very few European congregations to keep it in touch with colonial public opinion. Being also an *ad hoc* society, with neither organisation nor exclusive denominational tradition behind it, the London Mission attracted an unusual and even embarrassing variety of recruits. Besides Englishmen and Scots like David Livingstone, whose Lowland birth and upbringing disguised a Highland temperament which may explain a great deal, there were Hollanders like van der Kemp and not a few Germans. College-trained men were relatively few: artisans, gardeners and the like quite numerous. Some like the well-known Robert Moffat of Bechuanaland and John Brownlee, virtual founder of Kingwilliamstown, were of Scottish peasant stock, while Gottlob Schreiner was a Swabian artisan. These and some few others either themselves attained distinction or, having done their own work with credit, left notable families to follow them. Others, including even James Read—a carpenter originally, who served his Coloured people faithfully for fifty years—were so unreliable in emergency that Dr Philip had reason on occasion to complain of missionaries "with no quality but their piety". So far as it had denominational allegiance, the London Missionary Society was Independent or Congregationalist. This at times was a weakness. The Congregationalism of its members made against centralised control, where such variety of origin most needed it. Another element of independency was a lively tradition, in direct line of succession from the Puritans, of opposition to authority in Church or State. The personal ascendancy of even an outstanding leader being suspect, Dr Philip, as Superintendent, by no means had it all his own way. Directors in London, Robert Moffat and others on the spot often shied at his view that it was impossible to "preach the Word" effectively without regard to the political disabilities of the mission people. Moreover, where so much depended on individuals, particular stations might fall below standard for want of central control. But hostile generalisation is unjust.

Whatever criticism may lie against it, the London Missionary Society has had less than justice largely because the extent of its work in the Colony involved it from the beginning, almost single-handed, in the fight to secure and safeguard the rights of its Hottentot followers. Even before 1820 and for thirty years thereafter, till of set policy it left many of its "congregations" to stand or fall by themselves, there were London missionaries, and very few others, in every considerable town or village of the Hottentot area from Cape Town to Grahamstown, and from Algoa Bay to Graaff-Reinet, Colesberg, Philippolis, Griqualand, Bechuanaland and even in Namaqualand, as well as at highly important strategic points like the Kat River, the Keiskamma and Kingwilliamstown on the scene of actual conflict between colonists and Xhosas. For this very practical reason the London Missionary Society figures so largely in the internal "colour" politics of these early years.

It was at Bethelsdorp, certainly, that the fight began. In 1808, as we have seen,[1] James Read was alleging gross ill-usage of Hottentots, in general and in particular. One of his letters was published in No. 20 of the *Transactions* of his Society in London. With no great need of urging from Downing Street, the Colonial Government was at this time doing its best to strengthen the arm of the law. In the legislation of 1809, already described, there was one clause decreeing that in cases involving serious injury to Hottentots, "the Fiscal shall prosecute according to the common law in use in the Colony". That such express enactment should be necessary is significant of the anomalous status of the Hottentots. Even so, the Field-cornets, whose bias was generally recognised,[2] retained considerable powers of "domestic" discipline and could inflict corporal punishment without the formality of a trial. Masters, it is true, were subject to fine, but Hottentots were discouraged from making complaints—no easy matter when their movements were circumscribed by the necessity of securing a pass or permit, possibly from an unsympathetic Field-cornet—by the provision that those seeking redress from the officials might be detained

[1] *Vide supra*, p. 285.
[2] Collins's Report, *Records of Cape Colony*, VII, 107; VIII, 288. Report of Circuit Commission 1812.

in gaol till their case was heard and, if their complaint proved frivolous, suffer "such correction as the nature of the case shall require". Little wonder that abuses were possible.

So apparently thought van der Kemp and Read. Early in 1811 they moved again: the former in a letter to Earl Caledon, the latter once more to the London Missionary Society—Wilberforce in this instance bringing Read's charges to the notice of Lord Liverpool, who on August 9 ordered enquiry.[1] Again the Colonial Government had anticipated instructions. Not only had Colonel Cuyler, the Landdrost of Uitenhage, been ordered to investigate, but, as a fuller safeguard, by proclamation of 16 May 1811 an earlier suggestion was adopted and the local authorities were subjected to regular and close supervision by itinerant Justices of a Circuit Court. The first circuit in 1811 was uneventful, being handicapped by a state of war on the frontier. The second, which set out from Cape Town in September 1812, was destined to make history. Expressly charged with the investigation of numerous missionary complaints in addition to several Crown prosecutions, it has become well known as the Black Circuit. For the eastern districts the work fell upon two Judges, Messrs L. C. H. Strubbers and P. L. Cloete, with G. Beelaerts van Blokland, a well-known advocate, as public prosecutor for Uitenhage, in the place of Landdrost Cuyler, whose administration was deeply involved.

Van der Kemp having died in 1811, the burden of the Hottentot case fell on James Read. While there is no reason to doubt his sincere honesty, this good-natured artisan missionary was rather indiscriminate and even rash in accepting complainants' stories: a stronger and more cautious man would have realised the immense difficulty of substantiating charges in open court when many of the alleged injustices had been committed years earlier, and when, at best, the evidence was that of ignorant and easily confused Hottentots and slaves. The result was inevitable. Relatively few charges, none of them capital, were brought home against accused farmers; but in spite of the obvious difficulty even of bringing "more than a thousand" witnesses to court, at least eight of the sixty-two Europeans charged were convicted of crimes of violence against servants, several were found to have withheld wages, and several more were kept for trial at a later sitting of the court or remanded for trial at Cape Town. There one of the accused was condemned to death, but reprieved.[2] There was thus enough to show that abuses might and did happen, and that the effective legal protection of slaves and Coloured servants demanded the attention of any self-respecting Government. Naturally

[1] Cory, G., *Rise of South Africa*, I, 208.

[2] Theal, G. M., *History of South Africa*, I, 202; Cory, G., *Rise of South Africa*, I, 211–18; du Plessis, J., *Christian Missions in South Africa*, p. 133; Marais, J. S., *The Cape Coloured People*, p. 121. For a critical account of the affair see Reyburn, H. A., "Studies in Cape Frontier History", in *The Critic, October*, 1934.

enough, however, the much larger percentage of acquittals attracted public notice at the time and long afterwards. What rankled, as Henry Cloete put it in his lectures nearly half a century later,[1] was that "nearly a hundred of the most respectable families on the frontier were implicated" in charges, some of them frivolous or false, brought by Coloured servants—in a community, it should be added, where slavery was still the established order and Hottentots were esteemed more lightly even than slaves. To make things worse, the charges were apparently countenanced by Christian missionaries. The outcry was loud and long against those of the London Missionary Society and against most of their works.

Three years later the Slachter's Nek episode, described in an earlier chapter, showed the rising tide of feeling,[2] though here the missionaries were not directly implicated. The question of Hottentot status, the colour problem, had become a burning matter of colonial politics, revealing a sharp cleavage between Government and other supporters of the rule of law, and those who clung to the rule of the master.

The next few years proved nearly fatal to the London Missionary Society in South Africa. Read, though recognised by the Directors as van der Kemp's successor, ordinarily left most of the business of the society to be done by Dr George Thom, formerly a parishioner of Dr Philip's congregation in Aberdeen and now conveniently stationed in Cape Town. Dual control gave rise to faction. Since the missionaries were not wholly united even in their methods of attacking slavery,[3] an influential section readily blamed what seemed to them the imprudence of Read for having provoked violent conflict with public opinion in the Black Circuit affair. Now difficulties in procuring the military service of mission Griquas brought Institutions into disfavour with the Government itself, on the ground that the missionaries kept imperfect control.[4] When, in spite of this, Read took a leading part in the founding of two stations for Bushmen beyond the colonial frontier, the dissatisfied anti-Read faction held an irregular "synod" at Cape Town in 1817, where, after a general airing of skeletons from missionary cupboards, no fewer than five of them severed their connection with the Society, several, including Dr Thom, accepting from the Government patronage livings in the Dutch Reformed Church.

Complaint about the outlying Institutions having reached London, together with echoes of the dissident missionaries' allegations against some of their colleagues, the Secretary of State, Lord Bathurst, demanded that the parent Society should hold an enquiry and set its house in order. The answer was the appointment to a superintendency

[1] Cloete, H., *The Great Boer Trek*, 1856; reissued, Cape Town, 1900.
[2] *Vide supra*, p. 217.
[3] Macmillan, W. M., *The Cape Colour Question*, p. 93; and L.M.S. Records.
[4] *Vide infra*, p. 305.

of Dr John Philip, who on his arrival early in 1819 found the Government attitude almost actively hostile, at least to extra-colonial stations.[1] Since 1817 Robert Moffat and other new arrivals had been expressly prohibited from going beyond the frontier even to established mission stations. In 1818 Read's Bushman stations, one of them at Tooverberg (later Colesberg), had been summarily suppressed. A few months later, still dissatisfied with the position of the Griqua missions, Lord Charles Somerset reported to Earl Bathurst that since these stations harboured runaways and "subtracted that useful class of labourers" from employment in the colony, he had told Dr John Philip, the newly arrived Superintendent, that "Griquatown must be broke up".[2] Attention in fact was diverted from the status of Hottentots in general to the affairs of particular Institutions.

The first three years of Philip's mission were quiet enough. His first report, made jointly with his colleague, the Rev. John Campbell, a well-known African traveller, came very near to accepting the official view of the missionary Institutions and of the shortcomings of Read and van der Kemp. Reforms on the stations having been set in train, his relations with Sir Rufane Donkin, now Acting-Governor, were almost intimate. Though there were still vague suspicions of a "conspiracy against our missions", Philip's one "battle" at this time was bloodless.[3] By gentle persuasion Donkin was brought in 1820 to lift the ban on missionaries travelling beyond the borders of the colony, thus opening the interior, not only to Robert Moffat, but to the Wesleyans, whose wide activities date from this time.

Presently the very friendliness of Philip's relations with Donkin produced a new crisis. In May 1821 he availed himself of the Acting-Governor's offer to "do what he could for missions" when on tour by "thrusting into the governor's hand", at parting, a series of letters and statements for his consideration. The documents contained fresh allegations by Read—this time of forced labour, used for private ends, as well as of particular hard cases—Colonel Cuyler and other officials being directly implicated in charges of "oppressing" the Hottentots of Bethelsdorp. Philip, looking for an informal enquiry, foolishly took no steps to warn the missionaries. Donkin, for his part, regarded the aspersions on his officials as serious and personally examined Cuyler and others, who had little difficulty in clearing themselves: whereupon Philip reported to a friend that Read's charges "could not be proved" and that he had been "brought to much trouble by Read"[4]—to the detriment of his good relations with the authorities. In September, however, on the advice of his Evangelical friend, Sir Jahleel Brenton of the Simonstown naval station, he set out for Bethelsdorp to make his own investigations. There, in December, "in a corner of the missionary office", Philip discovered docu-

[1] *Vide supra*, p. 249.
[2] *Vide infra*, p. 305.
[3] Macmillan, W. M., *The Cape Colour Question*, pp. 128 *sqq*.
[4] *Ibid*. pp. 122 *sqq*.

ments "in the handwriting of Colonel Cuyler", which, he claimed, provided "not only the means of vindicating the calumniated missionaries, including James Read, but also the means of liberating the Hottentots from their cruel bondage". When on his return to Cape Town, Colonel Bird, the Colonial Secretary, called on Philip and read the papers, "his first words were, 'You have got strong things against us at last'".[1]

From this point a new chapter in the fight for Hottentot liberation began, In the course of 1821 Philip had been preparing a *Philosophical Review of Christian Missions*, recording his first rather complacent impressions; but early next year publication was stayed. His concern, he wrote, was no longer "about being an author", but "in what way I can most certainly and effectually secure the emancipation of the poor natives from their dreadful thraldom, and the Missions from the oppressive system they are groaning under". He had come to see, in short, that the very defects of the Institutions arose from the unsatisfactory legal position and disabilities of the Hottentots generally. Unlike Read and even van der Kemp, he also saw that, where the laws were defective, nothing was to be gained by a parade of particular hard cases, since inequity could readily be justified as being in full accordance with law. Keeping a close watch on the local authorities, he very shrewdly instructed missionaries to do as they were bidden by authority—but only on written orders—thus accumulating a mass of evidence on the working of the system.[2] Henceforth, Philip set to work on the principle that "our cause, if possible, had better rest on generals than on particulars", and that the aim must be a drastic revision and alteration of the laws governing Hottentot status in the Colony at large.

His first step in carrying this into effect was that appeal through Brenton and Wilberforce to Parliament and the public in England which helped to induce the Home Government to institute a Commission of Inquiry, whose scope and relevance to other colonial questions have already been described.[3] As soon as news of its institution reached the Cape, Philip set to work to prepare his case. From their arrival in July 1823 he maintained close personal contact with the Commissioners, interviewing them, handing in documents and entertaining them in his house on Church Square; at other times "riding out to breakfast" at Wynberg, and providing at least one of them with apparently satisfactory domestic servants from Bethelsdorp. He also rode ahead to Bethelsdorp and other stations to find that, with the Commissioners' visit in prospect, the local authorities were on their best behaviour. By 1824, however, there was little to be done about the Hottentots in face of the absorbing political struggle between the colonists, of whom Philip was

[1] Philip MSS.; and Letters in Philip, J., *Researches*, Appendix XI.

[2] Official and missionary correspondence in Philip MSS.

[3] *Vide supra*, p. 251.

one, and Lord Charles Somerset. In the end the Commissioners in their long-delayed report almost entirely supported Philip's contentions as to Hottentot disabilities; but their intervention did little more than provide the opportunity to ventilate the whole question.[1]

In 1825, with Lord Charles Somerset's term of office clearly nearing its end, Philip made one more wide tour of investigation preparing his case for the authorities in London and, in the last resort, for an appeal to British public opinion. Early in 1826 he sailed for England, where, refusing to become entangled in personal attacks upon Lord Charles Somerset, he applied himself assiduously to the case for the Hottentots. By the end of the year he had made a close ally of Thomas Fowell Buxton, Wilberforce's successor as leader of the anti-slavery party. In the course of 1827, with Buxton's help, he secured satisfactory interviews both with James Stephen, the powerful Permanent Under-Secretary at the Colonial Office, and with William Huskisson, for a short time Secretary of State for the Colonies. Asked by Huskisson, "Tell me in one sentence what you want for the Hottentots", he replied: "I require nothing for them but the power of bringing their labour to a fair market"—which, as Huskisson remarked, "includes everything else".[2]

After this promising success at the fountain-head of authority, Philip's appeal to the British public at large mattered less; but in April 1828, working at high pressure, he produced his two volumes of *Researches in South Africa*. The importance of this publication has been exaggerated. Sir George Murray, Huskisson's successor as Secretary of State, would appear to have read some of it; but, on Philip's own showing, Lord Brougham, who had received two copies, knew nothing about it, and Thomas Babington Macaulay, in spite of efforts by some of the Clapham connection, was not persuaded to review it. A Macaulay *Essay* might have helped. The first battle for non-European rights was, however, already won. On 15 July 1828, without debate, Sir George Murray, speaking on behalf of the Government, accepted a motion by Buxton for an Address to the Crown praying that "directions be given for effectually securing to all the natives of South Africa the same freedom and protection as are enjoyed by other free persons residing at the Cape, whether they be English or Dutch".[3]

Before this, the Cape Government had itself taken action. How far the Acting-Governor, General Bourke, was influenced by the discussions in London does not appear. Having previously assured the London Missionary Society of his zeal for the "improvement of the Hottentots", he had gone out to supersede Somerset in 1826.[4] "The necessity for an enactment of this nature", he wrote on 22 July 1828,

[1] *Parl. Pap.* 1830, XXI (584).

[2] Philip MSS. quoted in Macmillan, *The Cape Colour Question*, pp. 216 *sqq.*

[3] *Hansard*, 2nd Ser. XIX, 1694. *Parl. Pap.* 1835, XXXIX (252), p. 34.

[4] *Vide supra*, p. 257.

"has been apparent to me from a very early period after my arrival in the Colony."[1] After waiting in vain for a report from the Commissioners, "whose attention it had engaged", he at last took action on a memorandum prepared by Andries Stockenstrom, of whom, it is significant, Philip had written from Graaff-Reinet on 2 August 1825: "The Landdrost and I agree remarkably well on the subject of the Aborigines."[2] This official's suggestions were now embodied in Ordinance No. 50 "for improving the condition of Hottentots and other free persons of colour at the Cape".[3] This was promulgated at Cape Town on 17 July 1828.

At one sweep all former proclamations and enactments were repealed. By the second clause the immobilising law of passes was swept away, insomuch as Hottentots were no longer to be subjected to "any compulsory service to which other of His Majesty's subjects are not liable", nor "to any hindrance, molestation,...or punishment of any kind whatsoever, under the pretence that such person has been guilty of vagrancy, or any other offence, unless after trial in due course of law". Clause 3 finally set at rest any doubt remaining as to the competence of Coloured people to purchase or possess land. Other clauses sought to remove grave abuses attendant on the practice of apprenticeship: children might still be bound, but only by separate contracts and for no more than seven years in all; moreover, no claim for compulsory apprenticeship was to lie "under colour of [children] having been fed or clothed by their employer"; Hottentot servants were expressly allowed to keep their children on the premises of the employer without contracting them, and without giving the employer any claim to "the labour or services of such uncontracted children".

This Ordinance, while admitting the substance of Philip's case, fell something short of complete legal equality. When the published ordinance reached him from the Colonial Office, Philip, who had been pressing for an Order-in-Council to implement the Commons' resolution of July 15, hestitated for a time to accept it on the express ground that he disliked such separate or class legislation. In the end, after consultation with Dr Lushington, the eminent lawyer of the anti-slavery party, he agreed to be content with an additional clause—as he put it, "the seal of the King in Council"—prohibiting its repeal or amendment except with the express sanction of the Crown. Thus fortified, the Fiftieth Ordinance was confirmed on 15 January 1829.[4]

No legal provisions could at a blow override the hard facts of the Hottentots' economic helplessness. As little could reluctant colonists accept at large Philip's sound doctrine that Hottentots and backward people generally were to be thought of, not only as producers "furnishing a present accommodation to their master", but as consumers

[1] C.O. 1443 (Cape Archives), Bourke to Huskisson, 22 July 1828.
[2] Macmillan, W. M., *op. cit.* p. 213.
[3] *C.G.H. Govt. Gazette*, 25 July 1828. For text, see Eybers, *Select Const. Docs.* pp. 26–8.
[4] P.C. 2/210, pp. 67–138.

whose progress and prosperity were essential to the well-being of the community of which they formed a part. But greater freedom in "bringing their labour to a fair market" materially strengthened the reiterated provisions in restraint of truck in liquor and tobacco, and prohibiting the detention of goods or cattle. With the stringent vagrancy laws abolished, and oral contracts (to this day the general rule on South African farms) allowed to run only from month to month, Coloured people were more likely to be able than hitherto to leave bad employers and seek better conditions elsewhere.

A measure of such far-reaching social significance is not to be judged by the first few years of its operation, even if its immediate effects were certainly known. It was to be expected, as public clamour announced and cautious witnesses like the Wesleyan missionary, the Rev. William Binnington Boyce, testified,[1] that some of the Coloured people, released from the tyranny of pass-laws which had punished any free movement as vagrancy, should revert for a time to "roaming the country". Philip, who returned to the Cape at the end of 1829, possibly forgot in his protests that the lack of impressive figures to show an increase of crime might only justify the complaint that crime went unpunished;[2] but he was probably right in alleging gross exaggeration. On a tour through the country early in 1830 he noted that, wherever he went, crime was always said to be serious just over the hills, in the next district: "At Swellendam, it was at George, at George, in the Long Kloof"—and so on to Grahamstown.[3]

Dr Philip, however, was prepared for reasonable safeguards. If stock-theft was difficult to control, he would, he told Benjamin Moodie, a Swellendam farmer, stiffen the law even to the extent of admitting circumstantial evidence: he would in particular strengthen the machinery of government, appointing more magistrates and constables and building more prisons: he would even accept a law against vagrancy, provided always that it was accompanied by a "Poor Law Settlement" for the relief of the genuinely poor and distressed.[4]

The missionary leader was on strong ground. The position of the Hottentots, before 1828 morally doubtful, had been economically little calculated to promote the country's well-being. All the evidence suggests that slaves, as valuable property, were more highly regarded and better cared for than Hottentots, for whom, as at once cheaper and more easily replaced, masters took little or no responsibility. Whatever the opposition and consequences, slavery by common consent had to go, and the laws of 1809, the product of a slave-owning age, could hardly survive intact when slavery itself was challenged. But the removal of restrictions by the Fiftieth Ordinance demanded other measures to help the freed Coloured people to adapt themselves

[1] Boyce, W. B., *Notes on South African Affairs from* 1834 *to* 1838, pp. 122 *sqq.*
[2] Philip MSS., "Journal of Tour of 1830".
[3] *Parl. Pap.* 1836, VII (538), p. 763.
[4] *Ibid.* p. 725.

to new conditions. The Government itself had begun well in 1829 by enabling fully 2000 Hottentots, mostly from older stations, to settle in the very attractive Kat River Valley, where, for a time at least, they did very well.[1] Unfortunately, constructive measures stopped short. The Government, having unsuccessfully attempted to prevent the London Missionary Society from following its own people to the new settlement, stood aloof, hostile to the organisation best able to help it.

Early in 1830 came the distraction of Philip's trial for libel. Under the old system, which the *Researches* had been designed to expose, treatment of Hottentots might be arbitrary and yet quite legal. Now, to the satisfaction of his opponents, Philip was fined £200, with £900 costs, for having published in that book what the Court held to be a false and malicious libel on William Mackay, a frontier official. On another point of detail Philip was next involved in 1831 in a long dispute with the Government itself over an alleged encroachment on the lands of the Theopolis Institution. The truth would seem to be that the people of Theopolis had come to be more and more strictly confined within their original bounds, the Society at last being obliged to re-purchase from two grantees land, which, in roomier days, the Hottentots had been in the habit of using unmolested.[2]

These futile episodes absorbed energy which had been better used in co-operative efforts by Government, colonists and missionaries to find means of bringing the Hottentots through a difficult period of transition. They also threw Government and colonists into joint opposition to Philip, who, holding fast by the Ordinance of 1828, returned in 1833 from a long tour of the interior to find Governor Sir Lowry Cole and his successor, the Acting-Governor, Colonel Wade, completely committed to his opponents' view of what was necessary for the effective control of the Hottentots. Their ideas, as embodied in a Draft Vagrancy Law, were calculated to satisfy the old school. Even minor officials were required to "apprehend all persons" whom they might "reasonably suspect of having no honest means of subsistence"—an "honest" livelihood being so defined as to exclude "searching for and digging for roots...or wild honey...and taking and killing game" without the permission of the landowner. Anyone so found was liable to be set or assigned to labour, public or private, at the discretion of the magistrate or official concerned. In the course of 1834 this measure was actually carried by a narrow majority in the Legislative Council.[3] At once the missionaries, as a body, strongly supported by John Fairbairn and the *Commercial Advertiser*, were up in arms. Philip himself plied the new Governor, Sir Benjamin D'Urban, with memorials, Hottentot petitions and protests

[1] Opinions cited in Cory, *Rise of South Africa*, II, 388 *sqq.*
[2] Macmillan, W. M., *The Cape Colour Question*, pp. 226 *sqq.*
[3] *Parl. Pap.* 1837, VII (425), p. 174.

against a law, which, as drafted, was certainly wide enough to secure complete "control". The Institutions all over the country were crowded out by refugees, from veld and farms, apprehensive of a return to the conditions existing before 1828.[1] Theopolis quaintly expressed the Hottentot view of the new law as follows:

> [It was] to save themselves [the farmers] the trouble of keeping, if it were only an old woman, to protect their cattle and sheep from jackal, wolves, and tigers, whose sins have often been laid on the backs of Hottentots and Kaffirs, *memorialists not excepted*.[2]

In George and elsewhere Field-cornets were suspended for demanding passes from travelling Hottentots as if the draft were law.[3] Philip's insistence on the entrenchment of the Fiftieth Ordinance against simple amendment or repeal was therefore justified, and there is little doubt that it was by his influence also that D'Urban was persuaded of the unwisdom of the projected measure,[4] for in spite of the support it obtained in the Legislative Council, he reserved the Ordinance for His Majesty's pleasure. In a despatch of 11 March 1835 Lord Aberdeen approved of D'Urban's action, and disallowed the draft law. Ordinance 50 had survived this first and most formidable frontal attack, which proved also to be the last.

If the law of 1828 is to be judged solely by the reactions of farmer opinion it may be written down as disastrous, more fatal even than the more spectacular emancipation of slaves which took effect on 1 December 1834. To old-fashioned colonists, already disturbed by the attack on slavery, the veto on the Vagrancy Law was the last straw. The Boers who a few years later joined the Great Trek were very few of them slave-owners;[5] but probably no colonist was so poor that he had no Hottentot servants, and masters also set great store by the authority and prestige of enforcing such summary methods as the old law had permitted. The Fiftieth Ordinance unquestionably finds its echo in the Trek leader Retief's well-known protest that, wherever they went, the Trekkers were resolved to maintain "proper relations" between masters and servants. Hottentot emancipation was a prime factor in creating that dread of *gelijkstelling* (equality), which modern writers are agreed was a prime cause of the Great Trek itself.[6] Beyond the Colony the Trekkers had to deal with a more numerous and formidable coloured population, the Bantu—a people with no tradition of submissive farm labour and no experience of civilised ways of life. Their actual physical danger being greater, they remained confirmed adherents of the pre-1828 policy.

[1] Macmillan, W. M., *The Cape Colour Question*, pp. 238, 239.
[2] *Parl. Pap.* 1836, VII (538), p. 747.
[3] *Ibid.* p. 244.
[4] Macmillan, W. M., *Bantu, Boer and Briton*, p. 91.
[5] *Vide infra*, p. 327.
[6] See Gie, S. F. N., *Geskiedenis vir Suid Afrika*, II, 341; Walker, E. A., *The Great Trek*, pp. 90 *sqq*.

In the Colony, however, if only because of the disastrous trekking of so many of the malcontents, the storm blew over. On 11 August 1836, for example, the *Grahamstown Journal* was writing of Ordinance 50 that "no man condemned the Act itself: it was admitted to be founded on benevolence and justice, but...proper checks should have been provided". The principle of legal equality came to be generally admitted, more especially when, owing to frontier unrest caused by "Kaffir" refugees, Ordinance 2 of 1837 at last armed officials, not against what they might "reasonably suspect" to be vagrancy unsupported by "honest means of livelihood", but against actual criminal vagrancy.

Thereafter, with rare exceptions in such times of general excitement as marked the anti-convict agitation of 1849, there is little, if any, mention of any Hottentot "problem".[1] In the internal peace which reigned after the departure of the Trekkers, a new Governor, faced since emancipation by a great increase in the numbers of "free persons of colour", took the step for which Philip had hoped in 1828.[2] In 1841, a general Masters and Servants Law was put on the Statute Book without a word of comment either from missionaries or from colonists, and Ordinance 50 stood repealed as from August 1842. This consolidating measure, which introduced minor changes, for example the first extension of the length of farm contracts, applied chiefly in practice to Coloured servants; but it now brought all servants, black or white, under one law. This was in fact complete legal equality, clearing the way for a further step. The old objection to constitutional progress, that a large part of the population was in a state of dependence and subject to special class legislation, fell away. In 1849 Hankey and Kat River Hottentots cheerfully paid their subscriptions to the Anti-convict Association then battling to avert the social complications that were feared should the Cape become a convict station.[3] About the same time John Fairbairn and Andries Stockenstrom, equally unpopular of old as champions of "Kaffir" rights, became leaders once more in a colony whose dissensions no longer turned on colour policy. No one in 1853 was at pains to challenge a correspondent of Fairbairn's, who claimed that the new Parliamentary constitution of that year was designed to "ensure their right position to all citizens,...a constitution based on principles which forbid class government or class legislation".[4] The struggle which began in 1822 had resulted in the establishment in the old Colony of that policy of equal rights for civilised men, which is still known distinctively as "the Cape policy". In the long run, the vindication of Ordinance 50 and of the changes it initiated is that, not

[1] *Vide infra* p. 378 *sqq*, and see Macmillan, W. M. *The Cape Colour Question*, pp. 259–60.

[2] C.O. 1448 (Cape Archives), Napier to Russell, 30 January 1840.

[3] Lists and letters in Philip MSS.

[4] MS. in the Gubbins Collection in the library of the University of the Witwatersrand Johannesburg.

only the Hottentot problem, but the very name Hottentot, passed out of recognition.[1] The successors of slaves and Hottentots, known as "Cape Coloured", rank to-day as a civilised people.[2]

[1] It is still used in the form "Hotnot" as a term of contempt.

[2] They are increasingly less sure of that status since the accession to power of an Afrikaner Nationalist Government in 1948.

CHAPTER XIII

THE FRONTIER AND THE KAFFIR WARS

1792–1836

THE expansion of white colonisation in the eighteenth century has sometimes been spoken of as the "first Great Trek". Owing to geographical conditions, especially rainfall, the natural line of colonial advance ran eastward between the coast and the great escarpment which bounds the Karoo. By the seventeen-seventies the van of the colonists had reached the Great Fish River. There, for the first time, they met with serious resistance, and there, for virtually fifty years, the eastward advance was stayed, while a thinner stream was diverted north-east towards Graaff-Reinet and beyond. With only minor and temporary alterations and attempts at rectification, the Fish River remained the eastern boundary of the Colony from 1778 till as late as 1847. Out of range of Cape Town, lack of markets and of transport made the colonists wholly dependent on cattle-raising, which, if only for want of fencing, necessitated large farms and great reserves of pasture. The essential High Veld, the relatively well-watered grasslands of the modern Free State and southern Transvaal, had not yet been discovered, so that long before the Great Trek (1836) the virtual hold-up at the Fish River made land-hunger in Cape Colony a fact to be seriously reckoned with. Much the most attractive land for settlement lay just ahead of the eastern advance under the Winterberg and Katberg from the modern Bedford to Kingwilliamstown. The attractiveness of this area, and not the cover for "thieving" afforded by the rather arid Fish River bush, made it now the great objective of immigrant Xhosas and advancing colonists, as well as the scene of the continuous struggle of the so-called "Kaffir" wars from 1779 till at least 1853.

In 1778 Governor van Plettenberg made the first attempt at an eastern frontier agreement, but from the beginning the Fish River boundary was most ambiguously defined. For sixty miles the middle reaches of the river run parallel to the coast at right angles to any rational line of demarcation between the Cape Colony and "Kaffirland". Taken strictly, this was highly favourable to the Xhosas and should have left them in possession of the whole of the delectable districts of modern Bedford, Adelaide and Fort Beaufort, which were the real bone of contention. In practice, colonists and Governors came unmistakably to think of the Fish River as running its whole course conveniently at right angles to the coast through Fort Beaufort straight to the Amatola mountains beyond, whereas this was really the line of the Kat River, a northern tributary of the Fish. As late as 1819 the definition of the boundary was still vague, for example about "ridges west of the Chumie", so that there was some excuse for conflicting claims in the Kat River country.

Serious ambiguity attached also to the implications of the term "boundary". In 1778 Governor van Plettenberg had vaguely hoped to settle frontier troubles by drawing his line between the Colony and the Xhosa country, oblivious of the fact that then and long afterwards there were Kaffirs with homes west of any conceivable Fish River line. The Governor, true to the tradition of the Company, must have assumed that the Xhosas—since he was powerless to eject them—were to be, like the Hottentots, in the Colony but not of it. It followed that Kaffirs in the Colony had no "right" to be there, having certainly no organised "State" to insist on private rights of occupancy in the "annexed" country. In the very year after van Plettenberg's settlement, 1779, a quarrel arose and one of the Kaffirs, or Amaxosa, was driven "out of the colony". When his friends made not unnatural reprisals upon colonial cattle, the farmers banded themselves into a commando and drove more Xhosas across the Fish River—Xhosa cattle being seized and divided among the victors by way of compensation. Such was the "first" Kaffir war. But the Xhosas were by no means all cleared out of the Colony, and a "second" war broke out in 1789. This time, the Company government being weaker than ever and near its fall, a peace was eventually agreed upon which allowed the Amaxosa to remain in the Zuurveld—that is, the country towards the modern Grahamstown to the west of the Fish River—"without prejudice to the ownership of Europeans".[1]

Still the Company refused to recognise that some Xhosas had now no homes except within the Colony, and that, failing real expulsion, there must be some attempt to give them a clear status if they were to become peaceful subjects or citizens. This problem—the *damnosa hereditas* of the Company's policy—even the stronger British Governments of a later day long refused to face. Though in truth they had never been effectually removed, the theory was always that the Xhosas had "slunk back" into lands where they had no right to be, where also they undoubtedly made life dangerous for frontier farmers. During the disorders of the First British Occupation—a "third" war—they may even have reached further west than before, making the country in the neighbourhood of the new drostdy of Uitenhage (1804) very insecure. In 1809 Colonel Collins, reporting on the state of the interior,[2] recommended strong measures and an extension of the colonial frontier to the Koonap. This task fell to Earl Caledon's less patient successor, Sir John Cradock, who in October 1811 called out the burghers and gave Colonel John Graham a free hand to deal with the situation—using "persuasion if

[1] Theal, G. M., *History of South Africa before 1795*, III, 181.
[2] *Records of Cape Colony*, VII, 101 *sqq*.

possible". Early in 1812—in a "fourth" war—the chief Ndlambi and his followers were, this time more forcibly, though still probably far from completely, expelled from the Zuurveld—Grahamstown, Cradock and lesser strong places being established to hold the new-old line of the Fish River.

The Amaxosa tribes were in fact very loosely organised and could not easily be bound as a whole to any terms of agreement. Governors were prone to recognise as "Paramount" some Chief like Gaika, who, not being generally acknowledged as supreme, lost any influence he had when made responsible, as here, for bargaining away land which had never been his. Gaika, with whom General Janssens had treated about the Fish River boundary in 1803, was no doubt the hereditary "Great" Chief of the western Xhosas; but though he continued to be recognised by later Governors, Chief Ndlambi, thus expelled, was a formidable rival, being himself an uncle of Gaika, son by one of his wives of a more widely acknowledged chief, Rarabe. Ndlambi's predicament after 1812 inevitably emphasised the rivalry. By the usual account, some 20,000 of Ndlambi's people were "driven out of the Colony". This was only to make confusion worse confounded. It was impossible for Gaika or other Chiefs to the east of the Fish River to make room easily for such a host of newcomers, people who had long been settled elsewhere, and soon they were fighting among themselves. In times of crisis the Africans have sometimes produced "prophets". One of the most remarkable of the line now came to the front in the person of a certain Makhanda, who, obviously making a rallying cry of the Europeans' treatment of their people from the Zuurveld, presently threw his weight on the side of Ndlambi. In 1818 the rival factions fought a pitched battle on the Amalinde flats, near Kingwilliamstown, and Gaika, badly defeated, appealed to the Cape Government for support. The results were a European march to the rescue of Gaika, and a counter-attack, inspiringly led by Makhanda, in 1819. This attack—the only one to venture so far—was broken at the very gates of Grahamstown, the new capital of the east, and the colonial counterthrust was pushed as far east as the Kei River. Such was the "fifth" Kaffir war.

This traditional differentiation of first, second, third and fourth Kaffir wars, dated by Dr Theal as commencing in 1779, 1789, 1799 and 1812 respectively, is misleading. Disorders persisted throughout, especially in the period of republics and rebellions in Swellendam and Graaff-Reinet. Even in 1812 the war was said to be over by March;[1] yet the burghers called up for service in October 1811 were apparently disbanded only in July 1814, there being little difference between peace and war on that troubled frontier.[2] From 1778 till at least 1812 successive Governments were apparently too weak and unstable to

[1] Theal, G. M., *History of South Africa since 1795*, I, 196.
[2] *Records of Cape Colonv*, vols. for 1811–14 *passim*.

come near a settled policy for the control of relations between colonists and the Xhosas, who for good or ill were now their close neighbours. At most, as in their refusal to give any status to Africans inevitably within the Colony, they created bad precedents whose influence persisted.

Meantime the insecurity due to the resistance of the African tribes had diverted colonial emigration from the east to a northward line of expansion. Here, drought and distance were almost the only obstacles; Native resistance there was none. Physical barriers, such as mountains or rivers, were slight and the frequent droughts only one more incentive to an ever greater dispersal of the scanty population. Significantly, so widely scattered were stock-farmers in those parts that Graaff-Reinet on the Karoo had become a landdrostdy in 1786, considerably earlier than Uitenhage (1804) in the coastal or subcoastal belt, where climatic conditions were on the whole kinder. To the north, expansion continued without interruption, till in 1824 the upper Orange River became the recognised boundary. Close intensive settlement being here more impossible than ever, the area added to the Colony was considerable, but the number of people provided with the land and grazing they wanted was small, both absolutely and relatively. Political complications were at first unusually slight; but this northward expansion accentuated the loneliness of pioneer conditions, emphasised the independent spirit and self-reliance of the frontiersman, and helped to prepare the way for the second and greater Trek from 1836 onwards.

Save for occasional travellers' reports there is little record of happenings in this area, which was still in the eighteen-twenties vaguely spoken of as Bushmanland, till after 1800 missionaries began to take some notice of the scattered "Hottentots" of those parts. Many of the Coloured people (those at least who affected the course of development) were earlier refugees from the Colony itself, or the very mixed offspring of such refugees and aboriginal Hottentots or Korannas. This mixture often had some degree of sophistication, resulting from a dash of European blood, experience of life in the Colony, habitual use of the Dutch language, and sometimes the possession of horses and guns. Much the most important group were the Griquas, often significantly known as *Bastards*, but even as late as 1822 they amounted to no more than four thousand in all scattered along some 400 miles of the Orange River.[1] Nomads by origin, and in such country almost of necessity, some of these Griquas were gathered together after 1800 by the efforts of missionaries of the London Society, like Albert Kicherer and William Anderson, and in some sort settled at Klaarwater, later known as Griquatown, the headquarters of the second Adam Kok and soon afterwards of Andries Waterboer. In the following years, always with the guidance of London missionaries,

[1] Estimate by J. Melville in Philip MSS.

other settlements were established under Cornelis Kok at Campbell, and about 1825—to the gradual extrusion of earlier Bushmen—under the second Adam Kok at Philippolis. With the colonists of these days, and with officials and Governors, these outlying missionary settlements were far from popular.[1] About 1814 William Anderson of Griquatown roused sharp criticism by his failure, and virtual refusal to try, to act as recruiting sergeant and send a quota of Griquas to the distant drostdy of Tulbagh to serve on commando. This episode, together with insistent allegations that the mission stations "harboured" or even encouraged runaway slaves and "free" labourers from colonial farms, gave rise to the general charge that missionary "control" was ineffective. As Lord Charles Somerset once put it, the missionaries subtracted "the useful class of labourers of the Hottentots and Bastard tribes from those occupations to which they were best suited, without benefit to themselves and with great detriment to the public".[2] In 1818, therefore, Robert Moffat and others were refused permission to leave the Colony; two struggling London Missionary Society stations for Bushmen at Tooverberg and Hephzibah were suppressed,[3] and in 1819, as told above, Griquatown itself was threatened with being "broke up".[4]

The alleged danger from lawless Coloured men was insufficient, for example, to prevent speedy Boer occupation of the water-holes at the suppressed Tooverberg, which became the village of Colesberg about 1829. But there was unrest, and there were usually colonists—like a certain runagate named Coenraad Buys, who was active on the eastern frontier in the troubles of the seventeen-nineties—ready to do illicit trade in guns and ammunition. As a result the islands of the Orange River and the hills beyond became the resort of "banditti", Griquas and others; and these being inclined to use their guns indiscriminately in forays upon Bushmen or other neighbours, the northern frontier remained liable to sporadic disturbances. Afrikaner, a Namaqua Hottentot, at one time specially prominent as a freebooter, was softened by contact with the well-known Robert Moffat, and withdrew towards Namaqualand. But at last the Government decided to take some action. In 1822 John Melville, a surveyor and later a missionary of the London Society, was appointed Government Agent at Griquatown, the headquarters of Andries Waterboer, the ablest and most dependable of the Griqua captains. Melville's task proved well-nigh hopeless. As Dr Philip insisted, after a visit to the north in 1825, "Government ought to accompany the appointment with sufficient power to enforce its authority".[5] Assumption of responsibility was never the Government's strong point. Indeed

[1] Macmillan, W. M., *The Cape Colour Question*, ch. x.

[2] *Records of Cape Colony*, XII, 243. Somerset to Bathurst, 30 June 1819.

[3] Macmillan, W. M., *The Cape Colour Question*, pp. 128 *sqq.*

[4] *Vide supra*, p. 292.

[5] Letter of September 1825 to an unnamed official; cf. *Parl. Pap.* 1836, VII (538), p. 610.

its earlier fussy and ineffective attempt to conscript Griquas now added heavily to the embarrassments both of Waterboer and of the Agent, whose efforts to maintain order rather strengthened the Bergenaars, a section of the Griquas who took to the "mountains", protesting that the appointment of the Agent was but another scheme to enforce the plan of "making soldiers" of them.[1] About 1823 Waterboer and the Bergenaars were forced into some sort of temporary unity against the formidable bands of African marauders, who had been set in motion by the ferocious "Mantatees". Weary of getting scant backing, Melville, in 1826, resigned in despair, and the Government was thus again without even official representation beyond the Orange River, where critical years were at hand. In the light of later happenings and as showing the need for government in those parts, it is instructive to find among the Philip MSS. of 1827 a letter from Landdrost Stockenstrom of Graaff-Reinet requesting "Captain" Waterboer to apprehend a burgher named Joubert and send him *gevangen* (prisoner) to the drostdy.

Immediately after Melville's withdrawal there were fresh developments. As always, a new definition of the colonial boundary, like that in 1824 at the Orange river, was but a prelude to further movements. For the first time such expansion, involving as it did encroachment on native-held lands, had white witnesses. From 1826 onwards missionary letters tell the tale. Philippolis was the point at which travellers from several Orange River drifts were likely to meet. Now a shrewd missionary artisan, named James Clark, reported in every letter, first from this strategic centre and later from near Bethulie whither he followed the retreating Bushmen, that large numbers of Boers were crossing the boundary for pasture—in 1828, "this year as in former years"—depasturing the country of the Natives and driving the shy Bushmen ever further afield. Presently, in a crescendo, the complaint arose that the Boers were coming, not merely for temporary pasture, but to settle, extruding Bushmen and Griquas from their none too numerous *fonteine* (water-holes), or buying the lease of Griqua *burger* lands for an old song. These practices the missionary-guided Chiefs tried in vain to check; a "title-deed" survived in the Philip papers by which, in 1828, "Captain" Kok made a grant of land to one of his Griquas on the express condition that he should neither sell nor lease it to any white colonist. In the same year the Government itself reasserted an evergreen prohibition against burghers crossing the boundary. Political grievances had little influence here: as late as 1834 many of the Boers were riding all the way back to Colesberg to pay their colonial taxes.[2] But even had there been no official connivance at evasion,[3] prohibitions were

[1] Melville Correspondence *passim*, in Philip MSS.
[2] Chase, J. C., *History of South Africa*, II, 35, 255.
[3] Macmillan, W. M. *Bantu, Boer and Briton*, p. 45.

powerless against the pressure of even a scanty population on wide but still scantier pasture. Failing to take full responsibility and control, the Government did at least defer to missionary protests so far as to refuse with unprecedented sternness further extension of the boundary, refusing also to accede to Boer petitions for farms in what it recognised as Griqua country and even beyond.[1] The northern outlet for colonial expansion seemed almost as rudely closed as that on the Fish River.

Meantime there were momentous happenings in parts far beyond the direct influence of the European advance. Somewhere about 1817, in the lands beyond the Tugela river, there arose the famous Zulu tyrant warrior known as Chaka.[2] History, for want of serious and sufficient documentary evidence, must walk warily. A first-class military tyrant is such an uncommon phenomenon among African chiefs that Native oral tradition is likely to be highly coloured, and perhaps to have coloured occasional travellers' tales also. Even dates and places are uncertain. Though Delagoa Bay seems on occasion to have been used by slavers,[3] the effects of the slave trade upon the Africans in what is now called Zululand have never been considered. Nor is it possible to gauge the repercussions of the check administered on the Fish River to the coast tribes lying to the west of Chaka's sphere of action. Yet, whatever the circumstances of his rise, it is clear that in the years before his assassination in 1828 Chaka and his armies carried fire and slaughter over large parts of what are now Natal and Zululand and possibly Pondoland. The estimate that losses by death due to his devastations amounted to "more nearly two millions than one" has no statistical value;[4] but undoubtedly many tribes were scattered and broken, and as many scores of thousands are said to have perished from starvation and disease as were slain in actual fighting.

Some of the reactions among the refugees fleeing before Chaka's war bands, and themselves plundering, are more directly traceable than the main events of the time. Not all were mere raiders. One petty chief, Moshesh, who began in a northern corner of what is now Basutoland with a handful of followers, lived to show the capacity of Africans for peace and diplomacy. Selecting presently as his base the flat-topped natural hill-fortress which he made famous as Thaba Bosigo, he there defied attack, seldom himself provoking it. He it was who in 1832 sent an embassy with a gift of cattle to "buy" a missionary from Dr Philip, then on tour near the Orange River. The cattle were "lifted" by Griquas, but next year, on Philip's recommendation, the Paris Missionary Society accepted this unusual

[1] Sarel Cilliers, in Bird, *Annals of Natal*, I, 252; Philip MSS., Memo. on Causes of Boer Emigration.
[2] *Vide supra*, p. 38.
[3] Theal, G. M., *Records of S. E. Africa*, II, 477; IX, 23.
[4] Theal, G. M., *History of South Africa since 1795*, I, 396.

invitation. With French missionaries like Eugène Casalis as his advisers and staunch helpers, Moshesh showed great art and discretion in rallying his supporters and keeping the fragments together. By the 'forties his claims had extended and his authority was dominant far into the middle of the later Free State. The compact Basuto nation survives as his monument.

A very different fate befell the scattered tribes west of the Drakensberg, Bechuana of various sorts, speaking a dialect closely akin to that of the Basuto. The first blow fell from a marauding band of which we have already spoken, known from the name of an Amazon leader (Mntatisi) as "Mantatees". Pouring from Natal through Basutoland, where their pressure forced Moshesh to fall back on the hill-fortress of Thaba Bosigo, they seem to have pushed by way of the Caledon River far across the future Orange Free State towards Bechuanaland. They there broke up, but not before they had driven the fierce Bafoking down upon Kuruman. There these folk were broken in 1823 by a few hundred of Andries Waterboer's well-armed and mounted Griquas, who had been called in by the local missionary Robert Moffat. The vague term "horde" probably exaggerates the numbers and strength of the Mantatees, one fragment of whom straggled back to the Caledon River and survived under an undistinguished chief called Sikonyela, while others known as the Makololo seem to have penetrated as far as the Zambesi to the disturbance *en route* of the Bechuana country.[1] On the central High Veld, decimation and depopulation were carried a degree further by a more formidable warrior, Moselikatze (Mzilikazi), who, with a real Zulu army, emulated the methods of Chaka himself and overran much of the region round the Vaal. His following, famous as the Matabele, settled for a time on the Marico in the western Transvaal, whence they were driven by the Trekkers to find more permanent rest in Matabeleland (Southern Rhodesia).[2]

Devastating as these wars and raids undoubtedly were, it must have happened here, as in the "cleared" Zuurveld, that remnants of the dispossessed tribes took refuge in the high mountain kloofs or hid themselves in the bush and waited for the storm to pass. In 1836 Natal was reputed "empty"; yet in Natal, as we shall see later, before the republic of the Voortrekkers was two years old, Africans began to appear, almost as it would seem from every bush, to the serious embarrassment of the infant State. On the High Veld also, it is clear, the Voortrekkers soon found themselves vexed by the same problem of "surplus" Natives,[3] and to this day the detribalised Native population in the Free State, relatively small though it be, suggests that even there fragments of older tribes survived the slaughter of the

[1] Walker, E. A., *History of Southern Africa*, p. 176.
[2] *Vide supra*, p. 38, *et infra*, pp. 331, 409.
[3] Agar-Hamilton, J. A. I., *The Native Policy of the Voortrekkers*, pp. 53, 75, etc.

'twenties or 'thirties. It is certain that about 1836, when the effects were fresh, the apparent depopulation caused by the Chaka wars both encouraged the Boers to trek and determined in large measure the course of their exodus.

More immediately, the Chaka wars caused reactions in the already harassed country near the Fish River. From about 1820 onwards waves of refugees, who were at the same time raiders, began to appear: for example the Bacas and the Fetcani or Fingos, or new migrations like that of the Tembus, generally known at the time as "Tambookies". The unlucky Amaxosa soon found themselves between two fires, forced to find room not only for Ndlambis and others from the Colony, but for these newcomers from the east. This complication has not been sufficiently taken into account in judging the intractability of the tribes to the attempts of the colonial Government to establish order on the frontier.

Even after the clearing of the Zuurveld in 1812 unrest and cattle-stealing continued very much as before. The old tradition of the Dutch East India Company having been to avoid all possible contact with the blacks, the generally accepted line of policy was still little more than a vain attempt to keep black and white apart. Soldiers as most of them were, with a Home Government impatient of expense and with the idea of slavery insensibly colouring their attitude, frontier officials and Governors fought shy of experiments in civil administration. Instead of attempting to include the Africans as subjects within the sphere of colonial jurisdiction and protection, they were inclined to use their slender and inadequate forces to hold a fixed line of frontier. Kept together in relatively strong garrisons, the small number of troops available could not, as the better officials were still complaining much later, be used to full advantage as a mobile police force,[1] and there were no civilian administrative officers to keep in touch with the people and deal with grievances before they became serious. Frontier officers, and perhaps Circuit Commissioners also,[2] had for some time inclined vaguely to the device of maintaining a clear space between the Colony and the Kaffirs, in the hope that this might facilitate control, if not stop all intercourse. In 1819 the defeat of Makhanda and Ndlambi[3] seemed to give Lord Charles Somerset an opportunity of carrying out this policy. In October by an "amicable agreement", which was not committed to writing, Somerset made another "treaty" with the Paramount (Gaika): the country between the Fish River and its near neighbour, the Keiskamma, was to be kept entirely free—at least of Kaffirs.[4]

If the objective were really, as tradition has invariably asserted, to

[1] Macmillan, W. M., *Bantu, Boer and Briton*, p. 249.
[2] E.g. *Records of Cape Colony*, x, 94. Report of Circuit Court, 1813.
[3] *Vide supra*, pp. 228, 303.
[4] Theal, G. M., *Hist. of S. A. since* 1795, I, 282–3.

use the occasion to establish a neutral belt or "vacant tract", the bargain was not only vain but disingenuous, for apparently on the same day, in reporting the arrangement to Lord Bathurst, Somerset wrote: "The country thus *ceded* is as fine a portion of ground as is to be found, and with still unappropriated lands in the Zuurveld it might perhaps be worthy of consideration with a view to systematic colonisation."[1] Next year Sir Rufane Donkin, having consulted Gaika—as if about a modification of the bargain of 1819—pressed a scheme for a soldier settlement at Fredericksburg in the country between the Fish and the Keiskamma. Had the "neutral belt" been cleared of tribesmen some such planting of troops would have been essential to keep it "empty"; but by 1825 grants of farms were being so freely made at least in the country between the Fish and the Koonap that by 1827 the only point under discussion seems to have been whether or not the prohibition of slavery in Albany applied also to farmers in the "ceded" territory. This change of name is significant. It had gradually become normal; correspondence between Glenelg and Stockenstrom suggests that in 1836 no one very clearly knew when or how.[2]

Of course the territory never was effectively cleared nor the experiment seriously tried. One doughty chief, Maqoma, an elder son of Gaika, who presently played the role of Ndlambi to the next heir Sandile, had a favourite home in a delectable corner of the Kat River country. In 1812 the expulsion of Ndlambi from the Zuurveld had made that Chief restive under his grievances till he was overthrown with Makhanda.[3] Now it was Maqoma's turn. By 1822 he had "crept back" into the Kat River area, followed presently by his brother Tyali. Another chief, Pato, was formally allowed to graze his cattle there, nearer the sea, in what is now Peddie. Then, in 1829, Maqoma was again forcibly expelled—not for the last time—from the Kat River country—significantly enough, for interfering with the "Tambookies", who, as we showed above, were refugee immigrants from the east: and by a proclamation of 17 April 1829 the boundary of the colony was definitively extended to "heights west of the Chumie",[4] in other words almost to the line, not of the Fish River, but of the Keiskamma. Henceforth this attractive Chief, who had a genius for getting the good-will of his European guards—"Harry Smith can refuse Maqoma nothing", wrote one witness in 1836—was often to be the leader of "sedition".[5] The old struggle on the Fish River was merely carried one step further east to the Keiskamma.

Yet history has abundantly shown since that better relations were possible. Even the ten years of the "neutral belt" were marked by

[1] *Records of Cape Colony*, XII, 337 (15 October 1819).
[2] C.O. 49/27, Stockenstrom to Glenelg, February 1836.
[3] *Vide supra*, pp. 228, 303.
[4] Walker, E. A., *Historical Atlas of South Africa*, Plate 10.
[5] Macmillan, W. M., *Bantu, Boer and Briton*, p. 70.

some slight mitigation of the struggle. There was a period of relative peace during which the 1820 Settlers were able to consolidate their position—even if their presence also afforded more opportunities of cattle-stealing. Normal peaceful relations were somewhat extended. In Kaffraria there was a definite beginning of missionary work. Joseph Williams of the London Society settled with Gaika from 1816 till his death in 1818, and John Brownlee in 1820 went to the future site of Kingwilliamstown, first as a "Government" missionary, then after 1825 again under the London Society. Wesleyans settled on the lower Keiskamma and, still further afield, with Hintza, chief of the Galeka Xhosas, in the Transkei.

Trade, too, was developing. From 1817 onwards there were official "fairs" twice a year, first in Grahamstown and latterly at Fort Willshire on the Keiskamma; presently, in 1830, restrictions were removed and traders moved freely into Kaffirland itself. The tribesmen, moreover, were beginning to be useful to farmers, providing even cheaper labour than the Hottentots. After 1823 there is evidence of the employment both of refugee Bechuanas, fleeing from the north before plunderers like the "Mantatees", and even of eastern frontier Xhosas.

The handling of this new labour problem suggests that ideas of policy were in some confusion and administration lax. In 1828 General Bourke sought to take control by Ordinance, No. 49, which authorised Field-cornets to issue passes to Natives entering the Colony in search of work—thus curiously applying to the newcomers the pass-system which, by the very next Ordinance, No. 50, was abolished for the Hottentots of the Colony.[1] Natives were now habitually employed, though not without protest. Settlers wrote to the newspapers urging the danger to security:[2] missionaries complained that the already low Hottentot wage-rates were being under-cut.[3] Administration therefore was hesitant; indeed according to one authority the Ordinance was "suspended",[4] and by another account was "repealed" almost at once "on 25 August 1829".[5] In 1837, however, Stockenstrom, as Lieutenant-Governor, demanded a ruling from Governor D'Urban and was expressly assured that Ordinance 49 was valid.[6] Thereafter it was regularly enforced though it apparently clashed somewhat with arrangements made under the recent Kaffir treaties.[7] In 1849 therefore, doubts having again arisen, the Attorney-General was appealed to, and gave his opinion that on technical grounds the Ordinance had in fact lapsed soon after enactment, but

[1] *Vide supra*, p. 295.
[2] W. G. in *The Grahamstown Journal*, 14 February 1833.
[3] Macmillan, W. M., *The Cape Colour Question*, p. 253.
[4] Theal, *G. M. History of South Africa since* 1795, II, 11.
[5] Cory, G. E., *Rise of South Africa*, II, 361.
[6] C.O. 1353 (Cape Archives), Stockenstrom to D'Urban, 13 February 1837.
[7] Macmillan, W. M., *Bantu, Boer and Briton*, pp. 66, 67.

that it was inadvisable to make this fact known.[1] It was only repealed in 1867 after the annexation of British Kaffraria by the Colony.[2]

In face of such manifest failure to correlate the frontier problem with experience gained in the Colony itself it is not surprising that there was continued insecurity on the frontier, where indeed the problem of administration was still more complicated.

There was nothing yet to show how tractable African tribes normally are under a benevolent European administration, but at quite an early date it was discovered that they have a workable law of their own. Unhappily, "indirect rule" was yet unthought of; but in 1817, by agreement with Gaika, Governor Somerset hit on the promising plan of applying to the control of cattle-stealing a practice borrowed from the tribes themselves. So much do similar cases suggest similar remedies that the practice in question, familiarly known as the "spoor law", is almost exactly described in the Anglo-Saxon King Edgar's Ordinance of the Hundred,[3] itself closely paralleled among the earlier Franks. If cattle disappeared it was the duty of the complainant to track the animals as far as he could, and to throw on the headman of the kraal to which the lost animals were traced the onus of either proving that the tracks went on beyond, or returning the stolen beasts to their owner with compensation.

Unfortunately the Bantu spoor law was applied wholly from the outside without the safeguards customary in a homogeneous Bantu community. Among themselves, for example, according to a modern authority,[4] while "any attempt to obliterate the spoor would be sufficient proof of guilt", it was usual to make kraals *collectively* responsible over an area bearing some relation to the value of the property stolen, so that the number taken "should not exceed one or two for each kraal (household)". Safeguards of this kind, it is clear, were disregarded. Indeed, by throwing the whole onus on the tribes, the device absolved the Government from taking normal police measures for the protection of its own subjects. In practice, commandos of farmers did their own spoor-finding and, if they could, exacted compensation: sometimes military patrols and commandos acted together—not always with greater efficiency, as in the episode known as Colonel Henry Somerset's "blundering commando" of 1825, when twice over the wrong village was robbed of its cattle and some women and children were shot.[5] After this episode General Bourke, in 1828, decreed that patrols must not enter Kaffirland in tracing a spoor unless the stolen cattle were in sight. Sir Lowry Cole, on the other hand, yielding to outcry, allowed patrols to follow spoors wherever they led, though they were "not to seize Kaffir cattle

[1] Macmillan, W. M., *Bantu, Boer and Briton*, p. 67. [2] *Vide infra*, p. 426.

[3] Stubbs, W., *Select Charters of English Constitutional History* (Eighth Edition, 1900), p. 70.

[4] Memo. dated 1882, by the late Sir W. E. Stanford, preserved at Tsolo R.M.'s Office.

[5] Cory, G., *Rise of South Africa*, II, 239.

as compensation". In the end there is no reason to doubt the evidence of the Rev. John Brownlee of Kingwilliamstown, agreeing exactly as it does with that given to the Aborigines Committee of 1835 by Stockenstrom, recently Commissioner General of the Eastern Province, that "in most cases the guilty escape with impunity, while the innocent are deprived of the means of support and reduced to want and misery".[1]

In spite of the "spoor law", therefore, colonists certainly continued to be subject to devastating cattle raids from which these military methods, a poor substitute for a police system, were quite unable to protect them. As time passed, the "propensity to thieving" with which the Bantu have been generously credited rather increased. Provoked anew, especially by the expulsion of Maqoma from the Kat River in 1829, the tribesmen repeatedly in and from that year retaliated for the loss of their lands by raiding the dispersed and often isolated cattle-byres of the white farmers.[2] They were driven near desperation by continuous pressure both from the Colony and from Chaka refugees, despair being intensified by years of drought. The treatment meted out to Maqoma began to bring home to them the real danger of losing altogether their sole means of subsistence—their land. It was also of these same tribes that one witness reported significantly a little later that they were determined to "stand by the House of Gaika...lest we be broke up as the Hottentots were".[3]

In short, when for the first time missionaries and humanitarians, fresh from the liberation of the Hottentots of the Colony in 1828,[4] began at last to direct their attention to the state of the tribes on the frontier, the position was as unsatisfactory as it had ever been, In 1830, and again in 1832, Dr John Philip carried his "researches" into Kaffraria and quickly realised something of the truth. In Cape Town he moved with caution, being at that time on no very happy footing either with colonists or with the Governor, Sir Lowry Cole.[5] His appeal was rather to London, and to his new friend Thomas Fowell Buxton. In September Miss Buxton tells him that her father "has been with Mr Stanley several times" about "your horrid commandos". A few months later Edward Stanley, the Secretary for the Colonies, disturbed by these representations, refused his sanction to Ordinance 99, yet another commando law,[6] despite the fact that Sir Lowry Cole had urged this Ordinance as necessary to strengthen his call on the services of the burghers, not so much against the tribes, as against "bandits" who were still troublesome in the vast and sparsely populated northern districts.

[1] L.M.S. Report by Rev. J. Brownlee, 1830.

[2] Cf. list of alleged losses from November 1828 to September 1829. Cory, *Rise of South Africa*, II, 341.

[3] Capt. C. L. Stretch, 1845, quoted in Macmillan, *The Cape Colour Question*, p. 238.

[4] *Vide supra*, chapter XII.

[5] *Vide supra*, pp. 295 *sqq*.

[6] Macmillan, W.M., *The Cape Colour Question*, p. 83; *Parl. Pap.* 1835, XXXIX (252), pp. 60, 64.

The north, which was more completely within the sphere of his own missions, became the starting-point of Dr Philip's new campaign. This was to be quite as momentous, though in the end less successful, than that on behalf of the Hottentots. Returning in 1833 from a tour *via* Kaffraria to the Orange River and beyond, he began to urge upon the government the need for a more stable policy. Alarmed by the dangerous activities of the Matabele, he urged the potential usefulness of the Griquas as a frontier guard, and pointed out at the same time the disturbing effect of the Boer advance in those parts. On an earlier visit, in 1825, Philip's difficulties at Bethelsdorp and elsewhere had made him shy of bringing Griquas into a Colony where there was as yet no protection for Hottentots, but now in casting round for a remedy he came down emphatically in favour of incorporating Griqualand in the Colony.[1] In the changed conditions due to the Fiftieth Ordinance he was emphatic that the Griquas were ready for the change and needed the protection of the colonial laws; further, he maintained that to recognise and make use of them was the best remedy for their lawlessness, and even the best protection against the Matabele. A year later in December 1834 he succeeded in securing a treaty whereby Andries Waterboer, duly furnished with a salary, some arms and the guidance of an agent, the Rev. Peter Wright, was recognised and made responsible for law and order in the area of Griquatown—this treaty being the precursor of others, which were destined to give rise to a violent dispute a generation later in the days of the diamond discoveries in those parts.[2]

From these dealings in the north Dr Philip turned naturally to apply similar reasoning to the problems of the eastern frontier. This appears first in a letter to Buxton on and after his grand tour; later, more directly and in greater detail, in negotiations with a new Governor. Both the tone and the burden of Philip's complaint have been misrepresented. It was not that "innocent Kaffirs" were the victims of wantonly cruel colonists, but that, for the protection of either, the Government's purely military policy of patrols and commandos and reprisals was ineffective, if not stupid. Let the Government, he urged, try the effect of "something written", an adaptation of the new Hottentot policy, a stable agreement, security for personal rights and, above all, civil instead of military administration.[3]

It is clear that in London also new influences were at work, for the Ministry of Lord Grey, which had just been carried into power on the wave of liberal agitation for the Reform Bill, was open to suggestions for humanitarian reform in colonial policy as in other fields. The Secretary of State, as we have seen, received Fowell

[1] In detail, summarising earlier conversations, in a letter to Colonel Wade, 10 October 1833 (Philip MSS.); *Parl. Pap.* 1836, VII (538), pp. 623 *sqq*.

[2] *Vide infra*, ch. XVII.

[3] Macmillan, W. M., *The Cape Colour Question*, ch. VIII *passim*.

Buxton and listened to his complaints. Though it was done under some misapprehension, the revised Commando Law was vetoed with asperity.[1] At the end of the same year, 1833, the Government gave Sir Benjamin D'Urban unusually detailed instructions for reform. In particular, with regard to the frontier, Buxton's representations had undoubtedly produced an effect, for the commando system was judged dubious, if not "brutal"—and D'Urban was told that "it will be incumbent on you to devise such other measures as may appear calculated to protect colonists against unprovoked aggression".[2]

A very heavy task was laid upon the shoulders of the reforming Governor, and the way in which he carried it out has afforded much matter for controversy. To add to our difficulty in interpreting his work and times, D'Urban was inclined to be secretive as well as lax or even remiss in despatch-writing. So now, with constitutional innovations to be inaugurated[3] and excusable apprehensions as to the results of emancipation, which was due to be carried out in December, it was not till May 31, five months after his arrival, that the Governor at last braced himself to attend to his instructions about the frontier. "The time is now come", he wrote to Philip, "for me to take into my most serious consideration the whole of the frontier system." Philip, therefore, was asked to call and discuss a reasoned memorandum which he had submitted to the Governor in March.[4] In this document Philip had urged the injustice and ineffectiveness of the commando system, its disturbing effect on the tribes, the defects of the treaty with Gaika, and the necessity for "something written" so that Chiefs might know just where they stood—all this with a view to establishing a better order of things on the frontier. For several months D'Urban and Philip were in close collaboration on new plans and in June and July intimate letters passed between them—those of the Governor all in "confidential" holograph—containing frequent allusions to long interviews in which the matter was discussed. In August it was agreed that Philip should proceed to the frontier districts before the Governor to "prepare the way" for D'Urban's own projected visit. When he arrived there, Philip sent back to Cape Town much sound and reasonable advice which was favourably received. As the Governor himself wrote later,[5] having already (June 17) "caused communications to be made to the chiefs ...expressive of my disposition and intention to enter into a new order of relations with them", he now "availed himself" of Philip's visit "to explain to them more fully, and in detail, the nature" of such new agreements.

[1] Cory, G., *Rise of South Africa*, II, 447 *sqq*.
[2] *Parl. Pap*. 1835, XXXIX (252), p. 65.
[3] *Vide supra*, p. 264.
[4] Correspondence in detail in Macmillan, W. M., *Bantu, Boer and Briton*, pp. 87 *sqq*.
[5] C.O. 48/161, despatch of 5 January 1835.

From August to November 1834 communications still passed between the Governor and his agent. With needless secrecy, Lady D'Urban and Mrs Philip acted as intermediaries, and almost weekly Mrs Philip assured her husband of the Governor's reiterated intention of starting for the frontier himself "next month". To the end, whether in continued apprehension of the effects of the impending emancipation or from mere indecision of character, D'Urban procrastinated. By his delay he missed an opportunity which never fully returned.

On the frontier, in spite of a great drought, September and October 1834 were marked by "profound peace". The promise of a visit by the Governor in person helped to keep the tribes abnormally quiet. In November Philip felt that he had done all he could to prepare the way, and leaving it to the Governor to complete his own task, set out on his return. Yet, before he left the frontier, Philip himself saw "kraals burning".[1] The Chiefs were being rewarded, not by the visit that they expected from the Governor, but by an unprecedentedly severe application of the old reprisal system—"Border Law" as understood by Colonel Somerset.

Three European-owned horses and a foal had been stolen, and were made good, after delay, by forty Xhosa cattle, which according to frontier valuation were their equivalents. In the course of reprisals by patrols this fine was exacted twice over, till in the end the penalty for the theft amounted to a hundred cattle.[2] To some of the patrols the Xhosas made a show of resistance, whereupon unfortunate incident followed unfortunate incident. One petty Chief was wounded: some of the cattle seized belonged to a Chief who was not concerned in the matter—and by Bantu custom to seize a Chief's cattle was to declare war. By December 9 the missionary, James Read, who had accompanied Philip on his round of visits to the Chiefs, wrote in despair:

> Somerset came and collected all the troops and they are now clearing the country from Willshire to the sea....The old thing over again; for the act of one man, punish hundreds, and now again just in the time of harvest while the corn is in the field.... Can this be Sir Benjamin's order?...The chiefs will think we have deceived them.[3]

Alarm was justified. By Christmas Eve thousands of Xhosas had begun to pour into the Colony—not as in 1819 in one mass, but in raiding parties which carried fire, destruction and looting over the whole of the frontier districts. Their attack was skilfully made on a wide front, but the theory that the attack had been long premeditated is dubious despite all the evidence that was brought forward later. The Chiefs had the Governor's own word for it that reform was due; instead of the expected reform they suffered Somerset's intensive

[1] *Parl. Pap.* 1836, VII (538), p. 553.
[2] Cf. account in Cory, G., *Rise of South Africa*, III, 54 *sqq.*
[3] "Papers on Kaffir War, 1835." P.R.O., C.O. 48/165.

clearing of the country; whereupon Maqoma, Tyali and others lost all patience. The Governor, who had dallied so long with his plans for reform, was hardly justified in his complaint that the onslaught came "in a time of profound peace", or that the missionaries and others had failed to give any warning of the danger of a catastrophe.

Now and for many months the voice of reformers was stilled by the din of the sixth Kaffir war. On New Year's Eve Cape Town had the alarm. At once Colonel Harry Smith made his famous six-day ride from Cape Town to take charge and calm the panic in Grahamstown; he was followed less rapidly by D'Urban himself. Shocked at the devastation he found on every side, the Governor precipitately forgot his earlier plans for a reform of the frontier system. Very soon he had begun to lean to a project put forward in Albany by Duncan Campbell of carrying the boundary forward from the Keiskamma to the supposedly shorter and more defensible line of the Kei.[1] After some delay, due to swollen rivers, the territory of the hostile Chiefs was invaded. Here D'Urban readily accepted local suggestions that the "chief instigator of all the mischief" was the Transkeian potentate, Hintza, a Galeka, described as Great Chief of all the Xhosas. Nothing daunted by the ill-success of similar earlier treaties with Gaika, D'Urban decided that Hintza must be made to pledge himself for the good behaviour of his western neighbours. In April 1835, having by no means accounted for Maqoma and the rest, he pushed his troops forward with very little resistance across the Kei to the neighbourhood of Butterworth, whither, after repeated summons, Hintza came to the camp to parley—of his own free will.[2]

Among Hintza's people there were now some thousands of strangers, refugees of the Chaka wars known as Fingos. These, in the cattle-driving which accompanied the invasion, came to blows with their masters or protectors, Hintza's own people. Rather readily adopting their cause, D'Urban and Smith presently threatened Hintza with dire pains and penalties for his alleged ill-treatment of these people. Before long the unfortunate Chief became first a hostage, then a prisoner, and to him, thus constrained, D'Urban on May 10 dictated terms of peace. Maqoma and his colleagues were declared to be "expelled for ever" from the country west of the Kei, which now, as the Province of Queen Adelaide, became part of the Colony so "treacherously invaded and plundered" with the "countenance and concurrence" of Hintza. He, as "Paramount", having been "compelled to sue for peace and accept the terms of it", was now to be responsible for the maintenance of peace and of this treaty. A day or two later Hintza, who was detained until the appropriate fine in cattle should be paid, made a desperate attempt to escape and was shot; his body, moreover, was mysteriously mutilated. So, with their Chief's

[1] Approving notes in D'Urban's hand on a Memo. of 28 January 1835. C.O. 48/161.

[2] Soga, J. H., *The South Eastern Bantu* (Johannesburg, 1930) gives the Xhosa version.

unfortunate death rankling in the minds of the Xhosas, and with their now mortal enemies, the Fingos, taken under protection as British subjects to be planted on Xhosa land, the delusive peace was made and the war brought to an uneasy end.

This peace rather intensified the complications of the frontier, for the original culprits were uncaught and uncurbed. It was at this point, and not earlier, that missionary and humanitarian criticism again lifted its voice. Earlier in the year Philip, having urged his own mission Hottentots to their military duty, had contented himself with long private letters to Fowell Buxton trying to explain the causes of the war and feeling his way to suggestions of how in the end to "close the wounds".[1] "Alas", wrote Mrs Philip on February 16, "the poor infatuated wretches, goaded by oppression, appear to have put it out of the power of the missionaries to plead their cause." Loyal to the Governor, with whom he had so hopefully collaborated in 1834, Philip himself on February 27 was still confident. "We have put the saddle on the right horse", he wrote. On May 23, however, he changed his tone: "In former communications", he told Buxton, "I considered it my duty to support the governor"; now he insisted that the invasion was not, as D'Urban maintained, "without provocation, in a time of undisturbed peace", but was the inevitable result of the old bad frontier system. D'Urban's phrase "irreclaimable savages" roused his missionary ire, as was natural; but above all, the "sentence of extermination", supposing a prolonged campaign could indeed "expel" the "savages", was infallibly calculated to repeat on the Kei the same old struggle that had raged first on the Fish River and latterly on the Keiskamma. Here in particular Philip has been gravely misrepresented. In May and June 1835 he repeatedly emphasised: "I do not object to any of the countries beyond becoming part of the Colony provided the natives have their lands secured to them";[2] with this proviso as part of the Governor's plan, "England by extending her institutions over such provinces might have made her dominion a blessing." Still more clearly and emphatically, in a private letter to the younger James Read in October 1835 he wrote:

> On the subject of the Kaffirs...being retained as British subjects I have long made up my mind....They cannot otherwise be saved from annihilation.

In his evidence before the Aborigines Committee in 1836 he was still definitely for retaining the new province.[3] D'Urban, he agreed, was right in holding that in order to secure peace on the frontier the Government must take full control—even up to the Kei. Philip,

[1] Macmillan, W. M., *Bantu, Boer and Britain*, pp. 117 *sqq.*

[2] Philip to Buxton, 29 May and 4–28 June 1835. Philip MSS. Copies of some of these documents, lost in the Johannesburg fire of 1931, are among the Records of the L.M.S., London.

[3] *Report of Select Committee re Aborigines,...August* 1836. *Parl. Pap.* 1836, VII (538), p. 625.

however, saw further that this necessitated also giving the tribes security for their property in land and, so far as possible, the privileges of other subjects and citizens.

Completely justifying his critics, D'Urban found almost at once that the forcible expulsion of the Kaffirs from his new province of Queen Adelaide was too big a task for the troops at his disposal. New Wesleyan advisers may have influenced him; at all events, by July he was cautiously letting it be known, possibly through the Kaffir women,[1] that he was prepared for further negotiations with the tribes. As a result, on September 17 the Chiefs were assembled once more to agree to a new peace. Maqoma and his friends, with the ban removed, were now to remain very much where they were in "locations" approved by the Governor. As D'Urban reported to London, though not until November 19, the tribes were to be "settled by His Majesty's grace in a portion of the land conquered from them—of which meanwhile large tracts are still left open for the occupation and speculations of Europeans"—and this in such a way that the old clan spirit would be "rapidly subdued and forgotten", and "the whole brought under the power of the general colonial laws".

Unfortunately for this scheme, prompt and forcible despatch-writing was not D'Urban's strong point. His normal plan was to send a short letter with masses of enclosures to tell their tale, if they could. Two months had already passed since the revision of his treaties when he wrote to report to the Colonial Office, where, it will be remembered, the authorities were throughout 1834 awaiting his proposals for a new frontier system. They can hardly have been so surprised as D'Urban was when the old system brought about the disastrous Kaffir invasion. In the absence of full despatches from the Governor himself they were driven to seek information where they could. In May 1835 Fowell Buxton had on a second attempt secured the appointment of a Commons Select Committee, which had been refused earlier, to investigate this and other matters affecting the "Aborigines" of the Empire.[2] The evidence of Stockenstrom and others before the Committee in the summer was little favourable to the old frontier system. In September, when news of D'Urban's original May treaties had arrived, Buxton privately introduced to the new Secretary of State, Lord Glenelg, the Rev. W. Ellis, secretary of the London Missionary Society, who in the following months assiduously plied him with Philip's evidence on the fundamental causes of the war and with his criticisms of D'Urban's policy, especially of his resort to expulsion as a means of control.[3] Under such influences Glenelg's faith in the Governor was seriously shaken and, after giving

[1] Memo. of 28 July 1835 by Theophilus Shepstone, son of a Methodist missionary, who was then but a youth. Macmillan, *op. cit.* p. 121.

[2] See *C.H.B.E.*, vol. II, chapter IX.

[3] Philip MSS. quoted in Macmillan, *Bantu, Boer and Briton*, p. 137.

him a hesitant warning on October 20, he set himself—or probably the Permanent Under-Secretary, James Stephen—to the composition of the famous and devastating 150-page despatch of 26 December 1835.[1] Agreeing, at the outset, that it was D'Urban's duty to repel invaosin and to secure the Colony against a repetition thereof, he went on to suggest that hostilities "might have been more limited in their range", and, in words which roused bitter resentment, that the Xhosas had "ample justification" and more "right" on their side than their conquerors. At great length Glenelg demanded a full explanation of the old system and of all that had happened. While ostensibly leaving to the Governor a much qualified discretion, he directed D'Urban to "prepare the public mind" for the abandonment of the new province before the end of 1836.

This despatch reached D'Urban early in March 1836. A little earlier, in February, his own of 19 November 1835 had arrived in Downing Street with an account of his revised September treaties. Far from replying to the criticism of 26 December, this added fuel to the fire by explaining that the terms of the new treaties were "in conformity with those of May 12", which had already been so unreservedly condemned by the Secretary of State: worse still, as pencilled comments show, certain phrases, such as the reference to "speculations", and the suggestion that the Xhosas had been "chastised—not extremely but perhaps sufficiently", intensified the uneasiness already felt in the Colonial Office. At once (February 17) Glenelg informed the Governor that the King was not disposed to accept the allegiance of the Xhosas nor any accession of territory, and demanded further explanations.

D'Urban, with inexplicable folly, forgetting how he had himself glossed over the drastic difference between his May and September treaties, settled down to wait a more favourable reply to his November despatch. Lord Glenelg went unanswered, save for curt notes praising Colonel Harry Smith's successful frontier administration under what D'Urban called "the system". In May, so D'Urban told Smith, he was ready to overthrow Glenelg's "every argument and inference . . . . I shall send off my despatch in a few days."[2] Actually, the completion of this vital document was delayed until December or January—the final date is obscure—and reached London only on 15 March 1837. For a year and more Glenelg had had no "further explanations". Now, on 1 May 1837, he replied finally. Taking exception to "passages...of a declamatory nature, and upon which it can scarcely be incumbent on me to dwell", he concluded that cooperation was impossible and that he was "left no alternative" but to recall the Governor.

[1] For the text see Bell, K. N. and Morrell, W. P., *Select Documents on British Colonial Policy*, 1830–1860, pp. 463 *sqq.*

[2] Letter to Smith, D'Urban-Smith MSS., S. A. Public Library, CapeTown.

Meantime, in February 1836, Glenelg, who certainly adhered to the opinion of his original despatch, had appointed Andries Stockenstrom as Lieutenant-Governor of the Eastern Province with the express duty of "framing, consolidating, and carrying into effect such a system as may ensure the maintenance of peace, good order, and strict justice on the frontier". When the Lieutenant-Governor reached Cape Town from London in July, D'Urban received him with rather frigid politeness; but they seem to have agreed to maintain the D'Urban "system" a while longer, till the arrival of "further positive orders" from Glenelg. This "system", as ardently pursued by Colonel Harry Smith with some success, was in effect a benevolent despotism exercised under martial law. But now, on August 18, without previous warning to Stockenstrom, who had set out from Cape Town only the day before, and without further word to or from Glenelg, D'Urban suddenly took fright at the opinion of his law officers about the legality of his proceedings and abrogated martial law.[1] Thereupon Smith's "system" became impossible, and nothing remained for Stockenstrom but to make new treaties more in accordance with Lord Glenelg's expressed views. In December treaties were completed abandoning D'Urban's new province of Queen Adelaide, making over even the old Ceded (Fish River) Territory as a "loan in perpetuity" to certain Bantu Chiefs, and abrogating the commando system or anything resembling it. The principle of Stockenstrom's measures for establishing peace was in itself an advance—the "acknowledgment", as he wrote later,[2] "of the right to the territory of its then actual possessors", a recognition, before "reserves" other than mission "institutions" had been thought of, that the Xhosas must have a secure right to homes of their own. Ultimately, Stockenstrom hoped, the tribes, having learned the benefits of civilisation, would see the advantage of accepting British sovereignty. The fatal weakness was that for the present it threw on the Chiefs, with the help only of Diplomatic Agents of the Government, the whole responsibility for keeping the frontier in peace.

The happenings of this critical period were in truth not merely a South African affair but an acute early manifestation of a world problem which has perplexed many besides South Africans from that day to this. If any censure is called for, some must fall on Sir Benjamin D'Urban for his failure to justify the frontier control he instituted and for plain neglect of duty in the matter of despatch writing. Dr Philip, the traditional villain of the piece, the spokesman and executive agent of the British philanthropists, showed throughout a wider grasp of the essentials of this human problem. It was regrettable but inevitable that this should hurt and wound the feelings of suffering frontier colonists. Fowell Buxton's Aborigines Committee,

[1] Macmillan, W. M., *Bantu, Boer and Briton*, pp. 156–7.
[2] To James Read, Philip MSS.

which attracted much fire of criticism at the time, though its evidence is a mine for historians, had singularly little influence on the event. As we now know, a detailed South African report was drafted by Buxton and Philip working together in the winter of 1836–7. In June 1837, however, when Buxton began to read "our South Africa" to the Committee,[1] Sir George Grey, Under-Secretary of State—not to be confused with the later Governor of the same name—floored him by producing D'Urban's long-delayed reply to the Glenelg despatch of December 1835—"papers a yard high"—without which the Committee could not proceed. Thereupon, to make sure of some report before that Parliament died, Buxton was compelled in haste to hack away all the detail and leave only bare but not inopportune principles of policy, which had less influence than they deserved.[2] This humanitarian Committee uttered, for example, a reasoned warning against that policy of dealing with backward tribes by means of such unequal "treaties" as continued to be the first and last resort of Downing Street. "Exeter Hall", in short, the object of so much blame and fear, was a vague influence rather than an effective power in colonial policy.

Some blame may, indeed, rest on the broad shoulders of His Majesty's Government of the day. To its credit there are the emancipation of slaves in the British Empire and the lion's share of the burden of suppressing the slave trade; but in spite of honest concern for the welfare of backward races, Governments fought shy of taking responsibility and real control. As early as 1824 Dr Philip vainly urged the occupation of Delagoa Bay, among other reasons as a check on the activities of slave-traders.[3] In 1835 requests to take over the infant colony of Natal were politely declined. On the northern frontier of the Colony, in the so-called Griqua country, Waterboer had been recognised and a treaty concluded with him in 1834 for the protection of the remote and rather arid Griquatown. In Adam Kok's Philippolis, however, a strategically far more important centre further east, disputes and disorders, due directly and indirectly to the advance of white colonisation, were actually the occasion for refusing even a treaty.[4]

In 1836, on the other hand, a traveller, Dr Andrew Smith, was warmly commended for a handful of almost meaningless treaties of amity, which he had concluded with Native Chiefs,[5] among others with the formidable Matabele, Moselikatze. In the same year and in the same spirit the Cape of Good Hope Punishment Act made British

[1] Buxton letters in Philip MSS., quoted in full by Macmillan, *Bantu, Boer and Briton*, pp. 161 *sqq.*

[2] The Report "with comments", some of which may be Philip's, was published by the Aborigines Protection Society, London, 1839.

[3] C.O. 389 (Cape Archives), Philip to Somerset, 17 April 1824. *Records of Cape Colony*, IX, 23, 41 *sqq.*

[4] Macmillan, W. M., *Bantu, Boer and Briton*, pp. 51, 191.

[5] See list in Brookes, E. H., *History of Native Policy*, ch. I.

subjects liable to punishment, on their return to the Colony, for crimes committed anywhere south of lat. 25° South; at the same time the Government failed and refused to give either them or the tribes adequate "protection" beyond the frontiers and, as it seemed to colonists, even within the colonial boundaries.

By refusing, as we have seen, to grant Boer petitions for farms beyond the Orange River, the Government also closed the northward line of advance which had so long served to mitigate the effects of Xhosa resistance to colonisation in the east. When, in addition, the long-deferred hopes of new farms in the east, roused among the frontiersmen by D'Urban's plans, were rudely dashed to the ground, the cup was full. Even if there had been no slavery question and no grievance about Hottentot measures like the Fiftieth Ordinance, thwarted land-hunger was enough by itself to produce a serious explosion. This explosion, the Great Trek, is dealt with in our next chapter, but the failure to establish settled civil and political administration among the tribes had results which for long were hardly realised. The consequences will fill many of our pages.

CHAPTER XIV

THE FORMATION OF NEW STATES, 1835–1856

(a) THE GREAT TREK, 1835–1848

THE Great Trek of the Cape frontiersmen is still the central event in South Africa's history. It can be distinguished both from the slow dispersion of the sheep and cattle farmers that had preceded it since the last years of the seventeenth century, and from the steady drift into the more outlying parts of the Union that has followed it, by its size, its abruptness and, above all, its spirit and intention.

Everything that occurred during the six generations from the foundation of the Cape Colony to the beginning of the Trek had conspired to make of the Cape pastoralists the most highly specialised members of the Afrikaner people. They were the most characteristic product of that isolated history—one hundred per cent Afrikaners. Nevertheless, though they had long been conscious of interests and experiences that differentiated them from the agricultural community behind Cape Town, they had hitherto always taken their colony with them on their journeys. Now, many of them deliberately left the colony behind them. They trekked away, as the Pilgrim Fathers had done two centuries before and the Mormons were destined to do a few years later, to found a community of their own in the wilderness.

By their trek they determined the future course of South African history. Within a short decade the area staked out for European occupation was doubled and an already inadequate white population was dispersed still more thinly over vast territories: the social and political effects of that sudden rush are still apparent. The Trek also thrust Europeans in considerable numbers among Bantu tribesmen for the first time and thus began the South African native problem in its present form. It further faced the Government of the Cape Colony, the one organised Government in southern Africa other than the Portuguese in Mozambique, with the insoluble problem of ruling frontier territories much wider and far less accessible than the colonial frontier districts that were already overstraining its resources. The effort to rule, reluctantly undertaken, broke down, and rival Governments emerged from the confusion; South Africa was balkanised for sixty years to come. Finally, the Trekkers and their sons gained upon the High Veld a further lease of the rigid and circumscribed life that was fast passing in the Cape Colony. That way of life has since decayed, but its ideas, hallowed by memories of the Trek and of political independence, still dominate the northern parts of the Union of South Africa and profoundly influence the rest.

The Boers of the eighteen-thirties—and almost without exception the Trekkers were "boers", that is to say frontier stock-farmers—had a definite character of their own. They were religious-minded, self-reliant, patient of inanimate circumstance if not of their fellow-men, possessed as a rule of the family virtues, and good fighters in their own fashion if well led. But they had their faults. Sir Harry Smith, a soldier and Governor who knew them well and was respected by them in return, described them as "men... of strong prejudices, most credulous in all respects, especially where the Government is concerned, jealous to a degree of what they regard their rights, constantly at variance with one another, and evincing that want of mutual confidence",[1] which helps largely to explain why they had such frequent evil fortune on trek and in their early republics.

The Cape frontiersmen held firmly by three main traditions.[2] First, that a farm to be a farm must consist of 6000 acres or so of land, regardless of quality, and that each man was entitled to one such farm at least, taken at pleasure and held indefinitely on payment of a small and fixed annual "recognition" to the distant central government.[3] Secondly, they believed that the redeeming feature of the central government was that it was distant. Local government by landdrosts and semi-elected and wholly sympathetic farmer heemraden the frontiersmen understood; but the central government was to them a more or less alien thing whatever flag might fly over the castle at Cape Town. Experience had taught them that that government could usually be tired out, or else evaded by the simple process of edging further away from it. Thirdly, starting with an endowment of late seventeenth-century Calvinism and brought up for generations among slaves or Bushmen and Hottentot serfs and latterly Bantu barbarians, the Trekkers held as firmly as any politician in the Carolinas that there was a divinely appointed gulf between themselves and such as these.

The Great Trek took place when and how it did because all these three fundamental traditions were challenged simultaneously. The central government showed obviously that it meant to govern, and along new lines; economic conditions were changing rapidly and destroying the old isolation, and the apostles of humanitarianism and the Evangelical revival were pushing in to preach doctrines of Native rights that to the Boers seemed destructive of all security.

Changing economic conditions provided much of the driving force behind the Trek, though of themselves they could never have imparted to it its spirit of antagonism towards the Cape Colony and its

[1] Smith to Grey, 26 March 1849; *Correspondence re Sovereignty, Parl. Pap.* 1851, XXXVII [1360], p. 2.

[2] Walker, E. A., *The Frontier Tradition in South Africa.*

[3] *Records of Cape Colony*, ed. Theal, G. M., VIII, 106; *Report of the Surveyor-General of the Cape Colony* (G. 30–1876); and *vide supra*, p. 152.

British rulers. The mutual pressure of Europeans and Bantu in the eastern borderlands was becoming serious. The frontier had been advanced slightly further eastward three times between 1812 and 1831, but the relief thus afforded had been in great measure cancelled by the unpopular institution in 1813 of quit-rent tenure for new farms, and by the planting of British settlers and Hottentots in parts of the annexed territories. In the east Boers had little to hope for unless they were prepared to go in and live among the tribes of Kaffirland, as Louis Trigardt, the first of the future Voortrekkers, and some others did between 1829 and 1834.

Land-hungry men could hope for better things to the north-east. Ten years before the Trek was talked of seriously, cattlemen had reached the drifts over the middle Orange, and government had reluctantly followed them up. Now, in 1834, scores of families were scattered to the east of the new boundary between the Stormberg Mountains and the upper Orange; others were settled just beyond that river, and landless men within the colony were asking leave to take up farms in what is now the central Orange Free State.[1] Thus the line of least resistance on to the High Veld was already clearly marked out by 1832, when the Imperial Government proposed, as part of a general policy, to make land, its one great colonial asset, a source of revenue by auctioning Crown lands for cash.[2] Boers who already found variable quit-rents for farms of variable sizes irksome, survey expensive and the issue of title-deeds slow and uncertain, could not support such a radical change in land tenure in the midst of a prolonged drought. Substantial men were tempted to trek for the sake of their numerous sons, less substantial men for fear lest they themselves became landless, the many landless lest they sink to the level of poor whites, and all because they were harassed by the abrupt transfer of their colony from a servile to a free basis of society. In the latter part of 1834, the frontier districts were full of talk of a mass trek. Exploring parties rode out to South-West Africa, to the north-eastern Transvaal and along the coast belt to Natal, this last in the tracks of the soldier-explorer, Dr Andrew Smith, who had recently visited the ruling Zulu Chief in those parts.[3] These *kommissie trekke* reported early in 1835. The first had traversed desperate lands, but the other two had found vast tracts of fine open country that had been swept well-nigh clear of inhabitants by the Zulus, Matabele and Mantatees.[4]

These preparations are conclusive evidence against accepting the traditional idea that the two primary causes of the Great Trek were the inadequate compensation paid for emancipated slaves and the upsetting of D'Urban's settlement of the eastern frontier after the

[1] *Annals of Natal*, 1495–1845, ed. Bird, J., I, 252, 505.
[2] *Cape Government Gazette*, 18 May 1832.
[3] Kirby, P. R., (Ed.), *Andrew Smith and Natal.*; *vide supra*, p. 322.
[4] *Annals of Natal*, I, 231, 252, 504; Preller, G. S., *Voortrekkermense*, I, 275 *sqq.*

Kaffir war of 1834–5 by the combined forces of Downing Street and Exeter Hall. It is true that many Trekkers, and those the most vocal, came from the eastern frontier lands, but others came from the northern districts where there was no Kaffir menace. The overthrow of the D'Urban settlement was only a subsidiary cause, though a powerful one. So it was with compensation. Apart from the fact that the men from the northern and eastern districts, who formed the mass of the Trek, had never had many slaves, the unsatisfactory details of compensation only appeared in full two years after the Trek had been provisionally decided upon.

Emancipation was resented as one aspect of the revolution that had been sweeping through the colony since 1828. It was the steady and growing pressure of a government allied with philanthropy that bred in the frontiersmen a spirit hostile to the new society which was taking shape. To them the British Government at the Cape, newly organised under the reforms of 1828–34, was strange and its point of view still stranger. The landdrosts might survive as magistrates or civil commissioners, but the popular heemraden were gone and the field-cornets had been shorn of most of their powers. Not only did magistrates and the circuit judges use unfamiliar English as the language of their courts, but they were too few to make it easy for farmers to comply with the law, especially the law governing the disciplining of their coloured servants. And not everyone wished to comply in a community that nursed resentful memories of the Black Circuit of 1812[1] and hated the necessity of answering to the law for dealings with dependents who to them were something less than "Christian men".

The Fiftieth Ordinance of 1828 had abolished the pass-laws and had permitted free persons of colour to hold land if they could get it; laws vexatious to slave-owners[2] had culminated in emancipation, and there was the certainty that at the end of 1838 the ex-slave apprentices would join the Hottentots on a footing of civil equality with their late masters. The Imperial Government would not hear of a vagrancy law to hold these coloured folk in place as a reasonably stable and cheap labour supply for white employers,[3] and women resented even more bitterly than men this equality in their own houses with beings who had hitherto been their property or at most their humble dependants, and who might now become competitors for land with their own sons.[4]

In the confusion that followed the Kaffir war, the frontier districts were full of complaints of insecurity, of vagrancy, thieving, runaway servants, of armed "foreign Kaffirs" in the mountains with nothing

[1] *Vide supra*, p. 290.
[2] See Eybers, G. W., *Select Constitutional Documents*, p. 155.
[3] *Vide supra*, p. 298.
[4] *Annals of Natal*, I, 459.

but an inadequate pass-law to check them, and neither a garrison sufficient to give security nor permission to deal with the matter in frontier fashion. The abrogation in 1834 of Cole's Ordinance 99 reorganising the commando system had bred uncertainty: D'Urban's post-war attempts to overhaul the system gave rise to a scare that the Boers were about to be subjected to European military service. To make matters worse, many had suffered losses during the war and Government was slow to honour requisition notes; nor would it provide compensation for losses even to the extent of remitting taxes for a year or two. Instead of granting the farms in the Ceded Territory and the Queen Adelaide and Stormberg areas for which British and Afrikaner frontiersmen eagerly applied, the Government actually restored the lands to the tribes.[1] The disappointed applicants were bitterly resentful.

In such an atmosphere it was easy for an isolated and suspicious folk to believe the wild rumours that ran along the frontiers, some of them spread by speculators desirous of buying up deserted farms cheaply. The frontiersmen, too, believed that their philanthropic critics were stating their own side of the story in Cape Town and London unchallenged, and this "unjustifiable odium" cast upon them rankled and rankles still. Yet these were subsidiary causes. It was primarily land hunger and a determination to uphold white privilege that drove the Trekkers out of the colony in their hundreds to seek security and satisfaction in independence.

The Great Trek passed through two stages: first, the Trek proper, a more or less organised exodus north-eastwards from the Cape Colony, and then a drift still further inland from the areas occupied during the first stage. The movement began at the close of 1835, ran with ever-increasing strength throughout the later 'thirties, and slackened in the early 'forties. During the first two years the Trekkers remained on the High Veld, more particularly in what is now the central and northern Orange Free State. In November 1837, however, the main body went down into Natal. During the next six years Natal was the principal scene of action. To the Boers it was a desirable land offering a point of contact with the outer world, but to the colonial authorities it was the headquarters of a movement they were anxious to stop, sandwiched between tribesmen who constituted a threat to the vulnerable eastern frontier.

Towards the close of 1843 the Trek passed into its second stage. The Natal Republic submitted finally to the Crown and the centre of action swung back to the High Veld. By that time, after eight years, perhaps 12,000 Europeans had left the colony. Recruitment from the colony by no means ceased, for throughout the 'forties there was a flow, largely for economic reasons, from the more settled parts to the frontier districts and beyond; but now the Trek was essentially

[1] *Vide supra*, p. 326.

a movement away from Natal, away from the present Free State, northward, always northward and further out of reach of British influence and control. Those years saw the formation of communities on the High Veld, pure Trekker beyond the Vaal, Trekker in the main between the Vaal and the Orange. By the year 1856 both the Orange Free State and the Transvaal had won the independence the Trekkers had set out to seek, and isolated little Natal had become a Crown colony separate from the parent Cape Colony.[1]

Louis Trigardt, the first of the Trekkers, had been living for some time with a few friends in Kaffirland. Hearing that he was wanted by the military authorities for his real or supposed offences during the recent Kaffir war, he slipped across the Orange River towards the end of 1835. He journeyed northward at the head of a little party of fifty, keeping more or less in touch with a similar party under Johannes van Rensburg. The van Rensburgs were destroyed by hostile tribesmen in the lower Limpopo valley, but the Trigardts reached the Zoutpansberg in the far northern Transvaal, stayed there for a time, and then made their way down the breakneck passes of the Drakensberg to Delagoa Bay. Those of them who survived the fever sailed round by sea to republican Natal in 1839.[2]

The first considerable trek entirely from within the colony took place in February 1836, when Hendrik Potgieter, the founder of the Transvaal, led out some sixty families from the Tarka and Colesberg districts. Potgieter acquired the cession of the northern half of the future Free State from a petty local chieftain, and rode on with a few friends as far as the Zoutpansberg seeking in vain for a road down the mountains to Delagoa Bay. On rejoining his main party south of the Vaal, he found that one or two scattered groups had been destroyed by the Matabele. He himself only beat them off at Vechtkop with the loss of all his draught oxen; but he succeeded in making his way to Thaba Nchu, halfway back to the Orange, with the help of Moroko, Chief of that place, of Moroko's Wesleyan missionary, the Rev. Thomas Jenkins, and of Boers who had just arrived there from the colony (October 1836).[3]

The Trekker skirmishers had thus either disappeared into the blue or had been driven back by the Matabele. Henceforward the advance was more deliberate. The Potgieters found at Thaba Nchu a large party from Graaff-Reinet under Gerrit Maritz. The combined parties elected a Volksraad, a legislature that was also a court, appointed Maritz, a man of some wealth and education, Chairman and Landdrost, and chose Potgieter as commandant (December 1836).[4] They

[1] For a detailed account of the Trek, see Walker, E. A., *The Great Trek*.

[2] *Dagboek van Louis Trigardt*, 1836–8, ed. Preller, G. S.; Preller, *Voortrekkermense*, II, I *sqq.*; Fuller, C., *Louis Trigardt's Trek across the Drakensberg* (ed. Fouché, L.).

[3] *Annals of Natal*, I, 238 *sqq.*; Preller, *Voortrekkermense*, III, 4, 18, 41; *Natal Papers*, ed. Chase, J. C., I, 71 *sqq.*

[4] R 9/36 (Transvaal Archives); Preller, *Voortrekkermense*, I, 297.

then raided the Matabele kraals at Mosega beyond the Vaal and brought away the waggons and oxen lost during the recent fighting, and also a group of despairing American Presbyterian missionaries (January 1837).

The stream was now beginning to run strongly, for trekking had been stimulated by the abrogation of martial law and the final overthrow of D'Urban's frontier settlement. One by one trek parties came in to the rendezvous at Thaba Nchu numbering up to a hundred waggons at a time, led by the chief local official or the patriarch of the clan. But as numbers grew, difficulties multiplied and the nascent Boer republic was rent by the mutual jealousies of Potgieter and Maritz. Hopes of better things came with the arrival of Piet Retief. He had quarrelled with Andries Stockenstrom, the newly arrived Lieutenant-Governor,[1] and after publishing a manifesto setting forth the grievances and aims of the Trekkers,[2] he now came in with four hundred followers to join the laagers. Being well known as an able man with experience of local civil and military government and a wider knowledge of colonial affairs than the rest, Retief was elected Governor and Commandant-General. The United Laagers elaborated their camp regulations and confirmed them by the Nine Articles of Association (April–June 1837).[3]

Thus, by the middle of 1837, the Trek was well under way and was causing grave anxiety to the Colonial Government, for the Trekkers had gone into country where individual Europeans had preceded them and where, to a certain extent, official colonial interests might be affected. Wesleyan and other missionaries were already scattered throughout Kaffirland; further to the east, the British and half-breed ivory traders, who, since 1824, had been at Port Natal (Durban) for a dozen years past by leave of the Zulu king,[4] had recently been furnished with a magistrate under the Cape of Good Hope Punishment Act,[5] the one hold the Colonial Government had on its subjects beyond the borders; further east still, Anglican and American missionaries had appeared in Zululand. To the north, beyond the Orange River, the London Missionary Society men had long been with the Batlapin at Robert Moffat's Kuruman, and with the Griqua captains—with Adam Kok at Philippolis on the route to the High Veld, and, further west, with Andries Waterboer at Griquatown and Cornelis Kok at Campbell on the Missionaries' Road that led northwards towards Central Africa. Americans had travelled up that road to the warlike Matabele at Mosega in 1836, while north-eastward of the Colony, beyond Adam's Philippolis, Wesleyans were at work among the small Bantu or half-breed clans of the Caledon River valley, and Paris

[1] *Vide supra*, p. 321.
[2] *Grahamstown Journal*, 2 February 1837; Preller, G. S., *Piet Retief*, p. 78.
[3] Preller, *Voortrekkermense*, I, 299.
[4] The first pioneers of Natal were two ex-naval officers, Francis Farewell and James King.
[5] *Vide supra*, p. 322.

Evangelicals among Moshesh's Basuto.[1] There was risk of conflict here, a risk that was enhanced by the break-up of the United Laagers.

Retief ruled an undivided company for only five months. In September, when the United Laagers numbered perhaps three thousand folk, the leaders quarrelled irremediably. Potgieter and Piet Uys, who had just come up with a large clan, were furious that Retief and Maritz should have divided all the high offices in the company between them; nor could they agree on the destination of the Trek. Retief and Maritz intended to occupy Natal, a practically vacant territory furnished with a passable harbour, which Uys had already explored with his *Kommissie trek* in 1834 and the British Government had refused repeatedly to annex.[2] But Potgieter made up his mind to go to the Transvaal, and Uys repudiated the Trekker constitution and proposed to go down into Natal independently.[3]

Retief hurried on ahead with his own following and, leaving them at the head of the Drakensberg passes with orders to stay there till his return, rode down with a few friends to Port Natal, the only safe road for a stranger from beyond the Drakensberg to follow into Dingaan's Zululand. Taking one or two of the Natal English as guides, he rode on to Dingaan's "great place", and there obtained the promise of Natal on condition that he recovered royal cattle stolen by a rival Chief.[4] Returning to the High Veld to discharge his mission, he met the Trekkers pouring down the passes into Natal.

Retief also found that during his absence Potgieter and Uys had taken a line of their own. With 135 mounted men and a few Bantu followers they had gone against the Matabele, the one tribal enemy the Trekkers had to fear on the High Veld. They had beaten them in a nine days' running fight along the valley of the Marico River without the loss of a man (November 1837). Defeated thus in January and again in November by Boers and heavily assaulted by the Zulus in the interval, Msilikazi, the Matabele king, had drawn off northward into what is now Southern Rhodesia, leaving Potgieter to claim as his successor all the open country that lies between the eastern Transvaal mountains and the Kalahari desert, in addition to the northern half of the modern Free State which was already his.[5]

The High Veld was now in the hands of the Trekkers. If Retief could clinch his bargain with the Zulus, Natal would also be theirs and with it an outlet to the Indian Ocean free from British control. But their victory over the Matabele—Zulus like his own people—and their premature descent into Natal had thoroughly alarmed Dingaan, who had long been disquieted by the doings of these men with their

[1] *Vide supra*, pp. 307.
[2] Walker, *History of S. Africa*, pp. 185, 193, 198.
[3] *Natal Papers*, I, 103, 110.
[4] *Annals of Natal*, I, 359 *sqq.*; Preller, *Retief*, pp. 148 *sqq.*
[5] R 49/39 (Transvaal Archives), Bührmann Papers. See Walker, *The Great Trek*, pp. 158, 331.

guns and horses. He resolved to destroy them, and Retief soon gave him his opportunity.[1] When they had recovered the Zulu cattle, Retief and his men, a hundred all told including Hottentot attendants and a white lad from the Port as interpreter, rode down by the direct but forbidden route to claim the cession of Natal. They had been warned of the danger they ran, but they took the risk. Dingaan signed a document ceding to the "Emigrant South Afrikans" the country between the Tugela and the Umzimvubu rivers, and then, having thus enticed the over-confident Boers unarmed into his presence, he turned and slaughtered them all. On the same day, 6 February 1838, he dispatched his impis to fall upon the scattered Boer laagers in Natal.[1] In some cases the Boers put up a successful defence, but in others they were overwhelmed. Some of the English settlers moved up with their Native levies to bring help from the coast, and Potgieter and Uys came down from the mountains; but the English met with complete disaster, Uys was trapped and killed, and Potgieter withdrew. In April 1838 the Zulus reached the coast and actually occupied Port Natal.[2]

The fate of Natal, the main object of the Trekkers' ambitions, hung in the balance. Most of the British settlers and their magistrate, and all the missionaries, English and American, had fled the country: the Natal Boers, some 3500 in all, had lost fully 350 slain and were cooped up in laager, and the whole territory was at the mercy of the savages. This tragic series of events convinced the Cape Government that, to avert worse disasters, it would have to intervene.

Governor D'Urban, who had tried to stop the Trek by persuasion and such hasty measures of reform as were in his power, had failed, and early in 1838 had been superseded by Sir George Napier, like him a veteran soldier of Wellington's Peninsular campaigns. Though he had seen much military service, the governorship of the Cape was Napier's first important civil post. He brought to it common sense, balanced judgment and a strong sense of fair play, valuable qualities for dealing with the confused and dangerous problems arising out of the Trek which were to occupy him during the whole tenure of his office (January 1838–March 1844).

What had happened was already clear in broad outline. Europeans had dispersed themselves thinly in a great arc running up from the old Eastern Frontier border districts through the open plains of what is now the Free State and thence down to the sea in Natal. Already there was a scattering of Trekkers beyond the Vaal with the promise of more to follow, but the fact that mattered was that the thin European line curved round the solid mass of Bantu in Kaffirland and Basutoland and thrust down to the Indian Ocean between the

[1] For detailed references for this episode. see Walker, *History of S. Africa*, p. 215 n.
[2] *Annals of Natal*, I, 227, 233, 241, 370, 399 *sqq*.

tribesmen in Pondoland and Zululand. All along that line contact between Europeans and Bantu threatened to produce friction with inevitable trouble on the colonial frontiers now weakened by the departure of fighting Boers, whose commandos had furnished a mobile force for their defence.

Napier was determined to put a stop to trekking if he could, and at first he replied upon his predecessor's policy of enlisting the help of the Dutch Reformed clergy to check an exodus which they condemned as a barbarising process.[1] He did all he could to persuade the Trekkers to return home; but soon, realising that they would not listen, he proposed to stop the Trek, or at least to control it, by more forcible methods. He believed that the first step towards the achievement of either end must be the establishment of a British administration at Port Natal subordinated to the Government at the Cape. At first Lord Glenelg, the Colonial Secretary, refused to accept this new responsibility, but, when news of the bloodshed in Natal reached England, he gave way so far as to permit Napier to send a detachment of the 72nd Regiment to Port Natal to restore order.[2]

Napier's hundred Highlanders arrived at Port Natal too late to avert further fighting. Maritz was dead, but reinforcements had reached the laagers from the Colony and the High Veld, and Andries Pretorius of Graaff-Reinet had hurried to Natal to take the lead before the British could intervene. Just before the troops arrived, he invaded Zululand.

Pretorius's commando was less than five hundred strong, but in spite of the disasters of the early months of the year, it advanced with cautious confidence. The Boers knew their superiority in the field. They had two styles of fighting, either firing from the saddle in the open or from behind the cover of the laager, a ring of heavy waggons lashed end to end with thorn-bushes piled between the wheels. Their guns and horses gave them an advantage over Bantu tribesmen, who, with hardly an exception at that time, had no missile weapons other than their assegais. Even the smooth-bore Trekker flintlocks had twice the range of assegais and, loaded with slugs, were deadly at close quarters. The Bantu had no chance against the Boers unless they could surprise them, as the Zulus and Matabele had each done once, or trap them in broken country, as the Zulus had trapped Uys.

The affair at Vechtkop had been a running fight followed by a struggle round the waggons; the Mosega and Marico battles had been fought entirely in the open; the fight in which Pretorius now defeated Dingaan's main army was a laager battle followed by a mounted pursuit.[3] The commando advanced for several days into Zululand and

[1] Engelbrecht, S. P., *Geschiedenis van de Nederduits Hervormde Kerk in Zuid-Afrika*, I, 1839[4], Dryer, A., *Die Kaapse Kerk en die Groot Trek*, p. 9.

[2] C.O. 1327 (Cape Archives), Glenelg to Napier, 13 January 1839; *Annals of Natal*, I, 398, 418.

[3] *Annals of Natal*, I, 234, 243, 438, 492; Preller, *Voortrekkermense*, I, 48, 178, II, 261; III, 100.

formed laager in a strong position on the banks of the Blood River.[1] Two sides of the square were covered by deep water, the other two were strengthened by a couple of small canon. There, on December 16, a Sunday, the defenders beat off thousands of the fearless savage warriors for two hours and then routed them by a mounted sortie. They killed three thousand Zulus at the cost of only three of their own men wounded, a terrible revenge for the earlier Boer disasters.

The victory by no means ended the Zulu power; nevertheless, it was the turning-point of the Great Trek. It stimulated the emigration from the Cape Colony, gave the Trekkers confidence, and set the Natalians free to organise Natal as the first of the Trekker republics. The English survivors at Port Natal had already given up to them such rights as they had, and now Captain Jervis, the British officer commanding there, took steps to mediate peace between the republic and Dingaan. The Great Chief promised to hand over the guns and horses he had captured and a huge herd of cattle and, by a clause that was not disclosed to Jervis, St Lucia Bay and the southern half of Zululand also (May 1839). The Natalians founded their capital of Pietermaritzburg and one or two other villages; landdrosts and the other familiar frontier officials took office, a Volksraad assembled, and the Trekkers began to scatter cautiously to their farms.[2] Moreover, in terms of the oath of perpetual remembrance taken by Pretorius and his commando before the Blood River battle, they first built the little Church of the Vow, which survives in Pietermaritzburg as a Trekker museum, and thenceforward regularly celebrated the anniversary of their deliverance as Dingaan's Day, thereby setting up a tradition that was to be observed by many generations of South Africans.

In December, Napier reluctantly recalled the British troops from Port Natal.[3] Pretorius promptly played off the faction which followed Dingaan's brother, Panda, against that which followed the king, and had the satisfaction of seeing the Zulu military machine broken and Dingaan driven to his death in Swaziland (February 1840). Panda became a vassal king, and paid an even heavier indemnity in cattle than his brother had promised to pay a few months before. Pretorius then came to terms with Potgieter. The huge district of Potchefstroom north of the Vaal, in which Potgieter had fixed his headquarters, and his territory of Vet River (Winburg) south of that river, joined a loose federation under the hegemony of Natal. Thus for a few years was realised, at all events on paper, the dream of that High Veld republic with an outlet to the Indian Ocean which was to haunt republican presidents to the end.

The Natal Volksraad now asked Napier to recognise the new

[1] Pretorius had a good eye for a defensive position.

[2] For the history of republican Natal see *Voortrekker Wetgewing...*, *Notule van die Natalse Volksraad*, 1839–45 (ed. Preller, G. S.); *Annals of Natal*; *Natal Papers*; Walker, E. A., *The Great Trek*, pp. 166 *sqq*.

[3] *Annals of Natal*, I, 547.

republic. At the moment independence seemed to be within reach. It is true that both the Marquis of Normanby and Lord John Russell, Glenelg's successors in the office of Colonial Secretary in the reconstituted Melbourne ministry, had begun to swing away from the old policy of intervention alternating with withdrawal.[1] A growing realisation of the commercial value of Natal, especially of its coal in relation to the route to India,[2] and the knowledge that it was useless to expect the Trekkers to come home again had inclined them both towards annexation; then, the news of further bloodshed in Zululand and the comments of "Mr Over-Secretary" James Stephen thereon had impelled Russell to instruct Napier to occupy the Port again or, failing that, some commanding position near by.[3] To this, however, Napier had demurred. The situation on the eastern frontier of the Cape Colony was precarious; he could hardly hope to reoccupy the Port without fighting and for that he had no troops to spare. Hence, when the Natal Volksraad asked for independence, he invited them to put forward precise proposals (September-November 1840).[4]

At this stage the republic's handling of its native policy played its decisive part in bringing about, first, indirect and then direct British intervention.[5] The Natalians' problem was essentially the old problem of the colonial frontier districts. Some four thousand Europeans, men, women and children, must find means of living in security on widely scattered farms with just enough Native labour on the spot for their needs, but not so much as would embarrass them. The underlying principle of the policy was racial segregation. Subject Chiefs like Panda were allowed to rule their own people in reserves which they held during good behaviour, but they must keep them within those reserves and not make war without leave. Blacks who were not under the rule of a recognised Chief were held in check by a stringent pass-law, and were ordered to contract for service with new masters within a fortnight of leaving their old employers. No coloured person might carry a gun or ride a horse or take a drink of intoxicating liquor without leave of his master. Labour was to be shared out equally at the rate of five native families to each farm, save that the Head Commandant might have ten, and unwanted Natives must quit areas in which Europeans might settle.

Besides this source of labour there were the Native apprentices, that is, orphans or children hired out by their parents. This practice had long persisted in the Cape Colony, and the Natal Volksraad did its

[1] On imperial policy, see Morrell, W. P., *British Colonial Policy in the Age of Peel and Russell*; also Bell, K. N. and Morrell, W. P., *Select Documents on Brit. Col. Policy*, 1830–60.

[2] Uys, C. J., *In the Era of Shepstone*, p. 8.

[3] C.O. 1327 (Cape Archives), Russell to Napier, 23 Dec. 1839; *Annals of Natal*, I, 525, 605, 626.

[4] *Annals of Natal*, I, 618 *sqq*.

[5] For republican Natal native policy, see *Voort. Wetgewing...*, *Notule* (ed. Preller, G. S.) *passim*; Agar-Hamilton, J. A. I., *The Native Policy of the Voortrekkers*.

best to exercise the legal control that could alone prevent it from degenerating into "virtual slavery"; but the system, in common with other sides of Trekker native policy, called for administration of the strongest kind, and in Natal administration was weak and erratic.

It was abuse of the apprenticeship system, combined with an indirect threat to the peace of the weakly held eastern frontier of the Colony, that set the troops moving once more towards Port Natal. Pretorius led a commando to the south-west border of Natal to recover missing cattle. The commando ran amok, carried off cattle and child apprentices, and thereby drove a neighbouring Pondo Chief, Faku, and the Rev Thomas Jenkins, his Wesleyan missionary, to appeal to Cape Town for protection.[1] Napier was loath to intervene, but he could not ignore Faku, who had been a "friend" of the Cape Government since D'Urban's day, nor overlook the danger of strife in the coast belt. He sent a small force to occupy a position in Faku's country close to the Natal border, declined to consider further the Volksraad's request for recognition, and asked the Secretary of State for orders.[2]

Russell now gave Napier general frontier instructions authorising him to send Agents and promises of protection to such Chiefs as desired them, and also to offer the Natalians the commercial privileges that still remained under the Navigation Acts if they would admit the troops.[3] Napier, however, made no move till a further manifestation of Trekker native policy obliged him to act. The Natalians had long realised that their social system, which could only survive in fixity and isolation, was threatened by the influx of clans that came out of hiding as soon as the Zulus had been broken and by Zulu refugees who poured south-westwards across the Tugela. At last the Volksraad decided to draft redundant Natives wholesale into lands that were partially occupied by Faku's Pondos. At this renewed threat to the peace of the coast belt Napier ordered the detachment up from the Natal border to the Port.[4]

The British troops reoccupied Port Natal in May 1842, and this time they had to fight for it.[5] Potchefstroom and Winburg and even the northern section of Natal virtually stood aside, but the southern Natalians were reinforced by Jan Mocke and three hundred men from Transorangia, the unorganised territory that lay between the Cape Colony and Winburg. Encouraged also by expectations of Netherlands aid held out to them by Johan Smellekamp, supercargo of the *Brazilia*, a Dutch vessel that had recently visited the Port, they

[1] *Annals of Natal*, I, 249, 631 *sqq.*, 646; *Voort. Wetgewing*, pp. 76, 86.

[2] *Annals of Natal*, I, 634.

[3] *Annals of Natal*, I, 640, 643.

[4] *Ibid.* I, 660.

[5] For the second British occupation of Natal, see Bird, *Annals of Natal*, II, and Chase, *Natal Papers*, II, *passim*.

besieged the troops till the arrival of a relieving force by sea compelled them to disperse. The Rump Volksraad submitted in July.

It was doubtful for some time whether Great Britain would retain Natal. Lord Stanley, Secretary of State in the new Peel ministry, had gone back from Lord John Russell's policy to the policy of spasmodic intervention combined with prayers to the Trekkers to come home that Lord Glenelg had favoured. He had at first ordered Napier to withdraw the troops, but on hearing of the heavy fighting and perusing the Governor's singularly blunt protest, he bade him hold on for the time being.[1] The matter had to be handled carefully. The recent scramble for Western Australia, New Zealand, Tahiti and the Marquesas Islands witnessed to the fact that Anglo-French relations in Far Eastern seas were difficult, and the Foreign Office believed that there were French interests behind the *Brazilia*.[2] This knowledge, and the growing turbulence engendered north of the Orange by tidings of strife in Natal, decided Stanley to hold on and to strengthen the Cape garrison. Napier made a naval demonstration off the Natal coast and sent Henry Cloete, a Capetown lawyer of old family, to effect the promised settlement (May-June 1843).

Cloete had hard work to do this. The Hollander, Smellekamp, had appeared at Port Natal once more just before his arrival, and though he had been moved on to Delagoa Bay by Major Smith, the commander of the British troops, and had been disowned by the Netherlands Government, many Natalians and their friends on the High Veld still believed that he had help to offer them.[3] The terms Cloete had to propose were not tempting. There was to be no colour bar and no large grants of land, and it was precisely to make sure of abundant land and the maintenance of "proper relations between master and servant" that the Trekkers had trekked.

The Natal Government was rent by quarrels and might be going to pieces, but some of its burghers favoured resistance to Napier's demands. They were supported in this determination by their wives and by six hundred stalwarts from the High Veld. In the end, however, the High Velders withdrew as soon as they learned that Cloete proposed to stop short at the Drakensberg mountains; the Volksraad accepted the proffered terms, and Cloete, having secured from Panda the cession of St Lucia Bay, turned to face the interlocked problems of land title and the influx of Zulus from beyond the Tugela (August 1843).[4]

The Republican Government survived its submission for more than two years while British troops stood guard over the capital and the Port, and the imperial authorities discussed the nature of the future

[1] *Annals of Natal*, I, 701; II, 43, 46, 103.
[2] *Ibid.* II, 171; Morrell, *Brit. Col. Policy*, p. 142; Uys, C. J., *Shepstone*, p. 19.
[3] *Annals of Natal*, II, 169 *sqq.*, 239.
[4] *Ibid.* II, 265, 299.

administration. It was only in December 1845 that a Lieutenant-Governor arrived and the Natal Republic ceased to exist. The new British authorities were less ambitious than Pretorius had been. They abandoned to the Pondos a large block of land to the south-west of the Port, dropped the claim to suzerainty over Panda and fixed the boundary between Natal and Zululand along the Tugela and Buffalo Rivers. The claim to St Lucia Bay was not exercised but was allowed to lie dormant for a generation.[1] What remained of Natal after its boundaries had been thus restricted became a detached district of the Cape Colony with a subordinate administration of a simple kind.[2]

Though circumstances had compelled it to annex this new territory, the Imperial Government had limited its liabilities as far as possible. It had resolved to control the Trekkers in Natal because they might harm wide imperial interests, but elsewhere it disclaimed all responsibility for its errant subjects; the "emigrant farmers" beyond the Drakensberg and the Orange might do as they would. Such was the proclaimed attitude of unconcern as late as May 1844;[3] but long before that time, in actual fact, the reluctant British administration had embarked upon a long and irresolute process of intervention beyond the Cape Colony's northern border that was to reach its logical conclusion in Sir Harry Smith's proclamation of the Queen's sovereignty from the Orange to the Vaal in February 1848. The events which led to this intervention were contemporary with the events in neighbouring Natal which have just been described. Necessarily they had a mutual reaction.

Sir George Napier made the first move in September 1842. At that time the northern half of the present Orange Free State consisted of the unstable republican district of Winburg wedged in between Pretorius's Natal and Potgieter's Potchefstroom. But it was the southern half, Transorangia, that interested Napier more directly. Not only had Transorangians taken part in the recent fighting in Natal, but trouble was brewing up between them and their Native and half-breed neighbours in Transorangia itself. Trekkers and pre-Trek Boers competed with one another for farms in Adam Kok's Griqua state of Philippolis to the north of the Orange River,[4] while beyond the Griqua borders men subject to no Government whatever, even in name, occupied land as they chose right up to the Winburg frontier.

Confusion was spreading eastward, too, from Transorangia into the Caledon River valley where Moshesh the Basuto was the strongest

[1] *Vide infra*, p. 530.
[2] Letters Patent, 31 May 1844; Proclamation, 21 August 1845; *Annals of Natal*, II, 394, 465.
[3] *Ibid*, II, 381.
[4] For history of the Griquas, see Orpen, J. M., *Reminiscences of Life in South Africa*; Lindley, A. F., *Adamantia*; Arnot, D. and Orpen, F. H. S., *The Land Question of Griqualand West*; Stow, G. W., *The Native Races of South Africa*.

Chief.[1] He had long been gathering scattered clans round his impregnable rock fortress of Thaba Bosigo, and laying claim to a belt of land running northward to the Vaal, and to another strip of cornland to the west of the Caledon, the most desirable part of the future Free State. His outposts were already in the cornlands intermingled with the subjects of rival Chiefs and, on the outskirts, with Boers who had drifted up singly from the frontier districts of Cape Colony. In the upper Caledon valley Sikonyela's Batlokwa were at feud with his Basuto. In the middle valley half-breed and Bantu Chiefs, such as Moroko of Thaba Nchu, and their Wesleyan missionaries claimed land and independence, while Moshesh and the Paris Evangelical missionaries, on whose advice he sometimes relied, claimed, and in Bantu law claimed justly, that they were Basuto vassals. In the lower valley there were Boers who coveted the cornlands and even Basutoland itself for its immunity from the horse sickness, while Moshesh, on his side, insisted that the Boers were allowed in his lands only by his grace and began to give broad hints that they should resume their trek to the republican north.[2]

In such a troubled land there was clearly danger of serious conflict. Napier therefore appealed to Lord Stanley for permission either to annex Transorangia and so control it, or to make treaties with the leading Chiefs so as to offer them some support.[3] He had been driven to make this suggestion by the activities of Jan Mocke, the leader of the Transorangians, who had taken part in the fighting against the British at Port Natal in May 1842. On his return from that unsuccessful venture Mocke had boasted that help was coming from the King of the Netherlands, who was said to have appealed to France and other Powers,[4] and that then the Boers would take up arms against the redcoats. Presently, regardless both of the interests of the hostile pre-Trek Boers and of Adam Kok, he moved down to Alleman's Drift on the Orange River to proclaim a republic. He was forestalled by Judge William Menzies, who was holding the circuit court at Colesberg on the colonial side of the river. Well knowing that he was exceeding his powers, Menzies, in words carefully chosen to avoid committing the Governor, took possession for the Queen of all the lands within the limits of the Punishment Act save the dominions of Portugal and of native rulers (October 1842).[5]

It was a magnificent gesture, but it was not practical politics. Napier, faced with the unwelcome choice between disavowing Menzies' action and confirming it in defiance of his instructions to

[1] For history of the Basuto, see *Basutoland Records*, ed. Theal, G. M.; Orpen, J. M., *Reminiscences*, and *History of the Basutos of South Africa*.

[2] *Basutoland Records*, I, I *sqq.*, 36 *sqq.*

[3] C.O. 1450 (Cape Archives), Napier to Stanley, 15 September 1842; *Basutoland Records*, I, 49.

[4] *Annals of Natal*, II, 116, 138; C.O. 1362 (Cape Archives), Hare to Napier, 9 March 1843. Enclosure.

[5] C.O. 1374 (Cape Archives), Menzies to Napier, 16, 23 and 28 October 1842.

annex nothing, disavowed it.[1] But since Mocke persisted in proclaiming his republic and thereby disturbed both the Griquas on one side of the river and the colonial farmers on the other, Napier sent a strong force of regulars up to Colesberg and, when the main body was withdrawn, stationed detachments there and at Cradock in the restive border districts (December 1842–February 1843).[2]

This show of British force, the first so far to the north, had a quietening effect and so impressed the Caledon River Chiefs that when Potgieter came down from Potchefstroom to sound them, neither Moshesh nor his neighbour, Moroko, would work with him.[3] Then, at the close of April 1843, Napier not only received instructions from Lord Stanley, as we have seen, to arrange for the annexation of Natal, but also permission to make treaties with the Transorangian Chiefs if necessary.[4] In June the 7th Dragoons arrived to enable him to guard the lengthening eastern and north-eastern frontiers. The Governor, however, postponed action in the north for a time, while Mocke and his friends tried to prevent the Natalians from coming to terms with Henry Cloete. When, however, Natal had submitted and the pro-colony Transorangians had rallied, many of them later on even petitioning to be included in the Natal settlement,[5] Napier felt the time had come. In November and December 1843, he concluded treaties with Adam Kok and Moshesh similar to that which D'Urban had made with Waterboer in 1834. The borders of Basutoland were roughly defined for the first time, and both Chiefs undertook to preserve order and to enforce the Punishment Act in return for subsidies.[6]

The treaties solved nothing, and yet they committed the Colonial Government to intervene in the last resort in support of its Native allies. Intervention would almost certainly be called for if either Chief tried to exercise his new powers against white men. No Transorangian would submit to that without a struggle.

The treaties were followed by fifteen anxious months during which Mocke tried to unite Transorangia with Potchefstroom-Winburg, and Adam Kok clamoured for the protection of British troops. At length Kok tried to arrest a republican, as he claimed he had power to do in terms of his treaty. Even the pre-Trek Boers defied Griqua jurisdiction, a scuffling warfare broke out, and the Colesberg farmers in the north-eastern colony prepared to join in. To guard against this wide extension of disorder, British troops rode up post-haste from the eastern frontier in May 1845, crossed the Orange River, and scattered the hostile Transorangians at Zwartkopjes.[7]

[1] C.O. 1450 (Cape Archives), Napier to Stanley, 7 and 11 November, 13 December 1842.
[2] *Ibid.* 13 December 1842 and enclosures; Chase, *Natal Papers*, II, 266, 271.
[3] *Basutoland Records*, I, 51.
[4] C.O. 1331 (Cape Archives), Stanley to Napier, 15 January 1843.
[5] *Annals of Natal*, II, 329, 349.
[6] *Basutoland Records*, I, 55; *Papers re Kaffirs*, *Parl. Pap.* 1851, XXXVIII (424), pp. 214 *sqq*.
[7] C.O. 1451 (Cape Archives), Maitland to Stanley, 13 May 1845 and enclosures.

Hard on the heels of the dragoons came Sir Peregrine Maitland, the first Cape Governor to cross the Orange. Maitland, an Irishman who had seen much service during the long French wars and later in India, had relieved Napier in March 1844. He had had experience of civil administration as Lieutenant-Governor of Ontario and Nova Scotia, but he was apt to hesitate in the face of difficulties and then to act precipitately, and he was too old a man to be called upon to grapple with such a confused and dangerous situation as that on the High Veld.

The problem facing him was to give security to all the various new-comers in the disputed territory, to relieve white men of the hated jurisdiction of black and coloured Chiefs, and to provide some machinery for keeping the peace. He summoned the Transorangian Chiefs to Touwfontein in Kok's principality (June 1845)[1] and proposed that each should divide his territory into two parts: the one an inalienable reserve, and the other an alienable area in which Europeans might lease quit-rent farms. Each Chief should continue to rule his own people, but a British Resident was to deal with Europeans and keep the general peace with a few coloured troops and a stated number of warriors from each tribe. Short of the annexation of the territory and the assumption of complete responsibility to which the British Government would not consent, this was the best scheme that could be devised; certainly it marked the first partial extension of British authority beyond the Orange. A British Resident took up his quarters at Bloemfontein in the alienable portion of Philippolis in January 1846, but amid the mutual jealousies of the Chiefs and their missionaries, the scheme could not secure more than a very partial application. Only Adam Kok set aside any alienable territory worth mentioning.

Maitland hoped that his Touwfontein system might be extended over the whole area of the interior covered by the Punishment Act, for everywhere there was confusion caused by the second Trek that had been set in motion by Smellekamp's exhortations, the loss of Port Natal and St Lucia Bay, and the threat conveyed to Trekker independence by Napier's treaties. About the New Year of 1844 expeditions from all parts of the High Veld and from northern Natal tried to get through to Delagoa Bay, where Smellekamp was, or, failing that, to some other Portuguese east coast port. Fever and fly thwarted them. Undismayed, Potgieter set to work to build a republic from the Orange River to the limits of Portuguese pretensions.

Since Pretorius had failed in Natal, Potgieter stood out as the republican champion. His Potchefstroom-Winburg republic repudiated all connection with Natal and claimed a frontier that took in Transorangia "to the bank of the Great River", i.e. the Orange

[1] *Basutoland Records*, I, 93; C.O. 1451 (Cape Archives), Maitland to Stanley, 1 August 1845.

(April 1844).[1] Potgieter then made his way to Delagoa Bay without loss and, by arrangement with the Portuguese and a local Chief, acquired a great tract of land in the eastern Transvaal highlands where Lydenburg now stands.[2] He next tried to secure Transorangia and, failing in this, returned home to find that his Potchefstroomers had already begun to trek to the new lands. Thither he followed them in 1845. He set up his capital at Andries-Ohrigstad just beyond the sphere of the Punishment Act in touch with "Portugal" and, he hoped, safe from British interference.

Meanwhile the Natalians had begun to trek again. A few stalwarts had gone north after the Volksraad's submission in August 1843; then, as the months passed, as the tide of colour rose and as hopes of free land or even a share in their own government faded, others followed them by twos and threes. Some went only as far as Winburg or Potchefstroom, but the more influential of them pushed north to Ohrigstad. After the Zwartkopjes fight, the discontented Transorangians fled north to Winburg or even across the Vaal, and so, all along the line, 1845–6 saw Trekkers edging away northward towards the Transvaal, the refuge of the die-hards of the Great Trek.

While Natal, Basutoland and Transorangia were thus involved in mutual troubles, Maitland's hopes of extending his Touwfontein scheme northward were blasted by the outbreak of a new Kaffir war in the old storm centre on the eastern frontier of Cape Colony. Fear of such a war had hampered every successive governor in his handling of the problems raised by the Trek, and now, when war came, it tied the hands of the British authorities for two critical years.

This war, the War of the Axe (1846–7), marked the final breakdown of the so-called Stockenstrom treaty system that had been instituted in the abandoned Queen Adelaide Province and the Ceded Territory in December 1836. That system was really part of the general treaty system that D'Urban and Napier had set on foot. It presupposed military force sufficient to keep the peace, and time for civilising influences to permeate the tribes and perhaps to bring them at last willingly under British rule.[3] Troops were not forthcoming in sufficient numbers to keep the peace on such a difficult frontier, though so long as Stockenstrom was on the spot as Lieutenant-Governor the treaties answered better than has commonly been allowed. But, in September 1838, Stockenstrom handed over to the rather ineffective Colonel John Hare, and the system gradually collapsed.[4] It had many critics

[1] C.O. 1382 (Cape Archives), Maitland to Stanley, 16 July 1844. Enclosure.

[2] Minutes, Ohrigstad Volksraad, 20 Aug. 1845, 15 May 1846 (Transvaal Archives); Stuart, J., *De Hollandsche Afrikanen*, pp. 181–3; Cachet, F. L., *De Worstelstrijd der Transvalers*, pp. 292 *sqq*.

[3] *Report of Select Committee re Aborigines*, *Parl. Pap.* 1836, VII (538), pp. 183 *sqq*., 248; Stockenstrom to Fairbairn, 29 Oct. 1840 (Gubbins Collection in the library of the University of the Witwatersrand, Johannesburg), see Walker, *History of South Africa*, p. 221.

[4] For breakdown of Treaty system, see *Further Papers re Kaffir War*, 1851, XXXVIII (424), *passim*; also *S. A. Commercial Advertiser* and *Grahamstown Journal*, *passim*.

—some of the officials on the frontier and in Cape Town, the majority of the frontiersmen, both Afrikaner and British, and, at the last, Stockenstrom's own successor, who held that, since Kaffirland was now ringed round by Europeans, it ought to be broken up. The murders of Hottentot herdsmen and the much rarer murders of Europeans, inevitable on all such Native frontiers, were ascribed solely to the independent tribesmen, together with the still more inevitable losses of unguarded stock in a thinly peopled and unfenced land cut across by rocky valleys and infested with wild beasts.

Some of the Chiefs for their part lost heart after Stockenstrom's departure and made no attempt to restore stolen cattle; others failed to restrain their subjects, and all felt themselves threatened when frontier officials scored up against them missing beasts which could not lawfully be claimed under the treaties.

Napier visited the frontier twice. On the first occasion he allayed excitement by a show of force, and on both modified the treaties in detail with the consent of the Chiefs and with good results (December 1840). But he upheld the system as a whole. Doubtless there were thefts, but the average value of frontier farms was rising as sheep took the place of cattle and the general prosperity of the Colony increased.[1] In any event, time must be gained to give the civilising policy a chance, and the treaties were the only alternative to a renewed policy of reprisals, which would breed another war expensive to the British exchequer and irritating to the mass of the non-frontier burghers who were liable to be called out on commando. In June 1843, just when affairs in Natal were reaching a crisis, the situation on the eastern frontier became so serious that Napier, with the consent of Sandile, the Gaika Chief, expelled an unruly chieftain from the Ceded Territory, regarrisoned Fort Willshire on the Keiskamma, and built a new fort between that river and the Fish. Matters drifted on during the rest of his governorship, and soon after taking office Maitland visited the borderlands to examine the problem on the spot. Partly by persuasion and partly by a show of force he induced the Chiefs to agree to important changes in the treaties. The tribes were left in occupation of the Ceded Territory, but only during good behaviour and not of right. The door into Kaffirland was opened more widely to colonists in search of missing cattle, and troops were permitted to patrol and build forts as a protection against raiders right up to the borders of independent Kaffirland. To make things more secure Maitland also concluded treaties beyond the Kei with Kreli the Galeka, Paramount Chief of the Xhosas, and with the Pondo Chief Faku, whose rule he recognised over a large "treaty state" on the western confines of Natal (October 1844).[2]

[1] *Parl. Pap.* 1851, XXXVIII (424), p. 35; Stretch, L.S., "Memorandum", 1846 (Gubbins Collection), see Walker, *op. cit.* p. 221.

[2] *Parl. Pap.* 1851, XXXVIII (424), pp. 227 *sqq.*

All this treaty-making was in vain, for within a few months both sides, native and white, were moving rapidly towards war, a war avowedly for land. What was left of the treaty system went by the board bit by bit; Grahamstown rejoiced openly that the parcelling out of Kaffirland was coming soon; the Gaikas, Tembus and Galekas closed their ranks in fear of a break-up,[1] and the last of a series of border "incidents" precipitated open war. An old Kaffir thief charged with stealing an axe was being carried to Grahamstown for trial when he was forcibly rescued by a party of Natives from beyond the border, and a Hottentot who had been manacled to him was murdered (March 1846). The colonial forces marched into Kaffirland and "the War of the Axe" began.

The war ran its course much as D'Urban's Kaffir war had done, but it lasted longer and was waged on a much more extensive scale. The cost to the colony and the British taxpayer was very heavy, for the operations dragged on indecisively for twenty-one months and, at one time, Governor Maitland had 3200 regulars in the field besides some 11,000 burghers and friendly Natives. The forces, far from their base, were hampered by costly and defective transport, by lack of water, and by endless bickering between the colonists, whom the regulars despised for the lack of discipline, and the regulars, whom the colonists accused of stiffness and lack of adaptability. In this last respect at least the campaign resembled the fighting on the North American frontier a century before and the Maori wars that were just beginning in New Zealand.[2] Maitland laid down his command in January 1847, and Sir Henry Pottinger, another Irishman who had seen both diplomacy and fighting in the service of the East India Company, took over the leadership. He brought the operations to an inconclusive end in some eleven months of obscure fighting[3] before he was in turn superseded in December 1847 by a new Governor, Sir Harry Smith.

Smith, who was to leave his mark deep in South African history, was the last of the line of Peninsular veterans who held the Governorship. He was no new-comer to the problems of the frontier, for he had won his experience there as D'Urban's right-hand man in the thirties.[4] After eleven years' residence in the colony he had passed on to India as adjutant-general and now returned as the hero of the First Sikh War and as an old friend. He held greater powers than any governor before him, for he was also the Queen's High Commissioner in South Africa, authorised to deal with affairs in territories beyond the

[1] Stretch to Fairbairn, 7 Nov. 1844, and Stretch, "Memorandum", 1846 (Gubbins Collection), see Walker, *History of South Africa*, p. 235; Macmillan, W. M., *Bantu, Boer and Briton*, p. 238.

[2] See *C.H.B.E.* vol. VII, Pt. II, p. 136.

[3] For the War of the Axe, see *Correspondence...re Kaffir Tribes*, *Parl. Pap.* 1847, XXXVIII [786]; *Papers re Kaffirs*, 1847–8, XLIII [912, 969]; Pottinger's *Despatch* 154 *of* 1847 (Cape Blue-Book); Cory, G. E., *The Rise of South Africa*, vols. IV, V.

[4] *Vide supra*, pp. 317 *sqq*.

Queen's acknowledged dominion but "adjacent or contiguous to" the borders of the colony. The circumstances of the Trek had made this new office essential, and Pottinger had been the first High Commissioner to be appointed,[1] but Smith was the first who was free to use the new powers. With all the energy of his impulsive nature he availed himself of them to bring about a general South African settlement.

The High Commissioner's first task was to deal with the eastern frontier of the colony and here he largely re-established D'Urban's rejected scheme of twelve years before.[2] He annexed the remains of the Ceded Territory outright and named them Victoria East. Fingos were settled in the northern half and protected by a screen of villages of time-expired soldiers, and the rest of the land was sold as farms. Smith also annexed what had been Queen Adelaide Province as a separate imperial dependency under the name of British Kaffraria, and compelled the recognition of the Queen's sovereignty along the mission road beyond the Kei which ensured land communications between the Cape and Natal.

In the north the Governor carried the frontier of Cape Colony up to the Orange along nearly all its length,[3] and then, having thus rounded off the territory under his full administration, he took up the far more difficult task of dealing with the Trekkers beyond the river and the scattering of Griquas among whom they were dispersed. The ring of so-called "treaty states" just beyond the colonial border had no real existence save on paper, and the ill-defined authority of the British Resident in Transorangia was precarious. Not that republican institutions were in better state, for there was anarchy in Winburg; beyond the Vaal the scattered groups of Boers at Potchefstroom and Ohrigstad were at feud with one another and their Native neighbours alike, and some of them were already on the move again into the northern wilds of the Zoutspanberg, while the Trekkers who had remained in Natal were already retracing their steps up the mountain passes.

The confusion that reigned beyond the Orange convinced Smith that he must either withdraw the Resident from Bloemfontein or else make British rule a reality. After a momentary hesitation he chose the latter alternative.[4] His friendly welcome by Moshesh and many of the Boers in Transorangia and even in republican Winburg heartened him, and having first frightened Adam Kok into parting with the remnants of his jurisdiction over the Griquas in the alienable portion of his lands in return for a small pension, he passed on to deal with Pretorius and his Natalians. He found them camped in the

[1] For the terms of appointment of the High Commissioner, see *Papers re Kaffirs*, *Parl. Pap.* 1847–8, XLIII [912], p. 5.

[2] *Vide supra*, pp. 317 *sqq*; and see *Papers re Kaffirs*, *Parl. Pap.* 1847–8, XLIII [969], for Smith's Kaffrarian settlement.

[3] *Ibid.* pp. 22, 55.

[4] *Correspondence re O. R. Territory*, *Parl. Pap.* 1852–3, LXVI [1646], p. 22.

rain at the foot of the Drakensberg, angry and depressed. The same forces that had driven them from the old Colony ten or twelve years before were still working in their minds. To dismay at the refusal of their new British rulers to impose a pass-law or to recognise any colour-bar in a country where tribesmen were far more numerous and dangerous than they had been in the Colony, was added bitter disappointment at the land settlement arranged by Cloete;[1] while, over and above these general grievances was the wrath of Pretorius, who, towards the close of the War of the Axe, had journeyed to Grahamstown to state the Natalians' case to Sir Henry Pottinger, and had been refused an interview by the harassed Governor. However, Sir Harry Smith was popular with the Trekkers for old times' sake, and they listened courteously to what he had to say in the long conferences round the camp-fires. By the promise of the immediate grant of full-sized farms to all who could prove their claims, and of similar farms to others who engaged to remain on them for seven years, he induced a few of the Trekkers to turn back into Natal. But the great majority would not listen. A few turned eastward and crossed the Buffalo River to found a little republic (Utrecht) on land granted them by Panda; the rest plodded away up the mountain road either northwards to Ohrigstad or north-westwards with Pretorius to Potchefstroom.

While the Natalians were still hesitating on the banks of the Tugela, Smith took a decisive step, for he hoped that the High Veld Boers would still admit their British citizenship even after twelve long years in the wilderness. He persuaded Pretorius to sound the "emigrant farmers" beyond the Vaal; but before he received their answer, thinking the action would be popular, he proclaimed the Queen's sovereignty over all, white, coloured and black, in the territories between the Orange, the Vaal and the Drakensberg Mountains (February 1848).[2] The proclamation of the Sovereignty was avowedly the sequel to Maitland's Touwfontein scheme. Great Britain must either take full control of the Trek, or leave the Trekkers and the tribes to fight it out. Even Earl Grey, the Colonial Secretary, had had to face that fact a year before,[3] and now it fell to Smith to take the last definite step towards control, which was neither so impulsive nor so rash as has sometimes been alleged. He returned to Cape Town hoping that he had linked Natal to the parent Colony by a territory in which the Queen's writ would run unopposed. And so it might have been but for Pretorius.

As soon as the High Commissioner had left the north, Pretorius tried repeatedly to raise the Winburgers by urging that Smith had

[1] *Annals of Natal*, II, 191, 279, 450 *sqq.*; *Correspondence re...settlement of Natal. Parl. Pap.* 1847–8, XLII [980], pp. 184 *sqq.*, 196, 212.

[2] *Parl. Pap.* 1848, XLIII [969], pp. 56, 63.

[3] C.O. 49/40, Grey to Pottinger, 4 Dec. 1846; de Kiewiet, C. W., *British Colonial Policy and the South African Republics*, 1848–72, p. 30.

no right to annex them, and when his efforts at persuasion failed, he called in the Transvaalers to compel them to rise. Potgieter was opposed to any such adventure, but Pretorius won over enough adherents in Potchefstroom to add to his own Natalians and invade the Sovereignty in the republican cause. As he marched south, his force was gradually swelled with willing and unwilling recruits until some 1200 men in all were under his command. There was no resistance to his progress, for the British Resident, Major Warden, had no effective force at his disposal and surrendered Bloemfontein without a blow. Pretorius put Warden across the Orange River and evidently hoped that that would be the end of the Sovereignty. He was mistaken. Sir Harry was not the man to submit to open defiance. He marched north with a strong force of regulars, reinforced it with some Transorangian burghers and Griquas, and after a brisk action dispersed the dwindling commando at Boomplaats midway between the Orange and Modder Rivers (29 August 1848). Pretorius fled across the Vaal with a remnant of his followers, and Smith was left to proclaim the Orange River Sovereignty once more as part of the Queen's dominions.[1]

Thus, by August 1848, Sir Harry Smith had possessed himself of the southern reaches of the Trekkers' Road that ran up from the Cape Colony to the Vaal drifts and the passes of the Drakensberg. Below the passes, Natal, now practically emptied of its Boer inhabitants, was under British rule, while, beyond the Vaal, the most determined of the Trekkers had reached the northernmost limits of their dispersion by the occupation of the Zoutpansberg. The outlines of the new territories of Natal, the Orange Free State and the Transvaal were already discernible. So far as such a movement can be said to have had an end, the Boomplaats campaign marked the end of the Great Trek.

(*b*) Control or Withdrawal? 1848–1856

The half-dozen years that followed Sir Harry Smith's apparently permanent settlement were among the most fateful in the history of South Africa. Save for a few Griqua and Bantu territories and some scattered groups of cattle farmers beyond the Vaal, the whole of the future Union of South Africa was under British rule and, therefore, open to the influence of the liberal Britain of the day operating mainly through the more or less liberalised Cape Colony. That fact was potentially of the utmost political and social importance. Politically, the republican form of government by Volksraad had as yet had only a brief career; in Natal and Winburg it had been swept away, and in the Transvaal it hardly existed except on paper. The Cape Colony, on the other hand, was already on the way to achieving parliamentary government after the usual colonial pattern. It might be assumed that

[1] *Papers re Natal, Parl. Pap.* 1849, XXXVI [1059], pp. 43, 61.

this system, and probably something like the new responsible government that was being evolved in Canada, would be established in due time wherever the Union Jack flew in southern Africa, though the conditions of Natal and the Orange River Sovereignty were primitive enough to make even the most enthusiastic Liberals pause.

Socially, the possibilities were even more pregnant. In D'Urban's day, Europeans had only had to find a *modus vivendi* with ex-slaves and Hottentots, the two sections of the Cape Coloured Folk within their own community; their relations with the Bantu, according to the segregation policy traditional since van Riebeeck's coming, had been a mere matter of frontier police work. But now Europeans everywhere had to face the problem of living beside and ruling tribal Bantu within the expanding Cape Colony and the new States they were making beyond its borders. The question at issue for South Africa was whether these relations were to accord with the liberal rules already fairly established in the original Colony, or with the rigid frontier ideas which the Trekkers had departed from that colony to preserve.

The story of the development of the Cape Parliament is told in the following chapter. Here it is sufficient to note that it was the deliberate work of imperial policy based on the notable social and economic advances made by the Colony between 1836 and 1853. During that period, the European population doubled in spite of the Great Trek, and revenue and trade expanded. Merino wool and Ichaboe guano, the prospect of copper in Namaqualand and the opening of inland markets by the Trekkers warranted increased expenditure on the machinery of government in Church and State. This improved machinery was not purely official as it had been in the days immediately preceding the Trek. Municipal councils, road boards, school committees, the Dutch Reformed Synod to which autonomy was granted in 1843, all were wholly or in part elective, and together they provided the training in local government and the physical or spiritual communications on which alone a sound system of self-government could be based. Thus, in a South Africa where no community was as yet either rich or populous, the Cape Colony was far and away the largest, wealthiest, most stable and, as ever, most closely in touch with the invigorating forces of the outer world. By adopting a colour-blind franchise for its municipalities in 1836 and for its parliament in 1853, it indeed widened the gulf that lay between itself and the Trekker republics; but that franchise was accepted as a matter of course in the western districts of the Colony, and although some easterners desired a higher franchise to exclude Bantu voters, a vagrancy law to control Coloured labour and separation from the West as a means to these and other ends, neither the dominant West nor the Imperial Government in the background was prepared to agree.

The Cape franchise of 1853 completed, as far as a political device could complete, the liberal solution of the Cape's original native problem begun by the Fiftieth Ordinance of 1828.[1] In so far as the Colony had an internal Bantu problem at the time of Sir Harry Smith's settlement, it was practically confined to the Fingos in Victoria East.[2] There, the main principles on which the future Cape Native Territories were to be ruled were already being established. The Fingos, assured of the two essentials, that is, land and skilled guidance by missionaries and officials, made marked progress and presently became a stabilising factor on the troubled eastern frontier.

Beyond that frontier lay the separate imperial dependency of British Kaffraria. This was to all intents and purposes a tribal reserve. Small European settlements were permitted around the forts, but everywhere else the tribes were left secure in their lands and under the rule of their Chiefs. They were subject, however, to the High Commissioner as "Great Chief", and to the general control of magistrates charged with the duty of seeing that nothing was done "inconsistent with justice and humanity". The weakness of the scheme was that the Chiefs were stripped of much of their authority and, in the absence of any considerable revenue, were given very little in exchange, while the magistrates, unable to apply the Roman-Dutch law of the Colony to tribesmen, were debarred from recognising tribal law and custom. They had to fall back on a mixture of martial law and common sense, altogether too much like the "Smith law" which Sir Harry himself had administered feverishly in D'Urban's Queen Adelaide Province in days gone by.[3]

After a time this system of personal government broke down in British Kaffraria. The Gaikas grew restive at the news that the Sovereignty men were pressing hard on Basutoland, a country that was really one with their own; they had long been resentful that some of their white magistrates refused to recognise certain of their most cherished and fundamental customs; a prophet arose among them who pointed to the anti-convict agitation then raging in the Colony (1849) as evidence that the white men were not wholly loyal to the "Great Chief".[4] The explosion came when Sir Harry Smith deposed the Gaika chief, Sandile, for contumacy, and placed his powers in the hands first of a European magistrate and then of a Xhosa nominee. The tribes refused to obey either, and when the governor sent up troops to arrest Sandile, they broke out into armed rebellion (December 1850). They mauled a column of troops, wiped out three of Smith's military villages, and cooped up the Governor himself for a time in one of the frontier forts.[5]

[1] *Vide supra*, pp. 295 *sqq*.

[2] For Smith's policy in Victoria East and British Kaffraria, see *Papers re Kaffirs*, *Parl. Pap.* 1848, XLIII [969], 1850, XXXVIII [1288].

[3] *Vide supra*, p. 301.

[4] *Vide infra*, pp. 377 *sqq*.

[5] For Kaffir War of 1850–3, see *Correspondence re Kaffirs*, *Parl. Pap.* 1851, XXXVIII [1334, 1352, 1380]; *Papers re Kaffir Tribes*, 1852, XXXIII [1428] and 1852–3, LXVI [1635]; *Report of Select Committee*, 1851, XIV (635); Cory, *Rise of S. Africa*, vol. v.

Smith was thus faced unexpectedly with an ugly situation which rapidly grew uglier. His garrison had been weakened by the recent despatch home of a battalion, and now the rebel Gaikas were joined successively by some of the Tembus, by many of the Kaffir police and Coloured Cape Mounted Rifles, and by numbers of Hottentots, landless men for the most part,[1] from the Kat River, Theopolis and Shiloh mission stations. Smith was dismayed that the Hottentots should join the Kaffirs, their hereditary foes, for in previous campaigns they had always given invaluable aid to the colonial forces; but, after all, they were discontented because they had not been treated as well as the burghers by whose side they had fought in the War of the Axe, and they listened to one Willem Uithaalder, who taught them that the time had come to strike a blow for the "Hottentot nation" of his dreams. Worse still, the commando system, which had shown ominous signs of weakening during the War of the Axe, broke down altogether. The burghers of the western districts were not even called out, and those of the threatened eastern districts responded badly. Some said they dared not leave their homes for fear of Kaffir raids, others that they had no mind to fight the Gaikas and then see Fingos and suchlike reap the fruits of victory, others again that British Kaffraria was the affair of the imperial authorities and none of their business. Smith always claimed that but for the defection of the Hottentots and the dereliction of their duty by the burghers, he could have ended the war quickly.[2] As it was, he was left to do the best he could, during the long months that must elapse before reinforcements from overseas could reach him, with the 1700 British regulars already under his command, colonial volunteers, friendly tribesmen and those Hottentots who remained loyal.

Smith, optimistic as ever, refrained from asking for reinforcements, which he knew the home authorities could ill spare: but, as the weeks went by, the fatal reactions of the Kaffir war on his South African settlement as a whole became apparent. Just as the War of the Axe had done much to ruin Maitland's Touwfontein scheme, so now the War of 1850 prevented Smith from handling firmly the urgent problems beyond the Orange River. The eyes of the British Government and public might be fixed on the costly Kaffir war (the mounting pile of bluebooks witnessed to that fact), but Smith knew that the central factor of his South African problem was the Orange River Sovereignty. If a firm administration could be established there and a reasonable land settlement be granted to the jarring Europeans, Griquas and Bantu, the attempt to control the Trek would stand; if not, it must fail, not only upon the High Veld, but possibly also in the newly-acquired coastal dependency of Natal.

[1] Macmillan, W. M., *The Cape Colour Question*, pp. 279 *sqq.*

[2] Smith to Grey, 17 April 1852, *Parl. Pap.* 1852–3, LXVI [1635], p. 72; *Autobiography of Sir Harry Smith*, ed. G. C. Moore Smith (1903), p. 791.

The prospects of success in the Sovereignty were not and never had been good. The whole stream of British colonial policy was against its maintenance: the desire to avoid additional expense and responsibility, the difficulty of reconciling the acquisition of colonies with the abolition of what remained of the old colonial system, and the widespread belief that colonies of settlement must one day fall away. Nevertheless, Earl Grey had recognised the annexation complacently enough on the understanding that the bulk of the inhabitants of all colours desired it and were prepared to provide for local defence and to pay their own way.[1] At first, all promised to go well. Many of the anti-British burghers had followed Pretorius beyond the Vaal; of the burghers who remained, some were loud in their professions of loyalty, and the rest seemed to be content with any administration that promised them security. New men, some of them of British stock, were coming up from the Cape Colony, and as late as October 1850, Grey had visions of a South African federation similar to that which he had propounded recently to the Australasian colonies.[2] But by that time the Sovereignty had begun to totter.

Major Henry Warden, the Resident at Bloemfontein, was a good regimental officer but no statesman. Without even an Executive Council to advise him, he was hampered by a Legislative Council consisting of district magistrates and nominated burghers. He had no adequate revenue and he must keep the peace with a tiny garrison of British regulars and Coloured troops, a swarm of tribal levies, and Boer farmers serving under elected commandants and field-cornets. If the burghers failed him, he would be almost powerless.[3]

Warden dealt with the tangled land problem summarily. He had no difficulty in the west where inhabitants of any kind were scarce; in the south he left the Griquas to look after themselves, which meant that they gradually parted with their farms; but in the east he fell foul of Moshesh, the Chief on whom the stability of the Sovereignty most of all depended. He compelled Moshesh under threat of war to accept a southern boundary which cut off a large wedge from lands claimed and partially occupied by the Basuto, and then recognised the claims of Europeans and rival Chiefs to nearly all the cornlands to the west of the Caledon River (September–December 1849).[4] This Warden Line naturally failed to bring peace. The Basuto refused to move to their side of it and there was no power to move them. Then the outbreak of the war in British Kaffraria shook the whole rickety fabric of the Sovereignty, and Smith made matters worse by directing Warden to recognise Moroko of Thaba Nchu, one of the "Wesleyan" chieftains, as Great Chief in place of Moshesh, whom he suspected of

[1] *Papers re Kaffirs, Parl. Pap.* 1847–8, XLIII [969], pp. 67.
[2] de Kiewiet, *Brit. Col. Policy*, p. 34; *C.H.B.E.* vol. VII, Pt I, 426.
[3] *Correspondence re assumption of Sovereignty, Parl. Pap.* 1851, XXXVII [1360], pp. 3 *sqq.*
[4] *Basutoland Records*, I. 276 *sqq.*, III, 104.

intriguing with the hostile Kaffirs. Thus encouraged, Warden called out his motley forces to drive the Basuto behind the Line; but his burghers failed to support him fully and he was defeated at Viervoet (June 1851).

Viervoet was the beginning of the end of the Sovereignty. Warden was forced to stand on the defensive at Bloemfontein, while the Basuto advanced to the line they had long claimed and harried the farms of those burghers who had turned out in his commando. Other burghers negotiated openly with Moshesh for immunity, and both they and he called on Pretorius for aid. Meanwhile in the south the Kaffir war was going badly and was spreading dangerously. After nearly a year of fighting the Gaikas and Tembus were showing as much enterprise and vigour as at the beginning, and now Kreli's still independent Galekas beyond the Kei River were being drawn in and the Pondos further east were restive. Smith called for two more regiments to drive the Gaikas out of the Amatola mountains.

This appeal for more troops was ill hearing to a failing Ministry which had already sent considerable reinforcements unasked, all the more so as its South African policy, based on the High Commissioner's sanguine reports, was under heavy fire from the parliamentary Opposition, other critics led by *The Times*, and the Committee for Trade and Plantations.[1] The Cabinet was alarmed at the inadequacy of the army for home defence in face of growing European dangers, harassed by the constant demands of the Indian army for men, and persuaded that colonies ought to provide for their own local defence.[2] Only very grudgingly did Grey send more troops. At the same time he warned Smith that unless the Sovereignty men would support their own Government, the Queen's authority might, however reluctantly, have to be withdrawn after peace had been established and her honour vindicated.[3] An unmistakable sign that Grey was weakening in his support of the Governor was his appointment of Major William Hogge and Charles Mostyn Owen as "Assistant Commissioners for the settling and adjusting of the affairs of the eastern and north-eastern boundaries of the Colony of the Cape of Good Hope" with power to report to himself direct.[4] This practically halved Sir Harry's powers; but he had to acquiesce. As soon as he could, however, he sent the Assistant Commissioners north to save the Sovereignty, the keystone of his South African settlement, with the reminder that he had given more thought to it than to any other part of his administration, and the warning that abandonment must lead to grave trouble with the tribes wherever white men were settled

[1] Morrell, W. P., *Brit. Col. Policy*, pp. 285–95; de Kiewiet, *Brit. Col. Policy*, p. 34.

[2] See *C.H.B.E.* vol. II.

[3] Grey to Smith, 15 Sept. 1851, *Parl. Pap.* 1852, XXXIII [1428], p. 539; Bell and Morrell, *Select Documents*, pp. 523 *sqq.*

[4] Instructions, 31 May 1852, and Grey to Smith, 11 June 1851, *Parl. Pap.* 1851, XXXVIII [1380], pp. 62, 66.

from Panda's Zululand in the south to newly-discovered Lake Ngami in the far north.[1] He himself remained behind to grapple with the apparently endless war in the Amatolas.

Both Hogge and Owen had had previous South African experience, and both soon realised that the fate of the Sovereignty depended largely on what happened north of the Vaal. To explain this we must return to note what had occurred there since Potgieter had led his Trekkers north in 1845.[2] Events in the Transvaal during the past few years had contributed nothing to stabilise the chaos to the south of the river. Potgieter had at first exercised patriarchal powers over his followers at Ohrigstad and had claimed supremacy over the whole of the Transvaal as pioneer Commandant. His benevolent despotism was challenged almost at once by immigrants from Natal who set up a Volksraad at Ohrigstad (1845), and his supremacy was then attacked by Pretorius who gained the upper hand at Potchefstroom during and after the Boomplaats campaign (1848). Soon afterwards, Potgieter moved away northward to the Zoutpansberg, while his opponents abandoned fever-stricken Ohrigstad for the new village of Lydenburg close by and agreed with Pretorius's folk that there should be one Volksraad for the whole Transvaal (May 1849).[3]

For some years afterwards this union existed only on paper. The local patriotisms of Potchefstroom and Lydenburg, and the personal jealousies of their respective leaders, were inflamed by religious disputes. Not only were many Transvaalers, and notably Potgieter's adherents, Doppers who regarded the orthodox members of the Reformed Church as latitudinarians, but the orthodox were divided among themselves.[4] Colonial and Sovereignty clergymen had visited the Transvaal from 1847 onwards, but in spite of repeated invitations none had come to minister permanently from either the Colony or the Netherlands, and the Transvaalers feared that none would come unless they themselves submitted to the Cape Synod. The Lydenburgers were prepared to submit, but the Potchefstroomers would not, lest the sword temporal should follow the sword spiritual. Controversy raged.[5]

The authority and revenue of this distracted State were both nominal. Little revenue could be obtained from a community of subsistence farmers and ivory-hunters, who left tillage to lackadaisical and unreliable Native servants and gardening to their wives, relied on casual immigrants from the British colonies for skilled labour, and

[1] Smith to Assistant Commissioners, 11 November 1851, *Parl. Pap.* 1852, XXXIII [1428], p. 202.

[2] *Vide supra*, p. 342.

[3] For early Transvaal history, see *Volksraad Notule* (Transvaal Archives); Stuart, J., *De Hollandsche Afrikanen;* Cachet, F. L., *De Worstelstrijd der Transvalers;* Engelbrecht, *Geschiedenis*, I.

[4] McCarter, J., *Geschiedenis der Ned. Geref. Kerk in Zuid-Afrika*; Engelbrecht, I, 114 *sqq.*

[5] *Correspondence re Sovereignty, Parl. Pap.* 1851, XXXVII [1360], p. 2; *Verslag der Handelingen van de Algemeene Kerkvergadering...*, April 1859, p. 40; Engelbrecht, *op. cit.* I, 32; Dreyer, *Die Kaapse Kerk*, pp. 88 *sqq.*

traded with the tribes and each other mainly by barter.[1] Still less could authority be looked for from a Volksraad which was overshadowed and sometimes interrupted by the sovereign people, that is, the burghers in arms, or from an executive which consisted of three Commandants-General each supreme in his own district.

The weakness of an embryo State with a scattered population, the quota of runaways from more orderly communities inevitable in frontier territories, and no police other than the commando was revealed in the Transvaal's Native policy. On paper, it was in the main the policy of republican Natal; in practice, as the constant reiteration of the laws sufficiently proves, it was what each group or even each man thought best. There was no true slavery in the Transvaal except possibly in the wild Zoutpansberg in touch with the slave-dealing Portuguese, but the apprenticeship system was gravely abused. The sale and purchase of apprentices occurred successively in the Orange River Sovereignty, the Orange Free State and even in the north-eastern Cape Colony in the middle 'fifties, while the measure of the thing in the Transvaal may be gauged from the fact that it still existed there among leaders of the community a full ten years later.[2]

Such were the facts that the new officers, Hogge and Owen, prepared to face. The Traansvaalers must either be brought under effective control or they must be given their independence, and both Assistants were inclined towards the latter course. The only obvious argument for trying to control the Trekkers was that, left to themselves, they might press hard on the missionaries and the tribes, especially on those along the Missionaries' Road that ran by their western borderlands towards Central Africa. They had claimed the Road as theirs since 1840; latterly they had turned back hunting parties on it,[3] and they were now quarrelling over land and jurisdiction with Montsiwa, a Barolong chief, and his Wesleyan missionary in the Molopo River section (December 1851).

This argument carried little weight in official circles. The old Evangelical enthusiasm had waned, and with a Kaffir war raging and the heavy task of safeguarding Native interests in the Sovereignty and Natal on their shoulders, imperial officials were less sympathetically inclined towards the tribes than they had been. As for the missionaries, the growing opinion among them was that they had nothing to fear from Trekkers who owed much to some members of their body in the early days of the Trek, and who apparently did not object to missionaries as such, but only to politically-minded missionaries.[4] If that were so, it was an objection which the Boers shared with many past Cape Governors.

[1] Stuart, pp. 216 *sqq.*; Engelbrecht, I, XIV, cxlvi *sqq.*

[2] *Correspondence re Adjacent Territories*...1855–7 (Cape Blue Book), pp. 126, 183, 199; Walker, *History of Southern Africa*, p. 275 *sqq.*

[3] *Correspondence re Sovereignty, Parl. Pap.* 1851, XXXVII [1360], pp. 28, 34, 69.

[4] See Agar-Hamilton, J. A. I., *Native Policy of the Voortrekkers*, pp. 90 *sqq.*

On the other hand the arguments for recognising the independence of the Transvaalers were strong. These die-hards of the Trek, who had trekked furthest and most frequently, would never acknowledge their British citizenship without a struggle. They were far away, the nearest of them perhaps 750 miles from Cape Town, and in all their supposedly barren acres there was no centre like Port Natal or Pietermaritzburg at which the troops could strike with hope of decisive success. Though only some 20,000 in all, the assertion of control over them would call for enormous exertion and expense.

Finally, it was not so much a question of British intervention in the Transvaal as of Transvaal intervention in the Sovereignty. Pretorius had hinted that though he would much prefer to negotiate for independence, he was ready in the last resort to respond to the appeals of Moshesh and the Winburgers and to cross the Vaal in arms. That must be prevented at all costs, and, if the Transvaalers could be placated, the Winburg malcontents would be isolated or at least be given an adjacent independent territory to which they could easily migrate. With such considerations in mind, Sir Harry Smith consented to raise the ban he had laid on Pretorius after Boomplaats and to allow him and other Transvaal delegates to meet Commissioners Hogge and Owen at the Sand River in the northern part of the Sovereignty to discuss future relations.

It was a strange haphazard conference. The new Assistants had no precise instructions, Potgieter's Zoutpansbergers were not represented, and the Winburg die-hards accused Pretorius and the Lydenburgers of deserting them. Nevertheless the two sides succeeded in reaching an agreement, and on 17 January 1852 the so-called Sand River Convention was signed as "Minutes of a Meeting between ... H.M. Assistant Commissioners ... and a deputation from the emigrant farmers residing north of the Vaal River".[1] Informal though it was, the agreement is one of the fundamental documents of South African history, for it recognised the existence of a Boer State. Henceforward the Transvaalers, by the very fact of their independence, were destined to influence profoundly their fellow-countrymen in the British territories to the south.

Both parties promised to facilitate mutual trade, to extradite criminals, to allow free movement across the common frontier, and to abstain from encroaching on each other's territories. Slavery was forbidden in the Republic; the Transvaalers, but not their dark-skinned neighbours, were assured of an open powder market in the colonies, and H.M. Government disclaimed all alliances with "coloured nations to the north of the Vaal River".

While this decisive step was being taken in the remote interior,

[1] For text, see *Correspondence re O. R. Territory, Parl. Pap.* 1852–3, XVI [1646], pp. 3–6; Bell and Morrell, *Select Documents*, pp. 526–8; Eybers, G. W., *Select Constitutional Documents*, pp. 358–9.

Sir Harry Smith, in command of ten good battalions and a regiment of lancers, was at last beating down the resistance of the Gaikas in the mountainous Waterkloof, and the Pondos were attacking Kreli's Galekas from behind. But news of these successes reached London too late to save the High Commissioner. Smith's prestige with the Cabinet was gone, and his enemies, eager to attack the ministry through him, were in full cry.[1] In the Lords, the Duke of Wellington, as Commander-in-Chief, indeed defended his conduct of the war;[2] but Major Hogge, on the spot, criticised it adversely, and Grey accepted Hogge's verdict.[3] He lost patience with Smith's oft-repeated assurances that all would be well presently, and early in January 1852, on the eve of the fall of Russell's Whig ministry, recalled him.[4]

At the ministry's request, Wellington nominated, as Smith's successor, the Hon. George Cathcart, who had been one of his own aides-de-camp at Waterloo. The appointment, in the middle of a campaign, of a comparatively unknown man who had never held any civilian post of importance nor had had South African military experience occasioned some surprise; nevertheless, those who appointed Cathcart knew that he was an energetic soldier who could be trusted to finish the Kaffir war. That to them was the principal consideration. Not so to Smith. To him, the war, now apparently so nearly ended, was only one factor, and that not the most important, of the South African problem. The crux lay in the despised Orange River Sovereignty. And all the signs of the times pointed to the speedy abandonment of that territory. Grey, disillusioned, had admitted wearily that the maintenance of British authority over the desolate plains of the Trekkers was "Quixotic philanthropy",[5] and had let the Transvaalers go. Now he agreed with Russell, his political chief, that the Sovereignty ought to be abandoned sooner or later.[6] Sooner rather than later, Smith feared. In April 1852 he sailed home despairing.

Hogge and Owen, on the other hand, were determined to save the key position if they could. Given that, the Transvaalers might one day be drawn out of their isolation into the British system. Besides, there was something south of the Vaal to show for four years of British rule, feeble though that had been. There were fully ten thousand white inhabitants and four or five villages, of which Bloemfontein and Smithfield were chief; each village had its Dutch Reformed clergyman, church and school; the capital possessed also the beginnings of an Anglican cathedral and a newspaper, *The Friend*, an offshoot of the

[1] See Morrell, *Brit. Col. Policy*, pp. 287–93, for illustrative extracts.

[2] *Autobiography*, pp. 642–3. See Fortescue, J., *History of the British Army*, XII, 526 *sqq*. for a favourable estimate of Smith as a soldier.

[3] Morrell, *op. cit.* p. 292.

[4] Grey to Smith, 14 January 1852, *Parl. Pap.* 1852, XXXIII [1428], pp. 253 *sqq*.

[5] Morell, *op. cit.* p. 302.

[6] Grey to Smith, 21 October 1851, *Parl. Pap.* 1852, XXXIII [1428], p. 245.

Grahamstown Journal.[1] Abandonment without overwhelming cause would, the Commissioners held, be a breach of faith to those British citizens who had gone up to the Sovereignty after the annexation.

The Commissioners were doing their best to restore order when Hogge, the more far-seeing of the two, died. While Owen struggled on amid growing confusion, Moshesh fell upon his exasperating enemy Sikonyela and overran his lands, and Pretorius rode into Bloemfontein to be hailed as the man who would put the Basuto in their place. Moshesh, taking the hint, showed a willingness to come to terms, but Major Warden issued ammunition to Moshesh's half-breed neighbours who promptly swept off Basuto cattle and horses. It was the last straw. Earl Grey had already indicated that Warden was unfit for his post;[2] hence Owen dismissed him for mishandling a desperate situation and, abandoning all hope of holding the Sovereignty without a considerable garrison, anxiously awaited the coming of the new High Commissioner (July 1852).

Cathcart was held fast until nearly the end of the year among the last smouldering embers of the Kaffir war. Immediately after his arrival at the Cape he had taken drastic steps to end it. He disbanded the useless Native levies, raised Mounted Police, the first in South Africa, and brought out the burgher commandos in force by promising them a share in the spoil of cattle if they came, and threatening to withdraw the regulars if they did not. They came. Ten thousand of Kreli's cattle were taken, and, by December 1852, the shattered tribes could resist no longer. The High Commissioner was thus free to hurry northward leaving the settlement of affairs in Kaffraria to wait while he dealt with the troubles beyond the Orange.

He arrived with 2500 men at his back to impose peace on the Sovereignty.[3] With his accustomed decision he condemned the Warden Line as roundly as Hogge and Owen had done, and refused to accept at face value the endless list of missing stock charged against the Basuto. Then, recalling his recent threats which had brought the Cape Colonists into the field and the consequent rounding up of Kreli's cattle that had ended the war, he hinted that the Sovereignty might be given up unless its burghers supported their Government, and demanded of Moshesh a heavy indemnity of horses and cattle within three days. The impossible task was not half performed within the time, and Cathcart invaded Basutoland to collect the balance. He was severely checked at the Berea on the road to Thaba

[1] *Correspondence re O. R. Territory, Parl. Pap.* 1854, XLIII [1758], pp. 23 *sqq.*, 54; *Correspondence re Adjacent Territories*...1855–7 (Cape Blue Book), p. 20; Stuart, *Hollandsche Afrikanen*, p. 184; Orpen, *Reminiscences*, p. 97.

[2] Grey to Smith, 14 January 1852, *Parl. Pap.* 1852, XXXIII [1428], pp. 253 *sqq.*

[3] Cathcart to Pakington, 14 November 1852, *Correspondence re Kaffirs, Parl. Pap.* 1852–3, LXVI [1635], p. 183. For Cathcart in the O. R. Sovereignty see *Basutoland Records*, I, II, and *Correspondence re O. R. Territory, Parl. Pap.* 1852–3, LXVI [1646], pp. 92 *sqq.*; Orpen, *Reminiscences*, pp. 156, 164, 239 *sqq.*

Bosigo, Moshesh's stronghold, and, to the surprise of all, accepted a face-saving compromise that the astute Moshesh offered and marched away south leaving a garrison of only 300 men in Bloemfontein. Apart from the need for effecting a speedy post-war settlement in Kaffraria, Cathcart excused his hasty departure with the plea that all claims against the Government had been "sufficiently compensated" by the Basuto cattle he had taken, "all wrongs redressed", and peace established along the whole four hundred miles of the Kaffraria-Basutoland frontier.[1] But the blow to British prestige was heavy. Moshesh could boast that he had beaten the redcoats;[2] those burghers of the Sovereignty who desired its maintenance lost heart, and those who wished to see an end of it were encouraged to hope.

Back from his ill-starred dash to the Sovereignty, Cathcart set about clearing up the mess left by Harry Smith's Kaffir war.[3] In March 1853, he dictated terms to the beaten Chiefs. As far as concerned the Cape Colony, he decreed that the eastern frontier lands should be a buffer between the Colony and British Kaffraria. To that end, he took land from the defeated Tembus and rebellious mission Hottentots, planted Fingos and Europeans thereon as a border guard, and founded Queenstown as a rallying centre. As for British Kaffraria, he established picked Fingos on individual quit-rent holdings in the Amatola Mountains, and small groups of Europeans near the forts that ringed those mountains round. He did indeed forbid the Xhosas to re-enter the Amatolas, but, disregarding the frontier clamour that the tribesmen be pushed back bodily behind the Kei River, he left the rest of the country to the Xhosas and Tembus and, in great measure, restored the authority of their Chiefs.[4]

Cathcart's tentative experiment in "indirect rule" in British Kaffraria was being carried much further in distant Natal by Theophilus Shepstone, a man who was destined to play a notable part in South African history for the next thirty years. Shepstone was the son of a Wesleyan missionary, the Rev. William Shepstone. His upbringing on the parental mission station in Kaffirland had given him such knowledge of Bantu languages and mentality that he had served as D'Urban's interpreter during the Kaffir war of 1835, and, after becoming a Native Agent, had been transferred to Natal at the close of 1845. There his duties as Secretary of Native Affairs were heavy, for the governance of the little district was almost entirely a matter of Native policy. For some years Natal was hard put to it to make ends meet on the proceeds of the ivory traffic, customs and Native hut-tax, while it looked round anxiously for white inhabitants. So

[1] Cathcart to Pakington, 13 January 1853; *Basutoland Records*, II, 4, 7.

[2] *Basutoland Records*, II, 270–1.

[3] *Vide supra*, p. 356.

[4] *Correspondence re Kaffir Tribes*, *Parl. Pap.* 1852–3, LXVI [1635], pp. 222 *sqq.*; *Further Correspondence*, 1854–5, XXXVIII [1969]; *Minutes...on Frontier Settlement*, June 1853 (Cape Blue Book).

slight was the immigration, however, that it did little more than fill the gaps left by the departing Trekkers. Ten years after the annexation, British Natal, wedged between Zululand and Pondoland and overrun by fully 100,000 of its own Bantu, could boast of only 8000 European inhabitants.[1]

Shepstone wished to segregate the Bantu in a single large reserve in which they could be more conveniently civilised by magistrates, police and industrial teachers;[2] but he had to be content with several scattered reserves, in all about one-tenth of the country, which were set aside by a Commission. Into these he shepherded some 80,000 Bantu with the aid of a few white officials and black police, and left the rest scattered on Crown lands or European farms. For lack of money, he had to forgo most of the police and magistrates and nearly all the schools. He therefore relied on missionaries as civilising agents, and the revival of chieftainship as the one means, other than his own great and growing influence, of maintaining order and cohesion in the reserves. But he also made one great innovation which distinguished Natal's native policy from that of the Cape, British Kaffraria and the Republics. In 1849, after a fierce struggle with the Recorder, Henry Cloete, and other champions of the Roman-Dutch law, he won recognition for Native law and custom. So long as Natal's Bantu remained in the tribal stage, they were to be tried by that law even by European magistrates and, on appeal, by the Lieutenant-Governor and Executive Council as "Great Chief".[3]

Shepstone's policy of legal differentiation was as unpopular among most of his brother officials and nearly all the colonists as were his reserves. From settlers clamorous for cheap black labour to grow their cotton and coffee and, still more, the sugar that was being introduced from Mauritius, the old frontier cry went up that the reserves were a public danger and drain on the labour supply, and must therefore be broken up. However, the authorities held firm, allowed an unofficial Commission to talk itself out, and watched the agitation die away amid laments for the good old republican days that were gone. Nevertheless, the outcry turned Shepstone's thoughts more and more towards his scheme for leading the mass of Natal's Bantu into No-mansland, the fertile and almost empty countryside beyond the western frontier that had once been included in republican Natal but now formed part of the Pondo treaty state.

While Cathcart was wrestling with the problems of the eastern frontier, and Shepstone *more suo* was "ganging his ain gait" in Natal, Ministers in London were steadily inclining towards the abandonment of the Sovereignty. Sir John Pakington, Secretary of State in the

[1] *Vide infra*, p. 401; *Correspondence re Settlement of Natal, Parl. Pap.* 1847–8, XLII [980], *passim*.

[2] *Correspondence re Natal, Parl. Pap.* 1852–3, LXII [1697], pp. 22 *sqq*. For Shepstone's policy *vide* Brookes, E. H., *History of Native Policy in South Africa*.

[3] Eybers, *op. cit.* pp. 235 *sqq*.

short-lived Derby Cabinet, had come round to the views of his predecessor, Earl Grey, that British commitments must be limited[1]. With a Napoleon newly enthroned at Paris and relations with Russia far from easy, the British Government was in no mood for indefinite and costly adventures in the remoter parts of South Africa. As for the general public, they were sick and tired of trouble there. To them, all that the Empire really needed was the Cape Peninsula for the defence of the India trade; anything more was to be held only in the interests of loyal subjects and Native tribes.[2] Natal, British Kaffraria and the Sovereignty had been annexed one after the other primarily on those grounds, and within a few years the Government had been faced with Kaffir and Basuto troubles, which had actually involved or threatened to involve most of the tribes within its over-extended dominions, as well as others, like the Pondos and Panda's Zulus, outside them. There must be an end as far as possible of responsibility for these new and unruly settlements with their frequent wars in which the burghers supported the imperial authorities reluctantly, and the only people who prospered were produce and gun merchants, transport riders and land speculators.

That may have been, as indeed it was, a jaundiced view to take of the South African scene; but there was truth in it, and, according to Cathcart, it was especially true of the Sovereignty. The Resident, Green, headed the list of speculators who held more than half of the land outside the tribal areas; the administration was not paying its way, and the only thing on which all its burghers seemed to agree was that they ought not to be called out to maintain the general peace by intervening in tribal quarrels. As for the future form of government, long before the Berea battle the Legislative Council at Bloemfontein had favoured annexation to the Cape Colony, soon to have its own Parliament,[3] and a larger and more representative delegation than that Council had presently demanded a Volksraad backed by a strong imperial garrison, and the return to the old frontier system of reprisals by field-cornets' parties.[4] Cathcart had been ready rather to let them have independence with its responsibilities as well as its privileges and be done with it.[5] Even if they should join hands with the Transvaalers, it might be better to have one strong Trekker state to deal with than several weak ones. Now, after the Berea battle, he suggested that a Commissioner be sent to go into the whole question,[6] and the Duke of Newcastle, Secretary of State in the new Aberdeen ministry, consented. Five thousand good troops were already locked

[1] de Kiewiet, *Brit. Col. Policy*, p. 69.

[2] Grey to Cathcart, 2 February 1852, *Parl. Pap.* 1852, XXXIII [1428], pp. 256 *sqq.*

[3] Theal, G. M., *History of S. Africa since 1795* (ed. 1908), III, 316 *sqq.*; *The Friend*, 12 January 1852.

[4] *Parl. Pap.* 1852–3, LXVI [1646], pp. 57 *sqq.*

[5] Cathcart to Pakington, 20 September and 12 October 1852, *ibid.* pp. 69 *sqq.*

[6] Cathcart to Pakington, 13 January 1853, *ibid.* p. 106.

up at the southern end of Africa, and rather than send the 2000 additional men, who in Cathcart's opinion were necessary to hold the unwanted Sovereignty, H.M. Government, the Duke announced, had decided to withdraw to the south of the Orange River.[1]

The imperial authorities were thus apparently prepared to throw the Sovereignty into the arms of the Transvaal at the risk of bringing Transvaal ideas and methods officially down to the Colonial frontiers. Yet that prospect might well have given them pause. The course of events in the Transvaal since the Sand River conference had not been reassuring. There had been grave risk of civil war between the partisans of Pretorius and those of Potgieter when the Sand River Convention was submitted to the burghers for ratification. The two ageing champions had, however, been dramatically reconciled, the Convention had been ratified and the authority of the Volksraad reaffirmed. But there was still no executive other than the three Commandants-General, and the republic, wavering between a Trekker polity and a settled constitution, was drifting further away from the colonial south and splitting internally into factions. Potchefstroom, encouraged by the arrival of a clergyman from the Netherlands at last, refused definitely to have its Church incorporated in the Cape Synod, and rival Lydenburg therefore made ready to secede from the republican Church and State.[2] The deaths of Potgieter and Pretorius within a few weeks of one another did not mend matters, for their sons, Piet and Marthinus, succeeded to their offices and their hates (March–June 1853).

Meanwhile the Republic had been embroiled with the tribes to the east and also along the Missionaries' Road to the west. Though the Convention had named no boundaries other than the Vaal River, the elder Pretorius had at once claimed the Road and closed it so that traders must pass through Potchefstroom and there pay duty on their goods and guns.[3] He had then asserted his authority over certain of the local Chiefs, in one case with violence and loot of women, apprentices, cattle and property from the house of David Livingstone, the L.M.S. missionary, which had been standing vacant and already partly pillaged close by. For this and other reasons the cry went up from some of the London Missionary Society men that, unless some Power intervened, the tribes north of the Vaal would be reduced to ruin and slavery, and that on no account must the Sovereignty be given up lest these things be done south of that river also.[4]

The missionaries had a strong case, but they overstated it and thus gave the Transvaalers a chance of proving to the world and especially to Sir George Clerk, newly arrived as Special Commissioner to

[1] Newcastle to Cathcart, 14 March 1853, *ibid.* p. 118 *sqq.*

[2] Stuart, *Hollandsche Afrikanen*, pp. 197 *sqq.*, 255; Engelbrecht, *Geschiedenis*, I, 18, 33, 48 *sqq.*

[3] *Correspondence re O. R. Territory, Parl. Pap.* 1854, XLIII [1758], p. 6.

[4] *Parl. Pap.* 1852–3, LXVI [1646], pp. 116; Theal, *History of South Africa*, III, 347.

"adjust" the affairs of the Sovereignty,[1] that Boers were not so black as they had been painted.

The Duke of Newcastle had told the Special Commissioner before he sailed, and told him again after his arrival, that the Sovereignty might yet be upheld on good cause shown;[2] but Sir George Clerk, a thorough bureaucrat schooled in the governorship of Bombay, read his instructions literally and prepared to go forward, regardless of prayers, threats or other circumstances. In other words, he proposed to provide for speedy abandonment. He knew that Cathcart favoured that course; he was reassured by tidings that reached him of the moderate Native policy of Marthinus Pretorius, and he was convinced that he must hurry on with his plan if Britain was not to be involved in another serious Native war. The state of affairs in the Sovereignty was rapidly going from bad to worse. The clans, with European connivance and occasional assistance, were at each other's throats in the coveted cornlands, and Moshesh, throwing off the restraint he had displayed since the Berea battle, seized the lands of Sikonyela and another of his chief tormentors under Clerk's very eyes (October 1853).[3]

In September Sir George Clerk met a large elected delegation of Afrikaner and British burghers. The delegates asked for compensation for Basuto cattle thefts, a settlement of outstanding land disputes and the abrogation of treaties with Native Chiefs. They argued against abandonment, but demanded that, if abandonment must come, they should be released unequivocally from British citizenship and guaranteed against Transvaal and Native claimants to Sovereignty lands.[4]

Clerk, undismayed by this demand for better government under the Union Jack rather than for independence, moved up to Basutoland to settle the boundary question with Moshesh. He found that border burghers preferred, Transvaal fashion, to have no definite boundaries at all, and that Moshesh, who had at first been willing to compromise somewhat, was now standing out for the Napier Line of 1843.[5] This made any immediate agreement impossible, and so, after stating clearly that the Warden Line of 1849 was dead and done with, the Commissioner put the negotiations with the Basuto aside and returned to Bloemfontein to resume his discussions with the Sovereignty burghers.

There he found that the original deputation, the "land-jobbers" or "obstructionists", as he called them, had dwindled disheartened away, and that the party of independence, "the well-disposed",

[1] *Basutoland Records*, II, 45.

[2] Newcastle to Clerk, 14 November 1853, *Parl. Pap.* 1854, XLIII [1758], p. 88.

[3] Clerk to Newcastle, 3 December 1853, *ibid.* p. 53.

[4] *Parl. Pap.* 1854, XLIII [1758], pp. 34 *sqq.*, 42 *sqq.*

[5] *Basutoland Records*, II, 94, 281, 434; Orpen, *Reminiscences*, pp. 297 *sqq.* and *History of the Basutos*, p. iii.

encouraged by Transvaal supporters and by his own undisguised opinions, had steadily grown in strength. The British and even the few Afrikaner delegates, who had remained on the committee after the rest had gone home, protested that the allegiance of British subjects could not be extinguished against their will and then only by Act of Parliament. But neither their protest, nor the delegation they sent to plead their case in London, nor yet the eleventh-hour "discovery" of traces of gold at Smithfield moved the Special Commissioner.[1] The republican tide was flowing strongly, stimulated by anger at hotly worded petitions that poured in from the Cape Colony, many of them, it is true, from the commercial community, but one at least from influential Dutch Reformed Church authorities asserting that abandonment must lead to the moral degeneration of the Europeans and the grievous physical hurt of the tribes concerned.[2] There was truth in the charges; but, just as similar charges away back in the 'thirties had sent men out on the Great Trek with bitterness in their hearts against "unjustifiable odium", so now these wholesale accusations drove many hesitating burghers into the republican camp.[3] The Winburg enthusiasts were soon able to tell the Commissioner that they were ready to take over the government of the Sovereignty. Clerk therefore summoned a meeting of the "well-disposed" to Bloemfontein, and, on 23 February 1854, signed a Convention with them for which he gained acceptance more easily by giving £50,000 as compensation for losses and for the arrears of official salaries.

The Bloemfontein Convention was a more precise and detailed version of the Sand River Convention.[4] It was also a more revolutionary document. The Convention with the Transvaalers had been a recognition of facts, but the Bloemfontein Convention was the withdrawal of an existing sovereignty against the wishes of many British subjects and in face of the apathy of many more. It was also the overturning of a treaty system. Andries Waterboer's treaty of 1834 had lapsed already with the signature of the Sand River Convention and the death of the Chief a little later;[5] but now Moshesh's agreement of 1843 also ceased to be of effect, though Moshesh never understood that,[6] and Adam Kok's treaty was emasculated. The Convention safeguarded Kok in theory, but it also bound him to facilitate the acquisition by Europeans of farms in Philippolis. When the Griqua chief refused to agree, Sir George threw him over with a suggestion that if he could not come to terms with the new Government he might be given a reserve to the south of the Orange.[7] Clerk refused to bind the

[1] Theal, III, 352 *sqq.*; *The Friend*, 26 Nov. 1853, 18 and 25 Feb. 1854.
[2] *Parl. Pap.* 1854, XLIII [1758], p. 12.
[3] *Ibid.* pp. 61 *sqq.*
[4] For text, see Eybers, pp. 282 *sqq.*
[5] *Parl. Pap.* 1854, XLIII [1758], p. 2.
[6] *Basutoland Records*, II. 99.
[7] A. 118 of 1861 (Cape), pp. 1 *sqq.*

Queen's Government never again to make treaties with Native Chiefs north of the Orange, but agreed that no future treaties should be made that were prejudicial to the new Orange Free State. With this the Boer negotiators were content.[1]

The actual withdrawal was carried out without ceremony or expression of feeling on either side. Clerk's little garrison of three hundred men marched quietly out of Bloemfontein with no apparent realisation that they were making history. As they passed over the colonial boundary at the Orange drifts through which Sir Harry Smith had splashed with such high hopes and good intentions six years before, they were accomplishing perhaps the most momentous step in South Africa's history. They witnessed to the fact that South Africa was split along the line of the Orange River into two sections as sharply divided from one another as were the North and the South of the United States of those days. "We quit this colony", Piet Retief had written in February 1837, "under the full assurance that the English Government . . . will allow us to govern ourselves without its interference."[2] At last, seventeen years later to the month, the English Government was giving that assurance. But in the nature of things in South Africa, leave "to govern ourselves" meant power to govern others. Therein lay the significance of the Bloemfontein Convention, following so closely as it did upon the Sand River Convention of 1852. Henceforward Native policy, then as now the fundamental problem, was to be handled on radically different lines in the two halves of South Africa.

Such was the situation and outlook early in 1854. The old Cape Colony, endowed with a civilisation franchise and legal equality for all the Queen's subjects, and set upon giving its tribesmen adequate lands and some measure of European guidance, might still hope to dominate the southern half of the future Union of South Africa. In the nature of things it would absorb adjacent British Kaffraria sooner or later; but it must expect to see distant Natal become a separate colony now that that little district had been severed from itself by the abandonment of the Sovereignty. As for the northern half of the future Union, that had been left to the Trekkers, and the Cape and imperial Governments had estopped themselves from interfering therein. The most they could hope to do was to influence the republicans by precept and example, and to pray that probable wars between one or other of the many European Governments and their Bantu or Griqua neighbours might not involve all the rest. Balkanisation was by no means complete when, towards the end of the fatal year, Sir George Grey arrived as Governor of the Cape Colony and High Commissioner to point to a general federation as the way out.

[1] Theal, *History of S. Africa*, III, 353.

[2] *Vide supra*, p. 330, n. 2.

The measure of his failure to achieve that end was half-a-century of friction and strife, a confused and at times bloody commentary on the Great Schism of the eighteen-fifties.

CHAPTER XV

CONSTITUTIONAL DEVELOPMENT, 1834–1858

IN 1834 when Sir Benjamin D'Urban took up his commission as Governor and Commander-in-Chief of the Cape of Good Hope that colony was still very largely governed by prerogative. Letters Patent, Orders in Council, formal Instructions under the Royal Sign Manual and Signet were the instruments of authority over and above local proclamations and ordinances. The Governor was admonished to execute "such further instructions as may hereafter be given by us through one of our Principal Secretaries of State", but these further instructions contained in despatches were not legally binding upon him. The more exalted form of an Act of Parliament was seldom applied to the Cape. Nevertheless the reforms carried out in Great Britain told their tale. The recent revision of English criminal law had some bearing upon the Charter of Justice and the introduction of trial by jury. Catholic emancipation in the United Kingdom was followed the year after by similar relief in the Colony.[1] The Legislative Council of 1834, slave emancipation with the apprenticeship regulations arising therefrom, and the local government Ordinances of 1836 may legitimately be claimed as the first fruits of the great parliamentary Reform Bill in Great Britain in 1832. The Old Toryism had fought its losing battle at the Cape no less than in the Mother Country when Wellington made his last sortie upon the floor of the House of Lords.

The illuminating report of the Commissioners of Inquiry of 1823 had drawn attention to the despotic powers of the Governor.[2] The Charter of Justice of 1827 deprived him of appellate jurisdiction, and the Advisory Council of 1825 was intended to check his executive and legislative omnipotence. But this Council, which had come into being before the Commissioners had concluded their deliberations, was ineffective from the start,[3] and the addition of unofficial nominees in 1827 led to no improvement. The Commissioners were hesitant with regard to constitutional reforms. They recommended the division of the Colony into two provinces and looked forward to a time when a Legislative Assembly might be established in each, but said little as to the structure of the Council which they actually favoured. For the problems of the Cape were too varied to fit into the common pattern of the Empire. The Colony was extensive and thinly peopled; its communications were poor and slow. Cape Town, its strategic centre

[1] Ordinance No. 68 of 1830.

[2] *Vide supra*, pp. 251 *sqq*.

[3] *Report of the Commissioners of Inquiry upon the administration of the Government of the Cape of Good Hope, Parl. Pap.* 1826–7, XXI (282), p. 14.

for external defence and its commercial metropolis, was in the south-west corner, while the zone for internal defence was far away in the extreme north-east and east. How was it possible to reconcile the conflicting needs and interests of slaves about to be liberated, of Hottentots, of Kaffirs, of white masters and Coloured servants? How satisfy simultaneously British settlers complaining of lack of governance and Afrikaner farmers protesting against an all-embracing governmental authority? These were some of the problems that "Mr Mother Country" had to solve in his dingy room in Downing Street, three months' sail from the scene of operations. The policy of *festina lente* was, in the circumstances, the most prudent; but colonial opinion lashed into activity by a newly liberated press understood few of the complexities of governance and was impatient of delay.[1]

By Letters Patent, dated 23 October 1833, two separate Councils were constituted: an Executive Council of certain specified office holders, and a Legislative Council of five officials and from five to seven unofficial nominees. In both Councils the Governor was chairman *ex officio*.[2] Supplementary Instructions under the Sign Manual were issued to D'Urban on 8 November,[3] which may be regarded as the text of the Cape Constitution during the next twenty years. The slight variations contained in the commissions and instructions issued to D'Urban's successors until 1852 were merely of the nature of constitutional amendments.[4]

In the executive sphere the Governor was no longer an autocrat. He had to consult his Executive Council excepting on matters of trifling moment or of great urgency. Should he act contrary to its advice he must transmit his reasons to the Secretary of State. The Governor appointed subordinate officers, but his nominations for higher posts were subject to confirmation by the Crown. He was empowered on the advice of his Council to suspend superior officers and even Judges for proved misconduct, and he might accept resignations pending the royal pleasure. No death sentence might be executed without his *fiat*, but his pardoning powers were no longer as wide as in Somerset's day; he had to consult with his Judges and could not remit penalties in excess of £50.

The relations between the Governor and the Legislative Council were intimate. It was the Governor's duty to recommend Ordinances with respect to appropriation and supply, and such others as were requisite for the peace, order and good government of the Colony.

[1] See Debate in the House of Commons (24 May 1830) re Petition for Representative Government, *Hansard*, 2nd Ser., XXIV, 1005 *sqq*. Quoted in Eybers, G. W., *Select Constitutional Documents illustrating South African History*, pp. 30 *sqq*.

[2] C.O. 1725 (Cape Archives) (Government Notices and Proclamations).

[3] C.O. 1321 (Cape Archives) (Instructions to Sir Benjamin D'Urban).

[4] See Instructions to Napier, 1838 (C.O. 1326); to Maitland, 1843 (C.O. 1331); to Pottinger, 1846 (C.O. 1336); to Smith, 1847, *Letters Patent appointing Sir H. Smith Governor*, *Parl. Pap.* 1851, XXXVII (457); *Debates and Petitions on the Constitution Ordinance*, *Parl. Pap.* 1852–3, LXVI (130).

He summoned and prorogued the Council, nominated unofficial members, presided over meetings and interpreted rules of procedure. He possessed a deliberative vote and also a casting vote if need be. He might "negative" an Ordinance on the ground that it was prejudicial to the Crown or inexpedient, but he must transmit to the Secretary of State his reasons for doing so.[1]

The authority of the Crown was exercised in multiple form. Over and above its right of legislating directly for the Colony, D'Urban was instructed not to enforce any Ordinance "until the Royal pleasure be known", saving ordinary financial measures and matters which, in the opinion of the Legislative Council, could not admit of delay.[2] The right of the Crown to disallow or to amend any Ordinance was always reserved. Should anything still escape the net there was the further proviso that unless express confirmation be given within three years, an Ordinance, otherwise valid, should cease to have any force after that period.[3]

The long list of topics which fell outside the scope of the local legislature is instructive. The Governor was enjoined not to propose or assent to any Ordinance (1) abridging the royal prerogative; (2) relating to the constitution, proceedings, numbers or mode of appointing the Legislative Council; (3) for increasing or diminishing the number, salaries or allowances of public officers; (4) for issuing paper money; (5) establishing lotteries; (6) amending the law of divorce; (7) entitling aliens to own land without being naturalised; (8) for making grants of Crown land; (9) interfering with the free and orderly exercise of religion; or (10) whereby "persons not being of European birth or descent might be subjected or made liable to any disabilities or restrictions to which persons of European birth or descent would not also be subjected or made liable".[4] No Ordinance to which the royal assent had been formerly refused might be proposed or assented to. To guard the Peninsular veterans, who successively held the Governorship, from foundering in a legal morass, the Judges were called in before the third reading of any Ordinance—to determine whether it was *intra vires*. In addition to the oath of allegiance D'Urban had to subscribe to a further oath that the "several laws relating to Trade and Plantations be duly observed".[5] His successor, Napier, was relieved of this duty of paying lip service to a vanishing system by the general overhaul of colonial Instructions.[6] In his day the more modern oath for the "due execution of office and impartial administration of justice" was substituted.[7]

[1] § 14 of Instructions to D'Urban.
[2] § 30 of Instructions to D'Urban.
[3] Cf. Ord. 3 of 1853 declaring Ord. 9 of 1836 in force.
[4] § 21 of Instructions to D'Urban.
[5] § 2 of Instructions to D'Urban.
[6] See *C.H.B.E.* vol. II, chap. X, XI.
[7] § 2 of Instructions to Napier.

The Legislative Council began its ill-starred career in April 1834. During the twenty years of its existence it was often derided and seldom commended; indeed, as we shall see later, it was held in the highest popular esteem when it did not function at all. There is copious evidence even from official sources that the Council proved a dismal failure.[1]

One cause of this was inherent in the Council's constitution. The unofficial members were too few to outvote the officials in a full Council since the Governor never appointed the maximum number permitted. The officials voted solidly on all questions that had been agreed upon in the Executive Council. During the Governor's absence from Cape Town internal jealousies among officials led to more independent voting, but it was impossible to shake the rooted popular suspicion that the officials were inimical to and contemptuous of the public.[2]

There were also technical defects that raised doubts about the status of the Council and of its unofficial members. Under D'Urban's Letters Patent the unofficial members were to hold their seats during good behaviour, but all subsequent Letters Patent implied that they held during pleasure. The Council should have been established by a separate instrument in the manner of the Charter of Justice, for the coupling of its constitution with the Governor's Commission gave good ground for the opinion that the Council was recreated with every Governor.[3] In fact there was serious doubt whether the nominee Council was a legislature in the true meaning of the term.[4]

Among the most cherished privileges of the members were freedom of debate and the right to initiate such measures as were not exclusively vested in the Crown. In 1837 much heat was caused by the supposed design of the Crown to curtail these privileges when Napier's instructions were read in Council. The unofficial members lodged a protest, but in the end it transpired that by the mistake of a clerk the wrong instructions had been transmitted and that Lord Glenelg was not to blame. In 1838 amended instructions were issued and all was well again.[5]

When the Council opened its minute book in 1834 the unofficial element consisted of five Western nominees. At first the proceedings were private, but a clamour arose for the admission of the public and the press and in due course the Council yielded.[6] Thereafter its

[1] *Correspondence re the establishment of a Representative Assembly*, *Parl. Pap.* 1850, XXXVIII [1137], pp. 17, 95, and *Papers re Representative Assembly*, *Parl. Pap.* 1852, XXXIII [1427], p. 58.

[2] See *Cape Town Mail*, September 14 and 21. *Papers re proposed Representative Assembly*, *Parl. Pap.* 1851, XXXVII [1362], pp. 29 *sqq*.

[3] Cf. Keith, A. B., *Responsible Government in the Dominions* (ed. 1912), I, 103, for the form of the Letters Patent.

[4] A legal opinion given to Fairbairn in London (quoted in *Parl. Pap.* 1852, XXXIII [1427], pp. 60–2).

[5] Napier to Glenelg, 14 March 1838 (Cape Archives; C.O.a. 23); Glenelg to Napier, 8 August 1838 (Cape Archives; C.O. 1326).

[6] Kilpin, R., *The Old Cape House*, p. 6.

proceedings were regularly recorded in the local press which aided the growth of an informed public opinion.

While Cape Town and its vicinity took kindly enough to the Council, the frontier districts were hardly aware of its existence. Nor was it possible till 1847 to find from among their "greater landowners and principal merchants" one who was willing to neglect his farm or his business to attend the sessions in Cape Town. When a member did appear from the Eastern Province, he was a lonely figure in the Council chamber and, generally speaking, the "Easterns" enriched the records of the Council more frequently with "reasons for dissent" than with solid achievements.

The limited scope of the authority of the Council was an incurable bar to political enthusiasm. The benevolent despots at the Colonial Office had laid down with meticulous care how Ordinances should be framed and drafted: "that all such ordinances be drawn up in a simple and compendious form avoiding prolixity and tautology"; nor was the ruling, numbering and paragraphing forgotten. Duly tutored and instructed, the Council proceeded to give its attention to matters of a routine sort that were rarely of political importance. Its Vagrancy Ordinance of 1834,[1] a matter of much greater popular concern, proved abortive. First the Judges ruled that the draft could not stand against the Fiftieth Ordinance and, when the necessary amendments were made and the third reading carried, D'Urban negatived it as inexpedient and Lord Aberdeen approved of his action.[2]

Baulked of matters "above their reach and capacity" the Council devoted its energies to things more prosaic. There came first the provision of a system of local government, for there had been over-centralisation which brought with it many evils. The position, no doubt, at the Cape was not so acute as in Canada,[3] but even in South Africa, as a critical observer remarked, "the repairs of a town clock are discussed in the Council Chamber".[4] The abolition of Heemraden in 1827 had deprived the district centres of the small measure of popular representation they possessed, though by way of compensation juries were established to which the Afrikaner, unlike the French Canadian, took readily as soon as he was aware that ignorance of English was no bar to service thereon. In 1836, again, regulations were framed whereby twenty-five householders resident in a central place might take the initial steps for the establishment of a municipality in the area.[5] Occupancy of premises of an annual value of £10 qualified for voting and a payment of £1 a year in local taxes was the condition of eligibility for election. Subject to these qualifications men of colour were as eligible as white men. Led by Beaufort West

[1] Ord. 1–4 of 1834. *Vide supra*, p. 298.
[2] Aberdeen to D'Urban, 11 March 1835 (Cape Archives; C.O. 1322).
[3] See Durham, *Report*, pp. 112 *sqq*.
[4] Boyce, W. M., *Notes on South African Affairs* (London, 1838), p. 124.
[5] Ord. 9 of 1836.

in 1837 the country was soon dotted with units of village government. Cape Town obtaining its municipal system by a separate Ordinance three years later.[1] Thereafter its commissioners and wardmasters took the lead in all the political agitation that followed.

While the villages might thus gain experience in self-government by deliberating and deciding upon their local affairs, the rural areas still remained under nominated Field-cornets and Justices of the Peace. Above these were the Agents appointed by the Governor—Resident Magistrates in their capacity of Civil Commissioners as successors of the old Landdrosts, administering the police, fiscal and judicial business of the country districts.

The outstanding need of the country was for better means of communication, and a comprehensive ordinance for the construction of roads was passed in 1843.[2] A Central Road Board of three official and three unofficial nominees was set up and charged with the construction and maintenance of all main roads. It drew its revenue from a special grant and a road rate, and relied mainly upon convict labour. To provide local roads elective Divisional Road Boards were set up chosen triennially from property owners in the district.

These elective Municipal Councils and Road Boards afforded useful training grounds for subsequent political co-operation on a national scale. Similar training was acquired in the numerous societies that sprang up to promote Christian knowledge and Bible study and to further philanthropic, educational and cultural ends. The part played by the Churches, in particular by the Dutch Reformed Church, was of great significance. In the early 'forties new churches were founded in outlying parts and villages grew up around them. The clergy and elders came up periodically to the Synod at Cape Town and the popularity of the Synod gave good ground for supposing that an elected legislature would receive the same measure of support. From the first the Church had been controlled strictly by the State, but after 1830 the State became more liberal, and even the Roman Catholic clergy were included in the government grant towards clerical salaries. An Ordinance of 1843 gave a wide measure of self-government to the Dutch Reformed Church, the Church of the great majority. The Synods were freed from the embarrassing presence of Political Commissioners, and their resolutions could be questioned only in the Courts of law. Nor was it any longer necessary to submit the names of elders and deacons for official approval.[3] The Anglican Church was at first under the direct control of the British Government, but it later achieved considerable local freedom.[4]

[1] Ord. 3 of 1839 as amended and re-enacted by Ord. 1 of 1840. Cape Town had to be specially treated, because it was a garrison town.

[2] Ord. 8 of 1843. [3] Ord. 7 of 1843.

[4] In 1847 the bishopric of Cape Town was established with Robert Gray as its first Bishop. Under his leadership the Anglican Church expanded and, six years later, sees were established at Grahamstown and at Pietermaritzburg with Gray as metropolitan. But his

In the eighteen-thirties education was still the handmaiden of religion in South Africa, as it was in England. Local school committees of nominee members had vague supervisory powers, but strict centralised control was preserved and no books were to be used in schools except those distributed by the Governor through the Bible and School Commission.[1] By 1839 this Commission had become atrophied, and the educational system was recast in the scheme drafted by John Fairbairn and Sir John Herschel, the noted astronomer, for only by the proper provision of schools could the South African College, founded at Cape Town ten years previously, hope to achieve its avowed aim of becoming a university.[2] Even so, progress was slow. The new Department of Education consisted of one all-powerful Superintendent, who was "general inspector, general registrar, curriculum maker, selector of teachers and of text-books".[3] First- and second-class schools were under his immediate control; farm and missionary schools (mainly for Coloured children) merely received grants in aid. The schools, almost without exception, were one-teacher schools, and teachers were ill-paid. Even on the eve of representative government in 1853 the grant for the ecclesiastical establishment was four times as high as that for education. But this state of affairs was not to continue for long. The ecclesiastical grant, assailed by upholders of the "voluntary principle", remained stationary in amount until it was abolished in 1875;[4] the educational vote was supplemented by ever-increasing annual appropriations.

While the Colony was thus growing to healthy adolescence much had happened elsewhere to encourage a relaxation of imperial authority. Sydenham in Canada was seeking to implement Durham's

attempt to maintain control through a general Synod was challenged by some congregations and their attitude was upheld by the Judicial Committee in 1863 on the ground that, since the Colony had representative government, the Crown, could no longer "regulate religion or civil rights by the prerogative".

In Natal, Bishop John Colenso, the stormy petrel of the Church, took up a similar attitude of independence which resulted in a schism in his diocese until his death in 1883. The outcome was a far-reaching Privy Council decision (1882) that the Church of the Province of South Africa was a voluntary association and that its members, in the absence of a specific contract, were not subject to the jurisdiction of its ecclesiastical courts. See Walker, E. A., *History of S. A.*, 3rd edn. (1957), pp. 237, 300, 302.

[1] Malherbe, E. G., *Education in South Africa*, p. 66.

[2] Ritchie, W., *History of the S.A. College*; Walker, E. A., *The S.A. College and the University of Cape Town.*; Fergnson, W. T. and Immelman, R. F. M., (Eds.), *Sir John Herschel and Education at the Cape, 1834–40*.

[3] Malherbe, E. G., *op. cit.* pp. 72–3. Inspection was almost unparalleled in those days. The Superintendent was James Rose-Innes.

[4] The "voluntary principle" implied the abolition of State grants to the Churches. It was an echo of mid-nineteenth-century liberalism and came to be regarded as a sound principle of relationship between Church and State on the ground that it would give religious societies more freedom from State control when financial support was withdrawn. Its sponsor in the colony was Saul Solomon, an ardent Congregationalist of Jewish origin and a prominent member of the Cape Parliament. He brought the issue before Parliament almost annually from 1854 until it triumphed in 1875. The voluntary principle was accepted by Natal in 1869. Solomon, W. E. G., *Saul Solomon*, pp. 34–8, 64–6, 173–9; Walker, E. A., *History of S. A.*, pp. 298, 302.

memorable Report, and other British possessions had caught the democratic fever. New South Wales, Van Diemen's Land, South Australia, St Lucia and even Malta petitioned for representative institutions. The Committee for Trade and Plantations was losing its influence over the Cabinet and parliament, for *laissez-faire* was coming into fashion. Thus encouraged the citizens of Cape Town in 1841 petitioned once again for a Legislative Assembly on the ground *inter alia* of the successful working of municipal institutions.[1]

To Governor Napier the grant of an elective Assembly seemed advisable as a school for political training wherein the inhabitants could learn "to think and act for themselves", but Lord Stanley, the Secretary of State, saw many difficulties in the way. Rival local interests, conflicting prejudices, racial friction between British, Afrikaner and Aborigines—all these had to be faced, and the management of the Fingos and other "caffre" tribes included within the Colony, as well as the emancipated slaves, seemed too weighty a burden for untried hands.[2] The outward flow of the Great Trek was drying up, but a new source of perennial difficulty was arising in the rivalry between the eastern and western parts of the Colony.

From 1836 to 1839 the Eastern Province had experienced the rule of a strong Lieutenant-Governor in Captain Andries Stockenstrom, and had not liked it; but since his departure, it had liked an "absent and distant government" still less. The Easterners would not join in the demand for an Assembly unless it were accompanied by separation or the removal eastward of the seat of government. This suggestion had first been mooted by D'Urban, who believed that Cape Town, whose interests differed from all the rest of the Colony, had far too great an influence in its affairs. If the capital were placed, for example, at Uitenhage this would be remedied.

In general the economic condition was not promising. Exports and imports were still unprogressive; there was a shortage of labour; immigration was at a standstill; there was only a single post a week between Cape Town and Grahamstown, and road building was still rudimentary. It was still uncertain whether the Cape could bear the expense of an elected legislature. But it was the problem of the franchise that troubled Lord Stanley most—the problem which had damped down the West Indian agitation for self-government.

Downing Street waited four years for a reply to Lord Stanley's objections and at last it was Earl Grey who reminded Sir Henry Pottinger that he was still awaiting a statement on the constitutional question (2 November 1846). But Pottinger was too much immersed in a Kaffir war to take any action and left the problem to his successor, Sir Harry Smith.

[1] Napier to Stanley, 20 December 1841, *Applications from the Cape ... for representative government ...*, *Parl. Pap.* 1846, XXIX (400).

[2] Stanley to Napier, 15 April 1842, *Applications from the Cape ... for representative government ...*, no. 6, *Parl. Pap.* 1846, XXIX (400).

During the six years (1841–6) since the question had become one of practical politics, the force of Stanley's objections shrank rapidly. The accumulated experience gained in church meeting, school committee and board room had taken the sting out of John Philip's gibe against an earlier petition for an Assembly that "the alphabet must come before Montesquieu and Locke". The freed slaves, having served their apprenticeship, were gradually finding their places in the labour market. The relations between the colonists and the mission stations were improving, and the Masters and Servants Ordinance of 1842, which studiously avoided all reference to colour, was found by the Crown so comprehensive a safeguard of the equality of treatment of all races that the Fiftieth Ordinance was thereby repealed.[1] The fact that certain Coloured persons had qualified for the municipal franchise and that in Cape Town a Malay had even been elected as a ward master[2] proved that the difficulties in the way of a uniform parliamentary franchise were not insuperable.

New roads and bridges and improved mountain passes made the posts more frequent and expeditious and greatly facilitated communication between the country districts and the seat of government.[3] Steamship service to England, new jetties and wharves and some lighthouses—all promised well for economic progress: while banks, insurance and joint stock companies pointed in the same direction. Sheep farmers were filling up the gaps in the Colony left by the cattle farmers who had gone on trek.[4]

The political situation was not so satisfactory, for the Kaffir war of 1846–7 had been painful and costly; but the cost fell mainly upon the British taxpayer, and the war was not without profit to local speculators, while the annexations that followed gave the Colony a better frontier and some hope of a more lasting peace. Natal had been annexed, and though the proclamation of the Queen's sovereignty over the territory beyond the Orange (Feb. 1848) was disturbing, there were at least indications that Britain did not intend to pursue its unwilling subjects to far-off Ohrigstad or Potchefstroom.

Above all there had been great political changes in England and other parts of the Empire. The Government seemed to be as anxious to give the boon of representative institutions as the colonists were to receive it. Lord Elgin had solved the riddle that had baffled his predecessors in Canada; New South Wales was flourishing under a representative system, and the youngest colony of all, New Zealand, had been supplied by Earl Grey with a complete federal scheme, which Captain George Grey, its Governor, had characteristically taken it

[1] Order in Council, 27 August 1842. Cf. Macmillan, W. M., *The Cape Colour Question*, pp. 263–4.

[2] Memorandum by John Montagu, *Parl. Pap.* XXXVIII [1137], p. 16.

[3] *Report upon the operations of the Central Road Board* (1843–53), *Cape Votes and Proceedings* 1855, App. I.

[4] Walker, E. A., *Hist. of S. A.* p. 205.

upon himself to pigeon-hole.[1] In Great Britain itself the Corn Laws had gone in 1846 and the last roots of the old colonial system were soon to be pulled out by the repeal of the Navigation Laws (in 1849). It is not surprising that Earl Grey at the Colonial Office, impatient of the £1,000,000 spent on the War of the Axe, should remind the new Governor, Sir Harry Smith, that in future the Colony would be expected to bear its extraordinary military burdens, a warning that pointed unmistakably to a system of representative government.[2]

The nominated Legislative Council was sinking deeper and deeper into contempt and the lack of tact of some of the Governors did not mend matters. Napier had properly snubbed the memorialists from Port Elizabeth who presumed to advise him on military defence,[3] but his cavalier treatment of unofficial members—"Do not waste your breath, important matters are settled elsewhere"[4]—was ill-advised. The Governor's interpretation of his functions as chairman of the Council was not always flawless. When appealed to on a point of order Napier was apt to ask for the ruling of the Secretary to the Government or of the Attorney-General. Smith's similar reliance upon Attorney-General Porter's legal wisdom infuriated the unofficial members on more than one occasion.[5] When defeated by the solid phalanx of officials, the unofficial minority often fell back upon its defences, refused to concur, and recorded reasons for dissent. They objected to the introduction of Appropriation Ordinances without the three weeks' notice required by the standing rules; they complained that the rigidity of the Charter of Justice delayed or prevented necessary judicial changes and reforms. The Government met the first objection by pointing out that Appropriation Bills were not subject either in Great Britain or elsewhere to the same procedure as other Bills. The second objection they accepted by empowering the Council to amend the Charter of Justice provided that no such amending Ordinance should take effect until confirmed by the Crown, unless it had been carried by the unanimous vote of the Council.[6] Pottinger's instructions (1846) marked a further extension of the legislative authority of the Council; henceforth all Ordinances which in the opinion of the Judges were *intra vires* might be promulgated and enforced without waiting for the confirmation of the Crown.[7] But these concessions came too late to revive public confidence in the Council.

[1] See *C.H.B.E.*, vol. VII, Pt. II, ch. VI, pp. 93–6.
[2] Quoted in *The Cape Monitor*, 15 November 1850.
[3] Chase J. C., *Natal Papers* (1843), II, p. 13.
[4] Theal, G. M., *History of South Africa*. II, 239.
[5] Cf. *Parl. Pap.* 1851, XXXVII [1362], p. 29; Adderley, C. B., *Statement of the Present Cape Case*, p. 5.
[6] Letters Patent, 4 January 1844 (*Government Gazette*, 5 April 1844).
[7] § 31 of Pottinger's Instructions (Cape Archives; C.O.1336).

The memoranda submitted by Smith's official advisers in 1848 provide instructive reading.[1] While Porter's report found most favour with the Governor, the views of the Colonial Secretary, John Montagu, of Chief Justice Wylde, and of Judge Menzies were no less weighty and comprehensive. There was general agreement that in the new constitution there should be two legislative Houses, but much division of opinion as to their structure. Porter and Montagu favoured a Legislative Council nominated for life; Menzies suggested nomination during pleasure; Wylde made a hesitating proposal that the Council be partly nominated and partly elected "perhaps by the members of the Legislative Assembly". All agreed that the Assembly should be fully elective, but the Judges were dubious of the eligibility of office holders, who would presumably sit in the Legislative Council. All were conservative in demanding a high property qualification for members, for that was still the rule in England. But what of the franchise? There was no question of a colour bar; property and property alone was to determine the right to exercise the vote. Montagu was inclined to accept the existing municipal and road board qualification, for it would simplify registration and cause least disturbance. Porter was of opinion that the basis should be the *annual* value of occupied fixed property varying from £10 for owners to £30 for tenants-at-will; Wylde was inclined to go higher. Very few of Fairbairn's Coloured friends would have got on the electoral roll under any of these schemes, except perhaps that of Harry Rivers, the Treasurer, who proposed in all seriousness that the qualification should be "voluntary"; a payment of 10*s*. when appearing to record one's vote! Truly a Treasurer's scheme, which duly failed to convince his colleagues.

The completed draft, the "Attorney-General's Draft", was a compromise between these views.[2] A nominated Council holding seats during pleasure; an Assembly elected by £10 owners and £15 occupiers (annual value); members to possess unencumbered fixed property to the value of £500 or to be "in receipt of a salary from the Crown of at least £200 a year". On the advice of Menzies, paragraph 21 of the Governor's Instructions prohibiting differential legislation for non-Europeans was incorporated. A reserved civil list was approved by all. Sir Harry Smith sent forward all the documents to London with his blessing, and opened the flood-gates of public opinion by removing the vexatious restrictions upon the holding of public meetings.[3] In acknowledging the memoranda, Earl Grey admitted that most of Napier's apprehensions as to the grant of a more liberal constitution were no longer well founded,[4] and passed them on to the Committee of Trade and Plantations. The Attorney-General's Draft

[1] *Parl. Pap.* 1850, XXXVIII [1137], Enclosures 1–8.
[2] *Parl. Pap.* 1850, XXXVIII [1137], Enclosure 9, pp. 47–55.
[3] Ord. 15 of 1848.
[4] Grey to Smith, 12 February 1849, *Parl. Pap.* 1850 XXXVIII [1137], p. 100.

of 1848 was the parent of the Cape Constitution Ordinance of 1853, but it only bore a general family resemblance to its offspring, which was not born without much travail.

The storms of 1848, the Year of Revolutions, were not without their repercussions upon the Cape. Long before the Board of Trade had issued its report upon Porter's draft the anti-convict agitation had taken place, and left an indelible mark upon future developments. Whether this episode be judged from the dispassionate pages of the blue-books[1] or from columns of Fairbairn's *Commercial Advertiser*, there can be no escape from the conclusion that the Crown Colony system stood self-condemned. Thrice before had H.M. Government sounded the local administration about the advisability of sending out convicts to the Cape to meet the labour shortage. Russell and Stanley had received answers in the negative;[2] Gladstone, whose offer was more tempting in view of the Table Bay harbour works, was informed that there would be no objection provided such convicts were placed under proper restrictions and not liberated in the Colony.[3] Nothing more was heard of the matter until Sir Harry Smith wrote with misguided zeal, "I beg Your Lordship . . . to take measures for conferring this boon upon Your Majesty's subjects in this Colony with as little delay as possible."[4] Earl Grey who, like Grenville in days gone by, read colonial despatches with avidity, was guilty of the same fatal assumption that he understood the situation perfectly. As convicts were apparently welcome, he felt justified in including the Cape among penal stations,[5] and asked Smith whether the Colony would take ticket-of-leave men.[6] Then, without waiting for a reply, he ordered the *Neptune* to sail for the Cape with 288 such men on board, failing to realise that convicts who worked in gangs would be more acceptable than men under nominal supervision who would be allowed to mix freely with the inhabitants.

The opinion of the colonists was emphatically opposed to the introduction of ticket-of-leave men. Smith was inundated with memorials, petitions and protests against convict labour from towns and hamlets; from ministers of religion of all denominations; from missionary societies, including one from the once redoubtable Dr Philip; from the eastern as well as from the western districts.[7] The citizens of Cape Town in public meeting assembled claimed the "rights of free men". Past animosities were silenced. An Anti-Convict Association was formed which soon had many branches, and pledges were taken not

[1] *Papers re transportation to the Cape*, *Parl. Pap.* 1849, XLIII (217), and *Correspondence re reception of Convicts*, *Parl. Pap.* 1850, XXXVIII [1138].

[2] Stanley to Napier, 14 November 1842, *Parl. Pap.* 1849, XLIII (217), p. 236.

[3] Maitland to Gladstone, 10 September 1846 and Enclosure, *Ibid.* p. 6.

[4] Smith to Grey, 8 May, 1848, *Parl. Pap.* 1849, XLIII (217), p. 19.

[5] *Ibid.* p. 46.

[6] Circular, 7 August 1848, *Parl. Pap.* 1849, XLIII (217), p. 23.

[7] 37 Enclosures in Despatch No. 94, 24 May 1849, *Parl. Pap.* 1850, XXXVIII (1138), pp. 38 *sqq.*

to receive or succour the convicts. Cape Town was the heart and John Fairbairn the soul of the movement as much as Boston and Samuel Adams had been in the greater drama that had once been enacted across the Atlantic. Indeed the American parallel might be drawn closer since Grey gave as a reason for sending the convicts the £1,000,000 which H.M. Government had spent in the late Kaffir war,[1] extorting from Grahamstown the indignant cry, "Did we not pay, did we not suffer?"[2] In the House of Commons, C. B. Adderley was an indefatigable ally of the colonists. "We founded colonies", he jeered, "for the sake of our convicts, and now we pretend to transport convicts for the sake of the colonies."[3]

The Anti-Convict Association, through its executive committee, sat *en permanence* and issued almost daily admonitions to its members and the country at large. Sackcloth and ashes were to be the order, and good citizens declined an invitation to a Government ball on the ground that the occasion was unsuited for gaiety. Smith was urged to refuse to take over the convicts, and precedent was found for him.[4] But while the Governor, whose personal sympathies were with the people, hesitated to disobey orders, the situation was becoming alarming. Government contractors were threatened; Field-cornets and Justices of the Peace resigned office.[5] Then followed resignations of unofficial members from Road Boards, Prison Boards, School Committees, the Harbour Commission and finally from the Legislative Council. Others nominees were appointed to the legislature, but these likewise resigned under pressure: physical, moral and economic. On July 14 the *Advertiser* announced exultantly, "The Council adjourned—it is believed never to meet again!"

At length the Attorney-General ruled that the Governor was "within the law" if he retained the convicts on H.M. ships until the royal pleasure be known, and this Smith promised to do. The extremists, however, demanded that the convict ship be sent away as soon as it had been revictualled. They renewed their pledges, and when the *Neptune* hove in sight, extended the boycott to the Naval Department, the Commissariat and all concerned with the administration and management of the convicts. Smith could not tolerate open sedition. He prohibited mobs, crowds or meetings in any public street, and issued a theatrical appeal to the army reminiscent of Bonaparte in Italy.[6] Fortunately means were found for evading the boycott, and the Executive Council proved an effective brake upon hasty action.

[1] House of Lords, 15 February 1849. *Hansard*, 3rd Ser., CII, 746 *sqq*.
[2] Report of Public Meeting in Grahamstown, 4 July 1849, *S.A. Pamphlets*, S. A. Public Library, 575, f. 362 (10).
[3] Adderley, C. B., *Argument against compelling the Cape to become a penal station*, in *S. A. Pamphlets*, 575, f. 362 (9).
[4] *South African Commercial Advertiser*, 16 and 26 May, 2 June 1849.
[5] Smith to Grey, 29 June 1849 (Despatch No. 106).
[6] Proclamation, 16 October 1849, *Parl. Pap.* 1850, XXVIII [1138], p. 129.

Grey's scanty despatches during this period make painful reading. The slow means of communication, which often rendered instructions obsolete before they had reached their destination, cannot be made to shoulder all the responsibility. Smith's despatch of May 24 reached him on August 13, and with the batch of memorials enclosed should have left no doubt in his mind as to the gravity of the situation. Yet Grey sat Buddha-wise for nearly four months longer hugging the belief that, when faced with a *fait accompli*, Smith would find a way out of the impasse. It was only on November 30 that he wrote, "Had I been aware how strong was the feeling which existed at the Cape on this subject, I should not have advised the measure which was adopted."[1] The *Neptune* was ordered on to Van Diemen's Land and the obnoxious Order in Council of 4 September 1848 was revoked.

Passive resistance had gained the day, a surer indication of a people's fitness for self-government than open rebellion. The activities of the Anti-Convict Association and all its branches, the frequent public meetings, the outspoken resolutions were proof positive that the Colony had served its apprenticeship qualifying it for representative government.[2] At no time previously had there been such solidarity. "This is the first occasion", wrote Smith, "on which Dutch and English inhabitants coalesced in opposition to Government";[3] and again, "East and West clasp hands and stand shoulder to shoulder."[4] Well might Fairbairn rejoice on the eve of the *Neptune's* departure that "the people of the Cape of Good Hope have shown to the world what it is that constitutes a state".[5]

Before the tumult and the shouting died, the report of the Committee of Trade and Plantations upon Porter's draft arrived.[6] Three fundamental conditions were laid down by Letters Patent; that the legislature should consist of a Governor and two Houses, *both* elective; that the Chief Justice should be *ex-officio* President of the Legislative Council; that the Governor should have power to dissolve both Houses simultaneously or the Assembly alone.[7]

The report was explanatory of the Letters Patent and advisory in other respects. In Canada an agitation for an elective Council had arisen, and the failure of the existing Cape Legislative Council did not encourage the Committee to recommend another similarly constituted. To guard against radicalism or parochialism, the Upper House was to be elected for a longer period than the Lower, upon a higher property qualification and by more extensive constituencies.

[1] Grey to Smith, 30 November 1849, *ibid.* p. 148.
[2] Cf. *S.A. Commercial Advertiser*, 15 May 1850. Fairbairn in the Legislative Council, 20 September 1850, *Parl. Pap.* 1851, XXXVII [1362], p. 82.
[3] Smith to Grey, 30 September 1849, *Parl. Pap.* 1850, XXXVIII [1138], p. 95.
[4] *S.A. Commercial Advertiser*, 26 May 1849.
[5] *Ibid.*, 16 Feb. 1850.
[6] *Report of Committee of Trade and Plantations*, *Parl. Pap.* 1850, XXXVIII [1137], pp. 101–8.
[7] Letters Patent, 23 May 1850, *Parl. Pap.* 1850, XXXVIII [1234].

Being directly elected, it should have wider powers in matters of finance than were normally given to second chambers. Office-holders should not be eligible for election since eligibility was a feature of "parliamentary government" (i.e. Durham's new-fangled responsible government); but it might be convenient to permit certain office-holders to participate in the business of either House without a vote. The Committee did not approve of a reserved civil list greater than was necessary for providing that certain items of expenditure be met, as in England, by permanent Acts, and even so the colonial legislature was to have the power to repeal or amend such Acts subject to reservation by the Governor. In view of the mixed population the committee favoured Montagu's high franchise proposals.

The popular press greeted this report with a chorus of approval,[1] but Smith and his advisers were perplexed. The Governor had instructions to complete the Council and draft a constitution Ordinance taking the Letters Patent as a basis and the report and Porter's draft as guides, but public opinion could no longer be ignored in the choice of unofficial members. In view of his unfortunate experiences with unofficial members in the previous year and of the changed political atmosphere, Smith ventured upon the unusual step of inviting recommendations from the municipal bodies and the Divisional Road Boards before filling up the vacancies.[2] These bodies held unofficial elections and sent in their nominations, the first five on the list being Christoffel Brand, editor of the *Zuid Afrikaan*, Sir Andries Stockenstrom,[3] F. W. Reitz, John Fairbairn and J. H. Wicht. Acting on the advice of his executive, Smith appointed the four first-named "Popular Members" with the Easterner, Robert Godlonton, editor of the *Grahamstown Journal*, as the fifth, although his name was eleventh on the list. William Cock, the sitting Eastern member, of course retained his seat.

Smith, who had merely bound himself to select members "from the names to be submitted", was within his rights in choosing Godlonton, and certainly the choice was a wise one, since it was desirable to have in a Council summoned to frame a constitution the man who had the confidence of the separatist centre. Moreover, Godlonton's appointment had been anticipated even in the Cape Town press.[4] Yet the four Popular Members thought fit to charge the Governor most unwarrantably with a breach of faith. Outvoted on this and other points they fell back upon the tactics of the previous year. On September 20, Stockenstrom read out "eleven reasons for dissent", and promptly resigned his seat. He was followed by his three

[1] *The Observer*, 7 May 1850; *S.A. Commercial Advertiser*, 11 May 1850.

[2] Government Notice, 6 May 1850.

[3] Stockenstrom had been given a baronetcy on relinquishing the office of Lieutenant-Governor in 1839.

[4] *The Observer*, 11 June 1850; *S.A. Commercial Advertiser*, 15 June 1850.

colleagues. They, as the representatives of the people, refused to be regarded as "an impotent minority packed together merely to complete an otherwise defective machinery".[1] By their resignation the Council once more ceased to function, for unless there were ten sworn Councillors, there was no Council.

The four ex-members with the aggrieved Mr Wicht formed themselves into a *soi-disant* constituent committee and drew up the "people's draft". Smith constituted the rump Council into a commission and ordered it to proceed post-haste with constitution-making, while he himself carried on a newspaper war with Fairbairn.

Rival petitions and memorials poured in, while Smith clung pathetically to the view that the "more respectable (though they be in a minority)" were with the Government. Above the din was heard occasionally the voice of the dissenting East taking exception (under thirty-one heads) "to any form of representative government holding its sittings in Cape Town".[2]

Earl Grey[3] was fast losing patience with a Governor whose policy resulted in meetings and petitions beyond number "calculated to create and to keep a most mischievous agitation in the Colony".[4] But in urging Smith to carry on with the existing Council, Grey showed that he was totally unaware of the legal difficulties which Smith presently explained in a dignified defence of his conduct.[5] In due course Grey made the *amende honorable*. In the meanwhile the "people's draft", "A constitution adopted by some five municipal councillors, about fifty Malays and a few others",[6] had been taken to London by Fairbairn, and was not faring well. The indefatigable Fairbairn sat on Lord John Russell's doorstep, took legal opinion and haunted parliamentary lobbies; all without avail.[7] C. B. Adderley, a leading light in the Colonial Reform Society, did what he could in the Commons and tried to awaken public interest by a *Statement of the present Cape Case*, to which John Adamson, a pillar of conservative society in Cape Town and a Professor at the South African College, replied.[8]

Unlike the issue of 1849, the affair of 1850 was but a storm in a tea-cup which a little tact on both sides might have obviated. A comparison of the two drafts shows little disagreement.[9] For instance both laid down that the franchise should be based upon the occupation of

[1] *Parl. Pap.* 1851, xxxvii [1362], p. 92.

[2] *Ibid.* pp. 159–62.

[3] Smith to Grey, 24 September 1850, Despatch No. 138 with Enclosures, *Parl. Pap.* 1851, xxxvii [1362], pp. 11–87; also Despatches Nos. 176, 177, 178, all on November 30, *ibid.* pp. 97–141.

[4] Grey to Smith, December 10, *ibid.* p. 197.

[5] Smith to Grey, 19 February, 1851, *Parl. Pap.* 1851, xxxvii [1362], p. 192.

[6] *Cape Monitor*, 22 November 1850. Cf. Adamson, J., *Notes on Cape Affairs*, pp. 10 *sqq.*

[7] For correspondence between Russell and Fairbairn, see *Parl. Pap.* 1852–3, lxvi [1581], pp. 52–72.

[8] Adamson, J., *Notes on Cape Affairs*, 2 July 1851.

[9] The texts of these drafts are given in *Parl. Pap.* 1851, xxxvii [1362], pp. 90, 151–6.

immovable property valued at £25. In other respects the official draft was more conservative, e.g. it favoured a high property qualification and a long period of tenure for members of the Legislative Council, for property would not be safe in a House full of "Cobbetts and Hunts".[1]

In the meantime frontier troubles had put the clock back. At the close of 1850 the most devastating of all the Kaffir wars had broken out.[2] "Loyal" Hottentots rebelled and thereby caused a strong reaction against the proposed low franchise; the miserable condition of the frontier drew the Government towards the separatist camp[3] to which it had been strongly opposed in 1848.[4] Immersed in military duties and with nerves frayed by Grey's untimely despatches, Smith was determined to complete the Council, even if it were necessary to remove it to Grahamstown and to fill the vacancies with Easterners.[5] Forced to decide precipitately, Montagu, who was acting head of the civil administration, appointed four respectable nonentities who had the confidence of neither East nor West, and, in October 1851, the Legislative Council functioned again. At this stage public opinion was extremely complex. Cape Town, loyal to its "people's draft", could see nothing good in the new Council; the East clamoured for separation or the removal of the seat of government;[6] farmers petitioned against the low franchise; missionaries and Coloured persons counter-petitioned in its favour. Montagu's brusqueness annoyed several petitioners and led to an unavailing agitation for his removal from office.[7]

Much further agitation might have been avoided if H.M. Government, with ample information to go upon, had taken Fairbairn's parting advice and given the Cape a constitution by Act of Parliament. But Russell would not go behind the backs of his colonial advisers; hence a draft Ordinance was prepared to be passed by the Legislative Council with such amendments as it thought fit, provided the Letters Patent of 23 May 1850 remained untouched. The provisions of this draft were in substance identical with the Constitution Ordinance as finally enacted, save that in it the property qualification for members of the Council was a compromise between the "people's" and the commissioners' drafts.[8]

When this Ordinance came up for second reading the unofficial

[1] Porter, in Legislative Council, *ibid.* pp. 44–5.

[2] *Vide supra*, p. 349 *sqq.*

[3] *Memoranda by members of Executive Council*, 22 October 1851 (Duplicate Despatches, Cape Archives; C.O.a. 52).

[4] *Parl. Pap.* 1850, XXXVIII [1137], Enclosures 1–8.

[5] *Minutes of Executive Council*, 29 September 1851 (Cape Archives; Minute Book, Executive 3).

[6] See *Separation Pamphlets*, S. A. Public Library, 575, e. 907, 908, 909; cf. Wilmot and Chase, *History of the Colony of the Cape of Good Hope*, pp. 469 *sqq.*

[7] *Parl. Pap.* 1852–3, LXVI [1581], p. 138, and pp. 6 *sqq.*, 12, 26, 31, 40.

[8] Draft of Ordinance, 15 September 1851, *Papers re Representative Assembly*, *Parl. Pap.* 1852, XXXIII [1427].

members were in no hurry to proceed. Montagu was inclined to agree to delay, but Smith peremptorily instructed him to carry on. The revulsion of feeling against "Aborigines" caused by the war led to the deletion of the £25 occupancy clause and the substitution of the Municipal and Road Board franchise with a £50 wage qualification as alternative. "The £25 franchise", said Montagu in reply to Porter's protests, "would widen the breach between the farmer and his servant."[1] He was all along more sympathetic to the Afrikaners than most of the officials, and he alone questioned the wisdom of making English the sole medium of debate in the future Parliament in view of the fact that it would not be the mother tongue of many of its members.[2]

The third reading was carried at length through the Legislative Council on 26 March 1852, but there was little enthusiasm.[3] The constitution was complete in so far as the Cape could make it, but it had still to run the gauntlet in Downing Street with a shaky ministry and an inexperienced Colonial Secretary in Sir John Pakington, who was overburdened with the other difficult South African problems that we have discussed elsewhere.[4]

When Cathcart superseded Smith in March 1852, the Constitution Ordinance was formally re-enacted to avoid technical difficulties owing to the change of Governor, and Cathcart left Lieut.-General Darling, the newly-arrived Lieutenant-Governor for the Eastern Districts to handle the political situation while he devoted himself to the troubles on the frontier.[5] Darling took his policy from the masterful Attorney-General, Porter, and wrote home adversely to the new constitution;[6] but for six months Pakington did nothing. When he did reply, he hinted strongly at the separation of the East from the West and the transfer of the capital in a despatch that set the whole Colony agog.[7] Fortunately, however, before he could do anything, the Derby Ministry fell (December 1852), and the new Colonial Secretary, the Duke of Newcastle, soon proved himself less undecided and more efficient than his predecessor. The necessary amendments to the Draft Constitution were soon made, including Porter's £25 franchise, and on 11 March 1853 an Order in Council was issued embodying the Cape Ordinance.[8]

Seven separate drafts had thus contributed to the making of this constitution, which, with amendments, was to serve the Cape until

[1] *Parl. Pap.* 1852–3, LXVI [1581], p. 236.

[2] *Parl. Pap.* 1850, XXXVIII [1137], p. 21. Cf. Adamson, J., *Case of the Cape of Good Hope and its Constitution*, p. 28.

[3] *Parl. Pap.* 1852, LXVI [1581], pp. 286–7.

[4] *Vide supra*, pp. 357 *sqq.*

[5] *Vide supra*, p. 357.

[6] Darling to Pakington, 25 April 1852, *Parl. Pap.* 1852–3, LXVI [1581], pp. 174 *sqq.*

[7] Pakington to Cathcart, 4 September 1852, *ibid.* pp. 326–7.

[8] The Constitution Ordinance, *Parl. Pap.* 1852–3, LXVI [1640] (Ord. 2 of 1852). Eybers, pp. 45–54.

the Union of 1910. Two elective Houses, a low franchise balanced by a high property qualification for the Upper House, the use of the cumulative vote and the approximately equal representation of East and West were amongst its most distinctive features. The £25 franchise, based as it was upon the total value of premises and land occupied in the same constituency, was equivalent to an annual rental value of 30*s*.,[1] with the effect that about 80 per cent of the adult male population in the Colony were entitled to registration.[2] Voting was to be by word of mouth, no literacy test of any kind being required. Every person qualified to vote was eligible for election to the Assembly excepting bankrupts and office-holders. Prospective Legislative Councillors had, in addition, to be not less than thirty years of age, and to possess unencumbered immovable property worth £2000 or, with movables, a total value of £4000 over and above all debts.[3] The basis of representation, as in England, was still territorial. The unit for the Assembly was to be the electoral district returning two members; but, for the election of the Legislative Council, the Colony was divided into a western division returning eight members and an eastern division returning seven members. Each of these divisions formed a single constituency. Hence the Council expressed more clearly than the Assembly the conflicting aims and ideas of East and West. The cumulative vote which was used in the Council elections as well as in the election of the four members for Cape Town in the Assembly gave every facility for the adequate representation of minorities.

The traditional balancing between legislature and executive is illustrated in the financial provisions. All supplies were voted in Parliament, but only at the request of the Crown; hence Money Bills were initiated in the Assembly upon the recommendation of the Governor.[4] In view of its elective character, the Council was given the power of amending as well as rejecting Money Bills,[5] a clause that was to lead to immediate friction. The financial provisions of the constitution were supplemented by two separate Ordinances. To give stability to essential services and to secure vested rights, the Governor was empowered "until Parliament shall otherwise direct" to pay out of the revenue specified sums for the civil establishment, for pensions and public worship, and for border (aborigines) expenditure.[6] The effect of this so-called "reservation of the civil list" was that a sum which in 1856 amounted to about one-third of the total revenue was spent under the authority of a permanent Act, the Governor being instructed to reserve his assent to Bills repealing or

[1] Adamson, J., *Case of the Cape of Good Hope and its Constitution*, p. 5.
[2] *S. A. Com. Advertiser*, 6 September 1853.
[3] Constitution Ordinance, § 33.
[4] Constitution Ordinance, § 80.
[5] *Ibid.* § 88.
[6] Ord. 3 of 1852.

amending this Ordinance. But if the Crown retained this uncertain check over expenditure, it showed confidence in the colonial legislature in another direction by giving it full control over customs policy, provided no differential duties were levied.[1]

The termination of rigid Crown Colony rule implied greater freedom for the local executive as well as for the local legislature. The age of government by instruction was at an end. Henceforth the Governor's Instructions were to be less definite in substance, narrower in scope and admonitory in effect. The relations between executive and legislature were to a large extent defined in the constitution. The Governor might propose laws, and had the sole right of recommending appropriations;[2] he might likewise return Bills to either House with amendments and, finally, declare according to his discretion whether he assented thereto in the name of the Crown, refused his assent or reserved the bill for the signification of the royal pleasure.[3] To facilitate the relations between the executive and the legislature certain office-holders were permitted to participate in the deliberations of either House, but without the right to vote.[4] By resolution, the first Parliament interpreted this privilege to include eligibility to serve on Select Committees, and the right to move or second motions—great latitude for an irresponsible executive.

At the opening of the first Parliament considerable doubt existed as to the extent of its legislative competence. With natural exuberance the popular press claimed the fullest freedom;[5] with equally natural caution Lieutenant-Governor Darling stressed prerogative, when, at the close of the first session, he reserved the Bill extending trial by jury to civil cases on the ground that it amended the Charter of Justice.[6] Official despatches clarified the issue. Sir George Grey, the first Secretary of State for the Colonies since the divorce of that department from the War Office, enclosed an opinion of the Law Officers of the Crown to the effect that "when the Crown gives a Constitution and a local legislature to a Colony, the Crown is held to have abandoned its legislative authority except where it is expressly reserved".[7] Further, since the Cape Parliament had power to make laws for the peace, order and good government of the colony, it had also power of "repealing or modifying Orders-in-Council relating to the Settlement".[8] The ultimate sovereignty of the Crown-in-Parliament over the Colony remained unimpaired, but the era of direct legislation for internal

[1] Order in Council, 5 March 1852; Ord. 6 of 1853.
[2] Constitution Ordinance, § 81.
[3] *Ibid.* § 82.
[4] *Ibid.* § 79.
[5] *S. A. Com. Advertiser*, 20 May 1854.
[6] Speech of Lieutenant-Governor Darling on prorogation of Parliament, 26 September 1854 (*Cape V. and P.; L.C.* 1854).
[7] *Opinion of Law Advisers of the Crown* (Cape Archives; G.H. 37).
[8] Secretary of State, Sir G. Grey to Governor Sir G. Grey, 6 February 1855 (Cape Archives; G. H. 37).

affairs by prerogative instruments was at an end. Orders-in-Council, when used hereafter, were issued under the authority of Parliament and related to extra-territorial matters or those arising from international conventions with regard to which the local legislature had no competence.[1] The grant of a legislature did not, however, imply that there was a delegation of prerogative powers which are attributes of an executive: hence the Cape Parliament might not pass coinage Acts, or grant honours, or issue charters, or curtail the executive powers of the Governor. All these would impair the prerogative of the Crown.[2] Negatively the Crown retained some supervision over internal affairs by the power of disallowing any Act within two years,[3] and by instructing the Governor to reserve certain classes of bills, e.g. those which amended the constitution, or differentially affected coloured races, or which were prejudicial to the Crown. Non-observance of these instructions did not invalidate an Act which was not otherwise repugnant to an Imperial Act that had been promulgated in the colony.

The elections ran their leisurely course from January to May 1854. There were no parties, but many Eastern members subscribed to a programme which included separation or the removal of the seat of government eastward, a vagrancy law, and a revision of the franchise in an upward direction.[4] Solidarity on these issues was in view of its structure more pronounced in the Council than in the Assembly. The fears regarding the low franchise had little justification in fact. In the population of the Colony, estimated in 1853 at 225,000, the Coloured outnumbered the Europeans in the ratio of 55 to 45, but the ratio of registered voters was heavily in favour of the Europeans.[5] Outside Cape Town, the villages and the mission stations, few Coloured people got on the roll, since neither domestic servants nor squatters satisfied the conditions of the franchise.[6] Ignorance and apathy likewise kept away from the polling booths a great many more Coloured persons than Europeans. If the proportion of Coloured persons to Europeans was higher in the eastern districts, the proportion of unqualified Coloured persons in those districts was likewise higher. There is no evidence that the Coloured vote vitally affected the return of any member to the first Parliament.

The Houses settled down to business in July 1854 and framed rules of procedure modelled upon those of Westminster. The first statute provided for freedom of speech in Parliament and, remembering the *Stockdale* v. *Hansard* decision of 1839, for immunity from libel actions

[1] This corresponds in effect with the provisions of the Colonial Laws Validity Act 1865, which defines the legislative powers of Colonies having representative institutions.
[2] Keith, A. B., *Responsible Government*, I, 117 *sqq.*
[3] Constitution Ordinance, § 83.
[4] *S. A. Com. Advertiser*, 24 September 1853.
[5] *Cape of Good Hope Statistical Register*, 1853.
[6] Government Notice (*Government Gazette*, 30 June 1854).

of all publications printed under the authority of Parliament.[1] This freedom was not to degenerate into licence, as the eccentric Dr Tancred speedily found when he was committed for five days to the custody of the Sergeant-at-Arms.[2] In the first session there was a serious clash between the two Houses over Money Bills. The Assembly, having deleted certain items recommended by the Governor, refused to concur in an amendment by the Council for the restoration of some of these charges, e.g. for the Central Road Board, on the ground that such an amendment was in effect equivalent to initiation by the Council. Several conferences of "managers" proved abortive, and the Appropriation Bill was literally dropped by the Speaker when he refused to receive the Bill at the hands of the messengers of the other House.[3] The Governor saved the situation by withdrawing the obnoxious recommendations, and by incorporating two Appropriation Bills in one which the Council reluctantly accepted.[4] Victory did not always rest with the Assembly, however, for in the following session a minor Appropriation Bill (for £3600) failed to pass upon the Assembly's refusing to agree to the deletion of an item by the Council.[5] The independence of the Council was likewise upheld by the occasional rejection of measures passed by the Assembly.

Several useful consolidating Acts stand to the credit of the first Parliament. By the Divisional Council Act the whole Colony was mapped out into effective units of rural government based upon the parliamentary franchise.[6] These elected Councils inherited the powers of the Divisional Road Board and the Divisional School Commissions which were now abolished. The powers of these Councils were extended from time to time. In 1858 the Central Road Board was also abolished. Its main functions were to be discharged by a Government department under a Commissioner of Roads, and its subsidiary duties were handed over to the Divisional Councils.[7] In the same year provision was made for the creation of elective School Committees with somewhat inquisitorial powers over teachers, and with the right to frame regulations subject to the approval of the Divisional Councils.[8] A Board of Examiners was also set up to give a fillip to higher education. In the sphere of justice the structure created by the royal Charter still stood firm. Trial by jury was extended to civil cases, but the Eastern desire for a division of the Supreme Court was not satisfied. A Cape Town motion in favour of responsible government aroused all the jealousy of the Easterners at Western domination,

[1] Act 1 of 1854.
[2] Kilpin, R., *Old Cape House*, p. 35.
[3] *Cape V. and P.*; *L.C.* 1854, Minutes 33, 40, 42.
[4] *Ibid.* Minute 44 (22 September 1854).
[5] *Cape V. and P.*; *L.C.* 1855, p. 251.
[6] Act 5 of 1855.
[7] Act 9 of 1858; Eybers, G. W., *Select Const. Docs.*, p. 85.
[8] Act 14 of 1858; Eybers, *op. cit.*, p. 87.

but it led to a useful Select Committee, which reported that all that was necessary for its consummation was the amendment of Paragraph 79 of the Constitution Ordinance so as to render certain office-holders eligible for election to Parliament.[1] Equally fruitless were numerous petitions for the extension of ecclesiastical commitments. The Liberal cause led by Saul Solomon, member for Cape Town, small in stature but mighty of brain, successfully held out for the "voluntary principle" which was ultimately to triumph.[2]

The most vexed question before the Parliament was the old issue of separation.[3] It had been raised almost from the moment of the landing of the 1820 Settlers, recommended in the Commissioner's report of 1825, harped upon in monotonous refrain by the *Grahamstown Journal* from its first issue, and swelled in chorus whenever the frontier was ablaze. The proclamation of the Eastern Districts and the appointment of a Lieutenant-Governor proved utterly futile to silence the clamour. As Cathcart pointed out, the Eastern and Western Provinces were merely convenient electoral divisions and the Lieutenant-Governor could do no more on his own initiative than a secretary to the Government.[4] That the Lieutenant-Governor was a "sham, denuded of all power", was an old Eastern complaint.[5] But the call for separation in the early stages was really misleading. The East had neither the population nor the resources to maintain a separate government. What the frontier really wanted was devolution—a federal scheme. But federation implied a central government concerned with major issues, and all the problems of the eastern frontier were of this category: defence, treaties, war, commandeering, martial law. The case against separation was well put by Porter in 1848. "If you have separation you must have a General Assembly. Where should it meet?"[6]

During the War of the Axe (1846–7) the removal of the seat of government first suggested by D'Urban was put forward as a strong alternative to separation. Thereafter most petitioners prayed for either form of relief indiscriminately. A strong, if extravagant, plea for removal was made by John Paterson, editor of the *Eastern Province News* and member for Port Elizabeth in the first Parliament. He found in the distant and absent government the root of all the troubles with the tribes and the main cause of the Trek.[7] In reply to Earl Grey's anxious enquiries, Sir Harry Smith and his advisers wrote

[1] *Cape V. and P.; P.* (1855), Appendix I, 150.

[2] *Vide supra*, p. 372.

[3] For this issue see Taylor, N. H., "The Separation movement during the period of representative government of the Cape, 1854–72." (Unpublished M. A. thesis, University of Cape Town, 1938.)

[4] Cathcart to Secretary of State, 2 August 1854 (Cape Archives; G.H. 37).

[5] Wilmot and Chase, *History of the Colony of the Cape of Good Hope*, pp. 293, 405.

[6] *Parl. Pap.* 1850, XXXVIII [1137], Enclosure I.

[7] Paterson, J., *Dissertation on the absolute necessity of Resident Government in the Eastern Province*, 1851 (S.A. Public Library, 575, e. 907 (11)).

voluminous memoranda on the subject.[1] The Governor, than whom none knew the frontier better, was strongly opposed to the removal of the capital: "Distance is no consideration. India is governed from Calcutta and Russia from St. Petersburg. . . . A supreme Government in a wilderness is an embarrassment in time of war."[2] He was well supported by W. Field, the Collector of Customs: "In 1846 Lieutenant-Governor Hare at Grahamstown did not realise that war was imminent, while Maitland in Cape Town did."[3] Porter was undecided, but Montagu, Rivers the Treasurer, and William Hope the Auditor-General were in favour of removal as a panacea for frontier ills, Montagu adding that the settled West was better suited than the disturbed East for a subordinate administration under a Lieutenant-Governor.[4] Smith, however, was on firmer ground than the majority of his executive. Waging war is not a normal function of government, and in time of emergency the legislative capital, as frequent experience has shown, should be well behind the scene of operations.

But in 1851 Smith, who had been hitherto as pronounced an opponent of separation as of the removal of the capital, was, in view of frequent frontier troubles and constant friction between East and West, prepared to change his mind on the issue.[5] He wrote to Grey that "when the proper period shall arrive for doing so", he would favour the setting up of a separate government and a separate legislature for the Eastern Province (which should include British Kaffraria and the Sovereignty beyond the Orange), "provided the seat of Supreme Government remained at Cape Town".[6] We are left in the dark as to whether there was to be a real separation, for which the East was not prepared to pay, or a federation which would not solve the problems raised by Porter. The Executive was agreed that some form of separate government was necessary, but in view of the imminence of representative government, the question was held over until after the Cape Parliament had met.

By 1856 the separatists had much sounder arguments on their side. The population was increasing in consequence of post-Crimean immigration; wool exports were flourishing; there was the example of Natal which had just been constituted a separate Crown Colony in 1856. Their opponents might point to the enlarged Kaffraria as a satisfactory buffer; to the separation of the office of Governor from that of the Commander-in-Chief, who was now stationed on the border backed by a large garrison; to a revised burgher law which had so frightened north-western farmers as to reinforce the separatist cause

[1] Cape Archives; C.O.a. 52 (various Enclosures 22 October and 20 November 1851).
[2] *Ibid.* Smith to Grey, 7 November 1851.
[3] Memorandum by W. Field, 22 October 1851 (Cape Archives; C.O.a. 52).
[4] Memorandum by J. Montagu (*ibid*).
[5] Cory, G. E., *The Rise of South Africa*, v, pp. 167, 270–1.
[6] Smith to Grey, 14 June and 7 November 1851 (Cape Archives; C.O.a. 50 and 52).

from an unexpected quarter.[1] The Grahamstown party, dissatisfied with parliamentary appropriations for Eastern purposes, raised the issue of separation in 1856, but Saul Solomon, one of the members for Cape Town, carried the House with him in favour of unity.[2] The Grahamstown party had not with them half the Eastern districts which were predominantly Dutch. In claiming a separate and independent government coupled with Western contributions to their defence they were "suing for a divorce from bed and board only and not from community of property".

The aftermath of the cattle-killing episode in Kaffraria[3] (1856–7) revived the agitation, and resulted in the dramatic resignation of Godlonton and his five followers in the Council. And there the matter rested until Governor Sir George Grey's grandiose schemes of federation held out further alluring prospects in the same direction.

During the two decades in which the Cape Colony had moved from Crown Colony rule to the threshold of self-government, a group of little states had arisen beyond its borders. The Cape Colony had expanded into a white-governed South Africa. The story of the Trek is told in the previous chapter, but it has direct bearing on our present subject, for the activities of the Trekkers created problems in government and policy of far-reaching consequence to the constitutional development of South Africa. They left the Colony fortified by an opinion of Stockenstrom that he knew of no law forbidding any of His Majesty's subjects from leaving his dominions; to which opinion D'Urban had subscribed,[4] though the Attorney-General, more cautious, had stressed not the legal issue but the practical difficulty of preventing this emigration.[5]

In truth neither Stockenstrom nor D'Urban was sure of his ground. The writ *ne exeat regno* was as old as *Bates's case* (1606),[6] and the maxim *nemo potest exuere patriam* was a time-hallowed principle of jurisprudence. Napier wisely remembered Burke's warning upon a more historic occasion, and tried to arrest the Trek by persuasion rather than by force;[7] but to recall the Trekkers to the legal boundaries of the Colony was beyond the resources of colonial statesmanship. The logic of events pointed to two alternatives: either to proclaim the sovereignty of the Crown over the adjacent territories thus occupied, or to accept the claim of the emigrants that they had divested themselves of allegiance. Philanthropy pointed one way, *laissez-faire* another; parsimony suggested an ingenious *via media* by an insistence upon a

[1] Petitions against the Burgher Law, *Cape V. and P.; H. of A.* 1855.
[2] Separation Debate, *H. of A.* 1856 (S.A. Public Library, 575, e. 908 (9)).
[3] *Vide infra*, p. 412.
[4] Chase, J. C., *Natal Papers*, I, 36, 53, 78.
[5] Eybers, G. W., *Select Constit. Docs.*, pp. 145–6.
[6] Prothero, G. W., *Constitutional Documents*, p. 341.
[7] Chase, J. C., *Natal Papers*, II, 19; Walker, E. A., *Hist. of S.A.* pp. 207 *sqq.*

personal allegiance without territorial annexation. The Cape of Good Hope Punishment Act of 1836 was the result.[1] The frontiersman's strictures upon this—"a bungling piece of ultra-philanthropic legislation"—were not wholly undeserved. It caused much friction and bad blood and proved of little practical utility. Ultimately Natal was annexed; the Orange River Sovereignty proclaimed and then abandoned: the independence of the emigrants north of the Vaal was recognised. By 1854 the era of vacillation in colonial policy was succeeded by a period of comparative stability and there only remains for consideration the constitutional aftermath of these events.

By the end of 1836 the Trek was in full swing, but not until the settlement in Natal, two years later, was an effective republican State established. Neither at Thaba Nchu (December 1836) nor at the Vet River (April–June 1837) was anything in the nature of a fundamental law adopted. During these years the Trekkers were a nomadic pastoral community, autonomous *de facto*, knit together more closely than any organised community in modern times by ties of blood, language, religion, race, occupation and cultural outlook. If constitution they had, it was largely unwritten; based upon Biblical ethics and such laws and customs of the Colony as they regarded fit and proper to Trek conditions. Their laws were more truly "in their breasts" than the royal prerogative in that of Richard II. The people in arms was sovereign; the people assembled in public meeting made law. Direct democracy as in the older Swiss cantons was the only system. The "People's Council" formed a provisional executive and administrative body entrusted with the minimum of authority requisite for the welfare of the camp.[2] This *Burgerraad* functioned as a Council of Policy as well as a Court of Landdrost and Heemraden; the military needs were served by a *Krygsraad*—a Council of Commandants. Nor was there any material change when Retief was elected Governor. The Nine Articles of Winburg of June 1837 are barren of constitutional precepts.[3] Their tenor is negative: to exclude all heterogeneous elements from the *Maatschappij* (Association). The first true fundamental law of the Trekkers is the *Grondwet* of Natal (October 1838).[4]

The *Grondwet* of Natal defined with some care the structure and functions of the legislature and of the judiciary, but said little about the executive.[5] Direct democracy was discarded and all power was delegated to the Volksraad, a Council of "People's Representatives" elected by citizens of full age. The councillors must be citizens between the ages of twenty-five and sixty, men whose judgment must be ripe but whose vigour must not be impaired—an important consideration in a State which had but just emerged from an armed camp. No

[1] 6 and 7 William IV, c. 57.
[2] Preller, G. S., *Voortrekkermense*, I, 297; II, 67, 94, 97.
[3] *Ibid.* II, 300–1; R 10/37 (S.S. I, Transvaal Archives).
[4] *Voortrekker Wetgewing* (ed. G. S. Preller), 1924, XII–XVI.
[5] Bird, J., *Annals of Natal*, I, 376 *sqq.*, II, 207; Chase, *Natal Papers*, II, 28–35.

man might refuse election or resign without valid reasons. Attendance was a duty enforceable by a fine as in medieval England. The Volksraad appointed and removed all officials from the Head Commandant downwards; it made treaties and alliances; it granted public land; it heard appeals, confirmed, mitigated or quashed sentences. Its procedure was simple and informal. The constitution was sufficiently flexible to permit of structural amendment without undue delay. As a rule office-holders were debarred from membership of the Raad, but exceptions were sometimes made, e.g. in the case of the Harbour Master. The Raad rejected a proposal to admit the Head Commandant to the same privilege, and at one time showed its suspicion of the military power by abolishing this office save in time of war or emergency. When lacking a quorum it frequently co-opted the necessary members. The *Vox populi* was respected, but it was not allowed to drown the voice of the chosen representatives. There were complaints of irregularities at elections, and Volksraad resolutions were sometimes flouted, but these blemishes were due more to defective administrative machinery than to sinister influences.[1] The Volksraad met four times a year, but the sessions were brief, seldom exceeding one week in duration. Between sessions from March 1842 onwards a committee of about five functioned as a *Kommissie Raad*, dealing with emergency issues. Its decision had to be confirmed at the next session. The social freemasonry prevalent among the Trekker communities did not however prevent the adoption of high-sounding titles for the Volksraad and the more important functionaries,[2] for the State had to stand upon its dignity.

In the judicial sphere and in local government the Natal *Grondwet* borrowed freely from the laws of the Cape Colony. The Landdrost was both Magistrate and Civil Commissioner, as in the old days. Petty cases were dealt with summarily; more serious matters were determined with the aid of Heemraden, and graver offences with the addition of a jury of twelve, whose verdict of guilty had to be unanimous. The Field-cornet was the ubiquitous agent of local government, combining civil and military duties; his military superior was the Commandant, his civil head the Landdrost.

The Natal Volksraad functioned for nearly seven years, but the shadow of annexation was upon it almost from the start.[3] In 1840–1 it strove vainly to obtain recognition by Great Britain upon a basis of "reciprocal alliance".[4] When Port Natal was occupied in the following year diehards began to recross the Drakensberg as we have seen. Ever since Retief's election as "Governor" the unity of the

[1] Preller, G. S., *Voortrekker Wetgewing*, pp. 5, 13, 28, 31, 32, 40, 46, 120, 122, 272, 276.

[2] Stuart, J., *De Hollandsche Afrikanen en hunne Republiek in Zuid Afrika*, pp. 112, 141.

[3] Bird, J., *Annals of Natal*, I, 605, 610 *sqq.*, 649, 690; Chase, *Natal Papers*, II, 52, 101, 147–148, 157, 196.

[4] Bird, J., *Annals of Natal*, I, 612, 622, 627 *sqq.*, 642–3, 657 *sqq.*; Chase, *Natal Papers*, II, 166 *sqq.*

Trekker groups had been maintained in theory. The Natal Volksraad claimed jurisdiction over the organised bands that had remained on the Vet River (Winburg), and over those who had trekked with Hendrik Potgieter to the Mooi River (Potchefstroom). Through the personal efforts of A. W. Pretorius, the hero of Blood River, a loose federal union with these communities was achieved.[1] After 1840 these districts were entitled to send delegates to Pietermaritzburg. In February 1841 a subordinate representative assembly, styled an Adjunct Raad, was created for the district of Potchefstroom;[2] and a similar Raad for Winburg two years later.[3] The Adjunct Raad was to be regarded merely as a committee of the general Raad and was bound to submit its resolutions twice yearly for approval. One need not unduly stress the legalistic unity. Ties of sentiment rather than of law bound the Trekkers. In matters of civil government Winburg and Potchefstroom were virtually independent, but all the federated districts were expected to stand together in the face of common danger. In practice the scheme broke down. Hendrik Potgieter had offered aid to Natal in 1842 but sent none.[4] In the critical period of the negotiations between Commissioner Henry Cloete and the Natal Volksraad in 1843, some Transvaalers and a number of men from between the Orange and the Vaal under Jan Mocke did, however, ride down to Pietermaritzburg in the vain hope of preventing submission.

The Volksraad session of August 1843 was of unusual constitutional interest. The normal body was reinforced by the addition of five members from beyond the Drakensberg. *Het Publiek* in the person of hundreds of armed burghers was there to give moral backing to the delegates. The five from "across the mountain" were irreconcilables, and withdrew from the meeting when they realised that the majority were not with them, and that Cloete did not propose to intervene beyond the Drakensberg. Moderate counsels prevailed, and the Volksraad accepted British allegiance in the terms of Napier's proclamation of 12 May 1843;[5] but delay in the confirmation of land titles and dissatisfaction with the allocation of native reserves led to a steady exodus of Boers from the new colony.

Upon the submission of Natal, the Winburg-Potchefstroom districts disowned all connection with the Maritzburg Volksraad, and Potgieter informed Cloete accordingly.[6] The incoming of emigrants from Natal among the Loyalists on the Modder, Riet and Caledon Rivers complicated the situation there and made a policy of mere drift north of the Orange impossible. The Menzies annexation of

[1] R90ᵃ/51 (Transvaal Archives, S.S.1); Malan, *Die Opkoms van 'n Republiek*, pp. 29–30, 67.
[2] Preller, G. S., *Voortrekker Wetgewing*, pp. 101–3. [3] *Ibid.* p. 233.
[4] R911/42 (Transvaal Archives SS.1).
[5] Preller, G. S., *Voortrekker Wetgewing*, pp. 243 *sqq.*; Bird, *Annals of Natal*, II, 165, 251, 266 *sqq.*; Eybers, pp. 174 *sqq.*
[6] Malan, *Die Opkoms van 'n Republiek*, p. 70; H. Potgieter to H. Cloete, 3 October 1843.

1842 was premature and unauthoritative, but it was regarded as the most logical step even by a hostile critic.[1] There followed the skirmish at Zwartkopjes, the Touwfontein Convention, the appointment of a Resident, and finally Sir Harry Smith's proclamation annexing the territory between the Orange and the Vaal (3 Feb. 1848).[2]

The breach with Natal was the occasion for the adoption of the Thirty-three Articles by the Potchefstroom Raad (April 1844). These were a fragmentary code of law, civil, criminal, administrative, to be supplemented by the "laws of Holland".[3] In spite of these Articles centrifugal tendencies were becoming more prominent. For some years the Transvaal Boer remained more or less a nomad. Organisation was that of the armed camp rather than of the settled state; the Krijgsraad was more effective than the Volksraad, the Commandant more potent than the Landdrost; loyalty, in short, to one's trek leader was stronger than national unity. Empty spaces and grazing needs encouraged this tendency. Was not secession by emigration theirs as of right? In 1845 Potgieter abandoned Potchefstroom for Andries-Ohrigstad; it was nearer to the sea and indisputably outside the zone of the hated Punishment Act. The Ohrigstad Volksraad, under the influence of immigrants from Natal, modelled itself upon that of Pietermaritzburg. It built up a constitution piecemeal by resolutions and instructions. Drawing freely on de Mist's Ordinance of 1805,[4] it defined with care the multifarious duties of the Field-cornets, for efficient local government mattered more than central authority.[5]

It claimed jurisdiction over the whole Transvaal, but its supremacy was challenged by *Het Volk* tumultuously in public meeting, no matter how few were present, by the newcomers on the Mooi River and at Magaliesberg, and by the redoubtable Head Commandant, Hendrik Potgieter, the *pater patriae* of the Transvaal. Potgieter, as founder, was at first given a privileged position in the Ohrigstad Raad,[6] but the Raad forthwith complained of the dictatorial airs of the Head Commandant:[7] "The state was not a monarchy, there must be no "Oom Hendrik to tell them what to do."[8] After coming within measurable distance of civil war, the dispute was patched up in 1847,[9] and presently Potgieter trekked north to the Zoutpansberg and there founded still another republic at Schoemansdal. In the south, Pretorius had established an ascendancy at Potchefstroom. More diplomatic than Potgieter and a better parliamentarian in view of his experience in Natal, Pretorius succeeded in checking separatist

[1] Lion Cachet, *De Wortelstrijd der Transvalers*, p. 261.
[2] *Vide supra*, p. 346.
[3] Eybers, G. W., *Select Constit. Docs.*, pp. 349–56.
[4] Walker, E. A., *Hist. of S. A.* pp. 135, 248.
[5] R 111 c and 111 f/45 (Transvaal Archives S.S.1).
[6] R 108/45 (Transvaal Archives).
[7] *Ibid.* R 116 and 116c/46.
[8] Lion Cachet, *De Wortelstrijd der Transvalers*, p. 304.
[9] R 120i/47 (Transvaal Archives).

tendencies. By obtaining recognition by Great Britain he gave to the Transvaal a *de jure* character which Natal had lacked. The Derde Poort Conference (May 1849) between delegates from Ohrigstad and other parts of the Transvaal laid the foundation stone of the South African Republic;[1] the Sand River Convention in 1852 made the completion of the structure possible.[2]

In the Orange River Sovereignty a civil government was set up two months after the annexation of 1848.[3] Centrally the High Commissioner at Cape Town was supreme. Locally there was a Resident who acted as Chief Magistrate and with him two District Magistrates. Popular sentiment was met by elective Commandants and Field-cornets. Following the rebellion and the defeat of Pretorius at Boomplaats, a revised constitution was introduced in the Sovereignty.[4] A Council consisting of the four Magistrates and of eight unofficial nominees was given limited legislative powers. The official element acted as an informal Executive Committee and drafted Government Ordinances, which the same Magistrates might be called upon to interpret on the Bench—an undesirable mixture of legislative and judicial functions.[5] Other provisions were on familiar lines, saving that the Courts of the Sovereignty were not competent to deal with the graver crimes; these had to be determined in the Courts of the Cape Colony. Provision was made for teachers and predikants; soon a newspaper appeared and the Sovereignty began to take on the air of a settled State. But, before long, abandonment was decided upon, a development that was not altogether unexpected.[6]

When independence had been granted by the Bloemfontein Convention of 1854, a provisional government was set up, a Volksraad elected, and a new constitution drafted which was to prove the best balanced and the most liberal of the republican constitutions (April 1854).[7] The task of preparing it was entrusted to a committee of the Raad which had before it for guidance several drafts, among them one by a Hollander teacher, Groenendaal, who borrowed widely from the institutions of the Netherlands Kingdom and the *Code Napoléon*, and another by J. M. Orpen, who modelled his version upon the fundamental law of the United States. The legislators culled political wisdom from these sources, but in the main they drew from the common fount of Trekker political thought tempered by the experience of the past twenty years.

[1] R 178 and 179/49 (Transvaal Archives); R 190/50; Lion Cachet, *De Wortelstrijd der Transvaalers*, p. 315; Malan, *Die Opkoms van 'n Republiek*, p. 72.

[2] Botha, P. R., *Die Staatkundige Ontwikkeling van die Transvaal*, pp. 4–7.

[3] Proclamation 8 March 1848 (Eybers, pp. 273–5).

[4] Regulations, 14 March 1849 (Eybers, pp. 275 *sqq.*); *The Cape Observer*, 20 August 1850.

[5] Malan, J. H., *Die Opkoms van 'n Republiek*, p. 128.

[6] Adamson, J., *Cape of Good Hope and its Constitution*, p. 35; Orpen, J. M., *Reminiscences of Life in South Africa*, pp. 96, 280, 286, 338; Collins, W. W., *Free Statia*, pp. 46, 73.

[7] *Friend of the Sovereignty*, 1, 8, 15 April 1854; Malan, J. H., *Die Opkoms van 'n Republiek*, pp. 224–7. For English version as amended in 1866, see Eybers, pp. 286–96.

A sovereign Volksraad of a single House, the Roman-Dutch law, the State Church, the Landdrosts and Heemraden, the Commandants and Field-cornets, the liability to military service from the age of sixteen, a white franchise, are all familiar features of the Trekker State; but there was to be no Commandant-General save when elected by field officers in time of war, nor was *Het Volk* given direct authority. The Volksraad was to be supreme in legislation and taxation and to exercise a wide control over the executive. At the head of the executive stood the State President elected by direct popular vote for five years. He was assisted by a Council of official and unofficial members, the latter being elected by the Volksraad. The individual functions of the President were few and narrow. He nominated officials for the approval of the Volksraad; he might suspend them; he supervised the administration, but he had no veto over legislation; with the support of a majority of the Executive Council he could grant pardons; but the declaration of war, the making of peace and the framing of treaties required the approval of the Volksraad. The President, as well as other officials, might be removed from office upon impeachment provided there was a three-fourths majority against him. By the same majority in three successive annual sessions the constitution might be amended.[1] This procedure was respected throughout the lifetime of the Republic.[2] The influence of the United States Constitution was further to be seen in the recognition of "natural rights"—security, property, freedom of the press and of public meeting, and equality before the law. The weakest link was the judiciary, which as yet lacked a proper Supreme Court and a Court of Appeal.[3] The elaborateness of the constitution, however, was not to the liking of the typical trek-boer; "was not the law of Moses sufficient?" asked some.[4]

North of the Vaal, the Derde Poort Conference of 1849 had created a peripatetic central Volksraad. Though its authority was often flouted, the idea took root. A *Kommissie Raad* helped to transact urgent business. The greatest obstacle to unity was the presence (in 1851) of four and later three Commandants-General, each with an independent command. However, the reconciliation between Pretorius and Potgieter and the ratification of the Sand River Convention at Rustenburg in March 1852 was a step in the right direction.[5] The title of South African Republic was adopted in 1853, but ecclesiastical

[1] § 24 of Grondwet of 1854 was amended by § 26 of 1866 to read "two successive annual sessions".

[2] Thompson, L. M., "Constitutionalism in the South African Republics", p. 53 (article in Butterworth's *South African Law Review*, 1954).

[3] Such Courts were established in 1876 by ordinary law on the supposition that the amending provision was required to change an article of the Constitution but not for adding additional matter.

[4] Orpen, J. M., *Reminiscences of Life in S. Africa*, p. 340.

[5] R390/52 (Transvaal Archives S.S.3); Lion Cachet, *De Wortelstrijd der Transvalers*, p. 366.

strife seemed to put union back indefinitely.[1] In the circumstances it was sheer optimism on the part of Marthinus Wessel Pretorius, the son of Andries, to draft a new constitution for such as would accept it. Nevertheless, the Rustenburg *Grondwet* was the result, and this, after much hesitation, Lydenburg and Zoutpansberg accepted between 1858 and 1860.

The Rustenburg *Grondwet* was a long and unwieldy document containing much miscellaneous material alien to a fundamental law.[2] In general structure it resembled the Free State constitution, upon which it must have been closely modelled, but there were certain characteristics that reveal the traces of twenty years of trek history. There was an executive with an elected President, but the Commandant-General could not be eliminated; he remained the most important member of the Executive Council, second only to the President. The sovereignty of the people was emphasised; the homogeneity of the community made it possible to confine all offices and membership of the Raad to the Dutch Reformed Church. Not only was citizenship limited to white men, but there was a definite declaration that "the people desire to permit no equality between coloured people and the white inhabitants, either in church or state".[3] The Roman-Dutch law of the Colony as it had existed at the time of the British Occupation in 1806 was accepted as the common law.[4]

In Natal, meanwhile, constitutional progress proceeded smoothly after 1845. For two years the district of Natal depended upon the Governor and Legislative Council of the Cape Colony, its Lieutenant-Governor being merely an executive officer.[5] Provision was made for adequate judicial machinery and procedure and for elective municipal boards in urban areas.[6] There followed the institution of a nominee Legislative Council, which in practice was identical in composition with the Executive Council and thus found little favour with the inhabitants.[7] But in the opinion of Lieutenant-Governor Pine a wide measure of local government was a necessary preliminary for representative institutions:[8] a sound instinct instilled by Durham's Report.[9] These defects were remedied in 1854. Two Municipal

[1] Walker, E. A., *Hist. of S. A.* pp. 298 *sqq*.

[2] Eybers, pp. 363–410; Bryce, J., *Studies in History and Jurisprudence*, I, 442 *sqq*.

[3] *Grondwet* of the S. A. Republic, § 9.

[4] For a lucid analysis of this constitution see Thompson, L. M., "Constitutionalism", pp. 57–65. See also van der Walt, A. J. H., "Die Ontwikkeling van Boere-Bestuursinstallinge", in the *Geskiedenis van Suid-Afrika* (1951). II, 70–98.

[5] Letters Patent, 30 April 1845 (Eybers, G. W., p. 184).

[6] Ordinances of Cape Leg. Council, 12, 14, 18 of 1845; 6, 16, 26 of 1846; Ord. 5 of 1847.

[7] Letters Patent 2 March 1847 (Eybers, p. 186); Holden, W. C., *History of Natal*, pp. 172–3.

[8] Memorandum by Lieut.-Gov. Pine, 28 September 1852, *Parl. Pap.* 1852–3, LXVII [1697], pp. 78–81.

[9] *C.H.B.E.* II, 340 *et seq*.

Ordinances were passed, one urban, the other rural, of which the urban one defined every township with 1000 inhabitants as a "borough" entitled to a corporate life similar to that of English boroughs. The rural measure was less satisfactory and was subsequently suspended.[1] Encouraged by the Bloemfontein Convention, a memorial praying for the abandonment of Natal was submitted by some 300 persons whose arguments the administration found little difficulty in refuting.[2] Considerable increase in population, which gave the British element a majority, favoured more liberal measures; but the presence of a Native population variously estimated to outnumber the Europeans in the ratio of maybe twenty to one justified official caution, Sir George Grey pointing out that as the franchise could not be based upon a colour bar, a high property qualification was inevitable. The Colonial Office had the benefit of an illuminating despatch by Sir George Grey, and another by ex-Lieutenant-Governor Pine,[3] and Grey's recommendations were in the main adopted.

The constitution of 1856 followed the traditional lines of a colony having a limited form of representative government. The institution of a single House, partly elected and partly nominated, was based on experiments in New South Wales and in some of the West Indies. In Natal the ratio of elected to official members was unusually high—12 to 4. The property qualification for the franchise was sufficient to debar the Native population. The Legislature had power to amend the constitution, provided all measures altering the existing structure of the Legislative Council or diminishing the salaries of officials or limiting the prerogatives of the Crown were to be reserved. The Crown likewise retained the power of revoking the Letters Patent.[4]

Under the constitution the Governor was empowered to appoint judges and pardon offenders, but the colony had outgrown the judicial system of the early days, and therefore the Supreme Court was reconstituted in 1857.[5] It was to consist of three Judges holding office on good behaviour and having jurisdiction over all criminal and civil causes arising within the colony. Trial by jury was obligatory in indictable offences and optional in the more important civil disputes. Appeals to the Privy Council were allowed on the same basis as appeals from other colonial courts of like standing.

By 1858, therefore, the process of political differentiation that had begun in 1834 was complete. The four present provincial units—the

[1] Ord. 1 and 3 of 1854 (Natal).

[2] Memorial 15 April 1854; Pine to Secretary of State, 25 September 1854 (Cape Archives; G.H. 37).

[3] *Correspondence re the Cape Colony, Natal, and adjacent Territories*, 1855–7; *Parl. Pap.* 1857, x [2198]; Grey to Russell, 24 November 1855; Labouchere to Grey, 17 December 1855 (Enclosure from Pine).

[4] Letters Patent, 15 July 1856 (Eybers, pp. 188 *sqq.*).

[5] Act 10 of 1857. In the early days Natal had merely a Lieutenant-Governor.

Cape Colony, Natal, the Orange Free State and the Transvaal—had all consolidated their political institutions. In the same year Sir George Grey opened a new vista by raising the issue of federation in his efforts to remedy the difficulties that inevitably arose from the presence of so many diverse governments within what was in essence a single community.

CHAPTER XVI

THE PERIOD OF TRANSITION IN SOUTH AFRICAN POLICY, 1845–1880

THE reluctant annexation of Natal in 1843, the treaties with the Griquas and Moshesh, and the military demonstrations beyond the frontier, which had culminated in the annexation of the Orange River Sovereignty in February 1848, were successive attempts to cope with new developments. But it was not till the years 1852–4 that the British Government emerged from the confusion caused by twenty years of trekking and Kaffir wars and assumed for the first time an unambiguous attitude towards South African affairs. That attitude was revealed in the complete acceptance of the Great Trek and its results. By the successive Conventions of Sand River and Bloemfontein the British Government abandoned the thesis it had upheld since the passing of the Cape of Good Hope Punishment Act in 1836, that the trans-frontier Boers were British subjects amenable to British law. The Conventions undermined the whole humanitarian assumption that one of the main functions of British power in South Africa was to supervise and manage the relations between the whites and the Natives; for, however inglorious had been the actual record of Native policy within and without the limits of the Cape Colony before 1854, the leading motive of that policy, as envisaged in Downing Street, had been the maintenance of peace between Natives and Colonists, and not the extrusion of the Natives or the advancement of the colonial frontiers.

The heavy expense of the Kaffir War of 1850–3, the menace of a Native war in the Sovereignty and the collapse of British administration there caused a violent reaction in the United Kingdom in favour of that section of public opinion led by Richard Cobden and Sir William Molesworth which demanded that the colonists should undertake and pay for the conduct of their own internal affairs. While the grant of responsible government to Canada, the passing of the Australian Colonies Act (1850) and the New Zealand Constitution Act (1852), which took place during these years, were in the main liberal acts based upon a profound and widely held belief in the right of British colonists to political liberty, the part played by considerations of economy and the Free Trade conviction that colonies which were independent were less expensive and no worse customers must not be lost sight of. The series of catastrophes in South Africa gave to these latter considerations an abnormal influence. It was in the excitement they provoked that the Conventions were born.[1]

The grant of unequivocal independence to the Boers of the Transvaal and of the Orange River Territory abandoned a large Native population to the mercies of land-hungry farmers, who, intolerant of any form of equality between white and black, proceeded either to dispossess the Natives of their land and to absorb them as servants, or to confine them to inadequate areas, substituting a nervous military control for the tribal government which the shock of contact with the Europeans had seriously and inevitably weakened.

Great as was this swing in British policy it was not complete. In 1854 the undisguised intention of the British Government was certainly to turn its back *à tout jamais* upon Boers and Natives in the trans-frontier regions. Governor Sir George Cathcart affirmed that the Boers could only maintain themselves by exercising "a requisite supremacy" over the tribes, and that therefore "reciprocal non-interference" was inevitable,[2] while in England the Colonial Secretary, Sir William Molesworth, with even greater bluntness agreed that beyond the limits which had been put to British dominion in South Africa the Natives might "slaughter each other", and the Boers and missionaries might, if they felt so disposed, assist them without fear of imperial interference.[3]

But the demand in certain quarters had been for an even greater withdrawal from the responsibilities of dominion. There had been a moment when Earl Grey himself had considered the possibility of a withdrawal from the Eastern Frontier and the contraction of British influence to Cape Town and the naval base at Simonstown. Yet neither he nor his successors dared take so drastic a step for fear of exposing the Colonists to Native attack, or alternatively of precipitating a war of aggression against the tribes. Hence while the Cape constitution of 1853 was very liberal, the executive power was left in the hands of a Governor not yet responsible to the local Parliament. In order that Native policy might be kept more securely under its control, the British Government decided to maintain British Kaffraria, annexed in 1847, as a separate administration under the Governor in his capacity as High Commissioner.[4] For very similar reasons, only a Crown Colony constitution was in 1856 given to Natal, whose handful of colonists, living in the midst of a Native population of over 100,000 and being virtually surrounded by thickly populated tribal areas, could not support the burden of defence, and consequently could not assume the burden of governing. The creation of the

[1] de Kiewiet, C. W., *British Colonial Policy and the South African Republics*, 1848–72, ch. v, *passim*.

[2] C.O. 48/327, Cathcart to Pakington, 28 July 1852; enclosure, Cathcart to Price, 12 July 1852.

[3] C.O. 48/367, Grey to Secretary of State, 25 July 1855; minute by Molesworth.

[4] *Parl. Pap.* 1854–5, XXXVIII [1969], pp. 3, 28, 16, 31.

Republics had been an act of desperation, and thus left unsolved a sheaf of problems. Their harvesting was to take the rest of the century and to disturb successively the Colonial Office, Parliament and finally the whole Empire.

Briefly, the British Government had conferred independence upon men who were bound to the majority of the colonists in the Cape by the strongest ties of blood, religion and tradition, who were economically dependent upon the richer coastal communities, yet who were enabled by their relations with the Natives to keep the frontiers of their neighbours in a state of continual and dangerous disturbance. The African population of South Africa, even more than the white population, was one. From the Zoutpansberg mountains in the far north of the Transvaal down to the Eastern Frontier itself ran a practically unbroken line of Native settlement—Swazis, Zulus, Basutos, Pondos and Xhosas. Pressure at any point was felt over the whole area, but as it was the natural tendency of the Native populations to move from north to south, it was the southern and therefore British frontiers which were likely to be affected most by Native unrest wherever it might occur. Transvaal relations with Zululand could not leave Natal unconcerned, while, more serious still, the restless Xhosas of the Eastern Frontier had in their immediate rear the Basuto tribes upon whose borders pressed the land-hungry Free Staters.

For the next two decades, from the time of Earl Grey to that of Lord Carnarvon, South African history is concerned with the consequences of the political subdivision. Because the representative institutions of the Cape Colony were less advanced than those of the younger independent Republics, the Mother Colony could not assume of her own accord the position of leadership to which her experience and her superior wealth, population and prestige called her. The undivided authority of the Governor as High Commissioner in the conduct of relations with the Republics and the tribes inevitably meant a loss of vital contact between the popular bodies in the different States and the most important matters that would affect their well-being. On matters of high policy the elected representatives of the colonists had little voice; they were thrust back into a narrow parochialism of outlook and naturally failed to appreciate the complexity of the problems at issue. Thus the principal need of South Africa was the establishment of a unity of policy in vital matters. The policy was hard to find and to apply on sound and consistent lines, and innumerable mistakes were made in the search for it, as subsequent chapters will show; but at any rate by 1854 it was realised by some observers that the South Africa which their policy must take into account was no longer bounded by the Orange or even by the Vaal, but must extend into the remote interior that Livingstone was revealing away up to the Zambesi. Any major event from thence southward to Table Bay might affect the fortunes of the whole area.

In the Cape the new order commenced under the most favourable circumstances. The Trekkers, main elements of discontent, lay beyond the border. The two millions of money expended by the British Government during the recent Kaffir war had stimulated trade. Imports and exports flourished, and the Republics held out the promise of new markets. There was a demand for immigrants to fill the gaps caused by the losses of the Trek—a demand intensified by the significant fact that the frontier tribes by maintaining their tribal solidarity despite their recent defeats had not yet in any great numbers abandoned their own herds and fields to serve in the kitchens and till the fields of the Colony. So real had been the co-operation between the European races brought about by the anti-convict agitation of 1849 that the stipulation that all debates in the Cape Parliament were to be conducted in English aroused no opposition from the Afrikaners.

Governor Cathcart having departed for a high military command in the Crimea in December 1854, the execution of the policy of the Conventions—non-interference in Native disputes and the non-extension of the colonial frontiers—was entrusted to Sir George Grey, who had won a high reputation for handling the Maori troubles in New Zealand.[1] A policy of inaction was repugnant to the temperament of the new Governor, which was independent, constructive and restlessly enterprising. In all his previous experience in South Australia and New Zealand he had been allowed the most complete freedom to apply what measures he considered best suited to the problems of his administration. Furthermore, in New Zealand, where the Maori problem was acute and where the different European settlements were geographically separate like those in South Africa, he had had to grapple with problems very similar to those which immediately engaged his attention on his arrival at the Cape (December 1854). Thinking rather in terms of what he considered South African needs than in terms of instructions from Downing Street, Grey immediately applied his New Zealand experience to the conditions of his new government.

His first problem was presented by the Eastern Frontier tribes. Although Cathcart had so far yielded to colonial opinion as to grant to the Colonists the confiscated land of the Kat River and Theopolis Hottentots, and had pushed some of the Tembus across the White Kei in order to make room for Europeans, the main principle of his post-war settlement had been the strict segregation of white and black.[2] With more insight than most soldier-Governors he recognised that to dispossess the tribes of their land would only invite a repetition of the wars of 1846 and 1851; hence he planned to maintain British Kaffraria intact as a great tribal reserve in which European influence was to be restricted to little more than military occupation. This

[1] See *C.H.B.E.* VII, Pt II, ch. VII.

[2] *Vide supra*, p. 358.

system, admirable in its comparatively generous recognition of tribal land tenure, but open to the objection that it left the Chiefs without any real supervision or control, met with Grey's immediate disapproval. Instead of segregating the Natives and the Colonists, he planned the penetration of Kaffir territory by roads and public works, and the transformation of Kaffir society by means of schools, hospitals and "institutions of a civil character" calculated to hasten the progress of amalgamation with the whites and so eliminate the frontier.[1] To this end also he planned the immigration into the midst of the tribal population of British Kaffraria of European settlers, whose presence would check the Africans, and from whom the latter would learn those habits of industry which would fit them to live in the same civil and economic order as the whites.[2]

Grey's Native experiments required expenditure, but such was the eagerness of the Home Government to adopt any scheme that promised to avoid the recurrence of Kaffir wars, that an annual sum of £40,000 was placed at his disposal with the understanding that after three years the amount would be progressively reduced. The British Government envisaged a drastic limitation of responsibility and an unenterprising tranquillity—Grey was bent on ambitious achievement.

Conditions on the Eastern Frontier soon convinced the Governor that the success of his experiment depended upon the relations which prevailed between the Free State farmers and their Basuto neighbours. It was the signal merit of Grey's South African policy that he undertook the solution of difficulties which faced him in terms of co-operation and assistance. His first action, indeed, was to assure the Republics of his desire to maintain with them the most friendly relations,[3] and to remove from Bloemfontein the British Agent, John Burnet, lest he should be regarded by the Boers as set to watch their actions or become the focus of intrigue.

Events in the Free State itself soon demonstrated the new republic's need of assistance. At the start, all sections had proceeded amicably to the election of a Volksraad. This body drew up a constitution which provided for a Volksraad elected by universal male European suffrage, and an elected President, who, with three Volksraad members and two permanent officials, was the executive head of the State. The choice of the first President indicated that the Basuto problem was regarded by all as central, for Josias Philip Hoffman owed his election largely to his reputation of being able to manage Moshesh.

The Free State realised its weakness and the urgent necessity for a settlement of those dangerous Native questions on which the Conventions had been silent. Revenue was and remained too exiguous

[1] *Parl. Pap.* 1854–5, XXXVIII [1969], pp. 36 *sqq.*, Sir George Grey to Secretary of State, 22 December 1854.

[2] C.O. 48/365, Grey to Secretary of State, 17 March 1855; Enclosure, Address to Cape Parliament, 15 March 1855.

[3] Address to Cape Parliament, 15 March 1855.

for the proper maintenance of a border force. The illusion of quiet prosperity with which the republic had commenced its existence was soon dispelled. In all matters of government there was the most lamentable inexperience. With the British flag had gone some of the British capital invested in the Sovereignty, and the welcome Commissariat expenditure no longer supported the Bloemfontein shopkeepers. The scattered rural population was unaccustomed to paying taxes and, in any case, taxes were extremely difficult to collect. Exports did not even balance the importation of groceries and manufactured goods from the Cape and Natal; coin flowed steadily out of the country while debts increased.

The hope that Cathcart had expressed that the Transvaal and the Free State would unite under Pretorius into a single republic, strong enough to hold the tribes, could not be realised. In 1854 Marthinus Wessel Pretorius, intent on carrying out his father's design of forming a single republic on the High Veld, made an incursion into the Free State, hoping to find support there against the factions which opposed him in the Transvaal, and claiming that, as the son of the great Voortrekker leader, he was the rightful ruler of the Free State. But the men of the Free State were not of the same inclination and persuasion as the Transvaalers; he found only a few Winburgers and malcontent borderers in his favour.[1] The population even on the rich Basuto border was scanty and nervous in the face of superior numbers, and thus there was for a while a disposition to conciliatory measures. Moshesh on his side donned the resplendent uniform of a French general and entertained President Hoffman at Thaba Bosigo with much ceremony and firing of guns; but he nevertheless claimed that the departing British had taken the Warden Line away with them. Before long the Basuto determination to recover the land they regarded as theirs expressed itself in encroachment and cattle-thieving.

Hoffman soon fell foul of the nervous public opinion in the Free State. The frontiersmen, from whose ranks had come the partisans of Pretorius, sulked because he collected evidence and attempted persuasion, instead of proceeding to peremptory action. When he was ill-advised enough to send Moshesh a keg of powder as a present to replace what had been blown away in salutes, an indignant outburst forced him to resign. Yet the generality of the burghers were as yet afraid to resort to force against the Basuto. A plan that the field-cornetcies should each in turn provide fifteen men for patrol duty along the border received but lukewarm support; another scheme to build fortified camps by voluntary subscription likewise came to nothing, and at last an appeal was made to the friendly Grey to mediate.[2]

[1] Orpen, J. M., *Reminiscences*, pp. 387 *sqq.*
[2] C.O. 48/368, D. 121, Grey to Secretary of State, 1 October 1855.

In October 1855 Grey, on his way to Natal to examine Native conditions there, met Moshesh and Hoffman's successor, Jacobus Boshof, at Smithfield, where he succeeded in obtaining promises of good conduct from Moshesh and the signatures of both parties to a document recognising the *status quo*. Since, however, the aim of neither Boers nor Basuto was the *status quo*, and each party was working to secure the expulsion of the other from the debated corn lands, Moshesh's signature was merely intended to avoid antagonising the powerful Cape Government. In order to distract the attention of the Colony and to immobilise it in the event of war with the farmers, Moshesh followed up his signature by sending emissaries amongst the Eastern Frontier tribes to foment discontent.[1] And so the truce on the Basuto border itself rapidly disintegrated into the old disturbed round of alarums and thefts.

On the Eastern Frontier, Sir George Grey could gauge the confusion beyond by the discontent among the Chiefs. Here, too, the land question was vital. After the heavy losses of territory they had suffered in the two previous wars, the tribes suffocated in inadequate areas, and hungrily eyed the ground which Grey was keeping empty for the German Legionaries disbanded after the Crimean War and German peasants whom he intended to settle there, since his efforts to get British emigrants had failed. Another foundation of tribal economy was rudely disturbed by a terrifying disease called "lung-sickness" which devastated the Native herds. In the circumstances a spark might create a blaze amongst the irritable tribes, and to Grey it seemed that the spark might come from the friction over the border. Yet he was helpless to take action. The Conventions categorically enjoined upon him non-interference in the trans-frontier regions. Although the object of his appointment had been the maintenance of the order established in 1854, he now denounced the Convention policy as dangerous to the peace and well-being of the whole country, and demanded of the Home Government power to modify the agreements and a greater liberty of action.[2]

Conditions in Natal and the Transvaal bore out the High Commissioner's contention that until the Europeans and Natives of South Africa were governed by the same rules within the same political organisation, the country as a whole could enjoy neither peace nor prosperity. In both Natal and the Transvaal the settlers thought already in terms purely of their own immediate needs and tended strongly to develop particularism and localism.

In Natal local and central government had developed rapidly since its annexation in 1843. Control by the Cape authorities was steadily relaxed, and in 1856 Natal was created a separate Crown Colony with a Legislative Council on which the elected members were predominant;

[1] C.O. 48/377, Grey to Labouchere, 23 October 1856.
[2] *Ibid.* Grey to Labouchere, November 1856.

two years earlier Durban and Pietermaritzburg had become municipalities, each with a flourishing newspaper. Immigrants and goods entered the colony directly from the United Kingdom; the Lieutenant-Governor no longer submitted his despatches for approval, but merely sent copies of the more important to the Governor at Cape Town for information. Cape and Natal merchants were rivals for the inland trade on which Natal depended until the development of sugar in the coastal belt and of wool up-country. In the towns it was fashionable to express a dislike for the Cape Colony. What was more serious than political separation and commercial rivalry was the divergence of attitude and legislation in the all-important sphere of Native affairs. In the Cape the principle of political equality irrespective of race had been enshrined in the Constitution of 1853; in Natal the application of Native custom instead of Roman-Dutch law introduced the opposite principle of civil distinction. The Natal colonists were prejudiced against the tribes within their own borders; they felt them to be a menace and considered that they held too much land. In spite of the fact that a not inconsiderable portion of Natal's revenue was derived from Native taxes, the elective majority of the Council was annoyed that it could not dispose of the £5000 which had been set aside for purely Native purposes in the Royal Charter. Above all was the fear that the Natal Zulus might make common cause with their kinsmen in independent Zululand. So Natal's Native policy was directed by Shepstone's ideas, and, in order to give as little excuse as possible to the desire of the colonists to break up the reserves and make the inhabitants work, that policy was concentrated upon keeping them quiet instead of attempting to civilise them as Shepstone had wished, but for which he had not the means.

In the Transvaal after the Sand River Convention there was independence but no government. The party organisation of the Great Trek had persisted in the form of settlements in different districts, each with its own local leader. In one direction there was considerable unanimity, but paradoxically enough it was a unanimity signally illustrative of Transvaal chaos. The Native policy of the Transvaal derived directly from the order of things which Ordinance 50 of 1828 and the abolition of the commando system in 1833 had destroyed in the Cape. As in the Colony before 1828 and in the contemporary Free State, land-hunger and labour needs were the two principal factors governing the farmers' relations with their Native neighbours or subjects.[1] In principle the farmers claimed that all Natives within the limits of the republic, ill-defined as these were, were their subjects liable to taxation and commando service. The Government claimed and on occasion exercised the right to impose a labour tax on subject tribes; detribalised Natives were by law compelled to enter the service of a European master.

[1] Cf. Walker, E. A., *History of Southern Africa*, pp. 277 *sqq*.

The process of detribalisation proceeded apace. The quarrel between the Transvaal farmers and the missionaries was caused by the attempt of the former to satisfy their need for land and labour, and was thus continuous with the old feud in the Cape provoked by Dr Philip's efforts to secure political and economic freedom for the Hottentots and to prevent the extrusion of the Griquas and the Eastern Frontier Kaffirs from their land. The Transvaal always insisted upon inequality between whites and blacks, and refused membership of the State Church to the latter. The war in 1852 with the Bechuana Chief Sechele, whose cause was espoused by Livingstone, and the incessant friction in the Zoutpansberg proceeded chiefly from the failure of the Boers to recognise that the Africans were landholders much like themselves, as well as from the deeply ingrained belief that they were ineducable and preordained to serve the European. For that reason the tribes of the Transvaal were to the last treated as a military problem. Friction in the fertile lands, where the whites and blacks inevitably met, was settled by the force of a commando. If the commando were succesful, the result was commonly the expulsion of the tribe or the settlement of the whites over the heads of the tribesmen, who were in this wise reduced to what was to be the fate of a great mass of Transvaal Natives—rightless squatters or labour-tenants on European-owned land. Hence the *Krijgsraad* or War Council figured prominently in the *Grondwet* or Constitution, and the Commandant-General, next to the President the highest dignitary in the State, was elected directly by the burghers.

It is true that some effort was made, especially in the early years, to regulate the landholding of the Native tribes. Near Potchefstroom, in Lydenburg and the Zoutpansberg, and on the western limits of the Transvaal locations were set aside for various Chiefs;[1] but in the main the Transvaal did not, and owing to the extreme weakness of the central government, could not control the relations between the natives and its citizens. Like the Free State it had not the means to keep the peace on its extensive borders, where—in the Zoutpansberg, Zululand, Swaziland and the vaguely delimited West—the Natives were thickly concentrated. The "treaties" and "alliances" with the tribes never had a legal basis, nor was there an independent judiciary that might have dealt with disputes on other grounds than mere physical force. There is much reason to believe that had the Transvaal and the Free State been possessed in 1870 of strong and respected legal tribunals they might have been spared the abrupt British intervention in the Diamond Fields dispute, which is dealt with in our next chapter. In default of any centralised policy local bodies of farmers made their own terms with their tribal neighbours. Thus the Lydenburgers obtained from the Swazis a grant of land that was wedged between Swaziland and Zululand (1855), and the Utrecht farmers

[1] Cf. Walker, E. A., *History of Southern Africa*, p. 277.

settled themselves on a slice of land ceded to them by Panda, King of the Zulus (1848–1854).

The Transvaal's earliest serious border troubles were in the West. As in Griqualand, this country was less uniformly fertile than elsewhere. Boer settlement gathered at the springs that dotted the country, and such piecemeal settlement was more severely felt by the Natives in an irregularly watered country than a more scattered occupation would have been, for they never willingly pitched their kraals in the more arid areas where there was little wood and only indifferent pasture. The conflict between the two races had wider repercussions than it might have had if the Trek Boers had been dealing only with untutored savages. The Bechuana and Bakwena tribes were by no means in a purely primitive state, for they had for years been taught and guided by the self-sacrificing labours of the shrewd and capable missionaries of the London Missionary Society, Robert Moffat and David Livingstone. The missionaries feared for their stations the same fate that was overtaking the Griqualand missions, while Livingstone, with the eye of a geographer, had already distinguished the commercial and strategic value of the highway leading past Kuruman, the principal Bechuana centre, to the more remote northern interior. Because they in their turn feared that the missionaries and traders would put this "Missionaries Road" to ill use by supplying the Natives with arms and ammunition, the Boers were constant in their efforts to control it. In 1852 Andries Pretorius entered into a definite boundary treaty with the Barolong chief Montsiwa, which enabled him to declare the Road closed despite the vehement protests of the missionaries, and notably of Livingstone, who had but lately passed north along the track to the discovery of Lake Ngami.

Soon enough there was open conflict with the tribes. The followers of the Bakhatla Chief Moselele, apparently agitated by the same wave of Native unrest that swept from the Cape Eastern Frontier to Basutoland and onward to Lydenburg and the Transvaal's western border, raided the cattle of the encroaching farmers and then fled to Sechele for sanctuary. Sechele refused to give up the robbers; whereupon a commando fell upon him and expelled him from his country.[1] It was during this expedition that Livingstone's house was ransacked, and a number of women and children belonging to Sechele's tribe were captured and distributed amongst the farmers as servants—an incident which in the highly coloured pages of Livingstone's description did much to arouse the hostility of British opinion against the "emigrant farmers", to use the phrase of the time.[2]

Livingstone's protest to the British Government fell, however, upon ears that were deaf to his suggestions of intervention. The meaning

[1] Livingstone, D., *Missionary Travels*, p. 118; Chapman, J., *Travels*, ch. v.
[2] See the Sand River Convention, Eybers, G. W., *Select Constit. Docs.*, pp. 357–9.

of the Sand River Convention was unambiguous : whatever occurred beyond the colonial borders was no concern of the British Government. With this *laissez-faire* policy Cathcart had been in agreement, but it was not long before the new Governor, Sir George Grey, found himself entirely opposed to it. He had early realised that the unsettled state of the Eastern Frontier, the anxieties of the Basuto border, the congestion of Native population in Natal and the numerous Transvaal punitive expeditions had, if not a common cause, at least a common solution.

Although both the laws and the conditions of the Transvaal were opposed to predial slavery as it had existed in the Cape before 1834, at least part of the domestic labour of the Transvaal farmers was obtained by means which, being reported in the United Kingdom through divers and not always unprejudiced channels, very profoundly influenced the British official attitude towards the republics.[1] Commandos against Native tribes not infrequently returned with women and children, who, according to a vague law providing for the care of Native orphans, were apprenticed to farmers. The apprenticeship system was, however, not peculiar to the Transvaal. Before 1828 the law of the Cape Colony had permitted the apprenticeship of Hottentot children.[2] On the Cape frontier in the early 'twenties, when the commando system was still the sole means of defence, children captured in collisions with the tribes would be apprenticed to their captors as household servants. It was a characteristic South African frontier practice. It had appeared during Warden's Sovereignty administration,[3] and was even destined to reappear in a modified form in the Cape Colony under self-government. The lot of the apprenticed children was rarely hard; yet despite the occasional attempts of what responsible authority there was in the Transvaal to prevent injustice, the system was flagrantly abused.[4] The President of the Republic himself had such children in his household, and once at least Potchefstroom was appalled by the ease with which a waggon-load of children, mysteriously become "orphans", was unashamedly peddled in the streets. Landdrosts, especially in the frontier districts, asked few questions when children were brought to them for registration as "orphans". Once a child had been indentured, the indenture could be transferred or sold with impunity. In the Zoutpansberg district especially the anarchy which prevailed abetted black-birding and the traffic in Native children who had been declared "orphans". On the Swazi border children were obtained by sale and barter. At the same time the impression received by the Colonial Office was utterly disproportionate to the actual extent of the evil. The efforts of

[1] de Kiewiet, C. W., *British Colonial Policy*, p. 247.

[2] *Vide supra*, ch. IX.

[3] C.O. 48/374, D. 36, Grey to Secretary of State, 3 May 1856 and Enclosures.

[4] Cf. Mauch in the *Geographische Mittheilungen*, 1870, p. 9. C.O. 48/409, D. 41, Wynard to Newcastle, 14 November 1861; Enclosure.

Pretorius to put a stop to the worst abuses depended upon his ability to control the lawless elements in the Zoutpansberg. During the anarchy of the 'sixties he was helpless;[1] yet it is illuminating to find that, in 1870, when the British Government was using the apprenticeship system in the Transvaal as a reason for opposing the Transvaal's pretensions to the Diamond Fields, the number of Natives voluntarily offering themselves for employment with the farmers was high enough to check the further development of the system.

The confusion which permitted these abuses to flourish was increased by the refusal of Zoutpansberg and Lydenburg to co-operate with the hated Pretorius.[2] Because of the hostility of his rivals in the Transvaal, Pretorius made another determined though clumsy and unsuccessful bid, early in 1857, to realise his ambition for a union with the Free State. He was defeated by the resolution of President Boshof, a Natal "moderate", who belonged to that group of Free Staters whose affiliations were much more with the Cape and Natal than with the Transvaal, and who best represented Free State sentiment until at least 1871. He appealed to the Cape Colony for assistance, and in April energetically broke the back of the Winburg insurrection when he confronted Pretorius at the Rhenoster River with a Free State commando. It was not till much later that the Transvaal and the Free State developed a common nationalism which they opposed to British influences. Moderate counsels prevailed. Each republic agreed to recognise the independence of the other, and Pretorius withdrew his personal pretensions to authority within the limits of the Free State.[3]

Though clumsily executed, Pretorius's designs were nevertheless an attempt to counteract the growing tendency of the farmers to split up into ever more numerous independent groups. For the divided republics he contemplated what Sir George Grey was beginning to advocate with increasing urgency for the whole of South Africa—a union of governments and parties, not merely for aggression and defence, but for the more inclusive needs of civilised government. But Pretorius, like Grey, was in advance of his time.

The main need felt by the farmers beyond the Orange was the establishment of their superiority over the Native races. The only means they would recognise was the subjection of the latter by physical force. Grey indeed was aware that any fusion or alliance between the two republics, over which the terms of the Conventions and the monthly admonitions from the Colonial Office allowed him no control, would almost certainly express itself sooner or later in a concerted front againt the tribes. Just as a coast may be devastated

[1] de Kiewiet, C. W., *British Colonial Policy*, ch. xv *passim*.
[2] C.O. 48/382, Grey to Labouchere, 6 June 1857; enclosing Coetzee to Grey, 12 March 1857.
[3] Theal, G. M., *Hist. of S. A.* (1908 ed.), iv, 42 *sqq*.

by waves without having experienced the upheaval which caused them, so Grey feared the effects upon the Cape and Natal of the republican Native wars.

Yet if the union of the republics was dangerous, so too was subdivision. If an offensive alliance against the Natives was a menace, there was the opposite menace of anarchy, of a continued separation of the Europeans into groups following uncoordinated and conflicting policies. Too weak to govern, the Boers were nevertheless strong enough to continue gnawing at the tribal territories, exciting and perpetuating the febrile unrest which lay over the Basuto border, the Zoutpansberg and Zululand, and did not cease to affect the Eastern Frontier.

Grey warned the Colonial Secretary, Henry Labouchere, of all these dangers; the first work of a united Transvaal and Free State would be to fall upon the Basuto. What Grey did not so clearly realise was that it was not impossible that the Natal colonists might wish to join the republics in a "defensive" war. For the safety of its own frontiers the British Government must forestall Pretorius by uniting with the Free State beforehand.[1] But Labouchere was adamant.[2] He told Grey that, if the Free State were in difficulties, he was entirely free to offer his good offices; for the rest, the strictest neutrality must be his cue. If any vital British interest made it necessary to exercise pressure upon the republics, this could be done through the British control of the ports. Meanwhile, if the Cape could bring itself to be generous in handing over a share of the customs receipts, it might do much to secure the friendliness and co-operation of the republics. Their actual independence, he insisted, must be scrupulously observed.

The Eastern Frontier gave Grey reason for the deepest concern. Its whole unhappy history predisposed it to infection from any disturbance. The dislocation and unsettlement occasioned by the loss of the Xhosas' cattle through disease and of their land through the treaty settlements of the last half-century were inevitably preparing another outbreak. In the beginning of 1857, when Grey was most anxiously concerned with events in the republics, war on the Eastern Frontier would indeed in all probability have broken out and set fire also to the inflammable Basuto border, had not the tribes in British Kaffraria and beyond been swept by an incredible madness, such as could only attack a community profoundly disturbed, which led them to destroy their cattle and crops in the vain hope of destroying their enemies.

A young Xhosa girl named Nonqause and her uncle Mhlakaza professed that they had seen the spirits of dead warriors, and that these had commanded the tribes to kill all their cattle and destroy

[1] C.O. 48/381, D. 34, Grey to Labouchere, 20 March 1857.
[2] C.O. 49/50, Labouchere to Grey, 5 March 1857.

all their corn. On a certain day, when the destruction was complete, a plenty of cattle and corn would spring up from the earth and the white man would be swept into the sea. Immediately the order went forth to kill and destroy. Whether Kreli instigated the movement in the hope of inciting the tribes to aggression is uncertain. Moshesh certainly anticipated that a war on the Eastern Frontier would engage the attention of the Cape Colony and prevent it from coming between him and the Free State. Nevertheless, it remains perfectly clear that the recent heavy Native losses in land and cattle and the inroads made upon the authority of the tribal Chiefs were the final explanation of the readiness with which the superstitious tribal minds turned in desperation to magic to make good their losses and punish the Europeans. But the day of plenty never came. Famine swept through the land. Thousands perished; many more scattered into the Kaffrarian hinterland and thirty thousand entered the Colony to take service with the farmers there.

The depopulation of British Kaffraria in 1857 was, however, the result rather of dispersal than of an absolute loss of population through starvation.[1] Within the year the scattered tribal fragments came creeping back only to find that Grey had forestalled them. The former lands of the Xhosa chiefs were either confiscated or considerably diminished. In the place of the Natives came the German Legionaries and the German peasants whom the Hamburg firm of Caesar Godeffroy was exporting from Germany.[2] Although he was soon thankful to ship many of the Legionaries to India as recruits for the forces dealing with the Mutiny, and the British Government prohibited the further immigration of the peasants, Grey, with the best intentions in the world, abetted and advanced that great and disastrous revolution by which the Europeans were possessing themselves of tribal land, turning the former inhabitants into servants or forcing them into a hideous congestion. Had he been permitted to carry out his plans fully, Grey would have applied to the whole of the territory between Natal and the Cape Colony those measures which the self-immolation of the tribes enabled him to introduce in British Kaffraria. Fortunately for the future of South Africa, however, he was prevented from turning all Kaffraria into the rural slum that British Kaffraria was destined to become.[3] By 1860 the European population of British Kaffraria was 6000. Though the Africans were still overwhelmingly more numerous, the European system of landholding—a farm to a man—seriously limited the extent of land available for tribes who had already been cramped for room before ever the Europeans had settled amongst them. The old chief Kreli was especially restless, so

[1] See *Parl. Pap.* 1857–8, XL (389), p. 30.

[2] C.O. 48/388, D. 24, Grey to Secretary of State, 20 March 1858; minutes.

[3] The reports of the Civil Commissioners and Resident Magistrates contain the Cape Blue Books on Native Affairs between 1874 and 1880 and are especially illuminating on the point.

restless that Grey yielded to frontier clamour and expelled the unhappy man across the Kei,[1] where he suffered miserably for want of land.

In the midst of these difficulties the long-impending storm on the Basuto border burst at last. In February 1858 President Boshof, at the end of his patience, informed Moshesh that any further intrusion by the Basuto would be regarded as an act of hostility, and sent a commission to the Caledon river district to define the limits of certain farms on which the Natives had defiantly settled. The move was precisely what Moshesh had wanted.[2] Confident that the Free State had not the strength to hold him, and harried himself by the raids of a Chief named Jan Letele of whom the Free State had unwisely made a subject and an ally against his Basuto, Moshesh deliberately encouraged the sallies and encroachments of his followers while the Free State commandos were assembling to sweep clean the debated country.

The Free Staters lost the war before it had well begun. Their thinly distributed frontier settlements were extremely vulnerable to the mobile Basuto, and the burden of attack and defence fell mainly upon the frontiersmen. The financial condition of the country was precarious, for production and exports were little developed and it was impossible to raise revenue by import dues. The Cape Parliament had on two occasions rejected Grey's recommendation that the Free State be given a fair share of the customs receipts on the goods imported through its ports, a proportion of which was intended for sale across the Orange. Some few Cape Colonists indeed joined the Free State forces, but Grey's proclamation forbidding the enlistment of British subjects in the commandos deprived the Free State of any appreciable assistance from this source.

The Governor was very uneasy.[3] In the Transvaal Pretorius had succeeded in persuading the Zoutpansberg farmers to accept his constitution and leadership, and immediately justified Grey's fears of the results of republican union by crushing a rising of the Bamapela tribes and co-operating with the Free State in quelling a rising of the Batlapin. Boshof's predicament grew desperate. His only salvation appeared to be union with the Transvaal or with the Cape Colony. Despairing appeals were sent to both. Boshof's personal leanings were towards the Cape,[4] but when Grey refused to intervene,[5] he allowed the pro-Transvaal faction its head.

Grey knew that union with the Transvaal would strengthen the

[1] C.O. 48/388, D. 9, Grey to Labouchere, 11 February 1858.

[2] Cf. C.O. 48/388, D. 14, Grey to Secretary of State, 5 March 1858; enclosing Burnet to Bates, 22 February 1858.

[3] *Ibid.*

[4] *Ibid.* D. 53, Grey to Secretary of State, 20 May 1858; enclosing Boshof to Grey, 27 April 1858. *Basutoland Records*, II, 353.

[5] *Ibid.* Grey to Boshof, 22 April 1858.

war party in the Free State and result in an active continuation of the war. From India, in the throes of the Mutiny, came urgent calls for help, but till the conflagration on the Basuto border was extinguished Grey could not spare a man of his small regular garrison from South Africa. He therefore paralysed the war party in the Free State and scotched the project it had already brought before the Volksraad in favour of union with the Transvaal, by threatening to modify the Bloemfontein Convention if it were accepted.[1]

Moshesh himself did not allow his successes against the Free State to blind him to the dangers of an alliance between the republics, and when Grey proposed his mediation,[2] accepted it with profuse thanks. In September 1858 the Governor finally negotiated a peace between the Basuto and the Free State; but events rapidly proved the entire worthlessness of the arrangement, for the boundary established by this first Treaty of Aliwal North maintained practically the whole of the obnoxious Warden Line except an accession to the Basuto of some territory between the Orange and Caledon Rivers. Grey himself had no confidence in the arrangement and sought a better solution in another direction.

The embargo placed by the Governor on the Transvaal alliance once again caused Free State opinion to swing in favour of federation with the Cape,[3] especially amongst those who cherished an affection for the Mother Colony and believed that that richer and stronger community would be the better ally. The Cape Colony indeed was enjoying unwonted prosperity. The number of immigrants greatly exceeded that of emigrants. Exports of wool, copper ore, mohair and hides increased apace. Money was easy and circulated freely. Imports were considerable, and as the bulk of the Colony's revenue came from import dues, taxes were relatively light, mercifully sparing Grey the financial conflict with the Parliament that was to be the misery of his successor, Sir Philip Wodehouse. As Natal was prosperous, too, he felt that the Cape Colony was in a position to bear whatever increased burdens federation with the Free State might impose. The open favour that the Free State showed to the idea of federation thus encouraged him in what he now regarded with profound conviction as essential for the present and future good government of the whole of South Africa. "Nothing but a strong federal government", he wrote to the Secretary of State, "which unites, within itself, all the European races in South Africa can permanently maintain peace in this country and free Great Britain from constant anxiety for the peace of her Possessions here."[4]

The time was to come when identical sentiments were to be ex-

[1] *Basutoland Records*, II, 395.
[2] *Ibid.* Grey to Boshof; Grey to Moshesh, 6 May 1858.
[3] C.O. 48/387, D. 97, Grey to Stanley, 24 June 1858; Enclosures.
[4] Grey to [Labouchere], 9 June 1858. *Basutoland Records*, II, 396.

pressed by the Colonial Office, but in 1856–8 Grey met with nothing but opposition to his proposals from the Secretary of State. The expenses of the Crimean War with its incredible waste, the Indian Mutiny and the Chinese expedition made the reduction of national expenditure the most pressing problem before the British Government, and hardened its resolution, already expressed in the Conventions, not only to incur no new responsibilities in South Africa, but even to lessen those it already bore.[1] Thus, in 1858, the grant from the Exchequer of £40,000 for frontier affairs, which Grey had enjoyed annually since 1854, was summarily cut down by half, while the Governor was requested to report on a project formed by the Secretary of State, Sir Edward Bulwer Lytton, for a federation of British Kaffraria, Natal and the Cape, which it was suggested would lessen the cost of administration.[2] The single aim of the British Government was economy. So long as British Kaffraria was a Crown Colony, the cost of frontier defence must fall upon the Home Government, but federation, it was hoped, would throw it on the Cape and make possible a substantial withdrawal of British troops. Grey's reply to Bulwer Lytton's enquiry was his elaborate and now classic despatch on South African federation.[3] In it he set forth all the dangers of a continued subdivision of the South African communities and urged federation, in a form remarkably like what we now call "Dominion status", as the only remedy.

Regardless of the fact that the Secretary of State had categorically instructed him to take no steps without preliminary reference to Downing Street, Grey brought before the Cape Parliament a resolution in favour of federation which he had received from the Free State.[4] It was an act of disobedience that finally broke down the patience of the Colonial Office. To that office federation meant "either enormous expense or the independence of South Africa".[5] In 1858 self-government seemed hardly compatible with the maintenance of imperial ties, though some of the Colonists were anxious to obtain it, as we shall show later. To Lytton the reabsorption of the Free State could only mean that the Free State would thrust "her Dutch nose into all sorts of black squabbles, from which the British Giant would always have to pull her out with the certainty of more kicks than halfpence".[6] The idea of "independence" for South Africa was the more unpalatable as the British Government seriously feared that it would mean a combination of the whites against the blacks. "Enormous expense", the other alternative, was

[1] de Kiewiet, C. W., *British Colonial Policy*, pp. 124–7.

[2] C.O. 49/52, Lytton to Grey, 6 September 1858 (private).

[3] C.O. 48/390, Grey to Lytton, 19 November 1858 (separate).

[4] C.O. 48/390, D. 192, Grey to Lytton, 22 December 1858; C.O. 48/393, D. 8, Grey to Lytton, 31 January 1859; Enclosures.

[5] C.O. 48/390, Grey to Secretary of State, 14 August 1858; minute by Merivale.

[6] *Ibid.* Minute by Lytton.

entirely out of the question. Thus, in strange companionship, motives of economy and a sense of responsibility for the peace of South Africa alike enjoined the maintenance of the *status quo*. As for Grey, he was too uncompromisingly opposed to the policy of the Conventions to be allowed to stay in South Africa, and in 1859 Lytton summarily recalled him on the ground of his disobedience to express orders.[1]

Grey was ahead of his times with his federation scheme in the twofold sense that his conception of complete local self-government had not yet found a place in colonial practice, not even in British North America, where an imperial garrison was still maintained. Nor were local conditions ripe. Enormous distances, which the slowly crawling railway development was not destined to conquer for many years to come, and the utter weakness of government and the bankrupt finance of the Republics, which the Cape for all its momentary prosperity had neither the desire nor the strength to support, would probably have proved obstacles so great that only a heavy imperial expenditure over a considerable period could have overcome them.

Nevertheless the fact remained that the problems raised by Grey were not solved by the imperial veto. The supreme question of South African life still remained, demanding positive action. Ultimately the British Government would be forced either to assume the responsibility of establishing co-operation between the South African States or to allow them freedom to arrive at a settlement for themselves. To grant the South Africans freedom to manage their own affairs might be disastrous to themselves and the tribes; yet few opponents to the principle of self-government could be found in the Colonial Office, the more so as that principle alone promised to Great Britain relief from financial and military responsibility. Thus, until 1871 at least, the story of British South African policy is one of unhappy perplexity, checkered with compromise and inconsistency, a patchwork of blundering half-measures and far-sighted action.

Grey's disobedience, though it led to his recall, called attention to the crying need for leadership in South Africa, and British opinion began hesitatingly to veer round towards his views. When he arrived in England he found the Duke of Newcastle in Lytton's place at the Colonial Office. The new Secretary of State upheld the censure passed on the Governor, but he was more impressed than his predecessor by Grey's arguments.[2] The paralysis of British policy produced by the conflict of incompatible aims suddenly showed distinct signs of passing. Newcastle realised that complete separation could not for ever be maintained between affairs within and affairs beyond the colonial border. The Conventions and their restraint

[1] C.O. 49/52, D. 147, Lytton to Grey, 4 June 1859.
[2] Newcastle to Grey, 4 August 1859, *Parl. Pap.* 1860, XLV (216), p. 38.

upon the expansion of the frontier would ultimately have to be abolished or modified.[1]

Restored to his post in 1860, Grey returned to the assault. He now conceived the plan of driving forward the Cape frontiers and British influence throughout the length of Kaffraria right up to Natal. To that end he moved Fingos and Tembus from British Kaffraria eastward across the Kei, and proposed to push Kreli and his followers beyond the Umtata, in order to make room between the Bashee and the Umtata for white settlers who were to be interspersed amongst the tribesmen as in British Kaffraria.[2] Grey also persuaded the Griqua Adam Kok to abandon the Philippolis lands, which, since 1854, had steadily been passing into Free State hands, and to settle south of the Drakensberg in Nomansland (now Griqualand East) as an outpost of British influence and a buffer against the Basuto, who were already spilling over into that region. On the Natal side Grey's policy of Kaffrarian expansion met with enthusiastic support. The tribes on the southern Natal border were giving trouble. The little colony lived in mortal fear of the surrounding independent tribes, whose restlessness and agitation ever threatened to infect the great mass of Africans within its borders. In 1861 the white community was dreading the possible consequences of the fierce civil war that had broken out in Zululand. Consequently Theophilus Shepstone's demand that Natal should be allowed to extend its influence over the neighbouring tribes met with the support and approval of both Lieutenant-Governor Scott and the colonists.[3]

Newcastle revealed the extent to which he had departed from the policy of the last seven years by giving to the Cape Colony permission to annex the land between the Kei and the Bashee[4] from which Kreli had been expelled in 1858, and to Natal permission to annex the Alfred district, a portion of Kaffraria on her southern border, in order that she might the more effectively control the troublesome tribes therein.[5] He was even prepared to consider the annexation of Zululand, if he could be convinced of its expediency. In his eyes these extensions of the two colonies were the first step towards the junction of the Cape Colony and Natal. Of necessity they would force the British Government to reconsider its attitude towards the Republics, for it could no longer feign indifference to their relations with their Native neighbours.

Having failed to gain the support of the Cape, the Free State despairingly sought for a close alliance with its sister republic and elected to its presidency no less a person than Marthinus Pretorius, the Transvaal President, himself. Boshof had vacated the office in

[1] C.O. 48/407, D. 10, Grey to Newcastle, 9 February 1861; minute by Newcastle. C.O. 49/55, D. 262, Newcastle to Grey, 4 May 1861.

[2] *Cape Blue Book for Native Affairs*, 1, No. 6 *passim*.

[3] C.O. 179/59, D. 43, Scott to Newcastle, 5 July 1861.

[4] C.O. 49/55, D. 380, Newcastle to Wynyard, 5 December 1861.

[5] C.O. 405/3, Newcastle to Scott, 5 December 1861 (confidential).

disgust in 1859 to become a British subject once more and one of the strongest forces in the Natal legislature. But the hope of the Free State that the personal union would develop into a permanent political union was crushed, for Newcastle threatened to modify the Conventions to prevent it, while the Transvaal distrusted the Free State policy of its absentee President, for it had no wish to see its own independence compromised or the ban on the traffic in arms and ammunition with the Natives abolished by the British Government.

A new menace to the British colonies now arose. For some time the republics had felt with increasing discomfort their dependence upon the coastal communities for imported goods. So long as the British territories alone had access to the sea, they were in a position to strangle the Republics by withholding from them essential supplies, In 1861, Pretorius, as President of the Free State, caused anxiety amongst the Cape merchants by casting his eyes in the direction of Port St John's in Pondoland.[1] As President of the Transvaal he had long had his eyes on St Lucia Bay, and had planned to run a corridor to it between Zululand and Natal. In March 1861, Cetewayo, in violent process of establishing his ascendancy in Zululand, had ceded a strip of Zulu territory along the Blood River to the Transvaal in return for a nominal gift of cattle and the more important recognition by the Transvaal of his paramountcy in Zululand. In Natal this cession was regarded as the first step of the Transvaal's march to the coast, and the Lieutenant-Governor registered a strong protest,[2] because he was nervous of the disturbances that the too close contact of the Boers and Zulus might provoke. Newcastle upheld the protest, and once again expressed his willingness to resort to the annexation of Zululand if it were necessary to check the Transvaal. Finally, at the moment that the United Kingdom, relying on Captain William Owen's unconfirmed annexation in 1823,[3] was already disputing with Portugal the possession of Delagoa Bay, there came a report that the Transvaal had designs in that direction. The British Government promptly declared its prior right to the Bay, both because it was apparent that it might one day be of commercial importance, and also because it wished to baulk any possible understanding between the Transvaalers and the Portuguese for the cession or the use of the port in view of its strategical importance on the flank of the route to India.[4]

Newcastle restored Grey to his governorship and allowed him to return to South Africa in July 1860 on the distinct understanding that he would not again promote his federation schemes. The basis of the Duke's South African policy was a willingness that both the Cape

[1] C.O. 48/401, D. 21, Wynyard to Newcastle, 15 February 1860.
[2] C.O. 179/59, D. 43, Scott to Newcastle, 5 July 1861.
[3] *Vide infra*, p. 463.
[4] de Kiewiet, C. W., *British Colonial Policy*, pp. 148–53.

Colony and Natal should extend their borders as they showed themselves ready to assume the responsibilities of government and expenditure involved. This pointed to early self-government and the abandonment of the Convention policy; yet, at the very moment that the British Government began to raise the embargo on colonial extension, serious and prolonged constitutional deadlocks occurred.

In 1861 Grey was transferred from South Africa to New Zealand to cope with the difficulties of a new Maori war,[1] and his departure coincided with the disappearance of the prosperity which in Cape Colony had lubricated the imperfectly co-ordinated machinery of representative government. This was caused by a combination of general world conditions and circumstances peculiar to South Africa. The devastating War of Secession in the United States brought in its train widespread depression and injured South Africa by the loss of the wool market; in the United Kingdom there was financial stringency, and a growing feeling that, in view of the ominous trend of French and Prussian policies, less must be spent on the colonies and more on the defence of the Mother Country. The useful parliamentary grant on behalf of British Kaffraria was peremptorily and finally withdrawn. Drought and a severe winter killed off large numbers of sheep and cattle, and a sudden slump in trade and revenues followed.

The new Governor, Sir Philip Edmond Wodehouse, who was appointed to succeed Sir George Grey, was destined to struggle through almost eight years of depression within the Colony, and with chaos and Native wars without. His experience, however, had equipped him well to cope with the unusual problems with which he was confronted during his lengthy governorship. In Ceylon, where he had spent most of his official career, and in British Guiana he had faced serious Native unrest. The unpopularity which was to be his lot in South Africa was no novel experience to him, and, as Superintendent of British Honduras, the feuds of Latin-American republics had given him an object lesson of the dangers of political divisions between closely related States. When he arrived in Cape Town at the beginning of 1862, he found the Treasury almost empty, reckless expenditure on every side, an inevitable deficit and conflict preparing both within and without the Colony. Throughout the whole of his governorship those conflicts went on concurrently but almost independently, and it will facilitate our understanding of his extremely difficult task if we consider them separately.

From Wodehouse's assumption of office in 1862 until the annexation of the Diamond Fields in 1870 the Cape Colony was in a state of almost unrelieved constitutional deadlock, for the Governor and the colonists looked at affairs from quite different angles. A considerable section of the latter pursued their demands for what they proclaimed as their inherent right to constitutional freedom, as though

[1] See *C.H.B.E.* VII, Pt II, p. 136.

they were the sole denizens of South Africa and there were no such things as tribes or frontier dangers. Some Liberal statesmen in the United Kingdom also took this theoretical view and wished for responsible government for the white community at the Cape simply because the colonies in Australia and British North America had already received it. Like the colonists, they neglected to observe that in neither of those regions was there a Native danger and that in both the colonists were capable of assuming the whole burden of local defence. But to Wodehouse, accustomed as he was to the problems of Crown Colonies, things appeared differently. It was good government and sound defence that were needed rather than artificial constitutional propriety, and he felt almost a contempt for the particularist squabbles of Cape society.

In 1860 John Charles Molteno of Beaufort West had introduced a motion in the Cape Assembly in favour of responsible government, but the motion was obviously premature and was withdrawn. Thereafter the question was overshadowed for some years by an agitation for the separation of the Colony. Robert Godlonton, the leader of the Easterners in the Cape Parliament, reviving an idea as old as the Commission of Inquiry in 1825, had advocated in 1854 without success the separation of the Eastern and Western Provinces of the Cape Colony. Friction had then for some years been smoothed away by prosperity; yet on many points Eastern and Western interests continued to diverge. Their relationship was very much that of Upper and Lower Canada. The East was largely British, the West predominantly Afrikaner. Grahamstown was Cape Town's rival for the Free State and Native trade and so aggressively British that the Eastern Afrikaners feared its domination. Railway development in the West provoked the jealousy of the East, and at last, in 1861, the Eastern Province, refusing to pay for the flagrant extravagance of the West, declared for complete separation of the two parts of the Colony.

Wodehouse's position was one of great discomfort. From Westminster, Newcastle pleaded with him to resist the tendency of the Cape Colony to split asunder and to achieve the "union of all the British possessions in South Africa under one powerful Government".[1] Wodehouse, in reply, pointed out the unfairness of expecting him to carry through such an ambitious scheme when he had not a penny that was not controlled by the highly contentious Cape Parliament. "It is absolutely essential", he wrote privately to Newcastle, "that the person who holds the position of Governor of this Colony and High Commissioner should be unmistakably recognised by Her Majesty's Government as the chief authority primarily responsible for the policy of the whole of South Africa." Newcastle agreed heartily, but

[1] Wodehouse Papers, Newcastle to Wodehouse, 4 July 1862 (private). The bound volumes of those of Wodehouse's letters which were not destroyed are in the library of the Colonial Office and they throw interesting light on the controversies of the period.

would promise neither a renewal of the imperial grant for British Kaffraria nor any addition to the Cape defences. Unable to override the colonists, Wodehouse tried to co-operate with them. The Public Works Department had not only largely overspent its parliamentary grant, but had also spent £200,000 in constructing gaols that were unfit for use.[1] In the circumstances Wodehouse could not hope to escape unpopularity and conflict. Obliged to choose between the equally unpopular alternatives of increased taxation or retrenchment and economy, he suffered the fate of all colonial governors appointed to cope with representative institutions in times of financial and commercial stress.

At the outset he had to make it known that he intended to raise heavier taxes and to oppose the separation of East and West, and he suggested the early annexation of British Kaffraria while it was still weak and had no money. But every one of these measures was highly contentious, and there was thus hardly an interest or a party in the Colony that he did not antagonise. Collectively and separately, Easterners, Westerners, Kaffrarians and Responsibles declared war on the Governor. He made an ineffectual bid for Eastern support by proposing to establish an Eastern Districts Court at Grahamstown and alternate sessions of Parliament at Cape Town and Grahamstown. An open avowal that he needed the support of Parliament likewise availed him nothing. Nor did he win much support for the annexation of British Kaffraria by his arguments that an independent British Kaffraria would continue to hold the port of East London annexed to it in July 1859—a serious blow to the Cape Town merchants. One after the other the Cape Parliament threw out Bills for equalising the representation of East and West, for separation and for self-government, and refused to listen to any proposals for increased taxation.[2]

Meanwhile, beyond the frontier, Natal was planning under Newcastle's permissive despatch to annex such a generous piece of Kaffrarian territory that it encroached upon territory which Grey had given to Adam Kok. Throughout the whole of Kaffraria there was nervousness and strain. Kreli prowled about in his cramped quarters to the great disquiet of the frontier settlers, and refused to retire deeper into Kaffraria for fear of the Pondo tribes. Newcastle declined to allow Wodehouse to create a defence force of irregular horse instead of the Cape Mounted Rifles, while the Cape muttered at having its Police in territory it did not control. Wodehouse realised that his chances of solving the constitutional and financial problems of the Colony depended in the most immediate fashion upon a prudent management of relations with the adjacent tribes.[3] He decided to

[1] Wodehouse Papers, Wodehouse to his son, 20 March 1863.
[2] A. 2–63 (Cape), pp. 11 *sqq.*
[3] Wodehouse Papers, Wodehouse to Newcastle, 18 January 1862 (private).

abandon Grey's scheme of expansion and settlement in Kaffraria. The suggestion that the sale to settlers of the land beyond the Kei might serve to restrain the Natives he dismissed on the grounds that it would strengthen British Kaffraria and hinder its annexation to the Cape. He obtained from Newcastle a categorical assurance that in all matters of Native policy, except those internal to Natal, his authority as High Commissioner in South Africa was absolute, and forced the chagrined Lieutenant-Governor of Natal to curtail his pretensions to Kaffraria so that Adam Kok might settle down in peace and comfort. Then he turned his eyes to the Free State border.

The years following the Basuto War of 1858 had brought progress in the Free State. Land that had once been allocated as tribal reserves on the western and southern borders was purchased from the petty chiefs, Goliath Yzerbek, Jan Danser and Lepui, and immediately taken up by the farmers. In December 1861, as we saw above, the Free State acquired the Philippolis lands of the Griqua chief Adam Kok. New villages were founded and the number of magistracies increased. On the Basuto border, however, the land war became increasingly desperate. Moshesh was growing old and less able than ever to control the rival Chiefs in Basutoland, who wanted more land in order to increase their pretensions and the number of their followers. Within their own recognised territory there was a greater congestion of horses and cattle than the country could carry since the tribes had been deprived of free movement over the wide pastures of their other western frontier lands.[1] On the Free State side of the line there was some increase of population ever hungry for extensive farms and ever more clamorous to thrust back the expanding Basuto. There was much fishing in troubled waters. Cattle-stealing, though its main cause was the land dispute, was stimulated by a league between rascal traders and the chieftains.[2] The followers of Jan Letele pilfered from the Basuto, who, at one stage, were losing more cattle than the farmers themselves. White scallywags bought Letele's plunder and spirited it across the frontier by night.

Each side in turn appealed to the Cape, Moshesh ostensibly asking to be received as a British subject, but in reality for permission to buy guns and ammunition, Pretorius asking for a share in the Cape customs dues in order to establish a frontier force to control the Natives. Wodehouse refused Moshesh's request because he was bound to do so by the Conventions. The request of the Free State he similarly refused, not only because he had no money, but also because he was unwilling to strengthen the farmers against their enemies. Like Grey, his close preoccupation with Kreli and the Eastern Frontier revealed to him how commotion in the centrally-situated Basutoland could

[1] Casalis, E., *The Basuto*. p. 21.

[2] C.O. 48/412, Wodehouse to Newcastle, 1 February 1862; Enclosure, Burnet to Acting-Secretary to Government, 13 January 1862.

send out disturbing waves into Kaffraria and on to the Eastern Frontier. Wodehouse also followed Grey in conceiving an immediate objection to the Conventions and the policy they represented; but, unlike Grey, he departed from a policy of co-operation with the republics. "It is beyond question", he informed Newcastle, "that we are the paramount power in this part of the world." The British Government should not hesitate to claim the right of adopting for the protection of its colonists any measures which the "misconduct" of the republics might force upon it.[1] This new imperious note was to be the keynote of South African history for many years.

The Free State had finally to admit that the Pretorius experiment had been a failure. Union with the Transvaal was a broken reed. Even the borderers, who were the President's staunchest adherents, were disgruntled, because, instead of the forceful measures they had expected, Pretorius's Basuto policy had resolved itself into the old routine of threatening messages and unsatisfactory replies from Moshesh. A proposal to establish a joint Basuto and Free State Court to deal with cattle thefts came to nothing, as did the attempt to raise a police force. Pretorius was once again deeply involved in the Transvaal. Although the split between Lydenburg and the rest of the country was healed by its adhesion to Pretorius's South African Republic, yet the former jealousies and rivalries, notably in ecclesiastical matters, survived. A Gilbertian situation resulted, and in July 1860 Pretorius was forced to resign his Transvaal presidency by the opposing faction, partly because of their personal animosity and partly because the too close alliance with the Free State threatened the Conventions. He was promptly reinstalled by his partisans, one of whom, Stephanus Schoeman, thereupon nearly precipitated civil war by attempting a *coup d'état* on his own account. Such power as the Transvaal Volksraad might have had to restore order was destroyed by the tendency of the warring leaders to appeal directly to the sovereign people, as had been done in republican Natal, with the difference in the Transvaal that the rivals cheerfully ignored the distinction between the votes of their partisans and those of the whole electorate. A new presidential election in December 1863, in which Schoeman's followers ousted Pretorius, actually provoked bloodshed, and Pretorius finally judged it advisable to leave the Free State and devote his attention to the Transvaal, where, with the backing of Paul Kruger, then at the opening of his momentous career, he was again duly elected President (May 1864).

In the Free State which Pretorius left behind him the followers of Moshesh had encroached beyond the Warden Line to a distance of fifteen miles. His place in the Free State was taken by Jan Hendrik Brand, an advocate of the Cape Supreme Court, a member of the Cape Assembly and the son of the Speaker. Brand's first

[1] C.O.D. 9, Wodehouse to Newcastle, 1 February 1862; Enclosures.

action was to request Wodehouse to arbitrate in the Basuto border dispute.[1] Guided solely by the documents and the land titles that Warden had promiscuously awarded in 1848 and 1849, and taking little into account the numbers or needs of the rival border populations, Wodehouse found that he had no alternative but to uphold the greater part of the line claimed by the Free State.[2] The jubilant farmers called for the expulsion of the Basuto beyond the line. Awed by the decision of the High Commissioner, the Basutos retired for a while, only to come truculently trooping back determined to maintain their huts and harvest their cultivated patches. Both Wodehouse and Brand urged the frontiersmen to exercise patience;[3] but temper on both sides ran high. As soon as Moshesh felt that his winter supplies were assured, he showed himself openly bellicose. Friction reached a climax and in June 1865 war broke out.

In the colonies meanwhile conditions had not improved. There was, first, an ecclesiastical dispute, the outcome of which affected British colonies in every part of the world. For his expression of heterodox views in doctrinal matters, Dr John William Colenso, Bishop of Natal, was deprived of his see by a decision of the court of the Bishop of Cape Town. As his nomination depended not upon the Bishop of Cape Town but upon letters patent, Colenso refused to acknowledge the jurisdiction of the Cape ecclesiastical court. When the case was brought before the Judicial Committee of the Privy Council, it was ruled that colonial churches were voluntary associations independent of the Church of England as by law established, and that therefore no one colonial bishop had any *a priori* authority over another. Hence, Colenso remained Bishop of Natal till his death in 1883 in rivalry with a Bishop of Maritzburg consecrated by the Bishop of Cape Town and three other bishops.[4] Shortly afterwards the Dutch Reformed Church experienced similar doctrinal trouble.[5] The Cape Synod had met in 1862 to purge itself of liberal elements touched by the latitudinarian views then spreading in the theological schools of Europe. The liberals appealed to the Cape Supreme Court. Though they won on legal points, they were ultimately overwhelmed by the conservatives. Among other things, the Supreme Court decided that extra-colonial clergy had no right to sit in the Cape Synod. The Transvaal (Potchefstroom) Synod already stood apart, and in 1865 the Orange Free State formed its own Synod. In the following year Lydenburg, which had first joined with Natal, evinced its still active distrust of Pretorius by forming a

[1] C.O. 48/424, Wodehouse to Cardwell, 26 November 1864; enclosing Brand to Wodehouse, 5 February 1864.
[2] Wodehouse Papers, Wodehouse to his son, 7 November 1864.
[3] See *Cape Argus*, 23 February 1865.
[4] Walker, E. A., *History of Southern Africa*, pp. 300 *sqq*.
[5] See Engelbrecht, S. P., *Geschiedenis van de Nederduits Hervormde Kerk in Zuid Afrika*.

Synod of its own. Ecclesiastical division had gone even further than political division. It was a sorry portent.

In his struggle with the Colonial legislature Wodehouse succceeded for a time in winning over the Eastern members of the Parliament by a secret agreement with their leaders that the 1864 session should be held in Grahamstown, that a branch of the Supreme Court should be set up there and that military headquarters should be moved thither from Kingwilliamstown. He managed to pass his money bills, but his action angered the West, and Kaffrarian affairs soon lost him the short-lived tolerance of the East.

In Kaffraria there was congestion amongst the Fingo population, and Kreli still moved restlessly on the other side of the Bashee river, hungry to recross the river into his former land. Wodehouse discovered for himself that the old Chief was desperate for want of room. How serious the problem of frontier defence really was appeared in the middle of 1864, when Kreli's uneasy sentry-go on the Bashee's banks produced another of the periodical panics by which the frontier was apt to be swept. But from England there came a peremptory order for the reduction of four companies of the Cape Corps as a measure of economy, while Sir Percy Douglas, in command of the frontier forces, declared that the Bashee could not be defended without an increase of military expenditure, and recommended that Grey's plan of thrusting Kreli beyond the Umtata be adopted. Both measures were clearly impossible and the demands of the man on the spot could not be reconciled with the parsimony of Downing Street. Wodehouse toyed half-heartedly with the idea of offering the Transkeian lands to settlers at a price that would be acceptable to the lean purses of the farmers, but when Edward Cardwell at the Colonial Office heard of the possibility of a conflict, he immediately ordered the abandonment of the whole Transkeian territory.[1] With the Transkei once more in possession of the overjoyed Kreli and the Fingos from British Kaffraria, who poured into the vacant territory, Cardwell took the next step in the process of devolving the South African burdens of the British Government upon the colonists, by arming the Governor with an imperial Act for incorporating British Kaffraria within the Cape Colony. Protesting and furious, the Cape Parliament had no alternative but to pass a measure of its own effecting that annexation.[2]

It was just at the moment when Wodehouse was engaged in the delicate task of shepherding the tribes into the Transkei that war broke out on the Basuto border.[3] The outbreak served to deepen the economic depression in Cape Colony. In Natal the news fell upon a community in the depths of financial and commercial collapse. Like

[1] C.O. 49/57, D. 784, Cardwell to Wodehouse, 5 August 1864; Theal, G. M., *History of S.A. since 1795*, V, pp. 44, 69.

[2] C.O. 48/317, D. 39, Wodehouse to Cardwell, 7 June 1865.

[3] Wodehouse Papers, Wodehouse to his son, 14 July 1865.

the Cape, Natal had enjoyed nearly ten years of prosperity, but the bases of that prosperity had been less secure. Some little coffee was indeed grown, but not enough cotton could be raised to fill the gap caused by the American Civil War.[1] The farmers in the Natal uplands followed the Cape Colony and produced increasing quantities of wool, while yet more wool came from the Transvaal and the northern Free State. In the early 'fifties sugar had been introduced and within a few years had become the leading staple. At first the planters, like the rest of the farmers, had been greatly hindered by the insufficiency and irregularity of labour. Grey drew the main flow of European immigration to the Cape, and such immigrants as came to Natal became traders and farmers and thus employers of labour themselves. The Native population preferred to remain in the crowded reserves, where much poor land, congestion, lung sickness and periodical droughts did not allow them to become more than indifferent and unstable contributors to the wealth of the colony. Those who could find no home in the reserves sought room on the Crown lands and private farms. Neither the demand of the Europeans that the reserves be diminished in area, nor laws intended to expel the Natives from the Crown lands, nor even the burden of taxes brought out a sufficient number of African labourers. Finally, following the example of the similarly situated West Indian planters, Natal arranged in 1860 for the importation of coolie labour from India. With the coming of the Indians the success of sugar was assured; but since the coolies came with their womenfolk, and under conditions that after a normal term of service of four or five years they could remain in the colony and even acquire land, many stayed to create later an "Indian problem" side by side with the Native problem. Both as servants and small landholders they played their part in limiting Natal's powers of absorbing a larger European population.

An unusually large part of Natal's white population was concentrated in the towns and mainly engaged in trade. During the early 'sixties there was an altogether unjustifiable confidence in the trade of the interior.[2] Merchants laid in large stocks to sell the indigent Winburgers, Transvaalers and Natives. Between 1859 and 1863 imports increased 160 per cent; the corresponding increase in revenue went to build roads and span rivers, and to find salaries for the three Judges who constituted the new Supreme Court and several additional magistrates. A railway line was laid between the Point and Durban. But imports greatly exceeded exports; the interior was too unsettled for secure trade; even when it bought, it could not pay cash. The land which the merchants of Natal offered as security for loans, and in which there was consequently much speculation, had little real value.

[1] Cotton did not become a material export from Natal until after 1870.
[2] See C.O. 179/91, Keate to Secretary of State, 9 December 1868.

The greatest organised scheme for the introduction of new settlers had been carried out by an Irish speculator, Joseph Charles Byrne, who had lived at the Cape.[1] Though he knew little of Natal, he saw in its need for emigrants the opportunity of a profitable speculation, and by dint of widespread advertisement in England he succeeded in attracting about 2500 persons in the year 1849–50. The influx of these new settlers largely laid the foundations of English-speaking Natal, but the scheme soon collapsed and Byrne himself was declared bankrupt. There was too little immigration after 1851 to stimulate a demand for land and the white population grew very slowly.

At the moment that the Basuto war broke out and the Transvaal subsided into deeper anarchy, the London money marked tightened, the demand for wool suddenly fell and drought descended upon the Cape. The bonded warehouses were gorged with unsold goods. There were numerous bankruptcies. Revenue fell abruptly, and this prepared the way for the inevitable conflict between executive and legislature.

Strangely, however, opinion in the two depressed British colonies expressed no resentment against the republics. As yet republican independence did not suggest to the colonists any vital division. The feeling of common interests was stronger than at any other time before 1908. Popular opinion in both coastal colonies declared for the Free State, which in their judgment was fighting the battle of the whites against the "heathenish barbarians". Thus Wodehouse found himself faced with what Grey had so much feared—the threat of the whites concerting common action against the blacks. When a raiding party under the Basuto chief Lesoana,[2] entering Natal in pursuit of some fleeing Free Staters, attacked some Transvaal farmers and swept off a quantity of Natal stock, the Transvaal sent a contingent to the Basuto border, and in Natal a universal clamour was raised for participation in the war against the Basuto. To the emotional outburst of the Natal colonists were added the calculating design of Shepstone, who saw in the crisis an opportunity of attaching Basutoland to Natal, and the hopes of the merchants who trusted to make good their losses by Commissariat expenditure.[3]

The Native world was no less agitated. In the Zoutpansberg, white and black bands raided and counter-raided; there were high words between the Zulus and the Transvaal concerning the border strip which Cetewayo had ceded in 1861, and a Transvaal commando assembled in readiness for hostilities. This increased the agitation of Natal, which was doubly afraid of the effect of a Transvaal-Zulu conflict upon its own Natives, and of the possibility of the Transvaal's

[1] Hattersley, A. F., *The British Settlement of Natal*; Robertson, H. M., "The 1849 Settlers in Natal" (*S.A. Journal of Economics*, September–December 1949).

[2] C.O. 179/75, McLean to Cardwell, 4 July 1865; enclosing McLean to Wodehouse, 2 July 1845.

[3] Wodehouse Papers, Wodehouse to Cardwell, undated.

using a victory to advance to the coast at St Lucia Bay. To the south-east of Basutoland Adam Kok quarrelled with the encroaching Basuto. How desperately the tribes needed land was seen in the fact that although 40,000 Fingos had flocked into the Transkei in 1864 and 1865, the land they had left behind them was promptly filled up again by other Africans.

Wodehouse's position was almost desperate. Basutoland must be kept intact lest its dispersed fragments spread confusion throughout the Native world. To that end he made an effort to localise the war by refusing Natal permission to "recapture" the raided stock. When Brand issued an appeal for volunteers from the Cape and Natal, the High Commissioner threatened to cut off supplies of ammunition to the Free State and to impose severe penalties on colonists who joined the Free State forces. Happily, he discovered in January 1866 that the Natal claims against Lesoana's raiding party had been grossly exaggerated, so that his neutrality remained uncompromised, and he could calmly wait for the war to fizzle out and for the time to come when the British Government could interfere and assert itself as the paramount authority in South Africa.

The Free State forces were indeed making little apparent headway. The mountain strongholds of Berea and Vechtkop were stormed, but a strong commando failed to occupy the key fortress of Thaba Bosigo. In reality, however, the course of the war was determined by flying columns, which, like Colonel Somerset's patrols on the Eastern Frontier in 1835, scoured the country, burning the huts, seizing the Native grain stores and driving off cattle. A Transvaal commando joined the Free Staters for a brief but remunerative spell.[1] Such warfare soon rendered the frontier belt almost uninhabitable to the Basuto. Only the clumsiness of a too democratic *Krygsraad*, and the tendency of the farmers to return to their farms as soon as the rains fell and the ploughing season commenced in October, saved the Basuto from ruinous losses. Moshesh saw that the Free State intended to expel the tribesmen, not merely from the disputed border, but far beyond from the best arable land in all the Basuto country; for while the war was raging policy was determined by the extremist frontiersmen, who had old scores to pay off and knew how extremely fertile some parts of the Basuto territory were.

In sore straits and knowing Wodehouse to be favourable, Moshesh and his sons Letsie and Molapo petitioned for the British Government to annex their territory.[2] Wodehouse forwarded the petition to the Secretary of State with his strongest recommendation in its favour,[3] and while awaiting a reply offered his mediation to the combatants. In Downing Street, Cardwell had already made a declaration

[1] *Petermann's Geographische Mittheilungen*, Ergänzungsheft 37, 1874, p. 21.
[2] C.O. 48/428, D. 77, Wodehouse to Cardwell, 12 August 1865.
[3] C.O. 48/431, D. 6, Wodehouse to Cardwell, 13 January 1866.

of faith by ordering the abandonment of the Transkei; hence, he now replied to Wodehouse, that unless there were some "overruling necessity", which he doubted strongly, the annexation of Basutoland could not be considered.[1] The Free State answered Wodehouse's offer by ejecting the French missionaries from the "Conquered Territory" on the plea that they aided and abetted the Natives, and proceeded to a more systematic destruction of the crops the Basuto had sown during the lull in December and January. The threat of a winter of famine broke the Basuto resistance, and the Free State commenced to dismember Basutoland. By the Treaty of Imparani, Molapo was compelled to cede his land north and west of the Caledon River, and to become a Free State subject in what remained of northern Basutoland. Soon after, in April 1866, by the Treaty of Thaba Bosigo, Moshesh was forced to make cession of a border territory that contained half of the total arable area in all Basutoland.[2] It was by far the most disastrous "treaty" yet forced on the Native population.

The war had been caused by the attempted expansion of the Basuto; the Free State ended it by crowding them into less territory still. Consequently the commandos had hardly turned their backs when the Basuto returned to their homes in the Conquered Territory, where they reaped what had been spared and, being left unmolested owing to the Free State's lack of regular police, followed their reaping by another sowing. In March 1867, when the crops were again ripening, the commandos were back in the disputed lands; to save their food supply the Basuto capitulated again. This time the Free State made some attempt to regulate the situation by offering to settle certain of the Chiefs and their subjects in specified reserves; but the land the Free State was willing to set aside was not considered enough, nor did the Basuto Chiefs regard their losses as permanent. Probably encouraged by the French missionaries, Moshesh openly repudiated the Treaty of Thaba Bosigo, renewed his appeals to be taken over as a British subject, and begged that his territory might be joined to Natal.[3]

In Natal, Shepstone, the power behind the Lieutenant-Governor, favoured the request on the twofold ground that in Basutoland the British Government would hold the key to South African Native politics, and that the annexation of Basutoland to Natal was an essential step towards the fulfilment of his ambition of a "Greater Natal" controlling all the surrounding tribal territories. This time the Basuto request found favour in Downing Street; but the reason for the change of view lay not in South Africa but in general imperial policy.

The 'sixties are significant years in British colonial policy. The

[1] *Parl. Pap.* 1868–9, XLIII [4140], pp. 84–5, Cardwell to Wodehouse, 9 March 1866.
[2] C.O. 179/80, D. 54, Bissett to Cardwell, 2 May 1866.
[3] C.O. 48/438, D. 88, Wodehouse to Secretary of State, 17 September 1867; Enclosure.

agitation for a lessening of the burden of colonial expenditure steadily grew, as England's apprehension of foreign entanglements increased.[1] A Select Committee on colonial military expenditure reported in 1861 in favour of the reduction of colonial garrisons maintained at the expense of the Mother Country.[2] The application of this recommendation implied, as Gladstone was quick to point out, self-government for such colonies as became responsible for their own defence.[3] Sure enough, when the troops commenced to leave New Zealand in 1864, the settlers, though not without serious qualms on the part of the Duke of Newcastle, were given the control over Maori affairs which had previously been withheld from them.[4] Upon Canada likewise the British Government impressed the necessity of organising its own local defence, and one of the most acceptable consequences to the British Government of the federation of much of British North America by the Act of 1867 was relief from the burden of the defence of the new Dominion.[5]

The same policy, though with great hesitation, was applied to South Africa. Here the colonists were greatly outnumbered by what parliamentary orators described as "untamed savages", and there was fear of a war of races. Consequently, when Wodehouse met the demand of the Colonial Office in 1864 that part of the troops be withdrawn from South Africa with a description of the disunion within the Colony and the discord without, the attempt was postponed. When the demand for withdrawal was repeated in 1865, Wodehouse had merely to point to an even more critical position.[6] In the Cape Colony in 1866 revenue was still exceeded by expenditure; the Houses refused to vote adequate supplies and demanded retrenchment. To Wodehouse economy appeared more imperative than constitutional government. The unmitigated and stiff-necked opposition of the Parliament under Molteno's guidance was actually becoming a menace to the Colony's credit. The Colonial treasury was empty, the Governor had to resort to loans to keep the administration going, there was not even money for relief work and the drought was still unbroken. In the session of 1867 a proposed tax on wool was indignantly rejected, although six magistrates had been dismissed as a measure of economy. Wodehouse, autocratic by temper and experience, was more than ever convinced that constitutional government in the conditions that prevailed had nothing to recommend it. In his view the remedy was not increased responsibility in the hands

[1] Cf. *Hansard*, 3rd ser., CLVIII, 1841 *sqq.*

[2] See Chappell, M. G., "The Select Committee of 1861 on Colonial Military Expenditure", an unpublished thesis in the Library of the Univ. of London; and *Parl. Pap.* 1861, XIII (423).

[3] *Ibid.* p. 257, Q. 3781.

[4] See *C.H.B.E.* VII, Pt II, p. 141.

[5] See Stacey, C. W., *Canada and the British Army.*

[6] Wodehouse Papers, Wodehouse to Cardwell, 11 December 1865.

of local politicians, but increased control by experienced Governors. He wished to apply to the Cape the measures which had recently replaced the old representative constitution in Jamaica,[1] there the Legislative Council had been abolished and the Assembly made into a mere Council of Advice by the inclusion of official members. Such a reform would give the Governor and High Commissioner a most necessary freedom of action, The circumstances of the Cape and Jamaica were however, radically different. In the West Indian colony it had been necessary to exercise the overriding responsibility of the Imperial Government in the face of imminent danger of Negro risings and of the massacre of the dwindling white population; but at the Cape there was no such danger. The white colonists were compact and gradually rising in prosperity, and the perils of revolt and massacre lay only on the frontier. The Cape Parliament refused absolutely to consider the Governor's Jamaica scheme, and yet it could come to no agreement on the alternative proposal for responsible government which had been brought forward again by Molteno in 1865.

Once again the British Government refrained from pressing its demand for the withdrawal of troops.[2] It began to realise that such withdrawal depended upon peaceful conditions, and it began also to attach an increasing importance to Wodehouse's insistent warnings that peace could only be guaranteed by the assertion of British supremacy in South African policy. In 1866 Sir Charles Adderley, who had opposed the original abandonment of the Orange River Sovereignty, became Parliamentary Under-Secretary for the Colonies. Largely owing to his influence, the growing dissatisfaction with the Conventions and the independence they had conferred on the republics crystallised into the desire to control the policy of the republics and, if possible, to include them again under British dominion. Henceforth this became the chief aim of British South African policy and its adoption marks the close of the period of transition. As a first step Wodehouse was finally authorised to annex Basutoland[3] on the explicit and significant condition, however, that not the British Government but Natal should be responsible for the organisation and expenses of its future government.[4]

That Basutoland should be annexed to Natal was not what Wodehouse had desired at all, because that would deprive him of freedom to negotiate directly with the Free State, would add another legislature to his burdens, and would also deprive him of precisely that direct control over Native affairs at which he was aiming. He distrusted Shepstone's Native policy, and was perturbed at the talk in the Natal legislature of taxing the Basuto in order to swell the exiguous Natal

[1] See *C.H.B.E.* vol. II, p. 736.
[2] C.O. 49/60, Elliot to Under-Secretary for War, 9 December 1867.
[3] C.O. 49/59, D. 78, Buckingham to Wodehouse, 9 December 1867.
[4] Cf. C.O. 179/81, Bissett to Carnarvon, 8 September 1866; minute by Adderley.

revenues, and of setting aside parts of Basutoland for white settlement. He doubted strongly the wisdom of subjecting tribesmen to a self-interested European Assembly, which was not remarkable for generosity towards its own tribal subjects. He announced therefore to President Brand that Basutoland was to be annexed, but said not a word of the terms laid down by the Colonial Office. To add to his difficulties there was confusion all along the northern border from the Zoutpansberg to Damaraland, where war was raging while Germany was inquiring whether Great Britain would protect her Rhenish missionaries. Wodehouse had no force to spare for that.

Brand had no confidence in the High Commissioner's assertion that the British Government would guarantee peace on the Basuto border; moreover, the farmers were winning the war, and wanted the land from which they were expelling the Basuto. To restore their land to the latter was to restore to them their power; not till the tribes were crushed and punished could there be peace. On legal grounds Brand argued that the British Government had bound itself to neutrality by the Conventions, and must abide by its word;[1] but Wodehouse had waited too long for his opportunity. He was afraid that the commandos, emboldened by non-resistance, would either drive the Basuto into a congestion that would make them dangerous, and thus perhaps provoke the withdrawal of the British Government's sanction as in 1864, or else disperse them among the neighbouring tribes. As it was, John Austen, the Native Commissioner, was nervous at the steady stream of refugees from Basutoland that was pouring into the Wittebergen reserve. Wodehouse peremptorily cut off the Free State ammunition supply at the ports, and on 12 March 1868 formally proclaimed the annexation of Basutoland to the Crown.[2]

The High Commissioner wrung a reluctant consent to his action from the Colonial Secretary, the Duke of Buckingham, by using Grey's favourite trick of offering to resign.[3] He tried to win over the Free Staters by offering them three hundred farms along the border with British title, the proceeds of the sales to go to the republic's treasury; but although the Free State debt was a quarter of a million, imports heavily exceeded exports and the farmers owed the banks and mercantile houses of the British colonies upwards of £650,000, the Volksraad refused the offer and sent two delegates to the Colonial Office to protest. Buckingham, however, told them that he had full confidence in the Governor. Brand had then no alternative but to negotiate.

In February 1869 Brand and Wodehouse met at Aliwal North, both in conciliatory mood. Brand's commandos had gone home; the farmers were tired of the war and its privations, and those in safety

[1] C.O. 48/440, Wodehouse to Buckingham, 18 March 1868; Enclosure, Brand to Wodehouse, 3 March 1868.
[2] C.O. 48/440, D. 24, Wodehouse to Buckingham, 18 March 1868.
[3] Wodehouse Papers, Wodehouse to Barrow, 9 May 1868.

behind the frontier grumbled at the acquisition of blocks of new land, which, flooding the market, caused a slump in prices. Brand himself was afraid that too great an intractability might endanger the Convention, so often threatened. Wodehouse knew, too, that deadlock or the firing of a shot would assuredly cost him not only the Home Government's support, but Basutoland too. So it was agreed to "split the difference".[1] The Free State received a not ungenerous slice of the coveted Basuto sowing lands; the Basuto, though they and their French missionaries had confidently anticipated the restoration of all their lands, were given enough to preserve them from the worst effects of congestion. Yet that they had lost much of their best grazing and ploughing land was seen, not alone in the fact that they began to develop an economy that was more pronouncedly agricultural than pastoral, but above all in the fact that, henceforth, the Basuto, like their Eastern Frontier neighbours, began to supplement their production by means of wages earned in the service of the whites. Nothing is more indicative of the seriousness of their land losses nor more illustrative of the political expediency of Wodehouse's summary intervention. Nevertheless the missionaries indignantly maintained that the Free State had been accorded too much; in England the Aborigines Protection Society nearly provoked a crisis in Parliament, and Earl Granville, the new Secretary of State, being nervous as well as annoyed at Wodehouse's refusal to annex Basutoland to Natal, meditated forcing the republic to return what it had gained, and was only restrained by the opposite fear of reopening the conflict[2] and by Wodehouse's categorical assurance that the Basuto had all the land they needed. The Convention of Aliwal North therefore received Granville's consent, and was ratified in Cape Town in March 1870. In the same month Moshesh died.[3]

It is interesting to note how determined Wodehouse was to prevent the republics from coming down to the sea. The southern Basuto border, as fixed by him, cut off the Free State from a possible corridor down to Port St John's in Pondoland, and that this was designed we can see from the fact that, immediately after the signing of the treaty of Aliwal North, he went to Nomansland to try to persuade the Pondos to cede the port.

On the whole the annexation of Basutoland was favourably received in the British colonies. In Natal, despite the settlers' recent disappointment, a feeling prevailed that the republics had proved themselves too weak to stand alone, and that as long as they were torn by dissension and Native strife, there could be no development of the interior trade to which the merchant fraternity in particular looked

[1] C.O. 48/445, D. 13, Wodehouse to Granville, 14 April 1869.
[2] C.O. 48/445, Minutes.
[3] *Basutoland Records*, v, 236, 262, 268.

to rehabilitate Natal's shattered fortunes. Moreover, in 1867, gold had been discovered on the Tati River to the north-west of the Transvaal, and in the following year diamonds were discovered in the northern Cape Colony. Mineral wealth in the interior—there were the examples of California and Ballarat to quote—brought trade, and Durban looked to capture a lion's share. Basutoland had opened the question of annexations, and opinion in Natal demanded that in addition to Basutoland the whole of the interior should be placed under British influence, and that the republics should not only be prevented from expanding, but as soon as possible be brought under British dominion.

In the Transvaal Pretorius's plight was serious. In opening the Volksraad in 1867 he had made the humiliating confession that government was almost at a standstill for want of cash; prices were inflated; shopkeepers were refusing paper money. The blocks of land which the Government liberally set aside as security for its issues of paper money availed little, because land was not in demand and values were therefore low. When the Zoutpansberg chiefs, Makapan and Mapela, successively rose, public opinion in the Transvaal was so apathetic that many burghers refused to turn out on commando; hence, after an unsuccessful attempt in January 1868 to quell the rising with an insufficient force, Kruger had to abandon practically the whole of the Zoutpansberg. And when he had gone, the volcanic nature of the South African Native world, despite Wodehouse's pacification of Basutoland, was demonstrated by fierce and bloody raids launched by the Swazis and the Shangaans against the Zoutpansberg tribes.

Under these circumstances Pretorius was instantly awake to the value to the Transvaal of the reported gold discoveries. Mineral wealth, increased commercial activity and the control of a port might yet save the Transvaal. An imaginative and adventurous Scot named Alexander McCorkindale had since 1864 succeeded in convincing Pretorius of the possibility of forming a trading company, with steamers working in conjunction with river boats plying on the Maputa River between Delagoa Bay and a point of the Swaziland-Transvaal border. In March 1868 Pretorius astounded Wodehouse, Natal and Portugal by issuing a proclamation annexing to the Transvaal an enormous extent of territory to the north and west including the gold-fields and, on the east, a narrow finger of land down the line of the Maputa River to Delagoa Bay, ignoring thus both the Portuguese and British claims to that harbour.[1]

Portugal, Wodehouse and Keate, Lieutenant-Governor of Natal, all protested vehemently. Wodehouse objected to the proclamation because it threatened the Missionaries' Road to the north, and he distrusted the power of the Transvaal Government to keep order

[1] C.O. 48/441, D. 62, Wodehouse to Buckingham, 18 July 1868.

amongst what might, if the Gold and Diamond Fields proved rich, become a numerous digging community in close proximity to the Matabele and Bechuana tribes; but he objected chiefly because he believed that the British possessions must "inevitably take part in and control" the "relations of the interior".[1] In Natal there was an outcry for annexation. Lieutenant-Governor Keate and the Legislative Council, afraid of losing commercial advantages and believing that the worst reports of the wild doings in the Zoutpansberg were true, both demanded permission to intervene. At Westminster, Buckingham promptly refused to recognise Pretorius's proclamation,[2] but, though not wholly disinclined, he would not consent to annex any additional territory for the Crown. In 1869, nevertheless, mainly owing to the influence of Adderley, the British Government had at last come to favour the reinclusion of the republics under British dominion. Provided the new order of things would be self-supporting (and by "self-supporting" self-government was necessarily implied), a federation of the South African States would be a desirable consummation. In September 1868 Wodehouse had categorically expressed before the Cape Parliament his belief in federation; the Natal legislature was unanimously in favour of that policy, and in November 1868 Buckingham suggested to the Governor that he take into "serious consideration" any overtures which might be made to bring the republics "in some form or other under British authority".[3]

Nevertheless, the cause of federation could make no practical progress until the constitutional issues had been settled in at least the greater and stronger of the British colonies. In both the Cape and Natal throughout 1868 and 1869 there was no improvement in the financial position and the constitutional deadlock continued. In 1868 the new Gladstone administration renewed the demand for the withdrawal of troops from South Africa. The British Government was opposed to Wodehouse's scheme to apply Jamaican government to the Cape, and Granville, the new Secretary of State, intimated his willingness to accede to any demand from the Colony for self-government. Towards Natal, however, his attitude was significantly different. The expectations of profit from the mineral discoveries had not been realised; reports had greatly exaggerated the richness of the fields; floods in 1868 had wrought disastrous havoc, and the deficit continued unrelieved. Lieutenant-Governor Keate proposed additional taxation; the Legislative Council retorted that he could tax the Natives and dismiss some officials.[4] Keate was obstinate and tactless and a deadlock ensued. The Natal colonists, afraid of losing the British

[1] C.O. 48/441, D. 62, Wodehouse to Buckingham, 3 June 1868.
[2] C.O. 49/61, Confidential, Buckingham to Wodehouse, 9 November 1868.
[3] C.O. 49/61, D. 194, Buckingham to Wodehouse, 23 November 1868.
[4] C.O. 179/90, Keate to Buckingham, 7 September 1868.

garrison, did not ask for full self-government, yet Granville refused to make them any constitutional concession, being influenced by the serious difficulty which the Maori wars had caused in self-governing New Zealand throughout the 'sixties, and the fears expressed by Wodehouse that the withdrawal of troops would be prejudicial to the safety of Natal. Wodehouse strove more earnestly than ever to impress upon the British Government the necessity of elaborating a policy which did not regard Natal as separate and different from the Cape, and which envisaged some form of union for all the South African States. In his eyes the only feasible policy was to strengthen the power of the Governor in the Cape, and that of the High Commissioner in Natal and the trans-frontier territories.

In the Cape in 1869 the deadlock involved not only Governor and Parliament and the Eastern and Western parties, but the two Houses as well. Newly elected at the end of 1868, the House of Assembly vetoed proposals for retrenchment and additional taxation, and called for the withdrawal of the Cape police whom Wodehouse had sent to Basutoland. Unable to tax the wool of the Easterners, Wodehouse turned to the wine of the Westerners and was desperate enough even to suggest an income tax. In the face of this deadlock, Granville was forced to agree with the Governor that either the executive or the legislature must give way. Having told Natal that he would not give it greater freedom for fear of Native disturbance, he could hardly adopt an opposite attitude towards the Cape with its far from contented tribes on the Eastern Frontier and Basutoland manifestly destined to be added at the earliest possible moment. The alternatives still were a Crown Colony government, on the lines recently introduced in Jamaica, and responsible government. Granville inclined strongly towards the latter course, but, urged by Wodehouse, deferred once again the recall of the troops and gave him a reluctant permission to put his former project for the abolition of the Assembly to the country. Contrary to Wodehouse's expectations, the result of the election was an emphatic rejection of any limitation of the constitutional powers of the Legislative Council, and in May 1870 Wodehouse finally left South Africa unpopular as never Governor had been before.

For his successor Granville chose a Governor of an entirely different experience and outlook. Sir Henry Barkly believed in responsible government and had become familiar with its practical working in Australia; it seemed as though under him there might be a change of era in South Africa. Yet Wodehouse's work did not pass away with him. South Africa owed to him the salvation of Kaffraria and Basutoland from being overrun by European settlement. Had that happened, there must have followed a disruption of their African populations, which, already serious enough, would have been utterly disastrous. Wodehouse's opposition to responsible government was both natural in the circumstances of his governorship and, be it observed, showed that he recognised that self-government was far from being the most important problem in South Africa at the time. In Wodehouse's view the overmastering problem was the further development of British policy towards the republics. Later events were to prove that he was right.

CHAPTER XVII

THE ESTABLISHMENT OF RESPONSIBLE GOVERNMENT IN CAPE COLONY, 1870–1872

THE year 1847 when Canada acquired responsible government is far more important in her history than the corresponding year 1872 in that of the Cape Colony, for the Cape, unlike Canada, made no original contribution to constitutional progress in the direction of self-government. It is even misleading to suppose that the achievement of responsible government at the Cape marks the end of an era of development and progress. If in the history of Canada it is legitimate to see constitutional experiment and growth as the dominating feature of the nineteenth century, constitutional progress in South Africa is but one issue closely bound up with other and greater issues—Great Britain's costly error in allowing the Great Trek to result in the growth of independent republics, and the economic and social problems arising from the ubiquitous contact of white and black races. Thus Cape self-government can only be properly understood in relation to the further development of British policy towards the republics, which was now to be seriously influenced by the discovery of diamonds on the banks of the Vaal River. Eclipsing the gold of Tati, diamonds provoked a crisis that involved the major issues of South African history.

By the time diamonds had been picked up, first at Hopetown in the Cape Colony and then on the banks of the lower Vaal river, the British Government had come to the conclusion that the policy which had given the Orange Free State and the Transvaal their independence had been mistaken. The constantly recurring Native wars and disturbances in the republics and the anxious protests from the Cape and Natal Governments which they provoked had long since converted the Colonial Office to Sir George Grey's gospel that the close association of the different South African communities under the same flag alone could solve the common problems of native administration and commerce. Since 1866, the British Government, with the strong support of the Natal and Cape Governments, had been frankly on the look-out for a legitimate occasion for abrogating the Sand River and Bloemfontein Conventions. By annexing Basutoland in 1868, by quashing in the same year Pretorius's bid for the territorial aggrandisement of the Transvaal, and by refusing to recognise the right of either Portugal or the Transvaal to Delagoa Bay, the British Government made it clear that it no longer considered itself bound by the policy of the Conventions. Thus, when diamonds were discovered and a great population grew up on the Diggings, the resistance of Great Britain to the assumption of control over the Diamond Fields by the Orange Free State and the Transvaal was a foregone conclusion.

Before 1870, an imperialism which saw in expansion its own reward had no place whatever in British South African policy. Almost paradoxically the constant aim of successive British Cabinets was the antithesis of aggressive or acquisitive expansion, for they desired above all things to be relieved of the expense and burden of South African internal affairs. Since 1866, the formation of a federal system which would be self-governing and self-dependent had been devoutly desired. The British Government would place no obstacle in the way of self-government for the Cape Colony; it would have been equally ready to give Natal wider powers of self-government but for its abiding fear of leaving so small a community to cope alone with its overwhelming Native population. Finally, the constant alarums in and instability of the republics could not but compromise the success of whatever freedom it granted the coastal colonies. Only the federation of the republics and colonies within the Empire could satisfy the necessities of British policy—self-government for South Africa and relief from the heavy military and financial responsibilities for the Mother Country.

The theatre of critical events during the period 1858–68 had been the region where Basutoland touches the Cape Colony, the Free State and Natal; but, after the annexation of 1868, interest shifted once more further west to the districts where the relations between Trek Boers, Griquas, Bechuanas and missionaries had presented such difficult problems to the Colonial Office and the Cape Government in the time of Dr Philip thirty-odd years before.[1]

The territory which the discovery of diamonds brought into prominence, together with the Missionary Road with which the Diamond Fields question is closely connected, had already been the subject of earlier dispute. The road into the interior used by missionaries and traders passed through the territory which came to be known as Griqualand West. Subsequent developments were to prove that both the colonisation of a vast expanse of interior country and the connection of the interior to the coast depended intimately upon the control of this Missionaries Road.

Of those who appreciated the value of the road, David Arnot, an enterprising lawyer of poor reputation from Colesberg, was not the least. About 1862 he had conceived the idea of bringing the road under British control. His reward would be derived from speculation in the enhanced land values which that control would undoubtedly produce.

In 1860 Henry Harvey and David Arnot became joint attorneys for the Griqua chief Adam Kok intending to profit by speculation in

[1] *Vide supra*, ch. XIII.

his lands. Whether out of distrust of his colleague or from greed, Harvey persuaded Kok a little later to sign a new power of attorney in his favour alone. At first his plan was to purchase the Chief's lands himself, but when Kok was already on his way to Nomansland, either Harvey's courage or his funds failed him. Posting after the Griqua Chief, he obtained from him permission to negotiate a sale with the Free State Government instead. Accurately speaking, the lands under negotiation were the Philippolis lands in the southern Free State, which were bounded on the west by part of the line from Ramah on the Orange to Platberg on the Vaal. In 1857, however, Adam Kok had been bequeathed the adjacent lands of Cornelis Kok, Griqua Chief at Campbell. Of the nature or position of these lands Harvey had no knowledge, but in order to draw the Free State to a speedy purchase he threw in for good measure "the lands of the late Cornelis Kok". In December 1861 Adam Kok readily signed the receipt for the purchase price of £4000. He would presumably have gone his way indifferent to the Campbell lands had David Arnot not persuaded him to deny having sanctioned their sale. Thereupon Arnot prepared himself for his tussle with the Free State. He promptly deserted Adam Kok and claimed the Campbell lands for the Griqua chief Nicolaas Waterboer, whose agent he became, on the grounds that Cornelis Kok had not been an independent chief but a vassal of Waterboer, and that all claims by the Free State to any part of the Campbell lands to the west or the east of the Vaal River encroached upon the independence of Waterboer. Before 1867 it was annexation by the British Government and liberal profits from land speculation which he had in view, but, a little later, he changed his plans and flew at higher game.[1]

In view of the conditions of Harvey's sale of Adam Kok's lands in 1861, the Free State's claims beyond the Vaal River lay open to considerable doubt. As early as 1864 President Brand expressed his willingness to refer these lands to the arbitration of Governor Wodehouse. As to the land on the Free State side of the Vaal River he refused to admit that the claim of his republic depended upon the purchase from Adam Kok. Before the Bloemfontein Convention, in the days of Sir Harry Smith's Sovereignty, Major Warden had issued land titles to twenty-nine farmers in the territory between the Vaal and the Ramah-Platberg line.[2] When the Bloemfontein Convention was signed, Sir George Clerk had made it abundantly clear that the British Government had no longer any interest in arresting the expansion of the farmers on to the land of the Griquas, and in fact had openly recommended it.[3] At that moment there had not been

[1] See Wilmot, Count A., *Life of Southey*, pp. 216–17; *ibid.* p. 224, Arnot to Southey, 18 March 1876.

[2] *Vide supra*, p. 351.

[3] de Kiewiet, C. W., *British Colonial Policy and the South African Republics*, pp. 82–3.

above two hundred Griqua families in the whole of Cornelis Kok's territory; then, moving away as the game was driven north, they had soon sold another 110 farms to Free State farmers. In a country that was arid except for occasional *fonteins* or springs, this settlement of some 140 farmers and their families constituted effective occupation. The Philippolis lands themselves were already honeycombed with white settlement at the time of their sale in 1861. The claim of the Free State, at least to the land on its own side of the Vaal River, rested on the complete collapse of Dr Philip's Griqua Treaty States and the consequent tendency of the European farmers to possess themselves of the best land. On the Basuto border, where the land was fertile and the Natives numerous, this tendency had produced war; in Griqualand the soil was, for the most part, poor, and the Griquas few and indifferent cultivators; white penetration had consequently been more insidious. This irregular process of Free State settlement was not easily capable of documentary demonstration, whereas the unscrupulous Arnot skilfully revived the former claims of Griqua chiefs to a territorial sovereignty which had crumbled away, brazenly creating the impression that nothing had happened to break down the system of Griqua States which Dr Philip had laboriously striven to erect. Thus he made it appear that the Free State had deliberately ignored the "sovereign" rights safeguarded by the treaty of 1834 between Chief Waterboer and the Cape Government.[1]

It was Arnot's extreme good fortune that he worked better than he knew, for, in Cape Town as in Downing Street, men were beginning to look with deepening suspicion upon the Native policy of the republics, and regretting the day when they had promised them immunity from interference.

The first diamond seems to have been found in 1867 in the district of Hopetown just south of the Orange river in the Cape Colony itself. The earliest significant finds, however, were made in the following year in the debated territory on the banks of the Vaal River, and when in March 1869 a diamond was discovered of such weight and excellence that it finally sold for £25,000, it was realised that valuable deposits had been discovered. The rush began and the long-drawn-out dispute suddenly became of urgent importance.

The first area worked was the River Diggings between the Harts and the Vaal rivers. It was a part of Pretorius's sweeping annexation in 1868. Into the land between the Vaal and the Harts had come a thin trickle of Transvaal farmers; there had been some fighting and several Chiefs had "treaties" with the Transvaal Government. Frontier between the Transvaal and the tribes there was none, and

[1] For the most powerful defence of the Free State claim see Lindley, A. F., *Adamantia*. The matter has never been fully examined. British officials like Captain Charles Warren, R.E., and Colonel Crossman were amazed at the extent to which Brand's evidence had been ignored or misunderstood.

before Pretorius could negotiate a line with the Chiefs, Arnot, acting as agent for the chief Mahura, boldly claimed a line that not merely cut off debatable territory, but also territory that had been long inhabited by Europeans. Before the crisis came in 1870, Arnot had been displaced as Mahura's agent by Theodore Doms, a man without his brains but equally unscrupulous.

In 1864, Wodehouse had been willing to arbitrate in the dispute between the Free State and Waterboer; but, while the Free State was fighting on the Basuto border, nothing had been done. In 1870, when the news of rich finds was beginning to excite the villages and farms throughout the land, Brand and Waterboer finally agreed to refer the question of the Campbell lands to the Governor of the Cape. From his contact with Wodehouse during the Basuto negotiations of Aliwal North in 1869, Brand knew that he would be just. But Wodehouse now refused to come. Lonely and worn after eight years of unpopularity and incessant battling with the Colonists, the prospect of another year like 1869 was intolerable to him.[1]

In August 1870, President Brand, Pretorius, Waterboer and Arnot met at the farm Nooitgedacht in an endeavour to reach a settlement. Brand insisted on confining the discussion to the Campbell lands west of the Vaal River; Arnot as firmly refused to exclude the lands on the Free State side and demanded that the whole dispute be referred to the arbitration of the Governor of the Cape. On the fifth day of the discussions Arnot abruptly left. The time was ripe for an appeal to the Cape.

Pretorius on his side had already tried to steal a march on his opponents by rushing a concession to a company, covering the richest diamondiferous ground between the Vaal and the Harts, through a bare quorum of the Volksraad. According to their origin the diggers were divided between supporters of the Transvaal, of British control and of a free diggers' republic, but as long as they had not been molested in their freedom to dig, the question of jurisdiction had not seemed acute. Now, however, the action of the Transvaal President provoked an outburst of excitement and considerable resentment in the camps. A Union Jack made its appearance, and the motley community of diggers from the British colonies and the republics broke up into factions either favouring Pretorius or shouting for the High Commissioner and British interference. At Klipdrift, Stafford Parker, once a sailor, was elected President of a republic ruled by diggers for diggers,[2] and by forecastle methods he maintained a sort of order.

In these circumstances the presence of Pretorius at the conference between Brand and Waterboer could only be regarded by the diggers and official opinion in Cape Town as a conspiracy between the two

[1] *Vide supra*, p. 437.
[2] *Parl. Pap.* 1871, XLVII [C. 415], pp. 131–3, Barkly to Kimberley, 8 March 1871.

republics,[1] for the Free State agreed to recognise the rights of the Transvaal to the lands it claimed. Pretorius, it is true, did his utmost to hush the storm he had provoked. He withdrew the concession and promised the diggers control over their own affairs, if they would accept Transvaal sovereignty over the land. But Pretorius had fired a train of events that ultimately led to British annexation. The claims of Chiefs like Mahura or Waterboer were laughed at by the diggers. It was already evident that the real problem of the Diamond Fields was not the Natives, but the thronging Europeans who swayed to and fro regardless of any boundaries or claims whatsoever as the rumours and reports of new finds reached them.

The Free State Commission, after continuing the examination of Waterboer's claims in his absence, declared them insufficient, and issued a proclamation annexing the Campbell lands to the Free State.[2] Olof Truter, an experienced digger, who had been to the Australian gold-fields and who Brand shrewdly calculated would be acceptable to British and Afrikaners alike, was appointed as Landdrost at Pniel to maintain Free State authority.[3]

The appeal Arnot immediately made to the Cape Government was of course the inevitable first move in his scheme of British annexation, but the departure of Wodehouse from South Africa was a piece of sheer good fortune for the scheme. Though the Governor's belief in the destiny of Great Britain ultimately to control all South Africa was constant and firm, he had been eminently just in his dealings with the republics; but Charles Hay, whom he left behind him as Acting-Governor, was entirely in the hands of the permanent officials at Cape Town. Of these, Richard Southey, the Colonial Secretary, who had been Wodehouse's right hand and had fought his fiercest battles in the Cape legislature, lacked the Governor's detachment and restraint. Much like Shepstone in Natal, Southey believed that the Conventions were an intolerable obstacle to the legitimate exercise of British authority in the subcontinent.[4] In addition the business houses in Cape Town and Durban, sorely depressed by eight drought-stricken years the effects of which had been deepened by the Basuto war and civil anarchy in the Transvaal, had every reason to look with disapproval upon the efforts of the two republics, so heavily in debt that they were almost bankrupt, to possess themselves of the fields. From Grahamstown, equally dependent upon the trans-frontier trade, came petitions for British interference. The Cape's desperate need of revenue and trade, and Southey's own imperialist convictions, led him to see in Arnot's appeal on behalf of Waterboer a splendid occasion for peremptory action. Arnot, who

[1] *Parl. Pap.* 1871, XLVII [C. 415], p. 443, Hay to Brand, 19 September 1870.
[2] *Parl. Pap.* 1871, XLVII [C. 415], p. 37.
[3] *Ibid.* p. 39.
[4] Cf. Froude, J. A., *Two Lectures on South Africa*, p. 26.

knew, none better, how monstrous was his game of bluff, by eking out his evidence with relevant but inconclusive statements, found no difficulty in convincing Southey of the justice of the Griqua chief's pretensions. *Prima facie* Arnot presented a very strong case for Waterboer. That Southey was honestly convinced is unquestionable; there is no evidence of collusion with Arnot.

So utterly did Southey's mouthpiece, Acting-Governor Hay, prejudge the questions at issue, and so great was his eagerness to forestall the Free State, that he did not wait to receive a full statement from Brand.[1] He indeed informed the President of Arnot's appeal, but before Brand had even received the communication, he issued a Government notice encouraging the diggers to resist republican jurisdiction by promising them British support in all "lawful" proceedings.[2] Two months later, unimpressed by the stream of protests and documents that commenced to flow in from the Free State, he appointed John Campbell as a Special Magistrate under the Cape Punishment Act, i.e. practically Lieutenant-Governor, to wrest authority from Truter.

By his appointment of Campbell, Hay definitely committed himself to support the Griqua chief against the Free State. Not only was the Act under which Campbell was appointed a dead letter, but under its authority magistrates could be appointed only to Native territories. That the Campbell lands were such had still to be proved. Nor was Hay's reading of the documents presented by the Free State that of an impartial arbiter. On his side, Brand, however, produced his evidence badly. Time was needed to unearth all the possible evidence and his case was consequently incomplete, while evidence subsequently adduced failed to remove the doubt in the minds of Southey and Hay. Yet, far as it had gone in supporting the cause of Waterboer, the Cape Government could go no further. A final decision rested with the as yet unknown successor to Wodehouse, and he, fresh from England, would necessarily be powerfully influenced by the attitude of the authorities at home.

The Colonial Office could not be altogether indifferent to the importance of attaching the Diamond Fields to the British possessions, though never was it more resolutely opposed to new territorial acquisitions than in the 'sixties. As early as 1867 the British Government had seriously meditated the annexation of the territories to the north of the Cape Colony which were afterwards incorporated in German South-West Africa, where mineral discoveries had been reported. In that period such an inclination is nothing short of astounding. Yet it was the fear of irresponsible settlement and possible annexation by a foreign power rather than a desire for acquisition that had almost persuaded the Colonial Office to take the step. To attribute the ultimate annexation of the Diamond Fields to a simple

[1] *Parl. Pap.* 1871, XLVII [C. 415], p. 39, Hay to Brand, 19 Sept. 1870.
[2] *Ibid.* p. 38, Government Notice, No. 379, 1870.

urge for gain is to misconstrue utterly the singular complexity of the motives and aims of the British South African policy. The antagonism of Free Traders to the expense of maintaining troops in Canada, Australia and New Zealand as well as in South Africa, the belief of the War Office that the troubled state of Europe in the 'sixties made a concentration of imperial troops desirable, the strict economy programme of the Gladstone administration, the impossibility of withdrawing imperial troops unless there was an assurance of peace for whites and blacks in South Africa, the consequent conviction that South Africa must seek strength in federation and self-government, and a genuine feeling widely held and encouraged also by the success of the recent British North America Act that the proper fulfilment of colonial development was responsible government—such were the causes which determined British South African policy from 1861 to the eve of Gladstone's Midlothian campaign in November 1879.

If the British Government had any consistent purpose in South Africa after 1866, it was the organisation of the subcontinent under a single government; but its fatal weakness was that it made no comprehensive effort to achieve its purpose. As a result, Governors, unprepared for sudden emergencies, exceeded their instructions and resorted to arbitrary action, while an unscrupulous lawyer could exploit the prejudices of a Colonial Secretary in Cape Town and provoke disastrously the resentment of those without whose co-operation a united South Africa was impossible.

By making it appear that the republics were encroaching on Native territory guaranteed by the British Government, Arnot excited in the Colonial Office a moral indignation against Presidents Brand and Pretorius that deeply affected its thinking.[1] Ignorant that great arid stretches of the debated territory were almost destitute of any Native population, the Colonial Office saw in the understanding at which the two Presidents had arrived at Nooitgedacht in August 1870 a conspiracy to despoil a numerous Native population of its land and independence. The belief long held that the frequently reported irregularities in apprenticing Native children to the farmers in the Transvaal indicated the prevalence of slavery in that republic caused the Colonial Secretary, the Earl of Kimberley to write, a month before the bulk of the evidence had arrived in England, that "Her Majesty's Government would see with great dissatisfaction any encroachment on Griqua territory by these Republics".[2] Just as the British Government had vigorously opposed the acquisition of Delagoa Bay by the Transvaal as a port for its alleged slave-dealing operations, so was it now afraid that, if the Boers were allowed to control the rich Diamond Fields, the Transvaal would ere long become too strong to be controlled. Frankly enough admitting, as did Sir Frederick Rogers,

[1] C.O. 48/451, D. 25, Hay to Kimberley, 19 September 1870, minutes.
[2] *Parl. Pap.* 1871, XLVII [C. 415], p. 65, Kimberley to Barkly, 17 November 1870.

the Permanent Under-Secretary, that it would be "idle" to unravel the vast accumulation of evidence which the despatches brought, and that it would be useless to scrutinise a "matter on which we cannot possibly form a sound judgment",[1] the Colonial Office allowed itself to be guided by the despatches from Cape Town.

Before the new Governor, Sir Henry Barkly, had arrived in Cape Town, opinion in the Colonial Office was unanimous that the disputed area should be annexed, but that the British Government should not make itself directly responsible for another territory like Basutoland. The onus of annexation must therefore fall upon the Cape Colony. Kimberley was aware that such a responsibility could best be assumed by a self-governing colony. The device employed in 1865 to force the annexation of British Kaffraria upon an unwilling and helpless Colonial legislature by passing an *in terrorem* British Act could not be lightly resorted to again.

Sir Henry Barkly had been purposely chosen to reverse the policy of Sir Philip Wodehouse and to give every encouragement to the early adoption of responsible government by the Cape Colony.[2] With regard to the Diamond Fields, he left England strongly under the influence of Hay's despatches and the attitude of the Colonial Office. Even before he left, he had expressed the opinion that the people of the Transvaal had "no peculiar scruples on the subject of slavery or the treatment of natives".[3] Moreover, he had small respect for the mass of intricate legal documents, which obscured what he recognised as the central question, whether the republics or the United Kingdom were to control the new centre of population on the Diamond Fields.

Barkly indeed was from the beginning no more able than Hay to approach the dispute without preconceived opinions. To the arguments put forward by Brand, whom he found waiting for him at Cape Town, he returned almost unchanged the objections already raised by Southey and Hay.[4] Brand, like the lawyer he was, made matters worse by overreaching himself. In claiming that, at the abandonment in 1854, the whole of the former Sovereignty as annexed by Smith in 1848 had fallen to the Free State, he forgot that on numerous occasions the Free State had recognised the independence of Adam Kok and Moshesh. Southey triumphantly pointed to Free State evidence containing errors of transcription. When it was discovered that the date of the watermark on one document was later than the date of the transaction on it, Arnot's contention that some of Brand's documents were forgeries seemed to be justified. The evidence was contaminated in Barkly's eyes, and Brand's explanations, though just enough, did not succeed in dispelling the Governor's suspicions.

[1] C.O. 48/451, D. 41, 45, 46, minutes by Rogers, 24 December 1870.
[2] *Parl. Pap.* 1871, XLVII [C. 415], p. 66, Kimberley to Barkly, No. 29, 17 November 1870.
[3] C.O. 48/451, Hay to Granville, 2 August 1870, minute to Barkly.
[4] *Parl. Pap.* 1871, XLVII [C. 415], p. 100, Barkly to Kimberley, 18 January 1871; *ibid.* p. 107.

When the President informed the High Commissioner that the Free State was willing to submit the Campbell lands to foreign arbitration, but would consider no arbitration whatever on the lands east of the Vaal, Barkly felt he had no alternative but a flat refusal.

Throughout 1870 the rush of farmers, shopkeepers and clerks to the River Diggings went on. In the New Year of 1871 their number was fully ten thousand. In the fever of digging their passions were quickly aroused; any interference with their operations would inevitably lead to violence. Pretorius had already almost destroyed any willingness they had shown to accept Transvaal jurisdiction. "Jan" Brand, it is true, was personally popular in the new camps that sprang up on the River Diggings on the Free State side of the Vaal, and presently also to the south, on the new Dry Diggings on the farms Dorstfontein and Bultfontein; the Free State Landdrost was efficient and pleased the mob by his firm handling of the Natives. Nevertheless, the news that Hay had appointed a British magistrate to the Diamond Fields was received with general enthusiasm and settled the minds of the majority in favour of British annexation. When the absentee proprietors of the farm on which Dry Diggings were discovered attempted to claim licence fees from the diggers on the ground that their titles did not reserve mineral rights to the government, the swing in favour of British intervention was more marked still.

Towards the end of January 1871 Barkly left Cape Town on a tour that included Basutoland and the Diamond Fields. When he arrived at the shouting and cheering camps in February, he realised more clearly than ever before that what was in the balance was no longer a question of the rights of Waterboer and the Barolong chiefs against the republics, but the government of the growing population of the Fields and the political leadership of the subcontinent. Quite frankly he admitted that the espousal of Waterboer's rights by the British Government was nothing more than a useful fiction. "It appeared to me", he wrote to Lord Kimberley at the Colonial Office, "that the British Government had gone too far to admit of its ceasing to support the cause of either Waterboer or the diggers, and that it was quite clear that any appearance of faltering on my part would only encourage the Free State and Transvaal in upholding their claims."[1] Yet, although he was thus clearly bent on annexation, he met the disputants and once more proposed arbitration.

Pretorius was willing and accepted the High Commissioner's proposal. The hopes of the Transvaal President had suddenly become brighter. At the end of 1870 he had met the Native claimants to the land between the Harts and the Vaal. At the meeting Theodore Doms claimed for the Barolong a territory that included the whole diamondiferous area claimed by the Transvaal, on the grounds that the Voortrekker leader, Hendrik Potgieter, had guaranteed these lands

[1] *Parl. Pap.* 1871, XLVII [C. 415], pp. 98–9.

to the father of Montsiwa, chief of the Barolong. But Ludorf, a missionary, who had been with the Barolong at Thaba Nchu, opportunely produced a document, actually a forgery, which "proved" that Montsiwa had no rights to land east of the Harts. Pretorius fell into the trap and declared himself ready to refer all territorial disputes to the arbitration of the High Commissioner. The Transvaal Volksraad gave the necessary authority in December 1870. In March Pretorius accepted Barkly's proposals for a concurrent jurisdiction by British and Transvaal magistrates over the disputed ground, pending the reference of all claims to a joint commission composed of representatives of the Chiefs and the Transvaal, with Lieutenant-Governor Keate of Natal as the final umpire in the event of disagreement.[1]

More astute and more obstinate, Brand refused to budge from his position that there could be no arbitration on the Free State's rights to the land on the east Bank of the Vaal. John Campbell stayed at Klipdrift north of the Vaal while the diggers were rushing from the valley of the Vaal to the Dry Diggings, and in May 1871 Truter followed them as Landdrost to Dutoitspan, the great centre of activity in those diggings, to counteract his influence. For the Campbell lands Brand still insisted on foreign arbitration.[2] He not only felt that no local arbitrator could at this stage be without a *parti pris*, but that there was a deeper issue still—republican independence. In annexing Basutoland, in its repeated threats to throw open the gunpowder traffic to the tribes, and in sending a British magistrate on to Free State soil, the British Government had violated its promises of 1854 not to interfere in disputes between the Free State and tribes beyond the frontier, and had imposed a serious qualification on the independence of the republic. On such vital questions, Brand insisted that only a foreign arbitrator could pronounce.

The President's proposals were repugnant to Barkly on several grounds. That they sought to exclude from discussion the Dry Diggings where the great bulk of the diggers was congregating was a grave objection; but in addition, arbitration by the King of Holland or the President of the United States, whom Brand suggested, was certain to prove tedious and lengthy. The need to govern the camps was too present and too urgent for that course. When once the Free State had exercised jurisdiction over the Fields for any considerable period, it might, having taken root, be so difficult to dislodge that the Home Government would refuse to take any action.

A foreign arbitration on British policy in South Africa Kimberley condemned out of hand.[3] The European horizon was clouded. 1870 was a most difficult year for British diplomacy. The very critical

[1] *Parl. Pap.* 1871, XLVII [C. 415], pp. 140–1, Barkly to Kimberley, 8 March 1871.
[2] *Ibid.* p. 159, Brand to Barkly, 7 March 1871.
[3] *Ibid.* p. 183, Kimberley to Barkly, 3 June 1871.

arbitration on the *Alabama* dispute with the United States, in progress at that moment, made a second venture into arbitration distasteful. "The action of foreign powers in these South African questions might lead to very serious embarrassments",[1] the Colonial Secretary declared; the Diamond Fields dispute was local and domestic, to be settled by the parties directly concerned. Kimberley's attitude could only be interpreted as a reaffirmation of Wodehouse's constant belief that in the conduct of their external relations the republics were in effect hardly less subject to Her Majesty's High Commissioner for South Africa than were the British colonies themselves.[2] As to the Conventions and the independence they conferred upon the "emancipated Boers", the Colonial Office refused to admit that they had been treaties between equal and independent powers; they were an "act of Grace on the part of Her Majesty which left Her Government with every right to put its own interpretation upon them".[3] Brand might protest with complete justification that such a view was not borne out by the facts of 1852 and 1854. His protest was just but not expedient. His obstinacy made annexation all the more inevitable, for he was too much a lawyer to seek a compromise.

There is no doubt that the Free State President acted as he did in the firm belief that Barkly had no authority to annex the Diamond Fields. In his negotiations with Wodehouse on the Basuto border he had seen that the British Government was strongly averse to incurring heavy expense across the frontier; he therefore concluded, during his talks with Barkly at Bloemfontein, that a similar reluctance dictated the High Commissioner's conciliatory offer to withdraw Campbell provided he on his side would accept local arbitration. He was even persuaded that a hostile demonstration might call the High Commissioner's bluff. Events on the Fields soon provided both the occasion and the excuse.

In February Campbell had felt that his position was strong enough for more authoritative action. In an endeavour to cut the ground from under Truter's feet he invited tenders for the erection of a gaol at Pniel and for a supply of provisions for a hundred mounted police. He also forbade the diggers to pay licences to any but himself, and, nothing loath, many complied. Brand met the challenge by ordering a commando of burghers up to Pniel to support Truter's authority. Instantly the camps buzzed with excitement and alarm. Calling to Campbell for arms, the British faction paraded angrily in front of two useless but encouraging cannon. Barkly, just returned from a reassuring trip to Basutoland, did not wince. Much less averse to using force than Wodehouse, he rushed the Cape Frontier Police to

[1] C.O. 48/455, D. 57, Barkly to Kimberley, 2 June 1871, minute by Kimberley.
[2] C.O. 48/454, Barkly to Kimberley, 7 April 1871, minute by Knatchbull-Hugessen.
[3] C.O. 48/456, D. 92, Barkly to Kimberley, 26 August 1871, minute by Knatchbull-Hugessen.

Hopetown and kept them there in readiness while he sent one troop on to Klipdrift. The warning was sufficient. Realising that his failure to intimidate the High Commissioner had done his cause great damage, Brand withdrew his commando and repeated his demand for foreign arbitration, this time adding the newly elected German Kaiser to the list of proposed arbitrators. A country without a treasury, with the Basuto war so shortly past and its burghers sick of campaigns, could not risk an armed clash. Convinced of this, and with the Transvaal agreeing to local arbitration, Barkly knew himself to be master of the situation.

As early as the beginning of March he had written to Kimberley that there was no alternative to annexation.[1] The wisest course was to end the impasse by sharp and firm action. As long as the rivalry between Truter and Campbell compromised ordered government, so long the digger population was tinder to every spark. Lord Kimberley, however, was still hesitant. From Barkly's despatches he first assured himself that the population of the Diamond Fields was hostile to the Free State, and that the Free State would not resort to force. "The Free State President will only bluster and then give in", minuted Knatchbull-Hugessen, the Parliamentary Under-Secretary, "any vacillation on our part might encourage him, and our trumpet must now put forth no uncertain sound."[2] Knatchbull-Hugessen commented on the "folly" of the British Government "in ever abandoning the authority over the Orange River Territory and creating a standing nuisance to British colonists in the erection of this petty Republic". Kimberley sought the advice of the Prime Minister, Gladstone, and thus fortified at last gave his consent to annexation.

The consent of the British Government was accompanied by most significant conditions.[3] The Cape Colony would have to undertake the responsibility of governing the territory which was to be united to it, together with the entire maintenance of any force that might be necessary for the preservation of order and the defence of the new border, such force not to consist of British troops, but to be a force raised and supported by the Colony itself. Kimberley was clearly aware that his conditions involved self-government. The time was past when the British Government could maintain for an indefinite period the "present anomalous constitution" in order to protect the Native races. No further expense for frontier defence could fall on the British taxpayer; on the other hand, if the Colonists were to pay, "they must have a control over the policy of the Executive".[4]

Kimberley's despatch permitting the annexation of the Diamond Fields arrived in Cape Town in the midst of a determined new effort

[1] *Parl. Pap.* 1871, XLVII [C. 415], p. 131, Barkly to Kimberley, 8 March 1871.
[2] C.O. 48/454, Barkly to Kimberley, 17 April 1871, minute by Knatchbull-Hugessen.
[3] *Parl. Pap.* 1871, XLVII [C. 415], p. 172, Kimberley to Barkly, 18 May 1871.
[4] C.O. 48/455, D. 53, Barkly to Kimberley, 31 May 1871, minute by Kimberley.

by Molteno and his party to carry responsible government. This time they were aided by Governor Barkly, who, despite the unanimous opposition of his Executive, threw his weight on the side of those who demanded that constitutional advance. With trade circulation speeded up and consumption increased by the discovery of diamonds, the extreme poverty of the Colony, which had been Wodehouse's most telling argument against self-government, had disappeared. The opening of the Suez Canal in 1869 had greatly reduced the importance of the Cape Peninsula as a strong point on the old sea-route to India. It had, of course, not destroyed it, but trade and military reinforcements now began to take the new route. The drought that had crippled the Colony had departed with Wodehouse, the ostrich-feather industry was flourishing, and the deficit, gloomily expected for 1870, had turned into a comfortable surplus. The British Government was withdrawing its troops, and with them went another objection to self-government.

Good times greatly heartened the "Responsibles", as Molteno's followers were called. For the same reason, however, the Easterners hardened in their opposition, for they still feared Western "Dutch" domination and believed that under responsible government the Western majority would throw the burden of taxation upon them, and be wanting in the peculiar "expertness" of the frontiersmen in handling the tribes. There was, too, the problem of the diggers in the Diamond Fields; if they were to become Cape citizens, their attitude towards the future could not be ignored. Thus Molteno failed again. His Responsible Government Bill passed the Assembly without a division on the third reading, although the Eastern members were still adamant; but, although it was baited with the promise of a commission to consider a division of Cape Colony and a relinking of East and West in a federation,[1] it was thrown out by the Council by 12 votes to 9. The Federation Commission was appointed in June 1871 with Robert Godlonton, J. C. Molteno and John Henry de Villiers as its most important members.

In the terms of the commission on the federation of the Eastern and Western Cape districts, the republics were not mentioned, but, certainly under the influence of de Villiers, there appeared in the questionnaire of the commission an unobtrusive query inviting opinions on the federation of the South African States as a whole.[2] Even thus early in his career there were few so well fitted as he to see, beyond the rivalries of the moment, the urgent need of co-operation throughout South Africa.

While the struggle was still at its height and before the Legislative Council had yet debated the Responsible Government Bill, Barkly, in his impatience to proceed with the annexation of the Diamond

[1] *Parl. Pap.* 1871, XLVII [C. 415), p. 186, Barkly to Kimberley, 20 June 1871.
[2] Walker, E. A., *Lord de Villiers and his Times*, pp. 51–3.

Fields, brought a resolution before the two Houses affirming the expediency of annexing them to the Cape Colony. Opinion in the Cape was by no means indifferent to the advantages of annexation. In face of the clearly expressed determination of the Home Government to undertake no further frontier defence for the Colonists, it was generally realised, even on the Eastern Frontier, that the time had come for the Cape Colony to govern the frontier tribes by its own strength. Hence the Cape Houses finally consented to pass a Bill annexing Basutoland (August 1871). Yet, on the annexation of the Diamond Fields there was room for considerable difference of opinion. There were not wanting members who refused to share Southey's imperialist views, and others who were not convinced that the republics were without a case against Waterboer. These objected to an act which, by provoking the hostility of the republics, might compromise the success of Cape self-government. Molteno jumped up in protest against the untimeliness of Barkly's resolution. His own counter-resolution,[1] that the question of annexation could not be entertained at such a juncture, came within very few votes of winning the House. Southey actually carried a resolution to the effect that there should be annexation, provided that only the lands *properly* belonging to Waterboer were annexed. Realising that the risk of defeat if he introduced the annexation Bill was considerable, Barkly decided to hold his hand until a more propitious moment, contenting himself meanwhile with obtaining from the two Houses resolutions in favour of the adoption of measures for the better government of the Diggings. His policy had narrowly escaped coming to grief, for, if the Cape Parliament had pronounced against annexation, the chances were small that the Home Government would have taken action.

In England, indeed, Kimberley saw the danger of being saddled with the Diamond Fields, even as Wodehouse had saddled the British Government with Basutoland in 1868; but, far from the scene and weeks behind in his information for lack of telegraphic communication with the Cape, the Colonial Secretary could do nothing more than repeat his hope that the Governor at least would obey his instructions and carry out the general policy the Cabinet had laid down. The reception by the general public of the Cape Parliament's resolutions on the Diamond Fields made it clear that the establishment of good order in the camps and even annexation were merely preliminary issues to the great problem facing the whole sub-continent.

The question above all others was, how were the many different communities in South Africa—its colonies, Native territories and republics—henceforth to live at peace with one another. The events of the last six years had brought that question imperiously to the fore.

[1] C.O. 48/456, D. 87, Barkly to Kimberley, 15 August 1871, Enclosures.

"The Federation or Confederation of the four now distinct settlements in South Africa is the leading political idea of the moment", wrote the *Natal Witness* in May 1871. The imminence of responsible government in the Cape, Molteno's project of federation between the Eastern and Western Provinces, and the issue of the Diggings turned men's minds to the wider possibility of a federation to include also Natal and the republics. Of this there was indeed need. The republics both chafed under a feeling of unfair treatment, and in Natal much bitterness was felt at Granville's decision in 1869 not to increase the colonists' control over the executive.

To the north of Natal the old Zulu chief, Panda, was nearing his end. When he was dead who knew what mischief his son Cetewayo's unbaptised assegais, with all the restlessness and turmoil in Swaziland and the Zoutpansberg beyond them, might not seek to do? For twenty years Natal had attracted relatively little attention, but now the tide of events was rising which for the next decade was to make that colony the storm centre of South Africa. Cetewayo had long been giving the Natal colonists reason to be apprehensive. His road to the throne had been cleared by the ruthless suppression of his rivals, and, moreover, in 1861, he had entered into a treaty with the Transvaal, whereby, in return for a grant of land, he was recognised as Panda's successor. In 1871 there were all the signs of heavier republican pressure upon Zululand and of coming conflict between Transvaal and Natal interests in that region, so that far-seeing observers, both in England and South Africa, were already looking with anxiety at a colony where a few thousand white planters were divided from the most menacing savage power in Africa by nothing but a river defensible only in time of flood.

In Basutoland the Basuto were recovering slowly from the utter confusion and acute stress which the recent war with the Free State and the loss of their best lands had caused. Work at the Diamond Fields and on the farms of the Free State was literally forced upon them through the sheer inability of their lands to support them. The lack of land was to be the most constant and bitter complaint of the Basuto; meanwhile they bought guns with the money which they earned. In Kaffraria the scuffling amongst the cramped pack of Chiefs boded ill once more for the Eastern Frontier, while in the Native locations of the Cape itself there was a congestion so grave that a few seasons of drought would almost certainly bring rebellion.

On the other hand diamonds and the investments they attracted from Europe were bringing good business to the Cape and Natal; even the republics were beginning to feel the benefit, and the financial auspices at least were favourable. In the Free State it was held by many that the grant of responsible government to the Cape would remove the "chief stumbling block to union".[1] In June 1871 Brand

[1] Walker, E. A., *de Villiers*, p. 51.

had written to de Villiers in the Cape that while the Diamond Fields dispute remained unsettled the question of federation was necessarily in abeyance, but once that obstacle was removed, there could be no good reason why the Free State "should not in time enter into communication with the British Government and the Transvaal Government" with a view to federation.[1]

That discussion showed signs of leading to action gave the Colonial Office unaffected pleasure. "Every encouragement to such a proceeding should be given", exclaimed Knatchbull-Hugessen warmly, "and Sir Henry Barkly be assured of the support of Her Majesty's Government to any policy aimed at such a result."[2] Some time later, when he had read Barkly's favourable account of the state of Basutoland since annexation, he broke out vehemently against the "miserably short-sighted policy" that had abandoned the Orange River Sovereignty, and on account of a "pitiful economy" had crippled the British Government's power of dealing "wisely, calmly and generously with the native tribes" and absorbing all South Africa under one single government.

Yet how was federation to be consummated? As matters stood in South Africa the Cape Parliament was not competent without a permissive imperial enactment to legislate on a subject that concerned the independent republics. Kimberley, notwithstanding, was determined that the initiative should come from South Africa. In federation the British Government not only desired to set South Africa's house in order, but also sought an opportunity for Great Britain to beat a dignified retreat from direct internal responsibility.

To achieve this, the Cape Colony, the oldest and richest political community of them all, must first of all become self-governing. The "great argument" for responsible government, in the view of R. G. W. Herbert, the new Permanent Under-Secretary, was that it afforded the only basis for a consolidation of the colonies, republics and Native territories under one government.[3] Led by a self-governing Cape Colony, the South African communities, like the British North American colonies, should settle their own terms of association first. Upon them must fall the entire responsibility of carrying out the new order, for the British Government, Kimberley wrote to Barkly, would only consider proposals for federation if the "Confederacy was placed under responsible government which should undertake the duty of self-defence and the management of all internal affairs". And so Barkly was once more exhorted not to relax his efforts on behalf of self-government, and authorised, in the event of a favourable report from Molteno's federation commission, to place the subject before a convention of republican and colonial delegates.

[1] Walker, *de Villiers*, pp. 51–3, Brand to de Villiers, 6 April 1871.
[2] C.O. 48/456, Barkly to Kimberley, 30 Aug. 1871, minute by Knatchbull-Hugessen.
[3] C.O. 48/455, D. 53, Barkly to Kimberley, 31 May 1871, minute by R. G. W. Herbert.

The Diamond Fields, Free State penury, Transvaal anarchy, political deadlock in the Cape, Natal outgrowing its constitution—these were so many pieces in an intricate puzzle that needed skilful arrangement. It was a magnificent opportunity for statesmanship, but unhappily nobody had the skill or the foresight to appreciate fully the great issues involved. There was overmuch obstinacy on Brand's side and precipitancy on Barkly's. It must be remembered that neither Kimberley, nor even his successor Carnarvon, was ever convinced that the time chosen for the annexation of the Diamond Fields, or even the step itself, was opportune, and it is certain that a more conciliatory policy would have done much to mollify Brand.

Sir Henry Barkly, the spearhead of imperial government, on whose shoulders critical immediate decisions lay, was hampered by the lack of experience in Native matters that he never overcame. He was too prone to judge South African affairs in the light of his experience in Australia, where policy had only to be guided by the needs of the colonists and there were no Native difficulties of any importance. The Australian Natives were few, primitive and helpless, the South African relatively immense in number, shrewd and dangerous. Though he had much force of character and perfect self-control, he made such efforts to co-operate with the Cape Ministry, after responsible government had been introduced, that he ended by being over-influenced by the exigencies of local politics to the neglect of wider questions, and seriously compromised his independence as the representative of the Home Government. After the annexation of the Diamond Fields, which was his one outstanding act, Barkly practically sacrificed his wider opportunities as High Commissioner to the narrower function of Governor of the Cape. Thus, like both Kimberley and Herbert in England, he failed to see that the problems of the Diamond Fields and the constitution he was commanded to administer at the Cape were significant mainly in their bearing on the future of South African cooperation. Unfortunately, he could not assume a genuinely South African point of view, as Sir George Grey had so easily done, nor had he in his intimate entourage a South African statesman like de Villiers to point out the urgent need of placating the burghers of the republics.

Partly because he had committed himself, and partly because he had frankly lost control of the situation after the appointment of the Federation Commission, Barkly proceeded to do the very thing most calculated to drive the republics into an irreconcilable antagonism. Brand had yielded to the pressure of the High Commissioner at least so far as to suggest the appointment of a commission from the Free State to confer with another from the Cape on the Diamond Fields question; but he still insisted on foreign arbitration in the event of disagreement. It was useless. On 17 October 1871 Keate had given his award on the Transvaal claims. Ludorf's "treaty", from which the Transvaal had expected so much, was declared a forgery. On the evidence Keate felt that he had no alternative but to decide for the Chiefs against the Transvaal. Any doubts Barkly might have entertained on the validity of Waterboer's claims were dispelled by the close correspondence between the boundaries claimed by the different Chiefs and those assigned them by Keate.[1]

In October 1871 Barkly formally annexed the Diamond Fields and thereby ruined all prospect of federation.[2] Protesting bitterly, Brand withdrew his officials at the entry of the Cape Police. In the Transvaal the Volksraad forced the resignation of the hapless President, declaring that the deed of submission to arbitration on the lands claimed by the Barolong had been signed by the President alone and was therefore unconstitutional.[3] The Volksraad refused to be bound by the Keate Award.[4]

In a letter of studied sarcasm, Acting-President Erasmus hinted that the High Commissioner was too ready to interfere in Transvaal internal affairs, and, in a scornful phrase that measured all the depth of Transvaal anger, begged to be excused from the further receipt of communications in which the inhabitants of the Transvaal were referred to under the "opprobrious epithet of *Boers*". In March 1872 Molteno's Federation Commission summed up the results of annexation in the single disconcerting statement that for the present it appeared to the majority of the Commission that the prospects of federation were remote.[5]

The bad feeling was not confined to the republics alone. Barkly was severely criticised by John X. Merriman, hitherto a staunch opponent of the "Responsibles". In the House of Assembly sharp tongues spoke of the scurvy treatment the Free State had received. When Southey introduced the Bill for the annexation of Griqualand West to the Cape Colony, the onslaught was so vigorous that he had to withdraw it. Almost every voice was raised against the inexpediiency of compromising self-government by annexing a disputed territory. More significant still, the displeasure of the leading Cape politicians indicated the likelihood there had been of securing considerable Cape support for a policy of co-operation with the Free State, a possibility that had now been thrown away.

When Parliament assembled at Cape Town on 18 April 1872 the Governor in his opening address strongly urged a reconsideration of the question of responsible government. He was convinced, he said, that there was "no ground for mistrusting the use that the Cape colonists would make of political power", and that his experience during the past year had afforded him "the strongest proofs of the

[1] C.O. 48/457, D. 121, Barkly to Kimberley, 31 October 1871; so-called *Bloemhof Arbitration Bluebook*, 1871.

[2] *Ibid.* D. 123, Barkly to Kimberley, 31 October 1871.

[3] *Ibid.* D. 145, Enclosure, Pretorius to Barkly, 18 November 1871.

[4] *Ibid.* Barkly to Kimberley, 18 December 1871, enclosing protest by Erasmus.

[5] *Parl. Pap.* 1873, XLIX [C. 732], pp. 42–6.

thorough fitness of the colonists to be entrusted with the uncontrolled management of their own affairs". To the Eastern element he gave the strong hint that under responsible government they would find places in the Cabinet, and that Eastern representation in Parliament would be readjusted so as to balance the disproportion between East and West. On June 3 the Bill introducing responsible government, which had passed the critical second reading by thirty-five to twenty-five votes, received its third reading in the Assembly. In the Council the anti-Responsibles numbered twelve and the Responsibles nine, but so obvious was the widespread sympathy in the electorate for the changes already accepted by the assembly, that two of the Anti-Responsible group were induced to join their opponents. The Bill passed the Council by a single vote, but the satisfaction of the Home Government was much diminished by Barkly's failure to relieve it of the Diamond Fields.

In England Kimberley ruefully read the news of Barkly's failure. "I never doubted", he wrote, "that Sir Henry Barkly made a mistake in annexing the diamond fields before the Cape Parliament had passed the bill. He exceeded his instructions and departed from the line of policy which I believe would have succeeded . . ."[1]

On the Diamond Fields illicit diamond buying, drunkenness, robberies and lawless Native labourers indicated the nature of the burden the British Government had unwillingly assumed. Back to Basutoland, Natal, and even to the far-off territory of Sekukuni in the eastern Transvaal Natives carried the guns they had bought with their earnings. Their chieftains' armouries of spears were replaced by deadlier weapons, and he became the most powerful among his fellows who could lay up the greatest stores of powder and ball.

Into the Transvaal the new President, the Rev. Thomas François Burgers, a colonist who had been the minister of the Reformed Church at Hanover in Cape Colony and a man of higher education than the Trekkers, brought enthusiasm for the national idea. Under him republicanism was turned into nationalism, and the anti-British policy that was to be the dominant and tragic note of the future began. Before long to preach federation in the Transvaal was tantamount to treason and English-speaking folk would be "Uitlanders".

[1] C.O. 48/461, Barkly to Kimberley, 17 June 1872; minute by Kimberley. See de Kiewiet, C. W., *British Colonial Policy*, p. 299.

CHAPTER XVIII

THE FAILURE OF CONFEDERATION, 1871–1881

THE year 1871 opened a new era in African history. The annexation of Griqualand West in that year, following upon the proclamation of British sovereignty over Basutoland (1868), clearly indicated that the British Government could no longer maintain its self-denying ordinance against expansion in Africa. The northward movement had begun. In 1871 the Keate Award barred that extension of the Transvaal Republic across its south-west border which had threatened to cut off the Cape from the North. The opening of the Suez Canal (1869) had begun to divert eastern trade to the Red Sea. South Africa had ceased to be regarded merely as a port of call and a stepping-stone to the East, and attention was directed to the interior of the country itself instead of overseas. In 1871 Henry M. Stanley plunged into East Africa in search of Dr. Livingstone, thus taking the first steps towards carrying on the work of that great missionary and explorer of tracing the sources of the main rivers in the heart of the Dark Continent.

The publicity which attended the explorations of Stanley and Verney Lovett Cameron, and the intensification of missionary enterprise following upon the death of Livingstone, focused the attention of the world upon the new and mysterious subcontinent. Already, in 1871 Germany, flushed with the fruits of her victory over France, was begining to look abroad for new markets for her growing commerce; but, for the present, German undertakings were confined to private enterprise. For the next twelve years the field was open for Great Britain to extend her empire up to the Zambesi. She remained blind to the greatness and the urgency of her opportunity.

For over two centuries South Africa had been deemed a barren land by Afrikaner and British traders alike. Mountain barriers behind inaccessible shores and the dread of savage tribes delayed their advance. There was no Hooghly, Thames or Rhine to bear upon its broad bosom the ships of merchants eager to open up trade with the interior. But a sturdy rural population had taken root and multiplied on this stony ground, content with the fruits of the earth gathered in the bracing air of the High Veld. Suddenly, to the growing interest in exploration and missionary work in Central Africa was added the stimulus of the startling discoveries of gold and diamonds in the hinterland of the Cape Colony at a time when both Boer republics were hopelessly in debt to creditors in the hard-pressed coastal colonies.

In 1865 ancient gold workings were discovered in Mashonaland; gold was also found in the eastern Transvaal and in the Tati district on the southern border of Matabeleland, where the Monarch mine was being worked as early as 1869. Meanwhile, in the Cape Colony, in April 1867, a little girl picked up a diamond near Hopetown close to the Orange river.[1] Next year diamonds were found near the junction of the Vaal and Harts Rivers in the barren wastes of Griqualand West. No wonder Marthinus Pretorius, the then President of the Transvaal, had sought to restore the ruined finances of his republic by annexing the wide area in which Tati and these river diggings lay. Pretorius had been obliged to relinquish his prize and even to resign,[2] making way for the Rev. Thomas François Burgers, a somewhat heterodox Dutch Reformed minister from the eastern Cape Colony. Then in 1870, to the "River Diggings" along the courses of the Vaal and Orange were added the "Dry Diggings" in the long hill between the Vaal and Modder Rivers.[3] To the "New Rush", where the town of Kimberley now stands, came in 1871 a slender, blue-eyed immigrant from England, Cecil Rhodes. Seated upon an upturned bucket at the edge of a mine, or reading a book for his examination at Oxford, or sorting diamonds surrounded by Zulu labourers amongst the chaos of miners' tents and native kraals, he was already dreaming of a British Africa.

Within ten years the product of the mines had reached £20,000,000. This discovery of mineral wealth introduced an entirely new and subversive element into the hitherto pastoral and agricultural life of South Africa. Its political, economic and social consequences were manifold and far-reaching. Into the midst of scattered and partly nomadic Afrikaner farmers flowed a stream of emigrants from overseas drawn from France, Germany and America as well as from Great Britain and her colonies—men vigorous, alien, enterprising, eager for wealth, heirs of an industrial civilisation and some of them imbued with liberal ideas of self-government and progressive administration. Diggers and shopkeepers were followed by capitalists with large ideas of progress and ambition, personal and national, and with powers of organisation to carry them out. To a great extent these capitalists were cosmopolitan Jews. Their industry brought wealth to an impoverished land, and implanted there a new form of civilisation with all its vices and virtues. In the wilderness cities sprang up, which were at once the products and the means of this new industrial life. The sudden revelation of wealth enormously strengthened the desire of the Afrikaner republics to substantiate their claims to the territory about which they had been wrangling with the British for ten years

[1] *Vide supra*, pp. 437–442.
[2] *Vide supra*, p. 457.
[3] Williams, Gardner, *The Diamond Mines of South Africa*; Winter, James, *South African Notes*.

past without knowing that they had allowed riches to lie there untouched whilst they tottered into bankruptcy.

The need for rapid transport to and from the mines and the coast gave a new importance to the old roads and a new value to the old ports. There was an imperative demand for improved communications. The iron road must supplant rough tracks across the veld, and the steam-engine take the place of the old ox-waggon. The importance of the Missionaries' Road, the route between the more or less waterless Kalahari plateau and the Transvaal border by which hunters, traders and missionaries made their way to the interior and the new Tati goldfields beyond the Diamond Fields, was now greatly enhanced. The Griquas' land, where the diamonds were discovered, lay also upon the direct route from the Cape ports, and, as we shall see later, the Transvaalers, to loosen the Cape's selfish monopoly of customs, began to contemplate the construction of a railway to the harbour of Delagoa Bay, which would give them a short route to the sea "free from the trammels of British ports and influence". In the Cape Colony, railways had already been built from Cape Town to Wynberg and Wellington (1864). The diamond diggings now became the goal of the main line, which, however, was not to reach Kimberley till 1885. In 1872 the Cape Government took over the existing sixty-odd miles of railways. £5,000,000 was shortly afterwards voted for developing a new line from East London and Port Elizabeth towards the diamond fields (1874). Natal had already entered upon its long struggle to improve the port of Durban, and, by lowering its customs dues, to compete with the Cape ports. In 1876 a State railway was begun to connect Durban with Pietermaritzburg, the capital, but it was long before it was continued through Ladysmith to the Transvaal border and the Orange Free State. The aim of this new line was also to tap the trade of the interior in which it would rival the projected railway from the Transvaal to Delagoa Bay. Thus began, to some extent in rivalry and as an expression of separatism, the forging of those great links in the iron chain of communication which was destined to weld together, politically and economically, districts hitherto divided and inaccessible.

Politically, the effects of the discovery of mineral wealth in Griqualand West and Tati were not less far-reaching; for since the mines lay beyond the Orange River, they might well entail British expansion northwards, and the abandonment of the determination, announced by British statesmen in the Bloemfontein Convention of 1854, not to advance beyond that limit. No longer could they maintain that disputes between Boers and Natives were no concern of the Cape Colony. They could scarcely help advancing if only to establish law and order as British subjects rushed to the Diamond Fields, and as other States laid claim to tribal territory in which they were concerned. Such advance, however, must mean the hemming in of the

Boer republics. It was a process which both irritated and by irritation consolidated them, whilst stimulating their national sentiment against the British immigrant.

Griqualand was administered for a time by diggers' committees and a triumvirate of officials, who endeavoured, not very successfully, to cope with the claims and demands of unruly diggers and the problem of Native labourers, now released from the colour bar, by which they had been prohibited from owning or dealing in diamonds. As the Cape Parliament fought shy of its qualified undertaking to incorporate the Diamond Fields, Griqualand West was presently established as a Crown Colony. Sir Richard Southey was appointed Lieutenant-Governor with an Executive and small elective Legislative Council (1873).[1]

Conflicting titles to lands granted by the former claimants to the mining area contributed to the unsettled state of the new colony. The High Commissioner therefore presently appointed a Land Court to inquire into their validity.[2] The result was startling. The Judge, Sir Andries Stockenstrom, son of the famous Sir Andries, decided that all claims made in Waterboer's name north of the Modder River were void. The evidence was overwhelming that Waterboer had no right to make grants across the Vaal River, and that the Campbell lands were never within his jurisdiction (March 1876).[3] Much of the evidence upon which Keate had acted in making his award was found to be unreliable.[4]

Thus a British Court had torpedoed the award, in accordance with which Great Britain had taken the land from the Orange Free State. Brand, who had never ceased to protest against that action as a great wrong, went forthwith to London to press his claims on the Colonial Secretary, Lord Carnarvon. His case was strongly backed by the historian, James Anthony Froude, who had investigated it on the spot in 1874.[5]

Restoration of the disputed territory, however, was by this time out of the question. Nor was it really desired by the Free State. The European population was now almost wholly British. The republic, having made as much as was to be got out of the sale of the farms, was not, as Brand had to confess to Carnarvon, in a position to impose order upon a turbulent community, whose votes would, moreover, have swamped the Afrikaner burghers in a presidential election. He therefore accepted as satisfactory compensation the sum of £90,000,

[1] *Parl. Pap.* 1871, x [C. 459]; 1872, LXII [C. 508]; 1876, LII [C. 1631]; Wilmot, A., *The Life and Times of Sir Richard Southey*; Theal, G. M., *History of South Africa since 1875*, v, 266 *sqq.*

[2] *Parl. Pap.* 1875, LII [C. 1342]; 1876, LII [C. 1401]; Theal, G.M., *op cit.*, v, 286–91.

[3] Major Owen Lanyon, 5 December 1875, and 6 April 1876, in Carnarvon Papers, P.R.O. G.D. 6/36. The references to P.R.O., G.D. are to the Carnarvon papers deposited in the Public Record Office. See also *Parl. Pap.* 1876, LII [C. 1401].

[4] *Vide supra*, pp. 456–7.

[5] Froude, J. A., *Leaves from a South African Journal*; Brand to Froude, 7 September 1875, P.R.O., G.D. 6/23, No. 28.

with the promise of an additional £15,000 on condition that a railway either to Natal or the Cape was built within five years (July 1876).[1] This settlement removed the difficulty felt by the Cape Afrikaners, who had hitherto refused to offend their kinsmen in the Free State by annexing the Diamond Fields. But the Colony, under the advice of the Premier, J. C. Molteno, still held back from assuming the burden of a government to which was now added the sum due to the Orange Free State. Carnarvon, however, was able to exert the necessary pressure by refusing Molteno permission to annex Walvis Bay and Tembuland unless Griqualand West was incorporated in the colony. An Act to that effect was therefore passed in 1877. Ratified in 1879, it was not carried into effect before October 1880, and then only after Molteno had fallen.

The attempts of the Transvaal to secure a corridor to Delagoa Bay, its natural outlet to the sea, helped to focus attention upon that quarter. This fine harbour had always invited settlement, and the Portuguese, as the original European occupants of South East Africa, had naturally established a factory at Lourenço Marques. But fever triumphed over trade on those malarial shores. The factory was abandoned at the end of the seventeenth century. This experience was repeated by the Cape Dutch, who built a fort there, but dismantled it and withdrew in 1730. The Portuguese, who never relinquished their claim to the bay, then reasserted their title by erecting another fort. The bay narrows into an estuary. On the northern bank Captain W. F. Owen, on one of his surveying cruises along the coast in 1823, had found a small Portuguese trading establishment, Espirito Santo, where the town of Lourenço Marques now stands; but on the southern shore the Portuguese had made no settlement nor laid any claim to it. Owen therefore concluded treaties with the King of Tembe, who ceded the southern part of Delagoa Bay to Great Britain (1823). The Portuguese thereupon removed the flag which Owen had hoisted, but it was replaced in the following year. So matters remained, without effective occupation on either side. Then had come, first, McCorkindale's proposal in 1864 to run steamers from the bay to the Transvaal;[2] next, four years later, Pretorius's abortive annexation of the bay,[3] and finally the discovery of gold and diamonds in the distant hinterland. This key position had obviously become of such vital importance that the Portuguese and British agreed to submit their rival claims to the arbitration of the President of the French Republic (1872).[4] Portugal claimed both shores on the bay and estuary

[1] Lord Carnarvon to Queen Victoria, 14 July 1876, P.R.O., G.D. 6/3, No. 5; Eybers, G. W., *Select Constitutional Documents*, pp. 342 *sqq.*

[2] *Vide supra*, p. 435.

[3] *Vide supra*, p. 435.

[4] Lord Carnarvon to Queen Victoria, P.R.O., G.D. 6/2, No. 32.

and much territory to the south. Her claim to the territory north of the estuary was not disputed, but the British title to the southern shore and the territory beyond, by virtue of Owen's treaty and inheritance from the Dutch, would seem equally valid, for the argument of effective occupation was weak on both sides. President MacMahon's award, however, was wholly in favour of Portugal (1875);[1] but before the decision was announced, Great Britain had done her best to discount it and guarded herself from the intrusion of a third power by concluding an agreement with Portugal that she would not part with the disputed territory. The Transvaal was now secure of a port free from British influence, and its President, Burgers, raised an expensive loan in Holland for building a railway to the coast. He appointed Hollanders to office in the Transvaal, concluded a commercial treaty with Portugal, and began to angle for alliances with Germany, Portugal and Belgium.

Yet another effect of the discovery of Diamondland was the demand created both in the mines and on the railways for the labour of natives drawn from the surrounding countries. Too often these labourers succumbed to the temptations offered by high wages and the vices of the cosmopolitan riff-raff which always finds its way to a new miners' camp. Too often they proved a source of infinite trouble and unrest when they returned to their kraals, wealthy, unsettled and armed with guns, for there was much callous gun-running from Kimberley, Durban and Delagoa Bay. Orange Free State farmers grumbled at the rise in wages, and their Government, seeing the Basuto arming on their borders, tried in vain to check the gun-running.

This trade in guns caused an outburst in Natal, which nearly involved all South Africa. A quarter of a century had elapsed since the Hlubi clan had been driven by the Zulus into Natal. There, under their great Chief, Langalibalele ("the sun is shining"), they had been allowed to settle on the north-west frontier bordering Basutoland. The young men now went to work in the Diamond Fields of Kimberley. They brought back with them guns, the introduction of which without registration was forbidden. Langalibalele took no notice of a summons to Pietermaritzburg to answer to the Supreme Chief (Lieutenant-Governor Sir Benjamin Pine) for this breach of the law, and after a brush in the Bushman's River Pass with a force sent to arrest him, made good his escape into Basutoland.[2] Happily he found no support there, and whilst troops and volunteers were hurrying to the scene from all the neighbouring colonies and men in both republics stood to their arms, Langalibalele was quietly handed over by Molapo. Panic caused by the dread of a general Native rising found expression in fierce punitive measures. The lands and property of

[1] *Parl. Pap.* 1875, LXXIII [C. 1361]; Johnston, Sir H., *Colonization of Africa*, pp. 56–8.
[2] *Parl. Pap.* 1875, LIII [C. 1121], [C. 1158].

the tribe and a neighbouring clan were confiscated, and women and children were driven into servitude.

Langalibalele was tried before an anomalous tribunal consisting of the Lieutenant-Governor as both judge and prosecutor, and white colonists and heads of tribes hostile to the prisoner. The trial was conducted under a mixture of Native and English law. Langalibalele was convicted upon utterly inadequate evidence and sentenced to confinement for life, a sentence which it was beyond the powers of the Court to inflict. The Cape Colony showed its sympathy with Natal by passing an Act which made it possible to confine the aged Chief upon Robben Island.[1] Dr Colenso, Bishop of Natal, and other champions of the Natives agitated for the quashing of the trial and annulment of the Cape Act. Reversal of the sentence might be regarded as weakness by the Native population; the intervention of the imperial authority might be resented by the colonists; but Carnarvon decided that, if ever that authority was to be exercised, it should be now. Pine was recalled; compensation was ordered to be paid to the clan which had suffered for its sympathy with the rebels, and Langalibalele was removed to the Cape mainland as a prisoner of state.[2]

The whole episode had revealed the shortcomings of Native policy in Natal. Ever since 1845 Theophilus Shepstone, first as Diplomatic Agent of the Native tribes and afterwards as Secretary for Native Affairs, had ruled the men of the "Black House" single-handed by sheer force of character and understanding of native ways. As we showed in an earlier chapter,[3] without the aid of one trooper, Somtseu ("the Mighty Hunter") as he was called, had settled 80,000 Bantu refugees from Zulu tyranny in locations reserved for them in Natal. He had kept the peace amongst them and the Zulu hordes beyond, strong in the devotion with which they rewarded his sympathy and firmness. Since the policy of segregation, which he preferred, had been rejected, he had reconstructed the tribal system destroyed by the Zulu despotism and, as its corollary, recreated a fabric of Native institutions and laws to be administered by Chiefs whom he appointed, subject to the Lieutenant-Governor as their Supreme Chief.[4] He made no attempt to Europeanise the Bantu; the essence of his system was to lead them to develop their own civilisation.[5] Now it was deemed no longer wise to leave this enormous Native population under the almost unrestricted powers of its Chiefs. The effect of creating "black

[1] Lord Carnarvon, Speech in House of Lords, 12 April 1875, *Hansard*, 3rd ser., CCXXIII, 681; Carnarvon to Queen Victoria, 28 Nov. 1874, P.R.O., G.D. 6/32, No. 60; Froude, J. A., *Leaves from a South African Journal*, p. 511.

[2] Carnarvon to Sir Henry Barkly, 16 December 1874, P.R.O., G.D. 6/32, No. 25.

[3] *Vide supra*, p. 359.

[4] *Report of Native affairs Commission* (Natal), 1852–3, and 1881–2.

[5] Cf. Brookes, E. H., *History of Native Policy in South Africa*, p. 29; Sir Bartle Frere, Despatch, 3 February 1879, *Parl. Pap.* 1878–9, LIII [C. 2260], p. 23.

Alsatias" within the borders of a colony, without any attempt to civilise them, seemed to be, as a famous High Commissioner, Sir Bartle Frere, was to observe a few years later, that "the natives did not become less barbarous, but much more dangerous".[1]

Sir Garnet Wolseley, strong with the prestige of a successful campaign against the Ashanti[2] and backed by a warship, was now sent as Special Commissioner to revise the constitution and Native administration of Natal (April-September 1875). The effect of his measures was to give to the executive greater powers of control over the Natives. Natives were placed under the ordinary criminal law, whilst a Commission was appointed to codify the unwritten Bantu law. At the same time a Native High Court was instituted for trying civil cases in which Natives were concerned, and for hearing appeals from the magisterial courts in the locations. Appeals in serious cases lay to the Supreme Court. Thus, unwisely as many thought, the unique judicial powers of the Supreme Chief were abolished, and a step was taken towards raising the Bantu to the level of white citizens.[3]

The problem of how to deal with Native races had not proved easy to solve. The solutions tried in South Africa had been varied and vacillating, but hitherto the attempts to avoid bringing Natives and Europeans into close contact had proved a failure. No less difficult in practice was the adoption of equality of treatment and status demanded by the ardour of a few missionaries, who still held the old ideas of Philip's day that there was no fundamental difference between European and Native. For whilst the British Government pursued its traditional policy of insisting upon respect for the Native's rights, the prevailing instinct of South Africans, British as well as Afrikaner, was that the black man's proper status was that of servant to the white.[4] The ambition to make South Africa a "white man's colony" also involved a tendency to keep the Natives in a position of definite political and social subjection, and in the republics the latter policy was frankly adopted.

As we have seen in an earlier chapter,[5] the Voortrekkers who fled from British rule fled with a determination to pursue their own method of dealing with the Natives. That method was the subjugation of the tribal country they seized, and the establishment thereon of a white land-owning aristocracy resting on the labour of a black proletariat. Within the Transvaal no Native was allowed to

[1] Sir Bartle Frere to Sir Michael Hicks Beach, 14 December 1878, *Parl. Pap.* 1878–9, LII [C. 2222], p. 212.

[2] See *C.H.B.E.* vol. III.

[3] *Parl. Pap.* 1875, LIII [C. 1187]; 1875, LVIII [C. 1192]; Lord Carnarvon to Queen Victoria, 16 February 1875, P.R.O., G.D. 6/1, Nos. 88, 89; Hardinge, Sir A., *Life of Lord Carnarvon*, II, 166–71; Maurice, Sir F., and Arthur, Sir G., *Life of Lord Wolseley*, p. 79; Martineau, J., *The Transvaal Trouble*, p. 78; Brookes, *History of Native Policy in S.A.*, p. 65.

[4] Cf. Fitzpatrick, Sir Percy, *The Transvaal from Within*, p. 328; de Waal, B. C., *With Rhodes in Mashonaland*, p. 105.

[5] *Vide supra*, pp. 325 *sqq*.

own land. The Native population was left under its old tribal system in locations, which were held on a precarious tenure and subject merely to general governmental control, while a number of families were suffered to remain on each white man's farm as labour-tenants, in other words, as serfs.

The Langalibalele affair emphasised the danger of such divergencies of Native policy in the several States and the urgent need of a uniform, humane and intelligent system. A uniform system could, however, only be brought about through an amalgamation of interests, and that meant federation.[1]

After the mid-century ebb of "Little Englandism", the tide of imperialism had begun to flow. When Disraeli came back to power in 1874, he turned the attention of his countrymen away from the domestic problems upon which it had been concentrated under Gladstone's administration, and began to inspire them with something of his own perfervid imagination. By one brilliant stroke after another he revealed to them that Great Britain was an Asiatic Power; she was to resume her high place among the nations, and the great age of Elizabethan adventure was to begin anew. The policy of the Government was declared by its chief to be an imperial policy, and its object the maintenance of the British Empire.[2] Under the stimulus of such imaginative statesmanship the British people began once more to look abroad and to take stock of their heritage.

It was in these circumstances that Lord Carnarvon came back to the Colonial Office, determined to repeat in South Africa the success of his Canadian Confederation Act of 1867. He at once began to press the idea of confederation upon the South African States with a view to their more satisfactory relationship.[3] Federation, indeed, was in the air of the 'seventies. The recent examples of Canada, of Germany and of Italy inspired Disraeli's gospel of an imperialism based upon an imperial tariff, imperial defence and a representative imperial council sitting at Westminster.[4] And at the Cape the policy of closer union was being advocated by men so diverse as John Paterson, political leader of the Eastern Province, J. H. de Villiers, Chief Justice of the Colony,[5] and Jan Hendrik Hofmeyr, a leading Afrikaner journalist;[6] for whilst, thanks to the perversity of circumstances and men's minds, a policy of dismemberment had recently been pursued in South Africa, the ideal of reunion yet survived. The vision which inspired large-minded men, from Sir George Grey to Lord Carnarvon, and from Sir Bartle Frere to Lord Selborne, was that of a group of

[1] Lord Carnarvon to Sir Henry Barkly, 27 May 1874, P.R.O., G.D. 6/32, No. 6.
[2] B. Disraeli's last speech in the House of Commons, 11 August 1876, *Hansard*, 3rd ser., CCXXXI, 1138.
[3] Lord Carnarvon to Sir H. Barkly, 27 May 1874, P.R.O., G.D. 6/32, No. 6.
[4] B. Disraeli, Speech at the Crystal Palace, 24 June 1872; *Times*, 25 June 1872.
[5] Walker, E. A., *Lord de Villiers*, p. 51.
[6] Hofmeyr, J. H., *Life of J. H. Hofmeyr*, p. 133.

self-governing colonies, reaching from the Cape to the Zambesi, strengthened and consolidated by the union of Afrikaner and British settlers under the Union Jack and the formal headship of a Governor-General. They saw, clearly enough, the evils of a chaos of colonies, protectorates and republics. For the danger of small, weak and isolated States with divergent policies, attacking or being attacked by coloured tribes, with the attendant risk of a general rising in which every State was concerned, and the deleterious effect upon trade and commerce of intercolonial separatism and mutual jealousies, remained always what they had been when Sir George Grey wrote his famous despatch.[1] Since then, the truth of Grey's observations in the later 'fifties had been demonstrated by the experience of those who had wrecked his schemes. But other developments had supervened. The acceptance of federation was finally frustrated by the very evils which it was intended to remove. If the opportunity of establishing a federal system with provincial courts and a central legislature after his New Zealand model, which Grey had proposed, was lost by the Imperial Government in 1859, it was the Imperial Government which now began to urge confederation, and, as fate would have it, it was the South African States which rejected union under the British Crown; for unfortunately the moment chosen by Carnarvon was not propitious.

The position had been radically altered since Grey's time, when the Orange Free State had expressed its desire to be reunited to the Cape Colony. Distrust and division, the product of former mistakes and of present circumstances, had increased on every side. Wisdom, tact, and above all patience in abundance were needed, if the course of events were to be guided to a happy issue; in the event error was piled upon error. But not all the blame is to be laid on the enlightened and determined statesman who now strove for the unification of South Africa under the British flag. On the one hand, as we have seen, the annexation of Griqualand West had roused the resentment of the republics and drawn them closer together in racial and political antagonism to Great Britain, whilst the intervention of the latter in Basutoland had both relieved the Orange Free State from a pressing danger which had inclined it to reunion with the Cape, and also provided it with a grievance against British aggression.

Nor did the effect of the policy of the Imperial Government, which had led to an increase of the Native population of Natal,[2] lessen the fundamental objection of the republics to bringing their treatment of natives into conformity with British ideas. Rather, they took advantage of the discontent roused by the intervention of the Imperial Government in the case of Langalibalele and others to woo the "Garden Colony" to closer union with themselves, in preparation

[1] *Vide supra*, pp. 411, 415–6.

[2] Winter, James, *South African Notes. Thraldom of the Native Races*, p. 45.

for a confederation under a flag other than the Union Jack.[1] In the Cape Colony the grant of self-government had filled the hands of the politicians with local problems, not the least of which was the question of the subdivision of the Colony. There was a strong movement for the separation of the Eastern from the Western Province, which it was feared confederation might strengthen; nervousness was also felt at the prospect of the unification of customs and railway developments. The Cape Colony desired time to consolidate its own institutions, in order that it might be ready to take its natural place as leader of a general South African Dominion;[2] it shrank, moreover, from assuming responsibility for the defence of Natal and the burden of her enormous Native population.[3]

It was true that statesmen in the republics as well as in the British colonies, men like Brand, de Villiers and Hofmeyr, agreed with Grey that no single State could stand by itself in face of the Native danger. A uniform policy towards the Natives could only be secured through the authority of a single paramount power. It was true that a pooling of the port dues at Cape Town, Port Elizabeth, Durban and East London would prove a genuine economy and would benefit South Africa as a whole; but each State considered most what it might lose. Each shrank from shouldering the responsibilities of others. When, for instance, men looked northwards, they saw that Griqualand West, where the finances were chaotic, where miners and speculators were rioting over their claims, and Griquas, Koranas and Batlapin were rebellious at the loss of their lands, might well add to their liabilities at a time when repayment of railway loans was their first consideration.[4] To Carnarvon, on the contrary, the opportunity of settling the Griqualand question was an additional argument for confederation.[5]

Natal, again, was loath to sacrifice the advantages of her geographical position and her low tariff, and feared lest she should be called upon to carry out imperial policy at her own expense. For the withdrawal of the imperial troops from the great self-governing colonies under Gladstone's Government had been advertised as part of a federal scheme which would leave both the problems and the burden of defence to the colonists themselves, and which, whilst discouraging them from any tendency to rely upon the garrisons for attacking neighbouring Native tribes, would prepare them for that ultimate independence to which Lord Granville looked forward.[6]

[1] Sir H. Barkly to Lord Carnarvon, 25 January, 15 July 1875, P.R.O., G.D. 6/32, Nos. 31, 36.

[2] Sir H. Barkly to Carnarvon, 25 July 1874, P.R.O., G.D. 6/32, No. 74.

[3] Froude to Carnarvon, 23 April 1875; Sir H. Barkly to Carnarvon, 27 May, 6 July 1874, P.R.O., G.D. 6/32.

[4] *Parl. Pap.* 1875, LII [C. 1342]; Lord Carnarvon to Queen Victoria, 29 April and 21 December 1875, P.R.O., G. D. 6/2, No. 75; Carnarvon to Disraeli, 23 March 1875, *ibid.* 6/11, No. 33 a.

[5] Hardinge, *Life of Lord Carnarvon*, II, pp. 63 *sqq.*

[6] Cf. Fitzmaurice, Lord, *Life of the Second Earl Granville*, II, pp. 20, 22.

Disraeli's ministry contemplated a reversal of this policy, and Carnarvon, with Disraeli's warm approval, prepared a plan for restoring the regiments, to be paid for by the colonists, as part of general imperial defence.[1] But the War Office and the Treasury made difficulties, and the House of Commons clung to the principle of "self-defence for the colonies" in ordinary emergencies.

Such was the position of affairs when James Anthony Froude, the historian, visited South Africa at Carnarvon's request in September 1874.[2] He travelled through the north of the Colony, Natal, the Orange Free State, Kimberley and the Transvaal. Everywhere he made speeches, in some of them pouring oil on smouldering embers, praising the Boers in contrast with the Kimberley miners, and declaring that the independence of South Africa would come when they could reply to aggressors with shot and shell.[3] But whilst stirring up existing antagonisms in this way, Froude undoubtedly found considerable support for the policy of federation, though that was variously interpreted.

Stimulated by Froude's report, Carnarvon addressed to the High Commissioner the famous despatch (4 May 1875) in which he proposed a conference at the Cape of delegates from all the South African States to consider a comprehensive Native policy, control of the gun trade and, if opportunity offered, "the all-important question of a possible union of South Africa in some form of Confederation".[4] If that had been all, the result might possibly have been more successful; but Carnarvon in his despatch elaborated every detail of his scheme, and even suggested the delegates: Froude for Great Britain, J. C. Molteno, the Premier of the Cape, for the Western Province, and John Paterson, leader of the Separationists, for the Eastern.

Molteno at once set his face against the proposal. He had himself carried a motion in favour of confederation a few years before (1871);[5] but confederation meant for him gradual annexation of the younger States to the old Colony.[6] His ministry had resented the interference of the Imperial Government in the matter of Langalibalele, and had been attacked for submitting to it.[7] Here, he now complained, was another instance of internal interference without previous consultation with responsible ministers; the Secretary of State should have awaited

[1] Carnarvon to Disraeli, 30 November 1875; Disraeli to Carnarvon, 8 and 10 December 1875; Carnarvon to Gathorne-Hardy, 9 February and 12 December 1875; Carnarvon to Queen Victoria, 20 February 1875, P.R.O., G.D., 6/11, Nos. 50, 51; 6/12; and 6/11, Nos. 5, 50, 51. Froude, *Oceana*, pp. 5–7.

[2] *Parl. Pap.* 1875, LII [C. 1244]; 1876, LII [C. 1399].

[3] Greswell, W., *Our South African Empire* (1885), ch. IX.

[4] *Parl. Pap.* 1875, LII [C. 1244]; 1876, LII [C. 1399].

[5] *Vide supra*, p. 452.

[6] Molteno to Carnarvon, 2 October 1876, P.R.O., G.D. 6/23, No. 250.

[7] Molteno to Sir G. Barkly, 24 December 1874, 5 January 1875, P.R.O., G.D. 6/32, Nos. 27, 29.

the initiative of the Colony.[1] Following the lead of a ministerial minute to this effect, the Cape Parliament denounced Carnarvon's courteous and conciliatory despatch as an attempt to withdraw responsible government from the Colony, to throw on it the expense of defending Natal, and to provoke a Native war. J. X. Merriman, soon to be Molteno's Attorney-General, described the interference of the Imperial Government as "an agitation from abroad".[2]

It was eminently within the province of the Home Government to initiate a scheme affecting all the South African States alike; but it is evident that the representatives of the Colony, recently endowed with responsible government, were unduly exasperated by the appearance of dictation in this *longa et verbosa epistola* from London. Carnarvon's well-meant enthusiasm overreached itself. Froude, his unofficial representative, made matters worse. He landed just after the Assembly had rejected the proposed conference and, instead of retiring, turned a deaf ear to the Governor and proceeded to take sides against the Premier with the Eastern Separatists, who desired federation as a form of local self-government, and the Western Federalists led by Jan Hendrik Hofmeyr.

President Burgers agreed to attend the conference, though it was already sufficiently obvious that in the Transvaal federation meant primarily union with the Orange Free State in a single Afrikaner republic, the achievement of the idea of a republican federation which had run through the history of the Trekker republics at least since 1840. But it also meant an offensive and defensive alliance with the British colonies, and on that fact Carnarvon hoped to build. Wolseley, for his part, secured approval of the conference in Natal, and, on a hint from him that it was the suspicious and difficult Molteno who blocked the way, Froude opened a campaign in the Cape against the Prime Minister in favour of the imperial policy. It was so far successful that a motion condemning his agitation was rejected by the Assembly. The tide, apparently, was turning.[3] Then another ill-timed despatch arrived from Carnarvon, announcing a conference in London as the second stage.[4] This conference met in August 1876. The Transvaal was not represented; Brand, on behalf of the Orange Free State, was bound by his Volksraad not to discuss confederation; Molteno refused to attend. Natal alone was fully represented, and Griqualand West was represented by Froude. The meetings resolved themselves into general discussions on affairs of common interest.[5]

[1] Molteno to Carnarvon, 26 June 1875, P.R.O., G.D. 6/23, No. 50; Report by J. A. Froude, *Parl. Pap.* 1876, LII [C. 1399], pp. 58 *sqq.*

[2] Froude to Carnarvon, 23 September 1875; 1876, LII [C. 1399], pp. 41 *sqq.*; Walker, *Lord de Villiers*, pp. 123 *sqq.*; Froude, *Oceana*, pp. 44–6.

[3] *Parl. Pap.* 1876, LII [C. 1399]; Maurice and Arthur, *Life of Wolseley*, p. 86; Carnarvon to Sir H. Ponsonby, 27 July 1875, P.R.O., G.D. 1, No. 159 a; Froude, *Oceana*, p. 45.

[4] *Parl. Pap.* 1876, LII [C. 1399].

[5] *Ibid.*

Carnarvon, however, was not easily deterred. He at once began to prepare a Permissive Federation Bill. A draft was submitted for the consideration of Ministers in the Cape Colony and Natal.[1] The South Africa Act, usually called the Permissive Act,[2] was passed in the following year (August 1877) embodying the amendments desired by them. It was a statesmanlike measure providing machinery for the confederation, under one government and under the British Crown, of such colonies and States as might wish to come into it, and defining a federal system similar to that of Canada. In many respects it anticipated the South Africa Act of 1909.[3]

To carry this scheme into effect, Carnarvon replaced Barkly, who was wholly under the influence of Molteno, by Sir Bartle Frere as High Commissioner and Governor of the Cape.[4] Frere was a man of sterling character and great ability. Like Wodehouse, he had gained large experience as an administrator in India. Imbued with a burning faith in the mission of the British people as an imperial and civilising power, he looked to the ultimate extension of British sovereignty up to the Portuguese frontiers. On the attainment of that ideal he concentrated all the powers of a clear mind, a strong will, and a gifted pen. His far-sighted views have in the long run been approved by events; but in his own time he was doomed to failure, and to suffer from a campaign of calumny which overwhelmed him in apparent disgrace.

Frere arrived at Cape Town on 31 March 1877. He had sailed as the emissary of peace and union. A little over a fortnight after his landing, he was presented with a *fait accompli*, which was to bear fruit in a quarter of a century of disunion and intermittent warfare; for on April 16 he was informed, unofficially, by a press telegram from Kimberley, that on the 12th Theophilus Shepstone had proclaimed the annexation of the Transvaal. Owing to the slowness of communications—for letters took over a fortnight to reach Cape Town from Pretoria—he did not receive official notification till the 30th[5]. A week before Carnarvon had offered his appointment to Sir Bartle, he had given Shepstone an independent commission to annex and administer such territories as, after due consideration, he should think fit, provisionally and during the Queen's pleasure, provided that he should be first satisfied that "the inhabitants thereof, or a sufficient number of them, or the Legislature thereof, desire to be-

[1] *Parl. Pap.* 1877, LX [C. 1681]; Carnarvon to Queen Victoria, 11 April 1877, P.R.O., G.D. 6/3, No. 20; same to Disraeli, 15 October 1876, Buckle, *Disraeli*, VI, 415.

[2] 40 and 41 Vict., c. 47.

[3] *Vide infra* pp. 654 *sqq*.

[4] Carnarvon to Sir Bartle Frere, 13 October 1876, Martineau, J. H., *Life of Sir Bartle Frere*, II, 162; Carnarvon to Queen Victoria, P.R.O., G.D. 6/2, No. 92.

[5] Martineau, II, 179; Frere to General Ponsonby, 13 May 1877, in *Letters of Queen Victoria*, ed. G. E. Buckle, 2nd Ser., II, 536; Worsfold, W. B., *Frere*, pp. 49 *sqq*.; Uys, C. J., *In the Era of Shepstone*, p. 372, takes the view that Frere knew of Shepstone's intention and could have stopped it.

come Our subjects". If, however, he found that immediate annexation was not possible, he was to consult the High Commissioner.[1] For already events in the Transvaal had given to Carnarvon's policy a new orientation.

The Transvaalers' ill success against Sekukuni, a powerful Bapedi Chief in the north-eastern parts of their republic, and the risk that the flame might spread, moved Carnarvon to write to Frere that the war had "rapidly ripened all South African policy.... It brings us near to ... the union of the South African Colonies and States."[2] Whilst relying upon Frere to promote confederation, and, with it, a general Native policy for South Africa,[3] he had conceived that if the Cape Colony were slow in accepting his ideas, they might now be forced to do so through the Transvaal. By Shepstone's mission he hoped to avert the general Native war which seemed to be imminent and, by annexing the Transvaal, presently to absorb the Orange Free State. Thus a confederacy might be brought about in the north-east, which would inevitably compel the Colony to come in.[4]

The relations of the Transvaalers with the Natives had long been a source of anxiety to the whole of South Africa. On every side they were on bad terms with their coloured neighbours. By the Sand River Convention, slavery was prohibited; but it was said by unscrupulous propagandists that under pretence of apprenticeship or the sale of cart-loads of "black ivory", the prohibition was practically ignored.[5] "Three things distress me very much," wrote Khama, King of the Bamangwato, from Bechuanaland, "war, selling people, and drink. All these I shall find in the Boers." And he besought the protection of the Great White Queen against a Boer invasion.[6]

A quarter of a century of autonomy had brought the Transvaal to the verge of bankruptcy and anarchy. Civil dissension had been created by the presence of the Dutchmen of European birth, or "Hollanders", whom President Burgers had introduced, and whose advanced political and religious views conflicted with the rigid Puritanism of the majority of the Boers. These turned to Paul Kruger, the Vice-President, as their leader and the successor of their heretical President. Taxes were refused; the executive was powerless to enforce their collection, or to prevent the fraud and violence with which encroachments were made upon adjoining tribal territory. The

[1] Aylward, A., *The Transvaal of To-day*, p. 389; Noble, *South Africa, Past and Present*, App., p. 339.

[2] 13 October 1876, *ap.* Martineau, II, 161.

[3] Carnarvon to Queen Victoria, *Letters of Queen Victoria*, 2nd Ser., II, 502.

[4] Carnarvon to the Queen, 15 September 1876, *Letters of Queen Victoria*, 2nd Ser. II, 479, 480, and 479 n.; same to Disraeli, 15 September and 15 October 1876; same to General Ponsonby, 20 September 1876, P.R.O., G.D. 6/3 Nos. 31–45.

[5] Martineau, II, 174; Haggard, Rider, *Cetewayo and His White Neighbours*, ch. II. The "black legend" has been greatly exaggerated and it was really the Boers' pressure on the Natives' land that was the cause of trouble. Every bit of authentic evidence sent to Downing Street related to the period before 1865.

[6] *Parl. Pap.* 1877, LX [C. 1748], [C. 1776].

inevitable result was the Sekukuni war, to which Carnarvon had referred in his letter to Frere.

Sekukuni, chief of the Bapedi tribe, had established himself on the north-east frontier of the republic, among the Lulu Mountains in the neighbourhood of the Lydenburg gold-fields. He objected to the presence of gold prospectors, and refused to pay taxes or to give up lands which the Boers claimed as part of the Swazi concession of 1846,[1] and which Burgers intended to offer as security for a loan for constructing the Transvaal section of the railway to Delagoa Bay. Entrenched in the mountains, Sekukuni repulsed an attack led by Burgers, whose commando promptly dispersed. Left without money or armed forces, the Transvaal Government availed itself of the services of a body of "filibusters", as they were called, under Captain Konrad von Schlickman, an ex-officer in the Prussian army. They were authorised to pay themselves by land and cattle taken from the natives. The result was a war of massacre and unrestrained brutality. Women and children were murdered, and the wounded slaughtered by von Schlickman's orders. When, at his death, von Schlickman was succeeded by Alfred Aylward, an Irish Fenian, friendly Natives were robbed and butchered by order of Field-Cornet Abel Erasmus, whom Wolseley publicly denounced as a "fiend in human form".[2] Barkly protested to Burgers against these atrocities, but he doubted whether the South African Republic had the power, even if it had the will, to stop them.[3] When Carnarvon wrote that such a war menaced the whole country, and suggested that the people of the Transvaal should put themselves under the protection of H.M. Government, the High Commissioner warned him that the intervention of British troops would be necessary.[4]

Alarmed by the success of Sekukuni, the miners at Lydenburg had already appealed to Natal and the Cape for help before the fighting began. The demand that the Transvaal should be taken under the protection of the British flag grew loud. Both on the grounds of humanity and self-preservation Carnarvon felt bound to intervene.[5] He believed that the situation of the Boers was one of imminent peril. They were confronted with the possibility of civil war, and whilst the revolt of Sekukuni had revealed their military and administrative weakness, they were at daggers drawn with a far more powerful neighbour on their borders.[6] Cetewayo (Ketshwayo), King of the Zulus, the most warlike and aggressive of the Bantu tribes, was determined to maintain his claim to the so-called Blood River Territory

[1] *Vide supra*, p. 408.

[2] Haggard, *Cetewayo and His White Neighbours*, p. 98; Sir H. Barkly to Lord Carnarvon, 16 September 1876, P.R.O., G.D. 6/32, No. 128.

[3] Barkly to Carnarvon, 18 December 1876, *Parl. Pap.* 1877, LX [C. 1776].

[4] *Parl. Pap.* 1877, LX [C. 1748], [C. 1776].

[5] Carnarvon Cabinet Memorandum, July 1875; Carnarvon to Queen Victoria, 12 November 1876, P.R.O., G.D. 6/3, No. 54.

[6] Frere to General Ponsonby, *Letters of Queen Victoria*, 2nd Ser., II, 536, 537.

between the Blood and Pongola Rivers. The republic, basing its rights on Panda's concession (1861), had annexed this district by proclamation in May 1875 and proceeded to tax the Zulu occupants. In Swaziland, also, where Cetewayo claimed to be Paramount Chief, the Boers were intriguing with a view to extending their dominions in the direction of Delagoa Bay. There a treaty was concluded with Mbandeni, the republic's nominee, which practically made him a subject of the Transvaal.[1] Cetewayo prepared to drive the Boers over the Vaal, and massed three corps of his trained impis on the frontier. The Boers, with but twelve shillings and sixpence in the Treasury, no credit and no organised military force, apparently lay at his mercy.[2] It is, however, maintained by some that the Boers were in no danger from the Zulus; others admit the danger, but declare that it was engineered by Shepstone. The two arguments seem to cancel one another.[3] The truth may be that disaster threatened the Boer frontiersmen, but hardly the whole country, and Shepstone made the most of the danger for political purposes.[4]

Another reason for annexation, though not for premature action, was the danger of foreign intervention. Burgers' attempt to secure foreign alliances—Belgian, Portuguese and German—had left no room for doubt in Shepstone's mind that, if England declined to interfere, her place would be taken by Germany.[5] For the demand for colonies was growing louder in Berlin, and the Brussels Conference of 1876 was heralding the coming scramble for Africa.[6]

On 22 January 1877, Shepstone arrived at Pretoria, escorted only by twenty-five mounted police; for, though a strong battalion had been ordered to Natal and was soon to advance northward to Newcastle, it had not been sent with the intention of using force against the Transvaal, but of maintaining order when the Transvaal had come under the British flag.[7] Shepstone quickly decided that nothing but an immediate declaration of British sovereignty could save the republic and all South Africa from the direst consequences. He was well received by both Afrikaners and British. No public meetings were held to sanction the cession, but addresses, memorials and letters were received by the Commissioner, which satisfied him that a large

[1] *Parl. Pap.* 1877, LX [C. 1748]; Carter, T. F., *A Narrative of the Boer War*, p. 562; Leyds, W. J., *Transvaal Surrounded*, p. 507.

[2] Cetewayo to Shepstone, *Parl. Pap.* 1877, LX [C. 1883]; Memorandum by Col. A. W. Durnford, *ap.* Martineau, II, 182, 183 n.; Carnarvon to Queen Victoria, 13 December 1876, P.R.O., G.D. 6/3, No. 69.

[3] Reitz, F. W., *A Century of Wrong*, p. 27; Leyds, W. J., *First Annexation*, p. 198; Colenso and Durnford, *The Zulu War*, p. 98; Uys, C. J., *In the Era of Shepstone*, pp. 219–225, 233.

[4] Kotze, Sir J. C., *Biographical Memories and Reminiscences* (Cape Town, 1934), agrees that the frontiersmen were in danger, but shows that Shepstone never threatened to let the Zulus loose on the Boers.

[5] Frere to J. M. MacLean, 22 April 1881, *ap.* Martineau, II, 183 n.

[6] See *C.H.B.E.* vol. III.

[7] Carnarvon to Barkly, 20 September 1876; Shepstone to Carnarvon, 28 March 1877, P.R.O., G.D. 6/32, Nos. 129, 203; Carnarvon to Shepstone, 4 Oct. 1876, *ibid.* 6/23, No. 2.

proportion of the inhabitants desired the establishment of British rule, "delivery from the thraldom of petty factions", and from the danger of being overrun by Cetewayo's hordes.[1] He may have been right; but he certainly underestimated the influence and determination of the remainder of the burghers, who were unwilling to sacrifice their independence at any price. No less certainly, the methods he adopted were unfortunate in the extreme.

Carnarvon had insisted upon the supreme importance of the cession being the act of the Afrikaner part of the population, and the desirability of winning the consent of the Volksraad;[2] but when Shepstone, after consulting with President Burgers, interviewed the Executive Council, Kruger warned him not to tamper with their independence. The Volksraad repeated that warning, when Burgers in vain endeavoured to effect certain much needed reforms. Shepstone had promised to hold his hand if they were passed. On their rejection, and when the Volksraad refused to consider the Permissive Act, he declared that annexation was inevitable. The Volksraad, in alarm, passed some of the rejected reforms and dispersed. Shepstone then made an arrangement with Burgers which was as foolish as it was reprehensible.

The situation was characteristic of much in South African politics. Both the President and a majority of the Executive appear to have been convinced of the necessity for the change, but were afraid of openly expressing their views. Many of them stipulated for office or pensions under the new Government. Shepstone thereupon privately arranged with Burgers the terms of a proclamation for taking the Transvaal under the British flag, and at the same time agreed that the President should issue a protest against it "to keep the noisy portion of the people quiet". Shepstone demurred at first, on the grounds that the proposed protest appeared to pledge the people to resist by and by; but Burgers satisfied him that by the time British troops arrived—for as yet there was not a single British soldier in the country—all opposition would have died out. On April 12, then, Shepstone published two proclamations, one declaring the Transvaal British territory and the other announcing that he himself had taken over the administration.[3] Burgers issued his formal protest and retired to the Cape Colony, where he was subsequently granted a small allowance (July 1878), which hardly made up for what he had expended for the republic out of his own pocket. His Executive Council also protested against what they described as "an act of violence".

[1] Shepstone to [Sir] Robert Herbert, Under-Secretary for the Colonies, 11 April 1876; same to Frere, 3 April 1876; same to Barkly, 23 November, 13 December 1876, Cf. Uys, *Shepstone*, pp. 219–22.

[2] Carnarvon to Shepstone, 4 October 1876, P.R.O., G.D. 6/23, No. 2.

[3] Shepstone to [Sir] R. Herbert, 11 April 1877, *ap.* Martineau, II, 180, 181; *Parl. Pap.* 1877, LX [C. 1776]; Carter, T. F., *A Narrative of the Boer War*, p. 562; Eybers, G. W., *Select Constitutional Documents*, p. 446; Leyds, *The First Annexation of the Transvaal*, p. 179.

The fundamental error in this proceeding was Shepstone's secret dealing with the President, and his not insisting upon an open request from the Volksraad or an immediate vote upon his action. It was believed, even by his opponents, that such a vote would have confirmed the annexation; the absence of it supported the argument that Burgers' arrangement was not legally valid.[1] An English historian cannot but agree with the verdict of the well-known novelist who was about to travel in South Africa, that "a nation with a popular parliament can only be held to express its opinion to another nation by the voice of its parliament".[2]

Shepstone's precipitancy thus prepared the way for agitation by those who clung to independence, and by those who, whilst ready to accept British aid at the moment, might choose to repudiate the annexation after the occasion for it had been removed.[3] He was actuated by his eagerness to carry out the policy of annexation as a step towards confederation, and by his conviction that, if he delayed, the whole country would be devastated. The tension, he explained, was so great that an accidental shot might have annihilated the republic and cost England millions to retrieve her position with the Natives.[4] On the eve of issuing his proclamation he sent word to Cetewayo, warning him that the country would henceforth be under British rule. The Zulu king at once sent his impis home, declaring that it was to fight the Afrikaners that he had called them together;[5] but he felt very sore at having been restrained by "Somtseu" from having his way with the Boers.[6]

Frere was startled by Shepstone's proclamation and regretted the use of the word "annexation", but he thought it best to accept the situation.[7] At the same time he was well aware that the loss of their independence had caused alarm and regret both among the old orthodox Dutch party and "the Afrikanders and Neologians who sympathised with Burgers in his dreams of a great anti-English South Africa".[8] The Orange Free State was afraid lest its own turn should come next. In the Cape Colony, the Afrikaners, led by Hofmeyr, saw in the extinction of the republic the death-knell of their hopes of predominance under the aegis of the Imperial Government.[9]

[1] Frere to Carnarvon, 15 May 1877, *ap.* Martineau, II, 186; Jorissen, E. J., *Transvaalsche Herinneringen*, p. 34.

[2] Trollope, Anthony, *South Africa*, II, 51.

[3] Lord Carnarvon, Speech in House of Lords, 25 March 1879, *Hansard*, 3rd ser., CCXLIV 1645.

[4] Shepstone to Carnarvon, 23 July 1877, P.R.O., G.D. 6/23, No. 8.

[5] Cetewayo to Shepstone, *Parl. Pap.* 1877, LX [C. 1883], p. 19.

[6] Frere to Herbert, 18 March 1878, *ap.* Martineau, II, 183 n.

[7] Martineau, II, 179, 180. Uys, C. J., *In the Era of Shepstone*, p. 317, argues that Frere could not have been surprised.

[8] Frere to Carnarvon, 21 May 1877, *ap.* Martineau, II, 186.

[9] Hofmeyr, *Life of Jan Hendrik Hofmeyr*, p. 162.

In England, the annexation was generally approved by all parties.[1] Under British administration the trade and finances of the Transvaal rapidly improved. There had been no active resistance from the burghers. The back-veld Boers, indeed, remained sullen and silent, but many others signed addresses of congratulation. All the Executive Councillors retained their seats, but P. J. Joubert, until recently Commandant-General, at once began to organise a secret campaign against the annexation. Within a month, two members of the Council, Vice-President Paul Kruger and E. J. Jorissen, the Attorney-General, left for London to demand its repeal (May 9), though a memorial protesting againt their mission and approving the annexation received, amongst many other signatures, those of six members of the Volksraad.[2]

Carnarvon, frankly incredulous that the annexation had been contrary to the wishes of the inhabitants, refused to reconsider it; but he promised the delegates that the wishes and interests of the Dutch population should be consulted as far as possible, and that Dutch should be recognised as one of the official languages (January 1878). In return, the two delegates undertook to foster a spirit of content, asked to be employed in the service of the Government, and, after a sterile visit to the Continent, returned to Pretoria.[3] There they found that affairs had assumed a new complexion.

The proclamation had announced that the Transvaal would remain a separate Government, with its own laws and legislature.[4] Shepstone, however, had not thought it advisable to summon the Volksraad, and Frere, though anxious that a constitution should be granted at the earliest moment, thought that the leading burghers should first be consulted as to the form of government they desired.[5] In the meantime the legislature was dissolved and no representative assembly of any kind substituted for it; instead, Shepstone, as sole authority, made a number of alterations in the laws and administration of justice by proclamation.

To minds peculiarly jealous of legalities, such changes, so ordered, seemed a clear indication of bad faith. The cry was raised that the promises by which Shepstone had induced the inhabitants to surrender their independence had not been kept. Discontent increased when Sekukuni, encouraged by Cetewayo, again rose in revolt, and two campaigns failed to crush him. Seeing that the wind had changed, Kruger joined Joubert in his agitation for repeal, and was supported by Jorissen, who had been dismissed from the Attorney-Generalship

[1] Carnarvon to Shepstone, 14 May 1877, P.R.O., G.D. 6/23, No. 4.

[2] *Parl. Pap.* 1877, LX [C. 1883]; Martineau, II, 181 n., 185, 186; Carter, *A Narrative of the Boer War*, p. 41.

[3] Van Oordt, J. F., *Paul Kruger en de Opkomst der Zuid-Afrikaansche Republiek*, p. 204; *Parl. Pap.* 1877, LX [C. 1883], pp. 16, 36; 1878, LV [C. 1961], p. 147.

[4] *Parl. Pap.* 1877, LX [C. 1776], p. 152.

[5] Frere to Carnarvon, *ap.* Martineau, II, 184.

for incompetence. Memorials were circulated for signature. Shepstone issued a proclamation[1] warning the promoters that they were guilty of sedition, and troops were held in readiness to overcome a meeting at Pretoria. The memorials, nevertheless, were numerously signed. Of 8000 adult males in the Transvaal, 6591 enfranchised burghers now voted against annexation, and only 587 for it.[2] This apparent unanimity was, however, partly the result of intimidation. The pressure exercised by the malcontents was all the more effective because well-disposed Boers had no confidence that the British Government would not change its mind, as it had done before in the case of the Orange Free State in 1854 and in 1839 in Natal. They knew that they would have to pay the penalty, if the republic were restored.[3] Armed with these petitions, Kruger once more sailed for London, this time accompanied by Joubert.[4] We will return to the sequel later.[5]

Frere hoped that, as Carnarvon had intended, the annexation of the Transvaal would strengthen the cause of confederation;[6] but the sympathies of the Afrikaners in the Cape Colony, as well as the Orange Free State, had been alienated, and intercolonial jealousy saw in the annexation the advantage of Natal rather than that of the Empire. Molteno grudgingly passed the Act for annexing Griqualand West, but would have nothing more to do with the imperial scheme, and his Ministry took pains to avoid any appearance of responsibility for the actions in the Transvaal.[7] Natal alone approved of the Permissive Act.

Frere's further efforts for confederation were fatally compromised by the Native wars in which he became involved. Among the Xhosa clans, the Galekas had by this time recovered to a great extent from the devastation and depopulation caused by their cattle-killing delusion in 1857.[8] Driven back across the Bashee by Sir George Grey in 1858, they had since been allowed to return and occupy a strip of the Transkei next the coast. There Kreli, son of Hintza, ruled in a state of semi-independence with a British Resident to control him and a pension from the Government. Inland, and likewise under British protection, a strong colony of Fingos had been settled. Whilst the Fingos, under the sympathetic guidance of capable British magistrates,[9] were advancing rapidly along the paths of civilisation, the Galekas remained in a state of savagery. Cooped up in a small

[1] *Hansard*, 3rd ser., CCXLII, 2065–2068.
[2] *Hansard*, *loc. cit.*
[3] Frere to Hicks Beach, 6 and 9 April, 1877, *ap.* Martineau, II, 290, 291.
[4] *Parl. Pap.* 1878, LVI [C. 2144]; Leyds, *First Annexation*, p. 233.
[5] *Vide infra*, p. 491.
[6] Frere to Carnarvon, 21 May 1877, *ap.* Martineau, II, 186.
[7] *Parl. Pap.* 1878, LV [C. 1980]; Martineau, II, 189.
[8] *Vide supra*, p. 412.
[9] Frere to Carnarvon, 3 October 1877, P.R.O., G.D. 6/34.

portion of the Transkeian territory between the Bashee and Kei Rivers, they looked with jealous eyes upon the lands of the neighbouring Fingos, their former "dogs". Border brawls were followed by pitched battles. Frere summoned the Paramount Chief to his presence, but Kreli, remembering the fate of Hintza in D'Urban's war,[1] refused to come. His young warriors could no longer be restrained. War broke out. The Colonial police was insufficient and ill-organised. If imperial troops were employed, Frere held that the Colonial sorces must be under the command of the General acting under his instructions as High Commissioner. But Molteno was jealous of co-operating with General Cunynghame and regular troops, and refused to submit the Cape forces to imperial military control. He wished to conduct the campaign in his own way, and to transport the Galekas to St Helena Bay, replacing them with Fingos. Frere objected to the needless cruelty of a plan which would, besides, be a standing cause of unrest.[2] In the end, Colonial volunteers and Fingos and Tembus assisted the imperial troops to drive the Galekas over the Bashee. Kreli's "army" was crushed and his "Great Place" destroyed by the Transkei Field Force under Charles Griffith (September 1877).[3]

The war seemed to be over, but, taking advantage of the neglect to guard the fords, bodies of Galekas slipped back over the Bashee. Crossing the Kei, they entered the location of the Gaikas in the Cape Colony itself, and roused them to rebellion under their chief, Sandile. There were several sharp engagements in the war which ensued, and which was conducted successfully by Sir Arthur Cunynghame and General Thesiger (later Lord Chelmsford) with 2000 regulars, the Mounted Police and some volunteers. By the end of June 1878, Sandile had been shot, Kreli had taken flight and an amnesty had been declared.[4]

The Gaika rising was the occasion of a constitutional crisis of some importance. Molteno and Merriman had been eager to break up the Gaikas' location altogether. Frere could see no justification for such violent measures; good police measures and kindly government, he held, were what was needed. "The Gaikas are our fellow-subjects, not our enemies." Molteno raised the cry of "Imperial domination and military despotism", and appointed Griffith Commandant-General of the Colonial forces to conduct a campaign independently of the Governor and Commander-in-Chief. Frere objected that such procedure was both contrary to reason and illegal. Although Molteno was supported by a faithful majority in the House of Assembly, Frere took the strong, indeed the unique, step of dismissing the

[1] *Vide supra*, p. 317.

[2] Molteno, P. A., *Life and Times of Sir J. C. Molteno*, II, chs. XXVIII, XXIX; Martineau, II, 231; Frere to Carnarvon, 22 October 1877, P.R.O., G.D. 6/34; Gathorne Hardy to Carnarvon, May 1876, *ibid.* 6/12.

[3] *Parl. Pap.* 1878, LV [C. 1961]; Frere to Ponsonby, 17 October 1877, *ap.* Martineau, II, 197–202; P.R.O., G.D. 6/34.

[4] *Parl. Pap.* 1878, LVI [C. 2144].

Ministry rather than surrender an undoubted privilege of the Crown, and at the same time countenance the aggressive and deplorable methods with which Merriman's "amateur campaign under civilian soldiers" was being conducted.[1] Molteno was succeeded by Gordon Sprigg, who, with great courage and patriotism, came from his farm in British Kaffraria and undertook to form a Ministry in these difficult circumstances. He passed an Act (1878) for disarming the Native tribes. As a natural corollary of the wars, Galekas and Fingos alike were disarmed, and in 1879 Fingoland and Griqualand East were annexed to Cape Colony.

Frere's instructions had directed him both to defend the colonies from attack by the Native tribes, and to promote good order and civilisation amongst them by placing them under some settled form of government.[2] This forward policy, which he heartily espoused, he now proceeded to put into effect. If only with a view to confederation, he saw clearly that the establishment of settled and peaceful conditions among the Natives was a necessary preliminary to obtaining the consent of those colonies which shrank from the liability of keeping order among the frontier tribes. The Imperial Government, he urged, must no longer shirk responsibility; evasion only resulted in the substitution of gun-runners and canteen keepers for the English magistrate. British authority must be extended over all the tribes south of the Portuguese frontiers, in order to prevent their exploitation by traders and adventurers, and to avoid the heavy penalty in blood and treasure which had always to be paid for abdication of the "clear responsibility of sovereignty".[3] With these ends in view, Frere now pressed Carnarvon to proclaim a protectorate over Damaraland and Namaqualand.

For a full generation past traders and missionaries had been making their way northwards through Bechuanaland to the Zambesi and north-westwards to Lake Ngami and Damaraland. Intertribal wars there caused a risk of foreign intervention, for in 1868 the struggle between the Damara and the Hottentots of Namaqualand had caused some German missionaries, whose stations had been plundered, to appeal to the British Government to declared a protectorate. The memorial of the Rhenish Missionary Society was commended to the British Foreign Office by the Government of Bismarck's new North German Confederation. Trouble was also to be apprehended from the Transvaal, for Boers, fleeing from the heresies of Burgers, had begun since 1873 to trek across the eastern borders of Damaraland. Hence, a Commissioner, W. Coates Palgrave, was sent by the Cape Government to make enquiries and restore peace (1876). He made

[1] Martineau, II, 202–14, 220–22; Molteno, *Life of Sir J. C. Molteno*, II, 300 *sqq.*; *Parl. Pap.* 1878, LVI [C. 2079]; Todd, *Constitutional Government*; P.R.O., G.D. 6/33, 34.

[2] *Parl. Pap.* 1878–9, LIV [Cd. 2454], p. 133.

[3] Frere to Hicks Beach, 8 Feb., 10 August 1878; to Sir Garnet Wolseley, 15 September 1879; *ap.* Martineau, II, 260, 352, 355.

some arrangements with the principal Chiefs and reported that they were anxious to be taken under British protection.

Molteno had at first been inclined towards annexation, but now, reluctant to face the expense, and annoyed at Carnarvon's insistence that the acquisition of Walvis Bay and Tembuland should be dependent on the incorporation of Griqualand West in the Cape Colony, he hung back. Frere urged that the whole country as far north as the Kunene River, and including Walvis Bay in particular, should be declared a British protectorate, and at last Molteno, who had consented to take over Griqualand West (1877), agreed that the Home Government should be requested to order the hoisting of the Union Jack at Walvis Bay. The Government, recognising its strategic value as "the only door of entrance to very large regions in which the Colony is naturally interested", sanctioned the annexation of the bay and territory from thirteen to eighteen miles inland (March 1878). The expenses of a British Resident, whose powers were confined to the shores of the bay, were to be borne by the Colonial Government,[1] though Walvis Bay was not formally annexed to the Cape Colony until 1884. The declaration of a British protectorate over Damaraland and Namaqualand was, however, definitely forbidden by the Colonial Secretary, Lord Kimberley (1880).[2]

The Galeka and Gaika risings had been accompanied by outbreaks among other Native tribes. Sekukuni was still in arms; the Pondos, the Griquas of Griqualand, West and East, the Batlapin and Barolong on the Bechuanaland border rose in rebellion. These outbursts were suppressed with no great difficulty; but they convinced Frere that a movement was on foot amongst the Native Chiefs, from Sekukuni to Kreli, towards a general insurrection of the Bantu against the new civilisation. Armed with guns and conscious of their superior numbers, they believed themselves more than a match for the white man. Some believed that they were encouraged by promises of support from the powerful nation north of Natal,[3] which was said to be thirsting for war. Frere certainly believed that they were looking to these Zulu warriors, and to Cetewayo their ruler, as leader and champions. He did not hesitate to accept the presumed challenge. Like Grey, seventeen years before, he recognised that the presence of armed and barbarous savages on the frontier of a colony must be fatal to its prosperity. Peace and prosperity in the Transvaal, he argued, depended upon the removal of this constant and paralysing threat to settlers; peaceful civilisation could not be established until it had been demonstrated once for all who was to be master.[4] Action would be in accordance

[1] Carnarvon to Frere, 23 January 1878, *ap.* Theal, *History of South Africa since* 1795, chs. LXXX, LXXXI. [2] *Vide infra*, chap. XX.

[3] Shepstone to Carnarvon, 11 December 1877, P.R.O., G.D. 6/23, No. 12.

[4] Frere to Herbert, 18 March 1878, *ap.* Martineau, II, 223; same to same, 10 November 1878, *ap.* Worsfold, W. B., *Sir Bartle Frere*, p. 112; Parr, Hallam, *A Sketch of the Kaffir and Zulu Wars*, p. 101; Sir Henry Bulwer, Lt-Gov. of Natal, to Carnarvon, 2 November 1878.

with the policy which he had been instructed to pursue, and he had the means to enforce it, thanks to the reinforcements which had been sent to deal with the Gaikas and Galekas.[1]

Hitherto the British had more or less held the balance between the republics and the tribes; but now that they had annexed the Transvaal, they were, as Shepstone promptly warned Carnarvon, face to face with a martial folk, whose well-organised army of some 40,000 men was armed with guns as well as assegais.[2]

The Zulus, under the military rule perfected by their old Chief Chaka, were a nation trained for war, a fighting machine of drilled warriors unmatched in courage and physique by the other tribes of South Africa. Their military organisation was based upon a regimental system of celibate soldiery closely resembling that of the ancient Spartans. Young braves were not allowed to marry until they had "washed their spears" in the blood of an enemy. Their present chief was Cetewayo, son of Panda, the successor of Chaka and Dingaan. Panda lived till 1872, but Cetewayo had been the real ruler of the Zulu tribe ever since a battle royal in December 1856 on the banks of the Tugela had resulted in the defeat of his brother, Mbulazi, and a frightful massacre of his followers. Handsome, aggressive, highly intelligent and utterly ruthless, Cetewayo had restored the military discipline of his people. When Panda died, Cetewayo, fearing lest his brothers might be recognised by Great Britain or the Transvaal, sought to secure the support of the Natal Government as well as that of the Transvaal Republic. He sent to both, requesting them to instal him as King of the Zulus. The Natal Government appointed Shepstone for that purpose. Before crossing the Tugela, Shepstone informed Cetewayo that the ceremony of installation must not be stained by the customary shedding of blood. Cetewayo publicly agreed that indiscriminate shedding of blood should cease, and that no Zulu should be condemned without open trial and public examination of witnesses, though at that very moment his hands were red with the blood of Masipula, his father's Prime Minister. No sooner had he obtained recognition than he cast his engagements to the winds; murders were continued, missionaries forced to flee the country and their converts persecuted.[3] "Did I ever tell Mr Shepstone I would not kill? I do kill." So ran his truculent answer to the protest of the Lieutenant-Governor of Natal against a massacre of young girls who had married without leave. "I shall not agree to any laws or rules from Natal."

In July 1878, parties of Zulus carried off by force from a police

[1] Carnarvon to Ponsonby, 26 October 1877, 21 January 1878; P.R.O., G.D. 6/3, No. 198; same to Gathorne Hardy, 29 January 1878, P.R.O., G.D. 6/12.

[2] *Parl. Pap.* 1878–9, LII [C. 2222], pp. 35 *sqq.*; Shepstone to Carnarvon, 23 July and 11 December 1877, P.R.O., G.D. 6/23, Nos. 9, 12.

[3] Memorial on Zulu Affairs, by Charles Brownlee, Resident Commissioner for Native Affairs, Cape Colony, 12 November 1878.

kraal in Natal, two wives of the chief Sirayo, who had sought refuge there. The women were put to death. When Lieutenant-Governor Sir Henry Bulwer demanded that the leading offenders should be surrendered for trial in Natal, Cetewayo made excuses for the outrage and offered to pay, as he had done before, a small sum as compensation for violation of the frontier.

Not unnaturally, the British had inherited much of the hostility and distrust with which the Zulus had previously regarded the Afrikaners, for the Zulus were now surrounded by British territory and that of the Swazis, whom the British had taken under their protection. Cetewayo was annoyed when Shepstone refused to permit even "one small swoop" upon the Swazis.[1] Whilst the young braves chafed at being prevented from "washing their spears in blood", their King was further exasperated by the prospect of being cheated of his hopes of regaining the Blood River Territory adjoining Utrecht, which he had so long disputed with the Transvaalers. Shepstone, who had previously supported Cetewayo's claim, now took the Transvaal point of view and informed him that it was without foundation;[2] for it was found that the King had misled the Natal Government, and that a formal cession had indeed been made by Panda to the Transvaal in 1861.[3] Disgusted at what he regarded as "Somtseu's treachery", Cetewayo built a military kraal in the disputed territory from which the Boer settlers were forced to flee for their lives.[4] Not content with thus occupying the Blood River Territory, he proceeded to build a kraal north of the Pongola, and notice to quit was given in his name to some German settlers at Luneberg.[5] On receiving information to this effect from Frere, Colonel Evelyn Wood moved up two companies of the 90th Regiment from Utrecht to protect them (October 1878). Frere sent a naval squadron to the coast of Zululand, and wrote to Sir Michael Hicks Beach, who had succeeded Carnarvon at the Colonial Office, that the Zulus were now quite out of hand. He insisted that some measures must be taken to put an end to their pretensions, and asked for reinforcements (August 30, September 10, 14, 30), for, in the meantime, Cetewayo having been induced to submit the Blood River question to arbitration, Frere had received from the commissioners (June 20) a report which unexpectedly gave to the Zulu king even more than he had asked for. Frere thought the award unjust to the Transvaal, and feared that the Boers would rise if he enforced it. He therefore decided that his announcement of the award should be accompanied by an ultimatum to the Zulus.[6] Sir Michael at first

[1] Martineau, II, 232.
[2] *Parl. Pap.* 1878, LVI [C. 2079], p. 53.
[3] Theal, IV, 151–5.
[4] Shepstone to Frere, 25 December 1877, *ap.* Martineau, II, 235.
[5] Martineau, II, 244.
[6] Martineau, II, 242, 268, 327; Frere to Hicks Beach, 22 September 1879; Frere to Sir R. Herbert, 23 December 1878.

expressed a guarded approval of the High Commissioner's policy, writing on October 2, that "of course Cetewayo must be kept in order and compelled to give up Zulus who violated the Natal and Transvaal frontiers". On October 10 he promised reinforcements if, after consulting Bulwer and Thesiger in Natal, Frere decided that they were needed, but he hoped a Zulu war might not be necessary.[1]

A week later the Conservative Cabinet reversed its policy. In a despatch dated October 17, Frere was informed that his request for reinforcements was refused as there were already 6000 regular troops in South Africa. Money and men, in fact, were required by the situation in Afghanistan and eastern Europe, and the Government had become anxious to avoid war with the Zulus in order to limit their commitments. Peace, they were now confident in spite of Frere's repeated warnings, could be maintained by the exercise of a "spirit of forbearance and reasonable compromise".[2] But on November 21, after the receipt of an urgent cable from Frere dated October 28, the Ministers again changed their minds. Reinforcements were to be sent, but only to be used for the necessary protection of the colonists.

Before this decision reached him, Frere had received on November 30 a telegraphic summary of a letter from Hicks Beach (November 7) stating that in view of the situation in the Near East, the Government could not comply with his request for more troops. "We cannot now have a Zulu war in addition to other troubles."

Nevertheless, Frere issued his ultimatum to Cetewayo. He felt that the Government was committed to the removal of the Zulu menace by the movement of troops which had just taken place.[3] He had come to the conclusion, shared by the great majority of South Africans, that the danger was imminent, and that if the issue were not now faced, the struggle might have to be fought, not to the north of the Tugela, but among the homesteads of Natal and Cape Colony.[4] His military advisers assured him that they had an ample force for an invasion of Zululand.[5] The frontier incidents mentioned above were indeed trivial and might easily have been settled, but they were sufficient indication of Cetewayo's hostile attitude however sincerely his champion, Bishop Colenso, may have held that he was docile and innocent.[6] It is evident enough now that, fundamentally, the problem was whether the rule of law or the rule of the assegai was

[1] Worsfold, W. B., *Sir Bartle Frere*, pp. 103, 116.

[2] *Parl. Pap.* 1878–9, LII [C. 2220], p. 273; Sir M. Hicks Beach to Queen Victoria, 11 November; Beaconsfield to the Queen, 12 November 1878; *Letters of Queen Victoria*, 2nd Ser., II, 644–6.

[3] Martineau, II, 263; *Life of Sir M. Hicks Beach*, pp. 90–111.

[4] Speech by Sir B. Frere, 11 June 1879; Frere to Sir M. Hicks Beach, *ap.* Martineau, II, 251, 252.

[5] Sir William Butler, *Autobiography*, p. 212.

[6] Martineau, II, 233, 247; Colenso and Durnford, *The Zulu War*; Shepstone to Frere, 1 December 1877, P.R.O., G.D. 63/4.

to prevail on the borders of Natal and the Transvaal. If Africa was to be civilised, war with the Zulus at some time was, as Shepstone had declared, inevitable.[1] Only a military defeat could induce that nation of warriors to abandon their military organisation.

Frere had plainly intimated to the Colonial Secretary that in presenting the award he would add conditions calculated to ensure a final settlement of the Zulu question.[2] To this announcement therefore (11 December 1878), he attached a message which was in effect an ultimatum, and an ultimatum which Cetewayo was not likely to accept, for it was an application to Zululand of the Kaffirland policy of disarmament and control. It called upon him to disband his army and permit its celibate warriors to marry; to substitute for trial "by rifle shots" fair trial for his subjects; to make reparation for the Sirayo and other incidents; to protect missionaries and their converts, and to receive a British Resident, who should be "the eyes, ears and mouth" of the Governor.[3] This ultimatum was signed by the Lieutenant-Governor of Natal and approved by Bishop Colenso, who thought Cetewayo would accept it.[4] An answer was required within thirty days. No answer was given, and on January 11, British troops commanded by Thesiger, now Lieutenant-General Lord Chelmsford, advanced into Zululand. Though most of the Transvaal Boers refused aid, Piet Uys and some other Boers of the Utrecht district offered their services to Colonel Evelyn Wood.[5]

Chelmsford's plan of campaign was to advance with four columns, converging from points on a 200-mile front upon Cetewayo's kraal at Ulundi. By taking the offensive, he hoped to forestall threatened raids into Natal,[6] and by compelling Cetewayo to keep his army in the field, to involve him in difficulties of supply. Of the four invading columns, one, under Colonel Pearson, crossed the Lower Tugela near the coast; one, under Colonel Evelyn Wood and Major Redvers Buller, entered Zululand near Newcastle on the north-east; one, under Lieutenant-Colonel Durnford, consisting mainly of Natal volunteers and Native troops encamped at Rorke's Drift was to act in concert with the General. The latter crossed the Buffalo river at Rorke's Drift on 20 January 1879. After a march of some ten miles, camp was pitched under the southern face of a steep hill called Isandhlwana, "the Little Hand". Four days later two men, speechless with panic, hunger and fatigue, were brought to

[1] Shepstone to Carnarvon, 11 December 1877.

[2] Frere to Sir M. Hicks Beach and Sir R. Herbert, 10 November 1878; Worsfold, *Sir B. Frere*, pp. 108, 113.

[3] *Parl. Pap.* 1878–9, LII [C. 2222], pp. 210 *sqq.*; Frere to Ponsonby, *Letters of Queen Victoria*, 2nd Ser., II, 656.

[4] Sir H. Bulwer. Minute on Sir Bartle Frere's ultimatum, *Parl. Pap.* 1878–9, LII [C. 2242], p. 16. The ultimatum is printed in *ibid.* [C. 2222], pp. 201–9; Frere to Sir M. Hicks Beach, 23 December 1878.

[5] Martineau, II, 258, 264; Leyds, *First Annexation of the Transvaal*, p. 245.

[6] Martineau, II, 272.

Frere's bedside at Pietermaritzburg bearing news of a terrible disaster.

Isandhlwana is a lofty eminence shaped like a lion couchant. Three sides of it are inaccessible; the northern side slopes gradually down to a range of hills. Chelmsford's camp beneath it was pitched across the road with an open plain in front, a small kopje on the right flank, and a long range of hills to the left and rear. No position more favourable for a surprise attack could have been chosen.

Yet, in spite of previous warnings by Kruger and Joubert, no precautions were taken to guard against it, whether by laagering the waggons or systematic scouting. Early on the morning of the 22nd, Chelmsford marched out with his main force in pursuit of an impi, which lured him further and further away. In his absence, an immense body of Zulus issued from behind the neighbouring hills and completely surrounded the British camp. The soldiers of the 24th, a very gallant regiment, abandoned by their Native allies, fought with the utmost skill and bravery to the last, fought till their ammunition was exhausted and every man was assegaied from a distance. Before the main column returned, 800 white and some 500 Native soldiers had been massacred and the camp plundered.[1] Meanwhile another Zulu force some 3000 or 4000 men led by Cetewayo's brother had marched on to Rorke's Drift. There 130 men under Lieutenants Bromhead and Chard had been left to guard the depot and communications with Natal. Hastily constructing barricades of biscuit boxes and mealie bags, this gallant handful of men repelled the determined attacks of the Zulus for twelve hours. At last they compelled them to retire with the loss of some 350 killed.

The stubborn defence of Rorke's Drift dramatically retrieved the disaster of Isandhlwana. It did more. The losses inflicted by this garrison and by the men who sold their lives so dearly at Isandhlwana struck a shrewd blow at the aggressive power and confidence of the enemy. At Isandhlwana the Zulus had lost over 3000 of their bravest warriors.

For some time panic reigned in Natal. Everywhere there was a stir among the Natives.[2] But Natal was saved from being overrun by the severe punishment which the Zulus had suffered, combined with the Native ritual of retirement for purification after battle, the presence of the other columns in Zululand, and the dissensions which broke out among the Zulu tribes. Nor is it necessary to reject out of hand General Butler's explanation that it was due to Cetewayo's restraining influence, because he still clung pathetically to the belief that the British were his friends, especially as that view was shared by Colenso.[3]

[1] Cf. Colenso, F. E. and Durnford, R., *History of the Zulu War*, pp. 413 *sqq.*; Durnford, *Isandhlwana*; Memorandum by Sir Bartle Frere, 29 January, 30 June, 1879; Wilmot, A., *History of the Zulu War*; Official Narrative, *Parl. Pap.* 1878–9, LII [C. 2222]; 1878–9, LIII [C. 2260]; 1878–9, LIII [C. 2367]; Martineau, II, 269, 270; Coupland, Sir R., *Zulu Battle Piece: Isandhlwana.*

[2] *Parl. Pap.* 1878–9, LIII [C. 2318]; 1878–9, LIV [C. 2374].

[3] Butler, Sir William, *Autobiography*, p. 199.

The loss of so many British troops was very serious; but every regular soldier from Cape Town was sent up to Natal, troops were hastily brought over from St Helena and Mauritius, the Free State offered help, and, when the news of Isandhlwana reached England, reinforcements were hurried out, arriving in South Africa on March 17. In the meantime, Colonel Pearson's column strengthened by a naval contingent had advanced to Eshowe in the heart of the Zulu country, but with the loss of all its transport. There it remained entrenched, successfully repelling all attacks. The northern column held a strongly fortified position at Kambula. The mounted portion of this force met with a severe check at the Hlobane Mountain (March 28), where Piet Uys was killed; but on the following day a fierce onslaught by a Zulu impi upon the camp at Kambula was repulsed with heavy loss. That action probably turned the balance of the campaign. A few days later Chelmsford succeeded in relieving the garrison at Eshowe, after fighting a successful action at Ginghinhlovo (April 2). In June he resumed his advance into Zululand.

There was to be one more painful incident in this unfortunate war. Prince Louis Napoleon, the only child of the Emperor Napoleon III and the Empress Eugénie, a chivalrous youth, who had been educated at Woolwich, had insisted on serving in South Africa to prove his gratitude to the British nation.[1] A small reconnoitring party of which he was a member was surprised by Zulus, and the Prince Imperial was assegaied whilst endeavouring to mount a restive horse.

"A very remarkable people, the Zulus," observed Disraeli, "they defeat our generals; they convert our bishops; they have settled the fate of a great European dynasty." He might have added that they nearly upset his own Government, for his political opponents were strengthened by all the forces of the anti-imperialists and the Aborigines Protection Society, whilst others did not scruple to maintain that the wise policy would have been to favour the Zulus as a check upon the ambition of the Boers.[2] A forward policy, if it is to be popular, must be swiftly and undeniably successful. The advance of Russia towards Afghanistan had been answered by a forward policy on the part of the Government of India. Roberts's brilliant campaign had silenced opposition; but in Zululand a military disaster involved the Government in a blizzard of unpopularity. The "hedging" instructions given to the High Commissioner, as Gladstone described them, provided the Government with the much-needed scapegoat.[3] Upon Frere was visited the odium of a failure for which he was not responsible. Before Isandhlwana, Hicks Beach declared himself to be sanguine of the success of Frere's policy, and thought it could be

[1] *Letters of Queen Victoria*, 2nd Ser., III, 12.
[2] Froude, *Life of Beaconsfield*, p. 251; Worsfold, *Sir Bartle Frere*, p. 340.
[3] *The Times*, 26 November 1879. Cf. Worsfold, ch. XVI.

defended "without much difficulty" (January 13);[1] but after Isandhlwana, Frere was censured in a curious despatch for having taken action without exchanging full explanations with the Cabinet (March 1879), though he was asked not to resign;[2] for although Disraeli was furious and talked of impeachment, Queen Victoria was strongly opposed to the supersession of the High Commissioner.[3] A double-minded man may be unstable in all his ways, but his position is security itself compared with that of a single-minded man at the mercy of politicians. Frere suffered accordingly. For many years the reputation of this devoted servant of the Empire, whose policy was to be the policy of the future, was obscured by clouds of obloquy and abuse; but in South Africa he was trusted and honoured by men of all parties.

To pacify public opinion as the war dragged on, the Government, in spite of Queen Victoria's vigorous protests, decided to send out Sir Garnet Wolseley with supreme civil and military authority over Natal, the Transvaal and the territories to the north and east thereof (28 May 1879). This step had been partly called for by friction between the military authorities and the civil government of Natal, and Frere himself had suggested that Natal ought to be under the direction of a General of the army.[4] Wolseley reached Durban on June 28, but before he could take command in the field, Chelmsford, advancing upon Ulundi, gained a complete victory which practically put an end to the war (July 4). Cetewayo was captured by the end of August, and the military power of the Zulus was broken for ever.

The settlement which followed bears Wolseley's name, but was undoubtedly inspired by Shepstone. It was a policy of *divide et impera*. Zululand was split up into thirteen independent Native territories, governed by John Dunn and Chiefs of the tribes which had been united by Chaka into the Zulu nation and were now resuscitated and separated once more. But over them was set no Paramount Chief. Only a British Resident was installed to be the "eyes and ears" of the Government, to give advice to the kinglets, but, contrary to Frere's advice, without authority over them or power to enforce it.[5] In the absence of any central European control, which was due to the disinclination of Great Britain to annex Zululand directly, the thirteen petty Chiefs fought each other like Kilkenny cats. At length, in 1882, the British Government was forced to intervene; but instead of proclaiming British sovereignty over the country and installing

[1] Sir M. Hicks Beach to Beaconsfield, 13 January 1879, Monypenny, H. and Buckle, G. E., *Life of Disraeli*, CI, 423.

[2] *Parl. Pap.* 1878–9, LIII [C. 2260], p. 109. Frere to Sir M. Hicks Beach, 30 June 1879; *Letters of Queen Victoria*, 2nd Ser., III, 109.

[3] Monypenny and Buckle, *Life of Disraeli*, VI, 438.

[4] *Letters of Queen Victoria*, 2nd Ser., III, 24–6; Monypenny and Buckle, *Life of Disraeli*, VI, 429–33.

[5] Frere to Sir Garnet Wolseley, 15 September 1879; *ap.* Martineau, II, 354–6.

Resident as Paramount Chief, it restored Cetewayo to part of his original kingdom. Another part along the Natal border was constituted a Native reserve to which those who did not like his rule might retire, while yet another part was left in the hands of Sibebu. Cetewayo's ambition to extend his sway to its old limits soon involved him in war with this rival chieftain. Within a year he was defeated, and driven into the Reserve, where he surrendered to a British force at Eshowe. There he died in February 1884.

One important consequence of the Zulu War was to emphasise the need of a direct telegraph service to South Africa, hitherto refused on grounds of economy. Cables at that time had to be relayed from St Vincent in the Cape Verde Islands, and communications were accordingly disastrously slow.[1]

Since the annexation of Basutoland to Cape Colony in 1871 the Government had never succeeded in establishing satisfactory control of the territory owing to its failure to support its few officials there. After the Zulu War it was resolved to apply to the Basuto the Disarmament Act, which, as we saw above, had been applied to the Galekas and Fingos.[2] A determined and intelligent people, living in the inaccessible Maluti mountains, the South African Switzerland between Natal and the Free State, the Basuto had that love of independence which is characteristic of a mountain-bred race. Labourers returning from the Diamond Fields had brought with them guns. Thus armed and splendidly mounted, many of them thought that the time was at hand when they would be able to drive the white people into the sea.

Inflamed by exaggerated reports of the disaster of Isandhlwana, which represented the British people as conquered and powerless, the Quthing Chief, Morosi, rose in rebellion in the south of Basutoland.[3] Only after a long and difficult blockade did the Cape troops succeeded in capturing his mountain fastness (November 1879). The Opposition in the Cape Parliament fought strenuously against Sprigg's proposals for the disarmament of the Basuto, and was supported in England by the Aborigines Protection Society and a section of the Radicals, whilst the French Protestant missionaries encouraged the tribesmen not to part with their cherished guns. Lord Kimberley, now once more at the Colonial Office on the accession of the Liberals to power (April 1880), displayed his sympathy with the Basuto by repudiating all responsibility. He acquiesced, indeed, in the use of Colonial forces to compel disarmament; but whilst the imperial troops were strictly forbidden to take part in any operations against the natives,[4] H.M. Government reserved complete liberty of action in

[1] Lord Carnarvon to Sir Stafford Northcote, 23 May 1877, P.R.O., G.D. 6/7, No. 110; *Letters of Queen Victoria*, 2nd Ser., III, 11.

[2] *Vide supera*, p. 481.

[3] *Parl. Pap.* 1878–9, LIII [C. 2318], 1878–9, LIV [C. 2374].

[4] *Parl. Pap.* 1880, LI [C. 2569]. Frere to Sprigg, 21 Oct. 1880, Martineau, II, 380 *sqq.*

any settlement that was made. Sprigg doubled the hut-tax and proposed to confiscate part of Quthing as compensation for the expenses of Morosi's war. Letsie, the Paramount Chief, was willing to obey, but his son, Lerothodi, and others rose in rebellion (September 1880). The rising spread to Griqualand East, the Tembus and other tribes south of the Drakensberg. The war which followed was hampered by divisions among the politicians, and the Basuto emerged from the conflict undeniably victorious. A peace was patched up in April 1881, Sir Hercules Robinson, the successor of Frere as High Commissioner, acting as mediator. The Basuto, indeed, promised to surrender their guns, but actually only a few old muskets were given up and no penalty was exacted for the rebellion.[1] The successful resistance of the Basuto struck a shrewd blow at white prestige in South Africa and was resented accordingly. Sprigg's Government fell. His successor, Thomas Scanlen, endeavoured to make good by denouncing both the Disarmament Act and the Robinson Award. His policy was to settle Quthing and abandon the rest of Basutoland. We shall consider its results in a later chapter.[2]

On the day following the outbreak of the Zulu War, the Transvaalers, assembling in congress at Wonderfontein to hear the report of their delegates who had been to London,[3] entered into a solemn league and covenant to regain their lost independence (13 January 1879).[4] They invited Sir Bartle Frere to meet them in public conference.

The second deputation had met with no better success than the first. Hicks Beach told the delegates plainly enough that British sovereignty would be maintained; but he assured them that the policy of the Government was that the Transvaal should remain an integral and separate State, enjoying self-government and united with the neighbouring colonies, for purposes common to all, into a South African Confederation (16 September 1878).[5] Frere met the delegates at Pietermaritzburg, on their way home, and confirmed the promise of self-government. But for two years the Boers had been waiting for the fulfilment of that promise, whilst Shepstone's autocratic administration, his reticence and procrastination, grew increasingly unpopular and prepared the soil for fruitful agitation.[6] Shepstone was removed, but his successor, Colonel Sir Owen Lanyon, aloof and overbearing, proved still more unsympathetic. Deprived of their Volksraad, which was the symbol of their independence and

[1] *Parl. Pap.* 1881, LXVII [C. 2964].
[2] *Vide infra*, pp. 506, 514 *sqq.*
[3] *Vide supra*, p. 479.
[4] Martineau, II, 284; Leyds, *First Annexation*, p. 243; *Parl. Pap.* 1878–9, LIII [C. 2316].
[5] *Parl. Pap.* 1878–9, LII [C. 2220], p. 366.
[6] Frere to Sir M. Hicks Beach, 2 May 1879, *ap.* Martineau, II, 306, 307; Frere to Lady Frere, 20 April 1879, *ibid.* II, 311, 312.

self-government, the Boers were given no chance during this critical period of settling down as British colonists, while their delegates had learned in England that, however determined the present Government might be never to abandon the sovereignty of the Queen, there was another party which might soon come into power, many of whose supporters were loudly denouncing the annexation. Agitation in the United Kingdom encouraged agitation in the Transvaal. The oscillations of parties at Westminster had already provided disastrous precedents of reversal of policy. In short, the situation gave grounds for refusing to accept the annexation as a *chose jugée* and to make the best of it.[1]

Seeing that the British were in difficulties with the Zulus, and learning from their delegates that Great Britain's hands were full with complications in Europe and Asia,[2] the Boer farmers began to contemplate an appeal to arms. In every farmstead that doctrine was preached. Mothers encouraged their sons, wives their husbands, to act as men or die as patriots. Their predikants assured them that the Lord of Hosts was on their side, for now their leaders would be, not the heretical Burgers as at Steelport, but men of the true puritanical faith.

When, after the victory of Kambula,[3] Frere was at length free to visit the Transvaal, he was met by hundreds of armed Boers at Kleinfontein near Pretoria clamouring for independence. In such surroundings, with the issue of a peaceful settlement or civil war hanging upon his words, Frere entered, coolly and dispassionately, into argument with the Boer leaders at Erasmus Farm (April 1879).

Without yielding an inch on the point of annexation, Frere sketched out a constitution on the lines laid down by Hicks Beach, providing for the immediate creation of an Executive Council and a temporary legislature to prepare the way for a representative Volksraad. He ordered a fuller use of the Dutch language, recognised the use of the Vierkleur, the old Republican flag, and consented to forward to the Queen a petition demanding repeal of the annexation. He took steps to strengthen the administrative service, which he found exceedingly inefficient, and agreed to a survey of a railway line to Delagoa Bay. The repudiation of the contract for constructing this railway had been one of the grievances enunciated in the petitions of the preceding year.[4]

But Frere was not to have the ordering of events in the Transvaal, for at this moment news reached him that he had been censured by the Cabinet for his Zulu policy,[5] and that by Wolseley's commission his own jurisdiction was restricted to the Cape Colony and adjacent

[1] *Parl. Pap.* 1878–9, LIII [C. 2367], p. 18.
[2] *Ibid.* p. 91.
[3] *Vide supra*, p. 488.
[4] Martineau, II, 285–310; *Parl. Pap.* 1878–9, LIII [C. 2367], pp. 84 *sqq.*
[5] *Parl. Pap.* 1878–9, LIII [C. 2260], p. 109; 1878–9, LII [C. 2222], p. 115; 1878–9, LIV [C. 2454], p. 129.

territory. His authority in the Transvaal was gone. The immediate effect was to stimulate the demand for retrocession. Dutch Republicans and Hollanders in Natal and the Cape Colony raised their voices; the Orange Free State Volksraad declared its sympathy with the Transvaal, and the Rev. S. J. Du Toit of Paarl in the Western Province of Cape Colony, an Afrikaner predikant, began to follow up his Afrikaans-speaking campaign by proposals for instituting an anti-British league, the Afrikaner Bond.[1] In such circumstances it was merely beating the air for the British Government to direct Frere to devote himself to the achievement of confederation.[2] Sprigg's Ministry, indeed, was ready to submit proposals to the Cape Parliament for summoning a conference to consider it; but in the following May, Kruger and Joubert visited Cape Town and persuaded their sympathisers not to think of confederation until the wrongs of the Transvaal had been redressed.[3]

Under Lanyon's militaristic rule discontent in the Transvaal increased. The natural aversion of the Boers to paying taxes was increased by their having to pay them to a foreign Government. They continued to arm and pray for retrocession. Wolseley, having defeated and captured Sekukuni,[4] went to Pretoria in December and gave a Crown Colony constitution to the Transvaal, consisting of a nominated Executive Council and Legislative Assembly. Once more he assured the burghers that, so long as the sun shone, the sovereignty of the Queen would be maintained. The Boers, however, were not to be satisfied with anything less than their cherished Volksraad.[5] At a mass meeting held at Wonderfontein in December, they repudiated the sovereignty of the Queen.[6]

In the spring of 1880 Disraeli's Government fell and Gladstone came into power. The Liberal party had gained office largely by denouncing the foreign and imperial policy of the Conservatives in Turkey, Afghanistan and South Africa. Lord Hartington, as Leader of the Opposition, had declared that the annexation of the Transvaal was not a settled question;[7] Gladstone, fulminating in Midlothian, proclaimed that he would repudiate the acquisition of Cyprus and the Transvaal, because they were obtained by means dishonourable to the country.[8] He saw in the Zulu War merely a slaughter of Natives attempting to defend their homes and independence. These speeches were broadcast among the Boers.

[1] *Vide infra*, pp. 518–9; *Parl. Pap.*. 1878–9, LIV [C. 2454], p. 106; Frere to Hicks Beach, 28 August 1879, *ap.* Martineau, II, 346.

[2] Hicks Beach to Frere, 28 May 1879, *Parl. Pap.* 1878–9, LIII [C. 2318], p. 84; 1878–9, LIV [C. 2454], p. 51.

[3] *Parl. Pap.* 1880, LI [C. 2655], pp. 4 *sqq.*; Hofmeyr, *Life of J. H. Hofmeyr*, pp. 170 *sqq.*

[4] *Parl. Pap.* 1880, L [C. 2505], p. 42.

[5] Martineau, II, 362–5.

[6] Carter, *Narrative of the Boer War*, pp. 80–3.

[7] Speech, House of Commons, February 1880, *Hansard*, 3rd Ser., CCL, 92.

[8] Speech, Peebles, 30 March 1880, *The Times*, 31 March 1880.

In anticipation of favours to come, the agitators held their hand. Wolseley thought that the Boers were becoming reconciled to the inevitable.[1] On his advice, troops were withdrawn from South Africa, whilst he himself went home. Kruger and Joubert wrote to Gladstone begging him to satisfy the expectations roused by his Midlothian speeches.[2] Their request was presently backed by many of the new Premier's supporters,[3] but no immediate reversal of policy took place. Frere was continued in office with instructions to promote confederation, and was only recalled (August 12) when it was realised that there was no hope of obtaining it. Queen Victoria disapproved of this step, both as unjust to Sir Bartle and on the principle that it would create the impression that Governors were dependent upon the support of the political party which nominated them. As to the Transvaal, Gladstone replied that the necessity of maintaining order and the obligation contracted towards the Native population rendered it imperative to continue the Queen's supremacy. But a large and liberal system of self-government was once more promised.[4] There was a lull, and then the storm broke. The Boers rose in revolt.

A great meeting held at Paardekraal (Krugersdorp) elected a Triumvirate: Kruger, Pretorius and Joubert, to serve as an executive till the Volksraad resumed its functions. Heidelberg was chosen as a temporary capital, and at Heidelberg, on Dingaan's Day (December 16), the flag of the republic was hoisted. On the same day, Piet Cronje's men opened fire on Major Winsloe's detachment at Potchefstroom.[5] On the 20th, a column of 240 men, sent to reinforce the garrison at Pretoria, was shot to pieces by Joubert in attempting to cross Bronkhorst Spruit.

Sir George Colley, Wolseley's successor, was in a difficult position. He had little over 1000 men at his disposal. He might wait for reinforcements, but there was danger lest, if given time, the rebellion might spread into the neighbouring colonies. Colley decided to check the rising forthwith, and to relieve the scattered British garrisons beleaguered in the Transvaal. Doubtless he underrated the military prowess of the irregular forces he had to meet.

The Boers were a "nation of deerstalkers". Superior in numbers and vastly superior in marksmanship to the British troops, they awaited their advance in well-chosen positions.[6] Colley tried to force his way into the Transvaal from Natal through the pass at Laing's Nek. There on 28 January 1881, and again on 7 February at Ingogo

[1] Sir G. Wolseley to Hicks Beach, 10 April 1880, *Parl. Pap.* 1880, LI [C. 2676], p. 32.

[2] *Letters of Queen Victoria*, 2nd Ser., III, 247–8; Morley, Lord, *Life of Gladstone*, VIII, ch. II.

[3] Carter, *Narrative of the Boer War*, pp. 240, 241.

[4] Queen's Speech, 20 May, 1880, *Hansard*, 3rd Ser., CCLII, 65; Carter, *Narrative of the Boer War*, pp. 94–7; *Letters of Queen Victoria*, 2nd Ser., III, 96, 99.

[5] Leyds, *First Annexation*, pp. 265 *sqq.*; Carter, *Narrative*, pp. 116 *sqq.*

[6] Butler, Sir William, *Life of Sir George Colley;* Carter, *Narrative*, pp. 116 *sqq.*; *Parl. Pap.* 1881, LXVI [C. 2783].

River, Joubert repulsed him after severe fighting.[1] Reinforcements were at hand, but without waiting for them, Colley pushed resolutely on. Still with inadequate forces, he made a second attempt to force Laing's Nek from the west, where the steep and lofty Majuba mountain commands the position. The height was scaled on the night of 26 February. At dawn the Boers, looking up from their encampment below, beheld the British troops on the summit. Expecting to be devastated by shell fire, their first impulse was to retreat; but neither rockets nor gatlings had been brought up, and they decided to attack. They advanced skilfully under cover, swarming up in open order through gullies and undergrowth and firing as they advanced from terrace to terrace. They reached the brow unscathed, for the British troops were badly posted in a cramped position on a mountain top, convex-shaped. Nor did the untrained levies of Afrikaner farmers hesitate to charge when they came face to face in the open. Pouring in a series of murderous volleys, they drove the defenders in headlong flight with a loss of 280 men, killed, wounded and prisoners out of 554. Colley was killed upon the summit,

Majuba, from a military point of view, was a mere incident. Sir Evelyn Wood, with large reinforcements, was ready to retrieve it. Sir Frederick Roberts sailed from England to succeed Colley, but before he arrived, an armistice had been concluded (23 March). The Boers had agreed to disperse to their homes, when they had been guaranteed complete self-government under the suzerainty of the Queen,[2] for Lord Kimberley had opened negotiations before Ingogo, and had instructed Colley to arrange an armistice. Kruger's reply, accepting it, was not received till 7 March after the engagement at Majuba.[3] There were loud demands that the military situation should first be rectified, but the Cabinet, making the fond and frequent British mistake of judging other people by themselves, decided to ignore the Boer victories and to trust to the effect of an act of magnanimity. No doubt they were influenced by the dread of civil war throughout South Africa. Already Free State volunteers were coming to the aid of the Boers; their Volksraad had declared its sympathy with the objects of the Transvaal, and if the Orange Free State were to join the insurgents, their example would probably be followed by a large proportion of the Cape Colony Afrikaners in the endeavour to achieve a "United South Africa, free from British authority".[4]

If Gladstone's Government had restored the independence of the Transvaal Republic immediately after taking office, it might have been an act of wisdom and in just accordance with their criticisms of

[1] *Parl. Pap.* 1881, LXVII [C. 2837].
[2] *Parl. Pap.* 1882, XXVIII [C. 3114], p. 49.
[3] *Parl. Pap.* 1881, LXVII [C. 2837].
[4] Appeal from the Transvaal to the Orange Free State, 19 February 1881, *Parl. Pap.* 1881, LXVII [C. 2866].

their predecessors; but to refuse it at first, and then to concede it after defeat in the field to a people so ignorant of the real strength of Great Britain, had the most untoward results. Its effect was to fill the Boers with contempt for the nation they thought they had conquered. and overweening confidence in their power to push the British into the sea.[1] Loyal British subjects, left to bear the brunt of Boer arrogance, were filled with a bitter sense of humiliation and resentment. Queen Victoria expressed the intense dissatisfaction of a large part of her subjects at home and abroad when she told ministers that disastrous results would follow the humiliation of a peace made on the morrow of defeat.[2]

The terms of settlement were arranged by a Royal Commission acting under instructions from Downing Street. By the preamble of the Convention of Pretoria[3] (3 August 1881), the Transvaal was guaranteed "complete self-government, subject to the suzerainty of Her Majesty", and upon conditions laid down in thirty-two articles. Control of relations with foreign powers was secured by Article II. The boundaries of the Transvaal territory, including the eastern districts, were for the first time clearly defined (Arts. I and XIX). Native interests were carefully protected by a series of Articles (III, XIII–XV, XXI–XXIII), Article III providing that no enactment specially affecting them should have effect without Her Majesty's consent, and Articles XXI–XXIII creating a Native Locations Commission, which was to hold land on their behalf. A British Resident was to perform functions analogous to those of a chargé d'affaires and consul-general (Arts. XVII, XVIII). The independence of the Swazis was recognised (Art. XXIV). The Transvaal State was made liable for the debts of the South African Republic before the annexation and for expenditure since, as well as for compensation for specified damages during the war (Arts. VII–XI). Article XXV prohibited discrimination against British produce or manufactures. Articles XXVI and XXVII safeguarded the rights of persons other than Natives "conforming themselves to the laws of the Transvaal" as to immigration, trading, property, residence and taxation. No provision was made as to their political status; but in the conversations with H.M.'s representatives preliminary to the Convention, Kruger had definitely promised that, as before the annexation, British subjects should enjoy complete freedom of trade and that there should be no difference as to privileges between them and the Boers "so far as burgher rights are concerned", except perhaps "in the case of a young person who has just come into the country".[4]

[1] Reitz, F. W., *A Century of Wrong*, p. 32.

[2] *Letters of Queen Victoria*, 2nd Ser., III, 198, 201–5, 221, 229; Gladstone to the Queen, 12 March, *ibid.* p. 202; Lord Kimberley to the Queen, 17 March, *ibid.* p. 203.

[3] Eybers, G. W., *Select Constitutional Documents relating to S. A.* pp. 455–63.

[4] 10 May 1881; *Parl. Pap.* 1882, XXVIII [C. 3114]; [C. 3219], pp. 25, 53; Carter, *Narrative*, pp. 522–61; Leyds, *First Annexation*, ch. XX.

History would have been very different had he kept that promise in the spirit in which it had been understood by the Commissioners. Without it, the Convention would not have been signed.[1]

Whether the conclusion of peace in the face of defeat was wise or foolish may be an open question. What seems less doubtful is that twice, in little over a year, British statesmen had had the chance of recognising the Transvaal as a self-governing State under the effective paramountcy of the Imperial Government exercised by the High Commissioner acting through a local Agent with definite powers of control, and had twice thrown away that golden opportunity of uniting British and Afrikaners alike, without sacrifice of individuality, in loyal devotion to an Empire State, working cordially both for the good of a united South Africa and of the greater whole. Now the Transvaalers had virtually regained their independence. It remained to be seen how they would use it.

[1] De Villiers, Sir H. J. to President Steyn, 21 May 1899; same to Mr Fischer, 31 July 1899; *Parl. Pap.* 1900, LVI [Cd. 369]; *Milner Papers*, I, 394, 482, Cook, Sir E. T., *Rights and Wrongs of the Transvaal War*.

CHAPTER XIX

POLITICAL DEVELOPMENT, 1872–1886

DURING the fateful last quarter of the nineteenth century, the foreground of South African history is filled by all those issues which arose from the question how men of Dutch and English speech should live together in amity. Certain aspects of this drama now fall to be considered: the political development of Dutch South Africans; the attempts, successful in varying degrees in the several parts of South Africa, but chiefly in the Cape Colony, to guide that development in the direction of co-operation in a common South Africa, and then the progressive hardening of Afrikaner sentiment in hostility to British sentiment. All this fills the foreground; but in the background there is the abiding question of the relations between white man and coloured man. At times, when solid progress has been made towards the attainment of a united European front, that question takes a more prominent place, but for the most part, the gathering conflict between British and Afrikaner obscures men's vision of the more enduring problem, and in the republics and in Natal Native problems advance steadily towards that complexity which has made them issues of life and death for Western civilisation in twentieth-century South Africa.

On 28 November 1872 the Constitution Ordinance Amendment Act, which provided for the introduction of responsible government in the Cape Colony, was promulgated.[1] Next day the names of the new Ministers were published. The Colony's first Prime Minister was John Charles Molteno. Southey, the retiring Colonial Secretary, and William Porter had both declined the proffered honour, the former because the opposition he had tendered to the Colony's constitutional development made it impossible for him to secure the necessary support, the latter on personal grounds; Saul Solomon had put forward impossible conditions.[2] The post therefore fell to Molteno who had fought in season and out of season for responsible government.

The new Prime Minister was a man of honesty, energy and discretion, well fitted to guide the Colony in its new constitutional adventure. He appeased the bitter opposition which had been offered to the change by giving a seat in his Cabinet to one member who had strenuously opposed responsible government, and by providing for the representation of eastern as well as western interests.

Fortune favoured the new Government. The bad times of the

[1] Act No. 1 of 1872. Text in Eybers, G. W., *Select Constitutional Docs. relating to S. A.* p. 63.

[2] *Parl. Pap.* 1873, XLIX [C. 732], p. 141.

'sixties had come to an end; a tide of prosperity was setting in. Agriculture was advancing and the plumage of the ostrich was beginning to yield rich returns; the discovery of diamonds was bringing men and money into the land; there was expansion of trade and an increase in the Colony's revenues. On these foundations the Government hastened to build. It acquired the telegraphs and the sixty-three miles of railway then in existence from their private proprietors, thus establishing in both cases the principle of state-ownership;[1] it arranged for greater speed and regularity in steamship communications between South Africa and Europe; it set about the development of the Colony's very inadequate harbour facilities; it put in hand the construction of bridges over the Orange and the Kei, and in 1874 launched what was, for those days, an ambitious scheme of railway construction into the interior from the ports of Capetown, Port Elizabeth and East London.[2]

One of the first acts of the new Government, and a not inappropriate symbol of the Colony's advancement in political status, was the establishment by Act of Parliament in 1873 of the first university in South Africa, the University of the Cape of Good Hope, a purely examining body with power to confer degrees, which was, however, destined to serve the country well for forty-five years.[3]

On the strictly political side Molteno's policy had two main aims. He stood for the defence and maintenance of the Colony's constitutional privileges, and he sought to end the ancient feud between Easterners and Westerners, which had expressed itself in the constantly recurring agitation for separation. In keeping with the first of these aims was his appointment, when a vacancy occurred in 1873, of his thirty-one-year old Attorney-General, John Henry de Villiers, as Chief Justice, a singularly happy choice which ended the tradition that chief justices must be drawn from oversea. With the second object in view, Molteno recruited his fellow-ministers from all parts of the Colony and held the administrative balance even between East and West; and, in 1874, to remove the old lines of political cleavage, he reconstituted the Legislative Council, hitherto elected on the basis of two great constituencies, East and West, by dividing the Colony into seven circles, each returning three members.[4] At the same time the return of prosperity diverted men's minds into other channels, and so furthered the success of his policy.

Molteno's attitude in relation to the Carnarvon confederation despatch was a natural expression of his general policy.[5] That despatch threatened to revive the provincial feud which Molteno was trying to scotch by providing for the separate representation of East

[1] Acts 15 and 18 of 1872 and 19 of 1874.

[2] Act 19 of 1874.

[3] Act 16 of 1873.

[4] Act 18 of 1874. Text in Eybers, *op. cit.* p. 64.

[5] *Parl. Pap.* 1875, LII [C. 1244], pp. 1 *sqq.*; 1876, LII [C. 1399], pp. 58 *sqq.*

and West at the proposed Conference, and showed a singular lack of appreciation of the Colony's new status, not only by launching a proposal of vital importance to South Africa without prior consultation with its one self-governing British colony, but also by suggesting the names of representatives of both sections of the Colony. Moreover, the propaganda conducted by James Froude, an emissary of the Secretary of State, was definitely opposed to the policy of the Colony's responsible ministers. Molteno's opposition and the results of it have already been described;[1] here it is sufficient to emphasise the significance of his attitude as a vindication of the Colony's constitutional rights.

Molteno was destined to fight yet another battle in the same cause. In 1877 a Kaffir war broke out,[2] and constitutional issues were raised which led to a violent conflict[3] between the ministry and Sir Bartle Frere, who had succeeded Sir Henry Barkly as Governor in March 1877. Molteno, with his Commissioner of Lands and Works, John Xavier Merriman, who was acting virtually as War Minister, maintained that the rebellion in the Ciskei was a matter with which the Colony alone should deal, using its own troops and appointing its own commanding officer. Frere insisted that the imperial General must have control of all the operations in the war on both sides of the Kei, that is, in the Colony's Ciskei and in independent Galekaland, and claimed that, by virtue of his commission as Governor and Commander-in-Chief, he himself was not bound by the advice of Ministers in regard to the command of military forces of any kind. Hence, Molteno tendered his resignation, not for the first time. It was not at first accepted, but a few days later, after the decisive victory of the war had been won, the Governor dismissed his Prime Minister, and summoned J. Gordon Sprigg to succeed him. The action was strictly constitutional and legal in itself, but unparalleled in the annals of responsible government. As if to emphasise its significance as an effective diminution of the Colony's constitutional status, the Secretary of State, Sir Michael Hicks Beach, defended the attitude of the Governor in the matter of the military command on the ground that "in consequence of the peculiar conditions of the colony and the adjacent territories, responsible government, as established at the Cape, has necessarily been made subject to a limitation not elsewhere required".[4]

Molteno had fallen in the defence of the Colony's constitutional privileges; yet when his dismissal came up for discussion at the next session of Parliament, this aspect of the matter received scant attention. Other considerations were allowed to obscure it; the fluidity of parties, which, for lack of clearly defined issues, characterised the Cape House during this period, asserted itself; and, though in 1877

[1] *Vide supra*, pp. 470 *sqq.*
[2] *Vide supra*, pp. 479 *sqq.*
[3] *Parl. Pap.* 1878, LVI [C. 2079], pp. 77 *sqq.*, 90 *sqq.*
[4] *Ibid.* p. 215.

Molteno had enjoyed the support of a considerable majority, in 1878 his dismissal was endorsed by 37 votes to 22 in a House which no election had intervened to change.[1] Clearly the fight for the principle that the Colony was mistress in her own house was not yet won. It was only destined to be carried through to success by the co-operation of men who represented a wider range of public opinion than Molteno had voiced. First it was necessary that the Afrikaans-speaking majority in the Colony should find itself politically and, in alliance with representatives of their English-speaking fellow-colonists, should take up the defence of colonial privileges.

To a very large section of the population the constitutional change which took place in 1872 had been of no immediate significance. At that time most of the Afrikaner colonists were completely out of touch with political activities; indeed their interest in public affairs was practically confined to the hot disputes between orthodoxy and rationalism then raging in the Dutch Reformed Church. To the debates in Parliament, in which in actual fact they had little effective representation, they paid but scant attention, and to them it mattered very little whether they were under a system of representative or of responsible government. Successive systems of government at the Cape since the foundation of the settlement had done little to develop their political consciousness. Lacking responsibility, they lacked interest. Moreover, the progressive anglicisation since 1806 of all public activities operated in the same direction. In Parliament, in the Civil Service, in the courts, in education, English and English alone was recognised. For many of the Afrikaner colonists of those days, who knew but little, if any, English, there was no means of political expression, no organisation, and no inducement to participate in public affairs. Many qualified voters did not trouble to register; those who did register could only with the greatest difficulty be prevailed upon to vote, and in many of the constituencies the idea of putting forward a local candidate hardly seemed to merit consideration. For a great part of the country the three large towns, Capetown, Port Elizabeth and Grahamstown, supplied the parliamentary representatives. So it came about that though the European population of the Colony was to the extent of perhaps two-thirds Afrikaans-speaking, only one-fourth of the Members of Parliament bore Dutch names, and many of those belonged to more or less anglicised families living in the towns.

It was in the eighteen-seventies that this spell of apathy began to be broken. It may be that the grant of responsible government did something to cause a stirring in the dry bones—far more potent, however, were the increased activity of Dutch journalism at that time, and the wave of feeling which spread through the Afrikaans-speaking people of the Colony as a result of the annexations of

[1] *Parl. Pap.* 1878, LVI [C. 2144], p. 196.

Basutoland and the Diamond Fields. In both cases, but more especially the latter, they felt that injustice had been done to their brothers across the Orange. Public affairs at last came to have a meaning and significance for them, and the awakening of Afrikaner national sentiment commenced.[1]

For this new spirit new forms of expression were soon found. In the first instance, however, these were economic and cultural rather than political. In the Eastern Province from 1873 onwards *Boerenvereenigingen*, associations of Dutch farmers, began to be formed. Similar associations had long been in existence amongst the British settlers; now for the first time the Afrikaner farmers began to organise. A few years later an association of wine farmers was launched in the Western Province. Different in character was a movement originally cultural, but soon developing a political bias, which was presently launched at Paarl. In spite of experiments by Louis Meurant, founder of the *Grahamstown Journal*, and a few others, Afrikaans was not yet a literary language. Now, however, in 1872, a campaign was started by Arnoldus Pannevis[2] for the recognition of Afrikaans for literary and other purposes. As long as Dutch, for literary and public purposes, meant the Dutch of Holland, the cultural development of the average South African of Dutch descent, who spoke a language which diverged markedly from it, was very seriously impeded; but if once it were recognised that the language which he spoke could be used for all purposes, an immense extension of his facilities for self-expression would follow. Hence, in 1875, the Rev. Stephanus Johannes du Toit founded "di Genootskap van regte Afrikaners"—the Society of true South Africans, which had as its object "to defend our language, our nation and our people".[3] Among its first activities was the establishment in 1876 of *Di Afrikaanse Patriot*, a newspaper in Afrikaans, which was followed by the issue of several books in that language. In the first instance this movement attained only partial success, but in the fullness of time it was destined to have important cultural results.

Upon these economic and cultural expressions of new vitality there followed an organisation of a more definitely political character. To meet the cost of the Kaffir War, the Sprigg Government, which was predominantly Eastern, submitted to the House in 1878 proposals for additional taxation. One of these provided for an excise of 2*s.* per gallon on colonial brandy. The western wine farmers were stirred to vigorous protest. They secured the reduction of the proposed tax by one-half, but a more important result was the establishment by Jan Hendrik Hofmeyr of a *Boeren Beschermings Vereeniging* (Farmers

[1] These developments can best be studied in the files of the Dutch press at the Cape of this period, notably *De Zuid Afrikaan, De Volksblad, De Volksvriend*, and *Di Patriot*.

[2] *Het Zuid Afrikaansche Tijdschrift*, 1884, pp. 127–8.

[3] Constitution quoted in van Niekerk, L., *De Eerste Afrikaanse Taalbeweging*, p. 4.

Protection Association).[1] The personality and the ideals of its founder were destined to give the foundation of this association great significance in South African history, and to end the mute and expressionless inertia which had until then characterised the Afrikaner colonist.

Hofmeyr belonged to a Dutch family which had farmed in what were then the outskirts of Cape Town since the middle of the eighteenth century. He had played a prominent part in the journalistic activity that had marked the 'sixties, standing forward as a champion of religious orthodoxy, and he himself had joined the staff of *De Volksvriend*, a Dutch newspaper established in 1862 to champion the orthodox view in the religious controversy. He had become its virtual editor at the age of seventeen, and had at length after a most strenuous struggle developed it into a journal of sufficient strength to enable it to absorb the old-established *Zuid Afrikaan* in 1871.

In this and in other ways he won a position of influence and authority. From an early stage he had realised the essential unity of South Africa, and had set himself to work for that ideal. The annexation of the Diamond Fields had stirred him profoundly, since, for the moment, it rendered that ideal the more difficult of attainment, because of the alienation of the hitherto anglophile Free State. He was by temperament too conservative to desire to guide the awakening Afrikaner national sentiment along lines that would disturb the relations between the Colony and Great Britain, but to him the Griqualand West disputes brought home very forcibly the lesson that, for the maintenance of amity within the South African family and for the ultimate attainment of unity, it was essential that the Afrikaners in the Colony should find the means of political expression, so that Afrikaners and British might co-operate on equal terms. So it was that he launched the *Boeren Beschermings Vereeniging* not so much as an organisation to combat a particular tax, but as a means of stimulating the political activity of the Dutch farmer.

The new organisation met with immediate success. At the elections of 1879 several of its candidates were returned. Hofmeyr himself entered Parliament, and at once became leader of the so-called Afrikaner party of Afrikaans-speaking members. Meantime the annexation of the Transvaal had taken place with the result that the Afrikaner national movement entered upon a new phase. In 1879 S. J. du Toit launched in *Di Patriot* a project for the establishment of a new organisation to be called the Afrikaner Bond.[2] This differed from the *Vereeniging* in the greater comprehensiveness of its conception. It was to include within its scope citizens of the two republics as well as of the Colony, and its aim was to be a "united South Africa

[1] Constitution quoted in Appendix to Hofmeyr, J. H., *Life of Jan Hendrik Hofmeyr*, p. 643.

[2] *Di Patriot*, 20 June and 4 July 1879. See also articles from *Di Patriot* reprinted in pamphlet form under the title *De Transvaalse Oorlog* (English translation entitled, *The Birth of the Bond*).

under its own flag". At first the movement hung fire until the Transvaal War of Independence sent a new wave of sentiment sweeping through Dutch-speaking South Africa. The national consciousness was now fully awakened, the sense of national pride embracing republicans and colonists of Dutch speech as members of a single nation was stirred, and the stream started flowing strongly in republican channels. Of this du Toit took full advantage. A large number of branches of the Bond were established in the Colony and in the republics, and the *Vereeniging* was, so it seemed, being left high and dry. The situation was one of real danger for the peace of South Africa.[1] Had the anti-British sentiment engendered by the Transvaal troubles been allowed to find permanent expression in an avowedly separatist and republican organisation such as the Bond was at its inception, the consequences might have been exceedingly serious. This danger Hofmeyr averted. He himself had no sympathy with du Toit's separatist aims. He accepted the position that some day South Africa would stand apart from the Empire; but he believed that there was much to be done before it became practical politics even to contemplate such an ideal, and in the meantime he regarded its proclamation as a serious threat to the peaceful and harmonious development of the Colony. And so, since the *Vereeniging*, owing to the restriction of its objects, could not contend against the Bond, he threw himself into the latter movement, brought about its amalgamation with the *Vereeniging*, and secured the elimination from its constitution of anything that would suggest a separatist tendency, substituting self-dependence for independence as the ideal which it was to pursue.[2] The connection of the Bond in the Cape with branches in the republics was allowed to lapse into desuetude. In itself it came to be simply a party political organisation for the banding together of those whose desire it was that the Afrikaner Colonist should take his rightful place in political life, and that his ideals should make their contribution towards the shaping of colonial policies. At the election of 1884 the Afrikaner Bond sent Hofmeyr back to Parliament as leader of a party of thirty-two in the House, not in itself commanding a majority, but the largest individual section, enabling him, since he repeatedly refused to accept the premiership himself, to act as the maker and unmaker of successive Governments.

It is in the light of the growing influence of the Afrikaner party that the parliamentary history of the Cape Colony during this period can best be understood. The years of the Sprigg Government were

[1] For further study of these events reference should be made to the files of *Di Patriot* and *De Zuid Afrikaan*.

[2] See constitution of Afrikaner Bond (1883) quoted in Hofmeyr, *Life of Jan Hendrik Hofmeyr*, p. 649, also "Programme of Principles of the Afrikander National Party (1889)", *ibid.* p. 652. See also Reports of Annual Congresses of Afrikander Bond most conveniently accessible, together with other relevant documents, in Hofmeyr Collection, S. A. Public Library, Cape Town.

full of difficulty and confusion. The Colony had many troubles of its own, and to these were added the repercussions of events in the Transvaal and in Zululand.[1] Sprigg's position was soon so gravely weakened that only the absence of an organised Opposition and the fluidity of the party system enabled him to carry on. The first serious blow to his prestige was his failure in 1880 to carry a resolution for the summoning of a conference to discuss confederation.[2] For many members confederation had been shorn of its charms by the Zulu War; to the Afrikaner party it implied acquiescence in the annexation of the Transvaal: Kruger, Joubert and Jorissen came down from Pretoria to put their case to their well-wishers at the Cape, and the opposition organised by Hofmeyr was so effective that in the debate the Government accepted the previous question. Shortly afterwards Frere left South Africa, and Sir Hercules Robinson governed in his stead.

This blow to ministerial prestige, upon which followed several defeats sustained on points of detail in connection with its policy of railway extension, encouraged the formation of a regular Opposition; mismanagement in Basutoland provided the material for an attack.[3] At the commencement of the 1881 session a "No Confidence" motion was submitted and received the backing of the Afrikaner party.[4] It was narrowly defeated, but a few days later Sprigg was advised that he no longer had the backing of the Griqualand West members, who had entered the House that session in consequence of the annexation (1880) of their little colony to the Cape. As a result Sprigg tendered his resignation. The spokesmen of the Griqualand West members was Cecil John Rhodes.[5] For the first time Rhodes and Hofmeyr had co-operated towards a common end.

The new Prime Minister was Thomas Scanlen, and among his ministers were Molteno, Merriman and Hofmeyr. Molteno, however, soon retired owing to age, and Hofmeyr also left the Cabinet, mainly because of a dispute with Merriman; but for some time he and his party continued to give the Government the support on which it depended. As a result he was able to make considerable advances towards the satisfaction of the newly awakened Afrikaner national sentiment. In 1882 the Constitution Ordinance was amended so as to permit the use of the Dutch language in addressing either House of Parliament.[6] In that same session provision was also made for the use of Dutch as the medium of instruction in certain grades of schools. In the parliament elected in 1884, where the Afrikaner party was in a still stronger position, a Bill was passed placing Dutch and English

[1] *Vide supra*, pp. 481 *sqq*.
[2] *Parl. Pap.* 1880, LI [C. 2655], pp. 4 *sqq*.
[3] *Vide supra*, p. 490.
[4] *Cape Times*, 12 April 1881, and subsequent days.
[5] Williams, Basil, *Cecil Rhodes*, p. 63.
[6] Act No. 1 of 1882. Text in Eybers, *op. cit.* p. 66.

on an equal footing in magistates' courts,[1] and it was further agreed that all public Bills and other papers should be submitted to the House in both languages. Still later a substantial advance was made in the direction of requiring a knowledge of Dutch for appointment to most posts in the Civil Service. Nevertheless, the form of Dutch for which recognition was thus secured was the Dutch of Holland, not Afrikaans, for Hofmeyr was in by no means complete sympathy with the cultural ideals of Pannevis and du Toit.

The co-operation between Scanlen and the Afrikaner party did not last long. The breach came on a matter raising issues far wider than its immediate significance. The Scanlen Government had attained a considerable measure of success in the administration of the Colony, but as the wartime boom spent itself, the clouds of depression had gathered. There was a set-back in the prosperity of the Diamond Fields caused by extensive falls of rock which made small-scale mining impossible; a considerable shrinkage in population resulted. The Colony's agricultural industry had to endure the attacks of drought and disease. It was a measure taken by the Government in dealing with one of those diseases, phylloxera, which, technically, led to its fall;[2] the real cause was, however, its alienation of the Afrikaner party by its Basutoland policy.

Repeated failures in Basutoland, the resultant loss of prestige, and the Colony's financial difficulties induced Scanlen in 1883 to fall back on the policy of retrocession to the Imperial Government. He followed this up by announcing his intention of asking Downing Street to annex the Transkeian territories as well.[3] On this issue the Afrikaner party definitely broke with the Government. The reintroduction of the Imperial Government as a direct governing factor in lands hitherto within the Colony or on its borders was obviously in conflict with the Bond's ideal of colonial self-dependence. This policy of colonialism, as it came to be called, was based on a ready acceptance of the imperial connection with all its privileges and obligations, but also on the principle that the affairs of the Colony should, as far as possible, be settled in the Colony, and that if external assistance were required for the solution of South African problems, such assistance should not be sought overseas, but in South Africa itself by co-operation with the other South African communities. It was a policy with which many British colonists found themselves heartily in accord; hence, after an election fought mainly on the cession of the Transkei, Scanlen met the new House and found himself faced not merely with an enlarged and consolidated Afrikaner party, but also with a considerable British opposition. He therefore took the first opportunity of resigning. Hofmeyr declined to form a ministry lest Afrikaner

[1] Act No. 21 of 1884. This and similar legislation is given in Eybers, *op. cit.* pp. 133 *sqq.*
[2] *Cape Hansard, Legislative Assembly*, 1884, pp. 12 *sqq.*
[3] *Parl. Pap.* 1883, XLVIII [C. 3708], pp. 3, 22, 37.

rule should consolidate the British elements in the House against it and thus deepen the racial cleavage. Rather than that, he lent the support of the Afrikaner party to Thomas Upington, whose ministry took office with the declaration that its policy was to assume control of the dependencies on the Colonial borders, to exercise fully its rights of self-government, and to resist anything that would reduce the Colony's liberties by subjecting the management of its internal affairs to outside control.[1]

At a very early stage these principles were challenged in spirit, if not in letter, by the incidents which led to the acquisition of Bechuanaland by the Imperial Government. These events are recounted elsewhere;[2] here it is only necessary to refer to their reactions on Cape political developments. Two things are important. Firstly, these events led to an extension of direct imperial rule in South Africa, with which the policy of colonialism was clearly in conflict. The establishment of the two small republics of Stellaland and Goshen[3] in what is now Bechuanaland raised the question of the control of the route of northward expansion. The recent Convention of London ruled out the possibility of its annexation by the South African Republic.[4] The Imperial Government was disposed to favour direct imperial control. Hofmeyr and Upington, on the contrary, wanted annexation to the Colony, and the Cape House in its 1884 session accepted this in principle.[5] But the developments in Bechuanaland and especially the folly of S. J. du Toit, now a member of Kruger's Government, in hoisting the republican flag there in defiance of the Convention, caused a storm. If the annexation of the Transvaal had stirred Afrikaner colonial sentiment, the retrocession had left its mark on British colonial sentiment, a mark which had been deepened by the success of the Bond in stimulating Afrikaner national consciousness. Now, as a result of the incidents in Bechuanaland, an Imperial League was founded as a counterweight to the Bond, and a strong appeal was made for imperial military intervention with the scarcely concealed hope that the opportunity would be taken to "avenge Majuba". The result was the Warren expedition, the imperial annexation of British Bechuanaland, the extension of a Protectorate over the rest of the huge territory and a further blow to the policy of colonialism.[6]

The Bechuanaland episode had an even further-reaching effect on Cape politics in another way. It marked an important stage in the political development of Cecil Rhodes. He had followed Livingstone, Arnot and Mackenzie in urging the necessity of keeping open the road to the north.[7] Through Robinson he had secured the

[1] *Cape Hansard, Legislative Assembly*, 1884, pp. 20, 21.
[2] *Vide infra*, pp. 523 *sqq.*
[3] *Vide supra*, p. 523.
[4] *Vide infra* p. 521.
[5] *Cape Hansard, Legislative Assembly*, 1884, pp. 342 *sqq.*; *Parl. Pap.* 1886, XLVIII [C. 4643].
[6] *Parl. Pap.* 1884–5, LVII [C. 4432]; 1886, XLVIII [C. 4643].
[7] *Vide infra*, pp. 522 *sqq.*

insertion of a provision in the London Convention blocking the Transvaal's westward expansion. Though at first favouring the annexation of Bechuanaland to the Colony, he now showed himself not averse from imperial intervention, and he was one of those who pressed for the despatch of the Warren expedition. Later developments, however, were by no means to his taste. Warren's settlement aroused his bitter hostility and made him one of the foremost champions of colonialism, one of the most persistent in the demand that "the Imperial factor must be eliminated".[1] As he himself put it in 1887, though he had come down to the House in 1881 "a most rabid Jingo", he had since "passed through the fire of Bechuanaland".[2]

So then the stage was set for the co-operation of Hofmeyr and Rhodes. The representative of an organisation which had once threatened to become an anti-British separatist republican movement had drawn near to Rhodes, the "regular, beefsteak, John Bull Englishman",[3] the man who in his first will had bequeathed his fortune yet unmade for the extension of British rule throughout the world.[4] They had met on the common platform of colonialism, whose main planks were self-dependence and hearty co-operation between all colonists, whether of British or of Afrikaner descent.

Bechuanaland did not merely convert Cecil Rhodes; it also converted the High Commissioner. In 1883 Sir Hercules Robinson had pressed for imperial interference in Bechuanaland, and next year had shown so little regard for his responsible ministers at the Cape that, without consulting them, he had appointed Rhodes as Special Commissioner in Bechuanaland, although he had been a member of the Cabinet which they had just displaced. But in 1889 he was to declare publicly that of the three competing influences in South Africa—colonialism, republicanism, imperialism—imperialism was a vanishing quantity, "there being now no permanent place in South Africa for Imperial control on a large scale".[5]

The Hofmeyr-Rhodes alliance did not take concrete form immediately, for in the next few years Rhodes played but a small part in Cape politics. The difficulties attendant on the amalgamation of the diamond-mining enterprises, participation in the launching of the gold-mining industry on the Witwatersrand, and his attempts to gain a footing in Zambesia kept him fully occupied. Hofmeyr on his side was content to co-operate with Upington, "the Afrikaner from Cork", and from 1886, after a reshuffling of the Cabinet, with Sprigg. These were years of steady progress in the Colony. The financial depression gradually spent itself; the discovery of gold

[1] "Vindex", *Cecil Rhodes, His Political Life and Speeches*, pp. 66, 153.

[2] *Ibid.* p. 153. See also Speech at 1891 Afrikaner Bond Congress, *ibid.* pp. 265 *sqq.*

[3] See speeches of Hofmeyr and Rhodes, quoted in Hofmeyr, *op. cit.* p. 376.

[4] Quoted in Michell, *Life of Cecil Rhodes*, I, 68.

[5] Quoted in "Vindex", *Cecil Rhodes, His Political Life and Speeches*, p. XXXI in greater detail.

inaugurated an era of prosperity.[1] Agriculture prospered and, as the price of the support which the Government received from the Afrikaner party, a policy of agricultural protection was steadily pursued to which Rhodes gave his blessing.[2] Moreover, the racial passions which had been aroused in 1881 and again in 1884 were allayed, and with the support of the Government of the Colony and the backing Sir Hercules Robinson received in London, the policy of colonialism, as far at least as the Cape was concerned, definitely prevailed.

We must now consider the extent to which similar progress was made elsewhere in South Africa and the measure of success attained by that policy in the sphere of inter-state relationships. In Natal the advance along the path of political progress was at first exceedingly slow. The grant of responsible government to the Cape and the subsequent growth of the sense of colonial self-dependence produced little effect in the sister colony. Natal's relative imperviousness to influences emanating from its neighbours was due primarily to physical isolation, for she was sundered from the rest of South Africa either by mountains or by an almost solid block of tribal peoples, and her means of intercommunication were of the poorest. Again, Natal's European population was still very small. In 1873 it amounted to 18,000, as against some 280,000 Bantu. The little colony with its superabundant Native population and the powerful Zulu kingdom overshadowing its eastern frontier had not proved attractive to European capital, and there was a measure of justification for Merriman's acid description of Natal as a white forwarding agency in a native location. It is no wonder that there the plant of colonialism was of slow growth, or even that Natal was ready reluctantly to accept the curtailment of her constitutional liberties.

In 1873, as we saw in the previous chapter, on the colony's western border, a section of the Hlubi tribe, under the Chief Langalibalele, broke out into rebellion arising from the failure of some of the tribesmen to register guns they had acquired at the Diamond Fields.[3] Though at one time this outbreak threatened to kindle an extensive Native war, it was suppressed without any very great difficulty. The manner of its suppression, however, and the severity of the penalties meted out to the rebels did not receive the approval of the Imperial Government. The Lieutenant-Governor, Sir Benjamin Pine, was recalled, and Sir Garnet Wolseley was sent out in 1875 as Administrator to inaugurate a new Native policy.[4] In the event the main feature of his policy proved to be a change in the constitution of the Legislative Council. It is remarkable evidence both of his prestige and of his

[1] *Vide infra*, pp. 526, 537 *sqq*.
[2] "Vindex", *Cecil Rhodes, His Political Life and Speeches*, p. 139.
[3] *Vide supra*, p. 464; *Parl. Pap.* 1874, XLV [C. 1025]; LIII [C. 1121] and [C. 1158].
[4] *Parl. Pap.* 1875, LIII [C. 1187], pp. 5 *sqq*.

diplomatic skill, that he persuaded the Legislative Council, which had hitherto consisted of five officials and fifteen elected members and had, in 1874, actually voted for responsible government, to pass a Bill adding eight nominated members to its number for five years.[1]

The year 1875 was, however, to mark a turning-point in Natal's history. In that year, following on the resumption of the importation of Indian coolies, a policy of railway construction and harbour improvement was decided upon,[2] which increased the European population substantially. Immigration, too, was effectively encouraged by the financial boom brought about by the Zulu and Transvaal Wars, but in the political sphere advance continued to be slow. In 1880 the Legislative Council again petitioned for responsible government. It secured no more than a reversion to the pre-Wolseley constitution, and an intimation that the grant of responsible government would mean that the colony would have to provide for its own defence.[3] At an election held in 1882 the colonists, who frankly wanted the privileges without the responsibilities of an enhanced political status, decided against responsible government on such terms.

The increasing trade with the interior, however, and the resultant questions of customs duties and railway communication brought home to Natal its membership of the South African family, and turned its thoughts in the direction, at least, of closer co-operation. It is significant that in 1884 a conference was held at Harrismith between representatives of Natal and of the Orange Free State to discuss matters of common interest.[4]

During this period the Free State offered rather more evidence than did isolated and imperialistic Natal of an approach towards a broad South African sentiment based on the conception of self-dependence. Always closely associated with the Cape by tradition and ever ready hitherto to move towards the goal of South African unity, it had been diverted towards isolationist republicanism by successive conflicts with British imperial policy in Basutoland, Griqualand West and the Transvaal. But the Free State was fortunate in the wise leadership of President Brand. It was possible for him to contend that the annexation of Basutoland and the Diamond Fields had relieved the republic of the difficulties of administering an unruly digger community, and had moreover tremendously simplified its Native problem in that it alone among the South African States had no great preponderance of tribal inhabitants. Brand could represent the retrocession of the Transvaal as in large measure cancelling the annexation, while the advance of the Afrikaner party to authority at the Cape and the breadth of view which had come to characterise Sir Hercules Robinson's policy could

[1] Law No. 3 of 1875, quoted in Eybers, *op. cit.* p. 199.
[2] Law No. 4 of 1875.
[3] *Parl. Pap.* 1882, XLVII [C. 3174].
[4] *Natal Legislative Council, Sessional Papers*, 1884, No. 1.

be noted as offering inducements to co-operation. The extension of the colonial railways virtually to the borders of the republic, to Colesberg in 1884 and to Kimberley and Aliwal North in 1885, gave tangible evidence of the value of such co-operation. To all this was added the consideration that, whereas the Cape had hitherto retained the whole of the customs duties on goods in transit to the Free State, a policy of active co-operation must lead to the recognition of the republic's claim to a rebate which had been put forward time and again since 1854. There was thus no lack of willingness on the part of the southern republic to contribute towards the realisation of that ideal of a united South Africa of which Cape colonialism was a local manifestation.

In the northern republic on the other hand the position was different. There, not unnaturally, the feelings aroused by the annexation were more bitter than anywhere else; there the desire to co-operate with colonies under British rule was least likely to be displayed. The Convention of Pretoria had in large measure restored the liberties taken away in 1877, but it had not done so completely; and though the Convention of London undoubtedly allayed some of the bitter feelings, it brought no modification in the policy of which Paul Kruger had come to be the chief exponent.

Kruger had risen steadily to be the leading figure in the political life of the Transvaal. When in the reaction from the Keate Award[1] President Pretorius had resigned, the Rev. Thomas François Burgers, a clergyman of the Dutch Reformed Church in the Cape Colony and a man of considerable intellectual ability and high idealism, had been chosen as his successor. Burgers was one of the early exponents of the doctrine of a united South Africa from the Cape to the Zambesi, for he saw clearly the importance of the mineralised Transvaal in the greater South Africa of which he dreamed, a South Africa in which all civilised men were to enjoy equal rights. So Burgers had embarked with vigour and enthusiasm upon the task of fitting his republic for the rôle which he held it to be destined to play. Educational and administrative reforms had been introduced into the republic,[2] and the scheme of a railway from Delagoa Bay was launched.[3] Burgers's schemes failed because he did not take sufficient account of the characteristics of the people whom he had been called upon to rule. He lost sight of their essentially slow-moving conservatism and of fissiparous tendencies which had not yet lost their power.

Failure to appreciate these facts produced the inevitable consequences. Burgers's new ideas, too precipitately introduced, provoked first criticism, then opposition, and then, in accordance with

[1] *Vide supra*, p. 457.
[2] S. A. Republic, Law No. 4 of 1874.
[3] *Z. A. Republiek, Staatscourant*, 14 January 1873; Volksraads Besluit of 16 November 1874 (*De Locale Wetten der Z. A. Republiek*, p. 603).

Transvaal tradition, well-nigh open revolution. Nor was it forgotten that Burgers had been one of the leaders of the Liberals in the theological disputes of the Cape Dutch Reformed Church. Theologically, perhaps, even more than in any other respect, the Transvaal Boer was steadfastly conservative. Paul Kruger, who was the champion of the straitest theological sect as well as one of those who had been most prominent in the Transvaal's earlier political history, naturally enough became the leader of the anti-Burgers opposition.

Kruger had come to the front yet more prominently as popular leader during the period of British occupation, and when the old Volksraad had been reconstituted and the re-establishment of the republic proclaimed, he, Pretorius and Commandant-General Joubert were appointed as a Triumvirate to administer its affairs.[1] The campaign of Majuba had been the result, and the retrocession of the Transvaal. It was Kruger who had been the main motive force in the resistance which had been offered; it was Kruger who played the chief part in the subsequent negotiations, and so when in 1883 the Triumvirate gave way to a President, it was he who naturally and inevitably was elected to that post.

The keynote of Kruger's policy, equally naturally, was the determination to regain completely the republic's independence, which he had fought so hard to secure. For that reason he would have as little as possible to do with the British colonies in South Africa. The willingness of the leaders of the Cape Afrikaner party to acquiesce in their position within the Empire, and their opposition to the original separatism of the Bond, rendered them suspect in his view. Between his temperament and Hofmeyr's there was a fundamental incompatibility. So then his thoughts came to run definitely on lines counter to a wider South African policy. The men of education whom he required for the administration of his State he sought not from amongst the Afrikaners at the Cape or the Free State, but in Holland and Germany; for the rest the ideal which he set himself to realise was that of a single Afrikaner republic spreading northwards from the Orange, separated from the British colonies by a ring-fence, political and economic, and making contact with the outside world, not through British ports, but in the first instance by way of Delagoa Bay, and later through a Transvaal port on the east coast which he was determined to acquire. The South Africanism of Kruger took account of the Afrikaner element only—all who did not belong to it could never become South Africans. And so tariffs were imposed upon colonial produce,[2] monopolies were given to concessionaires with a view to the establishment of factories that would make his republic "economically independent", and the construction of a railway to Lourenço Marques

[1] *Parl. Pap.* 1881, LXVI [C. 2794], pp. 3 *sqq.*

[2] *De Locale Wetten, Volksraadsbesluiten*, 21 and 22 October 1881; *Z. A. Republiek, Staatscourant*, 11 October and 1 November 1881.

was actively pressed. In 1883 the Portuguese had given a concession to Colonel Edward McMurdo, a United States citizen, to build a railway from the port to the frontier; next year Kruger extended to a syndicate mainly financed in Holland and Germany the monopoly of railway construction within the Transvaal's borders.[1]

Yet, strangely enough, it was from Kruger that the first move towards South African economic co-operation came. To this he was driven by the severe set-backs which his policy sustained. The railway project advanced all too slowly; MacMurdo got into difficulties; the syndicate was inert. The sense of isolation increased within the republic. The post-war slump, with the restriction of credit and the decline in property values, hit it severely; the debt with which it had been saddled by the Pretoria Convention, even after it had been reduced by the Convention of London, crippled its finances; there were renewed troubles in Sekukuni's country, and a war lasting almost a year against the Mapoch tribes (1882–3); the development of the Lydenburg goldfields and of those which had been discovered in 1882 in the Kaap valley further south (soon to be known as the Barberton area) was hanging fire for lack of railway communication; marketing facilities for the produce of the farmers were inadequate. Kruger's policy seemed to have brought no good to the republic, and he himself became increasingly unpopular. And so, with almost dramatic suddeness, he telegraphed to the Cape Government on 30 July 1885 the enquiry, "How about the Customs Union? Is there no chance that we take off the duty on colonial brandy and colonial-made waggons, and you the duty on our tobacco?"[2] At the beginning of 1886 the enquiry was repeated, together with a suggestion that the Cape railways should be extended from Bloemfontein to Pretoria.

It was an opportunity which the Cape Colony might have been expected to seize with eagerness. As early as 1884 the Bond, under Hofmeyr's inspiration, had declared for a South African Zollverein on the lines of the Prussian Zollverein, which had become the German Empire, as the one immediately practicable step towards closer co-operation.[3] Rhodes, too, had urged the same idea, and the Imperial Government had furnished a precedent by insisting that the Cape should pay Basutoland its fair share of customs receipts. It was of importance on other grounds that the Colony should settle its ancient customs dispute with the Free State.[4] The competition of the low Natal tariffs was beginning to be felt, and in 1884 the Cape Parliament had accepted as a professedly temporary measure a proposal to make a rebate to Free State merchants to the extent of the difference between the Cape and the Natal tariffs.[5] For this problem also the

[1] *Parl. Pap.* 1890, LI [C. 5903], pp. 19 *sqq.*
[2] *Cape Parl. Pap.* 1886 [1342], pp. 1, 4.
[3] See Report of Graaff-Reinet Congress of Afrikander Bond (Provinciale Bestuur).
[4] See Article 8 of Bloemfontein Convention of 1854.
[5] *Cape Hansard, Legislative Assembly*, 1884, pp. 283 *sqq.*

establishment of a South African Customs Union offered a permanent solution. Unhappily, the Upington Government, hard pushed for money and blind apparently to the significance of the Transvaal's overtures from the point of view of South African co-operation, after long delay rebuffed the Transvaal in the matter both of railways and of customs.

Meanwhile the South African Native problem was taking definite shape. In 1872 there had still been great masses of Natives not under European control within the limits of the future Union of South Africa. The Native problem was constantly in men's minds, but it was regarded almost entirely as a problem of defence. For the most part, the policy followed in Native affairs was one of drift; in the Cape Colony alone was real progress made, and that largely as a result of the co-operation between British and Afrikaners which the Hofmeyr-Rhodes alliance represented.

In general terms the Cape policy during this period may be said to have been a development of that initiated by Sir George Grey,[1] whose chief aims were the assumption of responsibility by the Government for all Native peoples up to the Natal border, the positive encouragement of these peoples to advance along the path of civilisation partly by planting Europeans in their midst and, more directly, by substituting the authority of magistrates for that of the Chiefs. One serious set-back, however, the Cape experienced in carrying out its policy. That was in Basutoland.

In 1871 the Cape Parliament had agreed to take over the territory which Sir Philip Wodehouse had annexed.[2] It proceeded to administer it in anticipation of the system to be developed later in the Transkei, not as a corporate part of the Colony, but as a distinct administrative area to which colonial law did not apply. At the same time it followed the broad lines of the Grey policy by encouraging civilisation through the development of the magisterial system.[3] These two features taken together constitute an anticipation of the policy now known as differentiation in contradistinction to the policy of identity, which had hitherto prevailed at the Cape, the underlying conception of the policy of differentiation being that the Native should not be Europeanised, but be encouraged to advance by development along the lines of his own distinctive characteristics. In conception the Cape policy as pursued in Basutoland was sound, but the replacement of the chief's authority by that of the magistrate should have been more gradual, and too little account was taken of certain fundamental features in the structure of Bantu society. Discontent gathered

[1] *Vide supra*, pp. 403 *sqq*, and see Despatch of Sir George Grey, dated 22 December 1854 in *Further Papers relating to the Kaffir tribes*, *Parl. Pap.* 1854–5, XXXVIII [C. 1969], p. 38.

[2] Act No. 12 of 1873, quoted in Eybers, *op. cit.* p. 61.

[3] See Reports of Governor's Agent in Basutoland and of Resident Magistrates in successive issues of the Cape *Bluebook on Native Affairs*.

and at length the storm broke, when, after the suppression of a rebellion of the border chief, Morosi, the Sprigg Government in 1880 decided to apply to Basutoland the Peace Preservation Act (No. 4 of 1879). This had been passed, as a result of the general tribal unrest then prevailing, in order to enforce the surrender of the guns which had been acquired mainly on the Diamond Fields. The resistance of the Basuto was unexpectedly effective.[1] The war dragged on, a large number of burghers, weary of the lengthening struggle, deserted, and when a few of the Chiefs indicated their willingness to submit, the Government gladly availed itself of the offer of Sir Hercules Robinson to issue an award for the settlement of the dispute.[2] That award imposed a fine of cattle on the Basuto, but allowed them to retain their guns subject to registration and payment of a licence fee. The trouble, however, was not yet at an end. Many of the tribesmen failed to register their weapons, and the Scanlen Government, recognising in the light of the experience of its predecessor that it would be exceedingly difficult to enforce the award with colonial troops, decided in 1882 on the policy of recalling both the disarmament proclamation and the award,[3] and simply maintaining in Basutoland a force strong enough to support the authority of the magistrates. That policy also having failed, the Government early in 1883[4] decided to withdraw its magistrates, and to be represented merely by a Governor's Agent with a Native Council of Advice. By this time colonial prestige had been sorely shaken; the Basuto would have none of this new scheme, and in despair the Government arranged to hand over Basutoland to the imperial authorities, and to pay towards the cost of its administration a sum not exceeding £20,000 annually in lieu of customs duties collected by it.[5] That arrangement took effect in 1884, and thus ended an episode which had seriously weakened the prestige of the European colonist in the eyes of a section of the Native peoples, and had introduced, as a complication of the Native problem of the future, the factor of direct imperial rule in an important tribal territory in the very heart of South Africa.

Elsewhere, however, the Colonial Government was more successful. In 1877 the so-called Ninth Kaffir War broke out as a result of quarrels between Galekas and Fingos east of the Kei. At first the outbreak was confined to the Galekas under Kreli and was, so it seemed, speedily crushed. There was, however, a recrudescence of the trouble. Some of the Tembus joined Kreli; Gaika tribes under Sandile within the Colonial boundaries went into rebellion, and

[1] *Parl. Pap.* 1881, LXVI [C. 2755], [C. 2821]; LXVII [C. 2964]; 1882, LXVII [C. 3112]; 1883, XLVIII [C. 3493], [C. 3708].

[2] *Parl. Pap.* 1881, LXVII [C. 2964], p. 20. See also *Cape Parl. Pap.* 1881, A. 44.

[3] *Parl. Pap.* 1882, XLVIII [C. 3112], p. 129.

[4] *Parl. Pap.* 1883, XLVIII [C. 3708], pp. 1 *sqq.*

[5] For Order-in-Council, see *Parl. Pap.* 1905, LV (130), pp. 5–6; quoted in Newton, A. P., *Unification of South Africa*, I, 92.

though Kreli was crushed in a battle fought near Kentani in February 1878, the rebellion dragged on until July.[1] That war led to the first step in the carrying out of what had been Grey's policy of extending the direct authority of the colony over the Transkeian peoples. In 1879 Fingoland and the Idutywa district were formally annexed, and Galekaland, though not annexed, came to be administered to all intents and purposes as if it had been. It was indeed grouped with the other two areas to form the chief magistracy of the Transkei.[2]

Colonial authority was also extended to the northward in what were coming to be known as Tembuland and Griqualand East. In Griqualand East or Nomansland, Adam Kok had surrendered his authority in 1875. By 1877 seven colonial magistrates had been appointed in the area between the Umzimkulu and the Umtata Rivers, the Drakensberg and Pondoland. Technically they were little more than agents with the tribal Chiefs, but in 1879 their position was regularised by the annexation of Griqualand East to the Colony as a distinct chief magistracy. As for Tembuland, colonial authority had been established over the greater part of the territory in 1876; after the war of 1877–8 it was extended over Bomvanaland and Emigrant Tembuland, and a chief magistracy of Tembuland was created. It was, however, not formally annexed, but remained in the same position as Galekaland.[3]

It was not until the Upington Government assumed office in 1884, and announced as its policy the assumption of definite control over the dependencies beyond the colonial borders, that a further advance was made. In 1884 the Cape annexed the portion of Pondoland in the immediate vicinity of the mouth of the Umzimvubu at Port St Johns;[4] in 1885 it also annexed Tembuland and Galekaland,[5] and in 1886 it formally added the district of Mount Ayliff on the borders of Pondoland to Griqualand East.[6] Save for Pondoland, the boundary of the Cape now marched with that of Natal. Though a British protectorate over the Pondoland coast had been proclaimed in 1885,[7] Pondoland itself remained independent for a season; but disturbances on the frontiers and internal anarchy made it an awkward neighbour. For some time there was a question whether it should be annexed to Natal or the Cape, but Rhodes's view prevailed and with the consent of the Pondo chiefs it became Cape territory in 1894.[8]

Of greater significance than the annexation of the Transkeian Territories, whose three chief magistracies were in 1891 regrouped

[1] *Parl. Pap.* 1878, LV [C. 1961], pp. 66 *sqq.*; [C. 2000]; LVI [C. 2079], [C. 2144].

[2] Act 38 of 1877; Governor's Proclamation No. 110 of 15 September 1879. See also *Bluebook on Native Affairs* (Cape), 1879; 1884, p. viii.

[3] *Bluebook on Native Affairs* (Cape), 1884, pp. ix, x, xii.

[4] Act 35 of 1884.

[5] Act 3 of 1885.

[6] Act 37 of 1886.

[7] *Parl. Pap.* 1885, LVI [C. 4590], pp. 15 *sqq.*

[8] *Cape Parl. Pap.* S. 9 of 1894 and 8 of 1895.

as two, and in 1902 united under a single officer, was the system of government applied to this almost exclusively tribal area. The governing principle of this system was the differentiation to which we have already referred.[1] The Territories were not absorbed within the administrative system of the Colony. The Governor-in-Council became the normal legislative authority, which meant legislation by proclamation, Parliament retaining merely the right of veto. Acts of Parliament did not apply unless expressly stated. With a wise gradualness the magistrates took the place of the Chiefs. In terms of the admirable Report of the Native Laws and Customs Commission of 1883,[2] Native civil law was recognised and administered without being codified and a Transkeian Penal Code was drawn up. Agricultural development was encouraged and the practice of constant public consultation with Natives was instituted. In general what was aimed at was a "unique progressive policy, adapting itself to the varied stages of advancing civilisation". Thus was the way prepared for Rhodes's Glen Grey Act of 1894, which is dealt with in a later chapter.[3]

[1] *Vide supra*, p. 514.
[2] *Report of Commission of Native Laws and Customs*, *Cape Parl. Pap*. G. 4 of 1883.
[3] *Vide infra*, p. 558.

CHAPTER XX

THE RACE FOR THE INTERIOR, 1881–1895

THE retrocession of the Transvaal after the victory of the "embattled farmers" made a nation out of a caste. It not only intensified national sentiment among the burghers of the Boer republic, but spread it among Afrikaans-speaking inhabitants of all classes from Cape Point to the Limpopo, from the banks of the Tugela to the wilds of Damaraland. It stimulated the growth of the Young Afrikaner Party, whose ideal was a United South Africa "under our own flag".[1]

Much of the inspiration of this movement came from the Afrikaner Bond, which, as we saw in the last chapter, had been founded in 1879 by the Rev. S. J. du Toit, a minister of the Dutch Reformed Church at Paarl.[2] The idea was taken up with enthusiasm in the Cape Colony; but it met with less success in the Transvaal, partly because there its ideals had been to a great extent achieved, and partly because Kruger, soon to be President, regarded with suspicion and dislike any division of authority. In the Free State it was discouraged by the wiser statesmanship of the President, Jan Brand, and J. G. Fraser,[3] member of the Volksraad for Bloemfontein; but there it found support in a Judge, F. W. Reitz, who had been educated in Cape Town and London, and the German editor of a local paper, Carl Borckenhagen.[4]

The object of the Bond, as expounded by them, was the establishment of a Federated Afrikaner Republic and the expulsion of the "English usurper" by arms and the aid of foreign Powers, by boycotting English people and English trade, and by the assertion of the Afrikaans language.[5] Its main effect would be, as J. X. Merriman declared, "to make the Transvaal Republic the paramount Power".[6] These extreme views were modified according to time and place as expediency demanded, and as racial and political animosity waxed or waned. Thus, in the Cape Colony, under the controlling influence of J. H. Hofmeyr, the Bond assumed a constitutional and parliamentary aspect, and was used more and more as a weapon in party politics. Hofmeyr recognised that the independence of South Africa was at the mercy of any Power which held the command of the sea; he therefore had no hope that the ideal of a United South Africa, from which the

[1] *Vide supra*, pp. 495, 501 *sqq*.
[2] *De Transvaalse Oorlog*, 1881.
[3] Fraser, Sir J. G., *Episodes in my Life*, pp. 76–82.
[4] *Bloemfontein Express*, 7 April 1881; Theophilus Schreiner, *Cape Times*, 5 November 1899.
[5] Thomas, C. H., *The Origin of the Anglo-Boer War revealed*, pp. 64 *sqq*.
[6] Speech at Grahamstown, January 1885, quoted Michell, *Life of Rhodes*, I, 229.

power of Great Britain should be eliminated, could be immediately realised. He disliked, too, the prospect of the domination of the Transvaal by such men as Kruger and Joubert; nor had he any desire to substitute German for British dominion. Extremists, however, kept the original end in view, though among the rank and file of easy-going Afrikaner Colonial farmers the Bond meant little, except when some bone of contention over the Transvaal or treatment of Natives roused racial feeling.

The Boers of the Transvaal paid little heed to the boundaries fixed by the Pretoria Convention, or to the article which reserved to the suzerain Power the control of dealings with Natives outside them.[1] Unchecked by their Government, which was hardly able, even if willing, to restrain them, they trekked in search of new farms across the borders eastwards, and from 1882 onwards they penetrated into Zululand at the invitation of Dinizulu, son of Cetewayo, took up land for farming and, in due time, founded the New Republic there. On the western frontier in Bechuanaland, they fomented the quarrels of rival Batlapin and Barolong chiefs, and were rewarded with grants of land by those whom they supported. Other European adventurers, from the Diamond Fields and elsewhere, took the opposite side. The whole country was kept in a ferment. Mankorwane and Montsiwa sought British aid; Masau and Moshete that of the Transvaalers. By the end of 1882 the two former had been worsted, and the Boer supporters of their successful rivals carved out of their territory lands in which they set up two little republics named Stellaland and Goshen straddling the Missionaries' Road to the north.[2]

Thus, east and west, the expansion of the Transvaal had begun. It threatened to hem in Natal on its eastern side and to cut the Cape Colony off from the Missionaries' Road, the only trade route to the north and the interior, for already the protection of the Transvaal was being invited by the petty republics in Bechuanaland and urged by Commandant-General Piet Joubert, Kruger's chief rival for the presidency.[3] Already there was an attempt to secure a footing in Matabeleland, where the defeat of the British at Majuba was used as an argument to convince Lobengula that "Codlin, the friend, not Short".[4] Furthermore in Germany, even before interest in South Africa and sympathy with the Transvaal had been roused by the War of Independence, Ernst von Weber had suggested a German settlement in Matabeleland, where the Boers might join their German kindred in a colony free from British interference.[5]

[1] *Vide supra*, p. 496.

[2] *Parl. Pap.* 1883, XLIX [C. 3486], [C. 3686]; 1884, LVII [C. 4194]; Leyds, W. J., *The Transvaal Surrounded*, pp. 99–172.

[3] *Parl. Pap.* 1884, LVII [C. 3841].

[4] Piet Joubert to Lobengula, 9 March 1882; Fitzpatrick, Sir P., *The Transvaal from Within*, pp. 54–5. The researches of J. A. I. Agar-Hamilton in the Joubert Correspondence show that Joubert was supporting the Stellaland and Goshen filibusters.

[5] *Berlin Geographical Journal*, 1880.

The fixing of the Transvaal's frontiers by the Pretoria Convention barred such expansion, whilst the assertion of British suzerainty in the Preamble and Article II conflicted with the desire of the Transvaal for absolute independence and liberty to form alliances with foreign Powers. The hope of the Young Afrikaners to see the Vierkleur "waving from Table Bay to the Zambesi" was publicly endorsed by the recently elected President, Paul Kruger.[1] "Then it shall be from the Zambesi to Simon's Bay, Africa for the Afrikaners", he had written, in appealing for aid to President Brand in 1881; and in 1883 he led a deputation to London to demand the revision of the Convention of Pretoria. The Volksraad, he pointed out to Lord Derby, the new Secretary of State for the Colonies in Gladstone's administration, had been very reluctant to accept the Pretoria Convention, and had only ratified it when he had assured them that refusal would mean renewal of the war. Moreover, Lord Kimberley had hinted at the possibility of revision, when he urged them to ratify the Convention and trust to time and experience to prove the necessity of future concessions.[2] Relief from financial obligations imposed by the Convention and the rectification of the south-west frontier were therefore now requested. Furthermore, the delegates complained that the Transvaal had not had the status of a contracting party in framing the Convention. They, therefore, presented the draft of a revised treaty, embodying its claim to be a sovereign international State, with a provision for the consequent reference to foreign arbitration of such disputes as might arise out of the treaty. Thus a campaign was opened for an object never lost sight of until 1899.

Lord Derby was far from being an energetic guardian of imperial interests. His back was stiffened, however, by Sir Hercules Robinson and Scanlen, both of whom were in London, and he rejected both the draft treaty and the claim. Nor would he abandon the British suzerainty.[3] He consented, however, to waive specific mention of it. The word "suzerainty", in fact, was a vague term, which had never been authoritatively defined; for that reason, Derby explained, he was content to abstain from repeating the word whilst keeping the substance.[4] Repetition of the word was avoided by omitting the Preamble of the Pretoria Convention by which the self-government of the Transvaal was guaranteed subject to the suzerainty of the Crown; the new instrument merely provided that "the following articles of a new Convention" should be "substituted

[1] Jorissen, E. J., *Transvaalsche Herinneringen* (trans.), p. 101; Van Oordt, J. F., *Paul Kruger en de Opkomst der Zuid-Afrikaansche Republiek*, p. 419; Mackenzie, John, *Austral Africa*, ch. VIII.

[2] *Parl. Pap.* 1882, XLVII [C. 3098], pp. 95 *sqq.*; Walker, E. A., *History of Southern Africa* p. 386.

[3] *Parl. Pap.* 1882, XLVII [C. 3114]; 1884, LVII [C. 3947]; 1884, LVII [C. 4036]; 1899, LXIV [C. 9507]; cf. Cook, E. T., *Rights and Wrongs of the Transvaal War.* ch. XVI.

[4] Lord Derby. Speech in the House of Lords, 17 March 1884, *Hansard*, 3rd Ser., CCLXXXVI 7.

for the articles embodied in the old".[1] Legal opinion was subsequently divided as to whether the provisions of the Preamble were thereby waived,[2] but the substance of suzerainty was kept by Article IV, which asserted the supremacy of Great Britain by reserving to the Queen control over the republic's treaty-making power.

The Convention of London was signed on 27 February 1884,[3] and ratified unwillingly by the Volksraad in August. By Article IV the South African Republic (for the Transvaal State had regained its old name) was still restrained from making treaties with foreign States, other than the Orange Free State, and with Native tribes to the east or west without the consent of the British Government; it was, however, to have power to make treaties with tribes to the north. Though the missionary societies vehemently opposed any extension of Boer authority over Natives, the provision requiring the assent of the suzerain Power to any legislation affecting them was dropped. The debt secured by the Pretoria Convention was reduced by one-third (Arts. V, VI) and the functions of the Resident at Pretoria were limited to those of a consular officer (Art. III). Those articles intended to safeguard the status of European residents and to preclude differential duties upon British goods were repeated. By Article II the Government of the South African Republic undertook to adhere strictly to the new boundaries laid down in Article I and to prevent encroachments beyond them. The latter article amended the south-west boundary, in dispute ever since the Keate Award, by giving the republic the eastern parts of Stellaland and Goshen; but, as the result of the compromise by which specific mention of "suzerainty" was dropped, the Transvaalers were denied control of the Missionaries' Road.[4]

After visiting the Hague, Berlin, Paris and Lisbon, Kruger returned home taking with him Dr W. J. Leyds, who soon became State Attorney, leader of the Hollanders and Germans whom his President began to import to staff his administration, and a staunch advocate of complete independence at a time when Germany was planting strategic colonies in various parts of Africa. Hofmeyr and the Cape Afrikaners sympathised with the aspirations of the Transvaal to expand westward, but a new force had arisen in South African politics hostile to that aim. Cecil Rhodes had entered the Cape Parliament in 1881. Already on the Diamond Fields he had laid the foundation of a vast fortune; but with him, wealth and the power which it brought were merely means to an end, and that no selfish one. Rhodes's ambition took the larger form of a patriotism which was coming to be known as "imperialism", patriotism inspired by passionate faith, as

[1] *Parl. Pap.* 1884, LVII [C. 3914].

[2] Lord Ripon to Lord Kimberley, 15 February 1895, *apud* Wolf, L., *Life of the First Marquess of Ripon*, II, 228, 229.

[3] *Parl. Pap.* 1884, LVII [C. 3841], [C. 3914], [C. 3947]; Leyds, W. J., *The Transvaal Surrounded*, ch. XVI.

[4] Walker, E. A., *Hist. of S. A.* p. 398.

of a Crusader, in the destiny and proved fitness of his countrymen to carry the torch of Anglo-Saxon civilisation into the dark places of the earth. The objects at which he aimed, even thus early, were to open up new territory for workers from the overcrowded homeland, and new markets for British manufactures; to occupy the interior of Africa; to ensure that his "North" should one day fall to the Cape Colony, and to promote the federation of South Africa as a portion of the British Empire.[1] But he looked much further than this. Whilst the conviction that his countrymen were the guardians of the highest form of civilisation inspired his crusading zeal on their behalf, his ultimate dream was of a *Pax Teutonica* enforced by a federated British Empire, Germany and the United States. A man of action, Rhodes was essentially also a seer, a man of vision. Size inspired him: he saw big, thought big, talked big. The immensity of South Africa thrilled him, and the immensity of the opportunity to be seized or lost haunted him. Time was always a vital factor in the success or failure of his plans. He was only forty-nine when he died.

Rhodes's ambitions, therefore, were similar, yet exactly opposed to those of Kruger and the original Bond. Necessarily they involved him in a lifelong duel with a personality no less vigorous and a will no less stubborn, engaged in the pursuit of a national ambition in itself equally legitimate unless it should involve infringement of the Convention by which the independence of the Transvaal was guaranteed. For whilst Rhodes was determined to secure for his country the vast hinterland of South Africa, Joubert and his party among the Transvaalers were working for expansion to the north or west. Kruger's immediate concern, however, was for consolidation by linking the Free State to the Transvaal and securing a port on the east coast.

Rhodes soon realised that he could not pursue his policy without the support of the Cape Afrikaners.[2] He set before them the ideal of uniting the British and Afrikaners through community of commercial and economic interests, and thereby creating a United South Africa, in which local affairs would be administered by local Governments subject to as little interference as possible by the Imperial Government.[3] With this object in view he struck a bargain with the Bond. By this alliance, which was continued until the Jameson Raid,[4] Hofmeyr secured Rhodes's support in maintaining a protective system in the interests of the Afrikaner farmers and wine growers, a system which Rhodes also favoured as helping British manufacturers. In return, Hofmeyr pledged himself to "throw no obstacles in the way of Rhodes's policy of northern expansion".[5]

[1] Jameson, L. S., in *The Imperialist*, 1897; Mitchell, Sir Lewis, *Life of Cecil Rhodes*, I, 226; statement by Rhodes, *ibid.* I, 94; Speech by Rhodes, 18 July 1883; "Vindex", *Cecil Rhodes*, p. 44.

[2] Jameson. L. S., in *The Imperialist*, 1897; Michell, *Life of Rhodes*, I, 72.

[3] *Parl. Pap.* 1883, XLIX [C. 3686], p. 95.

[4] *Vide infra*, pp. 504 *sqq.*

[5] Statement by Rhodes, quoted *ibid.* p. 94.

Rhodes's hand was strengthened by the trekking of the Transvaal Boers into Bechuanaland. The imposition by the Transvaal of a tariff on all Colonial produce (1881) had already cooled the enthusiasm felt by Cape members of the Bond for their kinsmen there. Now fear lest the Colony should be cut off from the interior, with all its promise of mineral and agricultural wealth, tended to unite the Cape Afrikaners with the British in determination to prevent it. Rhodes had been quick to appreciate the significance of raids into Zululand and Bechuanaland undertaken in support of the Boer trekkers. He described Bechuanaland as the Suez Canal of the trade of the country, "the neck of the bottle", controlling the trade route to the Zambesi. In his eyes, the issue at stake was whether the Colony was to be confined to the Cape Peninsula, or to become the dominant State in a confederated South Africa.[1] He urged the Premier, Thomas Scanlen, to accept an offer of his whole territory made by Mankorwane. The alternative, Rhodes declared, was its absorption by the Transvaal and the stoppage of all Colonial trade with the interior by the imposition of heavy custom duties. Scanlen, however, acutely aware of an empty Treasury and afraid of offending his friends in the Transvaal, was unwilling to commit the Colony to annexation. The offer of Mankorwane and a petition from some of the white Stellalanders were alike rejected, whilst G. J. van Niekerk issued a proclamation formally establishing the Republic of Stellaland (6 August 1883).

The High Commissioner, Sir Hercules Robinson, realised that if Bechuanaland were lost, British development in South Africa would be at an end. Missionaries like Livingstone and John Mackenzie had anticipated the warning of Rhodes. Derby was roused to put pressure upon the Cape Premier. An agreement was made for the temporary acquisition of the territory on the joint account of the Imperial and Colonial Governments.[2] But Cape politicians still took a very parochial view of their obligations; the mists of Table Mountain obscured their vision of the north, and the Cape Parliament refused to sanction the agreement. Derby, however, sent Mackenzie as resident commissioner to Bechuanaland (April 1884). In this he acted prematurely for if he had waited until August, when the London Convention was ratified, it would have been possible to appoint commissioners, in accordance with its provisions, to co-operate with Transvaal officials in keeping the peace on the eastern and western borders. Mackenzie, anxious to assert imperial authority and to preclude annexation to the Cape, proclaimed a British protectorate over the territory of Montsiwa (who was fighting the Goshenites successfully),

[1] Rhodes, C. J., speech in Assembly, 16 August 1883, 16 July 1884, "Vindex", *Rhodes*, p. 62; *Cape Argus*, 16 July 1884; Rhodes to T. Scanlen, 26 May 1883; Michell, *Life of Rhodes*, I, 153–75.

[2] Rhodes, C. J., speech at Barkly West, 28 September 1888, "Vindex", *Rhodes*, p. 215.

raised mounted police, and hoisted the Union Jack at Vryburg in Stellaland.[1] Annexationists at Cape Town and Pretoria and the Afrikaner farmers of Stellaland, whose titles to land were derived from the South African Republic, were equally annoyed. Rhodes appealed once more, and this time with more success, to the Cape Assembly to save the hinterland for the Colony. "We must not have the imperial factor in Bechuanaland", he declared, with the object lesson of its recent performance in the Transvaal before his eyes. The High Commissioner sent him to supersede Mackenzie (July 1884).[2]

Rhodes met the Stellalanders at Commando Drift and by recognising their land titles, which Mackenzie had questioned, persuaded them to accept a British protectorate (September 8). He was less successful in Goshen. Fighting there had ended in the subjugation of Montsiwa, and Kruger issued a proclamation annexing, provisionally and subject to the consent of H.M. Government, the whole of his territory "in the interests of humanity" (September 16).[3] The challenge could not be ignored. Backed by the protests of Cape loyalists, H.M. Government denounced the proclamation as a breach of the London Convention, and demanded its withdrawal. It is a significant coincidence that just at this moment Germany was proclaiming a protectorate over Namaqua-Damaraland (August 1884) and thus arousing apprehensions lest, by joining hands with the Transvaalers or the Portuguese in East Africa, she might cut off the Cape from the interior.[4]

Steps were taken to strengthen the Cape garrison, and though the Bond leaders threatened armed resistance on the part of their friends, Sir Charles Warren was dispatched from England in command of a strong force to clear out the filibusters from Goshen, restore the evicted Natives and hold the country for the Crown (November 10). The South African Republic was warned that it would be held responsible for the cost of the expedition. Kruger was alarmed, for his finances were then at a very low ebb. When, therefore, Warren advanced at the head of some 5000 British and Colonial troops, the President met him and Rhodes on the border at Fourteen Streams, and agreed to beacon off the boundary as provided in the Convention (January 1885).[5]

Warren, reinforced by Cape Colony troops, pushed on to Mafeking to find the Goshenites dispersed, and thence beyond the Molopo, without a blow being struck. Warren and Mackenzie were anxious to establish over the northern regions a protectorate under imperial administration after the fashion of Basutoland. Rhodes would have none of it, for throughout he was keen to make sure of the land and the Road, and set little store by purely British interests. Further,

[1] *Parl. Pap.* 1884, LVII [C. 4194].
[2] *Parl. Pap.* 1884–5, LVII [C. 4213].
[3] *Ibid.* and 1884–5, LXII [C. 4251].
[4] *Vide infra*, pp. 526 *sqq.*; Lord Fitzmaurice, *Life of the 2nd Earl Granville*, II pp. 355 *sqq.*
[5] *Parl. Pap.* 1884–5, LVII [C. 4275], [C. 4310], [C. 4432], [C. 4588]; 1886, XLVII [C. 4643].

though even he had found that the imperial factor had its uses, he justifiably dreaded lest the tide might turn and that such a protectorate might presently be abandoned. He, therefore, worked unceasingly for annexation to the Colony. Unfortunately Warren was led by Mackenzie into an attempt to repudiate Rhodes's non-racial principles, and to limit grants of land to men of British descent. Rhodes protested, and his protest was upheld by the Colonial Office (16 September 1886).[1] But the hostility which had thus been aroused amongst the Afrikaner party rendered the co-operation of the Cape Ministry impossible; for so long as the intervention of the imperial factor was confined to preventing the establishment of European Powers exercising control with or over other South African States, that party was in agreement with it; but the moment the suspicion was aroused that Warren's expedition might lead to war with the Transvaal and the avenging of Majuba, and thus stir up the dying embers of racial antagonism, Rhodes and the High Commissioner had to make it plain that there was no room for the imperial factor in the management of South African internal affairs. Then, every Cape Afrikaner was in agreement with them.

The Home Government therefore proclaimed a British protectorate over Bechuanaland as far north as the 22nd parallel of South latitude and east of 20th East longitude (March 1885), while the territory south of the Molopo River including the country of Montsiwa and Mankorwane, as well as what was left of Goshen and Stellaland, was constituted as the Crown Colony of British Bechuanaland (September 30). Ten years later this was annexed to the Cape. A share of the land was reserved for the Bechuana tribes, whose rights the expedition had been sent to uphold.[2]

Thus a strong force, strongly led, had achieved its object without bloodshed, though at a cost of £1,500,000 to the British taxpayer. The sudden vigour displayed by the imperial factor, inspired mainly by the energy and clear vision of a notable Englishman and a scarcely lesser Scot, had proved effective. Germany had been warned, Boer aggression had been checked, and access to the north preserved.

The other side of the medal was equally true, and equally obvious to both parties. The occupation of Bechuanaland was necessarily part of that process of encircling the Transvaal, which the Boers feared and resented. Rhodes stated quite frankly that his main object had been to secure the interior and to prevent the expansion of the Transvaal in that direction.[3] The position was not unlike that of the French and English colonies in America in the eighteenth century.

Rhodes and Kruger were not unique in their desire for expansion. The belated activity of Great Britain in Bechuanaland had been

[1] Michell, *Life of Rhodes*, I, 199–205.
[2] *Parl. Pap.* 1884–5, LVII [C. 4588]; 1886, XLVIII [C. 4643].
[3] Rhodes to Lord Harris, 7 June 1885, *ap.* Michell, *Life of Rhodes*, I, 211–15.

stimulated in some degree by the unexpected appearance of European rivals on the scene.[1] The sequence of events was, in fact, directing the attention of all the great Powers to Africa. The discovery of diamonds, rumours of gold, and the reverberations of the Zulu and Boer Wars had all tended to advertise it. Missionaries, explorers and adventurers were blazing the trails through the Dark Continent. During the next decade, immense untrodden spaces of primeval forests, pestilential swamps, uncharted deserts and stupendous mountains, with all their potential wealth of fruits and minerals, were explored and partitioned amongst the European Powers.

The scramble for Africa began. There was now a newcomer among the great colonising nations. In Germany, united now and victorious in Europe, the ambition was growing to assert herself as a World Power with a great colonial empire. Outlets were needed for her increasing population, new markets and the control of resources of raw material for her rapidly growing manufactures. Germany, so the Colonial Party there insisted, must have colonies and a fleet to protect them, and lands for her own people to settle under her own flag. Germany must have a place in the sun. The enterprise and endurance of German traders, missionaries and explorers had already paved the way.[2]

For a quarter of a century the German missionaries in Namaqualand and Damaraland had made frequent complaints of ill-treatment by the Natives and of their internecine wars; but in reply to representations from the German Government, Granville had repeated in 1880,[3] and again in August 1881, the refusal of his predecessors to extend British jurisdiction north of the Orange River outside the narrow circle around Walvis Bay.[4]

At the beginning of 1883, the German Ambassador informed the Foreign Office that Franz Lüderitz, a merchant of Bremen, proposed to establish a factory on the coast between the Orange and Little Fish Rivers, where he had recently purchased lands (November 1882). The German Government desired to know whether Her Majesty's Government exercised any authority in that locality, and would afford him protection in case of need. If not, Germany would extend to the factory the same measure of protection as she gave to her subjects in remote parts of the world, but "without the least design to establish a footing in Africa" (7 February 1883).[5] Granville replied that he must consult the Cape Government (February 23). The Cape Government, however, showed no disposition to occupy the territory south of Walvis Bay.[6]

[1] *Parl. Pap.* 1884–5, LVII [C. 4310]. [2] See *C.H.B.E.* vol. III.

[3] Lord Granville to Sir Hercules Robinson, 30 December 1880. [4] *Vide supra*, p. 482.

[5] Minute by Sir Julian Pauncefote, 7 February 1883, of Communication by Count Herbert Bismarck.

[6] Cape Government to Lord Derby, 30 January 1884; Lord Derby to Cape Government, 5 February 1884; *Parl. Pap.* 1884, LVI [C. 4190].

Neither the murmurs of the missionaries nor the denials of the German diplomats apparently aroused the least suspicion that any acquisition of territory was contemplated. Very few people took the colonial movement in Germany seriously. The Foreign Office and the Cape Ministers alike remained content to defer until their own good time annexations of territory upon which might depend the possibility of a United South Africa.

Lüderitz, however, having been assured of his own Government's protection, sent a ship to Angra Pequeña 280 miles south of Walvis Bay. There his agent concluded a treaty with Frederick, the local Chief, who in return for 2000 marks and a few old muskets assigned to him 215 square miles of land, with his sovereign rights, and ten miles of sea frontage on the bay, which now bears the name of Lüderitzbucht (1 May 1883). Next day the German flag was hoisted for the first time in a German colony. A German gunboat was stationed in the bay (October 15).

Protests were entered on behalf of British concessionaires. H.M.S. *Boadicea* sailed from Cape Town to uphold their rights, but the commander, on being informed on his arrival that he was in German territorial waters, returned to the Cape (November 3). Count Hatzfeldt, in London, then made official enquiry whether the British Government claimed sovereignty over Angra Pequeña and the adjacent territory, and, if so, upon what grounds (November 12).

Granville replied that although the Queen's authority had only been proclaimed at certain points, such as Walvis Bay and the Guano islets opposite Angra Pequeña, yet H.M. Government would regard as an infringement of their rights any claim by a foreign Power to sovereignty or jurisdiction between the Portuguese frontier and that of Cape Colony.[1] Bismarck replied by a despatch on 31 December 1883 in which he insisted on the establishment of some civil and political jurisdiction, and inquired upon what title Great Britain could claim sovereignty over that wide territory, hitherto considered independent, and what steps she had taken to protect German subjects. Trusting to previous assurances that Germany had no desire for territorial acquisitions, Derby at the Colonial Office remained as completely blind as Granville himself to her real intentions. He regarded Bismarck's enquiry as merely a suggestion for British occupation or annexation. The British Government would consent to that, if the Cape Colony would bear the cost; the views of the Colony must therefore first be ascertained.[2] But for some months no answer was received from the Cape.

There a parliamentary crisis had arisen with the defeat of Scanlen's ministry.[3] It was not until May 29 following that a reply was

[1] Lord Granville to Lord Ampthill, 21 November 1883.
[2] Lord Derby, Memorandum, 7 October 1884; *Parl. Pap.* 1884–5, LVI [C. 4262].
[3] Molteno had already retired in July 1882.

sent by their successors. Thomas Upington, the new Prime Minister, then carried a resolution in favour of annexing the whole coast up to Walvis Bay. The despatch of a warship to Angra Pequeña was suggested, in order that German intervention might not be excused by the absence of British protection. Again, on July 16, the Cape Parliament voted unanimously for the annexation of all territory up to the Portuguese boundary. It was then far too late.[1]

On 24 April 1884, Bismarck had instructed the consul at Cape Town that Lüderitz and his settlement were under the protection of Germany. A German warship patrolled the coast. Yet on May 12, Granville stated in the House of Lords that, so far as he knew, Germany had never claimed sovereignty over any part of the territory in question, and that the subject was under discussion between the two Governments. Bismarck then threatened to make trouble in Egypt, which the British had recently occupied under anomalous conditions. The British Government yielded (June 21), and in August a German protectorate was declared over the whole coast between 26° South latitude and the Portuguese boundary, with the exception of Walvis Bay.[2] The stone which the British builders had rejected became the chief corner-stone of German power in southern Africa.

Subsequently, by the Anglo-German Agreement of July 1890, the inland boundaries of German South-West Africa, embracing 322,450 square miles, were defined, and free access from the protectorate to the Zambesi was conceded by the Caprivi Zipfel, a corridor 20 miles wide.[3]

The annexation of Angra Pequeña had come as a complete surprise to Granville. Up to the last moment he had been assured by H.M. Ambassador at Berlin that neither Bismarck nor the Reichstag would support the German Colonial Party.[4] Bismarck subsequently asserted that he had made his intentions plain, and that his despatch of 31 December 1883 was intended to elicit a formal acknowledgment from England that she had no pretension to that "strip of land". He complained that by referring it to the Cape Government, Derby and Granville had interpreted it as if it had been merely an enquiry whether England desired to annex that territory, not whether she had done so. He denied the doctrine of "spheres of influence", and protested againt England setting up "a sort of Monroe doctrine in Africa against the vicinage of other nations".[5] Flourishing a document before the eyes of the assembled Reichstag, he declared that he had been unfairly treated by the British Government, which had

[1] *Parl. Pap.* 1884–5, LVI [C. 4265].
[2] Lord Derby's despatch, 4 December 1884; 1884—5, LVI [C. 4263], [C. 4262], [C. 4265]; Lord Fitzmaurice, *Life of 2nd Earl Granville*, II, 349–54.
[3] *Parl. Pap.* 1890, LI [C. 6046].
[4] Lord Granville to Sir C. Malet, 7 February 1885.
[5] German *White Book*, 10 June 1884.

vouchsafed no reply to this despatch, dated 5 May 1884, in which he had explained his views. He did not add that, though he had sent it to Count Münster, he had himself forbidden the ambassador to present it to Granville.[1]

These peculiar transactions were the first of a long series of similar actions on the part of Germany. So far from being thwarted in her colonial enterprises, she was treated with extraordinary forbearance by British statesmen. They were influenced in part by difficulties in Egypt and the Russian danger in Central Asia, both of which could be fomented by Germany, and in part also by the feeling that Great Britain ought not to play the dog in the manger and to resist German claims to colonial empire. On the other hand, the appearance of new competitors in the field had a stimulating effect upon the British nation, both at home and overseas, and quickened once again its instinct for colonisation and expansion. Whereas, in 1881 after the Boer War, the British Government had been anxious to cut down its responsibilities in South Africa to the utmost limit, such was the urge of events and public opinion that by 1897 the area under British rule had been doubled.

Apprehensions were at once aroused lest the Germans, who began to press eastwards through Damaraland, should link up with Boers trekking west, and thus form a Teutonic belt across the continent confining the British to the south of the Orange River. The Transvaal delegates, who visited London in 1883, had visited also Holland, Germany, Lisbon and Paris, and negotiated for a loan in Berlin as well as for support in obtaining the revision of the Pretoria Convention.[2] Directly after the German flag had been hoisted over Lüderitzbucht, the survey for a railway eastward from Angra Pequeña was begun, and the Volksraad confirmed the concession then made (April 1884) to a group of German and Dutch capitalists of a monopoly of railway construction in the Transvaal (23 August 1884).

It was at this juncture that trekkers from the Transvaal intervened in chaotic Zululand. Upon the death of Cetewayo, they proclaimed his son, Dinizulu, king, and obtained from him a large concession of land (May 1884). Reinforced by Afrikaner settlers from the colonies and republics, they there formed the "New Republic" with Vryheid for capital (August 1884) and advanced towards the sea urging their claims to three-fourths of the Zulu territory.

Upon the Zululand coast lies St Lucia Bay. It was thought at that time that it might be made a fair harbour and the possible

[1] Speech in Reichstag, 2 March 1885. *Reden von Bismarck* etc., II, 61; German *White Book* (1884); *Hansard*, 3rd Ser., CCXCV, 596; cf. Lord Fitzmaurice, *Life of 2nd Earl Granville*, II, 353, 427–9; *British Documents on the Origins of the War*, III, 408, 422. A somewhat different account is given in Lovell, R. I., *The Struggle for South Africa*, 1875–1899, pp. 94, 104 *sqq.*

[2] Lord Fitzmaurice, *Life of 2nd Earl Granville*, II, 355 *sqq.*

terminus of a railway from the Transvaal. For Kruger it offered the long-coveted outlet from the Transvaal to the Indian Ocean, and here, working through the agency of Lüderitz and the South African Republic, Germany prepared to repeat the coup of Angra Pequeña. Colonel Schiel, a German in the service of the republic, had obtained from Dinizulu a concession of lands in the neighbourhood of the bay. But both the Home and Colonial Governments were now awake. Bismarck had begun to make fresh trouble over British annexations on the Middle Niger. Derby realised at last that yielding to Germany was not being rewarded by the good-will which the British Government sought. The despatch of the Warren expedition showed that he had stiffened his back,[1] and before the German preparations in Zululand could be completed, H.M.S. *Goshawk* was ordered to St Lucia Bay. By virtue of an old treaty with King Panda (1843), the British flag was hoisted there on 18 December 1884, and the only passable harbour between Durban and Lourenço Marques was annexed in the interests of Natal.[2] The New Republic appealed in vain to Holland, France and Germany. German claims were satisfied by concessions in the Cameroons.[3]

The hunt was up. Whilst Sir Harry Johnston raced with Dr Karl Peters for East Africa, the Imperial Government warned the Cape ministry that the time was ripe to annex what it could of the coast up to Delagoa Bay (January 1885). Northward the Colony had taken over Walvis Bay on the south-west coast in 1884; eastward, before the end of 1886, it formally annexed Tembuland, Bomvanaland and Galekaland (26 August 1885) and incorporated the Xesibe district of Mount Ayliff in Griqualand East (October 1886) as the only solution of chronic difficulties arising from encroachments by the neighbouring Pondos.[4] In Pondoland General Thesiger (later Lord Chelmsford) had occupied the port and tidal estuary of St John's (31 August 1878), and British sovereignty was proclaimed there by Sir Bartle Frere on September 4. Letters Patent had been issued as long ago as October 1881 permitting annexation to the Cape Colony when the Cape Parliament should pass an Act for that purpose. Such an Act was now passed (July 1884) and the annexation was proclaimed on 13 September 1884.[5]

Mqikela, the turbulent chief of East Pondoland, however, gave continual trouble. Apart from cattle-lifting and Native feuds, he attempted to establish at Port Grosvenor a rival harbour to St John's,

[1] *Vide supra*, p. 524; *Parl. Pap.* 1884–5, LVII [C. 4310].

[2] *Vide supra*, p. 337; *Parl. Pap.*, 1885, LVI [C. 4587], pp.12, 58, 76, 80, 89, 97.

[3] *Parl. Pap.* 1884–5, LVI [C. 4214]; 1884–5, LVI [C. 4274]; 1884—5, LIV [C. 4290]; 1884–5, LVII [C. 4310]; 1884–5, LIV [C. 4442]; 1884–5, LVI [C. 4587], [C. 4645]; Leyds, W. J., *The Transvaal Surrounded*, pp. 50–5.

[4] Theal, G. M., *History of South Africa since* 1875, v, 168–81.

[5] *Parl. Pap.* 1887, LXI [C. 5022]; 1888, LXXV [C. 5410]; G. 5 and 30–86; G. 12–87 (Cape) (quoted by Walker, E. A., *Hist. Southern Africa*, p. 404); Theal, *Hist. South Africa*, v, 215–17.

and to levy tolls upon the commerce of Natal and the Cape Colony where the great waggon road from Umtata passed through his country.[1] His claims were presently settled, and a British protectorate proclaimed over the Pondo coast by the High Commissioner (5 July 1885).[2] The two Pondolands retained their independence for a while, for the German Government raised claims on behalf of concessionaires in East Pondoland, and Natal also had turned longing eyes towards Mqikela's territory. It was not until 1894 that Rhodes annexed both Pondolands to the Cape Colony.[3] Thus, all, and far more than all, the territory which Wodehouse had prudently abandoned in 1864[4] was at length annexed. From the Kei to the frontier of Natal the whole country was now at long last a part of the Cape Colony mainly as a series of tribal reserves.

The pressure of similar forces compelled the Imperial Government to settle the problem of Zululand. Hitherto Natal's demand for annexation had been refused; but it became evident, as the Boer farmers spread over Zululand, either that British sovereignty must be proclaimed, or the whole country be allowed to pass into the hands of the South African Republic. The New Republic was now formally recognised, but its territory was limited (1886).[5] It was subsequently incorporated into the South African Republic as the Vryheid district (July 1888). Afrikaner farmers were allowed to retain their farms at a nominal quit-rent in the remainder of Zululand, which became a British colony in 1887 under the surveillance of the government of Natal.[6] Natal, however, did not take over the government till ten years later (1897). In the interval Zululand was imperial territory, governed by a Resident under the general control of the Governor of Natal as Commissioner. Some years elapsed before the inter-tribal wars of the chieftains were suppressed. The confines of Zululand were subsequently extended to the Portuguese boundary and the Lebombo mountains, the eastern limit of Swaziland (1895).[7]

The success of Bismarck's policy of twisting the lion's tail had depended largely upon co-operation with the French Government under M. Jules Ferry; but when it was seen that Ferry's ministry was tottering to its fall, he temporarily changed his tactics. The problems raised in the Anglo-Portuguese Congo-Zambesi Agreement of 1884 called for international settlement. A Conference was held at Berlin. The outcome of this conference was the Berlin Act[8] (26 February 1885), which settled the future of the Congo River and Basin, and

[1] Theal, *Hist. South Africa*, v, 217–22.
[2] *Parl. Pap.* 1884–5, LVI [C. 4590]; 1887, LXI [C. 4980], [C. 5143].
[3] Williams, Basil, *Life of Cecil Rhodes*, p. 207; Theal, *Hist. South Africa*, v, chs. LXXVI, LXXVII.
[4] *Vide supra*, p. 413.
[5] *Parl. Pap.* 1884, LVIII [C. 4037], [C. 4191]; 1884–5, LVI [C. 4214], [C. 4274]: 1886, XLVIII [C. 4645].
[6] *Parl. Pap.* 1887, LXI [C. 4980]; 1887, LXI [C. 5143].
[7] *Vide infra*, p. 541.
[8] Hertslet, L. and E., *Map of Africa by Treaty*, pp. 468–86.

established free trade and navigation on the Zambesi and its affluents. As to claims of sovereignty, whilst the Act itself prescribed "certain uniform rules with reference to future occupations on the coast", Lord Salisbury was able to affirm two and a half years later that all parties to the Act had by that time admitted in principle that a claim of sovereignty could be maintained by real occupation of the territory claimed.[1] By Article VI, the principle of a "sphere of influence", as distinct from territorial acquisition, was formally recognised. The demarcation of "spheres of influence" then became one of the chief tasks of European statesmen. Backed by a strong majority in Parliament and the country, the skilful and authoritative diplomacy of Lord Salisbury contributed during the next few years to the solution of the international problems of Africa (1887–90).[2]

All this time, Cecil Rhodes had been working for a railway and customs union with the Transvaal. In roads, railways and telegraphs he recognised the essential means of developing trade with the new countries he was determined to open up; in hostile tariffs and transit duties, the fatal obstructions. There was an evident danger lest the carrying trade with the interior might be diverted from the Cape to Natal or the Transvaal.[3] The strong feeling of inter-colonial jealousy and separatism which had characterised the American colonies in the eighteenth century, and in a less degree those of Australia in the nineteenth, was expressed and accentuated by tariff barriers. Rhodes hoped that, apart from the material advantages which would accrue to the Cape from the fusion of its economic interests with those of the republics, the closer union promoted thereby would prove the first step towards reunion of the white races in one confederation, a confederation not forced from home by another Carnarvon, but—and in this the Colonial Office has long concurred—arising from a spontaneous demand from the states and colonies concerned.

The expansion of the British Empire was the dream and the work of Rhodes's life; but he was anxious that the expansion at which he aimed should come through the British colonies in the way and at the time they desired. They were, he held, those best fitted to manage their own affairs. He was supported by the growing feeling in the country born of the constant vacillations of the British Government, culminating in the "grand renunciation" after Majuba, that the administration of South African affairs should no longer be the sport of English party politics, or decided by a House of Commons in which the colonists were not represented.[4] Even reform in the Transvaal was presently deemed by many too dear at the price of re-establishing control from Downing Street.[5]

[1] Hertslet, L. and E., *Map of Africa by Treaty*, p. 706.
[2] See *C.H.B.E.* vol. III.
[3] C. J. Rhodes, speech on the Budget, 1 August 1883, "Vindex", *Rhodes*, p. 54.
[4] Michell, *Life of Rhodes*, I, 94.
[5] Max O'Rell, *John Bull and Co.*; statement by J. Chamberlain, 4 February 1896.

Actually, colonial wisdom was hardly justified of her children. Whilst Rhodes preached inter-colonial free trade, the South African Republic, finding itself in financial straits after the grant of self-government, had imposed a duty on colonial produce.[1] The Cape retaliated by taxing Transvaal tobacco. Natal, nursing her own ports and lines, adopted an anti-Cape policy in favour of the Transvaal in the matter of tariffs and railways. Down to 1889, with the exception that Basutoland was given her share of the customs dues in 1884, both the coast colonies retained the whole of the customs duties collected at their ports in transit to the interior states.[2] By that short-sighted policy they encouraged the South African Republic to turn towards Delagoa Bay. Customs, tariffs, railways and loans to finance them were, in fact, destined to be used rather as weapons in a struggle for predominance than as instruments for promoting union. Rhodes's efforts to secure federation, not by interfering with the independence of the neighbouring states, but by obtaining "Customs relations, railway communication and free trade in products with them",[3] were frustrated partly by the narrow outlook of the Cape politicians, and partly by the opposing ambition of Kruger and the dislike and distrust felt by Transvaal burghers for British traders and the British Government. Kruger would have nothing to do with federation such as Rhodes desired, but worked for a federation of his own with the Orange Free State, whilst using tariffs and railways to play off Natal against the Cape.

There was, however, a time when Kruger, in need of funds, was ready to enter into such a union as Rhodes proposed. In 1885 the Cape trunk line from Cape Town ended at Kimberley just north of the Orange River, and the Port Elizabeth and East London lines ended south of the river. There were no railways in either of the republics. The South African Republic was exceedingly poor and barely able to raise a loan of £5000. The Netherlands Railway Company, outcome of the monopoly of railways construction within the Transvaal granted to the Hollander-German syndicate in 1884, was not successfully floated until 1887 after the discovery of gold on the Rand; and it was not till gold had begun to pour wealth into the lap of the Government that the Company got to work. Always championed by the President in spite of its failure to fulfil the terms of its contract, it then soon obtained complete and profitable control of the finances of the state, piling up the National Debt, imposing heavy burdens on the mining industry, and dictating relations with the neighbouring colonies by differential rates and customs.[4]

[1] *Staatscourant*, 10 November 1881.

[2] See Van der Poel, J., *Railway and Customs Policies in S. Africa*, 1885–1910, pp. 10 *sqq.*

[3] Cf. Rhodes's speeches at Kimberley, 30 March 1891, and Port Elizabeth, 17 September 1898, "Vindex", *Rhodes*, pp. 265, 611.

[4] Cf. Fitzpatrick, Sir P., *The Transvaal from Within*, pp. 51–6; also *Parl. Pap.* 1901 xxxv [Cd. 623].

The natural line of advance for the railways both of Natal and the Cape Colony was over republican soil; but the farmers of both republics looked askance at railways, which they dreaded as heralds of an alien civilisation and competitors with their waggon-transport business. Be that as it might, when the traffic of the Lydenburg goldfields rendered a railroad imperative, the Portuguese Government granted a concession to Colonel Edward McMurdo, an American citizen, who floated a company in London to build a line from Lourenço Marques to the Transvaal border (1883). Progress was delayed by unexpected difficulties of construction and finance.[1] In 1885, therefore, Kruger opened negotiations for a customs union with the Cape and an extension of the railway from Kimberley. Rhodes urged acceptance. But Rhodes was then only a rising force in the Assembly. The offer was rejected, and the opportunity was lost for ever, for in September 1886 gold was discovered on the Witwatersrand. Kruger found himself provided, as by a miracle, with all the funds he needed for prosecuting his desire to secure a seaport of his own. He returned, therefore, to the idea of a junction with Delagoa Bay, which was both nearer to the Transvaal and had for him the attraction of not being under British control. By the end of 1887 the survey of the line from Pretoria to the Transvaal border was completed, and when in the following year a customs conference was proposed by Brand and Hofmeyr, the South African Republic refused to attend.

If union with the Transvaal was thus no longer to be attained through the merging of railway and commercial interests, there remained the alternative policy of preventing its union with the Orange Free State. Much resentment was felt there at the policy of commercial isolation through protective tariffs pursued by the South African Republic. Watching the progress of the Transvaal railway, the Orange Free State urged the extension of the Cape line through its territory to the Transvaal, but though Rhodes pleaded for the policy advocated by Hofmeyr and Brand, he could not rouse the Colony to immediate action.[2] A golden opportunity was lost of stopping the further extension of the Pretoria line to Delagoa Bay and with it the loss of much of the carrying trade from the Cape.

In the matter of customs, Rhodes was at last partly successful. A customs union with the Orange Free State was arranged in 1888 and ratified in the following year. By it the inland state received from the Cape Colony three-quarters of the duties collected on goods in transit. Both the Transvaal and Natal refused to join the union; the latter, indeed, appealed to the Imperial Government to protect its interests against the Cape.[3] In the same year a Convention was concluded with the Orange Free State for the continuation of the

[1] See Van der Poel, *op. cit.* pp. 20 *sqq.*
[2] Cf. Rhodes's letter to the *Cape Argus*, 6 July 1887.
[3] Walker, E. A., *Hist. Southern Africa*, p. 409.

Port Elizabeth line through Bloemfontein to the Transvaal border on the Vaal River (June 1889). A check seemed to have been given to the closer union of the two republics. Kruger used every device to delay the extension of the railway from Bloemfontein whilst the Delagoa line was being completed. At all costs, he was also determined to prevent the passing of the Kimberley line through Johannesburg and Pretoria on its way to the north. But the Delagoa line had once more come to a standstill. Then the Portuguese came to the rescue. Seizing McMurdo's railway line, they carried it on themselves to the Transvaal border (June 1889). Junction with Pretoria was completed in 1894. McMurdo's claims for compensation were referred to arbitration at Berne.[1]

This incident had a curious sequel. As soon as Rhodes had formed his first Ministry at the Cape (July 1890), he began an attempt to purchase Delagoa Bay from the Portuguese. The Home Government refused to help,[2] but at one moment it seemed possible that a bargain might be struck on payment of £700,000. National sentiment in Portugal, however, was against it, and whilst the Berne arbitration delayed negotiations, a foreign competitor raised the price. German financial aid was promised to the South African Republic for the purpose of buying McMurdo's railway. When that offer failed Berlin demanded from Lisbon that, on the conclusion of the arbitration, Germany and Portugal should deal with the railway by common agreement.[3] Rhodes, in the end, had to abandon his scheme (1894), because the British Government warned him that Germany would not let him have the Bay even if Portugal were willing.[4] Thus was the way paved for endless trouble with the Transvaal.

Rhodes replied to Kruger's refusal to allow the Cape-to-Cairo railway to pass through the Transvaal by forming a syndicate to run it along the western border through Bechuanaland. The line from Kimberley had reached Fourteen Streams by the end of 1889, and by the spring of 1891 had got as far as Vryburg, whence it was continued to Mafeking by the Bechuanaland Railway Company under contract with the Protectorate Government (1894). The Cape Government's Port Elizabeth line reached Bloemfontein at the same time as the Kimberley line reached Vryburg.[5] It was extended to Pretoria in the following year (December 1892), for, in terms of the Sivewright Agreement, permission for this extension and the right to fix rates as far as Johannesburg had at last been purchased by a loan from the Cape to the Netherlands South African Railway

[1] See Van der Poel, *op. cit.* p. 18; *Parl. Pap.* 1890, LI [C. 5903].
[2] 23 May 1892.
[3] Cf. Sir Eyre Crowe's Memorandum in Good and Temperly, *British Documents on the Origin, of the War*, III, 408.
[4] Michell, *Life of Rhodes*, II, pp. 93–6; Walker, E. A., *Hist. of Southern Africa*, pp. 439, 442.
[5] Speech by Sir Henry Loch 26 May 1891, quoted Michell, *Rhodes*, II, p. 44.

Company, which needed funds to complete its line to Delagoa Bay.

Kruger, however, was far from having had the worst of the duel. Though the customs and railway conventions tended to draw the Orange Free State into the arms of the Cape Colony, politically it had been wooed and won by the Transvaal. Kruger had endeavoured to draw it into closer union by means of a commercial treaty and military alliance, whilst attempting to veto the advance of the Port Elizabeth line. His overtures were rejected on the advice of President Brand, who, like Fraser, was determined not to be led into the conflict with the paramount Power, which, he foresaw, would be the necessary consequence of such an alliance (1886–October 1887);[1] for the implacable hostility of Kruger and his burghers to the British Government was plainly evident.[2] Unhappily, Brand, that judicious statesman, "an Afrikaner of the Afrikaners, a true friend of the English", died in July 1888.[3] He was succeeded by his opponent, F. W. Reitz, the declared advocate of a Afrikaner Republic of South Africa. The new President speedily committed the little pastoral Free State to the ambitious policy of the Transvaal. On 9, 10 and 17 March 1889, three agreements were signed at Potchefstroom which tied the Orange Free State to Kruger's chariot-wheels. One was a railway agreement, another a provision for free trade, and the third a defensive treaty binding the two republics to assist each other whenever the independence of either was threatened or attacked, provided that the one thought the other's cause was just.[4] Thus did the two republics begin to draw together in face of the paramount Power.

By a curious stroke of irony the means by which both Rhodes and Kruger were enabled to pursue their ambitions were derived largely from the same source. The former acquired a vast fortune from his consolidation of the diamond industry and his gold-mines on the Rand. The latter drew immense sums from the immigrants to the gold-mining industry, whose presence he at first invited and then resented, refusing Brand's sagacious advice "to make them your friends".[5]

Whilst the early diamond diggers at Kimberley, working single claims independently, were passing through the difficult times described in an earlier chapter,[6] the Legislative Council of Griqualand West added to their embarrassments by passing a Bill resuming the right of the Crown to all diamonds found in the territory (1872). Only the disallowance of the measure by the Home Government prevented

[1] Fraser, Sir J. G., *Episodes in my Life*, pp. 83–166, 229–32; *Milner Papers*, I, ch. VII.

[2] Fraser, *Episodes in my Life*, p. 254.

[3] J. X. Merriman, speech at Grahamstown, January 1885, quoted Michell, *Rhodes*, I. 229.

[4] *Milner Papers* (South Africa), I, 199–203.

[5] General C. R. Beyers, speech at Burghersdorp, January 1908, quoted Michell, *op. cit.*, I, 227.

[6] *Vide supra*, p. 506.

a riotous outbreak.[1] The difficulties of the small holders and speculators were not destined to end until their precarious diggings had been absorbed by powerful corporations, which, as Sir Richard Southey had foretold from the beginning,[2] could alone exercise uniform control of labour and maintain prices by adjusting output to the capacity of the market. The importance of the formation of the De Beers Consolidated Mines Company was not limited to its immediate economic aspect.[3] The trust deed of this great corporation (13 March 1888) gave it immense powers, reflecting the enterprise and ambition of its dominant life governor, Cecil Rhodes. It was not confined to diamond mining, but was empowered to build and operate railways, to acquire any other asset, including tracts of country in Africa and elsewhere, and to expend thereon any sums required for their good government. It was, in fact, a company equipped with powers like those of the old East India Company to build that empire in the north which had long since fired Rhodes's imagination. Kimberley became the financial centre of South Africa. To its diamond interests was now added the business of floating mining and exploration companies for developing the recently discovered goldfields in the Transvaal. From them, as founder of the Consolidated Goldfields (1886) and other companies, Rhodes derived yet greater wealth and power.[4]

The discovery of gold in the Witwatersrand was an event of immense importance both in the history of South Africa and in the economic development of the whole world. In 1886, the year in which the famous Sheba mine was discovered near Barberton in the eastern Transvaal, two brother prospectors, Frederick and Hendrik Struben, found rich gold-bearing reefs on the high land between Pretoria and the Vaal River, the conglomerate series of the Witwatersrand. With Major Lys they extracted the first gold therefrom.

A great gold-rush began. Immigrants from Kimberley, from all parts of South Africa and the outer world, but mainly from Great Britain and the British colonies, hurried to the Rand. In its centre they built a great city, Johannesburg, the creation almost of a day, in which tin shanties jostled marble palaces, and which held "all the wealth of the world and the woe too".

Hitherto Kruger, ever faithful to the ideal of Pretorius, had been pursuing his ambitions "without a sixpence in his Treasury".[5] Now, suddenly, he was provided with the means of continuing the struggle for supremacy in which he had been checked at Fourteen Streams.[6]

[1] *Parl. Pap.* 1875, LIII [C. 1121], [C. 1158]; 1876, LII [C. 1342].

[2] Southey to Shepstone, 29 August 1870, quoted Wilmot, A., *Life of Sir R. Southey*, p. 190.

[3] For the economic aspect, *vide infra*, pp. 776–781.

[4] Wilmot, A., *Life of Sir R. Southey*, I, 177–86; Williams, Gardner, *The Diamond Mines of South Africa*, chs. IX, X; Williams, Basil, *Cecil Rhodes*, pp. 92 *sqq*.

[5] Hofmeyr, J. H., *Life of J. H. Hofmeyr*, p. 390; Rhodes, C. J., speech at Barkly West, 28 September 1888, "Vindex", *Rhodes*, p. 214.

[6] *Vide supra*, p. 524.

The revenue of the South African Republic, which had fallen just short of £178,000 in 1885–6, had risen to £638,000 in 1887 and by 1889 was over £1,500,000.

The annexations of 1884–6 had completed British possession of the coast from the mouth of the Orange River on the west to the Portuguese frontier on the east, with one small exception. That exception was Tongaland. In Tongaland, south of Delagoa Bay, the very indifferent harbour of Kosi Bay seemed to offer Kruger his last chance of securing a port of his own.[1] The way to it lay through Swaziland and the territory of two petty chiefs, Zambaan and Mbegisa, between the Pongola River and the Lebombo Mountains. With these chiefs the Boers made some agreements (1887). Zambili, the Queen Regent of Amatongaland, alarmed at signs of aggression by the Boers on one side and the Portuguese on the other, appealed for British protection. In return, she undertook not to cede any part of her territory to foreign Powers without the sanction of the High Commissioner (1887). The British Government included in this agreement the lands of Zambaan and Mbegisa, though they were not subject to Zambili. The whole area between Swaziland and the sea was declared to be within the sphere of British influence (February 1888).[2] The South African Republic protested, whilst the two Chiefs concerned appealed to it for protection.[3]

In the meantime the Transvaalers were proceeding unceasingly with the peaceful penetration of Swaziland. The usual method of expansion practised by the Transvaal Boers was to open with a series of hunting expeditions, preparatory to sending their cattle across the border to graze. A foothold being thus secured, concessions were extracted from the local Chiefs, sometimes in return for aid in their quarrels. In Swaziland, concessions were easily obtained from Mbandeni, the wretched, drunken King.

But where white men of different nationalities were rivals for favours and annexation was threatened, it was always easy for the Bantu Chiefs to play off one against the other. This happened in Swaziland, as it happened in Zululand and Matabeleland. The Swazis had long been friends and allies of the Transvaalers, as for example against the Zulus and Bapedi; they were also good friends and allies of the British and wished to remain so. Kruger, in order to secure access to the port of Kosi Bay, was anxious to renew the control over Swaziland which the Transvaalers had exercised between 1875 and 1881. He had a bargaining counter in a treaty of alliance, which Grobler, one of his agents, had recently arranged with Lobengula, ruler of Matabele-Mashonaland, giving Transvaal burghers special

[1] Botha, P. R., *Die Staatkundige Ontwikkeling, etc. onder Kruger en Leyds*, ch. XII.
[2] *Parl. Pap.* 1890, LII [C. 6200]; 1895, LXXI [C. 7780].
[3] Leyds, W. J., *The Transvaal Surrounded*, pp. 261, 262.

privileges under the jurisdiction of their own consul. Lobengula, upon whose consent would depend the exercise in his dominions of the powers which Rhodes hoped to gain for his projected British South African Company, had just repudiated the Rudd mineral concession on which that company was to be based.[1]

Kruger therefore intimated (April 1889) that he was willing to withdraw his claims in the north and west in return for a free hand in Swaziland, the lands of Zambaan and Mbegisa, and the right to come to terms with Zambili, queen of the Tongas.[2] But if there was to be annexation, Natal was as anxious to secure its fruits for herself as was Kruger for the South African Republic. The independence of the Swazis was expressly safeguarded by the London Convention (Art. II), whilst the right of the republic to make treaties with Native tribes to the east and west was subject to the approval of the British Government (Art. IV). When, therefore, Commandant-General Joubert and Smit obtained from Mbandeni a will making Kruger his heir, the British Government refused to recognise it.

Robinson, however, fully aware that Mbandeni was playing fast and loose with both sides, declared, on the eve of his retirement from the High Commissionership, that Swaziland must come under either British or Boer rule. When the majority of settlers declared themselves in favour of the Transvaal (July 1889), the British Government availed itself of Kruger's earlier suggestion for a joint commission, which set up a temporary joint administration of whites over whites (December 1889).[3]

On the arrival of the new High Commissioner, Sir Henry (later Lord) Loch, Kruger stopped a projected trek by Transvaalers into Mashonaland and proposed a discussion of the whole situation. Loch accordingly met Kruger and Rhodes in conference at Blignaut's Pont in March 1890.[4] It was agreed to continue the joint administration for whites, but Loch refused to purchase the withdrawal of Boer claims in the north by ceding the sovereignty over Swaziland to the republic, as Kruger had proposed.[5] He consented, indeed, to the annexation by the South African Republic of the Little Free State, which had been set up on land granted by Mbandeni to a Transvaal official; but he insisted that the concession of access by rail to Kosi Bay must depend upon the republic's joining a customs union with one or other of the British colonies and allowing either the Cape or the Natal railway to cross its borders. Kruger could not induce his burghers to ratify these terms, angry as they were at the insult offered

[1] *Vide infra*, pp. 543 *sqq*.
[2] *Parl. Pap.* 1890, LI [C. 5918].
[3] *Parl. Pap.*, 1890, LII [C. 6200].
[4] *Parl. Pap.* 1890, LII [C. 6201]; 1890–1, LVII [C. 6217]; 1895, LXXI [C. 7780]; Leyds, W. J., *The Transvaal Surrounded*, pp. 235–361, 514; Hofmeyr, J. H., *Life of J. H. Hofmeyr*, ch. XXIV.
[5] *Parl. Pap.* 1890, LI [C. 5918]; 1890, LII [C. 6200]; 1890–1, LVII [C. 6217].

to their flag by Johannesburg irresponsibles while Kruger was passing through their city on his way to the Pont. Therefore Loch made preparations to support by arms a British commissioner in Swaziland in accordance with the terms of the London Convention, whilst sending Hofmeyr as mediator to Pretoria to urge agreement.[1] The first Swaziland Convention was then ratified by the Volksraad as a temporary measure (August 1890). By this Convention the Boers were offered access to the sea by a line through Swaziland, and a port, on condition that the British should retain the right of pre-emption, and on the then terms provisionally agreed upon at the Pont. The South African Republic consented to withdraw its opposition to the extension of railways to its border, and even to consider their extension to Johannesburg. It also once more agreed to renounce all claim to extend the territory of the republic, or to enter into any treaties with any Natives to the north or north-west of its existing boundary. It undertook to support the recently formed British South Africa Company in the establishment of order there.[2]

In Swaziland, however, the Transvaalers were making the joint administration impossible, whilst the republic refused to take advantage of the offer of a port on the conditions prescribed. But from Mbegisa and Zambaan it secured rights for a corridor for its railways. Then, in accordance with the article which permitted either party to denounce the convention if its conditions had not been fulfilled within three years, the Volksraad gave notice of its termination in August 1893.

The Marquis of Ripon, a Liberal imperialist who had succeeded to the Colonial Office in Lord Rosebery's ministry, instructed Loch to reopen negotiations (June 1893).[3] By the second Swaziland Convention the President was permitted, not to incorporate that country forthwith as he desired, but to administer it as a protectorate, if and when the Swazis should have empowered him to rule the whites. The Swazis, however, not only refused to take this step, but declared against the continuance of the joint administration and sent a deputation to London. British and Boer concessionaires were at loggerheads, the former urging the maintenance of the *status quo*, the latter seeking a pretext for intervention by the South African Republic. As it was deemed out of the question to go to war over Swaziland, Ripon decided that by "manifest destiny" Swaziland must be placed under the control of the South African Republic, with provisions, embodied in the third Swaziland Convention, for safeguarding the interests of the natives (December 1894).[4]

Before the South African Republic had assumed its protectorate in

[1] Hofmeyr, J. H., *Life of J. H. Hofmeyr*, pp. 394–406.

[2] *Parl. Pap.* 1895, LXXI [C. 7611]; 1890, LII [C. 6200], [C. 6201]; 1890–1, LVIII [C. 6217].

[3] *Parl. Pap.* 1893, LXII [C. 7212].

[4] *Parl. Pap.* 1895, LXXI [C. 7611]; Lord Ripon to Lord Rosebery, 4 September 1894, Wolf, L., *Life of the First Marquess of Ripon*, II, 222–6.

the following February, Kruger made a startling speech. Germany was suspected of intriguing in and about the Transvaal. Some members of the German Colonial Party, who regarded the Boers as a Germanic people and dreamed of a broad belt of Teutonic territory stretching across Africa from east to west, sympathised openly with the republic's difficulties with the British authorities; organs of the German press, regardless of the fact that their country had nothing much in the way of a Navy, talked wildly of intervention, and pointedly drew attention to a couple of German light cruisers anchored in Delagoa Bay; a few Germans were undoubtedly employed in the arming of the Transvaal, which had been begun very tentatively in the latter part of 1894. While preferential terms were being arranged for German importers, Leyds set sail for Berlin, thus awakening British suspicions that he was going thither to ask for protection. Were Germany to promise this at a time when Great Britain's relations with France were severely strained, and thus threaten to invade a sphere in which Great Britain claimed to be paramount, the challenge could scarcely be ignored.

It was in these circumstances that Kruger, speaking at a banquet in honour of the Kaiser's birthday on 3 January 1895, virtually proclaimed that he was reckoning on Germany as a counter-weight to Great Britain in Southern Africa. "We are growing up", he said, "and, although we are young, we feel that if one nation tries to kick us, the other will try to stop it."[3] What, if any, assurances of support he had received from Berlin is not known, but the reply of the British Government was decisive. It promptly proclaimed Amatongaland, Kosi Bay and the lands of Zambaan and Mbegisa a British protectorate (May 1895); the "manifest destiny" of the Transvaal evidently did not reach to the sea. The President declared that the act was an unfriendly one. Germany warned Great Britain that the annexation was not recognised by the Transvaal, and presently, after intimating that Great Britain's "opposition to German interests at Delagoa Bay" was one of the legitimate causes of her ill-will, declared that the continued economic independence of the Transvaal was a German national interest.[4] The appearance of a strong British squadron in Delagoa Bay anchoring beside the German ships had a calming effect. This squadron had, in fact, been dispatched before the crisis to take part in the celebration of the opening of the Delagoa Bay railway

All these moves by the South African Republic towards the coast

[1] *Vide infra*, p. 505.

[2] Ripon to Kimberley, 21 October, 25 November 1894; Kimberley to Ripon, 25 November 1894, Wolf, L., *Life of the First Marquess of Ripon*, II 232–3.

[3] *Parl. Pap.* 1897, IX (312 ii), *Appendix to Report of Select Committee on British South Africa* p. 548.

[4] *Parl. Pap.* 1895, LXXI [C.7780], [C. 7878]; Leyds, *The Transvaal Surrounded*, pp. 346 *sqq.*; German *White Book* (1896); Botha, P., *Kruger en Leyds*, pp. 469 *sqq.*; Walker, E. A., *Hist. South. Africa*, p. 404, and *Lord de Villiers and his Times*, pp. 453, 454; Wolf, L., *Life of Ripon*, II, 231 *sqq.*

were, of course, attempts, which, if successful, involved revision of the London Convention, which defined the Transvaal boundaries, prohibited their enlargement, guaranteed the independence of the Swazis, and forbade the conclusion of treaties with the tribes east or west without the consent of H.M. Government. Moreover, whilst Kruger's desire to obtain a port on the east coast was very natural from his point of view, yet the acquisition of such a port would inevitably open the door to Europe, and for the security of the British colonies it was necessary that Europe should be kept out of South Africa. In working for the limitation of Transvaal ambitions in this direction, the policy of the Imperial Government was essentially a South African policy and a peace policy conceived in the interests of all Afrikaners. But expansion of the Transvaal to the north had not been specifically prohibited by the London Convention.[1] Kruger's policy of expansion was entirely consonant with his countrymen's ever-present *trekgeest*, the desire to trek with guns and waggons to new lands in the "vast spaces washed with sun" which beckoned them onwards into the Great Continent. Since his rebuff in Bechuanaland, he had been concentrating upon expansion eastwards; but Piet Joubert, his rival for the presidentship, was deeply interested in the establishment of a republic in the north.

Men of vision had for some time been looking northwards to where, beyond the Limpopo, lay fertile lands fit for European occupation, and where, in the fabled region of Ophir and "King Solomon's mines", rumour spoke of goldfields far richer than the Rand. From the Transvaal boundary to the Zambesi, and between Portuguese territory on the east and the country of the Bamangwato on the west, stretched the Matabele-Mashonaland of Lobengula. The kraal of that powerful potentate at Bulawayo became the Mecca of concession-hunters. Boers and British from the south, Germans from the west, Portuguese from the east began to press their claims. Yielding to pressure from the Joubert party, Kruger dispatched an emissary, Piet Grobler, to negotiate with the Matabele king. Grobler succeeded in obtaining from Lobengula a treaty upon which the South African Republic was preparing to base far-reaching claims (30 July 1887).[2]

At the end of the year Rhodes learned that Grobler had been sent to reside as consul at Bulawayo. He, therefore, urged the High Commissioner to proclaim Matabele-Mashonaland within the sphere of British influence. That, without instructions, Sir Hercules Robinson could hardly do; but he sent the Rev. J. S. Moffat, the Assistant Commissioner in the Bechuanaland Protectorate, on a mission to

[1] Sir H. Robinson to Lord Knutsford, 19 December 1888; *Parl. Pap.* 1890, LI [C. 5918].

[2] *Parl. Pap.* 1884–5, LVII [C. 4588]; Williams, Basil, *Cecil Rhodes*, p. 116; Leyds, *The Transvaal Surrounded*, pp. 383–91.

Bulawayo. Lobengula, like Cetewayo, ruled over a race of armed and disciplined savages, holding in subjection less warlike tribes such as the Mashona, the Makaranga and Banyai. Like the Zulu kings, Dingaan and Panda, and other Bantu chieftains in contact with white claimants for their favours, his diplomacy consisted in professing exclusive friendship for either side, and in making and repudiating treaties as occasion served. Presently, Grobler, venturing into territory between the Shashi and Macloutsie rivers, which was in dispute between the Matabele and Khama's Bamangwato, was killed by the Bamangwato, an ugly incident which was only closed when Khama in person paid compensation at Pretoria. Moffat had therefore no great difficulty in persuading Lobengula to repudiate the Grobler treaty, his signature to which, he subsequently declared, had been obtained by fraud, and to sign a treaty with the "Great White Queen" binding him not to enter into any treaty with a foreign state, or to cede any territory without the High Commissioner's sanction (11 February 1888).[1] Robinson ratified the treaty,[2] whilst, as a hint to the Boers and also to prevent hostilities in the disputed territory, he moved up a force of Bechuanaland Police to Fort Elebi. Matabele-Mashona land was thus barred to other than British enterprise.

But the Imperial Government would go no further. At the Cape, Kruger's policy of isolating the Transvaal whilst pushing his plans for the aggrandisement of the republic, his rejection of the customs union, his taxation of Cape imports, his opposition to the extension of the Cape railway, and his preference for Hollanders over the Cape Afrikaners had forfeited the sympathy of those who had been willing, a few years before, to leave expansion north of the Vaal to the South African Republic.[3] Cape politicians still shrank, however, from the expense of annexing more territory.

Yet Rhodes saw that immediate action was necessary for the fulfilment of his policy of making the Cape Colony the dominant state in South Africa by securing for it the reversion of the interior and its administration right through to the Zambesi. The North must be won by private enterprise, if possible under the aegis of the state. Rhodes and Beit sent agents from the Diamond Fields to Lobengula. Traders and representatives of rival syndicates were buzzing like flies about the badgered monarch, whilst his young braves wished to make short work of all intruders, but Rhodes's men, C. D. Rudd, Rochfort Maguire and Francis Thompson, won the day. On 30 October 1888, Lobengula affixed his mark to a concession by which, in return for £1200 a year, 1000 rifles, 100,000 cartridges and a steamboat on the Zambesi, he assigned to them all mineral rights within his dominions[4]

[1] Leyds, *The Transvaal Surrounded*, pp. 393–9; *Parl. Pap.* 1890, LI [C. 5904], [C. 5918]; Michell, *Life of Rhodes*, I, 240.

[2] 25 April 1888.

[3] Rhodes, C. J., speech in Committee, 23 July 1888, "Vindex", *Rhodes*, pp. 196 *sqq.*

[4] *Parl. Pap.* 1888, LXXV [C. 5363]; Michell, *Life of Rhodes*, I, 244; Hole, C. Marshall, *Lobengula*, ch. XVIII.

and undertook to grant no concession of land or mining rights in future without their consent. Rhodes then applied himself to the difficult and expensive task of buying out the claims of previous concession-hunters, and went to England (1888–9) to impress Lord Knutsford at the Colonial Office with his scheme for forming a single company to develop Matabeleland under a charter from the Imperial Government. The time was propitious. Imperial expansion was in the air; the prospect of the fabled gold-mines was tempting and romantic. Moreover, the system of incorporating chartered companies to administer concessions had recently been revived with success. With a Government still lagging behind the energy, enterprise and decision of imperial pioneers, a reversion to the Elizabethan methods of colonial development seemed natural. The British North Borneo Company had been incorporated in 1881, the Royal Niger Company in 1886, the British East Africa Company in 1888; Germany had adopted the same policy. Nevertheless Rhodes met with strong opposition in his quest for a royal charter. The Government at first received his project coldly. Opposition came not only from a rival syndicate which brought over two Matabele indunas to undermine the Rudd concession, but also from the Aborigines Protection Society, the London Chamber of Commerce, and the South Africa Committee of Members of Parliament led by Joseph Chamberlain, who, with the Rev. John Mackenzie, urged that here, as in Bechuanaland, direct Crown government was the only means of securing just treatment of the Natives.[1] A declaration by W. H. Smith, the Leader of the House of Commons, that British Bechuanaland would not be annexed to the Cape drew a strong protest from Sir Hercules Robinson. The High Commissioner, besides strongly supporting the project of a chartered company in order to put an end to the intrigues of rival concession-hunters, as in Swaziland, protested against "the amateur meddling of irresponsible and ill-advised persons in England . . . which converts many a colonist from an Imperialist into a Republican". He went so far as to say publicly that there was no room on a big scale for the imperial factor in the internal affairs of South Africa. Robinson was superseded.[2] But as to the Charter, the Government yielded when Rhodes and Alfred Beit came to terms with their rival syndicate. Knutsford recommended the incorporation of a chartered company on the grounds that its activities would thus be more directly subject to the control of H.M. Government, whilst relieving it of diplomatic difficulties and the heavy expenditure of a Crown Colony.[3]

On 29 October 1889, the British South Africa Company was granted a royal Charter, which gave it almost unlimited powers in a field of operations lying north of British Bechuanaland and the Transvaal

[1] Cf. Machford, Julian, *Khama, King of the Bamangwato*.
[2] *Vide supro*, p. 508; *Parl. Pap.* 1886, XLVIII [C. 4839], [C. 4890]; 1888, LXXIV [C. 5488].
[3] Lord Knutsford to Foreign Office, 16 May 1889, *Parl. Pap.* 1890, LI [C. 5918].

and west of the Portuguese possessions.[1] During the next few years, especially between 1889 and 1899, many millions were raised by the Company and spent upon the development of the country. No northern limit was set to its enterprise because its founder had long been dreaming of a British dominion which should reach from the Cape to Cairo; yet it was only fifteen years since Froude, expressing the opinion held by a large part of his countrymen, had recommended that a line of forts from Table Bay to False Bay should be the northern limit of imperial responsibility, and wished that Natal had been added to the Free State.[2]

While the discussions over the Charter were proceeding, Rhodes was planning with F. C. Selous, the famous hunter-explorer, an expedition to establish the occupation of the Company's territory.[3] There was no time to lose. A great trek was being prepared in the Transvaal; a large Portuguese force was believed to be on the eve of advancing from the east, and at Bulawayo, a group of German financiers, with political as well as commercial aims, were sowing distrust of the British in the mind of Lobengula. Already Rhodes had persuaded his devoted friend, Dr Leander Starr Jameson, to abandon his lucrative practice at the Diamond Fields to guard his interests at Bulawayo. Jameson was a man of singular charm and magnetic personality. Once and again he visited the Matabele king, cured him of his gout and won his confidence. He persuaded Lobengula to restrain his young braves from attacking the "pioneer" force when it assembled in his borders, and to permit its advance to Mashonaland, provided that all Matabele kraals and cattle-posts were avoided on the way.[4]

On 27 June 1890, 200 semi-trained Pioneers and 500 British South Africa Company's Police with Selous as guide began their march from Macloutsie River supported by imperial Bechuanaland Police at Fort Elebi. As they advanced, an attack was momentarily expected, for 20,000 Matabele hung on their left flank while they marched for 400 miles into almost unknown country, cutting a road through dense bush. At last, thanks to Selous, they found their way from the low to the high veld by Providential Pass through a frowning barrier of otherwise impenetrable hills and on September 12 the British flag was hoisted on the Mashonaland plateau, where Fort Salisbury was soon added to the chain of forts, Tuli, Victoria and Charter, which had been erected on the way. The Pioneers were quickly disbanded to become the first settlers of "Rhodesia", the name officially given to the chartered territory a few years later

[1] Michell, *Life of Rhodes*, I, 257–67 and 331; *Parl. Pap.* 1890, LI [C. 5918]; Eybers G. W., *Select Documents*, p. 559.

[2] Froude, J. A., *Leaves from a South African Journal.*; Walker, E. A. *Hist. of S.A.*, p. 388.

[3] Selous, F. C., *Travel and Adventure in S. E. Africa*, p. 312.

[4] Michell, *Life of Rhodes*, I, 294 *sqq.*; Lucas, Sir C., *Hist. Geog. of South Africa*, I, 314; Hole, C. Marshall, *The Jameson Raid*, p. 14.

(1895). The success of this daring march was due to the skill of its leaders, the courage of their followers, and the self-restraint of Lobengula.

Agreements were quickly made with tribal Chiefs towards the south and east, whilst far to the north-west, beyond the Zambesi, Rhodes secured from King Lewanika a mineral and trading concession over Barotseland (September 6).[1] "To protect his rear", Rhodes also busied himself in obtaining from the Native chiefs in the Bechuanaland Protectorate concessions of rights and territory, some of which, under certain conditions, were confirmed by the Home Government.[2] Dr Jameson, as Administrator with absolute power, devoted himself to exploring and settling Mashonaland, but, before assuming his duties as administrator, he had made his way from Fort Salisbury down the Pungwe River to its mouth,[3] where lay the new port of Beira. Immediate access to the east coast was essential for the development of Mashonaland, and although Beira lay within the Portuguese province of Mozambique, it was the best port available.

As the British South Africa Company advanced eastwards, there was an inevitable clash with the Mozambique Company about the vaguely defined sphere of influence claimed by the Portuguese, for Portugal had never wholly abandoned her settlements and claims made in the fifteenth century.[4] After the failure of the Anglo-Portuguese agreement of 1884,[5] she had made treaties with France and Germany which recognised her claim to all the territory right across the continent between Portuguese East and West Africa (1886),[6] but Lord Salisbury refused to recognise the sovereignty of Portugal "in territories not occupied by her in sufficient strength to enable her to maintain order, protect foreigners and control the natives" (1887). Portugal, however, defiantly continued to assert her right to a continuous dominion from Angola to Mozambique including Nyasaland, Gazaland, Manicaland (the territory of the chief Mutasa), Mashonaland and Barotseland, claiming that the Zambesi was within the Portuguese sphere of influence in East Africa and was closed to all but Portuguese vessels.[7] On the strength of these claims, Major Serpa Pinto annexed the Shiré highlands and opposed the navigation of the Zambesi and Shiré Rivers by the African Lakes Company, but Lord Salisbury refused to recognise pretensions based "on archaeological arguments only". A mild ultimatum was dispatched to Lisbon in

[1] Rhodes, C. J., speech at Kimberley, 6 September 1890; *Report of Directors, B.S.A. Co.*, 31 March 1891; "Vindex", *Rhodes*, p. 244.

[2] Michell, *Life of Rhodes*, I, 324–6.

[3] Colvin, Ian, *Life of Jameson*, I, pp. 149 *sqq.*

[4] *Vide supra*, ch. IV.

[5] *Vide supra*, p. 531.

[6] Hertslet, K. and E., *Map of Africa by Treaty*, II, 673, 703.

[7] *Ibid.* pp. 705, 706.

January 1890 and a British squadron moved to Portuguese waters. A Convention was then signed, delimiting the British and Portuguese spheres of influence. Much to the indignation of Rhodes, the Convention ceded to Portugal the whole of Manicaland to the line of the Sabi River and most of Barotseland. Ratification, however, was refused by that Power.[1]

Jameson and Selous on their march to Fort Salisbury had ascertained that Mutasa did not recognise Portuguese suzerainty, but desired British protection. A treaty was signed with him on September 14 assigning the sole land and mineral rights of Manicaland to the Company. There upon a strong force of Portuguese troops marched from their fort at Macequece, on whose existence their claim to the occupation of Manicaland was based, and occupied Mutasa's kraal. Captain P. W. Forbes promptly left Fort Salisbury at the head of some thirty police, arrested the Portuguese officers and dispersed their troops (November 15). A concession of mining and territorial rights was also obtained by the Company's representative from Gungunhana of Gazaland.[2] Its potentialities were great, for not only would it have given the Company the area around Beira, but it would also have cut Kruger's connection with Delagoa Bay.[3] The Portuguese commandant at Beira then closed the Pungwe River route and his customs officers seized a British vessel on the Limpopo with Dr Jameson, who had been landing arms for Gungunhana, on board. An attack upon the Company's camp at Massamessi near Umtali, during a truce in May 1891, was repulsed, and Macequece was occupied.[4]

Great Britain, however, had no intention of riding roughshod over a weaker Power, her ancient ally. Agreement was happily reached, and the Anglo-Portuguese Convention, signed in June 1891, defined the spheres of influence of the two Powers in East Africa.[5] Macequece and most of Gazaland were confirmed to Portugal, whose frontier was extended southwards "as far as a line following the parallel of the confluence of the river Pongola with the river Maputa to the sea-coast". Barotseland and a great part of Manicaland were now assigned to the Company. Nyasaland and Mashonaland were recognised as British. To Great Britain was reserved the right of preemption of any Portuguese territory south of the Zambesi. Navigation on the Zambesi was declared free, and access to the coast was secured for the Company by the reopening of the port of Beira. It was agreed that a railway should be built thence to Fort Salisbury.[6]

[1] *Parl. Pap.* 1890, LI [C. 5904]. Cf. Walker, E. A., *Historical Atlas of South Africa*; Hertslet, L. and E., *Map of Africa by Treaty*, II, 1018.

[2] Selous, F. C., *Travel and Adventure in S. E. Africa*, pp. 315 *sqq.*

[3] Walker, E. A., *Historical Atlas of South Africa*, Pl. 19.

[4] Hole, C. Marshall, *Making of Rhodesia*, ch. XVII.

[5] *Parl. Pap.* 1890–91, LVII [C. 6370].

[6] *Parl. Pap.* 1890–91, XCVI [C. 6375]; 1890–91, LVII [6495]; 1897, LXII [C. 8434].

Meanwhile the withdrawal by the Transvaal Government of all claim to extend its territory or influence beyond the Limpopo had enabled Rhodes to stop a migration of Boers into Matabeleland. Rhodes was as ready to welcome Afrikaner as British colonists, provided it were under the British flag; but the trek which was now being organised with the support of Joubert was advertised as a step towards the establishment of a Boer republic in the north. It was based on a worthless concession obtained from a minor chief of the Banyai nation by two Transvaalers, Malan and Adendorff. After an abortive attempt to sell the concession to Rhodes, 2000 burghers prepared to cross the Limpopo. The High Commissioner, however, had undertaken to assist the Company in repelling violations of its territory. The Bechuanaland Police moved north in support and the Company's Police patrolled the border. Pressure was put upon the Transvaal Executive by Hofmeyr's Bond, and Kruger prohibited the trek in accordance with the terms of the Swaziland Convention.[1] He was not at all inclined to imperil his own hopes of a port on the east coast by helping his rival, Joubert, in schemes for expansion northwards. When a hundred Boers prepared to cross the Limpopo on 24 June 1891, they were informed by Jameson, as Administrator of Mashonaland, that no one would be allowed to pass unless he signed a deed of submission to the Chartered Company.[2]

The final act in the occupation of Southern Rhodesia came two years later, when the Company picked a quarrel with Lobengula and mowed down his massed impis with the new-fangled maxim-guns. Rhodes had wished to send his Pioneer Column against Bulawayo at the start and had always held that a struggle was inevitable.[3] Undoubtedly the fertile pastures of Matabeleland afforded a temptation to the white settlers, as well as the gold claims they hoped to stake out, especially as the gold of Mashonaland had proved to be disappointing: the acquisition of a "New Rand", which was believed to run from Tati to Salisbury right through Bulawayo, was of vital importance to the Company, because its funds were running low. The attraction of a new goldfield would revive confidence in the Company, and enable it to raise the capital necessary for development and buying up the vital Rudd and other concessions, which its shareholders had recently learned to their dismay were not owned by themselves, but by Rhodes and other of their Directors organised as the United Concessions Company.[4] Apart from these considerations, the proximity of armed and trained savages accustomed to periodic raids upon the inoffensive

[1] *Vide supra*, p. 539.

[2] Hofmeyr, J. H., *Life of J. H. Hofmeyr*, pp. 409–20; Leyds, W. J., *Transvaal Surrounded*, pp. 311 *sqq.*; Fitzpatrick, *Transvaal from Within*, p. 45; Michell, *Life of Rhodes*, II, 31–3; Colvin, Ian, *Life of Jameson*, II, 206.

[3] Rhodes, C. J., speech at B.S.A. Co. Meeting, 18 January 1895.

[4] B.S.A. Co.'s *Reports*, and *Reports of Annual Meetings*, 1891–4; *The Economist*, 18 November 1893; Walker, *Hist. of S.A.*, pp. 413, 424.

Mashona was incompatible with the development of civilised government.

Lobengula was an intelligent Chief and would probably have been content to enjoy his monthly subsidy, but he had increasing difficulty in restraining his young braves, eager for plunder and the washing of their spears in blood, the ritual upon which depended their right to marriage. On 18 July 1893, a Matabele impi, sent to punish an unruly local Chief near the border, got out of hand and invaded the precincts of Victoria, burning, looting and killing some of the Mashona who were servants of the white men. They were attacked by the Company's Police, but made no resistance. Jameson decided that the time had come to take the offensive, and, in order to get the district High Commissioner's leave to move, reported that the Matabele had fired first. It was an undertaking of exceeding hardihood. Whilst a force composed of 225 Bechuanaland Border Police with guns and some 200 of the Company's troops, with 2000 Natives led by Khama, under Major Goold-Adams, moved forward from Tuli and Tati on the southern border, two columns advanced upon Bulawayo from the north-east leaving Forts Charter and Victoria on October 9. The first column, led by Major Forbes and Sir John Willoughby, and accompanied by Jameson himself, consisted of 220 settlers; the second, under Major Allan Wilson, numbered 414. They joined forces on the 16th, and after reaching the western plateau, were surrounded and attacked on the Shangani River by 5000 Matabele (October 25). Three fierce onslaughts were repulsed. Again, on November 1, in the neighbourhood of Imbembesi, the British camp was attacked by even larger numbers of picked troops; but furious courage proved of no avail against machine-guns. Lobengula's royal regiments were mown down, and when the Company's force reached Bulawayo two days later it found that the old king had set fire to his great kraal and fled. There they were joined by Rhodes, who had come up from Cape Town by way of Beira, dawdling till it was certain his columns could not be stopped.[1] A flying column of Volunteers and Imperial troops under Major Patrick William Forbes was sent in pursuit of the king. Lobengula was never captured, but in the chase a party of thirty men under Major Allan Wilson was cut off by his rearguard. They fought till their last cartridge was spent. "They were not afraid to die," said an Induna who was present, "they were men".

Thus, with a few hundred resolute and well-led men of its own and the indispensable aid of an imperial force, the Company had opened up the land for traders and settlers. Already the telegraph wires had been carried from Mafeking to Salisbury,[2] one-third of the way from the Cape to Cairo (February 1892), and within four years of the time when Lobengula was still squatting on a biscuit box within the

[1] Walker, E. A., *Hist. of S.A.*, p. 429.
[2] Rhodes, C. J., to F. Schnadhorst, 25 April 1892, Michell, *Rhodes*, II, 48–9.

bloodstained walls of his kraal, the Bechuanaland railway reached Bulawayo (December 1897). The occupation of Rhodesia marks the opening of a new era in the history of South Africa. The last representative of military barbarism had been wiped out. This dazzling feat of northern expansion had been largely the work of one great British pioneer. The claim made by Rhodes and his supporters, including his Cape Ministry, that his Company had won the war single-handed, and therefore deserved the spoils, was, indeed, gross exaggeration. At a cost of £80,000 to the British taxpayer, the Bechuanaland Border Police under Goold-Adams had contributed largely to the success of the expedition, and had brought up essential supplies after the occupation of Bulawayo; for the next six months the "imperial factor" was responsible for maintaining order by patrolling Matabeleland. Nevertheless, great are the uses of advertisement. Rhodes had his reward in the Matabeleland Order-in-Council of 18 July 1894 sanctioned by the Liberal imperialist, Lord Rosebury, who had recently succeeded the aged Gladstone.[1] By it, in spite of the protests of the Aborigines Protection Society and others, including Loch, who fought hard to retain strict imperial control, the Company was assigned, under the ultimate and fatally distant control of the High Commissioner, the administration of territory now defined as limited by the boundaries of the Portuguese east coast territories and the South African Republic to a point off the mouth of the River Shashi; by the River Shashi itself and the territories of Khama of the Bamangwato up to the Zambesi, and by that river as far as the Portuguese boundary on the west coast, including an area of ten miles round Fort Tuli, but excluding the district of Tati already dealt with in the original charter. Meanwhile, Chartereds had rocketed at the mere rumour of war, and now the shareholders had at last bought the vital concessions from the United Concessions Company at the price of doubling their own share capital.[2]

[1] B.S.A. Company, *Directors' Report for* 1892–4, pp. 31, 35; *Parl. Pap.* 1898, LX [C. 8773], pp. 13 *sqq.*

[2] Walker, E. A., *Hist. of S. Africa*, p. 429.

CHAPTER XXI

THE PROBLEM OF CO-OPERATION, 1886–1895

(a) Railways, Customs and the Native Question

We have noted in an earlier chapter that the overtures of the South African Republic for an agreement on customs policy were severely rebuffed by Cape Colony in the autumn of 1885, and that President Kruger was thus unable to secure any share of the duties levied at the Cape ports on goods destined for the Transvaal. Wherefore the republic reverted to its former exclusive policy. But circumstances were rapidly changing in its favour. The Delagoa Bay Railway tangle was beginning to straighten itself out, agricultural conditions were improving, and in 1886 the momentous discovery of the gold reef of the Witwatersrand pointed unmistakably to a radical change of conditions in the impecunious republic.[1]

When, in July 1886, the Cape Government issued invitations to a customs conference, the South African Republic turned the tables and replied that it did not think any good would come of the proposal, and when in 1887 the Cape, now thoroughly alive to the importance of inducing the Transvaal to look south rather than east, sent a delegation to Pretoria with offers of a railway extension northward and duty-free admission into the Colony of republican produce, it made no impression.[2] On the contrary, the Cape had to watch Kruger make a determined effort to win Brand over to his policy. To that end a conference between the two republican governments had been held at Bloemfontein in October 1887 at which the South African Republic pressed for a federal union and co-operation in railway matters, on the basis of the construction of a line to Bloemfontein as an extension of the Delagoa Bay line and the closing of the Free State to railway extension from the south.[3] These proposals, however, Brand rejected. It was possible therefore for the Cape to endeavour to secure the co-operation of Natal and the Free State. A customs conference representing these three states met at Cape Town on 30 January 1888, and came to terms both on the question of a customs union and on a policy of railway construction through the Free State based on junctions with the Cape line near Colesberg and the Natal line near Harrismith.[4]

[1] *Vide supra*, pp. 513, 533, 537.

[2] *Cape Parl. Pap.* 1887, G. 37.

[3] "Rapport der Commissie benoemd bij Volksraadbesluit van den 15 den Juni, 1887", dated 22 October 1887 (Parliamentary Library, Capetown).

[4] *Parl. Pap.* 1888, LXXIV [C. 5390], pp. 1 *sqq.*

This agreement did not, however, settle the question. The conference proposed a compromise between the tariffs of the Cape and of Natal. The Natal Legislative Council bluntly declined to ratify the increases of rates which this involved and, in view of the rapid development of the Transvaal, decided to risk the loss of its trade with the Free State and to extend its railway to the Transvaal border. In the Free State also the agreement met with unexpected opposition. Those who sympathised with the Transvaal's policy and those whose interests were likely to suffer from railway extension joined forces, and the Volksraad merely approved of a line to Bloemfontein, and that only by the chairman's casting vote. Still more serious was the death of President Brand on 14 June 1888.

The Cape Town Conference thus led to no definite result, and again the battle was joined between the Cape policy and the Transvaal policy with the Free State holding the casting vote. Kruger's position was also a difficult one. Once again there were heartbreaking delays in the construction of the Delagoa Bay line, and when the Cape threatened to extend its railways northwards from Kimberley along his republic's western border, he advised the Free State of his endorsement of the policy of constructing a line from Colesberg to Bloemfontein. Its further extension to the Vaal he still sought to delay, and he pressed his point vigorously at a conference held at Potchefstroom in March 1889, where he and Francis William Reitz, the new President of the Free State, concluded a defensive alliance between their two republics.[1]

Later in that month a second customs conference met at Bloemfontein.[2] It soon proved to be impossible to find a tariff basis which Natal could accept, but the Cape and the Free State agreed to form a customs union, which came into existence on 1 July 1889 and was joined shortly thereafter by Basutoland and Bechuanaland. At the same time arrangements were made for the construction of a railway by the Cape Government from the Orange to the Vaal.

So far then the Cape policy had achieved a limited triumph, but the defection of the Transvaal and its economic ally, Natal, from the cause of South African co-operation was a serious blow. One more attempt was made by Hofmeyr to bring the Transvaal in. The activity of Rhodes in the north[3] and his proposed Bechuanaland railway, with the resultant encirclement of the republic on the west and on the north, gave him an opening. He proposed to the President that, to check this move, he should offer the Cape free trade in colonial produce, on condition that it prevented the extension of the Kimberley railway to the north, and co-operated with the republic in a policy of railway extension through the republic from the Vaal to the

[1] *Staatscourant der Z. A. Republiek*, 20 March 1889. *Vide supra*, p. 536.
[2] *Cape Parl. Pap.* 1889, G. 26.
[3] *Vide supra*, pp. 543 *sqq*.

Limpopo with a view to the tapping of the resources of Zambesia.[1] On this basis Kruger indicated his willingness to negotiate, but his Volksraad could not be persuaded to accept the free trade proposal. That decision of the Volksraad represents a turning-point in South African history. It finally registered the determination of the Transvaal not to co-operate with its neighbours; it imposed an apparently insuperable check to the development of the policy of colonialism on broad South African lines; it left Hofmeyr with no alternative but to co-operate actively with Rhodes both in the Colony itself and in his schemes of developing the north. On 17 July 1890, Sprigg having come to grief over a programme of railway extension, Rhodes became Prime Minister of the Cape Colony with the active support of Hofmeyr and the Bond, always the one true source of his political power.

The years 1890–95 were on the whole years of steady progress in South Africa both towards material wealth and towards the ideal of South African co-operation. In Natal an important step was taken in the direction of the removal of the imperial factor and an approximation to the middle policy of colonialism by the grant of responsible government in 1893. Natal, like the rest of South Africa, prospered in consequence of the discovery of gold on the Witwatersrand and was thus enabled to face with equanimity the almost complete diversion of its trade with the Free State which followed the establishment of the customs union. It was content to push on its railways, which reached the Transvaal border in 1891, and to exploit the advantages of Durban's proximity to the goldfields as compared with that of the Cape ports. But when the Cape-Free State railway entered Pretoria at the end of 1892 and the Republican Government refused to sanction an extension of the Natal line, Natal trade began to languish. Not even the development of its northern coalfields, which the railway extension to the border made possible, could make good the decline. It was the realisation that Kruger would be better disposed towards a colony with responsible government than towards a community whose rulers were appointed from Britain that finally induced Natal to accept the constitutional change.

For some years after the 1882 elections the responsible government movement had been in suspense. It was only in 1890 that a new effort was effectively launched by John Robinson, assisted now by Harry Escombe, a former opponent.[2] Two elections were fought on the issue, until at last on 10 May 1893 the Council adopted a Bill "to provide for establishment of Responsible Government in Natal", which, having received the consent of the Imperial Government, became law on July 3.[3] In terms of its new constitution Natal received a

[1] Letter quoted in Hofmeyr, J. H., *Life of Jan Hendrik Hofmeyr*, p. 355.
[2] *Parl. Pap.* 1890–1, LVII [C. 6487].
[3] Act 14 of 1893 (Natal); see also *Parl. Pap.* 1893–4, LX (216), pp. 771–832.

bicameral parliament: a nominated Legislative Council of eleven members appointed for ten years, and an elective Assembly of thirty-seven members, having a life of four years, with a responsible ministry of not more than six members. Robinson became Natal's first Prime Minister, with Harry Escombe, to whom "the future Dominion of South Africa", as he phrased it, was an ever-present dream, as his Attorney-General.

It is significant that one of the first acts of the new Government was to sign a convention with the Transvaal early in 1894.[1] In October 1895 the Natal line reached Johannesburg, and the operation of the trade agreement which had been arrived at promised well for greater harmony and closer co-operation throughout South Africa. Thus then the constitutional gap between the republics and Natal had been narrowed, the geographical barrier between Natal and the interior had been surmounted, commercial and other relations were developing harmoniously, and there was a growing feeling in Natal in favour of entry into the customs union. This was, in the event, only consummated when, after the elections of 1897, the country party had defeated Escombe, who had in that year succeeded Robinson as Prime Minister. The Binns Government found it easier than its predecessor had done to compromise on the question of Natal's low tariff policy. At a customs conference in Capetown in 1898 a settlement based on mutual concessions was arrived at, and Natal entered the customs union.[2] But the events which had in the meantime taken place in the Transvaal robbed that fact of much of the significance which it would otherwise have had.

The Free State during this period pursued a happily eventless course. President Reitz followed in the broad lines of the policy of his predecessor. His country shared in the general prosperity of South Africa, and the new railway line under Cape control yielded large profits, thereby justifying the policy of co-operation with the Cape. At the same time the Free State maintained cautious but friendly contact with the northern republic. It was indeed the indispensable bridge in South Africa's inter-state relations, and became increasingly conscious of what Marthinus Theunis Steyn, Reitz's successor in 1896, described as its mission, "to unite in hearty co-operation the members of the South African family".[3] The ideals of South African unity had in those years nowhere more cordial supporters than in the Orange Free State.

Far more full of incident was the history of the South African Republic. Kruger's policy had encountered many setbacks. The Free State had rejected his advances; his republic was encircled by British territories on the west and on the north; the road to an

[1] *Natal Government Gazette*, 14 February 1894.
[2] *Cape Parl. Pap.* 1898, G. 66.
[3] Quoted in van der Merwe, N. J., *Marthinus Theunis Steyn*, I, 65.

independent outlet on the eastern sea was now barred by the recent annexation of Tongaland in 1895;[1] the railways of the British colonies of the Cape and Natal were tapping the rich Witwatersrand traffic in competition with the Delagoa Bay line, which had at last been completed.[2] Meanwhile the very circumstance which had brought wealth to the republic—the discovery of gold—also brought with it a large alien population, which implied a vital threat to the isolationist ideal. So then the Kruger policy came to be narrowed down to a dogged attempt to resist what the President regarded as the Uitlander menace.

The Witwatersrand discoveries brought about many changes in South Africa. Nowhere were they so great as in the Transvaal. The iron horse made its entry into the land, and the civilisation of the nineteenth century met with bewildering impact the slow-thinking conservatism of a still predominantly seventeenth-century community. Taken unwares as it was by a set of new problems for which it was entirely unequipped, the Republican Government met the situation, at least during the first few years, with what was in the circumstances surprising success.[3] The legislation necessitated by the birth of the new industry was well conceived; towards the town of Johannesburg the Government acted with a great deal of liberality, and in the choice of many of its chief officials on the Witwatersrand it was very fortunate. Thus for some years the relations between the Government and the industry were happy. The industry prospered despite slumps and setbacks, despite also the pessimism as to the life of the mines which prevailed until 1894 when the deep levels may be said to have proved themselves. The farming community was provided with a most welcome market; money became plentiful; land values rose, and the Government on its side enjoyed a rapidly mounting revenue. While in the financial year 1885–6 it had received only £177,877, that amount had increased to £1,557,445 in 1889 and to £3,912,095 in 1896. Native wars, such as that against Malaboch in the northern Transvaal in 1894, no longer disorganised the state's finances as in the old days. Important public works were undertaken. The machinery of government was in many ways effectively modernised.

In another way also the discovery of gold opened the way to progress. Not all the Uitlanders whom it brought to the Transvaal came from oversea. Many thousands were from the Cape, Natal and the Free State. Being South Africans, they promised to become an important factor in breaking down the isolationist policy of the republic. Of these immigrants from the rest of South Africa some participated in voicing the general grievances of the Uitlanders on

[1] *Vide supra*, p. 541.

[2] *Natal Government Gazette*, 14 February 1894 (Article 18); *Notulen eener Conferentie in zake een gemeenschappelijke Regeling van Spoorwegaangelegenheden in Zuid Afrika*, 4 *Nov.* 1895.

[3] See for details *De Locale Wetten der Z. A. Republiek*, 1886–9.

the Witwatersrand, others asserted their influence over a wider field and protested against Kruger's unsympathetic policy towards other parts of South Africa, and more especially against the dominant position of Hollanders in the public service. In this way much was done to stimulate the growth of a progressive party in the Volksraad and in the country, which championed a policy of greater liberality towards the Uitlanders and more sympathy with the ideals of a broader South Africanism. Under the impulse of the new ideas and the new influences which were coming into the country, this party grew steadily. At one time it very nearly secured a majority in the Volksraad and at the presidential election of 1893 its candidate, General Joubert, only failed to beat Kruger by the narrowest of margins.

At the Cape also the tide seemed to have set strongly in the direction of bringing about effective South African co-operation. The years 1890–5 were years of great progress in every way. The cabinet which Rhodes had formed in 1890 was described as a "Ministry of all the Talents". It included Merriman, Sauer, his lifelong friend and the ablest debater in the House, James Rose-Innes, and two Bondsmen, Sivewright and Faure. The opposition was weak and complacent, Sprigg having declared his general confidence in the Government. But the chief source of the ministry's strength lay in the alliance between Rhodes and Hofmeyr, the two men working in close co-operation and in almost daily consultation. That was no mere alliance of convenience formed under the stress of political need. It was founded on close personal friendship and on common political ideals, not only, as has already been shown, in external policy, but in domestic policy as well. Both men aimed at co-operation between the two white races on a basis of equality towards the ideal of a united South Africa, self-dependent but within the Empire. Both men desired economic federation as a stepping-stone to political federation. The Kruger policy of isolation had forced Hofmeyr into co-operation with the Rhodes policy of northern expansion of which he approved since it was based on the "elimination of the imperial factor". And in domestic politics, both men had the same general ideas. On questions of Native policy, the encouragement of agriculture, and the policy of protection of the products of the soil they were in hearty accord.

Thanks to Merriman's prudent finance, the Colony weathered the storm caused by the failure of some of the banks in 1890 and was guarded against a repetition of the worst features of the crash by the Bank Act of 1890.[1] A vigorous policy of agricultural development was initiated, Rhodes giving personal attention and direct encouragement by means of his own farming enterprises. In 1895 the Scab Act[2] was made universally applicable, a most important

[1] Act 6 of 1890.
[2] Act 20 of 1894.

measure, the acceptance of which by the rural Bond only Rhodes's alliance with Hofmeyr could have made possible. A sound and well-thought-out scheme of railway construction was pushed forward.[1] Round the person of Rhodes there gathered such loyalty and devotion of men of both British and Afrikaner stock as is given to few men to enjoy. In 1893, it is true, there was a cabinet crisis, caused by personal differences and a divergence of outlook on Native questions between Merriman, Sauer and Innes on the one side and Sivewright on the other, which came to a head when the latter gave out an important contract without going to tender. Rhodes, after an unavailing attempt to induce either Hofmeyr or Chief Justice de Villiers to take over the premiership,[2] reconstructed his government without the four ministers who had quarrelled, but (such was the friendliness of the atmosphere then prevailing in the House) with the aid of Sprigg, the leader of the Opposition. The good work was continued and, as a less tangible but none the less important result of the Hofmeyr-Rhodes alliance, feelings of hostility between British and Afrikaner seemed to have disappeared—the Bond itself was attracting many English-speaking members—the ideal of co-operation was being effectively realised.

The alliance had also a notable effect upon the development of Native policy. Once the rival policies of differentiation and assimilation had been clearly envisaged, especially in Cape Colony, the problem of reconciling the Transkeian policy of differentiation with the general policy of identity in the matter of the franchise had to be faced. It came up first in 1886 when the question of the extension of the franchise to the newly-annexed Territories was considered. Enfranchisement on the lines then prevailing at the Cape would have brought masses of barbarian Natives on to the roll. The realisation of this led to the insertion in the Parliamentary Voters Registration Act of 1887,[3] the Act which extended the franchise to the newly annexed areas, of a clause which prescribed that both there and in the rest of the Colony a share in communal occupation of property should not be a qualification. The policy of identity was therefore maintained in the matter of the franchise, but the amendment of the law implied a recognition of the difference between European and tribal conditions of life. Five years later the Rhodes-Hofmeyr alliance led to a further amendment of the franchise qualification, in response to the growing feeling that it was dangerous to include Native voters not approximating to European standards on a common roll with European voters. By the Franchise and Ballot Act No. 9 of 1892, the property qualification was increased from £25 to £75, and the would-be voter was required to give proof of his ability to write. The policy of

[1] Act 28 of 1895.
[2] A documented account will be found in Walker, *Lord de Villiers*, pp. 222 *sqq*.
[3] Clause 17 of Act 14 of 1887.

identity was thus still maintained, for the rules applied to Europeans and Coloured as well as to Bantu, but again there was a concession to the policy of differentiation in that the number of Natives who would in future exercise the same political rights as Europeans was substantially reduced.

In the Glen-Grey Act,[1] also a fruit of the Rhodes-Hofmeyr co-operation, a more comprehensive contribution to the solution of the problem was made. In the first instance only applying to the Glen Grey region west of the Kei, that measure, by virtue of a clause permitting of its extension by proclamation to other districts, was conceived by Rhodes as a "Bill for Africa". Its main features were an improved form of land tenure and the initiation of a system of partial Native self-government. The system of land tenure, which was based on perpetual quit-rent, gave individual ownership, but protected the Natives against the possibility of alienation of their land to Europeans. In this and other ways it was adapted to Native needs, and so, as a logical consequence of the policy of differentiation, such tenure was not to be a qualification for the franchise. The system of self-government provided for the establishment of village councils and district councils, and contained the germs of the important developments which have since taken place. Already in 1894 a proclamation was issued extending the Glen Grey system to the four Transkeian districts of Idutywa, Butterworth, Tsomo and Nqamakwe,[2] and the next year a general council was instituted; in 1899 the district of Kentani was brought within the scope of the Act,[3] in 1903 eight other districts were dealt with similarly,[4] and by later extensions the whole of the Transkei was brought in, with the result that the Bunga, the Transkeian Territories General Council with its not inconsiderable powers of self-government, which it exercised with wisdom, was, till its recent abolition, perhaps the brightest feature in the complex of relations between white and black in South Africa.

Thus in the Transkei during this period an important advance was made; but in other parts of the Colony there was an absence of any definite policy, and this fact operated in such a way as to accentuate subsequent friction between white and black in the political and economic spheres. *Laissez-aller* was also the dominant characteristic of Natal's Native policy during this period. There, as at the Cape, there was a steady increase in the area of tribal territory brought under European rule, but territorial advance was not reflected in any advance in the ideas animating Native policy.

The increase of territory did not follow, as might have been expected, immediately after the Zulu War. Cetewayo was banished,

[1] Act 25 of 1894.
[2] Proclamation No. 352 of 1894; *Cape Parl. Pap.* 1898, G. 5, pp. 84, 88, 90, 93.
[3] *Cape Parl. Pap.* 1890, G. 31, p. 81.
[4] Proclamation 152 of 1903; *Cape Parl. Pap.* 1904, G. 12, pp. 121 *sqq.*

but Zululand remained independent. With a view to the final destruction of its military system, it was divided by Wolseley into thirteen units, each under its own Chief,[1] and a Resident was sent to be "the eyes and ears" of the British Government.[2] He had, however, no effective powers, and for lack of a central controlling authority the system broke down, Zululand being split into warring factions. Early in 1883 Cetewayo was brought back to rule over a reduced kingdom with diminished authority.[3] He failed, however, to enforce peace and was driven out of his kingdom by some of his own people within the year.[4] These disturbances led to the entry into Zululand of a band of Transvaalers, who received, as the price of assistance rendered to Dinizulu, Cetewayo's son, a large block of land in north-western Zululand on which they established in 1884 the New Republic,[5] claiming authority over an area extending to the sea at St Lucia Bay. Fearful of the possibility of this entry into Africa from the east being ceded to Germany, the British Government promptly annexed St Lucia Bay[6] in terms of a forty-year-old treaty with Panda, the then Zulu king.[7] In 1886 it gave formal recognition to the New Republic,[8] which it had thus cut off from the sea, and saw it absorbed into the South African Republic a year later.[9] The rest of Zululand was annexed outright to the British Crown in 1887.[10] Only Tongaland and the lands of Zambaan and Mbegisa now remained independent between British and Portuguese territory. It was there that, as we have seen,[11] Kruger hoped for several years to establish his East Coast port, at Kosi Bay; but in 1895 the area was annexed to Great Britain.[12] Two years later, together with all that remained of Zululand, it was handed over to Natal.[13]

There was no advance in Natal in the field of Native policy corresponding to that in Cape Colony. During Shepstone's benevolent despotism, which came to an end in 1875, Natal's Native policy had rested on the personality of one man. Shepstone's achievement had been a remarkable one. With no military force and entirely inadequate magisterial and police resources, he had maintained peace and order among a Native population outnumbering the European population of Natal by almost fifteen to one. The foundations of his system, based as they were on an intimate knowledge of Native life and on the desire to govern the Native peoples with due regard to their distinctive characteristics and needs, were soundly devised. Unfortunately Shepstone lacked money and perhaps energy to build

[1] *Vide supra*, pp. 489, 529.
[2] *Parl. Pap.* 1880, L [C. 2482], pp. 255–60.
[3] 1883, XLIX [C. 3466], pp. 107 *sqq.*
[4] [C. 3864], pp. 53 *sqq.*
[5] 1884, LVIII [C. 4191], pp. 55 *sqq.*; 1884–5, LVI [C. 4214], pp. 60, 83, [C. 4274]; 1886, XLVIII [C. 4645]; 1887, LXI [C. 4913].
[6] *Vide supra*, pp. 337, 530.
[7] 1884–5, LVI [C. 4587], pp. 1 *sqq.*
[8] 1887, LXI [C. 4980], pp. 57 *sqq.*
[9] 1890, LII [C. 5892], pp. 71 *sqq.*
[10] 1887, LXI [C. 5143], pp. 40–1.
[11] *Vide supra*, pp. 538 *sqq.*
[12] 1895, LXXI [C. 7780], pp. 41 *sqq.*
[13] 1898, LX [C. 8782], pp. 23 *sqq.*

upon these foundations once they had been laid. He instituted no active policy of civilisation; he did little to encourage the Natives to tread the path of progress; he did not seek to give them any means of political self-expression. His successors followed in his footsteps. Where they departed from his system, as in the institution of a Native High Court[1] with its resultant division of authority which disturbed the Native mind, and in the rigid codification of Native law,[2] they made changes for the worse rather than for the better. For the rest the *laissez-aller* attitude of Shepstone's later years was maintained. On the other hand, the paternalism and accessibility of Shepstone disappeared and officialdom took its place. So it was that, while his successors, like himself, failed to civilise the Natives, they, unlike him, began to lose control of them. Tribal disintegration was allowed to proceed without any adequate substitute for tribalism being provided, and nothing was done to find, either by the scientific development of agriculture or the creation of a local government system, an outlet for the energies that had once been expended in intertribal strife. Thus was created the situation which was to produce the rebellion of 1906.[3]

In the republics also the seeds of future trouble were being sown. The Free State, it is true, was in the favoured position of having comparatively few Africans to rule apart from those in European employ. Yet even there practices grew up during this period which were to add their quota of complexity to the Native land problem when it came to be tackled seriously immediately after the Union of 1910.[4]

Much more difficult was the problem in the Transvaal, where there was a far larger Native population. Of the South African Republic it would not be unfair to say, that prior to 1872 it had no Native policy at all, save in the matter of defence against possible disturbances and the provision of labour, and that while President Burgers did lay down a policy,[5] he made little attempt to carry it out. During the period of the British administration also little definite progress was made. A Department of Native Affairs was, however, created, which was retained after the retrocession, and the appointment by Shepstone of his son Henrique as head of that department brought the ideas of Natal to influence the subsequent Native policy of the republic. Indeed, the Ordinance (No. 11 of 1881), which was passed at Henrique Shepstone's instance by the moribund Legislative Assembly of the Transvaal, though it was rendered inoperative by the

[1] In terms of Law 26 of 1875.

[2] Law 19 of 1891. See also *Report of Natal Native Affairs Commission*, 1906–7, *Parl. Pap.* 1908, LXXII [Cd. 3889], p. 14.

[3] The development of Natal native policy may be studied in the Report of the Natal Native Commission of 1881–2 and accompanying evidence, printed in *Natal Government Gazette*, 31 October 1882.

[4] *Vide infra*, p. 679.

[5] See Law 3 of 1872, Law 4 of 1873, Law 3 of 1876.

Pretoria Convention, served in many respects as the basis of subsequent republican legislation. Of that legislation the most important item was Law 4 of 1885. That law, which accepted in its preamble the principle of differentiation, gave recognition to Native law, appointed the President as Paramount Chief, created the office of Superintendent of Natives, and provided for the stationing of specially qualified officials as commissioners in areas with large tribal populations. Meantime a Locations Commission had been constituted in terms of the Pretoria Convention to deal with what was in the Transvaal the most pressing aspect of the Native problem[1]—the demarcation of areas as native reserves. This Commission did a great deal of useful work, but it did not complete its task, leaving many tribes unprovided for.[2] From this, and from the failure to enforce the removal of Natives to the new locations where these had been provided, has arisen the complexity of the Native land problem in the Transvaal to-day with its large number of Natives living on Crown lands and on European-owned farms. To that, too, coupled with the failure of the Republican Government to encourage agricultural development, was due the pressure on Natives to enter into industrial occupations, and so was created another most difficult problem of competition between black and white. Thus, while the Transvaal adopted some of the good points in the Natal system, it took over also many of its weaknesses and in some cases accentuated them. It would have been well for South Africa if the Republican Government had, during the last decade of its history, been free to give more attention to its Native problem, which was, almost unnoticed, steadily increasing in complexity and in difficulty.

Besides the problems arising from the contact between European and African there were developing those which resulted from the contact of European and Indian. Those were problems which concerned mainly Natal and the Transvaal. The Cape never attracted Indians in any great numbers; the Free State early in its history prohibited Asiatic immigration.[3]

The coming of the Indian to Natal was the result of the development of sugar-growing in its coast belt. The Bantu labour available in Natal did not satisfy the planters in respect of quantity or of quality; other sugar-producing countries had grown rich with the help of indentured Indian labour. Why not Natal? And so, with the approval of Sir George Grey, India, as we saw in an earlier chapter, was pressed to send indentured labourers to Natal.[4] After some

[1] *Parl. Pap.* 1882, XXVIII [C. 3114], p. 42 (Article 21 of Convention), quoted in Eybers, *op. cit.*, pp. 455 *sqq.*

[2] See *S. A. Native Affairs Commission*, 1903–5; *Parl. Pap.* 1905, LV [Cd. 2399], *Evidence*, IV, 427–8, Questions 39745–55.

[3] *Wetboek van den Oranje Vrijstaat*, 1891, Hoofdstuk XXXIII, 262 *sqq.*

[4] *Vide supra*, p. 427.

hesitation it agreed, and the first shipload of coolies was landed in 1860. In 1866 the permission was withdrawn by the Government of India, but by 1874 its scruples had again been overcome. In that year the Natal Legislative Council created an Indian Immigration Trust Board to which it was to contribute £10,000 annually.[1]

For many years Indian immigration was regarded on all sides as an unqualified boon to the colony, not merely because it made possible the growth of the sugar industry, but because it promoted the colony's economic development in other ways. The Government not only actively encouraged the introduction of indentured labour, but also held out inducements for the labourers to remain in Natal after the expiry of their contracts.[2] In the 'eighties the voice of criticism began to be heard as a result of the tendency for certain occupations, mainly commercial, that were previously in the hands of Europeans to pass over to "free" Indians, that is, either those whose indentures had expired or those who had entered the colony on their own account. In 1884 a motion was introduced into the Natal Legislative Council asking for a commission to "devise the best means to be adopted to bring the Asiatic population of the colony under more effective supervision and control".[3] In 1885 the Natal Government appointed an Indian Immigrants Commission presided over by Mr Justice Wragg, which revealed a preponderance of European opinion in the colony against the "presence of the free Indian as a rival or competitor, either in agricultural or commercial pursuits".[4] But the interests of the sugar planters were powerful, and it was not until 1894 that the first administration under responsible government secured parliamentary sanction for the abolition of the annual government grant in aid of Indian immigration.[5] About the same time, instead of the indenture-expired Indian being induced to stay, pressure began to be put upon him to return home. After a Natal deputation had visited India to discuss the position with the Indian Government,[6] an Act was passed (Act No. 17 of 1895) which was conceived with this object, and *inter alia* imposed an annual licence fee of £3 on every indenture-expired Indian who did not either renew his indentures or return to India. But Indian immigration still continued on a considerable scale, chiefly in the form of "free" Indians, until in 1897 public feeling rose so high that an attempt was made to prevent forcibly the landing of some five hundred free immigrants. As a result, Escombe, who deplored that the lack of South African unity made it impossible to deal with the

[1] Law 20 of 1874.

[2] Law 2 of 1870, Sect. 51.

[3] *Votes and Proceedings, Natal Legislative Council*, 1884, p. 242.

[4] Report printed as Supplement to *Natal Government Gazette*, 20 September 1887. See specially pp. 84 *sqq*. See also Andrews, C. F., *Documents relating to the New Asiatic Bill*, pp. 25 *sqq*.

[5] Act 37 of 1894.

[6] *Natal Departmental Reports*, 1893–4, pp. A, 19 *sqq*.

Asiatic problem in a more effective manner,[1] introduced and passed into law an Immigration Restriction Act (No. 1 of 1897), which, in effect, all but prohibited the entry of "free" Indians, and also a licensing law relating to dealers (No. 18 of 1897), which was intended to check Indian competition in trade. The Imperial Government reluctantly gave its assent, regretting the necessity for restrictions which would exclude British Indian subjects from South Africa, but accepting the prohibition in order to secure the fair treatment of those who were lawfully settled there. The Imperial Government went on to demand fair and equitable treatment, involving complete equality before the law, for the Indian residents of Natal. Thus the Act of 1897 practically ended the immigration of "free" Indians. Nevertheless, the importation of indentured Indian labour continued, and so great was the natural increase of Indians already in Natal that the Indian population soon came to exceed the European.

In the Transvaal meanwhile the Indian problem was developing on parallel lines, though on a much smaller scale. Here there was no question of the deliberate introduction of Indian labourers, and indeed at the time of the retrocession there were no Indians in the territory.[2] But from 1881 onwards Indian traders began to enter the republic from Natal. By 1884 they had begun to make their presence felt, and public representations were made to the Government to pass restrictive legislation, such representations being based not so much on trade rivalry as on the objection prevailing in the Transvaal to any suggestion of equality between white and coloured races. The Government's hands were tied, however, by Article 14 of the London Convention, which gave any person other than a Native full rights of residence and trade in the South African Republic,[3] and before taking any action it consulted the Imperial Government as to whether legislation such as it was being urged to enact would be held to be in conflict with that article. Having obtained what it held to be satisfactory assurances, it proceeded to pass Law 3 of 1885, which excluded all Asiatics from the franchise, empowered the Government to demarcate areas for Asiatics to live in, and forbade the acquisition of fixed property by them outside of such areas. The law did not, however, become effective before 1887. The imperial authorities contended that it went further than they had in the original correspondence been led to believe, and it was only on the strong representations of the Republican Government based on health grounds, and in consideration of certain amendments to the law, that they finally withdrew their opposition.[4] Even so, difficulties of interpretation soon arose. The Transvaal Government held that the law

[1] Escombe, H., *Speeches of the Late Rt. Hon. Harry Escombe*, p. 335.

[2] See statement by E. F. Bourke, quoted in *Report of Asiatic Inquiry Commission, Union Parl. Pap.* 1921, G. 4, p. 9.

[3] *Parl. Pap.* 1884, LVII [C. 3914], quoted in Eybers, *op. cit.*, p. 473.

[4] *Parl. Pap.* 1895, LXXI [C. 7911], pp. 50 *sqq.*

allowed them to limit Asiatics not only in respect of the areas in which they might reside, but also in respect of the areas in which they might trade, and the Courts confirmed this view. The British Government strongly contested this interpretation. There followed a long and wearisome correspondence during the course of which little was done to enforce the law, until finally the point was submitted to arbitration. The arbitrator, Justice Melius de Villiers of the Free State, gave his award in favour of the republic.[1]

Such then was the legal position in the Transvaal. Doubtless, if the Republican Government could have exercised untrammelled discretion, it would, like the Free State, have forbidden Asiatic immigration altogether; as it was, possibly because of its unwillingness to alienate the British Government in a matter which affected its Indian subjects, it never really enforced even the law which it had enacted in other than a half-hearted fashion.[2] Only in a few towns were locations demarcated; even there no serious attempt was made to compel the removal of Asiatics to those locations; the Asiatic population increased steadily, and in 1899 numbered several thousands. Already their competition was keenly felt by the European small trader with his higher standard of living, though they were popular with the poorer burghers. Thus another problem had been allowed to develop under cover of the disunion prevailing in South Africa.

(*b*) The Jameson Raid

Rhodes had by 1890 achieved a position of immense power and prestige. Premier of the Cape Colony, he was also the founder of Southern Rhodesia and the head of De Beers and the Chartered Company. As managing director of the Gold Fields Company, his interest in the good government of the Transvaal was very great. He was more eager than ever to hasten a customs and railway union, which, like the Prussian Zollverein, would, he was convinced, lead on to a federal union of the whole Empire through inter-imperial tariff preferences. In the Cape Colony, racial antagonism was dying down, for Hofmeyr, at the first Colonial Conference on the occasion of the Queen's Jubilee in 1887, had shown that he was at one with Rhodes in advocating an imperial Zollverein and Colonial Home Rule.[3] When Natal was granted self-government (1893)[4] the prospect of confederation grew still brighter, for the new ministry declared in favour of economic union. The Transvaal alone, with its policy of commercial isolation and political expansion as the predominant factor in a Federated Afrikaner Republic, stood in the way.

[1] *Parl. Pap.* 1895, LXXI [C. 7911], pp. 5 *sqq.*
[2] Report of Asiatic Inquiry Commission, *Union Parl. Pap.* 1921, G. 4, pp. 7–9.
[3] Hofmeyr, J. H., *Life of J. H. Hofmeyr*, p. 297.
[4] *Parl. Pap.* 1893–4, LX (216).

Together with the virtues and vices normally characteristic of a peasant class, the farmers of the veld had developed to a singular degree a love of isolation and personal independence. From Calvinist forbears, Dutch, German and Huguenot, and from long political experience they inherited a desire to be alone, a desire intensified by long years spent amidst the wide spaces and clear atmosphere of the Karoo, so that it was said that among them a man begins to feel crowded when he can see the smoke from an adjoining farmstead. The Transvaal Boers nursed a hatred of industrialism, commercialism and officialism. They were content and determined to rule in patriarchal fashion over their families and servants, the Bible in one hand and the sjambok in the other. Especially did they resent interference on behalf of the Natives as "working the destruction of the land"[1] and endangering the lives of the sparsely-settled farmers. The country into which they had trekked some seventy years before they regarded as theirs by right and might. Dour, unprogressive, rooted in the tradition of their forefathers and regarding themselves as a chosen people, they had no intention of sharing their republic with the cosmopolitan crowd of later immigrants on the Rand, whom they despised as townsmen and scions of alien races, whilst appreciating their merits as consumers of produce and payers of taxes. The original Transvaal trekkers, by nature independent and resentful of control, had gone forth into the wilderness to become rulers without any adequate training in self-government. Inevitably the Boers had acquired but little skill in the business of government; yet the industrial development of the Transvaal under these newcomers rendered wise administration both difficult and imperative. The result was that the administration passed largely into the hands of other strangers.

When Kruger returned from his visit to London and the Continent in 1884, he had brought with him a following of educated Dutchmen and Germans, chief of whom was Dr W. J. Leyds.[2] This able lawyer had soon become his State Attorney and then, in 1892, State Secretary. Such men as he naturally induced the President to bring out more of their kind and equally naturally stiffened him in his anti-British attitude. Kruger relied on them reluctantly because he knew how much many of his burghers disliked them; but since he would not call in Free Staters or Cape Afrikaners to supply the administrative ability and experience that were lacking in "the sons of the soil", he must rely on foreigners from overseas. These men encouraged the hope that European Powers would support an attempt to throw off such shreds of British control as still remained; they gave Continentals an interest in their state by borrowing their money; they founded national institutions such as the National Bank, and fostered the Hollando-German Netherlands Railway to render the Transvaal independent of British or South African trade and

[1] Noble, John, *Official Handbook of the Cape Colony*.

[2] *Vide supra*, p. 521.

capital. At the same time the system of concessions and monopolies adopted by the republic gave opportunities for corruption, whilst diverting the profits of the gold-mines to the Treasury and thus providing the means of arming the republic, albeit on a small scale for the moment. One such concession was the Dynamite Monopoly, which cost the mines over £600,000 a year and was described by the President as a part of independence, because though it made no dynamite, it could make small-arm ammunition.[1]

The discovery of gold had drawn to the Transvaal a new immigration of European, American and Australian miners, as well as mine-owners, by no means exclusively British. Within ten years of the day when the ground was first broken on the Rand, they numbered more than half the population.[2] By their labour and enterprise they converted a backward and almost bankrupt country into one teeming with riches, whose political importance in South Africa increased in proportion to its wealth. The new wine of a vigorous and progressive race was being poured into the old bottles of a seventeenth-century Calvinism. The wine was full-bodied and the fermentation strong, but the bottles were singularly tough.

Sooner or later it was inevitable that the newcomers would demand political equality. That demand was hastened by the maladministration and corruption of the system under which they had to live. For Kruger was as determined as his burghers to obtain as much as possible of the profits of their industry whilst denying them any share in the government. There was always present in his mind, as in theirs, the memory of the English-speaking agitations which had helped to bring about the annexation of Boer Natal in 1842 and of the Transvaal in 1877. On the other hand, the Uitlanders (foreigners), as they were called, were conscious that they contributed five-sixths of the taxation, but that in the disposal of the revenue and in the making of laws they were allowed no voice. In the British colonies, Afrikaners and British enjoyed equal rights, even though the Afrikaners were in a majority, at all events with Cape Colony. Kruger had promised in 1881 that British subjects in the Transvaal should have equal rights and privileges with the burghers, except perhaps in the case of a young person who had just come into the country;[3] but in spite of a British Commissioner's warning, he did not commit himself on the score of the franchise. But in defiance of the spirit of the Convention by which the independence of the republic was conceded, and the pledge without which it would not have been signed,

[1] *Milner Papers*, I, 128, 494; Fitzpatrick, Sir P., *The Transvaal from Within*, pp. 59, 254; *Parl. Pap.* 1899, LXIV [C. 9317].

[2] *Parl. Pap.* 1895, LXXI [C. 7633].

[3] *Vide supra*, p. 496; Cook, E. T., *Rights and Wrongs of the Transvaal War* (1902 ed.), pp. 260–1. *Parl. Pap.* 1882, XXVIII [C. 3219], p. 25; 1900, LVI [Cd. 396], p. 1. For a passage omitted from the *Parl. Pap.* see Walker, *de Villiers*, p. 336.

restrictions upon the franchise and the liberties of the Uitlanders had been imposed, and were tightened as their numbers grew. As early as 1882,[1] when the gold-rush to Lydenburg had begun, Kruger, then the dominating member of the Triumvirate, had begun a series of measures extending the period required for landless men to obtain the franchise. His object was to save himself from being swept from power by mildly progressive new voters likely to support his rival Joubert. He did indeed invite immigrants to enter his republic after his election as President in 1883;[2] but four years later, he told the newcomers, who came trooping up to the newly-discovered Rand goldfields, that though he would draw no distinction between them and his "old burghers" in other respects, he would not give them the vote.[3] His attitude is understandable. He had gone out on the Great Trek as a small boy; the republic was largely of his making; it was essentially a pastoralist community, and he wished it to remain so, and now here were these alien folk of diverse tongues, faiths and traditions setting up a sprawling industry on the burghers' grazing lands. Few as yet believed that the mines would have a long life. If, therefore, he argued, he gave these people the vote, not only might they put Commandant-General Piet Joubert or some other rival in his place, but run the state into heavy expenditure in their own short-term interests and then, when the gold gave out, leave the old burghers to shoulder the debt. Worse still, they might vote his country into Rhodes's railway and customs combines, or even under the dreaded Union Jack. Not unnaturally, he sought to cope with the first really big rush to the Rand in 1890 by a drastic franchise law.[4]

The new franchise law did not modify the oath of allegiance, nor reduce the tangle of registration regulations which cumbered the entry to the road to the vote. It did indeed create a Second Volksraad, and made the acquisition of the right to vote for members thereof and to sit therein comparatively quick and easy; but it directed this assembly to concern itself only with the affairs of the mining districts, gave it no powers of taxation, subjected its acts to review by the original legislature, now the First Volksraad, and provided that the franchise for this Second Volksraad should not carry with it the vote for the Presidency or the First Volksraad. Aspirants for this, the vote that mattered, must wait fourteen long years with no assurance that the law might not be altered suddenly to their disadvantage, for the First Volksraad by no means always legislated by the leisurely and well advertised process of *wet* (statute), but often at a moment's notice by mere *besluit* (resolution). Nor was remedy to be had in the Courts, for at that time not even the Chief Justice claimed the right to test the

[1] Eybers, *Select Documents*, *op. cit.*, p. 437, note 3.
[2] Fitzpatrick, Sir P., *The Transvaal from Within*, pp. 39, 59–62.
[3] Van Oordt, J. F., *Paul Kruger en de Opkomst der Z.-A. Republiek*, p. 473.
[4] Eybers, *Select Documents*, *op. cit.*, pp. 488, 495, 500.

validity of legislation by the touchstone of the written and presumably rigid *Grondwet* (constitution). If it was in the law-book, a *besluit* was as good law as a *wet*.[1]

It is impossible to say how many Uitlanders would have sought to qualify for the franchise if it had been offered to them on easier terms. Probably few British subjects would have done so, but many others would doubtless have applied, especially men born in other parts of South Africa. As it was, most Uitlanders had been too busy and excited, in the early days especially, even to try to register. As time went on, the mining magnates showed clearly that they did not "care a fig for the franchise".[2] What was it to them? They had not come to the Rand to settle for good, but to make money; taxation was not heavy; the Gold Law was far more liberal than, for instance, in Rhodes's Charterland; they did not mean to damage their great cosmopolitan industry by quarrelling with the authorities, and they found that, if it came to the worst, some at least of the officials could be bribed. Middle-class folk and miners, who, for the most part, meant to make the Rand their permanent home, looked at it differently. They were used to political and trade union liberties, and resented being virtually told that they were less good men than others, who, in their eyes, were a pack of backveld bumpkins, while those of them who were South Africans saw no reason why other South Africans should be privileged above themselves simply because they had been born sons of burghers or had friends in high places. It was South Africans such as these who could perhaps have made the best contribution to the Transvaal had they been given the chance.

Doubtless the franchise and other grievances were exaggerated, especially in bad times, for the Rand was a "nervy" excitable region because of its altitude, its dependence on a speculative industry and its curious isolation. Be that as it might, there were other grievances. Such were high railway rates, customs duties and monopolies, which sent up the cost of living for everyone; the dynamite monopoly, which increased working costs on the mines on which the whole community depended; difficulties placed in the way of recruiting Bantu labourers, and the liquor traffic, which corrupted them when they had been recruited. Most of these grievances affected the magnates more than the rest, and to protect themselves, they formed the Chamber of Mines, not without good results. Other grievances, however, affected mainly the rank and file, who suspected that the Bench was dominated by the Executive, distrusted the juries manned exclusively by burghers, and grumbled that English was given far too little recognition in the Legislature, the Courts and the schools.[3] It was these hum-

[1] Kotze, Sir J. G., *The Judicial Crisis in the S.A. Republic*; Walker, E. A., *Lord de Villiers . .*, pp. 287 *sqq.*

[2] *Report of Select Committee . . . on British S. Africa*, Appendix III; *Parl. Pap.*, 1897, XIX, 311–1.

[3] Fitzpatrick, *Transvaal from Within* (1899 ed.), pp. 90, 327.

bler folk who realised first that votes were the surest way of getting the reforms they desired. In 1892, they were given a lead by Charles Leonard, an able and voluble Cape attorney, who began to enrol them in his National Union to seek redress by constitutional means.[1] He failed to win over any of the magnates, but he recruited a fair number of lesser folk and duly presented their petition. Kruger rejected it "Tell your people", he growled, "I will never give them anything".[2]

Many of his more liberal-minded burghers warned Kruger of the error of his ways, and so also did Rhodes a few days after the repulse of Leonard's petitioners;[3] but if Kruger would not hearken to his own Transvaalers, why should he listen to Rhodes, the man who had done so much to bar him out of Bechuanaland and the North? On the other hand, Loch, the High Commissioner, might have to be heeded, for it virtually lay with him to say whether he should be shut up in a kraal or be allowed to break out by way of the sole remaining opening through Swaziland to Kosi Bay. Negotiations on that issue were now destined to drag the Uitlander question into the limelight and cast the shadow of the imperial factor over Kruger's republic.

Kruger and Loch had met in conference thereon more than once, and on two occasions Uitlanders had expressed their feelings unmistakably. In 1890, some of them had insulted the Vierkleur while Kruger was passing through Johannesburg to meet Loch at Blignaut's Pont;[4] three years later, they had naturally given Loch an uproarious welcome as he was returning home from Pretoria, if only because he was the first High Commissioner to visit them. Their chance came again in 1894. This time, negotiations were certain to be more delicate than usual, because matters other than Swaziland were on the agenda. There was, first, the commandeering issue, which had arisen because British subjects, unlike those of many other states, were not exempted by treaty from commando service. A few of them had just been compelled to serve in the latest of the Transvaal's recurrent Native wars in spite of their protests.[5] Secondly, the franchise. This issue was coming up in an inflamed condition, for not only had the First Volksraad recently rejected two Uitlander petitions one after the other, but it had codified the franchise laws in such fashion that no Uitlander could get the full franchise until he was forty years of age and must be denationalised during the now customary fourteen years of waiting. Moreover, even Uitlanders' sons born in the republic were to suffer these disabilities, unless their fathers had taken the oath of allegiance.[6] That oath the Volksraad had reworded in a form which

[1] Fitzpatrick, *Transvaal from Within*, p. 94.
[2] Leonard, C., *Papers on the Political Situation in South Africa, 1885–1895*, p. 44.
[3] Rhodes in Cape House of Assembly, 16 August 1892.
[4] *Vide supra*, p. 539.
[5] *Parl. Pap.* 1895, LXXI [C. 7611], pp. 5, 8; 1896, LIX [C. 8159], pp. 1, 9.
[6] Law No. 14 of 1893, and No. 3 of 1894; *Parl. Pap.*, 1894, LVII [C. 7554].

most British subjects held to be unnecessarily humiliating, especially those many who believed that British suzerainty still existed, and that they ought, therefore, to be allowed to become burghers and still remain British subjects. Ripon, the Colonial Secretary, authorised Loch to offer Kruger concessions in return for a five-year Uitlander franchise.[1] Loch approached his task with some trepidation. Like many others, he hoped and believed that the Union Jack would soon be flying again at Pretoria; he was as eager as Rhodes to see southern Africa federated. His experiences in 1893 had led him to expect a civil war in the Transvaal between rival burgher factions, a war in which the Rand must be involved. He had decided that, in that event, he, as High Commissioner traditionally responsible for the peace of South Africa, would step in and stop it.[2] Perhaps as a warning, he had now brought the Bechuanaland Police up to the republican frontier. He did not go through Johannesburg, but he did not thereby avoid an Uitlander demonstration. The Pretoria Uitlanders turned out in force, and one of them, flourishing a Union Jack, mounted the box of the carriage in which he and Kruger were seated.[3] In spite of this display of bad manners, a provisional agreement on Swaziland was reached and the commandeering problem was more or less disposed of; but Loch did not venture even to mention Ripon's franchise proposal.[4]

This was not, however, the full tale of Loch's doings. All that he saw and heard convinced him that there would indeed be civil war, if yet another intransigent Volksraad were returned at the next elections, but now it would be a war between burghers and Uitlanders. He therefore resolved that, if that came to pass, he would call upon Kruger to protect British lives and property, and, if he did not do so, do it himself. He held that it must be done in that way, because if the cosmopolitan Uitlanders were successful on their own account and felt that they owed nothing to Great Britain, they would simply set up a republic of their own as averse as Kruger's to federation under the Union Jack.[5] Much of this he gathered from various Uitlander deputations. He indeed advised them to keep the law, but in chat with one or two Pretoria Uitlanders he showed himself anxious to know how long they could hold out.[6] After hearing a vehement Johannesburg deputation, which assured him that his appearance in their city would be the signal for a unanimous demand for British annexation, he was tempted to take them at their word, and then showed how his mind

[1] *Parl. Pap.* 1893, LXII [C. 7212], pp. 3, 13 *sqq.*, 123 *sqq.*; Wolf, L., *Life of... Ripon*, II, 255.

[2] *Parl. Pap.*, 1893, LXII [C. 7212], pp. 153 *sqq.*; *Cape Law Journal*, 1894; pp. 173, 269; Walker, E. A., *Life... of de Villiers*, p. 221.

[3] Kruger, Paul, *Memoirs* (1902 ed.), II, 247.

[4] *Parl. Pap.* 1896, LIX [C. 7933], p. 92, and [C. 8159], pp. 18, 21.

[5] Van der Poel, *The Jameson Raid*, pp. 15 *sqq.*

[6] Scoble, J., and Abercrombie, H. R., *The Rise and Fall of Krugerism*, pp. 149 *sqq.*, 158–9, 591 *sqq.*

was working in confidential talks with Lionel Phillips, the partner of Alfred Beit, Rhodes's staunch friend, and one of the few magnates who was inclined to co-operate with Leonard's National Union. Him Loch asked whether Johannesburg could hold out for a week, and hinted that, if it could, he would go thither straight away.[1] Possibly Phillips and the Pretoria Uitlanders read into Loch's words more than they should; but the fact remains that it was only the advice of the unenthusiastic magnate and of Sir Graham Bower, the anxious Imperial Secretary, which dissuaded Loch from risking a riot in Johannesburg with himself as chief rioter. On his return to Cape Town, Loch told Ripon what he proposed and asked for reinforcements and instructions. The Colonial Secretary approved of Loch's general idea, though he did not send the reinforcements. *Faute de mieux*, Loch tried to keep spare rifles handy for possible use by Uitlanders when the time came.[2] No one would suggest that he envisaged the Jameson Raid that was to be; but no one can deny that he sketched the rough plan: uproar on the Rand to be answered by the High Commissioner's intervention backed by a force from outside and arms for Uitlanders. Doubtless, Rhodes took note.

Phillips was inclined towards the National Union largely because the recent proving of the deep levels promised the Rand an almost indefinite life and thus stressed the importance of good government. Such government could best be ensured by votes. Rhodes as a fellow-Rand magnate, as it were an Uitlander *in partibus*, also saw that point. He saw much more. He knew that few even of the British Uitlanders had much love for him, the Cape or his Company, and he feared that the republic based on unlimited gold and Uitlander votes would never come into his federation, whether it was dominated by rivals like J. B. Robinson and the so-called Continentals, or by still more hostile "*Sydney Bulletin* Australians". Apart from all that, once the Transvaal, reformed or unreformed, had got railway connection with Delagoa Bay and Durban, it would shake itself free from dependence on the Cape-Free State sytem and snap its fingers at him. It was thus all the more infuriating that he should just have lost his best hope of bringing the republic to heel by having to give up, in face of German opposition, his attempts to acquire vital Delagoa Bay for the Cape Colony.[3] Then there was his Company on which so much depended. Failing the discovery of a New Rand, Charterland must be off-loaded as soon as might be either on to the parent Cape Colony or, better still, on to a South African federation, for he did not intend that the Company should bear the heavy cost of administration with no

[1] Van der Poel, *The Jameson Raid*, pp. 14 *sqq*.

[2] Van der Poel, *The Jameson Raid*, p. 17; Walker, *de Villiers*, p. 274; Wolf, *Life of... Ripon*, II, 227; *Parl. Pap.* 1894, LVII [C. 7554], and 1895, LXXI [C. 7611]; A. 6–96 (Cape) Appendix, p. vi.

[3] Gardiner, A. G., *The Life of Sir William Harcourt*, II, 311 *sqq*.; Michell, Sir L., *The Life of... Rhodes*, II, 95.

return longer than it must. Something must be done about it. Hence, towards the close of 1894, he went off in search of this New Rand with Jameson and John Hays Hammond, his American mining engineer from Johannesburg. They did not find it, but Hammond warned his companions that the Old Rand was seething with excitement and that if Rhodes did not direct the coming storm, the Uitlanders would take their own way.[1] Rhodes would not commit himself; the most he would do was to send Jameson to Johannesburg to see how the land lay. "The Doctor" promptly reported that Hammond was right; whereupon Rhodes sent him back to Rhodesia post-haste to drill his Police and raise volunteers duly equipped with the new-fangled maxim-guns.[2] If these had settled the Matabele, they could surely settle the Transvaalers.

The dreaded Volksraad elections went overwhelmingly in Kruger's favour and, at the same time, the Kimberley line reached Mafeking. Rhodes reminded Ripon of promises that, when it had done so, the Cape should have British Bechuanaland and his Company should have the Protectorate, so that the railway might be carried on to Bulawayo. Ripon temporised on that score, but when Kruger hinted publicly at the possibility of German aid, he promptly cut the Transvaal off from the sea. He reluctantly decided that Swaziland must go willy-nilly to that republic, but annexed the little territories to the eastward, which included coveted Kosi Bay.[3] Thus was Kruger at last shut up in a kraal.

By this time, Rhodes had come round to the idea of an Uitlander rising backed by Chartered levies. He and Jameson went to London in the New Year of 1895 to prepare the way. After being lionised, appointed Privy Councillor, and told, to his immense pride, that his North was to be named "Rhodesia", Rhodes returned to the task in hand. He detailed Jameson to foretell, with the Prince of Wales in the chair, the speedy economic federation of Southern Africa, and then to buy arms for the Company on an unaccustomed scale.[4] He himself approached the Liberal Prime Minister. The ever-helpful Rosebery approved of his plan, always provided the troopers did not go in before the rising had started, and helped to remove one major obstacle by suggesting to Ripon that Loch, who had long wished to retire, should be brought home almost at once instead of some three months later. Rhodes's old friend, Sir Hercules Robinson, was appointed in Loch's stead, a man experienced in South African affairs

[1] Colvin, I., *The Life of Jameson*, I, 307; Williams, B., *Cecil Rhodes*, pp. 394 *sqq.*; Michell *Life of . . . Rhodes*, II, 118 *sqq.*

[2] *Parl. Pap.* 1897, IX [311], pp. 259 *sqq.*; "Vindex", *Cecil Rhodes ... Life and Speeches*, p. 355; Williams, *Cecil Rhodes*, p. 248; Colvin, *Life of Jameson*, II, 13.

[3] *Parl. Pap.* 1895, LXXI [C. 7780], pp. 41 *sqq.*; [C. 7878]; 1897, IX [311], p. 348; Leyds W. J., *The Transvaal Surrounded*, pp. 346 *sqq.*; Fitzpatrick, *Transvaal from Within*, p. 106; Botha, P. R., *Die S. A. Republiek onder Kruger en Leyds*, pp. 469, *sqq.*

[4] *B.S.A. Co., Annual Meeting*, January 1895, pp. 19 *sqq.*; Dugdale, E. T. S., *German Diplomatic Documents*, II, 366.

and believed to be acceptable to Kruger. He was certainly acceptable to Rhodes, if only because he was ageing and not in the best of health and, therefore, less likely than Loch to ask awkward questions.[1]

Before sailing, Rhodes made useful contacts with influential members of *The Times* staff. He could reasonably count on the support of the imperial authorities at headquarters and Government House, and, unasked, that of the fervent imperialist, Edmund Garrett, the new editor of the *Cape Times*; nor need he despair of the accustomed backing of the Bond in Cape politics, even though the ailing Hofmeyr had just resigned his seat in the Assembly.[2] It was well that he could do so, because an approaching railway deadlock suggested that there was little time to be lost. At the end of 1894, the Natal line had reached the Transvaal frontier, the Delagoa Bay line had been completed, and the Sivewright Agreement had run out, thus depriving the Cape of its right to fix through-rates to the Rand. The Cape promptly cut rates to keep as much traffic as it could; the Netherlands Railway Company riposted by tripling rates over the last short section from the Vaal to the Rand. After the failure of a railway conference to reach agreement, the Cape proceeded to off-load north-bound goods at the Vaal drifts on to ox-waggons and trek them into Johannesburg, where a Kaffir boom was rising to its climax.[3]

At this critical stage, towards the close of May, Sir Hercules arrived with instructions to act as mediator, if events in the Transvaal so demanded, and the promise of reinforcements to give his intervention weight.[4] Then came a shock which swept away much of Rhodes's careful work in London: Rosebery's Liberals went out and Salisbury's Conservatives came in with their redoubtable Unionist ally, Joseph Chamberlain, as Colonial Secretary. The new Prime Minister, little interested in colonies, might perhaps be disregarded, but not so his ex-Radical colleague. Rhodes knew that Chamberlain had no love for him or his Company, and that though he too was eager to see southern Africa federated, he meant to have it on imperial lines and not on the Home Rule principles to which Rhodes and Sir Hercules subscribed. Altogether he was likely to be a more difficult man to handle than his colourless predecessor.

However, sufficient unto the day. . . . Meanwhile, here was a Transvaal legislator challenging the Uitlanders to "come on and fight", and then helping to throw out a big franchise petition.[5] Rhodes and Alfred Beit took up the challenge. Urged on by the ever-

[1] Van der Poel, *The Jameson Raid*, p. 23; Bower, Sir G., *Letters*; Bell, E. M., *Flora Shaw*, p. 177; Saner, H., *Ex Africa*, p. 258; Williams, *Cecil Rhodes*, p. 252; Gardiner, *Life of Sir William Harcourt*, II, 338; Walters, *de Villiers*, p. 225.

[2] Hofmeyr, J. H., *The Life of J. H. Hofmeyr*, p. 474.

[3] Hofmeyr, *Life of Hofmeyr*, p. 484; Cook, E. T., *Rights and Wrongs of the Transvaal War*, p. 57.

[4] Information given to one of the editors of the late Sir G. Bower, who queried the promise. So also did the late Earl Buxton at that time Under-Secretary for the Colonies.

[5] Fitzpatrick, *Transvaal from Within*, p. 400.

sanguine Jameson, they got into touch with Leonard and Phillips, now chairman of the Chamber of Mines, and found them in favour of an Uitlander rising supported *vi et armis* from outside.[1] This done, they made financial arrangements, which would surely prosper if all went according to plan. They induced the Chartered shareholders to authorise the issue of half a million new shares at £3. 10*s*. apiece at a date to be determined to pay for a stable administration in Rhodesia, the carrying on of the railway from Mafeking and the meeting of deferred interest on the debentures raised after the Matabele war, which would fall due at the end of the year.[2]

The next steps were to make sure of the new Colonial Secretary and get a jumping-off ground for Jameson and his men nearer to Johannesburg than Tuli far away to the north. It is hard to say precisely how much Chamberlain learned of what was afoot, because he himself confessed privately that he could not say what he had known and what he had not, but that, in any event, he had not wanted to know too much.[3] However that may have been, Rhodes sent Dr Rutherford Harris, the Company's Cape Town secretary, hurrying off to Whitehall to ask him for the transfer of the two Bechuanalands and, pending that, the immediate transfer to the Company of a small block of land at Gaberones some hundred miles north of Mafeking and right on the Transvaal frontier, so that the Company's Police might be able to protect the as yet non-existent railhead against "the ferocious Bechuana". Harris did so, but when he began to make a guarded "allusion" to Rhodes's plan, the great man refused to listen. After poor Harris had withdrawn, however, he did listen to Albert Grey, one of the Company's Directors, who was "in the know".[4] Harris was, therefore, justified in cabling to his distant chief that the Colonial Secretary would do all he could to help "provided he does not know officially of your plan", and, a little later after another talk uninterrupted this time by guarded allusions, "Mr Chamberlain states Dr Jameson's plan must not be mentioned to him".[5]

Chamberlain had to delay the transfer of the Protectorate, because Khama and two other Chiefs from those parts were coming to London to beg the Queen not to hand them over to the Company, whose allocation of reserves to the neighbouring Matabele had been far from generous. While he thus delayed, Kruger, at the end of August, played right into his hands and Rhodes's by giving notice that he would close the Vaal drifts to overseas goods in a few weeks' time.[6]

[1] Van der Poel, *The Jameson Raid*, p. 41.

[2] *B.S.A. Co. Annual Meeting*, 18 January 1895, p. 9; *Extraordinary General Meeting*, 12 July 1895; *Notice*, 24 July 1895.

[3] Garvin, J. L., *The Life of Joseph Chamberlain*, III, 83. Pakenham, Lady E., *Jameson's Raid*, gives a much more pro-Chamberlain account than that which follows in the text.

[4] Van der Poel, *The Jameson Raid*, 27 *sqq*.; Garvin, *Life of Joseph Chamberlain*, III, 33–9; *Parl. Pap*. 1897, IX [311], Qq. 6220–3.

[5] Garvin, *Life of Joseph Chamberlain*, pp. 110, 111; Van der Poel, *The Jameson Raid*, pp. 30, 31.

[6] *Parl. Pap*. 1897, LXII [C. 8474].

If he did close them, he would be breaking the London Convention, which forbade discrimination against the United Kingdom, whence these goods came. He would thus present Chamberlain with an unimpeachable excuse for intervention with at least the acquiescence of Cape Colonists and Free Staters, whose joint railway interests would be harmed. Had he but known it, he would also relieve Rhodes of the distasteful task of going ahead with the rising and the raid.

Pleased though he was to see Chartered £1 shares surging up to nearly £9 at the mere prospect of war with the Transvaal,[1] Rhodes felt bound to go ahead in case of accidents. He therefore made sure of the local embodiment of the imperial factor by explaining his scheme under the seal of secrecy to the disapproving Imperial Secretary, Sir Graham Bower, and, on his advice, informing the High Commissioner of the circumstances in which he would be expected to fill the role of *deus ex machina* bringing order out of chaos. Sir Hercules proved amenable, though he was always to plead ignorance of Rhodes and Chamberlain and their "damned conspiracies".[2] Having thus secured his rear, Rhodes concluded a firm bargain with Leonard and Phillips. The arrangement was that he should arm the Uitlanders and hold Jameson ready to go in to support the rising; that the Uitlanders should seize Johannesburg and the casually-guarded arsenal at Pretoria, and that he would despatch the High Commissioner northward at the psychological moment. He at once sent up Frank, his soldier brother, to organise the rising, set about smuggling the promised arms into Johannesburg, and then made sure of a jumping-off ground for Jameson.

Rhodes knew that British Bechuanaland was on the point of coming to the Cape Colony, but that would not serve his purpose.[3] He must have territory under his Company's direct control, and he could not wait for Gaberones, which was inconveniently far from the Rand and could scarcely be his awhile. He therefore pressed for the immediate transfer of a small block of land and invaluable water-holes at Pitsani near Mafeking. This transfer was made on 20 October with the ready assent of the minor Chiefs concerned. Jameson, as Resident Commissioner, at once hurried down, drafted Police from Rhodesia thither, and began to enrol members of the Imperial Bechuanaland Police, who were so soon to be disbanded.[4] He varied his labours by dashing to Johannesburg, confirming the as yet tiny Reform Committee in their resolution, and, after much persuasion, obtaining from five leading Reformers an undated letter of invitation to come to the rescue of the women and children.[5]

[1] *B.S.A. Co. Directors' Report*, 1894–5, p. 2; *The Economist*, 28 September 1895.
[2] Van der Poel *The Jameson Raid*, pp. 34 *sqq.*; *Parl. Pap.* 1897, IX [311], Qq. 2503–25.
[3] Eybers, *Select Documents*, p. 76.
[4] Van der Poel, *The Jameson Raid*, p. 39; *Parl. Pap.* 1896, LIX [C. 7962], pp. 12–16, 19, 28; A. 6–96 [Cape], Appendix A, pp. xiv–xvii.
[5] *Ibid.* pp. liii ff.

At this stage, Kruger almost rendered these hectic plottings labour lost, for, after one postponement, he closed the drifts on 1 November. At once Chamberlain saw to it that troopships should call at Cape Town, secretly arranged with Rhodes's Cape ministry for joint imperial and Cape military and financial action, and sent Kruger a virtual ultimatum.[1] Then, once Khama and his fellow-Chiefs had seen Her Majesty, he marked off with his own hand reserves covering nearly the whole of the Protectorate, and gave the Company a railway strip in the remainder right along the Transvaal border linking Mafeking and Pitsani with Rhodesia. On that very day, 7 November, Kruger reopened the Vaal drifts.[2]

Kruger thus saved himself. But he had had his warning. Like most other folk in South Africa and London, he had long suspected that trouble was brewing on the Rand. Resolved to take no risks, he sent Leyds, his State Secretary, to Europe to purchase arms, and directed that at least the local commandos be fully armed and that plans be made for the safety of Johannesburg and the capital. Chamberlain, for his part, felt that it would not do to let loose the irregulars too soon from the jumping-off ground, which he had just transferred to the Company. Knowing that it was for Rhodes to say when, if at all, the rising should take place, he advised him, as Harris duly reported, to allow "decent interval and delay fireworks for a fortnight".[3] He, nevertheless, sent him a strong hint that he was still ready to play his part by asking the High Commissioner what should be done in the event of a rising "with or without outside support".[4] The reply, edited jointly by Rhodes and Sir Hercules, first made much of Uitlander grievances, and then went on to recommend that the High Commissioner, with the avowed support of the British Government, should call upon the combatants to desist, and that all concerned should be told publicly that large forces were ready to sail for the Cape.[5] Having ascertained that Rhodes warmly shared his own hopes of seeing the Union Jack flying once more at Pretoria, Chamberlain said in the course of his reply that, if the Uitlanders would vote for that flag, they could choose their own Governor. At the same time, he gave warning that there must be no rising unless success were assured, because "a fiasco would be most disastrous".[6]

Such would seem to be the extent of Chamberlain's complicity in a plot that aimed primarily at the annexation of the Transvaal and only by the way at Uitlander enfranchisement. In the event of a genuine

[1] *Parl. Pap.* 1897, LXII [C. 8474], pp. 15, 16; G. 76 of 1897, pp. 7–15, 19, 22–26; Van der Poel, *The Jameson Raid*, pp. 32, 33.

[2] *Parl. Pap.* 1896, LIX [C. 7962], pp. 21–4; G. 76 of 1897, p. 27; Van der Poel, *The Jameson Raid*, p. 49.

[3] Garvin, *Life of Joseph Chamberlain*, III, 111, 112; Van der Poel, *The Jameson Raid*, pp. 45 *sqq*.

[4] Garvin, *Life of Joseph Chamberlain*, III, 58, 59.

[5] *Ibid.* III, 58, 62.

[6] *Ibid.* III, 63, 111, 112; Van der Poel, *The Jameson Raid*, pp. 48, 56.

rising, he was ready to let the High Commissioner and the troops go in with maybe the Company's men as the spearhead, but all decently and in order. What neither he nor anyone else foresaw at that time was what actually happened: an unauthorised raid by the Company's troopers alone, presumably to force on imperial intervention after the rising had been called off. Whatever the truth of the matter, the whisperings in Whitehall and Cape Town and the rumblings on the Rand were now momentarily drowned by a thunder-clap in Washington. Grover Cleveland, President of the United States, by an unprecedented stretching of the Monroe Doctrine, threatened to intervene in a recurrent boundary dispute between Venezuela and British Guiana.[1] Nevertheless, leaving that somewhat weary Titan, Lord Salisbury, to avert the bolts of angry Capitoline Jove, Chamberlain, another Prometheus, went on playing with fire. He put Rhodes and, through him, the Reformers in the way of knowing that, in his judgment, they should either hurry up and have the rising before the American complication became serious, or else postpone it "for a year or two at least".[2] Then, for the first time, he let the Prime Minister know something of what was going on, and showed that he was all for speedy action by telling the High Commissioner that troopships were on their way to Cape Town.[3]

Jameson had, meanwhile, completed his share of the preliminaries. Half his little force was at Pitsani, half at Mafeking, and he rode from one to the other fretting and fuming at the intolerable delays, while in the middle distance his Rhodesian Horse drilled from time to time *sans* uniforms, *sans* rifles, *sans* well-nigh everything.[4] The unhappy Reformers had by no means done their share. Divided among themselves, some meaning business and others not, they were distracted by the Kaffir Boom and faced with a sad shortage of arms, for however ingeniously Rhodes's agents were smuggling these in, they had so far smuggled in far too few. They prudently postponed the rising for a week, because, on the day originally fixed, their city would be swarming with visitors up for the races; at last, they bickered so furiously as to whether the rising was to be under the Vierkleur or the Union Jack that they had to send a deputation to Groote Schuur to settle at least that issue with Rhodes.[5]

Kruger, hearing of squads drilling in the streets of Johannesburg

[1] Ensor, R. C. K., *England, 1870–1914*, pp. 229 *sqq.*; Mowat, R. B., *The Diplomatic Relations of Great Britain and the United States*, chap. XXIV; *Parl. Pap.* 1896, XCVII [C. 7926] pp. 920–33; Perkins, Dexter, *The Monroe Doctrine, 1868-1907*, Chap. III.

[2] Garvin, *Life of Joseph Chamberlain*, III, 72.

[3] *Ibid.* III, 76–9.

[4] A.6—1896 [Cape], pp. liii *sqq.*, and Appendix QQ. pp. ccxxxvii–viii; Harding, C., *Frontier Patrols*, p. 45.

[5] Garrett, E., and Edwards, E. J., *The Story of an African Crisis*, p. 81; Van der Poel, *The Jameson Raid*, pp. 73 *sqq.*; Williams, B., *Cecil Rhodes*, p. 267; *History of "The Times"*, III, 174–5; Fitzpatrick, *Transvaal from Within*, pp. 127–8; Phillips, L., *Some Reminiscences*, pp. 144–8; Van Oordt, *Paul Kruger . . .*, p. 679; Hammond, J. H., *Autobiography*, pp. 332–4; *Parl. Pap.* 1897, IX [311], Q. 6836.

and Uitlander families rushing the south-bound trains, expected an explosion at any moment. He stood his ground, however, calling on all to obey the law; but he also showed himself conciliatory by seeing to it that duties on foodstuffs should be abolished, announcing that he was always ready to hearken to complaints presented in proper form, and promising friendly deputations of magnates, merchants and Pretorians that railway rates should be reduced, English-medium schools be given subsidies, and all who showed themselves loyal during the current crisis be enfranchised.[1] It may be that the Reformers weakened in face of these concessions; it is certain that they began to back-pedal hard.[2] It was not only that all of them were loath to check the Kaffir Boom by anything so disturbing as a revolution, but many of them were so conscious that their long-term interests were not those of Rhodes that they talked of cutting him and Jameson out altogether, rising in their own good time, and holding Johannesburg till Kruger yielded or the British Government came to the rescue. For the moment they resolved to stand by Rhodes's programme and to mislead the authorities by naming 4 January as the date of the rising, summoning a mass meeting for the second day thereafter and directing Leonard to issue a fiery manifesto forthwith; but they also hurried Leonard and the editor of the *Star* off to Groote Schuur, there to make fresh plans with Rhodes, and on three successive days sent word to Jameson that he must not move on any account because the rising would not take place yet awhile.[3] Those messages reduced the "Doctor" to a state of frenzy, but they brought the Colossus much comfort. Rhodes had never liked the scheme, and now it seemed that Jameson might not have to go a-raiding after all. He therefore told the High Commissioner that his plan had "fizzled out", and the High Commissioner told the Colonial Secretary.[4]

Chamberlain had already heard rumours of a probable "fizzle" from businessmen in the City, where the long-expected rising was as much common talk as in Government circles in Pretoria, and where most of those interested in gold shares were as averse to disturbance on the Rand as were the majority of the Uitlanders. He was, however, justifiably alarmed when the Company's lawyer, who had no very high opinion of Rhodes, hinted that the latter might send Jameson in to "manipulate a revolution" without waiting for the rising.[5] He at once told the High Commissioner that anything of that sort would imperil the Charter.[6] He was too late. Jameson's scanty stock of

[1] Van der Poel, *The Jameson Raid*, p. 106; Fitzpatrick, *Transvaal from Within*, p. 136.

[2] *Ibid.* pp. 129–30; Van der Poel, *The Jameson Raid*, p. 77; Hammond, *Autobiography*, pp. 322, 333–4; "Mermeix", *Le Transvaal et le Chartered*, pp. 130, 154; *History of "The Times"*, III, 213.

[3] *Parl. Pap.* 1896, LIX [C. 7933], p. 65; A.6—1896 (Cape), p. lx; Fitzpatrick, *Transvaal from Within*, p. 136.

[4] *Parl. Pap.* 1896, LIX [C. 7933], p. 2.

[5] Garvin, *Life of Joseph Chamberlain*, III, 81.

[6] *Parl. Pap.* 1896, LIX [C. 7933], p. 2.

patience had evaporated in the arid wastes of Bechuanaland. Disregarding all attempts by Rutherford Harris to hold him back, and, hearing nothing from Rhodes, the one man he would have heeded, he had convinced himself that the Uitlanders would never rise, if left to themselves. At last, he had wired to Rhodes that, unless he heard to the contrary by a certain hour, he would go in. A chapter of accidents ensured that the fatal message did not reach Rhodes till after the telegraph line to Cape Town had been cut.[1] Thus, Rhodes's last-minute attempt to stop the Raid failed to get through.

Jameson rode into a republic of mounted infantrymen with three light field-guns, eight maxims and rather more than five hundred men, four-fifths of whom were mere lads virtually untrained.[2] As if further to ensure failure, he went in at the very week-end on which the Transvaalers were assembled at their church-places for the quarterly *Nachtmaal* (Communion) with rifles, horses, *biltong* and waggons complete. Kruger had news of the invasion almost as soon as it had begun, and ordered the calling out of the commandos along the Raiders' line of advance and round the capital.[3] On the other hand, some twenty-four hours passed before the indignant Reformers learned that Jameson was coming to rescue the women and children, whatever they might say. Putting a bold face on it, they co-opted a number of prominent Uitlanders to their little committee, swore allegiance to the Vierkleur and solemnly hoisted it, gave out what arms they had, set up a provisional administration, despatched a party to seize the Pretoria arsenal, which made no serious attempt to do so, opened peace negotiations with the authorities, and prayed that there might be no shedding of blood.[4] Nor was there throughout the rising. The Uitlanders had no intention of shooting, and they had no one to shoot at, because Kruger withdrew his police from the streets to the fort which dominated the city.[5] The President called upon his Free State allies in terms of the treaty of 1889, and heard that they were duly lining the southern bank of the Vaal; but he made no further appeal for external aid, not even to Germany, who, as Leyds had warned him, would not fight for the Transvaal, however firmly she might stand for the *status quo* in southern Africa.[6] He showed, moreover, that he did not mean to have armed Germans in his republic at any price, for

[1] A.6 of 1896 [Cape], pp. 56–65, and Appendix QQ. p. ccxlii.

[2] Garrett and Edwards, *African Crisis*, pp. 88–91; Fitzpatrick, *Transvaal from Within* Appendix H: *Parl. Pap.* 1896, LIX [C. 7933], p. 44.

[3] Garrett and Edwards, *African Crisis*, pp. 125–36, 142–6; Fitzpatrick, *Transvaal from Within*, pp. 134–6; Hammond, *Autobiography*, pp. 327–8; Van Oordt, *Paul Kruger* . . ., pp. 686, 693–4; Jorissen, E. J. P., *Transvaalsche Herinerringen*, p. 135; Hofmeyr, N. J., *De Afrikaner Boer* . . ., pp. 237–8; *Green Book*, No. 1 of 1896, p. 4.

[4] Fitzpatrick, *Transvaal from Within*, pp. 137 *sqq.*; Garrett and Edwards, *African Crisis*, pp. 136–7.

[5] Van der Poel, *The Jameson Raid*, p. 113.

[6] Dugdale, *German Diplomatic Documents*, pp. 370–1; *Green Book*, No. 1 of 1896, pp. 4, 5, 7; *Parl. Pap.* 1896 [C. 8063], p. 18; Langer, W. L., *The Diplomacy of Imperialism*, 299.

when the German consul asked leave to bring up marines from the cruiser at Delagoa Bay to protect his consulate, he gruffly offered him a burgher-guard, if he was afraid.[1]

Jameson's men took four days to complete their raid. While they trailed along eastward over the rolling veld, many widely dispersed men were trying to make up their minds what they should do now. *The Times* had no doubts, for it published the famous letter of invitation with an impossible date inserted by Harris and further emendations, which made it read like a desperate appeal by hard-pressed men.[2] Rhodes, meanwhile, was either wandering on the slopes of Table Mountain, or sitting on the edge of his bed lamenting again and again in his high-pitched voice to the horrified Bower and his admiring Attorney-General, William Philip Schreiner, that "old Jameson" had taken the bit between his teeth and upset the apple-cart.[3] In the small hours of the Monday, 30 December, Bower told the High Commissioner what had come of all these "damned conspiracies".[4] Sir Hercules rose to the occasion, as he was destined to do throughout. He telegraphed to Jameson ordering him back[5], began to debate whether or no he should go to Pretoria, and, as soon as Rhodes had more or less recovered his balance, asked him to carry on as Prime Minister until someone else could take over. Thereupon, Rhodes sought to save something from the impending wreck by keeping Chamberlain up to the mark. He cabled to *The Times* and other influential friends in London that he was "confident of success.... Inform Mr Chamberlain I shall get through all right, if he supports me.... To-day, the crux is, I will win and South Africa will belong to England."

The Colonial Secretary in far-distant Birmingham was not so sure. Immediate news of Jameson's criminal folly brought him to his feet resolved to crush this thing before it ruined him. Like Sir Hercules he kept his head. He told the High Commissioner that he approved of all he had done so far, bade him do what he could to "prevent mischief", and intimated that he took it for granted that Rhodes would disown Jameson. This done, he dashed off to London, arriving in the grey dawn of the Monday, to warn the Prime Minister that if his Government supported the Raiders, it would play into the hands of Germany and other rival Powers, and that fighting in the Transvaal might easily lead to war on a South African scale.[6] Next day, he expressed his regret to Kruger, ordered Sir Hercules to tell Jameson that

[1] Walker, E. A., *de Villiers*, p. 265; Kotze, *Judicial Crisis*..., pp. 235–7.
[2] *The Times*, 1 January 1896; *Parl. Pap.* 1897 [311], Q. 6318–23; Hole, *Jameson Raid*, p. 222.
[3] A.6 of 1896 [Cape], pp. 53–4, 76, 214–22; *Parl. Pap.* 1897 [311], Q. 3304–7, 3401–4.
[4] Van der Poel, *op. cit.*, pp. 93–4.
[5] *Parl. Pap.* 1896, LIX [C. 7933], pp. 3–5, 8; *Parl. Pap.* 1896, LIX [C. 8063], pp. 116–17.
[6] *Parl. Pap.* 1896, LIX [C. 7933], p. 41; 1897 [311], Q. 8878; Garvin, *Life of Joseph Chamberlain*, III, 89–90.

his raid was sheer "filibustering", and told the B.S.A. Company's Directors that their Charter was in danger.[1] Cooler reflection suggested, however, that something might yet be accomplished; he did not need Rhodes's reminder that he could "still turn situation to England's advantage" if he would only pack the High Commissioner off to Pretoria post haste. On New Year's Day, therefore, he asked Robinson whether the time had not come for him to "intimate" that he was going north to Pretoria to make peace and conclude "a reasonable settlement of grievances",[2] and showed that he hoped that the Reformers might still make a fight of it by suggesting that the Raid was possibly a "feint" to draw off the commandos and thus make it easier for them to seize Johannesburg and the Pretoria arsenal.[3]

Lastly, the Kaiser went into action. He at once despatched a cruiser from Zanzibar to Delagoa Bay and proposed to follow this up with troops to assert a protectorate over the Transvaal. Dissuaded with much difficulty from this desperate venture, he none the less sent a semi-ultimatum to Whitehall and called upon France and Russia to join with him in bringing pressure on Great Britain.[4]

To return to Cape Town. The High Commissioner needed no promptings whether from the now truculent Rhodes, the agitated Reformers or even his own chief to go to Pretoria;[5] indeed, he had already asked Kruger whether he should do so.[6] His offer was repeated by the cautious Hofmeyr, who had at once emerged from his retirement to damp down the conflagration. The cautious leader of the Bond first sent his best wishes to Kruger; next, he urged the High Commissioner to issue a formal proclamation repudiating and recalling the Raiders, and then, knowing that Sir Hercules wished to go, advised Kruger to invite him.[7] Overcoming his natural reluctance, Kruger duly asked the High Commissioner to come up to help him "prevent further bloodshed", which was only too likely with the Raiders nearing Krugersdorp on the western edge of the Rand, a mere twenty miles from Johannesburg.[8] Once Sir Hercules had obtained Chamberlain's approval and notice that instructions for a settlement would follow, he made ready to start accompanied by Bower, but not by Hofmeyr, who declined to leave Cape Town.[9]

Apart from other considerations, Hofmeyr had plenty to do where he was in rallying his Bond, which had latterly showed signs of breaking up and might well be shaken further at the prospect of dropping

[1] *Parl. Pap.* 1897 [311], Q. 9675–6, 9734–5, 9747–51.
[2] *Parl. Pap.* 1896, LIX [C. 7933], pp. 9 *sqq.*
[3] *White Book*, No. 501, p. 9.
[4] Dugdale, *German Diplomatic Documents*, pp. 370–2, 377–8, 380.
[5] Van der Poel, *The Jameson Raid*, pp. 101, 119; *Parl. Pap.* 1897, IX [311], p. 599; *White Book*, No. 505, p. 228; Garrett and Edwards, *African Crisis*, p. 180.
[6] *White Book*, No. 501, p. 9; *Green Book*, No. 1 of 1896, p. 11.
[7] Hofmeyr, *Life of Hofmeyr*, p. 492.
[8] *Green Book*, No. 1 of 1896, p. 11; *Parl. Pap.* 1896, LIX [C. 7933], p. 12.
[9] Hofmeyr, *Life of . . .*, p. 493; *Parl. Pap.* 1896, LIX [C. 8063], p. 39.

Rhodes, from whom its leader had just parted. Hofmeyr had urged his old ally to repudiate and dismiss Jameson. Rhodes would not throw the Doctor over after all these years.[1] "I quite understand", Hofmeyr had replied coldly, "you need say no more." There was indeed no more to be said. Rhodes could not look again for the invaluable support of the Bond, but must forgo the unique position which he, an Englishman born, had so long enjoyed in the predominantly Afrikaner political life of the Old Colony. Hofmeyr, for his part, had turned away from that distressing interview to extort from the Colonial Secretary a promise that there should be a "searching inquiry" into the whole affair.[2]

As Sir Hercules and his Imperial Secretary boarded the Pretoria train they heard that Jameson had failed to pull it off within a couple of hours' ride of his goal—as near as that—for all the good his saddle-sore handful could have done even it if had ridden into Johannesburg.[3] Saddle-sore they must have been, because their leader had driven them relentlessly, paying no heed to repudiations and orders to turn back. Shepherded by commandos at a prudent distance because of his maxim-guns, he had reached Krugersdorp. There he had failed to break through. Turning aside for a final effort burdened by the knowledge that the High Commissioner had outlawed him, he had watched for help from the Reformers. None had come, because they had tied their own hands by agreeing to an armistice for twenty-four hours and had, in any event, scarcely any mounted men to send. After a running fight of some miles, the dead-beat little force had made its last stand at Doornkop. There, with the commandos closing in on all sides and the republican artillery unlimbering, the maxims had jammed and someone had put up the white flag (2 January).[4]

There could be no question now of the High Commissioner's dictating terms; he would be lucky if he could piece together the broken china. As the train chugged over the dusty Karoo, Robinson's meditations on that score were interrupted by the crash of yet another thunder-bolt, this time from Potsdam. At the first news of the surrender, the Kaiser had recovered his semi-ultimatum from Whitehall, mercifully unread, and had compromised with his advisers by cabling his congratulations to Kruger on having successfully defended his independence "without appealing for help to friendly Powers".[5] Doubtless the Kaiser's telegram helped to decide Kruger to give the insistent Leyds grudging leave to see if he could arrange for a

[1] Hofmeyr, *Life of*..., pp. 499, 501.

[2] *Ibid.* p. 491; *Parl. Pap.* 1896, LIX [C. 8063], pp. 24, 34.

[3] Van der Poel, *The Jameson Raid*, pp. 121 *sqq.* For details of the raid see the works of Hole, Colvin, Garrett and Edwards, Fitzpatrick, J. H. Hofmeyr, and *Die Brandwag*, 15 September, 1913.

[4] The raiders' losses were 17 killed, 55 wounded and 31 missing. The Transvaalers' losses were 4 killed and 3 wounded. The white flag was a coloured maid-servant's apron.

[5] Dugdale, *German Diplomatic Documents*, pp. 387–8; Langer, *Diplomacy of Imperialism* pp. 234–8.

conference of the Powers which would guarantee the Transvaal's independence; assuredly it roused the British Government and the mass of the British public. The former promptly commissioned a flying-squadron, which had a restraining effect on Cleveland, for whom the warning was primarily intended, but was taken by "My dear William" as a challenge to build him a fleet at least as strong as that which flew the flag of "Most beloved Grandmamma".[1] The British public, taught by the letter of invitation and optimistic rumours to regard the Raiders as fine fellows who were winning against heavy odds, were cast-down and sore at Jameson's surrender. Not all of them would go so far as to proclaim with their new Poet Laureate that they "would rather have had that foray than the crushings of all the Rand", even though there might be "girls in the gold-reef city", but very few of them were prepared to be kicked unexpectedly by any jack-booted Kaiser.[2] Probably it dawned upon some of them for the first time that Germany might one day be the enemy, and not France. Nor was it only men of British stock who were stung to protest. Hofmeyr might send his congratulations to Kruger and beg him to be magnanimous in the moment of victory;[3] but neither he nor any other Cape Afrikaner had any desire to see the Transvaal sheltering under the wing of the German eagle. He sent a message to this effect to the President and a statement for publication in London newspapers, and publicly prophesied better than he knew that if Germany were to attack Great Britain, she would lose all her colonies, "including Damaraland, which would not be an unmixed evil for the Cape".[4]

Sir Hercules found Kruger civil though understandably aloof, and the Reformers voluble and helpless. His real difficulties came from his own chief, who did not seem to understand that Doornkop had given the President all the cards. The High Commissioner could not know that Rhodes was hammering away at Chamberlain telling him that feeling in the Cape Colony was "tremendous", urging him not to "abandon England position because of failure", but to push hard for an Uitlander franchise and federation, and assuring him that he could still "make his own terms".[5] Sir Hercules knew that that was the one thing the Colonial Secretary could not do now, and judged it positively dangerous to do anything more than hint at his haughty demand for a five-year Uitlander franchise, a less humiliating oath of allegiance, equal subsidies for Dutch- and English-medium schools, and fully elective municipal institutions for Johannesburg.[6] He ignored repeated orders to take a strong line and use "firm language"

[1] Dugdale, *German Diplomatic Documents*, II, pp. 369, 398–404; Van der Poel, *The Jameson Raid*, p. 137; Garvin, *Life of Joseph Chamberlain*, III, 64 *sqq.*

[2] *History of "The Times"*, III, 214.

[3] Hofmeyr, *Life of...*, p. 495; *Parl. Pap.* 1896, LIX [C. 8063], p. 39.

[4] Hofmeyr, *Life of...*, pp. 495–6.

[5] *White Book*, No. 501, pp. 26, 31–2, 37, 41–2, 46.

[6] *Parl. Pap.* 1896, LIX [C. 7933], pp. 18 *sqq.*

until Chamberlain suggested sending troops up-country to prevent a possible move by the Rhodesian Horse. He then used firm enough language, curtly telling his chief that Rhodes had long since ordered that scratch force to stand fast. When Chamberlain went on to talk of sending reinforcements to the Cape to provide for "all eventualities", he told him bluntly to stop thinking in terms of redcoats and leave him in peace to manage everything in his own way.[1]

There was little enough for Sir Hercules to manage beyond helping Kruger to induce the Uitlanders to hand in their arms. Once this had been done, Kruger arrested all the members of the enlarged Reform Committee within reach, though he failed to catch Leonard, who was still away in Cape Town. He then called upon his indignant burghers to "forgive and forget", and promised Sir Hercules that the Reformers should have a fair trial.[2] Moved thereto by the pleadings of the High Commissioner, prominent Free Staters and Hofmeyr, and by his own good sense, he showed the Raiders mercy, shrewdly pointing out to his more fiery commandants, who clamoured for drastic summary action, that it would be much better to embarrass the British Government by leaving it to puzzle out how best to punish them. Hence, he handed Jameson and the other survivors over to the Natal authorities, who quietly shipped them all off to England, save about one hundred who had South African domicile.[3] Long before the last of them was gone by the end of January, the harassed High Commissioner had returned to Cape Town. There he received the Colonial Secretary's belated and irritable demand to know what he proposed to do next, and orders to stay in Pretoria till fresh instructions reached him. What Sir Hercules proposed to do next, and did, was to give his chief a downright snub. He told him straight out that it was useless even to mention Uitlander grievances, until, at the very least, the leading Reformers had been tried.[4]

Thus was Chamberlain silenced for the moment. For the rest, Leyds and the Kaiser found the Continental Powers but little interested in the fate of the Transvaal;[5] the storm over the Caribbean subsided gradually; the new Chartered shares fell below the price of issue,[6] and all hope of a peaceful federation of southern Africa faded away.

[1] *Parl. Pap.* 1896, LIX [C. 7933], pp. 30, 34, 36, 38–40; LIX [C. 8063], p. 146; *White Book*, No. 501, pp. 37, 43; *Green Book*, No. 1 of 1896, p. 28.

[2] *Green Book*, No. 1 of 1896, pp. 33, 40–1; Garrett and Edwards, *African Crisis*, pp. 227–31.

[3] *Parl. Pap.* 1896, LIX [C. 7933], pp. 18 *sqq.*, 30, 43, 45, 47–8, 54–6, 77; *Green Book*, No. 1 of 1896, pp. 49, 50, 52–5.

[4] *Parl. Pap.* 1896, LIX [C. 7933], pp. 55–7, 59; Garvin, *Life of Joseph Chamberlain*, p. 100.

[5] Dugdale, *German Diplomatic Documents*, pp. 392, 398; Langer, *Diplomacy of Imperialism*, pp. 247–8.

[6] *The Economist*, 4 and 11 January 1896.

CHAPTER XXII

THE STRUGGLE FOR SUPREMACY, 1896–1902

THE Jameson Raid, petty and ineffective though it was, weakened Great Britain's position in South Africa and embarrassed her elsewhere. It had come upon her standing apart both from the Triple and the Dual Alliance. It had brought her within measurable distance of war with Germany at a moment when war with the United States had seemed possible as the outcome of American intervention in the long-drawn British Guiana-Venezuela boundary dispute. It left her with the knowledge that the Transvaal had been revealed to the outer world as never before, and that Germany was ready, if direct negotiations between the Transvaal and herself broke down, to press for an embarrassing conference of European Powers which should affirm the republic's neutrality.[1]

Joseph Chamberlain, the Colonial Secretary, had taken a high line immediately after the Raid; but he had soon changed his tone and, acting on the advice of one of Kruger's most influential financial friends, had invited the President to London to discuss outstanding issues.[2] There was much to be said for top-level talks. They would gain time for passions to cool, give the sentimental London public a chance of according Kruger a vociferous welcome, lead possibly to the settlement of differences, and even be accepted as an alternative to the promised and unwelcome enquiry into the genesis of Jameson's disastrous venture. Kruger naturally saw difficulties such as his own advancing years and dislike of London ways, his burghers' fears lest he be cajoled into surrendering something of their independence, and the hatred of the Hollanders and other Continentals of all things British. Nor did Chamberlain make it easier for him to come. He first ruled out all modification of Article IV of the London Convention, which gave the Queen final control of the republic's treaty-making powers, the one request the President was certain to make; he then cabled the mere gist of a despatch defending the British Government's conduct during the Raid, proposing a discussion of Uitlander grievances, and suggesting a plan for a "modified local autonomy" for the Rand, but published that despatch long before its full text could reach Pretoria. This he did "from considerations of policy", which doubtless covered the need to placate Rhodes, who was in London in a dangerous mood fulminating against the evils of Krugerism.[3]

[1] *German Diplomatic Documents*, 1871–1914, ... selected and translated from *Die Grosse Politik der Europäischen Kabinette*, 1871–1914, by E. T. S. Dugdale, II, 370 *sqq.*

[2] *Parl. Pap.* 1896, LXI [C. 7933], pp. 83 *sqq.*; [C. 8063], pp. 1 *sqq.*

[3] *Parl. Pap.* 1896, LXI [C. 7933], pp. 89–91; [C. 8063], pp. 1–3, 16.

Nevertheless, once Chamberlain had apologised for thus overstepping the bounds of diplomatic courtesy, Kruger accepted his invitation and sent him his own heads of proposals. These included a large indemnity for the Raid, the cancellation of Rhodes's Charter, the cession of a harbour on the Indian Ocean, the full incorporation of Swaziland in his republic, and not only the abrogation of Article IV, but the substitution of an ordinary treaty of commerce and friendship for the whole London Convention, which he held to be "injurious to the dignity of an independent republic".[1] Towards the close of March the scheme fell through partly because State Secretary Leyds sent a warning from Berlin, and partly because the perusal of the contents of a box, which had been picked up on the Transvaal veld, suggested that the full story of what lay behind the Raid was not known. This box belonged to Captain Robert White, one of several seconded regular officers who had ridden in with Jameson, and contained, besides the key to the cypher, communications which had passed between many of the plotters revealing Rhodes as the puppet-master and more than hinting at the complicity of the High Commissioner and even more highly placed personages than he.[2] In face of this, Kruger asked that his visit be postponed. Thereupon, Chamberlain withdrew the invitation.[3]

The abandonment of the projected talks meant that the British Government would have to work out its South African problem by means of diplomatic correspondence instead of friendly conference. If such correspondence led to misunderstanding, and misunderstanding to war, it must see the business through this time with large forces, and the knowledge that another Majuba followed by retrocession might well cost Britain her coast colonies. Even if it won, there would be the cheerless prospect of maintaining a large garrison in a disaffected country. In any event, as Chamberlain told a warlike group in the Commons, Great Britain could not very well go to war to enforce franchise reforms that were not covered by the London Convention.[4] Much better sit quiet, resting on that Convention, and see what reforms Kruger would effect of his own mere motion.

The problem which faced the imperial authorities at the outset was distracting. South Africa lay politically and economically in fragments. The Raid had reversed violently all the centripetal forces which had hitherto been at work converging on the person of Rhodes. Rhodes's credit had been shaken severely in official circles in London, where Lord Salisbury and others mistakenly suspected that the real aim of the Raid had been the creation of a great British South African

[1] *Parl. Pap.* 1896, LXI [C. 79337], p. 90; *Parl. Pap.* 1896, LIX [C. 8063], pp. 5, 13; *Green Book*, No. 2 of 1896, pp. 63–5, 69–71.

[2] Phillips, L., *Some Reminiscences*, p. 165; *The Star* (Johannesburg), 27 April, 1896.

[3] *Green Book*, No. 1 of 1896, pp. 104–7; *Parl. Pap.* 1896, LIX [C. 8063], p. 23; LXII [C. 8423], pp. 15 *sqq.*

[4] *Hansard*, 4th series, XL, 905 *sqq.*

republic on both sides of the Limpopo.[1] Rhodes was no longer Premier of the Cape Colony; the makeshift Sprigg ministry was weak and uncertain; the British and Afrikaners, who had been united in opposition to the railway and customs policy of the Transvaal and, less definitely, on the score of Uitlander grievances, had been driven rudely apart. Many of the British section, however unjustly, held that Rhodes was simply a plutocrat who had fouled their flag for the sake of filthy lucre,[2] while others cold-shouldered the unhappy Uitlanders as betrayers of "the Doctor". The Afrikaner Bond, still the one organised political party, had rallied round Hofmeyr. It condemned the Raid as a treacherous attack on Afrikaner nationality, and announced that in default of satisfactory explanations Rhodes must remain beyond the pale.[3]

In Natal federalism was destroyed so completely that, of all her leading politicians, Harry Escombe alone continued to dream of a "future Dominion of South Africa". Secure in her new-won self-government, Natal could be trusted more surely than ever to make her economic peace with the South African Republic at the expense of the shattered Cape Colony. Much more serious was the fact that the Orange Free State, which had hitherto gravitated southward towards the Colony from which it had sprung, had been thrust abruptly northward into the arms of its sister republic. Immediately after the Raid, Marthinus Steyn had been elected President. Steyn embodied Afrikaner tradition in a less extreme form than did Kruger; nevertheless, he stood for a greater measure of political, economic and cultural exclusiveness than had his predecessors, Brand and Reitz.[4]

In the South African Republic Kruger was rehabilitated and entrenched. The liberal opposition had been forced over to his side for the time being by the threat to their independence; the mining magnates were more divided than ever between the Chamber of Mines connected with the Reformers, and the Association of Mines composed of Continentals and personal enemies of Rhodes. The rank and file of the Uitlanders, dismayed, discredited and divided, were either confirmed in their suspicions of the magnates or, in so far as they had looked to the Reformers for guidance, were robbed of that guidance by the three years' political inactivity imposed on them as part of the price of their liberty. The old Transvaal was less willing than it had ever been to listen to anything that seemed to touch its independence, and more intent on drawing the Free State into its political and economic orbit. And if its authorities chose to arm to the teeth, they could always point to the Raid as their justification; if they were slow to extend political liberties to Uitlanders, they could plead for time

[1] *German Diplomatic Documents*, II, 381, 389, 477; Walker, *de Villiers*, p. 272.

[2] Walker, *de Villiers*, p. 269.

[3] Botha, P. R., *Die Staatkundige Ontwikkeling van die Zuid-Afrikaqse Republiek* ..., pp. 452, 456; Hofmeyr, J. H., *The Life of Jan Hendrik Hofmeyr*, pp. 500 *sq.*

[4] Van der Merwe, N. J., *Marthinus Theunis Steyn*, I, 56 *sqq.*, 112.

to reassure their burghers, and for still more time in which to settle outstanding questions with a Secretary of State, who, many of them were firmly persuaded, had been privy to the recent attempt to extort those liberties by the strong hand.

Charterland remained. Immediately after the Raid, Rhodes had given up his power of attorney in Africa for the British South Africa Company and Chartered shares had fallen abruptly. The Cape-to-Cairo railway, shut out definitely from the Rand and the fertile northern Transvaal by the recent failure to hurry the republic into Rhodes's economic federation, must go north, if at all, through the dry and bush-clad plains of the Bechuanaland Protectorate, the coveted territory which there was now no immediate hope of winning for the Company.[1] But what had sent Rhodes hurrying post-haste to London had been Chamberlain's reminder at the first news of the Raid that the Charter itself was in peril.[2] There he received a promise that his Charter was safe as far as the all-powerful Colonial Secretary was concerned, provided he withheld from any committee of enquiry certain telegrams which convicted that statesman of foreknowledge of the Rising and the Raid. Thus reassured, he appointed his fellow-director, Earl Grey, as Administrator of Southern Rhodesia and, since he had been "in the know", hurried him off out of harm's way to set about in good earnest the development of the one unmistakably British and pro-Rhodian province left in southern Africa.[3] He himself followed him thither in March 1896 and, for some two years thereafter, took but little part in Cape politics.

Hardly had Rhodes arrived in Southern Rhodesia than a storm burst which threatened to sweep away all his work. The warlike Matabele had long been watching for a chance to rebel. They had been by no means thoroughly subdued in 1893; but they had been deprived of their King and given nothing in exchange but a skeleton and hastily recruited white administration backed by arrogant black police. Two inaccessible and undesirable reserves were poor recompense for the loss of the best of their lands and many of their cattle. They had, moreover, been subjected to compulsory labour for private as well as public purposes and were now plagued by drought, locusts and rinderpest, for which they blamed the white men. The capture of the Company's white police at Doornkop gave them their opportunity. Seven months of fighting ensued, much of it in the impregnable Matoppo Hills near Bulawayo on which fully eighteen hundred Company men and imperial Police could make little impression. At last, Rhodes took his life in his hands, went into those hills unarmed with two or three companions, and induced the Chiefs

[1] *British South Africa Company, Report of Extraordinary General Meeting*, 12 July 1895; *Director's Report for* 1895, *p.* 14; *ibid. for* 1896–7, *pp.* 5 *sqq.*; *The Economist*, 28 December 1895 and 4 January 1896.

[2] *Parl. Pap.* 1896, LIX [C. 7933], p. 2.

[3] *German Diplomatic Documents*, II, 401.

to surrender on the promise of wholesale redress of grievances. True, the Mashona to the east had risen unexpectedly in June and were not finally quelled till a year later: but, after the *indabas* in the Matoppos in October 1896, all real risk of losing Charterland was over.[1]

The survival of Rhodesia confirmed Rhodes in his resolve to hold on to his seat on the Chartered board; but it was becoming a question whether he could thus "let resignations wait" much longer or, worse still, save his Charter from the storm that was beating up at Westminster. So much had come out of recent months that the dreaded "searching enquiry" could not be further postponed. First, the Pretoria authorities had published the contents of *die trommel van Bobbie White* in a most damaging Green Book.[2] Next, in May, Judge Rheinhold Gregorowski of the Transvaal High Court had condemned the four leading Reformers to death, and sentenced the minor members of the Reform Committee to fines, two years' imprisonment and three years' banishment thereafter. Kruger had remitted the death penalties at once, but had then, under pressure, doled out "magnanimity by inches". It was several weeks before he released the four leaders in return for the payment of fines amounting to £25,000 apiece, fines which Rhodes and Alfred Beit to their credit paid, and a promise to abstain from Transvaal politics for fifteen years to come. At the same time, he freed all the lesser prisoners, save two who refused the proffered terms, in return for the payment of fines and a promise to keep out of Transvaal politics during the next three years.[3] Then, a few weeks later, a Select Committee of the Cape Assembly, making good use of the Transvaal Green Book, had condemned Rhodes, and thus at last obliged him to resign his seat on the Chartered board.[4] Finally, the Court of Queen's Bench had sentenced Jameson and five of his officers to imprisonment. "The Doctor" had soon been released on the score of ill health; but his friends must serve their full terms and, together with Colonel Frank Rhodes, resign their commissions.[5] As if all this were not enough, bitter Radicals like Sir William Harcourt and Henry Labouchere, editor of *Truth*, egged on by the vindictive Hofmeyr, were now stigmatising the Raid-Rising as a shameless piece of stock-jobbing. Chamberlain

[1] *Instructions to Sir R. E. R. Martin re control....*, *Parl. Pap.* 1896, LIX [C. 8060]; *Report by Sir R. E. R. Martin ...*, 1897, LXII [C. 8547]; *Proposed changes in the administration of the B.S.A. Co....*, 1898, LX [C. 8732]; *B.S.A. Co.*, *Report of Extraordinary General Meeting*, 6 November 1896, and *Report on Native Disturbances ...* 1896–7; Stent, Vere, *A Personal Record of some Incidents in the Life of Cecil Rhodes*, pp. 27 *sqq.*

[2] *Green Book*, No. 1 of 1896.

[3] *Corresp. re disturbances in the S.A. Republic*, *Parl. Pap.* 1896, LIX [C. 8063]; *Corresp. re S.A. Republic*, 1897, LXII [C. 8364].

[4] *Report of Select Committee of Cape House of Assembly*, *Parl. Pap.* 1897, LXII [C. 8380]; *Corresp. re S.A. Republic*, [C. 8423], pp. 31 *sqq.*; *Votes and Proceedings of the Cape House of* 28 May, 17, 24 July, 1896.

[5] *The Times* 21–9 July 1896; Clarke, E., *The Story of My Life*, pp. 328–9; Colvin, *op. cit.*, II, 148–56; Hole *op. cit.*, p. 270; *Fortnightly Review*, 1 September 1896.

had no choice but to move for a Committee of Inquiry into the genesis of the Raid and the past administration of the Chartered Company. This Committee duly met early in August. It dispersed a couple of days later with the ending of the session.[1]

If the break-up of the Committee and the comparative leniency of the punishment meted out to the Raiders confirmed the Pretoria Government in its belief in Great Britain's bad faith, the course of events in the Transvaal caused increasing anxiety to the Secretary of State. During the months succeeding the raid, the cool counsel of Germany and of the prudent Leyds, State Secretary of the republic, silenced wild talk of throwing the Convention overboard.[2] There were, however, still those who exulted that the South African Republic would soon be able to arm all Afrikaners south of the Zambesi and there was no possible doubt that it[3] was trying to shake itself free from economic dependence on Britain and her colonies, and to make contact with rival Powers. Above all, at a time when Great Britain and Germany were quarrelling over Zanzibar and Mombasa further up the east coast, there came circumstantial reports of joint German and Transvaal activities at Delagoa Bay. Needy Portugal, faced with the prospect of finding a large sum of money to meet the expected award of the Berne arbitration court to which, at the instance of Great Britain and the United States, the case of McMurdo's confiscated Delagoa railway had been referred,[4] might be induced to make saleable a concession held by one of her subjects at Katembe on the southern shore of the coveted bay.[5]

Meanwhile the Rand was restless. Petty irritations at the hands of youthful burghers and minor officials, many of them Hollanders, probably irked the Uitlander rank and file more than the withholding of the franchise. Many of these slights were not so much real as imagined by men who were accustomed to look down on most things Afrikaner and found it hard to adapt themselves to a society in which the Afrikaner, and the frontier Afrikaner at that, was politically dominant. Most of the Uitlanders would have hesitated to give up their existing British or other citizenship even had the republican franchise been accessible to them on reasonable terms; nevertheless, the withholding of the franchise except as a favour was resented, especially by men from other South African territories, as an implication that they were less good men than the "old burghers". The copious legislation of the session of 1896 emphasised their helplessness. A few of the new laws, such as the Education Act, promised

[1] *Report from Select Committee on British South Africa, Parl. Pap.* 1896, IX (380), pp. 45 *sqq.*

[2] *German Diplomatic Documents*, II, 390, 399 *sqq.*; Leyds, W. J., *Tweede Verzameling* (*Correspondentie* 1899–1900), *Bijlagen*, pp. 10. 13.

[3] *Die Volkstem*, 26 September 1896.

[4] *Vide supra*, p. 535.

[5] Gooch, G. P., and Temperley, H. W. V., *British Documents on the Origin of the War, 1898–1914*, I, 323 *sqq.*; Botha, P. R., *Staatkundige Ontwikkeling*, ch. XV.

to give them some kind of return for the taxes they paid, and Johannesburg was promised something like municipal self-government; but others, such as the limitation of the right to petition, the Press Law, the Aliens Expulsion and Aliens Immigration Laws[1] and the prohibition of open-air meetings, put very wide discretionary powers into the hands of an executive which was inclined to push the letter of the law as far as it would go, and regarded British and colonial Uitlanders with a jaundiced eye.

As 1896 wore on into 1897, bad times frayed the nerves of all, burghers, Uitlander rank and file, and magnates alike. In spite of a generous gold law, mining languished. It was the one and only great industry of the republic. It had been hurried into existence extravagantly during the early days, and was now sinking costly and as yet unremunerative shafts to tap the deep levels. Wages and other working costs ruled high and could not be brought down in face of high railway rates and the state's protective policy. Mine-owners scrambling with farmers in an inadequate labour market blamed the Government for the chronic shortage of Native labour; they blamed it also, and with far more justice, for its failure to deal effectively with the dynamite monopoly, or with sellers of illicit liquor and buyers of stolen gold amalgam. These accusations were presently urged by newspapers in the colonies and in Europe, while, in the background, the farmers, unable to supply the growing market of the Rand in spite of the protection afforded to their products against those of the more advanced British colonies and the Free State, were perishing off the face of the land from rinderpest, droughts, locusts, famine and, in the northern districts, fever.[2]

It was a touchy and harassed Government that now heard at the New Year of 1897 that Rhodes had been accorded a rapturous welcome in the Cape Colony by many of the British of the towns and by not a few of the Afrikaners of the countryside as he had come down from the Matoppos by way of Beira and Port Elizabeth to take ship at Cape Town for Westminster, there to face the reconstituted Committee of Inquiry.[3] Soon followed the news that Chamberlain, who, in the eyes of the Transvaalers and many others, ought to have been in the dock, was seated prominently among the inquisitors and seemed to be much less interested in solving the mystery of the Raid than in joining with Rhodes to make much of the "admitted grievances" of the Uitlanders, the alleged German peril and Rhodes's achievements as an empire-builder.[4] Then, early in April, Chamberlain not only queried their very liberal estimate of Raid expenses, but refused bluntly to pass on to the British South Africa Company a

[1] *Parl. Pap.* 1897, LXII [C. 8423], pp. 44 *sqq.*, 56, 65, 93 *sqq.*

[2] *Report of the Trade . . . and Industry of the S.A. Republic, Parl. Pap.* 1898, LXIV [C. 9093].

[3] "Vindex", *Cecil Rhodes, His Political Life and Speeches*, 1881–1900, ch. XVI; Michell, Sir Lewis, *The Life of the Rt Hon. Cecil J. Rhodes*, II, 196.

[4] *Parl. Pap.* 1897, LXII [C. 8423], p. 16.

claim of £1,000,000 for "intellectual or moral damages".[1] To act thus was to convince Pretoria that Downing Street was hand in glove with London Wall. And now here was Rhodes returning to Capetown in triumph to be welcomed by many colonists of British stock as their prospective leader and, obviously with the Uitlanders in mind, to demand "equal rights for every white man south of the Zambesi". It was some consolation to the Transvaalers to hear that he had then betaken himself to his beloved North.

Meanwhile the Transvaal Executive had fallen foul of the High Court and the Rand press, the two chief and valued safeguards of voteless Uitlanders and the pentecostal hosts of overseas investors. At the end of a long test case arising out of the gold law, Chief Justice Kotze, a protagonist of the Afrikaner section against the Hollanders, not only gave judgment against the Government and saddled it with the payment of heavy compensation, but in spite of past decisions of his own and others to the contrary, denied the power of the Volksraad to alter existing law by hasty resolution (*besluit*) or by any means other than the slow and cumbrous process of act (*wet*). And on American analogy, Kotze claimed the right for his Court to test the law by the touchstone of the written constitution (*Grondwet*).[2]

Kotze's fellow-Judges were by no means agreed on the existence of the testing right. Nevertheless, his decision shook the legal foundations of the republic, faced the authorities with the prospect of further similar judgments and effusions of cash, frightened away sorely needed capital from the mines, and startled the Free Staters at the very moment that Kruger had brought Steyn to the point of entering a close alliance. The Executive therefore hurried a resolution through the Volksraad empowering the President to dismiss any Judge who, on being challenged, still claimed the testing right. The Judges, who had been appointed for life and were subject to removal only after formal trial, appealed to the sovereign people. At the end of an acute crisis, de Villiers, Chief Justice of the Cape Colony, mediated a truce under which the Judges promised not to exercise the doubtful testing right, while the President undertook to submit to the Volksraad, as soon as possible, a draft law establishing the independence of the Bench and safeguarding the constitution on Free State lines against hasty alteration.

The liberty of the Transvaal press, whether government or opposition, was at all times liable to degenerate into licence. Doubtless Kruger and his advisers, isolated as they were from the outer world, took it all too seriously; but they knew that this alien, restive, and, as they believed, still partially armed Johannesburg supplied the

[1] *Correspondence re S.A. Republic*, 1898, LX [C. 8721], p. 3.

[2] Kotze, (Sir) J. G., *Documents and Correspondence relating to the Judicial Crisis in the S.A. Republic*, and *Judgement . . . in the case R. E. Brown v. Dr Leyds N. O.*, Pretoria, 1897; Walker, *de Villiers*, pp. 287 *sqq.*

newspapers of that outer world with most of its impressions of the republic. Kruger now suppressed *The Critic* and the much more influential *Star*. The proprietors of both appealed to the imperial authorities against these alleged breaches of the London Convention.[1]

It was now that Chamberlain, drawing his conclusions from the reports of Conyngham Greene, an experienced diplomat who had recently gone to Pretoria as British Agent, abandoned his attitude of hopeful expectancy. The party at Pretoria, which he was henceforward convinced was anxious to denounce the Convention and even to take the offensive, was being strengthened by the increase of the state artillery and mounted police, and by the work proceeding day and night on forts around the capital.[2] He regarded the new Aliens Immigration and Expulsion Laws as actual or potential breaches of the Convention, and the recent irregular conclusion of treaties with Powers as a whittling away of the vital Article IV of that instrument.[3] In March, again, the Transvaal had concluded an offensive and defensive alliance with the Free State under which the two republics were to arrange a loose scheme of federation,[4] and the Transvaal stood to benefit by any treaties its ally chose to make without let or hindrance by the Queen. A protocol was appended to the treaty of alliance arranging details of cooperation, laying down the principle of interchangeable citizen rights, and providing for a permanent Council of Representatives of the two republics. This Council, the so-called *Federale Raad*, was to consist of the Presidents or their deputies and five representatives of each republic holding office for two years. It was to meet at least once a year at Pretoria and Bloemfontein alternatively, and was "to report to and advise the respective governments on matters of common interest concerning mutual protection and trade relations, proposals in regard to Federal Union and objections thereto, to make recommendations with a view to uniformity of legislation and such other matters as may be referred to it..." This did not mean that the republics were actually federated, but it pointed to federation as a possibility and thus added to British anxieties. To add point to these facts and fears, Leyds was sailing for Europe to make contact with Holland, France and Germany, to secure a non-British cable and a German steamship service to the east coast, and to raise a loan partly for railways and other public works, but partly also, it was believed, for the acquisition of some sort of control, direct or indirect, over Delagoa Bay and its vital railway.[5]

The Imperial Government decided to take no risks. It sent Sir Alfred Milner to Cape Town as High Commissioner, dispatched a strong squadron to Delagoa Bay to show that it stood there for the

[1] *Parl. Pap.* 1897, LXII [C. 8423], pp. 80 *sqq.*, 130.
[2] *Report of H.M. Commissioners ... on the War in South Africa, Parl. Pap.* 1903, XL [Cd. 1789].
[3] *Parl. Pap.* 1897, LXII [C. 8423], pp. 1, 41, 47, 62, 71.
[4] *Bloemfontein Gazette Extraordinary*, 22 March 1897.
[5] Botha, P. R., *Staatkundige Ontwikkeling*, ch. XV.

status quo, and while Pretoria rang with reports that Great Britain meant to bring the Transvaal to its knees by seizing the port, presented two despatches to President Kruger protesting against the recently concluded treaties and the Aliens Immigration Law.[1]

Excitement was not confined to Pretoria. In Paris, whose interest in Madagascar and Rand shares was now as deep as its hatred of England, men talked of drawing nearer to Germany and even of bringing in distant Russia, the ally of France, to squeeze a preoccupied Britain out of Egypt. Nor was the tension relaxed when Chamberlain announced that an additional battalion and three field batteries were being sent to South Africa to balance "the enormous and continued military preparations" of the Transvaal.[2]

The storm subsided gradually. Kruger first sent a very long but conciliatory reply to London asking for Swiss arbitration on the Convention issue.[3] The Volksraad then repealed the Immigration Law, ostensibly because it inconvenienced neighbouring states and colonies,[4] but really, as everyone knew very well, because the troops and the warships had shown that H.M. Government meant business. So the squadron steamed away, the reinforcements moved up to their new camp at Ladysmith in northern Natal, and the newly-arrived High Commissioner registered the repeal of the Immigration Law as the one substantial gain made by the imperial authorities since the Raid.[5] It was a gain made practically at the cannon's mouth.

Sir Alfred Milner, a man of forty-three and a staunch believer in the value to humanity of the British Empire, had taken up his "awful job" with the full intention of upholding British supremacy much more firmly than it had been upheld of late years, and of excluding foreign interference from the sphere of British influence in southern Africa. He believed indeed that there could be no permanent peace until the Transvaal's franchise had been reformed drastically; but that could wait. Even the steady and necessary pressure on the Transvaalers to set their house in order in other respects need not be applied by Downing Street, but rather by himself more or less semi-officially. Such direct approaches might induce the Republicans not merely to keep the letter of the Convention, but to deal with "everyday local differences" in a friendly fashion instead of regarding each as a matter for "diplomatic treatment, as between Sovereign States". If war must come in the end, the Transvaal must be so clearly the aggressor that the Imperial Government could be sure of the support of the British everywhere and the sympathy of at least many of the Cape Afrikaners.[6] The first step then must be to win the confidence

[1] *Parl. Pap.* 1897, LXII [C. 8423]. pp. 113 *sqq.*
[2] *Parl. Pap.* 1903, XL [Cd. 1789], p. 184.
[3] *Parl. Pap.* 1898, LX [C. 8721], pp. 6 *sqq.*
[4] *Notulen von den Eersten Volksraad der Z.A. Republiek*, 6 May 1897.
[5] *The Milner Papers*, ed. Cecil Headlam, I, 53, 72.
[6] *The Milner Papers*, I, 33, 53, 64 *sqq.*, 70, 73, 227; Walker, *de Villiers*, pp. 307 *sqq.*

of the colonially-minded British in the Cape Colony and of those many Afrikaners, who, Milner believed, were sick of the Bond but afraid to speak out.

For a time, the dawn for which Milner was watching seemed to be breaking. Pressure by Steyn, the indispensable ally, and other Afrikaner friends; the drawing together of the Chamber and the Association of Mines under stress of bad times and defective administration; and the knowledge that European financiers fought shy of risking their money in his state, impelled Kruger to do something to restore confidence. *The Star* was allowed to reappear under an editor who was prepared to meet the authorities halfway, and, in April 1897, two Commissions were appointed: one to show the President how he might implement his promises to the Judges of constitutional reform, the other to inquire into the needs of the gold industry.

In May again, Leyds, whom Milner already regarded as the stormy petrel, had entered into mutually satisfactory conversations with Chamberlain and his Under-Secretary, Lord Selborne, at the lunch table in London.[1] Then, in June, the Queen's Diamond Jubilee was celebrated with enthusiasm by the Cape Afrikaners and with fitting decorum by President Kruger, who marked the day by releasing the two last of the Reform prisoners. Presently Johannesburg was given a municipal government, which indeed fell far short of the home rule for the Rand that, from first to last, Chamberlain thought the most desirable solution of the Uitlander difficulty, but which did confer considerable local powers attainable on an easily accessible franchise. Finally, after much hesitation, an appeal to the Courts was promised to non-burghers under the Expulsion law.[2]

From time to time, however, clouds obscured the dawn. Leyds left Chamberlain's lunch table for Paris, there to discuss fruitlessly his Delagoa Bay schemes, while Chamberlain approached Lisbon direct and with a like lack of success.[3] In July the Parliamentary Committee of Enquiry reported on the Raid. It was a report which earned for its signatories the title of "The Committee of No Enquiry". Apart from leaving untouched the administrative record of the B.S.A. Company, the second part of their assignment, they had plainly never seriously tried to get to the bottom of the first part, the genesis of the Raid. Above all, they had allowed Rhodes to withhold the crucial telegrams, which would have told them the truth, too much truth perhaps for the ministerialist majority, who had no mind to bring down the Colonial Secretary and, with him, the Cabinet; too much also for the Liberals, who were intent only on getting a

[1] *The Milner Papers*, I, 68; also verbal information given by Lord Selborne to the writer (1921).

[2] *S.A.R. Law No.* 19 *of* 1897; *Parl. Pap.* 1898, LX [C. 8721], pp. 16 *sqq.*

[3] Gooch and Temperley, *British Documents*, I, 44 *sqq.*, 329; Botha, *Staatkundige Ontwikkeling*, p. 239.

verdict against Rhodes and feared to stir up mud which might stick to such good Liberals as Lords Rosebery and Ripon and Sir Hercules Robinson, the High Commissioner. Hence, as a Liberal cartoonist recorded of the committee, "It respected confidences. It discovered the obvious.... It compromised no man ...", except, of course, one or two subordinate officials, and notably Sir Graham Bower, the High Commissioner's Imperial Secretary, who was sacrificed to save his dying and still officially "ignorant" chief. It exonerated the imperial authorities at Whitehall and Capetown, and left the Charter untouched; the most it did was to reprove the Company's Directors for not having restrained the Colossus, and, as it was bound to do, censure Rhodes himself.[1] Then, a week or two later, Chamberlain minimised the censure which he had just signed by giving its victim a rousing public "testimonial" as to personal character and imperial achievement. The Transvaalers could not know that he had done so, because he knew that, if he refused, a Radical member would have read out to the Commons enough of the withheld telegrams to break him.[2] They did know, however, that bad as the Raid had been, it was as nothing to this hush-up, this "lying in state at Westminster". It was that which rankled, and rankles to this day. Transvaalers began to say openly that now that the Jubilee was past, Great Britain meant to make trouble.

Nor did negotiations for a South African Immigration Conference, which Steyn had inaugurated, progress favourably. Milner persuaded his chief to allow him to offer to represent Rhodesia and other non-self-governing British territories rather than the paramount Power as such; but after six months of increasingly difficult correspondence, Steyn's suspicion of that very paramountcy, his hatred of all that Rhodesia stood for, and his evident determination to bring in the Germans from South-West Africa as a counterpoise to the British ended all immediate prospect of a conference.[3]

Then, in October, Chamberlain replied to the Transvaal's request for Swiss arbitration, which Milner had stigmatised frankly as a "try-on",[4] by declaring that the London Convention of 1884 was not a treaty but a mere declaration of the Imperial Government's intentions, and that the Queen's suzerainty expressed in the preamble of the Pretoria Convention of 1881 still stood.[5] There was this to be said for Chamberlain's thesis that in 1884 the Earl of Derby had declined to cancel the claim in so many words, but had preferred to

[1] *Parl. Pap.* 1897, IX [64], [311–I, II]; *Hansard*, 4th series, LI, 1163 *sqq.*

[2] *Ibid.*, LI, 311–17, 479–506, 574, 1099–1182; Garvin, *Life of Joseph Chamberlain*, III, 125; *Annual Report*, 1897, pp. 169–70; MacNeill, J. G. S., *What I Have Seen and Heard*, p. 258; *Truth*, 11 October, 1900; *The Spectator*, 19, 26 October, 2 November, 1901. *Report of the Select Committee* [*on the Jameson Raid*], *Parl. Pap.* 1897, IX [64], (311–I, II]; *Hansard*, 4th series, LI, 1163 *sqq.*

[3] Van der Merwe, *Marthinus Steyn*, I, 147, 152; *The Milner Papers*, I, 56, 73 *sqq.*

[4] *The Milner Papers*, I, 68.

[5] *Parl. Pap.* 1898, LX [C. 8721], pp. 18 *sqq.*

"abstain from using" a word which could not be defined legally and whose substance was retained in the Queen's control over the republic's treaty-making powers.[1] On the other hand, the Transvaalers had then accepted an unwelcome western boundary as the price to be paid for the disappearance of the suzerainty.[2] Its revival now threw them into a fury of suspicion, presented them with a first class debating point, and embarrassed the High Commissioner, to whom suzerainty was only a word, in his efforts to restore paramountcy as a solid fact based on historical precedents and, as he held, present needs.[3]

Like most British statesmen since Carnarvon's day, Milner looked forward to federation under the British flag as South Africa's ultimate destiny; but he also believed that the loyal and united South Africa which should reduce his own office to an "anachronism" and enable H.M. Government to dispense with its considerable garrison and naval squadron, was "a thing of the very distant future". Meanwhile the High Commissionership must remain "a fighting post . . . fighting all the time".[4]

Milner had come to Cape Town fully expecting to have to face a Boer raid into the northern Colony at any time within the next six months;[5] but he soon found that his chief immediate anxieties sprang from quite other quarters. In the Cape Colony, the compromise Sprigg ministry was fast losing the confidence of the Bond, which still dominated political life there, without gaining the solid support of the mainly British groups.[6] The Progressive Group which followed James Rose-Innes held to the fullest liberal programme: a redistribution of seats in the Assembly which should reduce the marked advantage of the conservative rural Afrikaner constituencies, the repeal of the protective duties on foodstuffs which pressed hard on the predominantly British towns, and a generous Native policy. But there were Progressives also in the ranks of the ministerialists, the Rhodians and even of the Bond, who advocated some or all of these measures, notably the first. The extreme anti-Transvaal elements organised by the South African League had first hailed Rhodes on his return at the height of the Delagoa Bay crisis, and then the embarrassed High Commissioner, as the man who should put Kruger and the Bond in their places.[7] Both men disappointed them. Milner was not to be hurried, and Rhodes had as yet too much to do in the North. Nevertheless Rhodes would be sure of backing if a coherent

[1] *Correspondence re Status of the S.A. Republic, Parl. Pap.* 1899, LXIV [C. 9507], pp. 4 *sqq.*; *Hansard*, 3rd series, CCLXXXVI, 7, 8. *Vide supra*, p. 509.

[2] Walker, *de Villiers*, p. 180, and *History of S. Africa*, p. 510.

[3] *Parl. Pap.* 1899, LXIV [C. 9507], p. 6.

[4] *The Milner Papers*, I, 119.

[5] *Ibid*, I, 39, 41.

[6] *Ibid.* I, 52, 59.

[7] Walker, *de Villiers*, pp. 296 *sqq.*

Progressive party should actually take shape, and he himself could get over the difficulty that some of the heads of its programme would be in flat contradiction to his own past domestic policy. How much support there would be for an imperial policy remained to be seen.

Next were the Uitlanders, who might precipitate a crisis and thus deny to the reforming party among the Transvaalers the time necessary to gain the upper hand before the coming presidential election.[1] At the moment, there were signs that that party was gaining the upper hand. In August 1897 the Industrial Commission reported on the gold industry in terms which the Uitlanders could hardly have bettered, and with a grasp of the problem which gave Milner "quite a new idea of the *niveau intellectuel* of the Boer".[2] Kruger was alarmed, for Schalk Burger, chairman of the Commission, was the hope of many of the Transvaal liberals and of the Free Staters for the presidency. Moreover, Leyds had returned from Europe without the desired loan, and some of the Commission's recommendations would cause loss of revenue to the hard-pressed exchequer. A Volksraad committee was therefore appointed to modify the report.[3] In the event, railway rates were reduced considerably and the Netherlands Company was obliged to give the state a larger share of its takings; many customs duties were lowered, and the Volksraad declared against further monopolies. But the President fiercely and successfully defended the dynamite concession and declined to hear of the board of officials and mining nominees proposed by the Commission to supervise the working of the gold and Native pass laws. This refusal to implement some parts of the report, and the unavoidable delay in carrying out other parts in which negotiations with neighbouring railway administrations were necessary, drove the Chamber and the Association of Mines together at last in watchful hostility to an Executive divided against itself and at issue with a Volksraad which was showing unwonted independence.

Milner studiously avoided doing anything which might check this process of disintegration. He did indeed wage a sharp and partially successful campaign on behalf of the Cape Coloured Folk on the Rand, whom the Volksraad, against the President's wishes, persisted in treating in all things as if they were raw Africans.[4] On the other hand, he declined to take up various minor difficulties; he gave the British Agent a hint not to worry Kruger with one of Chamberlain's "curiously academic" despatches on the true meaning of the Convention;[5] above all, in spite of the wishes of his chief and of the Agent, he shelved the matter of the dynamite monopoly, though the law officers

[1] *The Milner Papers*, I, 103.

[2] *Ibid.* I, 83.

[3] *Parl. Pap.* 1899, LXIV [C. 9345], p. 14.

[4] *Parl. Pap.* 1899, LXIV [C. 9345], pp. 80 *sqq.*; *Notulen* (1st Volksraad), 11 August 1897; *Z.A.R. Groenboek* 8 *van* 1899.

[5] *The Milner Papers*, I, 83.

of the Crown had declared it to be a breach of that Convention. To claim anything as of right under that instrument would silence the growing opposition in the Transvaal and might well lead to war, and he had no mind to fight about "a capitalists' question pure and simple".[1]

Lastly, away to the north of the troubled Transvaal was Rhodes, the biggest man in British South Africa, "undaunted and unbroken ... but also untaught", quite capable, unless he were guided, of making "shipwreck of his own ambition and our permanent interest". His personal following, Milner well knew, was "itching" for a quarrel, and Rhodes himself was not averse to having "another slap" at Kruger, of course "by peaceful means".[2] Rhodes's immediate ambition, however, was to achieve the speedy economic integration of Africa south of the Zambesi, which should form the basis of a political federation ensuring "equal rights for every white man".[3] He was now demanding the Bechuanaland Protectorate, which he claimed had been promised to him shortly before the Raid, proposing to combine it with Rhodesia as one huge thinly-peopled, self-governing colony in all of which the British South Africa Company should retain the mineral and other commercial rights; in other words, as Milner noted drily, a vast northern "absolute monarchy with Rhodes as monarch".[4] Rhodes hoped soon to see Natal enter the Cape-Free State customs union, and himself to win the Cape elections. That done he would carry a redistribution of seats in the Assembly and a Permissive Federation Act, while Harry Escombe, an ardent federalist and Home Ruler and Premier of Natal, was to carry a similar measure at Pietermaritzburg. It would be hard if such an organised British mass could not counterbalance or, perhaps, absorb the allied republics.[5]

But Rhodes, with his dread of Crown Colony rule, was in no mind to have the effective checks upon the administration and police of Southern Rhodesia, which Milner, like Loch before him, desired. Milner intended to have his own men, his "eyes and ears", upon the spot. An elective element he was willing to have in the proposed Legislative Council, but not the elective legislature which Rhodes was advocating frankly on the grounds that whereas H.M. Government might bully a Company, it would never dare to bully the elected of the people.[6]

Milner found means to control Rhodes through his passion for "size ... that big map".[7] He determined to make him earn the Bechuanaland Protectorate by good behaviour. Late in 1897 he

[1] *The Milner Papers*, I, 129, 138.
[2] *Ibid.* I, 38, 78, 106 *sqq.*
[3] Michell, *Life of Cecil Rhodes*, II, 202.
[4] *The Milner Papers*, I, 105.
[5] "Vindex", *Cecil Rhodes*, p. 520; Williams, Basil, *Cecil Rhodes*, p. 296.
[6] *The Milner Papers*, I, 109 *sqq.*
[7] *Ibid.*, I, 106.

journeyed north to see for himself. He found Southern Rhodesia still "in a pretty handsome mess". On the other hand, he admitted that, in spite of the depletion of their resources by the recent Matabele rebellion, Rhodes and his Company had pushed the country forward where Treasury methods would have starved it. If they had wasted much, they had also spent much; the Cape-to-Cairo railway had just reached Bulawayo; the framework of a decent administration was at last being constructed.[1] At Umtali, far away on the Portuguese border, Milner ran Rhodes to earth and gained his confidence. He persuaded him to accept his flexible scheme of imperial control and satisfied him that, though the Protectorate could not go to him yet awhile, the Company's prior rights of acquisition should be recognised.[2]

Finally, the Native question, which underlay the piecemeal political and economic superstructure of white southern Africa, was much in Milner's mind during the later months of 1897. The Transvaal was beyond his reach, but he was able to do something to set matters right, where it was sorely needed, in Rhodesia; tact and firmness smoothed over trouble in Basutoland, which at one time had threatened to involve the Free State; in the self-governing Cape, he did what he could to moderate the Ministry's desire to confiscate large blocks of reserve land at the end of a dreary scuffle with some Bechuana. There were times when he felt that if he was to fail in South Africa, it would be because he might be obliged to take a line on the Native question which would drive British and Afrikaners together in common hostility to the imperial cause.[3]

Events now occurred which thrust the Native question below the surface once more. In February 1898, Kruger was re-elected President. His opponents, Schalk Burger and Commandant-General Joubert, split the Liberal vote; his own supporters made the most of Chamberlain's inopportune reiteration of the suzerainty claim, while the presence, just across the Limpopo, of Rhodes, the personification to the Boers of the hated "big money power", was worth hundreds of votes to him.[4] Kruger's triumph was a blow to Milner's hopes of rapid reform and to his dwindling faith in the efficacy of friendly approaches. The old President was convinced that his critics wanted not reform but his country, while there were many questions which Milner felt he could hold back no longer. Already he had become involved in a bickering correspondence with Pretoria on the delicate subject of British Indians, a correspondence destined to run on for many months without much effect beyond complicating the general

[1] *Parl. Pap.* 1897, IX [311–I], pp. 603 *sqq.*; *B.S.A. Co., Directors' Report*, 1896–7, pp. 8, 9, 18.

[2] *The Milner Papers*, I, 139 *sqq.*

[3] *Ibid.*, I, 178 *sqq.*

[4] Chaplin, (Sir) Drummond, Letterbooks, 1897–8 (unpublished), 25 April 1898; *Die Volkstem*, 20 Nov. 1897.

South African problem of control of immigration, and preventing the Transvaal from enforcing its drastic anti-Asiatic laws.

Meanwhile the Federal Raad of the two republics had met for the first time in January. Kruger had talked much of a republican union, but the Free Staters had been so lukewarm that it had been agreed that the time for that was not yet. On the other hand, it had been resolved to work for greater unity notably in the matter of legislation, judicial procedure and constitutions, to set up a joint court of appeal, to accept Transvaal currency as legal tender in the Free State, and to give full weight to the interests of both states in the framing of foreign policy.[1] For the rest, Middelberg, the active manager of the Netherlands Company, was seeking to get control of the railways which the Free State had taken over in the preceding year from the Cape Colony. Leyds, too, was reported to be busy drafting treaties which would link the Transvaal through the Free State with foreign Powers, and was certainly demanding money for an enlarged diplomatic service from a canny Volksraad, which, for the moment, preferred "a consul in each country and no high titles".[2] But Continental governments were evidently taking the republic seriously. The French and German consuls at Pretoria had recently become consuls-general, and a Russian consul had appeared at Johannesburg, whither Russian Jews were proceeding in considerable numbers.

A renewed threat to the independence of the Transvaal Bench brought matters to a head. The Expulsion Law was indeed amended, but the promised appeal was to lie not to the Judiciary but to the Executive.[3] Finally, at the end of February 1898, Kruger abruptly dismissed Chief Justice Kotze for reasserting the testing right on the plea that the promised legislation safeguarding the Bench ought to have been passed before the close of 1897, whereas the President and de Villiers the mediator held that the period of grace extended to the end of 1898.[4]

Milner now looked forward to a "final smash" sooner or later. On purely South African, as distinct from imperial, grounds he was ready to force matters to an issue at once by insisting on the redress of substantial wrongs, all the more as the dismissal of the Chief Justice imperilled the general interest so gravely as to give good cause for intervention. But Chamberlain refused to touch the Kotze case. He reminded Milner that the British public would never agree to war on so "academic" a question as the interpretation of a preamble, and warned him that, in face of difficulties half the world over, England's greatest interest in South Africa at the moment was peace.[5]

[1] *Notulen van den Eersten Volksraad der Z.A. Republiek*, 4 October, 1898, pp. 935 *sqq.*
[2] *Ibid.*
[3] *Parl. Pap.* 1899, LXIV [C. 9345], p. 61.
[4] Kotze, (Sir) J. G., *The Judicial Crisis* . . ., pp. 22 *sqq.*; Walker, *de Villiers*, pp. 316 *sqq.*
[5] *The Milner Papers*, I, 214, 222 *sqq.*

The French in West Africa, the Khalifa in the Sudan, Germans at Kiau-Chau, and Germans again seeking to oust British railway interests from the dominions of the Turk—there was no gainsaying the facts.[1] Forbidden to act, Milner had at least spoken. His daily experience in the western Cape Colony and a visit to the eastern districts had convinced him that the British section as a whole was well-affected though leaderless, but that the bulk of the Afrikaners were already "at heart fellow-citizens" with the republicans, quiescent enough in ordinary times but liable to flare up whenever trouble was brewing with either republic.[2] At Graaff-Reinet, early in March 1898, a provocative passage in a Bond address of welcome had given him the opening he desired. His speech was at once a rallying cry to those Afrikaners, whom, from the first, he had hoped to win over so that they might induce the Transvaalers to set their house in order for the good of South Africa, and a warning to all concerned that Great Britain was not prepared to give up the position she had so long held in South Africa from fear of a heavily-armed republic and its colonial sympathisers.[3]

Delivered as it was in the midst of a fierce general election for the Cape Upper House, the Graaff-Reinet speech convinced Bondsmen and republicans that the High Commissioner was supporting the now fully organized Progressives; but it at least induced far-sighted Cape and Free State friends to give the Transvaalers an increasing measure of good advice in private. Nor can there be any doubt that, by clearing the air, it helped to bring about better relations between Great Britain and Germany in southern Africa.

In the Far East, Great Britain had replied to Russia's seizure of Port Arthur by herself acquiring a lease of Wei-hai-wei, and had swung over to the German side of the balance. On the other hand, in spite of inspired newspaper warnings to the Transvaalers not to expect too much in the way of German support, the chilly reception by Berlin of his hint at an alliance, and the passage of the first German Navy Act in April 1898, reawakened all Chamberlain's fears for Delagoa Bay, fears also of the intentions of the republicans.[4] He called upon the War Office to provide at least military transport, the utter lack of which had been revealed during the recent minor troubles in Basutoland.[5] Then, in May, he repeated his offer of the preceding year to Portugal. Harassed Lisbon, desperately afraid of Germany's ambitions in Africa, was readier than it had been then to listen to a proposal of a loan on the London market and a British guarantee of her possessions, in return for a mortgage on her African colonies and the denial to the Transvaal of any access to the Indian

[1] Gooch and Temperley, *British Documents*, I, 2 *sqq.*, 34, 42 *sqq.*, 132 *sqq.*, 333.
[2] *The Milner Papers*, I, 87.
[3] *Ibid.* I, 242 *sqq.*; *The Cape Argus*, 4 March 1898.
[4] *German Diplomatic Documents*, III, 21, 26, 29.
[5] *Parl. Pap.* 1903, XL [Cd. 1789], p. 191.

Ocean other than by the existing Delagoa Bay line. Her section of that line was to be controlled by a semi-official Anglo-Portuguese Company.

Towards the close of June, however, Germany and France brought pressure to bear on Portugal. In the end, Great Britain agreed to admit Germany to the negotiations lest she summon a general conference on Africa, including Egypt, a conference which jealous France and her ally, Russia, must necessarily attend. After carefully excluding France from all participation, the two Governments, on 30 August 1898, agreed publicly to furnish Portugal with loans secured on the revenues of her African colonies and of the island of Timor in the East Indies, and, privately, to divide these possessions between themselves in the not unlikely event of Portugal's defaulting. Delagoa Bay was to be included in Great Britain's portion, but the lion's share was to go to Germany. It was, the Germans explained, the least they could accept in return for abandoning the Boers, a subject on which their public opinion was extremely sensitive.[1]

In face of this agreement three months of hard work availed Leyds nothing to move France or Germany or, in the last resort, Russia to see to it that if his republic could not acquire Delagoa Bay or its railway, these should at least be internationalised.[2] There was no hope of common action even though the nature of the secret clauses of the Anglo-German agreement were shrewdly suspected. The United States were grateful for England's good offices in face of German opposition at Manila during their recent war with Spain, and the Fashoda crisis following hard upon Kitchener's conquest of the Sudan passed away without the expected Anglo-French war.[3]

Great Britain's position in the outer world might thus be immensely improved, but her position in the little world of South Africa was worse than it had been. She had nothing there capable of opposing the Transvaal's armaments, and troubles with the republic were piling up once more. British Indians, Cape Coloured, suzerainty, dynamite, the whole vexatious array—and daily Milner was finding it "more difficult to deal with these people".[4] He made up his mind that he must go home as soon as might be to convince statesmen that they must insist on genuine reforms even at the risk of war. Otherwise there would be an end to all real claim to paramountcy in southern Africa.

In the middle of 1898, however, there came a change for the better in Milner's relations with the Transvaal. The Hollander group was weakened by the departure to Europe of Middelberg and of Leyds,

[1] Gooch and Temperley, *British Documents*, I, 29, 45 *sqq.*, 329; *German Diplomatic Documents*, III, 38.

[2] Botha, *Staatkundige Ontwikkeling*, ch. XV; Leyds, *Tweede Verzameling*, Bijlagen, pp. 137 *sqq.*

[3] Gooch and Temperley, *British Documents*, I, 100 *sqq.*, 159 *sqq.*, 330 *sqq.* See *C.H.B.E.* vol. III.

[4] *The Milner Papers*, I, 196.

now Minister Plenipotentiary. Afrikaner resentment against Hollander control, over education particularly, was rising high in the Transvaal,[1] and Kruger, by no means patient of reliance on Continentals and desirous of drawing the southern Afrikaners to his side, appointed F. W. Reitz, ex-President of the Free State, his State Secretary, and J. C. Smuts, a brilliant young Cape advocate, State Attorney. These two men, trained in the more or less anglicised western Cape Colony and thereafter at the Inns of Court and Cambridge, might be expected to understand British ways better than their predecessors and at least to see the necessity of reform. This was indeed so. Reitz's conduct of a long correspondence on Swazi affairs was such that Milner felt that he could change his view of the whole situation if only he could be sure that "the Reitz policy of peace" as contrasted with "the Leyds policy of aggravation" were to be permanent.[2] For, "We don't want the Transvaal, any more than the Orange Free State, but only fair treatment for British industry and capital in the Transvaal and an abstention . . . from intrigues with foreign powers".[3] Reitz actually suggested that he should come north to meet the old President. Milner had himself considered doing so, for he had met Rhodes thus and latterly Steyn, with good results;[4] but there were difficulties in the way of a British High Commissioner entering the Transvaal; besides, would not Reitz "either break his neck or become like the men he serves"?[5] So many other issues still remained; "a big row" over the commandeering of British subjects was looming up, and the Volksraad had just accepted most of the resolutions of the new Federal Raad.[6] These resolutions envisaged the mutual recognition of franchise rights and professional certificates, the foundation of a university for the two republics, the encouragement of the use of Afrikaans as distinct from High Dutch, the creation of a joint board to consider constitutional questions, and the uniform arming of the commandos.[7] None of them, save possibly the last, need cause a High Commissioner immediate anxiety; nevertheless, taken as a whole, they promised to draw the republics closer together, and further apart from the colonial South and the Chartered North.

Over against the loosely allied republics, however, the British economic federation was taking shape. In Southern Rhodesia, Salisbury and half a dozen other little towns had made good, some of the mines were producing indubitable gold, and Rhodes was back on the board of the Chartered Company.[8] In October 1898, the Rhodesia

[1] Malherbe, E. G., *Education in South Africa*, 1652–1922, pp. 273 *sqq*.

[2] *Z.A.R. Groenboek* 2 *van* 1899; *Correspondence re Swaziland, Parl. Pap.* 1899, LXIII [C. 9206]; *The Milner Papers*, I, 237; Walker, E. A., *W. P. Schreiner*, pp. 125–6.

[3] *The Milner Papers*, I, 191.

[4] *Ibid.* I, 160.

[5] *Ibid.* I, 237–8.

[6] *Ibid.* I, 197.

[7] *The Milner Papers*, I, 197; *Notulen der Verrichtingen van den H. Ed. Volksraad* (O.F.S.), 1899, pp. 124 *sqq*.

[8] *B.S.A. Co., Director's Report*, 1896–7, pp. 8, 29, 31; *Detailed Report*, 1896–7 and *Report on the Administration of Rhodesia*, 1897–8.

Order-in-Council set up the system of government under which, with minor changes, the country was destined to be ruled for the next quarter of a century.[1] By that instrument, the Board of Directors was deprived of its legislative powers, its representatives in Rhodesia were subjected to real imperial control especially in the matters of Native affairs and police, and a Legislative Council with an elective minority was established. But the minerals and other assets remained in the hands of the Company, and the new constitution included the Rhodes customs clause, which offered goods from all parts of the British Empire specially favourable terms and thus, as Rhodes hoped, set the pace for the South African Zollverein of the near future.[2] Already, in April 1898, Natal had at long last joined the Cape-Free State customs union leaving the Transvaal in economic isolation.[3]

On the other hand, the Transvaal still held the economic trumps, and Rhodes's hopes of political federation were fading. Escombe, his Natal ally, had lost office before the end of 1897, and though the Progressives in the Cape had gained a narrow majority in the Legislative Council early in 1898, they were as narrowly defeated in the much more important Assembly elections a few months later. And this despite the fact that Rhodes had at last "come out as a Progressive" and declared that the question to be decided was whether the Union Jack or the Transvaal Vierkleur was to fly over a federated South Africa.

Milner believed that Rhodes was right; nevertheless, he would not allow the Progressives to hold on in the hope that disputed elections would give them a bare majority.[4] The game must be played according to the rules. So, W. P. Schreiner, himself no Bondsman and much more sympathetic to the imperial idea than were most of his followers, took office in October at the head of an individually strong Bond-Moderate ministry, which was held together by fear of Rhodes's money-bags, determination to safeguard the peace of South Africa, which they believed Rhodes's policy imperilled, and suspicion of Milner's ideas of paramountcy.[5]

From such a Ministry, nothing more than neutrality could be looked for in "the great game between ourselves and the Transvaal for the mastery in South Africa".[6] For that, in Milner's eyes, was what it had come to. The policy of national segregation which the Transvaalers had practised, since Majuba days especially, was simply the natural reaction of a small people, intensely Afrikaner and still

[1] *Correspondence re B.S.A. Co., Parl. Pap.* 1898, LX [C.8732]; for text of Order-in-Council see *Papers re B.S.A. Co.* 1899, LXIII [C. 9318].

[2] *B.S.A. Co., Report of General and Extraordinary Meeting*, 21 April 1898, p. 11; *S. Rhodesia Order-in-Council*, § 47.

[3] *Minutes of Convention, Cape Parl. Pap.* 1898, G. 66.

[4] *The Milner Papers*, I, 274.

[5] Hofmeyr, J. H., *Jan Hendrik Hofmeyr*, pp. 519 *sqq.*; Walker, *Schreiner*, pp. 112 *sqq.*

[6] *The Milner Papers*, I, 267; II, 25, 37.

essentially pastoral, against the capitalist civilisation which was pressing in upon it from all sides under the British flag.[1] True, apart from the dangers arising from the restricted franchise, which such a policy demanded, and a lively desire to see the gold-mines produce revenue and other advantages, national segregation need mean nothing more than the inconvenience of divided counsels in a South Africa which was in so many respects actually, and in many more potentially, an indivisible whole. Again, the republic's repudiation of the British claim to suzerainty might be a matter for lawyers. Not so its denial of British paramountcy. That, at the very least, implied that care for the welfare of southern Africa was to be shared by Great Britain and the republics on equal terms. It was coming to mean much more. Once upon a time, the Imperial Government had been content, as the Young Afrikaners were now insisting that it ought to be content, to patrol the coasts with its warships and to leave South Africans to settle their own differences. But in those days the British and Afrikaners of the western Cape Colony, Rhodes and Hofmeyr together, had seemed to control the future. The Raid, followed by the opening up of the deep levels and the arming of the government which controlled the mines and the railways that served them, had ended that dream. The North was fast overshadowing the old divided South, and the North that was becoming dominant was not Rhodes's Charterland, but the Transvaal of the sons of the Trekkers. Already enthusiasts were claiming that Kruger was lawful heir to van Riebeeck in the governance of *Zuid-Afrikaners*.[2]

Milner was not enamoured of the Uitlanders as a body, still less had he any undue tenderness for mining magnates; but he held that "two wholly antagonistic systems—a medieval race oligarchy, and a modern industrial state"—simply could not exist permanently side by side.[3] To wait till Kruger was gone might be to wait a long time, and what was to be hoped from his probable successor, the pliable Joubert or the upright but rigid Schalk Burger, the chief exponent of the doctrines of Transvaal dominance, who was prepared to offer nothing more than a selective franchise? Experience had shown that such a franchise was apt to mean the partisan enrolment of government supporters at the height of contested elections. Milner held that the Transvaal must adopt, or be forced to adopt, a constitution as liberal as that of the Free State. There would then be some chance that the more or less British ideas of the colonies might leaven the lump before it was too late, some chance at least that a Transvaal "neutralised by an Anglo-Dutch race fight *on equal lines*" would cease to be a focus of "disaffection" in the British colonies.[4] For there were

[1] Leyds, *Tweede Verzameling*, I (1), 11; Walker, *Schreiner*, pp. 143–4.
[2] Cachet, L., *Die Worstelstrijd der Transvalers*, p. 2.
[3] *The Milner Papers*, I, 234.
[4] *The Milner Papers*, I, 359, 477.

many in those colonies who avowed openly the ideas on which the Transvaalers had based their polity: that the British were sojourners in the land, the Natives mere children of Ham, and their own folk "the People".

On 1 November 1898 Milner at last sailed for England. There was nothing of immediate urgency to keep him back, and since Chamberlain had cabled for him to come,[1] he hoped that an uncomprehending Imperial Government would listen to him now as "the man on the spot". In London, he convinced the Colonial Office of the soundness of his diagnosis of the South African situation.[2] But that was all. Some of the London newspapers, which took their news from South African papers controlled by Rhodes and his friends, as well as a section of the investing public were excited over Rand and Rhodesian shares, all the more as Rhodes himself was in England to stimulate official and private interest in his province and his schemes for a railway to Lake Tanganyika. The War Office indeed took the precaution, long overdue, of ordering the military authorities at the Cape to prepare a scheme in case of sudden war;[3] but the great public displayed not the slightest interest in Uitlanders or anything else South African,[4] and the Cabinet was clearly so set on pacific courses that Chamberlain and Milner wrote a mild despatch to Pretoria, which they hoped would wind up the dreary debate on suzerainty. The despatch was to the effect that, whether or no suzerainty still existed, the admitted relations of Great Britain to the Transvaal amounted to the substance thereof, and that if the preamble of the 1881 Convention had indeed been cancelled with all mention of suzerainty, all mention of independence had been cancelled too.[5]

Meanwhile, a pistol shot, as on a later and more world-wide occasion, had given the signal for the war that was to come. One of the cordially detested Johannesburg police, in self-defence, shot an Uitlander, Edgar, in the man's own house. The policeman was acquitted by the jury on police and Uitlander evidence, but with the pointedly expressed approval of the Judge. The local branch of the South African League took up the matter along with other grievances, notably those of the Cape Coloured Folk, and held an illegal open-air meeting of protest. Two speakers were arrested. On their speedy release on heavy bail, an officially authorised mass meeting in the Johannesburg Amphitheatre was broken up under circumstances which pointed straight at official connivance. The League thereupon organised a petition to the Queen.[6]

Milner doubted at first whether these incidents meant immediate

[1] Sir A. Milner to W. P. Schreiner, 1 November 1898 (Schreiner Papers).
[2] *The Milner Papers*, I, 298; Gardiner, A. G., *Life of Sir William Harcourt*, II, 466.
[3] *Parl. Pap.* 1903, XL [Cd. 1789], pp. 201 *sqq.*
[4] Walker, *Schreiner*, p. 125.
[5] *Parl. Pap.* 1899, LXIV [C. 9507], p. 28; *The Milner Papers*, I, 298–9.
[6] *Parl. Pap.* 1899, LXIV [C. 9345], pp. 108 *sqq.*, 185.

trouble,[1] and the acting High Commissioner, Sir William Butler, who, soldier though he was, believed throughout that South Africa needed "a rest cure and not an operation", upheld the acting British Agent in his refusal to send on to the Queen a petition that had been already published.[2] It was then that the road was opened up on to the broad ground of policy which should carry conviction at home and abroad. It was opened up by the Pretoria Government itself. Kruger proposed to force a fifteen years' renewal of "the d—d dynamite monopoly" through the Volksraad as soon as it should meet. Milner at last agreed reluctantly that a despatch should go forward condemning that monopoly as a breach of the Convention.[3]

The arrival of the dynamite despatch, the return of Leyds empty-handed once more from the counting houses of Europe, pressure by Cape and Free State friends, the public offer by some of the mining houses of a loan of £600,000 wherewith to buy out the dynamite concession, and the fear lest magnates, clamorous Uitlander rank and file and the dreaded imperial factor should form a triple alliance against his republic, led Kruger to attempt to come to terms with some of his potential enemies. Few of the magnates cared for politics; there were signs of better times and they wished to make the most of them in peace; but they had their grievances, and to them had recently been added a hastily passed 5 per cent tax on profits. Some of them were ready to talk business. At the end of February 1899, just after Milner had returned to Cape Town, the Transvaal authorities opened negotiations with a few of the leading firms, informally at first, through Lippert, the original dynamite concessionaire, and began to track down vigorously illicit liquor sellers and other pests of the gold industry.

Most of the subjects discussed at these so-called "capitalist" negotiations were naturally financial.[4] The capitalists were, however, asked to support certain items in the Government's programme on which it was at issue with the High Commissioner and, to their embarrassment, to accept a five-year burgher franchise on behalf of the Uitlanders. The Government's formal terms, which they were permitted to cable to their principals in London and to the Secretary of State, were less favourable than Lippert's original proposal on the score of the franchise. Perhaps this stiffening of the terms was due to the Netherland Railway Company's promise of a loan of £2,000,000 to the Government; in any case, the franchise was now to be given only after seven years' registration and the taking of a needlessly emphatic oath of allegiance, and was apparently not to carry with it

[1] Sir A. Milner to Spenser Wilkinson, 31 January 1899 (unpublished).

[2] Butler, Sir W., *Autobiography*, pp. 398, 401, 406 *sqq.*, 415.

[3] *The Milner Papers*, I, 300; *Correspondence re Explosives Monopoly*, *Parl. Pap.* 1899, LXIV [C. 9317], pp. 1 *sqq.*

[4] *Parl. Pap.* 1899, LXIV [C. 9317]; [C. 9345], pp. 213 *sqq.*; Fitzpatrick, J. P., *The Transvaal from Within*, pp. 326 *sqq.*

any redistribution of seats, any voice in presidential elections, or any security against cancellation by a subsequent hurried Volksraad resolution.

Chamberlain and Milner both suspected that this dealing with selected individuals was an attempt to forestall possible imperial action;[1] nevertheless, they decided that the negotiators must be given a clear field. Chamberlain shelved the plea that the dynamite monopoly was a breach of the Convention and acquiesced in the cutting down of even authorised military expenditure;[2] but he also warned the "London friends" to make sure that the reforms were genuine. They, for their part, approved generally of the scheme, but declined to commit themselves on the franchise until representatives of the main body of the Uitlanders had been consulted. After some hesitation, the consultation was permitted, and then an enterprising Johannesburg journalist "scooped" the proposals including the Uitlanders' adverse comments on the franchise.[3] The negotiators were swept asunder on a flood of mutual recrimination, State Secretary Reitz declaring that, in spite of the participation of highly placed officials, there had been nothing official about the discussions.

The breakdown of the "capitalist" negotiations was fatal. Henceforward, Chamberlain and Milner regarded any scheme put forward from Pretoria as utterly unacceptable without the closest scrutiny, while the Transvaalers believed that both men were seeking to use the franchise as an excuse to meddle with domestic affairs, which, not being covered by the Convention, concerned no one but themselves.

The tragedy precisely was that the Transvaal franchise concerned all South Africa, as did nearly everything else that happened in the economic heart of the country. On the morrow of the breakdown, working men's meetings all along the Reef demanded the capitalists' five-year franchise, while the President toured his state offering a nine-year franchise saddled with the limitations associated with his previous seven years' offer.[4] Left to himself he would doubtless have been more statesmanlike, and he did hold out hopes of better things in ten years' time; but he had to consider his "old burghers" and others whose power depended upon a close franchise. Even so, he spoiled the effect of his present proposals by hurrying home to make a determined effort to force the Volksraad to renew the universally detested dynamite monopoly.

By this time, Milner had in his hands another Uitlander petition, which had been organised after the rejection of the first. He sent it on at once with the comment that the situation was as strained as it well could be and that, Convention or no Convention, the paramount

[1] *The Milner Papers*, I, 323.
[2] *Parl. Pap.* 1899, LXIV [C. 9317], p. 17; Butler, Sir W., *Autobiography*, p. 423.
[3] Fitzpatrick, Sir J. P., *South African Memories*, p. 179.
[4] *Parl. Pap.* 1899, LXIV [C. 9345], p. 205.

Power must assert itself or lose every friend it had in South Africa.[1] But for a time he hesitated to express his sympathy with the petitioners openly. The agitation was serious, a repetition of the state of things before the disastrous Raid; but "money bags are apt to be shortsighted" and the record of the Uitlander rank and file for persistence had so far not been convincing.[2] If they collapsed after the paramount Power had openly given them its support, the shock must react disastrously on Britain's prestige everywhere. As April wore on, however, the cyclone on the Rand sent waves of pro- and anti-Transvaal feeling sweeping in conflict through the colonies. On 4 May 1899 Milner crossed his Rubicon. He telegraphed home a long despatch declaring it a matter of imperial concern that the "helots" of the Rand should be put in a position to work out their own salvation by ceasing to be British subjects and becoming Transvaal burghers.[3] And Chamberlain's prompt reply on May 10, dwelling on British paramountcy and hinting at strong measures,[4] proved that he at least was willing to support the High Commissioner in a policy which put the franchise, and with it the reality of the British paramountcy, to the touch.

The risk of war was not faced yet awhile nor were the two despatches made public. Schreiner, who knew something of Milner's mind, tried to avert the appeal to arms. He ascertained that the liberal leaders in the Transvaal, Reitz, Smuts and Schalk Burger, would support a settlement of the dynamite question and a full five-year franchise, provided all the British demands were made known to them. The upshot was that Steyn invited his fellow-President and the High Commissioner to confer together at Bloemfontein.[5]

The arrangments for the Bloemfontein Conference were attended by many difficulties. Steyn and various Cape friends acted as honest brokers and warned the Transvaalers again and again that this time they must meet the High Commissioner halfway. Leyds, back once more from Europe, impressed upon them, as he did to the end, that Great Britain's hands were exceptionally free and that nothing need be expected from the Continental Powers, except at the very most a Russian diversion in Asia. For Great Britain had come to terms with Russia in China and with France in Africa; Germany was only too eager to settle mutual differences with her in Samoa, and France was determined that nothing warlike should mar the coming Paris International Exhibition.[6]

[1] *Parl. Pap.* 1899, LXIV [C. 9345], pp. 104, 184; *The Milner Papers*, I, 343, 345.

[2] *The Milner Papers*, I, 324.

[3] *Parl. Pap.* 1899, LXIV [C. 9345], pp. 209 *sqq.*

[4] *Ibid.* pp. 226 *sqq.*

[5] *Parl. Pap.* 1899, LXIV [C. 9345], pp. 239 *sqq.*; Hofmeyr, *Jan Hendrik Hofmeyr*, p. 536; Walker, *de Villiers*, pp. 330 *sqq.*; Van der Merwe, *Steyn*, I, 174; Schreiner and Merriman Papers, 1899, *passim.*

[6] Leyds, *Eenige Correspondentie uit* 1899, pp. 9, 25, 81, 85, 171, 175; Gooch and Temperley, *British Documents*, I, 3, 40, 127 *sqq.*, 199 *sqq.*, 280 *sqq.*, 331; *German Diplomatic Documents*, III, 85 *sqq.*, 93, 98.

On the other hand, the Volksraad gave an indication of what an unentrenched franchise would be worth by cancelling, against its President's advice, some of the selective franchises given since the Raid,[1] and the State Attorney gravely unearthed a plot by so-called British ex-army officers to rush the Johannesburg fort and hold it till the troops could come up. This "conspiracy" presently faded away in the light of a public investigation, but it did not smooth the path of the peacemakers.[2] Worst of all, Leyd's final departure for Europe reawakened the British Government's fears of foreign complications, and left the conduct of the Transvaal's diplomacy in the inexperienced and downright hands of the patriotic Reitz. Reitz threw to the winds part of a cautious despatch left behind by the departing Leyds, and in one sweeping sentence challenged suzerainty, paramountcy and the very Convention by declaring that the rights of the republic were derived from its own inherent nature as a sovereign independent state.[3]

Milner regarded the proposed Conference as a device of the Free State and Cape Afrikaners to gain time. He would have preferred to see the "helot" and "grievance" despatches made public first, so that all the world should understand the situation as he saw it; but he agreed with Chamberlain that in that event there would be no Conference. Once in conference Kruger must either grant such a franchise settlement as would permit of other outstanding questions being discussed in a less strained atmosphere, or reveal an invincible obstinacy that would justify stronger measures.[4] So Milner set out for his first and last meeting with the old President.

The Bloemfontein Conference (31 May–5 June 1899) ended in deadlock.[5] Kruger offered a seven-year franchise for five of which the applicant would be denationalised, still without the vital presidential vote, with no immediate enrolment of new burghers, and no simplification of the customary formidable obstacles. This he tried to make contingent on the incorporation of Swaziland and arbitration on disputed points arising out of the Convention, in the end, "without the foreign element". Milner refused to make the franchise part of "a Kaffir bargain". He demanded a five-year retrospective franchise of the fullest kind, a modified oath to be followed by immediate enrolment, and a redistribution of seats. The Free Staters and some of his own Transvaalers begged Kruger to yield. He would not. Other notable supporters, the belief that such reform must rob him of his country, and a large Uitlander petition expressing satisfaction with his

[1] *Notulen van den Eersten Volksraad* . . ., 16 May and 15 June, 1899; *Correspondence re Political Situation* . . ., *Parl. Pap.* 1900, LVI [Cd. 369], p. 2.

[2] *Correspondence re Political Affairs* . . ., *Parl. Pap.* 1899, LXIV [C. 9521], pp. 1 *sqq.*

[3] *Parl. Pap.* 1899, LXIV [C. 9507]; p. 32; Leyds, *Eenige Correspondentie*, pp. 200 *sqq.*; *The Milner Papers*, I, 390.

[4] *Parl. Pap.* 1899, LXIV [C. 9345], pp. 226 *sqq.*; *The Milner Papers*, I, 376 *sqq.*

[5] *Correspondence re Bloemfontein Conference*, *Parl. Pap.* 1899, LXIV [C. 9404); *Z.A.R. Groenboek 4 van* 1899; Van der Merwe, *Steyn*, I, 180 *sqq.*

régime, all encouraged him to stand fast. So Milner broke off the discussions a few hours before Chamberlain's message reached him urging him to let the President talk on as his custom was. "Perhaps", he confessed, "extreme fatigue had something to do with it."[1] Be that as it may, the prospect of war came clearly over the public's horizon for the first time. Steyn began reluctantly to arm;[2] Chamberlain published the "helot" and "grievance" despatches and told the startled House of Commons that a new situation had arisen in South Africa,[3] and shares fell on the London Stock Exchange.

Milner neither expected nor desired an ultimatum at this stage; that would rather follow the rejection of a formal presentation of the Bloemfontein terms. But he took it for granted that, since the burghers of the two republics alone outnumbered the regulars on the spot by seven to one, the publication of the two despatches inaugurating a forward policy would be accompanied by the despatch of troops, 10,000 at least, to make Natal safe before the crash came. The two things he dreaded most were a long period of suspense, and serious British reverses in the opening stages of the campaign.[4] Either of these would mean a long war. In the event, South Africa was condemned to both, because, after some debate, the British Cabinet decided neither to send an ultimatum nor to mobilise an army corps. Lord Salisbury and Sir Michael Hicks Beach, Chancellor of the Exchequer, refused to be hurried, all the more as neither public nor Parliament were really interested.[5] It was only at the end of June that the Cape command was ordered to collect regimental transport.[6] For "three raging months of crisis" Milner was left without the military and political backing which his policy demanded.

In South Africa itself, Milner's Bloemfontein programme won over to his side many Cape moderates,[7] and his promise to Natal of defence by the full strength of the Empire stiffened the backs of the Hime ministry which had recently taken office at Pietermaritzburg.[8] Nevertheless, he had some difficulty in silencing Escombe and others in Natal who talked of a vote of no confidence if war came without colonial ministers being consulted. Interference by colonial ministers in imperial policy Milner would not suffer. Rather than that, he would appeal to their electorates.[9]

At this stage Kruger laid his carefully guarded seven-year scheme before the Volksraad.[10] That assembly approved the scheme, but with

[1] *The Milner Papers*, I, 424.
[2] Van der Merwe, *Steyn*, I, 191.
[3] *Hansard*, 4th series, LXXII, 637.
[4] *The Milner Papers*, I, 356, 401.
[5] *Ibid* I, 33, 430 *sqq.*, 474.
[6] Butler, Sir W., *Autobiography*, p. 440.
[7] *Correspondence re Political Reforms* ..., *Parl. Pap.* 1899, LXIV [C. 9415], p. 17.
[8] *Correspondence re Defence of Natal* ..., *Parl. Pap.* 1900, LVI [Cd. 44], p. 1.
[9] *The Milner Papers*, I, 402, 461 *sqq.*
[10] *Parl. Pap.* 1899, LXIV [C. 9415], pp. 8, 11, 39.

incredible short-sightedness, before adjourning to seek the assent of their constituents, taunted the Free Staters with trying to evade their treaty obligations, and proposed to reallocate seats with such an overwhelming advantage to the countryside that any Uitlander representation would be cancelled in advance.[1] This folly drove many more Cape moderates over to the High Commissioner's side, and led the Cape ministry to induce Abram Fischer, a leading Free Stater, to go to Pretoria. Fischer reported that Kruger was yielding enough, but that Schalk Burger and other of his advisers would hear of no concessions worth naming.[2] Thereupon Chamberlain at Birmingham (26 June 1899) announced that Kruger's terms were quite unacceptable, and Milner began to insist that any franchise scheme must be tested in detail if there was to be any guarantee of satisfaction and permanency.[3] In other words, the British Government must be a party to the settlement.

The strain was eased for a moment when Hofmeyr and Albertus Herholdt, a moderate Bond member of the Schreiner ministry, hurried north. In secret session they induced Volksraad and Executive to modify the Franchise Bill, especially in the direction of making the vote more certainly accessible, and to appoint a dynamite commission.[4] On receipt of newspaper reports of the revised Bill, the Cape Ministry expressed its satisfaction; Chamberlain remarked that no one would dream of fighting over two years' difference in the qualification period; *The Times* pronounced the crisis at an end, and Milner in desperation talked privately of resigning if H.M. Government was to become "quite flabby".[5] It was only a momentary hesitation. Fuller information raised doubts, and when Chamberlain asked the Transvaalers to take no final action till he had seen the complete scheme, he was met with a firm refusal.[6] The franchise was their business and none of Downing Street's; so while petitions sympathising with the Uitlanders poured in upon the High Commissioner from all the British colonies in South Africa, and Rhodes, back at the Cape once more, challenged public opinion, especially Afrikaner opinion, by declaring for "equal rights for every civilised man south of the Zambesi",[7] the law was published. So riddled was it with pitfalls that neither the grant of five seats to the mining areas in each Volksraad nor an explanatory memorandum by the State Attorney could atone for its defects.[8]

[1] *The Milner Papers*, I, 451.
[2] *Ibid.* I, 447 *sqq.*
[3] *Correspondence re Political Reforms ...*, *Parl. Pap.* 1899, LXIV [C. 9518], p. 14.
[4] *Ibid.* pp. 25 *sqq. et passim*; 1899, LXIV [C. 9415], p. 42; Hofmeyr, *Jan Hendrik Hofmeyr*, pp. 540 *sqq.*; Walker, E. A., *W. P. Schreiner*, pp. 163 *sqq.*
[5] *Hansard*, 4th series, LXXIV, 1373; *The Milner Papers*, I, 453; Sir A. Milner to Spenser Wilkinson, 26 July 1899 (unpublished).
[6] *Parl. Pap.* 1899, LXIV [C. 9518], pp. 18, 35 *sqq.*
[7] "Vindex", *Cecil Rhodes*, p. 647.
[8] *Parl. Pap.* 1899, LXIV [C. 9518], pp. 7, 45, 63; Walker, *de Villiers*, p. 345.

Milner had already warned his chief that "the franchise and every other question have merged in one big issue: Is British paramountcy to be vindicated or let slide?"[1] But Chamberlain also knew that Campbell-Bannerman's Liberals would divide the House and the country on any war issue. He therefore announced, amid general approval, that the Cabinet was resolved to exhaust all peaceful means of reaching a settlement, and asked for a joint enquiry into the new law as the necessary prelude to a conference between the President and the High Commissioner at Cape Town on such matters as arbitration "without the foreign element".[2] At the same time 2000 men were sent to Natal and pressure was brought to bear upon Portugal to stop the importation of arms into the Transvaal through Delagoa Bay.[3]

The quarrel now centred on the joint enquiry. Without that Milner would accept nothing; rather than submit to such an invasion of their independence, the Transvaalers were ready to fight, reluctantly or eagerly according to their respective ages and temperaments. They were confirmed in their resolve by the belief that the power behind the Imperial Government was Rhodes and the pro-Rhodian press, which demanded insistently force or at least the show of force. Meanwhile, deaf to the pleadings of Cape and English friends, they followed Leyd's cabled advice to play for time and neither to accept nor reject the enquiry in so many words.[4] With time, Johannesburg's nerve might give way, the English Liberals might checkmate Chamberlain, there might even be a settlement. In any event, they must stave off war till October, when the grass would be grown for their horses and masses of hastily ordered munitions be safely delivered for use in a struggle. Many reckoned on help from Colonial Afrikaners, and hoped for European complications when perhaps 200,000 English troops would be engaged six thousand miles from home.[5]

In the second week of August, Smuts, the State Attorney, opened pourparlers with the British Agent through Johannes Wilhelmus Wessels, the Liberal leader of the Johannesburg Bar. As a result, Greene sent on two telegrams to the High Commissioner. The first, initialled by Smuts and himself, intimated that provided the joint enquiry was dropped, the Transvaal would give a five-year retrospective franchise including the presidential vote and not less than one-fourth of the seats in each Raad to the mining areas, and would agree to discuss the details of the Bill with the Agent. The Transvaal would also assume that no more would be heard of suzerainty, that non-foreign arbitration would be conceded, and that the discussion of the Franchise Bill would not form a precedent for interference in

[1] *The Milner Papers*, I, 457.
[2] *Parl. Pap.* 1899, LXIV [C. 9518], pp. 11, 29.
[3] *Parl. Pap.* 1903, XL [Cd. 1789], p. 17; Gooch and Temperley, *British Documents*, I, 85 *sqq.*
[4] Leyds, *Eenige Correspondentie*, pp. 93 *sqq.*, 106, 137.
[5] Walker, *Schreiner*, p. 144.

internal matters. The second telegram contained Greene's explanations of certain points on which he thought Smuts and he were also agreed, and without which the proposed concessions would be robbed of much of their value.[1]

Milner, recalling the "capitalist" negotiations, was disturbed by these pourparlers. But Chamberlain was jubilant. The two telegrams taken together gave him more than even the Bloemfontein terms, while discussion of the franchise bill might well be accepted as a substitute for the joint enquiry. He at once agreed to consider the scheme on its merits.[2]

The Transvaal's formal proposal was not quite so good as that contained even in the first telegram (August 19). Then, two days later —it can hardly be doubted in response to an agitated cable from Leyds—Reitz pointed out that the five-year offer was strictly dependent on the acceptance of the three points which had hitherto been assumed. Without that, no steps would be taken to lay the scheme before the Volksraad (August 21).[3]

The Pretoria authorities were congratulating themselves that if Great Britain rejected the offer, there would be a revulsion of feeling against her; while if she accepted it, the elimination of suzerainty and the joint enquiry, and the granting of an arbitration court would be worth far more to them than a reduction of two years in the franchise qualification period. One-fourth of the seats was, in their eyes, a fair and necessary concession to the Uitlanders, who would soon form the large majority in the state, while an alteration in the rules for presidential elections and the exclusive use of Dutch in the Volksraad (the two main points which Greene thought he had guarded against in his explanatory message) would give the presidency and even some of the new urban seats to "old burghers".[4]

On the British side there was a stiffening at once. A promise to consider the five-year scheme on its merits could not be taken as a promise to accept it in its entirety, while Reitz's second note had transformed an attempt to make friends into a "Kaffir bargain".[5] Chamberlain accused Kruger publicly of dribbling out reforms "like a squeezed sponge", and foreshadowed steps "which once for all shall establish which is the Paramount Power in South Africa".[6] He declined to promise never again to intervene on behalf of the Uitlanders on the ground that he could not give up Convention rights nor the right of any Power to protect its citizens in foreign parts, and he

[1] *Correspondence re Political Reforms, Parl. Pap.* 1899, LXIV [C. 9521], pp. 44 *sqq.*; 1900, LXIV [C. 9530], pp. 19 *sqq.*; *Further Correspondence*, 1900, LVI [Cd. 43], pp. 45 *sqq.*; *Z.A.R. Groenboek* 9 of 1899.

[2] *Parl. Pap.* 1899, LXIV [C. 9521], p. 46; *The Milner Papers*, I, 490.

[3] *Parl. Pap.* 1899, LXIV [C. 9521], pp. 58–9; Leyds, *Eenige Correspondentie*, p. 114 and n.

[4] Leyds, W. J., *Tweede Verzameling*, pp. 123, 154; *The Milner Papers*, I, 496.

[5] *Parl. Pap.* 1899, LXIV [C. 9530], pp. 23, 57.

[6] *The Times*, 28 August 1899.

further reminded Kruger that, after the franchise, there were other matters to be settled at a conference between himself and the High Commissioner.[1] Nevertheless, Chamberlain intended his reply to be a "qualified acceptance", for he repeated his acceptance of non-foreign arbitration and his desire to drop the suzerainty debate, which Reitz's second letter had revived, and also suggested that the British Agent should make a unilateral enquiry into the five-year scheme in lieu of the joint enquiry.

Chamberlain's despatch found the Transvaalers more confident than they had been for some time past. It is true that Uitlanders were either fleeing the Rand or clamouring for far-reaching changes, and Baden-Powell was known to be organising forces on the western border; on the other hand, the Portuguese, who had of late been holding up munitions at Delagoa Bay, had given way under German pressure and let the vital consignments through at the end of August.[2] The Transvaal authorities therefore read the qualified acceptance as a definite refusal. Explaining that they had had no intention of ruling out Convention rights, they went back to their existing seven-year franchise law and accepted, for what it might be worth, the unilateral enquiry. And they also made up their minds that if Great Britain sent any considerable body of troops to South Africa, they would send their commandos over the Natal and western borders.[3]

Coming as it did at the end of five weary weeks of wasted negotiation, during which the pulsation of the Rand had died down bringing business to a standstill throughout South Africa,[4] Milner took this reply as a signal that the Boers meant to fight. But Chamberlain still had Parliament to deal with, and, in Lord Salisbury, a chief who hated the very idea of a costly war on behalf of people he held in low esteem.[5] The most the British Cabinet would do was to order up 10,000 troops from the Mediterranean and India, sufficient, it believed, to secure the colonies from invasion and to show that it meant what it said, and to declare that failing the five-year franchise, including the use of English in the Volksraad, it would begin *de novo* and formulate its own demands.[6] On the same day, the Transvaal, under strong pressure from Cape and Free State well-wishers, ambiguously accepted the joint enquiry (September 8).[7]

Or had it only accepted the subsequent conference? That was Milner's view; but views were ceasing to count now that armed

[1] *Parl. Pap.* 1899, LXIV [C. 9521], pp. 49 *sqq.*

[2] Gooch and Temperley, *British Documents*, I, 85, 88; Leyds, *Eenige Correspondentie*, pp. 109, 129, 175.

[3] *Parl. Pap.* 1899, LXIV [C. 9521], pp. 52 *sqq.*; Leyds, *Eenige Correspondentie*, pp. 102, 162, and *Tweede Verzameling*, I (1), 16.

[4] *Parl. Pap.* 1899, LXIV [C. 9521], pp. 38 *sqq.*, 51.

[5] Newton, Lord, *Lord Lansdowne: a Biography*, p. 157.

[6] *Parl. Pap.* 1899, LXIV [C. 9521], p. 64; *Minutes of Evidence . . . on the War in South Africa*, 1903, LX [Cd. 1791], Q. 21302–3.

[7] *Parl. Pap.* 1899, LXIV [C. 9521], pp. 52 *sqq.*; [C. 9530], p. 1.

men were moving. British Liberals might hold that the Transvaal had itself shown the inadequacy of its seven-year law by its subsequent offer; they and the Bond leaders might hail the *de novo* despatch as a hopeful sign.[1] As a matter of fact, war was rapidly approaching. Pretoria accused Downing Street of putting forward new terms, and alleged that Greene had hoodwinked the guileless Smuts in the August pourparlers. The Volksraad debated the resumption of mine lands, the confiscation of the property of non-resident traitors, and the stiffening of the Expulsion Law.[2] Small parties of British troops and war correspondents took the water amid the cheers of a populace ignorant of the meaning of serious war, to be welcomed vociferously at the excited colonial ports. Milner, against the wishes of the pacific Schreiner Ministry, sent up a few regulars to organise the defences of Kimberley;[3] the Free State promised to stand by its ally, and the British Government decided to mobilise an army corps and announced that its list of demands would be forthcoming shortly.[4]

The fact that the Free State had thrown in its lot with its sister republic was a relief rather than an additional anxiety to Milner and Chamberlain. A wedge of neutral republican territory screening the open southern approaches to the Transvaal would have presented a grave obstacle to the troops, and would have complicated the thorough-going settlement that must follow the war that was surely coming. For the Transvaalers would never have accepted anything like the terms which Milner desired and which, in the main, Chamberlain was ready to advocate: repeal of all franchise legislation since 1881, absolute political equality for all resident Europeans, recognition of British paramountcy including the right of interference in internal matters where the welfare of South Africa was involved, and, so that H.M. Government might reduce its garrison, the dismantling of the Pretoria forts and strict limitation of the republic's artillery.[5]

The British ultimatum was never sent. It was Great Britain's turn now to play for time until her troops could land. On September 26 the republicans drew up their ultimatum ready for presentation as soon as their burghers should be ready on the frontiers.[6] Thither they were already converging as the advanced British troops in Natal moved north to Dundee. Cape ministerialists petitioned for peace fruitlessly;[7] Steyn called vainly on the United States to mediate and strove to hold back the impatient Transvaalers.[8] It was unforeseen

[1] Cook, E. T., *Rights and Wrongs of the Transvaal War*, p. 206.
[2] *Parl. Pap.* 1899, LXIV [C. 9530], pp. 11, 14; Walker, *de Villiers*, p. 354.
[3] *Papers re the Defence of Kimberley*, *Cape Parl. Pap.* 1900, C. 8.
[4] *Parl. Pap.* 1899, LXIV [C. 9530], p. 16.
[5] *The Milner Papers*, I, 525 *sqq.*
[6] Leyds, *Eenige Correspondentie*, pp. 174, 176, and *Tweede Verzameling*, I (1), 24, 30.
[7] *Parl. Pap.* 1899, LXIV [C. 9530], p. 39.
[8] Leyds, *Eenige Correspondentie*, pp. 180 *sqq.*; Van der Merwe, *Steyn*, I, 266 *sqq.*

lack of transport rather than Steyn's restraining hand that prevented Reitz (who knew his Stevenson) from cheerfully "tipping the black spot to Long John Greene" on October 2 instead of a week, a vital week, later.[1] The first of the British troops from India landed at Durban on October 3; the republican ultimatum took effect on October 11. Then the commandos on the Natal borders rose in their stirrups cheering and rode forward confident at least of initial victories, which should dismay the foe, hearten their colonial friends, and—who knew?—see the beginning of the end of the British Empire.[2]

The long war that followed this sanguine advance is of great military interest.[3] It was fought out between radically different military organisations in a most difficult and sparsely peopled country, a vastly greater Spain, totally lacking navigable rivers and canals, and ill-supplied with railways or even with roads. Once away from the coast strip, days were often hot and nights bitterly cold, and long droughts alternated with torrential downpours on the wide barren plains intersected with mountain ranges or dotted with isolated kopjes, each a ready-made fort.

Such a country suited the Boers far better than the British. The republicans were mounted infantry, grouped in loosely framed district commandos and led as a rule by elected officers. Discipline was not, and men came and went much as fancy or opportunity dictated; but this arrangement consorted with their tradition and experience better than any other. They fought widely extended, under cover, with their horses handy in the rear. Man for man, they were not the crack shots their fathers had been, but their Mauser rifles were far superior to the weapons of Majuba days and even in some respects to the British Lee-Metfords of 1899. In each army the commandos were backed by a disciplined force of police fighting in Boer fashion, and by a small but competent corps of artillery. Some of their guns were old-fashioned, and many of those ordered recently from Europe had failed to arrive before the outbreak of hostilities; but, at the start, they had seventy serviceable pieces including four six-inch Long Toms.

Against them came part of the most highly trained professional army of the day. The marksmanship of the British infantry was not really good, but it was better than it had been a decade earlier; the field artillery and cavalry were as fine as any in the world, though the largest guns they had were a few four-point-sevens, and they were supported by some mounted infantry, a novelty in European armies.

[1] *The Times History of the War in South Africa* (ed. L. S. Amery), I, 360, 371.

[2] Leyds, *Tweede Verzameling*, I (1), 31 *sqq.*; F. W. Reitz to W. P. Schreiner, 6 March 1899 (Schreiner Papers); Reitz, D., *Commando: a Boer journal of the Boer War*, p. 23.

[3] For the military operations see *The Times History*..., I–VI index; Maurice, Sir J. F. and Staff, *History of the War in South Africa*..., I–IV; German General Staff, *The German Official Account of the War*... *from Oct.* 1899 *to Sept.* 1900 (translated by W. H. H. Waters and H. du Cane), I, II.

But the main mass of this army was infantry, drawn for the most part from the towns, and none of it had ever experienced European warfare.

The weakest spot in both the British and the Boer armies was the head. At the outset, none of the three Commanders-in-Chief were outstanding men, none of them had properly trained staffs, and none of them had ever before had to handle such large forces in the field. But here again the Boers' problem was the simpler. They at least knew the ground; their forces were smaller, more mobile and self-reliant, able to do with less in the way of supplies, and able also to draw those supplies from home close at hand, whereas their enemies must draw their supplies from the distant coast through colonies many of whose inhabitants were either actively or passively hostile. These advantages coupled with the possession of interior lines enabled the Boers to put the bulk of their men into the firing line. And this was well for them, since their numbers were strictly limited. During the two and a half years of war they contrived to put into the field, in round figures, 69,000 burghers, besides 2700 regulars, 2100 cosmopolitan volunteers and 13,300 colonial rebels.[1]

The British problem, in the first instance, was to move from England an army corps of 47,000 men under Sir Redvers Buller across six thousand miles of water, and then to supply them and the 20,000 additional troops from other sources which were held to be adequate for "wiping something off the slate". The problem, as it developed, proved to be very much more difficult. From first to last the British employed 366,000 regulars, 30,000 troopers from various colonies, and over 52,000 men raised in South Africa, a high proportion of whom were throughout tied to guarding the endless railways.[2]

Both sides had much to learn. Khaki, mobile six-inch guns, machine-guns and one-pounder pom-poms, field trenches and barbed wire, finely-sighted clip-loading rifles with a long and flat trajectory, all made the last great European campaigns of the 'seventies seem positively eighteenth-century affairs. The South African war was the first war of importance fought on modern lines.

If the war was to be a long one, British numbers and almost limitless sources of material replenishment would tell, even though the troops must go up against a strongly placed foe at a time when the defensive had stolen a long march on the offensive everywhere. The republicans could rely on the Netherlands Railway workshops and Kruger's cherished dynamite factory for small-arms ammunition and shells, but guns they could not replace. Nevertheless, on October 11, the odds were heavily in their favour. Numbers, superior equipment and initiative were theirs. Fully 48,000 republicans were under arms

[1] Maurice, *History of War in S.A.*, I, 457 *sqq.*, IV, 704 *sqq.*; *Appendices to Minutes of Evidence ... on the War in South Africa, Parl. Pap.* 1903, LXII [Cd. 1792], p. 445.

[2] *Return of the Strength of the Garrison ..., Parl. Pap.* 1902, LVIII [Cd. 990]; Maurice, *History of War in S.A.*, IV, 671; 1903, XL [Cd. 1789], p. 35.

as against 27,000 British troops of very varying quality. Rather more than 20,000 burghers lay around the northern apex of Natal. In that colony there were only 13,000 British regulars and 2800 local levies. Of these, 4000 were thrust far forward at Dundee, while some 8000 under Sir George White lay to the south of them at Ladysmith, the road and railway junction which he meant to hold at all costs, partly for moral effect but mainly to force the invaders to rely on distant Johannesburg as the nearest railway link between the two republics. Basutoland, the South African Switzerland, mountainous and by tacit agreement neutral, separated the Natal theatre from the long western front of nearly one thousand miles. There, another 20,000 burghers tolerably furnished with guns, faced 5200 regulars and 6000 colonial volunteers with no artillery worth speaking of. All the British could hope to do was to hold Mafeking, Kimberley, the Orange River railway bridge and the junctions of the cross-lines south of that river. If these were lost before Buller's army corps came up, there might well be a wholesale Afrikaner rising in the Cape Colony.

It was touch and go. The bulk of the troops from India had landed at Durban a week or so before the ultimatum expired, but a month must elapse before the first of the army corps could reach South Africa. The priceless opportunity was let slip. Joubert, old and notoriously averse from invading the Queen's dominions, came over the Natal passes gingerly, fearing mines. The Free Staters, slower off the mark than their allies in a war which was not directly their war, did not come into action effectively anywhere for some days.

After heavy fighting in northern Natal at Talana Hill (October 20) and Elands Laagte (October 21), the British concentrated at Ladysmith and left open the road to the south. The younger Boers, flushed with success at Nicholson's Nek (October 30), were eager to ride on; but Joubert insisted on first investing Ladysmith, and when he did advance, the troops pouring up the line thrust him back behind the Tugela River. On the western front the republicans at once closed round Mafeking and Kimberley, but it was only on November 1 that the Free Staters advanced south of the Orange upon Colesberg. At once, thousands of men, who except for British citizenship were indistinguishable from the invaders, rose in rebellion.[1] But for the restraining influence of the Schreiner Ministry the rising would in all probability have been far more widespread.

Everywhere the republican Governments went as near as they could, without definitely committing themselves, to annexing the occupied territories; their local commanders went still further so that the Cape men might join them with an easy conscience,[2] and the

[1] *Correspondence re Cape Colony, Parl. Pap.* 1900, LVI [Cd. 246], p. 5; *Further Correspondence*, 1900, LVI [Cd. 420], pp. 26 *sqq*.

[2] *Further Correspondence, Parl. Pap.* 1900, LVI [Cd. 43], pp. 99, 129, 166, 206, 217; 1900, LVI [Cd. 261], pp. 5, 95, 261; Van der Merwe, *Steyn*, II, 5.

British replied with the declaration of martial law in the invaded districts. The early Boer successes, however, led Buller to give up his original plan of advancing across the drifts of the middle Orange and so on to the High Veld by the old Trekkers' Road. Sorely against Milner's wish,[1] he led the bulk of his army corps to the relief of Ladysmith, and sent the rest up the Cape railways towards Colesberg and Kimberley. At first all went well. Then, in the second week of December, the "Black Week", the advance was rudely held up at all points: at Magersfontein on the left, at Colesberg in the centre, and on the right at Colenso on the Tugela.

The United Kingdom had few friends. It is true that in September 1899 she and Portugal had discussed an alliance which would have permitted British troops to use Delagoa Bay as a base. On the outbreak of war, however, Portugal had merely renewed her ancient treaties of mutual defence with England, and had promised to hold up republican supplies without declaring the formal neutrality which would have prevented British ships coaling at the port.[2] The United States had also taken charge of British interests in the Transvaal; but British opinion was divided on the war policy, and war had been greeted by a roar of anger from many Continental newspapers, especially those of Paris. In spite of that, so far were Governments from entertaining ideas of intervention, that the news of the British reverses led Japan to express anxiety lest Russia should be encouraged to invade Korea; Italy hinted at setting British troops free by herself garrisoning Egypt; shares fell on the Berlin Bourse, and the Kaiser, gratified by the recent Samoan settlement, ceremoniously visited the Queen. Great Britain's hands were still free.[3]

The "Black Week" awakened the British Government and people to a sense of realities. Reinforcements were hurried out from Britain herself and from many of her colonies, and Lord Roberts was appointed Commander-in-Chief with Kitchener of Khartum as his Chief of Staff. Meanwhile, French checked the spread of the rebellion in the north-eastern Colony, and the Ladysmith garrison beat off determined attacks on the dominating positions of Caesar's Camp and Waggon Hill (January 6). But to balance these successes, Cape rebels in the far west seized Kuruman as the British detachments drew in to join Roberts's Grand Army (1 January 1900), and the party of Transvaalers who joined them annexed Prieska and two neighbouring Cape districts. In Natal also, Buller was beaten twice in quick succession at Spion Kop (January 24) and Vaal Krantz (February 5–7).

At last Roberts was ready and struck up towards Kimberley. He relieved that town (February 15) and then rounded up Cronje, who

[1] *The Milner Papers*, II, 27.
[2] Gooch and Temperley, *British Documents*, I, 88 *sqq*.
[3] *Ibid*, I, 233 *sqq*.

had held on too long, and forced him to surrender with 4000 men at Paardeberg (February 17–27). Meanwhile in response to Roberts's decisive stroke, which was in Milner's opinion "the only *Strategy* of the war",[1] the Free Staters had come trooping back from the Cape Colony and Natal to defend their own territory. This weakening of the besieging force enabled Buller to fight his way into exhausted Ladysmith (February 18–28), but it failed to save Bloemfontein. Turning eastwards, Roberts thrust the Free Staters aside and entered their capital (March 13).

The Free State commandos dispersed, and Roberts, thinking they were out of the war, offered to allow all save their leaders to remain at home on parole.[2] Indeed, even before the fall of Bloemfontein, the two republics had called for help to the Continental Powers and the United States, and had offered to make peace provided they might retain their independence (March 5).[3] Both offer and appeal were vain. The relief of Ladysmith had sent shares up at Berlin, and now all the efforts of the Russian diplomat, Count Mouravieff, to induce the Powers to present identical notes to Great Britain failed. Germany spoke of a ten-year guarantee of existing European frontiers as the price of her participation, and it was then learned that Great Britain had already declined an independent offer of mediation from Washington. It only remained for the Berne Court to issue its belated award on McMurdo's much-sought-after Delagoa railway. By committing Portugal to the payment of substantial compensation, this award bound her more closely than ever to Great Britain (March 29).[4] Lord Salisbury would not hear of republican independence. The Boer invasion, he replied, was "the penalty which Great Britain has suffered for having in recent years acquiesced in the existence of the two Republics".[5] Never again must there be rival political systems in South Africa.[6]

Apart from the crushing of the Prieska rebellion, a prolonged lull followed the capture of Bloemfontein. Roberts remained there resting his weary horses, nursing the men who had gone down in hundreds with enteric, and calling in the pick of the Natal troops from Natal, where Buller, who had failed to capture the Boer guns and waggons as they trailed away from before Ladysmith,[7] was also marking time. The lull saved the Boers. Joubert died and made way for the young and energetic Louis Botha, the victor of Colenso (March 27), while Steyn's exhortations and Christiaan de Wet's successful attacks on detachments at Sannah's Post (March 31) and Reddersburg (April 4) brought the Free Staters out into the field once more.

[1] *The Milner Papers*, II, 51.
[2] *Parl. Pap.* 1900, LVI [Cd. 261], p. 62. [3] *Ibid*, p. 20.
[4] Gooch and Temperley, *British Documents*, I, 44, 245 *sqq.*; *German Diplomatic Documents*, III, 116 *sqq.*
[5] *Parl. Pap.* 1900, LVI [Cd. 261], p. 21.
[6] *The Milner Papers*, II, 98.
[7] Reitz, D., *Commando*, p. 90.

Early in May the British moved again. The rebellion in Griqualand West was quelled and Mafeking relieved (May 17). Buller reoccupied northern Natal, and Roberts, on the banks of the Vaal, proclaimed the Free State British territory as the Orange River Colony (May 24).[1] Crossing the river at Viljoen's Drift of famous memory, the main army entered half-deserted Johannesburg (May 31). One more short stage brought them to Pretoria, under the shadow of the silent and costly forts which had caused so much of the mischief (June 5).

Kruger, old and broken, had almost yielded when the British set foot in his republic; but though men and money were running short, Steyn, Reitz and Smuts had dissuaded him. Now, with Botha at Diamond Hill keeping open the eastward line of retreat with difficulty, the war council negotiated secretly with Roberts.[2] This time de la Rey ended it by threatening to set up a republic of his own in the western Transvaal; so the Government, still in being, retreated slowly down the Delagoa Bay line. Step by step, Roberts followed it up into the broken country of the eastern Transvaal, while the Natal troops swung westward into the Free State. There, they narrowly missed taking de Wet, but did capture 4000 of his men under Prinsloo in the Brandwater Basin (July 15), and another considerable force under Olivier near Winburg (August 27). In the week of Olivier's surrender, the Transvaalers fought the last battle of the war in which large forces were engaged, at Bergendal (Dalmanutha) (August 26). They then watched their old President go down to Lourenço Marques to take ship for Marseilles, and jettisoned the bulk of their heavy material on the Portuguese border. Roberts formally annexed the Transvaal (September 1) and declared the war ended.[3]

Milner was not so sanguine as Roberts, but he pushed on with the preparations for reconstruction. He had already laid the foundations of civil rule in the central and southern Orange River Colony; now, he sent Uitlanders and others to establish as much as might be of civil government at Pretoria. Meanwhile, in the Cape Colony, Schreiner and two of his colleagues had agreed reluctantly to the imperial demand that rebels should be disfranchised, and Merriman had headed a revolt in protest which wrecked the Ministry (June 13). In face of opposition so fierce that Milner thought of suspending the constitution, it thus fell to Sprigg to carry an Indemnity Act, to set up Courts to try men accused of rebellion, and to disfranchise rebels for five years. The Cape Parliament was then prorogued (October 15). It did not meet again for nearly two years.[4]

[1] *Parl. Pap.* 1900, LVI [Cd. 261], pp. 137, 144.

[2] *Parl. Pap.* 1900, XL [Cd. 1791], pp. 58, 71; Viljoen, B. J., *My Reminiscences of the Anglo-Boer War*, ch. XVI; Van der Merwe, N. J., *Steyn*, II, 61.

[3] *Proclamations by . . . Lord Roberts, Parl. Pap.* 1900, LVI [Cd. 426], p. 16.

[4] *Parl. Pap.* 1900, LVI [Cd. 264] *passim*; *Minutes* (Cape), A 1, 10, 12 of 1900; *Papers re Martial Law, Cape Parl. Pap.*, A 2 of 1900.

The Westminster Parliament, on the other hand, was dissolved two years before its time, primarily because the Government wanted public support for its resolve to depart from its original proposal to give all in South Africa full self-government, and instead, to subject the republicans to a period of Crown Colony rule during which they might get used to the change of allegiance.[1] The Colonial Secretary, however, had personal reasons for desiring an early election, because it might reduce the number of inquisitive Radicals in Parliament. Twice since the outbreak of war they had tried to make him show the skeleton in his cupboard. On the second occasion, in February 1900, they had been in a position to press him very hard, because a Continental newspaper, *L'Indépendance Belge*, had published correspondence stolen from the office of the Chartered Company's solicitor, which had passed between the solicitor and men connected with the Raid from May 1896 till August 1895.[2] The Liberal *Manchester Guardian* had been the only British journal of standing to draw attention to these revelations; but able editors and politicians on the Continent had jumped at them, not only because they were a stick with which they could belabour the intensely unpopular British Government, but because they gave substance to the widespread suspicion that the Colonial Secretary had known a vast deal more than he should have known about the whole unsavoury business, all the more that the letters did not make sense unless he had known. Chamberlain had been saved by loyal supporters, though only by a much smaller majority than usual.[3] He was resolved to have no more of it. Hence, the premature Khaki election was fought in October 1900 at the moment of apparent victory.[4] Though it only gave the Ministerialists three additional seats, it underwrote their Crown Colony policy and so took the heart out of the Radicals that they tried no more to "rake up the raid". On the other hand, it showed how deeply the nation was divided on the war issue, because for every eight votes given to the Ministerialists, seven were cast for the Liberals, or, as Chamberlain jeered, "given to the Boers". Be that as it might, the War Office scrapped its world-wide remount organisation; overseas contingents, South African volunteers, and many of the veteran regulars went home, and thither Roberts followed them leaving Kitchener to wind up the campaign (November 29).

Roberts had utterly misread the signs of the times. Already, in August, he had had to threaten with deportation the Boers who were breaking their parole in large numbers, and had stiffened the rules for the farm-burning which had been carried out sporadically

[1] *Parl. Pap.* 1901, XLVII [Cd. 547], pp. 1 *sqq.*

[2] Van der Poel, *The Jameson Raid*, pp. 250 *sqq.*; Garvin, *Life of Joseph Chamberlain*, pp. 551–2; Esher, Viscount, *Journals and Letters*, p. 193; Stead, W., *Joseph Chamberlain*, pp. 89 *sqq.*; Jeyes, S. H., *Mr. Chamberlain—His Life and Public Career*, II, App. IV.

[3] 256 to 152 as compared with 304 to 77; *Hansard*, 4th series, LXXIX, 599 *sqq.*

[4] Garvin, *Life of Joseph Chamberlain*, III, p. 554.

as a deterrent as early as June.[1] In September, again, small commandos had been active in the eastern Transvaal and the Free State. The truth was that the war had simply changed its character. Perhaps 60,000 burghers, rebels and foreign volunteers were still available either in the field or in their homes. Abandoning the paraphernalia of modern warfare, they were forming small mobile commandos of determined men ready to harass communications and detachments in the guerilla fashion of the Peninsular War ninety years before.

To the High Commissioner, this novel phase of the war was an exasperating interruption of the work of reconstruction. He looked to Kitchener to hold the vital areas while that work proceeded. Kitchener could not do it. He still had some 210,000 men, but half of these were tied to the railways, many more were immobilised on garrison or other duties, and others on no duty at all. He set to work resolutely with the men at his disposal, and called for a large force of mounted infantry from an England "denuded of troops".[2] This new mounted army could not be ready till April 1901. For five months to come the initiative would lie once more with the republicans.

The results of this military revolution were soon apparent. De la Rey advanced up to the outskirts of Pretoria from the fastnesses of the Magaliesberg; Botha struck, first, at Vryheid (December 1900) and then at the Delagoa railway; Smuts was successful at Modderfontein in the southern Transvaal (31 January 1901). Hertzog and others led small commandos into the Cape Colony once more, and some of them penetrated so far to the south and west that the British authorities called out local forces for home defence, and extended martial law over the whole Colony with the exception of the Native Territories and the ports (January 17).[3] Presently, Steyn and de Wet managed to invade the Cape Midlands with 1400 men (10–28 February 1901), and everywhere the Boers took heart when they learned that the Liberals who followed Campbell-Bannerman and the young Lloyd George had declared in favour of immediate self-government for them after the war, and that Liberal imperialists like Asquith and Sir Edward Grey were by no means set on unconditional surrender.[4]

The opinions of the Liberal imperialists were shared by Kitchener. Anxious to be gone to India, he agreed readily to discuss terms with Botha at Middelburg (February 28). The opportunity was apparently good. De Wet and the implacable Steyn were far away struggling to escape again from Cape Colony, and, during the actual negotiations, de la Rey was defeated at Lichtenburg (March 3). The

[1] *Proclamation . . . by Lord Roberts*, *Parl. Pap.* 1900, LVI [Cd. 426], pp. 11, 14 *sqq.*; *Correspondence re destruction of property*, 1901, XLVII [Cd. 582].

[2] *The Milner Papers*, II, 203.

[3] *Despatches by Lord Kitchener*, *Parl. Pap.* 1902, LXIX [Cd. 823], p. 11.

[4] Spender, J. A., *Sir Henry Campbell-Bannerman*, I, 319 *sqq.*

unwelcome prospect of ending the war by a compromise, which must give rise to difficulties later on, led Milner to take a decisive step.[1] Thinking in terms of the settlement that must follow the war, he wished to compel the Boers to surrender unconditionally and then to give them the most generous treatment. Under a commission which he had held since the preceding October, he transferred the headquarters of the High Commissionership from the Cape to the Transvaal, whose Governor he was to be as soon as the war ended, and hastened north to take part in the negotiations with Botha.

The terms offered at Middelburg were Crown Colony rule proceeding by easy stages to responsible government; £1,000,000 to meet the claims of burghers against their late Governments; no special war tax on farms, and possibly a loan to farmers. Coloured persons were to have legal rights similar to those which they already enjoyed in the liberal Cape Colony, but no African franchise would be considered till representative institutions had been granted and then only on terms that would ensure "the just predominance of the white race".[2] Finally, in spite of Kitchener's plea that an amnesty for rebels was a point of honour to the Boers, Milner insisted that they must be tried according to the laws of their respective colonies; otherwise rebels still in arms would fare better than those who had already come in, while the effect upon loyalists would be deplorable.[3] Whether it was, as Kitchener believed, that he would not abandon the rebels,[4] or, as Milner held, because he would not yet face the loss of independence,[5] Botha broke off negotiations abruptly (16 March 1901).

The war steadily became more bitter and destructive. Warfare against foemen in mufti, or sometimes, since the republicans were running short of clothing, in captured khaki uniforms, men who were on their stoeps one day and out on commando or cutting railway and telegraph lines the next, must, in Kitchener's opinion, entail more systematic farm-burning, especially as that was also to strike at the bases of "home supply".[6] But that in turn meant that an uprooted people must be transferred to concentration camps, an extension of the refugee camps that had been started in August 1900.

Neither Chamberlain nor Milner approved of this policy of making the country a desert ringed round with troops, both for its political effects on either side of the Equator and also because it must make reconstruction more difficult. Milner was only too anxious to get

[1] *The Milner Papers*, II, 207 *sqq.*

[2] There was then no bar to a Coloured and Indian franchise.

[3] *Papers re Negotiations, Parl. Pap.* 1901, XLVII [Cd. 528]; *Correspondence re South Africa*, 1901, XLVII [Cd. 547], pp. 55 *sqq.*; *Letter from ... Botha to ... Kitchener*, XLVII, 1901 [Cd. 546]; *Further papers re Negotiations*, 1901, XLVII [Cd. 663].

[4] Arthur, Sir G., *Life of Lord Kitchener*, II, 26.

[5] *The Milner Papers*, II, 219–20.

[6] *Further Papers re Refugee Camps, Parl. Pap.* 1902, LXVIII [Cd. 902], pp. 119 *sqq.*; cp. *The Milner Papers*, II, 193.

townsmen back to work and Boers back to their farms. He did extort leave from Kitchener for a few Uitlanders to go back north to restart some of the Rand mines on whose output reconstruction depended; but since Botha refused to allow "hands-uppers" to remain quietly in their farms, to get the Boers out of the concentration camps was quite another matter.[1]

Yet the camps were becoming an intolerable burden. Their number and cost were great and growing, their demands on transport exacting, and their record so far disastrous, whether under civil administration in the Orange River Colony, or joint civil and military control in the Transvaal, or purely military control in Natal.[2] Some were on ill-chosen sites and all of them were being crowded out. Nearly all those who flocked into them were the most independent-minded of country folk; many arrived in poor condition and entertained ideas on sanitation that were ill-suited to camp life;[3] many, again, were deeply suspicious even of those officials who were there in the interests of their comfort and health. The inadequate medical staffs, who themselves suffered heavily from disease and exhaustion, were unable to cope with the measles and pneumonia that played havoc with their charges. By October 1901 deaths were for a short time at the rate of 344 per thousand, the rate among the children alone being higher still. Meanwhile, in the field, fortune began to favour the big battalions. By May 1901, the new mounted army was coming into play: 80,000 mounted infantry, three-fifths of them from various British colonies, and behind them 160,000 other troops.[4] Against them, the Boers could still pit 44,000 mounted men; but their numbers were being whittled away and their movements hampered by the lines of blockhouses and barbed wire which Kitchener was stringing out along the railways and across country. As they were taken in successive "drives", they were usually shipped off to St Helena, Ceylon or Bermuda.

Such was the situation when, in May 1901, Milner sailed for England to discuss future Crown Colony rule and present concentration camp problems. During his absence some of the Transvaal leaders debated asking for an armistice. In the end, after consulting Kruger by cable, they met the Free State leaders at Waterval and agreed that there should be no peace without independence. They resolved that they must invade the Cape Colony in force, for there, if anywhere, independence was to be lost or won (June 20).[5]

In spite of these stout resolves, the commandos were kept on the run so continuously that Kitchener was emboldened to raise National

[1] *Parl. Pap.* 1901, XLVII [Cd. 663], p. 7; *The Milner Papers*, II, 164 *sqq.*

[2] Maurice, *History of War in S.A.*, IV, 659 *sqq.*; *The Milner Papers*, 225 *sqq.*

[3] *The Milner Papers*, II, 230.

[4] *The Times History* . . ., V, 246 *sqq.*; *Return of Military Forces, Parl. Pap.* 1901, XXXIX [Cd. 578].

[5] Kestell, J. D., *Met de Boeren Commandos* . . ., p. 158; Van der Merwe, *Steyn*, II, 69 *sqq.*

Scouts from among the Boers in the Transvaal, and Volunteers in the Orange River Colony, and to threaten to banish permanently all commandants who did not surrender within a fortnight and to debit the rank and file with the cost of the maintenance of their families in the camps (August 7).[1] The republicans' reply was to strike hard in all directions. Botha and de la Rey, at the head of truly formidable disciplined forces, either raided Natal or dominated the western Transvaal and, in September, Smuts invaded the Cape Midlands. With one-third of the Colony overrun, and rebels being recruited within sixty miles of Cape Town, martial law had to be extended even over the Cape ports to check the smuggling of ammunition (9 October 1901).

While the Boers were thus carrying on the war with renewed energy, Milner was devoting most of his time to looking after their women and children. He had returned from England with a free hand and a blank cheque. The camps were now at their largest, housing some 160,000 souls of all classes and colours.[2] Milner took over the Natal camps from the military, broke up the bigger camps wherever possible, and, by the end of the war, had improved all so vastly that the death-rate was down to 20 per thousand. What was done could not be undone; the deaths of at least 4000 women and 16,000 children, and the destroyed farms that lay behind those deaths, was bound to live in Afrikaner memories. But to set against these were facts more likely to be forgotten. Many of the inmates had come in of their own accord; Botha expressed resentment when the British made difficulties about taking in the families of fighting burghers, and Steyn himself could bid his men fight on with an easy mind since the enemy would care for their wives and little ones.[3] At the final peace conference Botha was destined to thank the British for all that they had done.

There had been times when the republicans had hoped against hope for foreign intervention. Anglo-German relations had been ruffled during the latter half of 1901, when Chamberlain had replied in spirited fashion to the aspersions which the Press and some members of the Reichstag, echoing Liberal criticisms, had cast on the conduct of the British troops, and once more when the Sultan of Turkey had given the concession for the Baghdad railway to a German company. But these things passed. Early in 1902, the Kaiser pointedly welcomed the Prince of Wales to Berlin, and expressed delight that Rhodes was making him nominator to fifteen of his new Oxford scholarships, while Great Britain secured her position in the Far East by concluding an alliance with Japan. The British Government was thus well

[1] *Correspondence re prolongation of hostilities*, *Parl. Pap.* 1901, XLVII [Cd. 732], pp. 6 *sqq.*

[2] *Further Papers re Concentration Camps*, *Parl. Pap.* 1901, LXVIII [Cd. 853], p. 131.

[3] Kestell, J. D., and Van Velden, D. E., *The Peace Negotiations*, p. 83; De Wet, C. R., *The Three Years' War*, p. 491; Van der Merwe, *Steyn*, II, 87.

able to decline an offer of mediation that was volunteered by the young Queen of the Netherlands (January 1902).[1]

But in the very act of declining foreign mediation, the British Government set the door ajar by hinting at negotiations between the British and republican authorities on the spot. Kitchener sent the correspondence without comment to Schalk Burger, acting-President of the South African Republic. In spite of de la Rey's capture of Lord Methuen at Tweebosch (March 7), Burger jumped at the opening. At his summons, the leaders of both republics met at Krugersdorp (April 9).[2]

At first it was doubtful whether the Boers would consent to negotiate. They knew that Ireland and other matters nearer home were claiming the attention of the disillusioned British electorate; they knew also that Rosebery's Liberal imperialists had declared for peace, provided the first move came from the Boers themselves. That move had now been made by the British. Here was a hint at negotiations and, with it, the implied recognition of the proscribed Governments. On the other hand, only 23,000 burghers and rebels still kept the field; supplies were almost entirely lacking in many districts, and the dreaded winter was coming on; meanwhile the British held the railways in the republics and were "driving" the country in all directions; in the Cape Colony, they were taking Smuts's subordinates one by one. They therefore agreed to meet Lords Milner and Kitchener at Pretoria. Undismayed by the defeat of Kemp, one of their stoutest commandants, at Roodewal (April 10), they asked for independence combined with the reforms which Milner had demanded at the Bloemfontein Conference long ago.[3] They were told firmly that the Middelburg terms must be taken as the basis and, in the end, they agreed, the majority of them with unfeigned relief, to consult the commandos without whose consent they could not give up their independence.[4]

So during the next four weeks, Kitchener gave every facility he could, short of a suspension of hostilities, and the Boer leaders put the facts before their scattered bands. On May 15 the members of their two Governments and sixty delegates with full powers met at Vereeniging on the Transvaal side of the Vaal, the common boundary of the two republics. It was a strange assembly of fighting burghers met to settle the fate of their people without consulting the great majority, who were either prisoners of war, inmates of the concentration camps, "hands-uppers" or even National Scouts in the service of

[1] Gooch and Temperley, *British Documents*, I, 263, 268 *sqq.*, 333 *sqq.*, II, 115; *German Diplomatic Documents*, III, 150 *sqq.*

[2] *Correspondence re Surrender*, *Parl. Pap.* 1902, LXIX [Cd. 1096]. For the negotiations see Kestell and Van Velden, *Peace Negotiations*; Kestell, J. D., *Through Shot and Flame*; De Wet, *The Three Years' War* (appendix); *Times History*, V, 509 *sqq.*, 564 *sqq.*

[3] *Parl. Pap.* 1902, LXIX [Cd. 1096], p. 2.

[4] *Ibid.* pp. 3 *sqq.*

the enemy. Generally speaking, the Transvaalers were in favour of coming to terms, the Free Staters for fighting on. In part this was because the Free Staters felt they had less to lose materially than their allies, who realised that the partially industrialised Transvaal could not be repaired easily; in part also because, whereas the Free Staters might reckon that they would predominate in their rural territory whatever happened, the Transvaalers feared that, if the war went on too long, they would find themselves thrust aside as intolerable disturbers of the peace by the "New Transvaal" that was rapidly taking shape under Milner's scheme of reconstruction. But the personal element goes furthest to explain the division of opinion.

All the long-standing jealousy of the Free Staters for the Transvaalers flared out, the anger of men who felt they had been dragged into a war that need never have taken place if their advice had been followed betimes, and who were now to be forced to make peace against their wish.[1] To Steyn, broken in body but inflexible of will, loss of independence meant loss of national self-respect and, with that, all hope of a future; to De Wet the struggle was now a "war of religion" in which God was seeking to make "a nation worthy of His name". Behind these two stood Hertzog, bitterly resenting Transvaal pressure, and Reitz, half Free Stater, half Transvaaler and wholly Afrikaner, determined to save something from the wreck even at the cost of letting the Witwatersrand and Swaziland go. Over against them were the Transvaalers: Schalk Burger first, admitting frankly that whatever else the war might be, it certainly had been a "war of miscalculation" in which the republicans, carried away by the war spirit, had underestimated their enemies and must now take the consequences.[2] Next, Louis Botha, patiently reiterating the military and economic facts, anxious for peace to "save the nation", and with him Smuts, newly come from the Cape Colony to report that there was nothing to be hoped for there, and to suggest, with a far-away look in his eyes, that present surrender was necessary to ensure a brighter future than ever before. Last of all, de la Rey, the big gentle man, who rarely raised his voice in anger and yet got more out of his men than any other except possibly Botha, insisting quietly that even if the leaders decided to go on with the war, the burghers would not follow them.

The final negotiations were left to a handful of men. On May 19 Botha, de la Rey, Smuts, De Wet and Hertzog went to Pretoria. There they met the High Commissioner and the Commander-in-Chief. Milner was hard put to it to conceal the fact that he disliked all negotiations, since "every concession we make means more trouble hereafter",[3] and in any event was determined not to jeopardise his policy of reconstructing Southern Africa on unmistakably

[1] Kestell and Van Velden, *Peace Negotiations*, pp. 27 *sqq.*; Van der Merwe, *Steyn*, II, 84.
[2] *The Milner Papers*, II, 362; *Times History*, V. 603.
[3] *The Milner Papers*, II, 211.

British lines; Kitchener, who for all his military training and heavy looks was a born diplomatist, "extremely adroit" and with "a kind side to him",[1] was resolved to make a clean-cut end to the interminable war. Possibly Kitchener did not look sufficiently to the political future that would follow the military settlement; "he does not care what he gives away",[2] groaned Milner. But it is equally possible that he saw further than his colleague, and realised that whatever settlement was made now, the ultimate fate of South Africa would depend upon the respective reproductive and staying powers of the British and Afrikaners, and their capacity for party discipline in the democratic future that was to be theirs sooner or later.[3] It was Kitchener who more than once saved the negotiations. On his suggestion the final drafting of terms was left to a civilian sub-committee consisting of the High Commissioner and his legal adviser, Sir Richard Solomon, on the one side, and Smuts and Hertzog in their capacity as lawyers on the other.

The outcome was a treaty which embodied the Middelburg terms modified in favour of the republicans to the extent of £3,000,000, supplemented by loans on easy terms, instead of £1,000,000, to help the burghers back to their farms and to meet war losses. Further, by an arrangement which Milner afterwards confessed was the greatest mistake of his life,[4] a decision on the African franchise was to be postponed beyond the stage of representative institutions till the achievement of full responsible government. The Coloured Folk and Asians were not mentioned.[5] Even so these liberal terms were not accepted unanimously by the delegates at Vereeniging. It is true that Botha and de la Rey won over De Wet; but Steyn resigned the shadow of his presidency rather than yield and took Reitz and four others with him. The rest accepted the terms. Near midnight, on 31 May 1902, the Treaty of Vereeniging was signed at Pretoria,[6] surely, Milner noted, "one of the strangest documents of history".[7]

Thus 22,000 soldiers had died and £223,000,000 had been expended to reassert British paramountcy in southern Africa and to make an end of the old Transvaal oligarchy.[8] The loss of life on the republican side cannot be stated precisely, but it was certainly not far short of 6000 fighting men, besides those many others who had died in the concentration camps.[9] It remained to be seen whether a new South Africa could be built up worthy of the effort and the cost,

[1] *The Milner Papers*, II, 215, 337.

[2] *Ibid.* II, 337.

[3] Cf. *Times History*, V, 573.

[4] *The Milner Papers*, II, 353.

[5] There was thus nothing to stop their getting the franchise.

[6] *Parl. Pap.* 1902 LXIX [Cd. 1096], pp. 12 *sqq.*

[7] *The Milner Papers*, II, 365.

[8] *Parl. Pap.* 1902, LVIII [Cd. 990]; *Times History* . . ., VII, 24 *sqq.*; Maurice, *History of War in S.A.* IV, 692 *sqq.*

[9] *Parl. Pap.* 1903, XLII [Cd. 1792], p. 445; Maurice, *History of War in S. A.* I, 457 *sqq.*, IV, 705.

and capable of refuting Lord Salisbury's gloomy prophecy before the war that if the Boers submitted without fighting, they would hate the British for a generation, and if they fought and were beaten they would hate them still longer.[1]

[1] Newton, Lord, *Lansdowne*, p. 157.

CHAPTER XXIII

THE FORMATION OF THE UNION, 1901–1910

IN approaching the problem of reconstruction after the war Lord Milner was actuated by a determination that never again should there be "two dissimilar and antagonistic political systems in that which nature and history had irrevocably decided should be one country".[1] The war had given the victory to the British system and the opportunity of reconstruction must be taken to make it permanently secure. The principal instruments to this end were the development of the gold-mining industry and the introduction of a British element into the farming population of the new colonies. In Milner's view the gold could not be extracted too rapidly, for the "overspill" of what was required to remunerate the capital invested in the industry would create other resources, would attract population, and would fill the coffers of the state; while British settlers would mitigate the old condition of things in which the race division coincided with a division of interest, the rural community being virtually Boer and the urban British.[2] The key to the position, therefore, lay in the north. To enable him to devote his undivided attention to it the High Commissionership was separated from the governorship of the Cape and attached to him personally, the new commission containing a clause empowering him to further the union of South Africa by inviting representatives of all the colonies and protectorates to confer with him on subjects of common interest, such as the treatment of the Natives and the working of the railways.[3] At the same time he was appointed Administrator of the new colonies and he left Cape Town on 28 February 1901 to assume this office. Sir Walter Hely Hutchinson, for many years Governor of Natal, became Governor of the Cape.

The fifteen months which now elapsed before the conclusion of peace allowed a great deal of preparatory work to be done before the real task of reconstruction began. The report of the Concessions Commission cleared away some of the least satisfactory relics of the old republican administration. Enquiries were held into land settlement, irrigation and the financial prospects of the new colonies.[4] The old statute book of the Transvaal was overhauled by Sir Richard

[1] *The Milner Papers*, II, 98. On the closer union movement *vide* Thompson, L. M., *The Unification of South Africa, 1902–1910*.

[2] Worsfold, W. B., *The Reconstruction of the New Colonies under Lord Milner*, I, 320–1; *Parl. Pap.* 1902, LXVII [Cd. 1163], p. 83.

[3] Commission dated 6 October 1900. Text in Newton, A. P., *The Unification of South Africa*, I, 172–6; *vide supra*, p. 626.

[4] *Parl. Pap.* 1901, XXXV [Cd. 623], XXIV [Cd. 626], XLVIII [Cd. 628].

Solomon and a mass of legislation was enacted by proclamation mainly on Cape lines. The administration of both countries was gradually taken over from the military authorities. Most important of all was the reopening of the gold-mines. The two obstacles in the way were deficiencies of labour and of rolling stock. The railways were fully employed coping with the transport requirements of the army and of the concentration camps, and Lord Kitchener would only agree to 150 of the 6340 pre-war stamps being restarted in April 1901. Before the end of the war the number had, however, risen to over 2000 and 45,000 white civilians had returned to the Rand.[1]

The gold-mining industry of the Transvaal was, as it had been before the war, dependent to a large extent for its labour on Africans from the Portuguese province of Mozambique, and this, coupled with the fact that the port of Lourenço Marques was the nearest and most convenient port for the importation of goods for the Witwatersrand, gave the Portuguese a powerful lever to ensure that it should receive the same treatment from the British Government as it had had from the South African Republic. The *Modus Vivendi* of December 1901,[2] which Lord Milner negotiated with them, accordingly provided that the customs duties on imported goods entering the Transvaal through Portuguese territory should be no higher than the duties on similar goods in transit through Natal and the Cape, that the railway rates should be relatively the same, that the traffic should receive equal treatment in the allotment of trucks and that the provisions of the treaty of 1875, which established free trade in local products between the Transvaal and Mozambique, should be maintained. On these terms a supply of labour was procured. It proved to be quite inadequate. At the same time some of the abuses to which the employment of African labour on the mines had been subject were reformed. Its recruitment was confined to labour agents licensed by the Government, the African pass system was made less onerous, the supply of intoxicants to any coloured person was prohibited and the living and working conditions on the mines were improved.[3]

While this preliminary work was going forward a political controversy developed in the Cape over the proposal to suspend the constitution. From Lord Milner's point of view the idea had much to recommend it. His control of the new colonies was supreme. He could rely on the Natal ministry, whose influence had been increased by the transfer to Natal from the Transvaal of the districts of Vryheid, Utrecht and part of Wakkerstroom. The Cape, in his opinion, was the "Achilles' heel" of British South Africa.[4] The last session of its Parliament in 1900 had been followed by an invasion of the Colony

[1] *Parl. Pap.* 1902, LXVII [Cd. 1163], p. 81.
[2] Text in Newton, *op. cit.* I, 176–8.
[3] Proclamations Nos. 11, 36 and 38 of 1901.
[4] *Parl. Pap.* 1902, LXIX [Cd. 941].

and the second rebellion. The case for suspension also rested on the fact that the constitution had already been violated wholesale. Parliament had been illegally prorogued beyond the last permissible date, the Government had been financed by Governor's warrants without parliamentary sanction, the biennial registration of voters due in February 1901 had not been carried out. But these lapses from constitutional propriety were due to temporary causes which would pass away when peace came, and were discounted by those who regarded Parliament as the best safety valve of public opinion. Moreover the movement could not be dissociated from the old controversy whether parliamentary representation should be calculated on voters or on population. The former was to the advantage of the urban or British community, the latter of the rural or Afrikaner. To settle this problem by granting a new constitution after suspending the old and on a basis which would satisfy the British would be, in the opinion of the Afrikaners, to ensure British hegemony. The attitude of the Home Government was that it would make no move until it was satisfied that the continuance of the existing constitution was a danger to the peace of the Colony and to the interests of the Empire and that a great majority of the white population favoured its suspension. Neither the petition signed by forty-two members of the Cape Parliament, which received the expressed sympathy of Lord Milner, nor that with 30,000 signatures which followed it, fulfilled these conditions. Moreover Sir Gordon Sprigg declared against suspension and carried his Cabinet with him with the exception of Dr Smartt, who resigned to lead the suspension movement. Rhodes was the only man capable of putting it through, but the condition of his health was now hopeless. The last few months of his life were spent in Great Britain and in Egypt, his restless spirit showing few signs of giving way. But on the voyage back to South Africa early in 1902 he suffered much from the heat in the tropics. On landing he went to live in his cottage at Muizenburg, where the air was cooler than at Groote Schuur. At Muizenburg he died on March 26.

The significance of Rhodes's career in South African history is not to be gauged by the events which followed the Jameson Raid, nor by such expedients as the suspension of a constitution, but rather by the Union which he did not live to see accomplished. He had a rooted dislike to the use of force as an instrument of policy, and was an unwearying advocate of negotiation. And although at times the means he employed to attain his ends were, as he himself admitted, open to question, he was never actuated in their use by sordid motives or by considerations of personal aggrandisement. His wide vision and the comprehensive range of his imagination left no room for such trivialities. Nor could he ever whole-heartedly share in the current particularisms and racial animosities, which were the chief obstacles to his schemes. His insistence on co-operation with the

Afrikaners was the negation of racialism, while his vision of the far north as the true hinterland of the Cape reduced intercolonial rivalries to their true proportions. He bequeathed these ideals as a legacy to those who survived him. His alliance with Jan Hofmeyr and the Bond was reborn in the friendship and mutual respect of Botha and Jameson; and the overcoming of the particularist and racial hindrances to union in the National Convention might not have been accomplished but for the memory of his inspiring personality. His advocacy of the exclusion of the "imperial factor" from the internal affairs of the country, coupled as it was with his conviction that its highest destiny lay within the British Empire, is reflected in the present status of the Union and of the other Dominions; while the Transkeian system of Native administration, in the development of which he played a prominent part, has pointed to perhaps the most hopeful approach to a rationalisation of the problem of the Africans.

After Rhodes's death the proposal to suspend the constitution was finally killed at the Colonial Conference, when Mr Chamberlain's objections to it were reinforced by those of Sir Wilfred Laurier and Sir Edmund Barton, Premiers respectively of Canada and Australia. Nevertheless some security was required that the necessary Act of Indemnity would be forthcoming on the withdrawal of martial law. Sprigg was confident of his ability to pilot it through; but his position was peculiar, for he had quarrelled with his own party and was maintained in office mainly by the Opposition. Mr Chamberlain, therefore, let it be known that the Imperial Parliament would pass the Act if necessary, and Sprigg agreed that martial law, though relaxed, should be maintained until it was passed. The Cape Parliament thereupon met on 20 August 1902 and passed the Bill and the estimates, and the position became again constitutional.[1] The Sprigg Ministry survived another year, but was then defeated on a motion for the investigation of martial law sentences, which it had undertaken to promote when the Act of Indemnity was passed, and the compensation paid to farmers for war losses. At the general election which followed early in 1904 the Progressives, under the leadership of Dr Jameson, were returned to power, thanks largely to the disfranchisement of the rebels, with a majority of 5 in the Lower House and of one in the Upper.[2]

In the meantime the Treaty of Vereeniging had opened the way to the complete assumption by the civil authorities of the governments of the new colonies. Lord Milner now became Governor of both, with Sir H. Goold-Adams as Lieutenant-Governor of the Orange River Colony and, in September 1902, Sir Arthur Lawley as Lieutenant-Governor of the Transvaal. The Letters Patent establishing

[1] *Parl. Pap.* 1902, LXVII [Cd. 1163]; Walker, E. A., *Lord de Villiers and his Times*, pp. 393–403; *Times History of the War in South Africa* 1899–1902, VI, ch. III.

[2] Colvin, I., *Life of Jameson*, II, 220–1.

the Governments allowed for nominated Executive and Legislative Councils, which at first were composed of the executive heads of departments, and reserved the control of the South African Constabulary to the High Commissioner. In him also was vested control of the railways of the two colonies operated as one system under the name of the Central South African Railways, assisted by a Financial Board of Control on which both colonies were represented.[1] The new Governments were proclaimed three weeks after the signing of the peace, the intervening period being occupied by the surrender of the burghers in the field.

The first task to be taken in hand was the repatriation of the civil population. Article X of the peace treaty required the appointment of a local commission in each magisterial district to assist the people to return to their homes and to provide food, shelter, seeds, stock and implements to those who could not supply themselves. A free grant of £3,000,000, known as "the ex-Burgher Fund", was made by the British Government for these purposes, and any additional funds required were advanced by the colonial treasuries as loans free of interest for two years and thereafter repayable over a period of years with 3 per cent interest. At first only the payment of relief was contemplated; the word "compensation" does not occur in Article X; in the end, however, the amount of war loss in each case became the measure of relief.[2] On the other hand the payment of relief could not be deferred until war losses had been assessed; to be effective it must be prompt. Therefore advances far in excess of the £3,000,000 were made while the assessment of war losses was proceeding, and the following scheme for the distribution of the free grant was adopted: credit for relief from the Repatriation Commission for proved war losses was granted to all ex-burghers up to £25, and those whose claims exceeded £25 received 2*s.* in the £ on the excess.[3] Thus a double process of relief and assessment had to be developed. The local commissions were responsible for both, but in their relief work they were under a Central Repatriation Board in each colony, and in their assessment work they were co-ordinated by a Central Judicial Commission. The latter body also administered the £2,000,000 given by the British Government for British subjects, neutral foreigners and Natives. It handed over £300,000 for the Natives to the Native Affairs Department and paid 17*s.* 4*d.* in the £ on the assessed claims of the British subjects and the foreigners. Another class requiring special treatment was "the Protected Burghers", who had either laid down their arms voluntarily or under Lord Roberts's proclamations of March 1900. They received 10*s.* in the £ on their assessed claims at a cost of £2,000,000. The whole cost of repatriation and compensation,

[1] Newton, *op. cit.* I, 182–205, 208, 220.
[2] *Parl. Pap.* 1903, XLV [Cd. 1551].
[3] *Milner Papers*, II, 373.

excluding £2,500,000 paid out on account of military receipts, amounted to over £14,000,000, half of which was charged to the British Exchequer and the other half against the public debt of the two colonies. Of this latter, £2,800,000 represented recoverable loans, more than half of which had to be written off in the end. Over 200,000 whites and 100,000 Africans had to be returned to their homes and helped until they could support themselves in a country which had been reduced to an absolute desert. The cost would have been less had not the severe droughts of 1902 and 1903 placed on the Government the burden of supporting the population for two years instead of one.[1]

The solution of many of the problems connected with this great operation was facilitated by the visit of Mr Chamberlain to South Africa. He landed at Durban on 26 December 1902 and spent from January 8–22 in Johannesburg in consultation with Lord Milner. During this fortnight the details of a guaranteed loan of £35,000,000 to pay for existing liabilities and future developments were settled. The former absorbed more than half of it, including the nationalisation of the Netherlands Railway Company system and the repayment of the old Transvaal debt. Of the balance, after providing £6,500,000 for repatriation and war compensation to the Cape and Natal, £1,500,000 were applied to capital expenditure on existing railway lines, £4,500,000 to new railway construction and £5,000,000 to land settlement and public works. The Transvaal had also to meet a request from Mr Chamberlain that it should make a substantial contribution to the cost of the war. Eventually a loan of £30,000,000 was agreed between him and Lord Milner to be issued in three instalments, the first of which was to be guaranteed by some of the South African mining houses and banks. It soon became apparent, however, that the two colonies, faced as they were with the task of reconstruction—a task aggravated by industrial depression and unfavourable seasons—could not be expected to bear the additional burden of an unproductive debt of this magnitude, and it was eventually abandoned by the Liberal Government in 1907.[2]

The guaranteed loan, being an intercolonial service like the railways and the South African Constabulary, required joint machinery to administer it. It could not be apportioned between the two colonies according to their several abilities to bear the burden, since their financial capacity was too unequal; unless it were spent on the basis of the work to be done, repatriation and development in the Orange River Colony would be starved. On the other hand the surplus revenue of the Central South African Railways more than

[1] *Parl. Pap.* 1906, LXXX [Cd. 3028]; Beak, G. B., "The Aftermath of War", in *Times History*, VI, 44–54.

[2] *Parl. Pap.* 1904, LXI [Cd. 2102] and 1903, XLV [Cd. 1552]; Worsfold, *op. cit.* I, 125–6, 181–8.

sufficed to meet the annual charges on the loan, and as the railways were already vested in the High Commissioner, assisted by the Intercolonial Financial Board of Control, it required only a development of this machinery to deal with the loan on the same lines. Therefore a new body was created in May 1903, called the Intercolonial Council,[1] which included unofficial representatives of both colonies. Its functions were to advise the High Commissioner on the financial administration of the Central South African Railways, on the expenditure on the South African Constabulary and on one or two other matters common to both colonies. It appointed a Standing Railway Committee every year to replace the Financial Board of Control and to prepare the annual railway budget. It decided on new railway construction subject to the consent of the Secretary of State. The net profits of the railways, after providing for the expenses of working, administration and maintenance, became its revenue against which the interest and sinking fund of the guaranteed loan were the first charge. Any deficit had to be made up by each colony in proportion to its revenue. A Railway Extension Conference, in which unofficial members were in a majority, had met in the previous March and had made recommendations on the spending of the sum provided in the guaranteed loan for railway construction; and at the first session of the Intercolonial Council in July an expenditure of £7,000,000 was authorised, £2,500,000 being assigned to bringing the existing system into repair and £4,500,000 to new construction.

No sooner were these plans adopted than the whole financial edifice on which they were built collapsed. Sir Arthur Lawley was acting as High Commissioner, Lord Milner having gone to Europe on leave, when the monthly returns of railway receipts made it apparent that the calculations on which the budget of the Intercolonial Council had been based were unreliable, the estimate of net railway revenue having to be reduced from £2,150,000 to £1,400,000. Two causes contributed to the deficit. First, the Customs Conference,[2] which had met in Bloemfontein in March 1903, had only managed to establish a customs union by agreeing to certain reductions in railway rates, which were demanded by the Transvaal in order to lower the cost of living. Owing to inaccuracies in the calculations on which the new rates were fixed, more revenue was sacrificed by the Central South African Railways than was bargained for. Secondly, the scarcity of labour and the drought seriously diminished traffic.[3] Lord Milner, on his return to the Transvaal, was obliged to report that the deficit on its budget, owing to the additional contribution required from it for the Intercolonial Council, might be £450,000. In the end a deficit was avoided, but work on some of the new lines had to be postponed,

[1] *Parl. Pap.* 1903, XLV [Cd. 1641]; Newton, *op. cit.* I, 220–31.
[2] *Parl. Pap.* 1903, XLV [Cd. 1599].
[3] *Ibid.* 1904, LXI [Cd. 1899], p. 9.

the South African Constabulary had to be reduced and other economies effected.[1] In October Sir A. Lawley had informed Alfred Lyttelton, who was now Colonial Secretary, that in his opinion, the only thing standing between the Transvaal and a general crisis was "the sanguine hope of the early immigration of Asiatic labour".[2]

The Bloemfontein Customs Conference had included in its agenda both the problem of the Africans and the question of alien immigration. It recommended that "in view of the coming federation of the South African colonies" a commission should be constituted to gather information and to make recommendations to the several Governments with the object of arriving at a common understanding on questions of policy for the Africans. The Native Affairs Commission of 1903–5,[3] to which this resolution gave birth, naturally discussed the problem of labour and made a series of suggestions calculated to improve the local supply by checking Africans squatting on farms except as farm labourers, by levying rents on those living on Crown lands, by enforcing municipal regulations against vagrancy, by encouraging a higher standard of education and by better facilities for travel. On alien immigration the Customs Conference declared that if industrial development positively required it, the introduction of unskilled Asiatic labourers under proper safeguards was permissible. This idea was not new to South Africa. It had been discussed during Mr Chamberlain's visit. Southern Rhodesia, where shortage of labour was a standing difficulty, had passed an Ordinance in 1900 making it possible, but Mr Chamberlain, in Johannesburg, would not agree to its being implemented, and Mr Lyttelton refused a similar request in December 1903.[4] On the other hand the Bloemfontein resolution justified the appointment of a Labour Commission in August to decide what the labour requirements of the country were and what supply was procurable from central and southern Africa. Meanwhile popular agitation in favour of the Chinese solution increased and when the majority of the Labour Commission reported in November that the demand for labour by all industries was far in excess of the supply, and that the mining industry alone was 129,000 Africans short,[5] public opinion, at any rate in the urban centres of the Transvaal, was almost unanimously in favour of it. The minority report of two Commissioners expressed the view that the shortage was due to temporary circumstances: the confusion caused by the war and the reconstruction work following it, the high wages paid by the military authorities during the war and the reduction of wages which had been rashly attempted after it by the mine employers. It also contended that the supply could be supplemented by European labour. An experiment in this

[1] *Parl. Pap.* 1904, LXI [Cd. 1895], [Cd. 2104]; *Intercolonial Council Minutes*, 1903–7; Worsfold, *op. cit.* I, 238–9, II, 8–23.

[2] *Parl. Pap.* 1904, LXI [Cd. 2102], p. 74.

[3] *Ibid.* 1905, LV [Cd. 2399].

[4] *Ibid.* 1904, LXII [Cd. 2028].

[5] *Ibid.* 1904, XXXIX [Cd. 1894].

direction had been conducted on the Village Main Reef gold-mine by F. H. P. Creswell, who argued that its success justified its wider application. In this contention he was not supported by other mining engineers nor by the mine employers, who, apart from the financial merits of his case, could not contemplate entirely reorganising the labour on the mines at a time when they were looking for a great expansion of the industry and were grievously disappointed that its return even to the pre-war level was so long delayed.

Lord Milner's point of view was a combination of both these opinions. The increase of the white population was of cardinal importance to him; he believed that only through it would the existing white prejudice against manual labour be overcome. But in order to secure it "things must move in the immediate future". Being now convinced that African labour was insufficient for the early future, he saw no alternative to calling in Asiatics as a temporary expedient;[1] he therefore advocated it while he was in England. On his return to the Transvaal in December 1903 he found the situation ripe for action. On December 30 the Legislative Council, which had been enlarged in the previous May to 16 official and 14 unofficial members, passed a motion by 22 to 4 in favour of the introduction of coloured labourers under indenture to be repatriated at the end of their contracts. On 16 January 1904 Mr Lyttelton assented to an Ordinance being introduced to give effect to it. After delays caused by the violent hostility which the measure evoked in England and in Australia and New Zealand, and by the Chinese Government's seizing the opportunity to secure a new convention, under the Treaty of Pekin of 1860, regulating Chinese emigration to all British colonies, it was passed and assented to.[2] The first Chinese started work early in July 1904. An improvement in the economic situation at once followed. The surplus shown by the Transvaal budget at the end of June 1905 was £347,000;[3] between March 1904 and March 1905 the European employees on the mines increased from 10,240 to 13,255, and the African labourers from 78,825 to 105,184; the number of Chinese employed at the latter date was 34,355, while in January 1907 it was 53,856.[4] Thereafter it declined, for the very success of the Asiatic labour importation movement had in it the seeds of its own destruction, for this so-called "Chinese slavery" played a leading part in the smashing defeat of the Conservative Government at the general election in Great Britain in January 1906. The new Liberal Ministry prohibited the issue of further importation licences and provided for the termination of the Ordinance one year after the first meeting of the self-governing Transvaal Legislature in 1907.[5]

[1] *Parl. Pap.* 1904, XXXIX [Cd. 1896], [Cd. 1897]; Worsfold, *op. cit.* I, 299.
[2] *Parl. Pap.* 1904, LXII [Cd. 1956]; Ordinance No. 17 of 1904.
[3] *Ibid*, 1905, LV [Cd. 2563].
[4] *Times History*, VI, 111–28.
[5] *Parl. Pap.* 1906, LXX [Cd. 2788].

So far we have not mentioned the attitude of the Afrikaner population towards Lord Milner's government. After the treaty of peace the men who had been the leaders in the field during the war and who had carried through the peace negotiations became naturally the political leaders of the people. They recommended them "to acquiesce in the peace and to obey and respect the new government" and they co-operated in every way in facilitating the surrender of those still under arms and in persuading the prisoners of war to accept the terms of peace. They took steps, however, to preserve some form of national organisation by appointing, at the meeting of the representatives of the commandos at Vereeniging, a head committee drawn from both countries, three of whom: Generals Botha, de Wet and de la Rey, were commissioned to go to Europe to collect funds for the widows and orphans of the war and to endeavour to secure modifications of the terms of peace.[1] They arrived in London on August 16, where they were given an immense ovation. They requested an interview with Mr Chamberlain and enclosed a list of subjects for discussion, which included, amongst others, a complete amnesty for all rebels, the reinstatement or compensating of all the old republican officials, payment for all losses occasioned by the British troops and for all properties used by them, and the taking over of all the obligations of the late republics and the restoration to the Transvaal of the districts transferred to Natal.[2] The Colonial Secretary replied that, in his opinion, these involved the negotiation of a new agreement and that he must decline to receive the deputation without a formal assurance that it would raise nothing inconsistent with the terms of peace. On this understanding an interview took place, which brought home to the Boer leaders that they must look for the recovery of their people within the four walls of the Treaty of Vereeniging. They were thrown back on the same conclusion by the failure of their appeal to "the civilised world" and of their continental tour to collect funds for the widows and orphans. This realised only £105,000, of which £20,000 was given by a citizen of the United States on condition that it should not be used for any purpose unfriendly to Great Britain. On their return to South Africa they were preceded by Mr Chamberlain and had further interviews with him at Pretoria and Bloemfontein, which only served to emphasise the conclusion already reached in London. Finding, therefore, that they could not secure a modification of the terms of the treaty, they assumed the position of detached critics of the British Government's action in fulfilling them.

They were not the only critics of the Crown Colony administration; a section of the British community on the Reef chafed under it and pressed for the introduction of responsible government. The Afrikaner

[1] *Parl. Pap.* 1902, LXVII [Cd. 1163].
[2] *Ibid.* 1902, LXIX [Cd. 1284].

leaders did not at first join in the demand. They held that not only was the time not ripe for self-government, but that even the appointment of unofficial members of the two Legislative Councils was inadvisable. They refused seats on these bodies when they were enlarged in 1903, and thus retained their freedom to criticise without assuming any responsibility for the actions of Lord Milner's government. Their criticism was directed especially against its education policy and the importation of Chinese labour. Education raised the problem of language. Article V of the peace treaty required that Dutch should be taught in the public schools where the parents of the children desired it. The Education Ordinance of 1903 limited the time to a maximum of five hours a week. This was considered inadequate.[1] In the Orange River Colony a compromise was reached in 1905, but the controversy was renewed, this time by the British South Africans, when General Hertzog, in 1908, after the grant of responsible government, established a system of compulsory bilingualism.[2] In the Transvaal the dispute was settled by General Smuts's Act of 1907, which provided for the use of the pupil's home language as the medium of education in the lower standards and, after standard 3, of English only, subject to adequate provision being made for the teaching of Dutch to every child, both Afrikaner and British, unless the parents objected. On the Chinese issue the Afrikaner leaders preserved their freedom of future action by declaring that the importation was a fatal mistake without popular consent, which they denied it had received.[3]

Lord Milner's policy had been to treat the new colonies as far as possible as if they were self-governing and to invite the advice and co-operation of leading citizens. He also recognized that full self-government could not be long delayed. On the other hand, if granted prematurely, it involved the risk of placing a still unreconciled Afrikaner majority in power. An intermediate stage was, therefore, decided upon and with this object the Lyttelton Constitution was drafted for the Transvaal, to come into force after May 1905 when the mandates of the nominated members of the existing Legislative Council expired. It provided for an Assembly of not more than 44 members all of whom were elective except the Executive officers, who would continue to be appointed by the Crown.[4] The preliminary announcement of this intention galvanised the country into political activity. The Transvaal Progressive Association supported the proposal. The Transvaal Responsible Government Association, which afterwards became the Nationalist Party, many of whose supporters were of British extraction, wished at once to go further, as its name implies. The Afrikaner leaders formed a party named "Het Volk" (The People) to

[1] *Parl. Pap.* 1904, LXI [Cd. 1895], p. 52.
[2] *Vide infra*, p. 663.
[3] *Ibid.* 1904, LXI [Cd. 1899], p. 21.
[4] *Ibid.* 1905, LV [Cd. 2400]; Newton, *op. cit.* II, 8–15.

support the latter course "in the event of a change being necessary".[1] Eventually this course was adopted, for a great change had come over the situation.

Lord Milner's tenure of office came to an end in April 1905. The chief feature of his record was the immense amount of permanent reconstruction work that had been accomplished, and he left South Africa worn out in labouring for what he believed to be her true welfare. He was succeeded by the Earl of Selborne. Towards the end of the year Sir Arthur Lawley was succeeded as Lieutenant-Governor of the Transvaal by Sir Richard Solomon, the Transvaal Attorney-General. Soon afterwards the Conservative Government in England was replaced by Sir Henry Campbell-Bannerman's Liberal Ministry, which at once introduced important changes of policy. It announced its intention of granting responsible government to both colonies, and Letters Patent were issued (Transvaal, 6 December 1906; Orange Free State, 5 June 1907) annulling the Lyttelton Constitution. Before this, however, the Government had stopped the issue of further licences to import Chinese, as Campbell-Bannerman had undertaken that they would.[2]

The Lyttelton Constitution, "in order not to revive and accentuate antagonisms between town and country", had settled the vexed question of the distribution of seats by allotting to each constituency an equal number of votes with a margin of 10 per cent in either direction to permit of local adjustments, and by providing for a periodic redistribution of seats. These principles were followed in the constitutions of 1906 for the Transvaal and 1907 for the Orange River Colony. In the Cape the same problem was being fought out with great bitterness by the introduction of a Redistribution Bill by the Jameson Ministry in 1906.[3] An average country constituency in the Cape contained 1161 voters compared with an average for Cape Town of 3426. The reform applied by the Act was that one member should sit for every 2000 town electors and one for every 1500 country electors. The constitutions of the Transvaal and Orange River Colony also departed from Cape and Natal precedents by adopting white manhood suffrage in accordance with the rigid colour distinction which was characteristic of the old republics, and by laying down that for the first four years, the Second Chambers or Legislative Councils should be nominative, the appointments being made in the first instance by the Governors and thereafter as vacancies occurred by the Governors-in-Council. Another special feature of both was the creation in each colony of an independent board to administer the affairs of the settlers who had been established under Lord Milner's land settlement schemes. These numbered 596 in the Transvaal and 660

[1] Newton, *Unification of S. Africa*, I, 281.
[2] Speech at Dunfermline. Newton, I, 235–9, quoting *Times* report, 18 November 1904.
[3] Act No. 29 of 1906; Colvin, *op. cit.* II, 239–40.

in the Orange River Colony and were occupying over two million acres. Though comparatively few in number, they introduced a new leaven into the rural areas and contributed to the improvements in agricultural methods which followed on Lord Milner's organisation of modern Agricultural Departments in both colonies. The British Government regarded itself as under a separate obligation to protect them against the possible effect on their position of the introduction of responsible government, and they were therefore removed from the control of the new Governments for a period of five years.

The elections were held in the Transvaal in February 1907 and resulted in Het Volk securing 37 seats, the Nationalists 6, the Progressives 21, and Labour or Independents 5. General Botha therefore was able to form a Ministry with a large majority. In the Orange River Colony no serious opposition to the Oranje Unie, the equivalent of Het Volk, was possible, and Abraham Fischer became Prime Minister in December 1907 with General J. B. M. Hertzog in control of Justice and Education. The Opposition numbered only 7 in a House of 38.

One of the first things with which the Transvaal Government had to deal was the Indian problem. The Treaty of Vereeniging had imposed no obligation on the British Government to continue the republican restrictions on Asians against which it had protested so strongly before the war. Nevertheless, in view of the strong public sentiment against their immigrating and trading, neither the law of 1885, which prevented them from acquiring citizenship or owning fixed property and bound them to enter their names with the magistrate of the District in which they lived and to reside in locations if required to do so, nor the law which excluded them absolutely from the Orange River Colony, was repealed.[1] Only those who were resident in the Transvaal before the war were allowed to return. The Peace Preservation Ordinance, which empowered the Government to prohibit anyone entering the new colonies, was used for this purpose.[2] This plan was designed to protect the existing rights of Asians and to postpone any decision on future policy until responsible government had been introduced. The difficulty of its application was to determine who were genuine pre-war residents. The rapid growth in the number of Asian traders, especially in the country towns, gave the impression that many were entering illegally, not only from India, but also from Natal, where a large Indian population existed, many of them brought in as indentured labourers between 1860 and 1911, when the Indian Government stopped their recruitment. In Natal by 1904 they numbered 100,000 against 97,000 Europeans. Their permanent settlement in that colony was deprecated, but the Indian Government consistently refused to agree to their compulsory repatriation on the expiry of their contracts. Therefore a £3 annual licence had been

[1] Transvaal Law No. 3 of 1885, § 2 (*c*). *Orange Free State Law Book*, ch. XXXIII.
[2] Ordinances Nos. 38 of 1902 and 5 of 1903.

imposed in 1895 on all who remained in Natal unindentured in the hope that it would encourage them to depart. Furthermore, in 1903, it had been applied to all their male children of 16 years or over, and to females of 13 or over, who did not either indenture or return to India. The collection of this tax had been perfunctory.[1] Faced with the growing public demand for legislation, with the position in Natal, with open land frontiers on all sides and with no share in the control of the oversea ports of entry, which they could only secure through unification, the Transvaal Government could adopt no other means of controlling immigration than registration, which, to be effective, had to be by finger-prints. An Ordinance was therefore passed in 1906 by the Crown Colony Legislature requiring all Asians to register and to carry certificates marked with their finger-prints. After the Imperial Government had refused to assent to it on the ground that the coming responsible government should deal with the question, the measure was re-enacted under responsible government in identical terms as the Asiatic Law Amendment Act of 1907.[2] The Asians responded with a passive resistance movement, under the leadership of Mohandas Karamchand Gandhi, a prosperous Johannesburg barrister, which filled the gaols to overflowing. Their objection to the law was to its compulsion and not to its requirement of finger-prints, and a compromise that they should be allowed to register voluntarily within three months and that all prosecutions should be suspended was arrived at in January 1908. It proved only a temporary suspension of hostilities, for Gandhi declared that he understood that the Act was to be repealed, which the Government refused to do.[3]

A still more serious crisis threatened in Natal. The development of democratic institutions in South Africa has too often been accompanied by a loss of personal touch between the Africans and their governors. This was particularly noticeable in Natal where the Africans remembered Shepstone's paternal administration. At the same time they were harassed by the rapid extension of European landownership. This caused them to become involved in accusations of stock-theft, and to be obliged either to pay what appeared to them to be exorbitant rents for land which they had hitherto occupied free of charge, or to work for its new owners or for others on conditions which were increasingly subject to legislative interference.[4] The war also had a disturbing effect on them, and they were inclined to attribute the withdrawal of the imperial troops to the King's displeasure with his European subjects. Emissaries of the "Ethiopian" movement

[1] *Parl. Pap.* 1903, XLV [Cd. 1683], [Cd. 1684].

[2] *Parl. Pap.* 1907, LVII [Cd. 3308].

[3] *Ibid.* 1908, LXXIII [Cd. 3892], [Cd. 4327].

[4] Acts 40 of 1894, 35 of 1899, 28 of 1902, 48 of 1903, 38 of 1905; Evans, M. S., *Black and White in South Africa*, pp. 132–7, 184 *et sqq.*; *Report of Natal Native Affairs Commission, 1906–7*, *Parl. Pap.* 1908, LXXII [Cd. 3889].

added fuel to the smouldering flames. The imposition of a poll tax of £1 on every European and Native male of 18 years and over, which brought those who did not pay the hut tax of 14*s*. within the grasp of the tax-collector, was the immediate cause of the outbreak. An attempt to collect the tax led to a conflict in the Richmond district in which two white policemen lost their lives.

Martial law was proclaimed. A colonial force was hastily mobilised and had no difficulty in arresting twelve Africans whose complicity in the deaths of the police was proved by a court martial. They were condemned to death. On receipt of this news in London, the Earl of Elgin, the new Liberal Secretary of State for the Colonies, instructed the Governor to stay the executions until further information had been supplied. The Natal Government thereupon incontinently resigned. It resumed office when the British Government announced that it had no intention of interfering with a colonial responsible government and that it was now satisfied with the explanations furnished by the Governor, but that the justification of its action lay in the presence in Pietermaritzburg of the 2nd Queen's Own Cameron Highlanders, who had been moved there at the request of the Natal Government, and in the necessity of the King's assenting to an Act of Indemnity. The convicted Natives were executed three days after the date originally appointed.

The rebellion then flared up in the north in the Mapumulo, Krantzkop, Umvoti and Nkandhla districts. It was a disorganised affair without leadership and had two phases. In the first the aged chief Sigananda, with a following upwards of a thousand, went into rebellion in the Nkandhla forest, while Bambata, with about five hundred, rose to the westward near the Qudeni mountains. A colonial force, two thousand one hundred strong, composed of Natal Police, militia and volunteers, with detachments of the Cape Mounted Rifles and of the Transvaal Volunteers, was mobilised under the command of Col. D. Mackenzie. It concentrated near Cetewayo's grave in the valley of the Insuzi River (a tributary of the Tugela), thus cutting the communications between the two rebel bodies. A force was left here, while Mackenzie with the remainder moved north to Nkandhla, from whence he carried out a series of drives into the bush. In due course Sigananda was located in a gorge of the Mome River, and at the same time information was received that Bambata intended to join him there. Both bodies of rebels could therefore be accounted for in the fight that took place in the Mome Gorge on 9–10 June 1906, in which Bambata lost his life. Soon afterwards Sigananda surrendered. The second phase started immediately afterwards in the Mapumulo district south of the Tugela River. Its centre was the kraals of two Chiefs, the one on the Insuzi River, a tributary of the Umvoti, and the other near the junction of the Insinsimbi and Tugela Rivers. The colonial forces had now increased to five thousand, and the rebels were variously estimated at from five to seven thousand. Mackenzie defeated them without much difficulty by a system of converging columns, and the revolt collapsed.

The comparative ease with which this rising was overcome did not minimise its menace to Natal and possibly to South Africa. It was accompanied by the murder of isolated Europeans, and by such mysterious symptoms as the slaughter of pigs and of white fowls and the discarding of European-made cooking utensils, which are typical of widespread Native unrest.[1] Had Dinizulu, Cetewayo's son and chief of the Usutu, openly supported it the situation would have been far more serious, but he used his great influence against it. Towards the end of 1907 the nervy Natal authorities suspected that he was plotting a further rising and again proclaimed martial law in Zululand. Dinizulu quietly surrendered on December 9. He was tried under a special Act of Parliament at the end of 1908. He was defended by one of the best advocates from the Cape, W. P. Schreiner, at the request of the British Government, and of the twenty-three counts of the indictment against him he was found guilty on only two and partly guilty on a third. He was sentenced to four years' imprisonment, the sentence to run from the date of his surrender, and was transported to St Helena.[2]

The Zulu rebellion made evident to South Africa that it was not self-governing so far as the Africans were concerned, so long as its control over them was divided between a number of governments. Action by one might at any time involve another in a crisis for which it had no responsibility. They could not deal independently with grave internal disorder nor with the wider problems of national defence. Natal had been proved unable to do so. She had been obliged to accept assistance from her neighbours and, to a less degree, from the Imperial Government and by calling in the latter had asked an outside authority to intervene in an internal question. The same lesson had been driven home by the Report of the Native Affairs Commission of 1903–5, which had made a number of far-reaching recommendations that could receive adequate attention only from a unified government. It had recommended, for example, that those Africans who desired it should be given the opportunity of owning land in individual tenure, that ownership of land by them, whether individually or collectively, should be confined to demarcated areas and should not be intermixed with European land ownership, that African locations for residential purposes should be established near labour centres, and that the representation of Africans in Parliament should be by Europeans elected on a communal African franchise, subject to the number of representatives, if any, and their qualifications being

[1] *Parl. Pap.* 1906, LXXIX [Cd. 2905]; Stuart, J., *History of the Zulu Rebellion*; Bosman, W. *The Natal Rebellion of* 1906.

[2] Walker, E. A., *Schreiner*, Chap. XIII; *vide infra.*, p. 654.

left to the decision of each separate colony.[1] All these proposals have attracted much attention since Union, but they could hardly be effected before Union.

The accession to office of General Botha and Abraham Fischer and the change of government in England were the visible signs of a reaction which had been gaining impetus as the years passed after the war. Lord Milner had always foreseen that this was inevitable. Time was of the essence of his policy and some of it was lost through the shortage of labour, the drought and the economic crisis. Moreover the optimistic estimates of the mining and agricultural prospects of the new colonies, which were so prevalent immediately after the war, were not justified in the event. Land settlement proved an arduous business in which nature was not very helpful; the only new mineral discovery of importance was the Premier Diamond Mine near Pretoria; the general development of the country, on which a real increase of the population by immigration depended, was disappointingly slow. The "Afrikaner revival", therefore, was all the more potent. It did not influence the character of the Natal Government, although there were three changes of ministries there between 1901 and 1909; the last, that of F. R. Moor, taking office in 1906. The local politics of Natal, apart from the African and Asian problems and the growing economic and commercial importance of Durban, had but a minor influence on the wider problems with which we are dealing. Its small European population being predominantly British, southern and central Natal was unaffected by the political reaction which swept the Transvaal and the Cape.

So also with Southern Rhodesia. It continued to be administered by the Chartered Company, with many signs, however, that a radical change would be necessary before long. It shared in the shortage of labour, in the economic depression and in the disappointment at the failure of early and too optimistic expectations. The settlers demanded an increasing voice in the government and that the Company should dissociate its commercial from its administrative activities. In order to meet them the elective element in the Legislative Council was increased in 1903 so that the Company retained only a bare majority. The two principal causes of dispute were the accumulated deficits, which the Company had been obliged to meet under its Charter and for which the settlers refused to be in any way responsible, and the ownership of the unalienated lands which the Company claimed under its original concession and on other grounds—a claim which the elected members refused to recognise. The British Government declined to take any action on either question before the first term of 25 years of the Charter expired in 1914. The effect of this deadlock was that the non-voting Rhodesian delegates in the National

[1] *Report of S.A. Native Affairs Commission*, 1903–5, *Parl. Pap.* 1905, LV [Cd. 2399], pp. 19 *sqq.*

Convention, which was destined to make the Union, found that their country could not possibly enter that Union until it had been resolved.[1]

In the Cape Dr Jameson's tenure of office daily became more insecure. He was faced from the start with a steadily diminishing revenue. During the four years of his government it fell from £11,701,000 to £7,147,000. "A beastly time of retrenchment and of a consequent growling public and a party at sixes and sevens" is his own description of it.[2] The retrenchment mostly hit the urban community, the mainstay of his "Progressive" party, which was also divided by the economic hostility of the interior and the coast. Kimberley, like Johannesburg, blamed the coast ports for the high cost of living; on the other hand it united with them in being free trade in sentiment, whereas the farming population was protectionist. This last division coincided with that between the two white races and the urban and rural communities, which Jameson persistently refused to exploit. The falling revenue necessitated additional taxation, which, when it took the form of a meat duty, alienated the free-traders, and, when an excise on brandy, was attacked by the farmers, who were less hit by his income tax than were his own followers. His scheme for settling the railway traffic problem was, as we shall see later, defeated by the jealousy between East London and Port Elizabeth.[3]

In May 1904 Jameson was robbed of his majority of one in the Legislative Council by the departure for England of a member, whose irregular appointment as railway refreshment contractor had helped to break up Rhodes's Ministry some twenty years before.[4] In September 1907 the same member brought about his defeat on the Appropriation Bill. The deadlock which ensued led to the dissolution of Parliament after the passing of a Partial Appropriation Act to cover the period until a new Parliament could meet. The election which followed added the coping stone to the Afrikaner revival. J. X. Merriman and the South African Party, the name which the Bond had adopted in 1903, were returned to power with large majorities in both Houses. To Jameson this seemed to imply that "in the meantime federation will have to wait", in the same way that the existence of his Ministry appeared to General Smuts in 1907 to be a serious obstacle to it.[5] But no one could foresee, early in 1908, the astonishing facility with which in the end Union was accomplished. The Cape elections put the responsibility squarely on the shoulders of the Afrikaners. They were not prepared to agree to unification under Progressive auspices. Would they realise that it was equally impossible of accomplishment if they failed to secure the full co-operation of the British?

The first organised movement towards Union was initiated by a group of young men, whom Lord Milner had brought out from

[1] *Vide infra*, p. 654.
[2] Colvin, I., *op. cit.* II, 248. [3] *Vide infra*, p. 652.
[4] *Vide supra*, p. 557; Kipling's "licensed vitteler".
[5] Colvin, *op. cit.* II, 270; Laurence, Sir P., *Life of Merriman*, p. 241.

England to work in his administration. They included Patrick Duncan, the Transvaal Colonial Secretary, and were led on by the prophetic inspiration of Lionel Curtis, who had been Town Clerk of Johannesburg and afterwards had been responsible, under Duncan, for establishing that system of municipal government in the Transvaal, which was not the least notable achievement of Lord Milner's reconstruction work. Curtis resigned from the public service in 1906 to devote himself to the cause of federation and, as a first step, prepared with the co-operation of the group a comprehensive and forcible statement of the case for it. Having accomplished this, he and his associates travelled through the country forming Closer Union Societies, organising conferences and enlisting the support and interest of local people. An official status was given to the Curtis Memorandum by Dr Jameson's submitting a request to Lord Selborne in November 1906 that, in his capacity as High Commissioner, he should undertake to review the general position in South Africa in order that its people might have an opportunity of expressing their opinion on the desirability of creating a central national government. Lord Selborne, having secured the approval of all the Governments concerned, including that of Southern Rhodesia, drew up the memorandum of 1 January 1907.[1]

The lesson inculcated in this highly important document was that South Africa would never be self-governing and might even drift into civil war so long as she was divided into separate states with no machinery other than the High Commissioner, who was responsible to the Imperial Government, to decide the inter-state disputes which her geographical and economic conditions made inevitable. A few changes, which had improved the position, without, however, materially affecting it, had followed after the war. All the states were now under one flag, with a High Commissioner having authority to invite them to discuss their differences and ready to act as mediator between them. Although the Intercolonial Council had been abolished after the grant of responsible government to the Transvaal and Orange River Colony, the railways of the two colonies were still administered jointly. Thus one railway boundary had been eliminated. The Customs Union Convention of 1903, which included Southern Rhodesia, had abolished inter-state tariff barriers; nevertheless the fiscal relations between the colonies were still far from satisfactory. Lourenço Marques remained the natural port of the "competitive area", as the gold-mining area of the Transvaal was called, and gradually the import traffic was being transferred to it. At the time of Union it was handling 67 per cent, while the Cape ports, which in 1894 dealt with 80 per cent, were getting only 11 per cent. This

[1] Newton, *op. cit.* II, 38–176, and Williams, Basil, *The Selborne Memorandum.* The Memorandum was first published, as an Imperial blue book, *Parl. Pap.* 1907, LVII [Cd. 3564], in July 1907.

diversion of the traffic benefited the Transvaal revenue, for the Central South African Railway owned 85 per cent of the railway from Lourenço Marques to Johannesburg as against 36·4 per cent of that from Durban and 55 per cent of the lines from Port Elizabeth and East London. It also encouraged the Portuguese to facilitate the recruiting of labour for the mines. At the same time it deprived the coast colonies of the revenue derived from the through traffic from their ports, the maintenance of which was, of course, equally dependent upon the Portuguese labour supply to the Transvaal mines.

The fairest division was obviously that the traffic should be distributed equally between the three competing systems. An agreement which would have made this possible was reached at Pretoria in February 1905, mainly through the influence of Lord Milner, who persuaded the Transvaal to make the sacrifice of revenue which it entailed. It was subject, however, to the ratification of the several Parliaments, and further involved the amendment of the *Modus Vivendi* of 1901, which led to protracted diplomatic negotiations with the Portuguese. Moreover the measure failed to pass the Cape Assembly, where it was defeated through the rivalry of East London and Port Elizabeth, for the scramble for the railway traffic caused disputes not only between the coast and the interior, but also between the rival Cape ports, and between the Cape and Natal. The construction of any new line in the interior might have the same effect. Thus the completion of the railway connection between Durban and Kimberley through Bloemfontein enabled Durban to challenge the hitherto undisputed control of the valuable Kimberley traffic by the Cape. The latter threatened forcibly to interfere by the erection of a fence along the border and had to be pacified by an agreement protecting its interests for a period of years. It is not surprising that the one unchallenged conclusion reached by the Pretoria Conference was that the only solution of these conflicts was the unification of all the railway and harbour interests.[1]

The same contentions arose over the customs. The interior advocated their revision in the direction of free trade in order to lower the cost of living; the Cape favoured increased protection in order to stimulate its own products, which the Customs Union now admitted to the interior free of duty. In order to secure this latter privilege, which had been enjoyed by the Portuguese since their treaty with the Transvaal of 1875, the Cape and Natal had been compelled to agree at Bloemfontein in 1903 to remissions of railway rates and to reductions of duties. The Transvaal was in the same position to dictate terms as it had been in 1895. The Convention was only ratified in the Cape Parliament by a majority of one. It was equally unpopular with the Transvaal farmers, who regarded the rich Transvaal market as their own preserve and wished others to be excluded from it. It

[1] Worsfold, *op. cit.* II, 45–55; Brand, R. H., *The Union of South Africa*, pp. 18–24.

was denounced by Natal in 1906. It had, therefore, to be patched up again at another Conference in such a way as to secure more revenue for the Cape and Natal, of which both were in sore need. This amended Convention[1] was in turn attacked in the Transvaal as needlessly increasing the cost of living. The Crown Colony Government defended it on the ground that it could not undertake the responsibility of breaking away from the Customs Union immediately before the grant of responsible government. As soon as General Botha was in office he gave notice of his intention of terminating it and another Conference had to be summoned to meet in Pretoria in May 1908.[2] The Transvaal demanded that rates and fares in all through traffic be arranged so as to "prevent the taxation of the people of the inland colonies by the coast colonies", that protection be by customs dues and not by railway rates, and that the carriage of raw materials be at the lowest possible rates and of manufactures at higher rates. The Cape proposed that rates should be so fixed as to secure that the through import traffic should be equally divided between the three competitors. Natal refused to be satisfied with less than a fixed proportion of 30 per cent. The Conference failed entirely to find a solution of these conflicting interests and had to be satisfied with continuing the 1906 compromise for twelve months to allow of the possibility of achieving political union being explored. With this object it passed a series of resolutions declaring that an early union of the several colonies under the British Crown was essential, and that their legislatures should be asked to appoint delegates to a national convention.[3]

Although these railway and customs disputes were the immediate cause of the meeting of the National Convention, other equally important problems were no more capable of being handled adequately otherwise than by a centralised administration. Indeed it was apparent that until South Africa had completed her political structure by adding this coping stone, none of the four self-governing states had complete control over its internal affairs. The Zulu rebellion was an apposite example of the inconveniences arising out of the existence of four separate Native Administrations. The recommendations of an important intercolonial commission, such as the Native Affairs Commission of 1903–5, were still-born through the same cause. The four separate legal systems were without a South African Court of Appeal to harmonise and co-ordinate the administration of justice. The existence of four Police and Defence Forces militated against their joint efficiency, and diminished the colonies' power of defence. The same disadvantage was an obstacle to an effective campaign against the numerous pests and plagues which are the accompaniment of South African farming. The development of the agricultural and

[1] *Parl. Pap.* 1906, LXXIX [Cd. 2977]; Newton, *op. cit.* II, 25–31.
[2] Brand, *op. cit.* pp. 25–7; Newton, *op. cit.* II, 217–18.
[3] Newton, *Unification of S. Africa*, II, 217–18.

livestock industries, in which the great majority of the population were permanently engaged, called for a unified Agricultural Department, as did also the mining industry for a single Minister of Mines. And all these considerations applied equally to Southern Rhodesia. It is not surprising in these circumstances that all the Parliaments concerned ratified the resolutions of the Pretoria Customs Conference, and so cleared the way for the meeting of the National Convention in Durban on 12 October 1908.

In accordance with these resolutions the Convention was composed of thirty members, of whom twelve came from the Cape, eight from the Transvaal, and five each from Natal and the Orange River Colony. Rhodesia was invited to send three delegates with no power to vote, but to hold a watching brief as to her admission to the Union "at such time and under such conditions as may hereafter be agreed upon". The personnel of this Convention reflected the preponderance of farmers and lawyers, which was noticeable in South African contemporary politics. The Afrikaners had always been predominantly a rural people: those of them who made their livings in the towns were usually more prominent in the legal and clerical professions and in the civil service than in commerce, mining or industry. Some delegates who could not properly be classed as farmers, such as Merriman, Dr Smartt, and General Smuts, were nevertheless intimately connected with that pursuit. There was but one prominent trader in the person of J. W. Jagger of Cape Town, while Sir George Farrar and Sir Percy Fitzpatrick were the only two members who were, or had been, responsible for controlling the gold-mining industry on which the economic future of the country largely depended. The chairman was Sir J. H. de Villiers, who afterwards became the first Chief Justice of the Union; two notable absentees were W. P. Schreiner, who, though appointed, resigned in order to defend Dinizulu,[1] and Jan Hofmeyr, who declined to serve mainly because he feared closer union had no chance of being achieved.

The prominence of farmers had as a natural corollary that the two European peoples were not equally represented. Excluding the Orange River Colony and Natal, in which the overwhelming Afrikaner predominance of the one was counterbalanced by the equally British composition of the other, the delegations from the Cape and the Transvaal comprised twelve Afrikaners as against eight Progressives. This inequality aroused some criticism but proved of no importance. The leaders of the British recognised that if Union was to come it would have to be under Afrikaner auspices; they also knew that it could not be secured without the co-operation of their own section. Therefore equality of representation was of no real importance. Moreover, the chances of success were greatly improved by the two parties in the Transvaal coming in advance to a working agreement

[1] *Vide supra*, p. 648; Walker, *Schreiner*, p. 291.

on the most controversial questions. The Transvaal delegation, therefore, attended as a united body, and also with a prepared plan of a constitution which had been worked out by General Smuts with the assistance of some of the Closer Union group. After sitting at Durban the Convention adjourned on November 5 to meet again in Cape Town on November 23. At the end of February 1909 it produced a report in the form of a draft South Africa Act, which was submitted to the four colonial Parliaments. The amendments proposed by them were then discussed at a meeting of the Convention in Bloemfontein in May, and the Act, in its final form, having been approved by each Parliament and by a referendum in Natal, was taken to London by a deputation appointed by each Government.

The obstacles which the National Convention had to overcome were economic and political. No unification was possible until the economic issues had been cleared out of the way, for the uniting of the railways by itself could not prevent rivalry between the ports, and Lourenço Marques had perforce to remain outside the Union. In the end the division of the through traffic to the competitive area was settled by an agreement concluded at Cape Town in February 1909,[1] by which Natal was allotted 30 per cent and Lourenço Marques a minimum of 50 and a maximum of 55 per cent, the Cape getting the balance of 15 per cent and the percentage by which the Lourenço Marques share might fluctuate below its maximum. The arrangement meant a new treaty with the Portuguese, since it was contrary to the *Modus Vivendi* of 1901. This was achieved by the Convention of 1909, which the Transvaal Government negotiated, guaranteeing to Portugal the minimum of 50 per cent for ten years.[2] The protection of the interior from taxation through the railways was attempted in the South Africa Act by incorporating in it the declaration that they and the harbours were to be administered "on business principles" with due regard to the encouragement of development in the interior by means of cheap transport. Their budget was separated from the general budget and, subject to the authority of the Governor-General-in-Council, their control was vested in a Board of three Commissioners in the hope that by this means the baneful effects of political interference in the management of public utilities might be avoided.

The political obstacles were equally formidable and were faced in a spirit of compromise and reasonableness which was a welcome novelty in contemporary South African politics. They can be classed under the two heads of provincial and racial. The first point to be settled was whether the new state was to be a federation or a union.[3]

[1] *South African Convention. Minutes of Proceedings*, pp. 269–70.
[2] *Parl. Pap.* 1909, LXI [Cd. 4587].
[3] Malan, F. S., *Die Konvensie-Dagboek van François Stephanus Malan* 1908–9, pp. 23–5.

The Convention decided on the latter, but had to make sacrifices to the natural desire of the four colonies to preserve their identity. Each, therefore, became a Province of the Union with a Provincial Council elected on the same franchise as the Union House of Assembly and dissoluble only by effluxion of time every three years, an Executive Committee elected by proportional voting by the members of the Council, and an Administrator appointed for five years by the Union Government. Their authority was confined to certain specified subjects, including education other than higher education, hospitals, municipal institutions and local works other than railways. Their Ordinances were subject to the consent of the Governor-General-in-Council. No question in law can arise between Provincial and Union jurisdiction, the Union Parliament having overriding powers in regard to all matters. Their taxing powers were limited to direct taxation in anticipation that their desire for popularity would discourage any tendency on their part to extravagance. The necessary financial adjustment between them and the central government was referred to a Commission to be appointed by the first Union Government. A discussion of the subsequent working of these unique combinations of parliamentary and municipal institutions does not belong to this chapter; their justification lies in the attempt through them to meet federal sentiment without weakening the authority of the central Parliament.

The rivalry between the Provinces to secure the capital of the Union was settled by making Pretoria the seat of government, Cape Town the seat of the legislature, and Bloemfontein the place of sitting of the Appellate Division of the Supreme Court. Bloemfontein and Pietermaritzburg also received some monetary compensation, and Natal received her much-desired 30 per cent of traffic to the "competitive area".[1]

Provincial sentiment also influenced the composition of the Union legislature. Each Province received an arbitrary and equal representation of eight members in the Senate, that total of forty being completed by eight others nominated by the Governor-General-in-Council, four of whom must be men acquainted with the wants and wishes of the non-Europeans. The representation of each Province in the House of Assembly was also settled arbitrarily. To allot the seats on the basis of the number of white voters in each Province was unfair to the Cape and to Natal, where the franchise depended upon a property qualification and, in the case of the Cape, an educational qualification also, while the Transvaal and the Orange River Colony had white manhood suffrage. Moreover, the Cape had a large Coloured, Asian and Bantu electorate which the adjective "white" excluded. The northern colonies would not agree to their inclusion. In the end a compromise was reached by taking the adult white male population as the basis

[1] Malan, *Die Konvensie Dagboek*, pp. 123–9, 185–95, 209–17.

of the calculation.[1] In the Transvaal and the Orange River Colony it was synonymous with the voters' register, for all white male adults were qualified, and in the Cape and Natal the term included those who were not. It meant, however, that the Cape had to agree to their non-European voters not counting and also to their non-European people losing the right to sit in the Union Parliament, though not in the Cape Provincial Council. On the other hand the franchise laws remained unaltered in each Province. Thus the Cape non-European voters retained the suffrage, which was entrenched by the provision that any Bill disqualifying them on racial grounds alone must be passed at its third reading by not less than two-thirds of the total number of members of both Senate and House of Assembly sitting together. On this basis the division of the seats was still unsatisfactory to the two smaller colonies and, to satisfy them, the two larger were obliged to transfer representation to them so that each should have 17 seats in a house of 121, the Cape having 51 and the Transvaal 36. The white male population basis was to become fully applicable only when the number of seats in the House of Assembly reached 150. A far more difficult problem was the division of the seats allotted to each Province between the urban and rural communities. It was, broadly speaking, a racial issue, for on it mainly depended the respective strengths of the British and Afrikaner representations. As we have seen, this was an old cause of friction. The South African Act follows the principle of the Lyttelton Constitution. The electoral divisions are demarcated by a Commission of Judges in such a way as to contain an equal number of voters, subject to a departure from equality being permissible to the extent of 15 per cent in either direction on the grounds of density or sparsity of population. After each quinquennial census a Commission redistributes the seats in each Province and provides for any additional number of members required to meet the growth of its population. When the total reaches 150 no further increase is provided for. The draft of the Act as it emerged from Cape Town had arranged that each constituency should return three members elected on the principle of proportional representation. This was deleted at Bloemfontein, mainly through the influence of Hofmeyr, and single-member constituencies were inserted instead.[2]

The language question was one of the first problems with which the Convention dealt. It was perhaps the most anxious and most difficult of all. The feeling that their language was in an inferior position as compared with English had been, as ex-President Steyn pointed out, the principal cause of the recent growth of Afrikaner racial sentiment. The Afrikaner Bond had been founded on it in the Cape; it had been used by the Boer leaders after the war as a chief instrument in the Afrikaner revival; General Hertzog had attempted to rectify it

[1] Malan, *Die Konvensie Dagboek*, pp. 41–3, 46–59.

[2] Hofmeyr, J. H., *Life of J. H. Hofmeyr*, p. 631.

in the Orange River Colony by means of legislative compulsion. At the National Convention all were agreed that both languages must be recognised as equal, but many difficulties arose in deciding what equality implied. Did it mean, for example, as the chairman of the National Convention ruled, that citizens of South Africa would have the right to speak either English or Dutch in public offices and Courts and to demand that they be answered in the one he preferred? Did this imply that every civil servant must be bilingual and that the general use of both languages was to be compulsory? Or did it mean that each individual should be free to use whichever he chose? General Hertzog's theory inclined to the former in that it required all officials to know both languages, but it was wholly unacceptable to the British. On the other hand the Afrikaner section feared that the absence of all compulsion might mean the gradual disappearance of Dutch owing to the overwhelmingly preponderating utility of English. In the end the Convention confined itself to embodying in the Act of Union a declaration that "both the English and Dutch languages shall be official languages of the Union and shall be treated on a footing of equality and shall possess and enjoy equal freedom, rights and privileges", and to protecting it against amendment by the same means as it did the non-European vote in the Cape.

The acceptance of this declaration did more than anything else to create an atmosphere favourable to Union; at the same time it left the problem connected with its application undecided, except as regards the Proceedings and Acts of Parliament and all government notices and publications in which the use of both languages was made compulsory. Attempts were made to apply it more specifically in other directions, but they were either too cumbrous or involved compulsion on individuals which the British would not tolerate. A field of controversy was, therefore, left open which bore fruit in the first Parliament after Union through the education controversy which had already arisen in the Orange River Colony. The National Convention, however, did not attempt to extinguish all the inflammable material with which the political atmosphere of South Africa was charged. It made no effort, for example, to find a solution of the Indian problem. It left the position as it was and preserved intact the barrier against the migration of Asiaans from Natal into the Transvaal and the Orange Free State. It left the various Native Administrations untouched. It did no more than specifically state that the administration of Native and Asian affairs should be vested in the central government, the full implication of this centralisation being emphasised by amendments accepted by the Union delegation in London. It confined itself mainly to contriving a governmental machine which would enable South Africa to grapple with her problems as a single state.

The National Convention centralised the administration of justice in a Supreme Court consisting of an Appellate Division and of Provincial Divisions formed out of the several Supreme Courts of the Cape, Natal, the Transvaal and the High Court of the Orange River Colony, and Local Divisions where necessary. It abolished the right of appeal to the Privy Council except in cases where special leave was granted by the Privy Council. It endowed the Parliament of the Union with full power to amend or repeal any provision of the constitution subject to the reservations in regard to the composition of the House of Assembly, the qualification of voters and the use of the two languages which have been noted above. It provided that Southern Rhodesia might be admitted into the Union by Order-in-Council, the terms and conditions of which should have the same effect as if they had been enacted by the Imperial Parliament.

As the draft South Africa Act had to pass through the Imperial Parliament the attitude of the Liberal British Government was of importance. It was primarily concerned with two matters: the non-European franchise, and the future of Basutoland, Swaziland and the Bechuanaland Protectorate. From its point of view the two questions were intimately connected. It could not hand over its trusteeship for the three High Commission Territories unless it were satisfied that the trust would continue to be fulfilled, and for this a reasonable non-European franchise would be a measure of security. Moreover Article VIII of the Treaty of Vereeniging, which precluded the introduction of an African franchise into the Transvaal and the Orange River Colony until after responsible government had been granted to them, had implied that the subject would be dealt with after this change had been effected.[1] Lord Selborne, therefore, suggested that Union was an admirable opportunity for carrying out the reform, and that it should take the form of a suffrage depending upon a civilisation qualification. We have already recorded, in connection with the representation of the four Provinces in the Union Parliament, the compromise which was eventually reached. The inherent difficulty of defining a test of civilisation, and also one which would not disfranchise Cape non-European voters or exclude others who might become possessed of the existing qualifications, caused the idea to be abandoned. In its place the Cape franchise was protected, as we have already stated, by a two-thirds majority[2] of the two Houses sitting together being required for its alteration, while for its extension to the other Provinces only a bare majority in each House sitting separately was necessary. Lord Selborne was able to express his confidence that in default of an agreement by the National Convention to extend it, the Imperial Government would be satisfied

[1] Malan, *Die Konvensie Dagboek*, pp. 47–59, in particular a speech by General Botha. Note that neither the Treaty nor the responsible government constitutions of the Transvaal and Orange River Colony barred a Coloured or Asian franchise.

[2] *Ibid.*, p. 73.

with this solution. Nor did he see reason to suppose that the Imperial Government would object to a limitation of the membership of Parliament to Europeans "as part of an otherwise satisfactory settlement".[1]

Although the Imperial Government regarded the decision of the National Convention on the general subject of the non-European franchise as an important factor in deciding the terms on which it would agree to hand over the High Commission Territories to the Union, there were also other conditions to which it attached so much importance that the Secretary of State for the Colonies informed Lord Selborne that it would be practically impossible to secure the assent of the House of Commons to any constitution which did not include the necessary safeguards. These were designed to preserve the separate identity of the Territories by placing their administration in the hands of the Prime Minister of the Union, advised by a Commission of three members, holding office for a term of years and irremovable except on addresses from both Houses of Parliament. The Governor-General-in-Council was constituted the legislative authority, his proclamations being laid before Parliament for its dissent if it saw fit. The revenues derived from each Territory were to be expended in it, the imposition of differential duties by the Union against them was forbidden, as also was the sale of intoxicating liquors. The alienation of any land in Basutoland, or of any land forming part of the tribal reserves in the Bechuanaland Protectorate and in Swaziland was prohibited. After some negotiation these terms were accepted by the National Convention, and were included in a Schedule of the Act of Union which was to become operative if and when the Territories were transferred.[2]

The Act was readily accepted by the Imperial Parliament in August 1909, in spite of the political colour bar which it contained, which naturally aroused opposition, and against which Schreiner, supported by many influential British, Afrikaner and non-European Cape Colonists, went to England to protest.[3] It came into operation on 31 May 1910, when Viscount Gladstone assumed office as the first Governor-General of the Union of South Africa, and General Botha became the first Prime Minister.

[1] Walker, *de Villiers*, p. 445–50.
[2] *Ibid.*, pp. 455–66.
[3] For the discussion concerning the measure in the Imperial Parliament and Great Britain see *C.H.B.E.* vol. III. pp. 374–5; Walker, *Schreiner*, pp. 320 *sqq.*

CHAPTER XXIV

SOUTH AFRICA AFTER THE UNION, 1910–1921

(a) THE UNION OF SOUTH AFRICA

THE result of the labours of the National Convention was received with genuine satisfaction throughout South Africa. It was confidently believed that the acceptance of a unanimously recommended settlement based on racial equality, at all events as far as concerned the Europeans, would put an end to the age-long struggle of conflicting ideals which had divided the white inhabitants into two antagonistic camps; it seemed, indeed, for a moment that a new spirit had been poured out upon the people; young men saw visions and old men dreamed dreams. But no sooner had the topmost peak of national sentiment been reached than the descent into the plain began. People began to realise that the past had not been obliterated by the magic wand of the National Convention, and that South African human nature remained very much what it had been before the Convention had met. Moreover, the removal of the many practical difficulties in bringing the new constitution into operation demanded more patience, tact and even sacrifice than had been generally anticipated.

The South Africa Act had hardly been passed by the British Parliament before the formation of the first Union Cabinet engaged the attention of the political leaders. The Act did not enter into details regarding the form of government, for the National Convention evidently assumed that the unwritten code and practice of the cabinet system of government, as it obtained under the British Constitution, were sufficiently known and understood in South Africa to be worked successfully if adopted by the Union.

This was assuming too much. True, that system had been in vogue in all four constituent colonies; but Natal's experience of it had been very short (1893–1910) and troubled by war and Zulu rebellion, while the Transvaal and Orange Free State had, as republics until 1900, been governed under a different system.[1] Under their republican constitutions the members of the Executive Council had been appointed, some by the President and the remainder by the Volksraad, for a definite period. They could be removed from office only by resolution of the Volksraad on a charge of misdemeanour or crime. The Executive Council had assisted the President in the government of the

[1] See Bryce, J., *Studies in History and Jurisprudence*; also Kotze, (Sir) J. G., *Documents and Correspondence relating to the Judicial Crisis in S. A. Republic*, 1892–3; Walker, E. A., *Lord de Villiers and his Times*, pp. 287, 316.

country, but unlike the British Cabinet and the United States Federal Cabinet, it had not consisted solely of heads of the great administrative departments, though several officials sat in it, nor had its members been necessarily in agreement either with the President's policy or with each other's.

From 1910 till 1924 the first three Prime Ministers of the Union and some of their most influential colleagues came from the late republics with a much longer and more intimate experience of the working of the republican than of the responsible government system, which they were now called upon to apply. Though the cabinet system did not work badly on the whole, it undoubtedly suffered during the early years of the Union from the want of a due sense of collective ministerial responsibility displayed by some of the Ministers. An instance of this occurred in 1912 when General Hertzog, while remaining Minister of Justice in the first Botha Cabinet, attacked the policy of racial conciliation to which the Prime Minister and his colleagues were definitely pledged. Even as late as 1925 Tielman Roos, then Minister of Justice in the Hertzog Cabinet, publicly expressed himself against the Native policy enunciated by the Prime Minister.

The lingering influence of the republican form of non-party government is plainly discernible in the Provincial constitutions. The members of the Provincial Executive Committees, as we have already seen,[1] are elected by the Provincial Councils for three years by proportional representation, and hence do not necessarily belong to the same political party nor resign office when they have lost the confidence of a majority of their Council. Perhaps this experiment of a non-party executive has not had a fair chance of proving its usefulness, seeing that the political party divisions of the Union have influenced the Provincial Councils from their inception; but it is certainly unpopular, especially in the two larger Provinces, the Cape and the Transvaal, where the Administrators have often exercised the decisive voice in evenly divided committees.

On the other hand the "best man government", which Starr Jameson mooted at the time of the formation of the first Union Cabinet, was not an attempt to introduce the executive system of the late republics.[2] What was intended was nothing more than a coalition Cabinet, consisting of the leaders of the pre-Union colonial majority and opposition parties, during the early formative years of the life of the Union. General Botha, then Prime Minister of the Transvaal and a candidate for the premiership of the Union, did not oppose the idea, but Merriman, Prime Minister of the Cape Colony, his rival for the Union premiership, delivered an address to his constituents at Victoria West in which he scouted the suggestion of a coalition

[1] *Vide supra*, p. 656.
[2] Jameson was knighted in January 1911

government and declared for a Union Cabinet on party lines. This destroyed whatever chance there had been of a "best man government", and when General Botha was called upon to form the first Union Cabinet he selected his colleagues from among the retiring colonial ministers only. This Ministry survived the first general election in September 1910, and General Botha met the first Union Parliament in November with a working majority of eleven votes in the Assembly, or of twenty-two counting in the Natal Independents.

By Article 137 of the South Africa Act it was provided that "both the English and Dutch languages shall be official languages of the Union, and shall be treated on a footing of equality, and shall possess and enjoy equal freedom, rights and privileges". The first definite indication that this enactment had not removed all outstanding difficulties between the two dominant European races was the revival immediately after Union of the controversy, which had centred round the Education Act (1908) passed by the legislature of the Orange River Colony during the short period of its existence.[1] That Act made compulsory both the study of the English and Dutch languages and their use as media of instruction in all Government schools. Though the power to legislate in connection with education, other than higher education, had been definitely assigned in the South Africa Act to the Provincial Councils,[2] the opponents of the principle of language compulsion brought the matter prominently before the public during the first Assembly elections, and when Parliament met, a motion condemning the compulsory clauses in the Education Act of the Orange Free State was tabled by the Opposition. The Prime Minister moved an amendment which was accepted, that a Select Committee be appointed to inquire into any language inequalities and compulsory provisions in the educational laws of the four Provinces, and to make recommendations thereon for the consideration of the Provincial Councils.

Thus it came about that for five months, while Parliament was laboriously engaged in shaping the necessary administrative and financial measures to carry on the affairs of the Union, a matter vital to the peaceful co-operation of the two races was being investigated behind closed doors in a committee room upstairs. The report of the Select Committee[3] was unanimous except for some reservations by one of the members, and was accepted by Parliament as a fair solution of a difficult problem. The Committee recommended that up to and including standard IV (average age of pupils 12 years) instruction should be through the home language, but that parents could claim that the other language be taught as a subject and also be introduced gradually as a second medium of instruction. Above standard IV,

[1] *Vide supra*, p. 643. [2] *Vide infra*, pp. 670.

[3] *Report of the Select Committee on Public Education*, S.C. 2, 1911 (Cape Town).

parents could either choose one language as the sole medium and the other merely as a subject, or both languages as media; but where no such choice was made by the parents, the child was to be instructed through the language best known and understood by him. These proposals were referred to the Provincial Councils, which gave full effect to them in every Province except Natal, where the parents' option of medium was retained in all standards. These education debates had proved that the racial fires were still smouldering; the sequel justified the fears of those who then predicted further trouble.

Ordinary Cabinet crises arising from the conflict of views of political parties on matters of policy are of more or less ephemeral importance. The breaking up of the first Union Cabinet stands however on a different footing as regards both the circumstances which led to it and its far-reaching consequences. Union had been brought about on the crest of a tremendous wave of faith and hope, but the rate of advance was too rapid for large sections of the community. Neither the slow-moving dwellers of the *platteland* nor the inhabitants of the cities, largely absorbed in business, fully realised all the implications of the new departure of co-operation on a national basis of equality as contemplated by the Act of Union, and two occurrences greatly strengthened the forces of reaction.

The first of these was the rejection of the education policy with which the name of General Hertzog had been identified during the short period of responsible government in the Orange River Colony. Though he served on the Union Select Committee above referred to and voted for its findings, he realised that his own policy had been discarded, for he presently sought to explain to the House of Assembly why he would not recommend the acceptance of the committee's findings to the Orange Free State.

As time went on General Hertzog convinced himself that the Afrikaans-speaking section was not getting the full benefit of the principle of racial equality as laid down in the South Africa Act, and that the Botha Cabinet, of which he remained a member, did not sufficiently stress the maintenance of that principle. This conviction found expression in a series of speeches culminating in one at De Wildt in the beginning of December 1912, in which he advocated the "two stream" policy over against the Botha policy of racial conciliation.

In Hertzog's eyes, the official conciliation policy was premature. Only by keeping the British and Afrikaner cultures apart could the latter, as the weaker and less fully-formed of the two, be saved from absorption.

The general tone of the De Wildt speech was interpreted as anti-British by one of the Ministers, Col. Leuchars from Natal, and induced him to tender his resignation. General Hertzog was now faced with the alternative, either of laying his views before the Cabinet and abiding by its decision, or of resigning. But he would do neither the one nor the other, and thus forced General Botha to put his own resignation as Prime Minister in the hands of the Governor-General. Lord Gladstone accepted it and immediately called upon Botha to form a new Cabinet. This he did, leaving both General Hertzog and Col. Leuchars out of the ministry.

After some hesitation General Hertzog drifted further apart from his former colleagues and ultimately found himself at the head of a new party under the name of the National Party, which arose from the clothing of cultural aims with political forms. This new party did not at first show much vitality and at the close of the session of 1914 seemed to be receding into the political background, when there broke over the Union like a thunderclap the declaration of the World War. By an overwhelming majority the Union Parliament decided to support General Botha's policy that the Union should take its full share in the defence of the cause for which the Allies had staked their all; but this decision was not acceptable to those who either were averse to helping the United Kingdom in any way, or who judged that the time had come to retaliate on her for having taken away the independence of the two late republics. The rebellion of 1914 followed, a rebellion whose fundamental cause was fear for the future of the Afrikaner way of life. These happenings greatly strengthened the opposition to the Botha Government and gave new life to the National Party.

Inspired by Tielman Roos, the then leader of the Nationalists in the Transvaal, the National Party carried on a vigorous republican propaganda throughout the war. After the Armistice it obliged Hertzog to lead a deputation overseas to ask for the "complete separation" of the Union from the Empire or, failing that, independence for the two ex-republics or, in the last resort, independence for the Free State alone. In Paris the deputation had an interview with the British Prime Minister, David Lloyd George, who reminded it pointedly that the Union was master of its own destiny. With this tactful rebuff the deputation was fain to be content.

After the signing of the Treaty of Versailles, Generals Botha and Smuts returned to the Union well satisfied that, as a result of the Union's war policy, their country had been raised to a status equal to that of Great Britain in the British Commonwealth of Nations and was recognised as a constituent member of the League of Nations. But General Botha was a dying man and did not live long enough to reap the fruits of his labours, nor long enough to regain the confidence of those who had repudiated his leadership.

The death of General Botha, in August 1919, removed in the eyes of many of his former followers the only obstacle in the way of the reunion of the Afrikaans-speaking South Africans into one political party, and as they considered such a reunion eminently desirable, a determined effort was made to attain the *hereeniging* or reunion of the

South African Party, now led by General Smuts as successor to General Botha, and the National Party under the leadership of General Hertzog. Hence, in September 1920, a congress of delegates from both parties was held at Bloemfontein for this purpose;[1] but the project failed because the Nationalists insisted on an active propaganda in favour of a republic and claimed the right of secession from the British Empire. A month later the Unionist Party, consisting almost exclusively of English-speaking South Africans led by Sir Thomas Smartt, decided to join the South African Party. A general election followed which gave General Smuts a substantial majority, and he proceeded to reconstruct his incomplete Cabinet by taking in three leaders of the former Unionist Party.

Opinion regarding these events was sharply divided. Those who took the racial view of nationalism were loud in regretting the division in the Afrikaner nation, while those who visualised a South African nation composed of all who accepted South Africa as their home, whatever their descent or country of origin, were convinced that the amalgamation of the South African and Unionist Parties was a most hopeful portent.

Although the formation of the Hertzog Government in 1924 as a result of the pact between the National Party and the South African Labour Party belongs to a later period than that with which we are here concerned, it may be pointed out that this coalition of an almost purely Afrikaner party (Nationalist) with a predominantly British political party (Labour) was also calculated to drive politics in the Union away from the racial line, that is as between Afrikaans and English-speaking whites, though in another sense the coalition was racial in that it was very largely directed against competition with non-European workers.

The most difficult administrative, legislative and social problems of the Union arise from the presence and contact of various heterogeneous elements in one community. According to official returns in 1929 the population of the Union consists of four main groups, viz. Europeans, 22·4 per cent; Coloured or mixed, 7·4 per cent; Asians, 2·3 per cent; and Bantu or Africans, 67·9 per cent.[2] Except in the Cape Province and to a very limited extent in Natal, the parliamentary franchise is confined to Europeans, but the Union Parliament is charged with the task of governing the whole population. The principal phases of this important task we must now consider in turn.

During the first twenty years of its existence the Union enjoyed a marked financial and economic success. Notwithstanding the interference caused by the Kaiser's War of 1914–18, the country rapidly developed in all directions, and its credit compared most

[1] *Report of the Hereenigings* (*Re-union*) *Congress* (Bloemfontein, 1920).

[2] *Official Year-Book of the Union of South Africa*, 1929.

favourably with that of the most prosperous member of the British Commonwealth of Nations.

In order to compare the revenue and expenditure of the four colonies in 1908–9 with that of the Union ten years later it is necessary to deduct the income of the railways and harbours from the revenue of the colonies, for under the South Africa Act the railways and harbours are treated as a separate concern of the Union, whose income is not added to the general revenue as was the case before Union.

The revenue figures[1] for the four colonies for the last complete year before Union and of the Union in the year 1920–1, are as follows:

1. Ordinary revenue of the four colonies for the financial year 1908–9, the last complete financial year before Union	£11,661,198	
2. Ordinary revenue of the Union for 1920–1 (excluding interest on Railway Capital)		£25,748,096
Revenue of the four Provinces for 1920–1	£8,079,033	
Less Subsidies from Union	£4,477,996	£3,601,037
Total		£29,349,133

From these figures it will be seen that the ordinary annual revenue of the Union had increased by over 151 per cent during the first eleven years of its existence. Part of this remarkable increase was derived from new taxes imposed during the First World War, but since some of these had been either reduced or repealed by 1921, the expansion of the resources of the country was the principal cause.

The figures for the ordinary expenditure are as follows:

1. Ordinary expenditure of the four colonies for the year 1908–9 (excluding interest on Railway Loan Capital)	£11,421,306	
2. (*a*) Ordinary expenditure of the Union for the year 1920–1 (excluding interest on Railway Capital)	£26,147,624	
Less Subsidies to Provinces	£4,477,996	£21,669,628
(*b*) Expenditure for the four Provinces for 1920–1		£8,417,858
Total		£30,087,486

An increase in the ordinary expenditure of more than 163 per cent in eleven years, as disclosed by these figures, seems in conflict with the confident expectations of those who recommended the adoption of union on the ground that the administration of one Union would cost less than that of four separate colonies. Such sanguine anticipations were not justified, for, not only had the old items of expenditure to increase *pari passu* with the rapid development of the

[1] *Vide Reports of the Controller- and Auditor-General* of each of the four colonies before Union and of the Union: *Cape of Good Hope*, U. 2—1911; *Natal, Times* Printing and Publishing Co., 1911; *Transvaal*, Government Printing and Stationery Office, 1911; *Orange River Colony, Argus* Printing and Publishing Co., 1911; *Union of South Africa*, U.G. 33—1922.

country, but the Union as a modern state was called upon to exercise many new functions of encouragement, control and regulation of various kinds of social and economic undertakings. No doubt elder statesmen, and in especial Merriman, were horrified at this departure from the old policy of *laissez-faire* of the days when states were supposed to exceed their proper functions if they went beyond the maintenance of law and order and the preparations for war; but it could not be otherwise, and the new activities had to be financed. Moreover, the outbreak of the First World War upset all the calculations of the pre-Union economists. The increase in pensions in 1919–20 over that in 1911–12, largely due to the payment of war pensions, alone amounted to £1,081,539, and in 1920–1 war bonuses of £1,922,082 were paid as against nil at the time of Union.

The increase in railway expenditure 1920–1 when compared with 1908–9 (from £9½ million to £28¼ million) is principally due to the opening of new lines, to heavier traffic with resultant increase in train mileage, to improved rates of pay, to allowances and general conditions of service granted to the staff, to the increased cost of material and to the additional provision made for depreciation. During the same period railway and harbour revenue increased from £10½ million to £27¼ million, so that the surplus of £1 million in 1908–9 was converted into a deficit of £1¼ million in 1920–1.

The strength of the financial position of the Union further appeared from the fact that notwithstanding the heavy expenditure incurred in connection with the First World War, the permanent debt of the Union was increased by less than £50 million during the first eleven years of its existence. The permanent debt of the Union at its inauguration was £109,336,834 and by 31 March 1921 it had risen to £158,359,541, an increase of £49,022,707.

The total expenditure on loan services during the same period amounted to £84,298,635, showing that over £35 million was obtained without addition to the permanent debt. The explanation is that the Union Loan Fund is regularly credited with large contributions from gold-mining leases, *bewaarplaats* leases, sales of Crown land, etc. ("*Bewaarplaats*" is the name given to land proclaimed under the Transvaal Gold Law, but which is not open for pegging.[1])

It may be of interest to note that the war expenditure of the Union, including the suppression of the rebellion of 1914, was from loan funds £32,173,094 and from revenue vote £5,839,461, giving a total of £38,012,555.

It will thus be seen that about 34 per cent. of the total loan expenditure was utilised for the war, and that over 15 per cent of the

[1] "Bewaarplaatsen" were defined under the Gold Law of 1898 as areas reserved from prospecting and digging and were roughly classified as: (*a*) localities used for public purposes or urban habitations; (*b*) sites on or near mines used for surface working; (*c*) water rights.

war expenditure was met out of current revenue. The remainder of the loan expenditure (66 per cent) went into loans for railways and harbours, irrigation schemes, advances to the Land and Agricultural Bank, housing loans and other reproductive undertakings.

Prior to the Union the British Government was responsible for important duties in connection with the defence of South Africa, in particular for the coast fortress defences of the Cape Peninsula and Durban. The Union Government from its inception held that the people of the Union should themselves undertake the defence of their country. To enable them to do so effectively the Defence Act of 1912 was passed. As the sequel showed, this step was taken none too soon.

The system laid down in that Act is based on the citizen army of Switzerland modified in accordance with the military tradition, experience and requirements of the Union. There was to be a small Permanent Force of 2500 Mounted Police with its own batteries of field artillery supplemented by a citizen-army organised more or less on the Swiss model. In time of war, every citizen between the ages of seventeen and sixty was to be liable to serve personally in the defence of his country "in any part of South Africa whether within or outside the Union". It would be for Parliament to say whether non-Europeans should be called upon to bear arms; meanwhile, European men were to be organised. Some 50 per cent of the white citizens between the ages of seventeen and twenty-five, say 25,000 in all, were to enrol in Defence Force regiments, descendants of the old volunteer organisations, either as volunteers or, in default, as conscripts chosen by lot on a district basis. During each of those four years, they were to drill regularly and put in a short period of continuous training. The rest were to join more free-and-easy Rifle Associations, virtually the commandos traditional to the countryside, making their own rules and, subject to ministerial approval, choosing their own officers. In grave emergencies, the Royal Naval Volunteer Reserve might be sent to serve with the Royal Navy anywhere, while the Cape and Durban Garrison Artillery and Fortress Engineers were to co-operate with their imperial opposite numbers, who still manned the forts at Cape Town, Simonstown and Durban.

Hardly had the organisation contemplated in the Defence Act been formed when the Kaiser's War broke out. The Union Government was able to inform the British Government promptly that if it desired to withdraw its troops from South Africa, the Union would be prepared to undertake its own land defences. This offer was readily accepted. The imperial infantry sailed for England immediately; the artillery were withdrawn early in 1916, and in 1921 the Minister of Defence on a visit to London agreed with the British Government that the Imperial Military Command in South Africa should be finally abolished. At the same time the Union ceased to pay the contribution to the Navy which had been originally granted by the Cape Colony and Natal in 1898, and undertook to furnish its own coast defence batteries and mine-sweepers. The British Government generously handed over to the people as a free gift all its land and buildings in the Union actually required for defence purposes, except, of course, the naval dockyard at Simonstown. The use of this small but vital dockyard was guaranteed to the King's ships at all times under the protection of Union batteries.

When the National Convention was considering the powers of the Provincial Councils, it provisionally decided that in view of its national importance education should be left to the Union. But on reviewing the results of its deliberations, the supporters of federation, as opposed to unification, found that comparatively minor functions had been assigned to the Provincial Councils, and they insisted on the reversal of the decision regarding education. This led to a compromise, the temporary and experimental nature of which is clearly reflected in section 85 of the South Africa Act, which provides that the Provincial Councils may make ordinances in relation to "Education, other than higher education, for a period of five years and thereafter until Parliament otherwise provides".

Since the South Africa Act does not define the term "higher education", a working definition had to be adopted on the establishment of the Union Education Department. It was decided that all education beyond the matriculation standard should be so regarded, this term being understood in the conventional sense derived from the well-known matriculation examination of the University of London which is taken at about the age of sixteen. The definition, however, gave rise to serious anomalies and difficulties, e.g. the institutions for the training of teachers were dealing with matriculated as well as non-matriculated students, and the institutions known as "industrial schools", erected for the care of waifs and strays and children committed by a magistrate under the Children's Protection Act, were being financed and administered by the Union. By an Act passed in 1925 the Union became responsible for the maintenance of all industrial and trade schools, those formerly under the control of the Provincial Administrations having been taken over as from 1 April 1925.

Higher education in the sense of education beyond the matriculation standard has made very rapid progress under the Union. The history of higher education in South Africa begins with the founding of the South African College in Cape Town in 1829, but it was not until 1858 that a Board of Public Examiners was established in the Cape Colony. Fifteen years later, in 1873, the University of the Cape of Good Hope was incorporated as an examining body on the model of the University of London as it then existed. This Cape Colony institution acted as the recognised authority on higher education for the whole of South Africa for more than fifty years. From 1897 the Orange Free State and Natal were represented on the University Council and in 1902 the Transvaal also joined it. With all its defects as a purely examining university, it served the needs of the time, and all attempts to form a teaching university for the training of students and for research failed for want of financial support or on account of geographical difficulties.[1]

Stimulated by the generosity of the late Alfred Beit, Sir Julius Wernher and Sir Otto Beit, who promised £500,000 for the erection of a teaching university on Rhodes's estate at Groote Schuur near Cape Town, provided the money was utilised before the end of 1916, the Government introduced a Bill in 1913 to found a federal university with headquarters at Groote Schuur. The suspicion and active opposition of the existing colleges, scattered over the whole Union, proved too strong for the adoption of this new proposal, while all the colleges, with the exception of the South African College, were as yet too weak to undertake the responsibility of becoming separate teaching universities. Another solution of the difficult problem had therefore to be devised; it was only after repeated efforts, supported by the enquiries of a Commission, that in 1916 success was attained.[2]

The scheme ultimately adopted provided for the founding of three universities: (*a*) the University of Cape Town, with which is incorporated the South African and Diocesan Colleges; (*b*) the University of Stellenbosch (formerly the Victoria College); and (*c*) the University of South Africa, a federal university consisting of six constituent colleges, two in the Cape Province, two in the Transvaal and one in the Orange Free State and Natal respectively. An additional College at Potchefstroom was incorporated in 1921 in the federal university, while the institutions at Johannesburg and Pretoria, hitherto members of that university, became full teaching universities in 1922 and 1930 respectively.

With five universities for a European population of less than two million there was danger that the competition for students between these universities might lead to the lowering of the standard of attainment, and that the multiplication of the faculties and the overlapping of facilities may result in wastage and inadequate financial support. But, in spite of this danger, it has to be admitted that the founding of these institutions has had a stimulating effect on the intellectual life of the Union, apparent not only in the great increase in the number of students, the expansion of the teaching staffs and the provision of magnificent educational buildings, but also in the deepening of public interest in education and the advance in all

[1] See Malherbe, E. G., *History of Education in South Africa*, 1652–1922. Also Walker, E. A., *The South African College and the University of Cape Town*, 1829–1929.

[2] *Report of the University Commission*, U.G. 42 of 1914.

fields of scientific research now being carried on at the universities.

Turning to higher education for non-Europeans, we may note that in 1905 the Inter-Colonial Native Affairs Commission recommended "that a central Native college or similar institution be established and aided by the various states, for training Native teachers, and in order to afford opportunities for higher education to Native students". However, the scheme did not become practicable till the founding of the Union. In 1914 the draft constitution of such a college was finally adopted and it was established as the South African Native College at Fort Hare in the Victoria East district, Cape Province. The Government of the Union made the College an annual grant, and since October 1923 it became eligible for the receipt of grants in aid of higher education on the same footing as similar institutions for Europeans. The College, which was ultimately to provide a liberal education of university standard, made steady progress and served in a measure to satisfy the reasonable aspirations of the non-European peoples of the subcontinent. Fort Hare was presently affiliated to Rhodes University, Grahamstown. This association resembled that of the University of Natal, whose centre is at Pietermaritzburg, but which had European and non-European sections in Durban. The "open" Universities of Cape Town and the Witwatersrand (Johannesburg) imposed no academic colour bar, but have latterly been compelled to fall into line with the racially exclusive and Afrikaans-medium Universities of Stellenbosch, the Orange Free State, Pretoria and Potchefstroom. Separate ethnic colleges, including Fort Hare, are now being provided for non-Europeans.

Primary and secondary education are administered by the Provinces. For the first few years after the Union the Provinces were financed from the Union Treasury, but in 1913 the Financial Relations Act was passed providing for a subsidy from Union funds of one-half of the ordinary annual expenditure of the Provinces. This provision, generally known as the "pound for pound" principle, undoubtedly encouraged the Provinces to spend liberally and, as time went on, more liberally than the Union could agree to, so that certain limitations as regards contributions towards the annual increase in expenditure had to be introduced. In 1925 Parliament made radical changes in the Financial Relations Act, *inter alia* substituting for the pound for pound basis of contribution an annual subsidy to each Province based on the number of European pupils in average attendance at primary and secondary schools.

In practice the application of the language-medium provisions of the law referred to above[1] has led to the establishment of parallel classes or, alternatively, of separate English- and Afrikaans-medium schools. The choice between these two systems largely depends on

[1] *Vide supra*, p. 664.

the number of pupils. Broadly speaking, the settlement has worked well by ensuring the spread of bilingualism among the rising generation, and thereby creating a better understanding between the English- and Afrikaans-speaking sections of the community.

The following figures indicate the progress of school education since the Union:

	No. of schools			No. of scholars				
Year	For European scholars	For non-European scholars	Total	Europeans	Non-Europeans	Total	No. of teachers	Normal State expenditure £
1910	3873	1999	5872	163,257	136,000	299,257	10,912	1,597,062
1926	4707	3408	8115	330,762	289,545	620,307	22,274	7,186,269[1]

From these figures it appears that whereas the number of scholars increased during the first sixteen years of the Union by 113 per cent, the state expenditure increased by 350 per cent, or more than three times as rapidly as the number of students. This disparity is accounted for mainly by four causes: (1) the betterment of the salary scales of teachers; (2) the provision of school facilities in the more sparsely populated parts of the Union, necessarily an expensive undertaking; (3) the introduction of the study of natural science, agriculture and housewifery in the curriculum of the schools, and (4) the increase of the inspectorate and the introduction of medical inspection of scholars.

The peace of the rapid progress of industrial life during the early years of the Union was unfortunately marred by considerable unrest and strife. Organised labour in the form of trade unionism had made its appearance in South Africa as early as 1881. These organisations, led by able and vigorous leaders from overseas, soon showed that they had come to stay and were determined to improve the conditions of European labour in the Union. The employers generally were not prepared to recognise these trade unions; hence, in time there followed conflicts and strikes. The Union was altogether unequipped to cope with these difficulties. Parliament had as yet not provided the machinery necessary to deal with industrial disputes, and what was even more ominous, the majority of its members, being totally unacquainted with industrial problems, were unsympathetic towards trade unions and their methods.

The Witwatersrand, with its extensive gold-mining industry, is generally recognised as the industrial storm-centre of the Union.

[1] The state expenditure in 1926 as between European and non-European scholars was as follows:

	Expenditure £	Cost per Scholar £ s. d.
European	6,358,852	18 18 7
Non-European	794,036	2 14 1

It should be noted that virtually all European children go to school; the majority of the non-Europeans do not.

There are to be found the ablest trade union leaders, while the peculiar conditions under which that industry is carried on favour the sudden development of dangerous industrial upheavals. The whole population of the Witwatersrand extending from east to west over a distance of some 60 miles, including Johannesburg, is practically dependent on one industry, namely gold-mining. If anything goes wrong in this industry, the whole Rand community, and indeed all South Africa, is vitally affected directly or indirectly. A more varied industrial centre can face a strike in any one industry with comparative equanimity, for while one of its activities may be temporarily paralysed, there are others in operation. A miners' strike on the Witwatersrand, however, is of the nature of a general strike.

Moreover, the labour force of the mines consists of white miners and Native workers in the proportion of about 1 to 10. The white miners are the skilled workers and supervisors. When the Union was established the majority of them were from overseas. They were well organised and ably led. Their trade union directed its energy mainly in two directions: to improve the pay and working conditions of the white miners and, as a corollary, to protect the position of the white miner by insisting on the maintenance of the colour bar, i.e. the provision that only white miners should be allowed to do skilled or semi-skilled work in the mines. A strike of white miners therefore means that some 300,000 Native workers on the mines automatically also become unemployed. To have so many Natives idle in the compounds creates a position fraught with difficulty and danger. To allow them to break away and wander aimlessly over the countryside is to court disaster. To keep them in the compounds both fed and occupied involves great expense, while to send them home means not only the cost of transportation, but also serious delay in restarting the mines when the strike is called off. And any attempt to continue mining operations with the Natives alone would only tend further to inflame the passions of the strikers, for the Natives would be regarded not merely as strike-breakers, but also as doing skilled work, which is zealously guarded as the prerogative of the white miner.

Industrial upheavals on the Rand marked the years immediately preceding the First World War.[1] The first of these strikes was in 1907, the second in May 1913. On the latter occasion, after a strike of their European miners had continued for a considerable time, the management of the New Kleinfontein Mine decided to take on new miners and to restart the mine. This led to a sympathetic strike on the other mines. The question at issue was really that of the recognition of trade unions. Johannesburg was soon filled with a seething mass of dissatisfied miners, who congregated there from all parts of the Rand,

[1] *Report of Judicial Commission* on Witwatersrand Industrial Disturbances, U. G. 55, 1913; also *Returns of Convictions under Martial Law*, Jan. 1914, U. G. 6, 1914; *Report of Economic Commission*, U. G. 12, 1914; *Return of Outrages . . .*, Jan. 1914, U. G. 8, 1914.

while the lawless hooligan element present in every mining centre was only too ready to take advantage of the unsettled state of affairs. Things became so serious that the Government was forced to intervene in July, and Imperial troops, the only forces available at that time, were obliged to fire on the crowd. In the end, it was agreed that the strike be called off on condition that the New Kleinfontein Mine should take the strikers back. Government provided some £48,000 to compensate displaced strike-breakers, and, after a judicial enquiry, recognised the trade unions and promised various remedial measures.

It was generally felt that this only meant a truce and not peace. An active propaganda was started by the railways and harbours employees' organisation. This introduced another dangerous element and made the position more critical. All the railways in the Union are state-owned and under one management. In the absence of navigable rivers and canals, and at a time before the advent of motor-lorries and aeroplanes, the large centres of population were dependent for their existence on the smooth and regular running of the train service. A railway strike therefore meant the stoppage of all mechanical transport, and the starving of many thousands should it continue for any length of time.

In January 1914 the storm broke. The Natal coal-miners struck in December 1913; the railway workers came out on strike on 8 January 1914, and the gold-miners were then worked up to the sympathetic-strike pitch by the most violent and outrageous speeches. This time the Government acted promptly. The recently established Union Defence Force was called up to assist in maintaining law and order, and the ringleaders who had overstepped the bounds of what was considered justifiable propaganda were arrested. The strike collapsed and Smuts deported nine of the leaders without trial.

The deportation of these men without trial was severely criticised by the Judges, Parliament and the Imperial authorities. The defence of the Government was that, under the existing law of the Union, the acts of which these ringleaders were accused were not crimes for which the common law made adequate provision. At last, with much difficulty, an Act of Indemnity was carried, the law was altered to deal with such cases, and the deportees were allowed to return within nine months, shortly after the outbreak of the First World War. An end was thus put to an unfortunate episode.

These events, as well as several further strikes in other industrial centres, deeply impressed the public mind and the legislature. Parliament was asked by the Minister of Mines and Industries, F. S. Malan, not only to pass measures enabling the Government to deal effectively with disturbances of the peace, but also to enact remedial legislation providing the necessary machinery both for the prevention of industrial disputes and for dealing with them should they unfortunately occur. These measures were not all immediately acceptable to Parliament, which had still to be educated up to the necessity of dealing sympathetically with labour organisations; but step by step the necessary measures were passed to provide the Union with an up-to-date industrial code modelled largely on corresponding legislation in Great Britain. Among these measures may be mentioned: the Workmen's Compensation Act (1914); the Miners' Phthisis Acts (from 1912 onwards); the Workmen's Wages Protection Act (1914); the Factories Act (1918); the Juveniles Act (1921); the Apprenticeship Act (1922), which repealed a previous Act of 1918, and the Industrial Conciliation Act (1924). The Union could thus claim to possess industrial laws as up-to-date and effective as those of any other country.

These measures are now administered by a separate Labour Department, more especially the application of the principle of the round-table conference of representatives of both employers and employees as embodied in the Conciliation Act. Their cumulative effect revolutionised the whole industrial outlook, and for the six years 1924–30 the Union became a very peaceful country from the industrial point of view, though in 1926 the so-called "Colour Bar Act" aroused fierce political controversy.

Notwithstanding this industrial unrest the development of the secondary industries in the Union has been remarkable. No doubt the isolation of the Union during the First World War from the large manufacturing centres, caused by the interference with shipping, compelled it to look to its own resources. Some of the industries that thus sprang into life during that period showed no vitality and disappeared when peace was declared, but the majority of them survived. Fostered by a policy of protection, which seeks to encourage local secondary industries without unduly handicapping the two primary industries of agriculture and mining, they spread in all directions. Many large oversea firms found it to their advantage to establish branch factories in the Union, which meant a welcome accession of capital as well as of technical knowledge and experience.

The policy of the Union with regard to immigration is based on the principle that each Dominion is master of its own destiny and therefore has the power to determine who shall be allowed to settle within its borders. The power of excluding immigrants is exercised even with regard to British subjects from other parts of the Commonwealth, and was freely recognised at the Imperial Conference of 1911. While welcoming desirable immigrants and assisting them to obtain land for settlement, the Union has so far not adopted any scheme of state-aided immigration.

The Immigrants Regulation Act of 1913 was passed to regulate the entry of newcomers. Certain classes of persons denominated *prohibited immigrants* may be excluded or even extruded from the country, or their residence may be circumscribed as to time and in other respects. Amongst such classes are persons who have been convicted of serious crimes; persons of ill-fame; the insane and diseased, including those who suffer from tuberculosis or are otherwise physically afflicted; persons likely to become a public charge, and in some cases illiterate persons. Further, by section 4 (1) (*a*) of the Act, the Minister of the Interior is empowered to certify as prohibited immigrants persons or classes of persons whose presence for economic or certain other reasons is considered undesirable. This clause has also been used to prevent the Union from being flooded by immigrants from eastern Europe at a time when the labour market was already unable to absorb the available local supply, and recent legislation (1929) has severely restricted immigration from the countries of eastern Europe by means of a quota. With regard to the immigration of Asians, South Africa, as we saw in earlier chapters, has had considerable experience of immigration from India and China, and is determined to prohibit any further immigration from Asia. In deference to the susceptibilities of the Governments of Eastern nations their people are not excluded by name.

By the provisions of the Immigration Act of 1913 the movement of Asians is restricted to the Province in which they are resident.[1] Except in the Cape Province, where Indians who possessed the necessary qualifications might be registered as parliamentary, provincial and municipal voters, Indians possessed neither the parliamentary nor the provincial vote. In 1924–25 Natal forbade their further enrolment on its local government electoral lists.

The passing of the Immigration Act in 1913 was the occasion for the Indians of Natal, led by a prominent Johannesburg barrister, Mohandas Gandhi, to start a passive resistance movement.[2] About 2700 Indians commenced a march to the Transvaal. Some 500 were detained on the border by the Natal police; the others continued their long tramp to Johannesburg until they were ultimately stopped and transported back to Natal. Negotiations followed between the Union Government and Gandhi, as a result of which an amending Act, providing for the recognition of Indian marriages and the abolition of the £3 poll-tax imposed on Indians by Natal before the Union as an inducement to their repatriation, was enacted. Gandhi soon afterwards departed for India.

[1] In 1921 the number of Indians in the Provinces and the Union was as follows:

	Total numbers	Born in South Africa
Cape	6,498	2,630
Natal	141,336	93,767
Transvaal	13,405	5,853
Orange Free State	100	73
Total for the Union	161,339	102,323

[2] *Vide supra*, 646.

Thus ended the passive resistance movement of 1913, but the vexed question of the relation between the Indians and European inhabitants of the Union was not thereby finally settled. As the competition of the Indian trader became more accentuated a persistent agitation was initiated among the Europeans of the Transvaal and Natal for a policy of ultimate repatriation, and in the meantime of their restriction for residential and trading purposes to prescribed areas within the municipal boundaries.

In 1924 a Class Areas Bill was introduced to set aside bazaars for Asians in towns where necessary, before the Bill could be dealt with a change of Government took place. Hertzog's new Nationalist-Labour Pact Government revived the Bill with slight amendments. The Indians received this proposed legislation with open hostility, and a deputation from the Government of India gave evidence before a Select Committee to which the matter was referred. The Committee reported in favour of the postponement of the further stages of the Bill pending the report of a reciprocal Union deputation to India.[1] As a result of the investigations of these deputations and the good offices of the imperial authorities, the Governments of India and the Union arranged for a Joint Conference in the Union to explore every possible avenue in order to arrive at a satisfactory solution of the Indian problem. The Conference met in Cape Town in December 1926, and an agreement was arrived at which was accepted by both Governments.[2] The main provisions of this agreement can be summarised as providing for: (1) the voluntary repatriation of Indians, the Indian Government co-operating by making suitable arrangements for their reception in India; (2) the advancement by the Union of the social and educational interests of those who decide to remain in the Union; and (3) the appointment by the Indian Government of an Agent[3] in the Union in order to ensure continuous and effective co-operation between the two Governments.

The problem of the relations between the European and the Native inhabitants of the Union is usually spoken of as the "Native question"—though it is also as much a European question. People still speak of a "solution" of the Native question; but no summary solution is possible, and it is necessary to think of the reply to the question in terms of a continuous adjustment and readjustment of relations, particularly in the fundamental matters of the occupation of land, employment and political representation.

In the Transvaal the squatting of Natives on privately owned farms, many of which are held by absentee speculators or companies for the sake of their mineral rights, has been a subject of contention for many years. The chief objections to squatting are that the lands so occupied

[1] *Report of Select Committee on Areas Reservation, Immigration and Registration (further Provisions) Bill*, S.C. 9, 1926.

[2] *Official Year Book of the Union*, p. 894 (Pretoria, 1929).

[3] Afterwards a High Commissioner.

remain undeveloped and become practically unauthorised Native locations, which seriously interfere with the occupation of the neighbouring land by Europeans. In the Orange Free State, again, a system of Native farming based on sharing the produce with the European owner of the land was at the time of the Union becoming more and more common, bringing with it all the disadvantages of the squatting system.

To the chronic dissatisfaction arising from these causes another was added shortly before the Union. In republican days of the Transvaal and the Orange Free State a Native was prohibited from holding in his own name any interest in land outside the tribal reserves. Something of a shock was caused in the Transvaal after the annexation, when the Supreme Court decided that the law on which reliance was placed for this prohibition did not effect its purpose. As soon as the Union was fairly in being, legislation was introduced to deal with these problems.

The Natives Land Act of 1913 purported to deal with the ownership and occupation of land by Natives and persons other than Natives, throughout the Union, on the basis of dividing the country into areas in which Natives only can acquire land or any interest in land, and other areas open only to persons other than Natives. Provision was further made for the appointment of a Statutory Commission to recommend, after due enquiry, where the dividing lines should be drawn. In the meantime the *status quo* as regards the ownership and occupation of land respectively by Natives and by persons other than Natives was to be maintained, while existing Native reserves were carefully scheduled in the Act. Until Parliament should make other provision, a discretionary power was given to the Government to allow a departure from the *status quo* in individual cases.

Those who assumed that this Act laid down the principle of land segregation for the Natives throughout the Union were soon to be disillusioned, for the Appellate Division of the Supreme Court decided that section 8 of the Act, which provided that nothing in the Act contained shall deprive the Native in the Cape Province of his political rights, excluded that Province from the operation of the Act. The occupation of land being one of the qualifications for the franchise in the Cape, the Court held that to apply the provisions of the Natives Land Act to the Cape Province would deprive the Natives of one means of acquiring the franchise.

A further difficulty in connection with the land segregation policy arose when the land had to be demarcated into Native and non-Native areas. The Commission reported in 1916, and in the following year General Botha introduced a Bill to give effect to its recommendations;[1] but the Bill, on being referred to a Select Committee, met with such determined opposition from the Europeans that it had to be

[1] *Report of Natives Land Commission*, vol. I, U.G. 19, 1916; vol. II, U.G. 22, 1916.

withdrawn. Local committees were then appointed to revise the recommendations of the Statutory Commission.[1] These furnished their reports in 1918, but again, and for the same reasons, no definite action was taken.[2]

Pending the enactment of legislation demarcating the areas, the Government freely used the discretionary power given to it in the Act of 1913 by allowing transactions whereby Natives were to acquire, by purchase or lease, land or an interest in land in areas recommended for Native occupation by one or other of the local committees. Thus some relief was afforded by administrative action from the rigidity of the Act of 1913, "until Parliament should make other provision".

The expression "colour bar" is normally applied to the exclusion of the non-Europeans and, more especially, Africans from any skilled or semi-skilled work. This prohibition had its origin on the goldfields of the Witwatersrand as a safety measure in connection with blasting operations underground. The dangerous nature of this part of mining, and the Africans want of knowledge in the use of explosives, led to the introduction by the Transvaal Republican Government of a mining regulation stipulating that blasting underground can only be performed by a qualified white person. Gradually, as the power of the Miners' Union increased, a tendency developed to extend this prohibition to other classes of skilled work, and to use it not so much as a safety measure, but as a protection for the employment of the more highly-paid white labour.

This was the position at the time of the Union. No legal colour bar existed in any Province other than the Transvaal. The Mines and Works Act, passed in 1911 to regulate the working and inspection of mines, works and machinery throughout the Union, gave to the Minister of Mines power to frame regulations (*inter alia* for the safety of mining operations). In accordance with this provision the old colour bar regulation of the Transvaal republican days was continued, though it was doubtful whether the Act covered a regulation of that nature. For a long time no one thought it worth while to test the legality of this regulation in Court, because it was well known that it was sanctioned by custom and the influence of the Miners' Union irrespective of the provisions of the law.

During the First World War a large number of white miners enlisted for active service, and, by consent, some latitude was then permitted so that non-Europeans might do semi-skilled work, like drill-sharpening, underground. When the war was over the attempt of the Miners' Union to go back to the *status quo ante* gave rise to a good deal of friction, which may be considered as one of the contributing causes of the great upheaval on the Witwatersrand in 1922.

[1] *Reports of Local Natives Land Committees*, Cape Province, U.G. 8, 1918; Orange Free State, U.G. 22, 1918; Natal, U.G. 34, 1918; Eastern Transvaal, U.G. 31, 1918; Western Transvaal, U.G. 23, 1918.

[2] Provision for additional Native lands was made, in a measure, by Act 18 of 1936.

Ultimately the legality of the colour bar regulation came to be tested in court, with the result that it was declared *ultra vires.*[1] After the change of Government in 1924 the Minister of Mines introduced the Colour Bar Bill, which legalised the old Transvaal colour bar regulation in so far as it applied to Africans but not to other non-Europeans, and enabled the Government by regulation to extend the new prohibition to all classes of skilled work throughout the Union. The Bill was most strenuously fought by the Opposition and rejected by the Senate. Reintroduced in the following Session, it was finally put on the Statute Book by a joint sitting of both Houses in accordance with the provisions of the South Africa Act (1926).

The Mandate and the Beginning of Civil Administration in South-West Africa

Article XXII of the Peace Treaty of Versailles created three classes of mandates. South-West Africa was placed in category (C) as a territory which "can be best administered under the laws of the Mandatory as integral portions of its territory".[2] Before the Peace Conference broke up, the Principal Allied and Associated powers agreed to confer this mandate upon the King "to be exercised on his behalf by the Government of the Union of South Africa". The final step in connection with the vesting of the mandate in the Union Government was the definition by the Council of the League of Nations, in accordance with the Peace Treaty, of "the degree of authority, control or administration to be exercised by the Mandatory". This document of seven short clauses adds little to the provisions of the Peace Treaty;[3] it was signed at Geneva on 17 December 1920.

After the surrender of the German forces in South-West Africa to General Botha on 9 July 1915, the territory was administered under martial law by an Administrator. By an Act of the Union Parliament in 1919 the exercise of the mandate was vested in the Governor-General, who by proclamation in 1921 delegated his powers to the Administrator. This was the beginning of civil administration. The Administrator now possessed the power of legislation by proclamation and controlled every form of governmental activity in the territory, except the railways which were placed under the direct control of the Union Department of Railways and Harbours. This form of autocratic government came to an end in 1925 by the passing of a Union Act providing for the creation of an Executive Committee, an Advisory Council and a Legislative Assembly.[4]

[1] Rex *v.* Hildick Smith, *S. A. Law Reports, Transvaal Provincial Division*, 1924.

[2] See *C.H.B.E.* vol. III, 657.

[3] *Official Year-Book of the Union of S.A.*, p. 979 (Pretoria, 1929).

[4] This Act is largely based on the *Report of a Commission on the future form of Government of South-West Africa*, appointed in 1921, U.G. 24, 1921.

Article CXXII of the Peace Treaty gave the Union full discretionary power to repatriate all the German nationals in the territory. The Government decided, however, to leave them undisturbed, unless there were special reasons to the contrary. In 1924 the South-West Africa Naturalisation of Aliens Act was enacted by which the Germans who remained were declared to be British subjects, unless they signified in writing that they were not desirous of being naturalised. Out of a total of 3489 persons who were eligible 3228 accepted British citizenship.

The insistence of the German inhabitants on retaining German as the medium of instruction in schools attended by their children caused some difficulty, until a concordat was concluded between the German and the Union Government, as a result of which thirteen of the seventeen elementary German schools were transferred to the Administrator.[1] The general principle of the concordat is that the transferred schools are to be financed by the Administrator and to retain German as the linguistic medium up to the end of the elementary course. All scholars above standard I are to receive a daily lesson in a Union official language, as chosen by the parents. This language becomes the chief medium of instruction after standard VI, when the pupils have attained the age of 14.

Thus, by 1921, the Union had already begun to achieve a *modus vivendi* with the Europeans of the mandated territory. The Natives remained, but it was only after this date that the Union was faced with the first real test of its fitness to discharge the chief of its duties as a mandatory.

(*b*) Southern Rhodesia: 1898–1924

The story of early explorations, of first contacts with the Mashona and Matabele, and of international competition for the lands between the Limpopo and Zambesi is told elsewhere in this volume. Here we are concerned to follow the development of Southern Rhodesia from 1898 to 1924, and to examine the conflict and co-operation of the principal parties involved: the British South Africa Company, the European settlers, the Imperial Government and the indigenous Africans with their missionary friends and champions. The struggle between the settlers and the Company for the control of the government and resources of the new territory supplies the dominant theme for the period, but the treatment and position of the African majority is important at every stage, and it is essential to keep constantly in mind the decisive events between 1890 and 1898 when the broad pattern of African and European land rights was determined, when the status and rôle of Africans was settled for years to come and when the foundations were laid for a new political, economic and social order.

[1] *Administrator's Report for the Year* 1921, U.G. 32, 1922.

Granted the "all-mastering thought that drove" Cecil Rhodes and the genuine idealism which inspired many who helped him to acquire his "North", the occupation of Mashonaland and the conquest of Matabeleland were marked by little of the "careful regard" for Native laws and rights which was expressly enjoined by the Royal Charter and early Orders-in-Council.[1] In the quest for gold to rival the riches of the Witwatersrand, the Pioneers and other frontiersmen did not scruple to destroy tribal institutions, to seize land, cattle and other "loot",[2] and to impress Africans for their labour needs, thus arousing the resentment which found violent expression in the uprisings of 1896/7. Yet constructive things were done in the crude foundation years, and no double standard of morality is required to pay tribute to the redeeming courage, generosity and personal leadership of Rhodes, qualities which endeared him to conquered warriors and disgruntled settlers alike. Rhodes it was who, unarmed, treated long and patiently with Lobengula's successors in their boulder-strewn Matoppo stronghold, and Rhodes it was who spent freely to compensate settlers for their losses during Rhodesia's "blackest hour".[3] It was Rhodes too who hastened the building of an ambitious network of railways and other communications, and who sought constantly to provide civic amenities for his tiny frontier community.

Sir Alfred Milner, the High Commissioner, was appreciative of Rhodes's generosity. During his 1897 visit to Southern Rhodesia he did not hesitate to stress its value in writing to Joseph Chamberlain: ". . . Treasury principles would starve Rhodesia—that is one great reason for keeping the Company up." But Milner found little to approve on the administrative side: "I am dead against any attempt to rip up the past, but, between ourselves, it is a bad story." In stating that the rebellion was largely due to the exercise of power by unfit people, Milner endorsed the findings of the recent Commission of Enquiry into the Native administration of the British South Africa Company,[4] and he concluded his report by declaring: "There will have to be a new Order-in-Council." In the body of his letter the High Commissioner had outlined the central provisions for the new constitutional instrument,[5] all of which were duly incorporated into the Southern Rhodesia Order-in-Council, 1898.

The principal innovations under the new constitution were the

[1] *Statute Law of Southern Rhodesia* from the Charter to 31 December 1898, pp. 3–13, *The Charter*, 29 October 1889, Article 14. See also pp. 15–18, the *Order-in-Council of 9 May 1891*, Section 4; and, pp. 21–31, the *Matabeleland Order-in-Council, 18 July 1894*, Sections 23–4, 27–8, 44–54.

[2] The reference is to paragraph 7 of Dr Jameson's "Victoria Agreement", 14 August 1893. Full text is given in Appendix A, pp. 92–92A, to the Privy Council Report, 1918, *vide infra*; substantially the same text is given in Harris, J. H., *The Chartered Millions*, pp. 82–3.

[3] Hole, H. M., *The Making of Rhodesia* (1926), p. 365. Several Europeans accompanied Rhodes to the Matoppos.

[4] *Report by Sir R. E. R. Martin, K.C.M.G., on the Native Administration of the British South Africa Company together with a letter from the Company commenting upon that Report. C–8547, 1897.*

[5] *The Milner Papers*, vol. 1, South Africa, 1897–9, pp. 139–46.

reservation of real and substantial powers to the High Commissioner, the creation of a Legislative Council with a representative element, at first comprising a minority of elected members, and the close regulation of Native affairs. To ensure that the High Commissioner was provided with information of the kind required for a proper exercise of his powers a Resident Commissioner was appointed with a seat but no vote in the legislature. This imperial officer took precedence after the Administrator and was thus assured of adequate seniority. Control of the police, an echo of the Jameson Raid, and supervision of African interests were made the most significant imperial concerns. Milner himself took a hand in the drafting of the Native Regulations, which were proclaimed in November 1898 in amplification of the already substantial Part V (Native Administration) of the new Order-in-Council.[1]

A new era of steady progress appeared to be open to Southern Rhodesia after the 1898 reforms; but, if there was now the prospect of a decent government for which Milner had worked, there was not to be the peace for which he hoped. In 1899 the South African War broke out to make great demands on the patriotic settlers, and to check grievously the development of the territory. To heighten depression, Cecil Rhodes died shortly before the Peace of Vereeniging ended the long and bitter struggle in 1902. Where there had been robust leadership and generous support to quieten misgivings and to assuage loss, there was now uncertainty and confusion among both settlers and Africans. Despite his "De Beers" approach to his vast new country as a whole, and his unorthodox methods of diplomacy and administration, Rhodes had been no less important to the Imperial Government. For Directors and shareholders too, the ending of the Rhodes era of direct personal control came as a shock; where hitherto they had been content to repose trust in a confident helmsman, the Company was now rudderless.[2]

Faced with the prospect of governing Charterland from remote London, the Directors sought guiding principles to substitute for empirical on-the-spot leadership, and commissioned Sir George Goldie, with a wealth of experience and achievement in Nigeria, to visit Rhodesia in 1904 on their behalf. But the milieu and history were vastly different from those of Nigeria, and Goldie failed to devise an acceptable scheme. The settlers were particularly incensed by his proposal that they should assume responsibility for the greater part of the administrative deficits incurred by the Company in the past. They were no less unhappy about the mining laws, which gave the

[1] *The Statute Law of Southern Rhodesia* (from the Charter to 31 December 1898), pp. 32–55. *The Southern Rhodesia Order in Council, 1898* (Part V, Native Administration, pp. 51–4), pp. 166–72, High Commissioner's *Proclamation* and *Schedule of Native Regulations*.

[2] On Rhodes see Walker, E. A., *Lord de Villiers and his Times, South Africa 1842–1914* (1925), pp. 491–2, and Williams, B., *Cecil Rhodes* (1938).

Company an undue share of hard-earned winnings, and the Company's claim to the ownership of the unalienated lands of the territory. "Administrative deficits" and "unalienated lands" were long to provide fruitful material for dispute and debate between Company and settlers, thus underlining Henri Rolin's acute diagnosis of the *contradiction interne* at the core of the being of a Chartered Company.[1] Saddled with governmental responsibilities to settlers well able to speak for themselves, and with commercial liabilities to equally critical and long-suffering shareholders, the administration had no easy task. The proddings of those concerned for the proper exercise of trusteeship towards the Africans were less urgent and insistent, but these too added their quota of harassment.

The confusion of the post-war years was brought to an end in 1907 when the Directors issued a Declaration of Policy,[2] at the heart of which was the decision to concentrate on the exploitation of the land resources of the territory by the encouragement of European settlement in the unalienated lands, especially in the areas adjoining the railways. Largely in consequence of this new policy, the European population, 12,600 in 1904, increased from 14,000 in 1907 to 23,600 in 1911. By 1907 there had come general recognition that the gold of Southern Rhodesia was present only in the modest amounts predicted by Sir James Bryce[3] and Milner rather than as portrayed in the early extravagant brochures of the Company; hence, with fewer limitations on their activities, the independent miners were allowed to play that more whole-hearted part in the production of the gold which made a significant contribution to economic development. But it was to land that the attention of the Company now turned, and until 1918 the Directors were confident that the unalienated areas were their private asset.

However, it was in 1908 that the Irishman, Charles Coghlan,[4] was first elected to the Legislative Council, and in the same year this new leader, who eventually was to approach the stature of Rhodes in the estimate of his fellows, gave effective voice to the settlers' views and pressed for Imperial arbitration on differences between the Company and the settlers. Coghlan's forensic ability had impressed the visiting Directors in 1907, and it was soon plain to all that in his rejection of the Company's claim to treat the unalienated lands as their own commercial asset, as well as in his powerful advocacy of the electors' case in other matters, the settlers had found a champion of great ability and integrity. In the course of his future career Coghlan was to meet and hold his own with men like Churchill, Smuts, Milner, Jameson and Drummond Chaplin in his successful endeavours to establish responsible government.[5]

[1] Rolin, H., *Les Lois et l'Administration de la Rhodésie* (1913), p. 167.

[2] *British South Africa Company*, Annual Report, 1907.

[3] Bryce, J., *Impressions of South Africa*, 3rd ed. (1899), pp. 270–2.

[4] Coghlan was born in King Williamstown.

[5] Wallis, J. P. R., *One Man's Hand, The Story of Sir Charles Coghlan and the Liberation of Southern Rhodesia* (1950).

Coghlan entered a legislature in which, in fulfilment of a promise by the visiting Directors, the nominated official element had been reduced. From their minority position in the first Council the settlers' representation had advanced, numerically, through a phase of parity, from 1903–7, to a majority position, which later, from 1914, became substantial when twelve, then thirteen, elected members faced six officials of the Company administration. Executive and financial power remained with the Company, but the settlers, led by Coghlan, constituted a formidable opposition whose views could not be ignored. Coghlan went with the Administrator, Sir William Milton, and Sir Lewis Michell as one of Southern Rhodesia's representatives at the National Convention, 1908–9, the assembly which framed the constitution of the Union of South Africa, from which Rhodesia remained apart, though the constitution provided for the possible future incorporation of the Company's territories;[1] it was Coghlan, again, who led the successful opposition to Dr Jameson's scheme to amalgamate the two Rhodesias (Southern and Northern) during the First World War. Coghlan was sympathetic to Southern Rhodesia's eventual political association with the "White South" rather than the "Black North", and in this he shared Milton's view of Southern Rhodesia's ultimate destiny; but to him it was essential first to resolve the conflict with the Company and to gain the freedom of choice and action which responsible government would confer.[2]

The land dispute provided the crucial constitutional and economic issue[3] and, with the twenty-five year period of the Royal Charter drawing to its end, it was to the land question that Coghlan returned early in 1914, when he drove through the Council a resolution asserting that the unalienated land of Southern Rhodesia was public property, not a private asset of the Company. In 1913 the settlers had rejected a not unreasonable land settlement scheme presented by Sir Starr Jameson, now President of the Company, and it was plain that a determination of the land dispute was essential in the interests of all parties. Thus, following the Legislative Council's resolution, the question of the ownership of the unalienated lands was in July 1914 referred to the Judicial Committee of the Privy Council with the support of the Crown, Company and settlers alike. Meanwhile the Colonial Office and the Company had reached agreement on the appointment of a commission to examine the Native reserves and to investigate African land needs. The Native Reserves Commission reported finally

[1] *South Africa Act*, 1909 (9 Edw. 7. Ch. 9), Section 150.

[2] Wallis, J. P. R., *One Man's Hand; vide supra*, pp. 100–109 and 141–5. For background see also Walton, E. H., *The Inner History of the National Convention of South Africa* (1012), especially pp. 17–30; *South African National Convention, 1908–09, Minutes of Proceedings and Annexures (Selected)*, pp. v–vi; Brand, R. H., *The Union of South Africa*, pp. 85–6; Walker, E. A., *Lord de Villiers*, p. 487 *sqq.*; Long, B. K., *Drummond Chaplin, vide infra;* Walker, E.A., *A History of Southern Africa, vide infra*, pp. 525–8, 555–8, 594–9.

[3] Birkenhead, Earl of, *Famous Trials of History*, 4th ed. (1926), pp. 207–15, the Southern Rhodesian Land Case.

in December 1915, and early in 1917 the Colonial Office informed the Directors that the Imperial Government had decided to accept its recommendations as a whole.[1]

The First World War (1914–18), in which Rhodesians of all races participated and in which white Rhodesians made an exceptional sacrifice, helped to delay the Judicial Committee's report and to bring respite in the constitutional struggle. In the face of many imponderables the settlers had agreed to a limited prolongation of Company rule; hence, in 1915 a Supplemental Charter was issued. This provided for the ten-year extension of Company government which had been made permissive by the original Charter; but this extension was made subject to the important proviso that, if at any time thereafter an absolute majority of the whole number of the members of the Legislative Council should pass a resolution praying the Crown to establish responsible government with supporting evidence to show that "the condition of the territory, financially and in other respects" justified this form of government, the Crown could accede to such prayer.[2] Thus was opened to the settlers of Southern Rhodesia the way which had been followed successively by the Cape Colony and Natal and, more recently, after Milner's departure in 1905 and the triumph of Campbell Bannerman's Liberals in 1906, by the Europeans of the Transvaal and Orange River Colony (Orange Free State).

On 29 July 1918 the Land Case was decided. Contrary to the Company's confident predictions, the settlers' main contention was upheld. So far from recognising that the unalienated lands were the commercial asset of the Company, the Judicial Committee of the Privy Council held that they comprised the public property of the Crown for whom the Company had acted as agent throughout the years. The Privy Council decision disappointed the champions of African interests, who had incurred large costs by engaging counsel to present the African claim to the unalienated lands and whose case was summarily dismissed, but the decision was not unwelcome to the other parties. For the Company, in particular, there was solace in the further opinion of the Judicial Committee that it was entitled to be reimbursed for administrative deficits necessarily and properly incurred during its years of agency.[3] In November 1918 the Company submitted a substantial claim to the Secretary of State, Walter Long, demanding interest on the money expended and making evident its desire for an early settlement.

[1] *Papers relating to the Southern Rhodesian Native Reserves Commission*, Cmd. 8674—1917.

[2] *The Statute Law of Southern Rhodesia* (from 1 January 1911 to 31 December 1922), pp. 36–8, *Supplemental Charter*, 2 March 1915.

[3] *In the Privy Council: Special reference as to the Ownership of the Unalienated Land in Southern Rhodesia*: Report of the Lords of the Judicial Committee of the Privy Council delivered 29 July 1918 [78] [141–308]. The Order-in-Council of 2 August 1918, containing the bare findings of the Judicial Committee, is given in *Statute Law of Southern Rhodesia* (1911–22), pp. 50–1; but see rather the full report with annexures of cases and counter-cases, with supporting documents.

In July 1919 Viscount Milner, now Secretary of State for the Colonies, appointed a Commission under Viscount Cave to assess the amount due to the Company as if its administration had been determined on 31 March 1918. The Company claimed £7,866,117; the Cave Commission, reporting on 15 January 1921, made an award of £4,435,225, rejecting the demand for interest. An additional sum was to be paid to the Company for the public works and buildings taken over by the new Government, but from the total there was to be deducted the value of lands which the Company had made over to itself for its own commercial purposes, and of those which it had granted in exchange for considerations other than cash. To determine the latter sums, the Cave Commission advised an independent valuation.[1]

The subsequent financial negotiations between the settlers, Company and Colonial Office were protracted and heated, and they exerted considerable influence on the constitutional struggle, especially after the intrusion of the "South African factor" discussed below. It is helpful, nevertheless, to draw together in one compass those elements of the financial issue relevant to the settlement which was finally reached only on the very eve of responsible government. The Colonial Office held that the new Territorial Government should meet the cost of the public buildings and movable assets acquired by the Company for administrative purposes, a principle which was not disputed by the settlers, though they questioned the Company's valuation of the buildings and sought impartial arbitration. The Colonial Office also proposed, following one of the alternative courses suggested by the Privy Council, that the outstanding sum due to the Company should be met from the sale of unalienated lands and, thereupon, recommended the appointment of a Crown Land Agent to supervise such sales.[2] There was, at the time, a reluctance on the part of His Majesty's Ministers to confront Parliament with the Privy Council's other proposal, namely that the Company be paid from British public funds.

To the Company, which had hopefully anticipated an immediate cash settlement, the proposed means of payment was deeply offensive, all the more because it felt that there would be indefinite postponement of the outstanding land questions by officials "impervious to the losses and inconveniences, caused by delay, which weigh with the ordinary litigant". The Company, therefore, submitted a Petition of Right in an endeavour to force the hand of the Imperial Government. Meanwhile pressure had arisen from another direction. In Southern Rhodesia deadlock gripped a legislature in which the elected mem-

[1] *Papers Relating to the Commission appointed to take an account of what would have been due to the British South Africa Company if the administration of Southern Rhodesia had been determined on 31st March 1918: Correspondence and Report*, Cmd. 1129—1921. See also *Minutes and Proceedings*, in continuation of Cmd. 1129—May 1918.

[2] *Draft Letters Patent*, Section 48, Cmd. 1573—1922.

bers, after a sharp budget clash with the Company's Treasurer, refused to vote supply. Nevertheless, in face of the widespread demand for self-government, the Imperial Government felt compelled to act. £3,750,000 was offered to the Company in full settlement of its claims, £2,000,000 of which was to come from the future Southern Rhodesian Government by 1 January 1924, together with the £300,000 which had been loaned by Milner's instrumentality in 1922 and 1923. In return, the unalienated lands, public works and buildings were to be transferred to the new Government of Southern Rhodesia. These conditions were promptly accepted and acted upon.[1] Thus ended a prolonged and acrid triangular controversy, which had been at times marked by a most bitter sense of grievance, but from which a saving humour had rarely been absent.

It is no easy task to attempt judgment on the financial controversy, let alone to hold in correct perspective the various political cross-currents and the many claims and counter-claims which were made, involving, as they did, even the war funds which had been expended heedlessly in a common cause. In the light, however, of the Privy Council's pointed stricture on the repeated failure of those responsible for Rhodesian affairs to define the respective rights of the parties engaged in the Company enterprise,[2] it is difficult to absolve successive Imperial Governments from a charge of neglect of the interests of its own citizens, as well as those of the peoples of Southern Rhodesia. The best defence is, perhaps, to be found in a comment of the Company's Administrator, Sir Drummond Chaplin, that "Rhodesian affairs cannot be the constant concern" of the Government of a great imperial nation. As to the charges of persistent parsimony on the part of the United Kingdom between 1918 and 1923, in sharp contrast to the generous treatment of the Transvaal and Orange Free State after 1902, there is the fact that Britain had been bled white by the First World War, and also the important fact that, at the last, the British taxpayers did duly perform their "appointed function".[3] In the event the Company emerged not unprofitably from the long-drawn financial encounter.[4]

[1] *Rhodesia: Correspondence regarding a proposed settlement of various outstanding questions relating to the British South Africa Company's position in Southern and Northern Rhodesia.* Cmd. 1914—1923. See also Cmd. 1984—1923: *Agreement between the Secretary of State for the Colonies and the British South Africa Company*, 29 September 1923, in continuation of Cmd. 1914; *Letters Patent providing for the constitution of Responsible Government in Southern Rhodesia*, 1 September 1923, Sections 48–9; *Statute Law of Southern Rhodesia*, 1923, Act No. 2, Southern Rhodesia Specific Loan Act.

[2] *Privy Council Report:* "In matters of business reticences and reserves sooner or later come home to roost. In 1894 a single sentence, either in an Order-in-Council or in a simple agreement, would have resolved the questions which have for so many years given rise to conflicting opinions . . .."

[3] Walker, E. A., *A History of Southern Africa* (1957), pp. 595–9.

[4] The Company retained large land holdings and the mineral rights as well as its control over the railways. For a sympathetic presentation of the views of principal Company and settler protagonists see Long, B. K., *Drummond Chaplin* (1941), pp. 242–9, 264–83; and Wallis, J. P. R., *One Man's Hand*, pp. 159–62, 170–2, 190–3, 215–18.

As Chaplin had predicted, on hearing the verdict of the Privy Council, the Company soon inclined to an early termination of their governmental responsibilities in order to be free to concentrate upon their specific commercial assets. The settlers were no less eager to assume control of affairs and, in May 1919, they hastened to ask Milner what evidence was required "financially and in other respects" to prove Southern Rhodesia's fitness for responsible government. The Secretary of State counselled caution and delay. He could not yet regard the territory as equal to the financial burden of responsible government and there was too "the important question arising out of the small number of White, as compared with the native population".[1] The General Election of 1920 enabled the settlers to make a spirited reply, for twelve of the thirteen successful candidates were pledged to secure immediate responsible government. In May 1920 the elected members again approached Milner. Again he advised delay, though he now made evident his approval of the principle of responsible government, provided that a sound constitution could be devised. No man knew better the dangers of a *solvitur ambulando* approach to the problems of the multi-racial societies of Africa, and the need for great care in the planning of political constitutions.[2] When, however, the settlers protested once more, it was Winston Churchill, Milner's successor and one of six Secretaries of State in the last decade of the Charter, who took command of the Rhodesian negotiations.

A committee under Lord Buxton, the recently retired Governor-General and High Commissioner in South Africa, was appointed in March 1921 to consider when and with what limitations, if any, responsible government should be granted to Southern Rhodesia. In May 1921 Buxton reported to Churchill advising a speedy end to the "present anomalous state of affairs". A responsible government constitution on the lines of that of Natal in 1893 was recommended and it was urged that a detailed scheme should be submitted to a referendum for outright acceptance or rejection by the electorate.[3] Churchill, however, now had other views. As a consequence the settlers were offered, not a straightforward vote on self-government, but a choice between responsible government or that entry into the Union of South Africa, which Milner and the Buxton Committee had noted was provided for by the South Africa Act of 1909. Smuts, Prime Minister of the Union, was in a precarious political position and would have welcomed the support of the settlers to whom he made the offer of generous representation and favourable economic development

[1] There were, in 1921, estimated to be 761,790 Africans of Southern Rhodesian origin and 100,529 aliens. The Europeans numbered 33,620.

[2] Worsfold, W. B., *The Reconstruction of the New Colonies under Lord Milner 1902–1905*, II, 260–1, quoting letter from Milner to Alfred Lyttelton, 21 February 1904.

[3] *First Report of Committee appointed by Secretary of State for Colonies to consider certain questions relating to Rhodesia:* Cmd. 1273—1921.

terms,[1] while the Company was attracted by the prospect of rewarding treatment in respect of the Rhodesian railways and other assets.[2]

This new challenge to the advocates of responsible government was formidable, for the issues raised were such as to cause deep heart-searching among honest men. Coghlan, like Rhodes, was from the Cape and was aware of the close bonds of history, kinship, law and trade which drew the peoples of South Africa and Rhodesia together, and he felt responsibility and concern for the course of political events in South Africa where rising nationalism and disruptive labour movements were threatening the whole compact and promise of Union. Chaplin, an able Administrator with a capacity for disinterested analysis, had no doubts about the desirability of entry into the Union, although in 1910 he had been firmly opposed to the "British" community in Southern Rhodesia losing its individuality in this way.[3] However, Chaplin now saw eye to eye with Smuts, and helped the latter to conduct an intensive personal campaign during his visit to Rhodesia. There were many who were attracted by the prospect of economic security which the Union offered, yet Coghlan and his followers remained firm to the end and chose not to surrender their identity. At the referendum in October 1922 the vote for responsible government was 8774 and for Union 5989, the substantial majority including the solid core of Rhodesians who shared with Coghlan all that was implied in his cry of "Rhodesia for the Rhodesians, Rhodesia for the Empire".[4]

The end of the long years of struggle was now at hand and generosity marked the concluding arrangements. Cordial messages from the Crown and Imperial Government wished well to the newly-annexed "Colony of Southern Rhodesia",[5] a full part at last of the King's dominions, and Sir Drummond Chaplin greatly facilitated the transfer of power. Wracked or no by internal contradiction, the Chartered Company had acquired Rhodesia and laid the foundations of the new order which had been unhesitatingly adjudged better than the old by the Judicial Committee of the Privy Council. On 1 October 1923 the new constitution was brought into being under the first Governor, Sir John Chancellor, and in April 1924 the seal was set on Sir Charles Coghlan's premiership by an overwhelming victory in the first general election under responsible government, when his Rhodesia Party won twenty-six of the thirty seats in the Legislative Assembly.

[1] *Inter alia* Rhodesia, with its small electorate, was offered ten seats in the Union House of Assembly, with the promise of increase, while at least £500,000 per annum would be guaranteed for the development of railway and other services.

[2] £6,836,000 was offered for the Company's "public" assets, including the railways; the Company to retain the mineral rights, and its immediate commercial holdings.

[3] Long, B. K., *Drummond Chaplin*, pp. 150 and 263.

[4] Walker, E. A., *A History of Southern Africa*, pp. 595–9, contains a valuable analysis of the Union or Responsible Government issue.

[5] 12 September 1923, see *Statute Law of Southern Rhodesia* (1923), pp. 11–12, the *Southern Rhodesia (Annexation) Order-in-Council* (1923).

Economic development after 1902 was steady, if very modest. There were more years of deficit than surplus, but revenue rose from £500,000 in 1903 to £1,500,000 twenty years later, while the deficit shrank to reasonable size as the years advanced. Minerals constituted the most important products, with gold far more valuable than all others combined. From 1903 onwards, after the Company had substituted a royalty system for its earlier attempt to dominate the companies which had alone been permitted to operate, the number of small workers increased so fast that, from 1907 onwards, the value of gold produced usually varied between £2½ to £3½ million per annum. Asbestos, chrome, coal and copper were also important, though their annual values were not above £500,000, save in the case of asbestos after 1920; there were, moreover, other minerals such as silver, lead, arsenic, mica and diamonds which made welcome additions to production. Maize, tobacco and cattle proved to be the most valuable agricultural and pastoral products, and after 1907 there was a substantial increase in the acreages under plough and pasture. Maize was first exported overseas in 1909, but the output was limited until the First World War provided a sharp stimulus, which also led to greater production of tobacco and to a marked increase in cattle herds and the improvement in breeding stock.[1] The fact that the Company paid no dividends before 1923 is an index of the lack of easily tapped sources of great wealth, and the data collected by various official cost-of-living investigators reveal the hardships which the small European population often endured in a remote region where amenities were few and railway charges high.[2] But the limited nature of the resources which were readily available on the new frontier was not an unmixed burden; the territory was spared the turbulence of Kimberley or the Witwatersrand, and a hardy and self-reliant community of patriotic white Southern Rhodesians gradually took shape. The generous bequests of Rhodes and Alfred Beit did much to solve educational problems and to supply some of the essentials of social and cultural life, while professional and technical officers of the administration undertook basic surveys and experiments of enduring scientific value.

The African economic contribution in labour, taxation, crops and cattle was always substantial, though few Europeans recognised its true magnitude and significance, while fewer still appreciated the nature of their own impact on African society or were overmuch concerned about their responsibilities for the government of Africans.[3]

[1] *Official Year Book of the Colony of Southern Rhodesia:* Statistics and General Information, No. 1, 1924. See also *Official Year Books*, Nos. 2–4, 1930, 1932 and 1952.

[2] *Southern Rhodesia: Report of Cost of Living Committee 1913.* (Chairman, Sir Edgar Walton). See especially comments on prices of town stands, pp. 14–16, 65; cost of building, pp. 16–20; high railway rates, p. 65.

[3] *British South Africa Company: Memoranda by H. Wilson Fox*, vol. III, Memorandum on

Like their forerunners in the older territories of European settlement in the south, as elsewhere in the world, they were preoccupied with ensuring for themselves adequate lands, with ample scope for possible future needs, and a sufficiency of labour. Labour and land certainly provide the main themes of European thought on Native affairs in the pre-1923 era, as indeed they were to do in the years after responsible government. With these very human and understandable, if dangerously self-centred, preoccupations uppermost in the minds of the settlers, it is important to examine the structure of government erected in 1898 and its working in regard to Africans.

Save for the Resident Commissioner, the imperial watch-dog, there was no special representation of African interests in the Legislative Council or the Executive Council, and it is unfortunate that the head of the Native Department was never accorded a seat among the official members so as to establish a tradition of direct local concern for the affairs of Africans at the heart of government at a time when few, if any, Africans were themselves capable of participating in a Western-type parliament. This was a step which was duly recommended by the Native Affairs Committee of Enquiry (1910–11),[1] and it is evident from an analysis of the debates on Native affairs that the presence of an informed officer would at least have prevented the repetition and entrenchment of major errors and misconceptions about African life. That there was real value in the Imperial Resident Commissionership is plain from that officer's successful halting of the endeavours of a united legislature to increase Native taxation during the slump which followed the South African war;[2] but though Southern Rhodesia was thereby possibly spared an uprising comparable with that of Natal in 1906,[3] the Resident Commissioner could scarcely intervene to protest or to invoke the High Commissioner and Secretary of State's power of disallowance on every occasion when African interests were disregarded or taken too little into account. The need for such robust and vigorous intervention seems clear today from the records of the statements and attitudes of the territory's early legislators, commencing from the first session of the first Council when the first move was made to abrogate the Africans' franchise rights inherited from the parent Cape Colony, and when other ill-considered

Problems of Development and Policy, 1910, contains an appraisal of the African rôle in economic life.

[1] *The Native Affairs Committee of Enquiry, 1910–11*, paras. 173 and 176. This committee was set up, with wide terms of reference, following a resolution in the Legislative Council. It had available the considered views of a conference of Superintendents of Natives convened in 1909 as well as the findings and recommendations of the inter-colonial South African Native Affairs Commission 1903–5 (Cmd. 2399—1905), which had included Rhodesia within its survey.

[2] *Southern Rhodesia: Correspondence relating to the Native Tax Ordinance, 1903; A2—1904.* See also *Legislative Council Debates:* 3rd Session, 2nd Council (1904), pp. 45–55.

[3] See Stuart, J., *A History of the Zulu Rebellion, 1906* (1913), and Natal Native Affairs Commission, 1906–7.

proposals on Native taxation and labour recruitment were put forward.[1]

Milner had insisted that the greatest care be taken in the recruitment and control of Native Commissioners; indeed, after 1898, there was a marked improvement in the quality of these, as of other, administrative officers. Many men with established reputations in the Cape and Natal Services came north to reinforce the Native Department, notably competent linguists from Natal, who, under the Chief Native Commissioner, Sir Herbert Taylor, introduced a number of the protective, if paternalistic, ideas and measures with which they were familiar.[2] The fact that the Native Commissioners were themselves protected under the 1898 Order-in-Council was important in that the more responsible and far-seeing of them could frankly express their views on vital issues, though the substance of power resided always with the central administration, with whose opinions on African affairs the settlers and their representatives were normally at one.

Land policy, perhaps the most vital issue, provided a major test of the efficacy of the safeguards of African interests. It is instructive, therefore, to examine the conflict between Company and settlers, Native Commissioners and missionaries, with the Imperial Government as intermittent arbiter. After the Matabele-Mashona rebellion of 1896/7, save for the remote and arid Shangani and Gwaai Reserves in Matabeleland already delimited in 1894,[3] Native reserves were roughly demarcated and confirmed by executive order in 1902, but their precise definition and formal safeguarding by means of Order-in-Council was to be delayed until 1920.[4] Meanwhile disputes were to rage over their size and suitability. In the event, though the advocates of African interests made significant gains, the balance undoubtedly lay with the Company and settlers. The total area of the reserves was pared down and there was no adequate fulfilment of the injunctions of early Orders-in-Council and the terms of reference of the Native Reserves Commission to ensure a sufficiency of water supplies and other natural resources. Nor could there be such fulfilment unless there was wholesale disregard for interests established after 1894, for, as the Native Reserves Commission and the Privy Council

[1] *Legislative Council Debates:* 1st Session, 1st Council (1899), pp. 3, 8, 12. See also *Report of Select Committee appointed to consider the System of Native Administration, 1899*, especially paras. 3 and 10.

[2] Rhodes's "Glen Grey" principles were accorded much lip-service and possibly provided a goal for policy in Rhodesia, but, as in Natal, little was done to implement the land and local government provisions central to the Cape Colony's Glen Grey Act of 1894. *Vide supra*, p. 558.

[3] *The Statute Law of Southern Rhodesia* (*From the Charter to December 31st 1898*), pp. 21–31; *The Matabeleland Order-in-Council, 1894*, Part IV, Land Commission; and Report of Land Commission, under Mr Justice Vintcent, dated 29 October, 1894.

[4] *The Statute Law of Southern Rhodesia* (from 1911–22), pp. 56–69. *The Southern Rhodesia* (*Native Reserves*) *Order-in-Council* (1920). This Order was incorporated into the Responsible Government Constitution Letters Patent, 1923 (Section 42 (1)).

acknowledged, "the rights and the system under which Southern Rhodesia has been since administered were in all essentials settled then".[1] The crucial question of African land rights outside the reserves had to await a decision till the early years of responsible government, though the segregationist intentions of the settlers were made plain beforehand, notably in their negotiations with Churchill.[2]

The labour abuses of the early years were largely mitigated after the rebellion, and Native Commissioners and industrial inspectors took care to regulate employer-employee relations, and, further, attempted to ensure reasonable attention to the needs of workers, especially of the many migrants from within as well as from without the borders. They were not always able to hold the balance, for not only were European artisans afraid of African competition and successful in enforcing their exclusive practices, but few employers engaged in precarious ventures in town and country were prepared to admit the Natives' right to, or need for, social cohesion, family stability, economic independence, education and welfare. Yet, while African traditions and values were neglected, to erode apace,[3] Africans learned much in the process and, fortunately, there were never wanting convinced Christians of all denominations to identify themselves with the African cause, and to bring to individuals and communities a powerful new integrating philosophy filled with purpose and hope.[4] The achievement of missionary educational and other endeavour was not to be generally apparent until after the Second World War (1939–45), but its firm foundations were laid in Chartered Company days by the successors of those courageous missionaries of an earlier age, Gonzalo da Silveira[5], Robert Moffat,[6] and David Livingstone.[7]

The Buxton Committee was inclined to agree with those who were satisfied with the latter-day Native administration of the Company and the race attitudes of the settlers, rather than with the severe critics who arose in force during the last years of the Charter;[8] but they nevertheless concluded that in the responsible government constitution there "should be somewhat strict reservations on behalf of the natives of Southern Rhodesia". These reservations, in many ways similar to

[1] *Privy Council Report;* see also *Native Reserves Commission*, Interim Report, para. 21, on difficulty "owing to the fact that so large an amount of the best land in the country was in the first days of the occupation alienated to syndicates and private individuals". On syndicates, etc., see Bertin, H., *Land Titles in Southern Rhodesia* (1912).

[2] *Southern Rhodesia: Report of the Land Commission* (1925), C.S.R. 3/1926, para. 41.

[3] See *Native Affairs Committee* (1910–11), and *Annual Reports of the Chief Native Commissioner(s)*.

[4] See especially references to Fr. Richarts, S.J., in Native Tax debates, 1904; Andrews, C. F., *John White of Mashonaland* (1935), and Cripps, A. S., *An Africa for Africans* (1927).

[5] *Vide supra*, pp. 94, 308, 409, and James Brodrick, S. J., *The Progress of the Jesuits* (1946), pp. 205–6.

[6] Wallis, J. P. R. (ed.), *Matabele Journals of Robert Moffat*, 2 vols. (1945).

[7] *Vide supra*, p. 409.

[8] Harris, J. H., *The Chartered Millions: Rhodesia and the Challenge to the British Commonwealth* (1920); *Southern Rhodesia: Correspondence with the Anti-Slavery and Aborigines Protection Society relating to the Native Reserves in Southern Rhodesia* (in continuation of Cmd. 8674—1917), Cmd. 547—1920.

those of 1898, were duly incorporated in the draft Letters Patent, and were accepted by the settlers in 1922, so to become part of the foundation law of the colony of Southern Rhodesia.[1]

In Northern Rhodesia, meanwhile, forces similar to those south of the Zambesi were beginning to stir. European settlers—ranchers, farmers and miners—were inspired by southern example to dispute the Chartered Company's title to the unalienated lands, while they otherwise challenged the administration and demanded an effective voice in affairs. Yet there could be no solution comparable with that of Southern Rhodesia, for the settlers were very few, the area vast and, in the words of the Buxton Committee, "Northern Rhodesia has no essential homogeneity either in population, geographical features, or history".[2]

The time-span of Company action before the Crown assumed responsibility for the government of Northern Rhodesia was much the same as that in Southern Rhodesia; but, from 1891 until 1911, when the separate administrations of North-Eastern and North-Western Rhodesia were fused,[3] and indeed until 1924, the Charter lands of the north were held in reserve while the southern estate was developed. The lead, zinc and vanadium brought the railway north in 1906 to Broken Hill, from whence it was extended to the Belgian Katanga in 1910; pioneer European farmers took up their holdings mainly along the line of rail, but also in the north-east at Fort Jameson and Abercorn; nevertheless, development was strictly limited, and only a handful of Company administrators were deployed throughout the territory, which was viewed then, as for years afterwards, principally as a labour reservoir.[4] Missionary and imperial endeavour, the latter aided by direct contributions from Rhodes, had also made secure the vital north-eastern sector of British Central Africa;[5] the achievement of H. H. (later Sir Harry) Johnston in contriving to establish a regime of law and order of benefit not only to Nyasaland but to North-Eastern Rhodesia was of the greatest significance.[6]

[1] *The Statute Law of Southern Rhodesia* (1923), pp. 12–32, *Southern Rhodesia Constitution*, see especially Sections 28; 39–47 (relating to native administration).

[2] *Second Report of the Committee appointed by the Secretary of State for the Colonies to consider certain questions relating to Rhodesia*, Cmd. 1471—1921, para. 18. In 1921 there were estimated to be 3634 Europeans and 979,704 Africans in Northern Rhodesia. (1911: 1497 Europeans and 821,063 Africans.) Among the Africans seventy-three different tribes and thirty different dialects have been distinguished, but there are three principal tribes, Lozi (Barotse), Bemba and Angoni, and six main language groups. The area, 285,130 square miles, is nearly twice that of Southern Rhodesia. Swamps, marshes, and deep valleys dissect and divide the land and make communications difficult.

[3] The *Northern Rhodesia Order-in-Council, 1911*, united the territories previously administered under the *Barotseland–North-Western Rhodesia Order-in-Council, 1899*, and the *North-Eastern Rhodesia Order-in-Council, 1900*.

[4] *Report of the Commission Appointed to Enquire into the Financial and Economic Position of Northern Rhodesia* (*Chairman Sir Alan Pim*). Colonial No. 145—1938. This report contains a valuable economic history.

[5] Hanna, A. J., *The Beginnings of Nyasaland and North-Eastern Rhodesia, 1859–95* (1956).

[6] Oliver, R., *Sir Harry Johnston and the Scramble for Africa* (1957).

Northern Rhodesia's direct involvement in von Lettow's campaigns during the War of 1914–18[1] helped to deepen its personality, while the Company's wartime attempts to unite the Rhodesias heightened a sense of distinctiveness among the Northerners, notably the Europeans, for Barotseland remained insulated by its treasured treaty,[2] while the Bemba, Angoni and other peoples saw little beyond their tribal horizons, notably the need to safeguard their ancestral lands from European penetration.[3] Thus it was the European settlers who applied the political spur to the administration, and this mainly after 1917 when an Advisory Council of five elected whites was constituted. In 1920 a petition was presented which demanded adequate information on revenue and expenditure and draft legislation. This petition was sympathetically received by the Secretary of State, but the whole question of the constitutional future of Northern Rhodesia was understandably referred to the committee responsible for advising on Southern Rhodesia.[4]

The Buxton Committee would have preferred that the dispute between the settlers and the Company over unalienated lands and administrative deficits be settled by the Judicial Committee of the Privy Council, and they acknowledged that the different circumstances attending the establishment of Company rule in Northern Rhodesia made it possible that argument on behalf of the Africans might reveal them to be the owners of the unalienated lands; but the Committee was at the same time firmly of the opinion that the termination of Company control should be effected simultaneously in both Rhodesias.[5] Hence, in view of the protracted and costly legal proceedings recently experienced in the case of Southern Rhodesia and the subsequent disputes, it is not surprising that it was decided to include Northern Rhodesia in the "Devonshire Agreement" of 29 September 1923.

Under this agreement the Company abandoned its demand for reimbursement of the administrative deficits and its more ambitious land claims, but retained substantial land as well as mineral rights.[6] The mineral rights, extending throughout Northern Rhodesia,

[1] *Vide infra*, p. 754.

[2] *Vide supra*, p. 546; Hailey, Lord, *Native Administration in the British African Territories*, Part II (1950), p. 80.

[3] *Ibid.* pp. 75–168. This section on Northern Rhodesia supplies detail on tribal land and administrative policy.

[4] The petition is printed as Appendix I to the *Buxton Committee's Second Report*, Cmd. 1471—1921.

[5] Cmd. 1471—1921. See especially paras. 10–12 and 17–19 in which the committee stresses the desirability of a court hearing for all interests and a binding legal decision on the many obscure and complex questions, and para. 15 in which it is urged that the Company administration be wound up simultaneously in both Rhodesias.

[6] Cmd. 1914 and Cmd. 1984 of 1923. *Vide supra*. The administrative deficits were estimated at £1,660,000. The Company retained a half-share in land sales in North-Western Rhodesia outside Barotseland until 1965, and it retained its 2,500,000 acres of freehold land in north-eastern Rhodesia. For a subsequent appraisal of the Agreement see Colonial No. 145—1938.

included the rich copper deposits adjoining Ndola, whose full promise was to be recognised shortly after the termination of Company administration. As to government, Northern Rhodesia became a Protectorate of the United Kingdom, with a constitution of the usual Crown Colony type, as from 1 April 1924. A Legislative Council containing a minority of elected European members was brought into being following a recommendation of the Buxton Committee, but executive power was concentrated in the hands of a Governor, responsible to the Crown, assisted by a wholly official Executive Council comprising members of the Colonial Service.[1] There was but little articulate African opinion at the time; but the new order was undoubtedly welcomed by the majority of the population, who shared that "preference for rule by the King's officers" which has been observed among the Africans of the High Commission Territories in South Africa.[2]

(c) The High Commission Territories

When the self-governing colonies in South Africa were united in 1910, the three High Commission Territories of Basutoland, Bechuanaland and Swaziland continued to be administered by Resident Commissioners as separate units under the South African High Commission. The maintenance of separate administrations was forced on His Majesty's Government by Native apprehensions—political necessity proving stronger than geography or economics. The Union Government took over from the Cape the collection of customs, paying a fixed percentage to each of the Territories by the Customs Agreement of 1910, and in Basutoland and Swaziland it also carried on the Post Office. The general law of the Union runs in all three Territories, as do Union statutes to some extent. Union currency is used, and so far as there are any such services as railways or even railway omnibuses, they are provided from the Union. The Territories gained by requiring no customs houses on their borders, and they were not ungenerously treated in the share of revenue allotted to them; but the benefits of the tariffs designed in later years to protect Union industries were more dubious.

The South Africa Act of 1909 provided, indeed, that on conditions laid down in a Schedule appended to that Act, the Territories might be transferred to the Union by the King with the advice of the Privy Council on address from the Union Parliament; indeed, immediately after inaugurating the Union in 1910 the Duke of Connaught visited Bechuanaland and, significantly, dealt at length with the question, which was so exercising the minds of the Bechuana, of the inclusion some day of the Bechuanaland Protectorate in the Union. When the

[1] Davidson, J. W., *The Northern Rhodesian Legislative Council* (1948). See also Cmd. 1471—1921, para. 16.

[2] Walker, E. A., *A History of Southern Africa* (1957), p. 269.

plan of separate administrations was originated to relieve the Cape from the embarrassment of trying to govern Basutoland in the 'eighties,[1] and later, in 1895, to save Khama and other Bechuana chiefs from subjection to Cecil Rhodes, whom they distrusted whether as Prime Minister of the Cape or as chairman of the Chartered Company, the ultimate authority of Downing Street was not seriously questioned even in Cape Colony. From the time of Union to the passage of the Statute of Westminster in 1931, however, there was a recognition of the virtual independence of the Dominion, even in Native policy. In 1930 the office of High Commissioner was separated from that of Governor-General, emphasising differences of policy, but leaving the Territories outside the Union, as the Natives preferred, yet also cut off from enjoying the ministrations of the regular British Colonial Service.

During this period several notable Chiefs gave place to new men. Letsie of Basutoland was succeeded by Griffith in 1912, and in Swaziland a long minority ended with the installation of Sobhuza II, a young Chief trained at the missionary station at Lovedale, who interested himself in the promotion of plans for a national school, while sturdily maintaining Native customs. In Bechuanaland Bathoen died in 1910, Sebele in 1911; in 1924 Linchwe, who had set a wise example by insisting on the conservation of three years' supply of food-corn and prohibiting sales below that amount, was succeeded by a capable regent, Isang, who co-operated actively with the Dutch Reformed Church in the establishment of a Bakhatla national school. Khama of the Bamangwato, perhaps the real originator of the Protectorate, died in 1923 at a very advanced age. In internal matters he was notable especially for his enforcement of temperance and for the promotion of Christianity among his people. He was succeeded by Sekgoma, on whose death in 1925 the regency passed to Khama's youngest son Tshekedi. Under all these Chiefs the Protectorate adhered to a form of "indirect rule", which consisted in the administration leaving extensive powers to the Chief and interfering as little as possible, as if on the theory that to keep order was the first essential and that no one could do this so effectively as the tribal Chief. The backing given by the administration tended to weaken old tribal checks and to make the Chief's rule autocratic. In 1912 a Special Court, with a Union advocate as President, was set up in Bechuanaland and Swaziland as a stronger substitute for the Resident Commissioner's Court, which was the earlier form of jurisdiction. This Court has jurisdiction in all civil and criminal cases, including the right to review the proceedings of inferior Courts and to hear appeals. In 1920 separate European and Native Advisory Councils were established in Bechuanaland, and in 1921 a European Advisory Council in Swaziland. Since 1928 Bechuanaland has had a Judicial Commissioner

[1] *Vide supra*, pp. 506, 515.

who sits either with or without the Resident Commissioner in the latter's Court. Appeal in all three territories lies direct to the Judicial Committee of the Privy Council. In Basutoland, the Pitso (National Council of Natives) consisting of ninety-five members nominated by the Chiefs and five by the High Commissioner, continued to meet periodically to "consult and advise" on domestic affairs.

Meantime the example of Northern Nigeria was beginning to suggest to the Colonial Office the possibility of something more constructive in the way of real local government with financial responsibility. Unfortunately the poverty of the Territories made it impossible to spare the money for the institution of Native treasuries. Since the visit in 1927 of Leopold Amery, Secretary of State, however, Resident Commissioners would appear to have been chosen from among men with experience in other colonies rather than, as formerly, from the services of the Protectorates themselves. Both in Basutoland and Bechuanaland proclamations were drafted intended to define the powers of the Chiefs and bring them under control, and to prepare for new developments of "indirect rule". Opposition has sufficed to hinder any real change, but a certain tension was thus set up. The views of the importance of Native interests authoritatively expressed by His Majesty's Government in a famous White Paper of 1930,[1] though shared by the new Dominions Office to which control had passed in 1925, hardly accorded with the trend of legislation in the Union and drew sharp comment from Union ministers. Neither did the newer policy altogether commend itself to old-fashioned Chiefs, who were accustomed to look to the Protectorate administration to uphold, rather than control, their own privileges. But in spite of all the disabilities of isolation, absorption by the Union came no nearer. The Natives valued the freedom of their position, and their distrust still inspired questions asked at frequent intervals. So late as 26 July 1933, an answer was given in the House of Lords to the effect that the British Government adhered to "pledges which have been given by successive Governments in the past" that the transfer contemplated by the South Africa Act would not be carried out without giving Parliament "an opportunity of discussing and, if they wished, of disapproving, any proposals for transfer". The Native population was to have "full opportunity of expressing their views", and His Majesty's Government would not "support any proposal of transfer if it involved any impairment of such safeguards for native rights and interests as the Schedule [of the SouthAfrica Act] was designed to secure."

Economically Basutoland is a highly attractive mountain country, with a few broad fertile valleys which are good for wheat. But though the rainfall is reliable, the growing season is short, and country which would be ideal for sheep farming with perhaps a score of people

[1] *Parl. Pap.* 1929–30, XXIII [Cmd. 3573].

to the square mile has to carry forty or fifty, sometimes up to a hundred, with serious deterioration. Of an estimated area of 11,716 square miles as much as 6000 square miles has been reckoned practically uninhabitable. There is no alienation of land to Europeans. The small export of wool, mohair and wheat, with some cattle, hides and skins, is far from sufficient to maintain a population reckoned in 1921 to be about half a million.

The enormous expanse of Bechuanaland, about 275,000 square miles, is all very dry and some of it virtually desert. Agriculture being precarious, the country is almost wholly dependent on cattle, with the beginnings of cream and dairy production and a small trade in karosses and curios. By agreement with the British South Africa Company, which also owns considerable blocks of farm land on and near the railway line, the Bamangwato country, the largest of the eight reserves, was at last thrown open in 1931 to prospecting for minerals. These, if found, might provide the supplementary revenue that is so much needed. Much land outside executive "reserves" is held as Crown land.

Swaziland is the most varied of the three Territories. The hills have a good rainfall as befits the home of the chief Native "rainmaker". The fertile plains, however, are less well watered and subject to malaria. There is some mineral wealth, not unimportant tin and a little gold. But during the interregnum of the 'eighties the ruling Chief made such wholesale concessions to Europeans that a Commission, whose decisions began to take effect in 1911, found that more than the total acreage of the country had been "conceded". Between 1911 and 1914, therefore, Natives were moved off concession areas and the Swazi population of some 120,000 was provided with reserves amounting to about a third of the country's total of 6704 square miles. Large areas in the south are actually farmed by Europeans, whose production, especially of tobacco, has added to the total wealth; but since the cost, for example, of education for these Europeans was a burden on the general revenue of the country, this did not simplify the problem of administering Swaziland as a predominantly African area.

Administration is no easy matter in any of the Territories, each of which is expected to maintain a full establishment out of its own resources. The Bechuanaland Report for 1915–16 noted that revenue for the first time slightly exceeded expenditure. This happened again in the following year, but in spite of starvation economy His Majesty's Imperial Treasury has repeatedly had to meet deficits. Basutoland was on the whole solvent, but in all three Territories the cost of the government to the Natives is high, the Native tax in each of them being quite as high as in the Union—and if the Chiefs' levies are included sometimes higher—although resources are proportionately less. The Natives have been dependent for revenue and even for livelihood on the export of their own labour. The Administrations have almost complacently treated this dependence on wage-earning as inevitable; Swaziland, for example, in 1920–1 reported that "labour though not plentiful is adequate for farming, mining, road-making, etc.", and it has been generally assumed in effect that all is well, since there are always the mines in the Union to fall back upon. But the annual reports of the various Administrations have noted the disturbing effects of upheavals such as the Rand strikes of 1913–14 and 1922, and in later years Basutoland, which has long depended markedly on employment in the diamond mines of Griqualand West, has been adversely affected by the misfortunes that have befallen that industry.

The First World War, which followed so closely after the Union, had little direct effect upon the Territories, but indirectly it emphasised the weakness of their economic position.[1] Though a Swaziland report noted an entire lack of Native interest in the course of the war, the other two Territories provided companies of a Native labour contingent, which did good service, Basutoland contributed £50,000 to war funds, and even Swaziland in the end furnished at least one aeroplane. The rise in prices added heavily to the costs of administration, even to the burden of such items as the equipment of the police; labour, on the other hand, was so plentiful that Native wages showed relatively little rise to balance rising prices, even if the better return for wheat and especially for wool brought some compensation and gave Basutoland a few years of comparatively elastic revenue.

By diverting energy from ordinary affairs the war undoubtedly retarded natural development, and in some respects there has been retrogression; Basutoland in particular has suffered from overcrowding with consequent over-grazing and disastrous soil erosion. Though enjoying an extremely healthy climate, this Territory was not only swept like the rest by influenza in 1918 with a death roll which was certainly under-estimated at 15,000, but in 1921–2 the Administrator reported that typhus, a disease of deficiency and dirt, "must be regarded as now endemic". Both in Basutoland and Bechuanaland medical reports indicated a serious spread of venereal disease, while the medical service to cope with these evils, and with the malaria of Bechuanaland and lower Swaziland, was a mere skeleton, there being only seven small hospitals as late as 1932 for the huge area of Bechuanaland. Basutoland indeed had a well-equipped leper settlement; but the burden of medical reports seemed to be that health must be regarded as "fairly good" so long as there is no epidemic.

[1] Conditions in these territories have improved of recent years.—(Editor).

CHAPTER XXV

THE UNION CONSTITUTION AND ITS WORKING[1]

THE Union Constitution is embodied in the South Africa Act.[2] In origin it resembles closely the constitutions of her sister Dominions. It was drafted by a National Convention appointed by the Parliaments of the four self-governing colonies; ratification by each of these bodies followed, save in Natal where a referendum was held; and finally the draft Bill was submitted by a South African delegation to the Imperial Parliament which gave to it the hall-mark of legal validity.

Technically, therefore, the fundamental law of the Union is a British Act amendable and repealable by the Parliament of Great Britain, for the wide powers possessed by the Union legislature in terms of the constitution did not detract from the supremacy of the Imperial Parliament. The well-known limitations on Dominion sovereignty found in the Crown's prerogative, the doctrine of repugnancy, the doctrine of territoriality *et hoc genus omne* clearly show that at the inauguration of the Union the South African Parliament was a non-sovereign legislative body.[3] The subject of the legal status of the Union does not enter here. More cogent is the question of the nature of the Union Constitution *qua* Union, i.e. from the South African angle alone[4]. After striving for federation since the eighteen-fifties South Africa in the end achieved a legislative union, but the spirit of compromise characteristic of the Convention left many traces of federalism. Among these were equal representation of the Provinces in the Senate[5] which has been extended by a convention to the nominated Senators as well; the acceptance of the Provincial franchise for Union purposes; the fixed minimum membership given to Natal and the Orange Free State in the House of Assembly; the Provincial constitutions and, as far as party politics permit, the representation of all the Provinces in the Union Cabinet.[6] Yet these federal features are merely superficial, for the Parliament of the Union has power to repeal or amend any of the provisions of the constitution, subject to

[1] No attempt has been made in this revision to embody in the text developments that have taken place since this chapter was originally written about 1935. but significant changes are alluded to in supplementary footnotes.

[2] South Africa Act (9 Edw. VII, c. 9).

[3] Keith, A. B., *Responsible Government in the Dominions*, II, 745 *sqq.*; Dicey, A. V., *Introduction to the Law of Constitution*, 8th ed. (1915), pp. 101–5.

[4] However, the resolutions of the Imperial Conferences of 1926 and 1930, the Statute of Westminster of 1931 and the South African Status and Seals Acts of 1934 that were based upon them gave to the Union the character of an independent state.

[5] This equality has been abolished by the Senate Act of 1955.

[6] South Africa Act, 1909, ss. 24, 25, 35, 53, 68–94.

certain time limits (which have now expired) or to special procedure or to reservation.[1]

The executive government of the Union is vested in the King, but may be administered by a Governor-General.[2] There is an assumption that the King would always be represented by a Governor-General, for all subsequent provisions relating to the exercise of executive government refer to the Governor-General and not to the King.[3] The Governor-General is appointed by the King, but the conventional usages as to advice given to His Majesty in this connection are common to all the Dominions and need not be elaborated here. The office of Governor-General for the Union was created by Letters Patent.[4] During the period 1910–21 the Governor-General was the executive head of the Union as well as High Commissioner, i.e. the agent of the British Government. His functions were limited by statute, his discretion guided by instructions, and he corresponded with and through "one of His Majesty's principal Secretaries of State".[5] While the Governor-General lacks the character of a Viceroy in his relationship with the British Government, he approaches more closely to a constitutional monarch in his dealings with his Union advisers. In neither case is he irresponsible. Political responsibility to the Secretary of State might lead to his recall;[6] legal liability might involve him in a suit at law. Hence, when the Government seeks indemnity for breaches of law, the Governor-General is covered likewise by such indemnity.[7]

Numerous provisions in the Union constitution vest functions in the Governor-General-in-Council, e.g. the nomination of Senators, the appointment of Administrators and of Judges.[8] Other clauses empower the Governor-General to choose Executive Councillors, appoint and dismiss Ministers, summon and prorogue Parliament, recommend appropriation or taxing bills, assent to, withhold assent

[1] South Africa Act, 1909, s. 152. Reservation was abolished in 1934. Since 1956 the special procedure applies only to the safeguarding of the equality of the two official languages.

[2] *Ibid.* s. 8. As amended by the Status Act the words "in regard to any aspect of its domestic or external affairs . . . acting on the advice of his Minister of State for the Union" were added.

[3] E.g. s. 12; cf. Keith, A. B., in *Journal of Comparative Legislation*, 2nd ser., XI (1909), 46. Nevertheless during his visit to the Union in 1947 King George VI exercised certain functions in person.

[4] 29 December 1909 (*Union Gov. Gaz.* 1 of 1910).

[5] All this is now obsolete. Since 1937 Letters Patent and Royal Instructions are issued under the Royal Great Seal and Royal Signet of the Union and countersigned by the Prime Minister.

[6] This is no longer the case.

[7] Act 1 of 1914, 2 (1) (a). Since 1931, the Governor-General has ceased to be the agent of the British Government. A separate High Commissioner has then and since been appointed to represent the United Kingdom Government in the Union in a quasi-ambassadorial capacity, and to exercise control over the High Commission Territories and, in a measure, over the two Rhodesias and Nyasaland.

[8] South Africa Act, 1909, ss. 24, 68, 100.

from or reserve a Bill for the signification of the King's pleasure.[1] In practice the distinction between the Governor-General-in-Council and the Governor-General sole is slight. A Union statute has in fact defined the term Governor-General as "the officer for the time being administering the government of the Union acting by and with the advice of the Executive Council thereof unless the context otherwise requires".[2] He is instructed to consult his Ministers on all topics, but his discretion is guided or limited with regard to reservation of Bills and the exercise of the prerogative of pardon;[3] for though the Crown's right of disallowance has not been exercised in the Union and is no more than a constitutional survival, the reservation of Bills (if statutory) is real and has been acted upon on several occasions.[4] All reserved Bills have been ultimately assented to by Order-in-Council.

The relations between the Governor-General and his Ministers have been pleasant, sometimes cordial. Botha and Lord Buxton had numerous, almost daily, informal discussions.[5] Buxton sometimes also consulted Merriman and other influential private members, the constitutional correctness of which Merriman himself doubted.[6] In public, the Governor-General must be more circumspect, since his Ministers alone are responsible for his political speeches.[7] Formal meetings between the Governor-General and the Ministers take place in Executive Council over which the Governor-General presides, but on at least one occasion Lord Buxton deliberated with his Ministers in Cabinet.[8]

The constitution empowers the Governor-General to summon an unlimited number of Executive Councillors and to appoint officers to administer such Departments of state as may be established.[9] Each of these officers, styled Ministers, must be sworn to the Council and must find a seat in Parliament within three months of taking office. A member of Parliament who takes ministerial office does not vacate his seat thereby. While in law the Executive Council may be wider than the Ministry, there is in fact no distinction between these bodies, because, so far, only Ministers have been sworn to the Council. In view of the smallness of the Ministry[10] all its members are in the

[1] South Africa Act, 1909, ss. 12, 14, 20, 62, 64.

[2] Interpretation Act, 5 of 1910; Nathan, M., *The South African Commonwealth*, p. 21.

[3] Royal Instructions, 29 December 1909, VII and IX (*Union Gov. Gaz.* 1 of 1910). The Governor-General's personal discretion has been limited by Section 4 of the Status Act to the choice of Executive Councillors, the appointment and dismissal of Ministers and the summons and prorogation of Parliament "subject to the constitutional conventions relating to the exercise of his functions".

[4] E.g. Electoral Acts, 12 and 31 of 1918; Financial Relations Acts, 9 of 1917 and 5 of 1921. The reserving power and the right of disallowance have been abolished by the Status Act (1934).

[5] Buxton, Earl, *General Botha*, pp. 217 *sqq.*

[6] Laurence, (Sir) P. M., *Life of J. X. Merriman*, p 402.

[7] Keith, *Responsible Government in the Dominions*, I, 279.

[8] On the peace terms with German South-West Africa; see Buxton, *Botha*, p. 224.

[9] South Africa Act, ss. 12, 14.

[10] Sixteen at present (1960).

Cabinet. There are no Parliamentary Under-Secretaries in the Union. The Governor-General's constitutional relations with his Ministers and the relations between Ministers and Parliament are in the Union broadly similar to those prevailing in Great Britain. But, as has been noted in an earlier chapter, the federal element was very marked in the earlier Union Ministries and Cabinet solidarity proved to be less effective than at Westminster.[1] The Ministers are the political heads of Departments and are not expected to be experts in departmental routine, a matter for permanent officials; but the smallness of the population of South Africa has made it possible for Ministers to obtain fuller knowledge and more control over actual administration than is practicable in Great Britain. Following the Cape practice, a Minister may sit and speak in both Houses, though he may vote only in that of which he is a member.[2]

The legislative power of the Union is vested in a Parliament consisting of the King, the Senate and the House of Assembly.[3] According to one commentator this clause is fundamental and unalterable,[4] but section 152 provides for the repeal or alteration of any of the provisions of the South Africa Act. Parliament has full power to make laws for the "peace, order and good government" of the Union—a convenient formula covering sovereign legislative power within the Union.[5] Its privileges are defined by statute and are narrower in scope than those of the British Parliament.[6] Each House may lay down rules of procedure which are in the main modelled upon those prevailing at Westminster.[7] In the conduct of parliamentary business there is little to choose between the Union and other Member States of the Commonwealth. There is the usual leisurely gait during the early part of the Session and the frantic rush at the end. There is the usual complaint of the Opposition that the Government curtails debate and stifles criticism. In 1914 the Indemnity and Deportation Bill was forced through Committee after thirty hours of continuous debate. These "third degree" methods to wear down opposition were followed by the adoption of the closure. There were complaints, even from the Government benches, that Ministers shifted the order papers about to suit their convenience without notice

[1] *Vide supra*, pp.662 *sqq*. Dr. Verwoerd has appointed four Deputy Ministers, who have no seats in the Cabinet.

[2] South Africa Act, s. 52.

[3] *Ibid*. s. 19.

[4] Nathan, *South African Commonwealth*, p. 36. This view is in conflict with present constitutional developments, e.g. the recognition of India as a "Republic within the Commonwealth" (1947) and the secession of Eire in 1948.

[5] South Africa Act, s. 59; *R*. v. *McChlery* ([1912] A.D. 199). Cf. sec 2 of the Status Act: "The Parliament of the Union shall be the sovereign legislative power in and over the Union."

[6] South Africa Act, s. 57; The Powers and Privileges of Parliament Act, 19 of 1911.

[7] South Africa Act, s. 58.

or regard for the members.[1] An interesting innovation is a joint rule, adopted in 1916, whereby any public Bill may be proceeded with in the next ensuing Session at the stage it had reached in the previous Session provided no dissolution has taken place in the interval.[2] Each House elects its own presiding officer, but the election is on party lines. For this reason, in contrast with British practice, the Speaker is opposed in his constituency and does not stand aloof from political addresses outside Parliament; yet withal the prestige of the Speakership stands high. The summons, prorogation and dissolution of Parliament are governed by the well-known conventional rules operating in Great Britain and the self-governing Dominions. The powers and prerogatives of the Governor-General with respect to legislation have already been mentioned.[3]

The South Africa Act provided for the constitution of the Senate for a period of ten years.[4] Four-fifths of the members were to be elected on the equal basis of eight from each Province; the remaining fifth were to be nominated—an unusual combination in an Upper House. In the vain hope that the Senate would be a non-party body, the elections were to be conducted on the principle of proportional representation;[5] but this hope was stultified *ab initio* by the fact that the electoral colleges were political bodies, being composed for the first election of the members of the existing Colonial Legislatures, and thereafter of the Provincial Councillors with the members of the House of Assembly for each Province sitting together. In practice the elections are rigidly controlled by the party caucus and the vagaries of the transferable vote have been minutely examined by party whips to give the best party results.[6] Indecent bargainings with "independents" have not been uncommon. Four of the eight nominees were to be selected "on the ground mainly of their thorough acquaintance by reason of their official experience or otherwise, with the reasonable wants and wishes of the coloured races in South Africa.". This elastic proviso has not deterred the Government from nominating good party men. The qualification of Senators included a higher age limit and the ownership of immovable property, well-known features of conservative Upper Houses.[7]

The House of Assembly is elected by direct popular vote for a period of five years, unless earlier dissolved. There must be a Session of Parliament once at least in every year. The franchise laws of the

[1] House of Assembly Debates, 1913, c. 1819.
[2] Kilpin, R. *Parliamentary Procedure in South Africa*, 3rd ed. (1955), p. 13.
[3] *Vide supra*, pp. 704–5
[4] South Africa Act, s. 24.
[5] *Ibid.* s. 134.
[6] *Cape Times*, 4 September 1929; *Cape Argus*, 3 September 1929.
[7] South Africa Act, s. 26. The composition of the Senate has been drastically altered by the Senate Act, 53 of 1955. Proportional voting and the equal representation of the Provinces have been deleted, and property qualification for elected members has also been abolished.

several colonies were to remain in force until Parliament otherwise decided. Elaborate safeguards were laid down for the retention of the non-European franchise in the Cape Province.[1] As an additional security, all Bills amending any of the provisions in the chapter headed "House of Assembly" were to be reserved.[2] Much amending legislation has been passed governing electoral procedure,[3] regulating press criticism during elections, providing for voting by post[4] and for enfranchising European women[5].

Much attention was given to the composition of the House. The Convention agreed upon a House of 121 members rising to a maximum of 150;[6] a happy mean, for the House is large enough to permit the party system to work smoothly and yet not so large as to delay business unduly and be a drain upon the country's purse. This has avoided the difficulties met with in the Commonwealth of Australia where the House is composed of only 75 members. The allocation of seats as between Provinces was broadly in proportion to the number of European male adults in the several Provinces with a more liberal treatment of the two smaller Provinces, whose representation was not to be reduced for ten years after union or until the House should have reached its maximum of 150, whichever was the longer period.[7] Adequate provision was made for increased representation, provided that no Province should be given any additional seats "until the total number of European male adults in such province exceeds the quota of the Union multiplied by the number of members allotted to such province for the time being".[8]

The National Convention, upon reconsideration, abandoned the idea of proportional voting for Assembly elections and decided upon single member constituencies to be mapped out by a Judicial Delimitation Commission and revised after every quinquennial census.[9] While each electoral division shall, as far as possible, be equal to the

[1] *Ibid.* ss. 35, 36. The safeguards have disappeared with the abolition of reservation (1934) and the deletion of the "entrenching" provisions in sec. 35 [see South Africa Act Amendment Act, 9 of 1956]. They had proved unavailing, as W. P. Schreiner had prophesied at the time. In 1936, the Cape Africans (Bantu) were removed from the common roll, and allowed to elect three Europeans to the Assembly. This privilege was taken away in 1959. In 1956, after the Senate had been ruthlessly packed to ensure the necessary two-thirds majority of the two Houses sitting together, the Cape Coloured and Indians were treated in the same way, and allowed to elect four Europeans to the Assembly. A few additional Senators were either nominated or elected to represent non-European interests. Non-Europeans may no longer sit in the Cape Provincial Council. Such is the end of the invaluable Cape civilisation franchise after a life of more than a hundred years.

[2] S. 152.

[3] Electoral Act, 12 of 1918.

[4] Electoral Act, 11 of 1926.

[5] Women's Enfranchisement Act, 18 of 1930.

[6] Total in 1958 is 163. The additions represent: six for South-West Africa; three for the Native voters at the Cape and four for the Coloured voters at the Cape. Native representation was abolished in 1959.

[7] South Africa Act, ss. 33, 152.

[8] *Ibid.* s. 34 (IV); for details see Nathan, *South African Commonwealth*, ch. IX.

[9] South Africa Act, s. 38.

quota of the Province, the Commissioners shall take into consideration *inter alia* "community or diversity of interests and sparsity or density of population", and shall have power to depart from that quota to a maximum of fifteen per cent in either direction.[1] Merriman all along fought against a mere counting of heads; "wealth, occupation and area" should be given weight. Though the Delimitation Commissions have not been guilty of gerrymandering, in practice the urban constituencies are heavily loaded and more remote rural areas have had the benefit of the minimum quota. Since Natal and the Orange Free State had smaller provincial quotas than the Cape and the Transvaal, it was not uncommon to find an urban division at the Cape having twice as many voters on the register as a rural division in Natal.[2]

When the first Union Parliament met, Upper Houses were somewhat out of favour. "All our experience goes to show", wrote Merriman to Lord Bryce, "that Upper Houses are either nuisances or nullities."[3] With the conflict raging in Great Britain between the Commons and the Lords before them, the Union House of Assembly was too ready to endorse this view. The Senate did not take kindly to this interpretation. In the first Session there were complaints (since often reiterated) that the time of the Senate was being wasted for the convenience of the other House. The unseemly rush at the end of the Session was resented;[4] on one occasion seven finance bills were taken through all stages in the Senate on a single day. Though by law all bills, save money bills, may be initiated in the Senate, the Government was loth to take advantage of this provision. Subsequently, some non-party measures were introduced first in the Upper House, but here again there were complaints that Ministers were too ready to change their minds in the Assembly after accepting certain amendments in the Senate.[5] In the first Parliament many Senators regarded themselves as non-party men with freedom to speak and vote "according to their convictions".[6] W. P. Schreiner, one of the nominated Senators, voted frequently against the Government.[7] The Senate protested against the tendency to legislate by regulation or by resolution,[8] and it considered itself slighted because the Government had made no reference in Senate to the circumstances of Hull's resignation.[9] The Prime Minister regretted the "unintentional slight", but Smuts bluntly told the Senators that the reconstruction of

[1] South Africa Act, s. 40; Laurence, *Merriman*, p. 274.
[2] Delimitation Commission Report (*Union Gov. Gaz.* 2 of 1910).
[3] Quoted in Laurence, *Merriman*, pp. 385–6.
[4] Senate Debates, 1913, cc. 245–51; Walker, *Schreiner*, p. 338.
[5] *Ibid.* 1912, cc. 779–86.
[6] *Ibid.* 1910–11, c. 254; 1912, c. 252.
[7] Schreiner was an Independent.
[8] *Ibid.* 12 December 1910; 1912, c. 804.
[9] Hull, the Minister of Finance, resigned in 1912 because of a dispute with Sauer, Minister of Railways, who pursued a policy of railway expansion without considering its effect on the Treasury.

the Cabinet was a "question that touched the prerogative of the Crown".[1]

The exact functions of the Senate with regard to money bills caused further difficulties. While accepting the constitutional limitations upon its powers of amending money bills,[2] the Senate by no means saw eye to eye with the Assembly as to what constituted a money bill, and claimed the privilege, possessed by the Australian Upper House, of suggesting amendments for the consideration of the Assembly by placing such suggestions in brackets with an explanatory footnote that these did not form part of the bill.[3] It refused to concur with the Assembly in regard to the payment of members on the ground that such a resolution was illegal,[4] and insisted with success that the Controller and Auditor General should submit his report to both Houses.[5]

Apart from the normal procedure governing legislation the constitution provided for joint sittings of both Houses for two distinct purposes. One is for amending certain clauses of the Act of Union, when the bill in question must be agreed to at the third reading by not less than two-thirds of the total number of members of both Houses sitting together.[6] Two of these clauses had entrenched the Provincial representation in the House of Assembly until such time as the total number of members should reach 150.[7] The remaining two aimed at safeguarding the equality of English and Dutch as official languages, and preventing the disqualification on the grounds of race or colour of persons otherwise qualified to become voters in the Cape.[8] The exigencies of the war of 1914 necessitated an amendment of section 34 and the first joint sitting took place in 1918.[9] The next joint sitting occurred in 1925 when Parliament voted that Afrikaans should be included in Dutch for official purposes.[10] Both these amendments were non-party agreements and were carried at the joint session without a dissentient. In 1929 another joint sitting to amend section 35 (which entrenched the voting rights of non-Europeans in the Cape Province) was fought fiercely on party lines and failed to secure the necessary two-thirds majority.[11]

Joint sittings may also be held to overcome deadlock between the

[1] Senate Debates, 1912, cc. 510, 692.

[2] South Africa Act, s. 60.

[3] Senate Debates, 1910–11, c. 300; *ibid.* 1912, cc. 131–7. For the whole question see *Memorandum* I of 1912, s. 35, S.C. 4—1918 (Minority Report, VI–VII) [s. 1—1917].

[4] Senate Debates, 1913, cc. 361–2.

[5] Exchequer and Audit Act, 21 of 1911, s. 40.

[6] South Africa Act, s. 152.

[7] *Ibid.* ss. 33, 34.

[8] *Ibid.* ss. 137, 35.

[9] Electoral Divisions Redelimitations Amendment Act, 31 of 1918.

[10] Official Languages of the Union Act, 8 of 1925.

[11] At later joint sittings Bantu were removed from the common roll by Act 12 of 1936, and Coloured voters likewise by Act 9 of 1956, in the latter case after the necessary two-thirds majority having been obtained by packing the Senate. The latter Act also deprived the Courts of their testing power save under section 137 (equal language rights).

two Houses.[1] If the House of Assembly pass a money bill and the Senate reject it, the Governor-General may convene a joint sitting in the same Session; if the Senate reject any other bill in two successive Sessions, a joint sitting may then be held. The fate of the disputed bill is determined by a bare majority of the total number present at the division at such joint sitting.[2] No provision exists for a joint sitting in regard to bills initiated in the Senate—a difficulty which has stood in the way of the introduction of contentious measures in the Senate as Government bills. No deadlock resulting in joint sittings occurred until 1925.

Before the first Senate had expired by efflux of time several enquiries had been held to report upon the future constitution of the Upper House.[3] These reports were all in favour of strengthening rather than weakening the Senate. It was proposed that the number of nominees be reduced; that the remaining Senators be directly elected by popular vote on a basis of proportional representation, each Province forming a single constituency; that Provincial equality in the Senate be retained; that the Senate should have wider powers with regard to suggesting amendments to money bills, and that the ratio in numbers between the Senate and the Assembly should be as 1 : 2 or 1 : 3. It may be noted that the ratio of 1 : 3 adopted in 1910 has since declined with the increase in the number of members of the House of Assembly to the detriment of the Senate at a joint sitting. The Government did not accept any of these suggestions, and the second Senate was constituted according to the provisions laid down in the Act of Union.[4]

While the Senate rejected several important public bills[5] before the Pact Government came into office in 1924, there was no real deadlock until then, and there was even a suspicion of collusion.[6] Since then party feeling in the Senate has become more acute. The rejection of the Colour Bar Bill[7] in 1925 led to an amending bill which ensured a docile Upper House for Governments of the future.[8] The most drastic provision of this bill enables the Government to dissolve the Senate within 120 days after a general election; upon such a dissolution and whenever a change of Government has occurred, the nominated Senators also vacate their seats. Before this bill came into effect there were sharp brushes between the Government and the

[1] The procedure discussed below has been repealed by the Senate Act, 53 of 1955, whereby joint sittings under section 63 are abolished, and give to the Senate a delaying power only on the lines of the British Parliament Act.

[2] South Africa Act, s. 63.

[3] S. 1—1917; S.C. 4—1918; Conference on future Constitution of Senate (*U.G.* 65 of 1920); *Journal of Comparative Legislation*, 3rd series, v (1923), 130–4.

[4] South Africa Act, s. 25. See also Beinart, B., "The South African Senate", *Modern Law Review*, November 1957, pp. 549–65.

[5] The Moratorium Bill, 1918; Wage Board and Apprenticeship Bills, 1922.

[6] Walker, *History of Southern Africa*, p. 572; *Round Table*, No. 46.

[7] "Mines and Works Bill" enacted at joint Sitting in 1926 (25 of 1926).

[8] Senate Act, 54 of 1926.

Senate, the Senate rejecting several bills, though all but one of these (the Flag Bill, which was settled by agreement) was carried subsequently at a joint sitting. The refusal of the Government to submit the German trade agreement to the Senate for ratification caused a great stir.[1] True to Merriman's prophecy, the Senate had become a nuisance; six months later, following a dissolution, it subsided into a nullity.

The decline of parliamentary authority in recent years, due partly to the complexity of the functions of Government and partly to the rigidity of party organisation and discipline, is no less noticeable in the Union than in Great Britain. The delegation of law-making powers to Ministers is a common characteristic.[2] While Ministers are politically responsible, the real framers of the numerous rules and orders are the permanent officials whom the Ministers consult.[3] Many pages of the Union statute book show evidence of the tendency to foster *droit administratif* and to detract from the majesty of the rule of law.[4] The extent of ministerial discretion may vary from refusing to issue a letter of naturalisation without cause assigned[5] to prohibiting an individual from residing in a certain locality on the ground of causing ill-will between black and white;[6] the measure of delegation may likewise vary from declaring decisions of an Immigration Board final on questions of fact[7] to the repeal or amendment by Proclamation of Acts of Parliament affecting Natives.[8] Nevertheless, the essential principles of the rule of law that officials are answerable before the ordinary Courts and are liable in damages for abuse of authority apply to the Union;[9] even a Native may obtain damages from a police officer for malicious arrest.[10] By statute the Crown may be sued upon contract or tort,[11] but no action lies unless proof of damage suffered is established.[12] In construing a statute which encroaches on individual rights, the Court will in case of doubt adopt the construction which favours liberty and the upholding of rights.[13] Regulations made under the authority of an Act of Parliament must

[1] *Journal of Comparative Legislation*, 3rd series, XI (1929), 252; *Cape Times*, 14 March, 1929.

[2] Lees-Smith, H., *Second Chambers*, pp. 26–8.

[3] Cf. Macassey, L., "Law-making by Government Departments", *Journal of Comparative Legislation*, 3rd ser., V (1923), 73 *sqq.*, and Hewart, Lord, *The New Despotism.*

[4] Article on "Administrative Law", *Cape Times*, 27, 28 Aug. 1928. This is particularly noticeable in the Department of Native Affairs where ministerial authority to govern by regulation is most pronounced.

[5] Act 4 of 1910, s. 5.

[6] Riotous Assemblies Act, 19 of 1930.

[7] Act 22 of 1913, ss. 2, 3.

[8] Native Administration Act, 38 of 1927. Since 1950 far-reaching statutory infringements have been made in the "rule of law", e.g. by the Suppression of Communism Act, the Natives (Urban Areas) Act, etc., Group Areas Act, and the Bantu Authorities Act, together with their Amending Acts.

[9] *Whittaker* v. *Roos and Bateman* ([1912] A.D. 92).

[10] *Ntisa* v. *Coetzee* ([1914] E.D.L. 504).

[11] Crown Liabilities Act, 1 of 1910.

[12] *Dalrymple and others* v. *Colonial Treasurer* ([1910] T.P. 372).

[13] *Joosub* v. *Immigration Appeal Board* ([1919] C.P.D. 109).

conform strictly to the provisions of the Act[1] and must be duly promulgated.[2] But the Courts are powerless against the wilful lawlessness of the Executive if Parliament condones such action. Thus in 1914, Parliament indemnified the Government for the surreptitious deportation of nine persons even though such action was described as "lawless kidnapping" by a Transvaal Judge.[3] Incidentally, this Act was also one of attainder, since the persons unlawfully deported were declared prohibited immigrants. That public opinion was against the Government was shown shortly afterwards in the Transvaal Provincial Council elections. The Government sought power to dispense with parliamentary indemnity under similar circumstances, but the good sense of Parliament foiled this effort.[4] It, however, obtained extensive control over public meetings and the right to set up Special Courts whereby certain offences against the state may be tried without a jury.[5]

War, which is always fatal to liberty, inaugurated in Great Britain the reign of D.O.R.A., and, in South Africa, the rebellion which was born of it greatly strengthened arbitrary authority.[6] Judges were too apt to remember the old tag *salus reipublicae suprema lex* and to forget one equally cogent, *fiat justitia ruat coelum*. Yet there were many precedents for the potency of martial law when war was actually raging.[7] A regulation under martial law was declared of retrospective validity;[8] a British subject interned by lawful authority[9] was declared a prisoner of war and not entitled to a writ of *Habeas Corpus*.[10] An Indemnity Act of 1915 validated all measures taken *or to be taken* for the maintenance of good order, and thus in effect condoned future breaches of the law without further indemnification.[11]

The judicial system of the Union is fully centralised. The Provincial Divisions are branches of the Supreme Court of South Africa and exist as mere geographical conveniences. Judges hold office during good behaviour;[12] Magistrates are subject to Civil Service

[1] *R.* v. *Nel* ([1913] E.D.L. 332).

[2] *R.* v. *Kombrin* ([1920] T.P.D. 414).

[3] House of Assembly Debates, 1914, c. 316; Indemnity and Undesirables Special Deportation Act, 1 of 1914; *Round Table*, No. 14 (March 1914).

[4] Peace Preservation Bill, *Round Table*, No. 15 (June 1914), pp. 578 *sqq.*; Walker, *op. cit.* pp. 551–2.

[5] Riotous Assemblies and Criminal Law Amendment Act, 27 of 1914.

[6] In consequence of a civil disobedience campaign on the part of some Natives, the Government hurriedly passed a Public Safety Act (3 of 1953) enabling the Governor-General to proclaim at any time a state of emergency for twelve months, during which time all measures that were deemed necessary to maintain order and public safety could be taken by regulation, even if they were in conflict with common law and the statutory liberties of the subject.

[7] *Krohn* v. *Minister of Defence* ([1915] A.D. 191); the case of *ex parte Marais* ([1902] A.C. 109) and *Van Reenen and Smit* v. *Att. Gen.* ([1904] A.C. 114 followed).

[8] *Ex parte Kotze* ([1914] T.P.D. 564).

[9] 5 (6) of Act 11 of 1915.

[10] *Nathan* v. *Union Government* ([1915] C.P.D. 353).

[11] Indemnity and Special Tribunal Act, 11 of 1915, s. 6 (c); *Journal of Comparative Legislation*, 2nd ser., XXXVIII (1917), 123.

[12] South Africa Act, s. 101; Judges' Salaries and Pensions Act, 16 of 1912.

Acts. Since Union, the rules of evidence and procedure have been codified.[1] That hoary English institution, trial by jury, has been subjected to much buffeting in South Africa. The grand jury has never existed, the civil jury has been abolished by statute,[2] and grave doubts exist as to the efficacy of the jury in criminal cases. As a bulwark of liberty against the Crown the jury no longer operates, since Special Courts may be set up for the trial of offenders without a jury.[3] These Courts have so far been utilised for political offences, but the Government has done nothing to prevent the miscarriages of justice arising from the frequent acquittals of Europeans when charged with offences against Natives, many of which have drawn stern comments from the Bench.[4] It should be added that since 1917 an accused person may elect to be tried by a Judge and Assessors without a jury.[5]

Since Union, the Privy Council has played but a small part in the South African judicial system. Appeals from a Provincial Division go to the Appellate Division and not to the Judicial Committee.[6] There is no appeal to the King-in-Council (excepting in maritime causes under the Colonial Laws and Admiralty Act, 1890) unless the King-in-Council grants special leave to appeal.[7] The appeals have been few and have invariably failed to disturb the judgment of the Appellate Division. The Judicial Committee will only entertain appeals if a broad principle of jurisprudence is involved.[8] Parliament may restrict grounds of appeal, but such bills must be reserved.[9]

In the National Convention a strong argument used in favour of a unitary constitution was that the validity of Union statutes would not depend upon judicial decisions,[10] for federalism, as Dicey neatly put it, "substitutes litigation for legislation".[11] This view must be qualified because the constitution is sufficiently federal under section 152 whereby special procedure must be observed for particular legislation. The Courts are competent to test whether such procedure has

[1] Administration of Justice Act, 27 of 1912; Criminal Procedure and Evidence Act, 31 of 1917; Magistrates' Courts Act, 32 of 1917.

[2] Act 11 of 1927.

[3] Acts 27 of 1914, 11 of 1915, and 6 of 1922.

[4] See article on Administration of Criminal Law in South Africa, 37 *South African Law Journal* (1920), pp. 131–8; Brookes, E. H., in *Coming of Age* (1930), pp. 388–90.

[5] Act 31 of 1917, s. 215. By an amending Act (21 of 1954) a long list of offences are enumerated wherein the Minister may direct that the offender shall be tried without a jury. In all other cases, trial shall normally be held before a Judge and Assessors unless the accused opt for a jury trial.

[6] South Africa Act, s. 104.

[7] *Ibid.*, s. 106.

[8] See *Journal of Comparative Legislation*, 3rd ser., II (1920), 331 for reference to *Whittaker* v. *Mayor and Councillors of the Borough of Durban* (1920); *de Villiers and Van Niekerk* v. *O.F.S. Law Society* in *Cape Times*, 17 October 1929.

[9] All Appeals to the Privy Council were abolished by Act 16 of 1950.

[10] Brand, R. H., *The Union of South Africa*, pp. 43–4; Walton, Sir E. H., *Inner History of the National Convention*, pp. 53 *sqq.*; Laurence, *Merriman*, p. 273; Nathan, *South African Commonwealth*, p. 200.

[11] Dicey, *Law of Constitution*, p. 175.

been followed.[1] Besides, the doctrine of repugnancy implies that the Courts have power to test the validity of statutes.[2] The South Africa Act specifically empowers the Superior Courts to decide the validity of Provincial Ordinances, but is silent as to statutes;[3] Inferior Courts which exercise these powers, as of right, were limited by later legislation.[4] Parliament may deprive the Superior Courts of such powers and may even abolish the Courts themselves.[5]

At the establishment of the Union all assets of the several colonies, actual and contingent, became the property of the Union;[6] the Union likewise took over their liabilities.[7] All revenues, save such as are derived from railways and harbours, are paid into a consolidated revenue fund. The rules governing appropriation, audit and control are similar to those prevailing in Great Britain. The Controller and Auditor-General holds on good behaviour and has far-reaching inspectorial duties.[8] He reports annually to Parliament.

Much cogent criticism has been levelled at South African financial administration—that the estimates are grossly inaccurate; that supplementary estimates are needlessly heavy and frequent; that special warrants are issued on flimsy grounds; that there is much irregularity in the manner in which authority is given for the spending of public moneys; that loan accounts are used indiscriminately for revenue purposes; that unauthorised expenditure is too readily condoned; that there is friction between the Treasury, which ought not to be a spending department, and the Auditor-General; that the Public Accounts Committee is slack in its supervision and that it is actuated by party motives; that Parliament, the ultimate arbiter, does not even consider the reports of its own Committee.[9] No one who watches contemporary politics can deny that much of this criticism applies to democratic systems in all countries. The root of the evil lies in the relationship between Cabinet and Parliament. The

[1] *Semble*, *R.* v. *McChlery* ([1912] A.D. 199); *Krause* v. *Commissioner for Inland Revenue* ([1929] A.D. 286). In 1952 the Supreme Court invalidated the Separate Representation of Voters Act [*Harris* v. *Minister of the Interior* 1952 (2) S.A. 428 (A.D.)] and the High Court of Parliament Act [*Minister of Interior* v. *Harris*, 1952 (4) S.A. 769 (A.D.)]. In both cases the decision of the A.D. was unanimous. In 1955 the enlarged A.D. declared the Senate Act valid by 10 votes to 1.

[2] Keith, *Responsible Government in the Dominions*, I, 351; Melius de Villiers in 36 *South African Law Journal* (1919), p. 365.

[3] South Africa Act, s. 98 (3).

[4] S. 104 of Act 32 of 1917; 37 *South African Law Journal* (1920), p. 408; 38 *S.A.L.J.* (1921), pp. 132, 190; *R.* v. *Thompson* ([1914] T.P.D. 426).

[5] The testing power has been abolished in 1956 save under sec. 137. In the High Court of Parliament Case (1952) the Appellate Division held that Parliament cannot constitute itself into a Court of Appeal.

[6] South Africa Act, ss. 117, 121, 122, 123, 125.

[7] *Ibid.* s. 124.

[8] *Ibid.* s. 132; Exchequer and Audit Act, 21 of 1911.

[9] See extracts from Auditor-General's Report (1927–8), *Cape Times*, 4 April 1929; Shannon, H. A., in *Cape Times*, 27 November 1930; *Cape Argus*, 27 November 1930; *Round Table*, No. 81.

sword of impeachment or attainder no longer hangs over the neck of a defaulting Minister. Even the high traditions of the British Public Accounts Committee have not enabled it to roar any louder than a sucking dove. Parliament is the ultimate judge, and, as long as it consents to register the ministerial will, no devices to control such will can work effectively.

Failure of adequate control is thus inherent in the parliamentary system. In the Union, during the years 1910–21, there were few glaring abuses. The chairman of the Public Accounts Committee was a member of the Opposition and the Committee often divided on non-party lines, but Parliament paid scant attention to its criticism and too readily acquiesced in authorising, *ex post facto*, unwarranted expenditure.[1] Unauthorised Expenditure Acts are hardy annuals in the Union. Courageous Auditors-General have had their spirits damped by the chilly receptions of their reports and the occasional open hostility of Ministers.[2]

The most valuable assets acquired at Union were the railways and harbours. The National Convention made a laudable effort to keep them out of politics; it separated their finances from ordinary revenue and laid down elaborate provisions to guard against extravagance and mismanagement.[3] Railways and harbours were to be administered "on business principles by a Board of which the Minister of Railways was Chairman".[4] But the Board was small, and its members lacked knowledge and strength to combat the Minister, who in turn was influenced by Cabinet and Caucus decisions. There were vague recommendations for the promotion of cheap transport, agricultural and industrial development, but no provisions for efficient management. General revenue was not to profit from the railways except during the first four years of Union, no less than £3,000,000 being paid into general revenue within two years.[5] In 1916 the Railway and Harbour Board was reduced to a purely advisory capacity.[6] There is much evidence that railway and harbour administration is in practice far different from what the framers of the South Africa Act had intended.[7]

The fathers of the constitution attempted to safeguard the public services of the Union from political patronage, favouritism and nepotism, which are invariable sign-posts on the road to graft, bribery and corruption. A Public Service Commission was to be set up with power to frame rules as to the qualifications of candidates and the

[1] House of Assembly Debates, 1913, cc. 2835, 3538.

[2] E.g. a bitter attack on the Auditor-General's Report by the Minister of Posts and Telegraphs (Walter Madeley), *Cape Times*, 30 May 1928.

[3] South Africa Act, ss. 117, 130, 131.

[4] *Ibid.* ss. 127, 141, 142.

[5] Acts 8 of 1910, 27 of 1911, 22 of 1912.

[6] Railway Board Act, 17 of 1916.

[7] *Journal of Comparative Legislation*, 2nd ser., XLI (1918), 167–9; Frankel, S. H., *Railway Policy of South Africa*.

classification of services, and to make recommendations as to appointments and promotions.[1] The salaries of the Commissioners were too low, the period of appointment (five years) too short, and the provisions for security of tenure inadequate.[2] The higher posts, part-time officials and the members of the numerous boards were not under its supervision. Though hampered by these difficulties, the Commission made a courageous effort to exercise its functions in the spirit of the Act of Union. There followed friction as to the interpretation of its powers, the Government claiming that the Commission had no voice in normal expansion of services but only as regards readjustment and reorganisation.[3] The Commission appealed to Parliament, but received scant sympathy.[4] Legislation followed to validate the action of the Government and to curtail the powers of the Commissioners;[5] protests were of no avail.[6] During the following years the Government did not even go to the trouble of keeping the Commission up to its statutory strength and more *ex post facto* laws were required.[7] A Commission of Enquiry, appointed in 1918, reported in favour of a stronger and more independent Public Service Commission.[8] The Government accepted recommendations for the increase of the salaries of the Commissioners and for giving them better security of tenure. Disputes between the Commissioners and the Ministers were to be settled by the Cabinet, the Commission having the option of reporting to Parliament.[9] While the Commission is undoubtedly stronger now than it was before 1918, the practice of appointing good party men to vacancies has led to a unanimity of a kind not contemplated. Cases where Ministers make nominations over the head of the Commission are still frequent.[10]

While the structure of the central government in the Union follows closely in its broad features that of the other Dominions, its Provincial organisation is unique. The National Convention, faced by the necessity of placating federal sentiment in Natal and by the need of some intermediate institution between the central legislature and municipal bodies, created a cross between a Canadian Province and a French Department.

[1] Public Service and Pensions Act, 29 of 1912.
[2] *Round Table*, No. 80, p. 896.
[3] Second Report of Public Service Commission, 1913 (*U.G.* 9 of 1914).
[4] Brookes, in *Coming of Age*, p. 337.
[5] Act 39 of 1914.
[6] Third Report of Public Service Commission, 1914 (*U.G.* 1916).
[7] Act 15 of 1916.
[8] Graham Commission, Fifth Report (*U.G.* 1920).
[9] Act 27 of 1923.
[10] See article on "Union Public Service", *Cape Times*, 5 February 1930; *Round Table*, No. 80 (September 1930). Political influence of this kind has not diminished. Of late there have been other factors that have lessened the efficiency of the public service, Among them are compulsory bilingualism which has the effect of debarring immigrants from posts for a considerable time, and the policy of *apartheid* which has resulted in an acute shortage of suitable personnel for all jobs reserved for white persons.

Each original colony was to retain its identity as a Province of the Union with an Administrator at its head. This officer is appointed for five years and may not be removed in the interim except by the Governor-General-in-Council for cause assigned, which must be communicated to both Houses.[1] This favourite device of the Convention to lessen party pressure has worked sufficiently well in so far as no case of removal has yet arisen, but no Government has reappointed any Administrator who was not in political sympathy with it.[2] The scrupulous moderation of Botha led him to consult those members of his Cabinet who were residents of the Province affected before making his choice;[3] but all that the constitution requires is that, as far as practicable, preference be given to persons resident in the Province.[4] The Administrator, like a Governor of a Crown Colony, serves in a dual capacity. As executive head of the Province he is chairman of the Executive Committee; he summons and prorogues but does not dissolve the Provincial Council. He may recommend legislation, sit and speak, but not vote, in the Council, and no moneys may be appropriated without his recommendation.[5] As the representative of the Union Government he administers matters entrusted to him which do not fall within the functions of the Provincial Council.[6]

An Executive Committee of four is elected by each Provincial Council by proportional voting, the effects of which have been, outside Natal and the Orange Free State where the opposition is very weak, to give the Administrator the balance of power. The members of this committee hold their seats during the full life of the Provincial Council and are thus impervious to votes of censure. The residuary functions of the executives of the several colonies are vested in them. There is rigidity in procedure in so far as all questions are determined by a majority of votes, the Administrator having a deliberative vote and also a casting vote if need be.[7] In recommending appropriations he may act without consulting the other members of the Executive.[8]

The Provincial Councils are elected for three years upon the same franchise as for the House of Assembly.[9] A person qualified to vote was also eligible as a member; there was therefore no colour bar in the Cape Province.[10] The Councils may make Ordinances upon a specified list of subjects provided they are not repugnant to any Act

[1] South Africa Act, s. 68.

[2] The appointment in 1958, as Administrator of Natal, of A. E. Trollip, an Opposition member for a Transvaal constituency in the last Parliament, is noteworthy.

[3] Engelenburg, F. V., *General Louis Botha*, p. 204.

[4] South Africa Act, s. 68.

[5] *Ibid.* ss. 74, 78, 79, 89.

[6] *Ibid.* s. 84.

[7] *Ibid.*, ss. 78, 81, 82.

[8] Hofmeyr, J. H., in *Coming of Age*, p. 301.

[9] Extended to five years in 1935.

[10] South Africa Act, s. 70. By Act 30 of 1956 members of Provincial Councils must be Europeans.

of Parliament.[1] No Ordinance has force until assented to by the Governor-General-in-Council, which means in effect that the Councils merely *recommend* legislation; such assent may be withheld or reserved. A reserved Ordinance falls away if not assented to within one year.[2] The field of provincial legislation is strewn with much litigation. The Courts have ruled that Provincial Councils, though non-sovereign, possess all the attributes of legislative bodies; hence the Courts cannot interfere with Ordinances merely because they are unwise, impolitic or unreasonable.[3] The Privy Council has upheld a decision that the Provincial Councils may invalidate contracts or pass *ex post facto* laws.[4] Power to regulate does not include power to prohibit (e.g. a Transvaal Ordinance prohibiting betting was declared *ultra vires*),[5] but it does include power to discriminate as between black and white.[6] A rule of procedure requiring the taking of the oath of allegiance as a condition precedent to the taking of a seat in Council has been held *ultra vires* as creating an additional qualification for membership of the Council, notwithstanding that such oath of allegiance is required from members of the Union Parliament.[7]

The financial relations between the Union and the Provinces constitute the most important factor in the provincial experiment. The Provinces were given general powers to raise revenue by direct taxation and to borrow money upon the sole credit of the Province,[8] but, pending the report of a Financial Relations Inquiry Commission, the provincial services were to be met by parliamentary subsidies.[9] Hence for several years the Provinces were pensionaries of the Union Government and did not tax themselves at all. The Commission duly reported in 1912, and an agreement was reached with the Provincial Executives upon the basis of the majority report.[10] Half the normal expenditure of the Provinces was to be met by subsidy subject to certain limits as to increase; their powers of direct taxation were

[1] *Ibid.* ss. 85, 86.

[2] *Ibid.* s. 90.

[3] *Middelburg Municipality* v. *Gertzen* ([1914] A.D. 544).

[4] *Marshall's Township Syndicate Ltd.* v. *Johannesburg Investment Co. Ltd.* ([1920] A.C. 420) quoted in 37 *South African Law Journal.*

[5] *R.* v. *Williams* ([1914] A.D. 460).

[6] *George* v. *Pretoria Municipality* ([1916] T.P.D. 501), but see *Journal of Comparative Legislation*, 2nd ser., xxxv (1916), 63–6. How far-reaching the ancillary powers of the Councils are may be judged from the following A.D. decisions. In *Abraham* v. *Durban Corporation* 1927, A.D. 444, the Court held that a Natal Ordinance limiting the municipal franchise to those who were eligible to be registered as parliamentary voters was valid; thereby Indian ratepayers were deprived of the municipal vote. And in *Swart and Nicol* v. *de Kock and Garner*, 1951 (3) S.A. 589 A.D., the Judges by 3 votes to 2 upheld a Transvaal Provincial Ordinance extending the mother-tongue medium to private unsubsidised schools, notwithstanding the equality of the two official languages, on the ground that this power was ancillary to provincial control over lower education. See also May, H. J., the *South African Constitution*, 3rd ed., pp. 356–90.

[7] *Conradie* v. *Vermeulen N.O.* ([1920] O.P.D. 203).

[8] South Africa Act, s. 85 (i, ii).

[9] *Ibid.* s. 118.

[10] Reports of Financial Relations Inquiry Commission (*U.G.* 11 and 14 of 1912).

limited as regards certain sources of revenue, which were to be assigned to the Provinces but levied under Union laws; provincial loans were to be raised from the Union Government alone; an additional grant of £100,000 was given to Natal and the Orange Free State.[1]

Although the Union was then only three years old, Parliament was inclined to regard the Provincial Councils as unwanted and unnatural. Their legislative efforts were considered as inroads upon the liberty of the subject. Creswell, leader of the Labour Party, hoped that the Government's veto would not be a dead letter, and Smuts explained that before assent was given to any Ordinance, the law advisers would be consulted. By a strange irony a Labour majority in the Transvaal was the first to feel the effect of the veto.[2] Smuts further stated that one of the principal reasons for setting up Provincial Councils was to keep elementary education out of the political arena;[3] but where elementary education ends and higher education begins it would now be well-nigh impossible to determine.[4]

Though possessing all the trappings of a Parliament: the caucus, the whips and the divisions, the provincial system lacks all the essentials of independent existence. There is no provincial judiciary, no police, no separate civil service or departments of state. The Council is little more than a shadow parliament. Its meetings are brief, its business dry, its powers weak. At the most, it is a stepping-stone to political promotion. In the exercise of its limited powers it has failed to gain much public support or sympathy.[5]

Constitutional conflicts within the Provincial Councils have been as frequent as they have been futile. In the Transvaal in 1914 the Labour majority on the Council declined to elect any members to the Executive Committee, because under the system of proportional representation the Administrator (in whom it had no confidence) would hold the balance of power. It also refused to vote the necessary appropriations; but the expenditure was met by the Administrator from advances made by the Union Government. The grant of this loan without the approval of the Council was contrary to law and had to be validated by subsequent legislation.[6] Attempts on the part of the Council to limit the powers of the Administrator resulted in three Ordinances being reserved and allowed to lapse.[7] In the Cape in

[1] Financial Relations Act, 10 of 1913.

[2] House of Assembly Debates, 1913, cc. 2891, 2903, 2910.

[3] Senate Debates, 1913, c. 239.

[4] Hofmeyr, J. H., in *Coming of Age*, p. 314 Much has been clarified by Act 38 of 1945. Higher education includes technical education and the training of teachers in secondary schools as well as university education. On the other hand elementary education of Natives has been transferred to the Department of Native Affairs (Bantu Education Act, 47 of 1953).

[5] *Cape Times*, 11 May 1928; *Round Table*, No. 52 (September 1923).

[6] Financial Adjustment Act, 42 of 1917, s. 2; Nathan, *South African Commonwealth*, p. 157.

[7] *Journal of Comparative Legislation*, 2nd ser., XXXVIII (1917), 131–2; Keith, *Responsible Government in the Dominions*, II, 724, footnote.

1928 there was the ludicrous incident of the Executive Committee unanimously recommending certain financial measures, which the Council as unanimously rejected without bringing about any crisis in the mutual relationship.[1]

A Commission of Inquiry which reported in 1916 had little good to say of the provincial system: "They are so constantly altering the law that no one knows what it is." The Commission recommended the abolition of the Councils, the transfer of education to the Union, and the creation of several administrative bodies for local purposes.[2] The solitary Natal representative, in a minority report, pleaded for wider powers for the Councils and pointed out, with some reason, that abolition would not diminish expenditure but increase it.[3] However, no action was taken on the report.

The subsidy basis of financial relationship, introduced in 1913 as a temporary experiment, was continued with variations until 1925, when the adoption of a *per capita* grant based upon school attendance was hailed with relief. The efforts of the Provinces to find new revenue have led to much litigation. The Courts held that the taxing of mining profits was *intra vires*,[4] but came to an opposite conclusion as regards the taxing of Natives.[5] Since 1925 the Provinces have lost the general power of imposing direct taxation and are limited to the specific taxes enumerated in the Provincial Subsidies Act of that year.[6]

Parliament may abolish the Provincial Councils or abridge their powers, but such bills had to be reserved.[7] Nearly all the Financial Relation Bills since 1913 have abridged their powers, but have been assented to after reservation.[8] The abolition of reservation by the Status Act (1934) was followed by an Act safeguarding the existing rights of Provincial Councils.[9]

No issue before the National Convention was of greater moment than the future political status of non-Europeans. Broadly speaking, there was antagonism between the traditional Cape view-point and that of the North, where the old Trekker principle that there shall be no equality between white and black survived as a complete colour bar. The Convention could do no more than accept the *status quo* as a basis for the Union with safeguards against the disfranchisement of non-Europeans in the Cape Province.[10] These safeguards included

[1] *Cape Times*, 11 May 1928; Hofmeyr, J. H., in *Coming of Age*, p. 316.
[2] Report of Provincial Administration Commission (*U.G.* 45 of 1916).
[3] *Ibid.* p. 50.
[4] *New Modderfontein Gold Mining Co.* v. *Transvaal Prov. Adm.* ([1919] A.D. 367).
[5] *Transvaal Prov. Adm.* v. *Letanka* ([1922] A.D. 102).
[6] Act 46 of 1925. By a consolidating Act (38 of 1945) the subsidy system was restored and the sources of provincial revenue were strictly defined.
[7] South Africa Act, s. 64.
[8] Acts 9 of 1917, 5 of 1921, 46 of 1925.
[9] Section 149 of the South Africa Act was amended so as to require a petition of the Provincial Council affected for the alteration of its boundaries or the abridgment of its powers. But as this section is not entrenched, it has no more than a moral value.
[10] South Africa Act, s. 35.

the reservation of repealing or amending bills, and there were hints in high quarters that such reservation would be real.[1] It was hoped that the four Senators nominated on the ground of special knowledge of Native affairs would also hold a watching brief.[2] On the whole the victory lay with the North and Natal. The Cape members have been by no means satisfied with the vesting of general administrative powers in the Governor-General-in-Council, in other words, in the Ministry.[3]

Since Union there has been an undoubted urge to segregate the Native, geographically, socially, economically and politically. The spirit of the North has so far prevailed that the view is generally accepted that Native development should proceed upon communal and not on individual lines. There has been much legislation—on the whole barren of results, but indicative of the ideas that prompt the legislators. In the first decade, Native policy was tentative, experimental; in the second it was more certain and definite. By various stages Parliament has delegated its powers over Natives to the Governor-General-in-Council.[4]

The coping-stone of administrative supremacy was not supplied until the passing of the Native Administration Act of 1927, whereby the Governor-General-in-Council was given very full powers to legislate by proclamation even to the extent of repealing Acts of Parliament, with the widest discretion in dealing with tribes or individuals.[5]

[1] *Journal of Comparative Legislation*, 2nd ser., XI (1909), 54.

[2] Senate Debates, 1912, c. 820. The four Senators who are elected to represent the Natives under the Native Representation Act of 1936 have proved more effective than the nominated Senators.

[3] South Africa Act, s. 147; Laurence, *Merriman*, p. 275.

[4] A systematic Native policy on a basis of *apartheid* (separateness) has been undertaken by the Nationalist Governments since 1948. The results so far have been mainly to create unrest and hardship.

[5] House of Assembly Debates, 1927, LX, cc. 5096 *sqq*.

CHAPTER XXVI

THE GERMANS IN SOUTH-WEST AFRICA 1883–1914

(a) The Military Occupation, 1883–1907

WE have seen in earlier chapters how, largely owing to geographical conditions, the territory lying to the north of Cape Colony along and behind the Atlantic seaboard did not attract settlers and, save for a few missionaries and traders, was left in its primitive state. The opening up of the region came late and was carried out by the German Empire independently of the rest of South Africa. The German régime lasted for thirty years, during which its story lies apart from that of the rest of the sub-continent and demands separate treatment.

The Native population of the region is akin to that originally found in Cape Colony; hence, the description given in an earlier chapter need not here be extended.[1] It is estimated that in the last quarter of the nineteenth century there were about 5000 of the Bushman tribes, 20,000 Namaqua-Hottentots, 27,000 Berg Damaras, 30,000 Hereros, 137,000 Ovambo and some 8000 Bastards living in the territory, but the figures are largely guesswork and do not indicate accurately much more than the proportions of the various tribes. The Namaquas live in the south, the Bastards and Hereros in the centre and the Ovambo in the remote north, while the Bushmen are now scattered throughout the east and north-east and the Berg Damaras live in separate groups in Namaqualand and Hereroland.

There was constant hostility between the Hereros and Namaquas leading to frequent and destructive wars, and the efforts of the missionaries who, by 1880, had been working in the territory for some forty years, had often to be exerted to bring about peace and prevent the complete destruction of the defeated tribes. Such a peace had been arranged in 1880 after a long Namaqua-Herero war when Germany first appeared on the scene. In 1883, as was stated above,[2] the Bremen merchant, F. A. E. Lüderitz, received the tacit approval of the German Government for his schemes for the purchase of lands from tribal Chiefs in the territory, and on 1 May 1883 he bought Angra Pequeña (later called Lüderitzbucht) and the lands lying five miles round it from the Hottentot chief, Joseph Frederick of Bethany. On 25 August 1884 he extended his nominal purchases from the same Chief to include a coastal strip of 20 miles wide from the Orange River northwards to 26° South latitude. By three further treaties with other

[1] *Vide supra*, Chapter II.   [2] *Vide supra* ,p. 526 .

chiefs this indefatigable promoter of German interests carried his claims further north over the whole coast up to 28° South, while on 24 April 1884 Prince Bismarck, Chancellor of the German Empire, announced to the German Consul at Cape Town that Lüderitz and his establishments were taken under the formal protection of Germany.[1] A new complication was thus introduced into the South African tangle.

The treaties of purchase were expanded into treaties of protectorate with the German Empire by Dr Gustav Nachtigal, the Consul-General for the west coast of Africa. In these treaties the Native Captains and their subjects were guaranteed protection of life and property, and the jurisdiction of the Captains over their own tribesmen was recognised. Disputes between Europeans, however, or between Europeans and Natives were to be subject to German jurisdiction. The right of entrance of German merchants and settlers was conceded. Further protectorate treaties were concluded in rapid succession between 1885 and 1890 by two official plenipotentiaries of the German Empire, Drs Göring and Carl Buttner.

The plan of the German Government for the colonisation of their new protectorate followed British and French models, and it was decided to establish chartered companies for its development. The first was the *Deutsche Kolonialgesellschaft*. When in 1886 Lüderitz was accidentally drowned on a journey to the Orange, this company entered into his inheritance and assumed possession of the whole coastal strip. To protect the inhabitants and keep the peace, the formation of a small armed force became an absolute necessity. Two officers and five non-commissioned officers were recruited in Germany, who, it was hoped, would be able to train a body of Native police for use in case of emergency.

Dr Göring, with a small staff of officials to assist him, acted as representative of the Empire, but having no force at his disposal, he was powerless in the event of a serious crisis such as arose in 1888. Maharero, the Herero captain of Okahandja, whose influence was felt throughout Damaraland, was hard pressed by Hendrik Witbooi, the Hottentot Captain of Gibeon, and Dr Göring found it impossible to give him the protection guaranteed by the treaty. In addition he was subject to the constant influence of a trader, Robert Lewis, who took it ill that South-West Africa had become a German colony and succeeded in persuading Maharero to repudiate his treaty with the German Empire (October 1888). The *Kolonialgesellschaft*, with its small police force, was unable to protect the highest official of the German administration or to establish his position, and Dr Göring and his officials had to withdraw to the protection of the Cape Government at Walvis Bay.

The German Government now recognised that effective colonial

[1] *Vide supra*, p. 528.

development was impossible without regular troops, and a force of specially recruited volunteers was therefore sent to the new colony in June 1889, and was placed under the command of Captain C. von François. It was still thought possible, with a small nucleus of German regulars, to drill and train a much bigger force from among the Natives, especially the Bastards of Rehoboth.

Since the Hereros had repudiated their treaty, it was too dangerous to place troops in their land, for though Hendrik Witbooi worried only the Hereros and refrained from hostilities against the Europeans, the Germans recognised in him their chief enemy, since he was striving to turn the other Chiefs also against them. Von François for the time being could not attack Hendrik so as to relieve the Hereros and rid himself of his enemies in Namaqualand, but he could at any rate intercept his supplies of munitions. He therefore issued a proclamation forbidding the importation of arms and ammunition, which until then had been carried on unhindered from Walvis Bay. To check this traffic of firearms into the interior Fort Wilhelm was built on the Bay Road at Tsaobis. Having thus gained a foothold in the interior, von François left a garrison at Tsaobis and then proceeded to Windhoek, where on 18 October 1890 the present flourishing capital of South-West Africa was founded. Lying as it did in the centre of the country between the warring Namaquas and Hereros, Windhoek was in a strategic sense admirably suited for military occupation, and from this vantage ground the establishment of German rule both to the south and to the north could be successfully undertaken.

Meanwhile Hendrik Witbooi had proceeded from Gibeon to Hornkranz, where he occupied a fortified position in an almost inaccessible neighbourhood with the double object of being nearer the herds of the Hereros and of securing himself against surprise. Although his attempts to persuade the Namaqua Captains to abrogate the Protectorate treaties were unsuccessful, he was reinforced by Namaqua tribesmen greedy for booty.

In the summer of 1893, von François, who had received reinforcements from Germany, attacked Hendrik Witbooi in his lair and compelled him to flee. But Witbooi's power was in no wise broken. He tried to conclude peace with Samuel Maharero, the son and successor of Maharero, in order to make common cause against the German troops. The new situation thus created demanded strong reinforcements, and in addition the transformation of the mercenary force into an imperial protectorate force. Major Theodor Leutwein was sent out as the commander, while von François, after building forts at Gibeon and Beersheba, returned to Europe on leave. Leutwein defeated Witbooi at Nankluft in August 1894 and compelled him to sign a treaty (14 September 1894) promising to return to Gibeon with his subjects, to receive a military force, and in case of necessity to place fighting men at the disposal of the Government. In return his chieftainship was confirmed and an annual salary was granted him by the German Government.

The object of the generous treatment given to Witbooi was to reconcile a dangerous opponent to his fate and, if possible, to convert him into a useful ally. But new difficulties arose, for the Namaqua tribe at Gobabis, always prone to plunder, rebelled in alliance with the eastern Hereros (Ovambanderu), who were embittered because Samuel Maharero of Okahandja had been appointed Paramount Chief of all the Hereros, a novelty to the tribe which down to that time had had no Paramount Chief. The Protectorate troops had to take up arms again in 1896, and the campaign closed with the complete subjection of both tribes. The Namaquas lost the right of choosing their own Chief and were placed under Hendrik Witbooi of Gibeon, while both the leaders of the eastern Hereros, Nikodemus and Kahimemua, were shot as rebels at Okahandja in June 1896. There were other risings between 1897 and 1901, but they were merely of local importance.

As the years passed both Namaquas and Hereros felt themselves cramped and injured by the advancing power of the Germans. Here and there immigrants began to settle as farmers. It is true that the farms were legally bought and that all the money received for them went to the Native vendors; but since land, both in Namaqualand and in Hereroland, was looked upon as the property of the tribe, the tribesmen found it impossible to submit to the new conditions under which large tracts of their grazing grounds became the property of individuals. Other grievances arose from the dealings of peripatetic traders, who sold merchandise to the tribesmen on credit. When the time for payment came, the traders often claimed those cattle, which, according to old tribal custom, the Hereros might not alienate. Everywhere inflammable material was collecting. The old feud between the Namaquas and Hereros was forgotten; all that was needed for a conflagration was the kindling spark. It fell late in 1900 and set the whole of South-West Africa ablaze.

At the end of that year a serious quarrel broke out at Warmbad in the extreme south of Namaqualand between the Namaquas and a German official stationed there. Both the official and the Namaqua Captain were shot, and this was the signal for the rising of the Bondels tribe. The Namaquas assembled at Zandfontein, on the Orange River, and received reinforcements from the Karas mountains under the leaders Morris and Morenga. It was necessary to concentrate all the forces in the Protectorate in order to quell the rising, which luckily remained local. After several engagements Leutwein succeeded in concluding peace with the insurgents at Kalkfontein on 27 January 1904, and the Bondels surrendered three hundred guns and returned to their lands.

The despatch of the troops to Namaqualand left the whole of the north practically without protection. This gave the Hereros a favourable opportunity to attempt to shake off the German yoke and win back the lands and water-holes (fountains) they had sold. Samuel Maharero gave the command that, while the missionaries, both British and Afrikaner, were to be spared, every German should be massacred. One hundred and twenty-three German male settlers were massacred, but the influence of Christianity among the insurgents was already so strong that the wives and children of the Germans, with three exceptions, escaped with their lives.

The rebellion broke out on 12 January 1904 at Okahandja, the seat of Samuel the Paramount Chief, and by the beginning of February all the Herero Chiefs were in the field. The few soldiers who had been left behind to protect the forts at Okahandja, Omaruru and other places dared not risk a fight in the open and were content to protect such of the colonists as had fled thither. No one knew when help would come, if it came at all. The telegraph wires had been cut and the railway lines torn up in several places, while Omaruru and Okahandja were closely besieged by the rebels.

At the end of 1903, the 40 officers and 730 men of the regular forces had been reinforced by men on the retired list, while the Bastards and Berg Damaras, who had remained loyal, rendered useful services to the troops in the way of wagon-driving and reconnoitring. The Berg Damaras had not forgotten that it was due to the Germans that they had been delivered from encroaching Hereros and Namaquas, and that it was through the exertions of the missionaries and the German Government that they had obtained the reserve at Okombahe as their first and only tribal possession. In spite of all this, however, German rule in South-West Africa was in extreme jeopardy in those days of January 1904.

In a few days, the beleaguered forts were relieved and the Hereros withdrew, driving off their cattle and those which had been seized from the massacred German farmers. Thus commenced the second stage of the rebellion.

Major Leutwein, having returned from the south and assumed the command of the troops, set to work. Reinforcements arrived from Germany and it became possible to take the offensive. After a good deal of fighting in which heavy losses were sustained on both sides, though chiefly on that of the rebels, the Hereros assembled at the Great and the Small Waterberg. To surround and subdue the whole people was not possible with the troops at Leutwein's disposal, and yet everything depended on his being able, not merely to crush individual clans but to end the campaign at one blow by means of a grand attack. At the command of the Kaiser, therefore, operations were suspended for the time being until sufficient troops had arrived. Leutwein proceeded to Germany and General von Trotha took over the supreme command. As soldier and as administrator Leutwein had gained the confidence of the people, both German and African, and it was questionable whether a new commander without knowledge of the country could reasonably be expected to do as well as he had done.

General von Trotha evolved an ambitious plan of attack, difficult of execution in an unsurveyed and bush-clad region against Hereros, who numbered between 40,000 and 50,000 souls and possessed about 6000 rifles. The idea was to deliver a series of converging attacks in the Waterberg, and in accordance with this plan the main battle was fought at Hamakari. The Hereros offered a stubborn resistance, but after a long struggle they recognised that they must either yield or break through somewhere with their women and children and cattle. They chose the latter alternative, but a serious difference of plan arose among them. The old men desired to break through towards the north-west in order to withdraw their great herds into the tropical Kaokoveld, the former abode of their fathers. The young men saw that this attempt would probably fail and looked to the waterless sandy desert to the east with the object of passing through it into British territory. Without coming to a definite decision, the Chief Samuel escaped with his personal followers through the gap still left open eastward towards Omaheke and escaped into British territory. His people, thus left to their fate, immediately followed. The retreat continued always in an easterly direction, and, in spite of the lack of horses and the impediment of the cattle, was so rapid that the weary German command failed to overtake the fugitives.

But what the troops had not succeeded in doing was accomplished by the sandy desert. Thousands of the Hereros died of thirst; the cattle perished wholesale, and only small fragments of the tribes reached British territory to find a new home in Bechuanaland on the shores of Lake Ngami. Other fragments roamed about the land—dangerous bands without internal cohesion. Thus the Hereros had been crushed, but there was no real peace in the land and the farmers did not dare resume operations; they had to be on their guard lest they should fall into the hands of some raiding band. The fact that numerous official raids against the marauders were made in all directions and many prisoners brought in was little satisfaction for the farmers. The soldiers who were stationed on their farms to protect them proved more effective, but in spite of all their exertions the Germans could not clear the bush.

General von Trotha was recalled and Herr von Lindequist undertook the administration of the colony as its first civilian Governor. While his predecessor had declared that "the destruction of all the rebellious tribes is the goal of my endeavours", von Lindequist recognised that the realisation of such an aim was against the interests of the land, since Native labour was a necessary factor in its development. The new Governor, who had already played a part in the affairs of South-West Africa as judge and administrator under Leutwein before 1900, knew how great was the influence of the missionaries on the Herero people. Though only a small proportion of the people had been converted to Christianity, the Christians were universally respected and the missionaries had the confidence even of the pagan Hereros, who never doubted their honesty. That had been proved at the beginning of the war by the fact that none of the German missionaries had been murdered, though in some cases they had been compelled to remain for weeks among the Hereros before they succeeded in reaching the forts. Von Lindequist therefore appointed three missionaries to control Herero encampments in various places, whither the fugitives could betake themselves without fear of punishment. The encampments were not under military control but were administered by the civil government, which supplied whatever was necessary for their maintenance. More than 12,000 Hereros came in during the following months and the raiding bands gradually disappeared. Farms could now be occupied once more without danger. The captured Hereros were supplied to the farmers as labourers, and in 1907 the system had been so far successful that the last prisoner camp was broken up and the Herero war was at an end.

Three ordinances regulated the relations of the Europeans with the Natives. The former chieftainships were abolished; tribal domains were declared Crown property and confiscated and, for the time being, the Hereros were forbidden to keep cattle, since they no longer possessed grazing land and everywhere there was a demand for them as labourers and herdsmen. In order to prevent injustice on the part of the employers, the rights of the labourers were laid down by law; they were allowed to choose their own employers and to move about subject to a pass law. So they resigned themselves to their hard lot till gradually they were permitted once more to acquire cattle.

In the meantime, while the Herero war was still raging, unrest had once more broken out in Namaqualand. It is true that Hendrik Witbooi, now nearly 80 years old, had by the terms of his treaty placed a considerable number of his men at the disposal of the German commander for the struggle at the Waterberg. On the other hand, Morenga, a leader of raiding bands, had surprised the small German force stationed in Dawignab (23 July 1904) and, later, the station at Wasserfall was taken. Hendrik Witbooi, who was himself subject to fits of religious ecstasy and stood under the influence of Stuurman, a "prophet" from the Cape Colony, formally repudiated his treaty of submission and declared war. Von Burgsdorff, the district officer at Gibeon, hoping to be able to avert hostilities with Witbooi by a personal interview, went to him without a guard, relying on his previous good relations with the Chief. On the way he was treacherously murdered and the Namaqua war commenced (4 October 1904).

The small German force, scattered in detachments in various parts of Namaqualand, suddenly found itself confronted by tribesmen with 600 rifles. Previous experience had shown that this new enemy must be taken seriously. Though the Bastards of Rehoboth, the Namaquas of Beersheba and a section of the Namaquas of Bethany held aloof from the war, yet even so the Germans could not move before their troops had been reinforced.

In November preparations had so far advanced that Colonel Deimling could attack the enemy. In the case of the Namaquas it was not possible, as it had been in that of the Hereros at the Waterberg, to bring off a combined attack. From the beginning the Namaqua war was of the guerilla type and thus proved most exhausting, particularly since the enemy knew the country much better than the Germans. The war consisted almost entirely of pursuits of isolated bands. In December 1904 the Witboois were beaten at Naris, and in January 1905 Simon Koper was defeated at Gochas.

In April 1905 General von Trotha, whose work in the north was completed, took command of the troops in Namaqualand. The main portion of the troops which had been concentrated at the Waterberg and in the north could be marched south. It was hoped that it would be possible to track down and defeat Hendrik Witbooi, the most dangerous of the rebels. Hendrik, however, had fled to the almost waterless Kalahari whither the troops could not follow him; but suddenly he appeared at Vaalgras not far from Keetmanshoop. During an attack on a hospital transport he was mortally wounded and died advising this followers to lay down their arms as further resistance would be useless. Hendrik's son and successor, Samuel Isaac, was ready to stop hostilities. Not so Simon Koper, who was somewhere in the Kalahari with his warriors, and other bands which were constantly threatening the security of south-eastern Namaqualand.

There was as yet no railway from Keetmanshoop to Lüderitzbucht, and serious difficulties arose in connection with the supply of provisions. It was not until March 1906 that it was possible to take the offensive once more. The dangerous Namaqua leader Morenga was beaten in May 1906 and driven over the border to surrender to the Cape Police, who interned him at Prieska; but he escaped, and once more collected a band around him until at length, on 20 September 1906, he was mortally wounded in a scuffle with British troops and his band dispersed.

The last rebel tribe surrendered their arms in December and returned to their lands at Warmbad and Kalkfontein South, where they were granted life and freedom under German sovereignty.

In the Kalahari, Simon Koper had still to be subdued. After long and careful preparation Captain Friedrich von Erckert succeeded in surrounding him at Seatsub. Von Erckert was slain, but the ever-threatening danger which had so badly hindered the settlement of the south was at length completely removed.

Thus, early in 1907, the state of war in South-West Africa could be declared at an end. The troops had fought 88 engagements against the Hereros and 295 against the Namaquas. The total number of Europeans killed in the north and the south together was 179 officers and 2169 men.

(*b*) Civil Administration and Economic Conditions

The constitutional history of the German colony of South-West Africa falls into three periods of which the first extends from the occupation down to 1891. This was a phase of purely mercantile administration when Bismarck's original plan of allowing commercial colonies to grow up unassisted by the state, save in matters of defence, was being worked out. This system in the end proved impracticable and was abandoned. The second period, extending from 1891 to the Herero rising in 1904, was one of military administration. During the first period there was already an armed force consisting of so-called "*Reiter*" or "troopers", though there were scarcely any horses. These "troopers" formed the nucleus of the colonial force organised in 1891 and raised in 1894 by Cabinet order to the rank of *Kaiserliche Schutztruppe*, i.e. Imperial defence troops. They were a body of German mercenaries especially entrusted with the duty of defending the life and property of the merchants and settlers who composed the infant colony, and designed also to open up and administer the country. The supreme command was given to an Imperial Commissioner, styled after 1893 *Landeshauptmann* (i.e. Provincial Administrator) and after 1898 Governor.

The first Governor was Theodor Leutwein, appointed as *Landeshauptmann* in 1893. He held office for eleven years. By his energetic and able government German supremacy was maintained at a trifling cost, supported only by a force of a few hundred men. He divided the colony into seven military districts with 35 posts. A small nucleus of mobile troops was retained in the capital, and the remainder of the forces, some 700 men in all, were apportioned to the scattered posts throughout the colony. Military, police and purely technical administrative duties were all entrusted to the same hands. In 1896 general conscription was introduced, though at the beginning of the Herero rising there were only some 750 merchants and settlers who could be considered fit for military service. In addition to the white settlers, Natives according to their ability were bound to serve as police or soldiers for a period of two years when called upon.

Leutwein sought to develop the colony by means of this primitive military system; he also introduced for the first time civil jurisdiction by districts to which civilian officials were appointed. If they had legal training they combined judicial with civil functions. In the districts advisory boards were set up, each composed as a rule of three persons chosen, if possible, by election, the idea being that a representative of each of the three groups of settlers—merchants, artisans and farmers—should be heard before any grave decision of policy was adopted. Here was a beginning of representative institutions, but it really had no influence.

The Herero rebellion marks the end of the Leutwein régime and also the end of the purely or preponderantly military period of administration. Leutwein was severely and often unjustly criticised, but responsible circles in Berlin realised that far more energy and money must be poured into the defended district of the colony if it were to be properly and usefully developed. For that purpose a civil administration adapted to all needs must be introduced. In 1906 a *Gouvernementsrat*, modelled on the Legislative Councils of the British Crown colonies, was set up. This consisted of eleven official and eleven non-official members having certain age and property qualifications and holding office for two years. The transactions of the *Gouvernementsrat* were purely advisory in character, for its resolutions were in no way binding upon the Governor; but the system was a distinct step forward, for it gave to the farmers and merchants some influence in the government of the colony.

Finally, in 1909, self-government was established in the districts of the *Schutzgebiet*,[1] where civil administration was thoroughly organised. All the German inhabitants were grouped together into *Gemeinde* or corporate communities, and Local Councils were elected in each. The *Bezirksräte* or District Councillors, however, were retained, meeting in district councils. Here, therefore, was the foundation on which to evolve a representative *Landesrat* or Legislative Assembly from the nominated *Gouvernementsrat*, that is to say a deliberative organ of parliamentary character.[2] There were then in German South-West Africa nine districts entirely under civil administration employing 824 administrative officers. They included all the principal colonial settlements. The remainder of the colony was divided into eight districts, the heads of which were military officers working in conjunction with the district constabulary. Three judicial districts had been established with a Supreme Court sitting at Windhoek.

Some 15,000 white inhabitants occupied the defended districts at the outbreak of the First World War. The defence force included some 2000, artisans and labourers numbered 2000, settlers and farmers 1600, engineers and technicians 300, and merchants and inn-keepers

[1] The term *Schutzgebiet* was coined by Prince Bismarck as a special technical expression to stress the difference from the old type of colony and to create a new sort of oversea dominion.

[2] *German Colonial Handbook for* 1913.

1000. There were small groups of clergy, lawyers and medical men, some 3000 women and about the same number of children. Thus the population of the settled districts of the colony showed the typical characteristics of early colonial development, In comparison with the number in civil and private occupations, the number in official and military employ was still large.

At this time the territory under direct administration contained some 80,000 Natives, of whom 60,000 were in the Ovambo section in the north and the remainder in the Caprivi strip, which carried the colony across to the Zambesi. The Ovambo section was the only fertile region which in favourable years with normal rainfall was capable of being self-supporting; the rest of the colony was arid and demanded special methods of cultivation. Nevertheless, cereals could be raised in isolated areas if technical care and knowledge were devoted to them. Dr Theodor Seitz, the last Governor before the occupation of the colony by the Union, in later years deplored the neglect of agriculture and the concentration of the colonists on cattle-raising.

The Natives of South-West Africa, Hereros, Hottentots and Bantu, had always been engaged in cattle-raising. As distinct from those in tropical regions, the races in the temperate South-West African upland showed a spirit of confidence and independence. Accustomed to a free, nomad life in this comparatively empty and partly desert land, they were only too ready to oppose the incoming white settlers with bitter animosity. Thus, while the agricultural Ovambo easily adapted themselves to German rule because their territory was not attractive to white settlers, the Hottentots were more intractable, while the Hereros, who were almost wiped out during their great rebellion of 1904–5, were most difficult of all. With the handful of other Bantu and the Bushmen, who led a miserable existence tending their scanty flocks, the Germans managed to come to terms without much difficulty; but as soon as a serious endeavour was made to develop the colony into a real settlement for a white population, the question of the protection of the widely scattered farms from Native assault became acute. It was impossible to allot to each farm a guard of six or eight troopers, for while a farm might yield 6000 marks per annum, six troopers would cost the government some 18,000 marks.[1]

The immigrant Boers played a special part in the colony. They first appeared as more than a few stragglers in 1895–6, and in larger numbers in 1900 as a consequence of the war that was then reaching its climax in South Africa. Their forward march was exactly of the same sort as in the other treks that have been common throughout South African history. Before 1914 there were in German South-West Africa some 2000 persons of white stock who were not of German nationality, and almost the whole of them were Boers. In the German

[1] A mark in 1914 was worth one British shilling.

colony they stood for a growing consciousness of South African nationality, and through their ancient colonial tradition and practical experience they performed epoch-making work in the cultivation of the arid country. Irrigation, transport, the organisation of traffic and mining, all owed an immense debt to their enterprise. The new German settlers certainly learned a great deal from the Boers, but there is no doubt that a main source of the spirit of opposition to the traditional red-tape of responsible German officialdom was to be found there also.

The so-called Bastards, who were the offspring of Boer men and Hottentot women, first appeared in South-West Africa in 1860. Their numbers were considerable and by 1913 amounted to 1647, so that they presented difficult problems to the German authorities. They retained their own administration and their own advisers, and under the German flag did much profitable business, particularly in hides, timber and transport. Many were casual labourers and their morals were notoriously lax, but they supplied deficiencies in the Native labour market and thus made themselves useful to the German Government. Always in close association with the Boers on both sides of the international frontier, they consistently refused to take up arms against either the British or the Afrikaners.

The economic history of South-West Africa is to a great extent the history of the *Deutsche Kolonialgesellschaft für Südwestafrika*.[1] Founded in 1885 the company purchased the property acquired in the country by the Bremen merchant, Lüderitz, for 300,000 marks, and proceeded to open up the territory with the modest capital of 500,000 marks. Lüderitz had already put more than 800,000 marks into the enterprise. The new company was not an ordinary joint-stock company, but a chartered corporation, working under the statutes of Prussia, with the primary object, not of commercial gain, but of political and economic work for the general welfare. The principal German banks, the wealthiest capitalists, many members of the princely houses and various well-known parliamentarians combined together expressly to support Prince Bismarck's policy. At the time of its foundation it was quite evident that none of the subscribers looked upon the company as an ordinary form of capital investment.

The high hopes of the founders were soon disappointed. It was realised that the development of the country must inevitably be a much longer process than was at first anticipated. The company strove to raise fresh capital, but the amount forthcoming was insufficient and again and again help had to be sought from the Government. The business men, who had to carry out the work of the company, desired to make money and so were constantly at logger-

[1] See a study from documentary sources, Sander, L., *Geschichte der Deutschen Kolonialgesellschaft für Südwestafrika*, 2 vols.

heads with the authorities. In the end the state had to bear all the cost of the colony, while any returns were claimed by the company. The free development of the colony into a self-supporting settlement was constantly obstructed by the special privileges of the company, until in 1910, after long wrangles, an arrangement between the state and the *Kolonialgesellschaft* was concluded.

The Government of South-West Africa took over the whole of the property of the company, which was then limited to purely commercial functions. Mining was included among these, and the *Deutsche Diamantengesellschaft*, the diamond-mining company which had been founded a few years before, was absorbed. The State Secretary for the Colonial Office, Bernard Dernburg, was severely attacked for his share in concluding this agreement on the ground that it was contrary to the interests of the state. He was compelled to retire, but from the commercial and legal point of view there is no doubt that the agreement was the best that could have been made in the circumstances. Historically, despite the good will of individual members of the company, it cannot be denied that the *Kolonialgesellschaft* impeded and hampered the progress of the colony.

In addition to the main company, several other smaller companies were founded as purely speculative ventures, amongst which were several of British origin or under British influence. The *Kolonialhandbuch* for 1913 listed five British companies, some with a head office in London and others in Cape Town. The most important were the Kharaskoma Syndicate and the South-West Africa Company. These were mainly concerned with land and mining development. Other enterprises were sandstone quarrying, a steam distillery, ostrich-raising, sealing, and sheep-rearing for the production of wool. At the beginning of the Herero rising these companies held at their disposal 20 per cent of the land suitable for colonisation and had mining rights covering 70 per cent of the whole colony. After the Herero rising, in connection with the agreement with the *Deutsche Kolonialgesellschaft* already discussed, there was a general clean-up, and the result was that the Government, which had also taken over the whole of the lands of the rebels, now possessed by far the greater part of the land in the colony. General freedom to prospect for minerals was now accorded, thus affording new opportunities for energy and initiative.

The development of South-West Africa into a prosperous settlement depended on whether land suitable for the purpose could be opened up by irrigation. Big schemes were designed by expert technical engineers; dams were planned for construction across suitable valleys and watering-places arranged for stock. Many of the plans were carried into effect; boring parties were set to work to tap the subterranean water-springs and the divining rod was used with a fair measure of success. Estimates of the number of Europeans to be settled differed widely, but, given normal conditions, the figure might be expected to reach 70,000. As is well known, there was considerable emigration from Germany in the years before the war. German South-West Africa was the only colony possessed by the Reich that was suited to receive large numbers of white settlers, and so the idea of concentrating effort upon it was very tempting both on patriotic and economic grounds.

Unfortunately, however, great practical difficulties were encountered. The soil of South-West Africa was well adapted to moderate and large-scale enterprise, but the German emigrants were of the small settler type, mostly sons of peasants with small resources, who were anxious to find cheap or free agricultural land. In South-West Africa small holdings to be tilled by methods approximating to those of horticulture were in most districts unobtainable.

The cost of laying out a farm of 5000 hectares approached 20,000 marks, one-tenth of its value being paid for the land in advance and the remainder together with the accruing interest being spread out in the form of rent.[1] In the capital cost of laying out the farm the expenses of maintaining the family and five Native labourers were included, for even under favourable conditions little return, let alone profit, could be expected before the third year. After the Herero rising a large cattle-ranch could not be opened up for less than 50,000 marks. At that period a person with sufficient resources to undertake such an expenditure could find ample opportunities in Germany itself. Thus the number of persons with the essential resources, who were attracted to begin in a new country a career that might in time make them into moderately prosperous farmers, was very limited. The best colonising material was to be found among the smallholders, each with 3000–5000 marks at their disposal, who were ready to work hard with their own hands. Thus it was clear that without state subsidies colonisation on any large scale was impossible.

The Imperial Government did what it could. Troopers and police, who by previous service were already familiar with the country, were settled on the land provided they possessed at least 2500 marks of their own. A German peasant family of four had to give evidence of their possession of 10,000 marks. Additions from various funds, given mostly in the form of loans without interest, defrayed the cost of transportation to the colony, the erection of temporary living accommodation, the supply of water and the purchase of cattle. The first years of such assisted immigrants were hard in any case, and they did not easily achieve independence.

One great evil at the beginning was the inflated price charged for what was often poor land. Unscrupulous petty Chiefs squandered the territory of their tribes, drawing a lucrative revenue for themselves and referring their aggrieved subjects for redress to the German

[1] A hectare equals nearly $2\frac{1}{2}$ acres.

Government. After the Herero rising the colonial administration set about forming reservations for the tribes, wherein either ownership or right of usufruct were assigned to them to the exclusion of white men. Since the Government decided to sell land only to actual settlers, no leasehold system came into existence. This may have had its good side, but there would have been advantage in special action in exceptional cases. Many persons of means in Germany might have been willing to purchase property in the colony, if they had been permitted to work the farms with properly qualified bailiffs. Even colonial members of the learned professions would have desired to purchase land with their own resources, if they had been allowed to employ managers for their holdings.

The first reported gold finds in South-West Africa were soon exposed as flagrant swindles, for the prospectors had "salted" the diggings with artificially introduced gold. Later, however, true deposits of copper, gold, tin, lead and iron were discovered in many places, but only copper was seriously exploited. Before the war the copper mines of the Otavi Mining Company produced 70,000 tons of ore per annum. A great sensation was caused by the discovery of diamonds in the colony. A native boy from the Cape and a railway station-master made the first discovery in 1908 in the hinterland of Lüderitzbucht. The diamonds were found near the surface of a vein some 40 kilometres long having a maximum depth of only 30 centimetres.[1] During the first year of the exploitation of the new field 40,000 carats of the value about a million marks were extracted. The diamonds were small, but they were of good water and therefore valuable. While in South Africa diamonds are extracted with great labour from a hard conglomerate, the method of procuring them from the sand dunes of South-West Africa was simple and cheap. The stones could be washed out through sieves, and machinery for the purpose was rapidly introduced. Immediately after the first discovery numerous diamond-mining companies were formed to exploit the fields; a diamond rush began, and as usual cosmopolitan adventurers flocked to the scene. The Government, however, quickly intervened with regulations to prevent indiscriminate exploitation. A maximum annual output was fixed for every person engaged in the new industry; a fixed tax of 10 marks per carat i.e. one-third of the average value was imposed, and export was only permitted by sea from the port of Lüderitzbucht. These measures called forth a storm of criticism.

Trade in German South-West Africa was generally speaking unrestricted; but traffic in alcohol was limited by special permit, licences to sell liquor were costly, and adherence to restrictive conditions was rigidly enforced. The sale of alcoholic liquors to the Natives was absolutely prohibited. Until 1890 the trade in arms was free, but from 1890 to 1897 it was partially restricted and, after that date, it

[1] A centimetre equals 0·3937 inch; a kilometre equals nearly $\frac{5}{8}$ mile.

became a government monopoly. Nevertheless, the Natives were easily able to procure arms from Cape Colony or through Walvis Bay.

At the outbreak of the First World War the colony possessed an excellent and extensive railway system; there were four state lines and two branch railways, while a new line to Amboland in the north was in course of construction. The value of these railways was estimated at 100 million Reichsmarks. In the country beyond the immediate reach of the lines communication was carried on by the traditional ox-waggon, though where made roads permitted the motor-car was already taking its place.

It is not easy to estimate the sum total of the expenditure of the German Reich upon the colony. During the period immediately preceding the war state subsidies amounted on the average to 250 million marks per annum. Education, hospitals, church building and missions, war against disease, and scientific surveys of the geology of the country swallowed up great sums, though to the benefit of the whole future of South-West Africa. From the purely economic point of view the colony was not paying its way in 1914. Imports very considerably exceeded exports, mainly owing to the large military and official organisation that was kept up, but the conviction that under normal conditions of development the disparity would in time be remedied was quite justifiable.

The colony was in no position to defend itself single-handed against serious attacks. The attitude of Berlin is best expressed by the slogan current at the time: "*Die Kolonien müssen in der Nordsee verteidigt werden*"—the colonies must be defended in the North Sea. The last governor, Seitz, was no friend of the colonial defence force; he wished to disband it and to send national troops to occupy the colony. The arms law introduced by him could not be put into force before the outbreak of war in 1914. Thus, although the struggle was honourably contested to the bitter end, the result against the vastly superior forces of the Union was a foregone conclusion.

German South-West Africa was the spoiled child among the German colonies. Many hopes were centred upon it, only to be bitterly disappointed. Many mistakes were made, but on balance the achievements of constructive enterprise outweighed them. It was the only German colony whose fate and fortunes were of real interest to the general public. This fact has found expression in the field of pure literature, for whereas the other colonies gave rise to nothing of any literary importance, South-West Africa produced at least two books of real literary merit: Gustav Frenssen's *Peter Moors Fahrt nach Südwest* and the *Südwestafrikanische Novellen* of Hans Grimm, himself a farmer in the colony.

CHAPTER XXVII

SOUTH AFRICA IN THE 1914–18 WAR

LIKE its sister Dominions of the British Empire, the Union of South Africa experienced the tension of feeling, which, since the opening of the twentieth century, revealed itself in the diplomatic exchanges between the leading powers of Europe and raised the nervous excitement of their subjects to a dangerous pitch. The gigantic military preparations which the Continental states had made, originally with a view to establishing national security, formed a standing temptation to indulge lust for gain or desire for revenge by recourse to war. Unfortunately, from 1904 onwards the points of difference between the various nations increased and the international situation became steadily more menacing. In these developments the Dominions took an anxious interest, for the mounting antagonism between the German Empire and Britain was one of the factors that made for war and impelled the Dominions seriously to consider the question of their own defence.

A war that involved the United Kingdom would involve the whole Empire. Each of the Dominions had the power to decide whether or not it would give active support to the mother country, but even a decision to remain passive would not insure it against invasion if the enemy chose to attack it. This was a contingency for which all the Dominions had to make provision, but the Union of South Africa was especially concerned, since it alone was bordered by German territory. Hence, even in the quiet atmosphere of the Union Parliament at Cape Town, a hint of the approaching storm in Europe might be detected in the speech with which General Smuts opened the second reading of the Defence Bill in February 1912.[1] It was regarded as needful for the Union Government to provide for its own defence by organising a force to serve "anywhere in South Africa within or outside the Union". No intention was expressed of using the force for service outside the subcontinent, but since the term "South Africa" was commonly held to cover all the territory south of the Zambesi, German South-West Africa was included within the range of its possible operations. The Bill was received with general approval and passed its third reading in May 1912. Few could have predicted from the nature and tone of the discussions the contumacy of circumstance that was to lead to rebellion when the conditions that prompted the Act's inception came into being.

Though it cannot be claimed that the conflict which commenced

[1] *Union of South Africa, House of Assembly Debates,* 2nd Session, 1912, pp. 619–46.

in 1914 was a colonial war in the same sense as the Seven Years War, yet colonial issues were by no means lacking. They were most prominent in Africa. There the colonial ambitions of Germany and Britain came most obviously into collision. The geographical distribution of the German colonies, situated on the opposite coasts of Africa, inspired the inevitable desire to link them up by a methodical expansion from east to west, but any endeavour to fulfil this object was bound to bring Germany into collision with Britain whose accepted line of development in Africa, summed up in the phrase "Cape to Cairo", ran from south to north. If their divergent interests should lead to a struggle between the two rivals, the hegemony of Africa would ultimately rest with the power which had the command of the sea. At the opening of the war in 1914, Germany, though she was aware that Britain would gain a military advantage in Africa by reason of her maritime ascendancy, realised that the general question of African supremacy would be settled by the issue of the war in the major theatres and hoped in the meantime to use its African possessions to support its military enterprises in Europe.

The outbreak of hostilities subjected the recently formed Union to a severe test. The loyalty of General Botha and his followers to the promises they had made at Vereeniging was above suspicion, but no one knew better than the Prime Minister that a section of the Afrikaner population was essentially hostile to the British connection. If the establishment of the Union had really meant the termination of racialism as between the British and the Afrikaners, the war need not have caused serious anxiety to the Government; but the flame of racial antagonism, which had never been entirely extinguished since 1902, had been fanned by the Free State group, led by ex-President Steyn, and from 1912 it was evident that this party, the strength of which it was impossible to gauge with precision, aimed primarily at furthering Afrikaner interest. Any possible advantages accruing from the imperial connection were to be utilised in the interests of a section of the community, but no obligations arising from this connection were to be acknowledged. This attitude, which was at bottom responsible for the outbreak of rebellion, was the logical expression of the fears and prejudices of many of the backveld Boers and of some who were by no means of the backveld. Their minds, passionately influenced by memories and experiences of years of resistance to what they deemed to be an exorbitant and overbearing power, inevitably saw their struggle with Britain as the central point of history. It absorbed them to the exclusion of all other considerations and led them to regard even the Peace of Vereeniging as merely an episode in a struggle that was not yet ended. General Botha, who shared the traditions of the Trekkers, could respect, if he could not approve these views, and he was naturally anxious to avoid any action that would stir the latent hostility of the irreconcilables into open rebellion.

His first idea was not to commit his Government, but circumstances soon made it impossible for him to maintain this negative attitude, for Africa proved to be a factor of considerable importance in the war. South-West Africa in German hands would be a constant source of danger not only to the Union but to the Empire as a whole, and the imperial authorities were anxious to effect its conquest as speedily as possible, for it lay athwart the ocean route between Europe and the East which had acquired a fresh importance through the fact of war. The conditions of naval warfare had changed enormously since the opening of the nineteenth century. Notably, the development of the submarine introduced a new menace to shipping and commerce and limited the scope of navigation in land-locked seas like the Mediterranean. Practically the whole of the Mediterranean littoral abounded in bases for submarine activity, and with the Suez Canal threatened from the east by Turkey, it was obvious that the historic route of Da Gama formed the safest if the longest line of communication between England and India. But Swakopmund and Lüderitzbucht, the two harbours of German South-West Africa, laid it open to attack, and if the German China squadron, commanded by Admiral von Spee, should enter the Southern Atlantic, it might destroy the wireless station in the Cape Peninsula, while it could count on receiving from the wireless stations in South-West Africa valuable information which might enable it to evade capture and to prey on British and allied shipping with serious effect. Hence for military and commercial reasons it was deemed essential to attack German South-West Africa without delay.

This was a project that directly concerned the Union, for the operations against German South-West Africa could be most easily directed from its territory and, as we have seen, this possibility had been noted when the Defence Act was framed. Owing to the attitude of the Afrikaner extremists, however, General Botha preferred at the outset to limit himself to the defence of the Union territories, and he informed the British Government that if the British regiments still in the country were required for duty elsewhere, the Union would provide for its own defence by substituting troops of its own newly-formed Defence Force for the imperial garrisons. In making this offer General Botha may have hoped to escape the possibility of having to organise an attack against German territory, but the words which he used did not rule out such a possibility, and the imperial authorities in gratefully accepting the offer requested the Government of the Union to undertake operations against the German colony in order to occupy its dangerous ports and to destroy the long-distance wireless station at Windhoek.[1]

The crisis which Botha had anticipated and dreaded was thus precipitated; but the request, he saw, was eminently reasonable,

[1] Walker, E. A., *Lord de Villiers and his Times*, p. 502.

for, since German South-West Africa could not be neglected, it was clearly in the interest of the Union that the invasion should be carried out by its own rather than by imperial troops. General Botha, therefore, though he had reason to dread the effect of the announcement, acceded to the request and made immediate arrangements for an attack. It was desirable to secure control of the two German harbours without delay. Swakopmund, fronting an unsheltered roadstead, was exposed to attack from the sea, and its wireless station and landing equipment were soon destroyed by a naval bombardment; Lüderitzbucht was more sheltered and possessed more abundant resources; it was, moreover, one of the termini of the slender railway system which formed a kind of quadrilateral within the colony. From the port the line ran practically due east to Keetmanshoop, whence, after throwing off a branch to Kalkfontein in the south, it veered northwards and, passing through Windhoek and Karibib, turned westwards to the other marine terminus at Swakopmund. A second line from Swakopmund passed through Karibib and ran in a northerly direction to Tsumeb and Grootfontein. The southern extension of the railway system from the quadrilateral to Kalkfontein had evidently been planned with the possible object of facilitating operations against the Union territories. It was decided to occupy Lüderitzbucht with a military force. Fortunately the Germans had taken no adequate measures to prevent this, and a force of 1824 men, commanded by Colonel P. S. Beves, which sailed from Cape Town on 15 September 1914, occupied the town without resistance on September 19. The scanty German forces withdrew inland, leaving a rearguard at Grasplatz where it was cut up and dispersed by Union troops in the first engagement of the campaign.

It was doubtful if Colonel Beves's small detachment was sufficiently strong to hold the harbour against the full force of the Germans in the colony; accordingly arrangements were made to support it by converging invasions from the Union. A force of nearly 2500 men under the command of Brigadier-General H. T. Lukin was landed at Port Nolloth and advanced with the purpose of seizing the drifts over the Orange River that separated the German territory from the Union. A second invading column of about 1000 men was assembled under Colonel S. G. Maritz at Upington on the Orange River. During the preliminary movements a small force under Colonel Grant was surrounded by Germans at Sandfontein on September 26 and compelled to surrender, the only reverse sustained by the Union arms in the South-West campaign.

The initial arrangements for the invasion of the German colony had been barely completed when the operations had to be suspended owing to the outbreak of a dangerous rebellion within the Union. Colonel Maritz gave the lead by throwing off his allegiance to the Government on 9 October 1914. General Botha had known for some time that a section of the Afrikaans-speaking population, especially in the Free State, was not to be relied on, and ample evidence had been brought to his notice that the invasion of German South-West Africa would be seized as a pretext for a rising. It soon became apparent that the views of the malcontents were shared by certain prominent leaders among the Afrikaners. General C. R. Beyers, who from his position as Commandant-General of the Defence force would in normal circumstances have been in charge of the operations against German South-West Africa, after some hesitation resigned his command and ultimately went into the rebellion. His example was followed by Major J. C. G. Kemp, who was in charge of the recently raised Defence Force units that had been collected in September at Potchefstroom, ostensibly for three weeks' peace training.[1] The adherents of the irreconcilable party also included such noted leaders as Generals de la Rey and de Wet, and the Government had strong reason to fear that their defection would lead to a very grave crisis.

Botha did everything in his power to avert the coming storm. His personal influence availed to prevent his old comrade in arms, General de la Rey, from committing himself to the initiation of a rebellious movement at Treurfontein in the Western Transvaal on August 15, but he never succeeded in gaining his unqualified support for the Government. De la Rey was in constant communication with the malcontents and had probably determined to throw in his lot with the rebels, when, on September 15, he set out from Pretoria with General Beyers for the Defence Force camp at Potchefstroom. Their car on nearing Johannesburg was ordered to halt by a small police post, part of a cordon that had been formed round the city in the hope of rounding up a gang of local ruffians, who were known to be trying to escape by car. The police had orders to fire, if their challenge was disobeyed. The challenge was ignored and Beyers's car held on its way; but at a village named Langlaagte it ran into a second post, and, when it again disregarded the summons to stop, a policeman fired at the tyre of the rear right wheel and the bullet, ricochetting off the road, killed de la Rey.[2] His death was due to a sheer accident, but many believed it to be a fortunate accident for South Africa. Colonel Maritz at Upington had never been wholly loyal to the Union and had for some time been engaged in treasonable correspondence with the German authorities of South-West Africa. Several interviews with the commandants of the Defence Force had convinced Botha that some of them were unwilling to participate in the campaign, and he went as far along the path of conciliation as he could safely go. Though the expedition to South-West Africa had been approved by Parliament and constituted the kind of duty which

[1] Walker, E. A., *op. cit.* pp. 559 *sqq.*

[2] A doctor who failed to stop was shot the same day at the other end of the Rand.

the Defence Force was designed to perform, Botha promised that only volunteers would be called on to take part in it. The Prime Minister used all his personal influence to dissuade Beyers from plunging into revolt, and had the Free State leaders raised their voices in his support, his efforts might have been successful. But ex-President Steyn and Hertzog maintained a deliberate silence, which was not unnaturally construed by the English-speaking population as well as by the rebels as an admission of essential disloyalty to the Empire.

It could not be denied that many persons in the Union were not as enthusiastic in the support of the Empire-Commonwealth as were the peoples of the other Dominions. In the past, allegiance could be cast off by the simple expedient of trekking beyond the established boundary, but since the days of the Great Trek boundaries had become stabilised and the repudiation of allegiance could no longer be represented as being other than an act of resistance to authority. The seriousness of this was probably not grasped by the rank and file who took up arms, but it was realised at least by their leaders, and the chief charge that falls to be made against them is that they said nothing to make the situation clear to their countrymen.

Thus the racial bitterness, which the Jameson Raid and the South African War had revived, became again a source of danger, for the political malcontents were encouraged to revert to the aims for which President Kruger had stood. They were elated by the news of the opening battles in Europe which went largely in favour of the Central Powers, and, the wish being father to the thought, believed that the downfall of Britain was assured. They saw in the difficulties of the British a renewed opportunity to repudiate all connection with Great Britain and to attempt to establish republican rule over the whole of South Africa. According to the report of the judicial commission of inquiry which was appointed in 1916, such was the principal cause of the rebellion.[1] Since sentiments of this type were widespread in what had been the old republics, it is not surprising that many of the Afrikaners really believed that General Botha and his ministers were secretly in favour of rebellion and were only awaiting a tolerable excuse to shake off British rule. The expedition to German South-West Africa was rather the occasion than the cause of rebellion, but it was sufficiently unpopular to enable the leaders of the extremists to stir up the country farmers into a dangerous state of unrest and disaffection; for they had always regarded Germany as a friend and, at the close of the South African War, several Afrikaner irreconcilables had become naturalised citizens in German South-West Africa.[2] It was quite in keeping with the ideas pervading the Free State and part of the Transvaal that the Prime Minister and

[1] *U.G.* 46–16, p. 101. For *Minutes of Evidence*, *vide U.G.* 42–16.

[2] *Vide supra*, p. 733.

General Smuts should be stigmatised as traitors to the national cause for organising the expedition against Germany territory.

How far a definite plan of campaign had been thought out by the leaders of the disaffected it is impossible to say. Their arrangements may have been dislocated by the accidental death of de la Rey, but the evidence produced before the judicial commission of inquiry, incomplete though it was, suggests that while rebellion was in the minds of many, no definite line of action had been agreed on. The comparative ineptitude with which the rising was conducted strengthens the opinion that the leaders had not advanced to the stage of a cut and dried plan. The crisis was precipitated by the action of Colonel Maritz, who, on October 9, having disarmed and handed over to the Germans those of his command who refused to be seduced from their allegiance, went into open rebellion. On receipt of these tidings the Government proclaimed martial law throughout the Union, and by means of negotiations and appeals did all in its power to prevent the rising from becoming general.

Forewarned by the ambiguous behaviour of Maritz, the Government had assembled a loyal force at Upington which moved against the rebels and drove them over the German border to Schuit Drift on October 24. By this time Beyers, Kemp, and de Wet were all in arms against the Government. The immediate object of the various rebel leaders was to collect as many men as possible with arms and ammunition and effect a junction with Maritz, but it was frustrated by the skilful activity of Botha. Beyers, harassed by Government forces and the commandos which had been called out, ultimately effected a junction with Kemp at Steenbokfontein in the western Transvaal. After being decisively defeated by a column under Colonel Alberts near Treurfontein on October 29, Kemp with about 2000 men set out on a daring ride across the desert to join Maritz. Seldom has a journey been more beset by perils and hardships, and it speaks volumes for the courage and tenacity of Kemp and his men that they succeeded in accomplishing their purpose; but they lost one-third of their strength in the effort and the survivors were too exhausted to undertake immediate military duty. Beyers, on the departure of his subordinate, moved south with over 1000 men in the hope of joining de Wet in the Free State, but his march was punctuated by disasters, and on November 17 his commando sustained a reverse near Bultfontein from which it was given no time to recover. The pursuit was carried on by the Government troops with such vigour that the rebel commando was utterly broken up and Beyers himself was drowned in attempting to swim the Vaal. The main Free State effort drifted to an equally humiliating conclusion. General de Wet had won such a high reputation as guerilla leader in the last days of the struggle of twelve years before that he was likely to attract many adherents to the rebel cause and, if he were given time to complete his arrangements, the rising might develop into a civil war on a large scale. General Botha accordingly so concentrated the Government forces as to bring de Wet to bay as speedily as possible. His tactics proved more than a match for his one-time war comrade. Driven from pillar to post the old General with his force was cornered and defeated at Mushroom Valley on November 12. He managed to escape with a few of his men, as he so often had done in earlier days, but he was ultimately run to earth and captured in the extreme north of British Bechuanaland on 2 December 1914.

The capture or dispersal of the main rebel forces appreciably strengthened the Government, and the smaller bodies of malcontents within the Transvaal and Free State were soon rounded up. By the end of 1914 the rebellion within the Union was at an end. Beyond its frontiers, Kemp and Maritz, discouraged by the discomfiture of their friends and the lack of support from the Germans, continued the losing struggle for a month longer. An attack on the Government column at Upington on 24 January 1915 was beaten off, and realising that the rising had no longer any hope of success, Maritz on January 30 signed an agreement providing for the unconditional surrender of the men under his command. Accordingly the main body of rebels, including Kemp, surrendered at Upington on 2 and 3 February 1915; but Maritz, with a few companions, preferring to become exiles rather than submit themselves to the laws of the Union, slipped away and ultimately found an obscure haven of safety in the wilds of Portuguese West Africa.

The manner in which Botha dealt with the rebellion stamped him as a statesman of consummate qualities. It was his supreme endeavour to prevent a recrudescence of the racial rivalry that had so long been the bane of South Africa, and though units of the Defence Force largely composed of men of British stock were in the field against the rebels, he so disposed his forces as to put the brunt of the work on his Afrikaner levies so that the struggle appeared to a large degree to be one between men of Afrikaner descent. At the same time Botha used every effort to capture or disperse the rebels and to avoid bloodshed as far as possible. Members of the Active Citizen Force who were captured were tried by summary court martial, but only one, "Japie" Fourie, was executed.[1] Never has rebellion been treated with greater clemency than in the case of South Africa. The rank and file were disqualified for ten years from holding government posts or serving in any public capacity, while the leaders were punished in addition by imprisonment and fines. Even these sentences were afterwards much reduced, but though this leniency was viewed with disfavour by many South Africans of British extraction, Botha refused to be

[1] Unlike the other rebel officers, Fourie had not resigned his commission. He was on active service under the Government when he went into rebellion and resisted strenuously to the last.

diverted from his statesmanlike course, for he firmly believed that the adoption of harsh measures would but increase the disaffection within the country. The total number of rebels who had taken up arms was only 11,472, of whom 7123 belonged to the Free State, but the Prime Minister suspected that it represented only a portion of those who were dissatisfied with his policy.

History has shown that the suppression of a rebellion generally adds to the immediate strength of a Government, and Botha strove with all his wide knowledge of his countrymen and his deep love of his fatherland to ensure that this rule should apply in the case of South Africa. At the best the country would gain in unity and harmony, and at the worst Britain would have no more cause to apprehend active opposition in the Union. Such hopes and expectations took no account of the fact that conditions in South Africa were exceptional. The unity that the country had attained only four years before was political rather than national, for the sense of racial divergence was still strong. Many who were not prepared to take up arms against the Government were yet unwilling to support any policy that promised active assistance to the British Empire, and they resented the feeling that South Africa was caught in the vortex of the World War and driven into activities of which they could not approve.

The suppression of the rebellion, however, left General Botha free to resume operations against the German forces which were still undefeated in South-West Africa. A Union garrison was in possession of Lüderitzbucht and other forces were collected near the borders of the colony. The country to be invaded was vast in extent and very difficult for military operations.[1] Roads fit for military purposes did not exist, and civilisation was practically confined to the railway system connecting the chief towns, Keetmanshoop, Gibeon, Rehoboth, Windhoek, the capital, and Karibib with the two ports. The Germans with their customary foresight had made extensive preparations for war. Their military establishment at the commencement of hostilities was 140 officers and 2000 other ranks, organised in mounted companies and batteries, and considerable reinforcements were available in the 7000 adult European male settlers, most of whom had undergone military training. Large stores of war material were established at various depots, most of them being, like Ukamas and Kalkfontein, near the Union frontier. Supplies of food, however, had to be carefully husbanded and from the outbreak of hostilities they were placed under a rigorous control by the German authorities. The chief difficulties to an invader were presented not by the numbers or efficiency of the German forces but by the barrenness of the country and the blistering heat of the sun. Moreover, the scarcity of water and roads virtually dictated

[1] *Vide supra*, p. 738.

the line of advance, so that the defenders could pollute the water or mine the roads that the invaders were likely to use. Further, the terrain was sufficiently broken to give great advantages to a resolute and well-trained defence. Altogether, the campaign involved a struggle with nature that might well have been too arduous for troops accustomed only to European conditions, and it proved extremely trying even to men who were inured to the conditions of South African warfare. It was obviously a difficult military problem to arrange how to employ large columns in a country so lacking in roads, water and food supply.

General Botha himself undertook the conduct of the campaign. It was a wise decision, for the Prime Minister had given repeated proofs of his skill in conducting military operations under South African conditions and he commanded the confidence of his Afrikaner and British troops alike. His plan of campaign was clear and simple. It was obvious that the capture of the railway system would involve the control of the best organised portions of the colony. Accordingly the main attack under the command of Botha himself was to be delivered against Windhoek from Swakopmund, which had been captured by a small detachment under Colonel P. C. B. Skinner on 13 January 1915. This movement was to be supported by operations in the south, where Union forces had been collected at Lüderitzbucht and Upington under Brigadier-General Sir Duncan Mackenzie and Colonel J. van Deventer respectively. In addition an eastern column under Colonel C. A. L. Berrange was to march against the railway from Kuruman. The principal attack was mounted in the north because it was known that the enemy drew most of his supplies from the region north of the Karibib-Windhoek railway line. Botha's object was not only to capture Windhoek and the railway but to destroy the enemy's forces and prevent them from escaping to the north, where with the resources of Central Africa to sustain them, they might carry on a prolonged guerilla struggle. The tactics employed by the Prime Minister were a skilful blend of Boer and British methods. The infantry units, consisting largely of British from the towns, maintained a steady advance along the centre, while the mounted burgher troops, accustomed to leave base and communications and to take with them such food and water as they required, carried out wide encircling movements which repeatedly put the enemy's forces in danger of capture.

Before Botha's arrival in February 1915 arrangements had been put in hand to construct a railway from Walvis Bay to Swakopmund, and another line from Upington in the north-western Cape Provinces linking up with the South-West African system. The first strategic objective was Karibib, since its fall would decide the fate of Windhoek and all the country to the south, and the enemy, realising its importance, had concentrated strong forces there. General Botha, with approximately 20,000 troops under his command, had a most difficult task to accomplish, for the country which he had to traverse supplied neither food nor water for his men, and the Germans were convinced that no advance from Swakopmund could be made with any hope of success. Botha proved that they were mistaken. After several preliminary operations he began his advance on 15 April 1915. The enemy's resistance was ineffective and, after successful actions at Trekkoppies and Otjimbingue, Botha's men occupied Karibib on May 5 and received the surrender of Windhoek a week later.

In the meantime the Union forces in the south had achieved considerable gains at the expense of the enemy. Colonel J. van Deventer, whose sterling leadership had been largely responsible for the surrender of the rebels under Maritz and Kemp, had seized control of the chief drifts across the Orange River before the end of the first week in March. Then, having reduced the German military posts to the south-east of the railway, he directed his march against Kalkfontein, the southern terminus of the railway system and an important military station. The most formidable obstacle to advance along the railway was presented by two considerable hills to the east of the line, and since a frontal attack could not have been successful without a heavy cost in life, van Deventer sent off a column under his brother, Colonel Dirk van Deventer, to effect a junction with Colonel Berrange's force, which had accomplished a wonderful feat of endurance in its march across the desolate and waterless Kalahari. On April 5 Colonel J. van Deventer entered Kalkfontein, where General Smuts arrived on April 11 to assume charge of the operations in the south. The junction of Dirk van Deventer with Berrange at Kiriis West on April 14 ensured the success of the turning movement and enabled Colonel J. van Deventer to continue his advance towards Keetmanshoop. These achievements materially facilitated the operations of Brigadier-General Mackenzie, who was in command of the column at Lüderitzbucht. Thanks to the energy of Sir George Farrar, who, having shown great organising capacity as the head of the East Rand Proprietary Mines, was employed by the Government to supervise the reconstruction of the railway destroyed by the Germans as they fell back, a large part of the railway line had been repaired, and Brigadier-General Mackenzie, having secured the station at Aus, turned off in a north-easterly direction with the intention of cutting off the Germans who were retreating before the southern and eastern columns. The enemy was encountered at Gibeon, where a stubborn fight took place on April 26, and though Mackenzie failed to round up the Germans, he put an end to the possibility of the enemy's maintaining an effective fighting force in the south. Had General Botha been able to reach Windhoek by this date, all the German troops in the south must have been compelled to surrender.

These achievements secured for the Union the control of nearly all the organised districts of the colony; but considerable enemy forces were still at large, and the remaining operations were now directed to encompass their capture or destruction. If they succeeded in escaping to the north, they would be in a position to cause great embarrassment to the Government from a political as well as from a military point of view.

From Karibib a railway line ran north-eastwards to Otavi, whence it threw off two branches to Tsumeb and Grootfontein. This formed the objective of the final operations. All the necessary preparations having been completed, the advance was begun on 18 June 1915. General Botha with two mounted brigades and an infantry brigade supported by artillery took the centre, while two burgher columns, under Brigadier-General M. W. Myburgh and Brigadier-General Coen Brits respectively, operated on the flanks. The enemy failed to take advantage of the defensive possibilities of Kalkfeld and was driven from that place on June 24. This allowed the pursuit to be carried on rapidly to Otavi. The advance guard of the central column under Brigadier-General M. Botha, in what has been described as "the most brilliant tactical operation of the campaign",[1] broke through the opposing resistance on July 1, captured the high ground at Otavi and thus put Botha in possession of the water supply of the district. This triumph virtually settled the campaign, for the flanking columns got astride of the German line of retreat and so caused the surrender of the main body of the enemy, consisting of 204 officers and 3166 other ranks, on July 9. The terms imposed by General Botha were generous. Commissioned officers were to keep their arms and to live under parole at any place they chose; non-commissioned officers retained their rifles without ammunition and were to be interned within South-West Africa wherever the Union Government might decide; the rank and file were allowed to return to their farms and keep their rifles for the purpose of self-defence against the tribes. Upwards of 40,000 Union troops had been engaged in the campaign, and of these 269 were killed in action or by disease and 263 wounded, a remarkably small casualty list for so brilliant an achievement.

These notable military successes were undoubtedly facilitated by the co-operation of the Navy without which troops could not have been landed at Swakopmund and Lüderitzbucht. The Navy kept the waters clear of mines and, without loss of a single ship or life, escorted and sometimes actually conveyed the Union forces from Cape Town to Lüderitzbucht, Walvis Bay and Swakopmund. In addition to protecting the ocean line of communications the Navy sent a squadron of armoured motor cars to assist the advance of the northern column. These cars gave valuable assistance in the action at Trekkoppies.

[1] *The Union of South Africa and the Great War*, 1914-1918, *Official History*, p. 32.

Thus was rounded off one of the neatest and most successful campaigns in the Great War. At small cost and with great credit to itself the Union had rendered an immense service to the Empire. The victory increased the security of the ocean line of communications between the United Kingdom and the East, and also added to the security of the Union itself. The expedition which had thus been carried out at the request of the Imperial Government was undertaken by the Union Government at its own expense, and its happy issue ended the concern of the Union for its own defence by land in the Great War.

The rebellion, the South-West Africa campaign, and the realisation that the war was going to be a long one led to a revolution in the Union's financial arrangements.[1] At the outbreak of war, the Government had at once taken steps to assist the producers and exporters of gold, wool and hides. Maize, then in its infancy, was left to fend for itself; the ostrich feather industry, owing to changes in fashion, was already dying, and nothing could be done for the great diamond industry, which, having overproduced even for the peace-time market, was forced by war to shut down for the time being. Parliament had met for a short special session in September. It had passed a Moratorium Act, given the Government powers, which it made no attempt to use for more than two years to come, to control food supplies, authorised the banks to issue notes of lower values than the customary £5, and finally voted £2,000,000, which it believed would be sufficient for all warlike needs until the end of the financial year in March 1915.

At the close of that financial year a totally new situation had to be faced. There was a deficit of £2,192,000; military expenditure already amounted to £8,750,000, and the Government was contemplating war on a considerable scale in German East Africa and the despatch of infantry and heavy artillery to Europe. A conference of leaders of all parties other than Labour, which declined to take part in what it held to be a conspiracy of the well-to-do, agreed upon a new financial policy. Estimates of expenditure for the year were limited to some £16,500,000; the sinking fund and the proceeds of land sales were diverted from loan account to the general revenue, and fresh taxation to the extent of £2,790,000 was raised by means of heavy increases in customs and excise duties, the lowering of the income tax exemption for married men from £1000 to £300, and a special levy of 4 per cent in addition to the existing 10 per cent on the profits of the gold-mines. Further, a loan of £16,000,000 was sanctioned for two more years of war, a heavy burden compared with those hitherto assumed by other Dominions. Finally, in December

[1] The best account of the Union's war-time finance, in its political setting, is given in *The Round Table*, 1914–18.

1915, the export of gold was forbidden, except to Mozambique. Having thus laid down the lines on which its share in the war was henceforth to be financed, the Union embarked in good earnest on the East African campaign.

German East Africa was less directly connected with South Africa than was South-West Africa, and responsibility for the operations in that region had been assumed by the imperial authorities. South African troops, however, were engaged in German East Africa from an early date, but the chief assistance from the Union was supplied after April 1915 when Lord Buxton, the Governor-General, suggested that in view of the satisfactory progress of the military operations in German South-West Africa, the Union might furnish assistance in other theatres. By that date the Imperial Government was becoming anxious about the strain on British man-power, and on 11 May 1915 the Secretary of State for the Colonies cabled that the British Government would gladly accept all the troops that South Africa could send. Accordingly an infantry brigade was formed and sent to Europe and a stronger force to East Africa, but in both cases the responsibility of the Union was limited to the despatch of troops.

German East Africa, a potentially wealthy territory, contained only 4200 Europeans at the outbreak of war. This immense territory, 384,000 square miles in area, was almost twice the size of the German Empire, and its boundaries touched those of British East Africa, Uganda, the Belgian Congo, Northern Rhodesia, Nyasaland and Portuguese East Africa. The three largest lakes in Africa: Victoria, Nyasa and Tanganyika, all touched the zone of the Protectorate. Practically the whole of the eastern margin of Lake Tanganyika formed its west boundary, while the northern half of the east coast of Lake Nyasa and the whole of the southern portion of Lake Victoria were also included in it. The strategic position of the Protectorate gave it a peculiar value in the eyes of the German authorities, for its possession put them in a position to dominate Central Africa. With the idea of developing its military as well as its commercial possibilities the Germans had constructed a railway from the port and capital of Dar-es-Salaam to Kigoma on Lake Tanganyika. The chief emporium of importance on this route was Tabora, the most populous town of the Protectorate in 1914, which had about 25,000 inhabitants. The only other railway in the Protectorate connected the port of Tanga with Moshi lying near the foothills of Kilimanjaro, the highest mountain in Africa. These railways formed the only easy means of communication within the country, for there were no metalled roads. The usual means of progress by foot was along narrow cleared tracks through dense bush, and these were incapable of bearing wheeled traffic of any description. Rivers are numerous, but none can be used for navigation. The largest is the Rufiji, which after following a north-easterly course runs into the sea opposite the island of Mafia. In the northern section of the Protectorate the largest river is the Pangani flowing into the sea south of Tanga.

The district falls into two main divisions: the coastal lowlands and the East African plateau, the former widening inland as one proceeds south. Isolated plateaux and mountain groups, such as the Nguru Mountains, diversify the whole territory, and the chief centres of population are found near the oases which interrupt the monotony of waterless bush. The climate is sub-tropical or tropical with considerable variations of temperature, and the rainy season is not uniform throughout the country. The land is not naturally adapted for white settlement, for malaria, malignant fevers and sleeping sickness carried by the tsetse fly are common. The most healthy stations are situated in the uplands. The natural resources of the Protectorate are abundant, consisting of plantation products and minerals. Most of the German inhabitants resided in the eastern portion of the protectorate, where, the two ports of Tanga and Dar-es-Salaam excepted, the principal towns were Wilhelmstal and Moshi.

The military resources of the protectorate were also considerable, for it was the home of predatory tribes, who had formerly earned a livelihood by selling slaves to Arab dealers. The Germans, seeing that these Natives were naturally warlike, formed and trained them into a very efficient army. The discipline of these Askari was admirable as is shown by the fact that they were able to maintain their morale until the close of a long and exacting conflict in which the odds were generally against them. Their mobility and independence of wheeled transport in a roadless country gave them an advantage over white troops who subsisted on rations imported from overseas, and they were practically immune from the endemic diseases which caused thousands of casualties among the Indian and European troops of the British.

At the outbreak of hostilities the Germans had a momentary superiority, for their army of 3000 Europeans and 11,000 Askari greatly outnumbered that of their rivals, which consisted of only the peace-time establishment of the King's African Rifles, a force barely adequate for the maintenance of order within its own territory. The size and character of the Protectorate were both an asset and a drawback to the enemy. Though open to attack from many sides, it yet offered abundant scope for protracted defence. Owing to British ascendancy at sea it was clear that the Germans could not permanently maintain the initiative which superior preparations and greater numbers momentarily gave them, and that it was only a question of time till the Lakes and the outlying portions of the Protectorate fell under the control of the British. These considerations were familiar to General P. von Lettow Vorbeck, a soldier of skill and determination, who had been in East Africa from the beginning of 1914. His task was to assist his countrymen in Europe by engaging the attention of as many British troops as possible. By husbanding his resources and taking full advantage of the defensive facilities presented by the terrain he expected to keep the field till the war was decided by the issue of the struggle in Europe.

Von Lettow, who had received an unexpected accession of strength in the men and guns of the German cruiser *Königsberg*, which had found refuge from the British fleet up the Rufiji river, used his temporary superiority to invade British East Africa, where, by capturing Taveta, he found himself in a position to threaten the Uganda railway between Nairobi and Mombasa. The safety of Mombasa was assured by the timely arrival of an infantry brigade from India, but even with this reinforcement the subsequent operations of the British were undertaken merely with the object of consolidating the defences of the colony. An attempt to capture Tanga from the sea was defeated disastrously in November 1915, and an attack on the German garrison of Longido was also unsuccessful. With the arrival of reinforcements, however, the position of the British steadily improved. British control of Lake Victoria was strengthened by the destruction of the German base at Bukoba, and in Nyasaland an enemy invasion was repulsed near Neu Langenburg. The German shipping on the inland lakes was gradually destroyed. The enemy had no strength to spare for ambitious expeditions against Northern Rhodesia, where a raid in July was severely punished.

Thus by the end of 1915 the British had gained the initiative. Strong reinforcements, consisting of two infantry brigades, a mounted brigade with an extra mounted regiment, five batteries of field artillery, a battalion of Coloured troops and a medical detachment arrived from the Union, the Government of which had been requested to permit General Smuts to take up the appointment of Commander-in-Chief. On 12 February 1916, just when he was embarking to assume his new duties, the British were repulsed with heavy losses in an attempt to storm Salaita Hill which commanded Taveta.

All the efforts against the German positions in the north-east of the Protectorate had hitherto been attended by failure, and General Smuts was therefore anxious to raise the morale of his command by snatching some military success before the rainy season set in. On his arrival he found the situation as follows. The strength of the German position was based on the control of the railway between Tanga and Moshi. This railway was protected on the east by the Pare and Usambara mountains, and while it remained in the enemy's hands, the British position in East Africa and Uganda could not be regarded as secure. It therefore formed the objective of Smuts' attack. Taveta, the key to the railway, was guarded by Salaita. The difficulties of a frontal attack had been demonstrated, as we have mentioned, and the most obvious way to turn the position was by the Ngulu gap in the Pare mountains to the south-east; but General

Smuts decided to gain Taveta by a turning movement to the north through Chala, at the same time deceiving the enemy by a reconnaissance against the Ngulu gap, while a column at Longido, which had been seized in January, was to advance down the western side of the Kilimanjaro foothills in an attempt to intercept the enemy's line of retreat near Kahé.

The all-important turning movement was brilliantly conducted by Brigadier-General J. van Deventer, and Taveta was occupied on March 10. This success cleared the way to the railway, and after heavy fighting the terminus at Moshi was reached on March 11. There the Commander-in-Chief was joined by General J. M. Stewart's force from Longido. Operations were resumed on the 18th, and by repeated use of enveloping tactics, which just failed to net the enemy's main force, General Smuts advanced along the railway as far as Kahé. Here a halt was made to complete preparations for a further advance, for in spite of the imminence of the rains, General Smuts was anxious not to allow the Germans a respite. Having reorganised his force into three divisions, he dispatched one under van Deventer south-westward against Kondoa Irangi. By a magnificent effort van Deventer forestalled the enemy and reached his objective on April 18, the small German garrison retiring to the south. Kondoa Irangi was the strategic as well as the commercial centre of the interior plateau, and von Lettow, leaving sufficient forces to hold the railway, made a great effort to recapture it. He was repulsed on May 9.

In the meantime the operations in the vicinity of the railway had to be postponed owing to the rains, but when these ceased near the end of May, General Smuts at once resumed his advance, his purpose being to clear the railway and the Pare and Usambara mountains as far as Handeni. There he would be conveniently situated for a thrust against the central railway, which was also to be the next objective of van Deventer. Handeni was reached on June 19, but the German forces evaded capture by a skilful use of the facilities for retirement afforded by the thick bush of the country. General Smuts now struck almost due south and, driving the enemy from Kangala, formed a camp near the Msiha river close to the Nguru mountains on June 23.

At this point a halt was necessitated owing to the exhaustion of the troops and the need for improving the lengthening line of communications. Meanwhile the coastal district to the rear of Msiha camp was cleared by troops of the Indian Army acting in co-operation with the Navy, and the ports of Tanga, Pangani, Sadani and Bagamoyo fell into British hands. The capture of Tanga provided General Smuts with a new line of communication to the coast. Moreover, in accordance with the general arrangements of the Commander-in-Chief, Allied forces in other parts of the Protectorate were closing in on the Germans. The Lake Victoria district was cleared of the enemy, and British and Belgian columns were bearing down on the Protectorate from the north and west in the general direction of Tabora, whose communications with Dar-es-Salaam had been cut by van Deventer, who advanced from Kondoa Irangi and reached the railway line at Kilimatinde and Dodoma near the end of July. About the same time another column consisting of the levies of Nyasaland and Rhodesia under the command of General (Sir) Edward Northey was invading the Protectorate from the south and was threatening the town of Iringa.

Thus by the end of July 1916 a large part of the organised districts of the Protectorate was in British hands. The main enemy forces under von Lettow, however, occupied a strong position in the Nguru mountains. Skilful flanking tactics ejected the enemy from this position after heavy fighting in August, and General Smuts with the chief British force bore down on Morogoro on the railway. These operations were facilitated by van Deventer's advance down the railway to Kilossa, which was captured after desultory fighting from August 15 to 22. Then, though exhaustion was now pressing hard on his men, van Deventer responded to a further demand of the Commander-in-Chief by driving the enemy from Uleia on August 26 and from Kidodi on September 10. General Smuts's purpose, however, of forcing a decisive action at Morogoro, formerly the administrative capital of the Protectorate, was frustrated by the retirement of von Lettow, who, though driven from position after position, never faltered and always punished carelessness on the part of the attack. By the middle of September 1916 the pursuers were too exhausted to carry the chase further and occupied an entrenched line in the vicinity of Kissaki. There they remained till January 1917, touch with the enemy being maintained by means of patrols.

During this interval a further reorganisation was made. One division was abolished and all the mounted South African troops still fit for service were posted to one brigade. All the unfit European troops were evacuated to the countries of their origin and, under these arrangements, about 12,000 South African troops left East Africa between October and December 1916, their place being taken by the Nigerian Brigade and new battalions of the King's African Rifles. The South African formations retained by the Commander-in-Chief consisted of the 2nd Division and the 2nd South African Infantry Brigade, which was in reserve under the immediate control of headquarters. In the meantime, Dar-es-Salaam surrendered to the Navy on September 3 and became the new sea base of the British forces. The occupation of Kilwa further south furnished another useful base, and there troops were collected for an advance into the hinterland. Thus a strong concentration was being brought into play against von Lettow. In August 1916 General Northey was at Iringa, and Tabora was occupied by British and Belgian troops; finally a Portuguese contingent crossed the Rovuma from the south to assist in rounding up the Germans. General van Deventer sent the 7th South African Infantry and a cyclist battalion under Colonel Fairweather to intercept a German force that was known to be retiring from Tabora, but the enemy, though roughly handled, succeeded in breaking through and continuing his retreat to the south. The vicinity of Iringa was the scene of several brisk encounters between opposing bodies of troops, the most notable success falling to General Northey's command, which captured an enemy detachment of over 300 men. After much confused fighting the Germans from Tabora, having eluded all efforts to surround them, eventually took up a position covering Mahenge. There they were confronted by the troops under Northey and van Deventer.

Before another organised advance was made, General Smuts relinquished his command in order to represent his Government at the Imperial Conference. His conduct of the operations had scarcely enhanced his military reputation, but though the enemy still kept the field, the success of the campaign was assured. His departure, followed by that of General Arthur Hoskins, left General van Deventer to direct the concluding stages of the campaign. The principal operations against the Germans were now directed from Kilwa and Lindi, and after a gallant resistance the enemy's last organised line was pierced, and near the end of November 1917 a large hostile force was compelled to lay down its arms.

The war now drifted into the guerilla stage and was fought out principally in Portuguese territory south of the Rovuma, von Lettow taking advantage of the defensive facilities of the country with skill and resolution. In the bushy, thickly forested country scored by numerous rivers, quite large contingents could be within a mile of each other without being aware of the fact. Von Lettow and his men were not tied down to any fixed locality; they could always obtain with ease the food of tropical Africa, and the interruptions caused by the rains afforded them a welcome respite lasting for almost half the year. Gradually, however, pressure and numbers began to tell, but though von Lettow was driven from the Protectorate, he gloriously fulfilled his purpose of keeping the field till the fate of East Africa was settled by the wholesale German surrender in Europe.

The Union of South Africa, by supplying troops and leaders for the campaign in East Africa, greatly assisted the cause of the Allies, enabling the imperial authorities to concentrate on the campaign in Europe. There white South Africa was represented by an infantry brigade, a medical corps, two brigades of heavy artillery, a signal company, two railway companies and a miscellaneous trades company. These troops were paid at Union rates by the British Government in return for a Union contribution of £1,000,000 to general war expenses, since General Botha, for fear of the growing Nationalist opposition and the restiveness of many of his own followers, could not undertake to pay them fully from Union funds. The infantry brigade, which arrived in England early in November 1915, was sent to Egypt in January 1916, where, under the command of Brigadier-General H. T. Lukin, it played the most prominent part in forcing the subjection of the Senussi, a tribe that was threatening Egypt from the west. This neatly conducted enterprise inspired the brigade with confidence for the severer test that awaited it in France, where after its arrival on 20 April 1916 it was attached to the 9th Scottish Division. Thereafter the history of this brigade is bound up with the story of the Western Front. It took part in most of the big battles in France and Flanders and acquired for itself a great reputation in a division that was noted for its hard fighting qualities. The epic struggle, which in July 1916 made Delville Wood known to the world, spread the fame of the South Africans throughout the Empire. The reputation that they then acquired was splendidly maintained by them in the subsequent engagements in which they participated with the 9th Division. After Delville Wood the brigade in 1916 and 1917 took part in a series of offensives at the Butte de Warlencourt (October 1916), Arras (April 1917) and Passchendaele (September and October 1917). During the retreat of the Fifth Army in March 1918 the brigade added to its laurels by a heroic stand at Marrières Wood, which, by delaying the German advance for seven hours, enabled the remainder of the 9th Division to continue its retreat in good order. Despite the terrible losses incurred in these efforts, the South Africans, now reduced to 1300 men, gave convincing proof by their exploits near Messines and Wytschaete in April that their fighting qualities were unimpaired.

After the repulse of the German offensives in 1918, the survivors of the South Africans were formed into a composite battalion and assisted in the capture of Meteren on July 19. Sufficient reinforcements having arrived to allow the brigade to be reformed, it was detached from the 9th Division and sent to join the 66th Division with which it remained during the rest of its service in France. In the victorious counter-attack of the Allies, it assisted in the capture of Beaurevoir and Beaumont and rendered valuable service by forcing the line of the Selle (October 12–19). When the brigade saw action again, the whole German front was obviously deliquescing in defeat, but the South Africans were faced by some of the toughest troops in the German army and were engaged in fighting until orders to cease fire were received on 11 November 1918. After the armistice the brigade served for a short time with the army of occupation in the Rhineland before returning to England in March 1919.

These services did not exhaust the military contributions of the Union during the war. The Coloured and African population of South Africa performed work of great practical value. The operations of white troops in the German West and East African campaigns were largely made possible through the African labour supplied by the Union. The only fighting unit furnished by the non-European peoples was the Cape Corps of two battalions, the rank and file of which were Coloured men drawn chiefly from the Cape Province. Its first experience of warfare was in East Africa where it acquitted itself with credit. The first battalion was then dispatched in April 1918 to Palestine where it maintained its reputation for good conduct and soldierly efficiency. Coloured men were also employed in the Cape Auxiliary Horse Transport, which was sent in 1917 to the Western Front in Europe, where 25,090 South African Bantu and a battalion of Cape Coloured men were employed in work that took place behind the lines.

The Union successfully vied with the other Dominions in organising arrangements for the comfort and welfare of its nationals engaged in the war. Three agencies, the Governor-General's Fund, the Red Cross (South Africa), and the South African Gifts and Comforts Organisation Committee, were formed to relieve the suffering and distress caused by the war. After the armistice the arrangements for the demobilisation of South African soldiers were carried out by a board under the presidency of the Chief of the General Staff and were so successful that the return of the men to civil employment was effected without causing any appreciable dislocation in the life of South Africa.

The heaviest casualties sustained by the South Africans occurred in the brigade that served in Europe, where 4648 men lost their lives. The total number of deaths in Egypt was 261, in East Africa 2141, in German South-West Africa 254, and in the Union, as a result of the rebellion, 409. These campaigns represented a military service far more varied than that contributed by any other Dominion and exposed the soldiers of the Union to conditions of warfare sufficiently divergent and exacting to form a severe test for the best of troops.

It has been estimated that over 136,000 white troops were sent by South Africa to the different fronts,[1] a proportion of the adult European male population that must be considered as remarkable in view of the fact that all were volunteers and that a large section of the people was averse to taking any part in the war.

The financial strain of the war was inevitably severe, but thanks to its gold-mines and excellent credit, the Union bore it well. In all, war and rebellion together cost the Treasury £38,012,555 of which all save £5,839,461 was borrowed money. Both the Treasury and the railways, however, fared surprisingly well on their ordinary budgets. Once at least the railways achieved a substantial surplus in place of the anticipated deficit by raising the rates on the bunkering traffic

[1] Buchan, J., *The South African Forces in France*, p. 260.

to the stream of shipping which was diverted from the Suez Canal to the old route round the Cape, by whittling down the amounts written off for depreciation, and by suspending renewals of track and rolling-stock for lack of the essential imported materials. It was only towards the close of the war that the deficit began to mount up seriously.

So it was with the general revenue and expenditure. Time and again the Treasurer budgeted for a deficit and found himself with a surplus, for borrowed money was pouring into the country, the output of gold was well maintained, farmers received unheard-of prices, the proceeds of customs, excise, posts and telegraphs rose and rose, and so fast did secondary industries spring up under the protection from foreign competition afforded by the preoccupations of Europe and North America, that, in 1917, the Union arranged for its first census of industrial production, and, a year later, organised a similar census for agriculture and passed its first Factory and Wage Regulation Acts.

On the other hand, expenditure could not be kept down to the old pre-war levels. It was swelled by the growing service of the public debt, the increasing demands of schools and universities to which the Government, to its credit, responded liberally, and the rising prices for goods of all kinds. Hence, taxation became progressively heavier along the lines laid down in 1915: increased customs duties, super-income tax, an export tax on diamonds as soon as that industry had revived sufficiently to be taxed; then, as the cry against profiteers rose louder, an excess profits tax and a "readjustment" of the income tax on companies. The proceeds of all these went into the general revenue, but the Government's half-share of the accumulated *bewaarplaatsen* fund[1] and the income which began to come in at last towards the close of the war from the state gold areas leased to companies were prudently paid into loan account.

By reason of her distance from the main sphere of hostilities, South Africa escaped most of the hardships of war-time. Some of her wool-farmers felt themselves aggrieved, and joined the Nationalist Party, when, in 1917, the Allies rationed shipping and faced them with the choice between accepting Great Britain's offer to take the whole of the 1917 clip at prices which were indeed lower than those of 1916 but none the less 55 per cent above pre-war rates, or finding an outlet for their wool, and much of the 1916 clip also, in the "open" but inaccessible markets of the United States and Japan.

South Africa knew nothing of food-cards, rent restrictions and the like. The cost of living did not rise markedly until May 1916, when the Government appointed a permanent advisory commission, and

[1] *Bewaarplaatsen* were storage areas and sources of water supply on which, in republican days, mining was not permitted. Deep-level mining made it possible to mine below them, and since 1908 the proceeds of the sale or lease of such areas had been paid into a special fund pending a decision. This was now taken. More than £2,000,000 were involved, of which the state took half and the owners the remainder.

presently, on its recommendation, fixed the price of sugar. Its next venture to exercise the controlling powers which it had taken away back in September 1914 was not so successful. At the close of 1917 it was faced with a shortage of wheat owing to the failure of part of the usual Australian supply. It feared its farmer supporters too much to fix a price, but decreed instead that bread must be made of wheaten flour mixed with barley, rye or maize. Thus, in the last year of the war, it began to conserve its wheat and earned the resentment of many of its urban supporters—and of their wives.

The Government failed even more definitely to control house-rents. In the middle of 1918 the cost of living in the principal towns had risen to 23 per cent above the pre-war level, rising working-costs were threatening some of the low-grade gold-mines with extinction, white and black workmen in Johannesburg were restive. The Government, therefore, proposed to take control of house-rents and to regulate the supplies of labour and material to industries essential to the public welfare. In spite of furious opposition from the most diverse quarters and open dissension in the Ministry, the Bill passed the Assembly at the very end of the session, but was adroitly shelved in the Senate. It was only during the short post-war boom of 1919 that house-rents were at last put under control.

On the economic plane, the Union emerged from the war in much better case than did most other states whose share in the struggle had been commensurate with her own; but politically the Union of South Africa was a house divided against itself. The suppression of the *opstand* of 1914 was followed by an increase of political opposition among the Afrikaners to the Botha Government, and the fact that at the election of 1915 the number of the Nationalists led by General Hertzog was doubled was proof that the men who had fought against the Government formed only a fraction of those who objected to a policy of active participation in the war. The traditional nationalism, which formed the political creed of General Hertzog, incompatible though it possibly was with the best interests of South Africa, obviously commanded considerable support from the Afrikaners, notably in the Free State, and encouraged by this he challenged every step of the Government to assist the imperial authorities. Asserting that the rebellion had been provoked by "the unconstitutionalism of a constitutional government",[1] he treated it as if it were a venial offence, and, basing his conduct on technicalities rather than principles, displayed parliamentary skill of a high order in extracting a political advantage from the Government's handling of the rebellion and the German South-West campaign, and thereafter from the Union's continued participation in the war and the Government's financial and social policies. This political conflict contributed more than the rebellion itself to bring about a recrudescence of racial strife.

[1] *Union of South Africa, House of Assembly Debates*, 6th session, 1915, p. 786.

A new determination to become independent of the Empire was aroused, and at the end of the war the Nationalists, encouraged by the enunciation of the doctrine of self-determination, put in a plea for the independence of the Union, failing that of both ex-republics, and, or, in the last resort, that of the Free State alone.

Thus, politically, the war was followed by a revival of racialism and saw the growth of a party which aimed at the rights of neutrality and secession from the Empire.

CHAPTER XXVIII

SOUTH AFRICA AND THE EMPIRE

THROUGHOUT the nineteenth and early twentieth centuries, the relations of the Imperial Power with South Africa were closer and more persistent than with British North America or Australia. This was so for three main reasons: the strategic importance of the Cape Peninsula; the existence, side by side with British colonies, of republics, the possessions of foreign Powers and tribal territories; and, lastly, the preponderance throughout the land of non-Europeans, African and Asian, for whom the British Government and electorate felt a real though fluctuating responsibility.

Great Britain had taken the Cape Peninsula to secure her road to India; she had kept the rest of the Cape Colony because she found it attached to the Peninsula. Until the completion of the Suez Canal in 1869, the Cape was the turning-point of that Dark Continent which cut in half Britain's growing Empire of the sea-ways. Even after that event such was its value as "the true centre of the Empire . . . clear of the Suez complications", a fine depôt for troops, a good market for provisions and a place for the repair of ships, that there were those who held that if the rest of South Africa were to become a self-governing federation, the Peninsula should be retained by Great Britain as a fortified Crown colony.[1]

The British occupation began in January 1806 when the redcoats entered Cape Town; it really ended in March 1916 when a dusty little column of Garrison gunners marched down from the forts on Table Bay to take ship for France. Since the Peninsula was throughout the only part of South Africa of "direct Imperial service", H.M. Government, to the dismay of energetic proconsuls and the fury of colonial annexationists, as a rule held to the policy, old as Van Riebeeck's day, of non-expansion. Throughout the nineteenth century it annexed only when Governors on the spot had taken some irrevocable step, or local officials and colonists had exercised irresistible pressure. These annexations within what is now the Union were more than once balanced by wholesale abandonments, or followed by the transfer of the annexed territories to one or other of the existing colonies, while further north, the Imperial Government preferred to help Rhodes's British South Africa Company with men, money and diplomatic action rather than itself to annex the Rhodesias. But the disaster of the Jameson Raid forced the Imperial Government to

[1] C.O. 48/455. Minute by R. G. W. Herbert on despatch No. 53, Sir H. Barkly to Sec. of State, 31 May 1871; Froude, J. A., *Short Studies of Great Subjects*, III, 373.

choose between letting matters take their own way, with the high probability of Transvaal predominance and the possibility of foreign intervention in southern Africa, and bringing direct pressure to bear on a land where political authority had been divorced dangerously from economic power. It chose the latter alternative and, during the war that followed, annexed the two Boer republics (1900). For a short space it exercised unexampled influence in southern Africa; but, from 1905 onwards, the course of events there and in Great Britain led it to relinquish its authority. After the Union of 1910, direct British rule persisted only in the High Commission Territories of Basutoland, Swaziland and Bechuanaland, and in the naval and military areas in the Cape Peninsula.

This long-continued British control, radiating from Cape Town, was rendered almost inevitable by the fact that South Africa was a microcosm of the state system of the world. Some authority was called for capable of safeguarding the interests of colonies, which, being colonies, could have little or no external policy of their own, capable also of looking at the affairs of South Africa as a whole. When, therefore, at the time of the Great Trek, states distinct from the Cape Colony took shape on the High Veld and in Natal, the Cape Governor was, in 1846, appointed also High Commissioner to exercise a restraining and mediatory influence over all that lay adjacent to the colonial borders. This new office was always held by the Governors at Cape Town until 1901, when Sir Alfred Milner took it away with him to the Transvaal, and, long before that happened, its vague authority had been extended beyond the Zambesi. For a decade, from 1897 onward, South African politics centred round the High Commissioners, till Lord Selborne, having powerfully assisted political union forward along the path which had been paved by Lord Milner, handed over the most effective of his powers to a South African Ministry (1910).

The Union cabinet and the legislature that lay behind it were based on British models adapted to local uses, in the main by the Cape Colony. The constitutional evolution of that colony and, *longo intervallo*, of Natal had followed the same general lines as that of Canada and Australasia; but though poverty, a sparse population, and poor means of communication had long been common to the British colonies in all three continents, the growth of parliamentary institutions in the South African group had been much slower than in the others. This arrested development was due primarily to the presence of a non-European and predominantly tribal majority either within or close to the colonies. South Africa has, indeed, always been the ornithorhynchus of Dominion politics. Geographically it belongs to the class of temperate colonies of settlement, ethnographically to that of tropical dependencies. It was only in 1872, when the liberal policy of equality of all before the law, an equality culminating in a colour-blind franchise, had stood the test of time in the Cape Colony, when the cutting of the Suez Canal and the collapse of the Second Empire in France had temporarily reduced the strategic value of the Cape Peninsula, and when the advent of gold and diamonds and ostrich feathers had given the Colony the wherewithal to pay its way, that H.M. Government virtually thrust autonomy upon a half-unwilling dependency. Natal, overwhelmed in a sea of Bantu, had to wait yet another twenty years for like privileges and only received them when Rhodes's scheme for a federation of the South African states and colonies seemed imminent (1893).

The main opposition to self-government came from officials and others within the Cape Colony. It arose from the fear that the withdrawal of the imperial garrison would leave the Europeans helpless in face of the tribes. As far as defence and external policy were concerned, the Cape entered upon self-government in a thoroughly "colonial" frame of mind. Its borderers might be scornful of imperial military men and methods; its new Ministers might, by their fierce suspicion of Downing Street interference, wreck Carnarvon's confederation scheme at the outset; but both ministers and frontiersmen still took it for granted that Great Britain would furnish that defence by sea which had seemed almost a law of nature since Trafalgar and, in the last resort, defence by land also. Therein lay the essence of colonialism: local control of policy and the final implementing of policy by the mother country.

It could hardly have been otherwise. Colonists everywhere had long been accustomed to count on British naval and military forces as a means of defence and a great source of gain. The Orange River Sovereignty men in the 'fifties, New Zealanders in the 'sixties, and Natalians as late as the 'eighties saw nothing incongruous in autonomy combined with the presence of a considerable imperial garrison. For ten years before the grant of self-government in 1872, the Cape authorities had protested vigorously against the reduction of the British garrison; afterwards, they took it hardly that they should be called upon to contribute to the cost of royal troops employed in the joint expeditions to which joint policy had given rise. The Imperial Government had great difficulty in persuading the Cape and Natal to pay something towards its expenses in the Kaffir and Zulu campaigns of 1877–79, in both of which the main burden had been borne by the regulars.[1] Warned by such experiences, Chamberlain, during the Drifts crisis of 1895, stipulated in advance that the Cape should bear half the cost of the projected expedition against the Transvaal, and, at the close of the Matabele rebellion of 1896, he obliged the Chartered Company to pay for imperial troops till it could raise a police force of its own to take the place of that which had been eliminated during the Jameson Raid. On the other hand, the British taxpayer alone financed the Warren expedition into Bechuanaland in 1885 and,

[1] *Correspondence re contributions*, *Parl. Pap.* 1882, XLVII [Cd. 3280], pp. 15 *sqq.*

except for the cost of local forces, the South African war of 1899–1902. And justly so; for, however loudly colonists may have called for intervention, both campaigns were the outcome of imperial policy.

It was this problem of mutual defence that brought the South African colonies into contact with portions of the Empire other than Great Britain and India. Among the colonial notabilities who met together under the presidency of the Colonial Secretary, on the occasion of Queen Victoria's Jubilee in 1887, to discuss almost informally the means of drawing together the scattered portions of the Empire, there were representatives both of autonomous Cape Colony and of Crown Colony Natal.

At this first Colonial Conference,[1] H.M. Government ruled out discussion of plans for closer political union such as that which the recently founded Imperial Federation League was propounding, and posited defence as the prime common concern. The colonists elected rather to dwell on the virtues of imperial trade preferences. Thus early were the lines laid down for all succeeding Conferences. There was much that interested the Cape vitally under both heads. An imperial *Zollverein* might well be in keeping with the proposals for a railway and customs union which Rhodes, Jan Hofmeyr, a rising power among the Cape Afrikaners, and the late President Brand of the Free State had long been urging in South Africa. Such arrangements were doubly desirable now that the Rand goldfields had been opened up a few short months before the meeting of the Conference. On the score of defence, the fortifications of Table Bay and the naval base at Simonstown were admittedly defective, and Germany had just planted herself to the northward of the colony in Damara-Namaqualand. After much discourse on hard times and Native responsibilities, the Cape undertook to bear half the cost of putting the Table Bay defences in order; but it declined to follow Australia's offer, an offer inspired by German activities in the Pacific, to make a contribution to the cost of the Navy in return for the presence of a considerable squadron in local waters. It was left to Hofmeyr, an ardent Cape Colonist, fully alive to the present value of the British connection whatever constitutional changes the next century might have in store, to attempt to solve the defence and preference problems together. Amid general expressions of interest, but with no tangible result, he proposed a surcharge of 2 per cent on existing duties on foreign imports throughout the Empire, and the allocation of the proceeds to the upkeep of the Queen's ships.[2]

Hofmeyr repeated his proposal at the next Conference.[3] This was

[1] *Proceedings of the Colonial Conference, Parl. Pap.* 1887, LVI [Cd. 5091], [Cd. 5091–1].

[2] *Parl. Pap.* 1887, LVI [Cd. 5091–1], pp. 463 *sqq.*; Hofmeyr, J. H., *Life of Jan Hendrik Hofmeyr*, ch. XVII.

[3] Hofmeyr, J. H., *Life of Jan Hendrik Hofmeyr*, ch. XXVII; *Report by the Earl of Jersey ... on the Colonial Conference, Parl. Pap.* 1894, LVI [Cd. 7553]; *Papers re the Colonial Conference, Parl. Pap.* 1895, LXX [Cd. 7632].

held at Ottawa in June 1894. It was a thoroughly colonial conference, summoned by the Canadian Government, which had long been eyeing anxiously the soaring McKinley tariff of the United States. The proposal won the warm support of Rhodes, Premier of the Cape Colony. South African politics were centring on Rhodes, Home Ruler of Home Rulers and sworn foe to "this free trade craze". The Cape and the Orange Free State had now made their railway and customs agreements, and several small British territories had adhered thereto; Rhodesia was taking shape, and Rhodes still hoped that the recalcitrant Transvaal and Natal would enter the customs union that was to make southern Africa one economic bloc, the foundation of a British bloc running the full length of Africa, an example and an incentive to the rest of the Empire. Self-governing Natal was not represented at the Ottawa Conference, but the Cape sent a strong delegation, including Hofmeyr. The Conference pressed for improved intercolonial cable and steamship services and then passed on to the question of imperial preference. Hofmeyr put forward his scheme again, thereby touching on the problem of defence which had hitherto been left severely alone. The great majority, however, preferred to ask boldly for what they wanted: the diversion of foreign trade into "British" channels "by a judicious adjustment of tariffs". It was an adjustment which the Free Trade British Government, mainly dependent on foreign trade, blandly declined to make.[1]

Much had happened in South Africa before the first regular Conference of Prime Ministers met in London in June 1897 at the time of the Queen's Diamond Jubilee. Rhodes had fallen, his alliance with Hofmeyr broken; the Transvaal was arming and rival national passions were rising fast. Nevertheless, Joseph Chamberlain, the high priest of Unionism at the Colonial Office, hoped for some marked advance towards imperial unity and the development of Empire resources. One or two tentative steps in this direction had already been taken since 1894. Legislation had set the Australian colonies free to offer intercolonial reciprocity; Canada had offered United Kingdom goods a slight preference; colonial Chief Justices had been admitted to the Judicial Committee of the Privy Council and, among them, de Villiers, Chief Justice of the Cape Colony, who had long taken a leading part in pressing for this desirable reform.[2] The Conference, however, effected little. Sir Gordon Sprigg, head of a highly insecure Cape Cabinet, and Harry Escombe, his Natal colleague, who represented a ministry that was nervous of Transvaal intentions, could merely join with their fellows in listening non-committally to Chamberlain's proposal that the colonies should be represented by plenipotentiaries in "a great council of the Empire". Both, however,

[1] *Papers re the Colonial Conference*, *Parl. Pap.* 1895, LXX [Cd. 7824]; Walker, E. A., *Lord de Villiers and His Times*, pp. 244 *sqq*.

[2] Walker, E. A., *de Villiers*, pp. 116 *sqq*.

promised to consider granting some preference to British goods in return for the defence and other services rendered freely by the Mother Country, and Sprigg, in a blaze of pure imperial spirit, offered Great Britain the gift of a cruiser. It was a gift which was presently commuted for an annual payment of £30,000 voted by the Schreiner ministry, which succeeded Sprigg's in 1898.[1] Natal followed suit with an annual subsidy of £12,000.

The next Conference met, in London again, in June 1902 to celebrate the close of the South African war and the coronation of Edward VII.[2] The war had been an imperial war in the sense that contingents had been forthcoming from many of the self-governing portions of the Empire; Milner's reconstruction policy was also imperial in that it was drawing on many parts of the British world for officials and experts. Chamberlain might well hope that imperialistic feeling would still run sufficiently high to make possible a far-reaching imperial reorganisation based on "ideas of kinship and mutual obligation" rather than on "mere pride of possession or of huckstering calculation".[3] In 1897 he had told the assembled Premiers that if they wanted a share in the privilege of control, they must also assume responsibilities, and they had replied that, at the moment, they desired neither the one nor the other. He now reiterated, more confidently, his proposals for a representative imperial council. The Premiers rejected the scheme unanimously, but expressed the hope that the Conference would meet every fourth year, and added that they ought to be consulted before Great Britain concluded commercial treaties with foreign Powers.

This new note was a warning that the Secretary of State had utterly misread the signs of the times, for it was sounded even by the delegates from a South Africa dominated by imperialism. Sir Albert Hime, Premier of Natal, most nearly approximated to the current conception of a true-blue imperialist, but Sprigg, representing the Cape once more, fell far short of that ideal. In other quarters, the tide of colonial nationalism ran still more strongly. It had been set in motion, as ever, by the experience of war and by the recent creation of the Australian Commonwealth;[4] it swept overwhelmingly through the discussions on imperial preference. Great Britain indeed had denounced long-standing most-favoured-nation treaties with Belgium and Germany which had stood in the way of full imperial reciprocity; Natal, since 1898, had been a member of the Cape-Free State customs union; since 1898, too, the Rhodes customs clause, rejected in 1894, had been embodied in the constitution of Southern Rhodesia, ensuring to British goods in the widest sense of the term easy entry into a territory

[1] *Vide supra*, p. 605; Walker, *Schreiner*, pp. 107, 121.

[2] *Papers re a Conference, Parl. Pap.* 1902, LXVI [Cd. 1299]; *Papers re Colonial Conference*, 1903, XLIV [Cd. 1597], [Cd. 1723].

[3] Boyd, C. W. (ed.), *Mr Chamberlain's Speeches*, II, 68–73.

[4] See *C.H.B.E.* VII, 453.

which Rhodes to the end had hoped would dominate the future South African *Zollverein*.[1] Nevertheless, when Chamberlain observed that the first object of the Conference should be "free trade within the Empire", the proposal found no favour with Premiers nearly all of whom were fostering nascent industries which feared above all things competition with the factories of Great Britain. Sprigg and Hime were perhaps not so directly interested in local protection as were some of their colleagues, for, though Milner's reconstruction looked to the creation of secondary industries financed by a ruthless exploitation of the gold-mines, those industries would arise in the Transvaal rather than in their respective colonies. Nevertheless, they agreed with their fellow-Premiers that imperial free trade was impossible at the moment, joined them in prayers for a change of heart in an unreciprocating Mother Country, and promised a preference of 25 per cent on United Kingdom goods.

Under the heading of naval defence, while Canada broke new ground by talking of a navy of her own, the rest were content to increase their contributions to the Royal Navy; the Cape to £50,000, and Natal to £35,000.[2] For a moment, Sprigg and Hime were inclined to fall in with the suggestion of Richard Seddon of New Zealand that each self-governing colony should set aside a special military force for general imperial service; but, on second thoughts, they went with the great majority who preferred rather to safeguard autonomy doubly by improving the general quality of local defence forces. So Seddon's warriors remained "the army of a dream".

On one other matter, closely touching South Africa, colonial nationalism showed itself unmistakably. Hime and Seddon brought forward the demand for the suspension of the Cape constitution which Milner and the Cape Progressives had been advocating for some time past in the interests of South African federation.[3] Chamberlain had never liked the scheme, for to touch even a colonial parliament was to threaten parliaments everywhere. Now Sprigg protested, Sir Wilfred Laurier of Canada and Sir Edmund Barton of the Commonwealth strongly supported him, and the matter ended.

The Colonial Conference of 1902 marked the point at which centrifugal forces began unmistakably to get the upper hand of centripetal. Everything that happened between its dissolution and the assembling of the next Conference in April 1907 conspired to promote the growth of nationalism within the Empire. This growing preoccupation with local interests and local freedom of action was revealed, not only in the colonies, but in the Mother Country also. There, South African events played an important part in furthering the

[1] Southern Rhodesia Order-in-Council, 1898, § 47; for text see Newton, A. P., *The Unification of South Africa*, I, 143; *Parl. Pap.* 1899, LXIII [Cd. 9138], pp. 3 *sqq.*

[2] Act (Cape) No. 14 of 1902, and (Natal) No. 5 of 1903.

[3] *Petition for the Temporary Suspension of the Cape Constitution, Parl Pap.* 1902, LXIX [Cd. 1162]; Walker, E. A., *de Villiers*, pp. 393 *sqq.*; *The Milner Papers*, II, 405 *sqq.*

process. In 1903, Chamberlain had returned from a tour in South Africa convinced that co-operation and not centralisation was the hope of the future, and, in the name of economic co-operation, had split the Unionist party and the nation on the issue of imperial preference.[1] That issue, the revelations of incompetence in the conduct of the late war, the education question and the storm that raged over Chinese labour on the Rand gold-mines had brought in the Liberals under Sir Henry Campbell-Bannerman at the end of 1905, pledged to end "Chinese slavery", to grant self-government to the two ex-republics in South Africa, to carry out sweeping domestic reforms and, above all, to defend "the big loaf" for the British electorate.

Meanwhile, Australia and New Zealand had angrily challenged the importation of Asiatics into a land in which their sons had shed their blood during the recent war. In South Africa itself a sense of unity and of the need for it was growing steadily. At the Bloemfontein Conference of March 1903, Milner had federated all British Southern Africa economically and induced it to give a 25 per cent preference to United Kingdom goods;[2] New Zealand had since arranged reciprocity with this new customs union, and Australia was taking steps to do likewise. Now, early in 1907, bad times, imperial counsel and the Afrikaner revival were all thrusting the jarring colonies along the road that led to closer union. But it would be a closer union with very little of an imperialist colouring. The Progressives in the Cape Colony were split, the colonial rebels had recovered their votes, and the Premier, Jameson, was no longer relying on the "Vote British" cry which had been raised inevitably at the 1904 elections so soon after the war. Natal had just passed through the strain of a Zulu rebellion, and though, by calling on Great Britain for help and then insisting on carrying out its own policy under threat of resignation, its ministry had merited Winston Churchill's stinging rejoinder that "so vehement an assertion of independence on the part of a colony was not altogether compatible and consistent with passionate appeals for the support of British troops",[3] the fact remained that the Ministry had defeated Downing Street and, following once more the example of the British South Africa Company after the Matabele war and rebellion of 1893–97,[4] was even now issuing a local medal to commemorate its victory over the Zulus. Further, Afrikaners were in power in a self-governing Transvaal, and it was certain that they would soon be in power also in the Orange River Colony. Transvaal self-government had been tested and not found wanting, for the royal assent had been given to stringent anti-Asian laws, which, combined with Natal's known attitude towards her Indians, had drawn

[1] Boyd, C. W., *Mr Chamberlain's Speeches*, II, 125 *sqq*.

[2] *Proceedings of Customs Union Conference, Parl. Pap.* 1903, XLV [Cd. 1599], [Cd. 1640].

[3] *Hansard*, Fourth Series, CLV, 275.

[4] *B.S.A. Company Directors' Report*, 1896–97, p. 13.

the attention of Delhi and Peking to southern Africa, where Gandhi, as yet the moderate lawyer, was beginning to organise passive resistance.

Thus, the Cape, Natal and Transvaal delegates to the 1907 Conference came from a rapidly changing South Africa to a political atmosphere in London very different from that of 1897 and 1902.[1] This time, the British Prime Minister, Sir Henry Campbell-Bannerman, and no mere Colonial Secretary opened the proceedings, declaring that "the essence of the British imperial connection" was freedom and independence, and its method regular Conferences interspersed with Subsidiary Conferences on matters which called for time and detailed discussion. That speech ended effectually the scheme which Alfred Lyttelton, then Colonial Secretary, had put forward in 1905, with the approval of Australia, the Cape and Natal, that the conference should be transformed into an Imperial Council, with a "purely consultative and advisory" permanent commission representative of all the self-governing colonies to prepare agenda and collect information. Jameson was still prepared to welcome the scheme "as a kind of seed which may grow";[2] but even he insisted that the Dominions—that title had come into use by 1907—were autonomous nations within the Empire and, though it be "a very disproportionate equality", equal to Great Britain. But that the seed might grow was precisely the danger in the eyes of the rest. Louis Botha, "the Benjamin of the Brotherhood", as Campbell-Bannerman called him,[3] had first electrified the assemblage by making his opening remarks in Afrikaans and then relieved it by proceeding quite satisfactorily in English, always to the point, always conciliatory and always commendably brief. He now insisted that the proper line was not centralisation but—blessed word—co-operation, and, mindful of the fate of hastily constructed political fabrics in his own country, counselled his hearers to "build slowly".[4] He ended, as usual, with a modest, "That is all I have to say"; but, indeed, it was all that needed to be said. The Conference decided that it should become for the future the Imperial Conference meeting every fourth year, no longer a concourse of Dominion Premiers under the chairmanship of the Colonial Secretary, but a conference between His Majesty's Government in the Mother Country and those in the "self-governing Dominions beyond the seas".[5] H.M. Government, in turn, promised to form a special Dominions department at the Colonial Office.

Having thus set out definitely along the road that led logically to the formal declarations of 1926 and 1930, which were to define independence within the Commonwealth, the Conference passed on to

[1] *Papers re Colonial Conference, Parl. Pap.* 1907, LIV [Cd. 3337], [Cd. 3340]; 1907, LV [Cd. 3404], [Cd. 3406], [Cd. 3523], [Cd. 3524].

[2] *Ibid.* [Cd. 3523], pp. 34–5.

[3] *Ibid.* [Cd. 3404], p. 4.

[4] *Ibid.* [Cd. 3523], p. 35.

[5] *Ibid.* [Cd. 3523], p. 70.

questions of defence. These did not detain it long, for the Liberals were still hopeful of checking the fatal race in armaments with Germany, and expected much from the Hague Peace Conference that was to meet on the morrow of the Colonial Conference. Led by Laurier, the Conference declined to accept the thesis of Sir Thomas Smartt, one of the Cape Progressives, that it was "the duty of the Dominions to help the Navy in some shape or form",[1] and somewhat grudgingly continued existing naval subsidies. On land, Botha looked forward to a South African military federation and, meanwhile, requested H.M. Government to maintain a considerable garrison in South Africa; Natal expressed itself satisfied with its own recent military achievements, and when Smartt revived Seddon's proposal of imperial service contingents, Jameson himself gently rebuked him for his "advanced ideas".[2] On the other hand, all welcomed the reforms outlined by Robert Haldane,[3] which included an Imperial General Staff, Dominion representation on the Committee of Imperial Defence, and the organisation of home defence forces everywhere more or less on the same lines.

South Africans, from whose colonies men were pouring out during the post-war depression faster than they were coming in, could add little that was fruitful on the score of immigration, nor, with their own customs union strained to breaking point, could they contribute anything to the preference debate which Alfred Deakin of Australia opened at interminable length. Jameson, always optimistic, hoped that preference would lead to Empire free trade and that, in turn, to world free trade; but Botha—perhaps with past franchise quarrels and present Indian legislation in mind—retorted that since "the mother country ought to leave us as much alone as possible", he for one found difficulty in interfering with her free trade arrangements.[4] But there was one matter on which all the South African delegates could co-operate heartily. Some members of the Conference were anxious to combine the House of Lords and the Judicial Committee of the Privy Council as an imperial court of appeal, a proposal too revolutionary for the legal authorities concerned. The Cape delegates and, to a less extent, their colleagues from other parts of South Africa were content to leave well alone, at least so long as Sir Henry de Villiers, the veteran Chief Justice of the Cape, was available to hear Roman-Dutch appeals on the Judicial Committee. But de Villiers had long advocated a federal court of appeal for all South Africa and, now, briefed by him, Botha, with the support of Jameson and the Natalians, carried a far-reaching resolution to the effect that wherever groups of colonies, whether federated or not, possessed a local appeal

[1] *Papers re Colonial Conference, Parl. Pap.* 1907, LIV [Cd. 3523], p. 541.
[2] *Ibid.* pp. 112–15.
[3] *Ibid.* p. 4; also *Papers re a Conference . . . on the Defence of the Empire, Parl. Pap.* 1909, LIX [Cd. 4948], pp. 32 *sqq.*
[4] *Parl. Pap.* 1907, LV [Cd. 3523], pp. 283, 304.

court, appeals to the Privy Council should lie only from that court.[1]

Botha's resolution foreshadowed one of the most decisive provisions of the South Africa Act of 1909,[2] whereunder all appeals from Provincial Divisions of the Union Supreme Court were to lie to the Appellate Division, and, except in cases arising under the Colonial Courts of Admiralty Act of 1890, no appeal should lie from that Division to the Judicial Committee save by special leave of the King-in-Council. Further, subject to reservation, the Union Parliament was to have the right to limit the cases in which such leave might be asked. That clause went much further than the parallel clause in the Australia Act of 1900.[3] It is true that the Commonwealth Parliament had then been given the same qualified powers of limitation, and that on high constitutional issues as between the federation and the states, or state and state, no appeal could be made to the Judicial Committee without leave of the Australian High Court; but in all other matters an appeal to the King-in-Council still lay as of grace and right from the High Court and, still more significantly, from the State Courts. The contrast was at once the measure of the difference between a unitary and a federal constitution, and of the progress that had been made between 1900 and 1909 towards Dominion independence within the Empire.

The South Africa Act was passing through the imperial Parliament when delegates from the four South African colonies, which it had been framed to unite, attended the first of the Subsidiary Conferences, on naval and military matters, in July 1909.[4] As representatives of a still disunited land, they could not, even if they would—and that to say the least of it was doubtful—follow Australia or New Zealand in undertaking to equip a local squadron. On the other hand, with ex-President Steyn urging on union in face of the growing German menace,[5] they could all agree readily that, for considerations of convenience, local military forces, equipment and transport should be on British models.

The first Colonial Conference, of May and June 1911,[6] was also the first to which the South Africans, led by Botha, came as representatives of a united Dominion. Before the Conference, Union public opinion had been focussed mainly on the Government's campaign against the mealie transport rates and the rebate system maintained

[1] *Ibid.* pp. 206 *sqq.*, 226.

[2] South Africa Act, 1909 [9 Edw. VII, c. 6], § 106; text in Eybers, G. W., *Select Constitutional Documents*, pp. 517 *sqq.*

[3] Commonwealth of Australia Constitution Act, 1900 [63 and 64 Vict. c. 12], § 74; text in Quick, J., and Garran, R. R., *Annotated Constitution of the Australian Commonwealth*, p. 272.

[4] *Papers re a Conference . . . on the Defence of the Empire*, 1909, LIX [Cd. 4948].

[5] Van der Merwe, N. J., *Steyn*, II, 220, 348.

[6] *Correspondence re Imperial Conference*, *Parl. Pap.* 1911, LIV [Cd. 5513]; *Precis* and *Proceedings of I.C.*, *Parl. Pap.* 1911, LIV [Cd. 5741], [Cd. 5745]; *Papers laid before . . . the I.C.*, *Parl. Pap.* 1911, LIV [Cd. 5746–1, 2].

by the Union-Castle line of steamships and its allies. Union, and the fact that the Union-Castle's mail contract was expiring, gave South Africa a much stronger bargaining ground than ever before. These matters received due attention in London, but the delegates soon found themselves launched on much deeper waters.

The general feeling at the Conference was that, in view of the Dominions' insistence since 1907 on their national individuality, requests for preference could hardly be pressed with decency. The Union delegates merely upheld the general principle of preference and the current practice, and concurred with their fellows in welcoming a Royal Commission to report on Empire resources and to recommend methods of extending mutual trade "consistent with the existing fiscal policy of each". As for immigration, Botha laid a rod in pickle for his own back when he should return home by expressing his willingness to spend money on importing good farmers, but not on importing men who would swell the numbers of the poor folk he already had on his hands, some of whom had proved hopeless failures in spite of governmental efforts to set them on their feet again.[1]

The attitude of the Union delegates on naval questions was much less equivocal from the imperial point of view than had at one time seemed likely. Before the Conference, the Botha ministry had proposed to deduct the cost of local naval services or of local coast defence from the old Cape and Natal contributions of £85,000, and to replace the preference on British goods by a grant in money or services to imperial naval and local defences.[2] It had, however, soon dropped the latter suggestion and, at the Conference, its delegates jettisoned the rest, undertook to continue the admittedly inadequate naval subsidy, and accepted the scheme of voluntary military co-operation recommended by the Imperial General Staff.

Constitutional issues were debated at considerable length at this Conference. Sir Joseph Ward of New Zealand pleaded earnestly for the creation of a representative Imperial Council of State to advise the King on all matters affecting the Dominions. Botha, among others, opposed the scheme with determination. Vested with authority—and to what representative body was the Council to be answerable?—it must, he held, limit Dominion autonomy; devoid of authority, "I fear very much that it would only become a meddlesome body".[3] Rather, to emphasise the rising status of the Dominions, he revived Deakin's proposal of 1907 that their affairs be transferred from the Colonial Office to the Prime Minister's department;[4] but, in response to Asquith's half-laughing remonstrance that a British Premier was already overburdened, he waived this suggestion all the more readily because the British Premier deprecated Ward's Imperial Council.[5]

[1] *Parl. Pap.* 1911, LIV [Cd. 5745], p. 159.
[2] *Parl. Pap.* 1911, LIV [Cd. 5513], pp. 12, 13.
[3] *Ibid.* [Cd. 5745], pp. 69–70.
[4] *Ibid.* 1911 [Cd. 5513], pp. 12, 13.
[5] *Parl. Pap.* 1911, LIV [Cd. 5746–1], pp. 112–14.

But when the Colonial Secretary in turn proposed that there should be a standing committee of the Conference manned by Dominion High Commissioners or other accredited representatives, Botha joined with Laurier to defeat even this mildest of potential checks on the beneficent development of liberty, decentralisation and co-operation. "We meet here as Prime Ministers," he said. "Sentiment and mutual interest bring us here together. Now it is sought to create committees."[1]

So this, the first serious attempt by the imperial authorities to provide means of continuous consultation on matters of imperial concern, was shelved. Yet the need for such consultation was becoming insistent. The condition of India pointed in that direction. Several of the Dominions had been exercised from time to time on the score of Asiatic immigration; at the moment none was more exercised than South Africa, which was not only wrestling with the intricacies of a general measure to regulate immigration, but was also involved in grave difficulties with its resident Indian population. Its policy towards them was such that feeling in India had risen to dangerous heights, and even the cautious Delhi Government had ventured to observe that "it does not appear to have been thoroughly considered that each Dominion owes responsibility to the rest of the Empire for ensuring that its domestic policy shall not unnecessarily create embarrassment in the administration of India";[2] At the Conference, the Earl of Crewe repeated this hardest of all truths, that no member of a group could live to itself alone.[3] But the Secretary of State for India had to be content with the well-worn reply that South Africa's Indian problem was not, as elsewhere, a mere question of labour, but a matter of self-preservation, and the hope that a settlement would be reached with the Indians on the spot.[4]

It was foreign policy rather than Indian difficulties that forced the problem of consultation to the front. Certain resolutions passed by the second Hague Conference had given rise to the Declaration of London, modifying the laws of war at sea (1908). This declaration had awakened an interest in foreign policy in several Dominions, especially in Australia. How were the new Dominion navies to be used: as separate units or as parts of a single combined fleet? More to the point, for what purposes were they to be used; in other words, what was to be the policy not of Great Britain only, but of the Empire?

International policy was naturally the last thing in which Dominions, with their long and sheltered colonial pasts, should take a direct interest. The South Africans alone had had any real experience of the meaning of war, *ultima ratio regum*; even so, the coast colonies had had little more than the usual colonial experience of external policy, and in the foreign politics of the republics there had always been

[1] *Parl. Pap.* 1911, LIV [Cd. 5745], p. 193.
[2] *Ibid.* 1911, LIV [Cd. 5746–1], p. 277.
[3] *Ibid.* [Cd. 5745], p. 399.
[4] *Ibid.* p. 409.

a strong element of make-believe as far as concerned Powers other than Great Britain. Both republics had been cut off from the sea; the Orange Free State had never had occasion to seek contacts with the outer world; the Transvaal's treaty-making powers had been restricted by the London Convention of 1884. But now that the Dominions asked for an exposition of the foreign situation and of imperial policy, Sir Edward Grey gave it them in secret session in such full measure that, as Botha was quick to note, he evoked an unexampled sense of solidarity.[1]

Solidarity inspired by the imminence of the German peril did not deter Laurier from demanding, nor Botha from successfully supporting him in the demand, that the Dominions should henceforward be to all intents and purposes free to make what commercial arrangements they chose with foreign Powers, unhampered by the most-favoured-nation clause in imperial treaties which might otherwise give their concessions an undesired universality.[2] For the rest, the Conference cordially approved the renewal of the Anglo-Japanese alliance and, less cordially, of the Declaration of London, Botha remarking that, whatever limitations the latter might impose, the Union would not suffer, as it could always import through neutral Delagoa Bay and export its own products to Great Britain through some neutral European port.[3] Then, passing beyond the commercial treaties which had hitherto been their prime concern, H.M. Government undertook to consult the Dominions on the policy to be pursued at future Hague Conferences and, "where time and opportunity and the subject matter permit", in other international negotiations also.

This last promise perhaps affected South Africa more nearly than other Dominions, because its territory marched with that of more than one European Power. It certainly obliged it to answer a question which at once arose now that the Dominions were claiming a voice in the shaping of imperial policy, for, if a breakdown of policy led to war, must the Dominions take part therein? Laurier had already announced that Canada would only do so actively if she thought fit. His words, pressed far beyond their meaning, touched a sympathetic chord in South Africa. The Natal republicans of 1840 had in a measure anticipated the question by asking for a treaty of alliance and the right of neutrality in time of war, leaving Great Britain free, in the event of a foreign threat to Natal by sea, to "interpose itself either in a friendly manner or to repel the same by force".[4] Thirty-five years later confederation had meant nothing more to the Transvaalers than an offensive and defensive alliance, while, on the eve of the South African war in 1899, W. P. Schreiner, Premier of the Cape, had raised

[1] *The Times*, 22 June 1911.
[2] *Parl. Pap.* 1911, LIV [Cd. 5745], p. 336.
[3] *Ibid.* p. 127.
[4] Bird, J., *Annals of Natal*, I, 611, 627; Walker, E. A., *The Great Trek*, p. 231.

the hopes of some of his followers and alarmed the High Commissioner by talking loosely of neutrality. Now, a Pretoria paper, *Die Volkstem*, argued that "an express declaration or Act" was necessary before the neutrality of "England or any other independent State of the Empire" could be broken.[1] But Botha replied curtly that "the enemy decides whether any part of the Empire is to be left alone".[2]

The Union delegates returned home from this momentous Conference to pass an Immigration Act in a form which gave no offence to national susceptibilities,[3] and to reach, not without riot and some little bloodshed, an apparently satisfactory settlement with their Indians. They also carried a Defence Act, which, in addition to a small permanent force, set up a modified form of compulsory service on the Swiss model and combined the existing urban volunteer regiments with the revived rural commandos.[4] But as an acknowledgment of the imperial importance of the halfway house to India, the Union authorities also agreed in case of serious war to draft their newly formed Royal Naval Volunteer Reserve into the King's ships, and to put the Cape Garrison Artillery and allied corps unreservedly at the disposal of H.M. Government for the defence of the Cape Peninsula and Durban.[5] In the event these forces were the first non-regulars in the Union to be mobilised in August 1914.

During the passage of the Defence Bill, Smuts had noted complacently that, however anxious H.M. Government might be to withdraw its attenuated garrison, the time had not yet come for that.[6] It had not; for, during the Rand strikes of July 1913, imperial troops, the only organised force available, had to be called out to fire on the rioters.[7] During the attempted general strike of January 1914, however, the new Defence Force came into play effectively, only to see Smuts throw away most of the fruits of a bloodless victory by summarily deporting nine syndicalist leaders to Great Britain.[8] The Secretary of State for the Colonies loyally reminded critics in the Commons that the Dominions with their freedom of action "are our constant pride, and only our occasional embarrassment";[9] but the fact remained that Smuts's illegal action had been a grave embarrassment and a warning of troubles that might be in store for such a novel type of political organism as the British Empire had now become. The Union had already strained the relations of one part of the Empire with another by its Indian policy; its Natives' Land Act of 1913

[1] *Die Volkstem*, 4 July 1911.
[2] *The Times*, 28 July 1911.
[3] Act No. 22 of 1913.
[4] Act No. 13 of 1912.
[5] *Ibid.*, §§ 13 and 22; De Villiers Papers, Diary, 2–6 August 1914.
[6] *Debates of the House of Assembly*, 1912, p. 1422.
[7] *Report of Witwatersrand Disturbances Commission, Parl Pap.* 1913, XLIX [Cd. 7112].
[8] *Correspondence re General Strike*, 1914, LIX [Cd. 7348].
[9] *Hansard*, 5th Series, LVIII, 378; also Keith, A. Berriedale, *Select Speeches and Documents . . . on British Colonial Policy*, II, 124.

pointed towards a Native policy that was all its own; now, it was flouting the liberty of white British subjects. Suppose it or some other Dominion used naval or military forces for its own ends against subjects of a foreign Power—what then?

The storm faded away on this note of interrogation and the deportees presently returned to a Union threatened with disruption. Botha had boasted at the recent Conference that the Union was a union of hearts as well as of Provinces.[1] The experience of the language and education quarrels during the parliamentary session just ended and, indeed, the whole course of South Africa's history should have taught him that the boast was premature. The British and Afrikaner sections respectively had long cherished radically different and largely erroneous readings of their joint history in each of which the opposite party was cast for the rôle of villain, and never more so than now while memories of the South African war were still fresh. In spite of the golden fruits of Milner's reconstruction policy, masses of the Afrikaners everywhere felt themselves harassed and worsted by new social, political and economic forces, which to their dismay had been pouring in upon them from the outer world even before that war, and had since poured in with redoubled force. This pressure was calling forth the resistance of a vigorous and suspicious nationalism whose more ardent champions looked for inspiration to the Voortrekkers' religion, manners, customs and traditions.

Co-operation with one another was still a novel experience for the South African states; co-operation with unknown states overseas was a leap in the dark, especially for the ex-republicans and those who felt with them. Popular apprehensions had once deterred Kruger from going to London to confer with Chamberlain; in those days also, criticism of domestic affairs by outsiders had been regarded as a threat to Transvaal independence. Now, ex-republicans must watch their Premier, himself a Transvaaler, going to Babylon to discuss the business of South Africa,[2] not with one Chamberlain only, but with seven others drawn from the four corners of the earth.

Botha's opponents held strong views on nearly everything that was discussed at the Imperial Conferences. The Transvaal had held aloof from Rhodes's economic federation only to be forced into Milner's; the British preference was to it at best a means of binding South Africa economically more closely to all that was British, at worst a veiled tribute to the imperial power. Immigration had been suspect since the early eighteenth century; now, it demanded that the poor whites be put back on the land, the appointed sphere of the Afrikaner, before newcomers were brought in at public expense to drag down the standard of living, to compete with sons of the soil for land and official posts, to overweight them with their votes and to endanger the

[1] *Parl. Pap.* 1911, LIV [Cd. 5745], p. 27.
[2] *Debates of the Union House of Assembly*, 1913, pp. 691–2.

as yet imperfectly held fortress of Afrikaner culture. As for defence, they frankly hated the khaki uniforms of the King's troops, while the Navy, the pride of their British fellow-citizens, was to them the instrument, operating in an utterly unfamiliar element, that had held the ring within which Great Britain had exercised her paramountcy, and in whose interests, as Botha himself had gently reminded the Conference of 1907, their republics had in times past been headed off from blue water.[1]

Many causes contributed to the ministerial *débâcle* of 1912, but the prime cause was the quarrel between Botha and Hertzog over the future relation of the Union to the Empire. Let be, in effect said Botha, anxious as ever to let half-sleeping dogs lie; do not raise the issue of imperialism now; whatever may have happened before 1902, Great Britain has behaved amazingly well since.[2] But Hertzog insisted on clearing up the issue forthwith. The interests of South Africa, he demanded, must be put first unmistakably and those of the Empire second; South Africa must be ruled by "pure Afrikaners". True, he included under that heading South Africans of British stock, who put South Africa first, but the British naturally lost sight of that fact when he went on to urge that the Afrikaner and British peoples must be kept apart in "two streams" as the proper means of achieving "the main object", the salvation of Afrikaner nationality.[3] In the ensuing storm, the Cabinet split, and Hertzog rallied to his standard all those who held that Botha and Smuts had sold the pass to the twin forces of capitalism and British imperialism.

Then came the Great War. The British infantry were withdrawn at once, though the gunners remained eighteen months longer; the Union assumed responsibility for its own defence by land and, after some division of opinion in its reconstituted Ministry,[4] invaded German South-West Africa. The expedition was the signal for a rebellion which gave life and bitterness to the new National Party. That party went from strength to strength, till, after the elections of October 1915, the South African Party, which clave to Botha, only held office by grace of the British Unionists on the tacit understanding that it would see the war through.

All the Dominions had at once followed Great Britain into the war. The strains and stresses of the long struggle forced to the front the problem of how to frame a common policy for half a dozen virtually independent governments. Dominion Ministers had some ground for complaint that they had had no timely warning of the rapid approach of war, and South African Ministers also that Sir Edward Grey had given them no hint of his highly confidential negotiations with Germany in 1913 for a possible partition of Portuguese Africa, a

[1] *Parl. Pap.* 1907, LV [Cd. 3523], p. 147.
[2] *Debates of the House of Assembly*, 1913, pp. 1998–9.
[3] *Ibid.* pp. 1971 *sqq.*
[4] Walker, E. A., *de Villiers*, p. 504.

partition which must have affected the Union directly.[1] On the other hand, though South African and New Zealand Ministers had visited London in that year on defence matters, no Dominion had done anything to ensure the close continuous consultation suggested by H.M. Government in 1911–12. The Botha Ministry had even declared itself satisfied with the existing conference machinery so long as control of foreign policy remained, as it must remain, with the imperial authorities.[2]

At the close of 1916, however, Lloyd George's National War Cabinet, as one of its first acts, summoned the Dominion Premiers and representatives of India to a special War Cabinet or Conference of the Empire. At once, the Nationalists took alarm. Those in the Transvaal had already raised the cry of out-and-out Sinn Fein, and now Hertzog foresaw an imperial federation in which the Union would be a tin attached to a cat's tail.[3] Imperial federation was, in truth, being freely discussed in Great Britain and the Dominions by enthusiasts who hoped that martial ardour and the realisation of common needs and perils would draw the bonds of empire tighter. At the Allied Economic Conference held in Paris in June 1916, Great Britain had for the first time gone very far towards committing herself to a post-war policy of imperial preference; the case for political federation, with dissolution as the alternative, had been put most clearly of all by Lionel Curtis early in 1916.[4] Curtis took sole responsibility for what he wrote; but there can be no doubt that his views were in the main those of the Round Table groups, lineal descendants of Milner's "kindergarten", which had done so much to further the reconstruction policy and then to strengthen the hands of the local imperial authorities and the Transvaalers at the National Convention of 1908–9. These groups were now striving to further the cause of imperial unity in diversity, and some at least of their members hoped that the War Conference would contribute powerfully to that end.

Botha declined to attend the special War Cabinet; the times were critical, and he believed he could do better service in South Africa than in London. He who, in earlier days, had valued the Conferences as a means of promoting "love and co-operation",[5] was now inclined to think that, at such a time, British ministers would find Dominion Premiers "a damned nuisance . . . fussing about without being of much practical value".[6] Nevertheless, he sent Smuts, fellow-conqueror of South-West Africa and part conqueror of German East Africa, who was at least free from the fatal taint of premiership. Smuts represented the Union on the War Conference (March 21–April 27)

[1] Keith, A. Berriedale, *Responsible Government in the Dominions*, II, 877 n.
[2] *Correspondence re Committee of Imperial Defence, Parl. Pap.* 1914, LX [Cd. 7347], p. 8.
[3] *The Round Table*, No. 25, December 1916, pp. 179–81.
[4] Curtis, L., *The Problem of the Commonwealth*, and *The Commonwealth of Nations*.
[5] *Parl. Pap.* 1911, LIV [Cd. 5745], p. 438.
[6] Buxton, Earl, *General Botha*, pp. 160–61.

and, on occasion, served as one of the two Dominion delegates whose presence transformed the British War Cabinet into the Imperial War Cabinet (March 20–May 2).[1] To Botha's great relief, Lloyd George himself ruled out all discussion of political consolidation, and Sir Robert Borden of Canada and Smuts emphasised that exclusion. At the conference proper, Smuts tried to limit debate to war and immediate post-war problems,[2] but the majority insisted on striking while the preferential iron was heating after these many years, and resolved that, "having due regard to the interests of our Allies", the Empire must make itself self-supporting in the matter of food supplies, raw materials and essential industries, and encourage Empire migration.[3] From this it followed that India as well as each Dominion should be accorded the right of practising reciprocity in the control of immigration.[4]

The Imperial War Cabinet and Conference dispersed; but Smuts, "special delegate from South Africa", remained in London at the service of the British Government and War Cabinet, while Botha, a tired man and a sick, held on at home in face of war weariness, recurrent rumours of rebellion, Native unrest, rising taxes, a soaring cost of living and the Nationalist hostility, which, in May 1917, found vent in the cry for a republic. That cry rose louder during the early months of 1918 when the Central Powers were making their last desperate bid for victory; but the tide of war was already on the turn when the Imperial War Conference met once more in June.[5] That assembly reaffirmed India's right to control her own immigration, agreed that Dominions might be represented in London by colleagues of their Premiers, and accorded to those Premiers the privilege, claimed by Botha in 1911, of corresponding directly with the British Prime Minister. Smuts's colleague, H. H. Burton, perhaps remembering Transvaal Uitlanders and disfranchised Cape rebels, also stood out manfully against the proposal that enemy subjects should for a term of years be debarred from naturalisation, political rights and the acquisition of lands or minerals. The proposal was shelved. Then the murmur of Cabinets, Councils, and Conferences was drowned in the crash of empires.

Immediately after the Armistice, Botha joined Smuts at the Imperial War Conference, which, in due time, became the British Empire peace delegation. He had laboured to beat the Germans and now hoped to give them terms as generous as those Great Britain had given the South African republics at Vereeniging, or he himself the Germans in South-West Africa. "Peace, you must know," he had said, "is perhaps a hundred times more difficult to make than war. . . . It takes

[1] *Papers re Imperial War Conference*, *Parl. Pap.* 1917–18, XXIII [Cd. 8566], [Cd. 8673].
[2] *Ibid.* p. 10.
[3] *Ibid.* p. 114.
[4] *Ibid.* pp. 117 *sqq.*
[5] *The Imperial War Conference*, 1918, XVI [Cd. 9177].

the wisdom of the world to make peace."[1] At the last, when he realised that the wisdom he sought was not to be found at Versailles, he scribbled on his agenda paper a prayer for charity and a warning that "God's judgments will be applied with justice to all peoples under the sun".[2] With Smuts he signed the treaty, lest by refusing he should put in jeopardy the Union's new status of a free state within the British Commonwealth and the League of Nations, and then returned home to die untimely. Smuts, now Prime Minister, did what his dead chief would surely have done by asking the Union Parliament to accept the treaty, but not necessarily to approve it.

Whatever Smuts may have thought of the treaty, he was convinced that nothing but good could come of the new-born League of Nations. In December 1918 he had powerfully summed up the proposals of the growing body of English-speaking men and women, more particularly those of the British statesmen and publicists with whom he was most closely in touch, who looked forward to a League which should not only perpetuate the naval, military and economic co-operation forced on the Allies by the facts of the war, and serve as a bulwark against future wars, but should function as "a great organ of the ordinary peaceful life of civilisation".[3] He found the working model of "the new machinery for the new situation", and the spirit that should animate it, in the British Commonwealth of Nations with its round table conferences, with its flexibility, which pretended to no "complete, definitive and final solution" of human problems, and with its reliance on the principles of nationality, autonomy and decentralisation, the only principles on which Europe "reduced to its original atoms" could be safely reconstructed. The sole departure from these principles that he would countenance in Europe and the Near East was in the provision to be made for the wreckage of the Austro-Hungarian, Russian and Turkish Empires. For "backward peoples" he prescribed the mandatory system with special emphasis on the ultimate authority of the League and its right to dismiss an unsatisfactory mandatory from its stewardship. As touching the colonies of Germany in Africa and elsewhere, he fell into line with the other Dominion representatives and advocated a policy of *uti possidetis* tempered by *pro forma* consultation of the Native inhabitants.

In most respects Smuts's scheme was an excellent forecast of the League that actually took shape. On the other hand, much that he desired was not achieved. The Peace Conference was not prepared merely to lay down the broad lines of the peace settlement and to leave it to the League to work out details; it did indeed guarantee Great Powers a vast majority in the Council of the League and thus

[1] Buxton, Earl, *General Botha*, p. 162.
[2] *Ibid.* p. 163.
[3] Smuts, J. C., *The League of Nations: a practical Suggestion.*

saved them from being swamped by the smaller and less effective Powers; but as against that, it demanded unanimity in the Council of the League instead of the 70 per cent majority he had proposed; it extended the mandatory system to Germany's colonies, even in Africa; it failed to abolish conscription, that "tap-root of militarism"; it brought no nearer the nationalisation of munition factories, and therefore left the purchase of arms from private sources open to "these small states, whose little fits of temper are too costly to the world". Nevertheless, there was the League in being, "the one guiding star of the future".

The Union Parliament accepted the treaty without, it was noted, first seeking the authority of the British Government to do so, and also the mandate for South-West Africa direct from the principal Allied and Associated Powers (September 1919). Smuts called on all for a fresh start on the basis of a frank acceptance of the British connection, and depicted South Africa's new political status in glowing colours.[1] It is true that between 1906 and 1914 this status had been foreshadowed, when H.M. Government had accorded separate representation to the Dominions through plenipotentiaries at more than one non-political international conference;[2] but it was none the less the services rendered by South Africa and the rest during the war that had extended and consolidated these humble beginnings for all the world to see, if not to understand. The essence of new status was that the British Empire was no longer a unit but a group in which the Union and the other Dominions stood on exactly the same footing as Great Britain. The British Parliament, Smuts claimed, no longer exercised sovereign powers over the Dominions; the latter would deal with foreign affairs through their own representatives; all parts of the self-governing Empire must be consulted on matters of peace and war; as in the Council of the League, no resolution could be taken "without the unanimous consent of all the nations of the Empire"; Dominions would have to decide whether they should or should not sign peace treaties and—here he drew perilously near to accepting the *Volkstem's* neutrality doctrine of 1911—"if a war is to affect them, they will have to declare it".

Smuts thus stood for South Africa as a free nation within two great international groups: "the British League of Nations...and the new world system". His rival, Hertzog, stood more definitely than ever for isolation as the one sure safeguard of Afrikaner nationality. Hertzog and his followers were by no means pro-German, but they were openly anti-imperial; indeed, during the Versailles sessions, Hertzog himself had led a deputation to Paris to demand, in keeping with Allied and Associated pronouncements on self-determination and the rights of small nations struggling to be free, the "complete

[1] *Cape Times*, 10 September 1919, 4 December 1920.

[2] Noel Baker, P. J., *The Present Juridical Status of the British Dominions*, pp. 46 *sqq*.

separation" of the Union from the Empire, failing that, independence for the two ex-republics, or, in the last resort, independence for the Orange Free State alone. At Botha's request, Lloyd George had met Hertzog and, among other arguments, had assured him that, as one of the British group "on a basis of complete equality", the Union would have far more influence in the League than any small isolated state. Neither this assurance, nor the South African Party's declaration that it stood for "constitutional developments which make the Union in an ever fuller sense a self-governing Dominion", satisfied the Nationalists. They held that the very existence of the imperial connection, frail though it now was, precluded true self-government. Fearful that South Africa might be dragged into another "British" war, they proposed the recognition of the right of secession as the incontrovertible proof that the Union was indeed master in its own house.

Smuts, who in so much else approximated closely to Nationalist views, was adamant on this one point. Again and again, during the war, he had dwelt upon the significance of the King. "You cannot", he told the British public, "make a republic in this country. . . . The King is not merely your King; but he is the King of all of us." That, now, was the burden of his defence of the imperial connection against Nationalist assaults. True, in the Union, His Majesty was to be in practice very much the King of South Africa; no one was to come between him and the Dominion authorities; his representative, the Governor-General, it was an open secret, was henceforward to be appointed on the recommendation of the local Ministry. The power to secede Smuts naturally did not deny; but he refused to admit the existence of a legal right to perpetrate a revolution however peaceful, a collusive royal divorce whereby the King should renounce the Union, or the Union the King.[1] Repeated efforts to reunite the South African and National Parties in a single Afrikaner phalanx, as at the time of Union, broke down on the secession issue, till at last Smuts turned away and joined forces with the predominantly British Unionists. At the elections of February 1921, the South African Party thus reinforced gained a substantial majority, and enabled its leader to attend the Imperial Conference of June secure of his home base.

Smuts's going to the Conference renewed the apprehensions of the Nationalists. They regarded the economic resolutions taken at Paris in 1916 and again at the War Conferences of 1917–18 as imperialist plots to fetter the trade and nascent industries of the Union; worse still, they knew that there was talk once more in many quarters of the constitutional reform of the Empire, which had been postponed in 1917 till the war should be ended. Haunted by Curtis's dilemma of federation or dissolution, they feared that the coming Conference would work out an imperial constitution limiting local autonomy.

[1] *The Round Table*, No. 37, December 1919, pp. 191 *sqq*.

There was no cause for that fear. During its first two years, the recent World War, for all its vast scope and destructiveness, had been simply a war; but after the deadlock on the Somme at the close of 1916, it became a revolution, the swift and violent culmination of forces and tendencies that had long been at work beneath the surface. Before the end of the gunfire on the main fronts two years later, most of the old land-marks were gone from all the world, swept away by the pitiless rain of high explosive. When so much else had been changed, the mutual relations of the United Kingdom and the Dominions could hardly remain unaltered. Nor had they. As in the North America of 1763, "the ties of common funk" had been loosened by the destruction of the mutual enemy. The waging of successful war had bred self-confidence in the Dominions; when, in 1919, the United Kingdom had given them a slight preference with the prospect of more to follow, they had gained something of what they had set their hearts on in the beginning, and, now that the post-war boom had collapsed, their domestic problems were insistent. The Imperial War Cabinet had ended with the war that had called it into being, and none of the Dominions had as yet taken the steps suggested in 1911–12, and again in 1918, to ensure even that "continuous consultation" which was so much less than the real share in responsibility and control envisaged by Chamberlain in 1897. In short, by 1921, the Dominions, members in their own right of the international League of Nations, were talking on constitutional matters in a language very different from that of 1917.

Throughout the long course of the Colonial and Imperial Conferences, Canada had as a rule competed with Great Britain for the distinction of first pointing the way to yet fuller liberties for all the Dominions; but, latterly, with the possible exception of Sir Robert Borden of Canada, no single man had done more to give currency to the ideas and phraseology of post-war imperial relations than Smuts. At the 1917 Conference he had eagerly welcomed the postponement of the constitutional issue as the deathblow to "the totally wrong" federal solution. Thereafter he had set himself with eloquent pertinacity to do away with the checks, relics of an outworn age, which the British Government still retained upon the absolute freedom of Dominion action. "Whatever we may say," he had said in 1917, "and whatever we may think, we are subject provinces of Great Britain."[1] All that would have to be changed; the theory if not the practice of equality would have to be considered more fully. The tone and the proceedings of the Conference of 1921 gave the measure of the change that had come about during four crowded years of revolution.[2]

[1] *Parl. Pap.* 1917–18, XXIII [Cd. 8566], pp. 46–7.
[2] 1921, XIV [Cmd. 1474] *The Prime Ministers' Conference.*

Before ever the Conference met, H.M. Government had announced that constitutional reform would not be debated; but since in South Africa some men still spoke of the Conference as the "Imperial Cabinet", Smuts before proceeding to its sittings took occasion to point out that it was nothing of the kind, but "a mere consultative body" with no executive powers whatever.[1] At the same time, in reply to Nationalist criticisms, he maintained, with the concurrence of the Labour Party which on many other grounds was drawing closer to the Nationalists, that imperial foreign policy was of first-class importance to the Union even from the domestic point of view. The Conference had, indeed, been summoned primarily to decide whether a renewal of the Anglo-Japanese alliance, which the Dominions had hailed with such satisfaction in 1911, would be compatible with the new conditions created by the advent of the League of Nations, or be possible in face of Australian suspicions and Canadian and United States hostility. In the Union Parliament, Smuts argued that the Empire should play the part of honest broker and avoid entangling alliances which might involve the Union, with the rest of the Empire, in war arising from incidents as apparently remote as the tragedy at Serajevo; at the Conference, he pleaded that private pacts were alien to the spirit of the League, which should be "specially sacred" to an Empire whose paramount needs were peace, disarmament and a good understanding with the United States.[2]

Smuts spoke as a South African conscious of the new forces pulsating through *Europe d'outremer*, above all through the United States, the greatest and most fully developed of that class of states to which his own country belonged. Clearly, he had revised his opinion of the importance of what had so long been rightly known as "the Continent". To him, the European stage was no longer of the first importance; rather, the focus of world politics had shifted to the Pacific across which America faces Asia.[3] Asia, at least, was in one sense as much an internal as an external problem to the Union. Transvaal traders and the Union Ministry were once more in difficulties with the local Indians, and India was espousing the cause of these men and of those in Kenya. The Conference resolved that the right to citizenship of Indians domiciled in the Dominions should be recognised. The Union delegates, faced with far more Indians than any of their colleagues and still under the erroneous impression that they were increasing faster than the Europeans, dissented resolutely. The Indian delegates, for their part, witnessed to their country's enhanced status under the Montagu-Chelmsford reforms[4] by mildly expressing the hope that a settlement might be reached by direct negotiation between Pretoria and Delhi.

[1] *Cape Times*, 21 May 1921.
[2] *Parl. Pap.* 1921, xiv [Cd. 1474], pp. 23–6.
[3] *Ibid.* p. 25.
[4] See *C.H.B.E.* v, 589 *sqq.*

This Conference marked a great change in the balance of power within the Empire. For the first time, in its collective capacity, it recommended policy to the King. It recommended close co-operation with France, provided France's policy made for the recovery of Europe; it recommended a tripartite understanding between the British Empire, the United States and Japan on naval armaments and the problems of the Pacific; it resolved that the Empire must have a fleet equal to that of any other single power, and left the British Government to see to it. That was its obvious weakness: it recommended policy and left the British taxpayer to foot the bill; it resolved that there should be in future "a united understanding and common action in foreign affairs", but proposed none of the improvements in existing machinery necessary to achieve that end.

Smuts's own actions revealed the true situation clearly enough. He insisted successfully that the Dominions should be represented at the Washington Naval Conference, which fixed the numbers of large warships which the United Kingdom, the United States and Japan were to be permitted to maintain;[1] then, having contributed valuable services to the cause of Anglo-Irish peace, he returned home to see the imperial South Africa military command abolished and imperial war property handed over to the Union. In common with other Dominion Premiers, he had long ago set aside Lord Jellicoe's scheme of naval co-operation, whereunder South Africa was to have undertaken the protection of traffic along the west coast of Africa and to have found some 4 per cent of the cost of a joint imperial navy.[2] Now, while guaranteeing Simonstown to the British Government as a naval base at all times, he undertook to man the coast batteries in the Cape Peninsula and at Durban and diverted the naval contribution of £85,000, that Delian tribute which the Nationalists had always resented, to local naval purposes conceived upon the most modest scale.

For South Africa and its sister Dominions, the Conference of 1921 marked the end of the British Empire that had grown up since the loss of the Old Thirteen.

[1] Keith, A. Berriedale, *Responsible Government in the Dominions*, II, 1204.
[2] *Ibid.* II, 1013.

CHAPTER XXIX

ECONOMIC DEVELOPMENT, 1795–1921

(a) 1795–1870. Agricultural and Pastoral Industries

THE white community which was settled at the Cape when the British forces arrived in 1795 numbered in all perhaps 16,000 people, nearly one-third of whom lived in Cape Town and the adjoining district. These five thousand, by reason of their proximity to the regular port of call between Europe and the East Indies, enjoyed a contact with external civilisations which the settlers in the more remote regions of the interior lacked. That advantage was reflected in the mode of life of the officials and licensed tradesmen of Cape Town and of their families. Their houses were well built and well laid out in long gardens and orchards. Their slaves, often skilled artisans and domestic servants, gave most of them the leisure enjoyed by more well-to-do families in Europe, although they lacked the opportunities which Europe offered for cultural employment of that leisure. Once outside the Cape Town district, the population thinned rapidly, especially to the barren north-west, where British troops found only five houses in the ninety miles between Cape Town and Saldanha Bay. In the fertile valleys immediately to the north-east, the homesteads clustered in villages: Stellenbosch comprised seventy houses, Paarl numbered thirty, and in the valley of Roodezand (now Tulbagh) there were forty families within thirty miles. But the northern regions of the district of Stellenbosch contained vast expanses of semi-arid country with barely a single inhabitant, and the farms growing corn for the Cape Town market and lying to the north of the wine farms, were rarely more than sixty miles or three days' journey away. Far away to the north-east, the district of Graaff-Reinet comprised about seven hundred families, whose grazing farms were scattered as far east as the Fish River and two hundred miles inland from the sea. The Cape Town folk saw little of these self-sufficient people, for the journey took one month by waggon and two or three months when driving their long-horned cattle or fat-tailed sheep; and the British commandant on arrival could find no one who knew the way to the Drostdy. In the eastern coastal district of Swellendam, extending nearly four hundred miles eastward to the Gamtoos River, there were perhaps five hundred farms grazing cattle and sheep, and some also producing corn and wine. The further from Cape Town in each direction, the more primitive and ephemeral were the farm dwellings and their equipment. Slaves in the legal sense were few outside the wine and grain districts, and the farmers relied on Hottentots and tamed Bushmen as herdsmen, giving them food and perhaps some clothing in return for their service.

The condition of the Cape community at the close of the eighteenth century, if not economically static, was at any rate such that material progress was hampered in almost every sphere by monopolistic restrictions on enterprise. There is perhaps a temptation to attribute too much of what was unprogressive in the economic outlook of the population to the policy of the Dutch East India Company. The geography of southern Africa—the inaccessibility of the immediate interior, the peculiarities of climate and vegetation and the aboriginal population—presented a problem of effective colonisation the very enormity of which may have contributed something to the weakening of the spirit of enterprise in a small and isolated community whose resources were entirely inadequate. Even the making of passable roads was too formidable a task: the provision of better transport facilities and of appropriate agricultural technique had still to wait upon invention. In such conditions a community may easily come to regard a bare subsistence and the minimum of trade as of the nature of things. But the Cape population suffered inevitably, too, from the absence of an identity of interest between the Government and themselves, and from the warping effect on development of rigid monopolistic institutions under the Company, which prevented the prompt and full adjustment of enterprise and resources to changing conditions. The nineteenth century saw the liberation in South Africa of the economic forces which, throughout western civilisation, have made for the material advancement of peoples.

Two kinds of restrictions upon internal and overseas trade must be distinguished: the system of monopolies and prohibitions, which kept the population in general out of the trading business, and, secondly, the system of taxation of trading transactions, which reduced the advantage from exchange generally and checked the transition from a mere subsistence economy. The monopoly concessions were abolished by the British authorities after 1795, the inhabitants securing both *laisser faire* and *laisser passer* within the borders. There were temporary difficulties in the early years, as, for example, when General Craig imposed trade restrictions in 1797 to relieve an acute bread shortage at Cape Town, and when monopolies and corrupt privileges were permitted to reappear under the governorship of Sir George Yonge; but the resolution of the Home Government was made clear by Yonge's recall, while the official instructions given at the end of 1796 to his predecessor, Lord Macartney, had been quite explicit.[1] The

[1] Theal, G. M., *Records of Cape Colony*, II, 7 (30 December 1796). Lord Macartney was explicitly instructed "without delay [to] afford such relief from the fiscal oppressions ... as you shall judge expedient, and particularly by abolishing monopolies, pre-emptions and exclusive privileges, and prohibitions and restraints to the free exercise of their

Batavian Government, guided by de Mist's report of 1802,[1] did not turn back from the new policy. Internal trade, if still taxed, was henceforward free from prohibitions.

Taxation of trade was another matter. In 1795 over one-fifth of the Government's revenue was derived from the duties paid at the barrier at Cape Town on wine, brandy and corn taken in from the farms; another quarter from the duties on sales at auctions and sales of immovable property and the stamped paper which was necessary for the most trifling transactions; nearly another fifth from the receipts from retail liquor licences. The duties paid on produce entering Cape Town were comparable with the octroi duties from which French municipalities still derive a considerable part of their revenues. They were retained for the sake of their revenue after the final cession of the Colony to England, and were not ultimately abolished until 1842, by which time the rapid growth of receipts from import duties had provided an adequate substitute. The stamp duties, however, were promptly abolished by the British Commandant on all purchases of amounts less than 100 rix-dollars.[2]

The embargo on overseas trade had already been lifted in part, before the British occupation, by the Commissioners-General, who in 1792 removed the restrictions on trade south of 30 degrees latitude (excepting that with the eastern territories of the Company), and permitted trade with the Netherlands either in ships sent back for overhaul or, as far as Cape produce was concerned, in foreign vessels. But the monopoly of the Company had been retained wherever it was effective, despite the abandonment of its dog-in-the-manger attitude; and the substitution of the restrictions of the Navigation Laws after the British Occupation constituted, in spite of all their prohibitions, a distinct gain in freedom for the colonists. Even these restrictions were relaxed to relieve temporary distress, foreign vessels then receiving special permission to trade; but trade to the East was normally reserved for the English East India Company.

As regards customs duties, the rates charged in the colony of Jamaica were applied to the Cape in 1796 as an interim measure, but no duties were to be levied on goods coming from any British possession. The Government in 1801 restricted the exemption from duty on imports into the Cape to goods from Great Britain and Ireland, however conveyed; henceforward goods from other British dominions carried in British vessels were to pay 5 per cent and all other imports 10 per cent. Between 1803 and 1806 the Batavian Government did not fully restore the former monopolies, and on the return of the British the complex Navigation Acts were again applied,

industry, either in agriculture, manufactures or other pursuits of interior commerce, and establishing in lieu thereof such reasonable duties or taxes as shall appear to you expedient".

[1] *Vide supra*, p. 195.

[2] A rix-dollar nominally equalled four shillings.

the customs duties on imports changing frequently. From 1807 to 1812 the products of Great Britain and Ireland were admitted free, those of the British dominions paying 5 per cent; while after 1813 a duty of 3 per cent on products of the United Kingdom was again levied for revenue purposes.

In 1820, the British Government recognised that Cape Town was "potentially the most important commercial port south of the equator"[1] by creating it a free port on a reciprocal basis side by side with declining Mauritius. The passage of Huskisson's two Reciprocity Acts of 1823 and 1824[2] was the beginning of the end of discriminatory duties on the basis of the nationality of shipping. In a few years many important countries completed treaties for reciprocal privileges. The Navigation Laws, which still confined British trade in specified commodities to British vessels,[3] were finally repealed in 1849; but they had already ceased to affect the Cape trade in 1832. Discriminatory rates of duty conferring a special preference on goods from the United Kingdom, and after 1832 on the produce of other British dominions, persisted till 1855. On such goods the import duty varied from 3 per cent in 1821 to 5 per cent after 1842, while on other imports the duty rose from 10 to 15 per cent apart from a few specific rates. The Cape Parliament in 1855 abolished the whole of the preferential duties on foreign goods following the spirit of the Act passed in 1854 by the Imperial Parliament.[4] The Act of 1855 fixed the general *ad valorem* rate at 7½ per cent and, to augment the revenue, the number of specific duties in the rated list was increased. The general rate remained unaltered until 1867, when it was raised.

After 1789 such export trade in Cape produce as was permitted by the Dutch East India Company was subject to an export duty of 5 per cent, and the freedom to export secured after the British Occupation was still limited by the terms of the Navigation Acts. In 1811 the export duty on colonial produce was finally abolished, and after 1820 the reciprocity treaties between the United Kingdom and foreign states allowed foreign vessels to engage in overseas trade with the Cape. The colonial policy of the United Kingdom, however, was not without a considerable compensating advantage to the Cape in the form of the preferential duties on wines and spirits. In 1800 the special rates of duty and drawback applicable to imports of spirits into Great Britain from the West Indian colonies were extended to Cape spirits, and at the same time Cape wines were admitted on the same terms as Portuguese, i.e. at two-thirds the rate of duty payable on French wine. By an Act of 1813 Cape wines were admitted at one-third the rate payable even on Portuguese and Spanish wines, a preference of 6*s*. 0¾*d*. per gallon over Portuguese and 16*s*. 8*d*. over French wines

[1] Manning, H. T., *British Colonial Government after the American Revolution*, 1782–1820, p. 435.

[2] 4 Geo. IV, c. 77 and 5 Geo. IV, c. 1.

[3] Including colonial ships.

[4] 16 and 17 Vict., c. 107.

which continued undiminished until 1825. Thereafter, although the duties on foreign wines were reduced more considerably than those on Cape wines and all rates were slightly increased in 1831 and again in 1840, the preferential rate was retained until 1860 at one-half the amount payable on the most favoured foreign wine. It was a period of unexampled prosperity for the wine industry of the Cape, but quality and reputation suffered in the scramble for quick profits. The Cape shared in the benefits from the reduction and abolition in the 'twenties and 'forties of the duties on the import of raw materials into the United Kingdom, particularly that of raw wool, which in the 'twenties was gradually reduced from 6*d.* per lb. to 1*d.* per lb. and was finally removed in 1844.

The revenues of the Cape Government did not suffer by the removal of the restrictions on trade. The importance in 1795 of the taxes on internal trade as a source of revenue has already been indicated. Another very important source, however, was found in the rents of lands leased out, which yielded one-quarter of the total receipts, while import and export duties amounted to less than one-tenth. By 1806, while the total government revenue and expenditure had trebled, customs receipts had increased ninefold and the simplified internal dues were yielding twice the revenue, so active had trade become. Thereafter for a generation the government revenues did not increase remarkably. With the steady increase in the responsibilities of the Government, expenditure in the 'thirties tended to outrun receipts. Gradually the customs duties took the place of the land receipts as the most considerable source of revenue.[1] Meanwhile the total revenue grew between 1830 and 1860 from £130,000 to £344,000. From 1860 until Union in 1910 the percentage of revenue derived from customs varied little, while the total increased fourteenfold.

Land revenues, stamp and transfer duties, and licences yielded increasing revenues as the Colony developed. Until 1814, local taxation consisted of a medley of special taxes in each district determined by local requirements. Following an enquiry, greater uniformity was then introduced, revenue in country districts being derived from a poll tax and taxes on livestock and on produce, and in Cape Town from an income tax, a house tax and a water rate. The *opgaaf* taxes collected by Landdrosts and Heemraden were taken over by the central Government on the supersession of these authorities in 1828 by the new system of Resident Magistrates and Civil Commissioners.[2] Since

[1] They provided an average of:

1821–30, 16 per cent
1831–40, 21 ,,
1841–50, 43 ,,
1851–60, 54·4 ,,

[2] *Vide supra*, p. 260. See also *Parl. Pap.* 1826–7, (282), (406), *Reports of the Commissioners of Inquiry into the Administration and Finances of the Cape of Good Hope*; *Records of Cape Colony*, XXVII, 342 *sqq*.

the introduction of elected municipal authorities in 1837, local taxation has been based on assessments of immovable property.

The Government finances were complicated until 1843 by the existence of its Loan and Discount Bank—the Lombard Bank—and of a paper currency, both legacies of the days of Company rule. While the rix-dollar remained merely a unit-of-account equivalent to four shillings, the currency of Cape Town and of such country districts as possessed any consisted of a medley of coins of gold (Dutch ducats, English guineas, Spanish doubloons, Portuguese Johannes, Venetian sequins, Indian pagodas and moguls) and of silver (Spanish dollars, Dutch guilders and schillings, English crowns and shillings and Indian rupees) rated in published tariffs. In 1782, however, the rix-dollar had become the unit of paper currency, and as the amount in circulation increased, gold and silver gradually disappeared from circulation. Under both the Batavian and British Governments inflation of the currency continued as a means of financing government expenditure, the circulation increasing from 1,291,000 rix-dollars in 1795 to over 3,100,000 rix-dollars in 1825. In 1825, in keeping with the general imperial policy, British silver coinage was made legal tender and the Cape was placed upon a gold exchange standard, convertibility of the rix-dollar being established at the low value to which it had fallen. There was inevitably discontent[1] at devaluation among those entitled by contract to fixed incomes in rix-dollars, but the other parties to those contracts secured the benefit. In 1832, the gradual substitution of sterling notes for the Cape paper currency was begun, and the exchange of old rix-dollar notes continued until 1841. By 1852 practically the whole of the sterling notes had themselves been replaced by specie. In 1881 gold became the only fully legal tender currency for the payment of any amount in the Cape.

The Lombard Bank had been established by the Government in 1793 on the simple plan of giving it a capital of inconvertible paper rix-dollars for loan to members of the community against security at 5 per cent, the profits accruing to the Government. In 1808 the rate was raised to 6 per cent, and a Government Discount Bank was then established to provide short term accommodation at the same rate and receive deposits. There were obvious limits, however, to the expansion of banking business on the basis of a capital of inconvertible paper and a government monopoly. Although the Government Bank continued to exist until 1842, a private joint-stock bank, the Cape of Good Hope Bank, began to operate in 1836, five years after the establishment of the Cape of Good Hope Savings Bank. It was the first of many small prosperous banking enterprises to spring up throughout the colony, the number in 1862 being twenty-nine, operating in twenty-one towns, with a total paid-up capital and reserves of over

[1] *Vide supra*, pp. 261 *sqq*.

£1,100,000 and deposits of nearly £2,000,000. The year 1860 saw the establishment of the London and South African and the Standard Banks, the first of the large-scale imperial banks.[1] There were already two banks in the Orange Free State and one in Natal.

Commercial banking developments denote an advanced stage of economic organisation, and show how considerable was the change in the productivity and trade of the Cape in the first half of the nineteenth century. Given freedom of trade, the colony of the Cape of Good Hope emerged during this period as an agricultural and pastoral community exporting wool, hides and skins, ostrich feathers and wine. Contributory causes were the improvement in transport, particularly the construction of passable roads into the pastoral regions of the interior, the reform of the system of land tenure, and improved knowledge of the appropriate methods of agricultural and pastoral farming.

The great obstacle to inland transport was the inaccessibility of the highlands of the interior to vehicular traffic, while to the north-west of the Cape coastal districts and across the isthmus of the Cape Peninsula itself, the shifting sand made going heavy. With so sparse a population to bear the expense, road construction was inevitably slow. A turnpike road through the Tulbagh pass was undertaken with convict labour in 1807, and during the next two decades a passable road was continued, avoiding the high land, as far as Worcester a hundred miles inland, thus improving communication eastward between the mountains to Swellendam and beyond. A more considerable undertaking completed in 1830 was the Sir Lowry Pass, which simplified the crossing of the Hottentots Holland range and made the eastern districts directly accessible for heavy traffic, avoiding the northern detour.

The most difficult trunk routes were finally tackled in the 'forties by the creation of a Central Board of Commissioners of Public Roads, financed by state grants, the levy of rates and loans raised on the security of future revenue from tolls. Between 1845 and 1853 the Montagu Pass in the eastern districts connecting Oudtshoorn with George and the coast, Michell's Pass from Ceres and the Bokkeveld region of the Karoo to the main Cape Town road, and Bain's Kloof avoiding the northern detour to Worcester, were all completed with the aid of convict labour or of British free labourers brought out at government expense. Once on the Karoo, the going was much easier throughout the Colony, so that, as soon as roads were made through the mountains, the farmers on the internal highlands were in a position to convey their agricultural and pastoral produce to the coast.

The improved roads made possible better postal services. After 1805 Hottentot runners were employed to convey letters between Cape Town and the Drostdies of each district; they were later replaced

[1] *Vide infra*, p. 810.

by horses and, in the 'twenties, by postcarts: a weekly postal service was set up in 1834. In 1852 there was a daily service from Cape Town to Paarl and Stellenbosch, thrice weekly to Grahamstown and twice weekly to the Karoo. The postcart also conveyed passengers. Following the issue of the famous three-cornered Capes in 1853, a penny post was established in limited areas in 1860 and four years later it was possible to extend it to the whole Colony. But, despite better roads, the ox-waggon remained the commercial vehicle and was still in use a century later.

Improvements in transport to and from Europe, however, waited more upon invention than upon finance. The Cape, an inevitable calling station on the most flourishing of the ocean-trading routes of the world, enjoyed indirectly the services of perhaps the finest sailing ships of the time—the East India armed merchantmen; but these lacked the speed of, for example, the much smaller Baltimore clippers, which American shipbuilders had been stimulated to evolve by the profits to be derived from West Indian trade whenever European warships could be successfully evaded. Whereas British legislation encouraged the building of slow vessels of large carrying capacity, the American shipbuilders had learned to build for speed. In 1797–8, the convoy which carried Lord Macartney and his staff to the Cape took only ten weeks on the voyage; yet at the end of 1815 the first of the monthly mail packets took 114 days (instead of 100) to reach Cape Town, and the vessels that conveyed the 1820 Settlers were over three months in reaching Simonstown. Only thirty years later the American clipper *Oriental* carried tea from Hong Kong to London in 97 days. When in 1825, the paddle-steamer *Enterprise* made her prize voyage to Calcutta in 113 days, she reached Cape Town in 58 days from Falmouth, and in 1847 another paddle-steamer covered the distance in 34 days. But those were exceptional performances. Not till 1855 was there a regular monthly steamship from England. In 1857 the Imperial Government concluded a mail contract with the Union Steamship Company, providing for monthly trips of 42 days' duration. After 1868 the mail service was run fortnightly, and, the Castle Company having begun to run ships in 1872, a mail contract for a regular weekly trip, to take 26 days, was made with the two companies jointly in 1876.

The volume of shipping calling at Cape ports was quadrupled between the 'twenties and the 'forties, and doubled again by the 'sixties. In 1860 a thousand vessels were entered annually inwards at Cape ports. Cape Town was still enjoying the privileges of a port of call on important trade routes, even after the opening of the Suez Canal in 1869, and already, and particularly after the 'forties, imports had increased rapidly in volume and the Colony had cargo of her own to offer as a return freight.

The development of an export trade in agricultural and pastoral produce of an equal volume would hardly have taken place without the changes that were made in the system of land tenure. In 1795, almost the whole of the quarter of the total revenue that the Government derived from land was in respect of the annual rent of loan farms or *leeningsplaatsen* of over 6000 acres each. Of these there were, judging by the revenue returns, between 1750 and 2000 leased out to farmers on a yearly basis at 24 rix-dollars per annum, or 12 rix-dollars if the land had very inferior soil or little water. No other variation in rent obtained in spite of great differences in fertility. Of land held under perpetual quit-rent tenure there were only about 4000 Dutch acres in all. The ease with which the farmers could change one holding for another militated against their taking the interest in the permanent condition of their farm which makes for improvements; it was always easier to exhaust the virgin qualities of the land and then move on, than to develop the holding from the outset with an eye to profitable, permanent occupation. Compensation was paid by the Government for improvements in the event of the cancellation of the lease, but, although cancellation was rare, the system of yearly renewal was not conducive to investment in well-constructed homesteads or elaborate development works.

There is much to support the view that the origin of the trek-boer's traditional mode of life is to be found in the Company's system of *leeningsplaatsen*.[1] In 1813, therefore, while Sir John Cradock was Governor, a proclamation announced that all new grants of land would be made upon a quit-rent basis, and that occupants of existing loan farms might have their tenure converted into perpetual quit-rent, which would be fixed, according to fertility, at anything up to a maximum of 250 rix-dollars per annum, the farms to be properly surveyed and limited to an area of 3000 morgen.[2] The higher rents were, however, too great a price for most of the farmers to pay for security against the small risk of cancellation of their loan leases, and in seven years less than one-fifth of the 2206 leases in existence were converted. The decision to lease no more Crown land on the old terms, moreover, compelled pastoralists, who refused to make their holdings permanently attractive to themselves, to move off to the north-east border where there was even better land and less chance of rent being demanded. Those who did not move out of the reach of the rent-collector were obliged henceforward to take a more permanent interest in their loan farms, even though they were slow to change the form of their tenure. After 1832, Crown lands were sold by auction, the quit-rent being generally fixed at 5 per cent of the sale price. In 1860 it was made possible to redeem quit-rents at fifteen years' purchase, changed in 1878 to twenty years' purchase.

Commissioner de Mist had urged in his Memorandum of 1802 that

[1] *Vide supra*, pp. 152–3.

[2] 1 morgen = $2\frac{1}{8}$ acres.

farms should be granted in freehold rather than on loan, that the fine grazing lands of the Graaff-Reinet district should be utilised to develop an export trade in pastoral produce, and that agriculture should be stimulated by experiments with new crops and prizes for proficiency. During the First British Occupation an agricultural expert, William Duckitt, was paid to conduct a model farm in the Malmesbury district for the encouragement of improved methods. De Mist himself, as an official of the Batavian Government, established an experimental Agricultural Commission in 1804, assisted by Duckitt and by a grant of land and a loan in paper currency. The Commission imported Spanish merino rams and bred wool sheep by crossing with the African hairy fat-tailed variety, procured a badly needed wine expert from the Rhineland, and obtained new olive plants from Portugual. Individual farmers had previously introduced merinos for the improvement of their flocks.

The Commission was encouraged to continue its work by the British Governors. Caledon endeavoured in 1807–8 to compel the use of merino rams in the Tulbagh district, and tried without success to encourage the breeding of merinos by the device of differential taxation. In 1818 Lord Charles Somerset imported merinos and maintained pure bred flocks at the government farms at Malmesbury, and in the east where Somerset East now stands. Horse-breeding was also encouraged.

Of the many attempts to assist farming developments, wine production provided the earliest spectacular success, mainly on account of the preferential duties granted by the United Kingdom.[1] The demand was for large quantity, rather than high quality, for the Cape product was used as a cheap adulterant of better European wines. In 1824, the year before the preferential duty was diminished, nearly three million gallons were exported; but naturally, as the preferential duty was gradually eliminated, the profit from the use of Cape wines disappeared, and as their quality had earned them no distinctive demand, the export fell off until after 1860 it was insignificant. Thereafter British taxation actually favoured foreign wines against the Cape product because of the heavy discriminating duty against wine of more than 26-degree proof spirit, although some relief was perhaps granted in 1886 by the raising of the limit to 30 degrees.

On account of insufficient knowledge of climatic conditions and their effects, although repeated efforts were made to develop wheat-growing, failures were continuous throughout the first half of the nineteenth century. Except in the south-western districts, where winter rains could be relied upon and where wheat was already a proven crop, and to a more limited extent in other parts of the country, where bitter experience had taught that wheat should be regarded as a winter dry-land crop produced with the aid of irrigation, the failures

[1] *Vide supra*, pp. 235, 791 *sqq.*

were universal. At no time had South Africa succeeded in becoming more than just self-sufficing in wheat.

The first small beginnings in the export of Cape wool were in the 'twenties, for the lessons from over thirty years of importation of and experimentation with merinos, and also with English, Saxon and French stock, were only slowly learned. Gradually, the suitability of particular breeds of wool sheep, either pure bred or crossed with the hardy native stocks, for the grazing lands of the eastern and north-eastern districts was determined and the ability of suitable breeds to thrive even on the dry Karoo was established. From the beginning, the pasturing of wool sheep was purely an export industry. By the 'forties there was no agricultural export equal in value to wool. The second quarter of the nineteenth century was the period of rapid development of the machine textile industry of Great Britain; the demand for raw wool, at prices attractive to growers, was insatiable.

Although outstripped by Australia, the expansion of Cape exports of wool was remarkable: 20,000 lb. in 1822; 200,000 lb. in 1832; 1,372,000 lb. in 1842; 25,000,000 lb. in 1862 (including exports through Cape ports from beyond the Cape borders). In value, wool became in 1840 the most important export, and remained so until overtaken by the diamond trade well on in the 'seventies: a striking testimony to the importance of road and pass construction between the high grazing lands and the coast. A handbook for settlers published in 1868[1] printed two wool-farmers' accounts, one showing a profit of £2860 in three years from the first investment of £1250 in sheep, the other a profit of £8065 in seven years from an investment of £2225.[2] Wherever production for export was physically possible, pastoral farmers went in for wool.

The development in sheep-farming was assisted by the arrival under the British administration of settlers who knew the requirements of Great Britain. The immigrants came in small parties, particularly during the distress after 1815, and included Scottish indentured labourers, some of whom were employed on farms growing corn and grazing flocks eastward from Mossel Bay. The most spectacular venture was the subsidisation by a British parliamentary grant of £50,000 of the immigration of the 1820 Settlers. Their original holdings in the new district of Albany, each of one hundred acres, were, as we saw in an earlier chapter, almost all doomed to disastrous failure.[3] Permission to move once secured, however, the new settlers soon showed initiative and resource. Among them were many skilled artisans, apart from agriculturists, and not a few with education and literary gifts, whose capacities at once found outlets in the new town of Grahamstown and elsewhere in the colony. Those who continued

[1] *The Cape Colony in 1868. A Handybook for Intending Settlers* (London, 1868).

[2] For the part played by the Jews in developing the wool trade, see Herrman, L., *The Jews in South Africa*.

[3] *Vide supra*, Chap. IX, p. 245.

to farm were responsible for the expansion, if not the introduction, of maize-growing as well as for the spread of wool-sheep farming, and to them South Africa is in this way indebted for what are to-day its two most valuable exports of farm produce.

The extent of cultivation of maize by the Natives of Africa before the nineteenth century is not known. The variety of sorghum known as Kaffir corn is on the other hand apparently indigenous to South Africa, and still forms in Native agriculture an important grain and forage crop and the basis for the brewing of Kaffir beer. The importance of the work done by the settlers in the Eastern Province in first developing those strains of maize which flourish easily in the north-eastern regions lies in the impetus which they gave to the adoption of that cereal as the main food crop for Native consumption both within the tribal territories and elsewhere. Thereby both the improvement of the standard of life of the Native peoples and the expansion of African economic life on the basis of Native labour have been greatly facilitated; and in our own day the highly valued special qualities of South African maize are an outstanding feature of the international grain trade.

Skilled artisans and European labourers have always been highly paid in South Africa as compared with unskilled African or Coloured workers. As urban life developed and buildings and roads had to be constructed, the Cape inevitably experienced an acute shortage of labour, which the supply of skilled Malays (who even while still slaves had been comparatively well paid) and unskilled Hottentot labourers could not meet. The immediate economic effects of the abolition of slavery in 1834 have been examined elsewhere.[1] The enforcement of annual contracts of labour, under a Masters and Servants Ordinance of 1842 and a Masters and Servants Act of 1856, ultimately restored regularity of supply of labour in the towns and agricultural areas. The pastoral farmers of the interior were not so much affected. In 1849 the Cape successfully resisted an attempt to meet the shortage by importations of convicts.[2] In the 'forties four or five thousand free labourers were brought from England at Government expense for road construction; and again in the late 'fifties over six thousand arrived, but many of them soon left for the new Australian goldfields. After the Crimean War four or five thousand German Legionaries and peasants were settled on farms in Kaffraria between the Keiskamma and Kei rivers, where their descendants still farm in the prosperous districts north of East London. But until the diamond discoveries in the late 'sixties, even these small waves of immigrants were exceptional and, unlike Australia, the increase in the European population consisted mainly of persons born in the Colony, and was barely affected by the small annual additions from the United Kingdom and Europe.

[1] *Vide supra*, p. 275.
[2] *Vide supra*, p. 377.

In the decade ending December 1845 some 12,000 to 14,000 souls went on trek from the Colony.[1] Many of them were already accustomed to frequent change of settlement. The census figures are admittedly defective, but if we take them as a basis and allow for severe loss of life owing to epidemics of measles and smallpox in 1839 and 1840, they show a general movement from the west to the northern and eastern frontiers. The Great Trek, taking it year by year, drained off almost all the natural increase of the white population of Cape Colony.[2] Economically there was little change of significance in the mode of life of the Trekkers wherever they and their descendants went, until the diamond and gold discoveries provided a local market for meat and maize and wheat to feed the populations of the mining camps, and a strong incentive to supply that need in the new opportunities to buy manufactured merchandise at the stores which quickly grew up there. During the years 1835–48, parties settled as far north as the Zoutpansberg and as far north-east as northern Natal. Most of the Natal Boers, as we saw in an earlier chapter, left Natal for the High Veld between 1844 and 1848, but a few remained in northern Natal.[3] In the years between the annexation of the Orange River Sovereignty by the British Government in 1848 and the Bloemfontein Convention of 1854, which established the independence of most of that territory, British settlers moved north and sheep grazing with an eye to the export of wool was rapidly extended beyond the Orange river.

The distribution of the population of the Cape Colony, in 1865, and their occupations are recorded in the report in that year of the first comprehensive census taken in the Colony. The white population numbered 181,000 out of an enumerated total of almost half-a-million people apart from Natives in reserves and independent tribes. Already less than half of this total population, and only fifty-eight per cent (105,000) of the Europeans, lived in the "Western Divisions", the regions of the earliest settlements. Seventy-five per cent of the occupied population was engaged in agriculture, only one-eighth pursued industrial occupations, and less than one-sixteenth was recorded as engaged in trade and transport. There were only eighteen towns all told with more than 1000 inhabitants each. Cape Town, with 28,000 inhabitants in the municipality (15,000 Europeans) and six suburbs of more than 500 Europeans each, was the only town with more than 5000 population in the older western divisions of the Colony. Both Port Elizabeth (nearly 9000 of all races) and Grahamstown (6000) in the much more recently settled eastern divisions were larger than Paarl (under 5000), and remote Graaff-Reinet (3700) was already the fifth largest municipality in the colony. About 60 per cent (110,000) of the European population were recorded as able to read

[1] *Vide supra*, chap. XIV.
[2] See *Cape of Good Hope Blue Books* (published annually from 1838 onwards).
[3] *Vide supra*, p. 346.

and write, as compared with less than 5 per cent (15,000) of the enumerated non-Europeans.

The more rapid development of the Eastern Province is explained by the returns of agricultural and pastoral produce. In 1865 the wool production from 8·37 million sheep was 18·9 million lb. compared with 8·2 million lb. in 1856, and not far short of three-quarters came from the Eastern Province, where in addition were three-fifths of the cattle and draught oxen (total 700,000) and more than half the horses and goats. Maize growing, predominantly suited to the Eastern Province, was already extending rapidly, although the total production was still below that of either wheat, barley or oats, all of which suited the older settlements better than the East. Wheat production showed no tendency to develop into a regular export business: occasional surpluses were sent abroad, but crop failures necessitated imports.

European South Africa in 1865, as we have seen, extended beyond the borders of Cape Colony, northward beyond the Orange River and the Vaal River, and north-east into what had become Natal. In the Orange Free State there were probably about 35,000 Europeans, already grazing possibly two million merino sheep, and there were perhaps between 20,000 and 30,000 Europeans in the Transvaal. Afrikaner families in the inland region of Natal tended during the 'forties to join their comrades across the Vaal River, while British immigrants settled in the coastal areas around Durban particularly after the last years of that decade. Between 1848 and 1851 Byrne's scheme alone introduced into Natal 4500 immigrants, who by arrangement with the Government received their passage and a grant of land for £10 per adult. In 1867 the European population of Natal was nearly 18,000, having doubled in ten years in spite of emigration to the Australian goldfields, and the estimated non-European population amounted to over 260,000. The growing of sugar cane was begun about the year 1850, and experiments were made with coffee and cotton. The large non-European population failing to provide a labour supply for the sugar estates, Indian indentured labourers were introduced from 1860 onwards, most of them to remain in the colony after completing their indentures. By 1865 Natal was sufficiently important for the regular European ocean mail service to be extended to Durban.

The progress of an agricultural community is dependent upon both natural and human causes, and this interdependence is well illustrated by the course of events between 1860 and 1870. The first of those years was marked by a severe drought and with one small break this persisted throughout the decade and caused great losses to the farmers. Their inability to pay their debts brought about depression which led in 1865 to a financial crisis followed by important banking consolidations.

The many local banks operating in Cape Colony had for some years enjoyed an extremely profitable business, which inevitably attracted competition from new and large branch banking corporations introducing capital from overseas. The London and South African Bank was incorporated by royal charter in 1860, and its decision in 1862 to transfer its head office from Cape Town to Port Elizabeth gave evidence of the growth of that port and the profitable nature of its business. The Standard Bank of British South Africa was registered in 1862 under the new limited liability provisions of the Imperial Act of that year, and it also established its head office in Port Elizabeth. The paid-up capital of these two banks approximately equalled the total capital of all the local banks then operating in the Colony and they both proceeded to open branches in all the principal business centres. The smaller institutions in both Cape Colony and the Orange Free State were gradually absorbed by them or consolidated with each other, a process that was hastened by the depression in the later 'sixties. While adversely affecting them all, it left the new banking companies with their many branches in a relatively strengthened position. Their establishment at this time was opportune; for providing as they did direct channels for the introduction of European capital to all settled parts of South Africa, their existence undoubtedly facilitated the sudden and wide expansion of business which came with the diamond discoveries at the end of the decade.

(*b*) 1870–1899. Railways and Mines[1]

The first of the new mining enterprises on a large scale that were to bring about such vast changes in South Africa was concerned with copper. The existence of rich copper deposits in the arid regions along the west coast had been known ever since the days of Governor van der Stel,[2] but the earliest mining boom only came with the opening of the Springbokfontein mines in 1852. The boom was rapidly followed by a slump in 1854–5, but the improved possibilities of securing capital from overseas led in 1863 to the flotation of the Cape Copper Company to work the deposits near Port Nolloth on the west coast of the colony. That venture immediately began a long period of profitable operation. Its success, however, was soon eclipsed by more spectacular discoveries.

In 1867 a Hopetown farmer was found to have in a collection of river pebbles a 21-carat diamond worth £500. Two years later another Afrikaner farmer purchased from a Griqua for £400 "The Star of South Africa", weighing over 83 carats rough. He resold it at once in Hopetown for £11,000 and in June 1870 its value estimated at £25,000. A measure of the rush of diggers to the River

[1] See also chaps, XIX–XXI.
[2] *Vide supra*, p. 134.

Diggings along Vaal River which followed is afforded by the record that early in 1870 there were already ten thousand adults searching for diamonds along the river around Barkly West and Pniel. There followed four new discoveries twenty to thirty miles away to the south-east, on the adjoining farms Dorstfontein (Dutoitspan mine) and Bultfontein, and in 1871 Vooruitzigt (De Beers) and Colesberg Kopje, the Kimberley mine). Beside the three farms on these Dry Diggings sprang up the town of Kimberley, quickly numbering 50,000 inhabitants and destined to overshadow similar settlements at Jagersfontein just across the border in the Orange Free State.

Diggers rushed the farms, and the owners had to be content with monthly licence fees, but they nevertheless sold at good prices. The original claim holders soon discovered indefinite depths of diamond-bearing "blue ground" below the surface yellow deposits, the extent of permanently bearing ground being indicated by the number of claims 31 feet square which each mine contained, viz. Kimberley 331, De Beers 591, Dutoitspan 1430, Bultfontein 886. Until amalgamation of claims was permitted, the separate quarrying of each to great depths soon became a ridiculously inefficient and hazardous enterprise.

The fact that some tens of thousands of people. who suddenly and without warning decided to congregate on a quarrying venture in a barren and hitherto rarely frequented part of South Africa 650 miles from Cape Town and nearly 500 miles from Port Elizabeth, could continue to do so indefinitely without starvation is evidence of the readiness of the still small farming and commercial community of South Africa to respond to the stimulus of lucrative trade offered by the prosperity of the diamond diggers.

A privately owned railway from Cape Town had been in operation since 1863 as far as Wellington, only 57 miles away, by a circuitous route. From thence onwards and from Port Elizabeth the journey to the Diggings had to be undertaken by coach, mule cart or ox-waggon. From Cape Town two transport companies began in 1870 to carry passengers, each of whom was allowed 40 lb. of luggage, to Pniel and Dutoitspan weekly in seven to nine days for £12; ox-waggons took six to eight weeks with their loads of supplies at £30 per ton. From Port Elizabeth, which, as we have seen, was already enjoying a prosperous export trade in wool and was now the most favourably situated port for the import of stores for Kimberley, a coach company began a service twice weekly, the trip taking about five days. Mule-waggons carried goods to the Diggings in fifteen days at about 20*s*. per 100 lb., ox-waggons took between a month and six weeks with ordinary supplies at £15 to £30 a ton according to season. It was no wonder that the mechanisation of mining progressed slowly in the early years.

Living, of a sort, at the diamond diggings was not dear. Until the permanence of the blue ground deposits was realised, the population lived under canvas, but iron stores and iron hotels were grouped around the market square within three months after the rush began. Streets were laid out by the end of 1871, although long after that galvanised iron houses were still frequently moved intact to new sites by gangs of Natives. Game was plentiful in the district; farmers round about found a ready market for meat at 6*d.* per lb., and the demand for maize for the Natives and wheat for the Europeans stimulated agriculture far and near; but vegetables were almost unobtainable. Fuel was a great problem. The whole country within a radius of 100 miles was denuded of its few trees in a very short time, for timber fetched £30 a load in the early days. Water at first cost 3*d.* a bucket, but was soon provided from the wells of the Diggers' Committee at 4*s.* per month for four buckets a day. Liquor and luxuries might fetch fantastic prices. Barnett Isaacs ("Barney Barnato"), who arrived at the Diggings in 1873 at the age of twenty from the East End of London, made his first working capital by the profitable sale of a stock of cigars which he took up with him.

The Kimberley mine being the richest and most rapidly developed, it was there that most of the early difficulties were encountered and the technique evolved by which they were overcome. Newcomers before 1873 were amazed at the primitive appearance of the workings: long narrow roadways 15 feet wide cut equally from adjacent lines of claims 31 feet wide, which yawned in chasms as much as 60 feet deep on each side as the quarrying proceeded. The workers (many of whom had only a quarter claim) descended by ladders or handholds to each claim, and hauled up their loosened ground in buckets to the road above them for removal by wheelbarrow or mule cart to the sorting grounds at the edge of the mine. When in 1873 the roadways fell in beyond repair, ropeways from each of many hundreds of claims up to derricks on the edge of the mine conveyed buckets to and fro. Horses replaced human labour to work the ropeways in 1874; engines not before 1875, on account of the cost of transport from the coast. Never was co-operation between independent workers so obviously advantageous but so completely absent. The reason was that in the early years the amalgamation of more than two claims was not allowed, but conditions in 1874 become so serious that as many as ten claims per digger were permitted. Thereafter the restrictions had soon to be entirely removed. In 1874, when the excavations were over 100 feet deep, a Mining Board was set up to deal collectively with the accumulation of water in the mine, and the young Cecil Rhodes and his partner took the pumping contract. The Board had also to deal with the removal of the reef, which was continually falling and sliding from the walls of the mine to bury the blue ground of many of the claims. Open working was continued to a depth of 400 feet and, as the mine deepened, the removal of fallen reef necessitated the levy of a steadily increasing general rate on the claimholders, for the burying of claims rendered large parts of the mine useless so that reef rates could not be paid. In 1882, following a year of financial difficulties, the local banks refused to finance more bills for the removal of reef, and the experiment was then successfully tried of sinking a timber shaft through the fallen reef, instead of attempting to remove it, and tunnelling into the blue ground. In that way the present method of underground mining of the blue ground was inaugurated.

By the end of the 'seventies the era of independent working of claims was past and, with the legal restrictions of amalgamation removed, exploitation by joint-stock companies began. Cecil Rhodes, who in 1871 as a lad of eighteen was making £100 a week on one of his brother Herbert's claims in the Kimberley mine, had by 1875, with his partner C. D. Rudd, transferred thence to the De Beers mine, and, profiting by the mistakes at Kimberley, was amalgamating claims there with a view to dominating the whole mine. By 1876 Barnato had made sufficient money out of trading, first in cigars and then in diamonds, to purchase four of the best claims in the Kimberley mine, and he also began to amalgamate with others. By 1880 the richest portions of all the four mines had been acquired by capitalists. The costs of working made the risk too great for small independent diggers, and joint-stock companies were floated to carry on operations. As many as seventy companies came into existence in the four mines in 1880 and 1881, nearly half of them lasting long enough to increase production by 50 per cent. In the Kimberley mine, Barnato Bros. in 1880 formed an amalgamation of claims under the name of the Barnato Diamond Mining Company, which in turn combined with the Standard Company and merged with the Kimberley Central Diamond Mining Company of which Barney Barnato became a leading shareholder. The chief competing business in the Kimberley mine was the Compagnie Française des Mines de Diamant du Cap de Bonne-Espérance. In the De Beers mine, Cecil Rhodes and his associates in 1880 founded the De Beers Mining Company with a capital of £200,000, and by 1885 further amalgamation had reduced the number of operating companies in that mine to seven and increased the capital of the De Beers Company to £840,000. The workings were then 650 feet deep, and, as in the Kimberley mine, open working had to be abandoned. With increasing depth came increased difficulties in operating several companies in one mine and increasing inducements to operate each mine as one unit. Underground tunnelling by one company threatened the workings of its neighbours. The Kimberley Central Mining Company and the French company each had two holdings in the Kimberley mine separated by each other's property, but neither permitted the other to tunnel through and shafts had to be duplicated. In May 1887 Rhodes completed the consolidation of the whole De Beers mine.

Production upon so large a scale by one company brought new anxieties. Profitable marketing of its output depended upon the activity of its competitors. The average price received per carat in the early days was £1 10*s*., but on occasion it had fallen below £1 as production increased. With the four mines likely to be operated each with the full economy of a single unit, the market could easily be glutted. Between 1882 and 1888 the cost of working was reduced at De Beers mine from 16*s*. 6*d*. to 7*s*. 2*d*. per carat found, and it was inevitable that similar economies would be achieved elsewhere. Rhodes applied himself at once to the task of controlling the output of his main competitor, the Kimberley mine. In London in 1887 he arranged with the firm of Rothschild for financial help in acquiring the French company, which had been built up by Messrs Jules Porges et Cie, a diamond-merchanting business founded in Paris in 1869. From 1871 the firm's Kimberley buyer was Julius Wernher, who became a partner in 1878, and in 1882 it was strengthened by Alfred Beit, who had arrived at the fields in 1875 as buyer for Lippert and Co. of Hamburg. With Beit's assistance and the co-operation of the firm of Lippert, Rhodes made an agreement to acquire the assets of the French company for £1,400,000, and, to avoid counter-bidding by Barnato, agreed to merge the French claims with the Kimberley Central Company in return for a fifth of its final share capital. In 1888, with the financial support of Beit and his associates and against the active opposition of Barnato, Rhodes set about acquiring a controlling interest in the Kimberley Mining Company. Barnato finally agreed to exchange his holding for De Beers stock, and De Beers Consolidated Mines Ltd thus secured control of the Kimberley mine. When the Kimberley Central Mining Company was formally liquidated later in the year, the Consolidated Company paid the sum of £5,338,650 for its assets. Barnato, Beit, Rhodes and Philipson Stow became life governors of De Beers Consolidated Mines, Ltd. In March 1888 the capital was £2,332,170, and it was kept low, properties being purchased by debenture issues.

There remained to be controlled the production of the Dutoitspan and Bultfontein mines, both of which had been developed along lines parallel with the two richer mines, although not so rapidly. Operations were severely limited by falls of reef in Dutoitspan in 1886 and in Bultfontein in 1889. It was, however, necessary for the De Beers Consolidated Company to acquire control of them in order to make restriction of production safe. Permanent working agreements were made with allied companies; the Griqualand West Company in Dutoitspan and the Bultfontein Consolidated Company, and other properties were acquired during 1889. In 1890 the Premier mine (Wesselton) was discovered on the adjoining farm of Benauwdheitsfontein and bought by De Beers Consolidated Mines for £303,000, on terms which gave the vendor a five years' working lease terminating in January 1896. The Consolidated Company secured in addition a large interest in the Jagersfontein mine in the Orange Free State, which had been discovered in 1871 and opened in 1878. Thus the production of diamonds was controlled with a view to permanence of profitable exploitation.

The activity at Kimberley had far-reaching reactions throughout South Africa, apart from the important stimulus that a large local market gave to grain and cattle farmers of the interior and to the languishing wine production of Western Province. The output of diamonds meanwhile rose from 102,500 carats in 1870 to 1,080,000 carats in 1872, 2,110,000 carats in 1879, and 3,841,937 carats in 1888. The value of the total output grew at the same time to more than £4 million annually. That achievement incidentally involved a revolution in trade and transport and a new mode of life for tens of thousands of tribal Africans. The diggers engaged in the first scrambles for diamonds, not believing that the good going would last, wanted labour at any cost, and offered high wages, firearms and ammunition. European agents would meet Africans on the roads leading to the Diggings, engage them at an agreed wage, and collect a commission of £1 per head on conducting them to employers on the look-out for African workers. Such news spread rapidly from kraal to kraal. In a few months there were collected at the Diggings among the thousands of Natives employed some who had come from north of the Zambesi, as well as large numbers from Bechuanaland and all parts of the future Union. They rarely stayed long after they had earned their gun and ammunition and a little money. It has been estimated that in each of the first seven years 30,000 Africans worked for a spell of perhaps four to five months on the Diamond Fields. Their insistence on coin rather than notes drained the banks of their specie, and large quantities had to be imported.

Great temptations were offered to the Africans by illicit diamond buyers to steal and sell part of the stones found, the losses being estimated at from £500,000 to £1,000,000 each year before the introduction of the compound system by De Beers in the 'eighties. With the African workers confined to the compound during the whole period of their term of service (normally from three months to one year) thefts were enormously reduced, and, as far as can be judged, the system had little effect on the willingness of Africans to go to Kimberley for employment, while with better food and medical attention their physical condition definitely improved. In 1892 there were about 10,000 Africans employed on the Kimberley mines.

The white population engaged in diamond digging was at first largely South African, but the discoveries inevitably attracted a stream of immigrants from Europe and as the mining operations became mechanised it became necessary to import technicians and skilled mechanics in considerable numbers, so that in 1894 only 33 per cent of the white employees of the De Beers Company were South African born. The presence of these skilled immigrants in South

Africa at the time of the gold discoveries in the Transvaal in 1886 accounts in part for the relative rapidity of the mechanical development of the Witwatersrand mines.

Importations of equipment for the diamond diggings showed themselves in the doubling of the average value of imports in the period 1870–4 as compared with the previous five years. The merchanting business flourished, and the main problem was to get the stores to the Diggings quickly enough. To hasten railway development the Cape Government in 1873 decided to raise the necessary loan itself and to acquire the existing private line to Wellington and develop it as a state railway. Political influences immediately compelled "equal treatment" of the three Cape ports, Cape Town, Port Elizabeth and East London; and legislation in 1873 and 1874 authorised construction to the interior from these three termini, a 3 ft. 6 in. gauge being adopted instead of the old 4 ft. 8½ in. By the end of 1879 eight hundred miles of often difficult construction had been achieved, and five years later, when Kimberley was reached, another thousand miles had been completed in Cape Colony and Natal. The Western System from Cape Town reached Beaufort West in 1880 and De Aar in 1884. The Midlands line from Port Elizabeth was opened to Cradock in 1881 and to Colesberg in 1883. In the following year the linking of De Aar with Naauwpoort established rail communication between Cape Town and Port Elizabeth and concentrated both lines upon the inland goal of Kimberley, which was reached from De Aar in 1885. An Eastern system from East London, in part strategic in design, the most expensive to construct and, because of ox-waggon competition, the least remunerative to operate, was opened to Aliwal North in the same year, but was not linked up with Kimberley via Stormberg and Rosmead until 1892.[1]

Government initiative undoubtedly secured more rapid railway construction through sparsely populated areas than would have resulted through private enterprise, but of the three routes the Midland system from Port Elizabeth was alone covering interest charges in 1885. The weakness of political control through a Railway Commission was very soon evident in rate policy. Cape Town, with the longer route to Kimberley, pressed against Port Elizabeth for lower ton-mile rates on long-distance traffic. But sharply tapering rates on inwards traffic could hardly be justified on a cost basis, for costs rose with the heavy gradients, the shortage of water, the absence of coal and the generally primitive conditions in the interior. Political control of three isolated systems, unconnected with each other in the early years except by sea or road, by a Minister in Cape Town who was harassed by questions from disappointed farmers was not likely to be an improvement on the decisions of the three local managers. Considerations of political peace resulted in the ignoring of cost and market

[1] For details see van der Poel, J., *Railway and Customs Policies in South Africa*, 1885–1910.

considerations and the application of uniform rates in 1883. Thereby the innocent Eastern system was further embarrassed. But colonial produce was carried to Kimberley at preferential rates, as compared with imported goods; and at an early stage the tapering rate was used, as it has been so extensively in later years, to neutralise the disadvantages of location of the more distant South African farmers.

Natal also was stimulated by the diamond discoveries and by their effect on the trade of the internal republics. Railway construction from Durban was begun by the Natal Government in 1876 to serve the new sugar estates by coast lines.

The sugar industry was by then about twenty-five years old. It had been begun perhaps in 1850 by a new settler introduced by Byrne, but had made little headway during the first ten years, for the local African labour supply was unsatisfactory; but in 1860 the importation of indentured Indian labourers was begun and in 1867 the new industry was favoured with a protective duty of 3*s.* 6*d.* per cwt. There were by then 5600 Indians in the Colony, and the output of sugar had reached nearly 10,000 tons annually at the time of the diamond discoveries. The new impetus which it then received attracted planters and mill-workers from Mauritius, railway construction was begun, and in 1879 the number of mill-plants had increased to 73. In the 'eighties, competition from Mauritius led to a rapid reduction in the number of mills and improvement in their efficiency, and in 1890 there existed no more than 37.

The difficult railway connection between Durban and Maritzburg was completed in 1880. Estcourt was reached in 1885 and Ladysmith in 1886. Thereafter the new gold discoveries in the Transvaal deflected attention to the northern route through Glencoe, while further construction westwards to Harrismith, the Orange Free State and Kimberley progressed more slowly. At this time Natal was pursuing deliberately the policy of maintaining her customs duties below those of the Cape in order to stimulate her transit trade with the two republics in the interior.

The effect of the diamond discoveries on the public finances of Cape Colony was not confined to borrowing for railway construction. At the middle of the century the Cape had been free from debt, and subsequent borrowing had been limited before the 'seventies to small short-term loans for public works. The public debt (mainly as the result of railway, harbour and other public works construction) increased in the diamond era to £11·4 million in 1880 and £23·75 million in 1890. The fall in interest rates from 6 to 4 per cent in the same period reduced the annual charge on these loans. Over half of the current revenue was derived from customs duties in 1870, and both revenue and expenditure expanded fourfold in the decade 1870–80 as the result of the general increase in business. The average rate of customs duty was raised in the 'sixties to about 10 per cent and it was raised again in the 'eighties. From 1888, on account of the gold-mining developments in the Transvaal, the Cape railways began to yield a net surplus after payment of interest charges, which was applied to the relief of general taxation.

The establishment of two dominating branch banking companies in the decade preceding the diamond discoveries[1] undoubtedly contributed to the rapid development of the Diggings. In 1873, with the rapid expansion of business, the Oriental Banking Corporation extended its operations to South Africa and established branches or absorbed existing local banks in several centres. On the failure of the main company in 1879 the Bank of Africa was established to take over its South African business. The Standard Bank had absorbed its rival the London and South African Bank in 1877, and its branches soon outnumbered all the other banks in the Colony.

A sharp depression developed in 1881, resulting only in part from the condition at that time of the diamond industry to which we have already referred; over-speculation in ostrich-farming was also to blame. During the 'seventies the invention of a satisfactory egg incubator had led to a rapid and profitable expansion of the new trade in ostrich feathers. Exports reached an annual value of over £1 million, but excessive production and deterioration in quality led to a sharp set-back in prices in the early 'eighties. A number of local banks failed. In Natal, several banks had been wound up in the 'seventies, and apart from branches opened by the imperial banks, the Natal Bank alone survived a set-back in 1890. From ninety-nine in 1883 the number of banks or branches in the Cape diminished to sixty-six in 1890, and the large banks themselves reduced the number of their branches during those years.

The depression was lifted by the extraordinary developments in the gold-mining industry that turned the eyes of the whole world to South Africa and brought about vital changes in its economic circumstances.

The proclamation by the Transvaal Government on 20 September 1886 of the Witwatersrand as a public goldfield under the Consolidated Gold Law of 1885 followed a series of minor discoveries and gold-rushes, and crowned a generation of persistent prospecting. Under the Transvaal Gold Law the landowner and the prospector were entitled to a certain number of claims, the remainder of the area being declared open to the public, subject to the payment of licence fees. Between the late 'fifties and 1865, in spite of governmental discouragement of prospecting, gold had been located and goldfields opened in the more remote northern, north-eastern and eastern districts of the Transvaal; in the Pietersburg district in 1870, and in Lydenburg to the south-east; in 1882 in the De Kaap valley in the Barberton district, to be followed in 1886 by the springing up of the

[1] *Vide supra*, p. 794.

town of Barberton near the rich Sheba mine. Already in 1872 there were over 1000 diggers on the Lydenburg field, and in the early 'eighties the reef and alluvial discoveries in the De Kaap and Barberton area attracted a cosmopolitan community of some 10,000 people, who included very few Transvaal Boers. In 1884 the new licence fees of £10,000 per month from the De Kaap goldfield, many times greater than the revenue of the South African Republic from all other sources, had already saved the state from bankruptcy.

The gold-bearing conglomerate reef of the Witwatersrand itself was first located near its north-west extremity by two brothers, F. and H. W. Struben, in 1884. By 1886 they had traced it eastward to the main reef at Langlaagte immediately west of where Johannesburg now stands. Samples were panned at Kimberley in July 1886, and immediately J. B. Robinson headed a race of wealthy diamond-mine operators northward to acquire farms in the new district. Bare pasture farms on the Witwatersrand which hitherto had sold for £350 to £750 each—and which could all have been acquired for £10,000—were sold by their owners within a few months for prices ranging from £7000 to £70,000 each, and still the buyers made enormous fortunes out of them. The Langlaagte and Robinson Companies alone, for instance, in five years from their flotation, produced from properties, which had originally cost their promoters £20,000, over £2,350,000 of gold, and paid £900,000 in dividends.

One farm was laid out as a township and auctioned on 90-year leases during 1886 and 1887 in 1800 lots for a total price of £50,000. In that way Johannesburg came early into being to replace the camp of waggons, tents and huts known as Ferreira's in which a mining population had promptly congregated in 1886, drawn from the diamond mines, the other gold-fields and soon from the ends of the earth. By the end of the century Johannesburg had 100,000 European inhabitants and a teeming population of African labourers. J. B. Robinson had been quickly followed from Kimberley by Hans Sauer, Cecil Rhodes, C. B. Rudd, Alfred Beit, Julius Porges and (later) Barney Barnato, so that all the financial groups already represented in Africa were at once concerned. Spectacular fortunes were made. Within ten years Rhodes was personally receiving between £300,000 and £400,000 a year from his share in the Gold Fields of South Africa, Limited, the company which in 1892 was renamed the Consolidated Gold Fields of South Africa.

From the beginning, reef mining on the Witwatersrand was predominantly a capitalistic venture for joint-stock companies. The "banket" reef had to be mined, crushed in stamps and pulped in order that its gold content could be extracted as far as might be by amalgamation with mercury. Much of the gold could not be recovered in that way, and it would not have been possible to deal with the vast lower-grade ores or to win the deep-level deposits by this process alone. The new McArthur-Forrest method of extracting almost all the residue of gold from the "tailings" (sand or slime) by dissolving it in cyanide solutions was not developed sufficiently for general use until the 'nineties. In the early years, shafts were sunk from the outcrop following the incline of the reefs as far down as the costs of working permitted. Thereafter, shafts were sunk to meet the reef lower down. The gold-bearing strata dip, very sharply at first, towards the south. The distance from the outcrop at which mining claims could be sold was determined by speculation as to the angle of dip, the richness of the deposit and practicability of working at great depths. Inevitably there were many failures and reconstructions of mining companies until knowledge of the geological and technical conditions could be acquired. Equally inevitably, no doubt, in the first few years the eager investing public proved an easy prey to unscrupulous company promoters. By 1889, when the first Chamber of Mines was established, confidence had been severely damaged by the flood of unreliable prospectuses, by over-capitalisation and by heavy losses due to these causes and to reckless management. The sinking of shafts to the deep levels involved risks of considerable loss. In the 'nineties mines were cut down to work reefs at 2000, 3000 and 4000 feet below the surface, and the progress of knowledge can be measured by the fact that before the end of the century the large financial groups had acquired properties at some places as far as four miles south of the outcrop and were contemplating mining ultimately to a depth of 7000 feet.

Apart from the obvious technical economies from expensive and heavy machinery, the risks involved in deep level prospecting and working entirely in one area and the need for maintaining the confidence of investors led to amalgamations into larger companies and group-working. As early as 1891, when 141 mining companies were working, twelve of them produced half the total output; in 1893, of 183 companies, 104 had yielded no gold. Before the South African War, the gold-mining industry had already become concentrated under the control of a few financial groups, and the foundations of the present-day system of group administration had been established. The extent of more recent improvements in technique can be gauged from the statement that in 1897 the average yield was 11·4 dwt. of gold per ton milled; the highest grade mine secured 32·3 dwt. per ton, while the lowest grade mine then worked yielded 7·6 dwt. Average working costs were then 29*s*. 6*d*. per ton milled. Thirty years later, when the annual output had increased nearly four times to £42 million, the average yield of all mines worked was 6·55 dwt., the highest grade mine giving 10·8 dwt. and the lowest only 4·0 dwt. Working costs had been reduced in the meantime to an average of 19*s*. 9*d*. per ton milled.

The figures of output of gold in the Transvaal showed a rate of growth far outstripping the most sensational development that South Africa had hitherto known—the diamond discoveries. In two years gold was being produced at the rate of 250,000 ounces or £1 million value per year; in ten years, by 1896, over two million ounces worth over £8½ million; in 1898, the last complete year before war suspended operations, over 3·8 million ounces valued at £16¼ million. About 750 tons of gold, worth over £80 million, had been secured by the close of the century. Thereby the economic system of the Transvaal and of the whole of southern Africa had been transformed.

It must be remembered that the habits of life of the greater part of the Transvaal farming population at the time of the Witwatersrand discoveries had changed little from those of the elders among them who had trekked away from Cape Colony perhaps half a century earlier. Many had literally never seen money; they traded by barter and paid taxes to the Government in kind. If they acquired money, they saved it, and saving meant hoarding, not investment. Their experience of the early mining prospectors had not usually encouraged business confidence; industry was confined by state concessions to favoured monopolists, and the rudimentary legal system afforded scant protection to those who cherished commercial aspirations. Small wonder, therefore, that the banks and financial houses found it uphill work to bring transactions with the farming population within the money and credit structure upon which capitalised mining enterprise was founded. When farmers sold estates, livestock or produce for money, payments had to be made in gold, which was generally hoarded, and a steady importation of specie became necessary.

Local banking ventures had not prospered in the early days of the Transvaal, but in the 'seventies the Cape Commercial Bank and the Standard Bank were operating branches and lending to the Government. The gold discoveries quickened banking development. The imperial banks and the Natal Bank opened more branches: a Holland bank—the Netherlands Bank of South Africa—began in 1888, and in 1891 the National Bank of the South African Republic was established, mainly by Dutch and German financiers, to enjoy special Government concessions and privileges. A State Mint, worked on concession by the National Bank, was also set up in Pretoria in 1891 to coin Transvaal gold. In 1895 a number of large investment businesses were floated under the title of banking companies, to provide capital for the speculative operations of several gold-mining magnates; but they transacted little or no ordinary banking business and were for the most part short-lived. The six principal firms engaged in real banking business increased the number of their Transvaal branches from 44 to 103 between the years 1894 and 1903.

In a community of predominantly subsistence farmers, the monopoly concessions to industrialists and traders caused little discontent except to disappointed concession-hunters. The new mining population took a different view of a dynamite monopoly, which lasted until the South African War and, without securing the ostensibly desired effect of obtaining the use of local materials, raised the price of explosives to the mines, as well as of cartridges to the farmers, considerably above that which would have yielded an equivalent revenue to the state by way of import duty.[1] That concession was typical of many secured by corruption, which raised the costs of construction materials, such as cement and bricks, and of many of the other requirements of the new industry, for the benefit, not of the government revenues, but of a favoured few. Without these handicaps mining development would certainly have been still more spectacular.

Of no less immediate concern to the gold-mining industry and of far wider significance throughout Southern Africa was the general transport and customs tariff situation.[2] When the Witwatersrand goldfields were proclaimed, the inland railheads were at Kimberley, Colesberg and Aliwal North in Cape Colony, and at Ladysmith in Natal. There were no railways in the Orange Free State and the Transvaal; all machinery and stores had to be conveyed from railheads by cart and ox-waggon. The fastest route for passengers and mails at the time of the Rand discoveries was by rail to Kimberley and thence by Cobb's "Australian" coaches, each drawn by ten to fourteen horses or mules changed every dozen miles, and capable of carrying fifteen passengers and about 1½ tons of mails, etc., reaching Pretoria in three days and nights from Kimberley.

Until 1888, the Cape Colony and Natal both exacted the full customs duty on transit trade to the Orange Free State and the Transvaal and passed none of it on, while the Transvaal herself secured only a trifling revenue on imports which entered by the more obvious routes. The average Cape tariff on all imports was considerably higher than that of Natal. Since 1875 the Transvaal had maintained a commercial treaty with Portugal, establishing free trade with Portuguese East Africa and admitting imports to the Transvaal through Delagoa Bay on payment of a 3 per cent transit duty, but the bulk of the trade was through Cape and Natal ports. A railway line had been long contemplated between Pretoria and Delagoa Bay, but finance had hitherto been the obstacle. The gold developments, however, created a keen rivalry between the two colonies and Portuguese East Africa for the carrying trade with important results which we have considered in earlier chapters.[3]

The height of the Cape revenue tariff was a disadvantage; her three railways, on the other hand, were truly offered a golden opportunity

[1] *Vide supra*, pp. 566.
[2] See van der Poel, J., *Railway and Customs Policies in South Africa*, 1885–1910.
[3] *Vide supra*, chaps, XX, XXI.

to justify their existence. The Cape had undertaken to give Basutoland its fair share of the customs revenue; now, in 1889, it agreed, in a customs convention with the Orange Free State which made free trade in South African produce secure, to remit 75 per cent of the customs revenue collected on transit trade. Apart from special duties, the general *ad valorem* rate was 12 per cent with a 3 per cent transit duty on traffic to the Transvaal. Under the Convention other South African states could apply for admittance to the Customs Union on adopting uniform tariff provisions. In the early 'nineties none but Bechuanaland and Basutoland did so. Natal's low tariff helped her to develop her trade with the Transvaal, while in the early 'nineties, the Transvaal Government broadly framed its customs tariff with an eye to obtaining as much revenue as it could from its flourishing new industrial population. There were high rates on flour and other foodstuffs to protect the burghers, and the industrial monopoly concessions were specially protected; but in the ten years 1889–98 the average rate on all imports was 10·6 per cent compared with at least 17 per cent levied in Cape Colony on imports for local consumption. In 1898 nearly 40 per cent of the revenue came from intoxicants, narcotics and jewellery—more than was raised on foodstuffs, tea, coffee and clothing. Irritating discriminations apart, the Transvaal tariff was not heavy.

In the meantime, railway construction was pushed ahead. After receiving a monopoly of railway construction in the Transvaal in 1887, the Netherlands South African Railway Company began to make slow progress at Komatipoort on the Portuguese border, and between 1890 and 1892 the whole Reef from Krugersdorp in the west was also linked by the "Rand Tram" with the new coal-mines of Boksburg and Springs in the east. The Cape lines were extended northward, that from Kimberley being laid in 1890 by the British South Africa Company as far as Vryburg in Bechuanaland, while through the Orange Free State the line from Colesberg was taken via Kroonstad to the Vaal River bridge by 1892. The work was performed under convention by the Cape Government, which also contracted under the Sivewright Agreement to continue the line on the Transvaal side and operate it until the end of 1894 as far as Germiston Junction on the "Rand Tram". In that way Cape Town and Port Elizabeth were linked with Johannesburg, and East London with both Kimberley and Johannesburg, in 1892. Between 1883 and 1894 the capital investment in the Cape lines increased from £10 million to £20 million.

The Cape ports had won the race, but their advantage was brief. In Natal, the Government extended its line from Ladysmith to the Transvaal border in 1891, and completed it to the Rand by arrangement in 1895. In the previous year, the connection with Delagoa Bay through Pretoria had been at last completed. The three lines were thus in active competition in 1895 as far as the Transvaal borders, and the Netherlands Company, operating within them, varied its rates on the Transvaal sections so as to divert traffic and secure the maximum profit from all inward consignments. When the Cape railway cut rates to the Vaal River, they were trebled on the Transvaal section. The Cape traders retaliated by transferring their consignments to ox-waggons at the frontier, and the Netherlands Company persuaded the Transvaal Government to attempt to prohibit that manœuvre. The course of political events associated with the failure of that attempt has already been considered.[1]

The profitability of the railways at this time can be gauged from the fact that in the best year, 1896, the Cape lines earned £8. 19*s*. 7*d*. per cent on the capital invested, while the Natal system (on which a debt of over £6 million had been incurred) earned £18. 4*s*. 0*d*. per cent. In that year Natal already carried slightly more of the through goods traffic (in value) to the Transvaal. In 1897 the general *ad valorem* tariff of the Customs Union was lowered to 9 per cent, and in 1898, when the rate was further reduced to 7½ per cent and the proportion of duties on transit trade passed on to the inland states raised to 85 per cent, Natal entered the Customs Union. The customs tariffs of the South African states were still framed mainly to yield revenue, and the necessity for importing foodstuffs, which originated with the growth of the population of Kimberley, was intensified by the growth of Johannesburg. The railways did not bring most South African farmers much nearer the market, and ox-waggon transport was in demand and more expensive than hitherto. A one-way trade developed from Australia in wheat, butter and meat. With the development of deep-level mining after 1895 imports of mining and other machinery from the United States, Germany and Belgium naturally began to grow rapidly, although in 1898 Great Britain still retained three-quarters of the import trade of British South Africa. As the years went by, there emerged ever more acutely the problem of finding coastward freights of any volume for the railways and outward cargoes for shipping.

One other repercussion of gold-mining in the Transvaal was at once felt throughout southern Africa and that was the demand for African labour. Recruiters, including traders, made a profitable business in the Native areas by persuading groups of Africans to make their first trip to Johannesburg, and the mines soon began to employ their own recruiters. From the first it was clear that the sources which served Kimberley and the Cape railways and public works could not meet also the needs of the Rand. The Cape Colony Government, concerned about the rising cost of labour in the colony, had in 1893 been advised by a commission on Native labour to levy a special tax on every adult male Native, to be remitted if he could prove that he had been absent from home in employment during the year. A clause in the Glen Grey

[1] *Vide supra*, pp. 573.

Act of 1894[1] gave legislative effect to this proposal, but steps were never taken rigorously to enforce it. From the early days in the Transvaal farm labour had in part been secured by the indenturing of Native children,[2] and in 1895 a Squatters' Law imposed a head tax on Natives who had not worked under Europeans.

Strenuous efforts were made by the gold-mining industry to attract Africans from Portuguese East Africa and the northern regions. Labour cost was between 50 and 60 per cent of the total cost of gold-mining. Surface boys were available from the Cape and the Native territories, but there was a great shortage at prevailing wage rates of underground workers. Competition between mine managers for labour inevitably forced up Native wages, and the new Chamber of Mines applied itself after 1889 to the task of minimising this effect. An attempt in 1892 to fix a maximum rate was abandoned on its being found to have simply the effect of curtailing the supply of labour, and in 1893 the Chamber established a special labour organisation under a Native Labour Commissioner. This soon yielded results. In 1896 it secured by concession from the Government of Portuguese East Africa the monopoly of the right of recruiting and of establishing depôts in that territory. But although during 1898 the number of mine Natives increased by 25 per cent to 70,000 by the end of the year, 100,000 were then required underground in existing mines, and the Chamber of Mines organisation, which had investigated possibilities of attracting labour not only from the whole of Africa, but also from China, India and Italy, had to report failure to do more. In July 1899 one hundred and fifty gold-mining companies employed a total of 108,000 Africans above and below ground. At that time the African workers were not barracked in compounds under regulations such as exist to-day.

Before the outbreak of war in 1899, the territories which had in 1895 been named Rhodesia were already beginning to assume economic significance to the civilised world on account of the small beginnings of a gold-mining industry. Baines in 1871 and Swinburne in 1872 had secured mining concessions from Lobengula, King of the Matabele, and in 1888 Rhodes's emissaries secured the so-called Rudd Concession of all mineral rights, which, as we have described elsewhere, was straightway made by Rhodes and his financial associates (particularly Alfred Beit and the Rothschilds) the basis for securing, in 1889, a royal charter for the British South Africa Company.[3] Rhodes's Pioneers of 1890 were given farms on condition of *bona fide* occupation, and in 1892 a number of South African farmers trekked from the Orange Free State, to be followed by other parties from the Transvaal, to settle in the new territory. In 1891 Rhodes also acquired for

[1] *Vide supra*, p. 558.
[2] *Vide supra*, p. 410, where the controversies over the local slave trade are discussed.
[3] *Vide supra*, pp. 545.

the Chartered Company a concession to sell land, which Lippert, a cousin of Beit, had secured from Lobengula in the previous year. A narrow-gauge railway from the port of Beira towards Salisbury was actually begun in 1892, but the Rhodesian border at Umtali was not reached till 1898. In the meantime Salisbury had been connected with Mafeking by telegraph, and the railway northward from Vryburg, commenced in 1893, reached Mafeking in 1894 and Bulawayo in 1897. The route northward from Kimberley skirted the Transvaal for political reasons and traversed poor traffic country. In 1899 Umtali was connected with Salisbury and the railway gauge was made uniform through to Beira in 1900. The war prevented further work on the northward line from the Bulawayo end, but materials were imported through Beira, and Salisbury was linked by rail with Bulawayo and the South in 1902. These lines were constructed for a number of railway companies, mainly under guarantee of interest and subsidy by the British South Africa Company, which raised the capital in ordinary shares or debentures as construction proceeded, and which was the ultimate rate-controlling authority. It was not to be expected that these railways, built mainly for strategic reasons, should yield a profit in the early years.

In the closing years of the nineteenth century, then, the South African people could look back on thirty years of unexampled growth and prosperity. From hardly more than a quarter of a million in 1865, the European population had risen to almost a million. In the meantime the barren regions of Griqualand West had been made to yield about £80 to £90 million of diamonds, and in the last decade there had been extracted from the Transvaal approximately the same value of gold. From the proceeds of their sale abroad the whole of South Africa had prospered. The mining operations had involved an enormous importation of capital and equipment and the establishment of important trading businesses. Three thousand miles of railway had been built to connect the mines with the five coast ports. Thereby a saving of literally months had been effected in the conveyance of stores from the coast, and the tempo of general business activity had been quickened. The mines and railways needed coal, and new coal-mines were producing at the rate of two million tons a year in the Transvaal and half-a-million tons in Natal after barely ten years of operation. The new populations of mine workers, white and black, had to be fed, and agriculture and trade prospered throughout South Africa, the cattle and sheep farmers and maize growers in particular. Already the wheat farmers could no longer produce enough flour for the increased population, and wheat and flour imports became a normal occurrence. The two colonies and two republics had in fact become bound by economic forces into one region. Rivalry between them, actuated by local business pressure and by concern for their budgetary stability and political independence, finding expression in railway competition and customs disputes maintained a superficial parade of separate interest and threatened war; but in reality the gold discoveries of the Transvaal had welded a more fundamental tie between them and made inevitable the speedy emergence of a national economic unit.

(c) 1899–1921. Economic Development and the Union of South Africa

The loss of life and destruction of farm and other equipment during the South African war 1899–1902 inevitably left their mark on economic development after the cessation of hostilities. In addition, the almost complete stoppage of gold-mining during the war involved considerable losses to the refugee Uitlander population and a cessation of dividends to shareholders. The growing of crops was dislocated in the republics, the northern districts of the Cape and Natal, and guerilla warfare ultimately interfered seriously with pastoral farming as far south as the Cape Midlands. The farming population of the republics lost also through the system of commandeering of provisions, sheep and cattle, horses and waggons by which means on their side the war was carried on. But much of the population of the Cape and Natal and of all districts occupied by British troops—farmers, traders, transport workers, builders, artisans and African labourers—prospered from the war expenditure of the Imperial Government as never before. Boom conditions prevailed so long as the spending continued.

Comparatively little of the cost of financing the war fell on the South African states. To the United Kingdom the total cost was over £200 millions, and colonial troops were paid liberally. South Africa put 50,000 men in the field, about one-ninth of the total force, and the Cape and Natal both maintained local forces, but the war was carried on mainly at the expense of the United Kingdom tax-payer on the one side and of the Boer farmers on the other. After the war, the Imperial Government distributed in free grants to British and Boer farmers in the two inland colonies a total of £7,000,000, and in 1903 a development loan of £35,000,000 was raised in England by the Transvaal Government for reconstruction and development in the Transvaal and Orange River Colony.[1] Of this sum, £6,500,000 was for compensation and repatriation, £13,500,000 for state acquisition of the railways, over £3,000,000 to take over existing debt, £2,500,000 for land settlement and £8,000,000 for further railway and public works construction. In 1908 the Transvaal issued a second loan of £5,000,000 to establish a land bank and provide for additional public works.

The early years after the war saw a continuance of prosperity as the result of the great expectations from the new colonies entertained by

[1] *Vide supra*, pp. 631, 637 *sqq*.

British and European capitalists and by British immigrants, and as a result of Government expenditure of the development loan in those colonies. But these hopes were not all realised and severe depression ensued, particularly in the Cape, which was afflicted by severe drought and in which the diamond industry was further affected by the American and European financial difficulties of 1907–8. The public revenue of Cape Colony fell in the five years 1902–3 to 1906–7 by over one-third, both the two main sources of income—the railway surplus and the customs receipts—falling sharply, whereas little reduction was made in expenditure, so that there was a series of Budget deficits. The public accounts of Natal showed less serious variations, railways receipts keeping up better than in the Cape. Customs and railway results depended largely, of course, upon the progress of economic developments in the Transvaal.

Little time was lost in starting the gold-mining industry again after the war, for the mining population was flocking back to the Rand before the end of 1901. The output for 1902 already reached nearly half the figure for 1898, and by 1904 new records of monthly output were again being made in spite of increased difficulty after the war in luring Africans back to regular work underground. Railway construction and operation, public works, industrial and farming developments throughout South Africa, all competed for African labour; and the scarcity was absolute, rather than relative to the scale of remuneration, in that many of the Africans worked to earn a more or less fixed sum to acquire wives and cattle and were liable to work less as competition among employers raised the rates of wages. The dependence of the gold-mining industry on Native labour from Portuguese East Africa, and the dependence in turn of the Transvaal Government on the gold-mining industry, resulted in questions of private trade becoming the subject of complex political bargaining, in which the strong bargaining position of the Portuguese Government enabled it to secure a guaranteed share of the transit trade to the Rand, and favourable customs treatment of such trade, as well as a revenue from the migration of Native labour. An agreement for a *modus vivendi* in December 1901 stereotyped the relation which existed before the war between the railway rates from Lourenço Marques, Durban and the Cape ports to the Transvaal, and, in addition to safeguarding the customs treatment of trade through Lourenço Marques, secured to the Portuguese Government a payment of a thirteen shillings fee for every African recruited, the fee to relate to a maximum contract period of one year. The agreement lasted until, in 1909, a Convention was agreed upon which continued broadly the same conditions in regard to African labour.[1] In 1903, when 89 per cent of the African labour on the gold-mines was already drawn from Portuguese East Africa and there seemed to be little prospect of augmenting the supply from other

[1] *Vide supra*, p. 655.

regions, three times as many African workers were wanted at once to operate existing equipment. The lack of labour upset the optimistic calculations which had been made, and difficult times ensued. From the beginning of 1904 the experiment was made of introducing indentured Chinese labourers. The number employed attained a maximum in 1906 of 50,000, but, thereafter, on account of political opposition, repatriation was begun, to be completed by 1910. Elaborate arrangements for accommodating, feeding and providing for the physical welfare of African workers were gradually built up, and the supply of labour improved. The system of centralised recruiting by the Chamber of Mines was continued, the recruits being allotted to mines on their arrival in the central compound at Johannesburg. By 1910 the number of Africans employed had been increased to nearly 200,000, the numbers from the four colonies having been increased to 26 per cent from the Cape, 7½ per cent from the Transvaal, 6½ per cent from Natal and Zululand, and 3½ per cent from the Orange Free State and Basutoland, as compared with 52 per cent from Portuguese East Africa.

In 1908 the Precious and Base Metals Act passed by the Transvaal Parliament inaugurated an important change in the terms on which gold-mining was permitted, as the result of which the Government (since 1910, the Union Government) has secured a considerable share of the profits of working the new areas thrown open. The Government was given power to lease any proclaimed land and divide it into suitable working areas, after which tenders for leases are invited by a Mining Leases Board from companies of approved financial strength, the tenders being in the form of offers of a sliding scale of percentages of profit which the company would pay the Government, in addition to rental of the claim and ordinary taxation. Beginning in 1910, wide tracts of the Far East Rand have in this way been opened up under lease by large mining companies. In that year the total gold output of the Transvaal was over 7½ million ounces, valued at nearly £32 million.

Railway rates in South Africa have been controlled by political rather than market considerations. The expansion of gold-mining induced an inwards traffic to the Rand from the competing ports, which kept railway rate policy and customs tariff policy in the forefront of South African politics. After the Treaty of Vereeniging the railway systems of the Transvaal and Orange River Colony were united under one administration, the Central South African Railways, with the effect that trade through the Cape ports traversed a much greater mileage of the inland system; nevertheless, it still remained in the interest of the new inland railway authority to stimulate the trade through Delagoa Bay, on which route its own net profit was greatest. Between 1902 and 1906 the share of the Cape ports declined from 45 per cent to about one-eighth and Durban barely kept one-third, while the traffic through Delagoa Bay rose from one-fifth to over one-half. An understanding reached in February 1905 at an Inter-Colonial Conference to share the traffic in certain proportions was held up by the terms of the *Modus Vivendi* of 1901.[1] The Transvaal-Mozambique Convention of 1909, which replaced that agreement, provided that railway rates should be adjusted to secure for Delagoa Bay a share of 50–55 per cent of the traffic, and this share was confirmed by a new Convention as recently as 1928. The 1909 Convention also secured Delagoa Bay against customs discriminations.

In 1903, following a Conference at Bloemfontein, the Customs Union[2] was extended to include for the first time all four colonies, the High Commission Territories and Southern Rhodesia, the coastal colonies abolishing their charges on transit trade and reducing the charge for collecting duties at the coast to 5 per cent. The new customs tariff rates embodied the beginnings of protection for local industries, and reintroduced preference for British goods after half-a-century; but revenue was the dominating object. Protection for agricultural produce was also secured by means of differential railway rates on colonial and imported produce. Preference for Great Britain was automatic, and the Dominions qualified for similar treatment as the result of reciprocity with Canada in 1904, Australia in 1906 and New Zealand in 1907. A Customs Conference in Pietermaritzburg in 1906 resulted in additional protection and higher revenue duties on the representations of the Cape and Natal, both of which were badly hit by the depression. The general *ad valorem* rate was raised from 10 to 15 per cent.

Railway construction went ahead rapidly in Cape Colony immediately after the declaration of peace. Between 1902 and 1906 about eleven hundred miles of new lines were completed opening up the old "Garden" waggon route from Cape Town through Mossel Bay and Oudtshoorn to Port Elizabeth, the wheat-lands of the Western Province, and the sheep and fruit districts lying between Port Elizabeth and East London. When in 1906 depression stopped further building elsewhere, the improved position of gold-mining enabled construction to proceed in the Transvaal. Of special importance was the opening in 1906 of the quick route to Johannesburg from Cape Town through Kimberley and Fourteen Streams, the finance having been arranged by the De Beers Company, and a more southerly route to Delagoa Bay from the Rand in 1908. The branch lines built through farming regions did not pay their way, and there was clearly a limit on the amount of such development which the Cape in particular could afford at a time when the transit trade was already ceasing to yield its contribution to the Colony's revenue. Since the 'nineties railway rates had been manipulated by the colonial Governments to

[1] *Vide supra*, p. 634.
[2] *Vide supra*, p. 639.

protect South African products by a system of preferential rates. Successive railway managers, select committees and inter-colonial conferences protested in vain against the use of the railways rather than the customs for such purposes, but the policy was continued after Union. Assistance to agriculture was by no means limited to railway construction and special railway rates. In all four colonies experimental farms and agricultural schools were established, and agricultural research was financed through special Agricultural Departments. Agricultural co-operation was encouraged in a number of ways; the Cape, for example, in 1905 authorised special loans to co-operative associations.

Transport costs inevitably loomed large in all trade questions, particularly during the years of depression, and the ocean shipping services with Europe came under severe public criticism. Mining development depended upon the importation of valuable machinery and manufactured stores, much of which needed speedy and regular shipping services. The shipping companies which provided such a service were therefore able to organise, in 1886, a Shipping Conference strong enough to enforce by means of a deferred rebate the carriage of all outward cargoes at profitable rates by their vessels, and the same restrictions were quickly applied to the smaller trade in South African exports. Shippers found it desirable to establish their own Association for collective bargaining in 1892: but the profitability of the shipping monopoly is manifest by the repeated attacks on its preserve by competing lines, which sought in particular a share in the trade in mining and agricultural machinery, and were readily supported by merchants in spite of the heavy penalty rates which the Conference exacted from them for spreading their business. The Conference weakened itself and aroused public indignation, but nevertheless maintained some of its power by admitting the German Hansa line in 1901, the Houston line in 1904 and the Prince line in 1905, following fierce freight wars. It was strong enough in May 1907 to upset the delicate balance of distribution of the transit trade to the Rand by suddenly raising its rates to Cape ports, so that an inter-colonial conference had at once to be called to adjust matters. After the appointment of the Royal Commission on Shipping Rings in 1907 it was clear that political union of the colonies would be promptly followed by legislation against the Shipping Conference.

The opportunities for economy in administration and extension of governmental activity created by the union, in May 1910, of the four colonies in one self-governing Dominion were greater than those which it offered for more effective economic co-operation between the people themselves.[1] Internal free trade had already been established, personal movement was already unrestricted so far as the

[1] South Africa Act, 1909 [9 Edw. 7, Ch. 9].

European population was concerned, and inter-colonial railway and customs conferences secured, if somewhat precariously, a South African rather than a narrowly localised view of trade and transport. From the standpoint of the individual citizen, Union affixed the seal of stability and permanence to conditions which had hitherto depended upon inter-governmental agreement. As regards government and administration, the substitution of one Parliament and four Provincial Councils for four small Parliaments may not have involved very large economies, and certain services which in any case require local administration, such as the provincial control of primary and perhaps secondary education, offered little possibility of economy; yet in the long run the replacement of four central administrations by one was bound to produce a gain not only in economy but also in efficiency. Reduction of staff could not result in an immediate large net saving of salaries, for all four colonies transferred generous pension and compensation commitments to the new Union Department of Finance; but at any rate the public servants and technical officers retained in the central administration were able by specialisation to accomplish much more than had hitherto been possible. To that fact one may attribute in part the great volume of legislation, regulation and information which has emanated, for instance, from the Union Department of Agriculture.

As regards governmental control of the railways, the South Africa Act in one respect widened the field for their use as an instrument of policy, and in another restricted the opportunities for so doing. With virtually the whole of the railways and harbours nationalised under one control, subsidy of one type of traffic from the receipts from another and discrimination between consignments according to their local or overseas origin or destination could be contrived on a still wider scale; but, on the other hand, the creation of a separate Railway and Harbours Fund, and the stipulation that the only permissible transfers from this account to the Consolidated Revenue Fund should be interest on invested capital, limited the use of the railways and harbours as a taxing instrument to such specific purposes of subsidy as could be secured within the railway and harbours accounts themselves. Thus, for example, the government monopoly of harbours has been made to yield a considerable net revenue which has been applied to railway purposes. Since Union the railway rates have continued to be used by successive Governments, exercising control through a Railway Board, to protect local produce in the inland markets, to subsidise branch lines, to subsidise the traffic in agricultural produce, industrial materials and exports by special "development" rates, to create inland centres of trade and industry by means of "distribution" rates, which penalise direct loading of small consignments from the ports to their destination, and finally to reduce the rates on long-distance traffic as compared with short-haul and high-rated consignments by enormously more than the difference in cost of carriage. The achievement of these aims has of course been dependent upon the possession of monopoly power to discriminate heavily against traffic which could "bear" a high rate. The disparity between high and low rates was already very wide in the first rate schedule of 1911. It was widened still further during and after the First World War, particularly in 1920, by the device of confining the lowering of rates, after the general war-time increases, to low-rated agricultural and mineral traffic, particularly for long hauls. These development rates had their desired effect of increasing the volume of traffic to which they applied, to such an extent that the railways have been compelled to incur heavy expenditure on specialised handling facilities at the terminals and specialised rolling stock (powerful locomotives and larger waggons), while at the same time the high-rated traffic, which hitherto bore the cost, failed to expand. Thus in 1928, 2,750,000 tons of high-rated goods brought in £19 million, while 19,000,000 tons of low-rated traffic yielded only £7 million. The continuance of this policy has proved to be dependent in recent years on the restriction of road-motor competition. New construction of branch lines into agricultural areas was embarked upon promptly after Union, the mileage of governmental lines being increased by over a third before the end of 1916 to a total of 9400 miles. Thereafter little new construction was added before 1923, in which year a new start was made with branch lines. In 1922 the 1400 miles of railway in South-West Africa came under Union Government control.

Little time was lost by the Union Government in legislating against the Shipping Conference, using as its weapon the attractive ocean mail contract. The Post Office Act of 1911 prevented the award of that contract to any shipping company adopting the deferred rebate system, with the result that the whole Conference abandoned this form of penalty clause and made a new agreement with shippers in order to permit a new mail contract in 1912. A share of the mail subsidy has been paid since 1883 by the United Kingdom. Though by 1883 the contract time for the voyage had been reduced to nineteen days, during the next forty years 1883–1923 little improvement was made on that speed. Better times were done in the 'nineties at a very high cost in fuel, but the contract time remained after Union at sixteen days fifteen hours. The mail contract must, however, be read in conjunction with freight agreements on government imports and on homeward produce, which have been negotiated together in one elaborate bargain, so that the terms of the mail contract have been sacrificed to secure concessions on commercial traffic. The whole character of South African trade has been transformed by the growth of a bulky export trade in produce in response to governmental encouragement of farming. In 1912 vessels sailing from Great Britain to South Africa were only filled with cargo to about one-third of their measurement capacity, and on the return voyage only one-fifth of their available space was occupied. In 1925 shipping proceeding from European ports to South Africa was approximately two-fifths full, while over two-thirds of the available space was occupied on the return journey. The outward trade from South Africa therefore attracted competing vessels, and the monopoly hold of the Conference lines was newly assailed.

The growth in the export of farm produce took place mainly in wool, sugar, hides and skins, maize and fruit. The fresh fruit trade is a new feature made possible since Union by refrigeration, encouraged by Government bargaining with shipping companies for maximum freight rates on fruit cargoes, and rigorously controlled by Government legislation. The earliest development after the war of 1899–1902 was in deciduous fruit—pears, grapes, peaches and plums—the trade expanding rapidly after the First World War to one million cases in 1922–3 and doubling again in five years. The citrus trade was almost negligible before Union, but its post-war expansion was even more rapid than that of deciduous fruits. In 1914 the Government took powers under the Fruit Export Act to provide for the inspection and grading of all fruit exports and for the registration of growers. Grading was further developed under an Agricultural Products Grading Act of 1922, and all exporters were required to pay a levy to finance a Fruitgrowers' Co-operative Exchange constituted under a Co-operative Societies Act of 1922. After 1925, by the terms of a Fruit Export Control Act, the whole business of shipment of fruit was conducted solely by a Control Board which reserved shipping space and spread the costs over exporters.

It has been observed that maize growing had been successfully introduced into the Eastern Province of the Cape before the period of the diamond discoveries. So well did it suit the regions of plentiful summer rainfall that maize rapidly came to be adopted as the staple crop and food of the African peoples in the Cape and Natal. The expansion of maize production was extraordinary. The local demand in the Transvaal for the feeding of the mine Africans on the Rand stimulated maize farming in the republic, and after 1902 the most suitable regions of the north and eastern Orange Free State, as well as the adjacent areas of the other colonies, were devoted increasingly to this crop under the combined stimulus of local demand, railway construction and favourable railway rates. After Union, government assistance and encouragement were redoubled. Experiment and research resulted in the introduction of improved types of maize, special railway rates were applied to develop a steady export trade, government grading was inaugurated, co-operative societies received special encouragement, and a chain of elevators at suitable points throughout the maize belt was linked by specialised rolling-stock to port elevators for bulk loading at Cape Town and Durban. In a good average post-war season nearly a million tons of maize were produced for local consumption and the same amount exported.

Wheat production, on the other hand, did not develop, despite a tariff, sufficiently to make South Africa self-supporting after the increase in population caused by the expansion of gold-mining in the 'nineties. Nor did the rapid expansion of maize-growing for export bring it to an importance comparable with that of the export trade in wool, which maintained throughout the period its predominant position among farm products. The demand of the worsted industry stimulated the improvement of merino strains, and the export of wool from Cape and Natal ports more than doubled in quantity between 1870 and 1898, mining development notwithstanding. The number of sheep was nearly halved by the South African War, setting back the exports from Natal for some years; but although the total number was not restored to the former figure of over twenty millions until about the time of Union, the yield of wool for export had by then increased 50 per cent as the result of improved breeding, the cultivation of drought feed-stuffs and the reduction of scab. Between 1910 and 1927 the exports of grease wool doubled again in weight and quadrupled in value, the trade in sheepskins keeping pace.

A growing export of hides and skins, particularly from Durban, testifies to the development of cattle-breeding in the interior since the last quarter of the nineteenth century, the rate of increase being particularly rapid since Union. The importation of pedigree cattle free of freight under the Ocean Mail Contract of 1912 tended to improve the general quality of stock and make possible the beginnings of an export trade in live cattle and meat.

In the sugar industry of Natal a variety of cane was introduced in the 'eighties which throve in the South African conditions, and the rate of expansion of the industry increased as a market developed on the Witwatersrand, particularly after 1902. The 1909 Customs Convention gave Natal an advantage in the internal market as against overseas competitors, although Mozambique sugar was admitted on equal terms under the *Modus Vivendi* and the 1909 Convention, and occasional competition from Mauritius was severe in the years before Union. Between 1910 and 1927 the output of sugar trebled, the acceleration after the First World War leading to a condition in which, with the price maintained at a high level in the Union by protection, there remained a growing surplus of production for export at the much lower world price. The dependence of the industry after 1859 on indentured Indian labour has already been noticed. The system of importing Indian coolies continued until 1911, since which time the industry has increasingly relied upon organised recruiting of Africans drawn from all over the Union. Since 1905 the Government, first of Natal and later of the Union, has involved itself in formal agreements arrived at by collective bargaining between the sugar planters and the millers concerning the terms of disposal of the crop. The basis of the successive agreements has in general been payment for cane by weight without reference to its sugar content, the price being dependent on the market price of sugar.

The Union Government soon turned its attention to the urgent problem of combating agricultural pests and livestock diseases. Neglect by any one farmer to deal at an early stage with a fresh outbreak brought to naught the best efforts of many others to eradicate these evils. Particularly where locusts were concerned, failure to report egg-laying and to destroy *voetgangers* repeatedly led to extensive loss of crops. The responsibilities of farmers were defined by an Agricultural Pests Act and a Diseases of Stock Act of 1911, and under subsequent legislation the Entomological Section of the Department of Agriculture was rapidly developed to conduct research and organise state assistance of a very varied character in the suppression of pests and in checking their dissemination.

One other governmental interest in farming must be noticed: the finance of land settlement and farming operations. The colonial and republican governments before the South African War had made it their object broadly to secure quickly as much revenue as possible from the lease and sale of public lands. After that war the four colonial governments endeavoured to combine this object as far as possible with the second one of encouraging land settlement by the offer of terms of payment adjusted to the nature of the farming to be undertaken. The Union Government supplemented the colonial legislation by its Land Settlement Act of 1912, giving power to Land Boards in each Province to advise in such matters as the value of land for disposal, the selection of settlers and the granting of financial assistance. The success of such schemes depends obviously upon the character and aptitude of the settlers who take up the land. It is fitting here to record the success since 1920 of the 1820 Memorial Settlers' Association in introducing suitable British settlers with capital, arranging for their training at appropriate farms and advising them in the selection of land for acquisition with the assistance of the Department of Lands. Between 1910 and 1927 over 12,500 settlers were allotted land, 26 million acres in area and £9 million in value, under the various Government Acts in force. Provision was made in each of the colonies before Union for advances of capital by a Government land bank to farmers on first mortgages of their land, and to agricultural co-operative societies. The land banks were absorbed by a Union Government Act of 1912 in a new Land and Agricultural Bank of South Africa, which commenced operations with a capital of nearly £3 million. The total capital fund was increased, mainly by additional Government appropriations, to over £10½ million by the end of 1927. In 1926 an Agricultural Credit Act provided for loans by the Land Bank to farmers against produce and personal security through the intermediation of regional loan companies and rural credit societies.

Parallel action to that concerning the land banks of the colonies was also taken on the subject of irrigation. Both the Cape and the Transvaal passed acts prior to Union in reference to irrigation schemes and the complex law of water-rights, and the Union Government in 1912 introduced legislation to provide for conserving and using the flow of rivers then largely running to waste, to control the distribution of water and preserve the vested rights of riparian owners. Regional Irrigation Boards were to be set up where the owners of two-thirds of an irrigable area were in favour, and the board could then proceed with schemes to be financed by rates on the land affected, loans being obtainable from the Government on the security of the rates. In 1928 there had been established one hundred and twelve Irrigation Boards mainly in the Cape and the Transvaal, and eighty-eight schemes had then been completed at a cost of £4½ million, the ratable area being 350,000 acres, in addition to a dam at Hartebeestpoort near Pretoria costing £1,600,000 and serving 40,000 acres. Many of the works constructed in 1919–23 proved unlikely to yield sufficient from rates to cover the high capital cost.

Railway and irrigation works and the financing of agricultural development increased the public debt of the Union steadily after 1910. South Africa's part in the First World War cost the Union about £38 million, most of which was added to the public debt. The Union Governments had resort increasingly to local borrowing, the external debt rising from £107 million in 1910 to £151 million in 1928, while the internal debt rose from £9 million to £87 million. The annual expenditure rose from £14¼ million in 1914–15 to nearly £30 million in 1920–21. A Currency Act in 1914 authorised the Government to declare the currency note issues of the commercial banks legal tender, and permitted an increase in the note issue on the deposit of securities with the Treasury. The circulation gradually increased thereafter to four times that of 1914. The issue of £1 and 10*s*. notes began early in the war, and an embargo on the export of gold became necessary in December 1915 (export to Mozambique being exempted until September 1919). South Africa did not return to the gold standard until 1925. Legislation in 1920 authorised the substitution of Treasury gold certificates, which were legal tender, for the gold reserves of the commercial banks, and these remained inconvertible so long as the South African currency remained below its gold par value. The Currency and Banking Act of 1920 also made provision for the creation on American lines of the South African Reserve Bank, to which was transferred the sole right of currency note issue in the Union. Reserve Bank notes were made legal tender in 1923 by an amending Act, which in addition prevented the commercial banks from exercising directing control over the central institution. The commercial banks were, however, required to maintain stipulated minimum reserves at the Reserve Bank against their liabilities. With the funds thus placed at its disposal the Reserve Bank earned considerably more than the maximum dividend which it might distribute to its shareholders, and the Union finances benefited from the surplus.

The gold-mining industry continued to prosper after Union. The output reached the figure of 9·3 million ounces in 1916, but thereafter it declined gradually until 1922, the year of a short but bitter strike of the white mine-workers, which is mentioned below. Nevertheless the proportion of the total world output of gold produced in the Transvaal rose steadily from one-third in 1910 to one-half in 1920, and that share has since been maintained. Falling costs of working, due largely to the increasing use of jack hammers in the mines, led to a steady expansion of production after 1922, the annual output reaching ten million ounces for the first time in 1927. Currency depreciation had involved an increase in working costs to the high figure of 25*s.* 8*d.* per ton of ore milled in 1920, but for the same reason the gold recovered realised 35*s.* 3*d.* per ton. After the return in 1925 to the former gold parity, the receipts per ton milled settled down in the neighbourhood of 28*s.*, while working costs were reduced once more to less than 20*s.*

The diamond-mining industry, successfully monopolised under one control by the beginning of the 'nineties, expanded its output rapidly in the twentieth century as the result of new discoveries. The rich Premier Mine in the Transvaal was opened up at the beginning of 1903, with the result that the production of diamonds in the Transvaal in 1908 (2,020,000 carats) actually exceeded for one year that of the Cape (1,590,000 carats), but the value (£1,550,000) was only one-half that of the Cape output. New mines were opened up between 1906 and 1912 just inside the Orange Free State border near Kimberley, and in 1913 the total production in the Union (5,160,000 carats) was valued at £11,390,000. South-West Africa had commenced production in 1909. The marketing of diamonds was in the hands of a diamond syndicate which endeavoured to avoid short period fluctuations in their value, and after the disturbances of the First World War the principal producers concluded an agreement to ration production and sell their agreed outputs through the syndicate. Their efforts to maintain values, despite forced sales in the post-war depression, stimulated new discoveries after the war in South Africa and elsewhere, and since the Union Government benefits greatly in revenue from the profitability of the industry, it began to concern itself with the selling policy of the producing companies. In 1925 it took powers to regulate the sale of mined diamonds, if necessary by conducting all marketing operations through its own board. Shortly thereafter new alluvial discoveries were made at Lichtenburg in the Transvaal and prices slumped, with the result that the government in 1927 included alluvial diamonds under its control and regulated new prospecting. Subsequent rich discoveries in Namaqualand were developed purely as a state concern.

The organisation of skilled workers into trade unions did not develop in South Africa on any significant scale until the gold-mining industry was well established. Wage-rates were high for the really skilled immigrant Europeans, and a strong incentive for collective bargaining did not present itself until, firstly, the introduction of Chinese labour and, secondly, the gradual acquiring of skill by the more experienced African workers aroused fears of the transfer of the less skilled tasks from Europeans to non-European labour working at the much lower rates of wages which employers offered them. Strikes on the mines in 1907, 1913 and 1914 led to the recognition of the South African Industrial Federation, as a representative organisation of white labour, by the Transvaal Chamber of Mines in 1915. The Union Parliament in 1911 issued regulations under a new Mines and Works Act to reserve thirty-two defined occupations on the mines for European labour, and in 1918 an additional nineteen occupations were added to the list by agreement. By this legal and conventional colour-bar European wage-rates were made at least temporarily secure.

Much of the skilled work was in fact increasingly left by the miners on occasion for African performance in contravention of the regulations, with the result that after the war the mine-owners' case for relaxation of the restrictions was strengthened by the knowledge that the Africans' capacity to undertake more skilled tasks could not seriously be questioned. In 1921, with the decline in the premium on the price of gold extracted, the Chamber of Mines proposed to terminate the agreement and open semi-skilled work to non-European labour. A fiercely contested strike followed in January 1922 involving both the coal-mines and the gold-mines and ending in bloodshed. The Chamber of Mines as a result limited its recognition of the trade unions to certain unions and applied its own ratio of white to black workers. At the end of 1923 the Courts in a test case declared the regulations which constituted the legal colour-bar under the Mines and Works Act of 1911 *ultra vires*; but the Chamber of Mines took no advantage of that judgment, and in 1925 the Government passed a regularising measure, which permitted the extension of the colour-bar by regulation to industrial as well as mining occupations.

Industry had by then become an important field for white employment. Lack of shipping and the concentration of the workshops of the world on munition work during the First World War had stimulated the manufacture in South Africa of consumption goods and productive equipment to meet local requirements. Wholesale prices of imported goods rose in the proportion 1000: 3185 between 1918 and 1920, while South African goods rose only in the ratio 1000:2249, and the combined index from 1000 to 2512. By 1922 the combined index had fallen again from 2512 to 1445. The renewed competition from overseas, with the fall in world prices in 1920, met with strong opposition from the organisations of employers and white employees which had grown up during the prosperous years. The white skilled workers were entrenched behind a series of statutory barricades against African encroachment upon their preserve. An Apprenticeship Act of 1922 and an Industrial Conciliation Act of 1924 made mandatory over every enterprise, in the industries covered, the agreements concerning conditions of entry into skilled trades and concerning wages and working hours and conditions, which were reached by representative committees of employers' associations and trade unions. A Wage Act of 1925 set up a Wage Board to regulate wages and working conditions in industries not covered by the Conciliation Act. The Wage Board was intended mainly to preserve minimum wage-rates for the lowest grade of "civilised labour", but it did not hesitate to fix rates and establish ratios of numbers of workers in all grades in the industries which it investigated. The average wage-rates of European men rose by 70 per cent between 1910 and 1920, and by 1922 fell again to about 40 per cent above the 1910 level, thereafter remaining fairly steady. Allowing for changes in the cost of living, there has been little change in the real wages of European workers during the whole period.

On the fruit, wine and wheat farms of the Western Province of the Cape agricultural labour remains predominantly Coloured or half-caste, working on long-term contracts for a daily wage varying from perhaps half-a-crown to one shilling with or without food and grazing or tillage rights. Throughout the rest of South Africa, the workers on European farms have always been Bantu and Indian, and the conditions of service are diverse in the extreme. There are at least one and a half million Africans living outside the Reserves on lands which have passed into European ownership. In many parts of the Transvaal and elsewhere European farmers simply settled on land on which Africans were already resident; in Natal the Africans themselves frequently came unchecked from the overcrowded Reserves to settle on European farms. Agricultural labour is of two types: wage-earners paid in cash or partly or wholly in kind, and labour-tenants giving service for the privilege of "squatting" with their families. As for the wage-earners, a hundred years ago and until recent times the customary payment for African workers from the Reserves was cattle—maybe, a cow and a calf and keep for a year's service. Gradually, wages other than cattle have become the general rule. The stream of young African men from the Reserves has grown for a number of reasons. Their demand for the merchandise offered by European traders has grown until the barter of surplus produce from the Reserves could no longer suffice to satisfy their needs, taxation has increased, and African women show a preference for husbands who have worked for a period outside the Reserves. Where wages are paid at all in cash, the amount for a male adult may be anything from five to forty shillings a month, the lower wages being supplemented by rations, the occasional carcase of a dead animal, old clothing and similar perquisites. A wage-earner may also be allowed to cultivate some land or graze some cattle on the lands of his employer. Where farming is carried on all the year round, labour contracts are for long periods and are sternly enforced under the Masters and Servants Acts; movement is difficult and local differences of wages may therefore persist indefinitely. More generally, however, hired labourers are required only from the ploughing to the reaping period. Reapers may be paid piecework, and sheep-shearers are frequently paid in this way (maybe ten shillings per hundred sheep, i.e. five days' work, with food).

The sugar industry of Natal maintains a recruiting organisation for its labour similar to that of the mines. Labour tenancy is widespread, particularly outside the Cape Province. It gives rise increasingly to dissatisfaction. From the Africans' side there is no security and therefore cultivation remains primitive. In Natal, the term of service is normally six months, and elsewhere ninety days. The whole family is bound to serve in return for the right to occupy and cultivate a piece of land and to graze such animals as they may possess. There may be other occasional perquisites. The European farmer expects the young adults to stay and serve, but, as parental control weakens, they tend to go off and the family may be evicted. If, on the other hand, the whole family wishes to move, the pass system and disputes concerning the service due impose impediments. Such mobility as remains tends therefore to be involuntary. In such conditions dissatisfaction is rife, and there is a growing measure of agreement that the introduction of wage-payment on the one hand and more precise terms of land tenure on the other must eventually work to the advantage of both sides.

Since the latter part of the nineteenth century new land had become increasingly scarce for the sons of farmers, and with the gradual transition from subsistence farming to production on a credit basis for a fluctuating market, existing farmers often became dispossessed by bankruptcy, particularly in areas which were liable to drought. For these reasons alone there emerged a landless class of Europeans, who lived as *bywoners*[1] on the farms of others or sought unskilled work in the towns and depended largely on sentiment for preferential treatment in their competition with Coloured and African workers. The magnitude and complexity of this Poor White problem was,

[1] Squatters, or tenants-at-will.

however, increased by a number of other causes, such as the attitude to life acquired through existence on alluvial diamond diggings, the dislocation and destruction of farms in the war period 1899–1902, the urban unemployment during the post-war depressions, and the wide gap between the earnings of skilled and unskilled workers on account of the concentration of the African and Coloured populations at the bottom. Estimates of the numbers of these unfortunate people varied widely on account partly of differing definitions of indigence, and the generally accepted figure of 8 per cent of the total European population has therefore to be used with reserve; but the existence of widespread destitution was undeniable, and many palliatives were inaugurated by private and public agencies. In addition to relief, government authorities responded to public insistence that government enterprises such as the railways should adopt a "civilised labour" policy, which implies the payment of higher wages to Europeans than their Coloured and African competitors would have been glad to accept for the work.

The wage legislation just described was also largely a response to the same pressure, and attempts were made to divert detribalised Africans from fields in which it was hoped to substitute Europeans. Gradually, however, it became more generally realised that cost-raising devices reduced the capacity of the rest of industry to give employment, and accentuated the pressure of the displaced non-European workers in those spheres. More attention was also paid to the possibility of eradicating the causes. The state encouraged and assisted existing church endeavour in this field; training centres in the form of agricultural labour colonies were maintained for those Europeans who might prove suitable for settlement on the land; special educational provision was made for juveniles, and co-operative institutions were encouraged, as we have seen, with the object of reducing the number of farming failures. Nevertheless, underlying the problem, "civilised labour" policies continued to exert an important and, viewed as a whole, a restrictive effect on the rate of economic development; and they worsened the unhappy lot of the urban Africans who subsisted at the very bottom of the social scale.

After 1920 the burden of high wages was in part transferred from the employers in the new industries to other sections of the population by increases in tariff protection, particularly that afforded by the customs tariff schedule of 1925 and subsequent years. Apart from specific duties, the Union Government in a Customs Tariff Act of 1914 levied a general *ad valorem* rate of 15 per cent, which was raised in 1915 to 20 per cent. After 1918 embargoes and special protective duties were applied to particular imports following the establishment of a tariff advisory board (the Board of Trade and Industries) in 1921, and the 1925 schedule greatly extended the range of protective duties. Imperial preference appeared in all the customs tariffs in the form of a 3 per cent rebate until 1925, when the amount of the rebate was made to vary with the commodity and at the same time the total extent of the concession was reduced. In the Tariff Act of 1914 special duties were authorised against dumping, and these provisions were considerably modified by the post-war legislation culminating in the Act of 1925.

Beyond the northern boundary of the Union, economic development took much the same course. The settlement of Southern Rhodesia proceeded steadily after the war and the completion of the railway to Salisbury in 1902. The European population increased from 12,500 in 1904 to 23,600 in 1911, but it is significant that in that year well over one-third lived in Bulawayo and the capital, Salisbury, and the same was still true in 1921, when the European population was 33,600. In that year a quarter of the occupied European population of 14,700 were engaged in agriculture, the next largest occupations being commerce, the public services and mining. There were, however, ten times as many male Africans in European employment, 40 per cent being engaged in agriculture and 30 per cent in mining. Early agricultural production consisted mainly of maize, grown as a foodstuff for local African consumption, and tobacco. The production of maize expanded until after 1918 the amount available for export normally equalled the local consumption, which itself had grown rapidly with the increase in the African mining population. Tobacco growing also increased rapidly under official encouragement, particularly after 1918, the bulk of the leaf being purchased by manufacturers in the Union of South Africa. Cattle-rearing by both European and African ranchers has developed steadily, yet by far the greatest contribution to the export trade has always been made by the mining industry. Following the promulgation of revised mining regulations in 1903, gold production proceeded in several parts of the country on the basis of royalty payments by the claim-holders to the British South Africa Company. Down to 1923 gold to the value of £57 million had been recovered, the annual export averaging well over £2 million in recent years. The discovery of extensive coal deposits at Wankie led in 1904 to the construction of the railway northward through Wankie over the Zambesi at the Victoria Falls into Northern Rhodesia. The line was extended to the Broken Hill zinc and lead mines in 1906 and to the Congo border in 1909. The coal-mining industry was rapidly developed for local consumption, particularly by the railways and mines, and for export northward to the Katanga copper mines. Since 1908 there has also occurred a rapid development of the production of high-grade asbestos and chromite.

This chapter opened with an account of the manner of life of the South African people at the end of the eighteenth century; it may well close with a similar view one hundred and thirty years later. In

1925 about one-third of the European population of nearly one and three-quarter millions were working for gain, and there were in the direct employ of Europeans about three times as many non-Europeans as European workers. The value of the national production in 1923 was estimated by an Economic and Wage Commission at £186 million. Farming contributed a quarter of the whole, and provided a living for over a third of the European men and three times as many other workers, but, whereas at the end of the eighteenth century the Cape population provided food not only for itself but also for the ships that called in Table Bay, by the opening of the twentieth century South African farming had ceased to produce enough wheat for the population; the country was no longer self-sufficient in food. Mining, employing only one-twentieth of the European workers but nine times as many Africans, yielded in 1923 one-fifth of the national income. Industry, with a fifth of the European men and one and a half times as many non-Europeans, produced one-sixth of the total. Only one-quarter of the entire population lived in towns or villages, but these included three-fifths of the Europeans and nearly one-half of the Coloured or mixed population. Of the urban districts, Johannesburg and Cape Town alone had more than 100,000 European inhabitants, and only fifteen towns numbered more than 20,000 population of all races. The Rand mining towns together comprised at least one-fifth of the entire white population.

Since the beginning of the twentieth century, the European population has grown mainly by natural increase rather than immigration. Less than one-sixth in 1921 was born outside the Union. The educational system has virtually abolished illiteracy among the Europeans, though not among the rest of the inhabitants of the country.

European farming and mining are alike dependent upon predominantly African labour, and the continuance of the supply has provided a major preoccupation for at least the past fifty years. The paradoxical situation in which a scarcity of African labour is accompanied by average wages of about one-quarter (including rations) of those paid to Europeans is explained in part by the peculiarities of the labour supply. So long as the African peoples remain out of contact with European modes of life, the wage incentive exerts only a limited influence upon their willingness to work for European employers. In so far as Africans work for only a more or less fixed sum, whether to pay taxes or to purchase commodities, higher rates of wages may for a period actually reduce the amount of work which they are willing to do. In so far, however, as the African peoples are encouraged to adopt European modes of life and to acquire new wants, it becomes more probable that higher rates of wages will have their more usual effect of increasing the labour supply.

CHAPTER XXX

SOCIAL AND ECONOMIC DEVELOPMENTS IN NATIVE TRIBAL LIFE

AMONGST the primitive cultures of the world that of the South African tribes at the time of their first contact with the European colonists takes a high place. Their languages and social organisation were highly developed. What Robert Moffat, the famous L.M.S. missionary of Kuruman, had said of the state of culture amongst the Barolong in the eighteen-twenties was very generally true of all South African Bantu tribes. Skill in the smelting and working of iron, in carving implements and utensils from wood, in weaving baskets and making pottery was widespread; most tribes depended upon agriculture as well as pasture for their subsistence.

Before ever the Africans were seriously menaced by European expansion into the interior, the picture of their tribal life was one of considerable turmoil. This confusion is usually attributed to the ravages of the Zulu, Matabele and Mantati tribes whom despotic Chiefs had drilled into efficient fighting organisations, but there is little doubt that an intense competition amongst the tribes for sowing and grazing lands was a universal cause of strife. In and near Moffat and Livingstone's Bechuanaland, tribal life was in an incessant commotion caused by the raids and migrations of tribes seeking to maintain themselves in a country of scanty rainfall and low fertility. In the more generously watered belt from the Zoutpansberg Mountains to Swaziland and thence by way of Natal to the Cape eastern frontier, a large tribal population had been packed, living there not in a land of wide and generous acres but in circumstances already of some discomfort. Contrary to accepted belief, the economic condition of most South African tribes was not one of savage or even "subtropical" ease; it was spare, with no great powers of resisting the pressure of advancing colonists.

Native policies in South Africa since the First World War have been too much influenced by the uncritically accepted belief that the Native population is increasing at a rate that threatens to overwhelm the whites within a relatively short period;[1] but the Native policies, such as they were, of much of the nineteenth century were based upon the opposite assumption. Throughout that century there was a gross underestimation of the Native population and there was therefore a belief that the tribes possessed more land than they could use, even though Transvaal farmers could speak of "surplus" Natives, and Cape

[1] See *Census Report*, 1921.

frontiersmen of tribal territories "teeming" with cattle without appreciating the contradiction.

Earlier underestimation caused later and more accurate enumeration to indicate an all too phenomenal increase. Precisely because of the unreliability of most nineteenth-century statistics it is impossible to compute even approximately the amount of error, though it is easily demonstrable that the increase in numbers of the African population was never such as to be alarmingly disproportionate to that of the whites. There is less value than may be supposed in the comment that the suppression by European influence of internecine strife meant a great increase in the rate of survival. The death roll in purely Native wars was never high, and there is even much reason to suppose that the devastation of the Zulu, Matabele and Mantati "hordes" was very greatly exaggerated. Even in their wars with the Europeans, although occasional commandos and military expeditions resulted in bloody encounters, it was notorious that the Natives lost few lives. Sir Harry Smith's "drive" on the Eastern Frontier in 1851 and the long agony of the Basuto wars were more cattle-raids than genuine warfare.[1]

The confusion of the eighteen-twenties saw much displacement of tribes and a surging hither and thither before the attacks of the warlike Zulus and Matabele. When these were broken, the fugitives poured back into their lands, for example in Natal and the western Transvaal, and a new mixing of peoples thus took place.

It is most unlikely that there has been any significant improvement in the conditions of life amongst the tribes within a recent period. Amongst the African women of the Eastern Frontier abortion was universally practised in the mid-nineteenth century,[2] and the practice, not limited to that Frontier, for women not to cohabit with their husbands during the period of suckling was well known as a limitation on population. Infantile mortality, always high amongst primitive societies, was stated by the French missionary Casalis to be much higher amongst the Basuto than in Europe.[3] The undermining effects of tuberculosis for which the greasy unabsorbent cotton clothing was partly responsible, measles, almost chronic typhus, much dysentery and widespread addiction to the smoking of Indian hemp were all seriously felt. There was more than mere reviling in the remark of Kreli, the Xhosa chief, that he hated the smell of Africans who kept European clothing on their unwashed bodies till it almost decayed. From certain indications it would even appear that deficiency diseases sapped the vitality of the young and weakened the old. When harvests were bad and often even when they were "normal", food shortage usually made itself felt every winter about the

[1] de Kiewiet, C. W., *British Colonial Policy and the South African Republics*, chap. III.

[2] Maclean, J., *A Compendium of Kafir Laws*, p. 62.

[3] Casalis, E., *The Basutos*, p. 193.

month of August,[1] becoming worse until December when the cows began to calve and gave milk. The maize was hardly fit for use before the middle of January. In the late 'thirties traders were already buying "surplus" corn which the tribesmen had to buy back later on.[2] Even when actual want was not experienced, a too continuous diet of maize produced scurvy, and Casalis made the suggestive observation that the Basuto always looked healthier in the season when the *imfe* or sweet reed ripened.[3] Meat, more especially after white hunters had driven off the game, was sparingly eaten.

Polygamy could not have been the cause of a great increase in population any more than the cessation of tribal wars. Not only did polygamy decrease in the course of the century, but it never was quite so universal as was frequently claimed by those to whom the practice was anathema. Tribal conditions were not in the main such as to affect profoundly the biological ratio between the sexes. The available evidence suggests that polygamy was somewhat more common in areas such as Natal that had suffered most from Zulu raids.[4] In one Natal district the magistrate counted 600 wives to 201 men, of whom, however, 54 had two wives and 52 only one. In Basutoland and on the Eastern Frontier it was common enough to attract attention, but it was far from universal. Its extent depended upon the fortune of the average individual, and the fortune of the Natives in cattle, even in the more spacious early days, was such as to limit very appreciably the possibilities of widespread polygamy. A census of the Ndlambi and Gaika districts of the Eastern Frontier in 1848,[5] even though its value is seriously limited by the inevitable inaccuracies of such counting as was possible by the handful of overworked Native officials and by the conditions that prevailed after the recent war, nevertheless gives an acceptable ratio between the numbers of men and women, the possible error being less intrusive in ratios between figures that are subject to the same defects. Counts in fourteen separate kraals gave only three kraals in which the number of wives was greater than that of the total men, with a ratio for the whole Gaika district of 100 wives to 107 men, and for the Ndlambi district of 100 wives to 101 men. The ratio of total men to total women tells practically the same story—in the Gaika district 100 men to 117 women. The number of males was less than it normally would have been on account of losses in the recent War of the Axe.

Although less validity can obviously be given to conclusions based upon a computation of the number of cattle so soon after a war, it is not without significance that in the Gaika district there was 0·74 head of cattle to every individual of the computed population, or 2·9 per

[1] Backhouse, J., *Extracts*, II, p. 43.
[2] *Ibid.*, II, p. 48.
[3] Casalis, E., *The Basutos*, p. 168.
[4] Holden, W. C., *Past and Future*, pp. 138–40.
[5] Maclean, J., *A Compendium of Kafir Laws*, pp. 149, 150.

head of the male population. The figures take on some increased value from the fact that other available ratios for different tribal areas show a reasonably close approximation, and do afford some reliable indication that the average fortune of the individual not only would not permit a universal plurality of wives, but actually that numbers of males were without the means to pay the bride-price for even a single wife. On the Eastern Frontier the majority of married men, according to the missionary William Shaw, had not more "than one lawful or recognised wife for each man".[1]

The conclusion that the South African Native population, not only on the Eastern Frontier but elsewhere as well, was consistently underestimated during the nineteenth century becomes even more important with the knowledge that at an early date the tribesmen were suffering from the hardships of too little land to a much greater degree than is usually conceded. Too little land in South Africa does not mean altogether a deficiency of acres; mere extent is a notoriously misleading index to the value of land in the subcontinent. Irregular and deficient rainfall, stretches of sandy, rocky or shallow soil greatly reduce the available arable land, and make it imperative for flocks to roam over wide areas. The scratching of the soil that passed for ploughing in African agriculture, the wasteful sowing of ungraded grain and an utter indifference to the use of animal manure exhausted the soil and necessitated continual alternation between tilled land and fallow.

Like the goats that nibbled away the grass and scrub from the gaunt slopes of ancient Greece, producing naked and eroded hill-sides and robbing Athens of its firewood, so the heavy demands of Bantu cattle on the limited resources of the reserves brought most of them to the extreme limit of overstocking. The heavy concentration of stock (overstocking being due rather to lack of space than to really large numbers of cattle) destroyed the natural covering of the soil, which tended to be blown off by the parching winds or washed away by heavy rain. The Natives, moreover, did not willingly live far from their source of firewood. One of the reasons which brought the Griquas together at the fountains was the comparative absence of firewood elsewhere in the land beyond the Orange River. In parts of Natal the lack of firewood was acutely felt, and much of Kaffraria was either naturally destitute of bush or it had been hacked and burned away in the course of generations.[2] And thus while to a colonist's eye the very conservative number of 300,000 Africans given in Maclean's *A Compendium of Kafir Laws* only peopled the Eastern Frontier thinly, closer observation in 1850 showed that the great number of Eastern Frontier Natives were so pressed for land that removals had become exceedingly infrequent. As early as 1833 the Eastern Frontier tribes were "so thronged upon

[1] Shaw, W., *Story of my Mission*, p. 420.
[2] Maclean, J., *A Compendium of Kafir Laws*, p. 4.

each other" that the missionary James Clark could make the startlingly true prophecy that the first drought would cause widespread starvation.[1] Everywhere the best land was occupied. Kraals in old and exhausted land had no good virgin soil on which to move, so that many kraals had occupied the same site for two and three generations[2] and had to fight hard to maintain themselves against their own neighbours.

In 1850 there was more land available than a decade later. The effect of the war of 1850 and the great cattle-killing of 1857 was to throw open the way to yet more dispossession. In 1858 Sir George Grey confiscated tribal lands almost gladly, leaving the tribes, who were temporarily dispersed in search of work with the farmers, to come back to lands so limited that their lot before 1850 seemed spacious by comparison.

Since the 'forties and earlier, the cow and calf with keep that had been the reward of a year's service with European farmers had already been a welcome addition to the reserve Natives' scanty resources. From the cattle-killing of 1857 onwards tribal organisation on the Eastern Frontier had to bear the full weight of a congestion so extreme that thenceforth the additional income derived from service with white colonists became essential to the maintenance of even the lowest level of subsistence. Even though the number of private locations on European farms relieved some of the congestion in the Native territories, there is evidence that in these very territories there was already a portion of the population without any land, and a distinction had arisen such as tribal economic organisation had never known between those who were fortunate enough to cultivate a patch of land, and those who, for lack of land, squatted on that of their fellow-tribesmen.[3] Their condition without doubt was much more miserable than that of the submerged tenth of the rural population in pre-revolutionary France with their cow, a fruit tree and a morsel of land. Without land for all in the tribe, one of the keystones of tribal life had been wrenched away. The tendency towards an unequal division of land weakened the communal organisation of the tribe without really producing a system of private ownership. Such later experiments as were tried in the Transkei after 1894 to introduce private ownership were seriously compromised by the heavy squatting of tribesmen on almost every available piece of land.[4]

In 1864 the frontier colonists still believed in the myth of "unsettled acres" behind the Eastern Frontier Kaffirs so spacious that thousands of Europeans might profitably and conveniently settle there without hardship to the tribal population.[5] Yet Governor Wodehouse

[1] Macmillan, W. M., *Bantu, Boer and Briton*, p. 73.
[2] Maclean, J., *A Compendium of Kafir Laws*, p. 150.
[3] Brownlee, C., *Reminiscences*, p. 71.
[4] *Vide supra*, p. 558.
[5] 50,000, according to one estimate; *vide* Theal, G. M., *Hist. of S. Africa since 1795*, v. pp. 65 *sqq*.

discovered on a personal tour beyond the Kei in 1862 that the territory beyond the Bashee, into which the hapless chief Kreli had been unceremoniously bundled for his "rebellious intentions" in 1857, could not maintain his followers. It was also seen that his removal still deeper into Kaffraria would be challenged by those already there. It was not then mere nostalgia that kept Kreli pacing the Bashee's banks like some caged beast. Throughout the length and breadth of Kaffraria there was indeed such a scuffling and jostling as competition for land alone could explain. Most fortunate for the fate of Kaffraria was it that Wodehouse restored a part of Kreli's former possessions between the Kei and the Bashee, and prevented the conversion of all Kaffraria into an area of mixed European and Native settlement like British Kaffraria.[1] Even then Kaffraria would assuredly have been deluged with Basuto after the disastrous second Basuto War, had not the Free State farmers and the opportune discovery of the Diamond Fields given employment to large numbers of them.

The story of the loss by the Basuto of their best grazing and sowing lands and their *refoulement* to the mountains and the narrow valleys of the Drakensberg has been told in an earlier chapter.[2] In the days of the Orange River Sovereignty the troubles of the unhappy British Resident Major Warden had been due partly to the apathy of the farmers and partly to the lack of financial and military support from the British Government. The main cause of his embarrassment, however, had been that at this early date the tribes of the Basuto border were trampling on each other's toes for want of room. His reckless distribution of largesse to the farmers in the shape of border farms, without regard to original Native settlement, had fiercely aggravated an already extremely dangerous situation. In 1853 after one glance at the Basuto border, Sir George Clerk, Her Majesty's Commissioner for regulating the affairs of the Sovereignty prior to abandonment, threw up his hands in despair at the inextricable confusion that met his eyes, and refused to burn his fingers by making any effort to separate the Europeans and Natives who lived there cheek by jowl.

If at first the new republican administration, conscious of exceeding weakness, was disposed to attempt an impartial settlement, it was soon clear that the expulsion of the frontier Natives from their land was the only solution the frontier farmers would accept. Again the familiar cry of cattle thieving was raised; unprincipled whites fished in troubled waters by smuggling guns[3] and buying stolen cattle; yet the Basuto wars of 1858 and 1865 were essentially land wars. Such fertile and well-watered land as that on the Basuto border could scarcely be found elsewhere in the Free State; yet for all its fertility the Natives' need for that land was so great that in 1861 the French missionaries

[1] de Kiewiet, C. W., *British Colonial Policy and the South African Republics*, p. 166.

[2] *Vide supra*, pp. 434.

[3] Casalis, E., *The Basutos*.

noticed a congestion of cattle and horses in Basutoland and frequent disputes arising from encroachments amongst the Natives themselves.[1] Though worsted in the war of 1858, the farmers succeeded in the conflict of 1865–8 in wresting from the Basuto so much of their best land, as well as such droves of cattle that Sir Harry Smith's description of the wars on the Cape Eastern Frontier as a sort of Smithfield cattle-driving was applicable on the Basuto border too. Consequently the Basutoland that Wodehouse annexed in 1868 was shorn of its finest arable land. Basutoland then joined the Eastern Frontier as a tribal area that could not support itself. The effect of the disaster upon Basuto life was evident in the crowds that sought work on the Diamond Fields and with the victorious farmers.

Diminished as it was, Basutoland was nevertheless guaranteed against further attack by the British annexation and remained a highly important reserve in probably the most important tribal area in South Africa. Henceforth, however, Basuto life had of necessity to undergo rapid transformation. With the loss of the Conquered Territory, Basutoland became a country covered over two-thirds of its area with the jumbled and inhospitable formation of the Maluti Mountains, with valleys so narrow that there was little ground that could be cultivated. To this country the Basuto had to adapt themselves. On land once used in extremity for summer pasturing, huts were built and crops grown, both at great expense of labour, for with the conquered lowlands had gone also the most plentiful supply of thatching material, and the patches on the hill-sides steadily lost their scanty soil by erosion to the same Conquered Territory. Erosion in Basutoland was accelerated by the need for fuel and the close cropping of the herds. Except in the extreme south-east portion nearly all the scrub and large timber was rapidly exhausted, and this combined with the close cropping of the Basuto livestock to deprive the soil of the protection the binding roots gave against the mountain torrents. In 1868 Basutoland was clearly unable to support its population; since then both the population and the number of cattle have increased, though the natural resources have decreased rather than increased. In a country a great part of which is useless for either cultivation or pasture there were, in 1920, 43 persons and nearly 300 head of livestock per square mile, figures that indicate an extreme degree of overcrowding, and that explain why, in 1911, 84,600 persons, about one person in every five and presumably mostly males, left Basutoland for periods averaging four months to earn the deficit in their country's production.

Of the motives for the British annexation of Natal in 1843 the need of protecting the Natives against the land-hungry farmers was strongly felt, even though Earl Grey thought that the areas to be set aside for tribal use should enable each European immigrant to "draw supplies

[1] See Galton, F., *The Narrative of an Explorer*, pp. 69–70.

of labour from the location in his more immediate proximity".[1] His intention was however a generous provision of land. The task, promptly assumed by the British administration, of setting aside enough land for Natal's tribal population was characteristically complicated by the gross ignorance on the part of colonists and officials of the number to be provided for. By the emigrant farmers it was claimed that Natal had been empty of Natives in 1838;[2] their demand that the "invaders" be segregated in the "empty" territory to the south of the colony was even at one time entertained by Shepstone. The reserves into which Shepstone in the end skilfully moved the Native population have usually been regarded as adequate at the time of their creation.[3] Even though the Natal Natives were better off than those on the Eastern Frontier, actually it was the almost unchecked squatting on European-owned land and the understanding rule of Shepstone that saved Natal for more than half a century from most of the discontents and evil consequences of a provision of reserve land that was inadequate from the beginning. The extent of squatting was at least 10 per cent, and most probably more, of the population. No small portion of the reserves was broken, precipitous and rocky, or sandy and barren. According to the American missionary Aldin Grout, whose knowledge was first-hand, it was land suited only to the habitation of "the owl and the eagle, the baboon and the jackal". Grout's probably too conservative estimate of 50,000 as the Native population of the three reserves, Inanda, Umvoti and Umlazi, gave nevertheless a density of 55 persons per square mile, or 11½ acres of mixed arable land and "baboon rock" per individual.[4] Of the Impofana location with 450,000 acres a considerable portion was, according to its magistrate, George Peppercorn, as worthless as the sands of Arabia. It was his opinion that no more than 2000 acres were available for the cultivation of the Native crops, while much of the pasture was unsatisfactory except in the summer months. Patches of good soil of more than five acres contiguous extent were rare enough to be remarkable, and he noticed that many small kraals were so placed that they could not cultivate at all, being therefore forced to barter their goats for the grain of those who were more happily placed. Such a situation contained the same distinction, already noticed in the tribal areas of the Cape Eastern Frontier, between those Natives who had land and those who had too little or none. The average extent of cultivation per hut of four or five persons was three-quarters of an acre. Only by constant change of pasture were the Natives able to keep up the numbers of their stock.[5] Such conditions, which were clearly not confined to the

[1] Quoted by Brookes, E. H., *History of Native Policy*, p. 327.

[2] Evidence of L. Grout in *Natal Native Commission*, 1852, pt. IV, p. 61; cf. also Holden, W. C., *op. cit.* p. 137.

[3] Cf. Macmillan, W. M., *Bantu, Boer and Briton*, p. 303.

[4] *Natal Native Commission*, pt. IV, pp. 50–3.

[5] *Ibid.*, pt. III, p. 66.

Impofana location alone, indicated a discomfort almost as extreme as existed on the older Eastern Frontier of the Cape Colony. Yet these were the reserves which Natal colonists clamoured should be reduced still further, so as to break down the tribal power of the Africans and force forth an "abundant and continuous supply of Kaffir labour".[1]

Wodehouse's annexation of Basutoland in 1868 had left the Free State without any Native problem of importance, but the Transvaal long lay beyond the limits of possible British interference. There the Trekkers were free, except for the interlude ended by Gladstone's Midlothian campaign (1877–1881), to apply their conception of the proper relations between Europeans and subject Native tribes. Their belief was that the Transvaal had been "captured" from the Matabele, and that by virtue of that conquest all tribes within the limits of the Transvaal held their land of the republic. From 1852 to 1899 the Transvaal Natives were treated mainly as a military problem. During the greater part of its existence the Transvaal Government had neither the strength nor the financial means to attempt the administration of the tribes. In the absence of civil control by magistrates rigorous military subjugation by commandos was the only alternative. Transvaal Native policy meant that the Natives were denied all civil and political rights. Such treaties as the Government signed with the Chief were instruments designed to legalise dispossession. Restrained only by the limitations of malaria and the tsetse fly, the farmers settled regardless of the Native population, turning whole tribes into rightless squatters. Resistance usually provoked a commando and the punishment of the "rebels". In the Zoutpansberg and in the Low Veld the climate and the resistance of thickly populated tribal areas somewhat checked the movement of dispossession; elsewhere the bulk of the Natives lost their land to such an extent that in the Transvaal a proportion of the Natives higher than elsewhere in South Africa came to be resident upon land owned by Europeans. And in the land boom of the decade before the South African War many farms in the little used and torrid Low Veld passed into the hands of land companies, even though they were inhabited by a numerous Native population.

Thus on the eve of the South African War (1899) the Native tribes throughout the length and breadth of South Africa lived on land owned by Europeans, or were huddled into reserves that were like islands in an ocean of European settlement.[2] This universal congestion of the Native population as the result of white pressure was followed inevitably by heavy inroads on Native stock. Even in the heyday of their independence, the Natives had not possessed "teeming" herds; their herds at all times were relatively small. But the place of cattle in the Native economy was of the greatest importance. They were the means of obtaining wives, the source of food and

[1] Brookes, E. H., *History of Native Policy*, p. 54.
[2] See Macmillan, W. M., *Complex South Africa*, p. 127, for modern figures.

clothing and the sole wealth. Whatever affected the cattle of the tribe affected its entire being.

The discontents that led to war on the Cape Eastern Frontier were not unusually associated with periods of hardship when drought caused the crops to fail and the cattle to perish. The crop failures of 1892, followed by a desolating plague of locusts in 1893, were not singular visitations. The droughts of 1834 and 1839, the hungry 'forties on the Eastern Frontier, the fearsome disease that decimated the herds in the 'fifties and the long agony of almost a decade of droughts in the 'sixties were bitter trials to the Native population. Only unwillingly did they eat or sell their cattle. In the early days of Native trading at the Fort Willshire fairs, the Natives brought gum, tusks and ostrich feathers, but no cattle. After 1850 trade in cattle was sometimes almost brisk; Basutoland, at all events, exported from 1860 onwards thousands of cattle to the Cape Colony every year.[1] Some of these could be exchanged for guns, "Cape smoke" and truck, but the Natives acted too often under the same compulsion as the brothers of Joseph, bartering their cattle for food that they might "live and not die".

New needs, blankets, truck, tea, coffee and sugar, occasional ploughs and waggons, and especially the growing burden of taxes were a heavy drain on cattle resources. So far from the truth were those who claimed that the Natives had merely to dispose of a few cattle to pay their taxes that in the Inanda reserve in Natal, "good scenery" but bad for cattle, the Natives early reached the point where they refused any longer to part with more of their herds. Out of a total of £1918. 7*s*. 0*d*. paid in taxes in 1851 only £35 was paid in cattle.[2] In the Impofana location, Magistrate Peppercorn indicated that this applied equally to the entire Natal Native population. The stock of this single location had been so seriously depleted in two years since 1850 that kraals of two and three huts no longer possessed any cattle.[3] For the larger kraals small herds of about twelve head were the average, so that the total population, which he estimated conservatively at about 6000 persons, actually possessed no more than 5000 head of cattle or 0·82 per head of estimated population. Granted the liability of such estimates to error, it is none the less striking that they tally with independent counts elsewhere. In the Gaika reserve on the Cape Eastern Frontier just after the war of 1846, there were, as was mentioned above,[4] 0·74 head of cattle per head of estimated population, in the Ndlambi location 1·02, while in British Kaffraria in 1864 the figure was still as low as 0·76. It is remarkable again that the Fingos of Peddie, accounted as unusually prosperous, should give a count of only 1·07. Error in counting cattle would be offset somewhat

[1] Casalis, E., *The Basutos*, pp. 169–70.
[2] *Natal Native Commission*, 1852 , pt. v, pp. 7 *sqq*.
[3] *Ibid*. pt. iv, pp. 9 *sqq*.
[4] Holden, W. C., *Past and Future*, pp. 134–5.

by errors in counting population, but not even the most generous allowance for error could disturb the fact that the number of cattle possessed by the Natives was at all times exceedingly low, and that as early as 1843 many of the Eastern Frontier Natives were entirely without cattle. The serious drain upon cattle resources rapidly reached the point where the equilibrium was upset with a resulting heavy strain on the social and economic life of the tribes.

Cattle played an essential part in marriage customs; *lobola* or the bride-price was paid in cattle to the family of the young man's bride.[1] At no time was either the wealth of the Natives or the disparity between the numbers of men and women such as to permit universal polygamy. What is more significant is that at an early date the young men on the Eastern Frontier and in Basutoland and Natal experienced difficulty in obtaining even one wife. While the *lobola* for Chiefs on the Eastern Frontier could be as high as twenty head of cattle, for an ordinary tribesman the amount lay between four and ten head. This figure would appear to hold for most Native tribes and does not seem to have varied greatly during the century; yet even such a low number of *lobola* cattle as four meant considerable waiting for the young man. One of the chief explanations of the growth of monogamy to the point in 1921 when the monogamous were ten times as numerous as the polygamous marriages was the dire poverty of the Reserves. It was this poverty, particularly in its effect upon marriage, that was one of the most efficient causes in forcing the African population out to work for the Europeans.

The inability of the land to assure many of the tribes an adequate food supply or to support the flocks and herds that were so essential to Native life was a severe strain upon Native social organisation. But this was merely one expression of the consistent strain that the different elements of the European population either deliberately or unconsciously exerted on Native life. The impact of the European upon the Bantu was a steady process of depression. Colonists, missionaries, magistrates and traders, whether their approach was friendly or hostile, were representatives of an alien culture. This was the product of Christianity, the Renaissance and the Industrial Revolution, and depended in short upon moral attitudes, social principles, economic motives and forces of social organisation, which, apart from an infinitely greater complexity, were completely alien to Native modes of thought.[2] Whatever the intentions of those agencies of European culture that came into contact with Native life, whether to "benefit" it by "improving" Native moral, spiritual or economic conditions, or to weaken and destroy Native military strength, their common basis was a disapproval of the Native mode of life. By precept and

[1] *Vide supra*, p. 40.
[2] Meinhof, C., *Die Religionen der Afrikaner*, pp. 10–11.

persuasion, aggression and annexation, these elements of European colonisation never halted in their work of betterment or destruction. Every trader who taught Natives to buy cotton blankets[1] and shirts, beads and all the range of kaffir truck (although he unexpectedly failed to sell Sheffield assegais!) added a new demand upon the scanty wealth and low productivity of the Natives. Every magistrate who pronounced judgment weakened the authority of the Chiefs and the validity of Native custom; every missionary who blessed a Christian marriage or taught his followers to clothe their nakedness hastened the warping and splitting of Native organisation.[2]

What may very reasonably be termed the introduction of a cash nexus into tribal life was one of the greatest factors in dissolving the original Native economic order. Before the expansion of the Europeans into the interior there was some barter amongst the tribes in dressed skins, feathers and iron implements. For the most part, however, Native economy was a subsistence economy in which trade and exchange played no significant part; much more than on the feudal manor of the Middle Ages the processes of production, distribution and consumption took place within the tribe. In such an order of society the possibilities of amassing individual wealth were small. Beyond the desire of the individual to accumulate enough cattle to increase and maintain his household, Native organisation offered small inducement to individual wealth. The Chief alone could accumulate such wealth as to mark him out from the rest of the tribe, but even his wealth was always tribal rather than personal.

European contact soon broke down the self-contained character of tribal economic existence. The activity of European traders had by 1834 built up a volume of trade on the Eastern Frontier alone that was valued at £40,000 per annum. This trade, originally in ivory, skins and gum, was expanded to include cattle and even agricultural products. In return the traders supplied the Natives with beads and buttons, wire, tobacco and bad brandy, progressively extending the range of goods to include pots and picks, axes, knives, blankets and clothing. By 1850 there was hardly a kraal south of the Zoutpansberg Mountains that was not visited by itinerant traders. These traders hastened the process that killed Native industries such as iron smelting, basket weaving and pottery making. By so greatly increasing the range of Native requirements, traders, as well as missionaries, threw upon the tribes a burden their subsistence economy could not bear. The burden was rendered all the more insupportable by the sudden shrinking in Native resources caused by the extensive European encroachments upon their land which we have been considering, and by wars and cattle disease. When the introduction of European magistrates enforced the payment of taxes even though

[1] Cf. Ward, H., *Five Years in Kaffirland*, p. 196.
[2] See remarks on native lore in Jacottet, H. A., *Treasury of Basuto Lore*, p. xxiii.

these might be as low as seven shillings a year in the Natal of 1850, the total accumulated pressure upon Native life broke down the self-sufficiency of the tribes. The Natives were forced to find the wherewithal to purchase their needs and to meet their obligations. Neither cattle nor the occasional surpluses of agricultural products could possibly meet these requirements. It was not merely that the Natives only parted with their cattle reluctantly, but also that their wealth in cattle and produce was normally not great enough both to pay their taxes and purchase goods from the traders. Where Natives did sell their produce, as was the tendency from the 'forties onwards on the Cape Eastern Frontier and in Natal from the 'fifties,[1] they did so at the risk of being compelled to buy back their grain during the lean winter months. The magistrate of one representative reserve in Natal reported in 1852 that if the hut tax were to be paid in cattle, 20 per cent of the reserve's cattle, equivalent to the total natural increase for a year, would be consumed.[2] To protect their cattle and to meet the needs their production could not satisfy, the Natives were forced to sell their remaining asset—their labour.

Beginning in the 'thirties, the stream of Natives who sought work with the Europeans on their farms and in their industries grew ever greater and stronger. From Kaffirland to the Zoutpansberg there could not have been a tribe that did not at the end of the century send its contingent to labour for the Europeans. It was the outward and visible sign of the disintegration of tribal life, the sign of a social and economic revolution that was without doubt the greatest event in South African history during the nineteenth century.

At first the earnings of the temporary labourers probably served to protect the Native herds from rapid depletion, and to preserve Native life from the corrosive effects of the money economy with which the Natives were becoming familiar; by three months' work the Natal labourer in the 'fifties might pay his tax and that of his parents. But inevitably the absence of large numbers of men, working for varying periods as farm labourers, domestic servants and in the last decades of the century as industrial workers, did violence to tribal life. In intimate contact with Europeans, the tribesmen acquired new tastes and habits that altered their whole attitude towards the life of the tribe. The introduction of currency favoured individualism in the ownership and disposal of property and undermined communal rights and clan control. Moreover, a vicious circle was created, for the absence of large numbers of tribesmen robbed the reserves of their labour force and diminished their productivity. With growing needs and increasing taxes, wage-earning became ever more imperative. By the end of the nineteenth century the Native population in the tribal areas was far on the way to becoming a class

[1] *Natal Native Commission*, 1852, p. 35.
[2] *Ibid.* pt. IV, p. 9.

of labourers so poor that in any ordinary year a great number of the male population was forced to go out to labour for the Europeans, and so congested that great numbers, destined to total over half a million, remained in the towns as a permanent labouring class, separated from the soil and utterly detribalised.

The story of change does not concern material circumstances alone. The depression in the economic condition of the Natives was followed by an equally profound change in the social and political conditions of their existence. Through the operation of the manifold influences of European life the Natives were to be attached to and partially absorbed by the new South African community that the nineteenth century produced; they were to lose their tribal independence and yet were to be denied what some writers rightly regard as the most important privilege in social and political existence; "For if men and women are to be attached to a society, they must look on it as something in which they have a part; a world in which what we may call the common mind finds in some degree, or by some means, scope, peace, comfort and self-respect; in which distinctions of class and fortune, however hardly and sternly drawn, do not forbid all ties of sympathy, all unity of sentiment."[1]

It is a far cry from the unhistorical equalitarianism of early missionaries, whose inexperienced enthusiasm thought to lead the "benighted heathen" to the Bible and ofttimes to Shakespeare,[2] to the practical latter-day missionary, versed in folklore and Native custom, who becomes common after the 'fifties;[3] yet both were constantly concerned in substituting European modes of belief and action for the old. To such institutions as polygamy, the bride-price (*lobola*), the *intonjane*[4] and circumcision rites of the youths, organised religion was antagonistic, indifferent to the fact that they were pillars of Native life and that Native life contains categories of thought utterly foreign to Europeans. To the average European the bride-price falsely appeared as the outright purchase of the woman,[5] who became the husband's chattel; Native marriage was revolting; polygamy was "nothing but a system of concubinage which existed in all heathen lands until the light of the Gospel shone upon them". The natural prejudice of the European mind attributed *lobola* and polygamy to an innate, though perhaps curable, immoral tendency.

The stability of Native society depended upon the principle that the social status and obligations of the individual were fixed, being conditioned by his precedence in the social group. A Native tribe partook somewhat of the nature of what Gierke has termed a *Genossen-*

[1] Hammond, J. L. and B., *The Age of the Chartists*, p. 5.

[2] Cf. Backhouse, J., *Extracts*, II, p. 51.

[3] Casalis, E., published his *Études sur la langue Sechuana* in 1841.

[4] See *Native Laws and Customs Commission Report*, 1883, p. 239.

[5] In 1848 Sir Harry Smith made the Chiefs of the Eastern Frontier promise "to abolish the sin of buying wives".

schaft in that it absorbed the entire individual, who was subjected to it in every activity and capacity. Within such a society customs and institutions were therefore so important, and took so central a place in the entire life of every member, that their disturbance affected the entire tribal organisation with a directness which was proportionate to the interdependence within that organisation. Because of such close and immediate interdependence tribal life was more vulnerable than would have been a higher social organisation. With the loosening of tribal ties there resulted a weakening of the collective responsibility that had been the chief guarantee against destitution, and against that special form of vagrancy that filled the towns with permanent Native populations. The very great changes in Native life cannot simply be explained by the mere violence of the white impact. The nature of the changes depended also upon the greater reliance of the tribe upon institutions that were more obtrusive and less differentiated than in more complex forms of social life, but that nevertheless carried in the Native bosom a very definite moral value. In striving to undermine such important practices as Native marriage customs, European effort weakened also the whole complex of ethical and ideological conceptions on which they were based. Whereas from the Christian point of view marriage contracts are individual and, to missionaries at all events, sacramental, *lobola* contracts bind the family groups of bridegroom and bride, and involve economic considerations of great importance. The fecundity of the marriage and the faithfulness of either party are of economic and social concern to both groups. Since the bride-price was quite often paid for the bridegroom by a father or an elder brother, and was received by the family of the bride as a substitute for her lost services, and could be forfeited by them in the event of barrenness or desertion on the part of the woman, the *lobola* contract carried with it important economic and, from the Native angle, ethical considerations affecting more than two individuals. Hence Christian marriages threatened to cut deeply into Native life. That the bulk of South African Natives remained unchristianised, though not uninfluenced, by missionary effort was due, not simply to lack of missionaries and funds, but to the natural resistance of customs deeply embedded in Native life. "Irredeemable" savagery and "imperviousness" to white teaching were frequently nothing more than unwillingness to adopt customs, which, however excellent in themselves, were subversive of familiar institutions. Such conclusions do not alter the fact that the Natives owed a great debt to missionary activity, if it be not measured by success in proselytising alone. The normal conditions of Native life were made impossible by the very process of European colonisation, and it was missionary activity that first struggled to prevent the dispossession of Natives from their lands, and missionaries who saw many of the consequences of white pressure and tried to prevent them. When they failed, the missionaries sought to soften the force of the impact, and strenuously strove to find the means whereby the Natives could live in the new order. And they knew that way could not be the reconstruction of the old; it must be the conscious encouragement of the process of change with the acceptance of the consequences of history.

No other feature of tribal organisation has suffered such rapid modification under white pressure as has the chieftainship. When the Natives were subject to their own laws, the Chief was the pivot of tribal life. Only rarely was the Chief superior to the law of the tribe. His authority was usually exercised according to established usage and the sentiment of the tribe as expressed by those councillors whom personal distinction and skill in tribal affairs rather than the will of the Chief had elevated to that position. So intimately was the life of the tribe bound up with the Chief, and so much was he the centre and expression of its institutions, that to a large degree the fate of the Chief was the fate of tribal solidarity.

Though Native ownership of land was group ownership, land was vested in the Chief. In a manner not unlike certain aspects of feudal tenure, the individual held of the Chief the land he cultivated. Consequently the power and prestige of Chiefs depended greatly on their power to distribute land amongst their followers. Obviously one of the first effects of the straits to which the tribes were reduced by white encroachment was to deprive the Chief of this important source of power.

Far more serious, however, was the sudden reduction of the Chief's authority by the appointment of magistrates in Native territories In 1848, after the War of the Axe, Governor Sir Harry Smith permitted the "reasonable exercise" of the Chief's authority over the members of the tribe, but made all his acts and decisions subject to revision by magistrates. To realise how unsettling such measures were, it is necessary to appreciate how greatly the manners and modes of primitive communities seem to them immutable and of the very nature of things. Acts such as that of Sir Harry Smith produced an effect of bewilderment and unjust treatment on the Native mind which was a main cause of the war that broke out in 1850.[1] After that war Sir George Grey struck a yet more swinging blow at the power of the Chiefs. Though still permitted to hear cases, they were assisted by magistrates, and in place of the revenues which they formerly derived from fines and confiscations they were given an annual stipend. The next and obvious development was the assumption of judicial powers by the magistrates and the reduction of the Chiefs to the position of assessors. Not even the greatest skill or tact could prevent the dissolving effects of such measures or prevent the impression of harsh and unjust treatment. To deprive any individual or class of individuals of the rank and authority which they possess by hereditary right could

[1] Brownlee, C., *Reminiscences*, p. 182.

only produce a feeling of degradation in the victim[1] and a sharp resentment in his loyal followers. The mass madness that overcame almost all Kaffirland in 1857, when the tribes slaughtered their cattle and destroyed their corn, happened because tribal life was shaken to its deepest roots by two severe wars, by the loss of land, the havoc of cattle disease and drought, and the assault upon the powers of the Chiefs. It was the collapse of an order that had been undermined and honeycombed for half a century by an aggressive European colonisation.

Of all the agencies that transformed Native life, one of the most powerful was the assumption of administrative control by the British Government over Native territories. So long as these had lain without the boundaries of the British possessions, the British Government could treat them, as the republics treated their Natives till the end, as presenting only military problems of defence, and at best could govern them "by despatch" from Cape Town. But no sooner had circumstances forced the tardy annexation of the lopped and diminished Native territories than the tribes were subjected more actively than before to European conceptions of justice and administration. The reluctance with which the successive annexations were undertaken stamped almost the whole subsequent trend of Native administration. As far as practicable, inexpensive and, preferably, self-supporting administrations were set up, with the results that the government of Native territories was, for almost the whole of the period under survey, inconsistent, halting, planless and disconcerting to Natives whose own laws were rooted in tradition. Dr Philip had envisaged a Native administration and a system of education that should designedly increase the share of the Natives in the life of the country;[2] but, instead, for safety's sake and because money and men were wanting, the practical aim of Native administration hardly rose higher than the maintenance of good order, liberty to work for the farmers and prevention of those crimes that were repugnant to principles of humanity.

The administrations were at all times understaffed. It is even surprising that the low salaries and arduous conditions did not burden the Natives with more ill-educated and ineffective officials than they in fact did. As it was, the Native territories enjoyed the services of not a few devoted and capable men, often of missionary stock. But if the missionary blood that ran in the veins of many officials gave them a valuable understanding, it also perpetuated in certain magistrates some intolerance of various "unchristian" practices and even, though more rarely, an unwillingness to realise the rough inroads upon Native confidence and morals which resulted from their more ill-considered decisions. Well as they understood the Natives, some, even of the best of them, believed that the Gospel could make no headway until the sword had broken up the tribes.

[1] Cf. Holden, W. C., *Past and Future*, pp. 393–4.

[2] *Aborigines Committee Report, Parl. Pap.* 1836, VII (538), pp. 635, 693.

Furthermore, there was an amazing uncertainty as to which law magistrates should apply in hearing Native cases. In Natal the Royal Instructions had laid it down that Native cases should be judged according to Native laws, but, in the territories under Cape jurisdiction, magistrates had considerable latitude in resorting to either Colonial or Native law.[1] Though exceptions were frequent, the rule was that, in purely Native matters, Native law should apply; but when Native law clashed with colonial law, Native law gave way.[2] It could happen that a Native claim, just under Native law and maintained by a Native court, was dismissed by a magistrate's decision. "I came here knowing the law," muttered one disgruntled Native, "I am judged by a law I do not know."[3] Already bewildered by the confusion and insecurity in their land tenure in which British annexation resulted, the lack of uniform legal policy could not but breed in them discontent and lawlessness. Thus, as dowry contracts were not recognised by colonial law, instances of magistrates who refused to entertain *lobola* cases, though predecessors had done so, were not unknown. European justice, being thus misunderstood and not always efficiently carried out, earned the contempt of many Natives and did much to prevent African litigiousness from finding its way to the magistrates' courts.

Native law was essentially customary law, little subject to innovation. Startling changes introduced by the Chiefs were at all times exceedingly rare. The opinion of the older men of the tribe and the sentiment of the tribe strongly influenced the Chief. Justice amongst Natives was of a spontaneous character; cases were public. Both pronouncements and punishments normally had an obviousness and naturalness to the Native mind that on occasion made it possible for a really flagrant offender to be punished without recourse to a process of legal trial. The familiarity on the part of every individual with the sanctions and prohibitions of tribal custom was as great a factor in maintaining equilibrium as the authority of the Chief. The unwritten laws of social usage in Bantu life were obeyed more spontaneously than is the case with written codes; the expression of tribal sentiment, contempt or indignation was usually an effective deterrent. This group sentiment, dependent on the submergence of the individual in the group, could not but accord ill with principles of social conduct based upon a far-reaching individualism that permitted the individual to own great acreages, even though he cultivated the merest fraction, and demanded that the punishment of murder be the death

[1] The Orange Free State and the Cape Colony proper never recognised Native law. In Basutoland (1877) and the Transkei (1879), Native law was recognised with certain qualifications. Natal recognised Native law. The position in the Transvaal was inconsistent and anomalous until the end of the century.

[2] Cf. Brookes, E. H., *History of Native Policy*, pp. 51, 180 *sqq*.

[3] Brownlee, *Reminiscences*, pp. 366 *sqq*.; *Native Laws and Customs Commission Report*, 1883, pt. II, p. 82.

of the killer. Not every administrator took the same care as Shepstone in Natal to explain to the Natives in language they could understand why a cattle-fine could no longer compensate for a murder.

Yet intolerance, disintegration of social solidarity and disrespect for tradition were not merely due to the prejudice or ignorance of individual officials, or to the incautious and unsystematic innovations of missionaries and administrators, or even altogether to the wide latitude given magistrates to hold that no Native law repugnant to humanity and civilisation could be valid; the shock of rapid conquest and the development of intercourse with Europeans introduced new and complicated questions for which the traditional customs of the tribe made no provision. It was inevitable that in issues where the "Ancients" themselves were nonplussed, the Natives should seek the decisions of magistrates, learn to abandon their own law on occasion by basing their pleading on points in colonial law, thus by their own action weakening the force of Native tribunals. The weakening of group sentiment had gone so far as to prompt Natives to bring up such cases as libel suits, even though Native law permitted the freest invective,[1] and to refuse to pay Native doctors their fees because they were not licensed according to colonial law.[2] What was so profoundly significant in such cases, and in many other evasions of Native law that never reached the Courts, was the clear evidence that all law was losing in the Native mind that ethical and social binding force that had distinguished it in tribal life. They indicated, too, the far more subtle and imponderable penetration of Native life by alien modes of thought and principles of conduct, notably conceptions of private property and private benefit.[3] Throughout, the solidarity of tribal life, the authority of tribal custom and practice over the actions of the individual progressively weakened. The refusal of Cape law to take cognisance of *lobola* cases caused Natives on the Eastern Frontier frequently and deliberately to affront their own laws by selling and reselling their daughters in the knowledge that the Cape law afforded them protection.[4] The effect of Proclamation 110 of 1879, which laid it down that the age of majority in the Cape Native Territories should be twenty-one, incisively illustrates the manner in which European policy lent its support to the forces of change in native life. Proclamation 110 made it possible for widows, who normally would pass under the control of the heir to the husband's kraal, to assert their independence and hold property in their own right.[5] It made it possible for the young men who had attained their majority to refuse obedience to the head of their kraal, to claim individual right in their cattle,[6]

[1] Warner, *Native Appeals*, pp. 6–7.
[2] *Ibid. Ndeon* v. *Bikani*, p. 24.
[3] Cf. Hobhouse, L. T., *Liberalism*, p. 43.
[4] See Brookes, E. H., *History of Native Policy*, p. 238.
[5] Warner, *Native Appeals*, *Sentanteni* v. *Nolanti*, p. 38.
[6] *Ibid. Jakeni* v. *Mbele*, p. 19.

and thus to undermine that collective responsibility that lay at the basis of Native economic and social life. A daughter of legal age was free to marry the man of her choosing.

What signified was not so much those Natives who deliberately threw off tribal control, but much more the menace to the system of interdependence and reciprocal obligation by which the members of the tribe were held together, the challenge to the conviction of tribes in the permanence and inevitability of their institutions, and the insidious impetus given to the movement of the whole Native population towards social and economic conceptions that were not their own. That the Native's attitude to his cattle and his land and his Chief should be modified under the pressure of European contact was as inevitable as that he should begin to use a plough where he had formerly used a hoe, and sigh for a gun to take the place of his assegai. With the magistrates came a new régime in the tribal areas. It was not only that the magistrates could not enjoy that intimacy with the tribesmen that made it possible for a Chief to receive a blow in a scuffle without being forced for dignity's sake to punish the striker; behind the magistrates the Natives were aware of "the chief called Government", distant, impersonal, inscrutable and to the Natives desperately inconsistent.[1] Old sanctions were weakened and new motives for conduct took the place of the old. The heavy weight of tradition that had made it inconceivable for the individual to regard himself as superior to the practices of the tribes became lighter. The immorality amongst the Eastern Frontier Natives, which Shepstone contrasted in 1883[2] with the temper of the tribes in the days when magistrates were not, was but the unescapable outcome when magistrates, with the best will in the world, could not always justify their decisions to the Native mind where strange laws were mixed with the old. From the Kaffir War of 1850 to the Zulu rebellion of 1906 the complaint is constant: "The young men of the tribe do what they will." The tragedy of 1857, which drove streams of Natives into the Colony looking for work, brought about more volcanically what the Basuto wars and the Transvaal commandos were doing with equal effectiveness elsewhere. From the time that the young men could leave the tribe to take service with the Europeans, the ties that bound them to Chief and tribe slackened; their former dependence upon the Chief and their elders for counsel and aid in marriage and every emergency went the way of respect and deference. Because they were no longer dependent, they lost their old respect for their Chiefs.

European colonisation put an end to intertribal conflict and to many cruelties in tribal life. It introduced missionaries and brought increasing attention to Native education, health and agriculture. It

[1] *Native Laws and Customs Commission Report*, 1883, pt. II, p. 82; and see also Shepstone's evidence.

[2] *Ibid.* pt. II, p. 51.

gave the Natives ploughs, waggons, clothes and new crops, and improved Native stock, even if only as the result of breeding with cattle stolen from the white farmers. Native administration developed high traditions of sympathetic and efficient effort. In the Cape the Natives were granted a fairly effective franchise and, in Natal, a technical right to the franchise. A British Governor saved the Transkei and part of Basutoland from being altogether swallowed up by the Europeans. In 1864 Letters Patent created the Natal Native Trust to administer and protect Native land rights. In the Cape the Glen Grey Act of 1894 initiated a policy that gave to about a million Transkei Natives a share in their local self-government with a local revenue, and introduced a very qualified and limited individual land tenure.[1]

But, despite these and other ameliorative acts, the social and economic development of South African Native life during the nineteenth century is a story of continuous depression and disintegration. The best efforts of European legislation have been either of merely local benefit, or expedients that did no more than patch the torn fabric of Native life. The principles of the Transkeian experiment were undoubtedly of the finest. In the reconstruction of Native life it was of the greatest importance that the Natives of the Transkei should be given a voice in their affairs, a revenue for carrying out their policies and the stimulus to enterprise that comes from individual ownership; yet unto this day the greatest stumbling block to the economic and social advance of the Natives is the fact that they had not enough land to maintain themselves or to progress.[2] The significance of the nineteenth century in Native history was that it produced a black proletariat, without independence or initiative, and with the growing "resentment of men convinced that there is something false and degrading in the arrangement and justice of their world".[3]

[1] *Vide supra*, p. 558.
[2] Macmillan, W. M., *Complex South Africa*, p. 121.
[3] Hammond, J. B., *The Age of the Chartists*, p. 2.

CHAPTER XXXI

THE ROMAN-DUTCH LAW IN SOUTH AFRICA

THE common law of South Africa south of the Zambesi, excluding Portuguese territory, is commonly stated to be the Roman-Dutch law as it prevailed in the Province of Holland during the existence of the Republic of the United Netherlands. For practical purposes this statement is sufficiently accurate, but it ignores a long period of historical development and masks a number of problems of theoretical and, occasionally, of practical importance. When the Dutch settlement at the Cape of Good Hope surrendered to the British forces in 1806, a stipulation that the rights and privileges which the inhabitants had heretofore enjoyed should be preserved to them was embodied in the Articles of Capitulation.[1] This included, in effect, if not by conscious intention, the preservation of the existing system of law. This Cape system was carried northward in the eighteen-thirties by the Trekkers who founded the republics and Natal, which, together with the Cape, now form the Union of South Africa. Cape law was presently applied to Southern Rhodesia, and after the Peace of Versailles (1919) Union law was extended to South-West Africa. Therefore, apart from modification by legislation or custom, the law of southern Africa is the law which was in force at the Cape in 1806.

The settlers at the Cape in 1652 brought with them the law of their homeland as the common law of the new settlement. It is generally accepted that this law was the law of the Province of Holland,[2]—the law of that province being preferred to that of the other provinces of the United Netherlands, no doubt, because of the predominant part it played in commerce and politics. The law of the Province of Holland was by the seventeenth century a fairly well-defined collection of legal principles consisting of statutory enactments—some having force throughout the Netherlands and other applying only to the province or even to a particular town—and the ancient customs of the people, supplemented by the Roman law, which after some centuries of infiltration had by the so-called *Instructie* of Charles the Bold been declared the ultimate source of law for the province.[3] During the sixteenth and seventeenth centuries the inconvenience and uncertainty caused by the existence of conflicting customs and local legislation had been ameliorated by legislation designed to introduce uniformity both in the law and in its administration. The most important of these enactments were the Perpetual Edict of 4 October 1540[4] and the Political

[1] See Eybers, G. W., *Constitutional Documents illustrating South African history,* 1795–1910, p. 16. [2] Wessels, J. W., *History of the Roman-Dutch Law*, p. 356.

[3] *Groot Placaat Boek*, III, p. 635, § 42. [4] *Groot Placaat Boek*, I, col. 311.

Ordinance of 1 April 1580.[1] The Perpetual Edict was a proclamation issued by Charles V; the preamble states that it was introduced to extirpate heresy, prevent the great expense and length of lawsuits and provide for the administration of justice throughout the land for the benefit of rich and poor alike. It dealt with divers subjects, including the evasion of liabilities by debtors, frauds on creditors, claims of wives on the insolvent estates of their husbands, monopolies, usury, reduction of local customs to writing, wills, notaries, limitations of actions, marriages of minors without consent of parents, etc. The Cape Prescription Act of 1861 is clearly adapted from this Edict of 1540, but, in regard to influence on South African law, the Political Ordinance of 1580 after the expulsion of the Spaniards was perhaps the most important law ever promulgated in Holland because it was a rough codification of the law upon so many subjects. The preamble recites that it was promulgated in order to put an end to the constant disputes which were caused by the uncertainty of the law governing marriage, succession, sale, mortgage, lease, registration of immovable property, etc., and it proceeds to deal explicitly with these subjects.

While legislation had thus consolidated the law, legal works dealing with the whole subject of Roman-Dutch law were published in which scattered laws were collected, arranged and expounded in logical order as a complete system of law. The greatest of these was that work of genius published in 1631 and commonly known as the *Introduction to Dutch Jurisprudence* by Hugo Grotius. The English translation of the title is misleading. Grotius wrote merely of the law of the Province of Holland, which was only one of the seven provinces forming the United Netherlands at that time;[2] but Grotius was followed by numerous other writers, two of the most important of whom dealt with the law of the Netherlands in general, namely, Simon van Leeuwen (1625–82) and Johannes Voet (1647–1713).

Broadly speaking, then, the common law introduced by the settlers into South Africa was the law of Holland as expounded by Grotius, van Leeuwen and Voet, and as they all quote freely from the Roman law, the starting point of many legal arguments in South Africa to-day is the *Corpus Juris* of Justinian, which, after nearly 1500 years, has not yet exhausted its inspiration of good sense and sound law.

Naturally the common law, thus introduced, has been considerably modified by subsequent legislation. Such legislation falls into two periods: the period of the Dutch occupation of the Cape and the period which has elapsed since the Cape was occupied by the British in 1806. During the Dutch period, there were four separate legislative bodies whose enactments might have had force and effect in the settlement at the Cape. These were the States General of the United Provinces, the States of Holland, the Government of Batavia and the Government of the Settlement at the Cape. All of them issued

[1] *Ibid.* I, col. 329.

[2] See Introduction to Maasdorp's translation of Grotius.

placaten, but it is still an open question whether some of these *placaten* ever had any legal force and effect at the Cape. At any rate the question has not yet been fully answered by judicial decision.

Dealing first with *placaten* issued at the Cape, it must be remembered that the Cape settlement was a mere out-station (*buiten comptoir*) of the East India Company's head-station at Batavia. Such out-stations were a familiar feature of the Company's method of government, and the Cape station, though considerably further from Batavia and nearer to Holland than any other, and consequently subject to occasional exceptional treatment by direct communication from the authorities in Holland, was governed from Batavia according to the familiar plan. Immediate control, however, was vested in the Governor and Council, who had power to legislate by means of *placaten*[1] which came into force on promulgation (usually by proclamation from the balcony of the Court House in Cape Town and posting up in some public place), but which were nevertheless subject to veto either from Batavia or from Holland. Of such *placaten* there was soon no lack; but inasmuch as no attempt was ever made to publish copies of them for general use or to collate them in one volume, they were generally as shortlived as they were numerous. They were usually re-enacted by succeeding Governors almost as if, like the Praetor's Edict at Rome, they lost validity with each new appointment. They are of little importance to-day because in 1857 a commission, consisting of four Judges, the Colonial Secretary and the Attorney General, appointed for the purpose of drawing up a collection of ordinances and laws in force in Cape Colony, issued a volume of statute law in 1862. The whole vast mass of *placaten* was then excluded, save nine only, of which six dealt with administrative and three with criminal matters. With the exception of these favoured nine, the *placaten* have to all intents and purposes since been ignored by the Courts and have thus had no influence on the Roman-Dutch law as now administered in South Africa. This attitude of the courts of law has, however, been criticised on the ground that the *placaten* contain provisions dealing with many points of law which have arisen for decision in cases heard in the courts.[2]

Among purely administrative provisions of the East India Company's period, the most notable were the introduction, or more properly the regularisation, in South Africa, by *placaat* of 8 July 1686, of the system, universal in Holland,[3] of registration of title to immovable property—a system of incalculable value to the country—and the complementary creation in 1714 of a debt registry for the registration of all mortgages over immovables.

[1] This legislative power has been challenged by Dr C. H. van Zyl in an article in the *South African Law Journal* (24 *S.A.L.J.* p. 132).

[2] Article by J. de V. Roos; 23 *South African Law Journal*, p. 242.

[3] See Placaat, 9 May 1529 (*Groot Placaat Boek*, I, col. 373).

With regard to Batavian legislation, the Dutch East India Company received its charter from the States General in 1602,[1] but the Charter did not state what law was to be administered in the Company's settlements, nor did it in specific terms authorise the Company to legislate for its settlements. Before the first settlement of the Cape the Governors-General in the East Indies had issued proclamations and *placaten*, and in 1642 Governor van Diemen promulgated a code of such laws, known as the Statutes of Batavia or Statutes of India, some of which were very similar in terms to laws appearing in the *Groot Placaat Boek*. It seems fairly clear that van Diemen's code was adopted at the Cape and applied by the Courts of law.[2] There is no doubt that in 1715 the court asked the Governor-in-Council to decide what laws should govern their proceedings, and the Governor-in-Council resolved that in future the Statutes of India should be observed in so far as they were not in conflict with *placaten* and ordinances promulgated by the Cape Government from time to time.[3]

In 1766 a new edition of the Statutes of India, called the van der Parra Code, was completed, but there is nothing to show that it ever came into force at the Cape.[4] The Statutes of India have not in fact influenced the development of the Roman-Dutch law in South Africa. They were used and quoted in the law courts prior to 1806, but from that date until quite recently practically no reference to them will be found in the law reports. This is probably due to the fact that they were not printed and copies of them were difficult to obtain. In 1827, on the suggestion of the Judges, an attempt was made to obtain from the Netherlands a collection of the laws in force at the Cape prior to 1806, but the official reply was that no such collection existed.[5] In recent years, however, the importance of these statutes has been recognised.[6]

So far as legislation in the Netherlands was concerned, all enactments by the States General became law at the Cape except those whose operation was limited to other territories by the intention of the legislature. In fact, such legislation as was applicable to Batavia and the Cape was normally incorporated in the Statutes of India which also embodied a good deal of matter taken over verbatim from the *placaat* books.

A more difficult question arises in respect of *placaten*, not of the States General of the Netherlands, but of the States of Holland. *Placaten* issued before 1652 were part of the law brought with them

[1] *Groot Placaat Boek*, I, 529.

[2] See article by C. Graham Botha in the *South African Law Journal*, 30 *S.A.L.J.* p. 292, in which references are given to the records in the archives showing how these statutes were used in the Courts of Law—*Rex* v. *Harrison and Dryburgh*, 1922 A.D. at p. 335 and the report of the 1857 Commission previously referred to.

[3] Resolution, *Raad van Politie*.

[4] See article in the *South African Law Journal* by J. L. W. Stock, 32 *S.A.L.J.* p. 328.

[5] Colonial Office Papers, Despatches Recd. 1315 C.A.

[6] See *Green* v. *Fitzgerald*, 1914 A.D. at p. 88.

by the founders of the settlement, but after 1652 the settlement was a dependency of the United Netherlands, not of the Province of Holland. The power of legislation for the new settlement therefore vested in the States General or, by delegation, in the East India Company, which had received its Charter from the States General and not from the States of Holland.

The question whether a *placaat* of the States of Holland and West Friesland of the 7 March 1754 had the force of law in South Africa arose in 1922.[1] Two persons were charged with contravening a provision of that *placaat* by publishing a defamatory leaflet in which the Government of the Union was accused of murdering unarmed Natives; the matter was taken to the Court of Appeal which held that the *placaat* never had the force of law at the Cape. The reasons for this decision were that the *placaat* had never been promulgated or acted upon in the Cape, but the larger question whether the States of Holland had power to legislate for the Cape was not decided. In theory the legislative power vested in the States General, but in practice post-settlement *placaten* of the States of Holland have been quoted in the Courts in South Africa and have been treated as binding.[2] In any event such *placaten* would not be of force without local promulgation, though proof of early recognition and enforcement would create a presumption of due but unrecorded promulgation. The provisions of a *placaat* may also have become incorporated into the law of the Cape by custom and by the adoption of institutional writers who rely on it.[3]

During the Company's period the Supreme Court at the Cape virtually consisted of the Council. As early as 1656, however, a distinction was drawn between the Council sitting in its administrative capacity as the *Politijcke Raad*, and the same Council sitting in its judicial capacity as the *Raad van Justitie*. The numbers of the *Raad van Justitie* varied from time to time; originally it consisted of six members, in 1783 it numbered thirteen, but at the date of the British annexation the number was nine, including the President. This court had plenary jurisdiction in all criminal and civil matters and was the court of appeal from inferior and district courts. From it an appeal lay to Batavia. The procedure was substantially that laid down for the Courts of Holland. In criminal matters it was regulated by an Ordinance of 1570. There was no right of private prosecution; the Fiscal or, in the case of country crimes, the landdrost of the district acted as public prosecutor; the system of preparatory examination was already in force; the accused was competent to give evidence and might be interrogated; testimony was not as a rule taken in open court.

[1] *Rex* v. *Harrison and Dryburgh*, 1922 A.D. at p. 320.

[2] A number of these are referred to in the case of *Rex* v. *Harrison and Dryburgh*, 1922 A.D. at p. 320.

[3] See *Estate Heinemann and others* v. *Heinemann*, 1919 A.D. at p. 114.

With the growth of the settlement the need was soon felt for a court to deal with petty cases. By a resolution of 31 August 1652 there was created a *Collegie van Commissarrissen van Kleine Saken* consisting of two officials, two burghers and a secretary.[1] In 1711 it was amalgamated with the Matrimonial Court, which had been founded in 1676, and at the end of the Company's government, in 1795, consisted of a President, who was a member of the Council, a Vice-President, who was a burgher, and four members as before. This Petty Court had jurisdiction up to 200 rix-dollars. It was abolished in 1809 on the creation of a Court of Landdrost and Heemraden for the Cape District.

Meanwhile the rapid expansion of the settlement beyond the boundaries of Cape Town had necessitated the creation of some system for administering the country districts. In Holland, there were in existence two typical Petty Courts: that of the *Schout* and *Schepenen*, which was regarded as the special court for the town and village, and that of the *Baljuw* and *Mannen*, which was rather the court for the countryside.[2] Of these two systems, the latter seems to have been selected for imitation, though with a change in terminology. In 1685 an official was appointed, corresponding to the *Baljuw*, known as the *Landdrost*, the first appointment being that of Johannes Mulder in 1685; while since 1683 the *Mannen* were represented by four Heemraden, of whom two were appointed yearly from among the principal local burghers. The Court of Landdrost and Heemraden became the recognised body for administering the country districts and in addition sat as a petty court of first instance, acting under instructions issued by the Governor. The district over which the landdrost had jurisdiction was known as the *Drostdy*, but the meaning of this word changed and, in later years, was only used to denote his official residence. The first district to be so controlled was Stellenbosch; by 1786 there were three such districts: Stellenbosch, Swellendam and Graaff-Reinet; in 1804 Uitenhage and Tulbagh were added.[3]

On the whole the administration of justice was not a success and gave rise to justifiable complaints. By the end of the eighteenth century it had fallen into a sorry plight and the Batavian Commissioner de Mist, who took over the Colony from the British in 1803, described the Department of Justice in the following terms: "A Council of Justice with no instructions except as regards the number, rank and salaries of its members; a Fiscal, independent of the Council to which he should be subordinate; the sentences of the Council which could be appealed against in India; the Fiscal responsible for his actions only to the directors in the Motherland; no statute book for the colony; no instructions for Landdrost and Heemraden who

[1] See an article by C. Graham Botha (38 *South African Law Journal*, p. 406).
[2] Wessels, *History of the Roman-Dutch Law*, pp. 162–3.
[3] Government Notices, *De Kaapsche Courant*, 12 May and 21 July 1804.

exercised minor jurisdiction in the District Courts, not without frequent complaints being voiced by the inhabitants;—this in brief is a picture of the miserable state into which justice and its administration had fallen in the colony, and in this disgraceful condition it remained right up to the time of the capitulation of the Cape to the English."[1] He pointed out that since 1779 the colonists had demanded that a complete collection of the laws in force in the Cape should be made, but that nothing had been done except that a resolution had been passed in 1783 directing the Government at the Cape to draft a General *Placaat* for the colony and instructions for the Council of Justice; it was not clear, however, that this resolution had produced any improvement in the administration of justice at the Cape.

The Dutch period was nevertheless one of vigorous legal growth. During this period, while the original victualling station became a colony, a system of law, which was soon to perish in the land of its origin, was so firmly implanted in the new soil that it could survive even the test of being administered by Judges trained both in a different system and in a different language.

The succeeding period, which opened with the Second British Occupation of 1806 and closed with the Union of 1910, saw the introduction of order and definition. At first the existing judicial institutions were continued. The Council of Justice continued its functions, but new members were appointed to it in place of the old whose services were terminated. In the country districts, the administration of justice by Landdrost and Heemraden was continued. In consequence of de Mist's report, their functions, as well as those of Field-cornets and gaolers, had been defined in a comprehensive Ordinance issued by Governor Janssens in 1805, and in 1809 a Court of Landdrost and Heemraden was established for the Cape district and its duties defined by special instructions published in 1809.

In 1827, however, the judicial system was entirely remodelled. In that year the first Charter of Justice was promulgated. This Charter, as modified by a second charter issued in 1832, is of vital importance in the history of legal institutions in South Africa, because it introduces entirely new ideas into the administration of justice. It created the Supreme Court of the Colony of the Cape of Good Hope and constituted it a Court of Record consisting of a Chief Justice and two Puisne Judges with jurisdiction in all causes, civil or criminal or mixed, arising within the colony; it appointed certain officers such as the Registrar or Keeper of Records, and the Master, who took over the duties of the Orphan Chamber in regard to the custody and care of the estates of deceased persons and minors, and the Sheriff, who had to carry into execution the judgments of the Court; it gave the Supreme Court power to admit to practice barristers and attorneys,

[1] *The Memorandum of Commissary J. A. de Mist, . . . 1802* [trans. Van Riebeeck Society, No. 3, pp. 234–5.]

power also to review the proceedings of all the inferior Courts; it instituted trial by jury; it empowered the Governor to constitute inferior courts with jurisdiction in civil and criminal cases, and it gave a right of appeal from the Supreme Court to the Privy Council in England.

About the same time the Government of the Cape promulgated a number of important ordinances dealing with the administration of justice. In 1827, Justices of the Peace were created and inferior courts of justice, called Courts of Resident Magistrate, were established,[1] whose very limited jurisdiction was presently considerably extended.[2] The office of Sheriff was regulated;[3] a Registrar of Deeds was brought into being and the duty was imposed upon him of keeping the registers of landed property and the Colonial Debt Registers.[4] A code of criminal procedure was introduced;[5] the legal age of majority was fixed at 21;[6] the English law of evidence was introduced;[7] the duties of the Master of the Supreme Court were defined and provision was made for the administration of the estates of deceased persons, minors and lunatics;[8] finally, a code for the administration and distribution of insolvent estates was enacted.[9]

The effect of all this legislation was revolutionary; it swept away the whole of the early machinery for the administration of justice and replaced it by a new system, which endured in the Cape Colony, with certain modifications, until the Union in 1910, and was frequently the model for legislation in the other provinces of the Union. Meanwhile, as the colony expanded, superior courts with local jurisdiction were set up: the Eastern Districts Court at Grahamstown in 1864 and the Griqualand West Court at Kimberley in 1882.

After the promulgation of the Charter of Justice the Cape Colony began to feel the steady and growing influence of English legal principles and ideas. Modifications of the old law were introduced, partly by legislation. Sometimes such legislation had the immediate effect of destroying the operation of great portions of the old law and of substituting in its place some corresponding portion of the English law; sometimes it merely repealed or modified old rules of law which were considered unsuitable to modern conditions, and sometimes it introduced new provisions, adapted from English legislation, to meet the needs of an advancing civilisation. The introduction of the jury system also made it necessary and convenient to adopt the English laws of criminal procedure and evidence.

[1] Ordinances 32, 33 of 1827.
[2] Ordinance 14 of 1847, Act 20 of 1856, Act 9 of 1857, Act 21 of 1876, Act 43 of 1885, Act 32 of 1917.
[3] Ordinance 37 of 1828.
[4] Ordinance 39 of 1828.
[5] Ordinances 40 of 1828 and 73 of 1830.
[6] Ordinance 62 of 1829.
[7] Ordinance 72 of 1830.
[8] Ordinances 103, 104, 105 of 1833.
[9] Ordinances 64 of 1829 and 6 of 1843.

The growth of commerce and the emergence of new conceptions, such as patents, trade marks, copyright and companies with limited liability, required new legislation. This was copied from English precedent. The Cape Insolvency Acts were largely copies from the English bankruptcy legislation, though they retained many of the principles of Roman-Dutch law.[1] In 1865 a Merchant Shipping Act was passed incorporating certain sections of the English Merchant Shipping Act of 1854. Under the old Roman-Dutch law a child could not be entirely disinherited by his parents, but Act 26 of 1873 and Act 23 of 1874 introduced freedom of testation. Section 2 of the former Act furnishes an interesting illustration of the living force and persistence of the Roman law. It reads as follows: "From and after the taking effect of this Act the sixth law of the ninth title of the fifth book of the Code of Justinian, commencing with the words *Hac Edictali*, and commonly called or known as the Law or *Lex Hac Edictali*, shall be and the same is hereby repealed." Again, in 1879, by the General Law Amendment Act, the English law was substituted for the Roman-Dutch law in all questions relating to maritime and shipping law, fire, life and marine insurance, stoppage *in transitu* and bills of lading, while certain legal rights recognised by the Roman-Dutch law were abolished, viz. the right of a lessee to claim a remission of rent in certain circumstances where he has suffered loss from inundation, tempest or other misfortune, and the right of one party to a contract of sale to cancel it when the price paid was more than double or less than half the value of the thing sold. Still later the Bills of Exchange Act of 1893 was passed which is practically identical with the English Act.

Legislation, however, was not the only means by which English law influenced the Roman-Dutch law. Many of the Judges appointed from 1828 onwards had been trained in the English law and some did not know the Dutch language; the Charter made provision for the admission as barristers only of men who had been admitted in England, Scotland or Ireland, or who had obtained degrees at Oxford, Cambridge or Dublin. Besides, the English law was a living system with text-books and law reports easily available, whereas the Roman-Dutch law had ceased to be administered in the Netherlands after the end of the eighteenth century. The Batavian and Cape statutes were difficult to obtain and were only available in manuscript, and the Netherlands statutes were in the Dutch language, whereas since 1828 the language of the courts was English.[2] The works of the Roman-Dutch commentators were in the Dutch language or in medieval Latin, many of them printed in black letter type and bound in bulky volumes. Human nature being what it is, the easy way in such circumstances was the way most often followed. Judges and lawyers,

[1] Ordinances 64 of 1829 and 6 of 1843.

[2] Section 32, Charter of Justice.

when confronted with a problem, had neither the time nor the energy for research into the Roman-Dutch authorities, and when a convenient English precedent was available, it was easy to follow it, with, perhaps, the qualification added, as a salve to the judicial conscience, that the English law was not in conflict with Roman-Dutch principles. The fact that the final court of appeal from the Cape was the Privy Council was another factor which assisted the incorporation of English principles into the Roman-Dutch law, because Judges were naturally inclined to give great weight to any decision or dictum in a judgment of that Court.

The disappearance of antiquated rules of Roman-Dutch law was also facilitated by the respect paid in Roman-Dutch law to custom. Custom can both create and destroy law, and even statute law may become inoperative through obsolescence, at any rate statute law prior to 1806.[1] Consequently, any Dutch statute or common law rule, which has fallen into disuse or which is inconsistent with modern customs, may be held by the courts of law to be no longer of force and effect in South Africa. This principle is a very powerful instrument in modifying the law, because it renders the courts free to discard obsolete rules of law and to adapt a medieval system to the needs of the present day.

The introduction of so many English law principles into the law of South Africa is not by any means a matter for regret; South African law has undoubtedly been strengthened and enriched thereby, but the slipshod legislative methods of its introduction have given rise to difficulties, some of which still await or defy solution.

It may appear a matter for legitimate surprise, in view of the assault upon it by the English system, that the Roman-Dutch law should have survived at all. But the Supreme Court was fortunate in its Judges, who showed not merely a loyal adherence to the direction of the Charter that the old law should be preserved, but also considerable skill and industry in understanding and interpreting that law. The example set in the early days by Menzies (1828–50), from whose notebooks the first Cape Law Reports were compiled, was followed with equal ability by Bell (1853–73), Cloete (1855–66) and Watermeyer (1857–67). Finally, with the appointment as Chief Justice, in 1873, of John Henry de Villiers (later Lord de Villiers) the battle was won;[2] for while the passage of time and the growth of legal research may have a little diminished his reputation as a master of Roman-Dutch law, it has served only to illuminate the more brightly his ability to harmonise its rules with the broad spirit of equity and the demands of the conditions of to-day, so that although particular judgments of his are now seen to have been wrong, his mark is nevertheless set upon the law of South Africa as indelibly as is that of Lord Chief Justice

[1] See *Seaville* v. *Colley* (9 S.C. at p. 39) and *Green* v. *Fitzgerald* (1914 A.D. at p. 88).
[2] See Walker, E. A., *Lord de Villiers and his Times*, chap. v.

Coke upon the law of England. The work which de Villiers did in the Cape Colony was carried on by a number of distinguished Judges on the Transvaal Bench, who, as barristers, had been influenced by the practice of the Cape Supreme Court.

With the Bench devoted to the maintenance of the Roman-Dutch law, it was inevitable that efforts would be made to facilitate the study and quotation of the older authorities, and thus, within the last fifty years, English translations of many works originally written in Latin or Dutch have appeared, and valuable South African textbooks on divers legal subjects have been published. These have made research easier and encouraged a proper study of the Roman-Dutch law. Perhaps there is an inclination to-day to delve too deeply into the past and in the decision of a case to place reliance upon the opinion of some medieval writer on Roman law, without a due appreciation of his importance or of the changes wrought by custom in the intervening centuries.

Until the early nineteenth century all development of the Roman-Dutch law in South Africa took place in the Cape Colony, but when settlers crossed the Orange River and founded the neighbouring states matters changed. In the Transvaal, the Thirty-three Articles of 1844 adopted, as the basis of their law, the Dutch law, "but in a modified form and in accordance with the customs of South Africa". In 1858, the *Grondwet* established courts of (*a*) landdrost, (*b*) landdrost and heemraden, and (*c*) a superior court of three landdrosts and twelve jurymen (*gesworen*). In September 1859, the Volksraad decided that van der Linden's Institutes should be the law book (*Wetboek*) of the Transvaal, and that when that work did not deal with the subject clearly or at all, then the *Wetboek* of van Leeuwen and Grotius' *Introduction to the Law of Holland* should be binding on the courts. Subsequently, by Proclamation 14 of 1902, the common law of the Transvaal was declared to be the Roman-Dutch law. In 1877 an Act was passed establishing a High Court of Justice consisting of three Judges; this was confirmed in 1883,[1] and thereafter the constitution and functions of the High Court were similar to those existing in the Cape Colony, while the functions of an inferior court were carried out by a landdrost. After the Peace of Vereeniging two superior courts were created, one in Pretoria and one in Johannesburg, and, instead of landdrosts, resident magistrates were appointed to act as inferior courts of justice in the different districts.

The Free State developed on similar lines. The Roman-Dutch law was adopted from the start,[2] and the courts were at first landdrosts and heemraden; then, in 1874, a High Court was set up as the superior court,[3] and landdrosts as inferior courts;[4] and then, after the annexation in 1900, a High Court and inferior Courts of Resident Magistrate.[5]

[1] Law 3 of 1883.
[2] *Law Book of 1901*, ch. I.
[3] *Ibid.* ch. II.
[4] *Ibid.* ch. IV.
[5] Ordinances 4 and 7 of 1902.

Natal was, in 1845, annexed to the Cape Colony, and an ordinance was promulgated introducing into Natal the Roman-Dutch law "as the same has been and is accepted and administered by the legal tribunals of the Colony of the Cape of Good Hope" and empowering the Governor to appoint magistrates in Natal.[1] In the same year an Ordinance was promulgated creating a District Court for Natal presided over by a Recorder. Local legislation has very largely followed Cape precedent, but the influence of English law has been greater; even the Statute of Frauds being thought worthy of imitation.

Southern Rhodesia has adopted the law of the Cape Colony as it was on 10 June 1891.[2] In 1919 the Roman-Dutch law as existing and applied in the Cape of Good Hope on 24 December 1919 was introduced into the mandated territory of South-West Africa.[3]

The Native Territories, forming part of the Union of South Africa, are subject to special legislation under which Native Custom is largely recognised and enforced by special courts, the broad general principle being that as between Europeans the Roman-Dutch law is enforced, while Native customs are applied to suits between Natives. The Transkei, however, possesses a penal code which came into force in 1886 and is in the main an accurate codification of the criminal law of the Cape Colony.

With the passing of the South Africa Act in September 1909 the period of primary development was at an end, and a period of assimilation and codification was ushered in. That Act created a Supreme Court for the whole of South Africa, consisting of an Appellate Division, a Provincial Division for each of the four Provinces, and a number of Local Divisions with jurisdiction limited to a part of their respective Provinces—the Eastern Districts Local Division at Grahamstown, that of Griqualand West at Kimberley, and that of the Witwatersrand at Johannesburg. The Appellate Division consists of a Chief Justice and four Judges of Appeal. It is the supreme court of appeal in both criminal and civil matters for the whole Union, as well as for the Mandated Territory and Southern Rhodesia. Each Provincial Division consists of a Judge-President and a number of Puisne Judges, sitting at the provincial capitals but regularly going on circuit through the larger towns. The Provinces are divided into a number of magisterial districts, each with a paid Resident Magistrate, who has jurisdiction, both civil and criminal, limited by amount (civil, £200 or more by consent; criminal, six months' imprisonment and fine of £50) and also by subject matter.

The Appellate Division sits to administer the Roman-Dutch law as it has been received in South Africa. In general, no Provincial decision is authoritative for the Union until it has received the sanction

[1] Ordinance 12 of 1845.
[2] Proclamation 21 of 1919.
[3] Proclamation, *Cape Government Gazette*, 16 June 1891.

of the Appellate Division. The task of interpreting an ancient code in the light of modern conditions is no easy one, and is made more difficult in South Africa by the rarity of some of the early legal works and the obscurity of many of their writers; but it is universally admitted that the Appellate Division has achieved a remarkable degree of success, avoiding, on the one hand, the perpetuation of ancient subtleties merely because they are ancient and, on the other hand, the abandonment of sound principles merely because they are not shared by other codes. The process, however, has still a long way to go. It is still possible for an apparently sound line of modern cases to be upset by reference to a seventeenth-century civilian, and for a doctrine which has been thought dead for a hundred years to rear its anachronistic head in the midst of the affairs of to-day.

The legislative output since Union has been profuse, most of it designed to repeal pre-Union Acts and consolidate the statutory laws of the different colonies upon various subjects into new comprehensive measures. The day is not far distant when pre-Union statutes, still in force, will fill only one very small volume.

It remains to say a word as to the content of the law. The Law of Persons is almost pure Roman-Dutch law. The age of majority is twenty-one for both sexes. Below that age, a minor is under the guardianship either of his parent, or of a tutor appointed by the father by will, or by the Court as "upper guardian", and is incapable of binding himself by contract except beneficially to himself. The common law effect of marriage is to create a community of all property in equal shares, the husband having the marital power which includes complete power of control over the property, the wife becoming a minor incapable of contracting except for necessaries or for trading. But though such marriages persist in the rural districts, the commoner form among educated people is by antenuptial contract, which usually excludes the marital power and leaves the wife in the same position in respect of her property as if she were not married. On the dissolution of a marriage in community, the property is divided into two equal shares, one of which goes to the side of the husband or according to his disposition, the other going to the side of the wife or according to her disposition. Divorce in South Africa is granted either for adultery or for malicious desertion after a preliminary order for restitution of conjugal rights, the latter ground in practice often amounting to consent. A remarkable feature of divorce practice in undefended cases is the facility with which the Courts assume jurisdiction on *ex parte* evidence of domicile by the plaintiff spouse.

With regard to the devolution of property on death, intestate succession was a subject on which the law of South Holland differed from that of North Holland. There being no reason why South Africa should favour either of the two sub-provinces, the matter was settled by a resolution of the Governor and Council dated 19 June 1714, which adopted the terms of the Charter for the East Indies of 1661. This charter represented a compromise between the two codes, incorporating the less fortunate provisions of both. Under it the widow, if she has any right of succession at all (which is doubtful), comes in only next before the Crown; there is no rule of primogeniture; representation is unlimited, and the rules as to succession where one grandparent survives are so obscure that they are still a matter of controversy. As for succession by will, the old limitations on freedom of testation, which the Roman and Roman-Dutch law imposed for the benefit of the children, were removed in the Cape as early as 1873, and later in the other three Provinces. The formalities for the making of wills are English. The most remarkable type of will is the mutual will of husband and wife, which frequently has the effect of leaving the surviving spouse in possession of one-half of the estate and in ownership of the other but without any power of testation in respect of either. A testator has power to impose *fidei commissa* on beneficiaries under his will, which are binding at any rate until the fourth generation. Hence complicated settlements by way of *fidei commissum* and substitution are not uncommon. But the law favours free power of disposition and the early vesting of rights, and in case of doubt will prefer the less to the more complicated interpretation.

With regard to the Law of Things, the ownership of land presents some interesting features. In the early days of the Cape settlement, although freehold tenure was not unknown, the commonest form of holding agricultural land was by precarious tenure, the holding being known as a "loan place". Gradually, however, there grew up a system of "perpetual quit-rent", the rights and obligations under which were substantially those of the Roman *emphyteusis*, and at the same time the precarious nature of the loan tenure was modified by custom in the direction of permanence and heritability. Finally, by a proclamation of Sir John Cradock (6 August 1813), leave was given to all holders of loan places to convert them into perpetual quit-rent tenure. Land at the present day in South Africa is therefore either unalienated Crown land, freehold, or quit-rent; the ninety-nine-year lease is almost unknown except for mineral rights. The conditions of quit-rent tenure vary from Province to Province, but generally the incidents consist in payment of a yearly sum to the Crown, incomplete power of alienation, and the reservation to the Crown of certain rights, the most important of which are the right to all minerals, the right to resume for public purposes (sometimes without compensation), and the right to take material for road-building. Title to land is registered in an office open to public inspection, in which are also registered all burdens on land whether of the nature of servitudes or of mortgage-bonds. The law of water-rights, which is statutory and based on Roman law, and the law of mining form special branches of extreme complexity.

The Law of Obligations is strongly individual. It has at last been established, after a long controversy between the Cape and the Transvaal Courts, that, in contract, neither form nor consideration is in general required; any agreement is actionable if made seriously and deliberately and with the intention that a lawful obligation should be created. Contracts may be made for the benefit of third parties, who by accepting them may sue upon them. Whether a contract is complete on acceptance of an offer or whether notification of acceptance is necessary, and whether such notification if sent by post must reach the offeror, are questions not yet authoritatively decided, though existing decisions favour the English rule on grounds based on Roman-Dutch authority. Among particular contracts, the law of sale exhibits certain peculiarities, which arise mainly from two sources. The one is the civil law rule as to the passing of ownership, *dominium* passing only on delivery coupled with payment of the price or the giving of credit. The other consists in the fact that the anomalies of Roman law in respect of remedies for breach of contract (anomalies arising from the history of the law of sale) have not yet been resolved in South Africa. Generally, it may be said that the law is more favourable to the buyer and less so to the seller than in English law, the maxim *caveat emptor* being of limited application only. The effects of fraud and mistake are substantially the same as in other systems.

In the Law of Delicts, South Africa has witnessed a very remarkable extension and development of the principles of the *Lex Aquilia*, comparable with and consequent upon the development achieved by the jurists of the Empire. The result has been to produce a generalised theory of negligence, which is not afraid to leave wide discretion to the tribunals in applying it to particular states of fact. The law of contributory negligence, and the effect of the concurrence of the negligence of two independent agents, have of late years been the subject of close analysis. Coupled with this there has been an interesting series of cases on the right of defendants to maintain an action for loss of support consequent on the death of the bread-winner, an action which is derived not from statute but from the common law. In other branches of the law of delict South Africa is less individual; her law of nuisance, for example, is almost pure English law.

In Criminal Law, the Transkei Native Code already referred to has not, as might have been expected, inspired any general measures of codification, though the unsatisfactory state of the early authorities (which seldom draw even the elementary distinction between crime and civil wrong) renders such codification every day more desirable. The principal peculiarity lies in the very wide scope of such crimes as fraud, *injuria* and theft, and, in matters of procedure, in the combination of English ideas with a system of state control of prosecutions. The Common Law is if anything more favourable to the accused even than is English law; but such statutory crimes as stock theft and liquor offences swing the balance well over to the other side. The principal requirement, apart from the question of a code, is a Court of Criminal Appeal on the facts, since the Appellate Division now has power to hear appeals only on points of law.

CHAPTER XXXII

CULTURAL DEVELOPMENT

THE mixed population of southern Africa consists of Bushmen, Hottentots, Indians, half-caste Coloured Folk, Europeans and Bantu in that ascending order of numerical magnitude. Folk of European stock number rather more than one in five in the Union of South Africa, one in ten in South-West Africa, and about one in thirty in the Federation of Rhodesia and Nyasaland; nevertheless, though they are thus in a minority everywhere, their culture is dominant. Hence, it will be best to consider that culture primarily and merely to mention the cultures of the other groups in so far as they have influenced it.

The European group in southern Africa is divided into two sections: the Afrikaners, whose home language is Afrikaans, a form of Dutch, and, for want of an individual name, the British, whose home language is English. The Afrikaners, who trace their descent mainly from the Netherlands, West Germany, Huguenot France and the Presbyterian Lowlands of Scotland, began to settle in Capetown some three hundred years ago and now constitute perhaps sixty per cent of the European group in the Union, the great majority of that group in South-West Africa, and a strong minority of that in the Federation. The British, who first began to come in any strength in 1820, are drawn from all parts of the English-speaking world and include many of the Jews from diverse countries. Difference of outlook and culture between Afrikaners and British are probably due far more to differences of occupation and interest than of descent. The Afrikaners, whether they be descended from the old-established landed families of the Western Cape Province, who form the aristocracy of southern Africa, or from less polished pastoralists or mealie-farmers up-country, have an agricultural tradition and, though they are nowadays moving into the towns, are still as a body closer to the soil than are the British. Numbers of the latter have indeed been on the land from the first and, to that extent, have shared the Afrikaners' main interest, but most of them have always lived in the towns and gone into business or the professions. The British have, moreover, as a rule taken a more lively interest in the doings of the outer world than have their Afrikaner fellow-citizens, and, not so long ago, many of them used to speak of Great Britain as "Home", meaning thereby the land that had given them their language, customs and ideals, and thus tempted nationalist-minded Afrikaners to accuse them of having a divided allegiance. There is little of such nostalgic talk nowadays, except possibly by a few newcomers; on the other hand, neither Afrikaners nor British, however real their loyalty to their common country, find it easy to draw inspiration for their art and literature from the sea and the soil and the factory machine. Nor can they, so long as they leave these things to be worked by non-European dependants. It will probably be a long time before white southern Africa can boast a tinker Bunyan or a ploughboy Burns, let alone a fisherman Peter.

There are, however, manifold signs that the two European sections will sooner or later share a genuinely common culture. Increasing bilingualism and intermarriage, a growing realisation of what each section can give to the country as a whole, pride in citizenship of the most influential state in all Africa and a determination to solve its problems jointly, an honest recognition by the British that southern Africa is their true home, all these things tend to draw the two sections closer together. This good work can be furthered by a general knowledge of the true facts of their common history, which records far more co-operation than antagonism. White southern Africa has very rarely been divided along Afrikaner *versus* British lines. Not a few of the British went out on the Great Trek, the Exodus of the Afrikaners, and more would avowedly have gone had they known how to live in waggons in the wilderness; during the South African War, the second great Afrikaner experience, many Afrikaners fought for the Crown, while many burghers of British stock fought for the republics; the Afrikaner Rebellion of 1914 was put down, not by the British, but by Afrikaners led by Louis Botha, one of themselves; more Afrikaners than British volunteered during the two world wars of the twentieth century. Again, after the balkanisation of the eighteen-fifties, the Orange Free State, with its many Scottish civil servants, worked as a rule with the parent Cape Colony against the Hollando-Afrikaner South African Republic and its economic appendage, ultra-British Natal. In the Cape, every Ministry was mixed Afrikaner and British, and nearly all of them were dependent on the Afrikaner Bond, which had many members of British stock; in the Union, the same salutary practice prevailed until 1948, when for the first time an exclusively Afrikaner Ministry took office. Afrikaners as well as British have been settled in Southern Rhodesia from the first; the same is true of South-West Africa, while men of both sections have long carried on much of the business of Portuguese Lourenço Marques.

It is undeniable that the "Afrikaans" and "English" cultures are drawing closer together, but, for all that, it is still necessary to distinguish between them without for a moment suggesting that they are entirely separate and, still less, contrasted developments. A short account of each in turn may serve to show that this is indeed so.

Afrikaans Culture

When the Cape Colony was founded in 1652, the parent United Provinces stood culturally in the front rank in Europe; yet for a long time to come little systematic attempt was made to acclimatise Netherlandish culture at the far end of Africa. It could hardly have been otherwise seeing that the higher officials, in many cases men of birth and education, looked on the struggling little colony as a mere stepping-stone to higher things either in Java or at home, while the rank and file were for the most part soldiers and sailors, husbandmen, artisans or clerks, very ordinary folk who simply brought with them what little they must have to earn a living and find their way about in a strange land. It is true that in the late sixteen-eighties a handful of Protestant French refugees, many of them of higher social standing than the earlier settlers, brought with them a leavening of civilisation that was destined to have a far-reaching influence; even so, many years later, the white community still consisted of a small group of harassed townsfolk in the capital and a scattering of farmers and pastoralists in the backveld, folk whose links with distant Europe were few and frail.

The centre of culture as of governance was the Castle at Cape Town, a fine Vauban fort and the first important European building in the land. Thence civilisation radiated outwards to later urban centres at Stellenbosch, Paarl, Swellendam, Graaff-Reinet and Uitenhage, nearly all of which became in due time the seat of a *landdrost* (magistrate), while each had its own *predikant* (minister). Formal education, however, was primitive, for though a few schools were opened in the little towns, most of the country folk must rely on *meesters* (itinerant teachers) and ministers of the Dutch Reformed Church, where these were within reach. Indeed, it was the latter whom nearly all the colonists had to thank that they could at least read the Bible and write their names.

Warm tribute must be paid to the civilising work of the Church. Nearly all the early settlers were members of the Dutch Reformed Church, which did its best for them with the hearty approval of the Company. *Predikants* were trained for the Company's service by the mother congregation in Amsterdam. None but men whose learning and character were vouched for by two Directors of the Company and two members of the Amsterdam *Classis* (Presbytery) were allowed to officiate in the Company's ships or stations, where they ranked next after the merchants. Only such fully qualified ministers were authorised to preach, to administer the sacraments of baptism and *Nachtmaal* (Holy communion) and to perform the ceremonies of marriage and burial. Where no such *predikant* was available, a *krankbesoeker* (sick-comforter) might conduct an ordinary service and read another man's printed sermon; but did such a one venture to preach a sermon of his own, he was liable to official reprimand. No *predikant* was resident at the Cape during the first thirteen years; hence, it is not surprising that, on his arrival in 1665, Johan van Arckel, the little colony's first regular minister, found merely a score of communicants among a total white population of perhaps one thousand souls. Van Arckel and his immediate successors, usually with official approval, followed the liberal policy prevalent in the Company's dominions of attempting to educate and convert the slaves, Hottentots and mixed-breed Cape Coloured Folk. In keeping with this policy, they summoned to the House of God not only Europeans, but folk of all colours; but here they found that the presence of slaves was a stumbling-block to some of their white parishioners, who objected to seeing them baptised, because no Christian could be held in bondage, and disliked having to sit next to them because of their dirt and servile status. Nevertheless, most of the burghers were liberal enough in their own homes. Besides attending church on Sundays when possible, each householder would conduct morning and evening family prayers at which all beneath his roof, regardless of colour, were expected to be present, the head of the house reading a portion from the Bible and putting up an extempore prayer, and all joining in the singing of a psalm from Pieter Datheen's rhymed psalmody or, in later times, a hymn or a psalm from Voet and Ghijsen's hymnology. This simple ritual, which is still followed on up-country farms, did much to keep alive that interest in reading and singing, which visitors noted with approval.

In the Company's sphere, the Church was subject to a dual control. The Company appointed, paid, promoted and transferred ministers and sick-comforters alike, while, at the Cape, the Council of Policy sent one of its members to hold a watching-brief at the meetings of each *kerkeraad* (consistory); but such a congregational council would sit under the chairmanship of its Minister and be manned by Deacons chosen by the Council from a double list submitted to it by the *kerkeraad*, and by Elders elected by the congregation subject to official approval. This complicated system worked well enough. The first congregation was formed at Cape Town in 1665 and, between 1685 and 1700, others were formed at Stellenbosch and Paarl, and at Drakenstein for the French refugees. Congregations were one thing, however, and ministers and church buildings quite another. Such was the shortage of the former that Stellenbosch and Drakenstein must share the services of a French-speaking minister and a Dutch-speaking sick-comforter till 1694, and Paarl must fill its pulpit as best it could for ten years thereafter. As for church buildings, the Cape Town congregation must worship in one or other part of the Castle till 1704, when it entered joyfully into a church of its own, the Groote Kerk in what is now Adderley Street, and that at Drakenstein must worship in a private house till the completion of its church in 1720. Thereafter, no new congregations were formed in the fast-expanding little colony for a quarter of a century, when churches were built at Roodesand (Tulbagh) in 1743 and at Zwartland (Malmesbury) two years later.

By the time these two frontier churches had been built, French had died out in the Colony and the Huguenot immigrants were being fast assimilated to the Dutch-speaking population, though the names of many of them were to survive to this day, often in a scarcely recognisable form, and with the names, a justifiable pride in French ancestry.[1] Far more fundamental changes were meanwhile taking place. As the eighteenth century wore on, lay and clerical liberalism wilted in face of the rising generation. White youngsters born in the Colony learned, like their parents before them, to rely on the services of dark-skinned folk who lived on a lower cultural level than themselves; they pressed successfully for stiffer slave laws and imposed a customary colour-bar on all non-Europeans, bond or free. Further, growing up in isolation at the far end of Africa, as they must once the Company had ceased to encourage immigration in 1717, and resentful also of restrictive rule by the Company's officials, they began to regard themselves as "Afrikaners" in contrast to these semi-foreign "Hollanders" at the Castle. And it was not only the colonial-born, but newcomers also, who felt that the Cape was their homeland. In this respect, the turning-point came in the mid-eighteenth century. As late as 1751, Hendrik Swellengrebel, for all that he was the first locally-born man to become Governor, retired "home" to the Netherlands, as so many genuinely Dutch officials had done before him. Then came a gradual change. Swellengrebel's successor, Ryk Tulbagh, a Hollander-born and friend of Linnaeus, the famous Swedish botanist, preferred to die where he had so long lived—in the Colony which he had done so much to advance. His example was widely followed, notably by the German immigrant, Joachim van Dessin, who, in 1761, bequeathed five thousand volumes to the Colony. These volumes, entrusted to the Cape Town Consistory of the Dutch Reformed Church, were handed over, sixty years later, to the now famous South African Public Library at Cape Town.

In spite of the influence of Tulbagh, van Dessin and their like, this new Afrikaner society gave little evidence of general cultural progress during the latter half of the eighteenth century. The young folk of the capital might pick up extravagant ideas from the sprigs of the nobility, who officered the French regiments in friendly occupation during the War of American Independence, but most of the rest were still just homely folk, wrapped up in their own day-to-day affairs and linked to the distant civilisation of their ancestral homeland by little more than a few ministers, sick-comforters and stray visitors from overseas. Nevertheless, though few of them had much book-learning and knowledge of the outer world, many were skilled builders, masons, carpenters, wood- and metal-workers, thatchers and so forth, who, having learned their crafts in a good school, could either reproduce or design for themselves whatever was needed in the house or on the farm. And not white colonists alone, but Malays and other non-Europeans, bond and free. The dignified churches, town houses,

[1] Botha, C. G., *The French Refugees at the Cape*.

drostdies (magisterial residences) and Western Province country-houses were the work of men of diverse colours and races working side by side.

Let it be recalled that, since the Church was the chief civilising influence, colonial craftsmen did much of their best work either for this or that church or *pastorie* (manse). Meanwhile, the ministers to whom the colonists owed so much were few and far between. As late as 1806 when the British finally took the Cape, there were only some dozen centres of organised Christian worship in the whole overblown dependency: seven Dutch Reformed churches at Cape Town, Stellenbosch, Paarl, Roodesand, Zwartland, Swellendam and Graaff-Reinet, a single Lutheran church in the capital, Roman Catholics celebrating Mass in the Castle by leave of the liberal Batavian officials, a privilege which the British at once withdrew, and newly-arrived missionaries of the Moravian Society at Genandendal and of the London Missionary Society at Bethelsdorp. From that time onwards, churches and mission stations multiplied fast within the Colony and without, but not before the Dutch Reformed Church had had to weather a grave crisis. Lacking means to train its ministers locally, it found that it could not get recruits from the Netherlands. At last, in 1822, and not for the last time, the situation was saved by the energetic Governor, Lord Charles Somerset, who called in half a dozen Scottish Presbyterians headed by the famous Dr. Andrew Murray. These learned, able and high-principled ministers undoubtedly saved the Church in the Colony; on the other hand, dour men that they were, they taught their flocks an intolerant puritanism and exaggerated reverence for the Sabbath that were foreign to the Dutch character; they were, moreover, the forerunners of so many other English-speaking ministers that at the time of the Great Trek in the late eighteen-thirties more than half the members of the Cape Synod were Scots, who, though they punctiliously preached in Dutch, saw to it that, as early as 1865, English should also be used in church. Their coming was a great gain to the Colony, because they encouraged education, ably seconded by Scottish schoolmasters whom Somerset also called in; they supported missionary enterprise, and they infused their work with a sincerity and spirit of self-sacrifice which have made their memories dear to their congregations for all time. Even to-day, Afrikaners, as a rule, feel that they have more in common with brother Presbyterians from Scotland than with the most staunchly Calvinistic "Hollanders".

There is no need to follow further in any detail the story of the Dutch Reformed Church in southern Africa beyond noting that it suffered disruption in the mid-nineteenth century shortly after its sister Established Kirk in Scotland had undergone a like fate. This disruption influenced Afrikaans culture, because the Afrikaners, who almost to a man were members of the Church, keenly followed in sermon and newspaper-article the struggle between the Liberals and the ultimately victorious Orthodox. There were soon at least three branches of Dutch Calvinism in southern Africa. The oldest and largest was and still is the *Nederduits Gereformeerde Kerk* (Dutch Reformed Church), which has 349 European congregations with a total membership of over 310,000, and 173 non-European congregations organised separately, since 1881, in the *Sendelings Kerk* (Mission Church) with a membership of some 50,000. Since 1859, it has had its Theological Seminary at Stellenbosch, where it trains its ministers, and has long had as its official organ *Die Kerkbode*, which has probably the largest circulation of any weekly publication in the country. The second branch is the *Gereformeerde Kerk* (Reformed Church), which has eighty-five congregations totalling over 43,000 souls, a Theological School at Potchefstroom and a bi-weekly journal, *Die Kerkblad*. Lastly, there is the *Nederduits Hervormde Kerk* (Dutch Reformed Church), which was once the state church of the South African Republic and now trains its ministers at the University of Pretoria and publishes its official opinions monthly in *Die Hervormer*. Taken together, these three branches can count fully 1,250,000 white adherents besides many thousands of non-Europeans, thus constituting the largest, though divided, Christian community in southern Africa. One further internal division remains, however, to be recorded. The Church in the Cape Colony had no colour bar for some two hundred years; but in 1857, the Cape Synod, still largely manned by Scots, reluctantly agreed that provision might be made for separate worship by Europeans and others because of "the weakness of some of its members". So fast did these weaker brethren multiply that, in 1881, it went still further and formed the separate *Sendelings Kerk*, avowedly for non-Europeans. This *Kerk* still remains under the general control of the parent body, which gives it much-needed financial aid, but such few non-European ministers as it has are all trained separately from and to a lower level than their white colleagues and receive smaller salaries than they. Separation on a colour basis has been the practice in the other local Dutch Reformed communions from the first.

There had been Lutherans among the earliest settlers, but the Company had disapproved so strongly of Churches other than the Dutch Reformed that they had been obliged to worship in private until 1780, when they were at last suffered to build their stately church in Strand Street, Cape Town. Even so, they had to wait many years before they were permitted to add thereto a much-disputed steeple. To-day they number some 261,000 souls.[1] The Roman Catholics, who were first allowed to organise themselves publicly in 1820, are about two-thirds as numerous. The Presbyterian Church of South Africa established its first congregation in 1813 and to-day counts

[1] This and subsequent figures include all adherents of whatever colour.

nearly 200,000 members; the Congregational Church, closely connected with the London Missionary Society for many years, began at much the same time as the Presbyterians and now numbers about 157,000; the Wesleyan Methodist Church of South Africa, whose main strength has long lain in the Eastern Province, dates from 1816 and has a present membership of 833,000.

The British naturally brought the Anglican Church with them in 1806, but for many years thereafter its handful of clergy were only colonial chaplains preaching in one or another Dutch Reformed or Wesleyan church by courtesy of the minister concerned. Better days dawned in 1847, when Robert Gray was consecrated first Bishop of Cape Town with a diocese covering most of what is now the Union with the tiny island of St Helena a thousand miles distant thrown in for good measure. Six years later outlying portions of this vast area were cut off as the dioceses of Grahamstown and Natal, their Bishops looking to the Bishop of Cape Town as their local primate. Then followed disruption. During the 'sixties some Low Church congregations, disliking the "Puseyite" High Church leanings of their brethren, insisted on keeping themselves apart as members of the Church of England as by law established *in partibus infidelium*. Undismayed by this unhappy division, which still persists, the main body organised itself between 1870 and 1875 on an autonomous basis as the Church of the Province of South Africa in communion with Canterbury. Some twenty years later the bishopric of Cape Town was elevated to the rank of an archbishopric. So fast has the Church of the Province grown that it now numbers 720,000 souls distributed over fully a dozen dioceses, the three most northerly of which have recently been grouped under an Archbishop of Central Africa with his seat at Salisbury. Like the Roman Catholics, the Anglicans exert great cultural influence through their training colleges and schools, several of which are organised on English public school lines and are excellent centres of education in book-learning, character, liberal thought and games. Beside these leading Christian denominations, there are numerous smaller Churches and, in addition, perhaps more than a thousand Bantu churches and sects, many of them very small and not a few frankly anti-European. Jews, by no means all of them conforming Jews, had found their way to the Cape almost from the first, but it was only in 1841 that a group of them founded the first synagogue in the country, at Cape Town. Half a century later, flourishing synagogues had been opened as far afield as Bulawayo and Salisbury. Moslems, again, had begun to come to the Cape in the early days, many of them being brought from the East Indies as slaves or political deportees. During long years they had to make shift to worship either in private houses or in the stone quarry near the well-known Malay Quarter in Cape Town, but during the eighteen-fifties they built them a mosque in that quarter and can now boast at least twenty-five in the

Cape Peninsula alone. There are now some 50,000 Moslems in Cape Town and other urban areas in the Western Cape Province. Most of South Africa's 441,000 Indians are Hindus, the overwhelming majority of them dwelling in coastal Natal. State aid has long been withdrawn from Churches of all kinds.

Full credit must be given to missions as a civilising force, all the more because missionaries from Dr John Philip, Robert Moffat, David Livingstone and John Smith Moffat downwards were often pioneers of Western settlement. Apart from a few sporadic efforts by Portuguese Roman Catholics on the lower Zambesi in days long gone by, little had been done till the last years of the eighteenth century. Then Protestants began to come in force led by Moravians to the Hottentots at Genadendal and Mamre, and closely followed by London Missionary Society men to the half-caste Griquas along the middle Orange valley, to the Bechuana further north, to the Hottentots again in the Eastern Province and to the Bantu beyond the Eastern Frontier. Long before the Great Trek, British missionaries had thrust a line of stations eastwards through still-independent Kaffraria, and a lonely Anglican missionary was found by the Trekkers holding on precariously just outside Dingaan's kraal in far-away Zululand. Nor was it only the British who came, for in 1816 Germans of the Barmen and Berlin Societies entered the field, the Paris Evangelicals arrived just in time to save Basutoland, while representatives of the United States Presbyterian Church (South) ventured, first, to the savage Matabele away to the north of the Bechuana and, failing there, to the kindred and equally ferocious Zulus.

The Moravian and other German missionaries were by no means unpopular, for they were well organised, they taught their dusky flocks the dignity of labour, and they maintained such a truly Teutonic discipline that friendly critics feared that their pupils would never learn to stand on their own feet. On the other hand, many missionaries and, in especial, politically-minded representatives of the London Missionary Society were looked at askance by officials and anathematised by Afrikaner and British frontiersmen, because they were alleged to be drawing off labour, too often failing to keep order among their heterogeneous disciples, and putting ideas into the heads of folk who had been divinely appointed to be mere "hands". Be that as it might, mission stations were little centres of civilisation and, in some cases, became the nuclei of towns by attracting thither white folk as well as non-European dependants. Butterworth and Windhoek played this rôle; somewhat further back in time, Worcester could boast a fine steepled church, an excellent brass-band, a large Native school and a model Native location long before 1824, when the local Europeans were numerous enough to acquire a pastor and school of their own. Undoubtedly, the influence of the missionaries was good in the long run. They themselves not only began the study of African philology and much else, but made a great contribution to the formation of a healthy national character. The descendants of many of them did fully as much, not indeed in the mission field, which few of them entered, but in the political and cultural life of the country, largely because they had been brought up in homes where good books and good talk were to be had, and had thereafter, as a rule, been sent to sound schools either in South Africa or the United Kingdom. Southern Africa, like Scotland, owes much to the sons and daughters of the manse.

New Ideas and Fresh Air

By the time the children of the first generation of missionaries had reached school age there were good schools in the Colony for them to go to. These were only one manifestation of the new ideas and fresh air let loose upon the isolated little colony by the British. The very coming of the British led, however, to social complications and, before long, there were signs that Afrikaner and British cultures might develop along divergent lines. The disheartened Afrikaners could not forget that they had been conquered by the newcomers in 1806, and were at first inclined to sit back, bickering on occasion among themselves. The British, on the other hand, were in much the same position as the Company's officials a hundred years back, unacclimatised newcomers with material interests differing in many ways from those of the older-established white folk, and without some of the spiritual and cultural amenities to which they had been accustomed. They, therefore, set about remedying that lack and were pleased to note that the Afrikaners followed suit. There was an inevitable divergence. It would be wrong to suppose that the Afrikaners started a sectional separatist cultural movement, but just as the British naturally drew on the culture of their own homeland, so the Afrikaners sought to strengthen their hold more systematically than hitherto on what remained to them of their ancestral Netherlandish culture, which was to them the symbol of intellectual independence. Hence began a rivalry between the English and Dutch languages, each of which could boast a fine literature and tradition. Awkward the situation might be politically and socially, especially after English had become the official language, but the cultural opportunities were great. Here, the Afrikaners, then and until quite recent times, stood to fare better than the British, because their children, virtually obliged to learn English, could become bilingual and thus have access to the treasures of both cultures, while the British youngsters as a rule suffered by only knowing their own language. True, these latter gained by speaking a world language, but that gain was comparatively slight and destined to be passing. Only to-day are the British in the Union and South-West Africa becoming bilingual under social and political pressure and thus equipping themselves to get the best out of both cultures.

The separatist tendencies of this strife of tongues were reinforced for a time by various exclusively Afrikaner associations. Afrikaners had been much given to forming groups, big and little, during the late eighteenth century. Such had been the Cape Patriots of 1779, a political party formed by burghers in the capital and the adjacent western districts to press for constitutional and economic reform; such, in more tumultuary fashion, had been the foundation in 1795 of the first Boer republic by a few hundred Afrikaner pastoralists on the far Eastern Frontier in rebellion against *Jan Compagnie*; such, again, had been the Masonic lodge, founded in 1772 in Cape Town and duly furnished with a temple in 1803; such, finally, were the many social clubs formed by Capetonians on the model of those in the East Indies. Now, Cape Town Afrikaners began to form literary and dramatic societies and, also, strong and exclusively Afrikaner social clubs, like the *Afrikaansche Societeit.* These fissiparous forces were, however, combated by others which made for co-operation. Social clubs were formed in English fashion to which all white men were eligible; folk of both sections jostled one another enthusiastically at the race meetings fostered by the sporting Governor, Lord Charles Somerset; they flocked to private theatricals, the fashion for which was set by visiting troupes of players;[1] they joined forces in a short-lived prohibition campaign during the eighteen-thirties; "all the principal Gentlemen and Ladies" competed eagerly for invitations to the frequent state balls at Government House, and many of their daughters found the less formal hospitality of the officers of the garrison and naval squadron so entrancing that they achieved their ambition of marrying into one or other of the services. In a much wider sphere, the emancipation of the slaves and the abolition of the legal colour bar between 1828 and 1842 had a civilising and unifying effect by gradually freeing Afrikaners from the slave-owners' mentality and thus bringing them closer to the liberty-loving British. Again, from 1837 onwards, town after town, led by Beaufort West, was given elective municipal institutions based on a simple economic franchise accessible to all male British subjects regardless of race. Hard on the heels of this institution of a civilisation franchise, the glory of the Old Colony till its destruction in our own day, came the long-overdue withdrawal of Political Commissioners from the Synod of the Dutch Reformed Church in 1842 and, a dozen years thereafter, the grant of representative institutions embodied in a Parliament both of whose Houses were elective on the now well-tried civilisation franchise. In 1855, elective Divisional Councils were created to teach the scattered countryfolk of all colours in the Colony that responsibility went with local powers.

There was, however, another side to the story. These liberalising forces were felt mainly in Cape Town and the parts adjacent. They

[1] Bosman, F. C., *History of the Theatre in South Africa.*

touched the up-country folk so little that, more than thirty years after the final British occupation, a shrewd and fair-minded British visitor could record that "the literary resources of the Boers are few, their opportunities of acquiring knowledge of other countries scanty, and their prejudices strong in proportion".[1] This summing-up was all too true. Some thousands of frontier Afrikaners and their wives, finding this social revolution more than they could stomach, went out on the Great Trek (1835–48) and set up republics in Natal, the Orange Free State and the Transvaal with the avowed intention of maintaining there the colour bar that was fading away in the parent Colony. They did so with such success that, after the union of the Cape with these new territories in 1910, their descendants, reinforced by conservative English-speaking Natalians, were strong enough to destroy liberalism in its South African stronghold.

Liberal ideas were spread throughout the Cape Colony mainly by the printed word. Thanks to the indefatigable Somerset, the South African Public Library, still "the bright eye of the Cape", was opened in 1822 in a small room in the old Slave Lodge, and was presently entrusted with van Dessin's five thousand volumes two generations after their donor's death. At the same time, Somerset took over a natural history museum collected by the army surgeon and explorer, Dr Andrew Smith, and housed it in a couple of adjacent rooms. There the neglected specimens slowly decayed; but the Library prospered and, in 1861, made a great step forward when it received from Sir George Grey, one of Somerset's most notable successors, his splendid collection of manuscripts, first editions and incunabulae. Housed at last in a dignified building of its own, it rapidly became the finest library in all Africa, standing in a class by itself for many years as something very much more than a mere circulating library. Latterly, however, other fine libraries have been opened in the chief cities of the Union and others of lesser pretensions, though of great value, in the larger towns.

Newspapers naturally did more at first than the new Library to spread the reading habit, if only because they could travel further and more cheaply than books. The first newspaper to be printed in Africa was *The Cape Government Gazette* issued by the British in 1800 during their first brief Occupation, but the first unofficial newsheet only appeared in 1824.[2] This was *The South African Commercial Advertiser*, a weekly paper printed in Cape Town by George Greig and edited jointly by the two Scottish friends, John Fairbairn and Thomas Pringle, the poet and sometime librarian of the Public Library. It was followed immediately by Pringle's *Journal* and the Rev. Abraham Faure's *Tydschrift*. Fairbairn's successful struggle for the freedom of the press against Somerset's restrictive policy engendered a cordiality between his Afrikaner and British supporters which did not die even

[1] Bunbury, C. J. F., *Journal of a Residence at the Cape*, p. 184. [2] *Vide supra*, pp 252.

after he had alienated many of them by refusing to press for representative institutions so long as slavery and the colour bar stood. Meanwhile, other newspapers had appeared in either English or Dutch, notably Christoffel Brand's *Die Zuid Afrikaan*, with its prophetic name, in 1830 and Louis Meurant's *Grahamstown Journal* a year later.[1] Both these papers were destined to live long, as also was *The Cape Argus*, which appeared four times a week in 1857 and presently became a daily and parent of the powerful Argus group. It is true that, in 1858, an experimental daily had managed to struggle along for a few short weeks, but it was not until 1876 that *The Cape Times* was launched, a daily from the start and still one of the most influential journals in southern Africa. Bantu readers had to wait for a paper of their own till 1884, when the able Xhosa, Tengo Jabavu, published *Imvo zaba Ntsundu*. Journalism, however, was not confined to the Cape. In Natal, *The Natal Witness* appeared in 1846 and *The Natal Government Gazette* three years later; north of the Orange River *The Friend* started its long and honourable career in 1850 as an offshoot of *The Grahamstown Journal*, to be followed in 1854 by the *Gouvernements Courant* of the newly-independent Orange Free State, while in 1857 the *Staats Courant* of the South African Republic appeared, the first such publication north of the Vaal, to be followed soon by *The Transvaal Argus*. In due time, a Kimberley press gave little Griqualand West the *Diamond Fields Advertiser*, and, at the turn of the century, Southern Rhodesia could boast *The Bulawayo Chronicle* and *The Rhodesia Herald*. To-day, there are well over three hundred Dutch, Afrikaans and English newspapers in southern Africa besides a score in one Bantu tongue or another. All dailies have good cable services, give excellent local reports and are well served by country correspondents; the standard of the dailies in the principal towns compares favourably with that of many journals in other Dominions and in the United Kingdom.

The Afrikaans press is naturally more consciously South African in tone than the English and, since it sets out to play a cultural rôle, tends to give the ideals of its own section of the public a prominence that their importance does not always warrant. Further, since it seeks to encourage local talent and finds it hard to recruit Afrikaans-speaking staff from overseas, its editors are nearly all South African-born, while those of the leading English papers, as a rule, are not. Possibly all southern African papers pay too much attention to politics and sport, but few of them completely ignore culture. Some even specialise therein. The Afrikaners are well served by *Die Brandwag*, an admirable journal devoted entirely to art and literature, by *Die Huisgenoot*, a very sound weekly, and by *Standpunte* and *Tydskryf en Letterkunde*, two of the best literary quarterlies in the country. The British, for

[1] There was as yet no "South Africa" in a political sense, but the term was coming into use, e.g. South African Public Library (1822), South African College (1829), *Die Zuid Afrikaan* (1830).

their part, have *Theorie*, a good quarterly produced by the University of Natal, and *English Studies in Africa* emanating from the University of the Witwatersrand. These two last-named publications, as well as *Standpunte*, welcome articles in either of the official languages.

Schools and Universities

Neither newspapers nor libraries can flourish without a multitude of readers. To-day, nearly all the white folk and very many others in southern Africa can read, but in the early nineteenth century this was no more so than it was then in the United Netherlands or United Kingdom of the day. The good Batavians had ascribed many of the shortcomings of young Cape Colonists to defective education, and had done what they could, in the short time allowed them, to remedy the lack. Their British successors had cautiously carried on the good work; but as late as 1822, though Cape Town could boast a few good schools like the *Tot nut van't Algemeen*, a private venture dating from Batavian days, a classical school run by an Anglican chaplain, and the "classical and commercial academy" started in that very year by Fairbairn and Pringle, the white countryfolk must still make shift with their customary scanty facilities for schooling and the non-Europeans continue to look to the missionaries. This was not enough. Hence, Somerset brought in half a dozen Scots and stationed them at district centres, there to give general education in English and religious instruction in Dutch free of charge, and, if desired, Latin also on payment of a small fee. Seven years later, a group of Afrikaner and British citizens of Cape Town floated the South African College as a company in the hope that it would speedily become a full-blown university. Alas, "Sacs", as the new college was destined long to be known, must be content to be little more than a school till the substructure of elementary and secondary schools throughout the Colony had become strong enough to bear such a weight. Meanwhile, the twenty-four "Somerset" schools showed signs of dwindling away as some of their Scottish masters departed and Afrikaner parents withheld their children because so much of the teaching was given in unfamiliar English. So rapid was the decay that, in 1839, Fairbairn and the famous visiting astronomer, Sir John Herschel, were invited to overhaul the educational machinery. Under the Herschel System, first-class English schools were to charge modest fees, second-class schools were to give free education in English or, if desired, in Dutch, and free third-class schools in the rural areas were to be assisted by state grants. Boards of subscribers, usually under the chairmanship of the local Dutch Reformed minister, were to provide buildings for the first- and second-class schools and, having duly elected the teachers, to supplement their meagre state stipends. Additional teachers were to be sought in Presbyterian Scotland, and the inspection of the whole system, a novel departure, was to be carried out by James Rose-Innes, the ablest of Somerset's Scots, as Superintendent of Education. In keeping with the Colony's civilisation policy, there was no formal colour bar, but Rose-Innes managed to keep most of the non-European children out of his schools by decreeing that scholars must be "decently clad and of good deportment". However, to atone in a measure for this exclusion, state grants were given to mission schools, an embryo Native college was founded by the Glasgow Missionary Society at Lovedale near the Eastern frontier, and in 1854 the Governor, Sir George Grey, began to pay state subsidies to Native industrial schools as part of his civilising policy. Presently, in 1865, just as English was finding its way into the services of the Dutch Reformed Church, that language was made the sole medium of instruction. It was only in 1881–2 that the use of Dutch, but not yet of Afrikaans, was permitted as a medium in the state schools at the discretion of the school committees and as a matter of right in Parliament.[1]

Meanwhile, secondary education had not been forgotten. Here the lead was given by the Churches. In 1842 the Dutch Reformed Church founded in Cape Town a Normal College for the training of teachers, and, seven years later Anglicans founded the Diocesan College, "Bishop's", a private school run on English public school lines at Rondesbosch near Capetown, and presently St. Andrew's also, a similar school at Grahamstown. In 1856, the Gymnasium, forerunner of Victoria College, was founded at Stellenbosch, and in 1874 the Huguenot Seminary for girls was established on United States lines at Wellington hard by. Nor was this advance confined to the parent Colony. Grey College was founded in 1854 at Bloemfontein, while state aid began to be given to lesser schools elsewhere in the newly-independent republic of the Orange Free State as well as in Natal and the poverty-stricken South African Republic. The problem of higher education was tackled first by the Cape Colony, as was only to be expected. There, in 1858, a Board of Examiners was set up to pave the way for the long-awaited university and, sure enough, in 1873, immediately after the discovery of diamonds and gold up-country and the grant of self-government to the Cape, this Board was superseded by the University of the Cape of Good Hope, not unfortunately a residential institution, but a mere examining university on the London model.[2] Next year grants-in-aid of professorial salaries and building grants on the pound-for-pound principle were provided.[3] Even so, as late as 1865, less than half the white children of the Cape Colony were at any kind of school, while the proportion was very much less in what were still the frontier societies of Natal and the two republics. It should, however, be remembered that South Africa was then still a poor country with a widely-scattered white population and scanty means

[1] Nearly all the schools in the Union are state schools. [2] Act No. 16 of 1873.
[3] Act No. 24 of 1874; Malherbe, E. G., *Education in South Africa*, p. 106.

of communication, and that even wealthy and densely-peopled England had not yet provided universal primary education. One other point: South Africa's educational system has been built up largely from imported ideas and methods. In the university sphere, Scottish ideas have prevailed; in the schools, Natal has borrowed almost entirely from England from the first; elsewhere, parents have been so eager to get schooling of some sort for their children that they have been ready to put up with almost any system that did not conflict with their "love of liberty, their deep religious sense, and their desire for self-government".[1]

The progress of education since Union has been rapid all along the line. However unhappy may have been some of the results of entrusting primary and secondary education to the Provincial Councils and "higher education" to Parliament, the record shows that there has been a growing desire for uniformity and a marked increase in the numbers of schools and pupils, especially after 1913, when primary education at least had been made compulsory for white children. Non-European children are not yet subjected to a like compulsion, but thanks to liberal grants from the Union's abounding revenue, a high proportion of them fare better in the matter of schooling than children of like race or colour in every other territory south of the Sahara. In the Union the advance of higher education has in some respects outrun the needs of the white population. The University Acts of 1916 abolished the examining University of the Cape of Good Hope, grouped the smaller and widely-dispersed University Colleges in the federal University of South Africa and chartered the South African and Victoria Colleges as the Universities of Cape Town and Stellenbosch respectively.[2] By 1950, all the smaller colleges received charters, with the result that there are to-day eight autonomous universities in the Union, a very liberal provision for so small a white population and the comparatively few members of other races who were permitted to attend any of them, all the more so, since the University of South Africa has been reconstituted as an examining body, which provides correspondence courses for its students. For many years, the autonomous universities fell into three groups, each distinguished by a different racial policy. The first group consisted of the universities at Stellenbosch, Bloemfontein, Pretoria and Potchefstroom, all with rigid colour bars. The second consisted of Rhodes University, Grahamstown, and the University of Natal. These followed the line of parallel development, Rhodes University, itself white, having affiliated to itself the non-European College at Fort Hare, a safe forty miles distant, and the University of Natal having established a separate non-European section at Durban some thirty miles from its white centre at Pietermaritzburg. The last

[1] Malherbe, E. G., *op. cit.*, pp. 7 *sqq.*
[2] Acts No. 12, 13 and 14 of 1916, all of which came into force in 1918.

group consisted of the Universities of Cape Town and of the Witwatersrand, Johannesburg. Here there had never been an academic colour bar; but though both admitted qualified folk of whatever colour to their lecture-rooms, laboratories and libraries, neither admitted them to its residences, nor, lest it should have to forgo important matches with *apartheid*-minded rivals, included them in its sports teams. The Nationalist Government has now imposed a colour bar on these two liberal institutions, removed Fort Hare from the University of Grahamstown and put it, together with projected Coloured and Bantu University Colleges organized as far as possible on a tribal basis, under the control of the Minister for Native Affairs. In contrast, Queen Elizabeth the Queen Mother has recently been installed as the first President of the newly-founded University College of Rhodesia and Nyasaland at Salisbury, which teaches for the London degree and has no colour bar other than that which, for the time being, excludes non-Europeans from its two experimental residences.

AFRIKAANS

If the proliferation of universities is one of the two events of cultural significance since 1910, the remarkable development of Afrikaans as a literary language has been the other. The Cape Colony, with its older cultural background, took the lead in both these developments and still retains it. The early settlers spoke and wrote seventeenth-century Dutch, a language no more standardised than was the French or German of that day; they found themselves living among folk of many different nationalities and tongues; hence, differences of idiom, pronunciation, vocabulary and spelling inevitably crept in, which, without destroying the stabilising influence of the Dutch of the pulpit and government office, gradually gave rise to Afrikaans, a form of Dutch differing in many ways from the Dutch now spoken in the Netherlands. Three main theories have been propounded to account for this change. The first is the so-called "Portuguese-Creole", that is the corruption of Dutch by the Malay-Portuguese or "Portuguese-Creole" *lingua franca* used by seafarers at Cape Town and other ports in the Company's sphere.[1] This *lingua franca* undoubtedly contributed some hundred words to Afrikaans, but in most cases it did so by way of Dutch or Indo-Dutch. Similarly, Hottentots, Malays and, much later, Bantu contributed a few words, mostly proper names or names of animals and plants. The second theory is the degenerative, that is, sheer mishandling by foreigners such as Germans and French Refugees. This process is not to be disregarded; on the other hand, it should be noted that neither the Germans nor the French were numerous and were from the first greatly outnumbered by the Dutch, that the French language had disappeared by about 1740 leaving hardly a trace, and that the Germans as a rule married Dutch or Afrikaner women, who

[1] Compare pidgin English.

would naturally teach their children their own tongue and not that of their fathers. The last theory is that of spontaneous development. This theory, which now holds the field, makes full allowance for corrupting influences, but maintains that just as the Dutch of the seventeenth century has suffered a sea-change, like many another tongue, so under new conditions Dutch became at the Cape something other than it had been. The late Professor Johannes Smith, an outstanding authority, concluded that: "The language change effected in South Africa forms an interesting parallel to the development of Anglo-Saxon to the English of the beginning of the twelfth century ... and the causes also were much the same in both cases".[1]

Be that as it may, there is ample evidence that Afrikaans was a distinct form of speech freely used by the middle of the eighteenth century. English, however, became the official language during the eighteen-twenties and, some forty years later, was made the sole medium of instruction in the schools in the Cape Colony, by which time it was the language of polite society, whether British or Afrikaner, in the Old Colony and, of course, in Natal. Where Dutch was still used, for instance in the pulpit or the press, it was the Dutch of the Netherlands, because Afrikaans was very generally despised as the patois of country bumpkins, mere *kombuis* Hollands incapable of conveying anything more than the most homely ideas. In those days and for long after, children in old Afrikaner families in the western Cape Colony were punished for using this "kitchen Dutch" in their parents' drawing-rooms.

Afrikaans was not used seriously as a literary vehicle till the last quarter of the nineteenth century. This is not to say that it had never been used before for workaday purposes. It had been used sometimes in correspondence during the later eighteenth century; it had likewise been used freely during the eighteen-thirties in his *Dagboek* (Diary) by the Voortrekker, Louis Trigardt;[2] stray specimens of Afrikaans verse and prose date back almost as far; during the 'forties, "Kaatjie Kekelbek" had relied on Afrikaans to air her caustic views on all and sundry in *Sam Sly's Journal*; a dozen years thereafter, Louis Meurant, magistrate of Cradock, had fought the cause of the Eastern Province against the Western in Afrikaans over the pen-name of "Klaas Waarzegger"; ten years later still, Francis William Reitz, future President of the Orange Free State, had written lively Afrikaans verse[3] and even translated some of Burns's poems into his native tongue. For some time past, articles in Afrikaans had been appearing in newspapers in the Cape, the Free State and the Transvaal, but the real beginning was only made in the mid-eighteen seventies, when

[1] Smith, J. J., *The Evolution and Recognition of the Afrikaans Language* ... Official Year Book of the Union of South Africa, No. 8, 1927, p. 18.

[2] *Dagboek van Louis Trigardt*, 1836–8 (ed. G. S. Preller).

[3] E.g. *Klaas Geswint en sy Paert* (*The Cradock News*, 1860), and *Steweltjeis van Sannie* (*Het Volksblad*, 1870).

Hollanders like Arnoldus Pannevis and C. P. Hoogenhout ("Klaas Waarzegger Jr") started an agitation for the use of Afrikaans as a distinct language. Led by the Rev. Stephanus Johannes du Toit ("Ware Afrikander"), the Dutch Reformed minister at Paarl, they founded an association, *Die Genootskap van Regte Afrikaners*, and in 1876 published the first Afrikaans newspaper, *Di Afrikaanse Patriot*.

This first Afrikaans campaign ran strongly for some twenty years, till du Toit's policy as Superintendent of Education in Kruger's Transvaal and, thereafter, his championship of Cecil Rhodes after the fatal Jameson Raid cost him the support of many Cape Afrikaners. In any event the campaigners had failed to win public recognition for the language, which is not surprising since such influential Afrikaners as Jan Hofmeyr, leader of the Afrikaner Bond, openly despised it and helped powerfully in 1890 to found the *Zuid Afrikaanse Taalbond* to further the interests of Dutch, and Sir Henry de Villiers, the Chief Justice, not only held that Dutch itself would in the end go down before English, but prophesied that the most Afrikaans could hope for was one day to find a "Cape Burns", who should "enforce the phrases of his homely dialect into literature and make them classical".[1] Nevertheless, "for a' that an' a' that", they broke down much of the opposition to the use of Afrikaans as a written language and thus paved the way for the triumphantly successful second campaign. This was inspired by the national consciousness awakened by the South African War. Undismayed by the competition of Simplified Dutch as well as the old charge that their language could not express abstract ideas, the champions of Afrikaans retorted that their own home-born language could do more to make Afrikaners culturally self-dependent than any new-fangled linguistic device, and, in 1905, boldly organised an Afrikaans language society as a dyke against the rising tide of English and a defence against the High Dutch of the *Taalbond*. A year or two later, they went still further by founding in Cape Town the influential Afrikaans Association to frame a policy which should convince their conservative opponents of the error of their ways.

Simplified Dutch thereafter steadily lost ground and Afrikaans began to be used regularly in the press. Then at last decisive proof was given that Afrikaans could do all that its protagonists claimed for it. That proof was given in 1906, when, in quick succession, J. F. E. Celliers published his poem, *Die Vlakte*, in a Pretoria daily paper, and the Rev. J. D. du Toit (Totius) followed it with his poem, *Bij die Monument*, an almost equally notable contribution for all that it was by no means free of Dutch idioms. These two men showed conclusively that Afrikaans could indeed be used for highly elaborate versification and could, moreover, express sublime thoughts quite as clearly and beautifully as either English or Dutch. There could thus be no doubt that Afrikaans had arrived as a literary medium, when the South

[1] Walker, E. A., *Lord de Villiers and His Times*, pp. 278 *sqq.*

African Academy for Language, Literature and Art was founded in 1909 to promote the interests of both Dutch and Afrikaans.[1]

The S.A. Academy has done much to standardise Afrikaans spelling and, generally, to further development of that language. The literary periodical, *Die Brandwag*, soon appeared and, from the first, had no difficulty in filling its pages with good material. Each succeeding year saw an increasing number of Afrikaans publications and, by 1914, mainly at the instance of C. J. Langenhoven, Afrikaans was recognised officially as one of the media of instruction in primary schools in all parts of the Union other than Natal. Five years later it became a permissible medium and a subject of instruction right through the Cape schools up to the standard of matriculation, while to-day it is the recognised medium in all "Dutch" schools and many secondary schools and technical colleges, and is also used freely in all the Union's universities, many of which have chairs in Afrikaans. Finally, in 1925, Afrikaans was entrenched in the South Africa Act as an official language on an equal footing with English and Dutch.[2] Official recognition, an excellent Afrikaans translation of the Bible in whose preparation "Totius" appropriately played a prominent part (1933) and the undertaking in 1926 of an authoritative Afrikaans dictionary on the largest scale have consolidated the position beyond all dispute. The Afrikaners' struggle for the frank acceptance of Afrikaans as their national tongue is at an end.

It remains to consider the value of Afrikaans as a cultural factor. No language can subsist indefinitely on official recognition alone; it can only survive by its own strength and on its own merits. To-day, Afrikaans stands in a favoured position as the visible sign of Afrikaner culture, the expression of the national ideals of fully half the white population of the Union. It has to some extent been pushed into that position by a political agitation inspired by the misleading slogan that "the language is wholly the people"; but having gained it, it can only keep it by showing that it can flourish alongside English, though not necessarily in opposition to that world-wide tongue. There are encouraging signs that it may do so, for, though it at present lacks some of the virtues of English, it can, as a branch of the same parent stem as modern Dutch, draw inspiration from the rich literature and culture of the Netherlands.

An Afrikaans literature is already taking shape, which, if allowance be made for its immaturity, compares well with that of any sister Dominion. Time alone will show whether it will develop along its present healthy lines or be content with a cultural mediocrity as ineffective as it is dangerous. That danger is real, because the language has thus far been nourished by a national sentiment more appreciative

[1] In 1959, Afrikaners celebrated the achievements of their language during the half-century since the foundation of the S.A. Academy.

[2] Act No. 8 of 1925.

of political advantage than of aesthetic distinction. Forced to supply reading matter at short notice for the schools and a public untaught by criticism to distinguish between genuine and spurious literary values, it lacks the stimulus that comes from open competition and the comparison of its own best with its rivals' best. Readers are still too often content with productions little better than the ephemera published in English; on the other hand, of late years, many Afrikaans writers have admitted the need of such criticism and have, to their credit, modelled their work on the best in three languages: English, Dutch and their own.

Whereas Afrikaans and Dutch have gone their separate ways, the English of the English-speaking community has scarcely diverged from that spoken in their homeland. The English of the white southern African community is in general as much standard English as that of any other Dominion, and if Afrikaners and British alike speak it with a variety of local accents and intonations, they do no more than do the diversified folk of the United Kingdom itself. The cultural influence of English has been very great. For half a century and more, the Dutch-speaking child learned at least the rudiments of what was then the official language, memorised the salient dates and facts of British history, and coloured his thoughts with a culture that was, if not alien, most certainly not home-grown. The English-speaking child, by contrast, had no incentive to learn anything outside his own tradition, language and customs. However that may have been, the fact that the importance of a study of English from the purely cultural point of view is now widely recognised by many who have hitherto feared it as a check on the evolution of Afrikaans culture is a welcome sign that the relative values of the two languages are being acknowledged in a hopeful spirit of partnership.

We must now briefly survey the development of southern African literature, science and art, taking the term "southern African" to mean not works on southern African subjects, but rather works by men and women born in southern Africa and by others who have lived so long in that country and have so thoroughly absorbed its spirit that they may justly be claimed both by southern Africa and their native lands. Thus defined, the matter may be conveniently considered under two heads: English and Afrikaans.

English Southern African Literature

Poetry. Poetry may fairly claim pride of place. Much of the work of the early "English" poets was bound by English literary tradition and showed little originality in thought or form; much of it, again, was merely descriptive and inspired by environment with a local rather than a general appeal. Nevertheless, it was soon sufficient in quantity to permit of the publication of anthologies. The first of these was

R. Stapleton's *South African Poems* (1828) consisting of poems culled from local newspapers and including some by Thomas Pringle, though not *Afar in the Desert* or other well-known poems of his colonial period, which appeared in his *Ephemerides* dedicated to his friend, Sir Walter Scott. Much later, in 1887, came Count Alexander Wilmot's *The Poetry of South Africa* containing selections from the works of twenty-two authors. Since then, the output has been considerable and, in an increasing degree, has won recognition throughout the English-speaking world. The quality of the work was long very diverse, though its technical correctness compared favourably with that of verse written in other parts of the Empire and Commonwealth. In any event, the quantity was so considerable that Edmund Crouch had a wealth of material on which to draw for his *Treasury of South African Poetry* (1907) and *Sonnets of South Africa* (1911), and Francis Carey Slater yet more for his *Centenary Book of South African Verse* (1925). Latterly, the quality of the poetry has improved markedly; for instance, there is much to admire in E. B. Watermeyer's excellent translations from Horace and Martial, Monsignor Kolbe's polished *Fancies and Thoughts*, Sir John Adamson's *Songs from the South*, Dr Charles Murray's *Hamewith* (1910), and Slater's *Drought* (1929), *Dark Folk* (1934) and later volumes.

The last of these scholarly men had almost ceased to write when, in 1924, Natal gave southern Africa her two most outstanding poets: Roy Campbell and William Plomer. Of the two, Campbell, the South African Byron, flamboyant, satiric and first of the Union's poets to be highly sensitive to the rightness and magic of words, deservedly has the higher reputation with his *Flaming Terrapin*, *Wayzgoose*, *The Zulu Girl* and other notable poems. He influenced Plomer, who showed his native understanding of the South African spirit in *Masondo's Dream* and *The Scorpion*. The two friends have been followed by younger men like R. N. Currey, Clarke Wade, Norman Clothier and Guy Butler, as well as by Anthony Delius, a wrestler with the unanswered problems of latter-day mankind. It is no small achievement that the comparatively small British section should have produced so many poets of this calibre in so short a time.

PROSE. During the First British Occupation, Lady Anne Barnard, authoress of *Auld Robin Grey*, gave promise of what English prose writers were to achieve in southern Africa in her delightful *Letters Written from the Cape*, 1797–1801. If it be questioned whether this charming bird of passage can be claimed as a local writer in spite of her warm-hearted efforts to understand Cape customs and conditions, it cannot be doubted that Thomas Pringle, a full generation later, is entitled to that distinction, though he too did not stay in the country for any great length of time. For some years after the publication of his *Narrative* in 1835, the best work was done by missionaries and other clergymen like William Boyce (*Notes on South African Affairs*,

1838), Robert Moffat (*Missionary Labours and Scenes in Southern Africa*, 1842) and Bishop John William Colenso (*Remarks on Polygamy* and *First Steps of the Mission*, 1859). Excellent works by travellers like Nathaniel Isaacs, David Livingstone, Charles Andersson, Gordon Cumming and others perhaps fall outside the scope of this chapter.

These early writers were followed by many others, notably by Charles Barter (*Dorp and Veld*, 1852) and Judge A. W. Cole (*Reminiscences of my Life*, 1896); but most of the latter's contemporaries merely produced romantic stories based on adventures during Kaffir wars or on the Diamond Fields and the Rand in their beginnings. Their works have a true enough South African ring, but few display much literary skill, save possibly those of Bertram Mitford (1864), who really knew his Zulus. Then, in 1883, Olive Schreiner wrote *The Story of an African Farm*. This novel, the first to have been built up entirely of local materials, and by a young woman living in an isolated dorp in the Cape Colony, was long held to stand alone as the high-water mark of southern African prose. Despite its gross sentimentality and sometimes absurd characterisation, it deservedly became a classic by reason of its sincere handling of such matters as the rights of women and doubt of God. Though it has now fallen somewhat from its high estate, it influenced its writer's immediate successors and more than held its own against those many who wrote of political events during the South African War, and even against others such as Ann Howart (*Jan: an Afrikander*), Perceval Gibbon (*Souls in Bondage*) and Francis Bancroft (*Of Like Passions*), who wrote on such tragic themes as mixed marriages and the woes of the half-caste. It maintained its lead comfortably over Daphne Muir, Ethelreda Lewis and Herman Charles Bosman, and even over Dorothea Fairbridge, whose *That Which Hath Been* (1910) was southern Africa's first historical novel, a most readable if not always historically sound defence of that unpopular Governor, Willem Adriaan van der Stel.

Latterly, Olive Schreiner's masterpiece has been run very close, to say the least, by Pauline Smith's *Little Karoo* (1905), the work of an authoress whom Arnold Bennett admired for her "strange, austere, tender and ruthless talent"; by Frank Brownlee's *Ntsukumbeni* (1929), a fine story of a Bantu cattle-thief, and by Sarah Gertrude Millin's *Dark River* (1920), *God's Stepchildren* (1924) and *Mary Glen* (1925), humourless but clear-sighted and logical studies of the complex psychology and frustrations of the Coloured Folk. Other contemporary novelists have won a deservedly high reputation. Such are William Plomer the poet, who has exalted the Bantu and cast down the white man in *Tarbott Wolf* (1925), Alan Paton, a fellow-Natalian, whose *Cry, the Beloved Country* (1948) tells the moving story of a devoted Zulu clergyman and his runagate son in Johannesburg, while in *Pack and Follow* (1945) and *Grey Mistress* (1949) "Joy Packer" records the trials of a naval officer's wife who is always on the move. In the same class are Laurens van der Post (*In a Province*, 1934), the Southern Rhodesian, Doris May Lessing (*The Grass is Singing*, 1950), and Nadine Gordimer, whose studies of psychological types in Johannesburg have won deserved recognition at home and abroad. Nor are all southern African novelists of European stock. Katie Hendricks in *The Bend in the Road* (1953) tells of life among her own Coloured Folk in Cape Town and among the Bantu elsewhere, while Peter Abrahams, a Coloured man, has dealt more generally with race relations.

There have been writers since the 'eighties in fields other than fiction whose work, critically considered, is in many respects superior to that of Olive Schreiner. Monsignor Frederick Kolbe's prose, for instance, has an exquisite clarity and his autobiography, *Up the Slopes of Mount Zion* (1924), ranks as a classic; the Rev. Ramsden Balmforth's *The Evolution of Christianity* (1898), *The Problem Play* (1929) and *The Ethical and Religious Value of the Novel* (1912) are valuable contributions to the discussion of ethics and religion, while Sir Percy Fitzpatrick's *Jock of the Bushveld* (1907), the immortal story of a dog, Sir John Adamson's philosophical writings, and Eric A. Walker's *Lord de Villiers and His Times* (1925) and *The Great Trek* (1936) may all be cited as examples of excellent prose.

The pioneer full-dress history up to the year 1884 is *The History of South Africa* (1910–19) by George McCall Theal, the Bancroft of South Africa, a massive series of volumes that is still regarded as the standard work, marred though it is by ungraciousness towards the imperial power, whether Dutch or British, and a scarcely concealed contempt for folk of other colours. Sir George Cory's *Rise of South Africa* (1910–30) covers much of the same ground, detailing mainly in similarly voluminous and even more disjointed fashion the doings of the 1820 settlers in the Eastern Cape Province and the parts adjacent until the middle eighteen-fifties. E. A. Walker's admirable *History of Southern Africa* (1928–1957) tells the story in far more compact form from the European beginnings almost to the present day. W. M. Macmillan, E. H. Brookes, J. A. I. Agar-Hamilton and J. S. Marais have dealt with the historical relationship between Europeans, Coloured Folk and Bantu; E. G. Malherbe has written on the history of education; P. Laidler and E. E. Mossop have interested themselves in antiquarian research, while Dudley Kidd has made first-class studies of Bantu life in *The Essential Kaffir* (1904), *Savage Childhood* (1906) and *Kaffir Socialism* (1908); J. Stevenson Hamilton and Deneys Reitz have written chapters of personal history in *Low Veld* (1929) and *On Commando* (1932) respectively, and Francis Bancroft and the vehement Olive Schreiner have fought for the cause of pacifism. Of philosophical works there are lamentably few and of outstanding dramatic works none as yet; but there are many good biographies, notably J. R. Wallis's *Fitz: the Story of Sir Percy FitzPatrick* (1955),

Oswald Doughty's life of Dante Gabriel Rosetti, *A Victorian Romantic* (1949) and E. A. Walker's *W. P. Schreiner. A South African* (1937) Some of the best prose written in the country lies half-hidden in newspaper files, for from the early days South Africa has had a sequence of literary journalists—men like John Fairbairn of the *South African Commercial Advertiser*, Frederick York St Leger and Basil Long of the *Cape Times* and Francis Dormer of the *Cape Argus* and the Johannesburg *Star*, who besides writing more or less polemical leaders, wrote essays of high literary merit. The development of English prose in southern Africa during the past few decades is an encouraging sign of a general cultural advance. The best of its exponents have no need to fear comparison with writers in any other part of the vast English-speaking world.

Afrikaans Literature

POETRY. The first South African poem we know of is the doggerel anonymous verse written in 1666 to celebrate the laying of the foundation stone of the Castle at Cape Town.[1] A century later, minor poets were singing of local events or venturing into the realms beloved of their kind everywhere, much of their work surviving in *Verzameling van Hollandsche Liederen*, an anthology compiled by J. de Kock in 1836. South Africa's first Dutch poet of any note was the Rev. Dammet Pierre Marie Huet, a man of culture and wide reading, whose *Paarlsche Gedigten* (1856) and *Afrikaansche Gedichten* (1868) are pleasing in thought and original in expression for all their imitative style. During the second quarter of the nineteenth century, the versatile Dutch Jewish immigrant, Joseph Suasso de Lima, not only opened the first Dutch bookshop in Cape Town, but discharged volleys of satirical rhymed verses and playlets against his rival, Charles Boniface, who replied in kind.[2] Apart from the light which it throws on the history of the drama in Cape Colony, the work of these two is of much less permanent interest than the attractive poems written by F. H. Schoon and Professor Hubertus Elffers during the 'eighties.

Until the middle of the nineteenth century virtually all Afrikaner poets wrote in Dutch, but they found it hard to do themselves justice in that medium. It was only when they realised that they had in Afrikaans a language of their own capable of being used for versification that they became truly vocal. The first volume of genuinely Afrikaans poetry appeared in 1860, but no copy now survives.[3] Ten years later, Francis Reitz began to write in an Afrikaans which differs in many respects from that now used; soon thereafter Melt Brink started his long career as a writer of short plays and humorous verse for the Aurora Literary Society, productions which were duly pub-

[1] For the text of this poem, *vide* G. M. Theal, *History of South Africa before* 1795, III, 144.
[2] Herrman, L., *A History of the Jews in South Africa*, pp. 94 *sqq.*
[3] Smith, J. J., *The Development... of Afrikaans*, Union of S.A. Year Book, No. 8, 1927, p. 91.

lished in *Grappige Stories en Andere Versies* and *Nationale en Afrikaanse Gedigte*, while during the early 'eighties "Oom Jan" and "Neef Jan" (J. D. Celliers) wrote occasional poems on local events. No Afrikaans poet, however, gave any indication that Afrikaans could rise to great heights till J. F. E. Celliers published *Die Vlakte* in 1906. This was the first poem of outstanding quality in the language, and though its thought and technique owe much to Jacques Perks's *Iris* and Shelley's *Cloud*, its originality of thought, beauty of diction and lyrical delicacy won almost instant recognition. Celliers afterwards published other notable poems, but this, his first great work, stands as his finest achievement. In contrast, the Rev. J. D. du Toit achieved a near equality with him when he published his volume of poems, *By de Monument*, in 1908, but he did not write his best work, *Trekkerswee*, till six years later. By that time, C. Louis Leipoldt had published *Oom Gert Vertel* in 1911 and, in due time, followed this with *Dingaansdag* (1920), the tragedy *Die Heks* (1924) and *Uit Drie Werelddele* (1924), while Eugene Marais had written *Winternag*, perhaps the finest Afrikaans poem yet published.

These poems, with their appeal to national sentiment and allusions to the psychological effects of the South African War, taught Afrikaners the literary value of their language and gave the necessary impetus to the second language campaign; they won the warm approval of competent critics in the Netherlands, who hailed them as contributions to Dutch literature as valuable as those which Guido Gezelle had recently made in his poems in cognate Flemish; finally, they inspired other Afrikaans poets. Prominent among these pioneers were the pessimistic Eugene Marais (1871–1936), H. H. Joubert (*Piet Retief en Andere Gedigte*, 1911, and *Dageraad en Sonneskyn*, 1918), A. G. Visser (*Gedigte*, 1925, and *Rose van Herrinering*, 1927), and D. F. Malherbe, the most prolific of the group and the first Professor of Afrikaans at any South African University, who followed *Karooblommetjes* (1910) with *Vergeet Nie* (1913), *Klokgrassies* (1917), *Vir Vryheid* (1919), *Die Timmerman* (1921), *Rivier en Veld* (1922) and *Skaduwee van 'n Vrou* (1925). Most of the works of these poets bear traces of the shock administered to traditional standards by the First World War, a shock which doubtless impelled C. J. Langenhoven to venture on his historical poem, *Die Stem van Suid-Afrika* (1921), and possibly as late as 1938 moved C. M. van den Heever to write his finest work, *Die Aardse Vlam*. By that time, younger poets were making their mark, men like N. P. van Wyk Louw, the first professional Afrikaans poet, with *Alleenspraak*; his brother, W. E. G. Louw, with *Die Ryke Swaas*, and Uys Krige with *Kentering*. Between 1936 and 1945, Elizabeth Eybers, the first Afrikaans poetess of note, revealed the thoughts and experiences of modern women in childbirth and other crises in *Belydenis in die Skemering*, *Die Stil Aventuur* and *Die Vrouw*. The Cape Coloured poet, S. V. Petersen, has shown that poetry in South Africa is not the monopoly of the white man,[1] while one or two poets of European stock have broken virtually new ground by translating from other tongues. Thus, the veteran C. J. Langenhoven rendered poems by Hesiod and Christina Rossetti into his native Afrikaans, F. van den Heever translated *The Rubaiyat of Omar Khayyam* and, a little later, Theodore Haarhoff made fine translations from the classics.

Afrikaans poetry is admittedly influenced by both Dutch and English literature, but the best of it is not merely imitative. It must be regarded as the spontaneous outpouring of original thought in a language that is peculiarly suitable as a vehicle for versification. The open vowel sounds, the absence of polysyllables and the simplicity of construction make Afrikaans verse sonorous and rhythmically smooth; they lend themselves best perhaps to the expression of ideas in the sonnet and blank verse, though most poets have adopted shorter metrical forms, especially for lyrics. The influence of Afrikaans poetry on the evolution of the language has been considerable and will doubtless continue to be so.

PROSE. Afrikaans prose has been struggling for many years to free itself from alien influences, and can hardly yet be said to have come into its own; indeed, it has developed much more slowly than Afrikaans poetry, especially during the generation that followed the South African War, when its most vigorous exponents were more concerned to defend their language and way of life than to polish their texts, and Afrikaners as a body were unable to decide between the rival claims of Dutch, Simplified Dutch and nascent Afrikaans. Dutch itself had never fared well at the hands of Afrikaners, for though they wrote in that language till at least the middle of the nineteenth century, they left little worthy of record unless it were the *Dagboek van Adam Tas* written about 1705 and published two hundred years later by Leo Fouche with a delightful translation by A. C. Paterson in the style of Samuel Pepys. In 1849, Pierre Huet, the pastor-poet, wrote good descriptive verse, but it was not until 1854 that the Hollander immigrant, Antoine Changuion, published his *Geschiedenis der Fransch-Protestantsche Vlugtellingen*, the first really important South African work in Dutch prose. Some thirty years later many books began to appear, some of them more or less historical accounts of the Trekkers. The best of these were the work of S. J. du Toit, J. D. Kestell, E. Godée-Molsbergen, J. Lion Cachet and W. Postma, all of whom wrote as a rule in academically correct High Dutch, though one or two of them occasionally experimented with Afrikaans. This they did, presumably, rather than try the short-lived Simplified Dutch, whose most voluminous champion was J. F. van Oordt, the author of what is still the best biography of President Kruger and of some twenty novels dealing with South African history in simple narrative fashion.

[1] In 1959, S. V. Petersen was awarded the annual medal for literature of the S.A. Academy, the highest honour any writer of Afrikaans can win.

Then at last, in 1907, Gustav S. Preller published his *Piet Retief* in Afrikaans, the first of several works of equal excellence, and was closely followed by Jan Hendrik de Waal.

Preller and de Waal achieved for Afrikaans prose what Cellier and Totius had achieved for Afrikaans poetry a short year earlier. Their work was a landmark in the history of the language, which thereafter speedily became the chief if not the sole medium in prose. Their immediate followers were G. R. van Wielligh and C. J. Langenhoven, both popular writers who did much to stimulate the love of reading among the Afrikaans-speaking public. It is true that they failed to produce work of permanent literary value if only because they were still feeling their way in a comparatively untried medium, but they did lay foundations on which others could build and win for themselves a definite place in Afrikaans literature. Such men and women were Eugene Marais, R. J. van Reenen, Marie Linde, Eric Stockenstrom, Nico Hofmeyr, Leon Maré, Hettie Smit, Jochem van Bruggen, P. de V. Pienaar and many others. Probably the best of these latter-day writers are "Sangiro" (A. A. Pienaar), whose *Uit Oerwoude en Vlakte* (1921) tells of the gradual extinction of a lion family, Jochem van Bruggen, whose *Ampie* (1942) is a sensitive character-study of poor whites struggling with unaccustomed life in an industrial town, and C. M. van den Heever, whose *Somer* (1935) and *Laat Vrugte* (1939) display a Wordsworthian sense of the power and beauty of nature. J. J. Smith's essays on the history of Afrikaans and its etymology are marked by a literary felicity which makes him a writer of arresting prose.

New books in Afrikaans, both original compositions and translations, are pouring from the press so fast that now they number at least ten thousand, but what Afrikaans stands in sore need of is competent honest literary criticism. Thus far, only a few critical works have been published, such as *Taal en Poesie van die Twede Afrikaanse Taalbeweging* by E. C. Pienaar, a detailed criticism of Afrikaans poetry, and a critical thesis on the prose of that same language campaign by P. C. Schoonees. Now that the spelling of Afrikaans has been more or less standardised and excellent examples of good Afrikaans are to be had, there is no excuse for tolerating shoddy works, least of all in the schools, where the authorities are still given to prescribing books of poor quality for examination purposes. Afrikaans literature must stand or fall in open competition with both Dutch and English literature. When that test is applied, there can be no doubt of its virility. Its development thus far is a fair indication of the cultural progress achieved by the public for which it caters during the past fifty years.

ART

Man has not expressed himself artistically solely in words; indeed, he painted before he wrote. After the Bushmen went out of business, however, there was to be no pictorial or plastic art that could be called distinctively southern African until about the middle of the eighteenth century. By that time colonial-born craftsmen, white and coloured, were showing that they could imitate and even surpass their teachers from Old Europe in the making of lovely tropical wood furniture, excellent metal and leather work, and splendid mural decorations. Even so, as late as 1780, it was the Company's German sculptor, Anton Anreith, who carved the magnificently ponderous pulpits of the Groote Kerk and Lutheran church in Cape Town, and adorned the gables of Groot Constantia and other famous buildings with graceful plaster work. Private citizens, it is true, owned good European paintings, but even when these were of local scenes, they had been executed either by birds of passage or by folk, who, never having been in the Colony, had had to rely on hearsay or sheer imagination.

The first signs of better things came with the new century when Samuel Daniel had the plates in his *African Scenery and Animals* lithographed after his return to Europe in 1804, and William Burchell, another English visitor, painted fine water-colour sketches on the spot. A little later, W. H. Langschmidt painted landscapes, and William Bowler, the gifted "gentleman's gentleman" and sometime assistant at the new Cape Royal Observatory, painted his delightful water-colours of land- and sea-scapes, ships and men, the originals of the much-sought-after Bowler Prints. Next came Abraham de Smidt with yet more landscapes, and Thomas Baines of King's Lynn, the first artist to visit and paint the recently discovered Victoria Falls and, thereafter, other southern African scenes as far afield as the lower Zambesi. In the early 'fifties, works by all these artists were hung in southern Africa's first art exhibition, appropriately enough in Cape Town, but most of the other exhibits were loan pictures by overseas artists. None of the sculptures were by local men or women.

Fifty years later it was a very different story. Exhibition catalogues then were full of the names of South Africans, nearly all of them locally born and many with high reputations in their own country and the outer world. At that time, the doyen was P. Hugo Naude, painter of portraits and the sparkling Cape scenery. After him came Neville Lewis, another outstanding painter of portraits and of dark-skinned Africans, Edward Roworth, whose best works were portraits again and landscapes, and P. Wenning, a pioneer of impressionism, whose renderings of old Cape buildings suggest that he would have become a great painter had he lived longer. Others were Gwelo Goodman, George Pilkington (sea-scapes), the veteran Hendrik Pierneef, Crosland Robinson, Ruth Prowse, W. J. Volschenk, a self-trained painter, W. M. Timlin, a black-and-white artist, and Nita Spilhaus, famous for her etchings. Irma Stern, a Transvaaler and foundation member of the German November Group, after unmerited ridicule for breaking away from conventional styles won recognition for her brightly coloured studies of Bantu; Rupert Shepherd, a Londoner, excels as a painter of portraits and red-blanketed Africans, while Gerard Sekoto, himself an African, paints life as seen through the eyes of his own folk. D. G. Boonzaier was a fine caricaturist; his son, Gregoire, is an impressionist; others have latterly ventured into the weird realms of post-impressionism, surrealism and abstract art. The chief southern African sculptors are F. Eloff, Mrs. Benson and I. Mitford Barberton; two others, Anton van Wouw and Moses Kottler, though born overseas, may justly rank as South African by adoption. One or two of the younger sculptors, notably the African Elsa Dziomba, incline towards highly modernistic abstract forms.

Art training is given in the Michaelis School of Fine Art in the University of Cape Town, in the University of the Witwatersrand at Johannesburg, and in Technical Colleges in some of the larger towns. Would-be artists can draw inspiration from the splendid collection of seventeenth-century Dutch art in the Michaelis Gallery, Cape Town, from works of good Victorian British artists in the Phillemore Ives Collection at Stellenbosch and from art galleries in Cape Town, Durban, Pietermaritzburg and Johannesburg. Nor are good modern statues lacking: of Dick King, a tired man on a tired horse at Durban, of General Louis Botha also on horseback, and President Kruger standing massive and four-square at Pretoria, of Jan van Riebeeck, Onse Jan Hofmeyr and Cecil Rhodes at Cape Town once more, of Rhodes again at Bulawayo and yet again, with his hands in his pockets, at Salisbury, and of Wilson's ill-fated patrol on the Shangani Monument near Rhodes's lonely grave in the Matoppos. Art interests are cared for, generally, by the newly-instituted state Art Advisory Council and, more specifically, by the South African Association of Arts, which *inter alia* arranges for touring exhibitions from overseas. Conversely, many South Africans go abroad for study and inspiration, and southern African art is regularly on view in the Venice Biennale and other exhibitions in Europe and America. The enthusiasm of the younger generation augurs well for the future of art at the far end of Africa.

Music and Ballet

Beyond simple hymn tunes and folk music from the various Mother Countries there was little musical life in southern Africa for fully two hundred years after the European settlement. During the last decades of the nineteenth century, however, several visiting musicians stayed on as teachers of their art and, after the South African War, a real start was made when the predominantly British public of some of the larger towns developed a taste for good concert music, a taste powerfully stimulated by the English pianist, Elsie Hall, who settled in Cape Town and made concert-going fashionable. The Cape Town

City Council sought to meet this demand by subsidising a municipal symphony orchestra with a generosity that was then unparallelled by any other city in the British Empire with the exception of wealthy and music-loving Manchester. By the time Johannesburg and Durban had followed Cape Town's example, a Capetonian had gone a step further, for in 1911 Professor W. H. Bell had founded the South African School of Music. This school, long since associated with the University of Cape Town, is probably unrivalled in the southern hemisphere with its Music Faculty in the University College of Music, Schools of Ballet and Opera and Little Theatre complete with cyclorama. It numbers on its staff four young neo-classicist Afrikaners who can stand comparison with their contemporaries the world over: Arnold van Wyk, Hubert du Plessis, Stefan Grove and John Joubert, the last of whom is recognised in Great Britain as the most talented composer southern Africa has yet produced.

Regular concerts and sometimes lectures also are given by the South African section of the International Society of Contemporary Music in association with the University of Cape Town, by the Cape Town Chamber of Music Society, by the outstanding Johannesburg Orchestra and by Musica Viva in Johannesburg; the Federation of Music Societies welcomes visiting musicians to the Eastern Cape Province, while first-class orchestras in Stellenbosch and other smaller towns and excellent programmes on the Afrikaans radio witness to the high standard of musical taste in Afrikaner society. Opera flourished until a few years back in Johannesburg and there are welcome signs to-day of its revival there, while to show that music knows no racial boundaries, Cape Coloured singers in Cape Town recently gave an admirable operatic performance in Italian, and Hugh Tracey's recordings of African music are revealing one of the world's great sources of music and rhythm. It is from such surroundings that increasing numbers of South Africans, musicians and dancers, by no means all of them white, are going out to make their marks overseas, some of them even in Covent Garden and the famous Sadler's Wells Ballet.

Architecture

Cape architecture was developed from the late Renaissance and Baroque styles prevalent in late seventeenth century western Europe. Presently, stately town-houses arose with pediments, curving gables and flat roofs, their sheer fronts painted white or green and protected from the road by narrow stoeps and gardens; but it was in the countryside that the characteristic "Cape Dutch" style was evolved, one of the very few outstanding "colonial" styles, finer even than that of the "great houses" of the Old South. During the eighteenth century, well-to-do farmers began to build these low white-washed houses usually of one storey below the *solder* (loft) and sloping roof, which was thatched for lack of tiles and adorned with high curving gables.[1] The walls were pierced by moderate-sized, deep-set windows with beautifully-proportioned little panes and furnished with heavy teak shutters, their fronts sheltered from the strong summer sun by wide pillared stoeps. The most famous architect of those days was the Frenchman, Louis Michiel Thibault, and the most skilled plasterer the German, Anton Anreith; but, for lack of such imported experts, much of the fine work was done by sensitive-fingered Malay slaves.

Georgian and Regency architecture came in with the British,—witness Lord Charles Somerset's Round House near Camp's Bay—but this was soon swamped by the increasingly chaotic styles of Victorian England. Taste touched rock-bottom during the last few decades of the nineteenth century, when far too many southern African towns disfigured themselves with abominably ornate civic buildings, and farmers replaced thatch with corrugated iron, ripped out their lovely old-fashioned windows to make way for windows of the sash variety, and banished their fine old furniture to the *solder* in favour of ponderous mahogany or sheer gimcrack. There was no one to stop the rot till Rhodes called in Herbert Baker from England to rebuild Groote Schuur in the old "Cape Dutch" style after the disastrous fire of 1896, and himself set the fashion by restoring the banished antique furniture to its rightful dignified setting. Baker, however, soon turned away to experiment with more ambitious styles, notably the imposing mixed architecture of the Union Buildings, which dominate Pretoria from a hill to the west of the city. Since his day, newer styles, among them those of le Corbusier and the Dutch and German modernists, have invaded the land often by way of the Schools of Architecture at one or other of the universities; inevitably, flat-topped sky-scrapers in United States style stand out boldly along the kaleidoscopic Rand, and match themselves with much success against the towering bulk of Table Mountain. Since 1945 much of the central part of staid Cape Town has been rebuilt in this impressive fashion. Ultra-modern architecture was first seen, perhaps surprisingly, in a few Dutch Reformed churches and Jewish synagogues in the Transvaal and Orange Free State. Corrugated iron *en masse* still defaces smaller towns like Kimberley and Mafeking except when for a few weeks it is mercifully masked by the delicate mauve of the jacaranda, but in the countryside the revived "Cape Dutch" style more than holds its own. Long may it do so.

Science

In a sense, scientific research began in southern Africa when the first European settlers explored their new country in haphazard

[1] There is a fine typically Cape Dutch curving gable dated 1671 in the Third Court of St John's College, Cambridge, a reminder that William of Orange was not the first Hollander to come to East Anglia in the seventeenth century.

fashion. Such systematic investigation as took place during the following two hundred years was carried out by visiting scientists and travellers, who came to study the country's flora and fauna, geography and heavens.

In this record of achievement, astronomy takes pride of place. Much work in this field was done in or near Cape Town, a settled centre in the southern hemisphere lying in a latitude not greatly different from that of western Europe, and blessed, as a rule, with clear night skies. In the middle of the eighteenth century, the Abbé Nicolas Louis de la Caille, the first serious astronomer to visit the Cape, worked for two years in a house in Strand Street, Cape Town, fixing the longitude of that town, starting a land survey northwards from Cape Town, cataloguing the southern stars and giving them the names they still bear. Nearly a century later, Sir John Herschel catalogued the southern galaxies and double stars, but he worked at Claremont and did not use the Royal Observatory, which had been founded in 1821 nearer Cape Town, where Sir David Gill, Cape Astronomer Royal, 1879–1907, was destined to take the lead in determining the parallaxes of the sun and southern stars, and to go far towards the mapping of the southern heavens by fixing the positions of some four hundred thousand of those stars by the then novel process of astronomical photography, and to carry de la Caille's land survey as far afield as Natal and Southern Rhodesia. Since Sir David's day, more than one of his successors has been appointed Astronomer Royal either at Greenwich or Hurstmonceaux; the present holder of that high office, Richard van der Riet Woolley, is a South African on his mother's side and a graduate of the University of Cape Town. Experts such as these have stimulated South African amateurs, notably Dr Alexander Roberts of Lovedale, who added to our knowledge of the fixed stars, and T. B. Blathwayt and G. E. Ensor, discoverers of new stars and comets.

To-day, there are five observatories in the Union besides the Royal Observatory. In the middle 'twenties, the University of Michigan and the Harvard College Observatory transferred respectively the Lamont-Hussey Observatory and the Royden Station to the neighbourhood of Bloemfontein; in 1937, the University of Oxford moved the Radcliffe Observatory to Pretoria and, with it, a seventy-four-inch telescope, the largest in South Africa. The Union Government has its own observatory at Johannesburg, which, in association with the University of Leyden's southern station, specialises in the study of double stars and the provision of an accurate time service. For the rest, South Africa boasts an Astronomical Society, one of the most active in the world.

Southern Africa has an equally remarkable record in botanical science, and well it may have, seeing that the original settlement was made in the Cape Peninsula, a region that has a unique flora and, though smaller than the Isle of Wight, has two hundred more species of wild flowers than the whole of England, and has given the world, among other garden plants, the geranium, pelargonium, gladiolus, freesia, erica and watsonia. The Dutch East India Company laid out a botanical garden at Cape Town, though this never achieved the success as a centre of research that crowned van Imhoff's greater venture, the Buitenzorg Botanical Garden in Java. Among the distinguished botanists who have worked in South Africa were Carl Thunberg, who spent three years in the country and published his *Flora Capensis* in 1807; William Burchell, whose *Travels in the Interior of Southern Africa* (1822–4) is a classic; Johan Drege, whose *Zwei Pflanzengeographische Dokuments* (1843), the fruit of several years' sojourn, first essayed to demarcate South Africa into botanical regions; William Henry Harvey, author of *The Genera of South African Plants* and first joint-editor, with a German colleague, of the still incomplete *Flora Capensis*; Peter MacOwen, Government Botanist and Director of the Cape Botanic Gardens; Harry Bolus, author of *The Orchids of the Cape Peninsula* and, in his day, the foremost authority on South African botany; Rudolph Schlechter, an indefatigable collector and field botanist; Rudolph Marloth, author of *The Flora of South Africa*, and H. H. W. Pearson, first holder of the Chair of Botany in the South African College, now the University of Cape Town, and founder of the magnificent National Botanic Garden at Kirstenbosch close by, a garden which now has a Karoo Garden as a sub-station near Worcester. The example of these men and the call of the country have encouraged many amateurs, who have done fine field work, especially among the aloes and mesembryanthema. There are to-day chairs of botany at each of the South African universities, and fully representative herbaria at Kirstenbosch and Pretoria in connection respectively with the University of Cape Town and the state Division of Botany. In 1921, Dr G. E. Pole-Evans started the serial publication of *The Flowering Plants of South Africa*, which now runs to many volumes and bears the more comprehensive title of *The Flowering Plants of Southern Africa*, while R. H. Compton, Professor of Botany in the University of Cape Town and Curator of the Kirstenbosch Botanic Garden, started *The Journal of South African Botany* and edited it for many years till his retirement in 1954. Generally speaking, since the beginning of the Botanical Survey of South Africa, researchers have paid more attention to distribution and ecology than to the traditional taxonomy.

Valuable additions to our knowledge of zoology were made by early travellers and collectors like Anders Sparrman (1772–5) and François le Vaillant (1780–5), both of whom studied, in particular, birds and mammals. During the first half of the nineteenth century, their work was carried on by Emil Holub, Dr Andrew Smith, Karl Anderson, A. J. A. Wahlberg and E. L. Layard, the famous ornithologist, all of whom undertook field work and classification with the help of such able collaborators as Benjamin Bradshaw, Frank Oates, R. Jameson and T. E. Buckley. Dr Andrew Smith formed an experimental museum at Cape Town as early as 1825, but this went to pieces after his departure and was only re-established as the South African Museum by Layard thirty years later. At the same time, a similar museum was founded at Grahamstown (1855) and, presently, at Bloemfontein (1877) and Pretoria (1893). To-day, half a dozen other centres possess good zoological collections. Zoological gardens were opened at Pretoria (1899), Johannesburg (1903) and Durban (1908), while in 1898 President Kruger proclaimed the Sabi River Game Reserve, which since 1926 has become world-famous as the Kruger National Park, the largest of several southern African game reserves.

The scope for zoological research in a country like southern Africa is immense, and it is encouraging to see that the universities have recognised this fact by providing ample accommodation and equipment in their zoological departments. Pioneer work on marine fauna by Professor J. D. F. Gilchrist in the University of Cape Town, has been expanded by his successors, L. Hogben and T. A. Stephenson, into an ecological study of the seashore life in which the Cape Peninsula is peculiarly rich; Professor C. de Villiers formed a flourishing school of cranial morphology in the neighbouring University of Stellenbosch, and Professor C. J. van der Horst served embryology equally well in the University of the Witwatersrand. Excellent research in entomology has been done by Roland Triman and J. H. Bowker in collaboration (*Rhopalocera Africae Australis*, 1862, and *South African Butterflies*, 1887), by van der Horst again, by Dr Louis Peringuey, Director of the South African Museum, on the Coleoptera especially, by F. Purcell and J. Hewitt on spiders and scorpions, by Austin Roberts on birds, and by Annie Porter on the internal parasites of man. Indeed, few fields have been altogether neglected and, as in the case of botany, research is steadily moving away from mere description to ecology and the study of behaviour.

The ancient rocks and abounding minerals of southern Africa have naturally invited geological research. The pioneer in this field was Andrew Geddes Bain, an 1820 Settler, who, stimulated by discoveries near Grahamstown in 1837, wrote a text-book on fossils and, some twenty years later, published the first geological map of the southern Cape Colony. The Cape Government presently appointed an official geologist and, soon thereafter, formed a Geological Commission just in time to profit by the discovery of diamonds in Griqualand West and gold in the Transvaal and Southern Rhodesia during the 'seventies. Dr Karl Mauch's discoveries in these two last-named regions were supplemented by those of Thomas Baines, the traveller-artist, and elsewhere by those of W. G. Atherstone, W. Anderson, G. A. F. Molengraaff, H. Merensky, E. T. Miller, J. Wagner, A. F. Williams and A. Young. After the discovery of gold on the Rand by the brothers Frederick Pine Theophilus and Hendrik Wilhelm Struben in 1886, research was encouraged in the Transvaal mainly by the Chamber of Mines; but little was done in Natal or the Orange Free State till the Union Geological Survey had been set on foot in 1912, a survey whose maps now cover some hundred thousand square miles of the Union and South-West Africa. Meanwhile, the Chamber of Mines had continued to preside over much promising research in mining, metallurgy and mineralogy, and several Technical Colleges had been established, one of which was destined to blossom forth into the University of the Witwatersrand. The Universities and the Geological Survey now carry out research, much of which has been subsidised by the Council for Scientific and Industrial Research since its formation in 1945 under the presidency of Dr B. J. F. Schonland. The most surprising of recent geological discoveries in southern Africa was, however, made almost casually thirty years ago when uranium was found in the "slimes" of Rand gold-mines. Since 1948, the Atomic Energy Board has supervised the growing production of this vital substance by the state and some of the mines, the necessary electrical current is supplied by huge plants, and Pretoria possesses the country's first cyclotron.

Much research has been devoted to physics and chemistry, thanks perhaps to their bearing on mining and metallurgy. At first applied physics fared better than pure physics, especially in the fields of astronomy, geomagnetism and metereology, because pure physics had to wait until men like Professor A. Ogg of the University of Cape Town had built up adequate laboratories and standards. To-day, each of the universities concentrates on one or other branch of this vast subject; the ubiquitous Council for Scientific and Industrial Research assists research throughout the Union and also specialises in research into nuclear physics, X-ray differentiation and biophysics in its own National Physical Laboratory; the Chamber of Mines likewise has its own laboratories and, besides tackling problems of ventilation and wood-preservation below ground, suggests problems and supplies data to the Bernard Pares Institute of Geophysical Research, which was founded in the mid-nineteen-thirties and is now attached to the University of the Witwatersrand; finally, the Fuel Research Institute concentrates on the problems of coal-mines. Two of southern Africa's leading physicists, Dr H. J. van der Byl and Professor R. W. James of the University of Cape Town, had made their reputations overseas before enhancing them in the Union; but the third, Dr B. F. J. Schonland, had done some of his best work on the mechanism of the lightning flash in his native land before becoming Director of the National Atomic Station at Harwell in southern England. As for chemistry, research is carried out in the universities with the support of the Council for Scientific and Industrial Research, the Metallurgical Society of South Africa, the South African Chemical Institute and the Cape Chemical and Technicological Society. Much of this work has always been done on soils and local products, but, latterly, an increasing amount is being done on mineral springs, a hitherto neglected subject.

Agricultural research has been encouraged by successive Ministries. Much attention has naturally been paid to soils and indigenous plants at the many research stations and the five agricultural colleges, the oldest and best known of which, the Elsenburg School of Agriculture, was founded in 1898 and incorporated in the University of Stellenbosch some thirty years later. On the other hand, in spite of the fact that the country depended in such great measure on its cattle and sheep, veterinary research was virtually non-existent in southern Africa two generations ago, such few official veterinary surgeons as there then were having all they could do in keeping an eye on outbreaks of animal diseases on the farms. Best known of these pioneers was Duncan Hutcheon, who was appointed Colonial Veterinary Surgeon of the Cape Colony in 1880 and, in 1906, became Director of Agriculture. Meanwhile (Sir) Arnold Theiler had been appointed State Veterinarian in the South African Republic in 1893 and, four years later, had set up his own little wood and iron laboratory at Onderste Poort near Pretoria. This, in 1908, became the State Veterinary Research Institute and has since won a world-wide reputation under its founder and Theiler's successor, Dr P. J. du Toit.

Of all the sciences studied in South Africa perhaps that of medicine has made the greatest advance there of recent years. Research in the basic or pre-clinical sciences has been active for three or four generations and has yielded valuable results, as evidenced in the reports of the South African Institute of Medical Research, established in Johannesburg in 1912, and in the publications of the University of Cape Town and the University of the Witwatersrand. Special mention might be made of research in human nutrition and, more recently, in virology. Valuable work has also been done in blood groups and their relationship to movements of primitive populations in the African continent. The two original medical schools in the Universities of Cape Town and the Witwatersrand have been supplemented by others in the Universities of Pretoria, Natal and Stellenbosch.

Since the institution of the Council for Scientific and Industrial Research with its medical and dental sub-committees after the Second World War, there has been spectacular advance in medical science and particularly in the clinical sciences. Research in human nutrition, especially in the rôle of protein malnutrition as a cause of widespread chronic disease, and in the rôle of dietary fat in relation to blood cholesterol and coronary heart disease, has been important.

Virology with special emphasis on poliomyelitis, and human parasitology with special reference to schistosomiasis and amoebiasis have also been productive fields of research.

Hospitalisation has made considerable progress. Hospitals of high quality are connected with each of the medical schools, where there is joint staffing by agreement between the local university and hospital authority. These hospitals are active centres for clinical research. The low *per capita* income of the country does not yet allow adequate hospitalisation in large rural under-privileged areas, but there missionary hospitals are widespread. A system of health-centres has been established to cater for ambulatory patients and to give some domiciliary service in selected under-privileged areas.[1]

The South African Medical and Dental Council, consisting of thirty members, controls the registration of medical practitioners, dentists, nurses and midwives, and has disciplinary powers. In 1952 the number of medical practitioners was 6160, of interns 597 and of specialists 1003.

Anthropology naturally awakens keen interest in southern Africa, not only because remains of various types of prehistoric man have been found therein, but because its present-day peoples are at very different stages of culture. The study owes its origins locally to missionaries or administrators like E. Casalis, H. C. Knudsen, H. A. Junod, E. Jacottet, P. Stapleton and Robert Moffat, who desired earnestly to know all that could be known about the folk committed to their charge. Of recent years, their pioneer work has been carried very much further by professionals assisted by many enthusiastic amateurs among whom the versatile Dr Louis Peringuey was outstanding. Perhaps the most notable worker in this field to-day is Professor I. Schapera, whose classic studies of the Tswana, of the Shona of Southern Rhodesia and of many other Bantu tribes show an increasingly sympathetic approach to such fundamental problems as tribal law and government, kinship relations, land tenure, ritual and witchcraft. Thanks largely to his labours and insight, such matters can no longer be contemptuously dismissed as "ye beastlie devices of ye heathen".

Alongside Anthropology goes Social Morphology for the study of which southern Africa offers a splendid field, because its rapid industrialisation, based largely on migratory labour, is drawing the Bantu majority wholesale into the towns, transforming them therein and then sending them back to influence tribal life profoundly. So also with Philology. Here, most of the pioneers were missionaries, and among later workers are still other missionaries, who either carry on

[1] In 1952 there were 570 hospitals in the Union, of which 238 were for whites only. There were also mine and factory hospitals, orthopaedic and infectious-diseases hospitals, missionary hospitals and general private nursing homes. One hundred or more of the private hospitals were state-aided. Government medical officers (district surgeons) do medical and public health work.

research themselves or encourage others to do so. During the eighteen-fifties, Bushman dialects were studied by W. H. T. Bleek (*Handbook of African, Australian and Polynesian Philology*, 1858), but few have followed him into this fast-disappearing field apart from Theophilus Hahn, Lucy Lloyd and his own daughter, D. F. Bleek, whose comparative dictionary of Bushman tongues is shortly to be published posthumously. Hottentot has fared somewhat better at the hands of the elder Bleek again and of D. M. Beach, an acknowledged authority on Bushman phonetics. Naturally enough, Bantu languages have been studied much more extensively, by Bleek once more during the 'sixties, when he earned the title of the "Father of Bantu Philology" thanks to the fundamental studies which he embodied in his *Comparative Grammar of the African Languages* (1862), and thereafter by Meinhoff, who, though his knowledge in this field was by no means really comprehensive, built up a school in Germany which still in great measure dominates African linguistics. Meanwhile, Dr Clement Doke had extended the work of his predecessors by prescribing fresh criteria for the classification and analysis of Bantu parts of speech, and D. Jones, leader of the "English" school of phonetics, had applied the principles of that school to Bantu tongues. Prominent workers in specific Bantu languages have been J. W. Appleby and A. Kropf (Xhosa), Bishop J. W. Colenso, A. T. Bryant, C. Roberts and W. Wanger (Xhosa and Zulu), A. Mabille and E. Jacottet (Southern Sotho), K. Endemann (Northern Sotho) and, far in advance of his time, W. Crisp (Tswana).

Africa is the richest of all continents in ancient man-made stone tools and weapons. This fact was hardly suspected by those few South African amateurs who dabbled in archaeology and human palaeontology a hundred years ago, inspired maybe by the publication in 1847 of the conclusions drawn by Boucher de Perthes from his discovery of prehistoric stone implements in the gravels of the Somme valley. The most notable of these pioneers was Inspector James Henry Bowker of the Frontier Armed and Mounted Police, who, in 1855, deposited in the South African Museum, Cape Town, the ancient stone implements he had collected along the Fish River on the Eastern Frontier. His finds were duly commented on, but it was only in 1868 that, after heated discussion, scientists in Europe agreed that man-made implements found in ancient deposits alongside bones of extinct animals were indeed part of the world's geological record. One direct result of this belated admission was that Dr Langham Dale, the Cape's Superintendent of Education, tried in 1870 to link the still living Bushmen and Hottentots with the old stone implements which abounded in the neighbourhood of the Cape Peninsula. Encouraged by Lord Avebury, a warm supporter of de Perthe's revolutionary thesis, he, his wife and sons and, on occasion, E. L. Layard, Director of the South African Museum, found many ancient stone artefacts and fragments of coarse pottery on the wind-blown surface of the Cape Flats, and deposited their finds either in the South African Museum or the British Museum.

Dale's enthusiasm inspired others to join in the search, among them E. J. Dunn and J. R. Gregory, the latter of whom concentrated on the ancient shell deposits around False Bay. Since, however, the science of Human Palaeontology was still in its infancy and everyone was deeply ignorant of nearly all that had happened in times long past in the vast area between the Sahara and South Africa, Dale and his immediate successors naturally applied the current and inappropriate European ideas of the sequence of archaeological ages to South African conditions. Neither they nor anyone else in their country had heard of the protests against this mistaken policy published in 1881 by the Englishman, J. C. Rickard, in an obscure English periodical.

The study aroused little public interest till after 1905, when the British Association paid its first visit to southern Africa. Forthwith, Dr Louis Peringuey, Director of the South African Museum, wrote a paper on *The Stone Age in South Africa*, a paper which he expanded into a book with the same title in 1911, still equating South African with European ages. This equation was, however, fast becoming impossible to maintain, for not only had Java yielded up, some twenty years back, fragments of the skull of *Pithecanthropus Erectus*, at that time the earliest known recognisably human type, but two years after the publication of Peringuey's book, the Boskop human skull was found near Potchefstroom, a very ancient skull whose owner was named *Homo Capensis* by Professor Robert Broom of Victoria College, Stellenbosch. Thereafter discoveries came in quick succession, of *Homo Rhodesiensis* at Broken Hill in Northern Rhodesia, a type even more bestial than Neanderthal or even than Java man, of further Boskop skulls as far apart as Zitzikamma near Port Elizabeth and Kalomo in Northern Rhodesia, and in 1924 fragments of an Early Pleistocene human skull in a limestone quarry at Taungs in Bechuanaland. Most experts held that this Taungs skull was merely that of an immature ape, but Professor Raymond Dart of the University of the Witwatersrand boldly named the new find *Australopithecus Africanus*, insisting that it was indubitably a human skull halfway between those of Java man and the highest living anthropoids.

It was now plain that, archaeologically speaking, southern Africa must cut loose from the European time scale and sequence. As a result of a survey of the Union started by the University of Cape Town in the year of the discovery of the Taungs skull, A. J. H. Goodwin of that university and Professor C. van Riet Lowe of the University of the Witwatersrand published in 1929 their *Stone Age Culture in South Africa* setting forth a scheme of "ages" adapted to local conditions, a scheme which received a ready welcome from South African scientists and the members of the British Association on their second visit in that very year. In due time, after Lowe had founded the Archaeological Survey of South Africa and seen it attached to his university, Broom and others discovered subhuman skulls like that of Taungs in numbers unparallelled anywhere else in the world, and at Sterkfontein in the western Transvaal found one associated with chipped pebbles. Broom, whose main achievement hitherto had been to deduce the descent of mammals from reptiles, turned aside to show that these Australopithecene discoveries proved that Dart was right in maintaining that the Taungs skull was indeed that of a *Hominid*, probably the oldest yet found. Broom even went so far as to suggest that the origins of *Homo Sapiens* himself must be sought in Transvaal deposits. Be that as it may, invaluable work has been done recently by W. H. Scheepers, J. Robinson, K. Oakley, Keith Jolly, Professor Mr. R. Drennan and others, who have discovered *inter alia* Saldanha Man, obviously a distant relative of Boskop Man and *Homo Rhodesiensis*, associated with animal bones and rough human artefacts.

One other field of archaeological research remains to be noted. Some half-century ago, much interest was shown in the great dry-stone buildings in Southern Rhodesia and the northern Transvaal, above all in those at Zimbabwe. The fashion then was to date the origins of the latter back to the distant days of King Solomon or even further back to those of ancient Dravidian Indians, and the exponents of these views were duly shocked when, in 1905, D. Randall MacIver declared that they were the work of mediaeval Bantu. Latterly, a strong British Association party led by Dr Gertrude Caton-Thompson of Newnham College, Cambridge, has proved that MacIver was right.

To-day many Southern African museums have good archaeological collections, while the University of Cape Town has long since provided a course in prehistoric archaeology, the University of the Witwatersrand is preparing to follow suit, and the examining University of South Africa offers diplomas in this subject. Maintenance of standards is helped by the archaeological survey centred in the University of the Witwatersrand and by the South African Archaeological Society, whose headquarters are at Cape Town. Valuable stimulus has been given by visiting scientists from Europe and North America, of whom the Abbé Breuil is probably the most famous. It is significant that the work of some white South African artists has already been influenced by their country's most ancient cultures.

To sum up, the progress made in science in most of its branches may to some extent be gauged by the multiplicity of flourishing scientific societies, of which there are at least thirty, headed by the Royal Society of South Africa. Meanwhile, the results of the work of the all-pervading Council for Scientific and Industrial Research are published in numerous journals and reports and, together with the output of the numerous state laboratories, are summarised quarterly in *The Research Review*.

Sport

No discussion of culture would be complete without mention of the sport in which southern Africans of all races take a keen interest. All have followed the Bushmen in their love of dancing, while more than one racial group has games and pastimes peculiar to itself, the frontier Afrikaners, for instance, playing *jukskei*, a rough-and-ready form of quoits, and performing folk-dances to the strains of the fiddle and concertina, and the Bantu dancing to the thud of drums and clapping of hands. All, however, either play or follow eagerly western European organised games. Hockey and Association football have comparatively few supporters; cricket, handicapped by lack of good turf pitches, is still confined mainly to a small English-speaking minority; rowing can find few suitable rivers, very rarely reaches the Henley standard, and has thus far produced only two Blues, both at Cambridge. Motor-cycling has its devotees; organised packs here and there hunt the jackal since no fox is to be had; horse-racing has been popular since the days of that sporting Cape Governor, Lord Charles Somerset, away back in the eighteen-twenties, and reaches its peak in the Durban July Handicap, South Africa's Derby. All these sports are on a comparatively small scale; on the other hand, there is widespread enthusiasm for boxing, rifle-shooting, golf and lawn tennis. Favoured by long spells of dry weather, a clear atmosphere and, as far as Europeans are concerned, abundant leisure, individuals and representative teams have won deservedly high reputations as far afield as St. Andrew's and Bisley and Wimbledon and wherever men do box. The South African sport *par excellence* is, however, Rugby football. This form of the game was brought direct from Rugby School in the eighteen-seventies by Canon George Ogilvie, for many years headmaster of the Diocesan College, Rondebosch. In spite of the fact that it has often to be played on hard stretches of sandy gravel, the game swept the country and has long held pride of place as the national sport. Four times between 1906 and 1952, South African Springbok teams have toured the United Kingdom, playing on each occasion a heavy sequence of international and club matches, and winning all save five matches lost and two drawn. In their own country, the Springboks have more than once dealt justly with visiting teams of New Zealand All Blacks and Australian Wallabies.

It is remarkable that South Africans should have achieved so many outstanding successes seeing that, in the name of *apartheid* (separation), their representative teams, even for such international events as the Olympic and British Commonwealth Games, are drawn only from the white minority, that is, from little more than one-fifth of the total population, Non-Europeans, especially the civilised Cape Coloured Folk, play the white man's games vigorously and, on occasion, excellently, and in most centres are allowed to watch white matches, provided they sit in segregated stands; but none of them may play as members of or against white teams, still less hope for inclusion in a national representative side. The non-European table tennis organisation has however been recognised internationally as the one and only body qualified to represent the Union in that game. Meanwhile, it says much for the sound physical quality of the European stock in South Africa that it can produce from its limited ranks so many teams of such notable excellence in so many fields of sport.

BIBLIOGRAPHY

PART I

COLLECTIONS OF MANUSCRIPTS IN PUBLIC AND PRIVATE ARCHIVES AND OFFICIAL PAPERS AND PUBLICATIONS

A. IN GREAT BRITAIN

By A. Taylor Milne, M.A., Librarian of the Institute of Historical Research, University of London.

1. PUBLIC RECORD OFFICE

(*a*) *COLONIAL OFFICE*

Chancery Lane, London, S.W.1.

At the time of the first British occupation of the Cape (1795), Henry Dundas (afterwards Viscount Melville), the newly-created Secretary for War, was nominally in charge of colonial affairs. It was not until 1801 that colonial business was officially transferred from the Committee for Trade and Plantations to the Department for War, Lord Hobart being created Secretary of State for the War and Colonial Department. A separate Secretary of State for the Colonies was appointed in 1854, whose office has continued ever since. A Secretary of State for Dominion Affairs was added in 1925, whose holder in 1947 became Secretary of State for Commonwealth Relations. These two last-named officials were responsible, in succession, for all business relating to the self-governing Dominions, or, as they are now called, the Member States, to Southern Rhodesia, to the High Commission Territories of Basutoland, the Bechuanaland Protectorate and Swaziland, and to the Imperial Conference, which, since 1944, has been renamed the Conference of Prime Ministers of the Commonwealth. When the Union of South Africa became a republic outside the Commonwealth on 31st May, 1961, the Secretary of State handed over the High Commission Territories to the Secretary of State for the Colonies, but retained his other responsibilities. Although papers relating specifically to colonial matters have been assembled in the "Colonial Office Records" at the Public Record Office, it should be remembered that a number may have lingered in the files of the Home Office, the Board of Trade, and the War Department.

Colonial Office Records relating to South Africa are usually bound in volumes systematically arranged. For each colony the most valuable series is that described as Original Correspondence, Secretary of State. One section of this contains the despatches, with their enclosures, from Governors and Lieutenant-Governors. It was the custom to note on incoming despatches the action taken or the nature of the reply. These minutes become very full as the nineteenth century advances, and in the 'seventies printed forms began to be used. Copies or originals of many despatches are in the Cape Town Archives or elsewhere in South Africa, but the minutes in the Public Record Office form an additional source of great value.

Another part of this series comprises the volumes labelled "Public Offices and Miscellaneous", which contain in-letters from government departments, officials and private individuals; also addresses, memorials and petitions.

The series of Entry Books contains copies of all outgoing correspondence down to 1873.

Since 1849 a Register of Correspondence has been kept for each colony. This contains brief summaries of the more important documents.

When the Entry Books were closed in 1873, an Index of Correspondence was started for each colony. The indexes to all classes of public records are now numbered in one series.

Colonial Governors were required to make periodical returns, the most important coming to be known as the "Blue Book". The Governor's covering despatch was in the nature of an annual report on the colony. It was usually presented to Parliament, and later the practice was extended to the Blue Book itself. The Blue Books and Statistical Returns are preserved and, together with runs of colonial newspapers, form a separate series.

The Acts of each colonial legislature form a separate series.

The Government Gazettes of each colony form a separate series.

Details of these records are contained in the *List of Colonial Office Records preserved in the Public Record Office* (*P.R.O. Lists and Indexes*, No. XXXVI, H.M. Stationery Office, 1911), which catalogues them down to 1837 and must be supplemented by the various typed lists kept at the Public Record Office. The same observation applies to the printed lists of other departmental records. M. S. Giuseppi's *A guide to the manuscripts preserved in the Public Record Office* (2 vols. H.M. Stationery Office, 1923–4) gives a general sketch of the different classes.

Colonial Office records are not open to public inspection until they are fifty years old. This restriction, however, does not apply to published records.

Note. The following lists of documents i–xx should be read in conjunction with those given in B i (*a*) which include some documents not to be found in the Public Record Office.

I. Africa, South: British South Africa Company

C.O. 3. Ordinances, 1 vol. (1891–9).
C.O. 417. Original Correspondence, vols. 1–137 (1884–94).
C.O. 455. Government Gazettes, vols. 1–4 (1894–1910).
C.O. 462 (Ind. 12964–6). Indexes, 3 vols.

II. Africa, South: Customs Union

C.O. 457. Miscellanea. Trade and shipping returns, 4 vols. (1906–9).

III. Africa, South: Intercolonial Council, Transvaal and Orange River Colony

C.O. 549. Minutes, papers laid, railway committee, vols. 2–11 (1903–8).

IV. Africa, South: High Commissioner

C.O. 548. Government Gazettes, vol. 1 (1901–8).
C.O. 550. Proclamations, vol. 1 (1906–8).

V. Africa, South, Union of

C.O. 552. Government Gazettes, vols. 1–4 (1910).
C.O. 553. Miscellanea. Statements of trade and shipping (including Northern and Southern Rhodesia), vol. 1 (1910). For earlier statements, *see* Africa, South: Customs Union, above.

VI. Amatongaland (Tongaland)

C.O. 4. Proclamations, 1 vol. (1896–7).

VII. Basutoland

C.O. 566. Blue Books of statistics, vols. 1–7 (1903–10).

VIII. Bechuanaland Protectorate

C.O. 576. Blue Books of statistics, vols. 1–4 (1896–1907).

IX. British Bechuanaland

C.O. 451. Government Gazettes, 1 vol. (1887–95).

X. Cape of Good Hope

C.O. 48. Original Correspondence, Secretary of State, vols. 1–524 (1807–94). Vols. 75–9, 100–15, 119–23, 128–9, 134, 160 are "Reports and papers of the Commissioners of Eastern Inquiry" (1825–34). *See also* C.O. 414 below.
C.O. 49. Entry Books, vols. 1–62 (1797–1872).
C.O. 50. Acts, vols. 1–11 (1825–1910).
C.O. 51. Sessional Papers, Votes and Proceedings, vols. 1–405 (1823–1910).
C.O. 52. Government Gazettes, vols. 1–104 (1823–1910).
C.O. 53. Miscellanea, newspapers, Blue Books of statistics, Statistical Registers, vols. 1–147 (1824–1909).
C.O. 336 (Ind. 12953–63). Register of Correspondence, vols. 1–11 (1850–85).
C.O. 462 (Ind. 12964–66). Register. Indexes, vols. 1–3 (1872–82).
C.O. 414. Commissioners of Eastern Inquiry, vols. 1–13 (1823–30). Papers supplementary to those in C.O. 48.

XI. Griqualand West

(Under Cape Colony after 1880)

C.O. 107. Original Correspondence, 1875–80. Nine volumes.
C.O. 344. (Ind. 13050), Register of Correspondence, 1875–80. One volume.
C.O. 522. Vol. I (Ind. 13051). Register of Out-Letters, 1876–80. One volume.
C.O. 108. Sessional Papers, 1873–80. Three volumes.
C.O. 109. Govt. Gazettes, 1876–80. One volume.
C.O. 461. Miscellanea, 1873. One volume.

XII. Natal

C.O. 179. Original Correspondence, Secretary of State, vols. 1–189 (1846–94).
C.O. 180. Acts, vols. 1–12 (1848–1910).
C.O. 181. Sessional Papers, Votes and Proceedings, vols. 1–68 (1846–1909).
C.O. 182. Government Gazettes, vols. 1–45 (1858–1909).
C.O. 183. Miscellanea, newspapers, Blue Books of statistics, Statistical Registers, vols. 1–58 (1850–1908).
C.O. 357 (Ind. 13189–97). Register of Correspondence, vols. 1–9 (1849–85).
C.O. 405. Entry Books, vols. 1–7 (1852–72).
C.O. 480 (Ind. 13198–200). Register. Indexes, vols. 1–3 (1872–85).

XIII. Orange River Colony

C.O. 224. Original Correspondence, Secretary of State, 2 vols. (1853–6).
C.O. 596. Acts (Ordinances, 1902–7; Acts, 1908–10), vols. 1–5 (1902–10).
C.O. 597. Government Gazettes, vols. 1–13 (1900–10).
C.O. 598. Miscellanea, Blue Books of statistics, vol. 1 (1905–6).
C.O. 599. Sessional Papers, vols. 1–19 (1902–10). Vols. 1 and 7, "Executive Council (Confidential), 1902–7", are not yet open to public inspection.

XIV. Rhodesia

C.O. 468. Sessional Papers (Administrative reports, mines reports), 3 vols. (1889–1902).

XV. Southern Rhodesia

C.O. 603. Sessional Papers, vols. 1–9 (1898–1910). Vol. 1, "Executive Council (Confidential), 1898–1909", is not yet open to public inspection.

XVI. Swaziland

C.O. 608. Miscellanea, Blue Books of statistics, vols. 1–4 (1906–10).
C.O. 609. Acts (Proclamations), vol. 1 (1904–6).

XVII. Transvaal

C.O. 291. Original Correspondence, Secretary of State, vols. 1–26 (1877–84).
C.O. 292. Acts (Ordinances, 1902–6), vols. 1–7 (1880, 1902–10).
C.O. 293. Sessional Papers, vols. 1–56 (1880–1910).
C.O. 294. Government Gazettes, vols. 1–46 (1869–1910).
C.O. 476. Miscellanea, Blue Books of statistics, vols. 1–7 (1878, 1902–9).
C.O. 477. Miscellanea, Green Books, vols. 1–3 (1884–98).
C.O. 510 (Ind. 13321–23). Register of Correspondence, vols. 1–3 (1877–84).
C.O. 511 (Ind. 13324–25). Register. Indexes, vols. 1–2 (1877–84).

XVIII. Zululand

C.O. 427. Original Correspondence, Secretary of State, vols. 1–19 (1887–94).
C.O. 322. Acts (Proclamations), vol. 1 (1887–97).
C.O. 472. Miscellanea, Blue Books of statistics, vols. 1–8 (1889–96).

XIX. Colonies (General)

C.O. 323. Original Correspondence, Secretary of State, vols. 1–399 (1784–1894). This class includes Law Officers' reports on colonial acts, applications for passports and colonial appointments, circulars and correspondence relating to the colonies generally. There are also private letters of Lord Bathurst and R. W. Hay. Index vols. are included in the series.
C.O. 324. Entry Books of commissions, warrants, instructions, petitions, grants, Orders in Council, etc., Series I, 175 vols. (to 1872). Vol. 47 is "Warrants, Cape of Good Hope, etc., 1795–1812". Vol. 69 is "Précis of correspondence, Cape of Good Hope, 1807–10".
C.O. 325. Miscellaneous Memoranda, etc., vols. 6–46 (1773–1858). Historical sketches of the colonies, returns of appointments, registers of appointments, précis and memoranda. Vols. 16, 32, 33 relate to South Africa.
C.O. 378 (Ind. 12855–64). Register of Correspondence, vols. 1–10 (1871–83).
C.O. 379 (Ind. 12866–70). Register. Indexes, vols. 1–5 (1871–83).
C.O. 380. Miscellanea. Draft letters patent, commissions, royal instructions, warrants, etc. Vols. 69–77 (1836–82) relate to South Africa.
C.O. 381. Entry Books, Series II. Vol. 25 is "Cape of Good Hope, vol. 1 (1854–72)". Vol. 50 is "Natal, vol. 1 (1836–70)".
C.O. 382. Daily Registers (Ind. 10625–37, 10686–98, 15561–72), vols. 1–39 (1849–72). A day-to-day register of letters received, each volume indexed.
C.O. 383. Act Registers, vols. 1–93 (1781–1894). These refer to the volumes of "Acts" which will be found under the various colonies.

C.O. 326. REGISTERS, Indexes, etc. This class includes a general register of colonial letters received in the Secretary of State's office between 1810 and 1849, after which letters were recorded in the several registers described under the individual colonies.

C.O. 432 (Ind. 12873–4). REGISTERS of miscellaneous correspondence, vols. 1–2 (1860–70).

XX. EMIGRATION

C.O. 384. ORIGINAL CORRESPONDENCE, Secretary of State, vols. 1–190 (1817–94). The earlier volumes contain correspondence relating to the 1820 settlers and other emigrants to South Africa.

C.O. 385. ENTRY BOOKS, vols. 1–30 (1814–71).

C.O. 428 (Ind. 13378–96). REGISTER OF CORRESPONDENCE, vols. 1–20 (1850–84). Includes Indexes.

Among the other miscellaneous series of the Colonial Office Records, there is probably much South African material, e.g. in C.O. 11 "General memoranda, vol. 1" (1842–50). In C.O. 412, vols. 92–105 are duplicates of papers presented to the South African Government. There is a certain amount of manuscript material retained at the Colonial Office, Whitehall, including No. 1472: "Sketches of the political and commercial history of the Cape of Good Hope to 1796, with suggestions relative to the colony submitted to the Cabinet, 1796." The private papers of Sir Philip Wodehouse, Governor of Cape Colony and High Commissioner, 1861–9, are also deposited there.

(b) *ADMIRALTY*

The Admiralty Office records are particularly interesting for South Africa during the period 1795–1815. They comprise papers brought together from the Secretary's Department, the Accountant-General's Department, and the Navy Board (abolished 1832).

AD. 1. SECRETARY'S DEPARTMENT. IN-LETTERS. Admirals' despatches. Vols. 54–86 (1758–1839) are from the Cape of Good Hope station; also vols. 5736, 5761, 5789, 5822, 5874, 5921, 5967, 6005 (1860–67). In this series there are a number of other sub-headings, such as "Letters relating to the colonies" (to 1839), "Letters from Secretaries of State" (to 1839), "Secret Letters" (to 1837). Vol. 5378 relates to the court-martial of Sir Home Popham, 1807; vols. 5487–8 are "Courts-Martial, Cape of Good Hope" (to 1837). From 1840 onwards the In-Letters are not arranged under sub-headings, but have an internal classification of letters from Admirals, Captains and other officers; also those from various departments, etc. The indexes noted below must be used to find the scattered South African items.

AD. 2. SECRETARY'S DEPARTMENT. OUT-LETTERS (to 1859). These are classified under about thirty sub-headings, such as "Orders and Instructions" (to 1815), "Secret Orders and Letters" (to 1820). South African material may be found by using the indexes.

AD. 7. SECRETARY'S DEPARTMENT. MISCELLANEA. This series contains a number of South African items: vols. 2–6, "Transactions of Sir Jahleel Brenton at the Cape of Good Hope" (1815–30); vols. 47–8, 53–4, "Correspondence with Admiral Nourse, Cape of Good Hope" (1822–4); vols. 320, 321, "Registers of Letters of Marque against Holland and the Batavian Republic" (1780–1801, 1803–1812).

AD. 12. INDEXES and COMPILATIONS, Series III (Ind. 4755–5091, 12142–604). These are digests and indexes of the Secretary's Department, In-Letters; the "digests" referring to subjects, "indexes" to names of persons and ships. Vol. 8 (Ind. 4762) is "List of Admirals' despatches, Cape of Good Hope" (1813–47).

AD. 13. SECRETARY'S DEPARTMENT. SUPPLEMENTARY collection of papers, vols. 1–63 (1814–80). Miscellaneous out-letters. Vols. 64–9 (Ind. 13897–902) are Registers of correspondence.

AD. 51 (Captains' Logs to 1852); AD. 52 (Masters' Logs to 1840); AD. 53 (Ships' Logs to 1885); AD. 54 (Additional Masters' Logs, 1837–71); and AD. 55 (Logs and journals relating to voyages of exploration, 1766–1861). These series all contain South African material.

AD. 106. NAVY BOARD. IN-LETTERS, OUT-LETTERS, MINUTES. 2003–7, "From Yards, Cape of Good Hope" (1795–1832); 3169–70, 3206, "Magazines of stores at Cape of Good Hope (1796, 1808, 1809–17)".

Of the Admiralty records, the Logs and Journals are open to public inspection without limit of date, but other classes are not open until they are fifty years old.

(c) *FOREIGN OFFICE*

Diplomatic correspondence between Great Britain and foreign powers relating to South Africa is to be found in various series arranged under countries. It should be remembered that the Embassy and Consular archives, though parallel with the Secretary of State's files, contain material which is not to be found in them.

F.O. 37. HOLLAND and NETHERLANDS, 884 vols. (1781–1905), is particularly interesting during the period 1793–1815.

F.O. 63. PORTUGAL. A series scarcely yet explored.

F.O. 64. PRUSSIA and GERMANY, 1654 vols. (1781–1905), is important during the eighteen-seventies and eighties for Anglo-Germany rivalry in Southern Africa. Vols. 1101–6 are "Annexation of Angra Pequena, 1883–5"; vols. 1145–50 are "Colonial Policy, 1876–1885".

F.O. 84. SLAVE TRADE. Besides the voluminous correspondence with foreign Powers, there is much with the Colonial Office concerning South Africa.

F.O. 97. SUPPLEMENTARY. Vols. 246–8, Holland (1781–96); vols. 300–322, Portugal (1782–1867).

F.O. 312. ARCHIVES OF COMMISSIONS, SLAVE TRADE: Cape Town. 43 vols. (1843–70). In-Letters, Entry-Books of Out-Letters, Registers, Accounts, etc. of the Mixed British and Portuguese Commission established under the Act of 3 July 1842. The seal of the Commission is F.O. 365/48.

Foreign Office records are open to public inspection after they are fifty years old. As far as possible the staff will answer questions on specific points arising at a later date.

(d) *HOME OFFICE*

H.O. 11. CRIMINAL. Convict transportation. Registers, vols. 1–121 (1787–1870). Lists, under the respective ships, of the names of convicts transported.

H.O. 30. DEPARTMENTAL. War and Colonial Office, 5 vols. and bundles (1794–1840). Vol. 5 is an Entry-book of Out-letters. There are scattered South African items.

Home Office records are open to public inspection to 1878. Records from that date until 1919 are at the Public Record Office and are, with certain exceptions, open to public inspection after they are fifty years old.

(e) *WAR OFFICE*

These records consist of official papers of the Secretary-at-War (an office abolished in 1863), the Secretary of State for War and Colonies, and the Commander-in-Chief. Between 1801 and 1855 letters on military matters will also be found in the "Colonial Office, Colonies General" series. *An alphabetical guide to certain War Office and other military records preserved in the Public Record Office* (*P.R.O.*

Lists and Indexes, No. LIII, H.M. Stationery Office, 1931) is one of the most valuable printed lists, since it includes material from other classes, such as Colonial Office and Home Office papers.

W.O. 1. CORRESPONDENCE. IN-LETTERS, to 1868. Vols. or bundles relating to South Africa are 178 (1796–7), 323–43 (1795–1812), 438–51 (1842–55) and 638, 657, 667, 695, 738, 740, 741, 749, 679, 784–5, 840, 841–2, 881, 893 (various dates).

W.O. 3. CORRESPONDENCE. OUT-LETTERS. Commander-in-Chief, 617 vols. (1765–1868). South African items include vol. 575, Appointment of Sir Harry Smith as High Commissioner and Commander-in-Chief in South Africa (1847).

W.O. 4. CORRESPONDENCE. OUT-LETTERS. Secretary-at-War (to 1861). Vols. 284–90 (1847–53), 717 (1813), 729 (1837–8) relate to South Africa.

W.O. 6. CORRESPONDENCE. OUT-LETTERS. Secretary of State for War, vols. 1–213 (1793–1859). South African vols. include 20–22 (1795–1806), 67 (1794–1807), 142 (1797), 176 (1798–1806), 196 (1856–7), 104–14 (1841–58).

W.O. 17. MONTHLY RETURNS of all Regiments at home and oversea, 2810 vols. and bundles (1759–1865). Since 1866 these returns have been abstracted and printed in part; the originals are not fully preserved. Nos. 1581–1646 are "Cape of Good Hope" (1795–1805).

Other War Office records containing South African material are: W.O. 31, Commander-in-Chief (1793–1870); W.O. 32, Miscellaneous papers (1855–1912); W.O. 33, Miscellanea; W.O. 43 (1809–57); W.O. 44, Ordnance Office, In-Letters (to 1873). All Pay-lists, Muster Rolls, and Monthly Returns are open to public inspection without restriction. Other classes are open only after they are fifty years old, while in the case of W.O. 1–8 and 31–33 all extracts made of documents dated later than 1858 are subject to official inspection.

(*f*) *INDIA OFFICE*

(These papers are deposited in the Library of the Office, Whitehall, London, S.W.1.)

Much material for South African history is to be found among the records of the (English) East India Company, preserved at the India Office. Within the series of "Factory records" is a "Cape of Good Hope" section of 24 volumes (vols. 1–5, Miscellaneous correspondence, 1773–1823; vols. 6–9, Letters from the Cape, 1795–1803; vol. 9a, Extracts from letters, 1808–31; vols. 10–17, Letters received at the Cape, 1808–36; vols. 18–24, Letters from the Cape, 1808–36). These volumes include papers of John Pringle who was the Company's Agent at the Cape between 1795 and 1815. See *List of Factory Records of the late East India Company preserved in the Record Department of the India Office, London*, H.M.S.O., 1897.

Other series containing scattered South African material are the "Marine Records" (journals of voyages from 1605; ships' logs; miscellaneous) and the "Home Miscellaneous Series", the description of which does not indicate the contents; vols. 88, 154, 155, 388, 726, 738, for instance, concern precautions taken at the Cape during the British Occupations of 1795 and 1806, and during the Indian Mutiny. See HILL, S. C., *Catalogue of the Home Miscellaneous Series of the India Office Records*, H.M.S.O., 1927. A general sketch is given in FOSTER, (Sir) W., *A Guide to the India Office Records, 1600–1858*, India Office. 1919.

Records in the Public Record Office are open to public inspection after they are fifty years old.

(*g*) *TREASURY*

T. 1. TREASURY BOARD PAPERS (to 1889). Chiefly In-Letters, with occasional minutes and reports.

T. 2. REGISTERS of PAPERS, alphabetical and numerical (to 1889).

T. 3. Skeleton Registers, 68 vols. (1783–1879).
T. 7. Out-Letters, Colonial Affairs, 26 vols. (1849–89).
T. 28. Out-Letters, Various. Vols. 41–59 are to Secretaries of State (1796–1856) and include material on colonial affairs.
T. 38. Accounts, Colonies (to 1838). A number relating to the Cape.
T. 64. Miscellanea, Various. Vol. 52 is "Cape Correspondence, with index to out-letters (1806–14)".
T. 70. African Companies. Vol. 68 contains "Letters (1749–51) and Description of the forts belonging to Europeans on the North, South and East coasts of Africa".
T. 71. Slave Registration and Compensation Records, 1630 vols. (1812–46). A great deal concerning South Africa. For further reference see Part II, Section vii.

These records are open to public inspection after they are fifty years old.

(*h*) *EXCHEQUER AND AUDIT OFFICE*

A.O. 1. Declared Accounts in Rolls (to 1828). Contains miscellaneous accounts, commissariat and general, relating to the Cape of Good Hope.
A.O. 2. Declared Accounts in Books (1829–48). Similar material to A.O. 1.
A.O. 3. Accounts, Various (to 1886). Occasional volumes of South African accounts.
A.O. 8, vols. 84–9, Colonial Drafts (1815–32) and A.O. 16, Miscellanea also contain South African material.

These records are open to public inspection to 1850.

(*i*) *BOARD OF TRADE* (*The name dates only from* 1861)

B.T. 1. In-Letters, 357 vols. (1791–1839). Of these vols. 34, 67, 77, 90, 111, 114, 127 contain references to the Second Occupation of the Cape, 1806–15.
B.T. 3. Out-Letters, 28 vols. (1786–1839). Entry Books, each indexed.
B.T. 4. Reference Books to In-Letters, 12 vols. (1808–39). Registers and subject indexes.
B.T. 5. Minutes of the Committee for Trade, 59 vols. (1784–1850). The Committee for Trade and Foreign Plantations only gradually lost responsibility for colonial affairs after 1794. Vols. 10, 17, 20, 21, 22, 23, 25, 26, 28 of this series concern the British Occupations of the Cape, 1795–1820.
B.T. 6. Miscellanea (to 1855). These include consular reports and returns, Orders in Council referring to colonial laws, etc. Vol. 19 is "African Accounts" (1795–1805).

The records of the Board of Trade are open to public inspection after they are fifty years old.

(*j*) *PRIVY COUNCIL OFFICE*

P.C. 1. Papers, etc., 141 bundles and vols. (to 1911). Scattered South African items.
P.C. 2. Registers (to 1836). They contain minutes of proceedings, Orders-in-Council, reports and papers. The later registers are still at the Privy Council Office, Whitehall, as are all the records of the Judicial Committee.

The Privy Council records preserved at the Public Record Office are open to public inspection to 1885.

(k) CHANCERY

The PATENT ROLLS contain the original enrolments of all grants, charters and commissions under the Great Seal. These extend into the twentieth century, and are open to public inspection—for records later than 1800 on payment of a fee. Records at the Public Record Office are open after they are fifty years old.

(l) GIFTS AND DEPOSITS IN THE PUBLIC RECORD OFFICE

G.D. 2. ALLAN PAPERS contain material on the ecclesiastical history of South Africa.

G.D. 6. CARNARVON PAPERS. The papers of the 4th Earl of Carnarvon are of the greatest importance for South African history, in particular vol. 23, South African correspondence—Shepstone, Burgers, Brand (1875–8); vols. 32–34, Cape correspondence—Barkly and Frere (1874–8); vol. 49, Cape memoranda (1814–77); vols. 80–84, 131, Publications, South Africa, Colonial Office, Confidential (1865–85) (vol. 84 concerns Froude's Mission); vol. 116, South Africa, Parliamentary (1866–75).

G.D. 8. CHATHAM PAPERS. Vols. 102, 140 contain correspondence between William Pitt the Younger and Henry Dundas, Viscount Melville.

G.D. 22. RUSSELL PAPERS. These include Cabinet memoranda and correspondence on colonial affairs (1855–67), preserved by Lord John Russell.

G.D. 29. GRANVILLE PAPERS. These contain Cabinet papers of the 2nd Earl Granville (1855–85). Vol. 135 is his correspondence with the Earl of Kimberley (1880–83).

It is not possible to give a general rule for freedom of access, but where these Papers are the private papers of the Minister concerned, they are open to inspection on the same terms as Records in the appropriate Department.

2. OTHER COLLECTIONS

(a) BRITISH MUSEUM

Among the Sloane, Egerton, and Additional Manuscripts preserved in the Department of Manuscripts are the following papers of South African interest:

EGERTON MSS. 1854. Memoirs and papers relating to the Dutch Colony at the Cape of Good Hope, by E. A. van Braam Houckgeest, 1789–92 (in Dutch).

EGERTON MSS. 1855. Danckelman's "Voyage dan l'intérieur de l'Afrique Méridionale", 1804.

ADD. MSS. 19824–5. Charts of the Cape and coasts of S. Africa, by J. Barrow, 1797–8.

ADD. MSS. 20226–8. Correspondence of Sir H. Lowe with Cape officials, 1816–21.

ADD. MSS. 23618. Plans of the Castle at the Cape, 1797, 1806.

ADD. MSS. 30096–7. Journal and memoranda of Sir R. Wilson on service at the Cape, 1805–6.

ADD. MSS. 33976. Map of the African coast from Cape Verde to the Cape of Good Hope, by Jan Vingboons, *c.* 1640.

ADD. MSS. 34184. A Dutch portolano containing coloured seventeenth-century maps of the Cape of Good Hope and the hinterland, soon after 1654.

ADD. MSS. 36590. Paper *re* Orange Free State, 1874–1900.

ADD. MSS. 36757. Boer Telegrams *re* S. African War, 1899–1900.

ADD. MSS. 37528. Thomas Edgar's journal of Captain Cook's Third Voyage, with a plan of Table Bay, 1776.

ADD. MSS. 37274–318. Wellesley Papers, Series II. Scattered South African material. Add. MSS. 37278 are letters from Governors and officials at the Cape, 1798–1802; 37308–10 are correspondence with the Barnards, 1797–1802.

ADD. MSS. 37842–935. Windham Papers. William Windham was Secretary for War and Colonies, 1806–7. He earlier corresponded with Lord Macartney and with the Barnards, 1796–1801. See Add. MSS. 37847, 37876, 37879, 37885–6, 37915–16.

ADD. MSS. 38190–489. Liverpool Papers. Lord Liverpool was Secretary for War and Colonies, 1809–12, thereafter Prime Minister, 1812–27. His correspondence with Melville and Bathurst is valuable, e.g. 38237–302.

ADD. MSS. 38734–770. Huskisson Papers. William Huskisson was Under-Secretary for War, 1795–1801; Agent for the Cape of Good Hope, 1799–1803; and Secretary for War and Colonies, 1827–8. Add. MSS. 38769 contains his correspondence as Agent.

ADD. MSS. 39299. Molteno Papers. Papers of Sir J. C. Molteno, first Premier of Cape Colony (d. 1886).

ADD. MSS. 39558. Letters from Capt. C. A. Lafone during S. African War, 1899–1901.

ADD. MSS. 39870. Journals, in Dutch, of Peter Vriezema, relating to the Lucas Expedition to the Cape, 1795–6.

ADD. MSS. 40100–2. Melville Papers. Papers of Henry Dundas, Viscount Melville, 1771–1801, supplementing those at Rhodes House, Oxford, and elsewhere.

ADD. MSS. 40181–617. Peel Papers, 1815–50. Most important during Sir Robert Peel's great ministry of 1841–6 (Add. MSS. 40432–603); in particular his correspondence with Stanley and Gladstone, his successive Secretaries for War and Colonies (Add. MSS. 40467–70); also general correspondence, 1841–6 (Add. MSS. 40485–597).

ADD. MSS. 43039–358. Aberdeen Papers. Now open to public inspection.

ADD. MSS. 44086—835. GLADSTONE PAPERS. Open to public inspection with special catalogue.

Printed *Catalogues* of the Sloane and the Additional (including the Egerton) Manuscripts may be consulted in the British Museum and other libraries.

(*b*) *BRITISH SOUTH AFRICA COMPANY*

11, Old Jewry, London, E.C.2

The majority of the older records of the British South Africa Company from 1889 onwards were destroyed by enemy action in May 1941. Fortunately, many administrative papers had recently been transferred to the office of the High Commissioner for Southern Rhodesia, and other papers relating to the early history of the Rhodesias to the National Museum of Southern Rhodesia, Bulawayo, Southern Rhodesia (*vide infra*. p. 953, under National Archives of Rhodesia and Nyasaland). After the Company had given up administration in 1923, all official administrative documents, including *Gazettes*, as well as Rhodes's own administrative papers, were transferred to the Office of the High Commissioner for South Africa, whence they were subsequently transferred to the National Archives of Rhodesia and Nyasaland (*vide infra*, p. 953). Hence, the Company now possesses very few of Rhodes's papers, and none of historical interest. Many of the Rhodes Papers are at Rhodes House, Oxford (*vide infra*, p. 927).

(*c*) *CHURCH MISSIONARY SOCIETY*

Salisbury Square, London, E.C.2

The records of this society, though not open to public inspection, may be examined by courtesy of the authorities. The bulk of incoming and outgoing correspondence is preserved, and there is a card-index to the various classes in the collection. Of South African interest are the journals and correspondence of the Rev. F. Owen's short-lived mission in Zululand (1837).

(*d*) *LONDON MISSIONARY SOCIETY*

Livingstone House, Westminster, S.W.1

The records of the society may be inspected with the sanction of the Directors. They include correspondence with missionaries in South Africa dating from 1799. Among these are the papers of van der Kemp, Read, Dr Philip and Robert Moffat. The journals of van der Kemp and Moffat are particularly interesting. The printed magazines, reports and accounts of the Society are a useful guide to the manuscripts, which are carefully collated for reference.

(*d*) *METHODIST MISSIONARY SOCIETY*

24 Bishopsgate, London, E.C.2

The archives of the society are not open to the general public, but special permission may be given to research students. The printed records, dating from 1816, are very full and well indexed. They consist of annual reports and a monthly publication entitled "Missionary Notices", in which missionaries' letters are printed. These provide a valuable key to the manuscripts, which comprise correspondence from Cape Colony, Natal, the Orange Free State and elsewhere, chronologically arranged.

(*f*) *RHODES HOUSE, OXFORD*

The library of Rhodes House, Oxford, is a department of the Bodleian Library and contains some 360,000 items. Among the South African manuscripts in the library are the following:

MACARTNEY PAPERS.
- Official letter-book of Lord Macartney while Governor of the Cape, 1797–8.
- Copies of proclamations and public papers, 1797–8.
- Letter-book, letters to statesmen, 1797–8.
- Letter-book, letters to Henry Dundas (later Viscount Melville), 1797–8.

A good many of the Macartney Papers, which were in the first Gubbins Collection at the University of the Witwatersrand, were destroyed by fire in 1931.

LORD CHARLES SOMERSET PAPERS, 1823–26.
SIR RICHARD BOURKE'S CORRESPONDENCE, 1825–48.
MISCELLANEOUS LETTERS, 1795–1900.
MAITLAND PAPERS: Letter-book of Sir P. Maitland, 1846–48.
ROBERT WHITE PAPERS, Cape Colony, 1795–1880.
DAVID LIVINGSTONE: photostats of 45 letters, 1841–72.
SIR JOHN MOLTENO. Correspondence, 1837–78.
SIR HENRY E. BULWER PAPERS, Natal, 1882–88.
CAWSTON PAPERS, re British South Africa Company, 1881–1911.
Selborne Memorandum as drafted by Lionel Curtis before emendation by Lord Selborne.
RHODES PAPERS: a section of the archives of the B.S.A. Company, in all 29 boxes including letter-books, telegrams and business correspondence. Also originals of Rhodes's wills, 1877–88 and miscellaneous documents. The permission of the Rhodes Trustees, Rhodes House, Oxford, is required before certain of these Papers can be consulted.

(*g*) *ROYAL EMPIRE SOCIETY*

Northumberland Avenue, London, S.W.1

The manuscripts in the library include:

Two letters from Moshesh, Chief of the Basuto, to Theophilus Shepstone and Lt.-Gov. Keate, 13, 16 May 1867.

Petition from the inhabitants of the Cape against the establishment of convicted felons in South Africa, 5 April 1849. [A large parchment.]

Narrative of a journey from Cape Town to Grahamstown, 1838, by Gen. W. C. E. Napier.

NEWNHAM MSS. F. J. Newnham was Secretary of the Native Location Commission in the Transvaal, 1905–6.

(*h*) *SOCIETY FOR THE PROPAGATION OF THE GOSPEL IN FOREIGN PARTS*

15 Tufton Street, Westminster, S.W.1

The new archives department of the Society contains a very large collection of material for colonial history. The *Digest of the Records* (1900 edn.) is now being superseded by a new inventory and the manuscripts are being arranged into the following classes:

(i) MS. Journals of the society, 1703– .
(ii) Minutes of the Standing Committee, 1702– .
(iii) Copies of letters received (originals disappeared). Cape Town, 1833– ; Natal, 1858– . Bound volumes, some indexed.
(iv) D. MSS. Letters received. Bound and indexed. The South African items date from 1850.
(v) E. MSS. Missionaries' Reports, 1850– . Annual reports, indexed since 1887.
(vi) Letters sent. Copies of out-letters. Africa and Mauritius, vols. 1 to 15, 1836–1927.

There are also numerous bundles of letters, etc., which are being sorted and have already revealed several early South African items.

Very little use has yet been made of the valuable material preserved by the Aborigines Protection Society, the American Board of Missions, the Glasgow (Church of Scotland) Missionary Society and the various French, German, Portuguese, Swiss and Scandinavian missionary societies. Some account of these may be found in the *Directory of Foreign Missions* (International Missionary Council), Revised edn., 1933.

3. LIST OF PARLIAMENTARY PAPERS

Parliamentary Papers relating to South Africa begin with the first British Occupation of the Cape of Good Hope in 1795. In preparing the list for the present volume of *The Cambridge History of the British Empire* a new plan has been adopted. By arranging all the papers chronologically and giving the briefest indication of their contents, it has been possible to present a much more comprehensive list than has yet appeared. From 1801 onwards details can be obtained from the sessional indexes and the following consolidated indexes published by the House of Commons: *Index to the Reports of Commissioners on Colonies* (1812–40) *and Emigration* (1812–47), *Parl. Pap.* 1847, LVIII (710–IV); *General Index to the Bills*, 1801–52, *Parl. Pap.* 1854, LXX (O. 8); *General Index to the Reports of Select Committees*, 1801–52, *Parl. Pap.* 1854, LXX (O. 9); *General Index to the Accounts and Papers, Reports of Commissioners, Estimates, etc.*, 1801–52, *Parl. Pap.* 1854; *General Index to the Bills, Reports, Estimates, and Accounts and Papers, etc.*, 1852–99, *Parl. Pap.* 1909; 1900–9, *Parl. Pap.* 1911, CIV (351); 1910–19, *Parl. Pap.* 1926, XXXI (169); 1920–28/9, *Parl. Pap.* 1930–1, XXXVII (8).

House of Lords' Papers, many of which are duplicates of those of the Commons, have sessional indexes from 1871, and a *General Index to the Sessional Papers printed by order of the House of Lords, or presented by special command*, 1801–37, *Parl. Pap.* 1859 Sess. 2, H.L., XXXI; 1859–70, *Parl. Pap.* 1872, H.L., LXVIII; 1871–84/5, *Parl. Pap.* 1890.

A classified list of "South African Imperial Blue-books" is given in S. Mendelssohn's *South African Bibliography*, vol. II, pp. 653–710, but it is selective and inaccurate. A more useful tool, though again selective, is M. I. Adam, J. Ewing and J. Munro, *Guide to the Principal Parliamentary Papers relating to the Dominions*, 1812–1911 (Edinburgh, 1913).

The references given below indicate in each case the session during which the paper was printed, the volume for that session into which it has been bound by the House of Commons or House of Lords, and the Sessional ( ) or Command [ ] number of the paper. It should be noted that the sessional numbers of *Bills* are a separate series from those of *Accounts and Papers*. Unless otherwise indicated references are to House of Commons' Papers.

1797–8, XLV (916). Cape of Good Hope, Accounts.
1814–15, XIII. Treaty between Great Britain and United Netherlands, 1814.
1816, XIII (214), (215). Cape, Civil Offices during 1796, 1815.
1817, XIV (225). Cape, Exports and Imports.
1819, II (206). 2nd Rept. from Select Com. on Finance (Army), 1819.
1819, II (529). 5th Rept. from Select Com. on Finance (Audit Office), 1819.
1819, II (539). Rept. from Select Com. on Poor Laws, 1819.
1819–20, IV (58). Cape, Return of Civil officers, revenues, 1819.
1819–20, IV (90). Cape, Exports and Imports, 1819.
1820, XI (34). Cape, Return of Civil officers, revenues, 1820.
1820, XII (35). Cape, Appt. of H. Ellis as Deputy-Secretary.
1821, XIV (45). Cape, Expense of conveying settlers.
1821, XVI (622). Cape, Return of pensions and allowances.
1821, XXI (374). Cape, Proposal to appoint two botanical collectors, 1 Sept. 1814.
1822, XX (92). Cape, Accounts.
1823, XIII (401). Cape, Estimate for facilitating emigration.
1823, XIV (343). Cape, Receipts and Disbursements.
1824, XVI (116). Cape, Estimate for facilitating emigration.
1824, XXIII (160). Cape, Acts *re* treatment of slaves.
1825, XVIII (131). Cape, Estimates of emigration costs.
1825, XIX (231). Cape, Acts *re* treatment of slaves.
1826, XXIII (438). Cape, Papers *re* British coinage order, 23 March 1825.
1826, XXV (431). Cape, Burnett's grievances, 1822–6.
1826, XXVI (332). Cape, Instructions for Commissioners of Inquiry.
1826, XXVI (350). Cape, Returns *re* population, 1812–20.
1826–7, XV (160). Cape, Estimated expenditure on Irish emigration.
1826–7, XXI (42). Papers *re* Cooke's memorial on prize slaves.
1826–7, XXI (202). Cape, Papers *re* slaves and aborigines, population since 1797.
1826–7, XXI (282), (406). Cape, Repts. of Commissioners of Inquiry on government and finances, 6 Sept. 1826.
1826–7, XXI (371). Cape, Papers *re* administration, 1821–6.
1826–7, XXI (444). Corresp. of Donkin with Colonial Dept.
1826–7, XXI (454). Corresp. of Somerset and Brink with Colonial Dept.
1826–7, XXI (470). Papers *re S. African Commercial Advertiser*.
1826–7, XXI (556). Papers *re* Carnall case.
1826–7, XXII (129). Cape, Slave trade and slavery.
1826–7, XXV (53), (347). Cape, Papers *re* slaves.
1829, V (300). Cape, Rept. of Commissioners on trade, harbours and navigation, 3 Oct. 1828.
1829, XXV (335). Cape, Repts. from Protector of slaves, 1826–7.
1829, XXV (339). Orders-in-Council *re* natives of S.A.
1830, XXI (8). Order-in-Council *re* colonial slave laws.
1830, XXI (352). Corresp. *re* colonial revenue and expenditure (H. C. Finance Com. of 1828).
1830, XXI (582). Return *re* slave population in colonies.

1830, XXI (584). Cape, Rept. of Commissioners on native tribes, 28 Jan. 1830.
1830, XXIX (650). Cape, Emigrants from Britain, 1820–30.
1830–1, XVI (230). Cape, Papers *re* slaves.
1831, H.L., CCXCIV (42). Cape, Representations *re* duties on Cape wines.
1831, H.L., CCXCIV (73). Cape, Account of imports from, 1812–31.
1831–2, XIX (678). Cape, Imports of raw silk from, 1814–32.
1833, XXVI (696). S.A., Emigrants to, 1825–32.
1834, VI (570). Rept. from Select Com. on colonial military expenditure, 1834.
1834, XLIV (617). Cape, Proclamations *re* aborigines.
1835, VI (473). Rept. from Select Com. on colonial military expenditure, 1835.
1835, XXXIX (50), (252). Cape, Papers *re* aborigines, 1834.
1835, L (278–II). Cape, Papers *re* abolition of slavery, 1834.
1836, I (471). Bill for the punishment of offences within certain territories adjacent to the Cape of Good Hope.
1836, VII (538). Rept. from Select Com. on aborigines, Aug. 1836 [Minutes, Appendix and Index only; see 1837, VII (238), (425)].
1836, XI (512). Rept. from Select Com. on disposal of land at Cape.
1836, XXXIX (279). Papers *re* Kaffir War and Hintza, 1835–6.
1837, VII (238), (425). Further Rept. from Select Com. on aborigines, 1830–6.
1837, VII (516). Rept. from Select Com. on colonial revenue and expenditure, 1837.
1837, XLIII (503). Papers *re* Kaffir War, 1835–7.
1837–8, XLVII [137]. Cape, Emigrants from Britain, 1832–6.
1839, XLVI (576). Imports of coffee from Cape, 1838–9.
1840, XXXIII (323). Cape, Governor's Rept. on children sent out by Children's Friend Society.
1840, XLIV (276). Imports of coffee from Cape, 1839–40.
1841, XIV (253). Cape, Abstracts of Commissioners' accounts, 1839–40.
1842, XXXIX [375]. Cape, Exports and imports, shipping, 1831–40. [There are periodical returns of this kind.]
1843, XXXI (91–IV). Cape, Estimate for Observatory. [There are periodical returns of this kind.]
1846, XXIX (400). Cape, Applications for representative government within the last ten years.
1847, XXXVI (253–II). Cape, Commissariat accounts, 1845–6. [There are periodical returns of this kind.]
1847, XXXVIII [786]. Corresp. *re* Kaffirs. 1845–6.
1847, XXXV (229–VII). Cape, Expense of erecting lighthouses.
1847–8, XLII [980]. Corresp. *re* settlement of Natal, 1844–6.
1847–8, XLIII [912], [969]. Papers *re* Kaffirs, 1846–8.
1847–8, XL (54). Supplementary Estimate for Kaffir War.
1847–8, XLVII (345). Cape, Land revenue and immigrants, 1837–46.
1847–8, LXIV (161). Papers *re* slave-ship *Bella Angela*, condemned at Cape, 1844.
1849, XI (86). Cape, Natal, Corresp. *re* immigration from Ireland.
1849, XXX (180). Rept. by Audit Board on Kaffir War expenditure, 1849.
1849, XXXVI (387). Corresp. *re* state of Kaffir Tribes.
1849, XXXVI [1056]. Corresp. *re* Kaffirs, 1848–9.
1849, XXXVI [1059]. Papers *re* Natal, Boer rising, 1848–9.
1849, XLIII (217). Papers *re* transportation of convicts to Cape, 1841–9.
1849, L (588). Cape, Emigrants from Britain, 1839–48.
1850, XXXVIII (104). Cape, Papers *re* convict discipline, 1849–50.
1850, XXXVIII [1137], [1234]. Cape, Corresp. *re* establishment of Representative Assembly, 1848–50.
1850, XXXVIII [1138]. Cape, Corresp. *re* reception of convicts, 1849–50.
1850, XXXVIII [1288]. Papers *re* Kaffirs, 1848–50.
1850, XXXVIII [1292]. Cape, Natal, Corresp., 1849–50.

1851, XIV (635). Rept. from Select Com. on relations with native tribes.
1851, XXXII (227). Estimate for Kaffir War.
1851, XXXII [1383]. Cape, Natal, Returns *re* emigration, settlements, etc.
1851, XXXIV (667). Cape, Natal, Customs duties.
1851, XXXVII (457). Cape, Appt. of Sir H. Smith as Governor, 1847.
1851, XXXVII [1360]. Corresp. *re* assumption of sovereignty over territory between Orange and Vaal rivers, 1849–51.
1851, XXXVII [1362]. Cape, Papers *re* proposed Representative Assembly, 1850–1.
1851, XXXVII [1417]. Cape, Natal, Corresp., 1850–1.
1851, XXXVIII (424). Papers *re* Kaffirs, 1837–46.
1851, XXXVIII (683). Troops employed in S.A. and expenditure by Britain since 1843.
1851, XXXVIII [1334], [1352], [1380]. Corresp. *re* Kaffirs, 1850–1.
1851, LVI, Part I [1424]. Cape, Corresp. *re* slave trade.
1852, XVIII [1499]. Cape, Natal, Papers *re* land and emigration.
1852, XXIX (107). Kaffir War, Estimate.
1852, XXIX (491). Cape, Convicts, losses sustained by Sir R. Stanford.
1852, XXX (89). Further papers *re* troops in S.A. since 1843.
1852, XXX (114), (413). Repts. *re* condition of troopship *Megaera.*
1852, XXX (426). Court Martial on loss of ship *Birkenhead.*
1852, XXX (516). Kaffir War expenses, Treasury minute, 24 Feb. 1852.
1852, XXX (544). Kaffir War expenses, Treasury minute, 22 June 1852.
1852, XXXII (355–1), pp. 10–35. Corresp. *re* church affairs in S.A.
1852, XXXIII (57). Cape, Six Ordinances of Legislative Council, Nov.–Dec. 1851.
1852, XXXIII (124). Cape and British Kaffraria, Return *re* population.
1852, XXXIII [1427]. Cape, Papers *re* Representative Assembly, 1851–2.
1852, XXXIII [1428]. Corresp. *re* Kaffir tribes, 1851–2.
1852, XLIX (451). Return *re* shipwrecks between Cape and Orange River, and Delagoa Bay, 1838–52.
1852–3, LIX (258). Cape, Troops in S.A. since 1849.
1852–3, LXII [1697]. Natal, Corresp., 1851–3.
1852–3, LXVI (130). Cape, Debates, petitions *re* Constitutional Ordinance, 1852–3.
1852–3, LXVI [1581], [1636]. S.A., Corresp. *re* Constitutional Ordinances, 1852–3.
1852–3, LXVI [1635]. Corresp. *re* Kaffir tribes.
1852–3, LXVI [1640]. S.A., Constitutional Ordinances, 1853.
1852–3, LXVI [1646]. Corresp. *re* Orange River Territory, 1851–3.
1852–3, XCV (120). Cape, Mail steamers.
1854, XXXIX [1743]. British exports to Cape, 1840–53.
1854, XLIII [1758]. Corresp. *re* Orange River Territory, 1853–4.
1854–5, XXXI (140–VII). Cape, Estimate for public works.
1854–5, XXXVI (444). Return *re* colonial bishoprics.
1854–5, XXXVIII [1969]. Corresp. *re* Gov. Grey and Orange River Territory, 1853–5.
1856, XXIV [2089]. 16th Rept. of Emigration Commissioners, Cape and Natal, 1856. [There are periodical returns of this kind.]
1856, XXXIX (223–VIII). S.A., Papers *re* care of natives, 1855–6.
1856, XLII [2050]. Cape, Rept. in part on present state, 1854.
1856, XLII [2096]. Corresp. *re* Gov. Grey and Orange River Territory, 1855–6.
1857 Sess. 1, X [2198]. Cape, Rept. on present state, 1855.
1857 Sess. 1, X [2202]. S.A., Corresp., 1856.
1857 Sess. 2, XXVIII (97). Corresp. *re* Parliamentary Grant for the civilization of native tribes.
1857–8, XXXV (475). Account of sums voted for Kaffir War, 1851–3.
1857–8, XXXVI (162–VII). Estimate for improvements in British Kaffraria and Orange River Territory, 1858–9.
1857–8, XL (119). Cape, Mail contract with Union Navigation Company.

1857–8, XL (389). S.A., German immigrants, 1856–8.
1857–8, XL [2352]. Corresp. *re* Kaffirs, 1856–7.
1857–8, XL [2403]. Cape, State of the colony, 1856. [There are periodical returns of this kind.]
1859 Sess. I, XIV (109). Corresp. *re* S.A. mail contracts, 1858.
1860, XLV (216), (357). S.A., Corresp., Grey's recall and re-appointment, 1858–60.
1860, XLV (596). Natal, Corresp., cotton-growing, 1857–60.
1861, XXXVI (117). Return *re* German Legion at Cape.
1862, XXXVI (293). Natal, Corresp., 1861–2.
1862, XXXVI (403). Cape, Corresp. *re* German settlers, 1860–1.
1862, XXXVI [3064]. Slave trade cases in Mixed British and Portuguese Court at Cape since 1843.
1863, XXX (434). Draft S.A. Mail contract with Union Steamship Co.
1863, III (113). Bill for punishment of offences committed in S. Africa.
1863, XXXVIII (430). Return *re* South African emigration, 1815–63.
1865, I (27), (45). Bill for incorporating territories of British Kaffraria with Cape Colony.
1865, XXXVII [3436]. Corresp. *re* annexation of British Kaffraria, 1864–5.
1865, XLI (450). Papers *re* expenses of Bishop of Cape Town in legal proceedings.
1865, L (487). Corresp. *re* Cape Town and Dock Railway.
1865, L (488). Corresp. *re* railways in Natal, 1863–5.
1866, XLIX (476), [3661]. Corresp. *re* Bishoprics of Cape Town, etc.
1866 [3689] *Not printed. Judgment of the Lords of the P.C., upon the Lord Bishop of Natal* [Colenso], *delivered* 20 *March*, 1865.
1867, XLVIII (307). Natal, Return *re* colonial chaplaincy.
1867–8, XLI (48). Natal, Treasury minute *re* superannuation of Col. Maclean, 1868.
1867–8, XLI (365). Corresp. *re* S.A. mail contract, 1868.
1867–8, XLVIII (454). Natal, Judgment in case of Bishop Colenso *v.* Dean of Pietermaritzburg.
1868–9, XLIII [4140]. Corresp. *re* status of Basutos, 1861–9.
1868–9, XLIII [4141]. S.A., Corresp., alleged kidnapping in Transvaal, goldfields in Mashonaland, 1866–8.
1870, XLIX [C. 18], [C. 99]. Basutoland, Corresp., 1869–70.
1870, XLIX (181), (181–I), (181–II). Corresp. *re* establishment of responsible government at the Cape and withdrawal of troops, 1867–70.
1871, XLVII [C. 459]. Cape, Corresp., 1867–71.
1872, H.L., XVIII (286). Cape, Petitions *re* responsible government.
1872, XLIII [C. 508]. Cape, Corresp., 1871–2.
1872, XLIII [C. 618]. Papers *re* Natal railway, 1871–2.
1873, IX (334). Rept. from Select Com. on Cape and Zanzibar mail contracts, 23 July 1873.
1873, XXXIX (61), (62), (84), (173), (199), (253), (334), (374). Postage, mails between Britain and Cape, 1860–72.
1873, XLVIII [C. 709–I]. Natal, Corresp., 1872–3.
1873, XLIX (C. 732]. Cape, Corresp., 1872–3.
1873, LIII [C. 778]. Return of consular establishments in Africa since 1815.
1874, XLIV [C. 882]. Cape, Corresp., 1873–4.
1874, XLV [C. 1025]. Papers *re* Kaffir outbreak in Natal, 1873–4.
1875, H.L., XIV (255). Papers *re* changes in Natal Constitution.
1875, LII (182). Papers *re* Mohamedan distress at Cape.
1875, LII [C. 1244]. Proposal for South African conference.
1875, LII [C. 1342]. Natal, Papers *re* Langalibalele.
1875, LII [C. 1342–I]. Cape, Corresp., Griqualand West, 1874–5.
1875, LII [C. 1348]. Papers *re* Orange Free State, Griqualand boundary.

1875, LIII [C. 1119], [C. 1121], [C. 1141], [C. 1158], [C. 1187]. Papers *re* Kaffir outbreak in Natal, 1873–5, Langalibalele.
1875, LIII [C. 1137]. Shepstone's rept. *re* Installation of Cetewayo, 1874.
1875, LIII [C. 1192]. Further Corresp. *re* Natal.
1875, LXXXIII [C. 1361]. Corresp. *re* Delagoa Bay.
1876, LII [C. 1399]. S.A., Proposal for conference, 1875–6.
1876, LII [C. 1401]. Cape, Corresp., Griqualand West, 1875.
1876, LII [C. 1401–1]. Natal, Corresp., 1875.
1876, LII [C. 1445]. Tristan d'Acunha, Corresp., 1875.
1876, LII [C. 1631]. Cape, Corresp., Griqualand West, 1876.
1877, H.L., VI (40), (40*a*), (67), (67*a*), (67*b*), (77), (174). South African Confederation Bill, 1877.
1877, LX [C. 1681]. Cape, Corresp., Griqualand West, 1876.
1877, LX [C. 1732]. Cape, Corresp. *re* Confederation bills, 1876–7.
1877, LX [C. 1748]. Transvaal, Native affairs, 1875–6.
1877, LX [C. 1776], [C. 1814], [C. 1883]. Papers *re* annexation of Transvaal, 1876–7.
1877, LX [C. 1815]. Papers *re* Shepstone Commission in Transvaal, 1877.
1878, LV [C. 1961], [C. 2000]. S.A., Corresp., 1877–8.
1878, LV [C. 1980]. S.A., Corresp. *re* confederation, 1877–8.
1878, LVI [C. 2079], [C. 2100], [C. 2144]. S.A., Further corresp., 1877–8.
1878, LVI [C. 2128]. Corresp. *re* letter from Kruger and Joubert, 10 July 1878.
1878–9, XLII (196). Agreement for telegraph to S.A., 9 May 1879.
1878–9, XLIII (68), (69). S.A. War, Vote of £1,500,000.
1878–9, XLIII (150). S.A. War, Return *re* arms and ammunition shipped to S.A. since 1874.
1878–9, XLIII (174). S.A. War, Return *re* troops embarked.
1878–9, XLIII (267). S.A. War, Return *re* Chicago tinned beef for troops, 1879.
1878–9, XLIII (326), (327). S.A. War, Supplementary Estimate.
1878–9, XLIII [C. 2310]. S.A. War, Return *re* troops embarked.
1878–9, LII [C. 2220], [C. 2222], [C. 2242]. S.A., Corresp., 1878–9.
1878–9, LIII [C. 2252], [C. 2260], [C. 2269], [C. 2308], [C. 2316], [C. 2318], [C. 2367]. S.A., Corresp., appointment of Wolseley, 1878–9.
1878–9, LIV (257). Return *re* military expenditure in S.A., 1871–9.
1878–9, LIV [C. 2234]. S.A., Corresp. *re* military affairs in Natal and Transvaal, 1878–9.
1878–9, LIV [C. 2374]. S.A., Corresp., 1878–9.
1878–9, LIV [C. 2454]. S.A., Corresp., Ulundi, 1878–9.
1880, XLI (68), (105). S.A. War, Supplementary Estimate.
1880, XLII (74), (95), (150), (220). S.A. War, Corresp. *re* conduct of troops in Transkei and Zulu Wars.
1880, XLII (85). S.A. War, Return *re* Chicago tinned beef for troops, 1879–80.
1880, L [C. 2482], [C. 2505]. S.A. War, Corresp., 1879–80.
1880, LI (148). Repts. on recent expenditure in S.A., 1180.
1880, LI [C. 2584], [C. 2586], [C. 2655], [C. 2676], [C. 2695]. S.A., Corresp., 1879–80.
1880, LI [C. 2569]. Corresp. *re* Basutoland, 1879–80.
1880, LI [C. 2601], [C. 2668]. Papers *re* Frere's allowances as High Commissioner, 1877–80.
1881, H.L., XII (14). Memorial from Paris Evangelical Alliance *re* native churches in Basutoland, 1880.
1881, H.L., XII (45). Copies of telegrams *re* Basuto War, and Kimberley's replies.
1881, LVIII (164), (165), (166). S.A. War, Votes of Credit, 1879–80.
1881, LVIII (412). Return *re* casualties and costs in S.A. Wars, 1875–80.
1881, LVIII [C. 2963]. Return *re* troops stationed in Natal and Transvaal, 1881.
1881, LXII (385). Transvaal, Estimates for 1881–2.

1881, LXVI [C. 2740], [C. 2783]. S.A., Corresp., 1880–1.
1881, LXVI [C. 2754]. Instructions to Robinson, 30 Dec. 1880.
1881, LXVI [C. 2755], [C. 2821]. Corresp. *re* Basutoland, 1880–1.
1881, LXVI [C. 2794]. Proclamations of Lanyon and Boer leaders.
1881, LXVII (292). Papers *re* native customs in Natal.
1881, LXVII [C. 2837], [C. 2838], [C. 2858], [C. 2866], [C. 2891]. S.A., Corresp., 1881.
1881, LXVII [C. 2892]. Instructions to Transvaal Commissioners, 31 March 1881.
1881, LXVII [C. 2950], [C. 2959], [C. 2961], [C. 2962]. S.A., Corresp., 1880–1.
1881, LXVII [C. 2964]. Corresp. *re* Basutoland, 1881.
1881, LXVII [C. 2998]. Convention of Pretoria, 3 Aug. 1881.
1881, LXXIV [C. 2984]. Repts. *re* colonial legislative assemblies.
1882, XXVIII [C. 3114], [C. 3219]. Rept. of Transvaal Commissioners, Parts I, II, 1881.
1882, XXXVIII (114). Zulu, and other Wars, Estimates, 1881–2.
1882, XLVII [C. 3098], [C. 3381], [C. 3419]. Corresp. *re* Transvaal, 1881–2.
1882, XLVII [C. 3112], [C. 3175]. Corresp. *re* Basutoland, 1880–2.
1882, XLVII [C. 3113]. S.A., Corresp., 1881–2.
1882, XLVII [C. 3174]. Natal, Bulwer's Instructions, 1881–2.
1882, XLVII [C. 3182]. Corresp. *re* Natal and Zululand, 1880–2.
1882, XLVII [C. 3247], [C. 3270], [C. 3293]. Corresp. *re* Zululand, 1881–2.
1882, XLVII [C. 3280]. Corresp. *re* Col. contrib. to Transkei and Zulu Wars, 1879–82.
1882, LXXX [C. 3410]. Treaty between S.A. Republic and Portugal, 11 Dec. 1875.
1883, XXXVIII (281). Colonial contributions to S.A. Wars.
1883, XLIII (11). Transvaal, Estimates for 1882–3.
1883, XLV [C. 3477]. Repts. *re* colonial legislative assemblies.
1883, XLVIII [C. 3493], [C. 3708]. Corresp. *re* Basutos, 1882–3.
1883, XLVIII [C. 3796]. Corresp. *re* Natal, 1881–3.
1883, XLIX [C. 3466], [C. 3616], [C. 3705]. Corresp. *re* Zululand, 1882–3.
1883, XLIX [C. 3486]. Corresp. *re* Transvaal, 1882–3.
1883, XLIX [C. 3635]. Repts. by Warren and Harrel on Bechuanaland.
1883, XLIX [C. 3654]. Corresp. *re* Transvaal debt, 1882–3.
1883, XLIX [C. 3659], [C. 3686]. Corresp. *re* Transvaal, 1883.
1883, XLIX [C. 3717]. Corresp. *re* Basutos, etc., 1883.
1884, H.L., XI (42). Copies of engagements with states or native tribes of S.A. (Sand River Convention, Bloemfontein Conference, etc.).
1884, LVI [C. 3855]. S.A., Corresp., 1883–4.
1884, LVI [C. 4190]. Corresp. *re* Angra Pequena, 1883–4.
1884, LVII (226). Corresp. *re* Transvaal 1876 debenture bonds, 1881–3.
1884, LVII [C. 3841]. Corresp. *re* Transvaal, 1883–4.
1884, LVII [C. 3914]. Convention of London, 27 Feb. 1884.
1884, LVII [C. 3947]. Corresp. *re* Convention of London, 1883–4.
1884, LVII [C. 4036]. S.A., Corresp., Jan.–May 1884.
1884, LVII [C. 4194]. Corresp. *re* S.A. Republic, 1884.
1884, LVIII [C. 3864], [C. 4037], [C. 4191]. Corresp. *re* Zululand, 1883–4.
1884–5, H.L., III (59). Bill to authorize advance to Cape Government.
1884–5, LV [C. 4224]. Corresp. *re* Bechuanaland expedition, 1884.
1884–5, LV [C. 4227]. Bechuanaland, Instructions to Warren, 10 Nov. 1884.
1884–5, LV [C. 4414]. Anglo-Belgian Convention *re* Congo, Berlin, 16 Dec. 1884.
1884–5, LV [C. 4442]. Anglo-German arrangement *re* spheres of action, Berlin, 16 Dec. 1884.
1884–5, LVI [C. 4214], [C. 4274], [C. 4587]. Corresp. *re* Zululand, etc., 1884–5.
1884–5, LVI [C. 4262], [C. 4265]. Corresp. *re* Angra Pequena.
1884–5, LVI [C. 4263], [C. 4589]. Corresp. *re* Basutoland, 1884–5.
1884–5, LVI [C. 4590]. Corresp. *re* Pondoland, 1884–5.

1884–5, LVII [C. 4213], [C. 4252], [C. 4275], [C. 4310], [C. 4432], [C. 4588]. Corresp. *re* S.A. Republic, etc., 1884–5.
1886, XLVII [C. 4889]. Rept. of Commissioners on land settlement in British Bechuanaland, 29 May 1886.
1886, XLVIII [C. 4644], [C. 4838], [C. 4700], [C. 4907]. S.A., Corresp.: liquor traffic, Orange Free State and Basutoland border, etc., 1885–6.
1886, XLVIII [C. 4643], [C. 4839], [C. 4890]. Corresp. *re* S.A. Republic, 1885–6.
1886, XLVIII [C. 4645]. Corresp. *re* Zululand, 1885–6.
1886 Sess. 2, XLVIII (52). Return *re* Expenditure on Zululand.
1887, LIX [C. 4956], [C. 5070], [C. 5237]. Corresp. *re* Bechuanaland, 1886–7.
1887, LX [C. 4959]. Corresp. *re* Tristan d'Acunha.
1887, LXI [C. 4913], [C. 4980], [C. 5143]. Corresp. *re* Zululand, 1886–7.
1887, LXI [C. 5022]. Corresp. *re* Pondoland, 1885–7.
1887, LXI [C. 5089]. Corresp. *re* Swaziland, Jan.–June 1887.
1887, LXI [C. 5180]. Corresp. *re* British claims in German S.W. Africa, 1884–7.
1887, LXI [C. 5238]. Clarke's rept. on Basutoland, 1886–7.
1888, LXXIV [C. 5390]. Corresp. *re* Cape Town conference, 30 Jan. 1888, on Customs Union and Railways, 1888.
1888, LXXIV [C. 5432]. Notification of acquisition of Zululand.
1888, LXXIV [C. 5488]. Corresp. *re* separation of High Commissionership from Governorship of Cape, 1887–8.
1888, LXXIV [C. 5588]. Rept. by H.M. Agent at Pretoria on session of S.A. Republic Volksraad, 1888.
1888, LXXV [C. 5331], [C. 5522]. Corresp. *re* Zululand, 1887–8.
1888, LXXV [C. 5363], [C. 5524]. Corresp. *re* Bechuanaland, 1887–8.
1888, LXXV [C. 5410]. Corresp. *re* Pondoland, 1887–8.
1888, LXXIV (157). Corresp. *re* railway between Kalk Bay and Simon's Bay.
1889, V (352). Basutoland and Bechuanaland Marriages Bill, 1889.
1889, LIV [C. 5620–II]. British Bechuanaland, Rept. of Acting Administrator, 1888–9.
1889, LVI (347). Zululand, Return *re* revenue, 1887–9.
1889, LVI (348). Zululand, Return *re* cattle seized, 1887–9.
1890, XLI (141). Papers *re* Cape railway bonds.
1890, XLVIII [C. 5897—13]. Papers *re* liquor traffic in Natal, 1888–90.
1890, XLVIII [C. 5897—32]. Loch's rept. on Basutoland, 1890.
1890, L [C. 6046], [C. 6048], [C. 6049], [C. 6049—I]. Brussels Conference, General Act and Protocols, 1889–90.
1890, LI [C. 5903]. Corresp. *re* Delagoa Bay railway, 1888–9.
1890, LI [C. 5904]. Corresp. *re* Portuguese in Mashonaland, etc., 1887–90.
1890, LI [C. 5918]. Corresp. *re* Bechuanaland, B.S.A. Co., 1888–90.
1890, LI [C. 6046]. Corresp. *re* Anglo-German agreement on Africa, 1 July 1890.
1890, LI [C. 6102]. Corresp. *re* liquor traffic, 1890.
1890, LII [C. 5892], [C. 5893], [C. 6070]. Corresp. *re* Zululand, 1888–90.
1890, LII [C. 6200]. Corresp. *re* Swaziland and Tongaland, 1887–90.
1890, LII [C. 6201]. de Winton's rept. on Swaziland, 25 Feb. 1890.
1890–1, LV [C. 6270–I]. Zululand, Rept. on forests.
1890–1, LVII (279). Hofmeyr's rept. on Pretoria mission, 18 Aug. 1890.
1890–1, LVII [C. 6212]. Corresp. *re* Anglo-Portuguese Convention, 20 Aug. 1890.
1890–1, LVII [C. 6217]. Corresp. *re* Swaziland Convention, 24 July 1890.
1890–1, LVII [C. 6313]. Extradition treaty between Great Britain and Orange Free State, 25 June 1890.
1890–1, LVII [C. 6370]. Papers *re* Lisbon Convention, 11 June 1891.
1890–1, LVII [C. 6487]. Corresp. *re* Natal, 1888–91.
1890–1, LVII [C. 6495]. Corresp. *re* Britain and Portugal in East Africa, 1890–1.
1890–1, XCVI [C. 6375]. Treaty of Lisbon, 11 June 1891.
1892, LVI [C. 6645]. Three Ordinances of B.S.A. Co., 1891.

1892, LVI [C. 6684]. Corresp. *re* Zululand boundaries, 1891–2.
1892, LXXIV [C. 6699]. Papers *re* slave-trading in Nyassaland.
1892, XCV [C. 6557]. General Act of Brussels Conference *re* slave trade, 2 July 1890.
1893–4, LX (216) *or* [C. 7013]. Corresp. *re* establishment of responsible government in Natal, 1891–3.
1893–4, LXI [C. 7043]. Corresp. *re* Boomplaats graveyard, Orange Free State.
1893–4, LXI [C. 7154]. Corresp. *re* railways in Bechuanaland, 1891–3.
1893–4, LXI [C. 7171], [C. 7190], [C. 7196], [C. 7290]. Corresp. *re* B.S.A. Co., Mashonaland, Matabeleland, Bechuanaland, 1891–4.
1893–4, LXII [C. 7212]. Corresp. *re* Swaziland, 1890–3.
1893–4, LXII [C. 7284]. Corresp. *re* Indunas' deaths at Tati, 1893.
1893–4, LXXI (467). Corresp. *re* B.S.A. Co. shareholders.
1894, LVII (177). Corresp. with B.S.A. Co. *re* customs, 1894.
1894, LVII (277). Treasury minute, 9 Aug. 1894, *re* agreement with British Bechuanaland Railway Co. for extension of Vryburg-Mafeking line.
1894, LVII [C. 7383]. Papers *re* Matabeleland and Mashonaland, 1889–94 (including Charter of B.S.A. Co., 29 Oct. 1889).
1894, LVII [C. 7504]. Johnston's rept. on administration of eastern portion of British Central Africa, 31 March 1894.
1894, LVII [C. 7554]. Petition from British subjects in S.A. Republic, Johannesburg, June, 1894.
1894, LVII [C. 7555]. Newton's rept. and corresp. on Matabele affray, 1893–4.
1895, LXXI [C. 7611]. Corresp. *re* Swaziland, 1893–5.
1895, LXXI [C. 7633]. Corresp. *re* number of British residents in S.A. Republic, 1894.
1895, LXXI [C. 7637]. Papers *re* British sphere north of Zambesi; agreements with B.S.A. Co., 1891–4.
1895, LXXI [C. 7780], [C. 7878]. Corresp. *re* Tongaland, 1888–95.
1895, LXXI [C. 7782]. Corresp. *re* customs and railway agreement (3 Aug. 1894), 1895.
1895, LXXI [C. 7911]. Papers *re* British Indians in S.A. Republic, 1895.
1895, CIX [C. 7594]. Accession of Orange Free State to General Act of Brussels Conference (2 July 1890), 3 Aug. 1894.
1896, IX (380). Rept. from Select Committee on British South Africa (Jameson Raid), 11–14 Aug. 1896.
1896, LVIII [C. 7925], [C. 8013]. Corresp. *re* slave-traders in British Central Africa, 1895–6.
1896, LVIII [C. 8254]. Johnston's rept. on B.C.A. Protectorate, 1895–6.
1896, LIX [C. 7932]. Corresp. *re* transfer of British Bechuanaland to Cape, 1895.
1896, LIX [C. 7933], [C. 8063]. Corresp. *re* disturbances in S.A. Republic, 1895–6 (Jameson Raid, etc.).
1896, LIX [C. 7946]. Papers *re* British Indians in S.A. Republic, 1895.
1896, LIX [C. 7962]. Corresp. *re* visit of Khama, etc. to England and future of Bechuanaland, 1895.
1896, LIX [C. 8060]. Instructions to Col Martin *re* armed forces in B.S.A. Co. territories, and to Gen. Carrington *re* operations against Matabele, 1894–6.
1896, LIX [C. 8130]. Rept. from Matabeleland Land Commission, 1894, and corresp., 1894–6.
1896, LIX [C. 8141]. Corresp. *re* rinderpest, 1896.
1896, LIX [C. 8159]. Papers *re* commandeering of British subjects in S.A. Republic and visit of High Commissioner to Pretoria, 1894.
1896, LIX [C. 8164]. Corresp. *re* retirement of de Wet, H.M. Agent at Pretoria, 1896.
1896, LXVIII [C. 8117]. B.S.A. Co., Power of attorney to Rhodes.
1896, XCV [C. 7971]. Anglo-Portuguese agreement *re* spheres of influence north of Zambesi, 20 Jan. 1896.
1896, XCV [C. 8014]. Anglo-Portuguese Notes *re* boundary of Tongaland, 1895.

1896, xcvii [C. 7926]. Corresp. *re* boundary of British Guiana.
1897, ix (64), (311), (311–i), (311–ii). Reports from Select Committee on South Africa (Jameson Raid).
1897, lxi [C. 8357]. Corresp. *re* Tristan d'Acunha, 1888–97.
1897, lxii (205). S.A., Return *re* spirits imported, 1890–4.
1897, lxii [C. 8346]. S.A. Republic, Corresp. *re* imprisonment of Davis and Sampson, 1896–7.
1897, lxii [C. 8380]. Rept. of Select Com. of Cape Assembly on Jameson Raid, 29 May–17 July 1896.
1897, lxii [C. 8404]. Despatch forwarding S.A. Republic's claim for damages by the Jameson Raid, 16 Feb. 1897.
1897, lxii [C. 8423]. Corresp. *re* S.A. Republic, 1895–7.
1897, lxii [C. 8434]. Papers *re* Article 2 of Manica Arbitration, 11 June 1891.
1897, lxii [C. 8474]. Corresp. *re* closing of Vaal Drifts, 1895.
1897, lxii [C. 8547]. Martin's rept. and corresp. *re* native administration by B.S.A. Co., 16 Jan. 1897.
1897, ci [C. 8308]. Accession of S.A. Republic to Geneva Convention (22 Aug. 1864), 30 Sept. 1896.
1897, ci [C. 8337]. Agreement between Great Britain and S.A. Republic *re* P.O. Money Orders, 1896.
1898, lx (161). Return *re* staff of B.S.A. Co., 30 Sept. 1897.
1898, lx [C. 8721]. Corresp. *re* S.A. Republic, 1897.
1898, lx [C. 8732]. Corresp. *re* proposed changes in administration of B.S.A. Co., 1898.
1898, lx [C. 8773]. Papers *re* B.S.A. Co.'s territories, 1889–94.
1898, lx [C. 8782]. Corresp. *re* Zululand, 1895–8.
1898, lx [C. 8797]. Corresp. *re* native disturbances in Bechuanaland, 1897–8.
1898, cv [C. 8680]. Accession of Orange Free State to Geneva Convention (22 Aug. 1864), 28 Sept. 1897.
1898, cv [C. 8833]. Corresp. *re* accession of Orange Free State to Postal Convention. Vienna, 4 July 1891.
1899, Sess. I, lii (52). S.A. War, Supplementary Estimate.
1899, Sess. II, lii (1). S.A. War, Supplementary Estimate.
1899, lii [C. 9531]. S.A. War, Memorandum showing heads of expenditure.
1899, lxiii [C. 9138]. Papers *re* B.S.A. Co., 1898–9.
1899, lxiii [C. 9206]. Corresp. *re* Swaziland, 1898.
1899, lxiii [C. 9223]. Reprint from *Board of Trade Journal* of articles on economic conditions in Africa.
1899, lxiii [C. 9323]. Corresp. with Rhodes *re* proposed extension of Bechuanaland railway to Lake Tanganyika, 1898–9.
1899, lxiii [C. 9428]. Accounts and estimates of B.S.A. Co., 1896–1900.
1899, lxiv [C. 9093]. S.A. Republic, rept. for 1897 on trade, commerce and gold-mining.
1899, lxiv [C. 9317]. S.A. Republic, Corresp. *re* explosives monopoly, 1899.
1899, lxiv [C. 9343]. Corresp. *re* S.A. Republic's claim for Jameson Raid damages, 1897–9.
1899, lxiv [C. 9345]. Papers *re* complaints of British subjects in S.A. Republic, 1897–9.
1899, lxiv [C. 9404], [C. 9415], [C. 9518], [C. 9521], [C. 9530]. Corresp. *re* Bloemfontein Conference and proposed political reforms, 1899.
1899, lxiv [C. 9507]. Corresp. *re* status of S.A. Republic, 1898–9.
1900, H.L., xii (231). Return *re* railways in Orange Free State and S.A Republic.
1900, v (114). S.A. War, Bill to provide for raising war loan.
1900, xlii [Cd. 196]. Rept. of War Funds Relief Committee, 28 May 1900.
1900, xlviii (36). S.A. War, Supplementary Estimate of men and money required, 1899.

1900, XLVIII (110). S.A. War, Sub-heads under which two supplementary estimates will be accounted for, 1900.
1900, XLIX (94). S.A. War, Return *re* army contracts and defective stores.
1900, XLIX (115). S.A. War, Return *re* Imperial Yeomanry companies.
1900, XLIX (158). S.A. War, Return *re* Members of Parliament serving.
1900, XLIX (268). S.A. War, Return *re* casualties from causes other than wounds.
1900, XLIX (279). S.A. War, Return *re* medical and sanitary arrangements, 1899.
1900, XLIX [Cd. 155]. S.A. War, Telegrams *re* publication of despatches, 1900.
1900, XLIX [Cd. 279]. S.A. War, Naval stores transferred to S.A. to Dec, 1899.
1900, XLIX [Cd. 421]. S.A. War, Return *re* military forces in S.A. 1899–1900.
1900, LI (184). S.A. War, Return *re* troopships, 1899–1900.
1900, LVI [Cd. 53], [Cd. 128]. S.A. War, Proclamations by High Commissioner *re* property in S.A. Republic and Orange Free State, 1900.
1900, LVI (310). Return *re Natal Witness* corresp. on censorship.
1900, LVI [Cd. 18]. S.A. War, Corresp. *re* despatch of colonial contingents.
1900, LVI [Cd. 33]. S.A. War, Corresp. *re* naval action with regard to foreign vessels (*Bundesrath*, *Herzog* and *General*), 1899–1900.
1900, LVI [Cd. 35]. Corresp. with Presidents of S.A. Republic and Orange Free State, March 1900.
1900, LVI [Cd. 43], [Cd. 261], [Cd. 369], [Cd. 420]. Corresp. *re* S.A., 1899–1900.
1900, LVI [Cd. 44]. Corresp. *re* defence of Natal, 1899.
1900, LVI [Cd. 122]. S.A. War, Telegrams from Roberts *re* abuse of White Flag.
1900, LVI [Cd. 230]. S.A. War, Telegrams *re* hospital arrangements.
1900, LVI [Cd. 264]. Cape, Corresp. *re* Cape rising, 1900.
1900, LVI [Cd. 426]. S.A. War, Proclamations by Lord Roberts, 1900.
1900, XCI [Cd. 353–1]. German steamers subsidized for S.A.
1900, CV [Cd. 34]. Corresp. *re* seizure of *Springbok* and *Peterhoff* by U.S. in 1863.
1901, H.L., XI (30). S.A. War, Return *re* soldiers invalided home.
1901, V (289). Rept. from Joint Select Committee on charitable agencies for relief of widows and orphans of soldiers and sailors.
1901, XXIV [Cd. 626], [Cd. 627]. Repts. of S.A. Lands Settlement Commission, 28 Nov. 1900.
1901, XXIX [Cd. 453], [Cd. 454]. Rept. of Commission on care and treatment of sick and wounded during S.A. campaign.
1901, XXX [Cd. 455]. Rept. of Commission on care and treatment of sick and wounded, Appendix to Minutes.
1901, XXXV [Cd. 623], [Cd. 624], [Cd. 625]. Rept. of Transvaal Concessions Commission, 19 April 1901.
1901, XXXVII (150). Return *re* estimated cost of Wars in S.A. and China.
1901, XXXVIII (293). S.A., Corresp. *re* telegraph agreement, 27 July 1901.
1901, XXXVIII [Cd. 465]. Memorandum on Army Estimates for 1901–2.
1901, XXXIX [Cd. 462], [Cd. 578]. Return *re* military forces in S.A., 1899–1901.
1901, XXXIX [Cd. 469]. Return *re* oversea colonial contingents in S.A.
1901, XL [Cd. 610]. Return *re* volunteers and drafts embarked for S.A. in 1900.
1901, XLII (142). Despatches *re* Naval Brigade in S.A.
1901, XLII (374). Return *re* troop transports.
1901, XLVII [Cd. 457], [Cd. 458], [Cd. 463]. S.A. War, Despatches *re* hostilities, 1900–1.
1901, XLVII [Cd. 461]. Corresp. between Roberts and Botha, June 1900.
1901, XLVII [Cd. 464]. Telegrams from Milner *re* reported outrage at Calvinia.
1901, XLVII [Cd. 467]. Corresp. *re* recall of Colvile.
1901, XLVII [Cd. 470]. Barberton Court of Enquiry on Spragge and other prisoners of war, 25 Sept. 1901.
1901, XLVII [Cd. 520]. Colvile's rept. on Paardeberg, 3 March 1900.
1901, XLVII [Cd. 522], [Cd. 605], [Cd. 695]. S.A. War, Kitchener's despatches, 1900–1.

1901, XLVII [Cd. 528], [Cd. 546]. Corresp. *re* Middelburg Conference, 1901.
1901, XLVII [Cd. 547]. S.A., Corresp., 1900–1.
1901, XLVII [Cd. 582]. S.A. War, Corresp. with Boer commanders *re* destruction of property, 1900.
1901, XLVII [Cd. 608], [Cd. 694]. S.A. War, Returns *re* persons in concentration camps, 1901.
1901, XLVII [Cd. 663]. Negotiations between Botha and Kitchener, 1901.
1901, XLVII [Cd. 693]. Dixon's rept. on Vlakfontein, 29 May 1900.
1901, XLVII [Cd. 732]. S.A. War, Corresp. *re* hostilities, 1901.
1901, XLVII [Cd. 781]. S.A., Proclamation by Kitchener *re* Land Contracts, 1 July 1901.
1901, XLVIII [Cd. 628]. Barber's rept. on Transvaal and Orange River Colony finances, 29 March 1901.
1901, XLVIII [Cd. 667]. Papers *re* finances of B.S.A. Co. 1899–1900.
1901, XLVIII [Cd. 714]. Papers *re* native legislation of S.A. Republic, 1898–9.
1902, XLIX (94). S.A. War, Return *re* defective stores.
1902, LV (155). Estimates for war charges in S. Africa and China.
1902, LVI (30). S.A. War, Papers *re* army.
1902, LVI [Cd. 885]. S.A. War, Estimates of sums still required.
1902, LVI [Cd. 996]. S.A. War, Revised estimates.
1902, LVII [Cd. 961]. S.A. War, Contract with Bergl & Co. for meat.
1902, LVII [Cd. 964]. S.A. War, Contract with Imperial Cold Storage Co. for meat.
1902, LVII [Cd. 981]. S.A., Papers *re* martial law.
1902, LVIII [Cd. 884], [Cd. 892], [Cd. 990]. Returns *re* military forces in S.A., 1899–1902.
1902, LVIII [Cd. 963]. S.A. War, Papers *re* army remounts, 1899–1902.
1902, LVIII [Cd. 993], [Cd. 994], [Cd. 995]. S.A. War, Proceedings of Court of Enquiry on Army Remount Dept. since 1899.
1902, LXVII [Cd. 789], [Cd. 793]. S.A. War, Returns *re* numbers in Concentration Camps, Aug.–Sept. 1901.
1902, LXVII [Cd. 893]. S.A. War, Rept. on Concentration Camps by Ladies' Committee appointed 12 Dec. 1901.
1902, LXVII [Cd. 903], [Cd. 1163]. S.A., Corresp., 1901–2.
1902, LXVIII [Cd. 819], [Cd. 853], [Cd. 902], [Cd. 934], [Cd. 936]. S.A. War, Repts. on Refugee Camps, 1901–2.
1902, LXVIII [Cd. 939], [Cd. 942], [Cd. 1161]. S.A. War, Statistics *re* Refugee Camps, 1901–2.
1902, LXIX (360). S.A. War, Return *re* troopships, 1901–2.
1902, LXIX [Cd. 820], [Cd. 823], [Cd. 824], [Cd. 890], [Cd. 965], [Cd. 970], [Cd. 984], [Cd. 986], [Cd. 988]. S.A. War, Kitchener's despatches, 1901–2.
1902, LXIX [Cd. 821], [Cd. 822], [Cd. 888]. Corresp. *re* Boer treatment of natives, 1901–2.
1902, LXIX [Cd. 904]. Papers *re* legislation affecting natives in Transvaal, 1900–2.
1902, LXIX [Cd. 906]. S.A. War, Corresp. with Netherlands Government, Jan. 1902.
1902, LXIX [Cd. 921]. Petition of Boer prisoners at Bermuda.
1902, LXIX [Cd. 933]. Letter from Tobias Smuts to Botha.
1902, LXIX [Cd. 941]. Corresp. *re* Natal, 1901–2.
1902, LXIX [Cd. 967], [Cd. 968], [Cd. 987]. S.A. War, Despatches (Spion Kop, Ladysmith, etc.).
1902, LXIX [Cd. 979]. S.A. War, Return *re* farms, etc., destroyed by Boers.
1902, LXIX [Cd. 1096]. S.A. War, Corresp. *re* Boer terms of surrender, 1902.
1902, LXIX [Cd. 1162). Papers *re* petition for suspension of Cape Constitution.
1902, LXIX [Cd. 1200]. Corresp. *re* labour supply in Southern Rhodesia, 1899–1902.
1902, LXIX [Cd. 1284]. Papers *re* interview between Secretary of State and Boer leaders, 1902.

1902, LXIX [Cd. 1329]. Corresp. *re* appeal of Boer Generals to the civilized world Nov. 1902.
1902, LXIX [Cd. 1363]. Papers *re* finances of B.S.A. Co., 1900–3.
1902, LXIX [Cd. 1364]. S.A. War, Rept. of Commission on martial law sentences, 28 Oct. 1902.
1902, LXIX [Cd. 1365]. Transvaal Liquor Licensing Ordinance, 1902.
1903, IV (189). South African Loan and War Contribution Bill, 1903.
1903, XXXVI (130). Estimates for war charges in S. Africa and China.
1903, XXXVIII [Cd. 1423]. Papers *re* martial law in S.A.
1903, XXXVIII [Cd. 1499]. S.A. War, Corresp. *re* proceedings of Board of Officers on supplies of unfit meat and vegetables at Pretoria.
1903, XLV (184). S.A., Return *re* taxation of natives, 1903.
1903, XLV (189). Ordinances *re* naturalisation in Transvaal and Orange River Colony, 1902–3.
1903, XLV (345). Rand Mines, Return *re* native mortality, sickness and desertion, 1902–3.
1903, XLV [Cd. 1463]. S.A., Corresp., 1902–3.
1903, XLV [Cd. 1531]. Corresp. *re* recruitment of labour in British Central Africa, 1903.
1903, XLV [Cd. 1536]. Rept. from H.M. Commissioner for B.C.A. on Anglo-Congolese frontier, 13 March 1903.
1903, XLV [Cd. 1551], [Cd. 1553]. Papers *re* Transvaal and Orange River Colony, 1903.
1903, XLV [Cd. 1552], [Cd. 1586]. Papers *re* finances of Transvaal and Orange River Colony, 1902–3.
1903, XLV [Cd. 1555]. Papers *re* Transvaal Criminal Procedure Code, 1903.
1903, XLV [Cd. 1599], [Cd. 1640]. Papers *re* Customs Union Conference, Bloemfontein, March 1903.
1903, XLV [Cd. 1635]. Memorandum *re* African Protectorates, June, 1903.
1903, XLV [Cd. 1641]. S.A., Papers *re* Inter-Colonial Council, 1903.
1903, XLV [Cd. 1682]. Papers *re* B.S.A. Co. finances, 1902–4.
1903, XLV [Cd. 1683]. Transvaal and Orange River Colony, Corresp. *re* proposal for Indian coolies on railways.
1903, XLV [Cd. 1684]. Transvaal, Corresp. *re* British Indians.
1903, LV (354). S.A. War, Return *re* troopships, 1899–1902.
1904, XXXIX [Cd. 1894], [Cd. 1896], [Cd. 1897], Repts. of Transvaal Labour Commission, 1903.
1904, XL [Cd. 1789], [Cd. 1790]. Rept. of Commission on War in S. Africa, 1903.
1904, XLI [Cd. 1791]. Rept. of Commission on War in S. Africa, Minutes, 1903.
1904, XLII [Cd. 1792]. Rept. of Commission on War in S. Africa, Appendices, 1903.
1904, XLIX (39). Treasury Minute *re* Transvaal Govt. Stock.
1904, LXI (205). Returns *re* mortality in S.A. mines.
1904, LXI [Cd. 1844]. Special Commissioner Birchenough's rept. on British trade in S.A., Nov. 1903.
1904, LXI [Cd. 1895], [Cd. 2104]. Corresp. *re* Transvaal and Orange River Colony, 1903–4.
1904, LXI [Cd. 1898], [Cd. 1899], [Cd. 1941], [Cd. 1986], [Cd. 2026]. Corresp. *re* Transvaal Labour question, 1904.
1904, LXI [Cd. 2102]. Transvaal and Orange River Colony, Corresp. *re* finances, 1903–4.
1904, LXI [Cd. 2103]. British Central Africa, Census returns.
1904, LXII [Cd. 1945], [Cd. 2025], [Cd. 2183]. Corresp. *re* introduction of Chinese into Transvaal, 1903–4.
1904, LXII [Cd. 1950]. Transvaal, Corresp. *re* recruitment of labour in B.C.A. Protectorate, 1903–4.

1904, LXII [Cd. 1956]. Anglo-Chinese Convention *re* Chinese labour in British colonies and protectorates, 13 May 1904.
1904, LXII [Cd. 2027]. Return *re* Transvaal magistrates, 1904.
1904, LXII [Cd. 2028]. Southern Rhodesia, Corresp. *re* proposed introduction of Chinese, 1903–4.
1904, LXII [Cd. 2163]. Memorandum *re* African Protectorates.
1905, V (257). War stores commission bill.
1905, IX [Cd. 2435], [Cd. 2436]. Rept. from Committee of Army Council on War contracts.
1905, LXVI (228), [Cd. 2433]. Corresp. *re* war stores, 1899–1901.
1905, XLVI [Cd. 2440]. Royal Commission on sick and wounded, Abstract of Minutes.
1905, LV (130). Return *re* High Commissioner's authority in British South Africa.
1905, LV [Cd. 2399]. Rept. of the S.A. Native Affairs Commission, 1903–5.
1905, LV [Cd. 2400], [Cd. 2479]. Papers *re* constitutional changes in Transvaal, 1904–5.
1905, LV [Cd. 2401]. Corresp. *re* labour in Transvaal mines, 1904–5.
1905, LV [Cd. 2408]. Memorandum *re* African Protectorates.
1905, LV [Cd. 2482], [Cd. 2563]. Corresp. *re* Transvaal and Orange River Colony, 1904–5.
1905, LVI [Cd. 2239]. Transvaal, Corresp. *re* British Indians, 1904.
1905, LVI [Cd. 2584]. Award of King of Italy *re* Barotse border, 1905.
1906, LVII [Cd. 3127], [Cd. 3128], [Cd. 3129]. Rept. of Commission on War stores, 31 July 1906.
1906, LVIII [Cd. 3130], [Cd. 3131]. Rept. of Commission on War stores, repts. by chartered accountants on S.A. War contractors.
1906, LXXVII (357). Return *re* coolie labour in British colonies or protectorates since 1901.
1906, LXXVII [Cd. 2785], [Cd. 2975]. Corresp. *re* future organization of colonial conferences.
1906, LXXIX [Cd. 2830]. Papers *re* B.S.A. Co.'s finances, 1902–6.
1906, LXXIX [Cd. 2905], [Cd. 2927], [Cd. 3027], [Cd. 3247]. Corresp. *re* native disturbances in Natal, 1906.
1906, LXXIX [Cd. 2977]. Draft Customs Union Convention, Pietermaritzburg, March, 1906.
1906, LXXIX [Cd. 3094]. Repts. by High Commissioner on visits to Basutoland and Bechuanaland, 1906.
1906, LXXX (114). Transvaal, Return *re* gold output for 5 years preceding Chinese labour.
1906, LXXX (156). Transvaal, Return *re* crimes committed by Chinese labourers since June 1905.
1906, LXXX [Cd. 2786], [Cd. 2788], [Cd. 2819], [Cd. 3025]. Corresp. *re* labour in Transvaal mines, 1905–6.
1906, LXXX [Cd. 2823], [Cd. 3028]. Corresp. *re* Transvaal and Orange River Colony, 1905–6.
1906, LXXX [Cd. 3250]. Papers *re* Transvaal Constitution of 1906.
1906, LXXX [Cd. 3251]. Transvaal Asiatic Law Amendment Ordinance (No. 29 of 1906).
1907, IV (314). Bill to authorize Treasury to guarantee Transvaal Loan.
1907, LVII [Cd. 3308]. Transvaal, Corresp. *re* legislation affecting Asiatics, 1906–7.
1907, LVII [Cd. 3338]. Transvaal, Annual rept. of Foreign Labour Dept. Johannesburg, 1905–6.
1907, LVII [Cd. 3405]. Corresp. *re* Chinese labourers in Natal, 1906–7.
1907, LVII [Cd. 3526]. Orange River Colony, Letters Patent and Instructions for Governor, 5 June 1907.

1907, LVII [Cd. 3528]. Transvaal and Orange River Colony, Corresp., 1906–7.
1907, LVII [Cd. 3563]. Corresp. *re* removal of native prisoners from Natal, 1907.
1907, LVII [Cd. 3564]. Selborne's despatches *re* S. African federation, 1907.
1907, LVII [Cd. 3621]. Papers *re* Transvaal Loan Act, 1907.
1908, LXX [Cd. 4119]. Sargant's rept. on native education in S.A., March 1908.
1908, LXX [Cd. 4323]. Herbst's rept. on Rietfontein area, 12 Feb. 1908.
1908, LXXII [Cd. 3888], [Cd. 3998], [Cd. 4001], [Cd. 4194], [Cd. 4195], [Cd. 4328], [Cd. 4404]. Natal, Corresp. *re* native affairs, 1906–8.
1908, LXXII [Cd. 3889]. Rept. from Natal Native Affairs Commission, 25 July 1907.
1908, LXXIII (39). Transvaal, Names of civil servants dismissed, 1907.
1908, LXXIII [Cd. 3887], [Cd. 3892], [Cd. 4327]. Transvaal, Corresp. *re* legislation affecting Asiatics, 1907–8.
1908, LXXIII [Cd. 3993]. Corresp. *re* recruitment of labour in Nyassaland for Transvaal and Southern Rhodesia mines, 1906–8.
1908, LXXIII [Cd. 3994]. Corresp. *re* Transvaal Indentured Labour Law Temporary Continuation Act, 1907.
1908, LXXIII [Cd. 4120], [Cd. 4121], [Cd. 4357]. Papers *re* native labour in Transvaal mines.
1908, LXXIII [Cd. 4353]. S.A., Return *re* Civil Service retrenchments.
1909, V (297). Bill, intituled, an Act to constitute the Union of South Africa.
1909, XLVII [Cd. 4686]. Rept. of sub-commission of Royal Commission on shipping rings *re* Evidence taken in South Africa.
1909, LIX [Cd. 4909]. Blyth's rept. on agriculture and viticulture in S.A., Oct. 1909.
1909, LX [Cd. 4525], [Cd. 4721]. Repts. from delegates to S.A. Convention *re* S.A. Constitution Bill, 1908–9.
1909, LXI [Cd. 4584]. Transvaal, Corresp. *re* Asiatics, 1908–9.
1909, LXI [Cd. 4587]. Convention between Transvaal and Mozambique, 1 April 1909.
1910, LXVI [Cd. 5099], Corresp. *re* referendum in Natal.
1910, LXVI [Cd. 5363]. Transvaal, Corresp. *re* legislation affecting Asiatics, 1909–10.
1911, LII [Cd. 5579]. S.A., Corresp. *re* bill to regulate Asiatic immigration, 1908–11.
1912–13, LIX [Cd. 6087]. Transvaal, Corresp. *re* British Indians, 1908–12.
1912–13, LIX [Cd. 6283]. S.A., Corresp. *re* bill to regulate Asiatic immigration, 1911–12.
1912–13, XCIII [Cd. 6405]. Sir R. S. Holland's rept. for 1911 on S.A. trade.
1913, XLV [Cd. 6940]. S.A., Corresp. *re* bill to regulate Asiatic immigration, 1912–13.
1913, LXVIII [Cd. 7023]. Holland's rept. on S.A. trade for 1912.
1913, XLV [Cd. 6941], [Cd. 6942]. Transvaal, Corresp. *re* Witwatersrand strike, 1912–13.
1914, XVIII [Cd. 7505]. Dominions Commission, 3rd interior rept. (South Africa), 1914.
1914, XLIX [Cd. 7112]. Rept. of Commission on Witwatersrand disturbances.
1914, XLIX [Cd. 7265]. Rept. of Indian Inquiry Commission (Strike in Natal).
1914, LIX [Cd. 7111]. S.A., Corresp. *re* legislation affecting Asiatics.
1914, LIX [Cd. 7213]. S.A., Text of Indemnity and Undesirables Special Deportation Bill.
1914, LIX [Cd. 7348]. S.A., Corresp. *re* general strike, 1914.
1914, LIX [Cd. 7508]. S.A., Corresp. *re* Natives Land Act, 1913.
1914, LX [Cd. 7264]. Southern Rhodesia, Corresp. between Sir S. Jameson and Colonial Office *re* constitution.
1914, LX [Cd. 7352]. B.S.A. Co., Return *re* revenue and expenditure in N. & S. Rhodesia, 1912–13.
1914, LX [Cd. 7509]. Southern Rhodesia, Papers *re* reference to Judicial Comm. of Privy Council of land ownership question.

1914–16, XIII [Cd. 7706], [Cd. 7707]. Dominions Commission, Minutes of Evidence taken in S. Africa, 1914.
1914–16, XLV [Cd. 7644]. S.A., Corresp. *re* Indians Relief Act.
1914–16, XLV [Cd. 7645]. B.S.A. Co., Corresp. *re* continuance of administrative provisions of Charter.
1914–16, XLV [Cd. 7648]. Holland's rept. for 1913 on S.A. trade.
1914–16, XLV [Cd. 7708]. B.S.A. Co., Return *re* revenue and expenditure, 1913–14.
1914–16, XLV [Cd. 7873]. Corresp. *re* proposed expedition against German South-West Africa.
1914–16, XLV [Cd. 7874]. S.A., Rept. on outbreak of Rebellion.
1914–16, XLV [Cd. 7970]. B.S.A. Co., Supplementary Charter, 3 March 1915.
1914–16, XLV [Cd. 8073]. Gauntlett's rept. for 1914 on S.A. trade.
1916, XX [Cd. 8306]. Papers *re* German atrocities and breaches of the rules of war in Africa.
1916, XX [Cd. 8371]. Paper *re* certain trials in German South-West Africa.
1917–18, XXIII [Cd. 8614]. Wickham's rept. for 1915 and 1916 on S.A. trade.
1917–18, XXIII [Cd. 8674]. Paper *re* Southern Rhodesia Natives Reserves Commission, 1915.
1918, XVII [Cd. 9146]. Rept. on natives of S.W. Africa and their treatment by Germany.
1918, XVII [Cd. 9155]. Wickham's rept. for 1917 on S.A. trade.
1918, XVII [Cd. 9210]. Corresp. *re* wishes of natives of German colonies as to their future govt.
1919, XXXVI [Cmd. 357]. Wilson Goode's rept. for 1918 on S.A. trade.
1920, XXXIII [Cmd. 547]. Corresp. with Aborigines Protection Society *re* native reserves in Southern Rhodesia.
1920, XXXIII [Cmd. 842]. Rept. by Wilson Goode on conditions and prospects for trade in South-West Africa Protectorate.
1920, XXXIII [Cmd. 956]. Wickham's rept. for 1919 on S.A. trade.
1920, XXXIII [Cmd. 1042]. Despatch to High Commissioner transmitting Order-in-Council, 9 Nov. 1920.
1921, XXIV [Cmd. 1129]. Papers *re* Commission on money due to B.S.A. Co.
1921, XXIV [Cmd. 1273], [Cmd. 1471]. Repts. from Committee on Rhodesian questions.
1921, XLIII [Cmd. 1204]. Mandate for German S.W. Africa.
1922, XVI [Cmd. 1573]. Papers and draft Letters Patent providing for reponsible govt. in Southern Rhodesia.
1922, XVI [Cmd. 1682]. Treasury Minute, 10 April, 1922, *re* S.A. debt reduction in connection with purchase of S.A. wool.
1923, XII [Cmd. 1988]. Imperial Conference, Appendices *re* position of Indians in S.A.
1923, XVIII [Cmd. 1914]. Corresp. *re* proposed settlement of outstanding questions relating to the position of the B.S.A. Co. in Southern and Northern Rhodesia.
1923, XVIII [Cmd. 1984]. Agreement *re* position of B.S.A. Co., 29 Sept. 1923.
1923, XXV [Cmd. 1888]. Anglo-Portuguese Agreement for renewal of Part I of Mozambique-Transvaal Convention of April 1909.
1924, XVIII [Cmd. 2177]. Treasury Minute, 19 June 1924, *re* issue of arms and ammunition to S.A. Govt. during War.
1924, XXVI [Cmd. 2220]. Memorandum *re* Germans in mandated territory of S.W. Africa.
1924–5, XXX [Cmd. 2568]. Anglo-Portuguese note *re* Angola-Rhodesia frontier.
1926, XXX [Cmd. 2777]. S.A., Agreement with Portugal *re* boundary between Angola and S.W. Africa.
1926, XXX [Cmd. 2778]. S.A., Agreement with Portugal *re* Kunene River.
1928, XVIII [Cmd. 3076]. Papers *re* Southern Rhodesia Native Juveniles Employment Act, 1926, and S.R. Native Affairs Act, 1927.

1928, xxvi [Cmd. 3066]. Notes exchanged between S. Africa and Portugal in settlement of Mozambique-Swaziland boundary.

1928, xxvi [Cmd. 3070]. Notes exchanged between S. Africa and Portugal in settlement of Mozambique boundary.

1928–9, v [Cmd. 3234]. Hilton-Young Commission, Rept. on dependencies in Eastern and Central Africa.

1929–30, xxiii [Cmd. 3573], [Cmd. 3574]. Papers *re* native policy and closer union in East Africa.

1929–30, xxxi [Cmd. 3487]. S.A., Treaty of commerce and navigation with Germany, 1928.

1929–30, xxxi [Cmd. 3495]. S.A., Convention with Portugal *re* native labour from Mozambique, railways and commerce, 1928.

1930–1, xix [Cmd. 3696]. Note by Secretary of State *re* contract with Imperial Airways, Ltd., for weekly service between England and S. Africa, 18 Oct. 1930.

1930–1, xxxvi [Cmd. 3676]. Commercial agreement between S.A. and Mozambique, Feb. 1930.

1931–2, xxvii [Cmd. 4082]. Notes exchanged between S.A. Govt and Germany *re* registration of patents, &c., 1930.

1931–2, xxvii [Cmd. 4111]. Notes exchanged between S.A. Govt. and U.S.A. *re* airworthiness certificates, 1931.

1932–3, x [Cmd. 4368]. Pim's rept. on financial and economic position of Bechuanaland Protectorate, March 1933.

1933–4, xx [Cmd. 4723]. Treasury Minute, 30 Oct. 1934 *re* repayment of Debentures by S.A. Govt.

1933–4, xxvii [Cmd. 4603]. Notes exchanged between S.A. Govt. and U.S.A. *re* licences to pilot civil aircraft, 1933.

1933–4, xxvi [Cmd. 4604]. Notes exchanged between S.A. Govt. and U.S.A. *re* air navigation, 1933.

1934–5 [Cmd. 4907]. Report of commission on financial and economic position of Basutoland, Jan. 1935.

4. SELECT LIST OF PARLIAMENTARY DEBATES

Summaries of British Parliamentary Debates previous to 1803 may be found in *Cobbett's Parliamentary History*, e.g. Pitt's reference to the first capture of the Cape, 1795, in vol. xxxii, col. 585, and the debate on the Treaty of Amiens, 1802, in vol. xxxvi, col. 692. From 1803 onwards much fuller summaries were given in the *Parliamentary Debates*, known until vol. xvi (1813) as *Cobbett*, thenceforward as *Hansard*. This publication has run through four series and a fifth is current. The figures given in the references below indicate the series, volume and column at which the more important debates on South Africa may be found. Unless otherwise indicated, the debates were in the House of Commons.

Motion *re* expense of Cape, 1795–1802; 11 June 1804. ii, 610.

Bill for regulating Cape trade; 14, 24, 26 March 1806. vi, 446, 523, 539.

Lords. Bill for regulating Cape trade; 28 March, 1, 2, 21 April 1806. vi, 563, 636, 640, 805.

Commons. Question *re* capture of Cape; 16 April 1806. vi, 753.

Lords. Debate on Peace Establishment, South Africa; 14 Feb. 1816. xxxii, 510.

Commons. Debate on Peace Establishment, South Africa; 12, 19, 25, 28 Feb., 6 March 1816. xxxii, 385, 671, 915, 992, 1255.

Lords. Motion *re* military establishment; 15 March, 5 April 1816. xxxiii, 356, 973.

Commons. Army estimates; 8, 11 March 1816. xxxiii, 76, 134.

Lords. Debate on emigration to Cape; 12 July 1819. xl, 1549.

Speech by Wilberforce on slavery at Cape; 25 July 1822. 2nd ser. vii, 1783.

Carnall's petition presented; 27 May 1825. 2nd ser. XIII, 903.
Motion *re* Burnett petition; 16, 22 June, 5 July 1825. 2nd ser. XIII, 1166, 1274, 1483.
Bird's petition *re* Cape currency presented; 19 May 1826. 2nd ser. XV, 1277.
Debate *re* Somerset's conduct; 7, 8 Dec. 1826. 2nd ser. XVI, 303, 320.
Motions for papers *re* Donkin; 17 May 1827. 2nd ser. XVII, 883.
Petition for responsible government at Cape; 8 June 1827. 2nd ser. XVII, 1168.
Motion for Somerset papers; 29 June 1827. 2nd ser. XVII, 1427.
Motion *re* S. African natives; 15 July 1828. 2nd ser. XIX, 1694.
Cape petition for representative government; 24 May 1830. 2nd ser. XXIV, 1005.
Lords. Petition *re* Cape wines; 2 Sept. 1831. 3rd ser. VI, 1022.
Motion *re* treatment of aborigines; 14 July 1835. 3rd ser. XXXIX, 549.
Colonial administration—S. Africa; 6 March 1838. 3rd ser. XLI, 498, 518.
Albany Petition presented; 10 July 1838. 3rd ser. XLIV, 114.
Lords. Debate on Cape petition; 21 June 1842. 3rd ser. LXIV, 272.
Cape petition *re* juvenile criminal immigrants; 7 Feb. 1843. 3rd ser. LXVI, 222.
Petition from Cape Dutch *re* representation; 2 June 1848. 3rd ser. XCIX, 249.
Motion for papers on Kaffir War; 20 March 1849. 3rd ser. CIII, 1031.
Motion *re* transportation to S. Africa; 27 March 1849. 3rd ser. CIII, 1371.
Lords. Two petitions from Cape *re* transportation; 12 Feb. 1850. 3rd ser. CVIII, 709.
Lords. Two petitions from Cape *re* Legislative Council; 6 Feb. 1851. 3rd ser. CXIV, 156.
Lords. Motion *re* Kaffir War; 6 March 1851. 3rd ser. CXIV, 1093.
Commons. Statement *re* Kaffir War; 10 March 1851. 3rd ser. CXIV, 1167.
Motion for Select Committee on Kaffir tribes; 15 April, 8 May 1851. 3rd ser. CXVI, 226, 732.
Lords. Question *re* Sir H. Smith's policy; 20 May 1851. 3rd ser. CXVI, 1153.
Commons. Cape petitions for representative government; 4 June 1851. 3rd ser. CXVII, 399.
Supply—Expense of Kaffir War; 13, 23 June 1851. 3rd ser. CXVII, 737, 1102.
Lords. Motion for committee on Cape representative government; 15 July 1851. 3rd ser. CXVIII, 694.
Lords. Debates on Kaffir War; 5, 6, 13, 19 Feb. 1852. 3rd ser. CXIX, 174, 187, 476, 746.
Question *re* recall of Sir H. Smith; 9 Feb. 1852. 3rd ser. CXIX, 251.
Supply—Kaffir War; 5 April 1852. 3rd ser. CXX, 734.
Lords. Petition *re* military emigration to Cape; 10 Dec. 1852. 3rd ser. CXXIII, 1204.
Supply—Kaffir War; 8 Aug. 1853. 3rd ser. CXXIX, 1455.
Motion *re* Orange River Territory; 9 May 1854. 3rd ser. CXXXIII, 52.
Supply—Cape; 31 July 1855. 3rd ser. CXXXIX, 179.
Supply—Cape, Orange River Territory; 6 June 1856. 3rd ser. CXLII, 1108, 1052.
Observations *re* German Legion at Cape; 22 May 1857. 3rd ser. CXLV, 753.
Supply—Cape, Orange River Territory; 5 Aug. 1857. 3rd ser. CXLVII, 1112.
Supply—Orange River Territory; 13 July 1858. 3rd ser. CLI, 1420.
Supply—Orange River Territory; 1 Aug. 1859. 3rd ser. CLV, 765.
Supply—Orange River Territory, British Kaffraria; 18 Aug. 1860. 3rd ser. CLX, 1518.
Supply—Orange River Territory, British Kaffraria; 16 July 1861. 3rd ser. CLXIV, 1029.
Supply—Orange River Territory, British Kaffraria; 12 June 1862. 3rd ser. CLXVII, 511.
Motion *re* Cape mail contract; 21 July 1863. 3rd ser. CLXXII, 1201.
Second Reading, British Kaffraria Annexation Bill; 16 Feb. 1865. 3rd ser. CLXXVII, 312.
Lords. Motion *re* colonial bishoprics; 18 June, 13 July 1866. 3rd ser. CLXXXIV, 503, 787.
Commons. Motion *re* Cape Town railway; 15 June 1866. 3rd ser. CLXXXIV, 501.

Motion *re* troops at Cape; 4 June 1867. 3rd ser. CLXXXVII, 1596.
Lords. Motion *re* troops at Cape; 18 June 1867. 3rd ser. CLXXXVIII, 5.
Observations *re* conditions in Transvaal and Orange Free State; 25 July 1870. 3rd ser. CCIII, 899.
Supply—Motion *re* S. African confederation; 3 March 1871. 3rd ser. CCIV, 1275.
Lords. Observations *re* Cape responsible government; 8, 11 March 1872. 3rd ser. CCIX, 1621, 1747.
Commons. Motion *re* S. African confederation; 28 May 1872. 3rd ser. CCXI, 806.
Motion *re* Cape responsible government; 29 July, 8 Aug. 1872. 3rd ser. CCXIII, 24, 698.
Questions *re* Delagoa Bay, Basutoland, etc.; 21 Feb. 1873. 3rd ser. CCXIV, 790.
Motion *re* Kaffir outbreak; 12, 20 April 1875. 3rd ser. CCXXIII, 664, 1285.
Motion *re* annexation of Transvaal; 7 Aug. 1877. 3rd ser. CCXXXVI, 545.
Motion *re* native policy in S. Africa; 18 March 1878. 3rd ser. CCXXXVIII, 1511.
Motion *re* annexation of Transvaal; 15 Aug. 1878. 3rd ser. CCXLII, 2061.
Lords. Motion *re* Cape Mounted Police; 6 Dec. 1878. 3rd ser. CCXLIII, 174.
Lords. Motion *re* reinforcements; 18, 24 Feb. 1879. 3rd ser. CCXLIII, 1400, 1640.
Commons. Motions *re* Frere and Zulu War; 14, 17, 24, 25, 27, 28 March 1879. 3rd ser. CCXLIV, 931, 1038, 1503, 1606, 1864, 1865, 1991.
Motions *re* Frere and Zulu War; 31 March 1879. 3rd ser. CCXLV, 20.
Debate on civil and military command in S. Africa; 26 May 1879. 3rd ser. CCXLVI, 1227, 1241.
Observations *re* Zulu War; 27 May 1879. 3rd ser. CCXLVI, 1364.
Statement *re* S. African expenditure; 31 July 1879. 3rd ser. CCXLVIII, 1713.
Motion *re* administration of native affairs; 1 Aug. 1879. 3rd ser. CCXLVIII, 1852.
Supply—S. African military expenditure; 4 Aug. 1879. 3rd ser. CCXLIX, 102.
Motion *re* telegraphic communication with S. Africa; 12 Aug. 1879. 3rd ser. CCXLIX, 908.
Motion *re* Basuto disarmament; 25 May 1880. 3rd ser. CCLII, 451.
Lords. Observations *re* Frere's salary; 10 June 1880. 3rd ser. CCLII, 1579.
Supply—S. African affairs; 31 Aug. 1880. 3rd ser. CCLVI, 839.
Lords. Observations *re* Zulu campaign; 2 Sept. 1880. 3rd ser. CCLVI, 1025.
Lords. Motion *re* Basutoland; 7 Jan. 1881. 3rd ser. CCLVII, 154.
Debate on Address—Basutoland; 20 Jan. 1881. 3rd ser. CCLVII, 1065.
Supply—Annexation of Transvaal; 21 Jan. 1881. 3rd ser. CCLVII, 1109.
Lords. Motion *re* Transvaal Triumvirate; 21 Feb. 1881. 3rd ser. CCLVIII, 1345.
Statement *re* Transvaal negotiations; 4 March 1881. 3rd ser. CCLIX, 326.
Lords. Observations *re* Basutoland; 24 March 1881. 3rd ser. CCLIX, 1789.
Lords. Debate *re* Transvaal peace arrangements; 31 March 1881. 3rd ser. CCLX, 249.
Lords. Debate *re* Gladstone's letter to Tomkinson; 10 May 1881. 3rd ser. CCLXI, 136.
Commons. Motion by Hicks Beach *re* Transvaal rising; 15, 20, 25 July 1881. 3rd ser. CCLXIII, 1009, 1368, 1756.
Supply—Motion *re* Cetewayo; 16 Aug. 1881. 3rd ser. CCLXV, 149.
Motion *re* Lieut.-Governor of Natal; 28 Feb. 1882. 3rd ser. CCLXVI, 1869.
Supply—Debate *re* Cetewayo; 17 April 1882. 3rd ser. CCLXVIII, 756.
Motion *re* policy in Transvaal; 13 April 1883. 3rd ser. CCLXXVIII, 202.
Motion *re* Transvaal Convention of 1881; 15 June 1883. 3rd ser. CCLXXX, 658.
Supply—Motion *re* Transvaal; 6 Aug. 1883. 3rd ser. CCLXXXII, 1659.
Lords. Motion *re* Angra Pequena; 12 May 1884. 3rd ser. CCLXXXVIII, 3.
Lords. Motion *re* Angra Pequena; 19, 30 June 1884. 3rd ser. CCLXXXIX, 787, 1653.
Lords. Debate on Address—S. Africa; 23 Oct. 1884. 3rd ser. CCXCIII, 27.
Commons. Debate on Address—S. Africa; 29 Oct., 4 Nov. 1884. 3rd ser. CCXCIII, 441, 959.
Supply—Bechuanaland; 13 Nov. 1884. 3rd ser. CCXCIII, 1655.

Civil Service Estimates—Angra Pequena; 12 March 1885. 3rd ser. CCXCV, 963.
Commons. Cape of Good Hope (Advance) Bill; 23, 24, 25, 27, 28 March 1885. 3rd ser. CCXCVI, 347, 377, 537, 807.
Lords. Cape of Good Hope (Advance) Bill; 26, 27, 28 March 1885. 3rd ser. CCXCVI, 621, 807, 963.
Commons. Motion *re* Stellaland; 1 May 1885. 3rd ser. CCXCVII, 1279.
Lords. Observations *re* death of Brand; 16 July 1888. 3rd ser. CCCXXVIII, 1351.
Lords. Liquor traffic among African natives; 6 May 1889. 3rd ser. CCCXXXV, 1194.
Lords. British missionaries in East Africa; 28 May 1889. 3rd ser. CCCXXXVI, 1224.
Commons. Motion *re* public works at Cape Town; 28 May 1889. 3rd ser. CCCXXXVI, 1240.
Lords. Motion *re* Delagoa Bay; 9 July 1889. 3rd ser. CCCXXXVII, 1793.
Lords. Observations *re* Portugal and East Africa; 16 May 1890. 3rd ser. CCCXLIV, 1094.
Commons. Anglo-German Agreement Bill; 24, 25, 28 July 1890. 3rd ser. CCCXLVII, 743, 917, 1077.
Lords. Observations *re* Swaziland; 4 Aug. 1890. 3rd ser. CCCXLVII, 1713.
Lords. Observations *re* Anglo-Portuguese African treaty; 11 June 1891. 3rd ser. CCCLIV, 137.
Civil Service Estimates—Zululand; 18 March 1892. 4th ser. II, 1258.
Debate on Swaziland affairs; 4 May 1893. 4th ser. XII, 131.
Supply—S. Africa; 18, 19 Sept. 1893. 4th ser. XVII, 1517, 1600.
Debate on Matabeleland; 9th Nov. 1893. 4th ser. XVIII, 537.
Question *re* Rhodes and Cape hinterland; 12 Jan. 1894. 4th ser. XX, 1446.
Supply—African companies; 15 March 1894. 4th ser. XXII, 391.
Bechuanaland Concession Commission; 15 March 1894. 4th ser. XXII, 405.
Supply—Matabeleland and Mashonaland Agreement; 31 July 1894. 4th ser. XXVII, 1480.
Supply—Transvaal; 17, 18 Aug. 1894. 4th ser. XXVIII, 1466, 1490.
Supply—Swaziland; 18 Aug. 1894. 4th ser. XXVIII, 1507.
Amendment to Address—Transvaal and Swaziland; 6 Feb. 1895. 4th ser. XXX, 133.
Adjournment—Swaziland; 14 March 1895. 4th ser. XXXI, 1064.
Supply—Appointment of Sir H. Robinson; 28 March 1895. 4th ser. XXXII, 426.
Supply—Swaziland affairs; 29 March 1895. 4th ser. XXXII, 487.
Debate on Address—Transvaal affairs; 13 Feb. 1896. 4th ser. XXXVII, 282.
Lords. Statement *re* Kruger; 27 April 1896. 4th ser. XXXIX, 1705.
Lords. Statement *re* Pretoria trials; 28 April 1896. 4th ser. XL, 1.
Lords. Personal explanation by Lord Loch; 1 May 1896. 4th ser. XL, 313.
Supply—S. African affairs; 8 May 1896. 4th ser. XL, 884.
Lords. Question *re* trial of Jameson; 2 July 1896. 4th ser. XLII, 516.
Motion for select committee on Jameson Raid; 30 July 1896. 4th ser. XLIII, 1057.
Select Committee on British S. Africa; 11 Aug. 1896. 4th ser. XLIV, 566.
Select Committee on British S. Africa; 21, 28, 29 Jan., 5 Feb. 1897. 4th ser. XLV, 171, 762, 801, 1417.
Supply—Africa and European Powers; 2 April 1897. 4th ser. XLVIII, 425.
Select Committee on S. Africa; 13, 26 July 1897. 4th ser. LI, 4, 1093.
Debate on Address—British S. Africa Co.; 8 Feb. 1898. 4th ser. LIII, 79.
Lords. Transvaal Mortgage Loan Bill; 14 Feb. 1899. 4th ser. LXVI, 811.
Lords. Transvaal Loan Bill; 21 Feb. 1899. 4th ser. LXVII, 2.
Motion *re* barracks in S. Africa; 24 Feb. 1899. 4th ser. LXVII, 539.
Lords. Transvaal Loan Bill; 13 March 1899. 4th ser. LXVIII, 510.
Supply—S. African affairs; 20 March 1899. 4th ser. LXVIII, 1348.
Supply, Army Estimates—Barracks in S. Africa; 21, 24 April 1899. 4th ser. LXX, 253, 310, 489.
Lords. Transvaal Loan Bill; 8 May 1899. 4th ser. LXXI, 3.
Lords. Transvaal Loan Bill; 6, 12 June 1899. 4th ser. LXII, 410, 828.

Lords. Question *re* Bloemfontein Conference; 8 June 1899. 4th ser. LXXII, 597.
Commons. Questions *re* Bloemfontein Conference; 8 June 1899. 4th ser. LXXII, 636.
Transvaal Loan Bill; 13 June 1899. 4th ser. LXXII, 1055.
Transvaal Loan Bill; 26 June, 5 July 1899. 4th ser. LXXIII, 582, 1514.
Transvaal. Explanation by J. Chamberlain; 6 July 1899. 4th ser. LXXIV, 40.
Transvaal Loan Bill; 10, 13 July 1899. 4th ser. LXXIV, 298, 663.
Cape. Statement by J. Chamberlain; 25 July 1899. 4th ser. LXXV, 278.
Lords. Debate on Transvaal affairs; 28 July 1899. 4th ser. LXXV, 621.
Supply—Cape, Transvaal; 28 July 1899. 4th ser. LXXV, 686, 1530.
Lords. Debate on Address—S. African crisis; 17 Oct. 1899. 4th ser. LXXVII, 3.
Commons. Debate on Address—S. African crisis; 17, 18, 19 Oct. 1899. 4th ser. LXXVII, 60, 181, 254.
Appropriation Bill—S. African crisis; 25, 27 Oct. 1899. 4th ser. LXXVII, 600, 765.
Lords. Debate on Address—S. African policy; 30 Jan. 1900. 4th ser. LXXVIII, 2.
Commons. Debate on Address—S. African policy; 30, 31 Jan., 1, 2, 5, 6, 7, 8, 9 Feb. 1900. 4th ser. LXXVIII, 71, 164, 295, 451, 590, 731, 830, 941, 1066.
Lords. Question *re* Butler's despatches; 1 Feb. 1900. 4th ser. LXXVIII, 244.
Lords. Debate on military measures; 12 Feb. 1900. 4th ser. LXXVIII, 1167.
Supply—Supplementary Army Estimates; 12, 13 Feb. 1900. 4th ser. LXXVIII, 1257, 1382.
Lords. Debate on S. African War; 15, 16, 20 Feb., 1 March 1900. 4th ser. LXXIX, 9, 196, 504, 1355.
Supply—Supplementary Army Estimates; 15, 16, 19 Feb. 1900. 4th ser. LXXIX, 134, 239, 396.
Commons—Committee on Jameson Raid; 20 Feb. 1900. 4th ser. LXXIX, 599.
Lords. Debate on S. African War; 6, 8 March 1900. 4th ser. LXXX, 168, 344.
Lords. Motion *re* S. African railways; 8 March 1900. 4th ser. LXXX, 337.
Supply—Army Estimates; 12, 15, 16 March 1900. 4th ser. LXXX, 602, 775, 1077.
War Loan Bill; 7, 13, 14, 15 March 1900. 4th ser. LXXX, 330, 745, 892, 986.
Lords. War Loan Bill; 16, 19 March 1900. 4th ser. LXXX, 1053, 1163.
Adjournment—S. African War; 6 April 1900. 4th ser. LXXXI, 1414.
Lords. Debate on Spion Kop despatches; 4 May 1900. 4th ser. LXXXII, 707.
Supply—Army Estimates; 4 May 1900. 4th ser. LXXXII, 768.
Motion *re* War Office; 8 May 1900. 4th ser. LXXXII, 1062.
Supply—Army Estimates; 19 June 1900. 4th ser. LXXXIV, 449.
Supply—Supplementary Army Estimates; S. African War, Hospitals, etc.; 29 June, 5 July 1900. 4th ser. LXXXV, 89, 648.
Lords. Debate on War Office; 17 July 1900. 4th ser. LXXXVI, 196.
Supply—S. African War; 25, 27 July 1900. 4th ser. LXXXVI, 1164, 1525.
Supplementary War Loan Bill; 1 Aug. 1900. 4th ser. LXXXVII, 320.
Lords. Motion *re* reserve forces; 3 Aug. 1900. 4th ser. LXXXVII, 584.
Lords. Motion *re* Commander-in-Chief; 3 Aug. 1900. 4th ser. LXXXVII, 592.
Lords. Debate on Address—S. Africa; 6 Dec. 1900. 4th ser. LXXXVIII, 19.
Commons. Debate on Address—S. Africa; 6, 7, 10 Dec. 1900. 4th ser. LXXXVIII, 97, 221, 359.
Supply—Supplementary Estimates; 11, 12 Dec. 1900. 4th ser. LXXXVIII, 512, 612.
Ways and Means—Transvaal railway; 12 Dec. 1900. 4th ser. LXXXVIII, 661.
Supplementary War Loan Bill; 3 Dec. 1900. 4th ser. LXXXVIII, 713.
Appropriation Bill—S. African situation; 13, 15 Dec. 1900. 4th ser. LXXXVIII, 761, 879.
Lords. Debate on Address—S. African War; 14 Feb. 1901. 4th ser. LXXXIX, 31.
Commons. Debate on Address—S. African War; 14, 15, 18, 19 25, 26 Feb. 1901. 4th ser. LXXXIX, 72, 180, 369, 501, 1069, 1239.
Supply—Army Estimates; 8, 11, 12 14 March 1901. 4th ser. XC, 1052, 1241, 1357, 1605.

Supply—Army Estimates; 15 March 1901. 4th ser. xci, 129.
Supply—Supplementary Estimates; Transvaal Concession Commission; 19, 25 March 1901. 4th ser. xci, 453, 1162.
Appropriation Bill—Peace negotiation; 28 March 1901. 4th ser. xcii, 95.
Supply—Army Estimates; 29 March 1901. 4th ser. xcii, 277.
Adjournment—Peace negotiation; 2 April 1900. 4th ser. xcii, 509.
S. African War; Concentration Camps; 17 June 1901. 4th ser. xcv, 573.
Transvaal Loan Bill; 4 July 1901. 4th ser. xcvi, 817.
Finance Bill—S. African affairs; 17 July 1901. 4th ser. xcvii, 699.
Supply—Army Estimates; 25 July 1901. 4th ser. xcviii, 97.
Supply—Grant to Lord Roberts; 31 July 1901. 4th ser. xcviii, 698.
Transvaal Loan Bill; 1 Aug. 1901. 4th ser. xcviii, 880.
Supply—Civil Service Estimates, Emigration; 2, 5, 6 Aug. 1901. 4th ser. xcviii, 1904, 1254, 1454.
Appropriation Bill—S. African affairs; 15 Aug. 1901. 4th ser. xcix, 978.
Lords. Debate on Address—S. African War; 16 Jan. 1902. 4th ser. ci, 4.
Commons. Debate on Address—S. African War; 16, 20 21 Jan. 1902. 4th ser. ci, 86, 324, 472.
Lords. Debate on S. African War; 27 Jan. 1902. 4th ser. ci, 906.
Supply—Supplementary Army Estimates; 31 Jan. 1902. 4th ser. cii, 49.
Lords. Statement *re* army meat contracts; 10 Feb. 1902. 4th ser. cii, 812.
Lords. Motion *re* Boer prisoners; 13 Feb. 1902. 4th ser. cii, 1188.
Lords. Debate on army remounts; 13 Feb. 1902. 4th ser. cii, 1189.
Lords. Debate on army remounts; 17 Feb. 1902. 4th ser. ciii, 155.
Lords. Debate *re* army meat contracts; 20 Feb. 1902. 4th ser. ciii, 554.
Lords. Motion for joint committee on war contracts; 24 Feb. 1902. 4th ser. ciii, 846.
Supply—Army Estimates; 4, 6, 7, 10 March 1902. 4th ser. civ, 366, 606, 734, 896.
Commons. Debate on concentration camps; 4 March 1902. 4th ser. civ, 402.
Lords. Debate on war contracts; 6 March 1902. 4th ser. civ, 553.
Lords. Debate on Methuen's reverse; 10 March 1902. 4th ser. civ, 835.
Lords. Debate on army remounts; 10, 13 March 1902. 4th ser. civ, 842, 1227.
Lords. Debate on martial law in S. Africa; 17 March 1902. 4th ser. cv, 123.
Commons. Debate on army remounts and other contracts; 17, 18 March 1902. 4th ser. cv, 185, 334.
Debate on S. African War; 20 March 1902. 4th ser. cv, 565.
Lords. Debate on state of military supplies; 21 March 1902. 4th ser. cv, 685.
Supply—Army Estimates; 21 March 1902. 4th ser. cv, 740.
Budget debate—S. African War; 15 April 1902. 4th ser. cvi, 291.
Lords. Debate on martial law in S. Africa; 24 April 1902. 4th ser. cvi, 1149.
Commons. Debate on martial law in S. Africa; 24 April 1902. 4th ser. cvi, 1208.
Finance Bill—S. African War; 12 May 1902. 4th ser. cvii, 1383.
Adjournment—S. African affairs; 16 May 1902. 4th ser. cviii, 487.
Lords. Debate on peace terms; 2, 5 June 1902. 4th ser. cviii, 1086, 1510.
Transvaal Loan Bill; 14 May, 4 June 1902. 4th ser. cviii, 251, 1457.
Supply—Grant to Kitchener; 5 June 1902. 4th ser. cviii, 1555.
Vote of thanks for peace; 5 June 1902. 4th ser. cviii, 1585.
Supply—Grant to Kitchener; 18 June 1902. 4th ser. cix, 1066.
Lords—Debate on Boer prisoners; 7 July 1902. 4th ser. cx, 905.
Lords. Facilities for British settlers in S. Africa; 15 July 1902. 4th ser. cxi, 219.
Supply—Buller's position; 17, 21 July 1902. 4th ser. cxi, 527, 788.
Lords. Debate on Transvaal Concessions Loan; 18 July 1902. 4th ser. cxi, 640.
Supply—Cape Constitution; 29 July, 6 Aug. 1902. 4th ser. cxii, 23, 810.
Supply—Vote for S. Africa; 4 Nov. 1902. 4th ser. cxiv, 79, 211, 338.
Observations *re* restocking S. Africa; 16 Dec. 1902. 4th ser. cxvi, 1312.
Supply—Transvaal and Orange River Colony; 3, 4 March 1903. 4th ser. cxviii, 1264, 1367.

Supply—S. African affairs; 19 March 1902. 4th ser. CXIX, 1240.
Appropriation Bill—native labour in S. Africa; 24 March 1903. 4th ser. CXX, 67.
S. African Loan Guarantee; 6 May 1903. 4th ser. CXXI, 1522.
Lords. Debate on S. African garrison; 20 July 1903. 4th ser. CXXV, 1094.
Appropriation Bill—S. African military works; 21 July 1903. 4th ser. CXXV, 1390.
S. African Loan Bill; 27, 31 July 1903. 4th ser. CXXVI, 339, 1141.
S. African Loan Bill; 7 Aug. 1903. 4th ser. CXXVII, 521.
Lords. S. African Loan Bill; 10, 11, 12, 14 Aug. 1903. 4th ser. CXXVII, 531, 799, 961, 1282.
Debate on Address—S. African War; 4, 5 Feb. 1904. 4th ser. CXXIX, 375, 489.
Lords. Chinese labour in Transvaal; 11, 12 Feb. 1904. 4th ser. CXXIX, 965, 1141.
Debate on Address—Chinese in Transvaal; 16 Feb. 1904. 4th ser. CXXIX, 1501.
Debate on Address—Chinese in Transvaal; 17, 22 Feb. 1904. 4th ser. CXXX, 26, 631.
Supply—Supplementary Estimates, S. African affairs; 22 Feb. 1904. 4th ser. CXXX, 526.
Lords. Chinese in Transvaal; 4 March 1904. 4th ser. CXXXI, 167.
Lords. Chinese in Transvaal; 18, 21 March 1904. 4th ser. CXXXII, 4, 117.
Commons. Motion *re* Chinese in Transvaal; 21 March 1904. 4th ser. CXXXII, 252.
Appropriation Bill—Chinese in Transvaal; 24 March 1904. 4th ser. CXXXII, 1484.
Adjournment—treatment of S. African natives; 5 May 1904. 4th ser. CXXXIV, 592.
Lords. Chinese in Transvaal; 20, 24, 28 June 1904. 4th ser. CXXXVI, 407, 1107, 1385.
Lords. Motion *re* Lovat's Scouts; 18 July 1904. 4th ser. CXXXVIIII, 231.
Lords. Debate *re* Transvaal Labour Ordinance; 11 Aug. 1904. 4th ser. CXL, 196.
Lords. Motion *re* Crown Agents in Transvaal and Orange River Colony; 11 Aug. 1904. 4th ser. CXL, 202.
Debate on Address—Chinese in Transvaal; 17 Feb. 1905. 4th ser. CXLI, 481.
Lords. Chinese in Transvaal; 27 Feb. 1905. 4th ser. CXLI, 1277.
Commons. Debate on Selborne's appointment as High Commissioner; 6 March 1905. 4th ser. CXLII, 491.
Lords. Debates on stores in S. Africa; 27 March 1905. 4th ser. CXLIII, 1149.
Lords. Chinese in Transvaal; 16 May 1905. 4th ser. CXLVI, 407.
Commons. War stores in S. Africa; 26 June 1905. CXLVIII, 106.
Lords. Flogging of Chinese in Transvaal; 20 July 1905. 4th ser. CXLIX, 1356.
Debate on Address—Chinese in Transvaal; 22, 23 Feb. 1906. 4th ser. CLII, 532, 624.
Lords. Debate on Transvaal and Orange River Colony; 26, 27 Feb. 1906. 4th ser. CLII, 706, 906.
Commons. Debate on treatment of S. African natives; 28 Feb. 1906. 4th ser. CLII, 1212.
Lords. Chinese in Transvaal; 5 March 1906. 4th ser. CLIII, 8.
Appropriation Bill—Chinese in Transvaal; 21 March 1906. 4th ser. CLIV, 399.
Motions *re* S. African High Commissioner; 21, 29 March 1906. 4th ser. CLIV, 464, 1410.
Lords. Land settlement in S. Africa; 27 March 1906. 4th ser. CLIV, 1019.
Motion *re* martial law in Natal; 2 April 1906. 4th ser. CLV, 245.
Supply—Civil Service Estimates, S. African affairs; 5 April 1906. 4th ser. CLV, 754.
Supply—Civil Service Estimates, S. African affairs; 8 June 1906. 4th ser. CLVIII, 620.
Lords. S. African labour; 29 June 1906. 4th ser. CLIX, 1240.
Lords. Transvaal Constitution; 31 July 1906. 4th ser. CLXII, 611.
Supply—Civil Service Estimates, S. African affairs; 31 July 1906. 4th ser. CLXII, 729.
Lords. British settlers in S. Africa; 14 Nov. 1906. 4th ser. CLXIV, 1382.

Lords. Transvaal and Orange River Colony Constitutions; 17 Dec. 1906. 4th ser. CLXVII, 939.
Commons. Transvaal and Orange River Colony Constitutions; 17 Dece. 1906. 4th ser. CLXVII, 1063.
Lords. Debate on ministerial speeches *re* S. Africa; 19 Feb. 1907. 4th ser. CLXIX, 676.
Supply—Civil Service Estimates, S. African affairs; 11 March 1907. 4th ser. CLXX, 1278.
Supply—S. African affairs; 20 June 1907. 4th ser. CLXXVI, 697.
Lords. Chinese in Transvaal; 27 June 1907. 4th ser. CLXXVII, 56.
Transvaal Loan Guarantee Bill; 19, 20, 21 Aug. 1907. 4th ser. CLXXXI, 161, 699, 923.
Lords. Transvaal Loan Guarantee Bill; 27, 28 Aug. 1907. 4th ser. CLXXXII, 337, 426.
Lords. Motion *re* British Indians in Transvaal; 4 Feb. 1908. 4th ser. CLXXXIII, 653.
Supply—Transvaal Civil Service; 6 Feb. 1908. 4th ser. CLXXXIII, 1179.
Appropriation Bill—Chinese in Transvaal; 23 March 1908. 4th ser. CLXXXVI, 1104.
Motion *re* S. African natives; 13 May 1908. 4th ser. CLXXXVIII, 1215.
Lords. Indians in Transvaal; 19 May 1908. 4th ser. CLXXXIX, 35.
Supply—S. African affairs; 28 July 1908. 4th ser. CXCIII, 1244.
Lords. Debate on Address—S. African Federation Convention; 16 Feb. 1909. 5th ser. (Lords) I, 3, 9, 20, 31.
King's Speech—S. African Constitution; 16 Feb. 1909. 5th ser. (Commons), I, 13.
Appropriation Bill—S. African affairs; 25 March 1909. 5th ser. (Commons) II, 1938.
Adjournment—S. African affairs; 27 May 1909. 5th ser. (Commons) V, 1378.
Lords. S. Africa Bill; 22, 27 July, 3 Aug. 1909. 5th ser. (Lords) II, 682, 753, 855.
S. Africa Bill; 16, 19 Aug. 1909. 5th ser. (Commons) IX, 951, 1533.
Lords. S. Africa Bill, Royal Assent; 20 Sept. 1909. 5th ser. (Lords) III, 1.
Question *re* S. African Union Bill; 27 July 1909. 5th ser. (Commons) VIII, 1023.
Supply—S. African affairs; 27 July 1909. 5th ser. (Commons) VIII, 1027.
Lords. Debate on Address—S. Africa Constitution; 21 Feb. 1910. 5th ser. (Lords) V, 4, 7, 13, 16, 30.
Lords. Debate on Address—Prince of Wales in S. Africa; 21 Feb. 1910. 5th ser. (Lords) V, 4, 7, 14, 16, 29.
Supply—Union of S. Africa; 29 June 1910. 5th ser. (Commons) XVIII, 956.
Lords. King's Speech—Duke of Connaught's visit to S. Africa; 28 Nov. 1910. 5th ser. (Lords) VI, 1014.
Lords. King's Speech—Duke of Connaught in S. Africa; 6 Feb. 1911. 5th ser. (Lords) VII, 4, 12, 15, 30.
Lords. Observations *re* S. Africa; 29 March 1911. 5th ser. (Lords) VII, 715.
Lords. Motion *re* Imperial Defence—S. African War lessons; 3 April 1911. 5th ser. (Lords) VII, 824, 835, 851, 857, 882.
Supply—Union of S. Africa; 27 June 1912. 5th ser. (Commons) XL, 572.
Questions *re* Liebig Co. and British S. Africa Co.; 18, 26 June 1913. 5th ser. (Commons) LIV, 961, 1225.
Motion *re* Rand strike; 7, 8, 14 July 1913. 5th ser. (Commons) LV, 35, 242, 879.
Lords. Debate on British Indians in S. Africa; 30 July 1913. 5th ser. (Lords) XIV, 1507.
Supply—Rand strike; 31 July 1913. 5th ser. (Commons) LVI, 801.
Debate on Address—Union of S. Africa Indemnity Bill; 12 Feb. 1914. 5th ser. (Commons) LVIII, 353.
Motion *re* Transvaal Elections; 19 March 1914. 5th ser. (Commons) LIX, 2371.
Lords. King's Speech—Rebellion in S. Africa; 11 Nov. 1914. 5th ser. (Lords) XVIII, 17, 32.

Lords. Debate on Great War—S. Africa; 6 Jan. 1915. 5th ser. (Lords) XVIII, 235, 244, 256.
Lords. Tribute to General Botha; 15, 21 July 1915. 5th ser. (Lords) XIX, 435, 545.
Lords. Debate on Great War—S. African Campaign; 15 Sept. 1915. 5th ser. (Lords) XIX, 816.
Supply—Colonial Office Vote—S. African affairs; 30 July 1919. 5th ser. (Commons) CXVIII, 2173–2243 *passim*.
Supply—Colonial Office Vote—S. African affairs; 26 April 1920. 5th ser. (Commons) CXXVIII, 891–956 *passim*.
Observations *re* S. Rhodesia Native Control Bill; 20 Dec. 1927. 5th ser. (Commons) CCXII, 368.
Supply—Colonial Office Vote—Rhodesias; 20 Feb. 1928. 5th ser. (Commons) CCXIII, 1281.
Supply—Colonial Office Vote—Rhodesias; 13 July 1928. 5th ser. (Commons) CCXIX, 2649.
Lords. Motion *re* S. African Protectorates; 26 July 1933. 5th ser. (Lords) LXXXVIII, 1121.
Lords. Motion *re* S. African Protectorates; 13 Dec. 1933. 5th ser. (Lords) XC, 466.

B. IN SOUTHERN AFRICA

By the late A. C. G. LLOYD, M.A., Librarian of the South African Public Library, Cape Town.

1. DOCUMENTARY MATERIAL

(*a*) *THE UNION (REPUBLIC) AND SOUTH-WEST AFRICA ARCHIVES*

There are five public Archive depots in the Union (now the Republic) of South Africa, and in addition, one in the Mandated Territory of South-West Africa. The Archives of the four Provinces which form the Republic, covering the period down to unification in 1910, are in the repositories situated in the administrative capitals of those Provinces; the South-West African Archives are at Windhoek. The records of the Cape Archives depot (Provincial) at Cape Town occupy 32,748 linear feet of shelving, those in the Natal Archives depot (Provincial) at Pietermaritzburg occupy 13,085 feet, those in the Orange Free State depot (Provincial) at Bloemfontein occupy 6,361 feet, those in the Transvaal Archives depot (Provincial) at Pretoria occupy 31,499 feet, and those in the Central Archives depot, also at Pretoria, occupy 12,039 feet, while those in the South-West African Archives depot at Windhoek occupy 2,202 feet. In terms of the Public Archives Acts of 1922 and 1953, government offices must deposit their records in the appropriate depot once they are thirty years old. Public access in the Republic is allowed once the records are fifty years old; but in South-West Africa access is only permitted up to and including 9th July, 1915, the date on which German administration of the Territory ended. The Minister entrusted with the administration of these Acts may, on grounds of public policy, refuse access to records of the age of fifty years or more.

For the documents relating to the Cape in the Algemeen Rijksarchief at the Hague see the bibliography to section V *infra*. The Archives Depot in Cape Town contains many transcripts of documents in European archives relating to South Africa and a list of them will be found in Appendix 6 of *A brief guide to the various classes of documents in the Cape Archives for the period* 1652–1806, by C. Graham Botha. In addition to official records considerable collections of semi-official and private papers have been deposited in the depots—notably, at Cape Town, the D'Urban

Papers, the Senator F. S. Malan Collection and the Sir Lewis Michell Collection; at Pretoria (Provincial) the Potgieter Papers, the Sir Owen Lanyon Collection, the Kruger Papers, the H. T. Bührmann collection, the Dr. W. J. Leyds collection the Lauts Collection, the General P. J. Joubert Papers, the Soutter Collection, and the Dr. G. S. Preller Collection; at Pietermaritzburg, the Fynn Papers, the Shepstone Papers, the Colenso Papers and the Goodricke Papers; at Bloemfontein, the Muller Documents and the M. T. Steyn Papers; at Pretoria (Central Archives), the General J. B. M. Hertzog Collection, the J. G. Strydom Collection and the semi-official Papers of Field Marshal J. C. Smuts.

(*b*) *PARLIAMENT*

In the custody of the Clerk of the Senate are:

THE MINUTES AND PROCEEDINGS OF H.M. COUNCIL OF ADVICE FOR THE CAPE OF GOOD HOPE, 1825–34. MS. 4 vols.

PROCEEDINGS OF THE LEGISLATIVE COUNCIL, 1834–57 AND 1866. MS. 7 vols.

Appendices to the above, 1826–53. MS. 32 vols.

(*c*) *THE NATIONAL ARCHIVES OF RHODESIA AND NYASALAND*

Salisbury, Southern Rhodesia.

The Central Archives are in Salisbury, Southern Rhodesia, and much smaller Regional Archives are in Lusaka and Zomba for Northern Rhodesia and Nyasaland respectively. The Central Archives house the papers of the High Commissioner for South Africa relating to Central Africa (1879–1923), the papers of the Resident Commissioner (1899–1923) and all the papers of the Southern Rhodesian Executive Council (1898–1953). These papers are open to public inspection until 1923 inclusive, the year in which the British South Africa Company gave up the administration. The historical records, chiefly private papers, were transferred to the Central Archives by the National Muesum, Bulawayo, in 1948.

(*d*) *NON-OFFICIAL PAPERS*

The Dutch Reformed Church Archives housed in the *Huguenoten Gedenkteken* at Cape Town contain, in addition to Synodical Papers, the records of many of the older congregations.

The LIBRARY OF PARLIAMENT, Cape Town, contains the Fairbairn-Pringle Papers and a few papers of Dr John Philip.

The SOUTH AFRICAN PUBLIC LIBRARY, Cape Town, contains original MSS. of the following:

Hofmeyr, Hon. J. H. Political papers and correspondence.

Merriman, Rt. Hon. J. X. Political papers and correspondence.

Rose-Innes, Sir James.

Schreiner, Olive, Correspondence (in part).

Schreiner, Rt. Hon. W. P. Political papers and correspondence.

Typescript copies of the more important of the D'Urban-Smith papers, arranged by G. M. Theal to follow on those published in his *Kaffir War of* 1835, and 1 vol. dealing with the Great Trek.

The JAGGER LIBRARY, UNIVERSITY OF CAPE TOWN, contains many of the letters of Sir John Herschel (1834–40), most of the Olive Schreiner Papers and the bulk of the J. C. Smuts Papers.

The PUBLIC LIBRARY, PORT ELIZABETH, contains the private letter-book of Sir Rufane Donkin, Acting-Governor of the Cape, 1820–1.

The Library of the University of the Witwatersrand, Johannesburg. This library at one time contained the first Gubbin's Collection, which consisted of many MSS. and books providing material for the history of South Africa. This Collection, to which frequent reference is made in both editions of this Volume, was almost totally destroyed by fire in 1931. The late Mr. J. G. Gubbins, however, made a second Collection, which is now with University Library. This Collection consists mainly of books and pamphlets, but it also contains original drawings by Frederick L'Ons and other South African artists as well as original letters of Lord Macartney, Mrs. Philip, wife of the Rev. John Philip, Robert Godlonton, A. G. Bain, E. A. Maund, the Rev. Thomas Jenkins and the diary of Owen Letcher. The Ernest Oppenheimer Institute of Portuguese Studies, which is situated in the University grounds, contains many books from the earliest period onwards dealing with Portugal's contribution to the civilisation of Africa.

The Library of Rhodes University College, Grahamstown, contains Dr Theal's transcript of the D'Urban-Smith Papers described above.

In Private Possession.

The papers of Sir J. H. de Villiers, first Baron de Villiers of Wynberg, are in the possession of the family at Stellenbosch.

2. OFFICIAL PUBLICATIONS: SELECT LIST

Note. The Annexures to the *Votes and Proceedings* of the Cape Parliament, the Union Parliament, etc., contain all Select Committee Reports, Departmental Reports and Papers ordered to be printed. In the list given below, U.G. signifies publication by order of the Union Government; A. signifies publication by order of the House of Assembly; S. by the Senate; S.C. signifies a Select Committee Report.

(a) *PROVINCES, HIGH COMMISSION TERRITORIES AND MANDATED TERRITORY*

Basutoland

Orders in Council, High Commissioner's proclamations and government notices, 12 March 1868–30 June 1913. Cape Town, 1913.

High Commissioner's proclamations, 1st July 1913–31st Dec. 1916. Pretoria, 1918.

High Commissioner's proclamations, 1917– . Pretoria, 1917– .

Bechuanaland

British Bechuanaland proclamations and the more important of the notices reprinted from the Cape of Good Hope Government Gazette, 1885–6. Cape Town, 1887.

British Bechuanaland proclamations and the more important of the notices reprinted from the British Bechuanaland Government Gazette, 1889–90. Vryburg, 1891.

Bechuanaland Protectorate and British South Africa Company's Territory. High Commissioner's notices and proclamations from April 1888 to June 1893. Cape Town, 1893.

Bechuanaland Protectorate. Orders in Council and High Commissioner's proclamations together with appendix containing the more important Government notices from 9th May 1891–30th June 1898, ed. by D. Ward. London, 1898.

High Commissioner's proclamations and notices, 1st July 1914–31st Dec. 1915. Mafeking, 1919.

High Commissioner's proclamations and notices, 1917– . Pretoria, 1919– .

British Bechuanaland Government Gazette, 1887–95.

BRITISH KAFFRARIA

Laws and regulations of British Kaffraria previous to its annexation to the Colony of the Cape of Good Hope. Cape Town, 1869.

British Kaffrarian Government Gazette, 1864–5.

CAPE COLONY

For Proceedings of the Council of Advice and of the Legislative Council before 1854, see under "Documentary Material" *supra*.

Treaties entered into by Governors of the Colony of the Cape of Good Hope and other British Authorities with Native Chieftains and others beyond the Borders of the Colony between the years 1803 *and* 1854. Cape Town, 1857.

The so-called Bloemhof Arbitration Bluebook. *Evidence taken at Bloemhof before the Commission appointed to investigate the Claims of the South African Republic, Captain N. Waterboer, Chief of West Griqualand, and Certain other native chiefs to portions of the territory on the Vaal River now known as the Diamond Fields.* Cape Town, 1871.

PARLIAMENT.

Minutes of the Legislative Council with Annexures, 1854–1910.

Votes and Proceedings of the House of Assembly with Annexures, 1854–1910.

Province of the Cape of Good Hope. Minutes and Ordinances, 1911– .

Cape of Good Hope. The Advertiser and Mail's Parliamentary Debates, 1854–5.

Debates in the House of Assembly, 1884–1909.

Debates in the Legislative Council, 1867–8, 1870–1, 1885–6, 1890–1909.

STATUTES, ORDINANCES AND PROCLAMATIONS.

Indische statuten ten tijde van . . . P. A. van der Parra. MS. 3 vols. This MS. is to be found in the Archives Depot at Cape Town.

Statuten van Batavia. MS. (*c.* 1700). Statuten van Batavia. MS. (*c.* 1715).

Statuten van Indien. MS. (*c.* 1820). 3 vols.

These three MSS. are in the South African Public Library, Cape Town.

Kaapsche Plakaaten, 1652–1795, 1803–6. MS. 8 vols. and index.

Statuten van Indien. MS. 3 vols.

Verzameling van wetten en regulation der Volkplanting de Kaap de Goede Hoop, 1652–1805. MS. 13 vols.

Index to the Statuten van Indien and to all ordinances, proclamations etc. to 1836. MS.

The above MSS. are in the Library of the Cape Provincial Division of the Supreme Court, Cape Town.

CHIJS, J. A. VAN DER. *Nederlandsch-Indisch plakaatboek*, 1602–1811. 17 vols. Batavia, 1885–1900.

The applicability of the Statutes of Batavia at the Cape is fully discussed in a series of articles by J. DE V. ROOS and C. H. VAN ZYL in vols. XXIII–XXV of the *South African* [*Cape*] *Law Journal*; also, by J. L. W. STOCK, "The new statutes of India at the Cape" in *South African Law Journal*, vol. XXXII, and by C. GRAHAM BOTHA in *South African Law Journal*, vol. XXX.

Proclamations, advertisements and other official notices . . . 1806–25. Cape of Good Hope, 1827.

HARDING, W. *The Cape of Good Hope government proclamations from* 1806 *to* 1825 *as now in force and unrepealed, and the ordinances* . . . 1825 *to* 1844. 3 vols. Cape Town, 1838–45.

Statute law of the Cape of Good Hope, comprising the placaats, proclamations and ordinances enacted before the establishment of the colonial parliament . . . *and still in force*. Cape Town, 1862.

Statutes, 1652–1909. 7 vols. and index. Cape Town, 1906–9.
Province of the Cape of Good Hope. Ordinances, 1911– . Cape Town, 1913– .

ADMINISTRATIVE AND STATISTICAL.

The Cape Town Gazette and African Advertiser, 1800–26, continued as *The Cape of Good Hope Government Gazette*, 1826–1910.
The Cape of Good Hope Eastern Province Government Gazette. 2 vols. Grahamstown, 1838–9.

From No. 2 onwards this title was changed to *Eastern Districts*.

Blue-Book for the Colony of the Cape of Good Hope. Cape Town, 1821–85, continued as:
Statistical Register of the Colony of the Cape of Good Hope. Cape Town, 1886–1909.
Province of the Cape of Good Hope. Official Gazette, 1910– . Cape Town, 1910– .

NATIVE TERRITORIES.

Transkeian Territories General Council. Proceedings and Reports of Select Committees etc., 1908– . Umtata and King William's Town, 1908– .
Statutes, proclamations and government notices in force in the Native Territories ... 1907 (ed. A. N. MACFADYEN). Cape Town, 1907.
Statutes, proclamations and government notices applied to the Transkeian Territories of the Cape of Good Hope ... 1907 (–1926). 3 vols. Cape Town, 1913–27.

GRIQUALAND WEST

Statute law. 2 vols. Cape Town, 1875–7. *Vide supra* p. 919.

NATAL

VOLKSRAAD.

Voortrekker wetgewing: notule van die Natalse Volksraad 1839–45, *met inleidinge en aantekeninge van G. S. Preller*. Pretoria, 1924.

The original documents from which this work is transcribed are in the Archives Depot at Pretoria.

PARLIAMENT.

Votes and Proceedings of the Legislative Council, 1857–93. Pietermaritzburg, 1857–93.
Votes and Proceedings of the Legislative Assembly, 1893–1910. Pietermaritzburg, 1893–1910.
Sessional Papers of the Legislative Assembly, 1893–1910. Pietermaritzburg, 1893–1910.
Debates of the Legislative Council of the Colony of Natal, 1879–93. Vols. I–XX.
Debates of the Legislative Assembly of the Colony of Natal, 1893–1910. Vols. XXI–XLIX.
Province of Natal. Minutes of the Provincial Council, 1911– . Pietermaritzburg, 1911– .

STATUTES, ORDINANCES AND PROCLAMATIONS.

HOWELL, J. M. *Ordinances, proclamations etc.*, 1836–47. Cape Town, 1848.
MOODIE, W. J. D. *Ordinances, proclamations etc. relating to the Colony of Natal*, 1836–55. 2 vols. Pietermaritzburg, 1856.
Statutes of Natal, compiled and edited by R. L. HITCHINS, 1845–1906. 4 vols. Pietermaritzburg, 1900–6.
Acts, 1907–10. 3 vols. Pietermaritzburg, 1907–10.
Ordinances of the Province of Natal, 1911– . Pietermaritzburg, 1912– .

ADMINISTRATIVE AND STATISTICAL.

The Natal Government Gazette, 1849–1910. Pietermaritzburg, 1849–1910.
Natal Blue Book, 1861–93. Pietermaritzburg, 1861–93. Continued as *Statistical Year Book of the Colony of Natal*, 1894–1909. Pietermaritzburg, 1894–1910.

Departmental reports were published as a supplement to the Natal Blue Book, 1884–93, and separately thereafter.

Province of Natal Gazette, 1910– . Pietermaritzburg, 1910– .

ORANGE FREE STATE

PARLIAMENT.

The MS. Minutes of Proceedings of the Legislative Council of the Orange River Sovereignty, 1849–52, are in the Provincial Archives Depot at Bloemfontein.

Notulen der Verrigtingen van den Hoogedelen Volksraad, 1854–98. Bloemfontein, 1869–98.

Minutes of Proceedings of the Legislative Council, 1903–7. Bloemfontein, 1903–7.

Minutes and Proceedings of the Legislative Council, 1907–9. Bloemfontein, 1907–9.

Votes and Proceedings of the House of Assembly, 1907–10. Bloemfontein, 1908–10.

Debates in the Legislative Council, 1903–7. Bloemfontein, 1903–7.

Debates of the Legislative Council and the Legislative Assembly of the Orange River Colony, 1907–10. Bloemfontein, 1907–10.

Inter-Colonial Council of the Transvaal and the Orange River Colony. See under "Transvaal", *infra*. p. 958.

Province of the Orange Free State. Votes and Proceedings of the Provincial Council, 1911– . Bloemfontein, 1911– .

STATUTES, ORDINANCES AND PROCLAMATIONS.

Wetboek, 1854–91. Bloemfontein, 1892.

Wetboek, 1892–99. Bloemfontein, 1899.

Statute law of the Orange River Colony, transl. by C. L. BOTHA. London, 1901.

Proclamations issued in the O.R.C. from the date of the Annexation to the Promulgation of the Constitution on 23rd June, 1902.

Ordinances, 1903–7. 4 vols. Bloemfontein, 1903–7.

Statutes, 1907–9. 3 vols. Bloemfontein, 1909–10.

Province of the Orange Free State. Ordinances, 1911– . Bloemfontein, 1913– .

ADMINISTRATIVE AND STATISTICAL.

Gouvernements Courant, 1857–1910. Bloemfontein, 1857–1910.

Province of the Orange Free State Official Gazette, 1910– . Bloemfontein, 1910– .

SOUTH WEST AFRICA

STATUTES, ORDINANCES AND PROCLAMATIONS.

The laws of South West Africa, 1915–22, edited by A. J. WATERS. Windhoek, 1923.

Proclamations and principal government notices issued in South West Africa, 1924–5. 2 vols. Windhoek, 1925–6.

Union legislation affecting South West Africa and proclamations, ordinances and principal government notices issued in South West Africa, 1926– . Windhoek, 1927– .

ADMINISTRATIVE AND STATISTICAL.

Amtsblatt für das Schutzgebiet Deutsch-Südwestafrika, 1910–Aug. 1914. Windhoek, 1910–14.

Official Gazette of South West Africa. Windhoek, 1915– .

SWAZILAND

Government Committee Laws, 1891–2. Cape Town, 1893.

Orders in Council, proclamations and principal government notices from 25 June 1903 to 30 June 1912. Cape Town, 1912.

Orders in Council, proclamations and principal government notices from 1 July 1912 to 31 Dec. 1915, edited W. W. USHER. Ermelo, 1925.

Orders in Council, Proclamations and principal Government Notices, 1922– . Pretoria, 1922– .

TRANSVAAL

PARLIAMENT.

Notule van die Volksraad van die Suid-Afrikaanse Republiek (South African Archives Records: Transvaal, 1844–5, 1851–3), 2 vols. 1950.

Notulen der Verrichtingen van den Hoog Edel Achtbaren Volksraad, 1889, 1890. Pretoria, 1889–90.

Before 1899 the Notulen were published in the *Staats Courant*.

Notulen der Verrichtingen van den H. Ed. Achtb. Eersten Volksraad, 1891–9. Pretoria, 1891–9.

Notulen der Verrichtingen van den H. Ed. Achtb. Tweeden Volksraad, 1891–9. Pretoria, 1891–9.

The Debates in the Volksraad, 1858–88, were published in the *Staats Courant* and in the *Notulen*, 1889–1899.

Inter-Colonial Council of the Transvaal and Orange River Colony, Minutes and Order Papers of Executive and Public Sessions, 1903–7. Johannesburg and Pretoria, 1903–7.

Inter-Colonial Council of the Transvaal and Orange River Colony. Debates, 1903–7. Johannesburg and Bloemfontein, 1903–7.

Minutes (and Proceedings) of the Legislative Council, 1902–10. Pretoria, 1902–10.

Notule van die Volksraad van die Suid-Afrikaanse Republiek (South African Archive Records: Transvaal, 1844–50; 1851–3. 2 vols., 1950).

Reports of Select Committees, Legislative Council, 1903–6. Pretoria, 1903–6.

Debates of the Transvaal Legislative Council, 1903–10. Pretoria, 1903–10.

Votes and Proceedings of the Legislative Assembly, 1907–10. Pretoria, 1907–10.

Reports of Select Committees, Legislative Assembly, 1907–10. Pretoria, 1907–10.

Annexures to the Votes and Proceedings of the Legislative Assembly, 1907–10. Pretoria, 1907–10.

Debates of the Transvaal Legislative Assembly, 1907–10. Pretoria, 1907–10.

Debates of both Houses of Parliament, Transvaal, 13 March, 1909–3 *April*, 1909.

Debates of both Houses of Parliament, Transvaal, 6 April, 1910–28 *April*, 1910.

Province of Transvaal. Votes and Proceedings of the Provincial Council, 1911–. Pretoria, 1911– .

STATUTES, ORDINANCES AND PROCLAMATIONS.

De locale wetten der Zuid Afrikaanse Republiek, 1849–97. 5 vols. Pretoria, 1887–97.

Statute law of the Transvaal, 1844–99. Pretoria, 1901.

Statutory proclamations of the Transvaal, 1900–2. 3rd ed. London, 1904.

Ordinances of the Transvaal Colony, 1902–6. 4 vols. Pretoria, 1903–6.

Statutes of the Transvaal, 1907–10. 4 vols. Pretoria, 1907–10.

Ordinances of the Province of Transvaal, 1911– . Pretoria, 1913– .

ADMINISTRATIVE AND STATISTICAL.

Staats Courant (Government Gazette), 1857–1910. Pretoria, 1857–1910.

Province of the Transvaal Official Gazette, 1910–. Pretoria, 1910– .

(*b*) *UNION OF SOUTH AFRICA*

PARLIAMENT.

Votes and Proceedings of the House of Assembly with printed annexures, 1911– . Cape Town, 1911– .

Minutes of Proceedings of the Senate, 1911– . Cape Town, 1911– .

Debates of the House of Assembly, 1910–15, 1924– .

The Senate of South Africa. Debates, 1910–15, 1924– .

Union of South Africa. Joint sitting of both Houses of Parliament. Debates, 1914. Cape Town, 1926– .

STATUTES.

Statutes, 1910– . Pretoria, 1911– .

ADMINISTRATIVE AND STATISTICAL.

The Union of South Africa Government Gazette, 1910– . Pretoria, 1910– .

Official Year Book of the Union and of Basutoland, Bechuanaland Protectorate and Swaziland, covering the period 1910– . Pretoria, 1918– .

(c) *THE HIGH COMMISSIONER FOR SOUTH AFRICA*

Orders in Council, Proclamations and Notices, 1916– . Cape Town, 1917– .
Official Gazette, 1901– .

(d) *RHODESIA, NORTHERN*

Statute law of North Western Rhodesia, 1899–1909. Livingstone, 1910.
Statute law of North Eastern Rhodesia, 1908–11, *N.W. Rhodesia*, 1910–11, *N. Rhodesia*, 1911–16. Edited P. J. MacDonell. Livingstone, 1917.

N. Rhodesia statutes for 1917–23 were published in the *Northern Rhodesia Gazette* as issued.

Proclamation and Ordinances of N. Rhodesia, 1924– . Livingstone, 1924– .
Northern Rhodesia Gazette, 1911– . Livingstone, 1911– .

(e) *RHODESIA, SOUTHERN*

Parliament.

Minutes of the Proceedings of the Legislative Council, 1899–1923. Salisbury, 1899–1923.
Votes and Proceedings of the House of Assembly, 1924– . Salisbury, 1924– .
Debates in the Legislative Council, 1899–1923. (Being a reprint from the reports of the *Rhodesia Herald*.)
Southern Rhodesia. Debates of the Legislative Assembly, 1924– .

Statutes.

Statute law of Southern Rhodesia from the Charter to 31*st Dec.* 1910, edited A. Speight. Salisbury, 1912.
Statute law of Southern Rhodesia from 1*st January*, 1911 *to* 31*st December*, 1922, edited A. Speight. Salisbury, 1923.
The Statute Law of Southern Rhodesia, 1922– . Salisbury, 1923– .

Administrative and Statistical.

British South Africa Company Gazette, 1894–1923.
Colony of Southern Rhodesia Government Gazette, 1923– .
Official Year Book, 1924– . Salisbury, 1924– .

PART II

OTHER WORKS

By the late A. C. G. Lloyd and A. Taylor Milne, arranged from material supplied by the authors of the several chapters

1. GENERAL BIBLIOGRAPHY

(a) *BIBLIOGRAPHIES AND GUIDES TO MATERIAL*

Adam, I. A., Ewing, J., and Munro, J., *Guide to the Principal Parliamentary Papers relating to the Dominions*, 1812–1911. Edinburgh, 1913.
Blaine, C. H. and Goad, C. F. *Consolidated index to the Statute law of the Union of South Africa*. Cape Town, 1924.
Bleek, W. H. I. *The Library of Sir George Grey*, vol. 1, part 1. 1858.

Botha, C. G. *A brief guide to the various classes of documents in the Cape Archives, 1652–1806*. Cape Town, 1918.

—— *The public Archives of South Africa, 1652–1910*. Cape Town, 1928.

British Museum. *Subject Index of the Modern Works added to the Library of the British Museum*, 1881– . 1902– .

Cape of Good Hope. *Index to the annexures and printed papers of the House of Assembly, 1854–1910*. 3 vols. Cape Town, 1899–1910.

—— *Index of Government proclamations and notices*, 1803–1901. 3 vols. Cape Town, 1881–1901.

For Catalogues of British Parliamentary Papers, see separate list above, Part I, A. 3.

Europeans and coloured races. *Guide to publications in the Library of Parliament . . . dealing with the relations between Europeans and coloured and backward races*. Cape Town, 1927.

The Fairbridge Library: a catalogue. 1904.

The Fairbridge Library now forms part of the South African Public Library.

Gids tot die publikasies in en oor Afrikaans in die Parlementsbiblioteek te Kaapstad. 2de uitgawe. Pretoria. 1934.

Goldman, P. D. A. *Beredeneerde inventarissen van de oudste archiefgroepen der Zuid-Afrikaanse Republiek*. Pretoria. 1927.

Haferkorn, H. E. *The South African War. A Bibliography*. Fort Humphreys, U.S.A., 1924.

Hahn, T. *An index to the Grey Collection in the South African Public Library*. Cape Town, 1884.

Huggins, W. N. *A Guide to Studies in African History*. New York, 1934.

Index der Staatscouranten, 1857–90. 3 vols. Pretoria, 1897–9.

Lewin, P. E. *Annotated bibliography of recent publications on Africa, South of the Sahara*. 1943.

Lewin, P. E. *Subject Catalogue of the Library of the Royal Empire Society*, vol. i. 1930.

Mendelssohn, S. *Mendelssohn's South African bibliography*. 2 vols. 1910.

—— *Additions*, 1910–1914. 3 vols., 1914. Typescript copies in British Museum and South African Public Library.

Port Elizabeth Public Library. *Catalogue*, vol. ii. 1906.

Schapera, I. Ethnographical research in South Africa. Appendix B. Select bibliography, in *Bantu Studies*, Sept. 1934, vol. viii, no. 3.

Theal, G. McC. *Catalogue of books and pamphlets relating to Africa south of the Zambesi in the English, Dutch, French and Portuguese languages*. Cape Town, 1912.

Union of South Africa. *Index to the Manuscript annexures and printed papers of the House of Assembly*, 1910–30. Cape Town, 1931.

—— *List of Union publications issued by the Government Printing and Stationery Department*. Pretoria, 1927.

Work, M. N. *A bibliography of the negro in Africa and America*. New York, 1928.

(b) *PERIODICAL PUBLICATIONS OF HISTORICAL AND OTHER SOCIETIES, ETC.*

Aborigines Protection Society. *Anti-Slavery Reporter*, 1825– . (Title varies.)

African Society, *Journal*. London, 1901– .

Linschoten-Vereeniging. *Werken*. 's Gravenhage, 1909– .

London Missionary Society, *Reports*, 1795– ; *Transactions*, 1795–1815, 4 vols.; *Quarterly Chronicle* for 1815–33, 1821–33; *Missionary Magazine and Chronicle* 1837–66, becoming the *Chronicle of the London Missionary Society*, 1867– .

Methodist Missionary Society, *Annual Reports*, 1816– ; *Missionary Notices*, 1816– .

Royal Geographical Society, London: *Journal*, 50 vols. 1831–80; *Proceedings*, 22 vols. 1856–78; *Proceedings . . . and Monthly Record of Geography*, 14 vols. 1879–92; *Geographical Journal including the Proceedings*, 1893– .
Royal Society of South Africa. *Transactions*, vols. 1– . Cape Town, 1909– .
South African Philosophical Society. *Transactions*, vols. 1–18. Cape Town, 1877–1909.
Van Riebeeck Society, *Publications*. Cape Town, 1918– .

There are many articles of South African interest in *Petermanns Geographisches Mitteilungen*. Gotha, 1855– .

(c) NEWSPAPERS

The most extensive collections of South African newspapers are to be found in the Library of Parliament and in the South African Public Library at Cape Town, the latter containing about 7000 volumes of bound newspapers.

The principal newspapers are arranged here under their place of publication and the dates of their issue are attached.

Bloemfontein. *De Express*, 1875–99; *Friend*, 1850– ; *Volksblad*, 1917– .
Cape Town. *Die Burger*, 1914– ; *Cape Argus*, 1857– ; *Cape Monitor*, 1850–62; *Cape of Good Hope Observer*, 1849–51; *Cape Times*, 1876– ; *Cape Town Mail*, 1841–53; *Ons Land*, 1892–1930 (combined with *Zuid Afrikaan*, 1830–94); *South African Commercial Advertiser*, 1824–69; *Standard and Mail*, 1869–79.
Durban. *Natal Mercury*, 1852– .
East London. *East London Despatch*, 1873– .
Graaff-Reinet. *Graaff-Reinet Advertiser*, 1861– .
Grahamstown. *Cape Frontier Times*, 1840–63; *Grahamstown Journal*, 1831–1919, when it was incorporated in *Grocott's Daily Mail*, 1920– ; *Het Kaapsche Grensblad*, 1844–61.
Johannesburg. *Rand Daily Mail*, 1902– ; *Star*, 1889– .
Kimberley. *Diamond Fields Advertiser*, 1878– .
King William's Town. *Imvo Zabantsundu*, 1884– ; *Kaffrarian Watchman*, 1866–99.
Paarl. *Die Afrikaanse Patriot*, 1876–1904.
Pietermaritzburg. *De Natalier*, 1844–6; *Natal Witness*, 1846– ; *Times of Natal*, 1851–1927.
Port Elizabeth. *Eastern Province Herald*, 1845– ; *Port Elizabeth Mercury*, 1850–9; *Port Elizabeth Daily Telegraph*, 1848–98, continued as *Cape Daily Telegraph*, 1898–1908.
Pretoria. *Ons Vaderland* (from *Die Vaderland*), 1915– ; *Pretoria News*, 1899– ; *Volkstem*, 1873– .
Queenstown. *Queenstown Daily Representative*, 1866– .

(d) COLLECTED HISTORICAL RECORDS

Andrew, C. F. (Ed.). *Documents relating to the New Asiatic Bill*. Cape Town, 1926.
Bell, K. N. and Morrell, W. P. *Select Documents on British Colonial Policy*, 1830–1860. Oxford, 1928.
Bird, J. *The Annals of Natal*, 1495 to 1845. 2 vols. Pietermaritzburg, 1888.
Chase, J. C. *The Natal Papers, a reprint of all notices and public documents*, 1488–1843. 2 pts. Grahamstown, 1843.
Eybers, G. W. *Select Constitutional Documents illustrating South African history* 1795–1910. 1918.
Foster, W. *British Rule in South Africa*. Cape Town, 1868.
A collection of official and other documents.
Godée-Molsbergen, E. C. (Ed.). *Reizen in Zuid-Afrika in de Hollandse Tijd*. 4 vols. 's Gravenhage, 1916–32.

HERTSLET, Sir E. *Map of Africa by Treaty.* Revised ed. 3 vols. 1909.

JEFFREYS, K. M. *Kaapse Archiefstukken lopende over het jaar* 1778, uitgegeven onder toezicht van de Kommissie van Uniearchieven, Kaapstad, 1926– (in progress).

LEIBBRANDT, H. C. V. *Précis of the Archives of the Cape of Good Hope*, 17 vols. Cape Town, 1896–1906, including *The Defence of Willem Adriaan van der Stel*, 1897; *Resolutien van den Commandeur en Raden van het Fort de Goede Hoop*, 1652–62, 1898; *Journal*, 1651–62, 3 vols. 1897; *Journal*, 1662–70, 1901; *Journal*, 1671–4 *and* 1676, 1902; *Journal*, 1699–1732, 1896; *Letters Received*, 1649–62, 2 vols. 1898–9; *Letters Received*, 1695–1708, 1896; *Letters Despatched*, 1652–62, 3 vols. 1900; *Letters Despatched*, 1696–1708, 1896; *Requesten* (*Memorials*) *A–O*, 1715–1806, 2 vols. 1905–6; the third vol. is in MS. at the Cape Town Archives Depot; *The Rebellion of* 1815 *generally known as Slachter's Nek.* Cape Town, 1902.

MOODIE, D. *The Record; or a series of official papers relative to the condition and treatment of the native tribes of South Africa.* Cape Town, 1838–41.

The periods covered are 1649–1720, 1769–95, 1808–19.

—— *Specimens of the authentic records of the Colony of the Cape of Good Hope, relative to the aboriginal tribes.* Cape Town, 1841.

NEWTON, A. P. *Select documents relating to the Unification of South Africa.* 2 vols. 1924.

PRELLER, G. S. *Voortrekkermense, 'n riftal. Oorspronkelike Dokumente oor die Geskiedenis van die Voortrek.* 4 vols. Kaapstad, 1918–25.

SPOELSTRA, C. *Bouwstoffen voor de geschiedenis der Nederduitsche-Gereformeerde Kerken in Zuid Afrika.* 2 vols. Amsterdam, 1906–7.

THEAL, G. McC. *Abstract of the debates and resolutions of the Council of Policy at the Cape from* 1651 *to* 1687. Cape Town, 1881.

—— *Basutoland records*, vols. I–III. Cape Town. 1883.

Vols. IV–VI are unpublished but exist in MS. prepared for publication in the Cape Town Archives Depot.

—— *Belangrijke historische dokumenten over Zuid Afrika.* 3 vols. Kaapstad, 1896–1911.

Vol. I contains *Instructie van den Commissaris Hendrik Adriaan van Rheede*, 1685; *Verscheidene dokumenten betrekking hebbende tot den oproermaker Estienne Barbier*, 1739; *Reis van den Gouverneur Joachim van Plettenberg*, 1778.

Vol. II, *The antiquity of Man in South Africa*; *Bushman Paintings*; *Reis naar Delagoa Baai in* 1688; *Reisen naar Inhambane in* 1732 *en* 1733; *Reis van den Vaandrig Beutler*, 1752; *Reis naar Inhambane*, 1770.

Vol. III contains documents copied at the Hague and in Berlin.

—— *Chronicles of Cape Commanders; or an Abstract of original manuscripts in the Archives of the Cape Colony dating from* 1651 *to* 1691. Cape Town, 1882.

—— *Documents relating to the Kaffir War of* 1835. Cape Town, 1912.

—— *Records of the Cape Colony from Feb.* 1793 *to April* 1831. 36 vols. Cape Town, 1897–1905.

—— *Records of South-Eastern Africa.* 9 vols. Cape Town, 1898–1903.

(*e*) *GENERAL HISTORIES AND WORKS OF GENERAL HISTORICAL INTEREST*

BOTHA, C. G. *The French Refugees at the Cape.* Cape Town, 1919.

BOTHA, P. R. *Die staatkundige ontwikkeling van die Suid-Afrikaanse Republiek onder Kruger en Leyds. Transvaal*, 1844–1899. Amsterdam, 1926.

BROOKES, E. H. *The history of native policy in South Africa from* 1830 *to the present day.* 2nd ed. Pretoria, 1927.

—— *The Colour Problem of South Africa.* Lovedale, 1934.

BRYANT, A. T. *Olden times in Zululand and Natal, containing the earlier political history of the Eastern-Nguni clans.* 1929.

BRYCE, J. (later Visct.). *Impressions of South Africa.* New ed. 1900.

CANA, F. R. *South Africa from the Great Trek to the Union.* 1909.

CORY, (Sir) G. E. *The rise of South Africa; a history of the origin of South African colonisation and of its development towards the East from the earliest times to 1857.* 5 vols. 1910–30.

A sixth volume (1857–72) was in progress at the time of the author's death in 1935.

Crockford's Clerical Directory.

DEHÉRAIN, H. *Le Cap de Bonne-Espérance au XVIIe Siecle.* Paris, 1909.

—— *L'expansion des Boers au XIXe Siècle.* Paris, 1905.

DU PLESSIS, J. *A history of Christian missions in South Africa.* 1911.

ENGELBRECHT, S. P. *Geschiedenis van de Nederduits Hervormde Kerk in Zuid-Afrika.* 2 vols. Amsterdam and Pretoria, 1920–5.

FAIRBRIDGE, D. *Historic houses of South Africa.* 1922.

—— *A history of South Africa.* Oxford, 1918.

GIE, S. F. N. *Geskiedenis van Suid-Afrika.* 2 vols. Stellenbosch, 1924–8.

GODÉE-MOLSBERGEN, E. C. and VISSCHER, J. *South African history told in pictures.* Amsterdam, 1913.

GOODFELLOW, D. M. *A modern Economic History of South Africa.* 1931.

HERRMAN, L. *A History of the Jews in South Africa from the earliest times to 1895.* 1930.

HOFMEYR, J. H. *South Africa.* 1931.

JOHNSTON, (Sir) H. H. *A History of the Colonization of Africa by Alien Races.* Cambridge. 1913.

KILPIN, R. *The Old Cape House, being pages from the history of a legislative assembly.* Cape Town, 1918.

—— *The Romance of a colonial Parliament.* 1930.

KNOWLES, L. C. M. and C. M. *The economic development of the British Overseas Empire.* Vol. 3. *The Union of South Africa.* 1936.

KOCK, M. H. de. *Selected subjects in the economic history of South Africa.* Cape Town, 1924.

LEWIS, C. and EDWARDS, G. E. *Historical Records of the Church of the Province of South Africa.* 1934.

LOVELL, R. I. *The Struggle for South Africa, 1875–1899.* New York, 1934.

LUCAS, (Sir) C. P. *A Historical Geography of the British Dominions,* vol. IV, pts. 1 and 2. Oxford, 1913–15.

MACKEURTAN, H. G. *The Cradle Days of Natal, 1497–1845.* 1930.

MACMILLAN, W. M. *Bantu, Boer and Briton: the making of the South African native problem.* 1929.

—— *The Cape Colour Question: an historical survey.* 1927.

—— *Complex South Africa: an economic foot-note to history.* 1930.

MALHERBE, E. G. *Education in South Africa, 1652–1922.* Cape Town, 1925.

MILLIN, S. G. *The South Africans.* 1926. New and enlarged ed., 1934.

SOGA, J. H. *The South-Eastern Bantu.* Johannesburg, 1930.

SPOELSTRA, B. *Ons Volkslewe.* 2de druk. Pretoria, 1924.

SPOELSTRA, C. *Het Kerkelijk en Godsdienstig Leven der Boeren na den Grooten Trek.* Kampen, 1915.

STOCKENSTROM, E. *Historiese atlas van Suid-Afrika.* Stellenbosch, 1928.

THEAL, G. McC. *Ethnography and condition of South Africa before* A.D. *1505.* 1922.

—— *History and Ethnography of Africa south of the Zambesi, 1505–1795.* 3 vols. 1927.

—— *History of Africa south of the Zambesi, 1795–1872.* 5 vols. 1926–7.

—— *History of South Africa from 1873 to 1884.* 2 vols. 1919.

TROLLOPE, A. *South Africa.* 1878.

WALKER, E. A. *Historical Atlas of South Africa.* Oxford, 1922.

—— *A History of Southern Africa.* 1957.

—— *The Great Trek.* 1934.

(*f*) *BIOGRAPHIES*

BARNARD, Lady ANNE. *South Africa a century ago: letters written from the Cape of Good Hope, 1797–1801.* Cape Town. 1925.

BEAZLEY, C. R. *Prince Henry the Navigator*. 1908.
BUTLER, (Sir) W. F. *Sir William Butler: an autobiography*. 2nd ed. 1913.
—— *The Life of Sir George Pomeroy Colley*. 1899.
BUXTON, S. C. B. (Earl). *General Botha*. 1924.
CHAMBERLIN, D. *David Livingstone*. 1930.
COLE, M. L. and GWYNN, S. (Eds.). *Memoirs of Sir Lowry Cole*. 1934.
COLLIER, J. *Sir George Grey, Governor, High Commissioner, and Premier. An historical biography*. Christchurch [N.Z.], 1909.
COLVIN, I. D. *The Life of Jameson*. 2 vols. 1922.
COX, Sir G. W. *Life of John William Colenso*. 2 vols. 1888.
ENGELBRECHT, S. P. *Thomas François Burgers, 'n Lewenskets*. Pretoria, 1933.
ENGELENBURG, F. V. *General Louis Botha*. Pretoria, 1929.
FAIRBRIDGE, D. *Lady Anne Barnard at the Cape of Good Hope*, 1797–1802. Oxford, 1924.
FULLER, (Sir) T. E. *The Right Honourable Cecil John Rhodes*. 1910.
GARVIN, J. L. *The Life of Joseph Chamberlain*. 3 vols. 1932–4.
GODÉE-MOLSBERGEN, E. C. *De stichter van Hollands Zuid-Afrika: Jan van Riebeeck*, 1618–77. Amsterdam, 1912.
GRAY, C. *Life of Robert Gray, Bishop of Cape Town*. 2 vols. 1876.
HENDERSON, G. C. *Sir George Grey: Pioneer of empire in southern lands*. 1907.
HOFMEYR, J. H. and REITZ, F. W. *The life of Jan Hendrik Hofmeyr* (*Onze Jan*). Cape Town, 1913.
JABAVU, D. D. T. *The life of John Tengo Jabavu, editor of Imvo Zabantsundu*. Lovedale, 1922.
JOURDAN, P. J. *Cecil Rhodes: his private life*, by his private secretary. 1911.
KESTELL, J. D. *Christiaan de Wet*. Kaapstad, 1920.
KRUGER, S. J. P. *The memoirs of Paul Kruger*. 2 vols. 1902.
LAURENCE, (Sir) P. M. *The life of John Xavier Merriman*. 1930.
LEIPOLDT, C. F. L. *Jan van Riebeeck, a biographical study*. 1936.
LE SUEUR, G. *Cecil Rhodes, the man and his work*. 1913.
LOMBARD, J. P. La G. *Paul Kruger, die Volksman*. Pretoria, 1925.
MCDONALD, J. G. *Rhodes: a life*. New ed. 1934.
MACKENZIE, W. D. *John Mackenzie*. 1921.
MARTIN, A. D. *Doctor Vanderkemp*. 1931.
MARTINEAU, J. *Life and correspondence of Sir Bartle Frere*. 2 vols. 1895.
MERWE, N. J. v. d. *Marthinus Theunis Steyn, 'n Lewensbeskrywing*. 2 dln. Kaapstad, 1921.
MICHELL, (Sir) L. *Life of the Right Honourable Cecil John Rhodes*. 2 vols. 1910.
MILLIN, S. G. *Rhodes*. 1933.
—— *General Smuts*. 2 vols. 1936.
MOCKFORD, J. *Khama, King of the Bamangwato*. 1931.
MOFFAT, R. U. *J. S. Moffat*. 1921.
MOLTENO, P. A. *Life and times of Sir John Charles Molteno*. 2 vols. 1900.
NATHAN, M., *Paul Kruger*. 1941.
NEAME, L. E. *General Hertzog*. 1930.
OORDT, J. F. van. *De Levensgeschiedenis van President J. H. Brand*. Amsterdam, Cape Town, 1914.
PIROW, O., *James Barry Munnik Hertzog*. Cape Town. 1957.
PLOMER, W. *Cecil Rhodes*. 1933.
PRELLER, G. S. *Piet Retief: Lewensgeskiedenis van die grote voortrekker*. 10de druk. Kaapstad, 1920.
REES, W. L. and L. *The life and times of Sir George Grey*. 2 vols. Auckland [N.Z.], 1892.
ROBINSON, (Sir) JOHN. *A life time in South Africa*. 1900.
ROSENTHAL, E., *General de Wet*. 1946.
SMITH, E. W. *The Life and Times of Daniel Lindley*. 1949.
SMITH, (Sir) H. G. W. *The Autobiography of Lt.-Gen. Sir Harry Smith*. 2 vols. 1901.

SMUTS, J. C. (junior). *Jan Christian Smuts.* 1952.
SOLOMON, W. E. G. *Saul Solomon.* O.U.P., 1948.
SPENDER, E. H. *General Botha: the career and the man.* 2nd ed. 1919.
STOCKENSTROM, (Sir) A. *Autobiography.* 2 vols. Cape Town, 1887.
VAN DEN HEEVER, C. M. *General J. B. M. Hertzog.* 1946.
WALKER, E. A. *Lord de Villiers and his times: South Africa, 1842–1914.* 1925.
—— *W. P. Schreiner. A South African.* 1937.
WILLIAMS, BASIL. *Cecil Rhodes.* 1921.
WILMOT, Count A. *The life and times of Sir Richard Southey.* 1904.
WORSFOLD, W. B. *Sir Bartle Frere.* 1923.

2. SELECT LIST OF WORKS RELATING TO PARTICULAR SUBJECTS

SECTION I. THE GEOGRAPHICAL ENVIRONMENT

(Chapter I)

(*a*) MAPS

1. *Physical Map of the Union of South Africa* 1:1,000,000. Geological Survey, Pretoria, 1931.
2. *Geological Map of the Union of South Africa* 1:1,000,000. Geological Survey, Pretoria, 1925.
3. *Map of Africa* 1:2,000,000. British General Staff No. 2871. Sheets; Benguella, Rhodesia Mozambique, South-West Africa, Transvaal, Cape of Good Hope, and Natal.
4. *Philips' College Atlas for South Africa.*
   Contains reliable maps of the Union on a scale of 1:2,000,000.
5. *The Times Atlas.*
   Gives the Union on 1:2,500,000 and the other South African territories on 1:5,000,000.

Since the appearance of the first edition of this work great improvements have taken place in official mapping. Very useful is the beautiful map of the Union 1:500,000 (21 sheets). The country is largely covered by a map 1:250,000, and completely by a topo-cadastral map 1:250,000 (49 sheets). Selected areas have been mapped on the scales of 1:100,000; 1:50,000; 1:25,000. Less elaborate maps exist for the other territories, but here too progress is being made. Many of the older large-scale maps were unsatisfactory from the geographical point of view, especially on acount of poor representation of relief; yet they may be valuable for historical research, as the best means of locating the numerous farms and small rivers mentioned in old documents.

(*b*) GENERAL WORKS

DU TOIT, A. L. *The Geology of South Africa.* 1926.
FITZGERALD, W. *Africa: a social, economic and political geography of its major regions,* 1934.
KING, L. C. *South African Scenery.*
NARATH, R. *Die Union von Südafrika und ihre Bevölkerung.* Leipzig, 1930.
Official Year Book of the Union of South Africa. Published annually.
Official Year Book of Southern Rhodesia. Published annually.
PASSARGE, S. *Die Kalahari.* Berlin, 1904.
—— *Südafrika.* Leipzig, 1908.
SERTON, P. *Zuid-Afrika, Land van Goede Hoop.* Meppel, 1953.
South Africa and Science. Handbook published for the meeting of the British Association at Cape Town and Johannesburg in 1929.

STEVENSON-HAMILTON, J. *The Low Veld.* 1929.

TALJAARD, M. S. *Oor Berge en Vlaktes* [English translation: *Glimpses of South Africa*]. 1948.

WELLINGTON, J. H. *Southern Africa*, vols. I and II. 1955.

(c) ARTICLES FROM PERIODICALS AND OTHER SPECIAL PUBLICATIONS

1. *Surveying, Geology, Landforms.*

DU TOIT, A. L. Crustal movement as a factor in the geographical evolution of South Africa. *S. Afr. Geog. Journ.* 1933, vol. XVI, pp. 3–20.

—— The evolution of the South African Coastline. *S. Afr. Geog. Journ.* 1922, vol. V, pp. 5–13.

HARGER, H. The underground erosion of the S.-W. Transvaal Dolomite. *S. Afr. Geog. Journ.* 1922, vol. V, pp. 55–65.

KRIGE, A. V. An examination of the Tertiary and Quaternary changes of sea-level in South Africa. *Annals of the University of Stellenbosch*, vol. V, 1927.

KUPFERBURGER, W. The geological basis of S.A. Geography. *S. Afr. Geog. Journ.* 1919, vol. III, pp. 30–4.

TREVOR, T. G. The physical features of the Transvaal. *Geog. Journ.* 1906, vol. XXVIII, pp. 50–65.

WATERMEYER, G. A. Surveying and Geodesy. *S. Afr. Geog. Journ.* 1929, vol. XII, pp. 5–13.

—— The Survey of the Union of South Africa. *S. Afr. Geog. Journ.* 1919, vol. III, pp. 20–30.

WELLINGTON, J. H. Notes on the Surface Features of Natal. *S. Afr. Geog. Journ.* 1932, vol. XV, pp. 45–50.

—— The topographical features of the Witwatersrand. *S. Afr. Geog. Journ.* 1924, vol. VII, pp. 17–28.

2. *Climate, Irrigation, Vegetation, Animals.*

ACOCKS, J. P. H. Veld Types of South Africa. *Botanical Survey Memoir*, 1951, No. 28.

BEWS, J. W. An account of the chief types of vegetation in South Africa with notes on the Plant Succession, in *Journal of Ecology*, 1916, vol. IV, pp. 129–59.

—— South African Phytogeography. *S. Afr. Geog. Journ.* 1917, vol. I, pp. 11–22.

CLIFFORD, B. E. H. *Report on a journey by motor transport from Mahalapye through the Kalahari Desert, Ghanzi and Ngamiland to the Victoria Falls.* Pretoria, 1928.

EVANS, I. B. POLE. The Veld: its resources and dangers. *S. Afr. Journ. of Science*, 1920, vol. XVII, pp. 1–34.

FANTHAM, H. B. The Animals of South Africa and their geographical relationships. *S. Afr. Geog. Journ.* 1920–1, vol. IV, pp. 5–20.

FORDE, C. DARYLL. Irrigation in South Africa. *Geog. Journ.* 1925, vol. LXV, pp. 342–9.

KANTHACK, F. E. Irrigation in South Africa. *S. Afr. Geog. Journ.* 1922, vol. V, pp. 13–24.

—— Notes on the Kunene River, Southern Angola. *Geog. Journ.* 1921, vol. LVII, pp. 321–36.

MAUFE, H. B. Climatic changes in Southern Rhodesia during later Geological times. *S. Afr. Geog. Journ.* 1930, vol. XIII, pp. 12–16.

PLUMMER, F. E. *Aspects of Rainfall in the Western Cape Province.* University of Pretoria Publications, series no. 1, 1932.

—— A preliminary investigation into the variability of the rainfall of the Transvaal. *S. Afr. Geog. Journ.* 1926, vol. IX, pp. 5–20.

—— A Note on South African rainfall in relation to topography. *S. Afr. Geog. Journ.* 1930, vol. XIII, pp. 47–54.

Rainfall normals up to the end of 1925. *With an introduction and brief summary of the rainfall of the Union of South Africa by* A. D. Lewis. (Department of Irrigation, Meteorological Office.) Cape Town, 1927.

Report of the Desert Encroachment Committee, U.G. 59, 1951.

Report of the Drought Investigation Commission. U.G. 20, 1922, and U.G. 49, 1923.

Robertson, C. L. and Sellick, N. P. *The Climate of Rhodesia, Nyasaland and Moçambique Colony.* 1933.

Schumann, T. W. G. and Thompson, W. R. *A Study of South African Rainfall.* Cape Town, 1935.

Schwarz, E. H. L. The control of Climate by Lakes. *Geog. Journ.* 1921, vol. lvii, pp. 166–81.

Serton, P. The Desert in Human Geography. *S. Afr. Geog. Journ.* 1929, vol. xii, pp. 26–31.

Sutton, J. R. Some notes on Rainfall and Run-off in South Africa. *S. Afr. Geog. Journ.* 1922, vol. v, pp. 41–4.

Wood, H. E. The Climate of South Africa. *S. Afr. Geog. Journ.* 1918, vol. ii, pp. 5–8.

3. *Settlement, Economic Geography.*

Bowman, I. The White Man's land of Southern Africa. Chapter xi of *The Pioneer Fringe.* American Geographical Society, 1932.

Hugo, C. F. The Location of South Africa and its economic consequences. *Economic Geography*, 1933.

Langhaus, P. Buren in Deutsch-Südwest-Afrika. *Petermanns' Mitteilungen*, 1900, vol. xlvi, pp. 18–19.

Obst, E. Das Deutschtum in Südafrika. *Geographische Zeitschrift*, 1934.

Schultze, J. H. Eine neue Wirtschaftskarte von Südafrika. *Petermann's Mitteilungen*, 1931, pp. 22–4.

Serton, P. Zuid-Afrika. Special number of *Tijdschrift voor Economische Geographie*, 1933.

—— De Zuid-Afrikaansche Spoorwegen. *Tijdschrift voor Economische Geographie*, 1927.

Theron, H. F. Geografiese Invloede op die Wynbou in Suid-Afrika. *S. Afr. Geog. Journ.* 1932, vol. xv, pp. 15–34.

Wellington, J. H. The Economic Development of the Eastern Cape Province. *S. Afr. Geog. Journ.* 1928, vol. xi, pp. 22–37.

—— Land Utilization in South Africa. *Geog. Rev.* 1932.

—— Pioneer Settlement in the Union of South Africa. *Pioneer Settlement.* American Geographical Society, 1932.

4. *Regional Geography.*

Burg, M. van den. A regional survey of the Pretoria District. *S. Afr. Geog. Journ.* 1931, vol. xiv, pp. 3–18.

Clarke, (Sir) M. Unexplored Basutoland. *Geog. Journ.* 1888, vol. x, pp. 519–25.

Crawshay, R. Basutoland and the Basuto. *Geog. Journ.* 1903, vol. xxi, pp. 645–55.

Davies, W. N. G. Southern Rhodesia. *S. Afr. Geog. Journ.* 1933, vol. xvi, pp. 50–5.

Dickins, V. Journeys in South-Eastern Mashonaland. *Geog. Journ.* 1907, vol. xxix, pp. 15–23.

Du Toit, A. L. The Mier Country. *S. Afr. Geog. Journ.* 1926, vol. ix, pp. 21–6.

Hall, A. L. The Transvaal Drakensberg. *S. Afr. Geog. Journ.* 1925, vol. viii, pp. 7–20.

Jollie, E. T. Southern Rhodesia. *Geog. Rev.* 1927, vol. xvii, pp. 89–106.

Mason, M. H. The Transkei. *Geog. Journ.* 1918, vol. lii, pp. 30–43.

Rouillard, R. A. The Development of Northern Natal and Zululand. *S. Afr. Geog. Journ.* 1925, vol. viii, pp. 21–38.

SCHWARZ, E. H. L. The Northern Kalahari. *S. Afr. Geog. Journ.* 1926, vol. IX, pp. 29–36.

SERTON, P. Basoetoland. *Tijdschrift voor Economische Geographie*, 1925.

—— Laingsburg. *Tijdschrift voor Economische Geographie*, 1929.

SNEESBY, G. W. Eastern Pondoland: a geographical study. *S. Afr. Geog. Journ.* 1933, vol. XVI, pp. 39–49.

STIGAND, A. G. Notes on Ngamiland. *Geog. Journ.* 1912, vol. XXXIX, pp. 376–9.

THIELE, E. O. and WILSON, R. C. Portuguese East Africa between the Zambesi River and the Sabi River. *Geog. Journ.* 1915, vol. XLV, pp. 16–39.

TÖNNESEN, T. The South-West Africa Protectorate. *Geog. Journ.* 1917, vol. XLIX, pp. 282–99.

WELLINGTON, J. H. The Middle Course of the Orange River. *S. Afr. Geog. Journ.* 1933, vol. XVI, pp. 58–68.

—— The physical and economic geography of the Central Magaliesberg Region. *S. Afr. Geog. Journ.* 1926, vol. IX, pp. 37–44.

—— The natural regions of the Transvaal. *S. Afr. Geog. Journ.* 1927, vol. X, pp. 5–24.

—— The Vaal-Limpopo Watershed. *S. Afr. Geog. Journ.* 1929, vol. XII, pp. 36–45.

SECTION II. THE NATIVE RACES

(Chapter II)

The references given below are confined to standard works and other important sources on the history and ethnography of the various groups of native peoples. More extensive lists will be found in references with the annotation "Bibl.", and in the following detailed special bibliographies:

GOODWIN, A. J. H. A commentary on the history and present position of South African Prehistory. *Bantu Studies*, vol. IX (1935), pp. 291–416.

HAMBLY, W. D. Bibliography of African Anthropology 1937–1949. *Fieldiana: Anthropology* (Chicago), vol. XXXVII, no. 2 (1952).

SCHAPERA, I. The Present State and Future Development of Ethnographical Research in South Africa. *Bantu Studies*, vol. VIII (1934), pp. 219–342 [Bibl. pp. 280–342].

—— (ed.). *Select Bibliography of South African Native Life and Problems.* London, 1941. [Physical Anthropology, pp. 1–22; Archaeology, 23–35; Ethnography, 36–109; Modern Status and Conditions, 110–204; Linguistics, 205–234.]

1. *GENERAL*

History.

BARTHEL, K. Völkerbewegungen auf der Südhälfte des afrikanischen Kontinents. *Mitt. Ver. Erdk. Lpz.* 1893, pp. 1–90; Bibl.

GALLOWAY, A. Man in Africa in the light of recent discoveries. *S. Afr. J. Sci.* vol. XXXIV (1937), pp. 89–120.

HEURICH, G. Restvölker und Rückzugsgebiete in Südafrika. *Mitt. Auslands-Hochschule* (Hamburg), vol. XXXIX, part III, pp. 46–110; Bibl.

KINGON, J. R. L. A survey of aboriginal place-names. *S. Afr. J. Sci.* vol. XV (1918), pp. 712–79.

LAING, G. D. The relationship between the Boskop, Bushman and Negro elements in the formation of the Native races of South Africa. *S. Afr. J. Sci.* vol. XXV (1926), pp. 905–8.

PETTMAN, C. *South African Place-Names Past and Present.* Queenstown (S. Africa), 1931.

STOW, G. W. *The Native Races of South Africa.* London, 1905.

TOOKE, W. H. Notes on the geographical distribution of the Hottentot and Bantu in South Africa. *Rec. Albany Mus.* (Grahamstown), vol. II (1913), pp. 353–90.

VEDDER, H. *Das alte Südwestafrika: Südwestafrikas Geschichte bis zum Tode Mahareros 1890*. Berlin, 1934. (Abridged English translation, 1938.)

Ethnography.

FRITSCH, G. *Die Eingeborenen Süd-Afrika's*. Breslau, 1872.
HUTCHINSON, H. and NANKIWELL, J. W. *South Africa. Its Land and Its Peoples*. 1934.
THEAL, G. M. *Ethnography and Condition of South Africa before A.D. 1505*. London, 1910.

2. *NON-BANTU PEOPLES*

(*a*) BUSHMEN

History.

STOW, G. W. *The Native Races of South Africa*. London, 1905, pp. 1–231.
VEDDER, H. *Das alte Südwestafrika*. Berlin, 1934, Part I, chaps. 2 and 3, and *passim*.

Ethnography.

BLEEK, DOROTHEA F. Bushmen of Central Angola. *Bantu Studies*, vol. III (1928), pp. 105–25.
—— *The Naron: a Bushman Tribe of the Central Kalahari*. Cambridge, 1928.
DORNAN, S. S. *Pygmies and Bushmen of the Kalahari*. London, 1925.
FOURIE, L. The Bushmen of South West Africa. In: *The Native Tribes of South-West Africa* (Cape Town, 1928), pp. 79–105.
IMMENROTH, W. *Kultur und Umwelt der Kleinwüchsigen in Afrika*. Leipzig, 1933, pp. 170–351; Bibl.
JONES, J. D. R. and DOKE, C. M. (eds.). *Bushmen of the Southern Kalahari*. Johannesburg, 1937.
KAUFMANN, H. Die Auin: ein Beitrag zur Buschmannforschung. *Mitt. dtsch. Schutzgeb.* vol. XXIII (1910), pp. 135–60.
LEBZELTER, V. *Eingeborenenkulturen in Südwest- und Südafrika*. Leipzig, 1934, pp. 5–105.
METZGER, F. *Narro and his Clan*. Windhoek, 1950.
PASSARGE, S. *Die Buschmänner der Kalahari*. Berlin, 1907.
SCHAPERA, I. *The Khoisan Peoples of South Africa: Bushmen and Hottentots*. London, 1930, pp. 75–220; Bibl.
WILHELM, J. H. Die !Kung-Buschleute. *Jb. Mus. Völkerk. Lpz.*, vol. XII (1953), pp. 91–189.
ZASTROW, B. VON and VEDDER, H. Die Buschmänner. In: *Das Eingeborenenrecht*, ed. E. Schultz-Ewerth and L. Adam (Stuttgart, 1930), vol. II, pp. 399–435.

(*b*) HOTTENTOTS

History.

DU PLESSIS, I. D. *The Cape Malays*. 1944.
HEWITT, J. Notes relating to the aboriginal tribes of the Eastern Province. *S. Afr. J. Sci.* vol. XVII (1920), pp. 304–21.
MAINGARD, L. F. The lost tribes of the Cape. *S. Afr. J. Sci.* vol. XXVIII (1931), pp. 487–504.
—— Studies in Korana history, customs and language. *Bantu Studies*, vol. VI (1932), pp. 103–62.
PETTMAN, C. Hottentot place-names. *S. Afr. J. Sci.* vol. XVII (1920), pp. 334–52; vol. XIX (1922), pp. 372–82.
STOW, G. W. *The Native Races of South Africa*. London, 1905. Pp. 232–315.
VEDDER, H. *Das alte Südwestafrika*. Berlin, 1934.

Ethnography.

ENGELBRECHT, J. A. *The Korana: an account of their customs and their history.* Capetown, 1936; Bibl.

HOERNLÉ, AGNES W. The social organization of the Nama Hottentots. *Amer. Anthrop.* vol. XXVII (1925), pp. 1–24.

KOLB(EN), P. *Caput Bonae Spei Hodiernum.* Nürnberg, 1719. New ed., entitled *Reise zum Vorgebirge der Guten Hoffnung*, ed. by P. Germann. Leipzig, 1922.

OLPP, J. Die rechtlichen und wirtschaftlichen Verhältnisse des Kowesi-Stämmes im Gross-Namaland. *Mitt. Ges. vergl. Rechts-u. Staatswiss.* vol. I (1896) pp. 162–88.

SCHAPERA, I. *The Khoisan Peoples of South Africa.* London, 1930. Pp. 223–418; Bibl.

—— (ed.). *The Early Cape Hottentots, described in the writings of Dapper, Ten Rhyne, and Grevenbroek.* Capetown, 1933 (Van Riebeeck Society Publications, no. 14).

SCHULTZE, L. *Aus Namaland und Kalahari.* Jena, 1907, pp. 170–549.

WANDRES, C. Ueber das Recht der Naman und Bergdaman. *Z. Kol. Pol.* vol. XI (1909), pp. 657–86.

—— Ueber Rechtsbewusstsein und Recht . . . der Hottentotten. *Z. Kol. Pol.* vol. XII (1910), pp. 269–81.

WIKAR, J. H. Report of a Journey along the Orange River, 1779. In: *The Journals of Wikar, Coetse and van Reenen*, ed. E. E. Mossop, pp. 20–219. Cape Town, 1935 (Van Riebeeck Society Publications, no. 15).

(*c*) BERGDAMA

History

VEDDER, H. *Das alte Südwestafrika.* Berlin, 1934.

Ethnography.

LEBZELTER, V. *Eingeborenenkulturen in Südwest- und Südafrika.* Leipzig, 1934, pp. 106–81.

VEDDER, H. *Die Bergdama.* 2 vols. Hamburg, 1923.

3. *BANTU-SPEAKING PEOPLES*

(*a*) GENERAL

History, Distribution, Groupings.

DOKE, C. M. *The Southern Bantu Languages.* London, 1954.

FOUCHE, L. *Mapungubwe: Ancient Bantu Civilization on the Limpopo.* Cambridge, 1937.

GREAT BRITAIN: WAR OFFICE. *The Native Tribes of the Transvaal.* London, 1905.

TRANSVAAL NATIVE AFFAIRS DEPARTMENT. *Short History of the Native Tribes of the Transvaal.* Pretoria, 1905.

VAN WARMELO, N. J. *A Preliminary Survey of the Bantu Tribes of South Africa.* Pretoria, 1935 (N.A.D. Ethnological Publications, no. 5).

—— *Language Map of South Africa.* Pretoria, 1952 (N.A.D. Ethnological Publications, no. 27).

Ethnography.

SCHAPERA, I. (ed.). *The Bantu-Speaking Tribes of South Africa: an Ethnographical Survey.* London, 1937; Bibl.

(*b*) NGUNI

History.

AYLIFF, J. and WHITESIDE, J. *History of the Abambo, Commonly known as "Fingos".* Butterworth, 1912.

BIRD, J. *The Annals of Natal, 1495–1845.* 2 vols. Pietermaritzburg, 1888.

BROWNLEE, F. *The Transkeian Native Territories: Historical Records*. Lovedale, 1923.
BRYANT, A. T. *Olden Times in Zululand and Natal*. London, 1929; Bibl.
GIBSON, J. Y. *The Story of the Zulus*. London, 1911.
KROPF, A. *Das Volk der Xosa-Kaffern im östlichen Südafrika*. Berlin, 1889, pp. 1–80.
MYBURGH, A. C. *The Tribes of Barberton District*. Pretoria, 1949 (N.A.D. Ethnological Publications, no. 25).
SOGA, J. H. *The South-Eastern Bantu*. Johannesburg, 1930.
VAN WARMELO, N. J. *History of Matiwane and the AmaNgwane Tribe*. Pretoria, 1938 (N.A.D. Ethnological Publications, no. 7).

Ethnography.

BRYANT, A. T. *The Zulu People*. Pietermaritzburg, 1949; Bibl.
CAPE OF GOOD HOPE. *Report and Proceedings . . . of the Government Commission on Native Laws and Customs*. Cape Town, 1883 (Parl. Papers G.4–1883).
COOK, P. A. W. *Social Organisation and Ceremonial Institutions of the Bomvana*. Cape Town, 1931.
FOURIE, H. C. M. *Amandebele van Fene-Mahlangu en hun religieus-social leven*. Zwolle, [1921].
GLUCKMAN, M. The Kingdom of the Zulu. In: *African Political Systems*, ed. M. Fortes and E. E. Evans-Pritchard (London, 1940), pp. 25–55.
HUNTER, MONICA. *Reaction to Conquest*. London, 1936. [Mpondo.]
ISAACS, N. *Travels and Adventures in Eastern Africa, descriptive of the Zoolus*. 2 vols. London, 1836.
KRIGE, EILEEN J. *The Social System of the Zulus*. London, 1936.
KROPF, A. *Das Volk der Xosa-Kaffern im östlichen Südafrika*. Berlin, 1889, pp. 80–209.
KUPER, HILDA. *An African Aristocracy*. London, 1947. [Swazi.]
—— *The Swazi*. London, 1952; Bibl.
LESTRADE, G. P. Some notes on the political organization of certain Xhosa-speaking tribes in the Transkeian Territories. *Trans. Roy. Soc. S. Afr.* vol. XXIV (1937), pp. 281–301.
LIENGME, G. Un potentat africain: Goungounyane et son règne. *Bull. Soc. neuchâtel Geogr.* vol. XIII (1901), pp. 99–135.
MACLEAN, J. (ed.). *A Compendium of Kafir Laws and Customs*. Mount Coke, 1858.
MARWICK, B. A. *The Swazi*. Cambridge, 1940.
SHOOTER, J. *The Kafirs of Natal and the Zulu Country*. London, 1857.
SOGA, J. H. *The Ama-Xosa: life and customs*. Lovedale, 1943.
SPECKMANN, F. *Die Hermannsburger Mission in Afrika*. Hermannsburg, 1876. [Zulu, pp. 88–178.]
WANGEMANN, T. *Die Geschichte der Berliner Mission im Zulu-Lande*. Berlin, 1875. [Ethnography, pp. 3–98.]

(*c*) TSONGA

History.

JUNOD, H. A. The Ba-Thonga of the Transvaal. *Addresses and Papers, Brit. and S. Afr. Ass. Adv. Sci.* vol. III (1905), pp. 222–62.
—— The condition of the Natives of South-East Africa in the sixteenth century, according to the early Portuguese documents. *S. Afr. J. Sci.* vol. X (1913), pp. 137–61.

Ethnography.

JUNOD, H. A. *The Life of a South African Tribe*. Revised ed. 2 vols. London, 1927.

(*d*) SOTHO

History.

BREUTZ, P. L. *The Tribes of Rustenburg and Pilansberg Districts*. Pretoria, 1953 (N.A.D. Ethnological Publications, no. 28).

BREUTZ, P. L. *The Tribes of Marico District*. Pretoria, 1953 (N.A.D. Ethnological Publications, no. 30).
—— *Die Stamme van die Distrik Ventersdorp*. Pretoria, 1954 (N.A.D. Ethnological Publications, no. 31).
ELLENBERGER, D. F. *History of the Basuto, Ancient and Modern*. London, 1912.
ELLENBERGER, V. F. History of the Ba-ga-Malete of Ramoutsa. *Trans. Roy. Soc. S. Afr.* vol. XXV (1937), pp. 1–72.
—— History of the BaTlôkwa of Gaberones. *Bantu Studies*, vol. XIII (1939), pp. 165–98.
HUNT, D. R. An account of the Bapedi. *Bantu Studies*, vol. V (1931), pp. 275–326.
KRIGE, J. D. Traditional origins and tribal relationships of the Sotho of the Northern Transvaal. *Bantu Studies*, vol. XI (1937), pp. 321–56.
KRÜGER, F. The Lovedu. *Bantu Studies*, vol. X (1936), pp. 89–105.
—— Tlôkwa traditions. *Bantu Studies*, vol. XI (1937), pp. 85–115.
LAGDEN, G. *The Basutos*. 2 vols. London, 1909.
LANGUAGE, F. J. Herkoms en Geskiedenis van die Tlhaping. *African Studies*, vol. I (1942), pp. 115–33.
MACGREGOR, J. C. *Basuto Traditions*. Cape Town, 1905.
MATTHEWS, Z. K. A short history of the Tshidi Barolong. *Fort Hare Papers*, vol. I (1945), pp. 9–28.
MOLEMA, S. M. *Chief Moroka: his life, his times, his country and his people*. Cape Town, [1951].
NETTELTON, G. E. History of the Ngamiland tribes up to 1926. *Bantu Studies*, vol. VIII (1934), pp. 343–60.
SCHAPERA, I. A short history of the BaKgatla-bagaKgafêla. *Communications from the School of African Studies* (University of Cape Town), n.s. no. 3 (1942).
—— A short history of the BaNgwaketse. *African Studies*, vol. I (1942), pp. 1–26.
—— Notes on the history of the Kaa. *African Studies*, vol. IV (1945), pp. 109–21.
SILLERY, A. *The Bechuanaland Protectorate*. Cape Town, 1952.
THEAL, G. M. *Basutoland Records*. 3 vols. Cape Town, 1882.
VAN WARMELO, N. J. *The Bakgatla ba ga Mosêtlha* (etc.). Pretoria, 1944 (N.A.D. Ethnological Publications, nos. 17–22).
—— *The Ba Letswalô or Banarene* (etc.). Pretoria, 1944 (N.A.D. Ethnological Publications, nos. 10–16).
—— *Die Tlôkwa en Birwa van Noord Transvaal*. Pretoria, 1953 (N.A.D. Ethnological Publications, no. 29).
ZIERVOGEL, D. *The Eastern Sotho*. Pretoria, 1954.

Ethnography.

ASHTON, H. *The Basuto*. London, 1952. Bibl.
CASALIS, E. *Les Bassoutos*. Paris, 1895.
DIETERLEN, H. and KOHLER, F. Les Bassoutos d'autrefois. In: *Livre d'Or de la Mission du Lessouto* (Paris, 1912), pp. 23–156.
HARRIES, C. H. L. *The Laws and Customs of the Bapedi and Cognate Tribes of the Transvaal*. Johannesburg, 1929.
HOFFMANN, C. Sotho-Texte aus dem Holzbuschgebirge in Transvaal. *Z. EingebSpr.* vols. XVIII, XIX, XXI, XXII, XXIII, XXIV, XXVIII (1927–38), *passim*.
KRIGE, EILEEN J. and J. D. *The Realm of a Rain-Queen*. London, 1943. [Lobedu.]
LANGUAGE, F. J. *Stamregering by die Tlhaping*. Stellenbosch, 1943. Bibl.
MACKENZIE, J. *Ten Years north of the Orange River*. Edinburgh, 1871. [Ngwato.]
MERENSKY, A. *Beiträge zur Kenntniss Südafrikas*. Berlin, 1875. [Pedi, pp. 90–141.]
SCHAPERA, I. *A Handbook of Tswana Law and Custom*. London, 1938; revised ed., 1955.
—— The political organization of the Ngwato in Bechuanaland Protectorate. In *African Political Systems*, ed. M. Fortes and E. E. Evans-Pritchard (London, 1940), pp. 36–82.

SCHAPERA, I. *Married Life in an African Tribe.* London, 1940. [Kgatla.]
—— *The Tswana.* London, 1953; Bibl.
SHEDDICK, V. G. J. *The Southern Sotho.* London, 1953; Bibl.
WILLOUGHBY, W. C. *Race Problems in the New Africa.* Oxford, 1923. [Tswana, pp. 46–138.]

(*e*) VENDA

History

LESTRADE, G. P. Some notes on the ethnic history of the BaVenda and their Rhodesian affinities. *S. Afr. J. Sci.* vol. XXIV (1927), pp. 486–95.
VAN WARMELO, N. J. *Contributions towards Venda History, Religion, and Tribal Ritual.* Pretoria, 1932 (N.A.D. Ethnological Publications, no. 3).
—— *The Copper Miners of Musina and the Early History of the Zoutpansberg.* Pretoria, 1940 (N.A.D. Ethnological Publications, no. 8).

Ethnography

LESTRADE, G. P. Some notes on the political organization of the Venda-speaking tribes. *Africa*, vol. III (1930), pp. 306–22.
STAYT, H. A. *The BaVenda.* London, 1931; Bibl.
VAN WARMELO, N. J. and PHOPHI, W. M. D. *Venda Law.* 4 vols. Pretoria, 1948–9 (N.A.D. Ethnological Publications, no. 23).

(*f*) SHONA

History.

CATON-THOMPSON, G. *The Zimbabwe Culture: Ruins and Reactions.* Oxford, 1931.
EDWARDS, W. The WaNoe: a short historical sketch. *Nada* (Salisbury, S. Rhodesia), vol. IV (1926), pp. 13–28.
MARCONNES, F. The Rozvis, or "Destroyers". *Nada*, vol. XI (1933), pp. 72–90.
SEED, J. H. A glimpse of Native history: the Vashawasha. *Nada*, vol. XIV (1936), pp. 5–16.
SICARD, H. VON. The origin of some of the tribes in the Belingwe Reserve. *Nada*, vols. XXV (1948), pp. 93–104; XXVII (1950), pp. 7–19; XXVIII (1951), pp. 5–25; XXIX (1952), pp. 43–64; XXX (1953), pp. 64–71; XXXII (1955), pp. 77–92. [In progress.]

Ethnography.

BULLOCK, C. *The Mashona and the Matabele.* Cape Town, 1950.
HOLLEMAN, J. F. Some "Shona" Tribes of Southern Rhodesia. In: *Seven Tribes of British Central Africa*, ed. E. Colson and M. Gluckman (London, 1951), pp. 354–95. Bibl.
—— *Shona Customary Law.* Cape Town, 1952.
POSSELT, F. W. T. *Fact and Fiction: a short account of the Natives of Southern Rhodesia.* Bulawayo, 1935.

(*g*) HERERO

History.

VEDDER, H. *Das alte Südwestafrika.* Berlin, 1934.

Ethnography.

FRANCOIS, H. VON. *Nama und Damara.* Magdeburg, [1896]. (History, pp. 100–5; ethnography, pp. 159–202).
IRLE, I. *Die Herero.* Gütersloh, 1906.
SCHINZ, H. *Deutsch-Südwest-Afrika.* Oldenburg-Leipzig, [1891]. Pp. 141–202.
ZASTROW, B. VON. Die Herero. In: *Das Eingeborenenrecht*, ed. E. Schultz-Ewerth and L. Adam (Stuttgart, 1930), vol. II, pp. 213–68.

(*h*) Ambo

History.

Vedder, H. *Das alte Südwestafrika.* Berlin, 1934. Pp. 66–77, 159–72.

Ethnography.

Hahn, C. H. L. The Ovambo. In: *The Native Tribes of South West Africa* (Cape Town, 1928), pp. 1–36.

Lebzelter, V. *Eingeborenenkulturen in Südwest- und Südafrika.* Leipzig, 1934. Pp. 188–252.

Tönjes, H. *Ovamboland: Land, Leute, Mission.* Berlin, 1911.

SECTION III. AFRICA IN ANCIENT AND MEDIEVAL TIMES

(Chapter III)

(*a*) Original Sources

Abulfeda. Géographie d'Aboulféda, Trans. M. Reinaud. Paris, 1848.

Breasted, J. H. *Ancient Records of Egypt.* Chicago, 1906–7.

Idrísí. *Description de l'Afrique et de l'Espagne.* Trans. R. Dozy and M. de Goeje. Leyden, 1866.

Herodotus. *Histories.* Books i–iii, ed. A. H. Sayce; Books iv–ix, ed. R. W. Macan. 1883–1908.

Note also How, W. W. and Wells, J. *A Commentary on Herodotus.* Oxford, 1912.

Masudi. (i) Meynard, B. de et Courteille, P. de. *Maçoudi. Les Prairies d'Or. Texte et Traduction.* Société Asiatique. Paris, 1861–77.

—— (ii) Sprenger, A. *El Masudi's Historical Encylcopaedia.* Oriental Translation Fund, 1841.

Müller, C. *Geographi Graeci Minores.* Vol. i (contains Hanno's "Periplus", "Scylax", and the anonymous "Periplus") and vol. iii (Tabulae). Paris, 1855.

Periplus of the Erythraean Sea. See Müller, *Geog. Gr. Min.* as above; also translation by W. H. Schoff. New York, 1912.

Pliny. *Natural History.* Ed. L. Ian and C. Mayhoff. Leipzig, 1870–1909.

Polo, Marco, *The Book of Ser Marco Polo.* Trans. and ed. H. Yule. 2 vols. 1903.

—— *The Travels of Marco Polo.* Translated from the Text of L. F. Benedetto by A. Ricci. 1931.

Pomponius Mela. *De Chorographia.* Ed. C. Frick. Leipzig, 1880.

Ptolemy. *Geography.* Ed. C. Müller. Paris, 1883–1901.

Strabo. *Geographica.* Ed. and trans. H. L. Jones. 1927–32.

Theal, G. McCall. *Records of South-Eastern Africa.* Vol. i. Cape Town, 1898.

Warmington, E. H. *Greek Geography.* 1934.

Contains passages translated from Greek geographical sources down to Strabo.

(*b*) Modern Works

Beazley, (Sir) C. Raymond. *The Dawn of Modern Geography.* 3 vols. 1897–1906.

Bent, J. T. *The Ruined Cities of Mashonaland.* 1895.

Berger, H. *Geschichte der wissenschaftlichen Erdkunde der Griechen.* 2nd ed. Leipzig, 1887–93.

Bunbury, E. *History of Ancient Geography.* 1879.

Cary, M. and Warmington, E. H. *The Ancient Explorers.* 1929.

Caton-Thompson, G. *The Zimbabwe Culture: ruins and reactions.* 1931.

Cipriani, L. *Le Antiche Rovine e Miniere della Rhodesia.* Florence, 1932.

Fouche, L. *Mapumgubwe.* 1937.

Gaffarel, P. Les voyages d'Eudoxe, in *Mémoires de la Société d'Emulation du Doubs,* N. Sér., vii, 17 *sqq.* Besançon, 1872.

HALL, R. N. and NEAL, W. G. *The Ancient Ruins of Rhodesia.* 1904.
HALL, R. N. *Great Zimbabwe.* 1905.
—— *Prehistoric Rhodesia.* 1909.
HENNIG, R. *Von rätselhaften Ländern.* Munich, 1925.
KEANE, A. H. *The Gold of Ophir.* 1901.
LA RONCIÈRE, C. BOUREL DE. *La Découverte de l'Afrique au Moyen Age.* 2 vols. Cairo, 1924–5.
MACIVER, D. RANDALL. *Medieval Rhodesia.* 1906.
MÜLLER, W. *Die Umsegelung Afrikas.* Rathenau, 1889.
OORDT, J. F. VAN. *Who were the Builders of Great Zimbabwe? A Study.* Cape Town. 1906.
PETERS, C. *King Solomon's Golden Ophir.* 1899.
—— *Ophir nach den neuesten Forschungen.* Berlin, 1908.
RENNELL, J. *The Geographical System of Herodotus.* 2nd ed. 1830.
TOZER, H. F. *History of Ancient Geography.* 2nd ed. Cambridge, 1935.
WHEELER, J. *The Geography of Herodotus.* 1854.

SECTION IV. THE PORTUGUESE IN SOUTH AFRICA

(Chapter IV)

(*a*) COLLECTIONS OF DOCUMENTS

Alguns documentos do Archivo Nacional da Torre do Tombo acerca das navegações e conquistas portuguezas. Lisbon, 1892.
Annaes Maritimos e Coloniaes. 6 vols. Lisbon, 1840–6.
Archivo Portuguez Oriental. 9 vols. Nova Goa, 1857–76.
Bullarium patronatus Portugalliae Regum, vols. I, II. Lisbon, 1868–70.
Livros das Monções. 4 vols. Lisbon, 1880–93.
Memorias do Ultramar, ed. L. CORDEIRO. 6 numbers. Lisbon, 1881.
PAIVA MANSO, VISCONDE DE. *Historia do Congo (Documentos).* Lisbon, 1877.
SILVEIRA, D. GONÇALO DE, *Cartas* in PAIVA E PONA, A. P. DE, *Dos primeiros trabalhos dos Portuguezes no Monomotapa.* Lisbon, 1892.
THEAL, G. McC. *Records of South-Eastern Africa.* 9 vols. Cape Town, 1898–1903.
WELCH, S. R. *Some unpublished Manuscripts relating to the history of South and East Africa.* Pretoria, 1930.

(*b*) CONTEMPORARY HISTORIES

BARBOSA, DUARTE. *The Book of*, trans. by M. L. DAMES. 2 vols. Hakluyt Society. London, 1918–21.
BARRETO DE RESENDE, P. *Livro do Estado de India Oriental.* Brit. Mus. Sloane MS. 197, with plans and descriptions of fortresses in Africa and Asia.
BARROS, J. DE. *Da Asia.* 8 vols. Lisbon, 1778.
BOCARRO, A. *Decada 13, da Historia da India.* Lisbon, 1876.
CASTANHEDA, F. L. DE. *Historia do descobrimento e conquista da India.* 4 vols. Lisbon, 1924–33.
CAVAZZI, PE. G. A. *Istorica descrizione de tre regni Congo, Matamba e Angola.* Milan, 1690.
Collecção de noticias para a historia e geographia das nações ultramarinas. 7 vols. Lisbon, 1812–41.
CONCEIÇÃO, A. DE. Tratado dos Rios de Cuama (1696) in *O Chronista de Tissuary*, vol. II. Nova Goa, 1867.
CORREA, G. *Lendas da India.* 8 vols. Lisbon, 1858–66.
COUTO, D. DO. *Da Asia.* 13 vols. Lisbon, 1778.
— *Soldado pratico.* Lisbon, 1790.
DURAN, A. *Cercos de Moçambique defendidos por D. Estevam de Attayde.* Madrid, 1633.

Espirito Santo, D. do. *Breve relação das Christandades que os Religiosos do nosso Padre J. Agostinho teem a sua conta nos partes de Oriente.* Lisbon, 1630.

Faria e Sousa, M. de. *Asia Portugueza.* 3 vols. Lisbon, 1666–74.

Figueiredo Falcão, L. de. *Livro em que se contem toda a Fazenda dos Reinos de Portugal, India e Ilhas.* Lisbon, 1859.

Freitas, S. de. *De justo Imperio Lusitanorum Asiatico.* Valladolid, 1625; republished 1925.

Goes, D. de. *Cronica do felicissimo Rei D. Manoel.* 2 vols. Coimbra, 1925–6.

Hakluyt, R. *The Principal Navigations, Voyages, Traffiques and Discoveries of the English Nation.* (Maclehose edn.) 12 vols. Glasgow, 1903–5.

Historia Tragico-Maritima. 2 vols. Lisbon, 1735–6.

Lopes, D. *Relatione del Reame di Congo . . .* per Filippo Pigafetta. Rome, 1591. Eng. trans. by M. Hutchinson, 1881.

Mariano, Luis. Exploração Portuguesa de Madagascar em 1613 in *Bol. da Soc. de Geog. de Lisboa*, vol. vii, p. 313.

Oliveira Cadornega A. de. *Historia Geral das Guerras Angolanas*, vol. ii. Lisbon, 1902.

Owen, W. F. D. "The Arab Chronicle of Mombasa," trans. in Owen, Captain. *Narrative of Voyages*, vol. i. 1833.

Pacheco Pereira, D. *Esmeraldo de situ orbis*, ed. E. da Silva Dias. Lisbon, 1905.

Salil-ibn-Razik. *History of the Imams and Seyyids of Oman*, ed. G. P. Badger. Hakluyt Society. 1871.

Santos, J. de. *Ethiopia Oriental.* 2 vols. Lisbon, 1891.

Silveira, F. R. *Memorias de um soldado da India*, ed. A. de S. S. Costa Lobo. Lisbon, 1877.

Sousa, Frei Luis de. *Historia de S. Domingos.* 6 vols. Lisbon, 1866.

Strong, S. A. "The history of Kilwa", Arabic text with introduction in *Journal of Royal Asiatic Society*, 1895.

(*c*) Modern Works

Almeida, F. de. *Historia da Igreja em Portugal.* 8 vols. Coimbra, 1910–24.

Almeida d'Eca. *Normas economicas na colonização Portuguesa.* Coimbra, 1921.

Azevedo, J. L. de. *Epocas de Portugal economico.* Lisbon, 1929.

Bordalo, F. M. *Ensaio sobre a estatistica de Moçambique.* Lisbon, 1859.

Botelho de Sousa, A. *Subsidios para a Historia Militar Maritima da India*, Vol. i (1585–1605). Lisbon, 1930.

Caton-Thompson, G. *The Zimbabwe Culture.* Oxford, 1931.

Chadwick, H. *Life of the Venerable Gonçalo da Silveira.* Roehampton, 1910.

Consiglieri Pedroso, L. *Catalogo Bibliographico das publicações relativas aos descubrimentos portugueses.* Lisbon, 1912.

Cordeiro, L. *Diogo Cão.* Lisbon, 1892.

Cortezão, J. *A expedição de Pedro Alvares Cabral.* Lisbon, 1922.

Costa Quintella, T. da. *Annaes da marinha Portugueza.* 2 vols. Lisbon, 1839–40.

Felner, A. de A. *Angola.* Coimbra, 1933.

Feo Cardoso, J. C. *Memorias . . . de Angola.* Paris, 1825.

Ficalho, Conde de. *Viagens de Pedro de Covilhã.* Lisbon, 1898.

Fonseca, Quirino da. *Os Portugueses no Mar.* Lisbon, 1925.

La Roncière, C. Bourel de. *La découverte de l'Afrique au Moyen Age.* 3 vols. Cairo, 1924–7.

Peringuey, L. *Inscriptions left by early European navigators on their way to the East.* Cape Town, 1913.

Prestage, E. *The Portuguese Pioneers.* 1933.

Ravenstein, E. G. *The strange adventures of Andrew Battell.* Hakluyt Society, 1901.

—— The Voyages of Diogo Cão and Bartholomeu Dias. *Geog. Journal*, December, 1900.

Rodrigues, F. *Historia da Companhia de Jesus na Assistencia de Portugal.* 2 vols. Oporto, 1931.
Sousa Viterbo, F. M. de. *Trabalhos nauticos dos Portugueses nos seculos XVI e XVII.* 2 vols. Lisbon, 1898–1900.
Teixeira Botelho, J. J. *Historia Militar e Politica dos Portugueses em Moçambique da descoberta a* 1833. Lisbon, 1934.
Theal, G. McCall. *The Portuguese in South Africa from* 1505 *to* 1795. 1927.
Welch, S. R. *Europe's Discovery of South Africa.* Cape Town, 1935.
Whiteway, R. S. *The rise of the Portuguese power in India,* 1497 *to* 1550. 1899.

SECTION V. CAPE COLONY UNDER THE NETHERLANDS EAST INDIA COMPANY

(Chapters V and VI)

(*a*) Documentary Material

Official (Dutch).

The papers of the Dutch East India Company are to be found in the Koloniaal Archief, a department of the Rijksarchief at the Hague. Important series of extracts have been published by J. K. J. de Jonge in *De Opkomst van het Nederlandsche Gezag in Oost-Indië,* 13 vols. 's Gravenhage, 1862–88, and by P. A. Tiele and J. E. Heeres, *Bouwstoffen voor de Geschiedenis der Nederlanders in den Maleischen Archipel,* 3 vols. 's Gravenhage, 1886–95.

Official (South African). See Part I, B 1; Part II, 1 (*a*), Part II, 1 (*d*).

The Union Archives at Cape Town contain all the papers of the Company addressed to, or originating in, South Africa (originals and copies respectively) from the foundation of the Colony to 1795. See Part II, 1 (*d*) above for details of the volumes of extracts and copies of documents in the Union Archives which have appeared in print. The Historisch Genootschap of Utrecht has published the official Diary of Van Riebeeck, *Dagverhaal van Jan van Riebeek,* 3 vols. Utrecht, 1884–93; the spelling has been modernised and there is no index.

(*b*) Contemporary Authorities

Barrow, (Sir) J. *Travels into the Interior of Southern Africa.* 2nd ed. 2 vols. 1806.
Boers, W. C. *Verantwoording gedaan maken, ende aan de Wel-Edele Hoog Achtbare Heeren Bewindhebberen der Generale Geoctroyeerde Oost-Indische Compagnie ... op ende jegens zodanige niet minder læsive, als disrespectueuse Memoire als door J. van Rhenen, B. J. Artoys ... T. Roos en N. G. Heyns ... geprœsenteert.* 1782.

A copy of the above is in the South African Public Library, Cape Town.

—— *Advies van de Juridische Faculteit te Leiden (over de Procedures, ongedecideert hangende voor den ... Raad van Justitie aan Cabo de Goede Hoop, tusschen ... W. C. Boers ... en den Burger Jan Smit Jurriaansz).* Amsterdam, 1783.

A copy of the above is in the South African Public Library, Cape Town.

Bogaert, A. *Historische Reizen door d'Oostersche Deelen van Asia.* Amsterdam, 1711.

Contains an excellent account of the troubles between the Colonists and W. A. van der Stel. The author was in active sympathy with the Colonists and obtained his information from them.

Brink, C. F. *Nouvelle Description du Cap de Bonne-Espérance.* Amsterdam, 1778.
Dapper, O. *Naukeurige Beschrijvinge der Afrikaensche Gewesten.* Amsterdam, 1668.
Fouché, L. (Ed.). *Uit die Journael van Gysbert Heeck, anno* 1655. Pretoria, 1910.
—— *The Diary of Adam Tas* (1705–6)*: with an enquiry into the Complaints of the Colonists against the Governor W. A. van der Stel.* 1914.

Gewigtige Aanmerkingen over de Klagten en Bezwaaren der Kaapsche Burgerij bij H. H. Mogenden de Heeren Staaten Generaal ingeleeverd. Delft, 1786.

GODÉE-MOLSBERGEN, E. C. (Ed.). *Reizen in Zuid-Afrika in de Hollandse Tijd.* 4 vols. 's Gravenhage, 1916–32.

KOLB[EN], P. *Caput Bonæ Spei Hodiernum.* Nürnberg, 1719.

LICHTENSTEIN, M. H. C. *Reisen im südlichen Afrika.* 2 vols. Berlin, 1811–12.

The references in the text are to the translation by A. PLUMTRE, 1812–15.

PALLANDT, Baron A. VAN. *General remarks on the Cape of Good Hope* [1803], translated from the French. Cape Town, 1917.

PRINS, J. *Das Württembergische Kaapsregiment,* 1786–1802. *Die Tragödie einer Söldnerschar.* Stuttgart, 1932.

REENEN, J. VAN, ARTOYS, B. J., etc. *Memorie, gedaan maken en aan den Wel Edele Groot Achtbare Heeren gecommitte de bewindhebberen, der Gernerale Geoctroyeerde Nederlandsche O.I. Compagnie, ter Vergadering van Zeventienen binnen Amsterdam. Overgegeven uit de Namen en van wegens Jacobus van Reenen ... Barend Jacob Artoys ... Tielman Roos en Nicolaas Godfried Heyns, alle Vryburgeren aan Cabo de Goede Hoop.* Amsterdam, 1783.

A copy of this book is in the South African Public Library.

—— *Nadere Memorie....* Amsterdam, 1782.

A copy of this is in the South African Public Library.

SPARRMAN, A. *A Voyage to the Cape of Good Hope.* 2 vols. 1785.

STAVORINUS, J. S. *Voyages to the East Indies* ... translated ... by S. H. Wilcocke. 3 vols. 1798.

STEL, W. A. VAN DER. *Korte Deductie van Willem Adriaan van der Stel.* Amsterdam, 1708.

—— *Contra Deductie ofte grondige Demonstratie van de Valsheit der uitgegevene Deductie bij ... W. A. van der Stel.* Amsterdam, 1712.

—— *De Regte en Waare oorsprong en gevolg der laatste Onlusten, aan Caab van Goede Hoop voorgevallen: Historieel opgemaakt uit de eigene Stukken en Bewijzen van den Edelen ... Heere Willem Adriaan van der Stel ... Bestaande kn Neutraale Gedagten over desself Deductie.* Amsterdam, 1712.

Copies of the above three volumes are in the South African Public Library.

VALENTYN, F. *Beschrijving van Oud en Nieuw Oost-Indien,* vol. V, pt. 2, Dordrecht, 1726.

Van Riebeeck Society Publications. 1. *The Reports of Chavonnes and his Council and of Van Imhoff on the Cape.* 2. *Life at the Cape in the Mid-Eighteenth Century, by O. F. Mentzel.* 3. *The Memorandum of Commissary J. A. de Mist.* 4 and 6. *A ... Description of the Cape ... by O. F. Mentzel.* 5. *Collectanea.* 10 and 11. *Travels in Southern Africa ... by M. H. C. Lichtenstein.* 12. *Journals of Olof Bergh* (1682) *and* 1683) *and Isaq Schrijver* (1689).

WATERHOUSE, G. (Ed.). *Simon van der Stel's Journal of his Expedition to Namaqualand,* 1685–1686. Dublin, 1932.

(*c*) LATER WORKS

See also Part II, 1 (*e*) and (*f*)

Archives Year Book, 1946: *Personalia of the Germans at the Cape,* 1652–1806.

BEYERS, C. *Die Kaapse Patriotte,* 1779–1791. Kaapstad, 1930.

BLOK, P. J. *Geschiedenis van het Nederlandsche Volk,* vols. VI and VII. Groningen, 1907.

BOTHA, C. G. The Dispersion of the Stock Farmers ... in the 18th Century, *and* Prices in the 18th Century. *South African Journal of Science,* vol. XX, 1923.

—— *Early Cape Land Tenure.* Cape Town, 1919.

—— *The French Refugees at the Cape.* Cape Town, 1919.

Brakel, S. van. *De Hollandsche Handelscompagnieën der Zeventiende Eeuw.* 's Gravenhage, 1908.
Colenbrander, H. T. *Koloniale Geschiedenis.* 3 vols. 's Gravenhage, 1925–6.
Dehérain, H. *Le Cap de Bonne-Espérance au XVIIe Siècle.* Paris, 1909.
Dominicus, F. C. *Het Ontslag van W. A. van der Stel.* Rotterdam, 1928.
Encyclopaedie van Neerlands Indië. 2 vols. 's Gravenhage, 1911.
Includes an excellent sketch of the Dutch E.I. Co. by J. E. Heeres. There is a new edition, 1917–21, but the references given in the text are to the first edition.
Fouché, L. *Onze Eerste Scholen.* Pretoria, 1910.
—— *Die Evolutie van die Trekboer.* Pretoria, 1909.
Geyer, A. L. *Das wirtschaftliche System der niederländischen ostindischen Kompanie am Kap der Guten Hoffnung*, 1785–95. München, 1923.
Klerk de Reus, G. C. *Geschichtlicher Überblick der administrativen, rechtlichen und finanziellen Entwicklung der Niederländisch-Ostindischen Compagnie.* 's Gravenhage, 1895.
Marais, J. S., *Maynier and the First Boer Republic.* 1944.
Müller, P. K. *Georg Schmidt.* 1923.
Nathan, M., *The Huguenots in South Africa.* 1939.
Robertson, H. M. Some doubts concerning early Land Tenure at the Cape. *S.A. Journal of Economics*, June 1935; The Economic Development of the Cape under van Riebeeck, *S.A.J.E.*, Dec. 1945.
Roux, P. E. *Die Verdedigingstelsel aan die Kaap* . . . 1652–1795. Stellenbosch, 1925.
Walt, A. J. H. van der. *Die Ausdehnung der Kolonie am Kap der Guten Hoffnung* (1700–1779). Berlin, 1928.
Wieringa, P. A. C. *De oudste Boeren-Republieken: Graaff-Reinet en Zwellendam van* 1775 *tot* 1806. 's Gravenhage, 1921.

SECTION VI. THE CAPE DURING THE REVOLUTIONARY AND NAPOLEONIC WARS, 1795–1815

(Chapters VII and VIII)

(*a*) Manuscripts

1. *Public Record Office*

See Part I, A 1, particularly B.T. 1/34, 67, 77, 90, 111, 114, 127; B.T. 5/10, 17, 20, 21, 22, 23, 25, 26, 28; P.C. 2/170, 173, 180, 192, 196, 202. The Colonial Office correspondence for this period, together with relevant despatches from the Admiralty, War Office and other departmental files, is printed in Theal's *Records of the Cape Colony*, but it is to be noted that marginal annotations by the Secretary of State and other officials are omitted.

2. *Other collections*

See Part I, A 2, particularly

Letters of Lord Macartney (South African MSS., Rhodes House Library, Oxford).
Miscellaneous Correspondence of Henry Dundas, 1st Viscount Melville (Melville MSS., Rhodes House Library, Oxford).

(*b*) Parliamentary Papers

See Part I, A 3, particularly

5th Report from the Select Committee of the House of Commons on Finance, 1819, *Appendix IV; Parl. Pap.* 1819, II (529).
Report from the Select Committee of the House of Commons on the Poor Laws, 1819; *Parl. Pap.* 1819, II (539).

(c) Printed Collections

Historical Manuscripts Commission. *Report on the MSS. of Earl Bathurst, preserved at Cirencester Park.* H.M. Stationery Office, 1923.

—— *Report on the MSS. of J. B. Fortescue, preserved at Dropmore* (13*th Rept., App.*, pt. III; 14*th Rept., App.*, pt. V; and *Rept.*, vols. III–X). H.M. Stationery Office, 10 vols. 1892–1927. Chiefly important in this connection for correspondence of Grenville and Dundas relating to the British occupation and retention of the Cape.

Leibbrandt, H. C. V. (Ed.). *The Rebellion of* 1815, *generally known as Slachter's Nek.* Cape Town, 1902.

Londonderry, Robert Stewart, Viscount Castlereagh, 2nd Marquis of. *Memoirs and Correspondence*, ed. C. W. Vane-Stewart, 3rd Marquis of Londonderry. 12 vols. 1848–53.

Navy Records Society. *The Keith Papers*, vol. I (*Publications*, vol. LXII). 1927.

—— The second capture of the Cape (in *Publications*, vol. LXIII). 1928.

Windham, William. *The Windham Papers*, ed. A. P. Primrose, 5th Earl of Rosebery. 2 vols. 1913.

(d) Contemporary Works

Barrow, John. *Some Account of the Public Life, and a Selection from the Unpublished Writings of the Earl of Macartney.* 2 vols. 1807.

—— *Travels into the Interior of Southern Africa.* 2nd ed. 2 vols. 1806.

Bird, W. W. *State of the Cape of Good Hope in* 1822, ed. H. T. Colebrooke. 1923.

Bird was Comptroller of the Customs at the Cape and supplies valuable economic data.

Burchell, William J. *Travels in the Interior of Southern Africa.* 2 vols. 1822–4.

Campbell, John. *Travels in South Africa.* 3rd ed. 1815.

De Mist, J. A. *The Memorandum of Commissary J. A. De Mist, containing Recommendations for the . . . Government at the Cape of Good Hope*, 1802 (Van Riebeeck Society, *Publications*, No. 3). 1920.

Fisher, R. B. *The Importance of the Cape of Good Hope.* 1814. 3rd ed. 1816.

Janssens, J. W. *Bepalingen en Instructiën voor het bestuur van de Buitendistricten van de Kaap de Goede Hoop*, 1805. Amsterdam, 1922.

Lichtenstein, M. H. C. *Travels in Southern Africa in the years* 1803–6. (Van Riebeeck Society, *Publications*, nos. 10, 11.) 1928–30.

Neethling, C. L. *Onderzoek van 't verhaal van A. J. Sluysken.* 's Gravenhage, 1797.

Pallandt, Baron A. van. *General Remarks on the Cape of Good Hope* [1803], *translated from the French.* Cape Town, 1917.

Percival, R. *An Account of the Cape of Good Hope.* 1804.

Popham, Sir Home. *Minutes of a Court Martial . . . for the Trial of Sir Home Popham.* 1807.

Sluysken, A. J. *Verhaal gehouden bij . . . A. J. Sluysken zeedert het arrivement der Engelsche vloot . . .* 1795. 's Gravenhage, 1797.

Stockenstrom, Sir Andries. *Autobiography*, ed. C. W. Hutton, 2 vols. Cape Town, 1887.

Theal, G. McC. (Ed.). *Belangrijke historische dokumenten.* 3 vols. 1896–1911.

Vol. III contains material for the period 1795–1806.

Van der Kemp, J. T. *Memoir of the late Rev. J. T. van der Kemp.* London Missionary Society. 1812.

(e) Later Works

Barnard, Lady Anne. *South Africa a Century Ago. Letters written from the Cape,* 1795–1801. Cape Town, 1925.

Cobban, A. B. C. *Ambassadors and Secret Agents: the diplomacy of the First Earl of Malmesbury at the Hague.* 1954.

EDWARDS, I. E. *The* 1820 *Settlers in South Africa.* 1934.
FAIRBRIDGE, D. *Lady Anne Barnard at the Cape of Good Hope*, 1797–1802. Oxford, 1924.
FURBER, H. *Henry Dundas, First Viscount Melville*, 1742–1811. 1934.
CRAWFORD AND BALCARRES, A. W. C. LINDSAY, Earl of. *Lives of the Lindsays.* 2nd ed. 3 vols. 1849.
HEERES, J. E. *De Overgang der Kaapkolonie van Nederland in Engeland's bezit.* 1897.
LEIBBRANDT, H. C. V. *The Rebellion of* 1815 *generally known as Slachter's Nek.* Cape Town. 1902.
MANNING, HELEN TOFT. *British Colonial Government after the American Revolution*, 1782–1820. New Haven, 1933.
MARAIS, J. S. *Maynier and the First Boer Republic.* Cape Town, 1944.
MARTIN, A. D. *Doctor van der Kemp.* 1931.
MERWE, J. P. VAN DER. *Die Kaap onder die Bataafse Republiek* (1803–6). 1906.
REYBURN, H. A. Studies in Cape Frontier History. *The Critic* (Cape Town), Oct. 1934; Jan., April, July 1935.
ROBERTS, M. *Lord Charles Somerset and the "Beaufort Influence".* Archives Year Book for S. African History, 1951. vol. II, pp. 1–34.
ROBSON, W. H. New light on Lord Castlereagh's diplomacy. *Jour. Mod. Hist.*, III (1931), pp. 198–218.
VAN OORDT, J. W. G. *Slagter's nek.* Amsterdam, Pretoria, 1897.
WILKIN, W. H. *Life of Sir David Baird.* 1912.

SECTION VII. SLAVERY AT THE CAPE 1652–1838

(Chapter XI)

(*a*) CONTEMPORARY AUTHORITIES

1. MANUSCRIPT SOURCES: Official. See Part I, B 1 (*a*)

The manuscript papers in the Archives Depot at Cape Town dealing directly with the subject of slavery consist, in the main, of records of the Slave Registration Office established in 1816 under the control of an Inspector of Slaves. From 1830, separate offices existed for the eastern and western divisions of the Colony, and in each division the officer in charge was henceforth officially described as "Registrar and Protector of Slaves". The Cape Town Office was retained until 1838 to facilitate the adjustment of claims to compensation under the Act of Emancipation.

There are 43 volumes of *Letters Received* and 13 of *Letters Despatched.* Statistical information as to the number, value and condition of slaves in the various districts is contained in the 34 volumes of *Returns of Slaves* and in the separate volumes designated *Sales and Manumission.* The *Reports* and *Confidential Reports* of the Protector of Slaves are largely concerned with the treatment of slaves and are supplemented by volumes of *Slave Complaints* and *Judicial Proceedings.* There are 9 volumes of *Compensation Claims* and a supplementary volume of *Awards.*

For the period before 1806 there are miscellaneous papers, chiefly concerned with Government-owned slaves and the administration of the Slave Lodge, which have been filed with the later records of the Registration Office. References to slavery and its regulation recur frequently in the records of other departments.

2. OFFICIAL DOCUMENTS: Printed. See Part I, A 3; Part I, A 4 and Part II, 1 (*d*)

DE MIST, J. A. *Memorandum of Commissary J. A. de Mist.* (Van Riebeeck Society, *Publications*, No. 3.) 1920.
Reports of Chavonnes . . . and of Van Imhoff on the Cape. (Van Riebeeck Society, *Publications*, No. 1.) 1918.

3. Newspapers. See Part II, 1 (*c*)

British.

Anti-Slavery Reporter, vols. I–VI, 30 June 1825–July 1836, contains articles and reports on Slavery at the Cape of Good Hope, viz. I, no. 28, pp. 289–96; II, no. 22, p. 444; III, no. 6, pp. 139–42; IV, no. 11, pp. 329–30; IV, no. 14, pp. 377–84; VI, no. 8, p. 339.

British Review, December 1821, no. XXXVI, contains an article on the state of the foreign slave trade.

South African.

Journal of Secondary Education, Transvaal, vol. XI, nos. 43–4, contains "Replies to the Questions on the importation, etc., of slaves into the colony; proposed by His Excellency the Earl of Macartney, etc., etc. by W. S. v. Ryneveld . . . 1797".

4. Books and Pamphlets

Account of the Cape of Good Hope. 1819.

Contains useful statistical tables.

Barrow, J. *Travels into the Interior of Southern Africa.* 2nd ed. 2 vols. 1806.

Bird, W. W. *State of the Cape of Good Hope in* 1822. 1823.

Cape of Good Hope Philanthropic Society. *Annual Reports.* Cape Town, 1828–32.

Chase, J. C. *Practical considerations on the exact position of the slave question.* Cape Town, 1831.

Fairbairn, J. *Five Papers on the slave question.* Cape Town, 1831.

Fawcett, J. *Account of an eighteen months' residence at the Cape of Good Hope.* Cape Town, 1836.

Fisher, R. B. *The Importance of the Cape of Good Hope as a colony to Great Britain.* 3rd ed. 1816.

The author, a brother of the Bishop of Salisbury, was a friend of Sir John Cradock.

Lichtenstein, M. H. C. *Travels in Southern Africa in the years* 1803–6. (Van Riebeeck Society, *Publications*, nos. 10, 11.) 1928–30.

Miller, T. *Considerations on the exact position of the slave question.* Cape Town, 1831.

Miller was acting-clerk to the Council. He makes a moderate appeal to Cape proprietors to emancipate their slaves.

Negro Apprenticeship in the British Colonies. 1838.

Discusses from the humanitarian point of view the conditions of apprenticeship 1834–38.

Percival, R. *An account of the Cape of Good Hope.* 1804.

Proceedings in the House of Commons on slavery at the Cape of Good Hope. 1822.

A pamphlet reprinting the substance of speeches in the House of Commons on Cape slavery, with some comments. In the humanitarian interest.

Remarks on the demoralising influence of slavery, by a Resident at the Cape of Good Hope. 1828.

In the Library of the Anti-Slavery and Aborigines Protection Society, London, and in the South African Public Library, Cape Town.

Rose, Cowper. *Four Years in Southern Africa.* 1829.

Slave Colonies of Great Britain. 1826.

Gives an abstract of various parliamentary papers, with comments on Lord Charles Somerset's Proclamation of March 1823.

Wright, W. *Slavery at the Cape of Good Hope.* 1831.

Reports many trials of owners for cruel treatment of slaves.

(b) Later Works

See Part II, 1 (e)

Burn, W. L. *Emancipation and Apprenticeship in British West Indies.* 1937.
Coupland, R. *The British Anti-Slavery Movement.* 1933.
—— *Wilberforce.* Oxford, 1923.
Dehérain, H. *Le Cap de Bonne-Espérance au XVIIe Siècle.* Paris, 1909.
—— *L'Expansion des Boers au XIXe Siecle.* Paris, 1905.
Edwards, I. E. *Towards Emancipation.* 1942.
Halèvy, E. *L'Angleterre en* 1815. Paris, 1923. English translation, *A History of the English People in* 1815. 1924.

Analyses the humanitarian movement in England.

Harris, (Sir) J. *A Century of Emancipation.* 1933.
Hattersley, A. F. The Emancipation of Slaves at the Cape. *History*, VIII (Oct. 1923), pp. 180–6.

Discusses the question whether slavery could have been abolished by action at the Cape without the intervention of the Imperial Parliament.

Klingberg, F. J. *The Anti-Slavery Movement in England.* 1926.
MacInnes, C. M. *England and Slavery.* 1934.
Macmillan, W. M. *The Cape Colour Question.* 1927.
Mathieson, W. L. *British Slavery and its Abolition.* 1926.
—— *British Slave Emancipation*, 1838–49. 1932.
Wastell, R. E. P. *History of Slave Compensation*, 1833–45. 1933.

An unpublished thesis in the Library of the University of London.

SECTION VIII. THE FIRST PERIOD OF BRITISH RULE IN SOUTH AFRICA, 1815–36

(Chapters XII and XIII)

(a) Manuscript Sources in England

See Part I, A 1, particularly

Public Record Office, London.

Series C.O. 48. Original Correspondence, Secretary of State, especially for Governors' despatches and for special topics, e.g. Censorship of Press 1824–6, vol. XCVI, and 1835, vol. CLXV, Papers relating to the Caffre War.

These papers are very largely from the London Missionary Society.

Series C.O. 49. Entry Books of Correspondence, letters from Secretary of State.

Originals of letters to Governors are of interest for changes made in draft, e.g. of Glenelg's to D'Urban, 26 Dec. 1835. Those received from the Cape sometimes have marginal comments; many are endorsed with official minutes. Enclosures are sometimes missing. London and Cape Town to some extent supplement each other.

Series C.O. 51. Sessional Papers of Cape Council.

Non-Official. See Part I, A 2.

The London Missionary Society, 48 Broadway, Westminster, has MSS. See above, Part I, A 2.

(b) Manuscript Sources in South Africa

Official. See Part I, B 1 (a).

In the Archives Depot at Cape Town will be found the Duplicate Despatches, etc. of the Cape Governors. These give the most complete picture, but, even with enclosures, need supplementing by reference to local reports from districts, especially the Albany and Somerset series and Agents' reports for all questions relating to the Frontier and the 1820 Settlers, and to the Ecclesiastical series: "Missionary Complaints", for Missionary and Hottentot matters.

Non-Official. See Part I, B 1 (*c*).

The originals of the Philip Papers, the papers of the Rev. John Philip, to which frequent reference is made in both editions of this volume, were included in the first Gubbins Collection (*vide supra*, p. 954). Together with the rest of that Collection, they were housed in the Library of the University of the Witwatersrand, Johannesburg, and were nearly all destroyed by fire in 1931. Fortunately, many of Philip's letters and memorials survive in various Archives, while duplicates of his reports and correspondence with members of the London Missionary Society and officials are still in the L.M.S. Archives in London (*vide supra*, p. 927). The lost material, however, included not only the drafts or copies of most of the aforementioned documents, but also a mass of letters received over thirty years from missionaries and men of affairs in the Cape Colony or overseas. It also included the unfinished *Life* based on these and family records, the work of Philip's son and grandson.

In 1920, Professor W. M. MacMillan, at that time Professor of History in the University of the Witwatersrand, was invited by a representative of the Philip family to study their hoard of documents. The working notes on which he based *The Cape Colour Question* (1927) and *Bantu, Boer and Briton* (1929) are virtually all that remain to show for the lost Philip Papers. Since they are strictly working notes, they are sometimes editorially scored and often written in indelible pencil. Luckily the pencilling has lasted well, and the two thousand slips are at least as legible as were many of the originals. They could not, however, be readily filmed.

After many years, thanks to the zealous kindness of the Librarian of Rhodes House, Oxford, this mass of notes has been put in order, foliated, bound and provided with a rough Index to what has been lost. Practically all the originals have at least been "noted", and many have been carefully "abstracted" with not a few significant quotations. This Index, for all its limitations, is particularly commended to the notice of serious students of the history of the period.

The Fairbairn-Pringle correspondence in the Library of Parliament is useful for the story of the Struggle for the Freedom of the Press. The D'Urban Papers in the Cape Archives and the D'Urban-Smith transcripts in the South African Public Library are indispensable.

(*c*) Official Publications: British

See Part I, A 3, particularly the Parliamentary Papers

Reports of Commissioners of Inquiry upon (1) *the Administration of the Government*, (2) *the finances of the Cape of Good Hope*, *Parl. Pap.* 1827, XXI (282).

Report of Commissioners of Inquiry upon Trade of the Cape of Good Hope, navigation of the Coast, and improvement of the Harbours, *Parl. Pap.* 1829, V (300).

Hottentot Population. Reports of Commissioners of Inquiry re *condition of the Hottentots, Bushmen, Kaffirs, and other native tribes*, *Parl. Pap.* 1820, XXX (584).

Report from the Select Committee on Aborigines (*British Settlements*): *with the Minutes of Evidence, appendix and index*. *Parl. Pap.* 1836, VII (538); 1837, (238), (425).

Despatches re *the late Kaffir War and the death of Hintza*, 1836. *Parl. Pap.* 1836, XXXIX (279).

Despatches re *the late Kaffir War*. *Parl. Pap.* 1837, XLIII (503).

(*d*) Contemporary Works

Aborigines Protection Society. *Report of Select Committee on Aboriginal Tribes reprinted with comments by the Aborigines Protection Society.* 1838.

Ayliff, J. *Memorials of the British Settlers: an address.* Graham's Town, 1845.

Bowker, J. M. *Speeches, Letters, and selections from Important Papers.* Grahamstown, 1838.

Boyce, W. B. *Notes on South African affairs* 1834–8. Grahamstown, 1838.

Burnett, Bishop. *A reply to the "Report of the Commissioners of Inquiry at the Cape of Good Hope", upon the complaints addressed to the Colonial Government and to the Earl Bathurst.* 1826.

Buxton, Sir T. F. *Memoirs . . . with selections from his correspondence.* Ed. by . . . C. Buxton. 1848.

Campbell, J. *Travels in South Africa.* 1815.

—— *Travels in South Africa . . . narrative of a second journey.* 2 vols. 1822.

Chase, J. C. *The Cape of Good Hope and the Eastern Province of Algoa Bay &c., &c. With statistics of the Colony.* 1843.

Clinton, D. K. The London Missionary Society in South Africa, 1795–1836.

An unpublished dissertation in the Library of the L.M.S.

Cloete, H. *Five lectures on the emigration of the Dutch farmers in* 1843. Cape Town, 1856. Republished as *The History of the Great Boer Trek and the Origin of the South African Republics. . . .* Ed. by . . . W. Brodrick Cloete. 1899.

Curtis, C. G. *An account of the Colony of the Cape of Good Hope, with a view to the information of Emigrants.* 1819.

Donkin, Sir R. *A Letter on the Government of the Cape of Good Hope.* 1827.

Gardiner, A. F. *Narrative of a journey to the Zoolu Country in South Africa.* 1836.

Godlonton, R. *A Narrative of the Irruption of the Kafir Hordes into the Eastern Province of the Cape of Good Hope,* 1834–5. Graham's Town, 1836.

—— *Case of the Colonists of the Eastern Frontier of the Cape of Good Hope, in reference to the Kaffir Wars of* 1835–6 *and* 1846. Graham's Town, 1846.

Grant, P. W. *Considerations of the State of the Colonial Currency . . . at the Cape.* 1825.

Griffin, J. *The Real Facts disclosed, or the only real Guide to the Cape.* 1819.

Isaacs, N. *Travels and Adventures in Eastern Africa.* 2 vols. 1836.

Philip, J. *Researches in South Africa.* 2 vols. 1828.

Phillips, T. *Scenes and Occurrences in Albany and Cafferland.* 1827.

Pringle, T. *Narrative of a Residence in South Africa.* 1835.

Report of the Committee of the Society for the Relief of Distressed Settlers at the Cape of Good Hope. 1824.

Thompson, G. *Travels and adventures in Southern Africa.* 1827.

(*e*) Later Works

Agar-Hamilton, J. A. I. *The Native Policy of the Voortrekkers: an essay in the history of the Interior of South Africa,* 1836–58. Cape Town, 1928.

Brookes, E. H. *The history of Native Policy in South Africa from* 1830 *to the present day.* Cape Town, 1924.

Bryant, A. T. *Olden times in Zululand and Natal, containing earlier political history of the Eastern-Nguni clans.* 1929.

Campbell, C. T. *British South Africa. A History of the Colony of the Cape of Good Hope . . .* 1795 *to . . .* 1819 *. . . with Notices of some of the British Settlers of* 1820. 1897.

Coupland, R. *Wilberforce.* Oxford, 1923.

Dugmore, H. H. *The Reminiscences of an Albany Settler.* Graham's Town, 1871.

Du Plessis, J. *A history of Christian missions in South Africa.* 1911.

Hodgson, M. L. The Hottentots in South Africa to 1828. *S.A. Journal of Science,* 1924, vol. xxi, pp. 594 *sqq.*

Leibbrandt, H. C. V. *The Rebellion of* 1815, *generally known as Slachter's Nek.* Cape Town. 1902.

LOVETT, R. *History of the London Missionary Society*, vol. I. 1899.
MACMILLAN, W. M. *The Cape Colour Question: a historical survey.* 1927.
—— *Bantu, Boer and Briton: the making of the South African Native problem.* 1929.
REYBURN, H. A. Studies in Cape Frontier History. *The Critic*, Cape Town, Oct. 1934, Jan., April, July 1935.

Examines in the light of Sir A. Stockenstrom's papers the Black Circuit, the Slagter's Nek rebellion and Erasmus Smit's Bushman mission.

SCHAPERA, I. (Ed.). *Apprenticeship at Kuruman*, 1820–28, *being the journals and letters of Robert nad Mary Moffat.*

SHAW, W. *The story of my Mission in South-Eastern Africa.* 1860.
SOGA, J. H. *The South-Eastern Bantu.* Johannesburg. 1931.
STEPHEN, Sir J. *Essays in ecclesiastical biography.* 2 vols. 1849.
WALLIS, J. P. R. (Ed.). *The Matabele Journals of Robert Moffat*, 1829–60. 2 vols. 1945.

For Clapham Sect, Wilberforce, etc.

SECTION IX. THE FORMATION OF NEW STATES AND CONSTITUTIONAL DEVELOPMENT, 1834–58

(Chapters XIV and XV)

(*a*) MANUSCRIPT SOURCES IN ENGLAND

See Part I, A 1, particularly:

Public Record Office, London.

Series C.O. 48, 49, 51 (Cape Colony), 179 and 405 (Natal).

(*b*) MANUSCRIPT SOURCES IN SOUTH AFRICA

Official. See Part I, B 1 (*a*).

The correspondence of the Cape Governors and High Commissioners is in the Cape Archives. Local records, especially those of Albany, Colesberg and Graaff-Reinet, throw much light on the Great Trek. See also Proceedings of the Legislative Council in the Senate House, Cape Town. The papers preserved in the Pietermaritzburg Archives Depot are fragmentary until 1845, especially as some of the republican papers were transferred to the Transvaal. The same general remark applies to those in the depots at Pretoria and Bloemfontein until 1849.

Semi-official and Non-official. See Part I, B 1 (*c*).

Bührmann Papers, Dutch Reformed Church Archives, and D'Urban Papers and D'Urban-Smith transcripts at Cape Town; Shepstone Papers at Pietermaritzburg; Lauts and Soutter collections at Pretoria.

(*c*) OFFICIAL PUBLICATIONS, BRITISH

See Part I, A 3 for the Parliamentary Papers covering the appropriate years.

(*d*) OFFICIAL AND OTHER PUBLICATIONS, SOUTH AFRICAN

(i) OFFICIAL.

See Part I, B 2 (*a*) under the heads of Cape Colony, British Kaffraria, Natal, Orange Free State and Transvaal.

Notule van die Volksraad van die Suid-Afrikaanse Republiek (South African Archives Records: Transvaal, 1844–50; 1851–53). 2 vols. 1950.

(ii) UNOFFICIAL.

1. *Newspapers.* See Part II, 1 (*c*), especially *The Cape Monitor* (semi-official); *The Friend of the Sovereignty* (*Free State*); *The Grahamstown Journal; The South African Commercial Advertiser; De Zuid Afrikaan.*

The annual *Cape of Good Hope Almanac and Annual Register* (1834–58) contains useful topical articles.

2. *Pamphlets.* These pamphlets are to be found in the South African Public Library, Cape Town.

ADAMSON, J. *Case of the Cape of Good Hope and its Constitution.* 1853.

—— *Notes on Cape Affairs.* 1851.

ADDERLEY, C. B. *Argument against compelling the Cape to become a Penal Colony.* 1849.

—— *Statement of the present Cape case.* 1851.

ATKINSON, R. H. *A Letter to the Rt. Hon. Lord Stanley . . . on the late events at Natal.* Cape Town, 1842.

BIRD, J. *Form of Constitutional Government of Natal as affecting the safety of the inhabitants.* Pietermaritzburg, 1869.

Convictism. Report of the proceedings of a public meeting held . . . at Grahamstown . . . on the subject of the Order in Council constituting the Cape of Good Hope a penal settlement. Graham's Town, 1849.

Eastern Province, Separation Agitation. *Catechism of the Eastern Province Separation League: a few plain questions and their answers.* Port Elizabeth, 1860.

—— —— *Minutes of Proceedings of the Meeting of Delegates of the Eastern Province Separation League held at Somerset East on the 19th, 20th and 21st Feb.* 1861. Grahamstown, 1861.

—— —— *Notes on the Separation of the Eastern from the Western Province and concession to the Former of its own local government.* 1860.

—— —— *Reply of Sir Henry George Wakelyn Smith, to addresses on Separation presented by Mr William M. Harris, at Port Elizabeth, and Mr Hamilton Ross, at Cape Town, in* 1848. Port Elizabeth, 1848.

—— —— *Report of the Separation Debate in both Houses of the Cape Parliament,* June 1861. Cape Town, 1861.

—— —— *Separation. Letters on separation . . . Eastern Province Separation League.* Port Elizabeth, 1872.

—— —— *Separation. Petition of the Inhabitants of the Eastern Province of the Colony of the Cape of Good Hope to her . . . Majesty the Queen praying for separation and local self-government.* Port Elizabeth, 1872.

—— —— *Zamenspraak tusschen Klaas Waarzegger en Jan Twyfelaar over het onderwerp van Afscheiding tusschen de Oostelyke en Westelyke Provincie.* (By L. H. MEURANT.) Cradock, 1861.

MENZIES, W. *Narrative of a Correspondence etc., etc., etc., between the Hon'ble Mr Justice Menzies and Sir Andries Stockenstrom.* Cape Town, 1840.

METHLEY, J. E. *The New Colony of Port Natal.* 1849.

MOLESWORTH, (Sir) W. *Materials for a speech in defence of the Policy of abandoning the Orange River Territory, May,* 1854. 1854.

PATERSON, J. *A dissertation on the absolute necessity of resident government on the Eastern Province.* Port Elizabeth, 1851.

Road Board Memoranda. Cape Town, 1853.

SMELLEKAMP, J. A. *Mijn wedervaren in de Zuid-Afrikaansche Republiek.* Kaapstad, 1854.

SMITH, Sir A. *Report of the expedition for exploring Central Africa from the Cape of Good Hope.* Cape Town, 1836.

STOCKENSTROM, Sir A. *Light and Shade . . . The Hottentots of the Kat River Settlement.* Cape Town, 1854.

(e) Collected Historical Records

See Part II, 1 (d).

Bell, K. N. and Morrell, W. P. *Select Documents on British Colonial Policy*, 1830–60. 1928.

Includes a good series on South African Frontier policy.

Bird, J. *The Annals of Natal*, 1495–1845. 2 vols. Pietermaritzburg, 1888.

Contains the bulk of the official and much other correspondence bearing directly on Natal, and also statements by Trekkers.

Chase, J. C. *The Natal Papers....* 2 pts. Grahamstown, 1843.

A valuable supplement to Bird's *Annals*, including material bearing on the Cape's eastern frontier and the present Orange Free State.

Eybers, G. W. *Select Constitutional Documents* ... 1795–1910. 1918.

Preller, G. S. (Ed.). *Voortrekker wetgewing: notule van die Natalse Volksraad*, 1839–45.... Pretoria, 1924.

Indispensable as showing the inner working of the first Trekker republic.

—— *Voortrekkermense*. 4 vols. Kaapstad, 1918–25.

Chiefly statements of varying date and value by Trekkers.

Theal, G. McC. (Ed.). *Basutoland Records*, I, II. Cape Town, 1883.

Besides despatches and enclosures, contains a mass of local correspondence, official and other, and statements by Europeans and Basuto which were never sent to headquarters.

(f) Biographies

See Part II, 1 (f) for biographies or autobiographies of Bishop Gray, Sir George Grey, P. Retief, Sir H. Smith and Sir A. Stockenstrom.

(g) Contemporary Works

Anon. *The Cape of Good Hope Government and Legislature considered.* 1851.

Arbousset, T. *Relation d'un voyage d'exploration au nord-est de la Colonie du Cap de Bonne-Espérance, entrepris dans les mois de Mars, Avril, et Mai*, 1836, *par MM. T. Arbousset et F. Daumas.* Paris, 1842.

Adderley, Sir C. B. (Lord Norton). *Review of "The Colonial Policy of Lord John Russell's Administration" by Earl Grey*, 1853; *and of subsequent colonial history.* 1869.

—— *Some reflections on the Speech of Lord John Russell on Colonial Policy.* 1850.

—— *Statement of the present Cape case.* 1851.

Backhouse, J. *A narrative of a visit to the Mauritius and South Africa.* 1844.

Borcherds, P. B. *An auto-biographical memoir ... being a plain narrative of occurrences from early life to advanced age.* Cape Town, 1861.

Bowker, J. M. *Speeches, Letters, and selections from Important Papers.* Grahamstown, 1864.

Boyce, W. B. *Notes on South African affairs from* 1834 *to* 1838, *with reference to the civil, political, and religious condition of the Colonists and Aborigines.* Grahamstown, 1838.

Bunbury, (Sir) C. J. F. *Journal of a residence at the Cape of Good Hope, with excursions into the Interior, and notes on the natural history and the native tribes.* 1848.

Casalis, E. *The Basutos, or twenty-three years in South Africa.* 1861.

Cathcart, Sir G. *Correspondence ... relating to his military operations in Kaffraria.* 1856.

Chase, J. C. *The Cape of Good Hope and the Eastern Province of Algoa Bay, etc. etc., with statistics of the Colony.* 1843.

Cloete, H. *Five lectures on the emigration of the Dutch Farmers from the Colony of the Cape of Good Hope, and their settlement in the district of Natal, until their formal submission to Her Majesty's authority in the year* 1843. Cape Town, 1856. Edited and republished by W. Brodrick Cloete under the title of *The History of the Great Boer Trek and the Origin of the South African Republics*. 1899.

Delegorgue, A. *Voyage dans l'Afrique australe, notamment dans le territoire de Natal, dans celui des Cafres Amazoulous et Makatisses, et jusqu'au tropique du Capricorne, exécuté durant les années* 1838, 1839, 1840, 1841, 1842, 1843, *et* 1844. 2 vols. Paris, 1847.

Düben, G. W. von, Baron. *A. J. A. Wahlberg: ett minnesblad.* Stockholm, 1857.

Ferguson, W. T. and Immelman, R. F. M., (Ed.). *Sir John Herschel and Education at the Cape*, 1834–40. Cape Town. 1961.

Freeman, J. J. *A tour in South Africa, with notices of Natal.* 1851.

Godlonton, R. and Irving, E. *A Narrative of the Kaffir War of* 1850–1. 1851.

Gray, C. N. *Life of Robert Gray, Bishop of Cape Town.* 2 vols. 1876.

Grey, H. G., 3rd Earl. *The Colonial Policy of Lord John Russell's Administration.* 2nd ed. 2 vols. 1853.

Harris, Sir W. Cornwallis. *The wild sports of Southern Africa, being the narrative of an expedition from the Cape of Good Hope through the territories of the chief Moselekatse to the tropic of Capricorn.* 1839.

Hattersley, A. F. *More Annals of Natal.* 1936.

—— *Later Annals of Natal.* 1938.

—— *The Natalians.* 1940.

—— *Portrait of a Colony. The Story of Natal.* 1940.

—— *The British Settlement of Natal.* 1950.

Holden, W. C. *History of the Colony of Natal . . . to which is added . . . a brief history of the Orange River Soverignty.* 1855.

Kennedy, R. F. (Ed.). *Journal of Residence in Africa*, 1842–1853. Baines, T. Vol. I (1842–9). Cape Town. 1961.

King, W. R. *Campaigning in Kaffirland, or Scenes and Adventures in the Kaffir War of* 1851–2. 1853.

Livingstone, D. *A popular account of missionary travels and researches in South Africa.* 1861.

Merriman, N. J. *The Kafir, the Hottentot, and the Frontier Farmer.* 1853.

Moffat, R. *Missionary labours and scenes in Southern Africa.* 1842.

Moodie, D. C. F. *The History of the Battles and Adventures of the British, the Boers, and the Zulus, etc. in Southern Africa.* 2 vols. Cape Town, 1888.

Orpen, J. M. *History of the Basutos of South Africa. By the Special Commissioner of the* "Cape Argus". Cape Town, 1857.

Owen, F. *The Diary of the Rev. Francis Owen, M.A., Missionary with Dingaan in* 1837–8. *Together with extracts from the writings of the Interpreters in Zulu, Messrs. Hulley and Kirkman. Edited by Sir G. E. Cory.* (Van Riebeeck Society, *Publications*, No. 7). Cape Town, 1926.

Porter, W. *The Porter Speeches. Speeches delivered . . .* 1839–45. Cape Town, 1886.

Sanderson, J. *Memoranda of a trading trip into the Orange River (Sovereignty) Free State and the country of the Transvaal Boers*, 1851–2. *Journal of the Royal Geographical Society*, vol. xxx, pp. 233–55. 1860.

Schapera, I. (Ed.). *Livingstone's First Journals*, 1851–53. 1960.

Shaw, W. *The story of my mission in South-Eastern Africa; comprising some account of the European Colonists, with extended notices of the Kaffir and other native tribes.* 1860.

Smit, E. *Uit het dagboek van Erasmus Smit, predikant bij de Voortrekkers.* Kaapstad, 1897.

—— *Dagboek van Erasmus Smit*, 1836–9, *edited by G. S. Preller.* (*Voortrekkermense*, vol. ii.) Kaapstad, 1920.

Stockenstrom, Sir A. *Narrative of transactions connected with the Kafir War of* 1846 and 1847; *embracing correspondence between Sir P. Maitland, Lieutenant-Colonel M. Johnstone, Sir A. Stockenstrom, and others.* Grahamstown, 1848.

Stuart, J. *De Hollandsche Afrikanen en hunne Republiek in Zuid-Afrika.* Amsterdam, 1854.

Trigardt, L. *Dagboek van Louis Trigardt* (1836–8), *met inleiding en aantekeninge van G. S. Preller*. Bloemfontein, 1917.

Wahlberg, H. J. F. Auszug aus einem Briefe des Ingenieurs H. J. F. Wahlberg ... Port Natal ... den 15ten August 1843. *Monatsberichte über die Verhandlungen der Gesellschaft für Erdkunde zu Berlin*, 1844, p. 126.

Wallis, J. P. R. (Ed.). *The Matabele Journals of Robert Moffat*, 1829–60. 2 vols. 1945.

(*h*) Later Works

Agar-Hamilton, J. A. I. *The Native Policy of the Voortrekkers; an essay in the history of the Interior of South Africa*, 1836–58. Cape Town, 1928.

Cachet, F. Lion. *De Worstelstrijd der Transvalers aan het Volk van Nederland verhaald.* Amsterdam, 1882.

Collins, W. W. "*Free Statia*", *or reminiscences of a lifetime in the Orange Free State* ... 1852 ... 1875. Bloemfontein, 1907.

Dehérain, H. *L'Expansion des Boers au XIXe siècle.* Paris, 1905.

Dreyer, A. *Die Kaapse Kerk en die Groot Trek.* Kaapstad, 1929.

Du Plessis, A. J. *Die Republiek Natalia*, Archives Year Book, Cape Town, 1943 (part 1).

Engelbrecht, S. P. *Geschiedenis van de Nederduits Hervormde Kerk in Zuid-Afrika.* 2 vols. Amsterdam and Pretoria, 1920–25.

Fortescue, Sir J. W. *History of the British Army*, vol. xii. 1927.

Fuller, C. *Louis Trigardt's Trek across the Drakensberg*, 1837–38, *edited by L. Fouché.* (Van Riebeeck Society, *Publications*, No. 13.) Cape Town, 1932.

Gray, C. N. *Life of Robert Gray, Bishop of Capetown.* 2 vols. 1876.

Hattersley, A. F. *Portrait of a Colony. The Story of Natal.* 1940.

—— *The British Settlement of Natal.* 1950.

Hofstede, H. J. *Geschiedenis van der Oranje-Vrijstaat.* 's Gravenhage, 1876.

Kiewiet, C. W. de. *British Colonial Policy and the South African Republics*, 1848–72. 1929.

—— *A History of South Africa, Social and Economic.* 1941.

Kilpin, R. *The Old Cape House.* Cape Town, 1918.

—— *The Romance of a Colonial Parliament.* 1930.

Kotzé, J. G. *Het stichten der Zuid-Afrikaansche Republiek en haare grondwet.* Pretoria, 1894.

Lindley, A. F. *Adamantia, the truth about the South African Diamond Fields.* 1873.

Mackeurtan, G. *The cradle days of Natal* (1497–1845). 1930.

Macmillan, W. M. *The Cape colour question: a historical survey.* 1927.

—— *Bantu, Boer and Briton: the making of the South African Native problem.* 1929.

Malan, J. H. *Die Opkomst van 'n Republiek, of, die Geskiedenis van die Oranjevrystaat tot die jaar* 1863. Bloemfontein, 1929.

Merensky, A. *Beiträge zur Kenntniss Süd-Afrikas.* Berlin, 1875.

Meurant, L. *Sixty years ago, or reminiscences of the struggle for the freedom of the Press in South Africa.* Cape Town, 1885.

Morrell, W. P. *British Colonial Policy in the Age of Peel and Russell.* Oxford, 1930.

Orpen, J. M. *Reminiscences of Life in South Africa from* 1846 *to the present day.* Durban, 1908.

Pelzer, E. A. *Geskiedenis van die Suid-Afrikaanse Republiek*, deel 1, Cape Town, 1950.

Preller, G. S. *Piet Retief: Lewensgeskiedenis van die grote voortrekker.* 10de druk. Kaapstad, 1920.

Russell, R. *Natal, the Land and its Story.* Pietermaritzburg, 1891.

Scholtz, G. D. *Die Konstitusie en die Staatsinstellinge van die Oranje Vrystaat*, 1854–1902. Amsterdam, 1937.

Theal, G. McC. *Willem Adriaan van der Stel and other historical sketches.* Cape Town, 1913.

Includes the stories of L. Trigardt and P. L. Uys.

UYS, C. J. *In the era of Shepstone, being a study of British Expansion in South Africa* (1842–77). Lovedale, 1933.

VAN DER WALT, A. J. H., WIID, J. A. and GEYER, A. L. *Geskiedenis van Suid-Afrika*. 2 vols. Cape Town, 1951 (relative to this chapter is vol. II, Bk. 2, ch. 4).

VOIGT, J. C. *Fifty years of the History of the Republic in South Africa* (1795–1845). 2 vols. 1899.

WALKER, E. A. *The Frontier Tradition in South Africa*. Oxford, 1930.

—— *The Great Trek*. 1934.

—— *A History of Southern Africa*. 3rd ed. Longmans, 1957.

WICHMANN, F. A. F. *Die Wordingsgeskiedenis van die Zuid-Afrikaansche Republiek*, 1838–1860, Archives Year Book. Cape Town, 1941.

(*i*) PERIODICAL PUBLICATION

Butterworth's South African Law Review, Durban, 1954. Article on *Constitutionalism in the South African Republics*, pp. 49–72, by L. M. THOMPSON.

(*j*) UNPUBLISHED GRADUATE THESES

DE WET, C. J. H. *Die Republikeinse Konstitusies van Suid-Afrika*. M.A. University of South Africa, 1936.

GRUNDLINGH, M. A. S. *The Legislative Council of the Cape of Good Hope*, 1834–1853. M.A. Stellenbosch, 1937.

LONG, E. P. M. *The Constitutional Settlement of Natal*, 1843–1856. M.A. University of South Africa, 1928.

TAYLOR, N. H. *The Separation Movement During the Period of Representative Government at the Cape*, 1854–1872. M.A. University of Cape Town, 1938.

VOGEL, J. A. *Konstitusionele eksperimente van die Boere*, 1836–1877. M.A. Pretoria 1932.

SECTION X. TRANSITION IN SOUTH AFRICAN POLICY, 1854–1872

(Chapters XVI and XVII)

(*a*) MANUSCRIPT SOURCES IN ENGLAND

See Part I, A 1, particularly the series C.O. 48/327–461, C.O. 49/50–62, C.O. 179/59–91 and C.O. 224/1–2 in the Public Record Office, and the "Wodehouse Papers" in the library of the Colonial Office, Whitehall.

(*b*) MANUSCRIPT SOURCES IN SOUTH AFRICA

See Part I, B 1 and Section IX, *supra*.

(*c*) OFFICIAL PUBLICATIONS: BRITISH

See Part I, A 3 and A 4 for Parliamentary Papers and Debates, and also *Report from the Select Committee on Colonial Military Expenditure, Parl. Pap.* 1861, XIII (423). There is an unpublished study of this committee's work in the University of London library: CHAPPELL, M. G., "The Select Committee of 1861 on Colonial Military Expenditure", 1932.

(*d*) OFFICIAL PUBLICATIONS: SOUTH AFRICAN

See Part I, B 2.

(*e*) NON-OFFICIAL PUBLICATIONS: BRITISH

See particularly the newspapers: *The Times, Morning Post, Daily Telegraph* (1855–), *Morning Chronicle* (to 1862) and *Manchester Guardian*.

(*f*) Non-official Publications: South African

See Part II, 1 (*c*), particularly the newspapers: *Cape Argus*, *Cape Monitor*, *Friend of the Free State*, *Grahamstown Journal*, *Natal Mercury*, *Natal Witness*, *S.A. Commercial Advertiser* and *De Zuid Afrikaan*.

(*g*) Collected Historical Records

See Part II, 1 (*d*), particularly.

Eybers, G. W. *Select Constitutional Documents illustrating South African history*, 1795–1910. 1918.

Foster, W. *British Rule in South Africa*. Cape Town, 1868.

Theal, G. McC. (Ed.). *Basutoland Records*, II, III. Cape Town, 1883.

(*h*) Biographies

See Part II, 1 (*f*) for biographies of Rev. D. Lindley, Lord de Villiers, Sir J. H. Brand, Bishop Colenso, Sir W. Butler, Sir G. Grey, D. Livingstone, R. Moffat, Sir J. C. Molteno, Sir J. Robinson, Sir T. Shepstone, and Sir R. Southey.

(*i*) Contemporary Works

Adderley, C. B. (Baron Norton). *Review of "The Colonial Policy of Lord Russell's Administration", by Earl Grey, 1853, and of subsequent colonial history*. 1869.

—— *Letter . . . on the Present Relations of England with her Colonies*. [1861].

Archives Year Book, 1945: *Die Anneksasie van Griekwaland-Ives*.

Arnot, D. and Orpen, F. H. S. *The Land Question of Griqualand West*. Cape Town, 1875.

"Ba-Mangwato", (*pseud.*). *To Ophir direct: or The Route to the South African Gold Fields*, 1868.

Casalis, E. *The Basutos, or Twenty-three years in South Africa*. 1861.

Chesson, F. W. *The Dutch Republics of South Africa; Three Letters to R. N. Fowler, Esq., M.P., and Charles Buxton, Esq., M.P.* 1871.

Colenso, W. *Trial of the Bishop of Natal for Erroneous Teaching*. 1863.

—— *First Steps of the Zulu Mission*. 1860.

Lindley, A. F. *Adamantia. The Truth about the South African Diamond Fields*. 1873.

Livingstone, David. *Missionary Travels and Researches in South Africa*. New ed. 1899.

Livingstone, D. and C. *Narrative of an Expedition to the Zambesi and its Tributaries*, 1858–64. 1865.

Mauch, C. *Carl Mauch's Reisen im Inneren von Süd-Afrika*, 1865–1872. *Mit einer Originalkarte* (*Ergänzungsheft* 37 *zu Petermanns geographischen Mitteilungen*). Gotha, 1874.

Merivale, H. *Lectures on Colonization and Colonies*. 2nd ed. 1861.

Mitteilungen aus Justus Perthes' geographischer Anstalt. Bd. 1–24. Gotha, 1855–78.

Molesworth, Sir W. C. *Materials for a Speech in Defence of the Policy of abandoning the Orange River Colony*. 1854 [reprinted 1878].

Rogers, Sir F. "South Africa." *Edinburgh Review*, cxlix, pp. 534–66. April 1879.

Wallis, J. P. R. (Ed.). *The Matabele Journals of Robert Moffat*, 1829–60. 2 vols. 1945.

—— *The Matabele Mission: a Selection from the Correspondence of John and Emily Moffat. David Livingstone and others*, 1858–78. 1945.

—— *The Northern Goldfields Diaries of Thomas Baines*, 1869–72. 3 vols. 1946.

—— *The Zambesi Journal of James Stewart*, 1862–63. 1952.

—— *The Southern African Diaries of Thomas Leask*, 1865–70. 1954.

—— *The Zambezi Expedition of David Livingstone*, 1858–63. 2 vols. 1956.

(*j*) Later Works

Bixler, R. W. Anglo-Portuguese rivalry for Delagoa Bay. *Jour. Mod. Hist.*, x (Dec. 1934), 425–40.

Botha, P. R. *Die staatkundige ontwikkeling van die Suid-Afrikaanse Republiek onder Kruger en Leyds*. Amsterdam, 1926.

Bourne, H. R. Fox. *Blacks and Whites in South Africa*. 1900.

Brookes, E. H. *The History of Native Policy in South Africa from* 1830 *to the Present Day*. Cape Town, 1924.

Casalis, E. *My life in Basutoland. Trans. from the French by* T. Brierly. 1899.

Chesson, F. W. *The War in Zululand: a Brief Review of Sir Bartle Frere's Policy*. 1879.

Egerton, H. E. (Ed.). *Selected Speeches of Sir William Molesworth*. 1903.

Ellenberger, D. F. and MacGregor, J. C. *History of the Basuto, Ancient and Modern*. 1912.

Ellenberger, V. *Un siècle de Mission au Lessouto*, 1833–1933. Paris, 1933.

Engelbrecht, S. P. *Paul Kruger's amptelike Briewe*, 1851–77. Pretoria, 1925.

—— *Geschiedenis van de Nederduits Hervormde Kerk in Zuid-Afrika*. 2 vols. Amsterdam. Pretoria, 1920–5.

Fisher, W. E. G. *The Transvaal and the Boers*. 1900.

Fitzmaurice, E. G. (Baron). *The Life of G. G. Leveson-Gower, second Earl Granville*. 3rd ed. 2 vols. 1905.

Froude, J. A. *Two lectures on South Africa*. 1880. New edition, 1900.

Greswell, W. *Our South African Empire*. 2 vols. 1885.

Halford, S. J. *The Griquas of Griquatown*. 1950.

Kiewiet, C. W. de. *British Colonial Policy and the South African Republics*, 1848–72. 1929.

—— *A History of South Africa, Social and Economic*. 1941.

Lagden, Sir G. *The Basutos*. 2 vols. 1909.

Leyds, W. J. *De eerste Annexatie van de Transvaal*. Amsterdam, 1906 (Trans. 1906).

Lucas, (Sir) C. P. *History of South Africa to the Jameson Raid*. 1899.

Malherbe, E. G. *Education in South Africa* (1652–1922). Cape Town, 1925.

Marindin, G. E. (Ed.). *Letters of Frederic, Lord Blachford*. 1896.

Markham, V. R. *South Africa Past and Present*. 1900.

Monypenny, W. F. and Buckle, G. E. *Life of Benjamin Disraeli, Earl of Beaconsfield*. 6 vols. 1910–20.

Morley, J. (Viscount). *Life of W. E. Gladstone*. 3 vols. 1903.

Morrell, W. P. *British Colonial Policy in the Age of Peel and Russell*. Oxford, 1930.

Nixon, J. *The Complete Story of the Transvaal from the "Great Trek" to the Convention of London* (1884). 1885.

Orpen, J. M. *Reminiscences of Life in South Africa from* 1846 *to the present day*. Durban, 1915.

—— *Some Principles of Native Government Illustrated*. Cape Town, 1880.

Reid, T. W. *Life of W. E. Forster*. 2 vols. 1888.

Theal, G. McC. *History of the Boers in South Africa*. 1887.

Uys, C. J. *In the Era of Shepstone*. Lovedale, 1933.

Van der Poel, J. The Basutos, 1854–71. (Unpublished thesis in the library of the University of Cape Town.)

Van der Walt, A. J. H., Wiid, J. A. and Geyer, A. L. *Geskiedenis van Suid-Afrika*. Vol. II, Book 2, chap. 4. Cape Town. 1951.

Walker, E. A. *Lord de Villiers and his Times*. 1925.

Wilmot, A. *The History of Our Own Times in South Africa*. 3 vols. 1897–99.

Worsfold, W. B. *South Africa. A Study in Colonial Administration and Development*. 1897.

SECTION XI. THE FAILURE OF CONFEDERATION AND POLITICAL DEVELOPMENT, 1872–1886

(Chapters XVIII and XIX)

(a) Manuscript Sources in England

See Part I, A 1, particularly the series C.O. 48, C.O. 179, C.O. 291 in the Public Record Office; together with the "Carnarvon Papers", G.D. 6/1–34, 80–84, 116, 131; and the "Granville Papers", G.D. 29/135.

(b) Manuscript Sources in South Africa

See Part I, B 1.

(c) Official Publications: British

See Part I, A 3 and A 4 for British Parliamentary Papers and Debates; also the reports of civil commissioners and resident magistrates, which enclose Cape Blue Books on native affairs, 1874–80: *Parl. Pap.* 1874, XLIV [C. 882]; 1875, LI [C. 1183]; 1876, LI [C. 1622–I], 1877, LIX [C. 1825], [C. 1869]; 1878, LV [C. 2149]; 1878–9, L [C. 2444]; 1880, XLVIII [C. 2598], [C. 2730]; 1881, LXIV [C. 2829], [C. 3094]; 1882, XLIV [C. 3218], [C. 3388].

(d) Official Publications: South Africa

See Part I, B 2.

(e, f) Non-Official Publications

See Part II, 1 (a), (b) and (c).

(g) Collected Historical Records

See Part II, 1 (d), particularly.

ANDREWS, C. F. (Ed.). *Documents relating to the New Asiatic Bill.* Cape Town, 1926.
EYBERS, G. W. *Select Constitutional Documents illustrating South African History*, 1759–1910. 1918.
NEWTON (A. P.). *Select documents relating to the unification of South Africa.* 2 vols. 1924.

(h) Biographies

See Part II, 1 (f) for biographies of Rev. D. Lindley, Lord de Villiers, Sir M. Hicks Beach, Sir J. H. Brand, T. F. Burgers, Sir G. Pomeroy Colley, Sir Bartle Frere, J. H. Hofmeyr, Sir W. Butler, Sir J. C. Molteno, C. J. Rhodes, Sir J. Robinson, Sir T. Shepstone, Sir R. Southey, John X. Merriman and the Rev. J. Mackenzie.

(i) Contemporary Works

AYLWARD, A. *The Transvaal of To-day.* 1878.
CAMPBELL-JOHNSON, A. R. *South Africa, its Difficulties and Present State.* 1877.
CARTER, T. F. *A Narrative of the Boer War; its Causes and Results.* New ed. 1896.
COLENSO, F. E. and DURNFORD, E. *History of the Zulu War and its Origin.* 1880.
CUNYNGHAME, Sir A. A. T. *My command in South Africa, 1874–8.* 1879.
DURNFORD, E. *Isandhlwana.* 1879.
FRERE, Sir H. B. E. *Afghanistan and South Africa, a Letter to the Rt. Hon. W. E. Gladstone regarding Portions of his Midlothian Speeches.* 1881.
—— *Correspondence relating to the Recall of the Rt. Hon. Sir Bartle Frere, Bart.* 1880.
—— "The Union of Various Portions of British South Africa." *Proc. Royal Colonial Institute*, XII, pp. 133–74. 1881.

FROUDE, J. A. "Leaves from a South African Journal" (in *Short Studies on Great Subjects*, vol. III, pp. 477–558). 1883.
—— *Oceana; or, England and her Colonies.* 1886.
—— *Two Lectures on South Africa.* 1880. New edition, 1900.
GRESWELL, W. *Our South African Empire.* 2 vols. 1885.
HAGGARD, (Sir) H. RIDER. *Cetywayo and his White Neighbours.* 1882.
NOBLE, J. *South Africa, Past and Present.* 1877.
PARR, H. HALLAM. *A Sketch of the Kafir and Zulu Wars.* 1880.
TRANSVAAL WAR. *De Transvaal Oorlog.* Grahamstown, [1900]. (English translation *The Birth of the Bond.*)
TROLLOPE, ANTHONY. *South Africa.* 2 vols. 1878.
WATSON, R. S. *Histoire du Gouvernement Anglais et de sa Politique dans l'Afrique Méridionale . . . publiée par le Comité Central pour les Intérêts du Transvaal.* Utrecht, 1881.
WILMOT, A. *History of the Zulu War, 1879.* 1880.
WINTER, JAMES W. *The Diamond Fields of South Africa.* 1877.
—— "*Gigantic Inhumanity.*" *South African Notes.* 1877.
Zuid Afrikaansche Tijdschrift, 1878–93. Kaapstad, 1878–93.

(*j*) LATER WORKS

AMPHLETT, G. T. *The History of the Standard Bank of South Africa, Limited*, 1862–1913. Glasgow, 1914.
BOTHA, P. R. *Die staatkundige ontwikkeling van die Suid-Afrikaanse Republiek onder Kruger en Leyds.* Amsterdam, 1926.
BROOKES, E. H. *History of Native Policy in South Africa from* 1830 *to the Present Day.* Cape Town, 1924.
BUCKLE, G. E. (Ed.). *The Letters of Queen Victoria.* 2nd series, 1862–85. 3 vols. 1926–28.
COOK, (Sir) E. T. *Rights and Wrongs of the Transvaal War.* 1901.
COUPLAND, Sir R. *Zulu Battle Piece: Isandhlwana.* 1948.
ENGELBRECHT, S. P. *Geschiedenis van de Nederduits Hervormde Kerk in Zuid-Afrika.* 2 vols. Amsterdam and Pretoria, 1920–25.
ESCOMBE, H. *Speeches of the Rt. Hon. Harry Escombe.* Maritzburg, 1903.
EVANS, M. S. *Black and White in South East Africa.* 2nd ed. 1916.
FITZMAURICE, E. G. (Baron). *The Life of G. G. Leveson-Gower, second Earl Granville.* 3rd ed. 1905.
FITZPATRICK, (Sir) J. P. *The Transvaal from within.* 1899.
HARDINGE, Sir A. H. *Henry Howard Molyneux Herbert, fourth Earl of Carnarvon,* 1831–90. Ed. Elizabeth, Countess of Carnarvon. 3 vols. 1925.
HOLE, H. M. *Lobengula.* 1929.
—— *The Making of Rhodesia.* 1926.
JOHNSTON, Sir H. H. *A History of the Colonisation of Africa by Alien Races.* New ed. Cambridge, 1913.
JORISSEN, E. J. P. *Transvaalsche Herinneringen*, 1876–1896. Amsterdam, 1897.
KIEWIET, C. W. de. *The Imperial Factor in South Africa, a study in Politics and Economics.* 1937.
KOTZE, Sir J. G. *Biographical Memoirs and Reminiscences.* Cape Town, 1934.
LAGDEN, Sir G. *The Basutos.* 2 vols. 1909.
LEYDS, W. J. *The First Annexation of the Transvaal.* 1906.
—— *The Transvaal Surrounded.* 1919.
MACKENZIE, J. *Austral Africa.* 1887.
MARTINEAU, J. *The Transvaal Trouble.* 2nd ed. 1899.
MAURICE, Sir F. B. and ARTHUR, Sir G. C. A. *The Life of Lord Wolseley.* 1924.
MONYPENNY, W. P. and BUCKLE, G. E. *Life of Benjamin Disraeli, first Earl of Beaconsfield.* 6 vols. 1910–20.
MORLEY, J. (Viscount). *Life of W. E. Gladstone.* 3 vols. 1903.

Niekerk, L. van. *Die eerste Afrikaanse Taalbeweging*. Amsterdam, 1916.
Oordt, J. F. van. *Paul Kruger en de Opkomst der Zuid-Afrikaansche Republiek*. Amsterdam, 1898.
Reitz, F. W. *A Century of Wrong*. 1900.
Smith, J. J. "The Evolution and Recognition of the Afrikaans Language", [in] *Official Year Book of the Union of South Africa, No.* 8. Pretoria, 1927.
Statham, F. R. *Paul Kruger and His Times*. 1898.
Uys, C. J. *In the Era of Shepstone*. Lovedale, 1933.
Walker, E. A. *Lord de Villiers and His Times*. 1925.
Williams, Gardner F. *The Diamond Mines of South Africa*. 1902.

SECTION XII. THE PERIOD OF CONFLICT, 1881–1902.

(Chapters XX, XXI and XXII)

(a) Manuscript Sources in England

See Part I, A 1.

(b) Manuscript Sources in South Africa

Official. See Part I, B 1 (*a*).

Semi-official and Non-official. See Part I, B 1 (*c*), particularly the Papers of Lord de Villiers, J. H. Hofmeyr, J. X. Merriman, Olive Schreiner and W. P. Schreiner in Cape Town, and the second Gubbins Collection in Johannesburg.

(c) Official Publications: British

For Parliamentary Papers see Part I, A 3, covering the appropriate years.

(d) Official Publications, South African

See Part I, B 2.

(e) Non-Official Publications: British

Newspapers. See in particular *The Times, The Daily News, The Daily Telegraph* and *The Manchester Guardian*.

(f) Non-Official Publications: South African

Newspapers. See Part II, 1 (*c*), particularly *The Cape Times, The Cape Argus, The Friend, The South African News, The Star, Ons Land* and *Die Volkstem*.

(g) Collected Historical Records

See Part II, 1 (*d*).

Eybers, G. W. *Select Constitutional Documents . . .* 1795–1910. 1918.
Newton, A. P. *Select Documents relating to the Unification of South Africa*. vol. 1. 1924.

(h) Biographies

See Part II, 1 (*f*) for biographies or autobiographies of Gen. L. Botha, Sir J. H, Brand, Sir W. F. Butler, Lord de Villiers, Sir M. Hicks Beach, J. H. Hofmeyr, J. T. Jabavu, Sir S. Jameson, Khama, S. J. P. Kruger, D. Lindley, J. Mackenzie, J. X. Merriman, C. J. Rhodes, Sir J. Robinson, W. P. Schreiner, M. T. Steyn. Sir R. Southey.

(i) Contemporary Works

Angra Pequena [German Official correspondence, etc.]. Berlin, 1884.
Bismarck-Schönhausen, Otto E. L., Prince von. *Die politischen Reden des Fürsten Bismarck*. 14 B. Berlin, 1892–1905.

BOURNE, H. R. FOX. *Matabeleland and the Chartered Company*. 1897.
BRYCE, J. (Viscount). *Impressions of South Africa*. New ed. 1900.
CARNARVON, H. H. M. 4th Earl of. "The Cape in 1888." *Fortnightly Reveiw*, vol. XLIX, p. 862. 1888.
CHAMBERLAIN, J. *Mr Chamberlain's Speeches*. Ed. by C. W. BOYD. 2 vols. 1914.
COLQUHOUN, A. R. *Matabeleland*. 1893.
COOK, (Sir) E. T. *Rights and wrongs of the Transvaal War*. 2nd ed. 1902.
DE LA REY, J. H. and SMUTS, J. C. *Official Reports . . . together with other Documents relating to the War in South Africa* . . . (translated). 1902.
DORMER, F. J. *Vengeance as a Policy in Afrikanderland*. 1901.
DOYLE, (Sir) A. CONAN. *The Great Boer War*. 1902.
DUGDALE, E. T. S. (Ed.). *German Diplomatic Documents*, 1871–1914. Selected and translated [from *Die Grosse Politik der Europäischen Kabinette*, 1871–1914]. 4 vols. 1928–31.
DU PLESSIS, C. N. J. *The Transvaal Boer speaking for himself: some passages from "Uit de Geschiedenis van de Zuid-Afrikaansche Republiek en van de Afrikaanders"* . . ., selected and translated by R. ACTON. 1899.
DU TOIT, S. J. *Rhodesia, Past and Present*. 1897.
FITZPATRICK, (Sir) J. P. *The Transvaal from Within*. 1899.
FRIPP, C. E. and HILLER, V. W. (Eds.) *Gold and the Gospel in Mashonaland, 1888*. 1949.
GARRETT, F. E. and EDWARDS, E. J. *The Story of an African Crisis; being the truth about the Jameson Raid*. 1897.
German White Book. (1884.)
GOLDMANN, C. S. *The financial, statistical, and general history of the gold and other Companies of Witwatersrand*. 1892.
GOOCH, G. P. and TEMPERLEY, H. W. V. (Eds.). *British Documents on the Origins of the War*, 1898–1914. Vols. I–III. 1927–8.
HEADLAM, C. (Ed.). *The Milner Papers*, 1897–1905. 2 vols. 1931–33.
HENDERSON, J. T. (Ed.). *Speeches of the Rt. Hon. Harry Escombe*. Maritzburg, [1903].
HOBHOUSE, E. *The Brunt of the War and where it fell*. 1902.
—— *Report of a visit to the Camps of Women and Children in the Cape and Orange River Colonies*. 1901.
IWAN-MÜLLER, E. B. *Lord Milner and South Africa*. 1902.
JORISSEN, E. J. P. *Transvaalsche Herinneringen*, 1876–96. Amsterdam, 1897.
KELTIE, J. SCOTT. *The Partition of Africa*. 2nd ed. 1895.
KNIGHT-BRUCE, G. W. H. *Memories of Mashonaland*. 1895.
KOTZE, (Sir) J. G. *Documents and Correspondence relating to the Judicial Crisis in the South African Republic* (translated). 1898.
LEONARD, A. G. *How we made Rhodesia*. 1896.
LEPSIUS, J., BARTHOLDY, A. M. and THIMME, F. (Eds.). *Die Grosse Politik der Europäischen Kabinette*, 1871–1914. 40 vols. Berlin, 1922–7.
LEYDS, W. J. *Eenige Correspondentie uit* 1899. 's Gravenhage, 1919.
—— *Tweede Verzameling* (*Correspondentie* 1899–1900). 2 vols. (vol. I in 2 parts). 's Gravenhage, 1930.
—— *Derde Verzameling* (*Correspondentie uit* 1900). 2 vols. 's Gravenhage, 1931.
—— *Vierde Verzameling* (*Correspondentie* 1900–2). Deel I. Eerste en Tweede Band, en Deel II, Bijlagen, Index (als Manuscript gedrukt). 's Gravenhage, 1934.
MACKENZIE, JOHN. *Austral Africa*. 2 vols. 1898.
"MERMEIX", *pseud*. (TERRAIL, G.). *Le Transvaal et la Chartered*. (*La révolution de Johannesburg et les mines d'Or*.) Paris, 1897.
MUELLER, A. *Kritische Betrachtungen über den Burenkrieg*. 2 vols. Berlin, 1901.
NOBLE, JOHN (Ed.). *Official handbook. History, Products . . . of the Cape of Good Hope* (Colonial and Indian Exhibition, London, 1886). 1886.
NORRIS-NEWMAN, C. L. *Matabeleland and how we got it*. 1895.

OORDT, J. F. VAN. *Paul Kruger en de Opkomst der Zuid-Afrikaansche Republiek.* Amsterdam, 1898.
O'RELL, MAX, *pseud.* (L. PAUL BLOUET). *John Bull and Co.* 1894.
[REITZ, F. W.] *A Century of Wrong.* 1900.
REUNERT, T. *Diamonds and Gold in South Africa.* 1893.
ROSE, E. B. *The Truth about the Transvaal.* 1902.
ROYAL ENGINEERS. *Detailed History of the Railways in the South African War,* 1899–1902. 2 vols. Chatham, 1902.
SCOBLE, J. and ABERCROMBIE, H. R. *The Rise and Fall of Krugerism.* 1900.
SELOUS, F. C. *Sunshine and Storm in Rhodesia.* 1896.
—— *Travel and Adventure in South-East Africa.* 1893.
THOMAS, C. H. *The Origin of the Anglo-Boer War revealed.* [1900.]
THOMSON, H. C. *Rhodesia and its Government.* 1898.
VICTORIA, Queen. *The letters of Queen Victoria; a selection from Her Majesty's correspondence and journal between the years* 1886 *and* 1901, ed. by G. E. BUCKLE. 3rd series. 3 vols. 1930–32.
VILJOEN, BEN J. *My Reminiscences of the Anglo-Boer War.* 1902.
VILLEBOIS-MAREUIL, Count G. H. DE. *War Notes* (translated). 1901.
"VINDEX", *pseud. Cecil Rhodes. His Political Life and Speeches.* 1881–1900.
WAAL, D. C. DE. *With Rhodes in Mashonaland.* Cape Town, 1896.
WALLIS, J. P. R. (Ed.). *The Barotseland Journal of James Stevenson-Hamilton,* 1898–9. 1953.
WILLIAMS, GARDNER F. *The Diamond Mines of South Africa.* New York, 1902.
WILLS, W. A. and COLLINGRIDGE, L. T. *The Downfall of Lobengula.* 1894.
WOOD, J. G. *Through Matabeleland.* Cape Town, 1893.

(*j*) LATER WORKS

AMERY, L. S. (Ed.). *The Times History of the War in South Africa,* 1899–1902. 7 vols. 1900–9.
ANDREWS, C. F. (Ed.). *Documents relating to the New Asiatic Bill.* Cape Town, 1926.
Many documents dealing with the past history of Indians in South Africa.
Archives Year Book, 1947. *Die Stemreg-Vraagstuk in die Zuid-Afrikaansche Republiek,* Hugo, M. J.
ARTHUR, Sir G. *Life of Lord Kitchener.* 3 vols. 1920.
BIXLER, W. *Anglo-German Imperialism in South Africa,* 1880–1900. Baltimore, 1932.
BLUNT, WILFRID S. *My Diaries: being a personal narrative of events,* 1888–1914. 2 pts. 1919, 1920.
BOTHA, P. R. *Die staatkundige ontwikkeling van die Suid-Afrikaanse Republiek onder Kruger en Leyds. Transvaal* 1844–99. Amsterdam, 1926.
BUCHAN, J. (Baron Tweedsmuir). *The African Colony.* 1903.
CACHET, F. L. *Die Wortstelstrijd der Transvalers.* Amsterdam, 1882.
CHIROL, Sir V. "The Boer War and the International Situation, 1899–1902." *Cambridge Hist. Brit. For. Policy,* III, pp. 263–93.
CLARKE, Sir Edward G. *The Story of my Life.* 1918.
COHEN, L. *Reminiscences of Kimberley.* 1911.
COLQUHOUN, A. R. *Dan to Beersheba.* 1908.
COOK, (Sir) E. T. *Edmund Garrett. A Memoir.* 1909.
DARTER, A. *The Pioneers of Mashonaland.* 1914.
FITZMAURICE, E. G. (Baron). *The Life of G. G. Leveson-Gower, second Earl Granville.* 3rd ed. 1905.
FITZPATRICK, (Sir) J. P. *South African Memories, prepared . . . from the manuscript of the author by G. H. Wilson.* 1932.
—— *Lord Milner and his work.* Cape Town, 1925.
FRASER, Sir J. G. *Episodes in my Life.* Cape Town, 1922.
GARDINER, A. G. *The life of Sir William Harcourt.* 2 vols. 1923.

GARVIN, J. L. *Chamberlain.* 3 vols. 1932–4.
GERMAN GENERAL STAFF. *Kriegsgeschichtliche Einzelschriften. Aus dem süd-afrikanischen Kriege,* 1899 *bis* 1902. Berlin, 1903–5.
The War in South Africa from October 1899 *to September* 1900. Authorised English translation by W. H. WATERS and H. DU CANE. 2 vols. 1904–6.
HAFERKORN, H. E. *The South African War. A Bibliography.* Fort Humphreys, U.S.A., 1924.
HAMMOND, J. H. *The autobiography of John Hays Hammond.* 2 vols. New York, 1935.
HICKS BEACH, Lady V. *Life of Sir Michael Hicks Beach (Earl St Aldwyn).* 2 vols. 1932.
HOLE, H. MARSHALL. *The Making of Rhodesia.* 1926.
—— *The Jameson Raid.* 1930.

A copy annotated in MS. by the late Sir Graham Bower is in the S.A. Public Library, Cape Town. (S.A. MSS. d. 11.)

HONE, P. F. *Southern Rhodesia.* 1909.
JEYES, S. H. *Mr Chamberlain: his life and public career.* 2 vols. 1904.
KENNEDY, W. P. M. and SCHLOSBERG, H. J. *The Law and Custom of the South African Constitution.* 1935.
KEPPEL-JONES, A. *Friends or Foes?* 1950.
KESTELL, J. D. *Met de Boeren Commandos. Mijne ervaringen als veld-prediker.* Amsterdam and Pretoria. [1903.]
—— *Through Shot and Flame.* 1903 [1902].
KESTELL, J. D. and VELDEN, D. E. VAN. *The Peace Negotiations between the governments of the South African Republic and the Orange Free State, and the Representatives of the British Government.* 1912.
KHAMA, T. *Bechuanaland and South Africa.* 1955.
KILPIN, R. *The Old Cape House.* Cape Town, 1918.
—— *The Romance of a Colonial Parliament.* 1930.
KRUGER, S. J. P. *The Memoirs of Paul Kruger.... Told by himself* (translated by T. DE MATTOS). 2 vols. 1902.
LEE, Sir S. *King Edward VII, a biography.* 2 vols. 1925–7.
LEYDS, W. J. *The first annexation of the Transvaal.* 1906.
—— *The Transvaal surrounded.* 1919.
LOVELL, R. I. *The struggle for South Africa. A study in economic imperialism,* 1875–99. New York, 1934.
MAURICE, (Sir) J. F. and Staff. *History of the War in South Africa compiled by direction of H.M. Government.* 3 vols. 1906–8.
MOLTENO, Sir J. T. *The Dominion of Africanderdom: recollections pleasant and otherwise.* 1923.
—— *Further South African Recollections.* 1926.
MORLEY, J. (Viscount). *Life of William Ewart Gladstone.* 3 vols. 1903.
NEWTON, T. W. L., Baron. *Lord Lansdowne, a biography.* 1929.
PERKINS, DEXTER. *The Monroe Doctrine,* 1868–1907). Baltimore. 1937.
REITZ, D. *Commando, A Boer Journal of the Boer War.* 1929.
SPENDER, J. A. *The Life of the Rt. Hon. Sir Henry Campbell-Bannerman.* 2 vols. 1923.
STENT, VERE P. *A Personal Record of some incidents in the Life of Cecil Rhodes.* Cape Town, [1925].
THOMSON, L. M. Constitutionalism in the South African Republics (*Butterworth's S.A. Law Review*). Durban, 1954.
VAN DER POEL, J. *The Jameson Raid.* 1951.
WALLIS, J. P. R. (Ed.). *The Barotseland Journal of James Stevenson-Hamilton,* 1898–9. 1953.
WET, C. R. DE. *The Three Years' War.* 1902.
WOLF, L. *The Life of the first Marquess of Ripon.* 2 vols. 1921.
WORSFOLD, W. B. *Lord Milner's Work in South Africa from its commencement in* 1897 *to the Peace of Vereeniging.* 1906.

SECTION XIII. THE UNION, 1901–21

(Chapters XXIII, XXIV (*a*) and XXV)

For British Parliamentary Papers and debates see Part I, A 3 and 4.

(*a*) Official Publications: South African

See Part I, B 2

The Annexures to the *Votes and Proceedings* of the Cape Parliament, the Union Parliament, etc. contain all Select Committee Reports, Departmental Reports and Papers ordered to be printed. In the following section U.G. signifies published by order of the Union Government, A. signifies published by order of the House of Assembly, S. signifies published by order of the Senate, S.C. signifies Select Committee Report.

1. Departmental and other Reports.

Controller and Auditor-General. *Reports on Union Finance Accounts.* (Annual.)
—— *Reports on S.A. Railways Finance Accounts.* (Annual.)
Memorandum by the Clerk of the Senate upon the position of the South African Senate with reference to matters relating to Public Money. S. 1, 1912.
Witwatersrand Disturbances. *Agreements between Government and Strikers and demands made by Strikers.* A. 4, 1914.
—— *Convictions under Martial Law.* U.G. 6, 1914.
—— *Secret outrages committed, and attempts to commit outrages by explosives.* U.G. 8, 1914.
Memorandum by the Clerk of the Senate relative to the question of the Senate of South Africa after the expiration of the period of ten years for which it was constituted in 1910. S. 1, 1917.
Natives Land Act, 1913. Local Committees. *Cape Province, report.* U.G. 8, 1918. *Eastern Transvaal, report.* U.G. 31, 1918. *Natal Province, report.* U.G. 34, 1918. *Orange Free State Province, report.* U.G. 22, 1918. *Western Transvaal, report.* U.G. 23, 1918.
Report of Speaker's Conference on the future constitution of the Senate. U.G. 65, 1920.
South West Africa. *Administrator's Report,* 1921. U.G. 32, 1922.

In this report reference is made to the Concordat regarding the German language and to the taking over of the German schools.

Southern Rhodesia. Correspondence relating to the terms upon which the Union Government would recommend to Parliament the inclusion of Southern Rhodesia in the Union of South Africa. A. 187, 1923 (not printed).
Union Parliament. House of Assembly. *Standing orders.* 2 vols. Cape Town, 1919.
—— Senate. *Standing orders.* Cape Town, 1913.

2. Select Committee Reports.

Public Accounts Select Committee. *Reports.* (Annual.)
—— *Epitome of reports and Treasury minutes thereon, with index,* 1910–16. U.G. 38, 1916.
Public Education. *Report of the Select Committee on.* S.C. 2, 1911.

This Select Committee was appointed to examine the educational systems of the four Provinces in South Africa with a view to ascertaining whether they were in harmony with article 137 of the South Africa Act. The Report throws much light on the dual language controversy.

Financial Relations Bill. *Report of Select Committee.* S.C. 8, 1913.
Public Service and Pensions Bill. *Report of Select Committee on.* S.C. 11, 1912.
Public Service Commission's Report. *Select Committee's Report on.* S.C. 7, 1914.

Native Affairs. *Fourth report of the Select Committee on Native Affairs Administration.* S.C. 6*a*, 1917.

This report deals with the Native Affairs Administration Bill, which *inter alia* proposed to ratify the recommendations of the statutory Natives Land Commission appointed under the Natives Land Act, 1913. This part of the Bill was not proceeded with.

Areas Reservation and Immigration and Registration (Further Provision) Bill. *Special report of Select Committee on.* S.C. 9, 1926.

The evidence of the deputation representing the Government of India is important. The Committee reported in favour of a conference between representatives of the Union Government and the Government of India. The conference met in Cape Town in December, 1926.

3. Commission Reports.

Delimitation Commission, 1909. *Report.* Pretoria, 1910.

Financial Relations Commission. *First report.* U.G. 11, 1912.

—— *Second report.* U.G. 14, 1912.

Public Service Commission. *Reports.* (Annual since 1912.)

—— *First-Fifteenth reports on reorganization.* 1911–12.

Witwatersrand Disturbances Commission. *Report.* U.G. 55, 1913. *Evidence.* U.G. 56, 1913.

Economic Commission. *Report.* U.G. 12, 1914.

This Commission was appointed in 1913, after the disturbances on the Witwatersrand, to report on the economic conditions of the Mines.

Indian Enquiry Commission. *Report.* U.G. 16, 1914.

University Commission. *Report.* U.G. 42, 1914.

This report contains the most complete and authoritative review of the development of higher Education in South Africa.

Natives Land Commission. *Report.* U.G. 19, 1916. *Evidence.* U.G. 22, 1916. *Minute by Sir W. H. Beaumont (chairman).* U.G. 25, 1916.

The minute addressed to the Minister of Native Affairs deals with the wider aspects of the land segregation policy.

Provincial Administration Commission. *Report.* U.G. 45, 1916. *Evidence.* U.G. 8, 1917.

Public Service Commission of Enquiry. *First report.* U.G. 54, 1918. *Second report.* U.G. 26, 1919. *Third report.* U.G. 46, 1919. *Fourth report.* U.G. 57, 1919. *Fifth report.* U.G. 6, 1921.

South West Africa Commission. *Report on future form of Government.* U.G. 24, 1921.

The present constitution of S.W. Africa, granted in 1925, is largely based on this report.

Provincial Finances Commission. *Report.* U.G. 19, 1923.

Transvaal Asiatic Land Tenure Act Commission. *Report* (Parts I and II). U.G. 7, 1934.

(*b*) South African National Convention.

Minutes of Proceedings with annexures (selected) of the South African National Convention. Cape Town, 1911.

Malan, F. S. *Die Konvensie-Dagboek*, 1908–1909, trans. and edited by J. F. Preller (Van Riebeeck Society, Cape Town, 1951).

Walton, Sir E. H. *The Inner History of the National Convention.* Cape Town, 1912.

(*c*) South African Law Reports

Appellate Division *Reports*, 1910– .

Cape Provincial Division *Reports*, 1910– .

Natal Provincial Division *Reports*, 1910– .

Orange Free State Provincial Division *Reports*, 1910– .

Transvaal Provincial Division *Reports*, 1910– .

(*d*) Special Articles in Periodicals

Amery, L. S. The Constitutional Development of South Africa. *Trans. Royal Hist. Soc.* 1918, 4th ser. vol. I, pp. 218–35.
Beinart, B. The South African Senate. *The Modern Law Review*, 1957, vol. xx, pp. 549–65.
Buxton, S. C. B. (Earl). South Africa and its Native Problem. *Journal of the African Society*, 1921, vol. xx, pp. 161–73.
—— The South African Senate and the Speaker's Conference. *Journal of Comparative Legislation*, 1923, 3rd ser. vol. v, pt. I, pp. 130–4.
Curtis, L. South Africa since the Union. *Atlantic Monthly*, 1927, vol. CXLVI, pp. 253–63.
Dawbarn, C. Lord Buxton in South Africa. *Contemporary Review*, 1920, vol. CXVIII, pp. 795–800.
Harris, J. H. General Botha's Native Land Policy. *Journal of the African Society*, 1916, vol. XVI, pp. 7–15.
—— General Botha—Statesman. *Fortnightly Review*, 1917, vol. CI, pp. 652–60.
Jones, R. South African Union and the Colour Question. *Nineteenth Century*, 1909, vol. LXVI, pp. 245–56.
Keith, A. B. South African Union. *Journal of Comparative Legislation*, 1909, new ser. vol. x, pt. I, pp. 40–92.
—— Ministerial Responsibility in the Dominions. *Journal of Comparative Legislation*, 1917, new ser. vol. XVII, pt. 3, pp. 227–32.
Langenhoven, C. J. The Female Franchise and the Native Franchise. *The State*, 1909, vol. II, pp. 58–65.
Macassey, Sir L. Law-Making by Government Departments. *Journal of Comparative Legislation*, 1923, 3rd ser. vol. v, pt. I, pp. 73–89.
Mandelbrote, H. J. The Royal Prerogative in the Union. *The South African Law Journal*, 1936, vol. LIII, pp. 426–40.
Matthew, E. L. South African Native Land Laws. *Journal of Comparative Legislation*, 1915, new ser. vol. XV, pp. 9–16.
Newnham, F. J. Native Franchise in South Africa. *United Empire*, 1910, vol. I, pp. 571–9.
Peace, W. The Unification of South Africa. *Nineteenth Century*, 1909, vol. LXV, pp. 904–8.
Pollak, W. The Legislative Competence of the Union Parliament. *The South African Law Journal*, 1931, vol. XLVIII, pp. 269–87.
Prevost-Battersby, H. F. The Issue in South Africa. *Nineteenth Century*, 1921, vol. LXXXIX, pp. 329–40.
Scully, W. C. The Colour Problem in South Africa. *Edinburgh Review*, 1919, vol. CCXXX, pp. 78–92.
Seward, F. J. Parties under Union. *African Monthly*, 1909, vol. VI, pp. 361–71.
"South African", *pseud.* Political Parties and Problems of South Africa. *Contemporary Review*, 1920, vol. CXVII, pp. 197–203.
[Stock, J. L. W.] South African Constitutionalism. *Round Table*, 1914, no. 15, pp. 484–500.
"Table Mountain", *pseud.* The First South African Cabinet. *National Review*, 1913, vol. LXI, pp. 159–73.

(*e*) Other Works

See also Part II, I (*e*); Part II, I (*f*)

Beak, G. B. *The Aftermath of War; an account of the repatriation of Boers and Natives in the Orange River Colony* 1902–4. 1906.
Bosman, W. *The Natal Rebellion* 1906. 1907.
Brand, Hon. R. H. *The Union of South Africa*. Oxford, 1909.

BROOKES, E. H. *The Political Future of South Africa.* Pretoria, 1927.

—— *The Colour Problems of South Africa, being the Phelps-Stokes Lectures,* 1933, *delivered at the University of Cape Town.* Lovedale, 1934.

Full discussion of the Union's native legislation, 1910–32.

BRYCE, J. (Viscount). *Studies in History and Jurisprudence.* 2 vols. Oxford, 1901.

BUCHAN, J. (Baron Tweedsmuir). *The African Colony: studies in reconstruction.* Pt. III, chaps. XII–XIX. 1903.

CAMPBELL, P. C. *Chinese Coolie Emigration to countries within the British Empire.* 1923.

CLOUGH, E. M. O. *The South African Parliamentary Manual.* 1909.

COWEN, D. V. *Parliamentary Sovereignty and the Entrenched Sections of the South African Constitution.* Cape Town, 1951.

Coming of Age. Studies in South African Citizenship Politics, by eight contributors. Cape Town, 1930.

DICEY, A. V. *Introduction to the study of the Law of the Constitution.* 8th ed. 1915.

EGERTON, H. E. *Federations and Unions within the British Empire.* 2nd ed. Oxford, 1924.

EVANS, M. S. *Black and White in South East Africa.* 1911.

FRANKEL, S. H. *The Railway Policy of South Africa.* Johannesburg, 1928.

—— *Government of South Africa, The.* 2 vols. Cape Town, 1908.

Hereenigingscongress. *Report.* Bloemfontein, 1920.

This pamphlet throws much light on the Republican propaganda. It gives the reasons why the attempt to re-unite the South African and National Parties failed.

JENKS, E. *The Government of the British Empire.* 1918.

Johannesburg Joint Council of Europeans and Natives. *Memorandum no.* 4. *In defence of the Cape Franchise.* Johannesburg, 1929.

KEITH, A. B. *Dominion Autonomy in practice.* Oxford, 1929.

—— *The Constitution, Administration and Laws of the Empire.* 1924.

—— *Responsible Government in the Dominions.* 2nd ed. 2 vols. Oxford, 1928.

KENNEDY, W. P. M. and SCHLOSBERG, H. J. *The Law and Custom of the South African Constitution.* Oxford, 1935.

KILPIN, R. *Parliamentary Procedure in South Africa.* 3rd ed. Cape Town, 1955.

KOCK, M. H. DE. *An analysis of the Finances of the Union of South Africa.* Cape Town, 1922.

KOTZE, (Sir) J. G. *Documents and correspondence relating to the Judicial Crisis in the S.A. Republic,* 1898.

LEES-SMITH, H. B. *Second Chambers in theory and practice.* 1923.

MALAN, Rt. Hon. F. S. *Die Konvensie Dagboek van sy Edelagbare François Stephanus Malan,* 1908–9. Van Riebeeck Society, vol. XXXII. With English translation.

MALHERBE, E. G. *Education in South Africa,* 1652–1922. Cape Town, 1925.

MARRIOTT, Sir J. A. R. *The Mechanism of the modern State.* 2 vols. Oxford, 1927.

MAY, H. J. *The South African Constitution.* 3rd ed. Cape Town, 1955.

MILNER, A. (Viscount). *The Nation and the Empire, being a collection of speeches and addresses.* 1913.

NATHAN, M. *The South African Commonwealth.* Johannesburg, 1919.

National Party of South Africa. *Beginsels, Konstitutie en Statuten van de Nationale Partij in Zuid-Afrika.* Potchefstroom, 1914.

—— *Programme of Principles.* Cape Town, 1921.

NEAME, L. E. *General Hertzog.* 1930.

NEUENDORFF, G. *The Union Senate.*

An unpublished thesis in the University Library, Cape Town.

ORPEN, J. M. *The Native Question in connection with the South Africa Bill.* Cape Town, 1909.

PALMER, W. W., 2nd Earl of Selborne. *The Selborne Memorandum; a review of the Mutual Relations of the British South African Colonies in* 1907; *with an introduction by Professor Basil Williams.* Oxford, 1925.

PITTIUS, E. F. W. G. VAN. *Die stelsel van prowinsiale Rade in Suid-Afrika*. Pretoria, 1926.
PYRAH, G. B. *Imperial Policy in South Africa*, 1902–10. 1955.
ROSE-INNES, Sir J. *The Native Franchise Question*. Cape Town, 1929.
SCHLOSBERG, H. J. *The King's Republics*. 1929.
SCHREINER, O. D. *Closer Union*. 1909.
SOLOMON, Sir R. Government and Finances of the Union. *The Oxford Survey of the British Empire*, 1914, vol. III *Africa*, pp. 175–200.
South African Labour Party. *Constitution and Platform*. Johannesburg, 1914.
South African Native Races Committee. *The Native Races of South Africa: their economic and social condition*. 1901.
—— *The Natives of South Africa; their progress and present condition*. 1909.
South African Party. *Programme of Principles and Constitution*. Cape Town, 1914.
SPENDER, J. A. *The life of the Rt. Hon. Sir Henry Campbell-Bannerman*. 2 vols. 1923.
STUART, J. *History of the Zulu Rebellion*, 1906. 1913.
THOMPSON, L. M. *The Cape Coloured Franchise*. S.A. Institute of Race Relations, 1949.
—— *The Unification of South Africa*, 1902–10. 1960.
Times History of the War in South Africa 1899–1902 (ed. L. S. AMERY), vol. VI, pt. I. 1909.
WALKER, E. A. *Lord de Villiers and his times: South Africa*, 1842–1914. 1925.
WORSFOLD, W. B. *Lord Milner's Work in South Africa from its commencement in* 1897 to the Peace of Vereeniging. 1906.
—— *The Reconstruction of the New Colonies under Lord Milner*. 2 vols. 1913.

SECTION XIV. RHODESIA

(Chapter XXIV (*b*))

(*a*) OFFICIAL PUBLICATIONS

For British Parliamentary Papers and debates see Part I, A 3 and 4.

For South African and Rhodesian Parliamentary Papers and debates and Statutes see Part I, B 2.

BRITISH SOUTH AFRICA COMPANY. *Directors' Reports and Accounts*. (Annual.) 1891– .
—— *Reports of the Ordinary General Meetings*. (Annual.) 1891– .
—— *Reports of Extraordinary General Meetings*. 1893– .

(*b*) OTHER WORKS

ACWORTH, W. M. *Report on the Railway Question in Southern Rhodesia*. 1918.
BERTIN, H. *What ails Rhodesia?* Salisbury, 1913.
COGHLAN, Sir C. *Responsible Government: two addresses*. Bulawayo, 1919.
COLVIN, IAN. *The life of Jameson*. 2 vols. 1923.
COLVIN, IAN and LONGDEN, H. T. The future of Rhodesia. *The Quarterly Review*, April, 1914.
DAVIDSON, J. W. *The Northern Rhodesian Legislative Council*. London, 1947.
EYBERS, G. W. *Select Constitutional Documents . . .*, 1795–1910. 1918.
FLETCHER, TREVOR. *Rhodesia and the Union*. Salisbury, 1919.
FOX, H. WILSON. *Statement to the Rhodesian Chamber of Mines*. Bulawayo, 1914.
HEADLAM, C. (Ed.). *The Milner Papers*, vol. II. 1933.
HOLE, H. M. *The Making of Rhodesia*. 1926.
HONE, P. F. *Southern Rhodesia*. 1909.
JAMESON, Sir L. S. *Speech delivered by the Rt. Hon. Sir Starr Jameson*. Bulawayo, 1914.
NEWTON, A. P. *Select Documents relating to the Unification of South Africa*. 2 vols. 1924.
Round Table, The. Nos. 29, 38, 43, 44, 45, 48, 49, 53, 56.
SHAPIRO, M. J. *The Burning Question of Rhodesia. Whose is the Land and whose should it be?* Salisbury, 1913.
WALKER, E. A. Southern Rhodesia, in *The Times*, 19, 21 and 22 May 1920.

SECTION XV. THE GERMANS IN SOUTH-WEST AFRICA, 1883–1914

(Chapter XXVI)

(a) Documentary Material

1. *Official* (British and Colonial).

Angra Pequena. *Correspondence respecting the settlement at Angra Pequena*, 3 pts. *Parl. Pap.* 1884, LVI [C. 4190]; LVII [C. 4194]; LVIII [C. 4191].

—— *Further correspondence respecting claims of British subjects in the German Protectorate on the South-West Coast of Africa. Parl. Pap.* 1887, LXI [C. 5810].

—— *Anglo-German arrangement re spheres of action, Berlin, 16 Dec. 1884. Parl. Pap.* 1884–5, LV [C. 4442].

Palgrave, W. C. *Report of his mission to Damaraland and Great Namaqualand in* 1876. [G. 50, 1877.]

2. *Official* (German).

Weissbuch dem Deutschen Reichstag vorgelegt. 1885.

(b) Contemporary and Later Works

Alexander, Sir J. *Expedition of discovery into the Interior of Africa.* 2 vols. 1838.

Andersson, C. J. Explorations in South Africa, 1855. *Journal of the Royal Geographical Society*, vol. xxv, pp. 79–107.

—— *Notes of travel in South Africa*, ed. L. Lloyd. 1875.

Auer von Herrenkirchen, H. *Meine Erlebnisse während des Feldzuges gegen die Hereros und Witboois.* Berlin, 1906.

Baines, T. *Explorations in South-West Africa.* 1864.

Barmer Missionsblatt. (Erscheint in Barmen, Rheinland. Enthält von 1840 an wertvolle geschichtliche Mitteilungen.)

Barth, P. *Südwestafrika.* Windhoek, 1926.

Bayer, M. Hauptmann im grossen Generalstabe. *Die Nation der Bastards.* Berlin, 1907.

—— *Mit dem Hauptquartier in Südwestafrika.* Berlin, 1909.

Belwe, M. *Gegen die Herero* 1904–5. *Tagebuchaufzeichnungen.* Berlin, 1906.

Berichte der Rheinischen Missionsgesellschaft. Barmen. (Seit 1850. Bieten viel geschichtliches Material.)

Bittrolf, R. *Der Krieg in Deutsch-Südwest-Afrika.* Karlsruhe, 1895.

Boethke, Hauptmann. *Die Verkehrstruppen in Südwest-Afrika.* Berlin, 1906.

Brincker, P. H. *Aus dem Hererolande.* Barmen, 1896.

—— *Die Eingeborenen Deutsch-Südwest-Afrikas nach Geschichte, Charakter, Sitten, Gebräuchen und Sprachen.* Berlin, 1899.

Bülow, F. von. *Im Felde gegen die Hereros. Erlebnisse eines Mitkämpfers.* Bremen, 1905.

—— *Deutsch-Südwestafrika. Drei Jahre im Lande Hendrik Witboois.* Berlin, 1897.

Bülow, H. von. *Deutschlands Kolonien und Kolonialkriege.* Dresden, 1900.

Burger, A. *Aus dem Kriegsleben in Südwest-Afrika.* 1906.

Calvert, A. F. *Southwest Africa during the German occupation*, 1884–1914. 2nd ed. 1916.

Cannstatt, O. *Der Hereroaufstand und dessen Einwirkung.* Berlin, 1904.

Carow, R. *Die Kaiserliche Schutztruppe in Deutsch-Südwest-Afrika unter Major Leutwein.* Leipzig, 1898.

Chapman, J. *Travels in the interior of South Africa.* 2 vols. 1868.

Deimling, Oberst von. *Südwest-Afrika. Land und Leute. Unsere Kämpfe.* Berlin, 1906.

Denkschrift betreffend das südwestafrikanische Schutzgebiet. (Beilage zum *Deutschen Kolonialblatt.* 1893–4.)

Denkschrift über Eingeborenen-Politik und Hereroaufstand. Berlin, 1904.

Denkschrift über die Entwicklung der Schutzgebiete in Afrika und in der Südsee. 5 Bde. 1906–9.

Dove, K. *Deutsch-Südwestafrika.* Berlin, 1913.

Eckenbrecher, M. von. *Was Afrika mir gab und nahm. Erlebnisse einer Ansiedlerfrau in Südwestafrika.* Berlin, 1906.

Engelbrechten, Leutnant von. *Der Krieg in Deutsch-Südwest-Afrika. Vorgeschichte, Entstehung des Aufstandes. Der Bondelzwartaufstand. Der Hereroaufstand bis zu den Gefechten am Waterberg.* Berlin, 1906.

Fabri, F. *Fünf Jahre deutscher Kolonialpolitik.* Gotha, 1889.

François, C. von. *Deutsch-Südwest-Afrika. Geschichte der Kolonisation bis zum Ausbruch des Krieges mit Witbooi.* Berlin, 1899.

—— *Der Hottentottenaufstand. Studie über die Vorgänge im Namalande vom Januar* 1904 *bis zum Januar* 1905. Berlin, 1905.

—— *Kriegführung in Südafrika.* Berlin, 1900.

François, H. von. *Nama und Damara. Deutsch-Südwestafrika.* Magdeburg, 1896.

Galton, F. *Narrative of an explorer in tropical South Africa.* 1853.

Hanemann, Dr. *Wirtschaftliche und politische Verhältnisse in Deutsch-Südwest-Afrika.* Berlin, 1907.

Hassert, K. *Deutschlands Kolonien. Erwerbungs- und Entwicklungsgeschichte.* Leipzig, 1910.

Henderson, W. O. The German Colonial Empire, 1884–1918. *History,* xx (Sept. 1935), 151–8.

Hennig, R. *Deutsch-Südwest im Weltkriege.* Berlin, 1920.

Henoch, F. A. *Lüderitz.* Berlin, 1909.

Hereroaufstand, Der. (60 Tafeln mit untergedrucktem Text.) Trier, 1904.

Hesse, H. *Die Schutzverträge in Südwest-Afrika.* Berlin, 1905.

Irle, J. *Die Herero. Ein Beitrag zur Landes-, Volks- und Missionskunde.* Gütersloh, 1906.

Jahresberichte über die Entwicklung der deutschen Schutzgebiete. Berlin, 1895–1906.

Kämpfe, die, der deutschen Truppen in Südwestafrika. Auf Grund amtlichen Materials bearbeitet von der kriegsgeschichtlichen Abteilung I *des Grossen Generalstabs.* (Band I. Der Feldzug gegen die Hereros. Band II. Der Hottentottenkrieg.) Berlin, 1906–7.

Kingon, W. L. *The Germans in Damaraland.* Cape Town, 1889.

Kolbe, M. *Unsere Helden in Südwest-Afrika.* Leipzig, 1907.

Külz, W. *Die Selbstverwaltung für Deutsch-Südwest-Afrika.* Berlin, 1909– .

—— *Deutsch-Südwestafrika im* 25. *Jahre deutscher Schutzherrschaft.* Berlin, 1909.

Leutwein, P. *Meine Erlebnisse im Kampf gegen die Herero.* Minden, 1905.

—— *Die Leistungen der Regierung in der Südwestafrikanischen Land- und Minenfrage.* Berlin, 1911.

Leutwein, Th. G. von. *Die Kämpfe der kaiserlichen Schutztruppe in Deutsch-Südwest-Afrika in den Jahren* 1894–96. Berlin, 1898.

—— *Elf Jahre Gouverneur in Deutsch-Südwestafrika.* Berlin, 1907. Dritte Auflage, 1908.

Leutz, H. *Die Kolonien Deutschlands, ihre Erwerbung, Bevölkerung, Bodenbeschaffenheit und Erzeugnisse.* Berlin, 1900.

Ritchie, M. *With Botha in the field.* 1915.

Oelhafen von Schollenbach, H. *Der Feldzug im Südwest* 1914–15. Berlin, 1923.

—— *Die Besiedelung Deutsch-Südwestafrikas bis zum Weltkriege.* Berlin, 1926.

Pfeil, J., Graf von. *Deutsch-Südwest-Afrika jetzt und später.* München, 1905.

Pohle, H. Bericht über die von Herrn Lüderitz ausgerüstete Expedition nach Südwest-Afrika 1884–4. *Peterman's Mitteilungen.* 1886. Bd. xxxii.

Preller, G. S. *Voortrekkers van Suidwes.* 1941.

Rayner, W. S. and O'Shaughnessy, W. W. *How Botha and Smuts conquered German South West.* 1916.

RHEINEN, O. *Die Selbstverwaltung der Gemeinden in Deutsch-Südwest-Afrika.* Jena, 1912.

RIDSDALE, B. *Scenes and adventures in Great Namaqualand.* 1883.

ROHDEN, L. VON. *Geschichte der Rheinischen Missionsgesellschaft.* Barmen, 1888.

RUST, C. *Krieg und Frieden im Hereroland.* Berlin, 1905.

SALZMANN, E. VON. *Im Kampfe gegen die Herero.* Berlin, 1905.

SANDER, L. *Geschichte der deutschen Kolonialgesellschaft für Südwest-Afrika von ihrer Gründung bis* 1910. 2 Bde. Berlin, 1912.

SCHANZ, M. *Das erste Vierteljahrhundert deutscher Kolonialwirtschaft.* 1910.

SCHINZ, H. *Deutsch-Süd-West Afrika.* Oldenburg; Leipzig, 1891.

SCHLETTWEIN, C. *Der Hereroaufstand, was hat ihn veranlasst und was lehrt er uns?*— 1905.

SCHMIDT, K. *Geographie der Europäersiedlungen im deutschen Südwestafrika.* Jena, 1922.

SCHWABE, K. *Mit Schwert und Pflug in Deutsch-Südwestafrika.* Berlin, 1904.

—— *Deutsch-Südwestafrika. Historisch-geographisch-militärische und wirtschaftliche Studien.* 1905.

SEITZ, TH. *Südafrika im Weltkriege.* Berlin, 1920.

—— *Vom Aufstieg und Niederbruch deutscher Kolonialmacht. Erinnerungen von Dr Theodor Seitz.* . . . Bd. 3. *Die Gouverneursjahre in Südwestafrika.* Karlsruhe, 1929.

SIMON, L. *Geschichte der deutschen Kolonialgesellschaft für Südwest-Afrika.*

SONNENBERG, E. *Wie es am Waterberg zuging. Ein Beitrag zur Geschichte des Hereroaufstandes.* Berlin, 1905.

STÜLPNAGEL, C. VON. *Heisse Tage. Meine Erlebnisse im Kampf gegen die Herero.* Berlin, 1906.

Südwest-Afrika deutsch oder britisch? Eine Streitschrift von einem alten Afrikaner. Leipzig, 1907.

Tätigheit, die, des Landungskorps S.M.S. Habicht während des Hereroaufstandes in Südwest-Afrika Januar-Februar 1904. *Auf Grund amtlichen Materials bearbeitet im Admiralstab der Marine.* 1905.

TINDALL, H. *Two lectures on Great Namaqualand.* Cape Town, 1856.

TOWNSEND, M. *The rise and fall of Germany's Colonial Empire,* 1884–1918. New York, 1930.

Veröffentlichungen der Wissenschaftlichen Vereinigung in Südwestafrika. Windhoek, 1927–9. (Bd. I, Dr C. Frey, *Jonker Afrikaner and his time.* Bd. II, H. H. G. Kreft, *The diary of Hendrik Witbooi.*)

The diary of Witbooi is also published as vol. IX of the Van Riebeeck Society's *Publications.*

ZIMMERMANN, A. *Geschichte der deutschen Kolonialpolitik.* Berlin, 1914.

SECTION XVI. SOUTH AFRICA IN THE WORLD WAR, 1914–19

(Chapter XXVII)

(*a*) DOCUMENTARY MATERIAL

The best available information regarding the Rebellion is given in three official publications of the Union of South Africa, namely, *Report on the Outbreak of the Rebellion and the policy of the Government with regard to its Suppression* (U.G. No. 10, 1915), prepared by Professor Leo Fouché from information supplied to him by the Government; *Judicial Commission of Inquiry. Minutes of Evidence* (U.G. No. 42, 1916), and *Report on the Rebellion* (U.G. No. 46, 1916). The debates on the German South-West campaign and the rebellion are printed in *Union of South Africa, House of Assembly. Debates for* 1914 *and* 1915.

As regards military operations few books that can be considered as authoritative have yet appeared. Copies of the War Diaries of the South African units and formations that took part in the campaigns in South-West and East Africa, Egypt, and Europe, are housed in the Department of Defence at Pretoria. Statistics relating to the war are published in the White Book issued by the War Office, March 1922, *Statistics of the Military Effort of the British Empire during the Great War*, 1914–20. The figures which it gives should be compared with those shown in the *Official Year Book of the Union of South Africa, No.* 5, 1910–21.

(*b*) Other Authorities

1. *Newspapers.*

See Part II, 1 (*c*).

2. *Periodicals.*

Round Table, Nos. 16–34.

United Empire (Journal of the Royal Empire Society, formerly the Royal Colonial Institute), vols. v–viii.

Both give suggestive comments on Empire politics during the War.

(*c*) Other Works

Beer, G. L. *African questions at the Paris Peace Conference*. Ed. L. H. Gray. New York, 1923.

Brawley, B. G. *Africa and the War*. New York, 1918.

Buchan, J. (Baron Tweedsmuir). *The South African Forces in France*. 1920.

Regarded by South Africans as the standard account of the work of the South African Brigade in France.

Buchanan, Capt A. *Three years of War in East Africa*. 1919.

Buxton, S., Earl. *General Botha*. 1924.

"Captain", *pseud. With the Springboks in Egypt*. 1916.

Clifford, Sir H. *The Gold Coast Regiment in the East African Campaign*. 1920.

Corbett, Sir J. S. *History of the Great War. Naval Operations*. 3 vols. 1920–1.

Croft, Lt.-Col. W. D. *Three years with the Ninth Division*. 1919.

Crowe, Brig.-Gen. J. H. V. *General Smuts' Campaign in East Africa*. 1918.

The author was in command of Gen. Smuts' artillery.

Dane, E. *British Campaigns in Africa and the Pacific*, 1914–18. 1919.

Dewar, G. A. B. and Boraston, J. H. *Sir Douglas Haig's Command*. 2 vols. 1922.

Doitsh, E. *The first Springbok in Germany*. 1917.

Dolbey, R. V. *Sketches of the East African Campaign*. 1919.

Edmonds, Brig.-Gen. Sir J. E. and Becke, Major A. F. *Official History of the Great War. Military Operations. France and Belgium*. (In progress.)

Engelenburg, F. V. *General Louis Botha*. 1929.

Ewing, J. *History of the 9th (Scottish) Division*, 1914–19. 1921.

Fendall, Brig.-Gen. C. P. *The East African Field Force*. 1921.

Hall, W. P. *Empire to Commonwealth*. 1929.

An American view of the effect of the war on the Empire.

Hennig, R. *Deutsch-Südwest im Weltkriege*. Berlin, 1920.

Johnston, Sir H. H. *The Black Man's part in the War*. 1917.

Johnston, R. E. *Ulundi to Delville Wood*. 1930.

An account of the career of Major-General Sir H. T. Lukin.

Letcher, O. *Cohort of the Tropics*. 1931.

Lettow-Vorbeck, General von. *My Reminiscences of East Africa*. 1920.

A good general account of the campaign and valuable as showing the German point of view. The author exaggerates the strength of his enemies, and his details should be compared with those given in *Union of South Africa and the Great War*, 1914–18.

Lewin, P. E. *The Germans and Africa*. 1915.

—— *German rule in Africa*. 1918.

LUCAS, Sir C. P. (Ed.). *The Empire at War.* Vol. IV. 1925.
MACMUNN, Lt.-Gen. Sir G. and FALLS, Capt. C. *Official History of the Great War. Military Operations. Egypt and Palestine.* Vol. I. 1928.
MOREL, E. D. *Africa and the Peace of Europe.* 1917.
NEAME, L. E. *General Hertzog.* 1930.
O'NEILL, H. C. *War in Africa* 1914–17 *and in the Far East* 1914. 1919.
RAYNER, W. S. and O'SHAUGHNESSY, W. W. *How Botha and Smuts conquered German South West.* 1916.
REITZ, Col. D. *Trekking On.* 1933.
RITCHIE, M. *With Botha in the Field.* 1915.
ROBINSON, J. P. K. *With Botha's Army.* 1916.
SAMPSON, P. J. *Capture of De Wet; with Conquest of German West Africa.* 1915.
SEITZ, TH. *Südafrika im Weltkriege.* Berlin, 1920.
SOLOMON, E. *Potchefstroom to Delville Wood.* Johannesburg, 1919.
SPARROW, W. S. *The Fifth Army in March* 1918. 1920.
SPENDER, H. *General Botha: the career and the man.* 1919.
STANDAERT, E. *A Belgian Mission to the Boers.* 1917.
Union of South Africa and the Great War, 1914–18. *Official History.* Pretoria, 1924.

A clear narrative of the part played by South Africa in the various theatres of war. The treatment of the Senussi campaign is inadequate.

WALKER, H. F. B. *A Doctor's Diary in Damaraland.* 1917.
WALPOLE, V. *The men in the Line.* Cape Town and Johannesburg, 1930.
WEBB, H. S. *Oorzaken van de Rebellie.* Pretoria, 1916.
YOUNG, F. B. *Marching on Tanga.* 1917.

Notable for its vivid descriptions of warfare in East Africa.

SECTION XVII. SOUTH AFRICA AND THE EMPIRE, 1885–1921

(Chapter XXVIII)

(*a*) OFFICIAL PUBLICATIONS: BRITISH

See Part I, A 3, particularly the Parliamentary Papers:—

Correspondence re *contributions, Parl. Pap.* 1882, XLVII [C. 3280]; *Proceedings of the Colonial Conference*, 1887, LVI [C. 5091–I and II]; *Report . . . on the Colonial Conference*, 1894, LVI [C. 7553]; *Papers* re *the Colonial Conference*, 1895, LXX [C. 7632], [C. 7824]; *Papers* re *a Conference*, 1902, LXVI [Cd. 1299]; *Papers* re *the Colonial Conference*, 1903, XLIV [Cd. 1597], [Cd. 1723]; *Proceedings of the S.A. Customs Union Conference*, 1903, XLV [Cd. 1599], [Cd. 1640]; *Papers* re *the Colonial Conference*, 1907, LIV [Cd. 3337], [Cd. 3340]; LV [Cd. 3404], [Cd. 3406], [Cd. 3523], [Cd. 3524]; *Papers* re *a Conference on Defence*, 1909, LIX [Cd. 4948]; *Correspondence, proceedings and papers* re *Imperial Conference*, 1911, LIV [Cd. 5513], [Cd. 5741], [Cd. 5745], [Cd. 5746—I and II]; *Report of the Witwatersrand Disturbance Commission*, 1913, XLIX [Cd. 7112]; *Correspondence* re *General Strike*, 1914, LIX [Cd. 7348]; *Rupture with Germany* (*White Paper*), 1914, CI [Cd. 7445]; *Correspondence* re *Imperial Defence*, 1914, LX [Cd. 7347]; *Correspondence* re *expedition against German S.-W. Africa*, 1914, XLV [Cd. 7873]; *Papers* re *Imperial War Conference*, 1917–18, XXIII [Cd. 8566], [Cd. 8673]; *Imperial Preferences*, 1917–18, XXIII [Cd. 8482]; *Treaty of Peace at Versailles*, 1919, LIII [Cmd. 223]; *League of Nations*, 1920, LI [Cmd. 1022]; *Mandate*, 1921, XLII [Cmd. 1195]; *Papers* re *Prime Ministers' Conference*, 1921, XIV [Cmd. 1474].

(*b*) OFFICIAL PUBLICATIONS: SOUTH AFRICAN

See Part I, B 2, and the select bibliographies of the preceding chapters covering the years 1885–1921.

(*c*) Non-Official Publications

Periodicals. The Round Table, 1910– , particularly Nos. 3, 4, 18, 24–7, 35, 38, 43–6. *Journal of the Parliaments of the Empire*. 1920– .

(*d*) Other Works

Argyll, J. G., 9th Duke of. *Imperial Federation*. 1885.
Baker, P. J. N. *The present juridical status of the British Dominions in International Law*. 1929.
Chamberlain, J. *Mr Chamberlain's Speeches*, ed. by C. W. Boyd. 2 vols. 1914.
Curtis, L. *The Problem of the Commonwealth*. 1916.
—— *The Commonwealth of Nations*. 1916.
Demangeon, A. *The British Empire*. 1925.
Dewey, A. G. *The Dominions and Diplomacy*. 2 vols. 1929.
Dilke, Sir C. W. *Problems of Greater Britain*. 2 vols. 1890.
Egerton, H. E. *A short history of British Colonial Policy*, 1600–1909. 1932.
—— *British Colonial Policy in the 20th century*. 1922.
Elliott, W. Y. *The New British Empire*. 1932.
Fiddes, Sir G. *The Dominion and Colonial Offices*. 1926.
Findlay, J. G. V. *The Imperial Conference of* 1911 *from Within*. 1912.
Hall, D. *The British Commonwealth of Nations*. 1920.
Hall, W. P. *Empire to Commonwealth: thirty years of British Imperial History*. New York, 1928.
Jebb, R. *The Britannic Question*. 1913.
—— *The Empire in Eclipse*. 1926.
—— *The Imperial Conference*. 2 vols. 1911.
—— *Studies in Imperial Nationalism*. 1905.
Keith, A. Berriedale. *Constitution, Administration and Laws of the Empire*. 1924.
—— *The Constitutional Law of the British Dominions*. 1933.
—— *Responsible Government in the Dominions*. 2 vols. 1928.
—— *The Sovereignty of the British Dominions*. 1929.
—— The War Government of the British Empire: the Imperial War Cabinet. *Times History of the War*, vol. xii. 1917.
Lucas, Sir C. P. *The Empire at War*, vol. i. Oxford, 1921.
Kennedy, W. P. M. and Schlosberg, H. J. *The Law and Custom of the South African Constitution*. Oxford, 1935.
Marriott, Sir J. A. R. *The Mechanism of the Modern State*. Oxford, 1927.
Parkin, (Sir) G. R. *Imperial Federation*. 1892.
Porritt, E. *The Fiscal and Diplomatic Freedom of the British Dominions*. Oxford, 1923.
Root, J. W. *Trade relations of the British Empire*. Liverpool, 1904.
—— *Colonial Tariffs*. Liverpool, 1906.
Schuyler, R. L. *Parliament and the British Empire*. Cambridge, 1929.
Smuts, J. C. *The League of Nations. A practical suggestion*. 1918.
Zimmern, A. E. *The Third British Empire*. 1926.

SECTION XVIII. ECONOMIC DEVELOPMENT, 1795–1921

(Chapter XXIX)

(*a*) Official Publications (arranged in chronological order)

(1) Cape.

Report of the Railway Commission, 1878. G. 3, 1878.
Report of the Railway Rates Commission, 1883. G. 112, 1883.
Report of Select Committee on Colonial Agriculture and Industries, 1883. A. 3, 1883.
Illustrated Official Handbook of the Cape and South Africa, 1886, ed. J. Noble.
Report of the Conference on Customs Union and Railway Extension, 1888. G. 8, 1888.

Report of Select Committee on Colonial Industries, 1891. C. 1, 1891.
Report of Select Committee on Railway Management, 1893. S.C. 8, 1893.
Report of the Labour Supply Commission, 1893–4. G. 39, 1893 and G. 3, 1894.
Minutes of Conference on Customs Union, 1897, G. 44, 1897.
Minutes of Customs Union Conference, and Customs Union Convention, 1898. G. 66, 1898.
Minutes of Customs Union Conference, and Customs Union Convention, 1903. A. 1 and A. 2, 1903.
Customs Union Convention, 1906. *Parl. Pap.* 1906, LXXIX [Cd. 2977].
Report of the Customs Tariff Commission, 1908. G. 11, 1908.

(2) NATAL.

Report of the Customs Tariff Inquiry Commission, 1908 [No number.]

(3) ORANGE RIVER COLONY (FREE STATE).

Report of the Customs Commission, 1906. [No copy in Cape Town.]

(4) TRANSVAAL.

Report of the Transvaal Labour Commission. Parl. Pap. 1904, XXXIX [Cd. 1894–6–7].
Report of the Transvaal Indigency Commission, 1908. T.G. 13, 1908.
Report of the Mining Industry Commission, 1908.
Report of the Customs and Industries Commission, 1908. T.G. 6, 1908.

(5) SOUTHERN RHODESIA.

Report of Brig.-General F. D. Hammond on the Railway System of Southern Rhodesia, 3 vols., 1925. C.S.R. 2, 1926.
Report of the Land Commission, 1928. C.S.R. 3, 1926.

(6) UNION OF SOUTH AFRICA.

Report of the South African Native Affairs Commission, Parl. Pap. 1905, LV [Cd. 2399].
Report of the Commerce and Industrial Commission. U.G. 10, 1912.
Report of the Economic Commission. U.G. 12, 1914.
Report of the Select Committee on the Embargo on the Export of Specie. S.C. 2, 1920.
Report of the Commission on the Low Grade Mines. U.G. 34, 1920.
Reports of the Unemployment Commission. U.G. 16 and 34, 1921, and U.G. 17, 1922.
Report of the Sugar Enquiry Commission. U.G. 22, 1922.
Report of the Drought Investigation Commission. U.G. 20, 1922 and U.G. 49, 1923.
Report of the Commission on the Resumption of Gold Payments.... U.G. 12 and 13, 1925.
Reports of the Irrigation Finance Commission. U.G. 29 and 44, 1925, and U.G. 15, 1926.
Report of the Native Economic Commission. U.G. 22, 1932.

(*b*) PERIODICALS

Annual Proceedings of the South African Association for the Advancement of Science [*Economics Section*].
Journal of the Economic Society of South Africa. 1926–32.
Journal of the Institute of Bankers in South Africa. 1933 onwards.
Round Table, The. 1910 onwards.
South African Journal of Economics. 1933 onwards. Important articles on economic development.

(*c*) OTHER WORKS

AMPHLETT, G. T. *History of the Standard Bank of South Africa*, 1862–1913. Glasgow, 1914.
Anon. *An Account of the Colony of the Cape of Good Hope with a view to the Information of Emigrants.* 1819.

Anon. *Notes on the Cape of Good Hope made during an Excursion in that Colony in the year 1820.* 1821.

Anon. *The Cape Colony in 1868; a Handy book for intending settlers.* 1868.

Arndt, G. H. D. *Banking and Currency Development in South Africa, 1652–1927.* Cape Town, 1928.

Baines, T. *Gold Regions of South Eastern Africa.* 1877.

Barclays Bank (D.C. and O). *A Banking Centenary, 1836–1936.* 1938.

Barrow, Sir J. *Account of Travels into the Interior of South Africa in the years 1797 and 1798.* 1801–4.

Bisset, J. *On the construction of Railways in the Colony of the Cape of Good Hope.* Cape Town, 1869.

Bleloch, W. *The New South Africa.* 1901.

Brounger, W. G. *The Cape Government Railways.* 1885.

Brown, A. S. and G. S. (Eds.). *The South and East African Year Book and Guide* (Union Castle M.S. Co.). 1892 onwards.

Bruwer, A. J. *Protection in South Africa.* Stellenbosch, 1923.

Cannan, E. South African Currency. *Economic Journal.* 1920.

Carnegie Commission, Report of a: *The Poor White Problem in South Africa.* 5 vols. Stellenbosch, 1932.

Chamber of Mines, Annual Reports of the Transvaal. 1889 onwards.

Conacher, J. *Report upon the distribution of traffic between the South African Railways.* 1908.

Davenport, D. E. *A Railway Sketch of South Africa.* 1882.

Davidson, B. *Report on Southern Africa.* 1952.

Davis, J. Merle (Ed.). *Modern Industry and the African.* 1933.

De Kiewiet, C. W. *History of South Africa, Social and Economic.* Oxford, 1941.

de Kock, M. H. *An Analysis of the Finances of the Union of South Africa.* Cape Town, 1927.

—— *The Economic Development of South Africa.* P. S. King, 1936.

de Mist, J. A. *Memorandum . . . on the Government of the Cape of Good Hope* (translation). Cape Town, 1920. Van Riebeeck Society, Publication No. 3.

Edwards, I. E. *The 1820 Settlers in South Africa. A Study in British Colonial Policy.* 1934.

Evans, S. Preference and Protection in British South Africa, in *The Burden of Protection.* 1912.

Fairbridge, D. *Lady Anne Barnard at the Cape of Good Hope, 1797–1802.* Oxford, 1924.

Frankel, S. H. *Cooperation and Competition in the Marketing of Maize in South Africa.* 1926.

—— *The Railway Policy of South Africa.* Johannesburg, 1928.

—— *Capital Investment in Africa.* Oxford, 1938.

Franklin, N. N. *Economics in South Africa.* 2nd ed. Oxford, 1954.

Geyer, A. L. *Das wirtschaftliche System der holländischen ostindischen Kompanie am Kap der Guten Hoffnung, 1785–95.* München, 1923.

Giffen, Sir R. Some Economic Aspects of the South African War. *Economic Inquiries and Studies.* 1904.

Glanville, T. B. *Guide to South Africa* (4th ed. 1877). 1881.

Goldman, C. S. *Financial, Statistical and General History of the Gold and other Witwatersrand Companies of South Africa.* 1892.

—— *South African Mines.* 3 vols. 1895–6.

Goodfellow, D. M. *A Modern Economic History of South Africa.* 1931.

Jeppe, C. W. B. *Goldmining in South Africa.* 1948.

Hailey, Lord. *An African Survey.* Oxford, 1938.

Kanthack, F. E. *The Principles of Irrigation Engineering.* 1924.

Knowles, L. C. A. and C. M. *The economic development of the British Overseas Empire.* Vol. 3. The Union of South Africa. 1936.

LEHFELDT, R. A. *Gold, Prices and the Witwatersrand.* 1919.
—— *The National Resources of South Africa: with a Preface by the Rt. Hon. J. C. Smuts.* Johannesburg, 1922.
LESLIE, R. Paper Money and the Gold Exchange Standard at the Cape, in *The S.A. Journal of Science*, vol. XIII. 1916.
LEUBUSCHER, C. *Der südafrikanische Eingeborene als Industriearbeiter und als Stadtbewohner.* Jena, 1931.
MACMILLAN, W. M. *The South African Agrarian Problem and its historical development.* Johannesburg, 1919.
MANNING, H. T. *British Colonial Government after the American Revolution*, 1782–1820. Oxford, 1933.
MURRAY, M. *Ships and South Africa.* Oxford, 1933.
OULD, C. W. *William Stapleton Royce: a memoir.* 1925.
PAULING, G. *Chronicles of a Contractor.* 1926.
PAYTON, C. A. *The Diamond Diggings of South Africa.* 1872.
PLANT, A. The Anti-Dumping Regulations of the South African Tariff. *Economica.* 1931.
—— The Relations between Banking and the State in the Union of South Africa, in *London Essays in Economics.* 1927.
REUNERT, T. *Diamonds and Gold in South Africa.* 1893.
ROBERTSON, H. M. *South Africa: Economic and Political Aspects.* Duke Univ. Press, N.C., 1957.
SCHUMANN, C. G. W. *Die Kredietmark in Suidafrika.* Rotterdam, 1928.
—— *Structural Changes and Business Cycles in South Africa*, 1806–1936. P. S. King, 1938.
SELBORNE, 2nd Earl of. *A Review of the Present Mutual Relations of the British South African Colonies to which is appended a Memorandum on South African Railway Unification. . . .* usually known as the Selborne Memorandum. 1907.
Also published with an Introduction by WILLIAMS, Basil. Oxford, 1925.
VAN DER HORST, SHEILA T. *Native Labour in South Africa.* Oxford, 1942.
VAN DER POEL, J. *Railway and Customs Policies in South Africa*, 1885–1910. 1933.
WALKER, E. A. *The Great Trek.* 4th ed. 1960.
WEINTHAL, L. (Ed.). *Story of the Cape to Cairo railway and river route from* 1877 *to* 1922. 4 vols. 1923.
WILLIAMS, GARDNER F. *The Diamond Mines of South Africa.* New York, 1902 and 1906.

SECTION XIX. SOCIAL AND ECONOMIC DEVELOPMENTS IN NATIVE TRIBAL LIFE

(Chapter XXX)

(*a*) OFFICIAL PUBLICATIONS

Most of the Official Publications dealing with the Native Tribes during the Nineteenth Century are political in character, dealing with such topics as frontier disturbances and wars, annexations etc. In these publications information on Native Customs and Economic life is incidental. The more important of these are:

For Parliamentary Papers and debates see Part I, A 3 and 4.

Official Reports dealing with Native Economic and Social Conditions.

Report of Natal Native Commission, 1846–7.
Report of Natal Native Commission, 1852.
Report of Natal Native Commission, 1881.
Report of Native Laws and Customs Commission [Cape], 1883.
Of first-class importance.

Report of the South African Native Affairs Commission, 1903–5.
Of first-class importance.

Report of the Natives Land Commission. U.G. 19, 1916.
Report of the Natal Native Affairs Commission, 1906–7.
Cape Blue Books on Native Affairs, especially 1876, 1884, 1887, 1889, 1893, 1896.
Natal Blue Books on Native Affairs, especially 1878, 1882, 1897, 1898.

Miscellaneous Publications.

BIRD, J. *Annals of Natal.* 2 vols. Pietermaritzburg, 1888.
THEAL, G. McC. *Basutoland Records.* 3 vols. Cape Town, 1883.
Three further volumes prepared for publication but unpublished are in the Cape Archives.

Official Year Books of the Union Government. 1918 onwards.
Report of the Economic and Wage Commission 1925. U.G. 14, 1926. Cape Town, 1926.

(*b*) OTHER WORKS

ADAMSON, J. *Notes on Cape Affairs.* 1851.
AGAR-HAMILTON, J. A. I. *The Native policy of the Voortrekkers. . . .* 1928.
ALEXANDER, Sir J. E. *Narrative of a voyage of Observation.* 2 vols. 1837.
—— *An expedition of Discovery into the Interior of Africa.* 2 vols. 1838.
ANDERSSON, C. J. *Lake Ngami.* 1856.
—— *Notes of Travel in South Africa.* 1875.
ARBOUSSET, T. and DAUMAS, F. *Relation d'un Voyage d'exploration au Nord-Est de la Colonie du Cap de Bonne-Espérance.* Paris, 1842.
BACKHOUSE, J. *Extracts from the Journal of J. Backhouse.* 1840–1.
BAINES, T. *Explorations in South-West Africa.* 1864.
BARROW, Sir J. *An account of Travels into the Interior of Southern Africa.* 2 vols. 1801–4.
BIRD, J. *An inquiry into the causes of the Zulu War.* Pietermaritzburg, 1888.
BOWKER, J. M. *Speeches, letters, and selections from important papers.* Grahamstown, 1864.
BOYCE, W. B. *Notes on South African affairs.* 1839.
—— *Memoir of the Rev. William Shaw.* 1874.
BROOKES, E. H. *The history of Native Policy in South Africa from* 1830 *to the present day.* Cape Town, 1924.
—— *The Colour Problems of South Africa. . . .* Lovedale, 1934.
BROWNLEE, C. *Reminiscences of Kaffir Life and History.* Lovedale, 1896.
CALDERWOOD, H. *Caffres and Caffre missions.* 1858.
CALLAWAY, H. *The Religious System of the Amazulu.* 1868–70.
CAMPBELL, J. *Travels in South Africa.* 2 vols. 1822.
CASALIS, E. *The Basutos.* 1861.
COLENSO, J. W. *Ten Weeks in Natal.* Cambridge, 1855.
DÖHNE, J. L. *Das Kafferland und seine Bewohner.* Berlin, 1843.
EDWARDS, J. *Reminiscences.* Grahamstown, 1883.
EVANS, M. S. *Black and White in South East Africa.* 1916.
FLEMING, F. *Kaffraria and its Inhabitants.* 1853.
—— *Southern Africa.* 1856.
GALTON, F. *The narrative of an Explorer in Tropical South Africa.* 1853.
GROUT, L. *Zulu-Land.* 1863.
HOLDEN, W. C. *The past and future of the Kaffir Races.* 1866.
JACOTTET, E. *The Treasury of Ba-Suto Lore.* 1908.
JUNOD, H. A. *Les Ba-Ronga.* Neuchatel, 1898.
—— *The Life of a South African Tribe.* 2 vols. Neuchâtel, 1913.
KIDD, D. *The Essential Kaffir.* 1904.
KIEWIET, C. W. DE. *British Colonial Policy and the South African Republics.* 1929.
KROPF, A. *Das Volk der Xosa-Kaffern.* Berlin, 1889.

LAGDEN, Sir G. *The Basutos.* 2 vols. 1909.
MACKENZIE, J. *Ten years North of the Orange River.* Edinburgh, 1871.
MACLEAN, J. *A compendium of Kaffir Laws and Customs.* Mount Coke, 1858.
MACMILLAN, W. M. *Bantu, Boer and Briton.* 1929.
—— *Complex South Africa.* 1930.
—— *Africa Emergent.* 1938.
MEINHOF, C. *Die Religionen der Afrikaner.* Oslo, 1926.
MERENSKY, A. *Beiträge zur Kenntnis Südafrikas.* Berlin, 1875.
MOFFAT, R. *Missionary labours.* 1842.
OLDHAM, J. H. *White and Black in Africa.* 1930.
PERHAM, M. and CURTIS, L. *The Protectorates of South Africa.* 1935.
ROBERTSON, H. M. 150 Years of Economic Contact between White and Black. *S.A. Journal of Economics.* Dec. 1934 and March 1935.
SCHAPERA, I. *Migrant Labour and Tribal Life: a study of conditions in the Bechuanaland Protectorate.* 1947.
SHAW, B. *Memorials of South Africa.* 1840.
SHAW, W. *The story of my Mission.* 1860.
STOW, G. W. *The Native Races of South Africa.* 1905.
VAN DER HORST, S. *Native Labour in South Africa.* 1942.
WARD, H. *Five years in Kaffirland.* 2 vols. 1848.
WIDDICOMBE, J. *Fourteen years in Basutoland.* 1891.

SECTION XX. THE ROMAN-DUTCH LAW IN SOUTH AFRICA

(Chapter XXXI)

For official collections of Ordinances, Law Reports, etc. see Part I, B 2 (*a*).

BODENSTEIN, H. D. J. English influences on the Common Law of South Africa. 32 *S.A.L.J.* 337 *sqq.*
BOTHA, C. G. The Common and Statute Law at the Cape of Good Hope. 30 *S.A.L.J.* 292 *sqq.*
—— The early Inferior Courts of Justice at the Cape. 38 *S.A.L.J.* 406 *sqq.*
—— The early influence of the English law upon the Roman Dutch law in South Africa. 40 *S.A.L.J.* 396 *sqq.*
Cape Law Journal, 1884–1900, then *South African Law Journal*, 1901– . In other entries abbreviated to *S.A.L.J.*
COWEN, D. V. *Parliamentary Sovereignty and the Entrenched Clauses of the South Africa Act.* 1957.
Groot Placaat Boek. 10 vols. s' Gravenhage and Amsterdam, 1658–1797.
GROTIUS, H. *The introduction to Dutch Jurisprudence with an appendix containing selections from the notes of William Schorer · translated by A. F. S. Maasdorp.* 2nd ed. Cape Town, 1903.
KOTZE, Sir J. G. Review of Wessels's *History of the Roman Dutch law* in 25 *S.A.L.J.* pp. 353–65, 441–59; vol. XXVI, pp. 53–80, 387–409, 491–512; vol. XXVII, pp. 28–54, 191–213.
LEE, R. W. *Introduction to Roman Dutch Law.* 1915.
LEEUWEN, S. VAN. *Commentaries on the Roman Dutch Law*, edited by C. W. DECKER. Translated from the originals by Hon. Sir J. G. KOTZE. 2nd edn. 1921.
MAASDORP, Sir A. F. S. *The Institutes of South African Law, being a compendium of the common law, decided cases and statute law of South Africa.* 4th ed. Cape Town, 1922–32.
ROOS, J. DE V. Plakaat Books of the Cape. 14 *Cape Law Journal*, 1 *sqq.*
—— Statute Law of the Cape in pre-British days. 23 *S.A.L.J.* 242 *sqq.*
STOCK, J. L. W. *New Statutes of India at the Cape.* 32 *S.A.L.J.* 328 *sqq.*
WALKER, E. A. *Lord de Villiers and his times. South Africa, 1842–1914.* 1925.
WESSELS, Sir J. W. *History of the Roman Dutch Law.* Grahamstown, 1908.

WILLE, G. *Principles of South African Law.* 1945.
ZYL, C. H. VAN. The Batavian and Cape Plakaten. 24 *S.A.L.J.* 132 *sqq.*
—— Sources of South African Law. 18 *S.A.L.J.* 126 *sqq.*
—— *The theory of the judicial practice of South Africa, with suitable and copious practical forms subjoined to and illustrating the practice of the several subjects treated of.* 2 vols. 3rd ed. Cape Town, 1921.
—— *The South African Law Reports.*

SECTION XXI. CULTURAL DEVELOPMENT

(Chapter XXXII)

BALKEMA, A. A. *A History of Medicine in South Africa up to the end of the 19th Century.* Cape Town, 1958.
BLEEK, DOROTHEA. *Rock Paintings in South Africa.* London, 1930.
BOSHOFF, S. P. E. *Volk en taal van Suid-Afrika.* Pretoria, 1921.
BOSMAN, D. B. *Afrikaans en Maleis-Portugees.* Groningen, 1916.
—— *Oor die ontstaan van Afrikaans.* Amsterdam, 1923.
BOSMAN, F. C. L. *Afrikaans as Skryftaal.* Kaapstad, 1929.
—— *Afrikaanse kultuur en kultuurbesit.* Kaapstad, 1931.
—— *Drama en toneel in Suid-Afrika.* Amsterdam, 1928.
BOUWS, J. *Musiek in Suid-Afrika.* Bruges, 1946.
BUNBURY, Sir C. J. F. *Journal of a residence at the Cape of Good Hope.* 1848.
Coming of Age. Studies in South African Citizenship, by eight contributors. Cape Town, 1930.
CUMMING-GEORGE, L. *Architecture in South Africa.* 2 vols. Cape Town, 1933–4.
DEN BOER, J. H. VERDUYN. *Botanists at the Cape.* Cape Town, 1929.
DOKE, C. M. *The Southern Bantu Languages.* London, 1954.
DRENNAN, C. M. *Cockney English and Kitchen Dutch.* Johannesburg, 1920.
DU PLESSIS, I. D. and LÜCKHOFF, C. A. *The Malay Quarter and Its People, Capetown.* Amsterdam, 1953.
DU TOIT, A. L. *The Geology of South Africa.* Edinburgh, 1954.
DU TOIT, S. J. *Geskiedenis van die Afrikaanse taalbeweging . . . bewerk deur 'n Lid van die Genootskap van Regte Afrikaners* (i.e. S. J. DU TOIT). Paarl, 1880.
—— *Suid-Afrikaanse volkspoësie.* Amsterdam, 1924.
FAIRBRIDGE, D. *Historic houses of South Africa.* 1922.
—— *Historic farms of South Africa.* 1931.
—— *Letters from the Cape by Lady Duff Gordon.* 1927.
FLINT, W. and GILCHRIST, J. D. F. (Ed.). *Science in South Africa.* Cape Town, 1905.
Gedenkboek ter eere van die Genootskap van Regte Afrikaners (1875–1925). Potchefstroom, 1926.
GOODWIN, A. J. H. and LOWE, C. VAN RIET. *The Stone Age Culture of South Africa.* Cape Town, 1929.
GORDON-BROWN, A. *Pictorial Art in South Africa during the centuries to* 1875. 1954.
Grove's Dictionary of Music and Musicians. BLOM, E. (Ed.). London, 1954.
HESSELING, D. C. *Het Afrikaansch.* Leiden, 1899.
HUXLEY, J. *Africa View.* 1931.
KIRBY, P. R. *Musical Instruments of the Natives of South Africa.* Johannesburg, 1953.
KRITZINGER, M. S. B. *Oor skrywers en boeke.* Pretoria, 1932.
—— *Plateatlas by die Afrikaanse letterkunde.* Pretoria, 1931.
LEIPOLDT, C. F. L. *Oom Gert vertel en ander gidigte, met 'n Inleiding deur J. J. Smith.* 1911.
LLOYD, A. C. G. *The Birth of Printing in South Africa.* 1914.
MACNAB, R. The Emergence of Afrikaans as a Literary Language. *Journal of the Royal Society of Arts*, no. 5000, vol. CV, March 1957.
MALHERBE, E. G. *Education in South Africa* (1652–1922). Cape Town, 1925.
—— *The Bilingual School.* 1943.

MALHERBE, F. E. J. *Humor in die algemeén en sy uiting in die Afrikaanse letterkunde.* Amsterdam, 1924.
MENDELSSOHN, S. *South African Bibliography.* 2 vols. (*Vide* Classified Lists, 1910.)
MEYER, H. *Die Sprache der Buren.* Göttingen, 1901.
Muzikale Ommegang. Nederlandsche Keurboekerij, Amsterdam, 1948.
NATHAN, M. *South African Literature.* Cape Town, 1925.
NIEKERK, L. VAN. *Die Eerste Afrikaanse Taalbeweging.* Amsterdam, 1916.
NIENABER, G. S. and NIENABER, P. J. *Geskiedenis van die Afrikaanse Beweging.* Pretoria, 1941.
PATTERSON, S. *Colour and Culture in South Africa.* 1953.
PEARSE, G. E. *Eighteenth-century Architecture in South Africa.* 1933.
PHILLIPS, E. P. *A Brief Historical Sketch of the Development of Botanical Science In South Africa.* (South African Association for the Advancement of Science, 1930.)
PIENAAR, E. C. *Taal en poësie van die twede Afrikaanse-Taalbeweging.* Kaapstad, 1926.
—— *Taal en Poesie van die Tweede Afrikaanse Taal Beweging.* Kaapstad, 1931.
—— *Die Triomf van Afrikaans.* 1946.
Quarterly Bulletin of the South African Public Library. Cape Town, in progress.
RIBBINK, P. *Gids tot die publikasies in en oor Afrikaans.* Kaapstad, 1932.
RITCHIE, W. *History of the South African College.* Cape Town.
Royal Society of South Africa *Transactions*, in progress.
SCHAPERA, I. (Ed.). *Western Civilization and the Natives of South Africa. Studies in Culture Contact.* 1934.
SCHONKEN, F. T. *De oorsprong der Kaapsch-Hollandsche Volksoverleveringen.* Amsterdam, 1914.
SCHOONEES, P. C. *Die prosa van die twede Afrikaanse Beweging.* Pretoria, 1927.
—— *Die Prosa van die Tweede Afrikaanse Beweging.* Pretoria, 1939.
SHEPHERD, R. H. W. *Bantu Literature and Life.* Lovedale, 1955.
SMITH, J. J. Recognition and Evolution of the Afrikaans Language (*Union Year Book*, No. 8, 1925).
SMUTS, J. C. *Africa and some World Problems.* Oxford, 1930.
SÖHNGE, P. G., VISSER, D. J. L. and LOWE, C. VAN RIET. *The Geology and Archaeology of the Vaal River Basin* (South African Geological Survey, Memoir 35. Pretoria).
South Africa in Print. Cape Town, 1952.
South African Archaeological Society *Publications*, in progress.
South African Council for Scientific and Industrial Research. Pretoria, 1955.
STAPLETON, R. J. *Poetry of the Cape of Good Hope.* Cape Town, 1828.
TROTTER, A. F. *The Old Cape Colony.* 1903.
—— *Old colonial houses of the Cape of Good Hope.* 1900.
VAN DEN HEEVER, C. M., and PIENAAR, P. DE V. (Eds.). *Kultuur-geskiedenis van die Afrikaner.* 3 vols. Kaapstad, 1945–50.
WALKER, E. A. *The South African College and the University of Cape Town.* Cape Town, 1929.
WHITE, B. *The Language Question: the motive forces underlying the treatment of the language question in the government schools of the Orange Free State during the first twenty-five years of the twentieth century.* Bloemfontein, 1926.
WORRAL, J. *Ballet in South Africa.* Cape Town, 1949.
WORTHINGTON, E. B. *Science in South Africa.* London, 1936.

INDEX

The following abbreviations are used: S.A. = South Africa; B.S.A. Co. = British South Africa Company; N.E.I. Co. = Netherlands East India Company.